Frommer's

S0-AZJ-070

Italy
from $90 a day

· 5th Edition

by Reid Bramblett & Lynn A. Levine ·

Here's what the critics say about Frommer's:

"Amazingly easy to use. Very portable, very complete."
—*Booklist*

"Detailed, accurate, and easy-to-read information for all price ranges."
—*Glamour Magazine*

"Hotel information is close to encyclopedic."
· —*Des Moines Sunday Register*

"Frommer's Guides have a way of giving you a real feel for a place."
—*Knight Ridder Newspapers*

WILEY

Wiley Publishing, Inc.

Published by:

Wiley Publishing, Inc.

111 River St.

Hoboken, NJ 07030-5774

ISBN 0-7645-7672-0

Editor: Alexis Lipsitz Flippin
Production Editor: Donna Wright
Cartographer: Nicholas Trotter
Photo Editor: Richard Fox
Production by Wiley Indianapolis Composition Services

Front cover photo: Gondoliers with San Giorgio Maggiore in background.
Back cover photo: Hotel Royal Victoria, Pisa.

For information on our other products and services or to obtain technical support, please contact our Customer Care Department within the U.S. at 800/762-2974, outside the U.S. at 317/572-3993 or fax 317/572-4002.

Wiley also publishes its books in a variety of electronic formats. Some content that appears in print may not be available in electronic formats.

Manufactured in the United States of America

5   4   3   2   1

Contents

(4) Florence: Birthplace of the Renaissance   180

by Reid Bramblett

(5) Tuscany & Umbria   241

by Reid Bramblett

(6) Bologna & Emilia-Romagna   323

by Reid Bramblett

(11) Liguria & the Italian Riviera   563

by Reid Bramblett

(12) Southern Italy: Campania & Apulia   599

by Lynn A. Levine

(13) Sicily   681

by Lynn A. Levine

Index   736

List of Maps

An Invitation to the Reader

In researching this book, we discovered many wonderful places—hotels, restaurants, shops, and more. We're sure you'll find others. Please tell us about them, so we can share the information with your fellow travelers in upcoming editions. If you were disappointed with a recommendation, we'd love to know that, too. Please write to:

Frommer's Italy from $90 a Day, 5th Edition
Wiley Publishing, Inc. • 111 River St. • Hoboken, NJ 07030-5774

An Additional Note

Please be advised that travel information is subject to change at any time—and this is especially true of prices. We therefore suggest that you write or call ahead for confirmation when making your travel plans. The authors, editors, and publisher cannot be held responsible for the experiences of readers while traveling. Your safety is important to us, however, so we encourage you to stay alert and be aware of your surroundings. Keep a close eye on cameras, purses, and wallets, all favorite targets of thieves and pickpockets.

About the Authors

Reid Bramblett has lived in Italy on and off since the age of 11, and is the author of *Frommer's Tuscany & Umbria, Frommer's Northern Italy,* and *Frommer's Portable Florence,* and *Europe For Dummies,* as well as a contributor to *Frommer's Europe from $70 a Day.* When not on the road, he splits his time between New York and his native Philadelphia.

Lynn A. Levine is the author of *Frommer's Turkey,* as well as a contributor to *Frommer's Southeast Asia* and *Zagat Survey's Europe's Top Restaurants.* When not at home in Jersey City, New Jersey, she splits her time between Turkey and Italy, accompanied by her faithful Jack Russell Terrier, Buster.

Other Great Guides for Your Trip:

Frommer's Italy
Frommer's Rome
Frommer's Florence, Tuscany & Umbria
Frommer's Northern Italy
Frommer's Portable Venice
Frommer's Portable Florence
Italy For Dummies

Frommer's Star Ratings, Icons & Abbreviations

Every hotel, restaurant, and attraction listing in this guide has been ranked for quality, value, service, amenities, and special features using a **star-rating system.** In country, state, and regional guides, we also rate towns and regions to help you narrow down your choices and budget your time accordingly. Hotels and restaurants are rated on a scale of zero (recommended) to three stars (exceptional). Attractions, shopping, nightlife, towns, and regions are rated according to the following scale: zero stars (recommended), one star (highly recommended), two stars (very highly recommended), and three stars (must-see).

In addition to the star-rating system, we also use **seven feature icons** that point you to the great deals, in-the-know advice, and unique experiences that separate travelers from tourists. Throughout the book, look for:

Finds	Special finds—those places only insiders know about
Fun Fact	Fun facts—details that make travelers more informed and their trips more fun
Kids	Best bets for kids and advice for the whole family
Moments	Special moments—those experiences that memories are made of
Overrated	Places or experiences not worth your time or money
Tips	Insider tips—great ways to save time and money
Value	Great values—where to get the best deals

The following **abbreviations** are used for credit cards:

| AE | American Express | DISC | Discover | V | Visa |
| DC | Diners Club | MC | MasterCard | | |

Frommers.com

Now that you have the guidebook to a great trip, visit our website at **www.frommers.com** for travel information on more than 3,000 destinations. With features updated regularly, we give you instant access to the most current trip-planning information available. At Frommers.com, you'll also find the best prices on airfares, accommodations, and car rentals—and you can even book travel online through our travel booking partners. At Frommers.com, you'll also find the following:

- Online updates to our most popular guidebooks
- Vacation sweepstakes and contest giveaways
- Newsletter highlighting the hottest travel trends
- Online travel message boards with featured travel discussions

What's New in Italy

ROME

WHERE TO STAY Several of our recommended hotels have been busy over the winter season, upgrading, renovating, and adding as many stars as the Ministry of Tourism will allow. Now boasting new rooms, fresh baths, and three stars are the friendly **Smeraldo,** Vicolo del Chiodaroli (© **06-6875929**), and the **Abruzzi,** Piazza della Rotonda (© **06-6792021**), with its stunning views of the Pantheon. Meanwhile, the owner/architect of the **Navona,** Via dei Sedari 8 (© **06-6864203**), continues to upgrade, adding new rooms along with a bracing red breakfast room. His sister hotel, the **Residence Zanardelli,** Via G. Zanardelli 7 (© **06-6864203**), enjoys much the same TLC and has undergone a complete overhaul as of 2004. You'll hit pay dirt at **Hotel Galli,** Via Milazzo 20 (© **06-4456859**), where pristine accommodations are yours at prices of a bygone era.

WHERE TO DINE New to this guide but not to neighborhood professionals is the cafeteria-style **Magnosfera,** Piazza Indipendenza 24 (© **06-44703694**), where good, fresh food is offered at affordable prices. Another neighborhood favorite, this time near the Colosseum, is the straightforward **Luzzi,** Via Celimontana 1–3 (© **06-7096332**), which bustles under a relentless stream of plates and pasta bowls—at dirt-cheap prices. Speaking of dirt cheap and delicious, **Da Felice,** Via Maestro Giorgio 29 (© **06-5746800**), has liberalized its selection process—whereas it used to be almost impossible to nab a table, now it's only *difficult.*

SEEING THE SIGHTS One of the biggest attractions of Rome has recently become bigger: A 2-year restoration of the **Colosseum,** Piazza del Colosseo (© **06-7004261**), was completed in 2003, opening up an additional 65% of the monument to visitors, including a subterranean corridor that served as a passageway for gladiators and animals. The excavation of a second corridor known as Commodus's Passage reveals newly exposed plaster carvings and mosaics.

A whiter, brighter *Moses* now greets visitors ambling through **San Pietro in Vincoli,** Piazza San Pietro in Vincoli 4 (© **06-4882865**). After undergoing a 5-year process aimed at removing 500 years of accumulated grime from the marble surface, Michelangelo's masterpiece is as good as new. **Villa d'Este** in Tivoli (© **0774-312070**) has also benefited from some much-needed TLC: The statues have been cleaned, and the long-dormant fountain-powered organ and the musical fountain are singing once again. See chapter 3 for complete information on Rome.

FLORENCE

WHERE TO STAY Several of the famously cheap hotels lining Via Faenza are renovating and going midscale on us. Luckily, rates have barely budged at the **Albergo Azzi** (© **055-213806**), even though they've added TVs, air-conditioning, and other amenities to the rooms.

Similar upgrade work on Albergo Azzi's neighbor **Mia Cara** (℡ 055-216053) was just getting started when the last edition went to press. The work to turn this comfy old shoe of a place into a two- or three-star property is just finishing up literally as I type this. The new rooms will all have private bathrooms with hair dryers, minibars, telephones, TVs, and air-conditioning, and there are even rooms fitted out for guests with disabilities. Just when this new version of the hotel will open, however, is at the mercy of Florentine bureaucracy—but the Noto family will be ready to start accepting guests again in 2005. The prices—though double what they once were—will probably not top 100€ ($115), including breakfast, for a double room. No matter what the final price, Signora Noto promises Frommer's readers "a good rate." And here's a plus: By moving the entrance, they finally can make use of the building's elevator.

Finally, I've added a section detailing our favorite **wine bars** in Florence.

SEEING THE SIGHTS In the spring of 2004, Italy's minister of culture announced plans to **double the size of the Uffizi Gallery** by opening up the first floor to exhibition space, allowing for the display of as many as 800 more works of art. In late spring 2004, it was announced that the work could be completed by 2006. The expansion is intended to make the Uffizi one of Europe's premier art museums, on par in size with Paris's Louvre and Madrid's Prado (although, in terms of quality of the art, the Uffizi is already at that level). In the meantime, however, it's not clear what effect—if any—the renovation work will have on visitation to the Uffizi.

On May 24, 2004, **Michelangelo's David** emerged from a thorough 7-month scrubdown that left the artistic icon sparkling clean just in time to celebrate his 500th birthday. We should all look so good after 5 centuries!

Santa Croce finally capitulated, becoming the last of Florence's three major churches to start charging admission, a disturbing trend that began with Santa Maria Novella and then San Lorenzo.

The **Orsanmichele,** for lack of staff, no longer keeps regular hours—odd, since it sits smack-dab on the main tourist thoroughfare of the city, halfway between the Cathedral and the Uffizi, so you'd figure it would get tons and tons of visitors. See chapter 4 for complete information on Florence.

TUSCANY & UMBRIA

PISA The main **tourist office** has moved for the third time in 4 years—luckily, this time to a much more convenient location right next to the Leaning Tower. However, the state-supported **private tourism consortium** that books hotel rooms—and that used to share space with the tourist office—has moved, for some reason, even farther away from everything.

SAN GIMIGNANO The **cumulative ticket** to most of the town's sights no longer includes admission to the Collegiata (main church), which itself started charging for entry only a few years ago.

The old Museo Etrusco has become a **Museo Archeologico** after expanding and moving across town into a historic medieval/Renaissance pharmacy, also adding to its attractions a modern art gallery (okay, so that doesn't seem to fit thematically, but what the heck?).

SIENA The **Santa Maria della Scala complex** has continued to increase its presence on the tourism scene, sponsoring ever more intriguing temporary exhibitions and incorporating into its structure the modest Museo Archeologico (which was already next door; a doorway was opened up to add rooms onto the rambling ones of the main museum).

MONTALCINO La Fortezza, a fantastic wine shop installed inside the tall stone chambers of the town's glowering fortress, has new owners and management. They have wisely decided not to change a thing about running the place, which remains one of the best, and most atmospheric, spots to get familiar with Tuscany's mightiest red wines.

AREZZO The famous *Crucifix* by Giotto's teacher Cimabue has been fully restored and returned to its rightful place above the High Altar of **San Domenico.** What's shocking, given the trends elsewhere in Tuscany, is that the powers that be have since dropped the admission fee charged during the restoration process (to help fund the restoration). Kudos, Arezzo.

PERUGIA The city has introduced a new **Perugia Città Museo** card, which acts as a cumulative admission card to all of the city's major museums and sights, including the Galleria Nazionale, Capella San Severo, Collegio del Cambio and della Mercanzia, the Pozzo Etrusco, Museo Archeologico, and more. You can pick it up at any of the participating museums for 7€ ($9) for the 1-day version that's good for four sights, or 12€ ($15) for a 3-day version good at all sights. Families will appreciate the full-year pass, good for up to four people, for just 35€ ($44). Is it a good deal? Well, admission to the Galleria Nazionale alone is 6.50€ ($8), so the card is a fantastic bargain! For more info, call ✆ 075-5736458.

See chapter 5 for complete information on Tuscany and Umbria.

EMILIA-ROMAGNA

RAVENNA Both the Museo Arcivescovile (Archbishop's Museum) and the Cappella di San Andrea have reopened following extensive renovations.

MODENA The city now offers **free bikes** to get around town.

VENICE

GETTING AROUND Even though the regular tickets for Venice's **vaporetto** system of public "water buses" are already outrageously expensive, at 3.50€ ($4) per ticket, even those overpriced tix are no longer valid on the popular Grand Canal routes (nos. 82 and 1). You are now forced to fork over 6€ ($6.90) on the Grand Canal to ride what is essentially the public bus—albeit one that takes you down a stunning and incredible "main drag."

WHERE TO STAY The wonderful family-run **Hotel Bernardi-Semenzato** has opened a second annex—just four rooms done in Venetian style, including a family suite, but any increase in the number of rooms available at this gem of a budget hotel is welcome.

SEEING THE SIGHTS You can now book tickets in advance for entry into the **Accademia Gallery** (✆ 041-5200345; www.gallerie accademia.org) for an additional 1€ ($1.15) per ticket—which should seriously cut down on the wait during the busy summer months.

Large bags are no longer allowed inside the **Basilica di San Marco,** and a left luggage office has been established at Ateneo San Basso in Calle San Basso 315Λ. It's open Monday to Saturday from 10am to 4pm and Sunday from 2 to 4pm. Please note that the basilica is experimenting with this service, and its location, hours, or other conditions may have changed by the time you visit Venice.

In other sightseeing news, the Associazione Chiesa di Venezia, which curates most of Venice's top churches, now offers **audioguides** at some of the churches for .50€ (60¢).

After years of construction, the famous **Teatro La Fenice** (San Marco 1965, on Campo San Fantin; ✆ 041-786562 or 041-786580; www.teatro lafenice.it) has finally reopened. In January 1996, the city stood still in shock as Venice's principal stage for world-class opera, music, theater, and ballet went up in flames. Carpenters and artisans worked around the clock to re-create the *teatro* (built in 1836) according to archival designs. Inaugural performances in December 2003 included appearances by Riccardo Muti, musical director of La Scala, and Elton John. That, however, was just the inaugural. The theater won't actually host a regular schedule until November 2004, at the earliest—though it is expected to open for visitors to tour in summer 2004. Until then, the Orchestra and Coro della Fenice are performing, as they have since 1996, in a substitute venue—a year-round tentlike structure called the **PalaFenice** (✆ **041-5210161**)—in the unlikely area of the Tronchetto parking facilities near Piazzale Roma, convenient to many *vaporetto* lines. (To say it ain't the same as La Fenice is something of an understatement.) Decent tickets for the PalaFenice start at about 20€ ($23; at 10€/$12 for those "partially obstructed view" seats), and the box office is open Monday to Friday 9am to 6pm.

See chapter 7 for complete information on Venice.

THE VENETO & SOUTH TYROL

PADUA I guess someone heard the complaints about the 15-minute time limit to visit the restored **Scrovegni, or Arena, Chapel** frescoed by that Gothic master Giotto because now you can buy a "double turn" ticket good for 30 minutes inside the chapel—but only in the evenings (7–9:30pm).

The refined premises of the **Caffè Pedrocchi** now host live music on some evenings, as does the **La Corte dei Leoni** restaurant (in summer only).

TRENT The city now offers a **Trento Card** cumulative ticket for admission to the city's museums and unlimited use of public transportation.

BOLZANO In August 2003, a research team determined that the final moments of **Otzi—the famous Ice Man** whose body and accouterments were preserved for 5,300 years inside a glacier and 5 additional years in a museum in Bolzano—were anything but calm. The Ice Man was apparently caught in a thrilling battle, shot at least once in the back by an enemy arrow, and dragged away by a valiant companion who patched up Otzi's wounds before our hero gasped his last in an icy crevasse high in the Alps. They got all that from a microscopic examination of blood and fibers and an anatomical analysis. Whoever said forensics isn't cool?

MERANO The **Castel Tirolo** has reopened with a new museum about this scenic castle's history.

The city-run **spa** had closed at press time for a massive overhaul set to end by the end of 2004, with a hotel added in 2005.

See chapter 8 for complete information on the Veneto and South Tyrol.

MILAN

WHERE TO STAY The Hotel Ullrich has, for some reason, been renamed **Hotel Aliseo.** They didn't do anything about the funky smell in the hallway, though. Ah, well. It's still a great deal.

SEEING THE SIGHTS The brilliant neo-Gothic facade of **Milan's Duomo** will remain swathed in scaffolding for a thorough cleaning that's likely to last through the end of 2005.

The formerly free **Archaeological Museum** has started charging admission (sigh!). On the bright side, there's now a **combination ticket** for admission to the Pinacoteca Ambrosiana, the Museo del Duomo, and the new Museo Diocesano. See chapter 9 for complete information on Milan.

LAKE COMO

SEEING THE SIGHTS In Mennagio, the **Albergo-Ristorante Il Vapore** has reopened its excellent little restaurant, which was closed for the past 2 years following the untimely death of the chef—and patriarch—of this family-run operation. See chapter 9 for details.

TURIN

SEEING THE SIGHTS Turin is gearing up to host the **2006 Winter Olympic** games, so expect some changes to come as the city is spruced up in preparation for worldwide attention. For more information, check out www.torino2006.org. See chapter 10 for more details.

GENOA

SEEING THE SIGHTS The city has greatly expanded the benefits of its **Card Musei (Museum Card),** which will get you into 20 city museums—including the recently reopened **Palazzo Bianco painting gallery**—and has an option that includes free transport on all public buses, trams, and Metros.

The world-famous **Aquarium of Genoa** has expanded, adding a section on Italy's protected marine areas, an Antarctic exhibit, and touch tanks for kiddies who just have to reach out and touch a ray. See chapter 11 for complete information on Genoa.

NAPLES

GETTING AROUND It will still take a while to complete—particularly when excavations recover ancient Roman busts and rowboats—but work on the **subway extension** that will connect Piazza Garibaldi with the Duomo and Capodimonte is progressing nicely. Prepare for the slight inconvenience of construction near the train station and intermittently along Corso Umberto.

WHERE TO STAY The **Ginevra** hotel, Via Genova 116 (© 081-283210), has added five new, completely renovated and upgraded rooms opposite the main entrance. With amenities like air-conditioning, pristine en-suite bathrooms, and refrigerators, these five units are more indicative of three-star accommodations. The hotel still features inexpensive pension-style rooms. See chapter 12 for complete information on Naples.

POMPEII

SEEING THE SIGHTS Visitors to this ancient city can now experience Pompeii in its final moments. **"Pompeii by Night"** is a multimedia voyage back that revisits the sights and sounds of the dramatic moments leading up to and in the wake of the eruption. For information on nighttime tours, contact Pompeii by Night (© 081-8575347; reservations 8616405; www.arethusa.net). See chapter 12 for complete information on Pompeii.

CAPRI

GETTING THERE/GETTING AROUND It's either an efficient means of moving tourists or just another moneymaking scheme: To use the island's public transportation, visitors must now purchase a magnetic **"souvenir card"** for a refundable 1€ ($1.15). You can obviously choose to keep the card—which displays some of Capri's most famous scenery—at the end of your stay. See chapter 12 for complete information on Capri.

BARI

SEEING THE SIGHTS The old city's two main piazzas, **Piazza Mercato** and **Piazza Ferrarese,** which serve as the heart of Bari and the bridge between ancient and modern, have undergone a complete overhaul. Gone are the roadblocks, replaced by a pleasing excess of outdoor cafes, restaurants, and pubs. See chapter 12 for complete information on Bari.

AGRIGENTO

SEEING THE SIGHTS Nothing lasts forever, especially not freebees. In order to access the main three temples, it is now necessary to buy an **entrance ticket**—formerly necessary only for entry to the Temple of Zeus. See chapter 13 for complete information on Agrigento and Sicily.

The Best of Italy from $90 a Day

by Reid Bramblett & Lynn A. Levine

Two authors. One country. A myriad of experiences. Deciding what to see and do in Italy is not easy—especially if you're on a budget. Here, we've put our heads together and come up with the best of what this diverse country has to offer.

1 The Best Travel Experiences for Free (or Almost)

- **Enjoying Rome's Best Nighttime Panorama:** After a leisurely 3-hour dinner at a tiny trattoria in Rome's working-class neighborhood of Trastevere, stroll the cobblestone alleyways, then climb the Gianicolo hill for a moonlit panorama of the Eternal City. See chapter 3.

- **Listening to the Vespers in San Miniato** (Florence): This is one of the few places left in Italy where Gregorian chant is still sung. Here, in one of Florence's oldest churches, late-afternoon vespers transport you back to the lost centuries of the hilltop Romanesque church's 11th-century origins. See chapter 4.

- **Biking Through the Town and on the Walls of Ferrara:** For spectacular views, bike on the wide paths along Ferrara's medieval walls, which encircle the city with an aerie of greenery. Many hotels offer guests free use of bicycles. See chapter 6.

- **Taking a *Vaporetto* Ride on the Grand Canal** (Venice): For a fraction of the cost of a gondola ride, the nos. 1 and 82 *vaporetti* (motor launches) ply the Grand Canal, past

hundreds of Gothic and Byzantine *palazzi* (palaces) redolent of the days when Venice was a powerful and wealthy maritime republic. Angle for a seat on the open-air deck up front. See chapter 7.

- **Cruising Lake Como** (Lake District): Board a lake steamer for the pleasant trip from Bellagio to other picturesque small villages on the section of the lake known as the Centro Lago. To the north, the lake is backed by snowcapped Alps, while the shorelines are lush with verdant gardens. As the steamer heads from one port to another, ocher- and pastel-colored villages will beckon you to disembark and explore their ancient streets and *piazze* (squares)—a good reason to purchase a day pass. See chapter 9.

- **Climbing the Flanks of the Matterhorn in the Valle d'Aosta:** An excellent trail leads from Cervina-Breuil up the flank of this impressive mountain. A moderately strenuous uphill trek of 90 minutes will get you to the breathtaking Lac du Goillet. From there, it's another 90 minutes to the Colle Superiore delle Cime Bianche, a plateau with heart-stopping views. See chapter 10.

- **Walking in the Cinque Terre** (Italian Riviera): While away your time in the Cinque Terre by strolling from one lovely village to another along the Mediterranean on trails with views that'll take your breath away. See chapter 11.
- **Exploring the Land of the *Trulli*** (Apulia): The Valle d'Itria is a lush, surreal landscape carpeted with vineyards and speckled with one of Europe's oddest forms of vernacular architecture: *trulli,* pointy whitewashed houses constructed without mortar and roofed by a cone of dark stones stacked in concentric circles. The capital of the region is Alberobello, a UNESCO World Heritage town made up of more than 1,000 *trulli*—you can even spend the night in one. See chapter 12.
- **Driving the Magnificent Amalfi Coast:** The 48km (30-mile) ride down the Amalfi Drive is one of the most awe-inspiring, character-building, and hair-raising experiences on record. This two-lane road clings to cliffs sometimes hundreds of feet high, twisting and plunging past verdant gorges, tiny fishing villages, posh resort towns, and sparkling isolated beaches washed by bright azure waters. SITA buses make the winding and wonderful journey from Sorrento to Amalfi for a mere 2€ ($2.30). Don't forget to bring Dramamine. See chapter 12.

- **Sailing the Amalfi Coast Through the Eyes of Anthony Minghella** (Ischia): In the film *The Talented Mr. Ripley,* Ischia's Castello Aragonese, the rock at Sant'Angelo, and the magnificent waters served as a backdrop for the unspoiled Italian coastal experience of a bygone era. For 15€ ($17) per person, the island's cooperative water taxi will take you on a tour that circles this stunning island. When you're done, a dip in a thermal pool awaits. See chapter 12.
- **Taking a Sunset Picnic to the Valley of the Temples** (Agrigento, Sicily): The setting is humbling, the view is inspiring, and, when you're propped up against an ancient column, the experience is unparalleled. The setting sun bathes the temples in a mystical warm glow; then, in succession, floodlights illuminate the valley's temples. See chapter 13.

2 The Best Small Towns

- **Lucca** (Tuscany): Protected from the new millennium by its remarkable swath of Renaissance ramparts (said to be among the best preserved in Europe), Lucca evokes the charm of an elegant small town. Within these historic parameters, local matrons tool around on bicycles (everyone does—Lucca is like a quaint hill town without the hill), young mothers with strollers walk the ramparts' promenade beneath the shade of centuries-old plane trees, and exuberant examples of Pisan-Romanesque architecture draw visitors to the Duomo and San Michele in Foro. Hometown boy Puccini would have no problem recognizing the city he always held close to his music-filled heart. See chapter 5.
- **Gubbio** (Umbria): This proud, austere, no-nonsense mountain town has only recently figured on the maps of the intrepid off-the-beaten-path trekkers. Blessedly hard to get to, Gubbio has slumbered through the centuries and today offers one of the country's

best-preserved scenarios of medieval architecture and ambience. Because Gubbio is built into the side of the forest-clad Monte Igino, a funicular up to the Basilica of its beloved patron, St. Ubaldo, provides a stunning panorama and a chance to consider the centuries-old serenity of the time-locked outpost that poet Gabriele D'Annunzio called the "City of Silence." See chapter 5.

- **Bressanone (Brixen)** (South Tyrol): It's hard to believe that this quaint town was the center of a large ecclesiastical principality for almost 800 years. It is rich in history and natural beauty, and you can explore vineyards, mountains, and impressive museums and monuments, as well as amble past the town's pastel-colored houses on narrow cobblestone streets. See chapter 8.

- **Bellagio** (Lake District): The prettiest of all the towns in Italy's lake country, Bellagio was peaceful enough for Franz Liszt to use as a retreat—and because it hasn't been inundated with throngs of tourists, it could work for you, too. See chapter 9.

- **Ravello** (Campania): The Amalfi Coast could be described as a parody of itself, particularly in August, but only 4.8km (3 miles) up into the hills is a lush retreat worlds away from the tourist crush below. Perched at the lip of the verdant Valley of the Dragon, the quiet beauty and sculpted gardens of Ravello provide the perfect venue for public concerts throughout the year, tempting newcomers to explore the scenery that inspired Wagner's *Parsifal*. See chapter 12.

- **Ostuni** (Salento, Apulia): It's easy for the uninformed to bypass this enchanting little town on the way through to the "major" stops in Apulia. So be informed: Ostuni is so much more than a day at the beach—an afternoon spent walking through the whitewashed medieval alleyways of the "White City" makes for serious poetry. See chapter 12.

- **Erice** (Sicily): Sitting on a cliff top that soars well above the cloud line, Erice is a medieval town that frequently meets thick tufts of fog that engulf the cobbled streets in a mysterious and romantic mist. This sacred city was established as a religious center in honor of the Earth goddess centuries before the Greeks and later the Romans showed up and renamed her Venus. See chapter 13.

3 The Best Cathedrals

- **Basilica di San Pietro** (Rome): A monument not only to Christendom but also to the Renaissance and baroque eras, this cathedral was designed by Bramante, decorated by Bernini, and crowned with a dome by Michelangelo. Within its walls are some of the world's most renowned treasures: *St. Peter,* by Arnolfo di Cambio; and Michelangelo's haunting *Pietà,* a masterpiece representation in marble of Christ in the arms of Mary at the deposition, carved when the artist was only 19 years old. If that's not humbling, then a glimpse of the pope will be. See chapter 3.

- **Pantheon** (Rome): This consecrated church is more like a cathedral to architecture, with its perfect hemispheric dome and flawless proportions. Expertly engineered by Emperor Hadrian in the 2nd century A.D., the Pantheon survived the test of time, until Pope Urban VIII had the bronze tiles of the portico melted down to make the baldacchino for St. Peter's and 80 cannons. Today you can pay your respects to genius, as well as to Raphael, whose tomb resides within. See chapter 3.

• **Duomo** (**Cathedral of Santa Maria del Fiore;** Florence): The red-tiled dome of Florence's magnificent Duomo has dominated the skyline for 5 centuries. In its day, it was the largest unsupported dome in the world, dwarfing the structures of ancient Greece and Rome. In true Renaissance style, it was and still is considered a major architectural feat and was the high point of architect Filippo Brunelleschi's illustrious career. In 1996, an extensive and elaborate 15-year restoration was finally completed on the colorful 16th-century frescoes covering the inside of the cupola and depicting the world's largest painting of the *Last Judgment.* See chapter 4.

• **Duomo** (Siena, Tuscany): Begun in 1196, this black-and-white marble-striped cathedral sits atop Siena's highest hill and is one of the most beautiful and ambitious Gothic churches in Italy. Its exterior's extravagant zebra-striped marble bands borrowed from Pisan-Lucchese architecture continue indoors. Masterpieces here include a priceless pavement of masterful mosaics; 56 etched and inlaid marble panels created by more than 40 artisans (now uncovered for public viewing in late summer and early fall); the octagonal pulpit, carved by master Tuscan sculptor Nicola Pisano; and the lavish Libreria Piccolomini, frescoed by Pinturicchio in the late 15th century with the life of the Siena-born Pope Pius II, quintessential Renaissance man and humanist, and still housed with that pope's important

illuminated manuscript collection. See chapter 5.

• **Duomo** (Orvieto, Umbria): Begun in 1290 and with a bold, beautiful, and intricately ornamented facade that stands out among Italy's Gothic masterpieces, Orvieto's Duomo is also known for one of the greatest fresco cycles of the Renaissance in its Chapel of San Brizio. The cycle, begun by Fra Angelico and completed by Luca Signorelli, depicts in vivid detail the *Last Judgment,* one that was said to have influenced Michelangelo in his own interpretation for the Sistine Chapel. See chapter 5.

• **Basilica di San Marco** (Venice): Surely the most exotic and Eastern of the Western world's Christian churches, the onion-domed and mosaic-covered San Marco took much of its inspiration from ancient Constantinople's Hagia Sophia. Somewhere inside the mysterious candlelit cavern of the 1,000-year-old church, which began as the private chapel of the governing doges, are the remains of St. Mark, revered patron saint of Venice's ancient maritime republic. His "mascot," the winged lion, is linked to the city as closely as the "quadriga," the four ancient magnificent chariot horses that decorate the open loggia of St. Mark's Basilica overlooking one of the world's great squares. See chapter 7.

• **Duomo** (Milan, Lombardy): It took 5 centuries to build this magnificent Gothic cathedral— the fourth-largest church in the world. It's marked by 135 marble spires, a stunning triangular facade, and some 3,400 statues flanking the massive but airy, almost fanciful exterior. The interior, lit by brilliant stained-glass windows, is more serene. Lord

Tennyson rapturously wrote about the view of the Alps from the roof. See chapter 9.

• **Cattedrale di Monreale** (Sicily): Nothing short of jaw-dropping, this awesome church stands as a testament to the craftsmanship of imported Greek artisans from Byzantium, who carpeted the interior with 28,900 sq. m (311,077 sq. ft.) of glittering mosaics. In the cathedral's serene cloisters, you can while away the hours contemplating the hundreds of one-of-a kind twisted and inlaid minicolumns. If you see anything in Sicily, make it Monreale. See chapter 13.

4 The Best Museums

• **Musei Vaticani (Vatican Museums;** Rome): Centuries of collections and "indulgences" had to come to something: one of the wealthiest collections of art and historic artifacts in the world. The Vatican Museum's origins are humble, beginning in 1503 with Pope Julius II della Rovere's placement of a statue of Apollo in the courtyard of the Belvedere Palace and culminating in a showpiece of 12 galleries and papal apartments filled with a veritable catalog of civilization. There's everything from the Raphael Rooms, with their *School of Athens* fresco, to Michelangelo's incomparable Sistine Chapel, with its fingers-almost-touching depiction of *God Creating Adam.* In between, you'll find that statue of Apollo, plus a surfeit of Greek and Roman statues, medieval tapestries, illuminated manuscripts, ancient Egyptian and Chinese art, Etruscan artifacts, and a painting gallery covering everyone from Giotto and Leonardo to Caravaggio's *Deposition* and Raphael's final work, the magnificent *Transfiguration.* See chapter 3.

• **Galleria Borghese** (Rome): Never has such a small space packed such an amazing punch: Reopened in 2002 after a 14-year restoration, the Galleria Borghese elicits an audible "wow" at every step. The Pinacoteca is a shrine to Renaissance painting, with works by Andrea del Sarto, Ghirlandaio, Pinturicchio, Fra Bartolomeo, and Lorenzo di Credi. Raphael makes an entrance with his *Deposition,* and Botticelli is represented by his *Madonna col Bambino e San Giovannino,* while Caravaggio's works simply provide a tease for his tour de force in the Sculpture Gallery. Here, along with some of Caravaggio's most poignant works, is a collection of marble masterpieces by Gianlorenzo Bernini, including the *Rape of Persephone, Apollo and Daphne,* and the lifelike *Pauline Bonaparte as Venus.* See chapter 3.

• **Museo Nazionale Etrusco di Villa Giulia** (Rome): This is the single greatest museum devoted to the ancient, pre-Roman Etruscan culture. These guys left behind painted vases and beautiful funerary art, including a terra-cotta sarcophagus lid bearing life-size—and remarkably lifelike—full-body portraits of a husband and wife, smiling enigmatically and wearing their finest togas, sitting back to enjoy one final, eternal feast together. See chapter 3.

• **Museo Nazionale Romano** (Rome): After languishing behind the closed doors of the Baths of Diocletian for years, the most extensive and comprehensive collections of Roman art anywhere in the world are finally open to public viewing, housed in four of the city's top museums: Palazzo Altemps, Palazzo Massimo alle Terme, the Aula Ottagona, and the restored Baths of Diocletian. This reorganization of exhibitions allows you to appreciate not only an astounding collection of sculpture, mosaics, coinage, jewelry, and never-before-seen frescoes, but also the glorious spaces, ancient and modern, in which they reside. See chapter 3.

- **Uffizi Gallery (Galleria degli Uffizi;** Florence): When the Medici were the affluent men about town, this was the headquarters of the Duchy of Tuscany. For today's visitor, it is the riverside repository of the greatest collection of Renaissance paintings in the world—Giotto's *Maestà*, Botticelli's *Birth of Venus* and *Allegory of Spring,* Michelangelo's *Holy Family*—bequeathed to Florence with the understanding that the collection would never leave the city of the Medici nor these hallowed walls. "Stendhal's Syndrome," the peculiar malaise of vertigo from the sheer overload of unparalleled culture, most likely was first experienced here. See chapter 4.

- **Museo Nazionale del Bargello** (Florence): The harsh, fortresslike Bargello, incarnated as the constable's headquarters and local prison, among other things, is to Renaissance sculpture what the Uffizi is to Renaissance painting. Within this cavernous medieval shell lies a handsomely displayed collection without equal in Italy, with early works by Michelangelo and magnificent pieces by the early Renaissance master Donatello. See chapter 4.

- **Galleria dell'Accademia** (Florence): Michelangelo's *David,* one of the world's most recognized statues, looms in stark perfection beneath the rotunda of the main room built exclusively for its display when it was moved here from the Piazza Signoria for safekeeping. After standing in awe before its magnificence, many visitors leave, drained, without seeing the museum's other Michelangelos, particularly four never-finished *Prisoners* (or *Slaves*) struggling magnificently to free themselves. See chapter 4.

- **Palazzo Pitti's Galleria Palatina** (Florence): The former residence of the Medici, the enormous Palazzo Pitti is home to seven museums, the largest collection of galleries in Florence under one roof. The Galleria Palatina section, 26 art-filled rooms on the first floor of the palace, is the star attraction, home to one of the finest collections of Italian Renaissance and baroque masters in Europe. The art of the 16th century is the forte of the Palatina, in particular that of Raphael and his many Madonnas. The museum's treasures also include a large collection of works by Andrea del Sarto, Fra Bartolomeo, Rubens (superb), Tintoretto (canvases), Veronese, Caravaggio, and Titian (stunning portraits). See chapter 4.

- **Galleria dell'Accademia** (Venice): The glory that was Venice lives on in the Accademia, the definitive treasure house of Venetian painting and one of Europe's great museums. Exhibited chronologically from the 13th through the 18th centuries, the collection is said to have no single hallmark masterpiece; rather, this is an outstanding and comprehensive showcase of works by all the great master painters of Venice—Veronese, Tintoretto, Titian—the largest such collection in the world. Most of all, though, the works open a window onto the Venice of 500 years ago. Indeed, you'll see in the canvases how little Venice, perhaps least of any city in Europe, has changed over the centuries. See chapter 7.

- **Collezione Peggy Guggenheim** (Venice): Considered one of the most comprehensive and important collections of modern art in the world, these paintings and sculptures were assembled by eccentric and eclectic American expatriate Peggy Guggenheim in her own home. She did an excellent job of it, showing particular strengths in Cubism, European Abstraction, Surrealism, and Abstract Expressionism since about 1910. See chapter 7.

- **Museo Archeologico** (Naples): If you've come all this way just to pass through Naples on your way to Pompeii, you're missing half the show. Anything that hadn't already been carted off from the ruins by looters is housed here, including a special exhibit of erotic art in the *Gabinetto Segreto,* or Secret Chamber. Not to be overshadowed is an extensive collection of ancient sculptural masterpieces, including the *Farnese Bull,* a 4m-high (13-ft.) ancient narration carved out of one gargantuan block of marble. See chapter 12.

- **Museo Archaeologico Paolo Orsi** (Siracusa): Inaugurated in 1988 to pick up the slack left by the now defunct archaeological museum in Piazza Duomo, this museum, home to about 18,000 artifacts, is the most extensive archaeological collection in Sicily and among the largest of its kind in Europe. It's also one of the most coherent. With many of the treasures displayed in their proper historical context, the collection details Sicily's prehistoric era, the period of Greek colonization, and all of the principal subcolonies of eastern and central Sicily, including large hauls from both Gela and Agrigento. See chapter 13.

5 The Best Ancient Ruins

- **Foro Romano** (Rome): This poetic collection of architectural dctritus marks the spot where an empire ruled the ancient civilized world. You can explore the Roman Forum in an hour or two, but whether you pack a picnic lunch or simply gaze down over the zone from street level, the Forum's allure will call you back. See chapter 3.

- **Colosseo** (Rome): A well-known symbol of the Eternal City, the Colosseum for many *is* Rome. That's a heavy responsibility to bear, but this broken yet enduring structure succeeds admirably. Built over Nero's private lake (see Domus Aurea, below), the arena accommodated up to 50,000 Romans who came for bloody gladiator matches and wild beast massacres. Practically speaking, it's the largest amphitheater in the world and a study for the classical orders of architecture. See chapter 3.

- **Domus Aurea** (Rome): After 20 years of study and excavations, the Domus Aurea, or "Golden House," is finally open to the public, revealing frequently mindblowing testament to how the richer half lived. No expense was spared in the construction of this 150-room palace that surveyed four of Rome's hills and included Nero's private lake, hunting grounds, pastures, and vineyard. Completely swathed in gold, jewels, and works of art, Domus Aurea is a brilliant masterwork of megalomania in ancient Rome. See chapter 3.

- **Arena di Verona** (Verona): One of the best-preserved Roman amphitheaters in the world and the best known in Italy after Rome's Colosseum, the elliptical Arena was built of a slightly pinkish marble around the year A.D. 100 and stands in the middle of town in the Piazza Brà. Its perfect acoustics have survived the millennia and make it one of the wonders of the ancient world, as well as one of the most fascinating venues today for live moonlit performances (opera here is fantastic) conducted without microphones. See chapter 8.

- **Pompeii & Herculaneum** (Campania): One of the most tragic events in recorded history occurred in A.D. 79, when Mount Vesuvius blew its top 19km (12 miles) into the air, claimed the lives of thousands, and annihilated two thriving and prosperous cities. In Pompeii, it was a high-speed tidal wave of volcanic ash and superheated gases that violently hurled itself upon the city; in Herculaneum, it was a steady flow of scalding mud that scorched the victims' bodies down to the bone. The quick, devastating burials, however, did preserve two ancient cities, with villas, shops, public baths, and brothels uncovered much as they were almost 2,000 years ago. See chapter 12.

- **Greek Temples at Paestum** (Campania): Who'd expect to see such awesome ancient Greek temples in the middle of mozzarella country? Only an hour south of Naples stands the 9th-century-B.C. Greek colony of Paestum, founded when *Magna Graecia* extended into Southern Italy.

Actually, Paestum has something even Greece can't claim: the only known examples of ancient Greek frescoes in the world. See chapter 12.

- **Greek Temples of Sicily** (Segesta, Selinunte, and Agrigento): These shockingly poignant remnants left by Greek colonies in the age of *Magna Graecia,* or the "Greater Greece," reside in some of the most fascinating settings in Sicily. The temple of **Segesta** glows in tones of warm gold, sitting on the edge of a deep ravine surrounded by rolling hills covered with jasmine and aloe. **Selinunte** retains much of its original mystery, with an anonymous jumble of re-erected temples stretched out over two hills that flow gracefully into the Mediterranean. Settled along a man-made ridge below the modern city of **Agrigento** is the Valley of the Temples, a string of Doric temples awash in olive groves and pink almond blossoms in spring. The exquisite Temple of Concord ranks as one of the two best-preserved Greek temples on Earth. See chapter 13.

- **Villa Romana del Casale at Piazza Armerina** (Sicily): In the little hamlet of Casale outside the town of Piazza Armerina lie the most extensive, intact, and colorful ancient mosaics in all of the Roman world. The grounds of the villa, probably built as a hunting lodge for Emperor Maximus, include a peristyled main house, a triclinium, a bath complex, and a vast number of rooms for entertaining and regurgitating. With the stables and kitchen yet to be excavated, the 11,500 sq. m (123,785 sq. ft.) of mosaics are just the tip of the iceberg. See chapter 13.

6 The Best Wine-Tasting Experiences

- **Montalcino** (southern Tuscany): This less-trod area south of Siena is sacred ground to wine connoisseurs for its unsurpassed **Brunello di Montalcino.** The picturesque hill town has *enotecas* (wine bars) and cantinas right in town; Montalcino's mighty Medici fortress has been reincarnated as a rustic wine bar. With a rental car, you can head into the highly scenic countryside outside of Montalcino to the Fattoria Barbi, one of the area's most respected wine-producing estates, for a tasting and country-style dinner, even an overnight stay. See chapter 5.

- **Enoteca Italiana** (Siena, Tuscany): Siena sits to the south of the Chianti-designated area, so there could be no better setting to showcase Italy's timeless wine culture. Set within the massive military fortress built by Cosimo dei Medici in 1560, this wine-tasting bar provides a wide selection. The emphasis is on Tuscan wines—many made in the fabled Chianti area of Siena's backyard—but this enoteca is a national concern owned and operated by the government to support the Italian wine tradition. See chapter 5.

- **Verona** (Veneto): The epicenter of the region's important viticulture (Veneto produces more D.O.C. wine than any other region in Italy), Verona hosts the annual VinItaly wine fair held every April, a highly prestigious event in the global wine world. A number of authentic old-time wine bars still populate the medieval back streets of the fair city of Romeo and Juliet fame. First opened in 1890, the **Bottega del Vino** boasts a wine cellar holding an unmatched 80,000-bottle selection. Belly up to the old oak bar and sample from five dozen good-to-excellent wines for sale by the glass, particularly the Veronese trio of Bardolino and Valpolicella (reds) and Soave (white). **Masi** is one of the most respected producers, one of many in the Verona hills whose cantinas are open to the public for wine-tasting visits. See chapter 8.

- **Barolo** (Piemonte Wine Country): This romantic town is full of shops selling the village's rich red wines, held by many to be the most complex, powerful reds in Italy. The highlight is the **Castello di Barolo,** which houses a wine museum and enoteca in its cavernous cellars. See chapter 10.

- **Monterosso** (Italian Riviera): At the **Enoteca Internazionale** in this small, charming town in the Cinque Terre, you can taste local wines from the vineyards that cling to the nearby cliffs. See chapter 11.

7 The Best Hotel Deals

- **Navona** (Rome; ✆ **06-68211391**): The rooms at the Navona are not only pristine, tasteful, and decorated with limited-edition artworks, but they are located a stone's throw from the baroque wonders of Piazza Navona and right in the center of the historic quarter. Doubles begin at 135€ ($155). See chapter 3.

- **Albergo Firenze** (Florence; ✆ **055-268301**): A former student crash pad and today a renovated two-star choice that appeals to all age levels, the Firenze is ideally situated between the Duomo and the Piazza della Signoria. A fresh overall look, great bathrooms for the price range, and an address that beats the best put this hotel on every insider's shortlist. But don't expect a staff that's too professional or accommodating, or you'll leave disappointed. Starting at 83€ ($95) for a double with a bathroom, this is one of the *centro storico*'s best values. See chapter 4.

- **Piccolo Hotel Puccini** (Lucca, Tuscany; ℂ **0583-55421**): If you're planning a stay in Lucca, Giacomo Puccini's hometown, look no further than this charming three-star hotel in a 15th-century palazzo in front of the building where the great composer was born. Some of the hotel rooms overlook the small piazza and its bronze statue of Puccini. Paolo and Raffaella, the young and enthusiastic couple who run the place, have lightened and brightened it up and do everything to make this a perfect choice for those who appreciate tasteful attention and discreet professionalism. Piazza San Michele, one of Lucca's loveliest squares, is two steps away. Doubles start at 80€ ($92). See chapter 5.

- **Piccolo Hotel Etruria** (Siena, Tuscany; ℂ **0577-288088**): This recently refurbished hotel is lovely enough to be your base in Tuscany—at 78€ ($90) for a double, it's too great a find to be used as a mere 1-night stop. The proud Fattorini family oversaw every painstaking detail of its most recent renovation, and the taste and quality levels are something you usually find in hotels at thrice the cost. See chapter 5.

- **Borgonuovo Bed & Breakfast** (Ferrara, Emilia-Romagna; ℂ **0532-211100**): Outstanding hospitality and charm is the name of the game here. Starting at 85€ ($98), you can stay on a medieval palazzo in a guest room decorated with an eclectic mix of antiques.

The breakfasts served in the garden are feasts. See chapter 6.

- **Cappello** (Ravenna, Emilia-Romagna; ℂ **0544-219813**): This hotel is a true deal, considering what you get for 93€ ($107) per double. The best rooms have been carved out of grand salons and are enormous. The bathrooms are clad in marble or highly polished hardwoods, with luxurious stall showers and tubs, and, like the bedrooms, are lit with Venetian glass fixtures. See chapter 6.

- **La Cascina del Monastero** (La Morra, Piedmont Wine Country; ℂ **0173-509245**): What better way to spend your time in the wine country than to stay at a bed-and-breakfast at a farm that bottles wine and harvests fruit? Housed in a converted old and charismatic farm building, the rooms have exposed timbers and brass beds. Doubles run about 70€ to 76€ ($80–$87). See chapter 10.

- **Da Cecio** (Cinque Terre, Italian Riviera; ℂ **0187-812138**): After walking through the Cinque Terre, relax in your room at this old stone house in the countryside as you gaze out at the ocean, olive groves, and the nearby hilltop town of Corniglia. Doubles cost just 55€ ($63). See chapter 11.

- **Bella Capri** (Naples; ℂ **081-5529494**): Bella Capri is a clean, simple budget hotel ideally located for exploring Naples. Your touring plans will be a snap because the welcoming staff has gone out of its way to see that everything you could possibly get at the tourist information office is right here at the reception desk. You can also take breakfast on a private terrace overlooking the docks, all for as low as 62€ ($71) for a double. See chapter 12.

- **Il Monastero** (Ischia; ✆ 081-992435): Pretend you're Rapunzel in this converted convent atop a medieval rocky fortress. Evening and nighttime access to the hotel is via a long corridor and elevator, plus the short walk past the Chiesa dell'Immacolata to the hotel entrance. It's like having an entire castle to yourself. All rooms enjoy a sweeping panorama of Ischia Ponte and the sea. Doubles start at 110€ ($126). See chapter 12.

- **Trullidea** (Alberobello, Apulia; ✆ 080-4323860): Some hotels are clearly a destination in themselves, especially when UNESCO has declared them a national monument. Trullidea, a series of independent efficiencies under the conical stone roofs of the ancient *trulli* (beehive-shape dwellings), truly offers a peek into the lifestyles of the Alberobellese without requiring us to sacrifice even a whit of comfort. When the tour buses clear out, there's nothing left but you, a chatty neighbor, and an infinite cluster of twinkling stars. Doubles cost about 78€ ($90). See chapter 12.

- **Gran Bretagna** (Siracusa, Sicily; ✆ 0931-68765): No longer the intimate family-owned pensione of days gone by, the Gran Bretagna may have sacrificed character but not quality. Some rooms are frescoed, some are unusually spacious, and all are charming. It's still as warm and welcoming as before, only now all rooms have bathrooms, air-conditioning, TVs, and plenty of water pressure. Check out the old Spanish fortress walls beneath the ground floor on your way down to breakfast. Doubles are 100€ ($115). See chapter 13.

- **Villa Nettuno** (Taormina, Sicily; ✆ 0942-23797): For the best price-to-quality ratio in Taormina, the Nettuno wins, with doubles as low as 50€ ($58) off season. Grab a room with garden-terrace access for 'round-the-clock enjoyment of the postcard-perfect vistas of Taormina's cliffs and turquoise coast. See chapter 13.

8 The Best Affordable Hideaways by the Sea

- **La Camogliese** (Camogli, the Riviera Levante; ✆ 0185-771402): Call it a hideaway by the sea. Not only is this popular hotel near a beach, but the owner will also direct you to more hideaways along the nearby coast. Its location near the train station makes this attractive hotel especially convenient, and double rooms cost only 70€ to 75€ ($80–$86). See chapter 11.

- **Villa Rosa** (Positano; ✆ 089-811955): Aside from the great prices and kindly family management at this former *affittacamere,* the real attraction here is the view from your own bougainvillea-arbored sitting terrace across the inlet to a postcard-perfect shot of Positano's most photogenic quarter, the whitewashed and pastel cube houses climbing the headland in a jumble of balconies and flowers. The best part is realizing that you're paying only about 140€ ($160) for your double. You're getting a better view than the one from the famous Hotel Sireneuse across the street, for less than one-fifth the price. See chapter 12.

- **Villa Eva** (Anacapri; ✆ 081-8371549): Located in the hills above Anacapri and nowhere near Capri center, Villa Eva is the Isle of Capri's slice of paradise—a lush, exotic jungle thick with flowering vines and vegetation. If you don't stay here, you'll be sorry, even if the sea is a 20-minute walk away, just close enough for that pretwilight swim in the Blue Grotto. Doubles begin at 85€ ($98). See chapter 12.

- **La Tonnarella** (Sorrento; ℂ 081-8781153): Terraced below the quiet road leading out of town, La Tonnarella enjoys a stunning position high above the Bay of Sorrento, with views of the Sorrento headlands from almost every corner. Access to the beach at the base of the cliff is by elevator or via a lovely wooded path, and the grounds feature pine-shaded terraces and gardens for wandering about or enjoying a quiet meal. The hotel retains a 19th-century feel, with Oriental runners, loads of wood, and plenty of ceramic tile that give even the humblest of hotels a crisp elegance. Doubles cost 145€ ($167). See chapter 12.
- **Arathena Rocks Hotel** (Giardini-Naxos/Taormina, Sicily; ℂ 0942-51349): Set dramatically on the extreme tip of Punto Schisò, the Arathena Rocks Hotel is comfortably removed from the resort crowds of Giardini-Naxos, enjoying its private and jagged lava "beach." The terrace pool, set in a traditional sculpted Italian garden, provides an alternative to the rugged lava stones. It's only a 20-minute bus ride up to the colorful gardens and medieval streets of hilltop Taormina, where a hotelier would balk at the 55€ ($63) per person you're paying for such luxury, dinner included. See chapter 13.

- **Villa Nettuno** (Taormina, Sicily; ℂ 0942-23797): One of the last family-owned gems remaining in overdeveloped Taormina, Villa Nettuno retains its genteel, 19th-century character. The kindly Sciglio family is able to keep prices down—doubles are easy to take at 50€ to 70€ ($58–$80)—because they refuse to work with agencies and thus avoid having to pay commissions. The private and overgrown gardens climb the terraced hillside to an isolated stone gazebo, with its perfect panorama and savory solitude. With the cable car across the street, it's a quick and easy descent to the beaches of Mazzarò and Isola Bella. See chapter 13.

9 The Best Affordable Restaurants

- **Fiaschetteria Beltramme** (Rome; no phone): If you can find an empty table at this ultra-traditional seven-table bistro, it won't take long for you to become a parody of the 1950s caricature on the wall—the one of the rotund man pronouncing in Italian, "I can't believe I ate all that!" The recipes are hallowed, the service is consistent, and the decor is humble. See chapter 3.
- **Ditirambo** (Rome; ℂ 06-6871626): Run by a group of affable and handsome entrepreneurs, Ditirambo deviates from the nuts and bolts of traditional Roman cuisine, opening its palate to innovative and outstanding dishes representative of Italy's regional cooking. Reservations are essential. See chapter 3.
- **Il Latini** (Florence; ℂ 055-210916): Il Latini works hard to keep the air of an archetypal trattoria—long shared tables, hammocks hanging from the beamed ceiling—even if it has expanded to multiple rooms and tourists now know to flock here to join the local regulars in line for a table. There's no official set-price

menu—the waiters are inclined to simply serve you as much as you can eat and drink of their delicious crostini, thick soups and pastas, platters of roasted meats, desserts, bottomless wine and mineral water, even after-dinner grappa, and then just charge everyone at the table 28€ ($32) a head, an amazing price for a meal that will leave you stuffed for days and filled with fond memories for years. See chapter 4.

• **Da Giulio** (Lucca, Tuscany; ℭ 0583-55948): Delighted foreigners and locals in uncompromising allegiance agree that this big, airy, and forever busy trattoria is one of Tuscany's undisputed stars. Although casual, it's not the place to occupy a much-coveted table for just a pasta and salad. Save up your appetite and come for a full-blown home-style feast of *la cucina toscana,* trying all of Giulio's traditional rustic specialties. Waiters know not to recommend certain local delicacies to non-Italian diners, unless you look like the type that enjoys tripe, *tartara di cavallo* (horsemeat tartare), or veal snout. See chapter 5.

• **Osteria le Logge** (Siena, Tuscany; ℭ 0577-48013): This convivial and highly recommended Sienese trattoria is two steps off the gorgeous Piazza del Campo and a well-known destination for locals and well-informed visitors who join the standing-room-only scenario of those who keep this place packed. Its delicious *pasta fresca* (fresh homemade pasta) launches each memorable meal, with entrees that are all about the simple perfection of grilled meats. The excellent choice of extra-virgin olive oil is enough to confirm the affable owner's seriousness, seconded by a small but discerning wine list that

is topped by his own limited production of Rosso and Brunello di Montepulciano. See chapter 5.

• **Olindo Faccioli** (Bologna; ℭ 051-223171): This intimate, inconspicuous restaurant has a limited but delightful menu. The specials lean toward a light, vegetarian cuisine, but the starter of tuna carpaccio will satisfy fish eaters as well. You can linger here as you decide which of the 400 vintages of wine will go best with your meal. See chapter 6.

• **Al Brindisi** (Ferrara; ℭ 0532-209142): This just may be the oldest wine bar in the world—it's been around since 1435. The two timbered dining rooms are stacked to the ceiling with wine bottles, and, for 1.50€ ($1.70) and up, you can choose a glass from this overwhelming selection. Have some appetizers, sausage, or pumpkin ravioli with your wine, or go for the whole shebang with one of the many tourist and tasting menus, which include a feast of appetizers, a special main course of the day, dessert, and a carafe of wine, all for 9€ to 40€ ($10–$46). See chapter 6.

• **Osteria dal Duca** (Verona; ℭ 045-594474): There are no written records to confirm that this 13th-century palazzo was once owned by the Montecchi (Montague) family, and thankfully the discreet management never considered calling this place the "Ristorante Romeo." But here you are in "fair Verona," nonetheless, dining in what is believed to be Romeo's house, a characteristic medieval palazzo, and enjoying one of the nicest meals in town in a spirited and friendly neighborhood ambience fueled by the amiable family that keeps this place abuzz. It will be simple, it will be delicious, you'll probably make friends with the people sitting next to you, and you'll always remember your meal at Romeo's restaurant. See chapter 8.

- **Cantine Sanremese** (San Remo, Italian Riviera; ℰ **0184-572063**): Old habits die hard at the Cantine Sanremese, so come here to sample traditional, homemade Ligurian cuisine. Instead of ordering main dishes, sample the *sardemaira* (the local focaccia-like bread), *torte verde* (a quiche of fresh green vegetables), or any of their delicious soups, including minestrone thick with fresh vegetables and garnished with pesto. See chapter 11.

- **De Mananan** (Corniglia, Italian Riviera; ℰ **0187-821166**): In this intimate restaurant, which is carved into an ancient stone cellar, the owners/chefs use only the finest ingredients to prepare homemade specialties such as pesto, *funghi porcini* (wild porcini mushrooms), mussels, grilled fish, fresh anchovies stuffed with herbs, and *coniglio nostrano* (rabbit roasted in a white sauce). See chapter 11.

- **Cucina Casareccia** (Lecce, Apulia; ℰ **0832-245178**): Dining at this tiny trattoria makes you feel as if you should have brought along a bottle of wine: Concetta Cantoro treats customers as if they were guests in her own home, and

husband Marcello is a fine host. Leave the menu selection to the experts, and sit back and enjoy. See chapter 12.

- **Antica Focacceria San Francesco** (Palermo, Sicily; ℰ **091-320264**): "Slumming it" has never been so fun. This over-lit, high-ceilinged joint resembles a waiting room more than a restaurant and serves up some of the heaviest, greasiest, finger-lickingest food I've ever eaten (though I'll probably pass on the spleen next time). You won't get much more authentic Palermitano then this. See chapter 13.

- **La Forchetta** (Agrigento, Sicily; ℰ **0922-596266**): Every inch the traditional neighborhood trattoria, La Forchetta has true Sicilian character and excellent home cooking. Matriarch Mamma Giuseppa is a genuine blast, haranguing the waitstaff (often her sons) one minute and graciously greeting you the next. See chapter 13.

- **Zza** (Siracusa, Sicily; ℰ **0931-22204**): I will never have the opportunity to thank the train conductor for recommending this overlooked gem. The authentic fare—detailed in local dialect (with translations)—provided one of my most memorable meals in Sicily, at a price so low I'm sorry they don't ship overnight. See chapter 13.

10 The Best Cafes

- **Sant'Eustachio** (Rome): Famed for its froth, Sant'Eustachio is consistently packed at least three deep at the bar, with everyone clamoring for a shot of the special blend. No one ever leaves, and it's no wonder: There's so little coffee beneath all that foam that you have to keep getting refills to get a decent amount of coffee! While

you wait, the shop obliges with a tiny glass-case display of delectable coffee paraphernalia, all reasonably priced. See chapter 3.

- **Caffè Rivoire** (Florence): The pudding-rich hot chocolate of Florence's premier historical cafe is second to the real reason for a visit: its dead-on view of the city's greatest piazza and a front-row seat for people-watching. The ambience is Old World inside and out: The stately Palazzo Vecchio looms in front of outdoor tables and the piazza's most celebrated statue, a copy of Michelangelo's fabled *David.* Inside it's cozy and elegant, and no one raises an eyebrow if you nurse a tea for several hours. See chapter 4.

- **Historic Cafes of Piazza San Marco** (Venice): The nostalgic 18th-century **Caffè Florian** is the most famous cafe on this stunning piazza. But the truth is, if the weather is lovely and the other three cafes have moved their hundreds of tables outdoors, the piazza becomes one big Bellini-sipping, people-watching stage, with St. Mark's Basilica as its singular backdrop. Around the corner, just in front of the Palazzo Ducale, is the **Caffè Chioggia,** the only cafe with a view of the water and the Clock Tower, whose bronze Moors began striking the hour again after a 5-year renovation in 1999. Each of the piazza cafes has its own three- or four-piece orchestrina, but the music at the Chioggia is held to be the best and least commercial (no "New York, New York" here). See chapter 7.

- **Antico Caffè Dante** (Verona): The interior of Verona's oldest cafe is rather formal and expensive, but set up camp here at an outdoor table in Verona's loveliest piazza, named for the early Renaissance man of letters whose statue commemorates his love for the city and the ruling Scalageri family who hosted him during his years of exile. If you're lucky enough to hold tickets for the opera in the city's 2,000-year-old Arena amphitheater, this is the traditional spot for an after-opera drink to complete, and contemplate, the evening's magic. See chapter 8.

- **Antica Pasticceria Gelateria Klainguti** (Genoa): Verdi enjoyed Genoa's oldest and best bakery. You probably will, too, for its Falstaff (a sweet brioche) and stupefying selection of pastries and chocolates. See chapter 11.

- **Gran Caffè Gambrinus** (Naples): This courtly 19th-century bastion of Neapolitan society recaptures the golden age of Naples. See chapter 12.

2

Planning an Affordable Trip to Italy

The days when Italy was an idyllic, dirt-cheap destination for good food and countless treasures have passed, but there are still inexpensive ways to enjoy its wonders as well as its incomparable *dolce vita*. With some flexibility and advance planning, a moderate budget can go a long way. This chapter shows you how to get your trip together and get on the road.

1 Fifty Money-Saving Tips

This chapter is full of money-saving hints, insider information, contacts, and expertise accumulated over the authors' innumerable fact-finding trips. You'll enjoy your trip even more knowing that you're getting the biggest bang for your buck, easily keeping your costs for accommodations (let's say breakfast is included), lunch, and dinner to as little as $90 per day. (We assume that two adults are traveling together and that, between the two of you, you have $180 to spend. Traveling alone has other pluses and drawbacks but usually turns out to be slightly more expensive, mostly due to the hotel factor.) The costs of transportation, activities, sightseeing, and entertainment are extra, but we have plenty of insider tips to save you money on those activities as well.

It's hard to go wrong in Italy and so easy to go right if you give some heed to the following tips.

WHEN TO GO

1. So the weather isn't always a perfect 75°F and the skies aren't always cloud free. But **off-season Italy** promises the biggest cuts in airfare, the beauty of popping up at small hotels (more discounted rates) without needing a reservation confirmed 3 months in advance, enjoying the blessed absence of lines at the museums, and finding the local people less harried and more accommodating. For more details on high- versus low-season travel, see "When to Go," later in this chapter.

PACKAGE DEALS, INTERNATIONAL & DOMESTIC TRAVEL

2. An enjoyable, affordable trip begins long before you leave home. Do your cyber homework: Surf the **Internet** and save. There are lots and lots of Web pages and online services designed to clue you in on discounted airfares, accommodations, and car rentals. See "Planning Your Trip Online," later in this chapter, for some sites that offer real deals.

3. Prefer the face-to-face help of a professional? No problem. Visit a reliable **travel agency;** they often have access to deals and packages you wouldn't find on your own. It doesn't cost you a thing, and there's no obligation to buy. It never hurts to ask.

4. When calling the airlines directly, always ask for the lowest possible fare. Be flexible in your schedule—flying on weekdays versus weekends, or even at a different time of day, can make a substantial difference. Find out the exact dates of the seasonal rates; these differ from airline to airline even though the destination stays the same. Some flights into or out of Rome versus Milan may differ in price. Don't forget to ask about discounts for seniors, students, or children.

5. Buy your ticket well in advance. Most airlines discount tickets are purchased 7, 14, or 21 days before the departure dates.

6. Or buy your ticket at the last minute—something best recommended if you have a flexible schedule and are traveling off season when availability is more probable. See "Planning Your Trip Online," later in this chapter, for information on last-minute Internet airfares.

7. Be an educated traveler. Read the travel section of your local newspaper (especially weekend editions) for special promotional fares and discounts.

8. Check your newspaper for consolidators or wholesalers, once more frequently known as "bucket shops." These companies operate by alleviating blocks of unsold tickets from the major international airlines. It's still not a bad idea to check their records first with the Better Business Bureau, but most operate firmly aboveboard and offer substantial savings, particularly off season: See those we list in the section "Flying for Less: Tips for Getting the Best Airfare," later in this chapter.

9. Check escorted trips and package deals. Escorted tours are structured group tours, with a group leader. They are ideal for those who prefer the security of traveling with a group and don't want to be bothered with the details. Even if you're not a groupie, the air and hotel savings alone make escorted tours worth considering; in fact, many trips are unstructured enough to let you split from the group and do your own thing. You might even wind up preferring the companionship of the others on board and the luxury of having every day's bothersome details prearranged. Air/hotel packages (often offered by the airlines themselves) also offer great savings, though hotels are sometimes on the outskirts of towns (hence the big discounts); check their locations first if this is important to you. See "Packages for the Independent Traveler," "Escorted General-Interest Tours," and "Special-Interest Vacations," later in this chapter, for a list of operators that offer trips to Italy.

10. Domestic or one-way flights within Italy (or Europe) can be killers. The most distant flights within Italy (Venice to Palermo, for example) might be contenders for air travel, but opt for the train at a fraction of the cost, breaking up your travel times with overnight stops planned along the way. There is never a shortage of sights between any two points.
    All major airports have rail or bus service to get you to and from downtown—Rome and Pisa's convenient trains pull right into the airport itself. Taxis are expensive though tempting to jet-lagged travelers laden with luggage.

11. Which reminds us: Travel lightly! You'll never wear or need half of the stuff you're convinced you can't live without. The inconvenience you'll find at every turn is what you'll remember long after

your trip! What you'll save on cabs, porters, and energy can be considerable. Never take more than you can carry single-handedly when running for a bus or train.

12. Train travel in Italy has improved immeasurably since the 1970s and 1980s. The newer **Intercity** trains are clean and efficient enough to make second-class travel a near first-class experience. The fancy, fast-paced **EuroStar** trains can cut speed, but is a 1-hour (or less) difference worth the extra cost?

13. Map out your strategy before you leave to see if a **rail pass** will save you or cost you money (you can find a list of the various Italian ones offered, as well as purchase them, at www.raileurope.com). On long international stretches of train travel, the former is usually true. Within Italy, buying second-class point-to-point tickets as you go may save you money. Most rail passes are cheapest when purchased at home before you leave.

14. Use **public transportation** in cities rather than taxis. It offers a peek into the daily lifestyles of the local residents. Most concentrated historical districts make sightseeing most enjoyable when done on foot; in the large cities like Rome or Milan, consider daily or weekly passes for unlimited travel on buses or subways.

CAR RENTALS

15. Call around to all the major car-rental agencies; promotional rates sometimes make the big boys the best. Make a reservation before you leave home, but make one last inquiry before getting on the plane to see if any new, lower rates have been introduced in the meantime. Making your reservation before you leave for Italy is almost always a guaranteed money saver.

16. Ask questions about waivers and insurance suggested and required by the rental agency, and then check with your **credit card company** to see what they offer before booking. Don't wind up paying for the same coverage twice or getting charged for extraneous coverage that is recommended but not obligatory.

17. Aim for the least expensive economy car category (unless you'll be driving long autostrada stretches when it will seem you're standing still as virtually every other vehicle zips by). If you're told an economy car is unavailable in an attempt to have you book the next most expensive model, call elsewhere. Know in advance that almost all rental cars in Italy are stick shift; booking an automatic transmission—if any are available—will hike the price considerably. Air-conditioning will also cost extra, so consider the weather you'll be encountering.

18. Book the weekly rates to save—but keep in mind parking costs inside the cities. Booking a car for just a day or so sojourn in the country can be an expensive venture. But booking for a longer period, only to have the car sit in an expensive parking lot (almost all historic centers now ban car traffic entirely), makes little sense either. Weigh the variables to see what's most economical for you. If you plan to spend a week in a city and a week in the country, have your car booked for the day you leave the city.

19. **Parking** is a nightmare in Italy, and the police are serious about enforcing tow-away zones. Don't try to conserve parking-lot costs by parking on the streets if you're not sure what the street signs say (a red slashed circle filled in with blue means no parking; spaces

painted with blue lines mean you have to pay, either at a meter or to a parking official; yellow lines mean handicapped parking; white lines mean you need a local permit, which, only if you're lucky, your hotel can supply). The cost of retrieving a towed car is only half as bad as the hassle of trying to find it and get it back without the incident ruining your entire trip.

20. If you decide to rent once you're already in Italy, check out the prices and then call a friend back home and ask him or her to book for you from there if the rates are less; they almost always are.

21. Always return your rental car full of gas, or the rental agency will charge you for it, usually at top euro. Don't have heart failure at the cost of gas *(benzina)* in Italy: It is some of Europe's most expensive. The cars get excellent mileage, however, and you won't have to fill up often.

22. The largest cities may have car-rental offices at both the airport and downtown. There is often an extra charge to pick up at one and drop off at another; using downtown branches is almost always cheaper. To pick up and drop off in two different cities is even worse. In two different countries—better take the train.

ACCOMMODATIONS

23. If you're traveling during high season (roughly Easter through Sept or Oct), book early. You won't get any discounts, but you won't be forced to spend more by upgrading just to find a vacancy in town.

24. If the idea doesn't faze you, consider a less expensive room with a shared bathroom instead of an en suite private bathroom. Ask how many rooms will be sharing the bathroom—sometimes it is as few

as two; if the other room is vacant, the bathroom will be yours alone.

25. Many of the hotels listed in this book don't advertise seasonal rates, but some discount is usually offered during the slow periods. Always ask. The more nights you stay, the more you're likely to get a discount. The way you approach the subject is very important: A smile and a pretty-please upon check-in is always more successful than a hard-nosed demand. If it's a slow month and late afternoon, the advantage is yours.

26. Don't underestimate the power of Frommer's. Mention of this book in your faxed request or a flash of the book upon check-in will notify the hotel from whence you come. Most of the worthier hotels we list year after year are very appreciative of the volume and quality of travelers (that's you) that we bring to their establishments, and they're apt to do their best to accommodate you when and if possible.

27. Is your room so dismal you could just cry? Keep cool and polite, but voice your disappointment and ask if you can be shown another room. Be specific about what bothers you—a different room might have a firmer mattress or brighter lighting that would better meet your needs. You might even get upgraded at no extra cost. Don't resort to drama and histrionics.

28. Single rooms in Italy can be downright minuscule. If you're traveling alone and it's off season, ask if the management might be so kind as to offer you a double room at a single occupancy rate. Many of them will if the rooms are available; always ask.

29. Before arranging your own parking, check first with your hotel. Hotels often have a standing deal with a nearby parking facility. In

Venice, hotels will give you a voucher to present at the parking lots on the outskirts of town.

30. **Breakfast.** Is it included or not? Always ask, and ask if it is continental or buffet. If they expect you to pay 5€ ($5.75) per person (for example) for a prepackaged month-old *cornetto* (croissant) and cup of mediocre coffee, check out the charming outdoor cafe down the block instead. If the self-service, all-you-can-eat buffet of cold cuts, fresh rolls, juice, yogurt, and—well, you get the drift—is offered in a *simpatico* setting and will keep you going till dinner, dig in, enjoy yourself, and grab an apple for the road.

31. Never make **telephone calls** from your room if you can avoid it, especially long-distance ones. The service charge and taxes tagged on to the briefest call home will ruin the moment of enjoyment it brought. Use calling cards at public phones or arrange to have your family call you at designated hours. Or rent or buy a cellphone with global-roaming capabilities.

32. The "frigo bar" **(minibar)** is a mixed blessing. That Diet Coke *(Coca Lite)* and Toblerone candy bar can set you back an easy $10. Check the price list before giving in to hunger pangs, and know what you're about to eat—it might not taste that good.

33. Each hotel's policy regarding **children** is different, so be specific regarding your kids' ages when you book: Generally speaking, children under 12 (sometimes 10) stay for free in the parents' room. Remember: There's no fudging the children's age with the obligatory presentation of the passport upon check-in.

EATING

34. Take advantage of Italy's cornucopia of excellent bakeries and food stores, and make every lunch a picnic. Yes, you'll save more to spend on dinner, but you'll also wind up enjoying a four-star lunch in an opera-set piazza.

35. It's lunchtime and it's rainy or cold, or you just need to sit indoors for a while, but an expensive meal is out of your budget. Italy is slowly leaning toward the affordable quick lunch. Bars and cafes are serving informal lunches of pastas and salads as much to local merchants and workers as to cost-conscious travelers, usually for 6€ to 7€ ($6.90–$8.05) or less.

36. If you're running over your day's budget (sometimes it's hard to stay away from that Italian leather!), remember that this is the country that gave us pizza and wine. Find a pizzeria with outdoor seating, order a carafe of the house wine *(vino della casa),* and eat like a king (spend like a poor man). Save your three-course trattoria meal for a more solvent day.

37. Tourist menus *(menu turistico)* or fixed-price menus *(menu a prezzo fisso)* sound like a good deal and often are. But portions may be smaller, choices less varied or uninspired (expect the ubiquitous spaghetti with tomato sauce and roast chicken). Menus are usually posted in restaurant windows, so peruse your choices before entering and ordering.

38. If you aren't accustomed to eating so much but want to taste it all, order a *mezza porzione* (half portion) of pasta for your first course so you have room left for your second course—and be charged accordingly. Most restaurants will gladly oblige.

39. The rule of thumb in this cafe society: Always expect to pay more at a table than at the bar, more at an outdoor table (consider it your

cover charge for the free piazza-life entertainment). That said, don't expect to be rushed: For the cost of an iced tea or mineral water, you can sit and write postcards for hours and never overstay your welcome.

40. If you've been snacking all day and would be happy with just a good plate of pasta and not a full-blown repast, make sure you choose your restaurant well. You might anger some establishments if you occupy a table for a single-course dinner and not the full 9 yards. Casual, informal neighborhood joints won't give a second thought if you want to linger over a simple pasta, salad, and glass of wine.

   House wines can be surprisingly good and inexpensive. Enjoying a good bottled wine will bring your bill up a notch, but hey, that's probably what you're visiting Italy for anyway. Stick with wines of the region, and experiment with some of the small-time, lesser-known (but not necessarily less sophisticated) wine producers of the area. If you're really strapped for cash, go with the mineral water, then stop off at a wine bar after dinner and choose one very special cru-by-the-glass in a con-vivial *ambiente*.

SIGHTSEEING

41. Make a beeline for the **Tourist Information Office** to check out special events, free concerts, arts festivals, and so on, to maximize your (always too brief) stay in town. Some museums offer one evening a week free. Outdoor evening or church concerts are free, not infrequent, and lovely. Ask your hotel staff; they are often more helpful and informed than the tourism people.

42. To get the most out of always-increasing **museum admissions,** see if you can buy tickets in advance to eliminate waiting in line. Always ask about senior and student discounts. Extended hours for summer months are often confirmed at the last minute (and, therefore, are not reflected in guidebooks) and are not widely publicized: If you're in the know, you might have Florence's Uffizi Galleries to yourself at 10 in the evening—put a price on that! Speaking of which, many muse-ums are often open for free 1 day a month (it'll be crowded but, well, free). You can find this info and more like it at www.europe forfree.com.

43. More and more cities are offering joint tickets or passes for both major and minor museums. You might be able to get admission to as many as 10 museums over an open period of time. But study which museums are included—they are often obscure and esoteric collections that are of little interest or inconveniently located for the tourist on a tight schedule.

44. Free, do-it-yourself walking tours are a viable substitute for the expensive, escorted tours. But the latter are worth your while if your time in town is extremely limited and the sites are many. Before signing up for a half- or full-day tour, find out exactly which sites will be visited so you don't miss those of most interest to you.

45. Don't shortchange yourself on **people-watching** in Italy, the sin-gle great pastime that has been perfected here as an art form, and the best free entertainment you're bound to see anywhere. Pull up a cafe chair and settle in; to avoid any charge at all, a piazza bench will do fine.

SHOPPING

46. Before splurging on that fragile glassware from Venice or hand-painted ceramic platter from

Deruta, consider the cost of **shipping,** which can double an otherwise respectable price. Do you really want to carry a package around for the rest of your trip? Some stores don't offer shipping at all, and doing the job yourself (buying packing supplies and so on) can be troublesome and time consuming. Insurance hikes the cost even further.

47. Pay by credit card as often as possible: The fewer transaction fees (incurred by ATMs or changing traveler's checks to cash) incurred, the more saved.

48. Alas, **bargaining** in Italy, once a theatrical and generally enjoyable part of every purchase, is fast becoming a dying animal. But if you're buying more than one item, paying by cash or traveler's checks, are in an open-air market, and/or have struck up a friendly banter with the merchant, give it a shot. The best time to test your talents is during the slow months, when the shop looks like it's hungry for business.

49. Don't forget to cash in on your **value-added tax (VAT; IVA** in Italy) if you qualify. Millions of dollars of unclaimed refunds are the result of forgetful or uninformed tourists.

50. By now the world is a village. Be realistic about what you can and cannot find back home among the legion of made-in-Italy **souvenirs** you're dying to snatch up. Do you really want to spend a precious afternoon in Florence tracking down a pair of black leather gloves that are a dime a dozen at home, when your time could be far better spent gazing upon the wonder of Michelangelo's *David?*

2 The Regions in Brief

Italy as we know it was united only in the 1860s, and people still tend to identify themselves more as, say, Romans, Tuscans, or Sicilians than as Italians. Regional dialects are so diverse and strong that for a Neapolitan to converse with a Milanese, he has to resort to the common "textbook Italian" learned in school.

Here's a quick rundown of the regions covered in this guide to help you understand the country and aid you in deciding where you want to visit.

ROME & LAZIO
Lazio (Latium) and its capital, **Rome (Roma),** are at the center of Italy and, some say, of the Western world. Rome is where the philosophy and traditions of the ancient Greek east met the pragmatism of the robust west to form one of the world's greatest empires. Rome is an intricate layering of ancient, medieval, Renaissance, baroque, and modern cities. You can scramble about the Colosseum and Forum, explore churches filled with baroque paintings by Caravaggio, gawk at Michelangelo's Sistine ceiling frescoes, or simply enjoy a gelato under the shade of a Bernini-designed fountain.

FLORENCE & TUSCANY
Beautiful, magically lit **Tuscany (Toscana)** was the cradle of the Renaissance, producing such artistic geniuses as Giotto, Leonardo, Michelangelo, and Botticelli. From the rolling vineyards of the Chianti and wide valley of the Arno River rise one wonder after another: **Florence (Firenze),** capital of the Renaissance; **Siena,** city of Gothic painters and medieval palaces; **Pisa,** with its Romanesque cathedral and famously leaning tower; and dozens of other art-filled hill towns.

The Regions of Italy

UMBRIA

St. Francis was born in **Umbria,** the green heart of Italy, and perhaps his gentle nature derived from the region's serene hills and valleys, a sun-blessed landscape similar to that of its neighbor, Tuscany. The capital city of **Perugia** strikes a happy balance between medieval hill town, Renaissance art center, and bustling modern university city. Other Umbrian towns include such marvelously medieval centers as **Gubbio** and **Spoleto,** as well as that early Renaissance gem **Assisi.**

BOLOGNA & EMILIA-ROMAGNA

History has left its mark on the central region of **Emilia-Romagna,** riding along the north of the Apennine Mountains to the Po Valley. **Ravenna** was the last capital of the empire and later the stronghold of the Byzantines and the Visigoths. **Ferrara** was a center of Renaissance art and culture, while **Parma,** one of the most powerful duchies in Europe under the Farnese family, is a famed producer of parmigiano reggiano cheese and prosciutto ham. **Bologna** has been renowned for its university since the Middle Ages, and for its fine cuisine throughout history.

VENICE, THE VENETO & SOUTH TYROL

The Po River created the vast floodplain of the **Veneto** under the brow of pre-Venetian Alps to the north and the Dolomites in the west. What draws visitors to these agricultural flatlands are the art treasures of **Padua (Padova),** the Renaissance villas of Palladio in **Vicenza,** and—rising on pilings from a lagoon on the Adriatic coast—that year-round carnival and most serene city of canals, **Venice (Venezia).** The **Dolomites,** bordering Austria, cap the eastern stretches of the **South Tyrol** region with sharp pinnacles straight out of a fairy tale, while the peaks of the Alps crown the west. This region is home to legendary resorts like **Cortina d'Ampezzo** and **Merano,** as well as cities like **Trent (Trento)** and **Bolzano** that lie at the crossroads of the German and Italian worlds.

MILAN & LOMBARDY

Lombardy **(Lombardia)** is Italy's wealthiest province, an industrial, financial, and agricultural powerhouse named for the Lombards, a Germanic people who migrated south over the Alps in the Dark Ages. Beyond its Po Valley factories and cities, the scenic diversity of this prosperous region ranges from legendary lakes like **Como** and **Maggiore** backed by Alpine peaks to the fertile plains of the Po River. The region's capital, **Milan (Milano)**—hotbed of high fashion, high finance, and avant-garde design—is a city of great art and architecture as well (Leonardo's *The Last Supper* is but the beginning), and the region's Renaissance past is still much in evidence in **Cremona, Mantua,** and the other cities of the Lombard plains.

PIEMONTE & THE VALLE D'AOSTA

Piemonte (Piedmont) means "foot of the mountains," and the Alps are in sight from almost every parcel of Italy's northernmost province, which borders Switzerland and France. The flat plains of the Po River rise into rolling hills clad with orchards and vineyards. North of **Turin**—the historic, baroque capital of the region and host of the 2006 Winter Olympics, and, with its auto factories, a cornerstone of Italy's "economic miracle"—the plains meet the Alps headon in the **Valle d'Aosta,** with its craggy mountains, craggy mountain folks, and year-round skiing.

LIGURIA & THE ITALIAN RIVIERA

The **Italian Riviera** follows the Ligurian Sea along a narrow coastal band backed by mountains. At the center of the rocky coast of **Liguria** is **Genoa (Genova),** the country's first port and still its most important—a fascinating city that greets visitors with a remarkable assemblage of Renaissance art and architecture. Some of Italy's most famous seaside retreats flank Genoa on either side: from the tony resort of **San Remo** on France's doorstep all the way down to the picturesque string of fishing villages known as the **Cinque Terre** that line the coast just above Tuscany.

CAMPANIA

Welcome to the good life: **Campania** has been a refuge for the world-weary for over 2,000 years, from imperial Roman villas to modern resort towns. Campania wraps around **Naples (Napoli)**—that chaotic but beautiful city often overlooked on the grand tour—and is rimmed by the gorgeous **Amalfi Coast** with its necklace of comely villages: ravishing **Ravello,** historic **Amalfi,** and posh **Positano.** The seductive isles of **Capri** and **Ischia** lie just offshore. In A.D. 79, Campania's menacing volcano Mount Vesuvius rained tons of ash on the Roman port of **Pompeii,** preserving it as an evocative ghost town offering a unique glimpse into ancient civilization.

APULIA

This is the very sole of Italy, the bottom of the boot. **Apulia (Pulia),** running the length of the boot heel, puts the lie to the "poor south" reputation of southern Italy—10% of the world's supply of olive oil comes from here, and its ports are some of the Mediterranean's busiest. The region's austerely beautiful scenery, whitewashed buildings, and serene beaches have begun attracting visitors in much larger numbers.

SICILY

A mountainous triangle at the crossroads of the Mediterranean (and its largest island), **Sicily (Sicilia)** sits just a few kilometers off the tip of Italy's toe—and only a few dozen from Tunisia, swept by both the cold *tramontana* winds from the north and the parched, sandy *scirocco* winds off the Sahara. A landscape at once fertile and foreboding, lush and harsh, Sicily has hosted every Mediterranean civilization from the Greeks and Islamic North Africans through the Spanish Bourbons to today's Italians (with the Romans, Normans, Austrians, and, yes, the Mafia, in between). The past 3,000 years have imparted upon this island of lemons, olives, and almonds a rich heritage to enjoy, from Greek temples to mosaic-filled Norman cathedrals, Moorish palaces to tony seaside resorts.

3 Visitor Information

TOURIST OFFICES

For general information in your home country, try your local branch of the **Italian Government Tourist Board (ENIT)** or the ENIT-sponsored website www.enit.it. The North American site is www.italiantourism.com. Some Frommer's readers have reported that the office isn't really that helpful.

In the United States: 630 Fifth Ave., Suite 1565, New York, NY 10111 (© **212/245-4822** or 212/245-5618; fax 212/586-9249); 500 N. Michigan Ave., Suite 2240 Chicago, IL 60611 (© **312/644-0996** or 312/644-0990; fax 312/644-3019); and 12400 Wilshire Blvd., Suite 550, Los Angeles, CA 90025 (© **310/820-1898** or 310/820-9807; fax 310/820-6357).

In Canada: 175 Bloor St. East, Suite 907, South Tower, Toronto, ON

M4W 3R8 (© **416/925-4882;** fax 416/925-4799; enit.canada@on.aibn. com).

In the United Kingdom: 1 Princes St., London W1B 2AY England (© **207/399-3562;** italy@italian touristboard.co.uk).

USEFUL WEBSITES

Each city and town in this book lists its own websites for visitor information, and you can find plenty of other official links at the **Italian Government Tourist Board**'s site, **www.italiantourism.com**.

Good general websites include **In Italy On-line (www.initaly.com)**, with details on accommodations, tours, festivals, shopping, and more; the **Italian Tourist Web Guide (www. itwg.com)**, with online hotel reservations and information on art and history; and **Italy in a Flash (www. italyflash.com)**, offering hotel information, railway and airline schedules, the latest exchange rates, weather, and current news.

4 Entry Requirements & Customs

ENTRY REQUIREMENTS

U.S., U.K., Irish, Canadian, Australian, and New Zealand citizens with a **valid passport** don't need a visa to enter Italy if they don't expect to stay more than 90 days and don't expect to work there. If after entering Europe you find you want to stay more than 90 days, you can apply for a permit for an extra 90 days, which as a rule is granted immediately. Go to your home country's consulate.

In these halcyon days of the European Union, there are no more border controls between countries within the E.U. (except for the island nations of the U.K. and the Republic of Ireland), or when crossing into Norway or Iceland (neither of which are E.U.). That said, in these security-obsessed times, airport arrivals are often scrutinized regardless.

Switzerland, however—which is not a member of the E.U., nor even of the U.N.—does keep border guards, making it one of the few places where you still must undergo a passport check even when driving into the country. The same holds for the three Eastern European nations—Bulgaria, Romania, and Turkey—that are still waiting in the wings for E.U. membership.

No matter where you are, if your passport is lost or stolen, head to your consulate as soon as possible for a replacement.

Passport specifics, and downloadable applications, can be found on the Internet at the following sites: **www.travel.state.gov** (U.S.), **www. ppt.gc.ca** (Canada), **www.passports. gov.uk** (U.K.), **http://foreignaffairs. gov.ie/services/passports** (Ireland), **www.passports.gov.au** (Australia),

---

Tips Passport Savvy

Allow plenty of time before your trip to apply for a passport; processing usually takes 3 weeks but can take longer during busy periods (especially spring). And keep in mind that if you need a passport in a hurry, you'll pay a higher processing fee. When traveling, safeguard your passport in an inconspicuous, inaccessible place like a money belt and keep a copy of the critical pages with your passport number in a separate place. If you lose your passport, visit the nearest consulate of your native country as soon as possible for a replacement.

and **www.passports.govt.nz** (New Zealand).

CUSTOMS

WHAT YOU CAN BRING INTO ITALY Foreign visitors can bring along most items for personal use duty free, including fishing tackle; a sporting gun and 200 cartridges; a pair of skis; two tennis racquets; a baby carriage; two hand cameras with 10 rolls of film; and 200 cigarettes or 50 cigars or pipe tobacco not exceeding 250 grams. There are strict limits on importing alcoholic beverages. However, limits are much more liberal for alcohol bought tax paid in other countries of the European Union.

WHAT YOU CAN BRING HOME For U.S. Citizens Returning U.S. citizens who have been away for at least 48 hours are allowed to bring back, once every 30 days, $800 worth of merchandise duty free. You'll be charged a flat rate of duty on the next $1,000 worth of purchases. Any dollar amount beyond that is dutiable at whatever rates apply. On mailed gifts, the duty-free limit is $200. Be sure to have your receipts or purchases handy to expedite the declaration process. *Note:* If you owe duty, you are required to pay on your arrival in the United States, by either cash, personal check, government or traveler's check, money order, or, in some locations, a Visa or MasterCard.

To avoid having to pay duty on foreign-made personal items you owned before you left on your trip, bring along a bill of sale, insurance policy, jeweler's appraisal, or receipts of purchase. Or you can register items that can be readily identified by a permanently affixed serial number or marking—think laptop computers, cameras, and CD players—with Customs before you leave. Take the items to the nearest Customs office or register them with Customs at the airport from which you're departing. You'll

receive, at no cost, a Certificate of Registration, which allows duty-free entry for the life of the item.

With some exceptions, you cannot bring fresh fruits and vegetables into the United States. For specifics on what you can bring back, download the invaluable free pamphlet *Know Before You Go* online at **www.cbp.gov**. (Click on "Travel," and then click on "Know Before You Go!" online brochure.) Or contact the **U.S. Customs & Border Protection (CBP)**, 1300 Pennsylvania Ave. NW, Washington, DC 20229 (© **877/287-8667**), and request the pamphlet.

For British Citizens **Citizens of the U.K.** who are **returning from a European Union (E.U.) country** will go through a separate Customs exit (called the "Blue Exit") especially for E.U. travelers. In essence, there is no limit on what you can bring back from a E.U. country, as long as the items are for personal use (this includes gifts) and you have already paid the necessary duty and tax. However, Customs law sets out guidance levels. If you bring in more than these levels, you may be asked to prove that the goods are for your own use. Guidance levels on goods bought in the E.U. for your own use are 3,200 cigarettes, 200 cigars, 400 cigarillos, 3 kilograms of smoking tobacco, 10 liters of spirits, 90 liters of wine, 20 liters of fortified wine (such as port or sherry), and 110 liters of beer. For more information, contact HM Customs & Excise at © **0845/010-9000** (from outside the U.K., 020/8929-0152), or consult their website at www.hmce.gov.uk.

For Canadian Citizens For a clear summary of **Canadian** rules, write for the booklet *I Declare,* issued by the **Canada Customs and Revenue Agency** (© **800/461-9999** in Canada, or 204/983-3500; www.ccra-adrc.gc.ca). Canada allows its citizens a C$750 exemption, and you're allowed to bring back duty free one carton of cigarettes, one can of tobacco, 40 imperial ounces of liquor, and 50 cigars. In addition, you're allowed to mail gifts to Canada valued at less than C$60 a day, provided they're unsolicited and don't contain alcohol or tobacco (write on the package "Unsolicited gift, under C$60 value"). All valuables should be declared on the Y-38 form before departure from Canada, including serial numbers of valuables you already own, such as expensive foreign cameras. *Note:* The $750 exemption can be used only once a year and only after an absence of 7 days.

For Australian Citizens The duty-free allowance in **Australia** is A$400 or, for those under 18, A$200. Citizens can bring in 250 cigarettes or 250 grams of loose tobacco, and 1,125 milliliters of alcohol. If you're returning with valuables you already own, such as foreign-made cameras, you should file form B263. A helpful brochure available from Australian consulates or Customs offices is *Know*

Before You Go. For more information, call the **Australian Customs Service** at ℭ **1300/363-263,** or log on to www.customs.gov.au.

For New Zealand Citizens The duty-free allowance for **New Zealand** is NZ$700. Citizens over 17 can bring in 200 cigarettes, 50 cigars, or 250 grams of tobacco (or a mixture of all three if their combined weight doesn't exceed 250g); plus 4.5 liters of wine and beer, or 1.125 liters of liquor. New Zealand currency does not carry import or export restrictions. Fill out a certificate of export, listing the valuables you are taking out of the country; that way, you can bring them back without paying duty. Most questions are answered in a free pamphlet available at New Zealand consulates and Customs offices: *New Zealand Customs Guide for Travellers, Notice no. 4.* For more information, contact **New Zealand Customs,** The Customhouse, 17–21 Whitmore St., Box 2218, Wellington (ℭ **04/473-6099** or 0800/ 428-786; www.customs.govt.nz).

5 Money

Italy falls somewhere in the middle of pricing in Europe—not as expensive as, say, London, Switzerland, or Scandinavia, but not as cheap as Spain or Greece. Northern Italy—especially Venice, Milan, and Tuscany—is one of the costliest regions to travel through, but the advice in this book should steer you to the best options to fit any budget.

Luckily, ATMs (automated teller machines) are now found just about everywhere, even in the smallest towns, so cash is readily available and, as luck would have it, banks in Italy do not (as of yet) charge you a fee for using their bank—though your home bank probably will for using an out-of-network ATM, as well as a premium for withdrawing foreign currency (for more, see "ATMs," below).

It's a good idea to exchange at least some money—just enough to cover airport incidentals and transportation to your hotel—before you leave home so you can avoid lines at airport ATMs. You can exchange money at your local American Express or Thomas Cook office or your bank (often, though, only at the major branches). If you're far away from a bank with currency-exchange services, American Express offers traveler's checks and foreign currency for a $15 order fee and additional shipping costs (www.americanexpress.com or ℭ **800/ 807-6233**).

CURRENCY

In January 2002, Italy retired the lira and joined most of Western Europe in switching to the euro. Coins are issued in denominations of .01€, .02€,

Tips Dear Visa: I'm Off to Italy!

Some credit card companies recommend that you notify them of any impending trip abroad so that they don't become suspicious when the card is used numerous times in a foreign destination and block your charges. Even if you don't call your credit card company in advance, you can call always the card's toll-free emergency number (see "Fast Facts: Italy," later in this chapter) if a charge is refused—a good reason to carry the phone number with you. But perhaps the most important lesson is to carry more than one card on your trip; if one card doesn't work for any number of reasons, you'll have a backup card just in case.

.05€, .10€, .20€, and .50€, as well as 1€ and 2€; bills come in denominations of 5€, 10€, 20€, 50€, 100€, 200€, and 500€.

Exchange rates (see box below) are established daily and listed in most international newspapers. To get a transaction as close to this rate as possible, pay for as much as possible with credit cards and get cash out of ATM machines.

Traveler's checks, while still the safest way to carry money, are going the way of the dinosaur. The aggressive evolution of international computerized banking and consolidated ATM networks has led to the triumph of plastic throughout the Italian peninsula—even if cold cash is still the most trusted currency, especially in smaller towns or mom-and-pop joints, where credit cards may not be accepted.

You'll get the best rate if you **exchange money** at a bank or one of its ATMs. The rates at "Cambio/Change/Wechsel" exchange booths are less favorable but still a good deal better than what you'd get exchanging money at a hotel or shop (a last-resort tactic). The bill-to-bill changers you'll see in some touristy places exist solely to rip you off.

ATMS

The ability to access your personal checking account through the **Cirrus** (© 800/424-7787; www.mastercard. com) or **PLUS** (© 800/843-7587;

www.visa.com) networks of ATMs—or get a cash advance on an enabled Visa or MasterCard—has been growing by leaps and bounds in Italy in the last few years. It works just like at home. All you need to do is search out a machine that has your network's symbol displayed (which these days is practically all of them), pop in your card, and punch in your PIN (see "A PIN Alert," below). It'll spit out local currency drawn directly from your home checking account (and at a more favorable rate than converting traveler's checks or cash). Also keep in mind that many banks impose a fee every time a card is used at a different bank's ATM, and that fee can be higher for international transactions (up to $5 or more) than for domestic ones (where they're rarely more than $1.50). However, as I mentioned above, banks in Italy do not (at least yet) charge you a second fee to use their ATMs. To compare banks' ATM fees within the U.S., use www.bankrate. com. For international withdrawal fees, ask your bank.

An ATM in Italian is a *Bancomat* (though Bancomat is a private company, its name has become the generic word for ATMs). Increased internationalism has been slowly doing away with the old worry that your card's PIN, be it on a bank card or credit card, need be specially enabled to work abroad, but it always pays to check with the issuing bank to be sure (see "A PIN Alert" below). If at the ATM you get a message saying your card isn't valid for international transactions, it's likely that the bank just can't make the phone connection to check it (occasionally, this can be a citywide epidemic); try another ATM or another town.

When you withdraw money with your **bank card,** you technically get the interbank exchange rate—about 4% better than the "street rate" you'd get exchanging cash or traveler's checks. Note, however, that some U.S. banks are now charging a 1% to 3% "exchange fee" to convert the currency. (Ask your bank before you leave.)

Similarly, **Visa** has begun charging a standard 1% conversion fee for cash advances, and many credit card–issuing banks have begun tacking on an additional 1% to 3% (though, as we go to press, Visa is currently being taken to court over this practice in a class-action lawsuit, so keep tuned into the news to see what the future holds). Basically, they've gotten into the "commission" game, too. And, unlike with purchases, interest on a credit card cash advance starts accruing *immediately,* not when your statement cycles. Both methods are still a slightly better deal than converting traveler's checks or cash and considerably more convenient (no waiting in bank lines and pulling out your passport as ID). I use credit card advances only as an emergency option and get most of my euros with my bank card.

ATM withdrawals are often limited to 200€ ($230), or sometimes 300€

($345), per transaction regardless of your cash advance allowance. **American Express** card cash advances are usually available only from the American Express offices in Florence (see "Fast Facts: Florence," in chapter 4, "Florence: Birthplace of the Renaissance," for more information).

CREDIT CARDS

Visa and **MasterCard** are now almost universally accepted at most hotels, restaurants, and shops; the majority also accepts **American Express. Diners Club** is gaining some ground, especially in Florence and in more expensive establishments throughout the region. If you arrange with your card issuer to enable the card's cash advance option (and get a PIN as well), you can also use them at ATMs (see "ATMs," above).

If you **lose your card,** call toll-free *in Italy:* **Visa** (© **800/819-014**), **MasterCard** (© **800/870-866**), or **American Express** (collect © **336/ 393-1111** from anywhere, or toll-free in Italy © **800-872000**).

TRAVELER'S CHECKS

Traveler's checks are something of an anachronism from the days before the ATM made cash accessible at any time. Traveler's checks used to be the only sound alternative to traveling with dangerously large amounts of cash. They were as reliable as currency but, unlike cash, could be replaced if lost or stolen.

These days, traveler's checks are less necessary because most cities have 24-hour ATMs that allow you to withdraw small amounts of cash as needed.

A PIN Alert

Make sure the PINs on your bank cards and credit cards will work in Italy. You'll need a **four-digit code** (six digits often won't work), so if you have a six-digit code, play it safe by getting a new four-digit PIN for your trip. If you're unsure about this, contact Cirrus or PLUS (see "ATMs," above). Be sure to check the daily withdrawal limit at the same time.

The Euro, the U.S. Dollar & the U.K. Pound

At this writing, US$1 = approximately .87€ (or 1€ = $1.15)—the lowest the dollar has ever been (over the past 2 years, the two currencies were more on a par with each other). The rate fluctuates from day to day, depending on a complicated series of economic and political factors, and might not be the same when you travel to Italy.

Likewise, the ratio of the British pound to the euro fluctuates constantly. At press time, £1 = approximately 1.43€ (or 1€ = 70p).

These are the rates reflected in the table below, and the ones used to translate euro amounts into ballpark dollar figures throughout this book, rounded to the nearest nickel for amounts under $10, to the nearest dollar for amounts $10 and above (though this table will be precise to the penny).

Euro €	US$	UK£	Euro €	US$	UK£
0.50	0.57	0.35	30.00	34.50	21.00
1.00	1.15	0.70	40.00	46.00	28.00
2.00	2.30	1.40	50.00	57.50	35.00
3.00	3.45	2.10	60.00	69.00	42.00
4.00	4.60	2.80	70.00	80.45	49.00
5.00	5.75	3.50	80.00	92.00	56.00
6.00	6.90	4.20	90.00	103.00	63.00
7.00	8.05	4.90	100.00	115.00	70.00
8.00	9.20	5.60	125.00	144.00	87.50
9.00	10.35	6.30	150.00	172.00	105.00
10.00	11.50	7.00	200.00	230.00	140.00
15.00	17.24	10.50	300.00	345.00	210.00
20.00	23.00	14.00	400.00	460.00	280.00
25.00	28.75	17.50	500.00	575.00	350.00

However, keep in mind that you will likely be charged an ATM withdrawal fee if the bank is not your own, so if you're withdrawing money every day, you might be better off with traveler's checks—provided that you don't mind showing identification every time you want to cash one.

Most banks issue checks under the names of **American Express** (© 800/721-9768 in the United States and Canada, or 1-801/945-9450 collect from anywhere else in the world; www.americanexpress.com) or **Thomas Cook** (© 800/223-7373 in the U.S. and Canada, or 44/1733-318-950 collect from anywhere in the world; www.thomascook.com)—both offer versions that can be countersigned by you or your companion—**Visa** (© 800/227-6811 in the U.S. and Canada, or 44-171-937-8091 collect from anywhere in the world; www.visa.com); or **Citicorp** (© 800/645-6556 in the U.S. and Canada, or 1-813/623-1709 collect from anywhere in the world). AAA will sell Amex checks to their members without a commission. Note that you'll get the worst possible exchange rate if you pay for a purchase or hotel room directly with a traveler's check; it's better to trade in the traveler's checks for euros at a bank or the American Express office.

Call the numbers listed above to report **lost or stolen traveler's checks.**

WIRE SERVICES

If you find yourself out of money, a wire service can help you tap willing friends and family for funds. Through **TravelersExpress/MoneyGram,** 3940 S. Teller St., Lakewood, CO 80235 (*©* **800/666-3947;** www.money gram.com), you can get money sent around the world in less than 10 minutes. Cash is the only acceptable form of payment. MoneyGram's fees vary based on the cities the money is wired to and from, but a good estimate is $20 for the first $200 and $30 for up to $400, with a sliding scale for larger sums.

A similar service is offered by **Western Union** (*©* **800/CALL-CASH**), which accepts Visa, MasterCard credit or debit cards, or Discover. You can arrange for the service over the phone, at a Western Union office, or online at www.westernunion.com. A sliding scale begins at $15 for the first $100. A currency exchange rate will also apply. Additionally, your credit card company may charge a fee for the cash advance, as well apply as a higher interest rate.

6 When to Go

May to **June** and **September** and **October** are the most pleasant months for touring Italy—temperatures are usually mild and the hordes of tourists not so intense. But starting in mid-June, the summer rush really picks up, and from July to mid-September, the country teems with visitors.

August (with July a close runner-up) is the worst month. Not only does it get uncomfortably hot, muggy, and crowded, but the entire country goes on vacation from at least August 15 to the end of the month—and a good percentage of Italians take off the entire month, leaving the cities to the tourists. Many hotels, restaurants, and shops are closed—except along the coast and on the islands, which is where most Italians head.

From **late October to Easter,** most sights have shorter winter hours or close for renovation periods, many hotels and restaurants take a month or two off between November and February, beach destinations become padlocked ghost towns, and it can get much colder than you'd expect (it may even snow). The crowds thin remarkably, especially outside the Big Three tourist cities (Rome, Florence, and Venice).

In **mountain towns and ski resorts,** high season is from mid-December through mid-March; low season is June, when many hotels are closed (which is a shame, for there's great hiking in the mountains during June's warmer days).

High season on most airlines' routes to Italy usually stretches from June to the end of September plus Christmas/New Year's week. This is the most expensive and most crowded time to travel. **Shoulder season** is from the Easter season (usually late Mar or Apr) to May, late September to October, and December 15 to December 24. **Low season** is generally January 6 to mid-March, November 1 to December 14, and December 25 to March 31.

WEATHER

It's warm all over Italy in **summer,** especially inland. The high temperatures (measured in degrees Celsius) begin in May (sometimes later for the Alps), often lasting until some time in late September. July and August can be impossible, which explains why life in the cities slows down considerably (and life in the coastline resorts comes alive). Few budget hotels have air-conditioning (and just a handful of hotels in all of Italy have discovered mosquito screens, so when you open the windows for some respite from the heat, you tend to invite dozens of tiny bloodsuckers in as well). The November rains kick off Venice's *acque alte,* when the lagoon backs up a few times each month, flooding the central city with .6 to 1.8m (2–6 ft.) of water (no joke).

Winters in the north of Italy are cold, with rain and snow, and December through February can often be unpleasant unless you're skiing in Cortina. In the south, the weather is mild in the winter months, averaging 4°C and up (in the 40s F). Sicily's citrus and almond trees are already in bloom in February—but nights can be cold, and Italian hotels' heating systems can be . . . frustrating. Purpose-built, modernized hotels in their own buildings often have independent heating/cooling systems you (or they) can control, but in older hotels and in small ones that take up only part of a building, the heat can often be turned on for the winter only on a pre-established date dictated by the local government and can be left on only during certain hours of the day (just one of the many lovely laws still hanging on from the Fascist era). Some of the cheapest hotels in Southern Italy

and Sicily don't even have heating systems, so the rare cold snap can leave you shivering.

For the most part, it's drier in Italy than in North America. Since the humidity is lower, high temperatures don't seem as bad; exceptions are cities known for their humidity factor, such as Florence and Venice. In Rome, Naples, and the south, temperatures can stay around 90°F (32°C) for days, but nights are most often comfortably cooler. It's important to remember that this is not a country as smitten by the notion of air-conditioning and central heating as, say, the United States. And remember that the inexpensive hotels we list in this book are often the very places that will remind you of the pros and cons of ancient stone palazzi built with about 1m (3-ft.) thick walls. Don't expect the comfort of the Ritz.

HOLIDAYS

Offices and shops in Italy are closed on the following dates: **January 1** (New Year's Day), **January 6** (Epiphany, usually called *La Befana* after Italy's Christmas Witch, who used to bring the presents until Hollywood's version of Santa Claus moved the gift-giving to December 25 by

Italy's Average Daily Temperature & Monthly Rainfall

	Jan	Feb	Mar	Apr	May	June	July	Aug	Sept	Oct	Nov	Dec
Florence												
Temp. (°C)	7	8	10	16	19	24	25	21	18	17	13	8
Temp.(°F)	45	47	50	60	67	76	77	70	64	63	55	46
Rainfall (in.)	3	3.3	3.7	2.7	2.2	1.4	1.4	2.7	3.2	4.9	3.8	2.9
Naples												
Temp. (°C)	10	12	14	17	21	26	28	29	24	19	16	11
Temp.(°F)	50	54	58	63	70	78	83	85	75	66	60	52
Rainfall (in.)	4.7	4	3	3.8	2.4	.8	.8	2.6	3.5	5.8	5.1	3.7
Rome												
Temp. (°C)	9	11	14	17	22	28	31	30	23	18	13	8
Temp. (°F)	49	52	57	62	72	82	87	86	73	65	56	47
Rainfall (in.)	2.3	1.5	2.9	3.0	2.8	2.9	1.5	1.9	2.8	2.6	3.0	2.1

Hot Tickets
For major events where tickets should be procured well before arriving on the spot, check with **Global Tickets** in the United States at ℂ **800/223-6108** or www.globaltickets.com/GTS/INDEX.HTM. In Italy, call ℂ **02-54271.**

---

popular kiddie demand, though a few presents are always held over for *La Befana*), **Easter Sunday, Easter Monday, April 25** (Liberation Day), **May 1** (Labor Day), **August 15** (Assumption of the Virgin—much of Italy takes its summer vacation **Aug 15–30**), **November 1** (All Saints' Day), **December 8** (Feast of the Immaculate Conception), **December 25** (Christmas Day), and **December 26** (Santo Stefano); most Italians' **Christmas** holidays last from December 24 though January 6.

Closings are also observed in the following cities on feast days honoring their patron saints: Venice, **April 25** (St. Mark); Florence, Genoa, and Turin, **June 24** (St. John the Baptist); Rome, **June 29** (Sts. Peter and Paul); Palermo, **July 15** (St. Rosalia); Naples, **September 19** (St. Gennaro); Bologna, **October 4** (St. Petronio); Cagliari, **October 30** (St. Saturnino); Trieste, **November 3** (St. Giusto); Bari, **December 6** (St. Nicola); and Milan, **December 7** (St. Ambrose).

ITALY CALENDAR OF EVENTS

For more details on each event below, contact the **tourist office** of the city or town where the festival is held (see the individual chapters).

January

Epiphany celebrations, nationwide. All cities, towns, and villages in Italy stage Roman Catholic Epiphany observances and Christmas fairs. One of the most festive celebrations is the Christmas/Epiphany Fair at Rome's Piazza Navona. From Christmas to January 6.

Festival of Italian Popular Song, San Remo (Italian Riviera). A 3-day festival where major artists and up-and-comers perform the latest Italian pop songs and launch the newest hits. Late January.

Foire de Saint Ours, Aosta, Valle d'Aosta. Observing a tradition that's existed for 10 centuries, artisans from the mountain valleys come together to display their wares—often made of wood, lace, wool, or wrought iron—created during the long winter months. Late January.

February

Carnevale (Carnival), Venice. Venice's Carnival evokes the final theatrical 18th-century days of the Venetian Republic. Historical presentations, elaborate costumes, and music of all types in every piazza cap the festivities. The balls are by invitation, but the cultural events, piazza performances, and fireworks (Shrove Tuesday) are open to everyone. See chapter 7 for more information. From two Fridays before Shrove Tuesday to Shrove Tuesday.

Almond Blossom Festival, Agrigento (Sicily). This folk festival includes song, dance, costumes, and fireworks. First half of February.

April

Holy Week (Settimana Santa), Rome. The pope, passing the Colosseum and Roman Forum up to Palatine Hill, leads the most notable procession. A torch-lit parade caps the observance. Week between Palm Sunday and Easter Sunday; sometimes at the end of March, but often in April.

Good Friday & Easter Week observances, nationwide. Processions and age-old ceremonies—some from pagan days, some from the Middle Ages—are staged. The most colorful and evocative are in **Trapani** and other towns throughout **Sicily.** Beginning on the Thursday or Friday before Easter Sunday, usually in April.

Pasqua (Easter Sunday), Piazza di San Pietro, Rome. In an event broadcast around the world, the pope gives his blessing from a balcony overlooking a packed St. Peter's Square.

Scoppio del Carro (Explosion of the Cart), Florence. An ancient observance: A cart laden with flowers and fireworks is drawn by three white oxen to the Duomo, where at noon Mass a mechanical dove detonates it from the altar by means of a wire that passes through the Duomo's open doors. Easter Sunday.

Festa della Primavera (Feast of Spring), Rome. The Spanish Steps are decked out with banks of azaleas and other flowers, and later orchestral and choral concerts are presented in Trinità dei Monti. Late April or early May.

Maggio Musicale Fiorentino (Musical May Florentine), Florence. Italy's oldest and most prestigious festival presents opera, ballet, and concerts. It takes place at th Teatro Comunale, the Teatro della Pergola, and various other venues, including Piazza della Signoria and the Pitti Palace courtyard. Maestro Zubin Mehta is the honorary director, often conducting Florence's Maggio Musicale Orchestra, and guest conductors and orchestras appear throughout the festival. Schedule and ticket information is available from Maggio Musicale Fiorentino/Teatro Comunale, Via Solferino 16, 50123 Firenze (*©* **055-211158;** www. maggiofiorentino.com). Late April to June or July.

May

Calendimaggio (Celebration of Holy Week), Assisi. This pagan celebration of spring is held according to rites dating back to medieval times. First weekend after May 1.

International Horse Show, Rome. This show is held on the Villa Borghese's Piazza di Siena. Usually May 1 to 10, but dates can vary.

Sagra di Sant'Efisio (Festival of St. Efisio), Cagliari (Sardinia). At one of the biggest and most colorful processions in Italy, several thousand pilgrims (wearing costumes dating from 1657) accompany the statue of the saint on foot, on horseback, or in a cart. May 1 to 4.

Corso dei Ceri, Gubbio. In this centuries-old ceremony, 454-kilogram (1,000-lb.), 9m (30-ft.) wooden "candles" *(ceri)* are raced through the streets of this perfectly preserved medieval hill town in Umbria. Celebrating the feast day of St. Ubaldo, the town's patron saint, the candles are mounted by statues of the patron saints of the town's medieval guilds and are raced through the narrow streets and up a steep hill to the monastery—where Ubaldo always wins the race. May 15.

Voga Longa, Venice. This 30km (19-mile) rowing "race" from San Marco to Burano and back again has been enthusiastically embraced since its inception in 1975, following the city's effort to keep alive the centuries-old heritage of the regatta. The event is colorful, and every local seems to have a relative or next-door neighbor competing. For details, call *©* **041-5210544.** A Sunday in mid-May.

Cavalcata Sarda (Sardinian Cavalcade), Sassari. Traditional procession with over 3,000 people in Sardinian costume, some on horseback. Next-to-last Sunday in May.

June

Estate Ficsolana (Summer in Fiesole), Fiesole. For this festival, the Roman theater in Fiesole (north of Florence) comes alive with dance, music, and theater. Most of the performances take place in the remains of the 1st-century A.D. Roman theater. You can get information and tickets through **Agenzia Box Office,** Via Alamanni 39, Firenze (© **055-2100804** or 055-2616049), or at the Roman theater itself on the day of the performance after 4:30pm. A.T.A.F. bus no. 7 travels to Fiesole from Florence's train station and Piazza del Duomo. Late June to August.

Calcio Storico (Ancient Football Match), Florence. For this revival of a raucous 16th-century football match, teams representing Florence's four original parishes, identified by their colors and clad in 16th-century costume, square off against one another in consecutive playoffs on dirt-covered Piazza Santa Croce. It's preceded by an elaborate procession. Afterward, fireworks light up the night sky. See the tourist office for ticket information about numbered seats in the bleachers lining the piazza. There are four matches, usually culminating on June 24, feast day of St. Giovanni (St. John), beloved patron saint of Florence.

San Ranieri & the Gioco del Ponte (Bridge Game), Pisa. Two Pisa traditions: First, Pisa honors its own St. Ranieri with candlelit parades, followed the next day by eight-rower teams competing in 16th-century costumes. June 16 and 17. Second, the Gioco del Ponte takes place with teams in Renaissance garb taking part in a hotly contested tug-of-war on the Ponte di Mezzo spanning the Arno River. First Sunday of June.

Spoleto Festival, Spoleto. Dating from 1958, this festival, until recently known as the Festival dei Due Mondi (Festival of Two Worlds), was the creation of American-born Maestro Gian Carlo Menotti. It's now the country's biggest and most prestigious arts festival. International performers convene in this lovely Umbrian hill town for 3 weeks of dance, drama, opera, concerts, and art exhibits. For more information, contact **Associazione Spoleto Festival,** Piazza del Duomo 8, 06049 Spoleto (© **800-565600** toll-free in Italy, or 0743-220032; **0743-44700** from outside Italy; fax 0743-220321; www.spoletofestival.it). Also try the **Teatro Nuovo** (© **0743-40265**). Mid-June to mid-July.

Festa di San Giovanni (Feast of St. John), Rome. This festival is still celebrated with throngs of people singing and dancing and consuming large amounts of stewed snails and artery-clogging *porchetta* (pork) on Piazza San Giovanni in Laterano. June 23.

Festa di San Pietro e Paulo (Feast of Sts. Peter and Paul), Rome. The most significant Roman religious festival is observed with a street fair on Via Ostiense and Masses at St. Peter's and St. Paul Outside the Walls. Usually June 29.

Events That Last Throughout the Summer

Regatta of the Great Maritime Republics, Venice or Genoa. Every year, the four medieval maritime republics of Italy celebrate their glorious past with a boat race that rotates among Venice, Amalfi,

Genoa, and Pisa. Call the tourist offices for details.

Biennale d'Arte, Venice. This is Europe's most prestigious—and controversial—International Exposition of Modern Art, taking place in odd-numbered years only. More than 50 nations take part, with art displayed in permanent pavilions in the Public Gardens and elsewhere about town. Many great modern artists have been discovered at this world-famous show. Contact the board at ℂ **041-5218711** (www. labiennale.org) for more information. June to October.

Son et Lumière, the Roman Forum & Tivoli, Rome. These areas are dramatically lit at night. Early June to the end of September.

Shakespearean Festival, Verona. Ballet, drama, and jazz performances are included in this festival of the Bard, with a few performances in English. June to September.

Il Palio, Piazza del Campo, Siena. Palio fever grips this Tuscan hill town for a wild and exciting horse race from the Middle Ages. Pageantry, costumes, and the celebrations of the victorious *contrada* mark the well-attended spectacle. It's a no-rules event: Even a horse without a rider can win the race. Tickets (impossible to come by for non-Sienese) usually sell out by January, but consider joining the non-ticket-holding crowd that stands in the middle of the square. See the box in chapter 5 for more information. July 2 and August 16.

Arena di Verona (Outdoor Opera Season in Verona), Verona. Culture buffs flock to the open-air, 20,000-seat Roman amphitheater, one of the world's best preserved. The season lasts from early July to August for awesome productions of *Aïda* and others.

Music & Drama Festival, Taormina, Sicily. July and August are the most important months for performances held in the resort town's gorgeously sited ancient Greek amphitheater, with Mount Etna looming in the distance. The local tourism board distributes tickets.

July

Festa de' Noiantri (Festival of We Others), Rome. Trastevere, the most colorful quarter of Old Rome, becomes a gigantic outdoor restaurant, as tons of food and drink are consumed at tables lining the streets. A street fair is held on Viale Trastevere, and concerts and plays are performed on Piazza Santa Maria in Trastevere. This feast was immortalized near the end of Fellini's film *Roma* (the scene in which he interviews Gore Vidal). Mid-July.

Umbria Jazz, Perugia. The Umbrian region hosts the country's (and one of Europe's) top jazz festival featuring world-class artists. Mid- to late July.

Festa del Redentore (Feast of the Redeemer), Venice. This celebration marking the July 1576 lifting of a plague that had gripped the city is centered on the Palladio-designed Chiesa del Redentore on the island of Giudecca. A bridge of boats across the Giudecca Canal links the church with the banks of Le Zattere in Dorsoduro, and hundreds of boats of all shapes and sizes fill the Giudecca. It's one big floating *festa* until night descends and an awesome half-hour *spettacolo* of fireworks fills the sky. Third Saturday and Sunday in July.

August

Festa della Madonna della Neve (Festival of the Madonna of the Snows), Rome. The legendary founding of the Basilica di Santa

---

Tips **Dog Days of August**

Try to avoid traveling to Italy in August, as this is when most Italians take their vacations *(ferie)* and many shops and restaurants in the cities will be closed. Also keep in mind that many of the lodgings that are open in August do not have air-conditioning.

Maria Maggiore is reenacted with a pretty "snowfall" of rose petals over the congregation during Mass. August 5.

Torre del Lago Puccini, near Lucca. Puccini operas are performed at this Tuscan lakeside town's open-air theater, near the celebrated composer's former summertime villa. Contact the tourist office in Lucca. Throughout August.

Rossini Opera Festival, Pesaro. The world's top bel canto specialists perform Rossini's operas and choral works at this popular festival on the Italian Adriatic Riviera. Mid-August to late September.

Venice International Film Festival. Ranking after Cannes, this film festival brings together stars, directors, producers, and filmmakers from all over the world. Films are shown day and night to an international jury and to the public at the Palazzo del Cinema, on the Lido, and at other venues. Contact the tourist office or the Venice Film Festival (© **041-2726501** or 041-5241320; www.labiennale. org). Two weeks in late August to early September.

September

Sagra dell'Uva (Festival of the Grape), Rome. For this festival, grape growers from the region come to the Basilica of Maxentius in the Roman Forum and party in the shade of its half-ruined vaults. Costumed musicians accompany this harvest festival of half-price grapes

and other market stalls. First week in September.

Regata Storica, Grand Canal, Venice. Just about every seaworthy gondola, richly decorated for the occasion and piloted by *gondolieri* in colorful livery, participates in the opening cavalcade. The aquatic parade is followed by three regattas that proceed along the Grand Canal. You can buy grandstand tickets through the tourist office or arrive early and pull up along a piece of embankment near the Rialto Bridge for the best seats in town. First Sunday in September.

Giostra del Saracino (Joust of the Saracen), Arezzo. A colorful procession in full historic regalia precedes the 13th-century-style tilting contest with knights in armor in the town's main piazza. First Sunday in September.

Partita a Scacchi con Personnagi Viventi (Living Chess Game), Marostica. This chess game is played in the town square by living pawns in period costume. The second Saturday and Sunday of September during even-numbered years.

International Antiques Show, Florence. More than 100 internationally noted dealers hawk their most exquisite pieces—the crowd is as interesting as the wares. The historically potent setting of the massive Renaissance Palazzo Strozzi couldn't be more appropriate, but check for a possible change of venue. Admission is about 8€

($9.20). For information, visit the tourist office. Mid-September in odd-numbered years.

October

Sagra del Tartufo, Alba, Piedmont. The truffle is the honoree in Alba, the truffle capital of Italy, with contests, truffle-hound competitions, and tastings of this ugly but precious and delectable (and expensive) fungus. Two weeks in mid-October.

Maratona (Marathon), Venice. The marathon starts at Villa Pisani on the mainland, runs alongside the Brenta Canal, and ends along the Zattere for a finish at the Basilica di Santa Maria della Salute, on the tip of Dorsoduro. For details, call C **041-950644.** Usually the last Sunday of October.

November

Festa della Salute, Venice. For this festival, a pontoon bridge is erected across the Grand Canal to connect the churches of La Salute and Santa Maria del Giglio, commemorating another delivery from a plague in 1630 that wiped out a third of the lagoon's population; it's the only day La Salute opens its massive front doors (a secondary entrance is otherwise used). November 21.

December

La Scala Opera Season, Teatro alla Scala, Milan. At the most famous opera house of them all, the season opens on December 7, the feast day of Milan's patron St. Ambrogio, and runs into July. Though it's close to impossible to get opening-night tickets, it's worth a try; call C **02-860787** or 02-860775 for the box office, 02-72003744 for the information line (www.teatroallascala.org).

Christmas Blessing of the Pope, Piazza di San Pietro, Rome. Delivered at noon from a balcony of St. Peter's Basilica. It's broadcast around the world. December 25.

7 Travel Insurance

Check your existing insurance policies and credit card coverage before you buy travel insurance. You may already be covered for lost luggage, cancelled tickets, or medical expenses. The cost of travel insurance varies widely, depending on the cost and length of your trip, your age, your health, and the type of trip you're taking.

TRIP-CANCELLATION INSUR-ANCE Trip-cancellation insurance helps you get your money back if you have to back out of a trip, if you have to go home early, or if your travel supplier goes bankrupt. Allowed reasons for cancellation can range from sickness to natural disasters, to the State Department declaring your destination unsafe for travel. (Insurers usually won't cover vague fears, though, as many wary travelers discovered when they tried to cancel their trips in Oct 2001.)

In this unstable world, trip-cancellation insurance is a good buy if you're getting tickets well in advance—who knows what the state of the world, or of your airline, will be in 9 months? Insurance policy details vary, so read the fine print—and especially make sure that your airline or cruise line is on the list of carriers covered in case of bankruptcy. A good resource is **"Travel Guard Alerts,"** a list of companies considered high-risk by Travel Guard International (see website below). Protect yourself further by paying for the insurance with a credit card—by law, consumers can get their money back on goods and services not received if they report the loss within 60 days after the charge is listed on their credit card statement.

Note: Many tour operators, particularly those offering trips to remote or high-risk areas, include insurance in the cost of the trip or can arrange insurance policies through a partnering provider, a convenient and often cost-effective way for the traveler to obtain insurance. Make sure the tour company is a reputable one, however: Some experts suggest you avoid buying insurance from the tour or cruise company you're traveling with, saying it's better to buy from a "third party" insurer than to put all your money in one place.

For information, contact one of the following recommended insurers: **Access America** (② 800/284-8300; www.accessamerica.com); **Travel Guard International** (② 800/826-1300; www.travelguard.com); **Travel Insured International** (② 800/243-3174; www.travelinsured.com); or **Travelex Insurance Services** (② 800/228-9792; www.travelex-insurance.com).

MEDICAL INSURANCE Most health insurance policies cover you if you get sick away from home—but check, particularly if you're insured by an HMO. For travel overseas, most health plans (including Medicare and Medicaid) do not provide coverage, and the ones that do often require you to pay for services upfront and reimburse you only after you return home. Even if your plan does cover overseas treatment, most out-of-country hospitals make you pay your bills upfront and send you a refund only after you've returned home and filed the necessary paperwork with your insurance company. As a safety net, you may want to buy travel medical insurance, particularly if you're traveling to a remote or high-risk area where emergency evacuation is a possible scenario. If you require additional medical insurance, try **MEDEX Assistance** (② 410/453-6300; www.medexassist.com) or **Travel Assistance**

International (② 800/821-2828; www.travelassistance.com; for general information on services, call the company's Worldwide Assistance Services, Inc., at ② 800/777-8710).

Again, most health insurance plans covering out-of-country illnesses and hospital stays require you to pay your local bills upfront—your coverage takes the form of a refund after you've returned and filed the paperwork. However, **Blue Cross/Blue Shield members** (② 800/810-BLUE or www.bluecares.com for a list of participating hospitals) can now use their plans and cards at select hospitals abroad as they would at home, which means much lower out-of-pocket costs. There are member hospitals in most cities across Europe.

LOST-LUGGAGE INSURANCE On international flights (including U.S. portions of international trips), checked baggage is automatically covered at approximately $9.07 per pound, up to approximately $635 per checked bag. If you plan to check items more valuable than the standard liability, see if your valuables are covered by your homeowner's policy, get baggage insurance as part of your comprehensive travel-insurance package, or buy Travel Guard's BagTrak product. Don't buy insurance at the airport, as it's usually overpriced. Be sure to take any valuables or irreplaceable items with you in your carry-on luggage, as many valuables (including books, money, and electronics) aren't covered by airline policies.

If your luggage is lost, immediately file a lost-luggage claim at the airport, detailing the luggage contents. For most airlines, you must report delayed, damaged, or lost baggage within 4 hours of arrival. The airlines are required to deliver luggage, once found, directly to your house or destination free of charge.

8 Health & Safety

STAYING HEALTHY

There are no special health risks you'll encounter in Italy. The tap water is safe, and medical resources are of a high quality. In fact, with Italy's partially socialized medicine, you can usually stop by any hospital emergency room with an ailment, get swift and courteous service, be given a diagnosis and a prescription, and be sent on your way with a wave and a smile—and you won't even have to fill out any paperwork.

WHAT TO DO IF YOU GET SICK AWAY FROM HOME

In most cases, your existing health plan will provide the coverage you need. But double-check; you may want to buy **travel medical insurance** instead. (See the section on insurance, above.) Bring your insurance ID card with you when you travel.

If you suffer from a chronic illness, consult your doctor before your departure. For conditions like epilepsy, diabetes, or heart problems, wear a **MedicAlert** identification tag (℃ **888/633-4298,** or 209/668-3333 outside the U.S.; www.medic alert.org), which will immediately alert doctors to your condition and give them access to your records through Medic Alert's 24-hour hot line.

Pack **prescription medications** in your carry-on luggage, and carry prescription medications in their original containers, with pharmacy labels— otherwise, they won't make it through airport security. Also bring along copies of your prescriptions, in case you lose your pills or run out. Don't forget an extra pair of contact lenses or prescription glasses. Again, carry the generic name of prescription medicines, in case a local pharmacist is unfamiliar with the brand name.

Contact the **International Association for Medical Assistance to Travelers** (**IAMAT;** ℃ **716/754-4883** or 416/652-0137; www.iamat.org) for tips on travel and health concerns in the countries you're visiting, and lists of local, English-speaking doctors. In **Canada,** contact them at 40 Regal Road, Guelph, ON N1K 1B5 (℃ **519/836-0102;** fax 519/836-3412); and in **New Zealand** at P.O. Box 5049, Christchurch 5 (fax 643/352-4630).

The United States **Centers for Disease Control and Prevention** (℃ **800/311-3435;** www.cdc.gov) provides up-to-date information on necessary vaccines and health hazards by region or country. Any foreign consulate can provide a list of area doctors who speak English. If you get sick, consider asking your hotel concierge to recommend a local doctor—even his or her own. You can also try the emergency room at a local hospital. Many hospitals also have walk-in clinics for emergency cases that are not life-threatening; you may not get immediate attention, but you won't pay the high price of an emergency room visit. We list hospitals and emergency numbers under the "Fast Facts" section for each major city.

STAYING SAFE

Italy is a remarkably safe country. The worst threats you'll likely face are the pickpockets that sometimes frequent touristy areas and public buses; just keep your valuables in an under-the-clothes money belt, and you should be fine. There are, of course, thieves in Italy as there are everywhere, so be smart; don't leave anything in your rental car overnight, and leave nothing visible in it at any time, to avoid the temptation to a passing would-be thief.

Avoiding "Economy Class Syndrome"

Deep vein thrombosis, or, as it's know in the world of flying, "economy-class syndrome," is a blood clot that develops in a deep vein. It's a potentially deadly condition that can be caused by sitting in cramped conditions—such as an airplane cabin—for too long. During a flight (especially a long-haul flight), get up, walk around, and stretch your legs every 60 to 90 minutes to keep your blood flowing. Other preventative measures include frequent flexing of the legs while sitting, drinking lots of water, and avoiding alcohol and sleeping pills. If you have a history of deep vein thrombosis, heart disease, or other condition that puts you at high risk, some experts recommend wearing compression stockings or taking anticoagulants when you fly; always ask your physician about the best course for you. Symptoms of deep vein thrombosis include leg pain or swelling, or even shortness of breath.

9 Specialized Travel Resources

TRAVELERS WITH DISABILITIES

Italy certainly won't win any medals for being overly accessible, though a few of the top museums and churches are beginning to install ramps at the entrances, and a few hotels are converting first-floor rooms into accessible units by widening the doors and bathrooms.

Other than that, don't expect to find much of the landscape easy to tackle. Builders in the Middle Ages and the Renaissance didn't have wheelchairs or mobility impairments in mind when they constructed narrow doorways and spiral staircases, and preservation laws keep modern Italians from being able to do much about this.

That said, recent laws in Italy have compelled rail stations, airports, hotels, and most restaurants to follow a stricter set of regulations about wheelchair accessibility to restrooms, ticket counters, and so on. Many museums and other sightseeing attractions have conformed to these regulations, and even Venice has now installed wheelchair elevator platforms on many of the hundreds of bridges over the city's canals, effectively opening up well over half the historic center to mobility-impaired visitors (the tourist office map highlights the zones now accessible). **Alitalia,** as Italy's most visible airline, has made a special effort to make its planes, public areas, restrooms, and access ramps as wheelchair-friendly as possible.

Buses and trains can cause problems as well, with high, narrow doors and steep steps at entrances. There are, however, seats reserved on public transportation for travelers with disabilities.

Luckily, there's an endless list of organizations to help you plan your trip and offer specific advice before you go. Many **travel agencies** offer customized tours and itineraries for travelers with disabilities. **Flying Wheels Travel** (© 507/451-5005; www.flyingwheelstravel.com) offers escorted tours and cruises that emphasize sports and private tours in mini-vans with lifts. **Access-Able Travel Source** (© 303/232-2979; www.access-able.com) offers extensive access information and advice for traveling around the world with disabilities. **Accessible Journeys** (© 800/846-4537 or 610/521-0339; www.disabilitytravel.com) caters specifically to slow walkers and wheelchair travelers, and their families and friends.

Organizations that offer assistance to travelers with disabilities include **MossRehab** (www.mossresourcenet. org), which provides a library of accessible-travel resources online; **SATH** (Society for Accessible Travel and Hospitality; ✆ 212/447-7284; www. sath.org; annual membership fees $45 adults, $30 seniors and students), which offers a wealth of travel resources for all types of disabilities and informed recommendations on destinations, access guides, travel agents, tour operators, vehicle rentals, and companion services; and the **American Foundation for the Blind** (**AFB**; ✆ 800/232-5463; www. afb.org), a referral resource for the blind or visually impaired that includes information on traveling with Seeing Eye dogs.

GAY & LESBIAN TRAVELERS

Since 1861, Italy has had liberal legislation regarding homosexuality, but that doesn't mean being gay is always looked on favorably in a Catholic country. Homosexuality is legal, and the age of consent is 16. Condoms are *profilatici* (pro-feel-*aht*-tee-chee).

Luckily, Italians are already more affectionate and physical than Americans in their general friendships, and even straight men regularly walk down the street with their arms around one another—however, kissing anywhere other than on the cheeks at greetings and goodbyes will certainly draw attention. As you might expect, smaller towns tend to be less tolerant than cities. Homosexuality is much more accepted in the big cities and university towns, though in Italy only Milan has a significant gay community.

In fact, **Milan** considers itself the gay capital of Italy (though Bologna is a proud contender) and is the headquarters of **ARCI Gay** (www.gay.it), the country's leading gay organization, which has branches throughout Italy. A gay-operated, English-speaking

travel agency in Rome, **Zipper Travel** (V. Francesco Carletti 8, Rome 00154; ✆ 06-4882730; fax 06-4882729; www.zippertravel.it) can help create itineraries in both large and small cities, as well as make reservations for travel and hotel.

The International Gay and Lesbian Travel Association (**IGLTA;** ✆ 800/448-8550 or 954/776-2626; www.iglta.org) is the trade association for the gay and lesbian travel industry and offers an online directory of gay- and lesbian-friendly travel businesses; go to their website and click on "Members."

Many agencies offer tours and travel itineraries specifically for gay and lesbian travelers. **Above and Beyond Tours** (✆ 800/397-2681; www.abovebeyondtours.com) is the exclusive gay and lesbian tour operator for United Airlines. **Now, Voyager** (✆ 800/255-6951; www.nowvoyager. com) is a well-known San Francisco–based gay-owned and operated travel service.

Out and About (✆ 800/929-2268 or 415/644-8044; www.outandabout. com) offers guidebooks and a newsletter 10 times a year ($20/year) packed with solid information on the global gay and lesbian scene.

SENIORS

Italy is a multigenerational culture that doesn't tend to marginalize its seniors, and older people are treated with a great deal of respect and deference throughout Italy. But there are few specific programs, associations, or concessions made for them. The one exception is on admission prices for museums and sights, where those over 60 or 65 will often get in at a reduced rate or even free (see "A Cultural Note for Families & Seniors," above). Special train passes and reductions on bus tickets and the like are also offered in various towns (see "Getting Around," later in this chapter). As a senior in

Italy, you're *un anciano* (*un'anciana* if you're a woman), or "ancient one"—look at it as a term of respect, and let people know you're one if you think a discount may be in the works. Members of **AARP** (formerly known as the American Association of Retired Persons), 601 E St. NW, Washington, DC 20049 (© **888/ 687-2277**; www.aarp.org), get discounts on hotels, airfares, and car rentals. AARP offers members a wide range of benefits, including *AARP The Magazine* and a monthly newsletter. Anyone over 50 can join.

Sadly, most major **airlines** have in recent years cancelled their discount programs for seniors, but you can always ask when booking. Of the big **car-rental** agencies, only National currently gives an AARP discount, but the many rental dealers that specialize in Europe—Auto Europe, Kemwel, Europe-by-Car—offer seniors 5% off their already low rates. In most European cities, people over 60 or 65 get reduced admission at theaters, museums, and other attractions, and they can often get discount fares or cards on public transportation and national rail systems. Carrying ID with proof of age can pay off in all these situations.

Grand Circle Travel, 347 Congress St., Boston, MA 02210 (© **800/ 959-0405** or 800/321-2835; www. gct.com), is one of the literally hundreds of travel agencies specializing in vacations for seniors. But beware:

Many packages are of the tour-bus variety. Seniors seeking more independent travel should probably consult a regular travel agent. **SAGA Holidays,** 1161 Boylston St., Boston, MA 02115 (© **800/343-0273;** www.sagaholidays.com), has 40 years of experience running all-inclusive tours and cruises for those 50 and older. They also sponsor the more substantial **"Road Scholar Tours"** (© **800/621-2151**), fun-loving tours with an educational bent.

Many reliable agencies and organizations target the 50-plus market. **Elderhostel** (© **877/426-8056;** www.elderhostel.org) arranges study programs for those age 55 and over (and a spouse or companion of any age) in the U.S. and in more than 80 countries around the world. Most courses last 5 to 7 days in the U.S. (2–4 weeks abroad), and many include airfare, accommodations in university dormitories or modest inns, meals, and tuition. **ElderTreks** (© **800/741-7956;** www.eldertreks. com) offers small-group tours to off-the-beaten-path or adventure-travel locations, restricted to travelers 50 and older. **INTRAV** (© **800/456-8100;** www.intrav.com) is a high-end tour operator that caters to the mature, discerning traveler, not specifically seniors, with trips around the world that include guided safaris, polar expeditions, private-jet adventures, and small-boat cruises down jungle rivers.

A Cultural Note for Families & Seniors

At most state-run museums, children under 18 and seniors get in free, *but only if* they hail from one of the countries that has signed a reciprocal international cultural agreement to allow children and seniors this privilege. These countries include England, Canada, Ireland, Australia, New Zealand, and indeed much of the world—but *not* the United States. (However, many museum guards either don't ask for citizenship ID or wave kids and seniors on through anyway.) Children and seniors, no matter what their nationality, also get discounts on trains (see "Getting Around," later in this chapter).

FAMILY TRAVEL

If you have enough trouble getting your kids out of the house in the morning, dragging them thousands of miles away may seem like an insurmountable challenge. But family travel can be immensely rewarding, giving you and your children exciting new ways to see the world. As an added plus, little helps mature the kids faster than international travel.

Italians expect to see families traveling together and tend to love kids. You'll often find that a child in tow guarantees you an even warmer reception at hotels and restaurants.

At **restaurants,** ask waiters for a half-portion to fit junior's appetite. If you're traveling with small children, government-rated three- and four-star hotels may be your best bet—**babysitters** are on call, and such hotels have a better general ability to help you access the city and its services. But even cheaper hotels can usually find you a sitter. Traveling with a pint-size person usually entails pint-size rates. An **extra cot** in the room won't cost more than 30% extra—if anything—and most museums and sights offer **reduced-price** or free admission for children under a certain age (ranging 6–18). Kids almost always get discounts on plane and train tickets.

Familyhostel (© **800/733-9753;** www.learn.unh.edu/familyhostel) takes the whole family, including kids ages 8 to 15, on moderately priced domestic and international learning vacations. Lectures, field trips, and sightseeing are guided by a team of academics.

WOMEN TRAVELERS

Women will feel remarkably welcome Italy—sometimes a bit too welcome, actually. Yes, it seems as if every young Italian male is out to prove himself the most irresistible lover on the planet; remember, this is the land of Romeo and Casanova, so they have a lot to live up to.

From parading and preening like peacocks to wooing each passing female with words, whistles, and, if they can get close enough, the entirely inappropriate butt-pinch, these men and their attentiveness can range from charming and flattering to downright annoying and frustrating. The more exotic you look—statuesque blondes, ebony-skinned beauties, or simply an American accent—the more irresistible you become to these suitors.

And, as everyone around the world knows from watching Hollywood movies, American women are all uninhibited and passionate sex kittens. Alas, this falsehood doesn't make much of a dent in Italian boys' fantasies.

Flirting back at these would-be Romeos, even mildly, only convinces them that you're ready to jump into bed. Heck, mere eye contact encourages them to redouble their efforts. Unless you want all this attention, take your cue from Italian women, who may wear tight skirts and fishnets but, you'll notice, usually ignore the men around them entirely unless it's someone they're already walking with.

If you find yourself moderately molested on a bus or other crowded place—mostly the infamous bottom-pinching and rather inappropriate rubbing—tell him to "*Smetti la!*" ("Stop it!") and proceed to pinch, scratch, elbow, and so on to further discourage him or enlist the aid of the nearest convenient elderly Italian woman to noisily chastise the offender and perhaps whap him with her purse.

Note that all of this is kept to verbal flirtation and the occasional inappropriate touching that deserves a slap in the face. These men want to conquer you with their charm, not their muscles; rape is nearly unheard of in Italy. Most women report feeling far safer wandering the deserted streets of an Italian city back to their hotels at 2am than they do in their own neighborhoods back home, and that feeling is largely justified. You'll probably get tons of ride offers, though, from would-be chivalrous knights atop their Vespa or Fiat steeds. **Women Welcome Women World Wide (5W; ℭ 203/259-7832** in the U.S.; www.womenwelcomewomen. org.uk) works to foster international friendships by enabling women of different countries to visit one another (men can come along on the trips; they just can't join the club). It's a big, active organization, with more than 3,500 members from all walks of life in some 70 countries.

Check out the award-winning website **Journeywoman** (www.journey woman.com), a "real life" women's travel information network where you can sign up for a free e-mail newsletter and get advice on everything from etiquette and dress to safety; or the travel guide *Safety and Security for Women Who Travel,* by Sheila Swan and Peter Laufer (Travelers' Tales, Inc.), offering common-sense tips on safe travel.

STUDENTS & YOUTHS

If you're planning to travel outside the U.S., you'd be wise to arm yourself with an **International Student Identity Card (ISIC),** which offers substantial savings on rail passes, plane tickets, and entrance fees—note that your own school's ID will often *usually* suffice to snag you those discount admission at sights and museums across Europe; you need the ISIC for discounts on the rest. It also provides you with basic health and life insurance and a 24-hour help line. The card is available for $22 from **STA Travel** (ℭ 800/781-4040, and if you're not in North America there's probably a local number in your country; www.statravel.com), the biggest student travel agency in the world.

If you're no longer a student but are still under 26, you can get an **International Youth Travel Card (IYTC)** for the same price from the same people, which entitles you to some discounts (but not on museum admissions). (*Note:* In 2002, STA Travel bought competitors **Council Travel** and **USIT Campus** after they went bankrupt. It's still operating some offices under the Council name, but it's owned by STA.)

Travel CUTS (ℭ 800/667-2887 or 416/614-2887; www.travelcuts. com) offers similar services for both Canadians and U.S. residents. They also have a London office, 295A Regent St., London W1B 2H9 (ℭ **0207/255-2082**); or try **USIT Campus,** 52 Grosvenor Gardens, London SW1W 0AG (ℭ **0870/240-1010;** www.usitcampus.co.uk), Britain's leading specialist in student and youth travel. Irish students should turn to USIT (ℭ **0818/200-020;** www.usitnow.ie).

The Hanging Out Guides (www.frommers.com/hangingout), published by Frommer's, is the top student travel series for today's students, covering everything from adrenaline sports to the hottest club and music scenes.

If you enjoy meeting other young travelers on the road—and want to save money—consider staying in **hostels.** Some are quite nice and charge only $10 to $35 per night for what's generally a bunk in a dormlike room (often sex-segregated) sleeping anywhere from 4 to 50 or more and with a single big bathroom down the hall, college dorm–style. Happily, the recent trend at hostels has been away from gymnasium-size dorms and toward smaller shared units of four to six, often with a bathroom attached to each. There's usually a lockout from morning to midafternoon and a curfew of around 10pm to 1am—which

---

Tips Book 'em Early

Most youth hostels fill up in the summer, so be sure to book ahead.

---

can seriously cramp your evening plans, especially since many hostels are at the edge of town, meaning you have to finish dinner rather early to catch that long bus or Metro ride back out.

There are usually lockers for your bags, and you often must bring your own sleep-sack (basically a sheet folded in half and sewn up the side to make a very thin sleeping bag) or buy one onsite. For many, you need a **Hostelling International (HI) membership card** (see below)—at some, the card is required for a stay; at others, it gets you a discount; and at some private hostels, the card doesn't matter at all.

Membership in **Hostelling International,** 8401 Colesville Rd., Suite 600, Silver Spring, MD 20910 (© **301/ 495-1240;** www.hiusa.org), an affiliate of the International Youth Hostel Federation (IYH), is free for those under 18, $28 per year for people 18 to 54, $18 for those 55 and older, and $250 for a lifetime membership. HI sells the annual *International Guide—Europe* for $13.95. But in the days of the Internet, the official website of **Hostelling International** (www.hihostels.com) and that of independent **www. hostels.com** are free, more up-to-date, and far more useful than any print book. For more resources and direct links to the hostel organizations in each European country, check out the independent **www.europehostels.org.**

10 Planning Your Trip Online

SURFING FOR AIRFARES

The "big three" online travel agencies, **Expedia.com, Travelocity.com**, and **Orbitz.com**, sell most of the air tickets bought on the Internet. (Canadian travelers should try www.expedia.ca and www.travelocity.ca; U.K. residents can go to www.expedia.co.uk and www.opodo.co.uk.) Each has different business deals with the airlines and may offer different fares on the same flights, so it's wise to shop around. Expedia and Travelocity will also send you **e-mail notification** when a cheap fare becomes available to your favorite destination. Of the smaller travel agency websites, **SideStep** (www.sidestep.com) has gotten the best reviews from Frommer's authors. It's a browser add-on (you have to download it) that "searches 140 sites at once," saving you the trouble of doing so independently, but it works only on PCs. Also check out Web-based www.cheapflights.com for major airline fares, consolidator offers, and other great deals.

Also remember to check **airline websites,** especially those for Europe's 40-odd **low-cost/no-frills carriers** like easyJct (www.easyjet.com) and Ryanair (www.ryanair.com), whose fares are often misreported or simply missing from travel agency websites. You can find them all gathered at **www.nofrillsair.com.** Even with major airlines, you can often shave a few bucks from a fare by booking directly through the airline and avoiding a travel agency's transaction fee. But you'll get these discounts only by **booking online:** Most airlines now offer online-only fares that even their phone agents know nothing about. For the websites of airlines that fly to and from your destination, go to "Getting There," below.

Frommers.com: The Complete Travel Resource

For an excellent travel-planning resource, we highly recommend Frommers.com (www.frommers.com). We're a little biased, of course, but we guarantee that you'll find the travel tips, reviews, monthly vacation giveaways, and online-booking capabilities indispensable. Among the special features are our popular **Message Boards,** where Frommer's readers post queries and share advice (sometimes we authors even show up to answer questions); **Frommers.com Newsletter,** for the latest travel bargains and insider travel secrets; and **Frommer's Destinations Section,** where you'll get expert travel tips, hotel and dining recommendations, and advice on the sights to see for more than 3,000 destinations around the globe. When your research is done, the **Online Reservations System** (www.frommers.com/book_a_trip) takes you to Frommer's preferred online partners for booking your vacation at affordable prices.

Great **last-minute deals** are available through free weekly e-mail services provided directly by the airlines. Most of these are announced on Tuesday or Wednesday and must be purchased online. Most are valid only for travel that weekend, but some can be booked weeks or months in advance. Sign up for weekly e-mail alerts at airline websites or check megasites that compile comprehensive lists of last-minute specials, such as **Smarter Living** (www.smarterliving.com). For last-minute trips, **site59.com** and **lastminutetravel.com** in the U.S., and **lastminute.com** in Europe often have better air-and-hotel package deals than the major-label sites. A website listing numerous bargain sites and airlines around the world is **www.itravelnet.com**.

If you're willing to give up some control over your flight details, use an **opaque fare service** like **Priceline** (www.priceline.com; www.priceline.co.uk for Europeans) or **Hotwire** (www.hotwire.com). Both offer rock-bottom prices in exchange for travel on a "mystery airline" at a mysterious time of day, often with a mysterious change of planes en route. The mystery airlines are all major, well-known carriers—and the possibility of being sent from Philadelphia to Chicago via Tampa is remote; the airlines' routing computers have gotten a lot better than they used to be. But your chances of getting a 6am or 11pm flight are pretty high. Hotwire tells you flight prices before you buy; Priceline usually has better deals than Hotwire, but you have to play their "name our price" game. If you're new at this, the helpful folks at **Bidding-ForTravel** (www.biddingfortravel.com) do a good job of demystifying Priceline's prices. Priceline and Hotwire are great for flights within North America and between the U.S. and Europe. But for flights to other parts of the world, consolidators will almost always beat their fares. *Note:* In 2004, Priceline added nonopaque service to its roster. You now have the option to pick exact flights, times, and airlines from a list of offers—or opt to bid on opaque fares as before.

For much more about airfares and savvy air-travel tips and advice, pick up a copy of *Frommer's Fly Safe, Fly Smart* (Wiley Publishing, Inc.).

SURFING FOR HOTELS

Shopping online for hotels is much easier in the U.S., Canada, and certain parts of Europe than it is in the rest of the world. If you try to book a Chinese hotel online, for instance, you'll probably overpay, but for Europe, the system is as svelte as is it in the U.S. However, note that most smaller hotels and B&Bs (especially outside the U.S.) don't show up on these booking engine websites at all—a shame since, by and large, those smaller places tend to be the most charming and least expensive. In other words, it can be a good resource for booking a room in a four-star, multinational chain hotel, but not so good for that cheap local B&B or pensione.

Of the "big three" sites, **Expedia** offers a long list of special deals and "virtual tours" or photos of available rooms so you can see what you're paying for (a feature that helps counter the claims that the best rooms are often held back from bargain-booking websites). **Travelocity** posts unvarnished customer reviews and ranks its properties according to the AAA rating system. Also reliable are **Hotels.com** and **Quikbook.com.** An excellent free program, **TravelAxe** (www.travelaxe.net), can help you search multiple hotel sites at once, even ones you may never have heard of—and conveniently lists the total price of the room, including the taxes and service charges.

Another booking site, **Travelweb** (www.travelweb.com), is partly owned by the hotels it represents (including the Hilton, Hyatt, and Starwood chains) and is therefore plugged directly into the hotels' reservations systems—unlike independent online agencies, which have to fax or e-mail reservation requests to the hotel, a good portion of which get misplaced in the shuffle. More than once, travelers have arrived at the hotel only to be told that they have no reservation. To be fair, many of the major sites are undergoing improvements in service and ease of use, and Expedia will soon be able to plug directly into the reservations systems of many hotel chains—none of which can be bad news for consumers. In the meantime, it's a good idea to **get a confirmation number** and **make a printout** of any online booking transaction.

In the opaque website category, **Priceline** and **Hotwire** are even better for hotels than for airfares; with both, you're allowed to pick the neighborhood and quality level of your hotel before offering up your money. Priceline's hotel product even covers Europe and Asia, though it's much better at getting five-star lodging for three-star prices than at finding anything at the bottom of the scale. On the downside, many hotels stick Priceline guests in their least desirable rooms. Be sure to go to the Bidding-forTravel website (see above) before bidding on a hotel room on Priceline; it features a fairly up-to-date list of hotels that Priceline uses in major cities. For both Priceline and Hotwire, you pay upfront, and the fee is nonrefundable. *Note:* Some hotels do not provide loyalty program credits or points or other frequent-stay amenities when you book a room through opaque online services.

---

11 Getting There

BY PLANE

FROM NORTH AMERICA   From North America, direct flights are available only to Rome and Milan, though you can usually get a connecting flight to Venice, Florence, Palermo, Naples, or other major city. **Flying time** from New York is roughly 8 hours, from Chicago 9¼ hours, and from Los Angeles 11½ hours.

Online Traveler's Toolbox

Veteran travelers usually carry some essential items to make their trips easier. Following is a selection of online tools to bookmark and use.

- **Airplane Seating and Food.** Find out which seats to reserve and which to avoid (and more) on all major domestic airlines at www.seat guru.com. And check out the type of meal (with photos) you'll likely be served on airlines around the world at www.airlinemeals.com.

- **Visa ATM Locator** (www.visa.com), for locations of Plus ATMs worldwide, or **MasterCard ATM Locator** (www.mastercard.com), for locations of Cirrus ATMs worldwide.

- **Foreign Languages for Travelers** (www.travlang.com). Learn basic terms in more than 70 languages, and click on any underlined phrase to hear what it sounds like.

- **Intellicast** (www.intellicast.com) and **Weather.com** (www.weather. com). Give weather forecasts for all 50 states and for cities around the world.

- **Mapquest** (www.mapquest.com). This best of the mapping sites lets you choose a specific address or destination, and in seconds, it will return a map and detailed directions.

- **Universal Currency Converter** (www.xe.com/ucc). See what your dollar or pound is worth in more than 100 other countries.

- **Subway Navigator** (www.subwaynavigator.com). Download subway maps and get savvy advice on using subway systems in dozens of major cities around the world.

- **Time and Date** (www.timeanddate.com). See what time (and day) it is anywhere in the world.

- **Travel Warnings** (http://travel.state.gov/travel_warnings.html, www. fco.gov.uk/travel, www.voyage.gc.ca, www.dfat.gov.au/consular/ advice). These sites report on places where health concerns or unrest might threaten American, British, Canadian, and Australian travelers. Generally, U.S. warnings are the most paranoid; Australian warnings are the most relaxed.

The Major Airlines   Italy's national airline, **Alitalia** (© 800/223-5730; www.alitalia.it), offers more flights daily to Italy than any other airline. It flies direct to both Rome and Milan from New York, Newark, Boston, Chicago, Los Angeles, and Miami. You can connect in Rome or Milan to any other Italian destination.

British Airways (© 800/247-9297; www.ba.com) flies direct from dozens of U.S. and Canadian cities to London, where you can get connecting flights to Milan. **Air Canada** (© 888/ 247-2262, or 800/361-8071 TTY; www.aircanada.ca) flies daily from Toronto and Vancouver to Rome. **Continental** (© 800/231-0856; www.continental.com) doesn't fly to Italy itself, but it's partnered with Alitalia for the Newark-to-Rome and New York JFK-to-Milan flights, so if you're a Continental Frequent Flyer, you can reserve through Continental and rack up the miles. **Delta** (© 800/ 241-4141; www.delta.com) flies daily out of New York JFK (you can connect from most major U.S. cities) to Rome and Milan.

Possibly less convenient alternatives are **American Airlines** (℗ 800/ 433-7300; www.aa.com), whose flights from the United States to Milan all go through Chicago; **United** (℗ 800/528-2929; www.ual.com), which flies once daily to Milan out of New York, Newark, and Washington, D.C. Dulles; or **US Airways** (℗ 800/622-1015; www.usairways. com), which offers one flight daily to Rome out of Philadelphia. (You can connect through Philly from most major U.S. cities.)

FROM GREAT BRITAIN & IRELAND British Airways (℗ 0845/ 773-3377; www.ba.com) flies twice daily from London's Gatwick to Pisa. **Alitalia** (020-87458200; www.alitalia.it) has four daily flights from London to both Rome and Milan. **KLM UK** (formerly Air UK; ℗ 08705/074-074; www.klmuk. com) flies several times per week from London Heathrow to Milan (both airports) and Rome. In each case, there's a layover in Amsterdam.

No-frills upstart **Ryanair** (℗ 0871/ 246-0000 in the U.K.; www.ryan air.com) will fly you from London to Rome, Milan-Bergamo, Bologna, Genoa, Pisa, Trieste, Turin, Venice-Treviso, Venice-Brescia, Alghero, Ancona, Palermo, Pescara, Bari, or Brindisi. Its competitor, **EasyJet** (www.easyjet.com), flies from London to Rome, Milan, Venice, Bologna, and Naples. Both usually charge less than 36€ ($40) each way for such service. The East Midlands-based **bmibaby** (www.bmibaby.com) flies to Milan-Bergamo as well as Pisa.

There are more than 40 no-frills airlines in Europe these days, the roster constantly changing as some upstarts prosper and grow, and others wither and die. Independent websites **www.lowcostairlines.org** and

www.nofrillsair.com keep track of the industry. Another site, **Applefares. com,** will do a pricing metasearch of some two dozen low-cost European airlines, including some, but not all, of those listed above, plus some other, smaller ones. That way, you can see the going rate for, say, a London-to-Rome ticket—though it's not a booking engine, just a search engine.

The best and cheapest way to get to Italy from Ireland is to make your way first to London and fly from there (see above; to book through **British Airways** in Ireland, dial ℗ 800/626-747). **Aer Lingus** (℗ 0818/365-000 in Ireland; www.aerlingus.com) flies direct from Dublin to both Rome and Milan about 5 days a week. **Alitalia** (℗ 01-6775171) puts you on a British Midland to get you to London, where you change to an Alitalia plane for the trip to Rome. For **RyanAir,** call ℗ 0818/ 303-030 in Ireland.

FROM AUSTRALIA & NEW ZEALAND Alitalia (℗ 02-99221555; www.alitalia.it) has a flight from Sydney to Rome every Thursday and Saturday. **Qantas** (℗ 13/1313 in Australia or 0649/357-8900 in Auckland, New Zealand; www.qantas.com) flies three times daily to Rome via Bangkok, leaving Australia from Sydney, Melbourne, Brisbane, or Cairns. Qantas will also book you through one of these Australian cities from Auckland, Wellington, or Christchurch in New Zealand. You can also look into flying first into London and connecting to Italy from there. (There are more flights, and it may work out to be cheaper.)

GETTING THROUGH THE AIRPORT

With the federalization of airport security, security procedures at U.S. airports are more stable and consistent than ever. Generally, you'll be fine if you arrive at the airport **2 hours** before an international flight; if you show up late, tell an airline employee and she'll probably whisk you to the front of the line.

Bring a **current, government-issued photo ID** such as a driver's license or passport. Keep your ID at the ready to show at check-in, the security checkpoint, and sometimes even the gate. (Children under 18 do not need government-issued photo IDs for domestic flights, but they do for international flights to most countries.) In 2003, the TSA phased out **gate check-in** at all U.S. airports. And e-tickets have made paper tickets nearly obsolete. Passengers with e-tickets can beat the ticket-counter lines by using airport **electronic kiosks** or even **online check-in** from your home computer. Online check-in involves logging on to your airline's website, accessing your reservation, and printing out your boarding pass—and the airline may even offer you bonus miles to do so! If you're using a kiosk at the airport, bring the credit card you used to book the ticket or your frequent-flier card. Print out your boarding pass from the kiosk and simply proceed to the security checkpoint with your pass and a photo ID. If you're checking bags or looking to snag an exit-row seat, you will be able to do so using most airline kiosks. Even the smaller airlines are employing the kiosk system, but always call your airline to make sure these alternatives are available. **Curbside check-in** is also a good way to avoid lines, although a few airlines still ban curbside check-in; call before you go.

Security lines are getting shorter than they were during 2001 and 2002, but some doozies remain. If you have trouble standing for long periods of time, tell an airline employee; the airline will provide a wheelchair. Speed up security by **not wearing metal objects** such as big belt buckles or clanky earrings. If you've got metallic

body parts, a note from your doctor can prevent a long chat with the security screeners. Keep in mind that only **ticketed passengers** are allowed past security, except for folks escorting disabled passengers or children.

Federalization has stabilized **what you can carry on** and **what you can't.** The general rule is that sharp things are out, nail clippers are okay, and food and beverages must be passed through the X-ray machine—but security screeners can't make you drink from your coffee cup. Bring food in your carry-on rather than checking it, as explosive-detection machines used on checked luggage have been known to mistake food (especially chocolate, for some reason) for bombs. Travelers in the U.S. are allowed one carry-on bag, plus a "personal item" such as a purse, briefcase, or laptop bag. Carry-on hoarders can stuff all sorts of things into a laptop bag; as long as it has a laptop in it, it's still considered a personal item. The **Transportation Security Administration (TSA)** has issued a list of restricted items; check its website (www.tsa.gov/public/index.jsp) for details.

Airport screeners may decide that your checked luggage needs to be searched by hand. You can now purchase luggage locks that allow screeners to open and relock a checked bag if hand searching is necessary. Look for Travel Sentry certified locks at luggage or travel shops and Brookstone stores (you can buy them online at www.brookstone.com). These locks, approved by the TSA, can be opened by luggage inspectors with a special code or key. For more information on the locks, visit www.travelsentry.org. If you use something other than TSA-approved locks, your lock will be cut off your suitcase if a TSA agent needs to hand-search your luggage.

FLYING FOR LESS: TIPS FOR GETTING THE BEST AIRFARE

Passengers sharing the same airplane cabin rarely pay the same fare. Travelers who need to purchase tickets at the last minute, change their itinerary at a moment's notice, or fly one-way often get stuck paying the premium rate. Here are some ways to keep your airfare costs down.

- Passengers who can book their ticket **long in advance,** who can **stay over Saturday night,** or who **fly midweek** or **at less-trafficked hours** may pay a fraction of the full fare. If your schedule is flexible, say so, and ask if you can secure a cheaper fare by changing your flight plans.
- You can also save on airfares by keeping an eye out in local newspapers for **promotional specials** or **fare wars,** when airlines lower prices on their most popular routes. You rarely see fare wars offered for peak travel times, but if you can travel in the off months, you may snag a bargain.
- Search **the Internet** for cheap fares (see "Planning Your Trip Online," earlier in this chapter).
- **Consolidators,** also known as bucket shops, are great sources for international tickets. Start by looking in Sunday newspaper travel sections; U.S. travelers should focus on the *New York Times, Los Angeles Times,* and *Miami Herald.* For less-developed destinations, small travel agents who cater to immigrant communities in large cities often have the best deals. *Beware:* Bucket shop tickets are usually nonrefundable or rigged with stiff cancellation penalties, often as high as 50% to 75% of the ticket price, and some put you on charter airlines that may leave at inconvenient times and experience delays. Several reliable consolidators are worldwide and available on the Net. **STA Travel** is now the world's leader in student travel, thanks to their purchase of Council Travel. It also offers good fares for travelers of all ages. Destination Europe, the airfares branch of car renter **Auto Europe** (www.autoeurope.com), consistently offers the some of the best transatlantic fares at any time of year. **ELTExpress** (**Flights.com;** ✆ **800/TRAV-800;** www.eltexpress.com) started in Europe and has excellent fares worldwide, but particularly to that continent. It also has "local" websites in 12 countries. **FlyCheap** (✆ **800/FLY-CHEAP;** www.1800flycheap.com) is owned by package-holiday megalith MyTravel and so has especially good access to fares for sunny destinations. **Air Tickets Direct** (✆ **800/778-3447;** www.airticketsdirect.com) is based in Montreal and leverages the currently weak Canadian dollar for low fares; it'll also book trips to places that U.S. travel agents won't touch, such as Cuba.
- Join **frequent-flier clubs.** Accrue enough miles, and you'll be rewarded with free flights and elite status. It's free, and you'll get the best choice of seats, faster response to phone inquiries, and prompter service if your luggage is stolen, if your flight is canceled or delayed, or if you want to change your seat. You don't need to fly to build frequent-flier miles—**frequent-flier credit cards** can provide thousands of miles for doing your everyday shopping.
- For many more tips about air travel, including a rundown of the major frequent-flier credit cards, pick up a copy of *Frommer's Fly Safe, Fly Smart* (Wiley Publishing, Inc.).

Travel in the Age of Bankruptcy

Airlines go bankrupt, so protect yourself by **buying your tickets with a credit card,** as the Fair Credit Billing Act guarantees that you can get your money back from the credit card company if a travel supplier goes under (and if you request the refund within 60 days of the bankruptcy.) **Travel insurance** can also help, but make sure it covers "carrier default" for your specific travel provider. And be aware that if a U.S. airline goes bust midtrip, a 2001 federal law requires other carriers to take you to your destination (albeit on a space-available basis) for a fee of no more than $25, provided you rebook within 60 days of the cancellation.

GETTING THERE BY CAR

You'll get the **best rental rate** if you book your car from home instead of renting direct in Italy—in fact, if you decide to rent once you're over there, it's worth it to call home to have someone arrange it all from there. You must be over 25 to rent from most agencies (although some accept 21).

Though it once was smart shopping to see what rates Italian companies were offering, they're all now allied with the big agents in the States: **Avis** (© 800/230-4898, or in Italy toll-free 199-100133; www.avis.com), **Budget** (© 800/527-0700; www.budget.com), **Hertz** (© 800/654-3131 or 800/654-3001; www.hertz.com), and **National** (© 800/227-7368; www.nationalcar.com).

You can usually get a better rate by going through one of the rental companies specializing in Europe: **Auto Europe** (© 888/223-5555; www.autoeurope.com), **Europe by Car** (© 800/223-1516, or 212/581-3040 in New York City; www.europebycar.com), **Kemwell** (© 800/678-0678; www.kemwell.com), and **Maiellano** (© 800/223-1616 or 718/727-0044). With constant price wars and special packages, it always pays to shop around among all the above.

When offered the choice between a compact car and a larger one, always choose the smaller car (unless you have a large group)—you'll need it for maneuvering the winding, steeply graded Italian roads and the impossibly narrow alleyways of towns and cities. Likewise, if you can drive stick shift, order one; it'll help you better navigate the hilly terrain—and it's cheaper to rent and more common, to boot. It's also a good idea to opt for the **Collision Damage Waiver (CDW),** which for only $10 to $20 a day gives you the peace of mind and nerves of steel that driving in Italy requires; you pay only $7 per day for this service if you buy it through a third-party insurer such as Travel Guard (www.travelguard.com). Although the 19% IVA value-added tax is unavoidable, you can do away with the government airport pick-up tax of 10% by picking up your car at an office in town.

For more on driving in Italy, from road rules to maps, to gasoline, see the "Getting Around" section later in this chapter.

GETTING THERE BY TRAIN

Every day, up to 14 **Eurostar** trains (reservations in London © 0875/186-186; www.eurostar.com) zip from London to Paris's Gare du Nord via the **Chunnel** (Eurotunnel) in a bit over 4 hours. In Paris, you can transfer to the Paris Gare de Lyon station or Paris Bercy for one of three daily direct trains to **Milan,** overnight to **Venice** (15 hr.), and to a few other cities. Some of the Milan runs are high-speed TGV trains, a 6½-hour ride requiring a seat reservation. At least one will be an overnight Euronight (EN) train, with reservable sleeping couchettes; the Euronight leaves Paris around 10pm and gets into Milan around 8:45am.

If you plan on doing a lot of train travel, the definitive 500-page book listing all official European train routes and schedules is the *Thomas Cook European Timetable,* available in the United States for $27.95 (plus $4.50 shipping and handling) from Forsyth Travel Library, P.O. Box 2975, Shawnee Mission, KS 66201 (© **800/ 367-7984**), at travel specialty stores, or online at **www.thomascooktime tables.com**.

You can get much more information about train travel in Europe, plus research schedules and fares (largely for major routes) online, at **Rail Europe** (© **877/257-2887;** www. raileurope.com). For more on using Europe's trains, including resources for finding each country's national railway website—which will include much more detailed schedule and fare info than RailEurope, sometimes even in English!—check out **www.europe trains.org**.

EUROPEAN-WIDE RAIL PASSES
If Italy is only part of a larger European tour for you, the famous Eurailpass or new Eurail Selectpass may be useful (see below). The granddaddy of passes is the **Eurailpass,** covering 17 countries (most of Western Europe except England). It has recently been joined by the more modest but flexible Eurail Selectpass (an improvement on the old Europass), which can be

customized to cover three to five contiguous countries.

If, however, you're traveling only in the regions covered by this guide or just in Italy, these passes will be a waste of money. Similarly, if you're merely coming straight to Italy by train from another point within Europe, it'll be cheaper to buy just a regular one-way ticket. If this is the case and you're **under 26,** get a BIJ (Billet International de Jeunesse, or youth ticket, known as BIGE in Italy), which gets you a 30% to 50% discount on the second-class one-way fare. It also allows you a full month to get to your destination, during which time you can hop on and off the trains as often as you wish, so long as you stay headed in the direction of your final destination. BIJ tickets are sold only in Europe, under the names of Wasteels and Eurotrain, but you can get further information on them at **Wasteels Travel** (www.wasteels.com). In London, you can get the tickets at the Wasteels office at Victoria Station (© **020/7834-7066**).

For the Eurailpass and Eurorail Selectpass described below, you need to scribble the date on the pass as you hop on the train; you don't need to wait in line at the ticket window. However, you will need to go to the ticket window if the train you want to take requires you to reserve a seat (such as the Pendolino, which, as a first-class train, doesn't accept the second-class youth passes) or if you want a spot in a sleeping couchette. The Eurailpass gets you only a 33% discount on the TGV train through the Chunnel from London to Paris. The

---

Countries Honoring Train Passes
Eurail Countries: Austria, Belgium, Denmark, Finland, France, Germany, Greece, Hungary, Ireland, Italy, Luxembourg, the Netherlands, Norway, Portugal, Spain, Sweden, and Switzerland. *Note:* Great Britain isn't included in any pass.

passes below are available in the United States through **Rail Europe** (© **877/257-2887;** www.raileurope. com). No matter what everyone tells you, they *can* be bought in Europe as well (at the major train stations) but are more expensive. Rail Europe can also give you information on the rail-and-drive versions of the passes.

Rail passes are available in either **consecutive-day** or **flexipass** versions (in which you have 2 months to use, say, 10 or 15 days of train travel of your choosing as you go along). Consecutive-day passes are best for those taking the train very frequently (every few days), covering a lot of ground, and making many short train hops. Flexipasses are for folks who want to range far and wide but plan on taking their time over a long trip and intend to stay in each city for a while. There are also **saverpasses** for families and small groups, and **rail/drive** passes that mix train days with car-rental days.

If you're **under age 26,** you can opt to buy a regular first-class pass or a second-class youth pass; if you're 26 or over, you're stuck with the first-class pass. Passes for **kids 4 to 11** are half-price, and kids under 4 travel free. The rates quoted below are for 2004:

- **Eurailpass:** Consecutive-day Eurailpass $588 for 15 days, $762 for 21 days, $946 for 1 month, $1,338 for 2 months, and $1,654 for 3 months.
- **Eurailpass Flexi:** Good for 2 months of travel, within which you can travel by train for 10 days (consecutive or not) for $694 or 15 days for $914.
- **Eurailpass Saver:** Good for two to five people traveling together, costing $498 per person for 15 days, $648 for 21 days, $804 for 1 month, $1,138 for 2 months, and $1,408 for 3 months.

- **Eurailpass Saver Flexi:** Good for two to five people traveling together, costing $592 per person for 10 days within 2 months, or $778 per person for 15 days within 2 months.
- **Eurailpass Youth:** The second-class rail pass for travelers under 26, costing $414 for 15 days, $534 for 21 days, $664 for 1 month, $938 for 2 months, and $1,160 for 3 months.
- **Eurailpass Youth Flexi:** Only for travelers under 26, allowing for 10 days of travel within 2 months for $488, or 15 days within 2 months for $642.
- **Eurail Selectpass:** For the most tightly focused of trips, covering three to five contiguous Eurail countries connected by rail or ship. It's valid for 2 months, and cost varies according to the number of countries you plan to visit. A pass for three countries is $356 for 5 days, $394 for 6 days, $470 for 8 days, and $542 for 10 days. A four-country pass costs $398 for 5 days, $436 for 6 days, $512 for 8 days, and $584 for 10 days. A pass for five countries costs $438 for 5 days, $476 for 6 days, $552 for 8 days, $624 for 10 days, and $794 for 15 days.
- **Eurail Selectpass Saver:** Same as the Eurail Selectpass (and slightly less expensive), but for two to five people traveling together. Per person, the three-country pass is $304 for 5 days, $336 for 6 days, $400 for 8 days, and $460 for 10 days. A pass for four countries is $340 for 5 days, $372 for 6 days, $436 for 8 days, and $496 for 10 days. A five-country pass is $374 for 5 days, $406 for 6 days, $470 for 8 days, $530 for 10 days, and $674 for 15 days.
- **Eurail Selectpass Youth:** Good in second class only for travelers

under 26. Cost varies according to the number of countries you plan to visit, but all passes are valid for 2 months. For three countries, it's $249 for 5 days, $276 for 6 days, $329 for 8 days, and $379 for 10 days. A four-country pass costs $279 for 5 days, $306 for 6 days, $359 for 8 days, and $409 for 10 days. A five-country pass is $307 for 5 days, $334 for 6 days, $387 for 8 days, $437 for 10 days, and $556 for 15 days.

- **EurailDrive Pass:** This pass offers the best of both worlds, mixing train travel and rental cars (through Hertz or Avis) for less money than it would cost to do them separately (and one of the only ways to get around the high daily car-rental rates in Europe when you rent for less than a week). You get four first-class rail days and 2 car days within a 2-month period. Prices (per person for 1 adult/2 adults) vary with the class of the car: $452/$409 economy, $481/$423 compact, $496/$431 midsize, $531/$447 small automatic (Hertz only). You can add up to 6 extra car days ($49

each economy, $64 compact, $75 midsize, $95 small automatic [Hertz only]). You have to reserve the first "car day" a week before leaving the States but can make the other reservations as you go (subject to availability). If there are more than two adults, the extra passengers get the car portion free but must buy the 4-day rail pass for about $365.

- **Eurail SelectPass Drive:** This pass, like the EurailDrive Pass, offers combined train and rental car travel, but only for very focused trips: within any three to five adjoining Eurail countries. A flexipass, it includes 3 days of unlimited, first-class rail travel and 2 days of unlimited-mileage car rental (through Avis or Hertz) within a 2-month period. Prices (per person for one adult/two adults) are $335/$291 economy, $365/$305 compact, $392/$315 midsize, and $429/$331 small automatic. You can add up to 7 additional rail days for $39 each and unlimited extra car days for $49 to $95 each, depending on the class of car.

12 Packages for the Independent Traveler

Before you start your search for the lowest airfare, you may want to consider booking your flight as part of a travel package. Package tours are not the same thing as escorted tours. Package tours are simply a way to buy the airfare, accommodations, and other elements of your trip (such as car rentals, airport transfers, and sometimes even activities) at the same time and often at discounted prices—kind of like one-stop shopping. Packages are sold in bulk to tour operators—who resell them to the public at a cost that usually undercuts standard rates.

One good source of package deals is the airlines themselves. Most major airlines offer air/land packages, including **American Airlines Vacations** (© 800/321-2121; www.aavacations.com), **Delta Vacations** (© 800/221-6666; www.deltavacations.com), **Continental Airlines Vacations** (© 800/301-3800; www.covacations.com), and **United Vacations** (© 888/854-3899; www.unitedvacations.com).

The single best-priced packager to Europe, though, is the Internet-only travel agent **Go-Today.com** (www.go-today.com), which offers excellent 4- and 6-night air/hotel packages throughout the continent, as well as airfare/car rental deals. Its up-and-coming rival **Octopus Travel** (© 877/330-7765; www.octopuspackages.com) sometimes undercuts Go-Today.com's rates, but look carefully at the hotels you get. Often with Octopus, the lodgings are located way on the outskirts of town. By the time you "upgrade" to a property near the historic center and take a look at the new rate, Go-Today.com turns out the real price champ. **Italiatours** (© 800/845-3365; www.italiatourusa.com) is the tour operator branch of Alitalia airlines and offers package and escorted tours at extremely attractive prices. **TourCrafters** (© 800/ITALY95** or 847/816-6510; www.tourcrafters.com) offers escorted, hosted, and independent tours throughout Italy. Among the more traditional travel agencies, **Liberty Travel** (© 888/271-1584; www.libertytravel.com) is one of the biggest packagers in the Northeast and usually boasts a full-page ad in Sunday papers. **American Express Vacations** (© 800/241-1700; www.americanexpress.com) is one of the most reputable national operators. Several big **online travel agencies**—Expedia, Travelocity, Orbitz, Site59, and Lastminute.com—also do a brisk business in packages. If you're unsure about the pedigree of a smaller packager, check with the Better Business Bureau in the city where the company is based, or go online at www.bbb.org. If a packager won't tell you where it's based, don't fly with it.

Travel packages are also listed in the travel section of your local Sunday newspaper. Or check ads in the national travel magazines, such as *Arthur Frommer's Budget Travel, Travel & Leisure, National Geographic Traveler,* and *Condé Nast Traveler.*

Package tours can vary by leaps and bounds. Some offer a better class of hotels than others. Some offer the same hotels for lower prices. Some offer flights on scheduled airlines, while others book charters. Some limit your choice of accommodations and travel days. You are often required to make a large payment upfront. On the plus side, packages can save you money, offering group prices but allowing for independent travel. Some even let you add on a few guided excursions or escorted day trips (also at prices lower than if you booked them yourself) without booking an entirely escorted tour.

Before you invest in a package tour, get some answers. Ask about the **accommodations choices** and prices for each. Then look up the hotels' reviews in a Frommer's guide (note, however, that most hotels offered with package tours are cookie-cutter chain places very short on atmosphere, hence they might not appear within this book; use the Internet to check them out and see some pictures) and check their rates for your specific dates of travel online. You'll also want to find out what **type of room** you get. If you need a certain type of room, ask for it; don't take whatever is thrown your way. Request a nonsmoking room, a quiet room, a room with a view, or whatever you fancy.

Finally, look for **hidden expenses.** Ask whether airport departure fees and taxes, for example, are included in the total cost.

Finally, if you plan to travel alone, you'll need to know if a **single supplement** will be charged and if the company can match you up with a roommate.

13 Escorted General-Interest Tours

Escorted tours are structured group tours, with a group leader. The price usually includes everything from airfare to hotels, meals, tours, admission costs, and local transportation.

One of the most famous Italy tour specialists, **Perillo Tours** (© 800/431-1515; www.perillotours.com), offers many good itineraries. You can also get good tours from **Italiatours**

(℗ **800/845-3365;** www.italiatour usa.com), the tour branch of Alitalia airlines, and **TourCrafters** (℗ **800/ ITALY95** or 847/816-6510; www. tourcrafters.com).

Many people derive a certain ease and security from escorted trips. Escorted tours—whether by bus, motor coach, train, or boat—let travelers sit back and enjoy their trip without having to spend lots of time behind the wheel. All the little details are taken care of, you know your costs upfront, and there are few surprises. Escorted tours can take you to the maximum number of sights in the minimum amount of time with the least amount of hassle—you don't have to sweat over the plotting and planning of a vacation schedule. Escorted tours are particularly convenient for people with limited mobility. They can also be a great way to make new friends.

On the downside, an escorted tour often requires a big deposit upfront, and lodging and dining choices are predetermined. As part of a cloud of tourists, you'll get little opportunity for serendipitous interactions with locals. The tours can be jam-packed with activities, leaving little room for individual sightseeing, whim, or adventure—plus they also often focus only on the heavily touristed sites, so you miss out on the lesser-known gems.

Before you invest in an escorted tour, ask about the **cancellation policy:** Is a deposit required? Can they cancel the trip if they don't get enough people? Do you get a refund if they cancel? If *you* cancel? How late can you cancel if you are unable to go? When do you pay in full? *Note:* If you choose an escorted tour, think strongly about purchasing trip-cancellation insurance, especially if the tour operator asks you to pay upfront. See the section on "Travel Insurance," earlier in this chapter.

You'll also want to get a complete **schedule** of the trip to find out how much sightseeing is planned each day and whether enough time has been allotted for relaxing or wandering solo.

The **size** of the group is also important to know upfront. Generally, the smaller the group, the more flexible the itinerary and the less time you'll spend waiting for people to get on and off the bus. Find out the **demographics** of the group as well. What is the age range? What is the gender breakdown? Is this mostly a trip for couples or singles?

Discuss what is included in the **price.** You may have to pay for transportation to and from the airport. A box lunch may be included in an excursion, but drinks might cost extra. Tips may not be included. Find out if you will be charged if you decide to opt out of certain activities or meals. The sections on accommodations choices, hidden expenses, and single supplements discussed above under "Packages for the Independent Traveler " apply here as well.

14 Special-Interest Vacations

PARLA ITALIANO?

Language courses are available at several centers around the Italian peninsula. You can contact any of the following for information about programs across Italy, which vary in length, location (city versus rural), short or long term, and price: **Italian Cultural Institute** in New York (℗ **212/879-4242**), **American Institute for Foreign Study** (℗ **800/727- AIFS;** www.aifs.org), and **Institute of International Education** (℗ **800/ 445-0443** or 212/984-5413; www. iie.org).

BIKE TOURS

The Italian countryside has always been legendary for its beauty and architectural richness, and bicycle tours are a particularly memorable way to experience it.

Bike-it-yourselfers should arm themselves with a good map (see "Getting Around," later in this chapter) and make use of the resources of the **Club Alpino Italiano,** 7 Via E. Petrella 19, 20124 Milano (© **02-2057231** in Italy; www.cai.it). You can rent a bike by the week or longer at outlets in most cities.

The best tour resource is the annual **Tourfinder** issue of *Bicycle USA.* A copy costs $15 from the League of American Bicyclists, 1612 K St. NW, Suite 401, Washington, DC 20006 (© **202/ 822-1333;** www.bikeleague.org). Membership is $30 per year and includes the Tourfinder and the annual almanac with information on European bicycling organizations.

Hindriks European Bicycle Tours (formerly Holland Bicycling Tours), P.O. Box 6086, Huntington Beach, CA 92615-6086 (© **800/852-3258;** www.hindrikstours.com), leads 8- to 12-day tours throughout Europe. **ExperiencePlus!,** 415 Mason Ct., Suite 1, Fort Collins, CO 80524 (© **800/685-4565;** www.xplus.com), runs bike tours across Europe; **Ciclismo Classico,** 30 Marathon St., Arlington, MA 02174 (© **800/ 866-7314;** www.ciclismoclassico.com), is an excellent outfit specializing in tours through Italy.

COOKING SCHOOLS

Learn to make those incredible recipes you spent your vacation gaining 10 pounds on.

Cuisine International, P.O. Box 25228, Dallas, TX 75225 (© **214/ 373-1161;** www.cuisineinternational. com), brings together some of the top independent cooking schools and teachers based in Italy, France, Portugal, Greece, and England. Here are some Italy-specific cooking schools worth checking out: **Divina Cucina,** Via Taddea 31, 50123 Florence, Italy (© **925/939-6346** in the U.S., or 055-292578 in Italy; www. divinacucina.com); **Lorenza de' Medici's Cooking School,** contact Louise Owens, 3128 Purdue, Dallas, TX 75225 (© **214/739-2846** in the U.S., or 0577-744832 in Italy; www.coltibuono.com); and **Giuliano Bugialli,** 252 Seventh Ave., #7R, New York, NY 10001 (© **646/638-1099;** www.bugialli.com).

WALKING TOURS

If you don't feel the need to cover so much territory, you can appreciate even more of the countryside by walking or hiking (called "trekking" in Italian). Italy's resource for everything from countryside ambles to serious mountain trekking is the **Club Alpino Italiano** (see "Bike Tours," above).

Tips **Specialty Travel Websites**

At **InfoHub Specialty Travel Guide** (www.infohub.com), you can find tours in Italy (as well as other countries) centered on just about any and everything: antiques, archaeology, art history, churches, cooking, gay life, nudism, religion, wineries, and much more. If this sounds expensive to you, don't worry—while searching the site, you can even set your own price limit. Two other good resource sites for specialty tours and travels are the **Specialty Travel Index** (www.specialtytravel.com) and **Shaw Guides** (www.shawguides.com).

Wilderness Travel, 1102 Ninth St., Berkeley, CA 94710 (✆ **800/368-2794;** www.wildernesstravel.com), specializes in walking tours, treks, and inn-to-inn hiking tours of Europe. **Sherpa Expeditions,** 131A Heston Rd., Hounslow, Middlesex, England TW5 ORF (✆ **44-(0)20/8577-2717;** www.sherpaexpeditions.com), offers both self-guided and group treks through off-the-beaten-track regions. Two long-established, somewhat upscale walking tour companies are

Butterfield & Robinson, 70 Bond St., Suite 300, Toronto, ON M5B 1X3 (✆ **800/678-1147** in North America, or 416/864-1354 elsewhere; www.butterfield.com), and **Country Walkers,** P.O. Box 180, Waterbury, VT 05676 (✆ **800/464-9255** in North America, or 802/244-1387 elsewhere; www.countrywalkers.com). The bike tour companies **Experience-Plus!** and **Ciclismo Classico,** listed above under "Bike Tours," also do walking tours.

15 Getting Around

This book covers plenty of rural areas made up of small towns, so budget plenty of travel time for winding roads, slow local trains, and long layovers. The twisty roads aren't the kindest to motion sickness sufferers, but, fortunately, Italy's pharmacies are blessed with a miraculous chewing-gum medicine called **Travelgum** that, unlike Dramamine, starts working within a minute or two. Also, be warned that town-to-town coach drivers, in particular, seem to be trained to drive in such a way as to disturb even the most iron stomachs.

MAPS A city street plan is a *pianta;* a map of a region or larger area is a *mappa* or *carta.* Before you leave home, you can pick up one of the **Touring Club Italiano's (TCI)** enormous pristine maps of Italy's regions at 1:200,000 scale. You can find regional maps ("Toscana," "Veneto," "Sicilia," and so on) at some bookstores and most map and travel specialty stores in the United States, Canada, and the United Kingdom. TCI also publishes some pocket-size street maps of cities and makes laminated bound map booklets (if you don't like sheets), both regional and collections of city plans. **Edizione Multigraphic** covers Italy in varying scales with contour-lined maps so detailed that some actually

show individual farms. Their "Carta Turistica Stradale" 1:50,000 maps are perfect for exploring back roads, while the 1:25,000 "Carta dei Sentieri e Rifugi" sheets include hiking trails and alpine shelters for those hoofing it or on bike. The maps are widely available at bookstores, newsstands, and souvenir shops. **Litografia Artistica Cartografica** makes very complete and large foldout city maps with searchable indices. They also publish 1:150,000 province maps that are less detailed than the Edizione Multigraphic sheets but, because of this, are easier to glance at while driving.

Note that, even with a map, you are going to get lost in Venice (even Venetians get lost repeatedly if they venture outside their own little section of town). Accept this, and view it as part of the adventure.

BY PLANE

Italy's domestic air network on **Alitalia** (see "Getting There," earlier in this chapter) is one of the largest and most complete in Europe. Some 40 airports are serviced regularly from Rome, and most flights take less than an hour. Fares vary, but some discounts are available. Tickets are discounted 50% for children 2 to 12; for passengers 12 to 24, there's a youth fare. Prices are still astronomical for domestic flights, and you're almost always better off taking a train, except for long-distance hauls (like Venice down to Palermo in Sicily) where you'd rather spend the money than the time—unless you can stop off along the way: In Italy, there's never a shortage of major sights to see.

BY CAR

Italy is best explored by car. In fact, one of the most common and convenient ways to take a tour of this area is to fly or take a train into, say, Milan, see the city, then pick up a rental car to wend your way through whichever bit takes your fancy before ending up in Venice, Florence, or Rome, where you can drop off the car and fly home.

That said, driving in Italy is also expensive and notoriously nerve-racking—both for the winding roads and for the Italian penchant for driving a Fiat like a Ferrari. Both rental and gas prices are as high as they get in all Europe. Before leaving home, apply for an **International Driver's Permit** from the American Automobile Association (AAA; Ⓒ **800/222-1134** or 407/444-4300; www.aaa.com). In Canada, the permit is available from the Canadian Automobile Association (CAA; Ⓒ **613/247-0117;** www.caa.ca). Technically, you need this permit, your actual driver's license, and an Italian translation of the latter (also available from AAA and CAA) to drive in Italy, though, in practice, a license

alone often suffices. (Take all three along, to be on the safe side.)

Italy's equivalent of AAA is the **Automobile Club d'Italia (ACI),** a branch of the Touring Club Italiano. They're the people who respond when you place an emergency 116 call for road breakdowns, though they do charge for this service if you're not a member. If you wish, you may join at the border as you're driving into Italy or online at **www.aci.it.**

DRIVING RULES Italian drivers aren't maniacs; they only appear to be. Actually, they tend to be very safe and alert drivers—if much more aggressive than Americans are used to. If someone races up behind you and flashes her lights, that's the signal for you to slow down so she can pass you quickly and safely. Stay in the right lane on highways; the left is only for passing and for cars with large engines and the pedal to the metal. If you see someone in your rearview mirror speeding up with his hazard lights blinking, get out of the way because it means his Mercedes is opened up full throttle. On a two-lane road, the idiot passing someone in the opposing traffic who has swerved into your lane expects you to veer obligingly over into the shoulder so three lanes of traffic can fit—he would do the same for you.

Autostrade are superhighways, denoted by green signs and a number prefaced with an *A,* like the famous

---

Tips Prime Sightseeing Hours

One mistake many people make when scheduling their hopping from hill town to hill town is getting up early in the morning to travel to the next destination. Because many of Italy's sights are open only in the morning and almost all close for *riposo* (afternoon rest) from noonish to 3 or 4pm, this wastes valuable sightseeing time. I do my traveling just after noon, when everything is closing up. There's often a last train before *riposo* to wherever you're going or a country bus run (intended to shuttle schoolchildren home for lunch). If you're driving, you can enjoy great countryside vistas under the noonday sun.

A1 from Naples to Milan via Rome and Florence. Occasionally, these aren't numbered and are simply called *raccordo,* a connecting road between two cities. On longer stretches, autostrade often become toll roads. **Strade Statale** are state roads, usually two lanes wide, indicated by blue signs. Their route numbers are prefaced with an *SS* or an *S. Strade Provinciale* (SP) are similar provincial roads. On signs, however, these official route numbers are used infrequently. Usually, you'll just see blue signs listing destinations by name with arrows pointing off in the appropriate directions. Even if it's just a few miles down on the road, the town you're looking for often won't be mentioned on the sign at the appropriate turnoff. It's impossible to predict which of all the towns that lie along a road will be the ones chosen to list on a particular sign. Sometimes the sign gives only the first miniscule village the lies past the turnoff; at other times, it lists the first major town down that road, and some signs mention only the major city the road eventually leads to, even if it's hundreds of miles away. It pays to study the map and fix in your mind the names of all three possibilities before coming to an intersection.

The **speed limit** on roads in built-up areas around towns and cities is 50kmph (31 mph). On rural roads and the highway, it's 110kmph (68 mph), except on weekends, when it's upped to 130kmph (81 mph). Italians have an astounding disregard for these limits. Be aware, however, that police can ticket you and collect the fine on the spot. Although there's no official blood alcohol level at which you're "legally drunk," the police will throw you in jail if they pull you over and find you soused.

As far as *parcheggio* (parking) is concerned, white lines on streets indicate free public spaces and blue lines

pay public spaces. Meters don't line the sidewalk; rather, there's one machine on the block where you punch in how long you want to park. The machine spits out a ticket that you leave on your dashboard. Sometimes streets will have an attendant who will come around and give you your time ticket (pay him or her when you get ready to leave). If you park in an area marked PARCHEGGIO DISCO ORARIO, root around in your rental car's glove compartment for a cardboard parking disc (or buy one at a gas station). With this device, you dial up the hour of your arrival (it's the honor system) and display it on your dashboard. You're allowed *un ora* (1 hr.) or *due ore* (2 hr.), according to the sign. **Parking lots** have ticket dispensers but usually *not* manned booths as you exit. Take your ticket with you when you park; when you return to the lot to get your car and leave, first visit the office or automated payment machine to exchange your ticket for a paid receipt you then use to get through the automated exit.

ROAD SIGNS Here's a brief rundown of the road signs you'll most frequently encounter. A **speed limit** sign is a black number inside a red circle on a white background. The **end of a speed zone** is just black and white, with a black slash through the number. A red circle with a white background, a black arrow pointing down, and a red arrow pointing up means **yield to oncoming traffic,** while a point-down red-and-white triangle means **yield ahead.** In town, a simple white circle with a red border or the words *zona pedonale* or *zona traffico limitato* denotes a **pedestrian zone** (you can drive through only to drop off baggage at your hotel); a white arrow on a blue background is used for Italy's many **one-way streets;** a mostly red circle with a horizontal white slash means **"do not enter."**

Any image in black on a white background surrounded by a red circle means that image is **not allowed** (for instance, if the image is two cars next to each other: no passing; a motorcycle means no Harleys permitted, and so on). A circular sign in blue with a red circle-slash means **"no parking."**

GASOLINE   *Benzina* (gas or petrol) is even more expensive in Italy than in the rest of Europe. Even a small rental car guzzles between 30€ and 50€ ($34–$58) for a fill-up. There are many pull-in gas stations along major roads and on the outskirts of town, as well as 24-hour rest stops along the autostrada highways, but in towns, most stations are small sidewalk gas stands where you parallel-park to fill up. Almost all stations are closed for *riposo* and on Sunday, but the majority now have a pump fitted with a machine that accepts bills so that you can self-service your tank at 3am. Unleaded gas is *senza piombo.*

BY TRAIN

Italy has one of the best train systems in Europe, and even if you're traveling on a regional level, you'll find many destinations connected. Most lines are administered by the state-run **Ferrovie dello Stato,** or **FS** (© **892-021** for national train info, or 199-166177 to buy tickets; www.trenitalia.com), but private lines take up the slack in a few places. About the only difference you'll notice is that these private lines don't honor special discount cards or passes (see "Special Passes & Discounts," below).

Italian trains tend to be very clean and comfortable. Though trains are increasingly of the boring straight-through commuter variety, on many long-haul runs you'll still be blessed with those old-fashioned cars made up of *couchette* compartments that seat six or occasionally eight. (Try to find one full of nuns for a fighting chance at a smoke-free trip.) First class *(prima classe)* is usually only a shade better than second class *(seconda classe),* with four to six seats per couchette instead of six to eight. The only real benefit of first class comes if you're traveling overnight, in which case four berths per compartment is a lot more comfortable than six.

Few visitors are prepared for how **crowded** Italian trains can sometimes get, though with the increase in automobile travel, they're not as crowded as they were in decades past. An Italian train is full only when the corridors are packed solid and there are more than eight people sitting on their luggage in the little vestibules by the doors. Overcrowding is usually a problem only on Friday evenings and weekends, especially in and out of big cities, and just after a strike. In summer the crowding escalates, and any train going toward a beach in August all but bulges like an overstuffed sausage.

Italian trains come in six varieties, based on how often they stop. The **ETR/Pendolino** (P) is the "pendulum" train that zips back and forth between Rome and Milan, stopping at Florence and Bologna along the way. It's the fastest but most expensive option (first class only, a meal included); it has its own ticket window at the stations and *requires* a seat reservation. **Eurostar/Eurocity** (ES/EC; EN if it runs overnight) trains connect Italian cities with cities outside the country; these are the speediest of the standard trains, offering both first and second class and always requiring a supplement (except for Eurailpass holders, though the conductors won't always believe you on this one); **Intercity** (IC) trains are similar to Eurocity trains, in that they offer both first and second class and require a supplement, but they never cross an international border.

Of the regular trains that don't require supplements—often called *Regionale* (R) if they stay within a region (the Veneto) or *Interregionale* (IR) if they don't (the Veneto through Lombardy to Piemonte)—the **Espresso** stops at all the major and most of the secondary stations, the **Diretto** stops at virtually every station, and the snail-paced **Locale** (sometimes laughingly called *accelerato*) frequently stops between stations in the middle of the countryside for no apparent reason.

When buying a **regular ticket**, ask for either *andata* (one-way) or *andata e ritorno* (round-trip). If the train you plan to take is an ES/EC or IC, ask for the ticket *con supplemento rapido* (with speed supplement) to avoid on-train penalty charges. On a trip under 200km (124 miles), your ticket is good to leave within the next 6 hours; with trips over 200km (124 miles), you have a full day. (This code isn't rigorously upheld by conductors, but don't push your luck.) On round-trip journeys of less than 250km (155 miles), the return ticket is valid for only 3 days. This mileage-time correlation continues, with an extra day added to your limit for each 200km (124 miles) above 250 (the maximum is 6 days). If you board a regular train without a ticket (or board an IC/EC without the supplement), you'll have to pay a hefty "tax" on top of the ticket or a supplement the conductor will sell you. Most conductors also get extremely crabby if you forget to **stamp your ticket in the little yellow box** on the platform before boarding the train.

Schedules for all lines running through a given station are printed on posters tacked up on the station wall. *Binario (bin.)* means "track." Useful schedules for all train lines are printed biannually in booklets (which are broken down into sections of the country—you want *nord e centro*

Italia, north and central Italy, or simply *centro*) available at any newsstand. There are official FS-published booklets, but the better buy is the *Pozzorario,* which not only is cheaper but also lists private lines (and is just as accurate). Or simply download official schedules (and more train information, some even in English) from the Internet at **www.trenitalia.com**.

Stations tend to be well run and clean, with luggage-storage facilities at all but the smallest and usually a good bar attached with surprisingly palatable food. If you pull into a dinky town with a shed-size or nonexistent station, find the nearest bar or *tabacchi,* and the man behind the counter will most likely double as the "station master" to sell you tickets.

SPECIAL PASSES & DISCOUNTS
To buy the **Italy Flexi Railcard,** available only outside Italy, contact **Rail Europe** (www.raileurope.com). It works similarly to the Eurailpass, in that you have 1 month in which to use the train a set number of days; the base number of days is 4, and you can add up to 6 more. For adults, the first-class pass costs $239; adults traveling together can get the Saver version for $203 each. The second-class version costs $191 for adults ($163 on the Saver edition), or for youths under 26, the price is $160. Extra days cost $24 ($20 for Saver passes) in first class, $19 in second class ($16 for Saver), and $16 for youths.

A 4-day **Trenitalia Pass** is 447€ ($514) in first class, 357€ ($411) in second; a 5-day pass is 492€ ($566) in first class, 393€ ($452) in second; a 6-day pass is 536€ ($616) in first class, 428€ ($492) in second; a 10-day pass is 716€ ($823) for first class and 570€ ($656) for second. The **Youth Pass** version (for ages 16–25) is available for second-class travel only. A 4-day pass is 229€ ($263); a 5-day pass is 329€ ($378). Each additional day (up to 10 days) is an additional 30€ ($34). A **Saver Pass** allows two to five people to ride the rails for 4 to 10 days in either first or second class. A 4-day pass is 379€ ($436) in first class, 305€ ($351) in second class; a 5-day pass is 417€ ($480) in first class and 335€ ($385) in second class; a 10-day pass is 604€ ($695) for first class and 484€ ($557) for second class. Children ages 4 to 11 pay 50% of the adult fare.

The **Italy Rail 'n Drive** pass combines train and car travel throughout Italy, allowing you to visit some of the smaller towns—or anywhere else in Italy. The pass gives you 4 days of first- or second-class train travel within Italy and 2 days of car rental. Prices for 1 adult (first class/second class) are $375/$329 in a compact, $339/$289 in an economy, and $389/$345 in an intermediate or small automatic; for 2 adults (first class/second class), it costs $638/$538 in a compact, $590/$490 in an economy, and $650/$550 in an intermediate or small automatic. Additional car days are $49 economy, $65 compact, and $75 midsize.

When it comes to regular tickets, if you're **under 26,** you can buy at any Italian train station a 26€ ($30) **Carta Verde (Green Card)** that gets you a 15% discount on all FS tickets for 1 year. Present it each time you go to buy a ticket. The same deal is available for anyone **over 60** with the **Carta d'Argento (Silver Card).** Children under 12 always ride at half-price (and can get the passes mentioned below at half-price), and kids under 4 ride free.

BY BUS

Regional intertown buses are called *pullman,* though *autobus,* the term for a city bus, is also sometimes used. When you're getting down to the kind of small-town travel this guide describes, you'll probably need to use regional buses at some point. You can get just about anywhere through a network of dozens of local, provincial, and regional lines, but schedules aren't always easy to come by or to figure out—the local tourist office usually has a photocopy of the schedule, and in cities some companies have offices. Buses exist mainly to shuttle workers and schoolchildren, so the most runs are on weekdays, early in the morning, and usually again around lunchtime. All too often, however, the only run of the day will be at 6am.

A town's bus stop is usually either the main piazza or, more often, a large square on the edge of town or the bend in the road just outside a small town's main city gate. You should always try to find the local ticket vendor—if there's no office, it's invariably the nearest newsstand or *tabacchi* (signaled by a sign with a white *T*), or occasionally a bar—but you can usually buy tickets on the bus. You can also flag a bus down as it passes on a country road, but try to find an official stop (a small sign tacked onto a telephone pole). Tell the driver where you're going, and ask him courteously if he'll let you know when you need to get off. When he says *"E la prossima fermata,"* that means yours is the next stop. *"Posso scendere?"* (*poh*-so *shen*-dair-ay?) is "May I please get off?"

16 Tips on Accommodations, Villa Rentals & Farm Stays

Alas, Italy is no longer the country of dirt-cheap *pensione,* boardinghouse-style lodgings with shared bathrooms and swaybacked beds. Most hotels have private bathrooms in the rooms now (if not, my reviews state this), and regulations and standardization have become much stricter—which is all fine and good; the only problem is that prices have soared because of it, in most cases doubling and often tripling over just the past 5 years.

Many **bathrooms** are still dismal affairs—often a closet-size room with a sink, toilet, and bidet and just a shower head on the wall, a drain in the floor, and no curtain (rescue the toilet paper from a drenching before you turn on the water). Towels are often flat, pressed cotton sheets, though terry-cloth towels are coming into style. Soap isn't a given, but the water is safe to drink.

In place of Italy's old *pensione* system, hotels are now **rated** by regional boards on a system of one to five stars. Prices aren't directly tied to the star system, but, for the most part, the more stars a hotel has, the more expensive it'll be—but a four-star in a small town may be cheaper than a two-star in Milan . . . and probably even less expensive than a one-star in Venice. The number of stars awarded a hotel is based strictly on the amenities offered and not how clean, comfortable, or friendly a place is or whether it's a good value for the money overall. That is why you need this book!

A few of the four- and five-star hotels have their own private **garages,** but most city inns have an arrangement with a local garage. In many small towns, a garage is unnecessary because public parking, both free and pay, is widely available and never too far from your hotel. Parking costs and procedures are indicated under each hotel, and the rates quoted are per day (overnight).

The **high season** throughout Italy runs from Easter to early September or October—peaking June through August—and from December 24 to January 6. Of course, in ski resorts such as Cortina and Courmayeur, the peak is from Christmastime through mid-March (and they can become ghost towns in June). You can almost always bargain for a cheaper rate if you're traveling in the shoulder season (early spring and late fall) or winter off season (not including Christmas). You can also often get a discount for stays of more than 3 days. Always ask.

Supposedly, Italian hotels must quote the price for **breakfast** separately from the room and can't force it on you if you don't want it. However, most hotels include breakfast automatically in the room rate, hoping you won't notice, and many also argue that breakfast is required at their hotel. I've tried to include the separate per-person breakfast price for each hotel. With very few exceptions, Italian hotel breakfasts tend to consist of a roll or *cornetto* (croissant) and coffee, occasionally with juice and fresh fruit as well. It's rarely worth the 3€ to 15€ ($3.45–$17) charged for it because you can get the same breakfast—and freshly made instead of packaged—for around 2€ ($2.30) at the bar down the block. Ask for your room quote with a *prezzo senza colazione* (pretz-zoh *sen*-zah coal-lat-zee-*oh*-nay), or price without breakfast.

The Italian term **albergo** is more and more commonly being replaced by the international word *hotel*. *Locanda* once meant a rustic inn or carriage stop, though it's now used sometimes to refer to a place quite charming or fancy. The *pensione* system has pretty much disappeared, and with it the obligation to share bathrooms and eat three meals a day prepared by the families that owned them. These are now one- and two-star hotels, with many of them retaining the word *pensione* in their names to connote a small, often family-run hotel of character or charm (not always the case!). In 2000, Italy also introduced *"il Bed and Breakfast"* classification to encourage more of the smaller *pensioni* or larger rental-room operations to stop hiding from the tax collector and officially incorporate as a business.

Single travelers stand to be the most underserved: Rarely are single rooms anything to write home about (usually wedged into the space between the hall and the building's airshaft), and rarely is the rate charged actually half that of a double. Closet-size rooms are not uncommon; if it is a slow month, see if the hotel owner will consider renting a double room at a single-occupancy rate.

Reservations are always advised, even in the so-called slow months of November to March, when you might find towns such as Verona (not to mention the large cities) booked solid with conventions and trade fairs. Travel to Italy peaks from May through October, when many of the best (or at least best-known) moderate and budget hotels are often filled up a few days to a few weeks in advance.

Italy's keeping-up-with-the-Jones's approach to approval by its E.U. neighbors and government-imposed restrictions has done a tremendous amount to improve the status of its hotel situation—and it accounts for soaring prices. Still, the clean-as-a-whistle conditions that are a given in Switzerland or Germany's least expensive hostelries are not such a guarantee as you head south—all the more reason to rely on our suggestions. For more information and resources on hotels in Europe, check out **www.hotels-in-europe.org**.

APARTMENTS, VILLAS & PALAZZI

Local tourist boards and the provincial tourist office in the city or town where you expect to stay are not much help. Information on villas and apartments is available in daily newspapers or through local real-estate agents in Italy and some international travel publications. Millions of properties are put up for rent by their Italian owners—and to find them, you'll have to do your own homework and legwork. Single travelers will find the option of rentals expensive, couples less so. Groups or families of four to six people (the more, the merrier) may find villa or apartment rental an enjoyable

savings. Everyone fantasizes about that dream villa amid the vineyards; but remember that photos do not always a thousand words tell. Research a potential rental thoroughly to make sure you're not getting a dump; what looks like a gem may end up being right next to the train tracks.

Each summer, thousands of visitors become temporary Italians by renting an old farmhouse or "villa," a marketing term used to inspire romantic images of manicured gardens, a Renaissance mansion, and Barolo martinis, but in reality one that guarantees no more than four walls and most of a roof.

Actually, finding your countryside Eden isn't that simple and may require considerable research. Occasionally, you can go through the property owners themselves, but the vast majority of villas are rented out via agencies (see below).

Shop around for a trustworthy agent or representative (I've listed my top recommendations below). Often several outfits will list the same property but charge radically different prices. At some you sign away any right to refunds if the place doesn't live up to your expectations. Expect to pay $10 to $25 for a copy of each company's catalog; most refund this expense if you rent through them. Make sure the agency is willing to work with you to find the right property. Try to work with someone who has personally visited the properties you're considering, and always ask to see lots of photos: Get the exterior from several angles, to make sure the railroad doesn't pass by the back door, as well as pictures of the bedrooms, kitchen, and baths, and photos of the views out each side of the house.

If you're traveling with several couples, ask to see a floor plan to make sure access to the bathroom isn't through one couple's bedroom. Find out if this is the only villa on the property—some people who rent the villa for the isolation find themselves living in a small enclave of foreigners all sharing the same small pool. Ask whether the villa is purely a rental unit or if, say, the family lives there during winter but lets it out during summer. Renting a lived-in place offers pretty good insurance that the lights, plumbing, heat, and so on will be in good working order.

The following organizations rent villas or apartments, generally on the pricey side; stipulate your price range when inquiring. One of the best agencies to call is **Rentvillas.com** (formerly Rentals in Italy), 700 E. Main St., Ventura, CA 93001 (© **800/726-6702** or 805/641-1650; fax 805/641-1630; www.rentvillas.com). Its agents are very helpful in tracking down the perfect place to suit your needs. A United Kingdom agency—and one of the best all-around agents in Britain— is **Chapters by Abercrombie & Kent,** Sloane Square House, Holbein Place, London SW1W 8NS (© **08450-700618;** www.villa-rentals.com). Marjorie Shaw's **Insider's Italy,** 41 Schermerhorn St., Brooklyn, NY 11201 (© **718/855-3878;** fax 718/855-3687; www.insidersitaly.com), is a small, upscale outfit run by a very personable agent who's thoroughly familiar with all of her properties and Italy in general.

Also in the United States, **Parker Company Ltd.,** Seaport Landing, 152 Lynnway, Lynn, MA 01902 (© **800/280-2811** or 781/596-8282; fax 781/596-3125; www.theparkercompany. com), handles overseas villa rentals.

For some of the top properties, call the local representative of the **Cottages to Castles** group. In the United Kingdom, contact **Cottages to Castles,** Tuscany House, 10 Tonbridge Rd., Maidstone, Kent ME16 8RP (© **1622-775217;** fax 1622-775278). In Australia and New Zealand, call

Italian Villa Holidays, P.O. Box 2293, Wellington, 6015, New Zealand (© **800/125-555** in Australia, or 800/4-TUSCANY in New Zealand; fax 64-4-479-0021). At press time, the organization was searching for a representative in the United States.

One of the most reasonably priced agencies is **Villas and Apartment Abroad, Ltd.,** 370 Lexington Ave., Suite 1401, New York, NY 10017 (© 212/897-5045; fax 212/897-5039; www.vaanyc.com). **Homeabroad.com,** formerly Vacanze in Italia, 22 Railroad St., Great Barrington, MA 02130 (© **413/528-6610;** www.homeabroad. com), handles hundreds of rather upscale properties. A popular but *very* pricey agency is **Villas International,** 4340 Redwood Hwy., Suite D309, San Rafael, CA 94903 (© **800/221-2260** or 415/499-9490; fax 415/499-9491; www.villasintl.com).

For more on nonhotel accommodations options in Europe—including villas, *agriturimso* farm stays (see below), hostels, castles, B&Bs, and more— check out **www.beyondhotels.net.**

AGRITURISMO—STAYING ON A FARM

Italy is at the forefront of the *agriturismo* movement, whereby a working farm or agricultural estate makes available accommodations for visitors who want to stay out in the countryside. The rural atmosphere is ensured by the fact that an operation can call itself *agriturismo* only if (a) it offers fewer than 30 beds total and (b) the agricultural component of the property brings in a larger economic share of profits than the hospitality part—in other words, the property has to remain a farm and not become a glorified hotel.

Agriturismi are generally a crapshoot. They're loosely regulated, and the price, quality, and types of accommodations can vary dramatically. Some are sumptuous apartments or suites with hotel-like amenities; others are a straw's width away from sleeping in the barn on a haystack. Most, though, are miniapartments, often furnished from secondhand dealers and usually rented out with a minimum stay of 3 days or a week. Sometimes you're invited to eat big country dinners at the table with the family; other times, you cook for yourself. Rates can vary from 15€ ($17) for two per day all the way up to 250€ ($288)—as much as a four-star hotel in town—though most hover around the thoroughly reasonable rates of 50€ to 100€ ($58–$115) for a double. I've reviewed a few choice ones throughout this book, but there are hundreds more.

If you feel handy enough with Italian, you can avail yourself of the three independent national organizations that together represent all *agriturismi* (or, at least, all the reputable ones).

Go to the website of **Terranostra** (www.terranostra.it) and click on "La Tua Vacanza," then "Ricerche." A map of Italy will pop up. Click on the region you want, and you'll get hundreds of choices, arranged, unfortunately, alphabetically by name of the actual property (not by, say, town, which would make selecting one so much easier), with price categories of *basso* (low), *medio* (medium), and *alto* (high). When you click on the property name, you get a review with pictures and symbols (in Italian, but understandable enough), plus contact info and a link to the lodging's own website, if available.

At the website of **Turismo Verde** (www.turismoverde.it), click on "La Guida Agrituristica On-line." On the search page that pops up, you can choose to search by Regione (Lombardia, Veneto, Piemonte, and so on) or by Provincia (Como, Padova, Treviso, Asti, and so on). The results that come up based on your criteria are pretty much like the ones at Terranostra, only this time it returns all the results on a single page (rather than by pages of 10 each), so it's a bit easier to quickly find, say, all the lodgings near Aosta. Again, click on a property name to learn much more about it.

The easiest website to navigate is that of **Agriturist** (www.agriturist.it)—you simply click on a region on the map or text list, and the next page gives you the option of continuing in English. Unfortunately, the site fails after that. You can indeed find hundreds upon hundreds of individual properties via a search engine. Stupidly, though, they do not then provide each farm's own website (possibly because they want you to book via their own site), so tracking the *agriturismi* down is that much more difficult; plus the info provided about each is far skimpier than that given by other resources.

In the States, a few agencies are popping up to help you track down a perfect *agriturismo* in Italy, including Ralph Levey's **Italy Farm Holidays,** 547 Martling Ave., Tarrytown, NY 10591 (© **914/631-7880;** fax 914/631-8831; www.italyfarmholidays.com), which represents many of the more upscale *agriturismo* properties.

17 Tips on Dining

For a quick bite, go to a **bar**—although it does serve alcohol, a bar in Italy functions mainly as a cafe. Prices at bars have a split personality: *al banco* is standing at the bar, while *à tavola* means sitting at a table, where they'll wait on you and charge two to four times as much for the same cap-puccino. In bars, you can find *panini* sandwiches on various rolls and *tramezzini,* giant triangles of white-bread sandwiches with the crusts cut off. These run 1.50€ to 5€ ($1.75–$5.75) and are traditionally stuck in a kind of tiny pants press to flatten and toast them so the crust is

Getting Your VAT Refund

Most purchases have a built-in **value-added tax (IVA)** of 17.36%. Non–E.U. (European Union) citizens are entitled to a refund of this tax if they spend more than 154.94€ ($173; before tax) at any one store. To claim your refund, request an invoice from the cashier at the store and take it to the Customs office *(dogana)* at the airport to have it stamped *before* you leave. **Note:** If you're going to another E.U. country before flying home, have it stamped at the airport Customs office of the last E.U. country you'll be visiting (if you're flying home via Britain, for example, have your Italian invoices stamped in London).

Once back home, mail the stamped invoice back to the store within 90 days of the purchase, and they'll send you a refund check. Many shops are now part of the Tax Free for Tourists network. (Look for the sticker in the window.) Stores participating in this network issue a check along with your invoice at the time of purchase. After you have the invoice stamped at Customs, you can redeem the check for cash directly at the tax-free booth in the airport, or mail it back in the envelope provided within 60 days. For more info, check out **www.globalrefund.com**.

crispy and the filling hot and gooey; unfortunately, microwaves have invaded and are everywhere turning *panini* into something that resembles a very hot, soggy tissue.

Pizza à taglio or ***pizza rustica*** indicates a place where you can order pizza by the slice, though Venice is infamous for serving some of Italy's worst pizza this way. They fare somewhat better at ***pizzerie,*** casual sit-down restaurants that cook large, round pizzas with very thin crusts in wood-burning ovens. A ***tavola calda*** (literally "hot table") serves ready-made hot foods you can take away or eat at one of the few small tables often available. The food is usually very good, and you can get away with a full meal at a *tavola calda* for well under 15€ ($17). A ***rosticceria*** is the same type of place, with some chickens roasting on a spit in the window. In Venice, you can often get *chichetti*—finger food, snack on sticks, pâtés on bread—at a number of bars in the early evening (5–7pm), each morsel costing a modest .50€ to 1€

(55¢–$1.15). Milan and Turin have the same thing, only they don't have a special name for it, and it almost always comes free—so long as you're drinking something.

Full-fledged restaurants go by the name *osteria, trattoria,* or *ristorante.* Once upon a time, these terms meant something—***osterie*** were basic places where you could get a plate of spaghetti and a glass of wine; ***trattorie*** were casual places serving simple full meals of filling peasant fare; and ***ristoranti*** were fancier places, with printed menus, wine lists, waiters in bow ties, and hefty prices. Nowadays, though, fancy restaurants often go by the name of *trattoria* to cash in on the associated charm factor, trendy spots use *osteria* to show they're hip, and simple inexpensive places sometimes tack on *ristorante* to ennoble their establishment.

The ***pane e coperto*** (bread and cover) is a cover charge of anywhere from .50€ to 15€ (55¢–$17) that you must pay at every Italian restaurant for the mere privilege of sitting at

Country & City Codes

The **country code** for Italy is **39**. In 1998, Italy incorporated what were once separate **city codes** (for example, Rome's was 06, Venice's was 041) into the numbers themselves. Therefore, you must dial the entire number, *including the initial zero*, when calling from *anywhere* outside or inside Italy and even within the same town. For those of you familiar with the old system, this means that now, to call Rome from the States, you must dial **011-39-06-xxx-xxxx**. Increasingly, you'll notice Rome numbers beginning with prefixes other than 06; these are usually cellphone numbers. Fixed-line phone numbers in Italy can range anywhere from 6 to 12 digits in length.

the table. Most Italians eat a full meal—appetizer and first *(primo)* and second *(secondo)* courses—at lunch and dinner and will expect you to do the same, or at least a first and second course. You may also have a *contorno* (side dish) and *dolce* (dessert). To request the bill, ask *"Il conto, per favore"* (eel *con*-toh pore fah-*vohr*-ay). A tip of 15% is usually included in the bill these days, but if unsure, ask *"E incluso il servizio?"* (ay een-*cloo*-soh eel sair-*vee*-tsoh?).

Many restaurants, especially larger ones and those in cities, offer a *menù turistico* (tourists' menu) costing from 10€ to 35€ ($12–$40). This set-price menu usually covers all meal incidentals, including table wine, cover charge, and 15% service charge, along with a first and a second course. But it almost invariably offers an abbreviated selection of rather bland dishes: spaghetti in tomato sauce and slices of roast pork. Sometimes better is a *menù a prezzo fisso* (fixed-price menu), which usually doesn't include wine but sometimes covers the service and *coperto* and often has a wider selection of better dishes, occasionally including house specialties and local foods. Ordering a la carte, however, offers you the best chance for a memorable meal. Even better, forgo the menu entirely and put yourself in the capable hands of your waiter.

Many restaurants that really care about their food—from *osterie* to classy *ristoranti*—will also offer a *menù degustazione* (tasting menu), allowing you to sample small portions of the kitchen's bounty, usually several antipasti, a few primi, and a secondo or two (and sometimes several local wines to taste by the glass). They're almost always highly recommendable and usually turn out to be a huge feast. Prices can vary wildly, anywhere from 20€ ($23) to over 100€ ($115), though about 40€ ($46) to 50€ ($58) is most common.

The *enoteca* (wine bar) is a growingly popular marriage of a wine bar and an osteria, where you sit and order from a host of local and regional wines by the glass while snacking on finger foods and simple primi. It's also possible to go into an *alimentari* (general food store) and have sandwiches prepared on the spot, or buy the makings for a picnic.

FAST FACTS: Italy

The following list provides general info to cover all of Italy. You can find more specific information for major cities in the "Fast Facts" sections of their own chapters, including the local American Express offices.

Area Codes As noted in the "Country & City Codes" box above, Italy no longer uses separate city codes. Dial all numbers exactly as written in this book, and you should be fine.

Business Hours General open hours for **stores, offices,** and **churches** are from 9:30am to noon or 1pm and again from 3 or 3:30pm to 7:30pm. That early afternoon shutdown is the *riposo,* the Italian *siesta.* Most stores close all day Sunday and many also on Monday (morning only or all day). Some shops, especially grocery stores, also close Thursday afternoons. Some services and business offices are open to the public only in the morning. Traditionally, **museums** are closed Monday, and though some of the biggest stay open all day long, many close for *riposo* or are open only in the morning (9am–2pm is popular). Some churches open earlier in the morning, but the largest often stay open all day. **Banks** tend to be open Monday through Friday from 8:30am to 1:30pm and 2:30 to 3:30pm or 3 to 4pm.

Use the *riposo* as the Italians do—take a long lunch, stroll through a city park, cool off in the Duomo, travel to the next town, or simply go back to your hotel to regroup your energies. The *riposo* is an especially welcome custom during the oppressive afternoon heat of August.

Car Rentals See "Getting Around," earlier in this chapter.

Currency See "Money," earlier in this chapter.

Driving Rules See "Getting Around," earlier in this chapter.

Drugstores You'll find **green neon crosses** above the entrances to most *farmacie* (pharmacies). You'll also find many *erborista* (herbalist) shops, which usually offer more traditional herbal remedies (some of which are marvelously effective) along with the standard pharmaceuticals. Most *farmacie* of any stripe keep everything behind the counter, so be prepared to point or pantomime. *Note:* Most minor ailments start with the phrase *mal di* in Italian, so you can just say "Mahl dee" and point to your head, stomach, throat, or whatever. Pharmacies rotate which will stay open all night and on Sunday, and each store has a poster outside showing the month's rotation.

Electricity Italy operates on a 220-volt AC (50 cycles) system, as opposed to the United States' 110-volt AC (60 cycles) system. You'll need a simple adapter plug (to make our flat pegs fit their round holes) and, unless your appliance is dual-voltage (as some hair dryers and travel irons are), a currency converter.

For more information, call or send a self-addressed stamped envelope to **The Franzus Company,** Customer Service Dept., B50, Murtha Industrial Park, Box 142, Beacons Falls, CT 06403 (© **800/706-7064** or 203/723-6664; www.franzus.com). It'll send you a pamphlet called *Foreign Electricity Is No Deep Dark Secret,* with, of course, a convenient order form for adapters and converters on the back. You can also pick up the hardware at electronics, travel specialty stores, luggage shops, and airports, and from **Magellan's** catalog (www.magellans.com).

Embassies & Consulates Embassies and their consulates (consulates are for citizens—lost passports and other services; embassies are mostly only for diplomats) are all located in Rome, though such other major cities as

Milan often also have consular offices. Each major city chapter in this book has a "Fast Facts" section listing local embassies/consulates and their open hours for the U.S., Canada, the U.K., Ireland, Australia, and New Zealand.

Emergencies Dial ⓒ **113** for any emergency. You can also call ⓒ **112** for the *carabinieri* (police), ⓒ **118** for an ambulance, or ⓒ **115** for the fire department. If your car breaks down, dial ⓒ **116** for roadside aid courtesy of the Automotive Club of Italy.

Holidays See "Italy Calendar of Events," earlier in this chapter.

Hospitals The emergency ambulance number is ⓒ **118**. Hospitals in Italy are partially socialized, and the care is efficient, very personalized, and of a high quality. There are also well-run private hospitals. Pharmacy staff also tend to be very competent health-care providers, so for less serious problems, their advice will do fine. For non-life-threatening but still concerning ailments, you can just walk into most hospitals and get taken care of speedily—no questions about insurance policies, no forms to fill out, and no fees to pay. Most hospitals will be able to find someone who speaks English.

Information See "Visitor Information," earlier in this chapter.

Internet Access Cybercafes are in healthy supply in most Italian cities. In smaller towns, you may have a bit of trouble, but, increasingly, hotels are setting up Internet points. In a pinch, hostels, local libraries, and often pubs will have a terminal for access.

Language Though Italian is the official language, English is a close second, especially among those below age 40—they all learned it in school— and most people in the tourism industry. But most Italians will be delighted to help you learn a bit of their lingo as you travel. To get a leg up, go to the list of key phrases and terms in the appendices of this book.

Liquor Laws Driving drunk is illegal and not a smart idea on any road— never mind Italy's twisty, narrow roads. Legal drinking age in Italy is 16, but that's just on paper. Public drunkenness (aside from people getting noisily tipsy and flush at big dinners) is unusual except among some street people—usually among foreign vagabonds, not the Italian homeless.

Lost & Found Be sure to contact your credit card companies the minute you discover your wallet has been lost or stolen, and file a report at the nearest police precinct. Your credit card company or insurer may require a police report number or record of the loss. Most credit card companies have an emergency toll-free number to call if your card is lost or stolen; they may be able to wire you a cash advance immediately or deliver an emergency credit card in a day or two.

If you **lose your card,** call the following *Italian* toll-free numbers: **Visa** (ⓒ **800/819-014**), **MasterCard** (ⓒ **800/870-866**), or **American Express** (ⓒ **800/872-000,** or collect 336/393-1111 from anywhere in the world). As a back-up, write down the phone numbers that appear on the back of each of your cards (*not* the U.S. toll-free number—you can't dial those from abroad—but rather the number you can call collect from anywhere; if one does not appear, call the card company and ask).

If you need emergency cash over the weekend, when all banks and American Express offices are closed, you can have money wired to you via

Western Union (℗ 800/325-6000; www.westernunion.com). Identity theft and fraud are potential complications of losing your wallet, especially if you've lost your driver's license along with your cash and credit cards. Notify the major credit-reporting bureaus immediately; placing a fraud alert on your records may protect you against liability for criminal activity. The three major U.S. credit-reporting agencies are **Equifax** (℗ 800/766-0008; www.equifax.com), **Experian** (℗ 888/397-3742; www.experian.com), and **TransUnion** (℗ 800/680-7289; www.transunion.com). Finally, if you've lost all forms of photo ID, call your airline and explain the situation; they might allow you to board the plane if you have a copy of your passport or birth certificate and a copy of the police report you've filed.

Mail The Italian mail system is notoriously slow, and friends back home may not receive your postcards or aerograms for up to 8 weeks (sometimes longer). Postcards, aerograms, and letters weighing up to 20 grams (.7 oz.) to North America cost .52€ (60¢), to the United Kingdom and Ireland .41€ (29p), and to Australia and New Zealand .52€ (A$.90).

Newspapers & Magazines The *International Herald Tribune* (published by the *New York Times* and with news catering to Americans abroad) and *USA Today* are available at just about every newsstand, even in smaller towns. You can find the *Wall Street Journal Europe,* European editions of *Time* and *Newsweek,* and often the *London Times* at some of the larger kiosks. For events guides in English, see each individual city's "Visitor Information" listing.

Passports **For Residents of the United States:** Whether you're applying in person or by mail, you can download passport applications from the U.S. State Department website at **http://travel.state.gov**. For general information, call the **National Passport Agency** (℗ 202/647-0518). To find your regional passport office, either check the U.S. State Department website or call the **National Passport Information Center** (℗ 900/225-5674); the fee is 55¢ per minute for automated information and $1.50 per minute for operator-assisted calls.

For Residents of Canada: Passport applications are available at travel agencies throughout Canada or from the central **Passport Office,** Department of Foreign Affairs and International Trade, Ottawa, ON K1A 0G3 (℗ 800/567-6868; www.dfait-maeci.gc.ca/passport).

For Residents of the United Kingdom: To pick up an application for a standard 10-year passport (5-year passport for children under 16), visit your nearest passport office, major post office, or travel agency; or contact the **United Kingdom Passport Service** at ℗ 0870/521-0410 or search its website at www.ukpa.gov.uk.

For Residents of Ireland: You can apply for a 10-year passport at the **Passport Office,** Setanta Centre, Molesworth Street, Dublin 2 (℗ 01/671-1633; www.irlgov.ie/iveagh). Those under age 18 and over 65 must apply for a 12€ 3-year passport. You can also apply at 1A South Mall, Cork (℗ 021/272-525), or at most main post offices.

For Residents of Australia: You can pick up an application from your local post office or any branch of Passports Australia, but you must schedule an interview at the passport office to present your application materials. Call the **Australian Passport Information Service** at ✆ **131-232,** or visit the government website at www.passports.gov.au.

    For Residents of New Zealand: You can pick up a passport application at any New Zealand Passports Office or download it from their website. Contact the **Passports Office** at ✆ **0800/225-050** in New Zealand or 04/474-8100, or log on to www.passports.govt.nz.

Police For emergencies, call ✆ **113.** Italy has several different police forces, but there are only two you'll most likely ever need to deal with. The first is the urban *polizia,* whose city headquarters is called the *questura* and who can help with lost and stolen property. The most useful branch—the cops to go to for serious problems and crimes—is the *carabinieri* (✆ **112),** a national order-keeping, crime-fighting civilian police force.

Restrooms Public toilets are going out of fashion in Italy, but most bars will let you use their bathrooms without a scowl or forcing you to buy anything. Ask *"Posso usare il bagno?"* (*poh-*soh oo-*zar-*eh eel *ban-*yo). *Donne/signore* are women and *uomini/signori* men. Train stations usually have a bathroom, for a fee, often of the two-bricks-to-stand-on-and-a-hole-in-the-floor Turkish toilet variety. In many of the public toilets that remain, the little old lady with a basket has been replaced by a coin-op turnstile.

Safety Other than the inevitable pickpockets, especially in touristy areas, random violent crime is practically unheard of in the country. You won't see quite as many **gypsy pickpocketing children** in other places as is found in Rome, but they have started roving other major tourist cities. If you see a small group or pair of dirty children coming at you, often waving cardboard and jabbering in Ital-English, yell *"Va via!"* (go away) or simply "No!," or invoke the *polizia.* If they get close enough to touch you, push them away forcefully—don't hold back because they're kids—otherwise, within a nanosecond, you and your wallet will be permanently separated.

    There are plenty of locals, of course, who prey on tourists as well, especially around tourist centers like the Piazza San Marco in Venice and the Piazza del Duomo in Milan. In general, be smart. Keep your passport, traveler's checks, credit and ATM cards (if you feel the need to), and a photocopy of all your important documents under your clothes in a money belt or neck pouch. **For women:** There's occasional drive-by purse snatching in cities by young moped-mounted thieves. Keep your purse on the wall side of the sidewalk and sling the strap across your chest. If your purse has a flap, keep the clasp side facing your body. **For men:** Keep your wallet in your front pocket and perhaps loop a rubber band around it. (The rubber catches on the fabric of your pocket and makes it harder for a thief to slip the wallet out easily.)

Taxes There's no sales tax added onto the price tag of your purchases, but there is a **value-added tax** (in Italy: IVA) automatically included in just about everything. For major purchases, you can get this refunded (see the box earlier in this chapter). Some five-star and four-star hotels don't include the 13% luxury tax in their quoted prices. Ask when making your reservation.

Telephones & Fax **Local calls** in Italy cost .10€ (11¢). There are three types of public pay phones: those that take coins only, those that take both coins and phonecards, and those that take only **phonecards** (*carta* or *scheda telefonica*). You can buy these prepaid phonecards at any *tabac-chi* (tobacconists), most newsstands, and some bars in several denominations from 1€ to 7.50€. Break off the corner before inserting it; a digital display tracks how much money is left on the card as you talk. Don't forget to take the card with you when you leave!

For **operator-assisted international calls** (in English), dial toll-free ℂ **170**. Note, however, that you'll get better rates by calling a home operator for collect calls, as detailed here: To make **calling card calls,** insert a phonecard or .10€ coin—it'll be refunded at the end of your call—and dial the local number for your service. For **Americans:** AT&T at ℂ **172-1011,** MCI at ℂ **172-1022,** or Sprint at ℂ **172-1877.** These numbers will raise an American operator for you, and you can use any one of them to place a **collect call,** even if you don't carry that phone company's card. **Canadians** can reach Teleglobe at ℂ **172-1001. Brits** can call BT at ℂ **172-0044** or Mercury at ℂ **172-0544.** The **Irish** can get a home operator at ℂ **172-0353. Australians** can use Optus by calling ℂ **172-1161** or Telstra at ℂ **172-1061.** And **New Zealanders** can phone home at ℂ **172-1064.**

To **dial direct internationally from Italy,** dial ℂ **00,** then the country code, the area code, and the number. Country codes are as follows: the United States and Canada 1, the United Kingdom 44, Ireland 353, Australia 61, New Zealand 64. Make international calls from a public phone, if possible, because hotels charge ridiculously inflated rates for direct dial, but take along plenty of *schede* to feed the phone.

To call free national **telephone information** (in Italian) in Italy, dial ℂ **12.** International information for Europe is available at ℂ **176** but costs .60€ (70¢) a shot. For international information beyond Europe, dial ℂ **1790** for .50€ (55¢).

Your hotel will most likely be able to send or receive **faxes** for you, sometimes at inflated prices, sometimes at cost. Otherwise, most *cartoleria* (stationery stores), *copista* or *fotocopie* (photocopy shops), and some *tabacchi* (tobacconists) offer fax services.

Time Zone Italy is 6 hours ahead of Eastern Standard Time in the United States. When it's noon in New York, it's 6pm in Florence.

Tipping In **hotels,** a service charge is usually included in your bill. In family-run operations, additional tips are unnecessary and sometimes considered rude. In fancier places with a hired staff, however, you may want to leave a .50€ (55¢) daily tip for the maid, pay the bellhop or porter 1€ ($1.15) per bag, and give a helpful concierge 2€ ($2.30) for his or her troubles. In **restaurants,** 10% to 15% is almost always included in the bill—to be sure, ask *"E incluso il servizio?"*—but you can leave up to an additional 10%, especially for good service. At **bars** and **cafes,** leave a .10€ coin per drink on the counter for the barman; if you sit at a table, leave 10% to 15%. **Taxi** drivers expect 10% to 15%.

Water Although most Italians take mineral water with their meals, tap water is safe everywhere, as are any public drinking fountains you run across. Unsafe sources will be marked ACQUA NON POTABILE. If tap water comes out cloudy, it's only the calcium and other minerals inherent in a water supply that often comes untreated from fresh springs.

3

Rome: The Eternal City

by Lynn A. Levine

Appropriately dubbed "The Eternal City," **Rome (Roma)** grew out of a myth, developed into a powerhouse of antiquity, and became one of the greatest, most democratic and culturally rich civilizations in the history of the world. Its influence has been felt on civilizations all over the world, be it on religion, architecture, art, anthropology, or a hearty red sauce of pancetta and onions.

The city is a phenomenon of romanticism and timelessness, and exploring Rome is like walking through the pages of a life-size pop-up book. Rome's artistic legacy can become overwhelming in a city whose ancient streets are lined with medieval, Renaissance, and baroque churches designed by the likes of Bramante, Bernini, and Borromini, and enriched by Byzantine-era mosaics or frescoes, sculptures, and paintings by such masters as Giotto, Michelangelo, Raphael, Leonardo, and Caravaggio. But the wonder of Rome is that the works of these hallowed names only skim the surface of the city's rich art, architecture, and culture that is Rome. Its legacy is so thoroughly monumental that no matter how deep you dig (and as the public works people learn on a regular basis), it's inevitable that you'll come up with something to add to the annals of history. Discovering the city's secrets is an adventure in itself, a

test of patience and ingenuity in navigating crowds and insane traffic circles.

Rome's magnetism for the first-time visitor inevitably turns to the distant past, to the celebrity lineup of rulers considered sanctified (Augustus, Claudius, Octavian, Vespasian, Trajan, Hadrian) and schizophrenic (Tiberius, Caligula, Nero, Domitian). Challenging this order was the church, from its earliest stages as a rebellious pagan movement rejecting the emperor as the embodiment of religious power, to the potent empire that would direct the progression of religious, cultural, artistic, and political thought for centuries to come.

Obviously, if you're planning to "do" Rome in a week, you're going to be grievously disappointed, especially if you focus only on the city's top draws. Just as important as those 3 hours spent trudging through the Vatican Museums is the 3 hours spent dining and sipping local wine on the cobblestones of Campo de' Fiori or picnicking among the joggers and Frisbee-catching dogs on the Circus Maximus. And don't be discouraged by the often last-minute variations in hours and schedules—this is all part of the Roman experience of constant surrender to the unpredictable, to an ordered chaos even locals can't comprehend.

1 Arriving

BY PLANE

Most international flights land at **Leonardo da Vinci International Airport,** also called **Fiumicino** (© 06-65951; www.adr.it), 30km (19 miles) west of the city. Beyond Customs is a **visitors' info booth** with good free maps and brochures, open daily from 8:15am to 7:15pm. If you've booked a charter flight or are flying in on a budget airline, chances are, you'll land at the smaller **Ciampino Airport** (© 06-79340297), 15km (9⅓ miles) south of the city.

GETTING FROM THE AIRPORTS TO ROME   To get downtown from **Fiumicino,** follow the signs marked TRENI for one of the half-hourly **nonstop trains** (30 min.; 9.50€/$11) to Stazione Termini, Rome's main rail station. If the temperamental ticket machines are on the fritz, you can buy your ticket at the **Agenzia 365** at the head of the tracks. If you're really pinching euros, take one of the **local trains** marked ORTE or FARA SABINA (45 min.; 5€/$5.75) leaving from the same track and get off at Rome's Stazione Tiburtina, the secondary train station, where you can catch the Metropolitana (subway) line B to Termini station. You can also catch line B by getting off the train at the Ostiense stop and walking to the Piramide Metro stop, or you can hop on bus no. 175 to Termini. The amount you save by taking the local isn't worth the inconvenience unless your hotel is in Trastevere (20 min.; 5€/$5.75; get off at the Trastevere stop) or the Aventine (get off at Ostiense). For arrivals between 11:30pm and 5am, a **night bus** leaves Fiumicino for Tiburtina hourly (9€/$10). If you're headed to Termini, the no. 40N bus connects Tiburtina and Termini at night.

To get downtown from **Ciampino,** catch one of the **COTRAL buses** (1.30€/$1.50) leaving from outside the terminal every half-hour (6:50am–12:15am) for the 20-minute trip to Anagnina, the terminus of Metro line A, where you can grab a subway to Stazione Termini (1€/$1.15). Buses headed back to Ciampino leave from Via Marsala in front of Royal Santina Hotel (Mon–Fri 10:15am and 5:35pm; Sat and holidays 10:10am and 5:35pm). Tickets are 8€ ($9.20).

Taxis to and from either airport should cost around 40€ ($46), plus around 2.50€ ($2.85) for bags during the daytime (more at night and on Sun).

GETTING TO FIUMICINO FROM ROME   At track no. 22 in **Stazione Termini** is an **Alitalia/Fiumicino desk,** open daily from 6:30am to 9pm. The first airport train (30 min.; 9.50€/$11) leaves Termini at 6:50am (arriving 7:23am), while the rest run hourly on the 20-minute mark. If you have no luggage to check, you can check in for most Alitalia flights here as well (*except* flights AZ640/AZ642 to Newark or AZ650 to Toronto).

There are two options if you are arriving or departing between 11:30pm and 5am. The first local train out of Rome's **Stazione Tiburtina** leaves at 5:04am (48 min.; 5.55€/$6.40), then continuously every 20 minutes. There's also a night bus leaving Fiumicino for Stazione Tiburtina (where you will have to transfer for a local train to Termini) at 1:15am, 2:15am, 3:30am, and 5am; night buses for Fiumicino leave Tiburtina at 12:30am, 1:15am, 2:30am, and 3:45am.

BY TRAIN

There are at least three trains an hour from **Florence,** running anywhere from 1½ to 3½ hours, depending on whether you ride one of the state-run **(FS)** trains (some depart from Stazione Campo di Marte) or opt for one of the high-speed

---

A Train Station Tip

When arriving in Rome by train, stock up on bus and Metro tickets at the *tabacchi* (tobacconists) located inside the platform area just before passing into the main hall. There's no point in heading straight to the bus terminus empty-handed, and the automated machines in the Metropolitan are often on the fritz.

---

trains (**Eurostar** or **Intercity**). The fare is 15€ to 29€ ($17–$34). There are 10 direct and night trains daily from **Venice** (4½–7 hr.; 45€/$52) and hourly departures from **Milan** (4½–9 hr.; 46€/$53). From **Naples** (1½–2½ hr.; 14€–22€/$16–$26), there are two to three runs hourly and limited service on Sunday.

Rome's main train station is **Stazione Termini** (© **1478/88088** toll-free, or 06-47306599), at the northeast corner of the *centro storico* (historic center). A few long-haul trains stop only at Rome's secondary **Stazione Tiburtina,** in the southern part of the city (see "By Plane," above). Termini is divided into three sections: You'll be exiting the train in the area of the **tracks** or platforms, where, on Track 4, you'll find a small **tourist office,** open daily from 8am to 9pm; the **main hall,** filled with shops and services like newsstands, eateries, banks, the **Metro** entrance, and a 24-hour pharmacy; and then the **ticketing hall.** Outside the ticketing hall is Piazza del Cinquecento, a huge square containing **taxi stands** and Rome's major **bus terminus,** where some two dozen routes converge. If you have questions about how to get where you're going, check with the tourist information kiosk just beyond the taxi rank to the right.

BY BUS

Rome has coach connections with every major city in Italy, but train travel is invariably the more comfortable choice, as buses take longer, are less comfortable, and cost about the same. They can, however, be handy (but crowded) when the rail system goes on strike (a frequent occurrence). For 24-hour info on all bus lines into and out of Rome, call toll-free © **800-431784.** Most intercity buses arrive either near Stazione Termini (the main train station) or at one of several suburban bus stations (each near a Metro stop).

BY CAR

The saying "all roads lead to Rome" still rings true in Italy, even if none of them leads you directly (or logically) into the center of town. The capital is at the convergence of a dozen highways, including the **A1 autostrada,** which connects Rome with Florence, Milan, and Naples. The **Grande Raccordo Annulare,** called the **"GRA,"** is a highway ring around the greater Roman urban area into which all incoming roads feed. As Rome is such a headache to drive in, it's best to use the GRA to circle around to the side of the city closest to your final destination rather than try to cut across downtown. For **parking,** see "Getting Around," below.

2 Essentials

VISITOR INFORMATION

TOURIST OFFICES   The **main tourist office** (© **06-48899253;** fax 06-48899228; www.romapreview.it; Metro: Repubblica) is off Piazza della Repubblica at Via Parigi 5, behind the Baths of Diocletian; it's open Monday through

Friday from 8:15am to 7:15pm (Sat to 1:45pm). There's an **information booth** in the International Arrivals terminal at Fiumicino Airport, open daily from 8:15am to 7:15pm, as well as a **small office** on Track 4 at Stazione Termini (© **06-48906300**), open daily from 8am to 9pm (it's often difficult to find behind the mass of people).

For the lowdown on **events,** see "Newspapers & Magazines," under "Fast Facts: Rome," later in this chapter.

INFORMATION KIOSKS   There are a number of helpful information kiosks located conveniently around town, open daily from 9am to 7pm. Look for them on **Piazza dei Cinquecento,** outside Stazione Termini's main entrance, past the taxi stand and to the right (© 06-47825194); on **Piazza di Spagna/Largo Goldoni** (© 06-68136061); on Via Nazionale in front of the **Palazzo delle Esposizioni** (© 06-47824525); on **Piazza Tempio della Pace,** near the Fori Imperiali (© 06-69924307); on **Piazza Navona/Piazza Cinque Lune** (© 06-68809240); at **Castel Sant'Angelo/Piazza Pia** (© 06-68809707); on **Piazza San Giovanni** in Laterano (© 06-77203535); in Trastevere on **Piazza Sonnino** (© 06-58333457); and outside **Santa Maria Maggiore** (© 06-47880294).

ENJOY ROME   The private firm of **Enjoy Rome,** Via Marghera 8/a, near Stazione Termini (© **06-4451843** or 06-4456890; fax 06-4450734; www.enjoyrome.com; Metro: Termini), has expanded into a full-service travel agency. It began as a walking tour outfit in the early 1990s but soon became the first stop in Rome for budget travelers, students, and backpackers. In addition to offering walking and bike tours of the city, the Enjoy Rome people dabble in the hotel business and run a convenient bus trip to Pompeii. The young staff, from English-speaking countries, provides lots of info on the city and a free room-finding service (see "Accommodations You Can Afford," later in this chapter). The agency is open Monday through Friday from 8:30am to 2pm and 3:30 to 6pm, and Saturday from 8:30am to 2pm.

WEBSITES   Rome's official sites are **www.comune.roma.it** and **www.roma turismo.com.** There are also several good privately maintained sites. Try **Dolce Vita** (www.dolcevita.com), **Enjoy Rome** (www.enjoyrome.com), **Virtual Rome** (www.virtualrome.com), **Christus Rex** (www.christusrex.org; views of the website do not necessarily reflect ours), **the Vatican** (www.vatican.va), and **Time Out** (www.timeout.com/rome). The site **www.roma2000.it** hasn't been updated since June 2000, but it's chock-full of info.

FESTIVALS & EVENTS   Not to be missed are **Carnevale (Carnival),** ending on Martedi Grasso (Fat Tuesday); the **Festa di Primvera (Feast of Spring),** when the Spanish Steps are covered with azaleas; **Holy Week,** when pilgrims flood the city to attend church, see the pope say Mass at the Colosseum on Good Friday, and hear him speak a blessing from his balcony in the Vatican overlooking St. Peter's Square on Easter Sunday; **Rome's Birthday** on April 21, celebrated with ceremonies on the Campidoglio and candles set to flicker along the city's stairways and palazzo rooftops; the **International Horse Show;** the

---

Calling for Tips

Suggestions on restaurants and shopping tips are but a phone call away. Useful travel tips and general information on arts, culture, and entertainment are now available in five languages from **Call Center Rome** at © **06-36004399** (daily 9am–7pm).

May Day (May 1) free rock concert on the piazza in front of San Giovanni in Laterano; the **Estate Romana**'s summertime lineup of outdoor concerts, exhibits, movies, and performances; the outdoor performances of the **Rome Opera;** the **Festa di San Giovanni (Feast of St. John)** and **Festa di San Pietro e Paolo (Feast of Sts. Peter and Paul);** the **Festa dei Noiantri (Festival of We Others),** immortalized near the end of Fellini's film *Roma* (the scene in which he interviews Gore Vidal); and the pope's **December 25 Urbi et Orbi** blessing from his Vatican window overlooking St. Peter's. See the "Italy Calendar of Events" in chapter 2 for more details.

CITY LAYOUT

Rome is strung along an S-shape bend of the **Tevere (Tiber River),** with the bulk of the *centro storico* (historic center) lying east of the Tevere. While there are official administrative districts, the Romans themselves think in terms of an address being near this piazza or that major monument, so I'll do the same.

The north end of the *centro storico* is the oval **Piazza del Popolo.** From this grand obelisk-sporting square, three major roads radiate south: **Via del Babuino, Via del Corso,** and **Via di Ripetta.** The middle one, Via del Corso (usually just called the Corso), divides the heart of the city in half.

To the east of the Corso lie the **Spanish Steps** (where V. del Babuino ends) and the **Trevi Fountain.** Surrounding these monuments are Rome's most stylish shopping streets—including the boutique-lined **Via dei Condotti,** running straight from the Spanish Steps to the Corso. To the west of the Corso spreads the medieval Tiber Bend area, home to landmarks like the long, bustling **Piazza Navona,** the ancient **Pantheon,** the market square of **Campo de' Fiori,** countless churches, a few small museums, and the medieval **Jewish Ghetto.**

The Corso ends at about Rome's center in **Piazza Venezia.** This major traffic circle and bus juncture is marked by the overbearing garish white (locals call it the "wedding cake") **Vittorio Emanuele Monument.** Leading west from Piazza Venezia is **Via Plebescito,** which, after passing through the archaeological site and major bus stop **Largo di Torre Argentina,** becomes **Corso Vittorio Emanuele II.** Corso Vittorio Emanuele is a wide street that effectively bisects the Tiber Bend as it heads toward the river and the Vatican. (Piazza Navona and the Pantheon lie to the north, Campo de' Fiori and the Jewish Ghetto to the south.)

If you're at Piazza Venezia and facing south, go to the right around the Vittorio Emanuele Monument—behind which stretches the archaeological zone of the **Roman Forum**—to see the stairs leading up to **Capitoline Hill,** ancient Rome's seat of government. Around the left side of the monument is **Via dei Fori Imperiali,** a wide boulevard that makes a beeline from Piazza Venezia to the **Colosseum,** passing the Roman Forum on the right (slung into the low land

---

Mapping It Out

The maps in this chapter will help you orient yourself and find sights, hotels, and restaurants. For a more detailed map, get **Michelin map no. 38,** a large sheet map of Rome with a street finder (9€/$10). If you're searching for an address, stop into any bar or ask your hotel if you can look at their *Tuttocittà,* a magazine mapping every little alley (only Rome residents can obtain it). The bookstore chain Feltrinelli carries a commercial equivalent of a *Rome A to Z;* look in the Rome or Italy travel sections, usually a prominent display near the registers.

between the **Capitoline** and **Palatine hills**) and the **Imperial Forums** on the left. South of the Forum and the Colosseum rises the shady residential **Aventine Hill,** beyond which is another hill, the old working-class quarter **Testaccio,** which has become a trendy restaurant and nightclub district.

Those are the areas of Rome where you'll spend most of your time. But the grid of 19th-century streets surrounding the main train station, **Stazione Termini,** defines the eastern edge of the *centro storico.* You may also want to venture out at mealtimes to the area east of Termini to the university and intellectuals' district of **San Lorenzo,** home to some fantastic restaurants.

To the northwest of Termini (east of the Spanish Steps area) is a boulevard zone where many foreign embassies lie, the highlight being the cafe-lined **Via Veneto,** of the fashionable 1950s *La Dolce Vita* fame. Via Veneto ends at the southern flank of the giant **Villa Borghese** park, studded with museums and expanding northeast of the *centro storico* (it's also accessible from Piazza del Popolo).

Across the Tiber are two major neighborhoods you may be interested in. Mussolini razed a medieval district to lay down the wide **Via della Conciliazione** linking the Ponte Vittorio Emanuele Bridge with **Vatican City** and **St. Peter's Basilica.** South of there, past the long, parklike **Janiculum Hill,** lies the once medieval working-class, then trendy, and now touristy district of **Trastevere,** with lots of bars, restaurants, and movie theaters.

NEIGHBORHOODS IN BRIEF

Around Ancient Rome This catchall category covers the heart of the ancient city, from the **Colosseum** through the **Roman Forum** and **Imperial Forums** to the **Capitoline** and **Esquiline Hills, Piazza Venezia,** and the streets surrounding them to the river. Antiquity buffs will want to spend a lot of their visit in this vast archaeological zone, but it offers few good hotels and even fewer decent restaurants (most cater to entire tour buses with bad food at high prices).

Around Campo de' Fiori & the Jewish Ghetto This working-class neighborhood of the Tiber Bend, strung between the river and Corso Vittorio Emanuele II, has lots of good restaurants, a daily market on **Campo de' Fiori,** Renaissance palaces lining Via Giulia, and a burgeoning nightlife scene. More impressive is that many of the area boutiques are bucking the trend to close at lunchtime. The eastern half of the area—between Via Arenula and Via di Teatro Marcello and below Largo di Torre Argentina—has been home to Europe's oldest Jewish population ever since it was a walled **ghetto** in the 16th century. Roman Jewish cooking is some of the city's best, and you'll find delicious and relatively inexpensive examples in trattorie scattered throughout this zone.

Around Piazza Navona & the Pantheon This is the true heart of medieval Rome, with a host of sights and monuments like the lively **Piazza Navona,** the ancient and beautiful **Pantheon,** churches hiding Caravaggio paintings or Michelangelo sculptures, and plenty of pedestrian-only elbow room. It has a host of excellent restaurants, lots of nightlife possibilities, and a few choice hotels that won't break the bank. You're also within easy walking distance of both the Vatican and the ruins of ancient Rome. It's a toss-up between this and the Spanish Steps area when it comes to choosing the absolute best place to base yourself in Rome (sightseeing fanatics will want to book here, and shoppers nearer the Spanish Steps; hard-core budget-seekers may have to look elsewhere).

Around the Spanish Steps & Piazza del Popolo Since the 18th century, this has been one of the most popular expatriate areas, full of Brits and Germans and lots of *passeggiata* (evening stroll) action. Today the streets around **Piazza di Spagna** comprise the heart of Rome's shopping scene, with boutique-lined streets like Via de' Condotti sporting the biggest names in Italian and international fashion. It's also one of the most tourist-laden areas of the center, with "public living rooms" and universal tourist magnets like the baroque off-center sweep of the **Spanish Steps** and the gushing mountain of white marble called the **Trevi Fountain.** It's no coincidence that Rome's top hotels cluster at the Spanish Steps' summit or that American Express is on Piazza di Spagna itself (and that Italy's first McDonald's opened a few doors down in 1986). Moving about this neighborhood is often an exercise in weaving among large clots of camera-clicking tour groups, but the area certainly stays animated and most roads are blessedly closed to cars.

Around Via Veneto & Piazza Barberini In the 1950s, this was the heartbeat of *La Dolce Vita* ("the sweet life") made famous by Fellini films. **Via Veneto** still has the cafes of its heyday, but today they're overpriced and patronized mainly by tourists, and its grand old hotels are similarly expensive and booked mostly by guided and packaged tours. The area around Via Veneto and **Piazza Barberini** is also full of baroque and 19th-century palazzi, today home to everything from embassies to one of Rome's best painting galleries (in Palazzo Barberini), to newspaper headquarters.

Termini Aside from some churches and a great museum, the 19th-century neighborhood around the main train station is a pretty boring part of town and too far from the bulk of Rome's sights for even a comfortably long walk. However, it's hard to discount the abundance of cheap hotels in this area, which has actually improved dramatically in recent years. The streets just to the **north of Termini** have undergone the most noticeable improvements, but the immediate Termini area in general still has a ways to go.

The Aventine & Testaccio The **Aventine Hill** south of the Palatine and next to the river is one of central Rome's quietest, leafiest, and most posh residential sections, with a couple of ancient churches set on curving roads. Few tourists venture here, where Rome's urban sprawl becomes a distant memory. It's a good place to stay if you want a vacation from the urban chaos but still want the convenience of proximity to a nearby bus or Metro stop.

South of the Aventine and up against the river where it turns south again is one of Rome's greatest working-class neighborhoods, **Testaccio,** home of the old slaughterhouse and once Rome's port on the Tiber. Its name means "ugly head" and refers to the small manmade hillock that hems in the neighborhood on the east. Just as the Tiber did docklands in ancient times, Testaccio received countless barges carrying amphorae full of wine and olive oil. These ceramic vases were off-loaded and their merchandise measured into smaller, more salable containers; then the amphorae were discarded onto a pile that eventually grew into the 50m (165-ft.) hill of Testaccio, now covered with grass. Since all that ceramic keeps constant temperature and moisture levels, grottoes were dug into the mound for storing wine and food, and many of Rome's most authentic restaurants still line Testaccio, their dining rooms and cellars burrowed back into the artificial hill of pot shards and their kitchens turning out ultratraditional cuisine. The area has also become rather fashionable, and most of Rome's hottest nightclubs appear here in old warehouses (and often disappear after a few months).

Trastevere Trastevere (across the Tiber) was another of Rome's great medieval working-class neighborhoods, one that spoke its own dialect and had a tradition of street fairs and poetry—still echoed in the July **Festa de' Noiantri (Feast of We Others).** But after Trastevere became trendy in the 1970s and 1980s, popular with both the Roman upper middle class and lots of expat Americans, it sold out to tourism in the 1990s. It always had lots of restaurants and excellent tiny trattorie, but this boom in popularity has filled it beyond bursting with eateries, pubs, dance halls, funky boutiques, sidewalk vendors and fortunetellers, and a stifling crush of "trendoids" and tourists. Trastevere has become a requisite stop for coach tours and a guided walk in travel books. It's still one of Rome's most colorful quarters, much like Paris's Latin Quarter and New York's SoHo, and the best place to come if you just want to wander into a good restaurant at random.

Around the Vatican Called the **Borgo,** the area surrounding the **Vatican** and **St. Peter's Basilica** is full of overpriced restaurants and businesses that cater to the tour bus crowds, but you'll also find many modestly priced (if mostly boringly modern) hotels. Expanding north and northeast of the Borgo is the residential and shopping zone of **Prati**—no sightseeing, just a good glimpse into the daily life of middle-class Romans.

GETTING AROUND

Rome is a town to explore on foot. From little baroque churches with ancient columns to a roving knife sharpener working the pedal of his portable grindstone, you never know what you may come across while walking down a Roman street. Rome, however, isn't quite a walker's paradise—the sidewalks are too narrow (or often nonexistent) and the traffic far too heavy. Fortunately, much of the historic center has now been pedestrianized, save for a few main thoroughfares.

Beware: Rome's hard, uneven cobblestones are rough on your feet, your shoe soles, and your ankles.

All city transport uses the same 1€ ($1.15) *biglietto* (ticket). This simple one-way ticket gives you unlimited transfers for a maximum of 90 minutes within the city of Rome, including Ostia Antica but not the airport or Tivoli (you can enter the Metro system only once). There's also a **daily pass** (4€/$4.60), a 3-day pass (11€/$12), and a weekly pass (16€/$18), good for use on all buses, the Metro, and regional trains to Ostia and Cotral buses. Tickets for all expire at midnight of the day of expiration.

Tickets and passes for buses, trams, and the Metro are available from *tabacchi* (tobacconists), most newsstands, Metro stations, or machines at major bus stops (the machines, which are without exception consistently out of order, accept only coins). Children 10 and under ride free on all public transportation.

Validate That Ticket

Always remember to validate your ticket *before* you enter the Metro or board a bus or tram (on buses, stamp your ticket in the orange box) and hold on to it until you're off the bus or out of the Metro station. While the ticket costs only 1€ ($1.15), the fine will set you back 50€ ($58)!

BY METRO (SUBWAY)   Rome's **Metropolitana** (Metro, for short) isn't very extensive, with only two lines etching a rough X, with Termini at the intersection. **Line A** runs from Ottaviano (a dozen blocks from the Vatican), through such stops as Flaminio (near Piazza del Popolo), Spagna (Spanish Steps), Termini, and San Giovanni (Rome's cathedral). **Line B** is most useful to shuttle you quickly from Termini to stops for the Colosseo (Colosseum), Circo Massimo (Circus Maximus), and Piramide (at Rome's Tiburtina train station and near Testaccio). The Metro runs daily from 5:30am to 11:30pm.

BY BUS & TRAM   Rome's bus and tram system is much more extensive than the Metro, and you usually don't have to walk far for a connection. The tourist offices no longer distribute free bus maps, but you can pick up an equivalent *mappa degli autobus* at newsstands for 6€ ($6.90). You can also download the latest bus map from **www.atac.roma.it**.

One of the most useful lines is no. **64,** making a beeline from Stazione Termini to the Vatican (heavily used by tourists and, thus, thieves, and known as the Pickpocket Express). The no. 64 stops at Piazza Venezia (with the Vittorio Emanuele Monument), near to the "back door" entrance to the Roman Forum and within walking distance of the Colosseum along Via dei Fori Imperiali.

Nos. **492** and **175** from Stazione Termini will run you over to Via del Tritone near the Trevi Fountain and the Spanish Steps; if you're coming from the Vatican, hop on no. **62.** Bus nos. **116, 117,** and **119** are electric minibuses designed to navigate the narrow cobbled pedestrian streets of the *centro storico,* but not on Sunday. For bus information, call 🕐 **800-431784** or go to **www.atac.roma.it** on the Web.

Most buses run daily 5:30am to midnight, with a separate series of night buses whose route numbers are prefaced by an *N* (or look for the cute little owl over the phrase BUS NOTTURNO). For **bus information,** call 🕐 **800-431784** Monday through Friday from 8am to 6pm, or 🕐 06-46954444. Many buses start their routes at the large **Piazza dei Cinquecento** in front of Stazione Termini. There are also four major spots in the *centro storico* where multiple bus lines converge for easy transfers: **Largo di Tritone/Piazza Barberini, Piazza Venezia/Via Plebescito, Via Plebescito/Largo di Torre Argentina,** and **Piazza San Silvestro** (just off the Corso, between the Spanish Steps and the Trevi Fountain). For all of these squares, some buses pause at one of several stops arranged around the piazza itself, many others at a series of stops near the outlets of tributary streets feeding into the square.

BY TAXI   Generally you don't hail a cab in the street, but you summon one by calling a licensed taxi company and providing your location (call 🕐 **06-4994,** 06-3570, 06-6645, 06-5551, or 06-4157). You'll be given the ID name and number of the taxi that will pick you up (like Bologna/177), but since the dispatch systems are often voice recordings in Italian, you may want to have a local make the call for you (ask your concierge or even the barman). Sticker shock is augmented by the fact that the meter begins running as soon as you make the call, encouraging many an unscrupulous driver to drive around for a bit before picking you up. For this reason, it's often better to hail a taxi on the street (good luck) or, better yet, find a taxi at one of the **designated stands** at major piazze, including Piazza Venezia and Largo Argentina; at the Pantheon; and in front of Stazione Termini. The approximate (on the high end) fare from the airport to the center of Rome is about 40€ ($46; no more than 50€/$58 plus supplements for bags and night travel); from Termini to Rome center 10€ to 12€ ($12–$14); from Termini to the Vatican 16€ ($18); from Termini to the Colosseum 10€ ($12); and from Termini to Aventino 10€ ($12). Still, no matter what the meter says at the end of the ride, you'll likely wind up paying more. The initial charge is 2.35€ ($2.70) for travel between 7am and 10pm, 3.35€ ($3.85) on Sunday and holidays between 7am and 10pm, or 4.90€ ($5.65) between 10pm and 7am, plus .10€ (10¢) per kilometer. There is also an additional charge for luggage (1.05€/$1.20 per bag), and even a supplement for bringing your dog along.

BY CAR   Having a car in Rome is a pain, so if you have a choice, don't drive here. Not only are Italian drivers even more manic in the city, but the system of one-way roads seems specially designed to keep you from driving anywhere near your destination. Much of the historic center is pedestrian-only anyway, but you are allowed to drive in to your hotel to drop off luggage. Meanwhile, finding a parking spot is almost impossible, unless you don't mind dropping 20€ ($23) per day at a garage. If you plan to rent a car in Rome to tool about the countryside, wait to pick it up until the day you set out, and make your first stop back into town the rental agency lot.

Your hotel may have its own garage or an arrangement with one nearby, or you may be lucky enough to be staying in one of the few parts of the historic center that haven't yet been designated a *zona blu.* Most parking spaces have been painted with blue stripes, meaning you must pay a parking meter (usually a box at the end of the block that issues a time slip) or buy a parking "ticket" (1€/$1.15 per hour 8am–8pm) at the nearest *tabacchi* (tobacconists) or newsstand and place it on the dashboard—note that the meter maids are out in numbers, checking that you're back before your time runs out. **Public garages** are generally cheaper, the biggest being **Parcheggio Borghese** (3.45€/$3.95 the first 3 hr., then 1.15€/$1.30 per hour up to a maximum of 14€/$17 per day) under the Villa Borghese park. The entrance is on Viale del Muro Torto, which leads off into the park from the traffic circle at Porta Pinciana, where Via Veneto, Corso d'Italia, and Via Pinciana converge.

BY BICYCLE OR SCOOTER   The best prices on rental bikes or scooters are offered at **Bici e Baci,** Via del Viminale 5 (© 06-4828443; www.bicibaci.com; Metro: Termini), and **I Bike Rome,** Via Veneto 156 (© 06-3225230), in section 3 of the underground parking lot near Villa Borghese. Lowest rates advertised for scooters are for the dinkiest 50cc model, around 35€ ($40) per day, but note that *few shops actually have this model or this price.* Expect to pay at least 50€ ($58) per day. Scooters come with a helmet (required by law) and lock.

Warning: Rome's chaotic traffic, widespread pedestrian zones, and one-way streets make getting around challenging, if not downright dangerous, so even with a helmet, this should definitely not be your first time on a scooter.

FAST FACTS: Rome

American Express The office is just to the right of the Spanish Steps at Piazza di Spagna 38 (© 06-67641; Metro: Spagna), open Monday through Friday from 9am to 6:30pm and Saturday from 9am to 2:30pm; it closes an hour earlier during the 2 weeks of Ferragosto (Aug 15–Sept 1). To report lost or stolen traveler's checks, call © 1678-72000; for lost or stolen Amex cards, call © 722-80371.

Business Hours As in most of Italy, almost all shops and offices, most churches, and many museums observe a siesta-like midafternoon shutdown called *riposo,* about 12:30 or 1 to 3 or 4pm (or as late as 5pm in summer). Capitalism (or demand) has recently begun to show its ugly but irresistible head, as more and more stores in the center have adjusted to *orario continuato* (nonstop open hours). Nevertheless, it's a good idea to figure out the few sights in town that remain open during *riposo* to maximize your sightseeing—or you can just give in to the rhythm and enjoy a leisurely lunch to fill this time. Shopkeepers ease into the week by opening on Monday from about 3 or 4 to 8pm. "Normal" hours are Tuesday through Saturday from 9am to 1pm and 3 or 4 to 8pm. Not so for food or gastronomy stores, which open on Monday mornings but close Thursday afternoons.

Doctors & Dentists The **U.S. Embassy** (© 06-46741) keeps an updated list of English-speaking doctors and dentists, though you'll find that most doctors have some proficiency in English. First aid is available 24 hours in the emergency room *(pronto soccorso)* of major hospitals (see "Hospitals," below) or by calling the **24-Hour Medical Service** hot line at © 06-4826741. You can also try the **International Medical Center,** Via Giovanni Amendola 7 (© 06-4882371; Metro: Termini).

Embassies & Consulates The **U.S. Embassy** is at Via Vittorio Veneto 121 (© 06-46741; Metro: Barberini; Bus: 52, 53, 61, 62, 63, 80, 95, 116, 116T, 204F). For passport and consular services, head to the consulate, to the left of the embassy's main gate at no. 119, open Monday through Friday from 8:30am to 1pm and 2 to 5:30pm. The **Canadian Consulate** is at Via Zara 30, fifth floor (© 06-445981; Bus: 36, 60), open Monday through Friday from 8:30am to noon and 1:30 to 4pm. The **U.K. Consulate** is at Via XX Settembre 80/A (© 06-852721 or 06-4825441; Metro: Repubblica; Bus: 910), open Monday through Friday from 8am to 1pm. The **Australian Consulate** is at Via Alessandria 215 (© 06-852721; Tram: 3; Bus: 19, 38, 80, 88, 313), open Monday through Thursday from 9am to noon and 1:30 to 5pm, and Friday from 9am to noon. The **New Zealand Consulate** is at Via Zara 28 (© 06-4402928; Bus: 36, 60), open Monday through Friday from 8:30am to 12:45pm and 1:45 to 5pm.

Emergencies Dial © 113 in any emergency for the police. You can also call © 112 for the *carabinieri* (the military-trained and more useful of the two police forces); © 118 or 5100 to summon an ambulance; or © 115 for the fire department. *Pronto Soccorso* means first aid and is also the word used for emergency rooms. Call © 116 for roadside assistance (not free).

Hospitals In an emergency, go to the nearest emergency room *(pronto soccorso)* of any hospital *(ospedale).* Convenient ones in the historic center include **San Giacomo,** Via Canova 29, off Via del Corso, 2 blocks from Piazza del Popolo (⟨℃ **06-36261**); **Fatebenefratelli,** on Tiber Island (⟨℃ **06-6837299**); and **Ospedale Santo Spirito in Sassia,** Lungotevere in Sassia 1 on the river just south of Castel Sant'Angelo (⟨℃ **06-68351**). The new H bus line makes a circular route of all the major hospitals.

English-speaking doctors are always on duty at the **Rome American Hospital,** Via Emilio Longoni 69 (⟨℃ **06-22551**), and at the privately run **Salvator Mundi International Hospital,** Viale della Mura Gianicolensi 67 (⟨℃ **06-586041**). Most hospitals will be able to find someone to help you in English, and with Italy's partially socialized medical system, you can usually pop into an emergency room, get taken care of speedily without dealing with insurance forms, and be sent on your way with a prescription and a smile. Just for the record: European Union citizens in possession of an E111 form are entitled to free health care; Australians must present a valid Medicare Card.

Laundry Self-service *lavanderie* (laundromats) are all over town. Try the **Laundromat and Internet cafe,** Via Milazzo 20, where you can do your wash and check your e-mail (3€/$3.45 per hour) at the same time. They'll also do the wash for you in an hour for 6€ ($6.90), soap included. For coin-operated laundromats, hit the **Ondablu chain,** with central locations at Via Principe Amadeo 70b (south of Termini) and Via Vespasiano 50 (near the Vatican); or the **Lavarapido** self-service chain, with locations at Via della Peliccia 35 (near Piazza Santa Maria in Trastevere) and at Via della Chiesa Nuova 15/16. The cost is 6€ ($6.90), soap not included.

The bulk of the *lavanderie,* though, are full-service, charging ridiculous by-the-piece rates to wash, dry, press, and wrap up your T-shirts and undies like a Christmas present. Always ask first if service is *a peso* (by weight, the cheap way) or *al pezzo* (by the piece). However, these full-service joints also usually provide *lavasecco* (dry-cleaning) service at prices comparable to those in the U.S. Your hotel (which will invariably have its own service at equally extortionist prices) will be able to point out the nearest one.

Mail & E-mail The Italian mail system is notoriously slow, and friends back home may not receive your postcards for anywhere from 1 to 8 weeks (if ever). Postage for international postcards and letters costs .65€ to .70€ (75¢–80¢), depending on the destination. Stamps are available at the numerous post offices around town as well as any *tabacchi* (tobacconists; signs have a white T on a brown or black background), which have longer hours than the post offices. The **main post office** is at Piazza San Silvestro 19, 00187 Roma, Italia (off V. del Corso, south of the Spanish Steps); it's open Monday through Friday from 9am to 6pm, Saturday from 9am to 2pm, and Sunday from 9am to 6pm. Enter and head around to the right to buy *francobolli* **(stamps)** at windows 22 and 23. If you want your letters to get home before you do, use the **Vatican post office** instead. It costs the same—but you must use Vatican stamps, available only at their post offices. There are three offices: to the left of the basilica steps, just past the information office; a less crowded branch behind the right colonnade of Piazza San Pietro (where the alley dead-ends beyond the souvenir stands); and upstairs in the Vatican Museums entrance, near the gift shop.

To **receive mail** while in Rome (for a modest pick-up fee), have it sent to the main post office above, addressed to Your Name, FERMO POSTA, Roma, Italia. Holders of Amex cards can get the same service for free by having mail sent c/o American Express, Piazza di Spagna 38, Roma, Italia. Have the sender specify on the envelope that it's "Client Mail."

Most hotels now offer Internet access as a paid perk. You also can log onto the **Internet** in central Rome at **Thenetgate,** Piazza Firenze 25 ((✆ 06-6879098), open in summer Monday through Saturday from 10:30am to 12:30pm and 3:30 to 10:30pm, and in winter daily from 10:40am to 8:30pm. Thenetgate also has branches at Via delle Grazie 4, near the Vatican ((✆ 06-68193238); in Stazione Termini near Via Marsala ((✆ 06-87406008); and in Stazione Tiburtina at Via Cluniacensi 26/28/30 ((✆ 06-43535214). **Internet Point,** Via Gaeta 25 (exit Termini to the right onto V. Marsala, turn left onto V. Marsala, and follow to V. Gaeta; (✆ 06-47823862), is heavily frequented by students and backpackers and open daily from 9am to midnight. North of Castel Sant'Angelo is **Xplore,** Via dei Gracchi 85 ((✆ 06-3202072), stocked with 20 computer stations. You can order off a typical pub menu (which in Italy includes stuffed *focaccie,* thank heavens), plus beer, wine, and cocktails. It's open Monday through Saturday from 3pm to 1am. Keep your eyes open for **call centers** as well, some of which have added Internet access at rates cheaper than that found at the locations mentioned above.

Newspapers & Magazines Expatriate magazine *Wanted in Rome* (1€/$1.15; www.wantedinrome.com) has a calendar-of-events section along with classified ads and articles on Rome and Italy from the foreigner's point of view. You'll find it at most newsstands, especially around tourist areas like the Vatican. Free at tourist offices and kiosks is *L'Evento,* a bimonthly published by the city of Rome with information on exhibits, concerts, theater, and other special events. *Un Ospite a Roma* is free at the finer hotel desks around town (they won't throw you out if you act like you belong) and has details on what's going on around town, including a list of free music concerts and church recitals. If you want to try your hand at Italian, the Thursday edition of the newspaper *La Repubblica* contains the indispensable magazine insert *TrovaRoma* (www.repubblica.it), a complete guide to entertainment, events, galleries, and show listings for the coming week. Two other prime resources are the excellent weekly magazine *Roma C'è* (1€/$1.15), which has a "This Week in Rome" section at the end in English, and the Rome edition of *Time Out* (2€/$2.30), which comes out every 2 months; both are available at newsstands.

Pharmacies **Farmacie,** recognizable by the green semineon cross, follow a rotation schedule for night, Sunday, and holiday hours, so there's always a pharmacy open in every neighborhood. The rotation schedule is posted in the window of every pharmacy, or you can head to a 24-hour pharmacy. **Farmacia della Stazione** is on Piazza dei Cinquecento, in front of Stazione Termini at the corner of Via Cavour ((✆ 06-4880019; Metro: Termini); **Piram,** at Via Nazionale 228 ((✆ 06-4880754); and **Internazionale,** at Piazza Barberini 49 ((✆ 06-4871195; Metro: Barberini), which returns to a rotation schedule on weekends.

Police Dial (✆ **113** in emergencies (see also "Emergencies," above).

Safety Random violent crime is extremely rare in Rome, but pickpocketing runs rampant in tourist areas, where a desperate thief may go as far as slitting open purses or backpacks with knives. Thieves favor buses that run between Stazione Termini and the major sites (particularly bus no. 64 to the Vatican), so try to maintain a healthy distance between you and your traveling companions. Other pickpocketing areas are near the Forums and the Colosseum, in Piazza del Popolo, around the Vatican, and around Termini, though the station is now staffed with private security officials. The Porta Portese flea market in Trastevere is another prime target. Men should keep their wallets in their front pockets and their hands on it while riding buses; women should wear their purses diagonally across their chests with the flaps facing in. It's all too common for young thieves on Vespas to effectively pull off a drive-by purse snatching. Keep your purse on the wall side of the sidewalk and try not to walk too close to the sidewalk's edge.

Gypsy children present an unexpected face of crime, working in packs around tourist areas. These kids aren't physically dangerous, but whenever they're around, a tourist and his money will soon be parted. They approach looking pitiful, begging and occasionally waving scraps of cardboard scrawled with a few words in English. If you see a group of dirty kids headed your way, yell *"Va via!"* ("Scram!") or loudly invoke the *polizia*. If they get too close, shove them away—don't hold back just because they're kids. They congregate outside Stazione Termini by the bus depots, at the Colosseum, at the Forum entrances, and in subway tunnels. Gypsy mothers usually stick to panhandling, but I've heard of Oliver Twist–type tales of scams involving swaddled babies flying through the air. The mother tosses what appears to be her baby, usually a doll in blankets (but sometimes the real thing!) at you. When in your surprise you rush to catch it, they or their accomplices are poised to empty your pockets.

Telephone **Local calls** in Italy cost .10€ (10¢). There are two types of public pay phones, those that take both coins and phone cards and those that take only **phone cards** (*carta telefonica* or *scheda telefonica*). You can buy these prepaid phone cards at any *tabacchi* (tobacconists), most newsstands, and some bars in denominations of 1€, 2.50€, 5€, and 7.50€ ($1.15, $2.85, $5.75, and $8.60). Break off the corner before inserting it and don't forget to take the card with you when you leave the phone.

To make calling-card calls, insert your card or coin—which will be refunded at the end of your call—and dial the local number for your service: **AT&T** at ☎ **172-1011, MCI** at ☎ **172-1022,** or **Sprint** at ☎ **172-1877.** These numbers will raise an American operator. You can also use any one of them to place a collect call, even if you don't carry that particular phone company's card.

Italy has recently introduced the **TIME** card for calling overseas, sold at the same outlets as regular phone cards, in increments of 5€, 10€, and 25€ ($5.75, $12, and $29). Calls to the United States, Canada, Western Europe, and Australia cost only .04€ (5¢) per minute. You don't insert this card into the phone; merely dial ☎ **1740,** then push *2 for instructions in English when prompted. If you use this card for national calls within Italy, keep in mind that these are billed at a slightly higher rate than the normal *scheda telefonica*, at .18€ (20¢) per minute (.33€/35¢ for calls to cellphones).*Tip:* Calls to a cellphone from within the country (numbers beginning with 0338, 0330, 0347, 0335, 0339, 0368, and so on) no longer require you to dial the first zero. Keep the zero for calls made from outside of Italy. Also remember that calls to a mobile phone are charged at a higher rate than calls made to a land line, so keep it short.

Tipping Increasingly in restaurants, a *servizio* (service charge) of 15% is automatically added to your bill, so always ask, *"E incluso il servizio?"* ("Is service included?") when you get the check. If not, leave 15%; if yes, it's still customary to leave an extra .50€ (55¢) per person at the table. At a bar, put a .10€ or .20€ (10¢ or 20¢) piece on the counter with your receipt when you order your espresso or cappuccino; if you're ordering at a table, leave about .50€ (55¢) per person. Tip taxi drivers about 10%.

Travel Agencies In Stazione Termini, you'll find a desk for **CTS** (✆ 06-4679254), offering discounts (under age 26) and assistance (all ages), but only for *international* train travel. Their main office is located at Corso Vittorio Emanuele II 297 (✆ 06-6872672), open from 8:30am to 8:30pm. **Agenzie 365** (✆ 06-46624471), a network of 18 agencies located in the train stations and airports of Italy's major cities, is a full-service agent offering tickets, hotel reservations, car rentals, city tours, excursions, money change, and money transfers; it's open daily from 8:30am to 9pm. Another discounter, **Wasteels,** Via Milazzo 8c (✆ 06-4456679), is geared to the under-26 crowd.

3 Accommodations You Can Afford

Even as a budget-conscious traveler, you don't have to settle for the cheap, often squalid rooms surrounding the train station. (Although there are several good ones recommended below, the location leaves something to be desired.) You can still stay well within budget in a small but comfortable room overlooking the Pantheon, near the Spanish Steps, or hidden in Trastevere. If you're having trouble finding a place, many of the budget establishments in Italy work regularly with the hotel booking website **www.hostelworld.com**.

Hotels claim to have high and low seasons, with prices quoted accordingly, with high season usually from Easter to October (excluding Aug) and Christmas. Unfortunately, "high season" seems to be getting longer and longer, while "low season" has withered to a few weeks in January and February. Be flexible, and you might just get a better rate. Finally, rates quoted below are subject to the time limitations characteristic of print, so don't be astonished (and don't blame me) if the rate quoted by the hotel differs from the one here by 5€ ($5.75; the average rate of per-person increases).

ROOM-FINDING SERVICES The **tourist offices** (see "Visitor Information," earlier in this chapter) will help you track down a room but are often loathe to do so when there's a long line behind you. Tourist offices aren't allowed

Country & City Codes
The **country code** for Italy is **39**. The **city code** for Rome is **06**; use this code when you're calling from outside Italy, within Rome, and within Italy.

⌒Tips A Note on Buses & Trams

In each review's list of buses and trams that pass near the hotel, **boldface** indicates lines you can take directly from the main train station, Stazione Termini (from either the bus terminus on Piazza del Cinquecento out front or from a stop on the streets ringing the piazza).

---

to play favorites regarding specific hotels, so the employees will arbitrarily look for any available room in your price range. (Some people are kind enough to try to stick you close to the center.)

You may have more luck and certainly better service at **Enjoy Rome** (see "Visitor Information," earlier in this chapter), which specializes in finding budget accommodations, even at the last minute. The English-speaking staff will help you for free via phone, in person, or via e-mail. The clerks often try to convince you to stay in hostels or other dormlike rooms (often in their own hostel), especially if you're under 30—just remind them you're willing to pay a bit more for a private room.

AROUND ANCIENT ROME

Perugia   This well-run inn is located on a side street a block behind the Forum entrance. Everything's kept clean (the white tile floor isn't something that can hide dirt), and small pictures hanging on the walls add some color. A few of the rooms get the benefit of air-conditioning (10€/$12 extra per night), while table fans are provided to guests in the others. Room no. 26 overlooks a minuscule courtyard full of hanging ivy, but the street's fairly quiet, so you can open the windows for light in the front rooms.

Via del Colosseo 7 (near the corner of V. Tempio della Pace), 00184 Roma. ⓒ **06-6797200.** Fax 06-6784635. www.hperugia.it. 13 units, 7 with bathroom. 30€–60€ ($35–$69) single without bathroom, 45€–100€ ($52–$115) single with bathroom; 65€–135€ ($75–$155) double with bathroom. 10€ ($12) per night A/C. See website for last-minute rates. Rates include breakfast. AE, DC, MC, V. Parking 25€ ($29) in nearby garage or free on street. Bus: 40N, 60, **75**, 85, 87, **115**, 117, **175**, 186, 271, 571, 810, 850. Metro: Colosseo. **Amenities:** Internet access. *In room:* TV, hair dryer.

WORTH A SPLURGE

Hotel Lancelot ⓡ *Finds*   Friendly, convenient, and comfortable, the Lancelot boasts the one thing most hotels covet: loyal, interesting, repeat guests. The entrance is a welcoming shaded inner courtyard off a tranquil side street just steps from the Colosseum, Forum, and Domus Aurea. The welcoming tone set by the hotel's convivial and multilingual family permeates this seven-story hotel (with elevator), especially in the dining room, where a three-course meal is served nightly at oversize round tables to encourage interaction with other guests. Rooms have either marble or bare wood floors covered with Oriental rugs, while all have a tasteful mix of traditional contemporary and antique furniture. There are several wheelchair-accessible rooms on the ground floor, and room nos. 10 and 11 have showers specifically designed for those with mobility problems. In the summer, guests have a choice of relaxing on the flowering rooftop terrace or in the rear garden shaded in vines.

Via Capo D'Africa 47. ⓒ **06-70450615.** Fax 06-70450640. www.lancelothotel.com. 61 units. 95€–110€ ($109–$127) single; 152€ ($175) double; 172€ ($198) triple; 190€ ($219) quad; 225€–255€ ($259–$293) suite. Half-board available for an additional 15€ ($17) per person. Parking 10€ ($12) available on request. Metro: Colosseo. Bus: 40N, 60, **75**, 85, 87, **115**, 117, **175**, 186, 271, 571, 810, 850. **Amenities:** Restaurant (for guests); bar; concierge; 24-hr. room service; laundry service; dry cleaning. *In room:* A/C, satellite TV, hair dryer.

Rome Accommodations

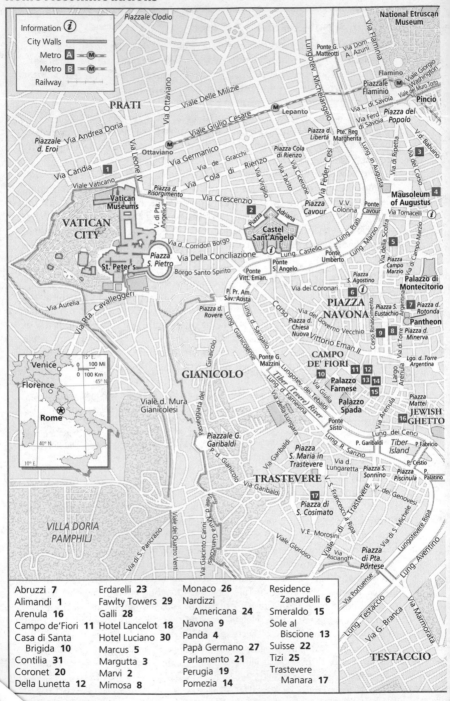

Information ⓘ
City Walls
Metro Ⓐ Ⓜ
Metro Ⓑ Ⓜ
Railway

Piazzale Clodio

National Etruscan Museum

PRATI

VATICAN CITY

Vatican Museums

St. Peter's

Piazza S. Pietro

GIANICOLO

VILLA DORIA PAMPHILJ

Venice
Florence
Rome

15° E.
0   100 Mi
0   100 Km
45° N.
40° N.
10° E.

TRASTEVERE

TESTACCIO

Castel Sant'Angelo

PIAZZA NAVONA

Pantheon

CAMPO DE' FIORI

Palazzo Farnese

Palazzo Spada

JEWISH GHETTO

Mausoleum of Augustus

Piazza del Popolo

Pincio

Flamino

Abruzzi **7**	Erdarelli **23**	Monaco **26**	Residence
Alimandi **1**	Fawlty Towers **29**	Nardizzi	Zanardelli **6**
Arenula **16**	Galli **28**	Americana **24**	Smeraldo **15**
Campo de'Fiori **11**	Hotel Lancelot **18**	Navona **9**	Sole al
Casa di Santa	Hotel Luciano **30**	Panda **4**	Biscione **13**
Brigida **10**	Marcus **5**	Papà Germano **27**	Suisse **22**
Contilia **31**	Margutta **3**	Parlamento **21**	Tizi **25**
Coronet **20**	Marvi **2**	Perugia **19**	Trastevere
Della Lunetta **12**	Mimosa **8**	Pomezia **14**	Manara **17**

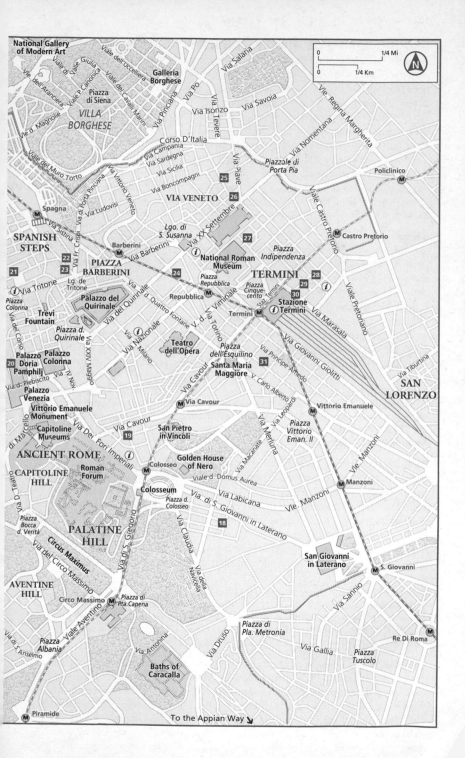

AROUND CAMPO DE' FIORI & THE JEWISH GHETTO

Arenula   Located on the fringes of the Ghetto, the friendly Hotel Arenula is perfectly placed, within an easy walk of many of Rome's main attractions. The hotel is located on four floors in a 19th-century *palazzo;* the entrance is as grand as you might expect of Rome's former aristocracy, but unfortunately, there's no elevator. Accommodations are composed of respectably-sized rooms containing the requisite (but pleasing) armoire, desk, and chair. The white tile floor doesn't allow for lax housekeeping, and the hotel is indeed clean and well maintained. The bathrooms boast the hopeless lip-shower setup, but for these prices, I suggest you get used to a wet bathroom floor for the duration of your stay.

Via Santa Maria de' Calderari, 47, 00186 Rome. ☎ **06-6879454.** Fax 06-6896188. www.hotelarenula.com. 50 units. 70€–92€ ($81–$106) single; 95€–121€ ($109–$139) double. Rates include breakfast. AE, DC, MC, V. Bus: H, 8, 23, 63, 271, 630, 780. *In room:* A/C (10€/$12 extra), satellite TV, hair dryer.

Campo de' Fiori ☆   The units vary greatly at this central inn, from rustic ones with brick arches and wood-beamed ceilings to those in a more romantic (read: floral) decor. Although only nine rooms come with private bathrooms, it's also possible to book a room with a shower, so that only the toilet in the hall is shared. Some rooms are just big enough to fit a double bed, but most are sizable, and all the shared facilities are clean. The main downside is the lack of an elevator, and the appearance of wear on the carpet increases the farther up you go. The reward for making it up to the top is that the duplex roof terrace affords a 360-degree vista of the city's rooftops and domes (room no. 602 enjoys a private view). The nightly party noise wafting up from the piazza can be annoying, so request a room off the front if you want to sleep more soundly.

Via del Biscione 6 (off the northeast corner of Campo de' Fiori), 00186 Roma. ☎ **06-6874886** or 06-68806865. Fax 06-6876003. www.hotelcampodefiori.com. 27 units, 9 with bathroom. 80€ ($92) single without bathroom, 90€ ($104) single with bathroom; 100€ ($115) double without bathroom, 150€ ($173) double with bathroom. 30€ ($35) discount in low season. Rates include breakfast. MC, V. Parking 25€ ($29). Bus: 46, 62, **64**, 116, 116T. **Amenities:** Concierge; courtesy car (pay); babysitting. *In room:* Hair dryer (ask at desk).

Della Lunetta   The Della Lunetta's accommodations may feel a bit institutional, with ranks of two to three cots and modular furnishings, but this hotel has the best prices in the neighborhood. Most bathrooms have enclosed shower stalls, but a few suffer from the curtainless-spigot-in-the-wall and drain-in-the-floor arrangement. Also, it has no elevator, a deterrent for those looking for a modicum of convenience. Except for the quiet roof terrace that sits in the oversize shadow of St. Andrea Church, this is a last-choice option in this cluster of hotels above Campo de' Fiori, though it's quieter than those closer to the campo itself.

Piazza del Paradiso 68 (off Via del Paradiso, a block from Corso Vittorio Emanuele II), 00186 Roma. ☎ **06-6861080.** Fax 06-6892028. 35 units, 21 with bathroom. 60€ ($69) single without bathroom, 70€ ($81) single with bathroom; 90€ ($104) double without bathroom, 120€ ($138) double with bathroom; 120€ ($138) triple without bathroom, 150€ ($173) triple with bathroom. No breakfast. MC, V. Free parking on piazza (if you can find a spot). Bus: 46, 62, **64**, 116, 116T. No phone.

Pomezia *(Value*   This spare but comfortably furnished inn has been in the same family since 1932, and the current generation of three brothers keeps it in pretty good shape. The most recent update shows in the reception and breakfast room, though the labor would have been put to better use in the dismally outdated (but clean) shared bathrooms. The rooms with private bathrooms were renovated in the mid-1990s, and it's worth springing for them. You may not have an elevator to help you reach the top-floor rooms, but they do catch some rooftop views and a little less street noise. In fact, the double-paned windows don't do much good, and the walls are thin, so a room on the *cortile* air shaft is best for light sleepers. The Pomezia has also added a freshly renovated room for travelers with disabilities on the ground floor.

Via dei Chiavari 12 (between Largo Pollaro and V. Giubbonari), 00186 Roma. ℂ/fax 06-6861371. 25 units, 22 with bathroom. 65€ ($75) single without bathroom, 105€ ($121) single with bathroom; 80€ ($92) double without bathroom, 125€ ($144) double with bathroom. Rates 10% lower in winter. Rates include breakfast. AE, DC, MC, V. Bus: 46, 62, **64**, 16, 116T.

Smeraldo 𝕣   The Smeraldo offers the utmost comfort and lots of amenities at reasonable prices. The hotel was entirely renovated in preparation for the 2004 season, so all rooms have fresh and comfortable mattresses, spanking new bathrooms, and pleasant faux-antique furnishings. The rooms are extremely quiet, except for some distant traffic rumble on the Via Monte della Farina side. A sunny rooftop offers a panorama of Rome, and there's also a shady fourth-floor terrace.

Vicolo dei Chiodaroli (between V. Chiavari and V. Monte della Farina), 00186 Roma. ℂ 06-6875929. Fax 06-68805495. www.smeraldoroma.com. 50 units. 75€–100€ ($86–$115) single; 110€–135€ ($127–$155) double. Rates include breakfast. AE, DC, MC, V. Parking 35€ in nearby garage. Bus: H, 46, 62, 63, 64, 70, 80, 81, 87, 186, 492, 628, 640, 780, 810. Tram: 8 to Largo di Torre Argentina, 116 to Campo de' Fiori. **Amenities:** Bar; concierge; tour desk; car-rental desk; 24-hour room service. *In room:* A/C, satellite TV, hair dryer, safe, ISDN line.

Sole al Biscione 𝕣   Founded in 1462, Rome's oldest hotel has always worked toward self-improvement, and all rooms with bathrooms were renovated for the 2000 Jubilee. Those not redone in that round are still in pretty good shape, and the big old-fashioned wood furnishings are nicely tooled or inlaid. However, even the double-glazed windows on the street-side rooms can't block out the late-night revelers, so request one overlooking the garden courtyard. Fourth-floor rooms boast a rooftop view encompassing a few domes and hundreds of TV aerials. Check out the basement garage, where bits of Pompey's Theater (55 B.C.) remain. This inn is popular, so book ahead.

Via del Biscione 76 (half a block north of Campo de' Fiori), 00186 Roma. ℂ 06-68806873. Fax 06-6893787. www.solealbiscione.it. 62 units, 47 with bathroom. 65€ ($75) single without bathroom, 83€ ($95) single with bathroom; 95€ ($109) double without bathroom, 110€–125€ ($127–$144) double with bathroom, 140€ ($161) double with bathroom on top floor with A/C, minibar, and panoramic view. Ask about discounts in low season. No credit cards. Parking 21€ ($24) in garage. Bus: 46, 62, 64, 80 to 1st stop on Corso Vittorio Emanuele; 116 to Campo de' Fiori. **Amenities:** Concierge; tour desk; laundry service; dry cleaning. *In room:* A/C (in 3 units on top floor), TV, minibar (in 4 units).

WORTH A SPLURGE

Casa di Santa Brigida 𝕣𝕣   Rome's best (and poshest) convent hotel is run by the curt sisters of St. Bridget in the house where the Swedish saint died in 1373. The location is optimal, across from the Michelangelo-designed Palazzo Farnese and a block from the daily market and nightlife of Campo de' Fiori. The splurge prices are a bit high but justified by the comfy and rather roomy old-world rooms with antiques or reproductions on parquet (lower level) or carpeted (upstairs) floors. The bathrooms are a little old but at least have shower curtains, and the beds are firm. There's a roof terrace, library, and church. This retreat is highly requested, so reserve as far in advance as possible.

Via Monserrato 54 (just off Piazza Farnese). Postal address: Piazza Farnese 96, 00186 Roma. ℂ 06-68892596. Fax 06-68891573. www.brigidine.org. 24 units. 95€ ($109) single; 170€ ($196) double. Rates include breakfast. DC, MC, V. Bus: 23, 40, 46, 62, 64, 116, 280. **Amenities:** Restaurant. *In room:* A/C, hair dryer (on request), iron (on request).

AROUND PIAZZA NAVONA & THE PANTHEON

Coronet *@@* *Finds*   Here's your chance to live like an aristocrat in a high-ceilinged room in the 15th-century Palazzo Doria-Pamphilj. Simona Teresi and her son preside over baronially sized rooms with modest but comfortably mismatched tasteful furnishings—some functional, others antique style. Most rooms have orthopedic mattresses. There are three hall bathrooms for the three rooms without private facilities. Room nos. 34, 35, and 45 have wood ceilings and sitting corners with sofas. The piazza isn't very noisy, but use whatever excuse you need to request a room overlooking the private gardens.

Piazza Grazioli 5, 00186 Roma. *©* **06-6792341.** Fax 06-69922705. www.hotelcoronet.com. 13 units, 10 with bathroom. 75€–140€ ($86–$161) double without bathroom, 115€–170€ ($132–$196) double with bathroom. Rates include breakfast. MC, V. Free parking on piazza (ask hotel for permit). Bus: 46, 62, 64, 70, 81, 87, 186, 492, 628, 640, 810 to Via Plebescito; then turn up Via della Gatta. **Amenities:** Concierge; tour desk; babysitting; 24-hr. room service; laundry service; dry cleaning; nonsmoking rooms; safe at desk. *In room:* TV (free on request), hair dryer.

Marcus *@@* *Kids*   This updated pensione in a central 18th-century palazzo is easily one of Rome's best two-star hotels. Care for visitors shows up in the occasional classy antique furnishing, the firm beds, the Persian rugs on the patterned tile floors, the walls hung with Roman prints and Art Deco lights, and windows with formidable double glazing. The recently renovated bathrooms are small but functional, although, like those in most Italian pensiones, the showers tend to leak water onto the floor. The highest rate includes use of the air-conditioning, and the larger rooms have futon chairs that can sleep an extra person.

Via del Clementino 94 (in the renamed final block of V. Fontanella Borghese before Piazza Nicosia, just south of Augustus's Mausoleum), 00186 Roma. *©* **06-68300320.** Fax 06-68300312. www.albergomarcus.com. 18 units, 17 with bathroom. 70€–100€ ($81–$115) single bathroom; 85€–135€ ($98–$155) standard double bathroom; 95€–150€ ($109–$173) large double (2 with marble fireplace) with bathroom. Rates include breakfast. 10% discount for cash payment. AE, MC, V. Parking 16€ ($18) in nearby garage. Bus: 70, 87, 116, 186 to Via di Monte Brianzo; 70, 81, 186, 628 to Lungotevere Marzio. **Amenities:** Concierge; tour desk; car-rental desk; courtesy car (pay); room service (breakfast); babysitting; laundry service; dry cleaning; nonsmoking rooms. *In room:* A/C, TV, minibar, hair dryer, safe.

Mimosa *Kids*   This friendly little pensione offers a fantastic price for such a central location, but prepare for a trip back to the trappings of the local frat house. Things are a bit threadbare but well cared for, and the Cappelletto family has promised to redo some of the rooms very soon. The room furnishings are built in or modular, with multiple beds (springy yet firm) for families on a budget. The welcoming atmosphere and homey touches separate this modest inn from the real student dives. All rooms are nonsmoking.

Via Santa Chiara 61, 00186 Roma. *©* **06-68801753.** Fax 06-6833557. www.hotelmimosa.net. 11 units, 7 with bathroom. 55€–77€ ($63–$89) single without bathroom; 75€–88€ ($86–$101) single with bathroom or double without bathroom; 75€–118€ ($86–$136) double with bathroom. Breakfast 6€ ($6.90). No credit cards. Parking: Few free spots on piazza (ask for permit). Bus: 116 to Piazza della Rotunda; H, 46, 62, 63, 64, 70, 80, 81, 87, 186, 492, 628, 640, 780, 810. Tram: 8 to Largo di Torre Argentina, turn up Via delle Torre Argentina, then left on Via Santa Chiara. **Amenities:** Courtesy car from airport (pay). *In room:* A/C, no phone (pay phone in lobby).

Navona *@@* *Finds*   Boasting Versace bath tiles, made-to-order furnishings, and smart curtains and bedspreads you might easily choose for your own home, the three-star-worthy Navona is the product of the discerning in-house Natale family, whose son and architect, Cory, is perennially renovating this 15th-century *palazzo*. Rooms are located on several floors, and almost all exhibit some historic detail, like an exposed Roman column or 15th-century rosette. Rooms 15A through E, which have wonderful exposed ceiling beams, are the divided former residence of Keats and Shelley. Amenities like a TV and phone are available in about half of the rooms, and a top-floor suite with a kitchenette is available on a weekly basis. The hotel accepts credit cards only to hold reservations. All rooms are nonsmoking.

If the Navona is full, the Natales may accompany you up to the equally nice **Residence Zanardelli,** Via G. Zanardelli 7 (near Piazza Tor Sanguigna, north of Piazza Navona), 00187 Roma (℃ **06-6864203;** fax 06-68803802).

Via dei Sedari 8 (off Corso del Rinascimento, between Piazza Navona and the Pantheon), 00186 Roma. ℃ 06-6864203. Fax 06-68803802. www.hotelnavona.com. 30 units. 95€ ($109) single; 135€ ($155) double; 170€ ($196) triple. Rates include breakfast. AE, DC, MC, V. Free parking on street (ask hotel for permit). Bus: 70, 81, 87, 116, 186, 492, 628 to Corso del Rinascimento; 46, 62, 64, 80 to 1st stop on Corso Vittorio Emanuele II. In room: A/C (15€/$17), no phone (pay phone in lobby).

WORTH A SPLURGE

Abruzzi   When you can look out your window and see the Pantheon less than 30m (100 ft.) away, you've found something special. Of course, after a complete overhaul in 2003 and the addition of a couple of stars, it's not as cheap as it used to be. Not all rooms are blessed with the view (the three singles are on the back courtyard), but each is now outfitted with marble bathrooms, new cherrywood furniture, and shiny laminate flooring. Because the piazza is a popular hangout until late, the noise can get annoying, but with this location and that view, who cares? Keep in mind that off-season rates can go as low as 150€ ($172), so check the hotel website for special deals.

Piazza della Rotonda 69, 00186 Roma. ℃ 06-6792021. Fax 06-69788076. www.hotelabruzzi.it. 25 units. 130€–155€ ($150–$178) single; 175€–195€ ($201–$224) double. Rates include breakfast. AE, DC, MC, V. Bus: 116 to Piazza della Rotunda; H, 46, 62, 63, 64, 70, 80, 81, 87, 186, 492, 628, 640, 780, 810. Tram: 8 to Largo di Torre Argentina and walk 4 blocks north. Amenities: Concierge. In room: A/C, satellite TV, hair dryer, safe.

AROUND THE SPANISH STEPS & PIAZZA DEL POPOLO

Erdarelli   The authentic image of a family-style pensione is alive and well at the Erdarelli, welcoming guests since 1935 only yards to the Spanish Steps. One of the Erdarellis will greet you with a warm welcome before shooing you down the narrow lobby corridor for access to the elevator. Although some of the rooms have been renovated, the pensione is still, for the most part, characterized by mismatched wooden furniture and old garret-style showers or bathrooms in the units. The dorm-style TV room is dressed in red vinyl. Book at least a month in advance and considerably more for one of the four rooms with private terraces.

Via due Macelli 28, 00187 Rome. ℃ 06-6791265. Fax 06-6790705. erdarelli@italyhotel.com. 28 units, 22 with bathroom. 65€ single without bathroom; 75€ ($86) single with bathroom; 85€ ($98) double without bathroom, 100€ ($115) double with bathroom. A/C 10€ ($12) per day extra. Rates include breakfast. AE, DC, MC, V. Parking 21€ ($24) in neighboring garage. Bus: 116, 116T, 117, 119, 175. Metro: Spagna.

Margutta   The Margutta isn't for those who need a lot of elbow room, but it offers reliability and a touch of style for an inexpensive central choice. The hard-working management likes to joke around, providing efficient service with a smile in rapid-fire English. Curly wrought-iron bed frames give the rooms a classy feel, but the lumpy beds barely pass muster for firmness. Most rooms are immaculate but on the small side of cozy, and some bathrooms are positively minuscule. The double-glazed windows keep the street noise down, but since you're already on a side street, things are pretty tranquil.

Via Laurina 34 (2 blocks from Piazza del Popolo between V. Babuino and V. del Corso), 00197 Roma. ℃ 06-3223674. Fax 06-3200395. 24 units. 104€ ($120) single; 115€ ($132) double; 150€ triple ($173). Rates include breakfast. AE, DC, MC, V. Bus: 117, 119 to the end of Via del Babuino; 81, 628, 926 to Passeggiata di Ripetta. Metro: Flaminio (not the closest, but most direct from Termini). Amenities: Concierge; tour desk; car-rental desk; room service (breakfast); babysitting. In room: Hair dryer.

Panda This hotel is just 2 blocks from the Spanish Steps, but you'll have to trade comfort for location—there are no amenities like phones and an elevator, and there are few private bathrooms. The linoleum-floored second-floor rooms are decidedly inferior and no-frills, so request a first-floor room (with touches like frescoed ceilings, wrought-iron fixtures, and firm beds set on terra-cotta floors). All rooms are clean, but none is very large. The rooms facing the (mostly pedestrian) street have double-glazed windows, so at least you won't be counting cherubs in those lower front rooms.

Via del Croce 35, 00187 Rome. ℂ **06-6780179.** Fax 06-69942151. www.hotelpanda.it. 20 units, 12 with bathroom. 42€–48€ ($48–$55) single without bathroom; 62€–65€ ($71–$75) single with bathroom; 65€–68€ ($75–$78) double without bathroom; 93€–98€ ($107–$113) double with bathroom. AE, MC, V. Bus: 116, 117, 119 to Piazza di Spagna. Metro: Spagna. **Amenities:** Concierge; tour desk; car-rental desk; wireless Internet. *In room:* A/C.

Parlamento ⟨⟨⟨ The Parlamento has four-star class at two-star prices. After a few stairs, there's an elevator to the third floor and a friendly reception area. The room furnishings are antique or good reproductions and firm beds backed by carved wood or wrought-iron headboards. A *double set* of double-glazed windows blocks out the street traffic. Fifteen rooms have air-conditioning (installation is tentatively planned for additional rooms; try to negotiate out of the charge), and the bathrooms were recently redone with hair dryers, heated towel racks, phones, and (in a few) marble sinks. You can enjoy the *trompe-l'oeil* breakfast room or carry your cappuccino to the small roof terrace with its view of San Silvestro's bell tower (several upper-floor rooms share this vista). Some larger units are great for families, including the triple no. 82 with big old antiques and no. 108 with two bedrooms and a small terrace.

Via delle Convertite 5 (at the intersection with V. del Corso, near Piazza San Silvestro), 00187 Roma. ℂ/fax **06-69921000.** 23 units. 70€–115€ ($81–$132) single; 90€–152€ ($104–$175) double. Rates include breakfast. AE, DC, MC, V. Parking 15€ ($17) in nearby garage. Bus: 52, 53, 61, 71, 85, 116, 160, 850 to Piazza San Silvestro; 62, 80, 95, 119, 175, 492 to Largo Chigi/Via Tritone. **Amenities:** Concierge; tour desk; car-rental desk; room service (breakfast only). *In room:* A/C (in 15 units), satellite TV, hair dryer, safe.

Suisse ⟨⟨⟨ A long block down a quiet street from the astronomically priced hotels atop the Spanish Steps, the sterile Suisse is run like a tight ship—probably in no small part due to the frau at the head of this small third-floor hotel. Renovations on all 12 rooms were completed as of 2001, leaving restored antique furniture on pleasantly creaky parquet floors; new, if smallish, bathrooms characterized by accordion shower doors; and even a few original ceiling stuccoes. Most of the rooms are arranged around an inner stone courtyard, making for a blissfully quiet night's sleep (four face V. Gregoriana). To top it off, breakfast is served in your room. The Suisse is popular, so book ahead. You can pay only half your bill with a credit card, and there's no one at the desk to buzz you in from 2 to 6am.

Via Gregoriana 54 (near the intersection with V. Capo le Case), 00187 Roma. ℂ **06-6783649.** Fax 06-6781258. 13 units. 81€–95€ ($93–$109) single; 126€–148€ ($145–$170) double. Rates include breakfast. MC, V. Bus: 52, 53, 56, 58, 58/, 60, 61, 62, 95, 116, 117, **175,** 492. Metro: Barberini. *In room:* Hair dryer.

AROUND VIA VENETO & PIAZZA BARBERINI

Monaco ⟨Value⟩ Maria Tomassi, her sister Elena, and her grown children run this bare-bones hotel at the edge of an upscale neighborhood. Most rooms are quite sizable, with just a few pieces of mismatched functional furniture and tiny bathrooms (no shower curtains). The mattresses range from thin and stiff to soft and springy, so you may want to test a few before choosing your room. It's all a bit institutional, with shared bathrooms straight out of a college dorm, but the friendly Tomassis keep it clean and the prices are low. The streets can be noisy by day, but they quiet down at night. There's sometimes a midnight curfew, so ask before heading out.

Via Flavia 84 (parallel to V. XX Settembre, near V. San Tullio), 00187 Roma. ℂ **06-42014180.** Fax 06-4744335. 12 units. 52€ ($60) double; 70€ ($81) triple. Rates include breakfast. No credit cards. Free parking on street. Bus: **16,** 37, **38,** 60, 61, 62, 136, 137, **319, 360,** 910.

Tizi The family-run Tizi is in a posh neighborhood just south of Villa Borghese park. A few antique-style pieces in the reception hall give way to modular furnishings in the rooms, but the orthopedic mattresses rest on old-fashioned metal bed frames. The ceilings are high and airy, some with stuccowork, and the private bathrooms are in good working order, with box showers. There's one shared bathroom for every two rooms. This inn is a favorite with young travelers in search of peace and a friendly atmosphere rather than beer and parties.

Via Collina 48 (east of Piazza Sallustio and west of V. Piave), 00187 Roma. ℂ **06-4820128.** Fax 06-4743266. 24 units, 10 with bathroom. 42€ ($48) single without bathroom; 55€ ($63) double without bathroom, 72€ ($83) double with bathroom. Extra person 30% more (but small children can squeeze in for free). Breakfast 7€ ($8.05). No credit cards. Parking about 18€ ($21) in nearby garages. Bus: 92, 217, 360 to 1st stop on Via Piave, after crossing Via XX Settembre; 80 to Via Boncompagni; 910 to Via D. Sella; 16, 36, 38, 60, 61 to Via XX Settembre; 490, 495 to Via Lucania. **Amenities:** Nonsmoking rooms. *In room:* No phone.

NORTH OF STAZIONE TERMINI

Bus information is included for the hotels below, but you'll notice none is boldface. Each hotel is within a few blocks of the Termini train station.

Fawlty Towers This hotel/hostel is a fave of students and the younger international set who are primarily of the clean-scrubbed variety. It's owned by Enjoy Rome, staffed by a crew of friendly English-speakers, and has the cleanest and most comfy hostel-style accommodations in town. The shared dorms are on the fifth floor (there's an elevator) and private rooms on the sixth. The hostel rooms sleeping three or four are as bare as you'd expect but not squalid (no bunk beds, just soft cots). The simple singles and doubles have firm mattresses and functional furnishings. Four bathroomless rooms have at least a sink and a shower. There's a solarium with a TV, fridge, and microwave, as well as a small terrace. No curfew.

Via Magenta 39, 00185 Roma (a block north of Termini, between V. Milazzo and V. Marghera), 00185 Roma. ℂ **06-4450374** or 06-4454802. Fax 06-49382878. www.fawltytowers.org. 16 units, 5 with bathroom. 47€ ($54) single without bathroom; 55€ ($63) single with shower and sink (no toilet); 65€ ($76) double without bathroom, 70€ ($81) double with shower and sink (no toilet), 80€ ($92) double with bathroom; 86€ ($99) triple with shower, 93€ ($107) triple with bathroom; 20€ ($23) bed in dorm without bathroom, 23€ ($26) bed in dorm with bathroom. No credit cards. Metro: Termini. Bus: Any to Termini. **Amenities:** TV lounge with fridge, microwave, and Internet access (1€/$1.15 for 30 min.; 3€/$3.45 per hour). *In room:* Fridge, no phone (pay phone in lobby).

Galli 🅰🅰 *(Finds)* You'll find only bright rooms and the smell of freshly mopped floors in this little gem located on the second and fourth floors of an old building near the train station. Rooms on the fourth floor were renovated in 2002 and outfitted in a fresh decor with new furniture, so you may want to opt for one of these. Rooms on the second floor are slightly more worn, but they're still head and shoulders above others in this hotel's class; what's more, room nos. 206 and 208 have the benefit of a small and characteristically European step-up balcony. And there's more good news: At the time of this writing, an elevator was being installed in the building. Plus, a life-saving self-service laundry/Internet cafe is next door at street level.

Via Milazzo 20, 00185 Roma. ℂ **06-4456859.** ℂ/fax 06-4468501. www.albergogalli.com. 12 units. 25€–65€ ($29–$75) single; 40€–85€ ($46–$98) double; 65€–105€ ($75–$121) triple. AE, DC, MC, V. Closed Christmas, New Year's Day, Easter, May 1. Parking 12€–14€ ($14–$16) in nearby garage. Metro: Termini. Bus: Any to Termini. *In-room:* A/C, TV, minibar, hair dryer, safe.

Hotel Luciano   In these days of the irrepressible euro, it seems the best bargains are found around the train station. Case in point: the Luciano, an unexpectedly well-appointed hotel just a stone's throw from Track 1. The hotel, originally a hostel and in this location since 1950, was completely renovated and upgraded to two stars in 2000. Room size varies, but bathrooms and even shower stalls are generally ample. Decor ranges from bare golden-hued walls to triangular headboards and some Venetian touches. Although the renovations prevented the installation of air-conditioning units in all the rooms, the management provides portable units on request.

Via Milazzo 8, 00185 Rome. ⓒ 06-490659. Fax 06-491327. www.hotelluciani.it. 38 units. 45€–75€ ($52–$86) single; 75€–110€ ($86–$127) double. Rates include breakfast and reflect season. **Amenities:** Bar; meeting room; laundry; Internet access. *In room:* A/C, satellite TV, hair dryer at reception.

Papà Germano 𝄐𝄐   Gino is a terrifically friendly guy who loves to help visitors settle in to Rome. As the owner of the Germano, he holds cleanliness in the highest regard and repaints or repapers every year or two. The mattresses are firm to the point of being hard, but just about everything—from the built-in units and box showers to the double-glazed windows and hair dryers in every room—is spotless and either new or kept looking that way. The shared bathrooms are great, but units with private bathrooms also have satellite TVs. Six bathroomless rooms can become dorms (you can save by bunking with two or three strangers). All the guidebooks list this inn, so call ahead.

Via Calatafimi 14a (4 blocks west of Stazione Termini, on a dead-end street off V. Volturno), 00185 Roma. ⓒ 06-486919. Fax 06-47825202. www.hotelpapagermano.com. 17 units, 7 with bathroom. 32€–45€ ($37–$52) single without bathroom; 50€–75€ ($58–$86) double without bathroom, 57€–90€ ($66–$104) double with bathroom; 59€–83€ ($68–$95) triple without bathroom, 77€–105€ ($89–$121) triple with bathroom; 23€–27€ ($26–$31) bed in shared room (3–4 beds) without bathroom. Cash payment 5€ ($5.75) less. 10% discount Nov 10–Mar 10. AE, DC, MC, V. Parking 12€–14€ ($14–$16) in nearby garage. Metro: Repubblica. Bus: 16, 38, 86, 92, 217, 360 to Via Volturno; 36, 60, 61, 62, 63, 84, 90 to Via Cernaia; 75 to Piazza Indipendenza. *In-room:* TV, minifridge (newest rooms), hair dryer, safe.

SOUTH OF STAZIONE TERMINI

Contilia ⟨Value⟩   As the automatic doors part to reveal a stylish marble lobby of Persian rugs and antiques, you may find yourself double-checking the address. The old-fashioned pensione Contilia has taken over this building's other small hotels and gentrified itself into one of the best choices in this dicey neighborhood. The rooms have been redone in modern comfort with satellite TVs and safes. The double-glazed windows keep out traffic noise, and the rooms overlooking the cobblestone courtyard are even quieter. The unrenovated bathrooms are a bit small and lack shower curtains; those with Jacuzzis cost 15€ ($17) extra.

Via Principe Amadeo 79d–81 (2 blocks south of Termini between V. Gioberti and V. Cattaneo), 00185 Roma. ⓒ 06-4466942. Fax 06-4466904. www.hotelcontilia.com. 41 units. 60€–135€ ($69–$155) single; 75€–165€ ($86–$190) double; 100€–225€ ($115–$259) triple. Rates include breakfast. AE, DC, MC, V. Parking 18€ ($21) in garage. Metro: Termini. Bus: Any to Termini. **Amenities:** Concierge; tour desk; car-rental desk; courtesy car; 24-hr. room service; babysitting; laundry service; dry cleaning; nonsmoking rooms. *In room:* A/C, TV, minibar (on request; only 5 to go around), hair dryer, safe.

Nardizzi Americana 𝄐⟨Value⟩ The Nardizzi has always been a steal, and even through renovations, Nik and Fabrizio have managed to keep the rates reasonably low (quote this guide for the best prices). The style is inspired by ancient Rome, with street lamps on the narrow terrace and a patterned tile decor giving an inlaid stone look to the walls and floors of the public areas.

The rooms have tiled floors and updated bathrooms, and a few have wood-beam ceilings; the smaller ones contain built-in dressers and the larger ones walk-in closets. In 2001, direct Internet service was installed in every room (it operates via the TV with an infrared keyboard); the only cost is the connection fee. Note that low-season rates are applied from June 16 to August as well as in winter.

Via Firenze 38 (just off V. XX Settembre, 2 blocks from V. Nazionale), 00184 Roma. ℂ 06-4880368. Fax 06-4880035. www.hotelnardizzi.it. 22 units. 60€–110€ ($69–$127) single; 95€–130€ ($109–$150) double. Rates include breakfast. Frommer's readers get 5% discount (but you must show them the book); if paying in cash, the discount rises to 10%. AE, DC, MC, V. Parking around 15€ ($17) in nearby garage. Metro: Repubblica. Bus: H, 60, 63, 64, 70, 116T, 170, 640 to Via Nazionale/Piazza della Repubblica; 36, 60, 61, 62, 63, 84, 86, 90, 175, 492, 910 to Largo Santa Susanna/Via V. E. Orlando. **Amenities:** PlayStation and VCR in lounge; concierge; tour desk; courtesy car (more for departures than arrivals); 24-hr. room service; babysitting; laundry service; dry cleaning; nonsmoking rooms. *In room:* A/C, TV, hair dryer (ask at desk), safe.

IN TRASTEVERE

To get to your Trastevere hotel from the airport, hop on the local train toward Tiburtina (instead of the express into Stazione Termini), which will stop at Trastevere's train station, where you can catch tram no. 8 up Viale Trastevere.

Trastevere Manara ℝ (Value)   In 1998, what was Trastevere's dingiest hotel was transformed into the classiest and is now one of Rome's best bargains. It offers cushy amenities at fantastic prices, a location at the heart of Trastevere's restaurants and nightlife, and a nearby daily market for fresh picnic pickings. The gentrified rooms are still pensione cavernous but now boast tiles and painted stucco, massive modular wood furnishings, and renovated bathrooms. All except smaller (and dreary) nos. 1 and 2 overlook the market square of San Cosimato—be prepared for a dawn wake-up. The hotel management also has three efficiency apartments for four or five people for rates comparable to those above. Hotel transfers are provided on request for 52€ ($60) for two people.

Via Luciano Manara 24a–25 (just behind Piazza San Cosimato; it's the continuation of V. di Fratte di Trastevere off Vle. Trastevere), 00153 Roma. ℂ 06-5814713. Fax 06-5881016. www.hoteltrastevere.com. 9 units. 80€ ($92) single; 103€ ($118) double (plus 2€/$2.30 with view); 130€ ($150) triple. Rates include breakfast. AE, DC, MC, V. Free parking on street (ask for permit) or 18€ ($21) in nearby garage. Bus: H, 780, tram 8 to Viale Trastevere (get off at the 2nd stop after you cross the river); 44, 75 to Viale Trastevere. **Amenities:** Concierge; tour desk; courtesy car (pay); room service (breakfast; also drinks to 11:30pm); babysitting; laundry service; dry cleaning. *In room:* A/C (only in no. 12), TV, hair dryer.

AROUND THE VATICAN

Alimandi   This is a tour group–style hotel, but one of the better ones, and that probably explains the *free airport transfer* (pickups according to a specific timetable). The location is great for the district, 3 blocks from Rome's best daily food market (on V. Andrea Doria) and a short staircase down from the Vatican Museums entrance. The rooms are modern and comfortable, holding few surprises in the built-in wood units and newish bathrooms. The firm beds sport fresh foam mattresses. There's a faux medieval bar, a billiards room, and a roof terrace with no particular view but good sun and caged exotic birds.

Via Tunisi 8 (at V. Veniero and the base of the steps up to Vle. Vaticano), 00192 Roma. ℂ 06-39723941. Fax 06-39723943. www.alimandi.org. 35 units. 80€–125€ ($92–$144) single; 135€–150€ ($155–$173) double. Rates include breakfast. AE, DC, MC, V. Free parking. Metro: Cipro. Bus: 49, 492. **Amenities:** Concierge; tour desk; car-rental desk; courtesy car (free for airport); babysitting; laundry service; dry cleaning. *In room:* A/C, TV, hair dryer, safe.

(*Fun Fact* **To Pick a Pope**

Fox News has the roof terrace of the Alimandi booked as its lookout for the next papal selection—the top cardinals lock themselves into the Sistine Chapel for closed deliberations; the world knows a new pope has been decided only when the black smoke issuing from the chapel chimney turns white.

Marvi   Since 1969, a friendly guy from Orvieto has run this clean little hotel on a side street of the Borgo (the zone between the Vatican and the river). His rooms are simple, and some of the hodgepodge furnishings are actually quite nice; the bathrooms, though, are tiny. Cot springs support stiff foam mattresses covered by fashionable bedspreads. Room nos. 10 and 14 have stuccoed ceiling decorations, and no. 11 gets lots of light from windows on two sides. The third-floor rooms tend to be pretty quiet.

Via Pietro delle Valle 13 (off V. Crescenzio a block west of Piazza Adriana, the north arm of Castel Sant' Angelo's star-shape park), 00193 Roma. ⓒ/fax **06-68802621** or 06-6865652. 8 units. 80€ ($92) single; 90€ ($104) double; 120€ ($138) triple. Rates include breakfast. No credit cards. On-street metered parking. Bus: 34, 40, 49, **70**, 87, 186, 280, **492**, 913, 926, 990. Metro: Ottaviano–San Pietro.

4 Great Deals on Dining

Dining out is an event for Italians, and it's unheard of not to have at least two plates, generally a *primo* (first course) and a *secondo* (second or main course). Sometimes you can slide by with an antipasto and primo, but in Rome, even these tend to be of exaggerated portions. Don't be bullied into eating more than you can realistically hold, and don't be intimidated by that incredulous *"E dopo?"* or *"Basta così?"* (meaning "Then what would you like?" or "That's all you're having?").

With so many courses expected of you, it's easy to drop 25€ ($29) and upward of 50€ ($58) in overpriced tourist trattorie in the center. Stick to your guns and order only what you want, except in finer restaurants, when ordering only one plate is considered bad form.

At *osterie* (cheap eateries frequented by locals) and *fiaschetterie* (old-fashioned wine bars serving a few inexpensive dishes), you can get basic, filling Roman meals for under 15€ ($17). Many are just steps from the most touristy sights of the *centro storico,* so if you can resist the temptation to live *la dolce vita* along Via Veneto, you'll have no problem on a budget. If you want to wander and find a restaurant on your own, be aware that the strongest concentration of eateries is in Trastevere. In addition, all around town you'll find trendy **"wine bars"** (called that even in Italian) where you can drink remarkable wines by the glass and nibble on cheese platters, salamis, and often inventive small dishes all pretty cheaply. And if you're looking for a simple but meal-size salad, try one of **Insalata Ricca**'s outlets (see below), or pop into a *"caffeteria"* or **"snack bar"**— essentially a local bar that sets out premade pastas and salads to nourish the neighborhood workers.

A typical Roman meal begins with an *antipasto* (appetizer or "before the pasta"), which most often means a simple *bruschetta* (slab of peasant bread grilled, rubbed with garlic, drizzled with olive oil, and sprinkled with salt; *al pomodoro* adds a pile of cubed tomatoes on top). If you see *carciofi* (artichokes), *alla giudea* or otherwise (especially if you're in the Jewish Ghetto), snap up one of Rome's greatest specialties—tender and lightly fried in olive oil. A favorite that found its way across the Atlantic some time ago is *prosciutto e melone,* a surprisingly good combination of salt-cured ham draped over a slice of sweet cantaloupe (in summer, it may be figs instead of melon).

Your primo could be a soup—try *stracciatella* (egg and Parmesan in broth)—or a pasta. Available on just about every Roman menu are traditional favorites like *bucatini all'Amatriciana* (pasta in a spicy tomato sauce studded with pancetta and dense with onions), *spaghetti alla carbonara* (spaghetti mixed with eggs, bacon, and loads of black pepper—the heat of the pasta cooks the eggs), and *pasta al pomodoro* (pasta in a plain tomato sauce). Also try *penne all'arrabbiata* ("hopping mad" pasta quills in a spicy tomato sauce), *tagliolini alla gricia* (thin egg noodles with Parmesan and pig's jowl, which is sort of like bacon), *tagliolini* or *spaghetti cacio e pepe* (with black pepper and grated pecorino cheese), *pasta e fagioli* (pasta with beans), *pasta e ceci* (pasta with chickpeas), or *gnocchi* (potato-based pasta dumplings).

Secondi include traditional local dishes like the eyebrow-raising but delicious *coda alla vaccinara* (braised oxtail with tomatoes), *pajata* (calves' intestines still clotted with mother's milk and often put in tomato sauce on rigatoni pasta), and *trippa* (good old-fashioned tripe). Less adventurous main courses include *involtini* (veal layered with prosciutto, cheese, and celery and then rolled and cooked with tomatoes), *polpette* (meatballs), *bocconcini di vitello* (veal nuggets, usually stewed with potatoes and sage), *pollo arrosto* (roast chicken, often excellently sided *con patate,* with roast potatoes), *pollo e peperoni* (chicken smothered in roasted red and yellow peppers), *straccetti con rughetta* (strips of beef tossed with torn rughetta lettuce), *arrosto di vitello* (simple roast veal steak), and *abbacchio a scottaditto* (grilled tender Roman spring lamb chops, so good the name declares you'll "burn your fingers" in your haste to eat them). One of the best Roman secondi is *saltimbocca* ("jumps-in-the-mouth"), a tender veal cutlet cooked in white wine with sage leaves and a slice of pro-sciutto draped over it.

Roman **pizza**—the kind from a cheap sit-down pizzeria or *pizza al forno*—is large, round, flat, and crispy (unlike its breadier Neapolitan cousin). A "plain" tomato sauce, mozzarella, and basil pie is called *pizza Margherita.* The adventurous may want to try a *cappriciosa,* a selection of toppings that often includes anchovies, prosciutto, olives, and an egg cracked onto the hot pizza, where it fries in place. You can also get the Roman version of pizza by the slice, *pizza rustica* (aka *pizza à taglio*) from hole-in-the-wall joints.

The *contorni* (sides) on the menu are vegetables dishes (*melanzana* is egg-plant, *fagioli* are beans, *patate* are potatoes, and *zucchini* are obvious). End your meal with *tiramisu* (a layer cake of espresso-soaked lady fingers and sweetened, creamy mascarpone cheese dusted with cocoa), a *tartufo* (the mother of ice-cream balls—a fudge center, then vanilla, then chocolate, dusted with cocoa or bittersweet chocolate chunks), or simple *biscotti* (twice-baked hard almond cookies).

AROUND ANCIENT ROME

Birreria Peroni ⊛ BEER HALL/BUFFET   At few places in the historic cen-ter can you get good food so cheap, fast, and filling. This Italian beer hall has been in this vaulted space since 1906, and the edges of the room were frescoed in the 1940s with Art Nouveau sportsmen drinking beer and espousing homi-lies like "Beer makes you strong and healthy." The buffet includes prosciutto, goose salami, stuffed or piccante olives, beans with tuna, and marinated

Rome Dining

Al Piedone **21**
Antica Taverna **13**
Antica Caffè del Greco **44**
Antico Caffè della Pace **14**
Arancia Blu **50**
Armando's Café **3**
Babington's Tea Rooms **43**
Birreria Peroni **42**
Cafe Doney **45**
Cafe Rosati **4**
Cantina Cantarini **46**
Checchino dal 1887 **41**
Da Augusto **37**
Da Benito **29**
Da Felice **39**
Da Giggetto **31**
Da Gino **9**
Da Pancrazio **28**
Dar Filettaro a
  Santa Barbara **27**
Dar Poeta **35**
Ditirambo **25**
Fiaschetteria Beltramme
  (da Cesaretto) **8**
Edy **7**
Enoteca Corsi **22**
Giolitti **10**
Grappolo d'Oro **16**
Hosteria Romanesca **26**

Il Brillo Parlante **6**
Il Ciak **34**
Il Delfino **23**
Il Duca **36**
Il Matriciano **2**
Il Mozzicone **12**
Insalata Ricca II **18**
Insalata Ricca VI **1**
Ivo a Trastevere **38**
L'Angolo Divino **24**
La Piazzetta **52**
La Tana di Noiantri **33**
La Torricella **40**
Lilli **11**
Luzzi **53**
Magnosfera **49**
Pasticceria Strabbione **47**
PizzaRé **5**
Pizzeria Baffetto **15**
Pommidoro **50**
San Crispino **54**
Sant'Eustachio **20**
Sora Margherita **30**
Sora Lella **32**
Taverna della Scala **37**
Terra di Sienna **17**
Tram Tram **51**
Tre Scalini **19**
Trimani Il Wine Bar **48**

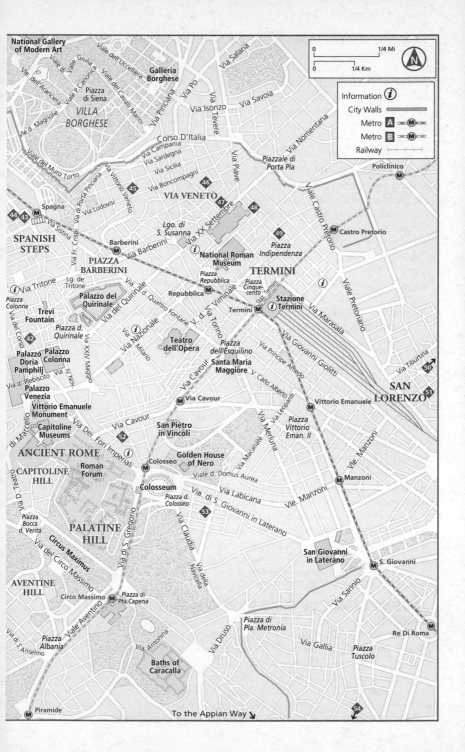

National Gallery
of Modern Art

Galleria
Borghese

VILLA
BORGHESE

Piazza
di Siena

Viale dell'Uccelliera

Viale Giulia
Vie dell'Aranciera
Viale P. Canonica
Viale dei Cavalli Marini

Vle d. Magnolie

Viale del Muro Torto

Via Salaria

Via PO

Via Pinciana

Via Isonzo

Via Tevere

Via Savoia

Corso D'Italia

Via Campania

Via Sardegna

Via Sicilia

Via Boncompagni

Piazzale di
Porta Pia

Via Plave

Via Nomentana

Policlinico

45

46

VIA VENETO

47

48

Spagna

Via di Porta Pinciana

Via Vittorio Veneto

Via Ludovisi

Via XX Settembre

49

SPANISH
STEPS

44 43

Via Sistina

Via Fr. Crispi

Via Barberini

Barberini

PIAZZA
BARBERINI

Lgo. di
S. Susanna

National Roman
Museum

Piazza
Indipendenza

Viale Castro Pretorio

Castro Pretorio

Via Tritone

Lg. de
Tritone

Palazzo del
Quirinale

Via del Quirinale

Via d. Quattro Fontane

Piazza
Repubblica

Piazza
Cinque-
cento

TERMINI

Viale Pretoriano

Piazza
Colonna

Trevi
Fountain

42

Via del Corso

Piazza d.
Quirinale

Via Nazionale

Via Milano

Repubblica

V. d. Viminale

V. d. Torino

Repubblica

Termini

Stazione
Termini

Via Marsala

Palazzo
Doria
Pamphilj

Palazzo
Colonna

Via XXIV Maggio

Via IV Nov.

Teatro
dell'Opera

Piazza
dell'Esquilino

Santa Maria
Maggiore

Via Principe Amedeo

Via Giovanni Giolitti

Via Tiburtina

50

Palazzo
Venezia

Via d. Plebiscito

Via Cavour

V. Carlo Alberto

SAN
LORENZO

51

Vittorio Emanuele
Monument

Via Cavour

Via Cavour

Vittorio Emanuele

V. Leopardi

Via Merulana

Vle. Manzoni

Capitoline
Museums

di Marcello

Via Dei Fori Imperiali

52

San Pietro
in Vincoli

Piazza
Vittorio
Eman. II

ANCIENT ROME

Roman
Forum

Golden House
of Nero

Via Macanate

Via Labicana

Manzoni

CAPITOLINE
HILL

Colosseo

Viale d. Domus Aurea

Vle. Manzoni

V. D. Teatro

Colosseum

Piazza d.
Colosseo

Via. di S. Giovanni in Laterano

53

Piazza
Bocca
d. Verità

PALATINE
HILL

Via di S. Gregorio

Via Claudia

San Giovanni
in Laterano

S. Giovanni

AVENTINE
HILL

Circus Maximus

Via del Circo Massimo

Via della Navicella

Via Sannio

Circo Massimo

Piazza di
Pta. Capena

Viale Aventino

Piazza
Albania

Via di S. Anselmo

Piazza di
Pla. Metronia

Re Di Roma

Via Antonina

Via Druso

Via Gallia

Piazza
Tuscolo

Baths of
Caracalla

Piramide

To the Appian Way

54

0   1/4 Mi
0   1/4 Km

N

Information
City Walls
Metro A
Metro B
Railway

113

artichokes, while plates cover the requisite *bucatini all'amatriciana, trippa,* and *pollo arrosto con patate.* The indecisive should try the *arrosto misto alla Peroni* (a huge mix of lots of German beer hall–style eats, like sausage with sauerkraut and goulash with potatoes). To wash it all down, order a Peroni beer or the "blue ribbon" Nastro Azzurro label.

Via San Marcello 10 (north of Piazza SS. Apostoli). © **06-6795310.** Dishes 3.50€–13€ ($4–$15); buffet items 3.50€–6.50€ ($4–$7.45). MC, V. Summer Mon–Fri 12:30–11:30pm, Sat 8pm–midnight; winter Mon–Fri 12:30–3:15pm and 7:30pm–midnight, Sat 7pm–midnight. Closed up to 4 weeks in Aug. Bus: H, 40, 60, 62, 63, 64, 70, 81, 85, 95, 117, 119, 160, 170, 175, 492, 628, 850.

La Piazzetta *Finds* ROMAN La Piazzetta is a breath of fresh air for anyone looking for a serene setting and optimum fare just steps (and worlds) away from the travel-weary area around the Colosseum. The management accommodates just about any request, including those that extend their lunchtime hours (within reason), assuming you won't mind feasting on what's left of their savory *antipasti* or the day's special *paste.* Try the chef's *mezze maniche alla vegitariana* ("short sleeve" pasta with tomatoes and goat cheese) or, my favorite, the *raviolone* with sage, butter, and saffron. For heartier fare, you can dine without overdoing it on *polpette di carne* (not just your average meatball) or succulent *tagliata di manzo* (rare beef topped with Parmesan and arugula). The chef outdoes himself in the dessert area, crafting delicacies like *millefeuilles, sfogliato* (with custard and pignoli nuts), and *baba* dripping in limoncello.

Vicolo del Buon Consiglio 23/A (near V. del Colosseo). © **06-6991640.** Primi 8€–10€ ($9.20–$12); secondi 11€–18€ ($13–$21). AE, DC, MC, V. Mon–Sat noon–3pm and 7–11pm. Bus: 40N, 60, 75, 84, 85, 87, 117, 175, 186, 810, 850. Metro: Colosseo.

Luzzi *Finds* ROMAN Luzzi's appeal is in its ability to provide the perfect combination of desirables in an Italian restaurant: The kitchen cranks out top-notch Roman favorites, the staff is almost stereotypically animated, and it all comes dirt cheap. The restaurant, which expands into a covered sidewalk cafe in summer, is tucked down a side street between the Colosseum and the Basilica di San Clemente. The service staff bustles through packed lunches and dinners to feed the hordes of locals and tourists who flock here. There are also lots of single diners in the evening, perhaps from one of the handful of nearby hotels. A sampling of the menu above and beyond the typical includes *consommé con tortellini* (soup with tortellini), *risotto alla crema di scampi* (shrimp risotto), *gamberoni alla marinara* (shrimp in marinara sauce), *carpaccio rughetta e parmigiano* (carpaccio of beef with arugula and parmigiano), and *abbacchio al forno* (lamb chops).

Via Celimontana 1–3. © **06-7096332.** Primi 3.50€–6€ ($4–$6.90); secondi 4.50€–8€ ($5.15–$9.20). AE, DC, MC, V. Thurs–Tues 12–3:30pm and 7–11pm. MC, V. Closed 2 weeks in Aug. Metro: Colosseo. Bus: 40N, 60, **75,** 85, 87, **115,** 117, **175,** 186, 271, 571, 810, 850.

AROUND CAMPO DE' FIORI & THE JEWISH GHETTO

Da Benito *Finds* ROMAN/ITALIAN Da Benito, a humble, working-person's trattoria, offers no-frills tables that fill with regulars looking for good food at great prices. Near the door hangs a handwritten menu to use as a guideline for when you step up to the food case, since they'll make whatever you want (within reason). You may want to stick with a salad, like the plate of smoked salmon and mini mozzarella balls on a bed of potatoes and arugula, or combine it with a *tramezzino* (sandwich sliced in a triangle) or a simple primo of *penne al ragù.* Heartier fare leans toward *saltimbocca all romana* (veal cutlet with prosciutto, sage, and Marsala wine) or *salsiccia con contorno* (sausage with a side dish, generally potatoes). The friendly staff will help if you don't know how to order or pay (at the cashier on your way out).

Via dei Falegnami 14 (near V. Arenula). C 06-6861508. Primi 3€–10€ ($3.45–$12); secondi 3€–6€ ($3.45–$6.90). No credit cards. Mon–Sat 6am–7pm. Bus: H. Tram: 8, 23, 40, 46, 62, 63, 64, 70, 87, 186, 204F, 280, 630, 780, 810.

Da Giggetto 𝓡𝓡 ROMAN JEWISH   This third-generation eatery in the ghetto is one of the classics of Rome dining. In room after room under brick arches and wood beams, drying herbs and spices hang from the ceiling until the time comes to drop a sprig into one of the traditional recipes. The starters rely on fried dishes like *carciofi alla giudia* (flattened fried artichokes) and *fiori di zuccine ripieni* (fried zucchini flowers stuffed with mozzarella and anchovies). Expect well-prepared Roman dishes as well, like *bucatini all'amatriciana, penne all'arrabbiata, saltimbocca,* and *costolette di abbacchio a scottaditto*. With so much excellent food, it's easy to go overboard, so keep an eye on that mounting bill. Call ahead if you want one of the coveted tables wedged between the ancient Roman temple columns sprouting out of the sidewalk.

Via del Portico d'Ottavia 21–22. C 06-6861105. Reservations recommended. Primi 7.50€–10€ ($8.63–$12); secondi 8€–12€ ($9.20–$14). AE, MC, V. Tues–Sun 12:30–3pm and 7–11pm. Closed Aug. Bus: H, 8, 23, 63, 116, 280, 780.

Da Pancrazio ROMAN/ITALIAN   It doesn't get more atmospheric than a restaurant with basement rooms set into the restored arcades of Pompey's 55 B.C. theater. Though tour groups often book these historic downstairs rooms, try your darnedest to get a seat there—though there's nothing wrong with the coffered wood ceiling and brick arches upstairs (in warm weather, everybody sits out on the piazza). For a touristy restaurant, the cooking is surprisingly excellent. Among the top dishes are *spaghetti alla carbonara,* delicious *cannelloni alla Pancrazio* (pasta tubes stuffed with spinach and meat), and *spaghetti con la bottarga* (with gray mullet eggs). Follow up with *involtini, abbacchio al forno con patate, tournedos di filetto alla Rossini* (beef tournedos in Madeira sauce with liver pâté), or fresh fish.

Piazza del Biscione 92 (just off the northeast corner of Campo de' Fiori). C 06-6861246. Reservations highly recommended. Primi 9€–12€ ($10–$14); secondi 9€–20€ ($10–$23). AE, DC, MC, V. Thurs–Tues 12:30–2:30pm and 7:30–11pm. Closed 25 days in Aug. Bus: 40, 46, 62, 64, 116.

Dar Filettaro a Santa Barbara *Value* SALT COD   You can join the line of people threading to the back of the bare room to order a bargain-basement filet of *baccalà* (salt cod) fried golden brown and *da portar via* (wrapped in paper to eat as you *passeggiata*). But after all that walking, and with a peek at the rock-bottom-price sides, you may just decide to eat in.

Largo dei Librari 88. C 06-6864018. Primi and secondi 3€–5€ ($3.45–$5.75). No credit cards. Mon–Sat 12:30–3:30pm and 7:30–10:30pm. Closed August. Bus: 40, 46, 62, 64, 116.

If It's Tuesday, It Must Be . . .

In addition to their regular offerings, the menus of many smaller Roman eateries still follow the traditional weekly rotation of dishes: Tuesday *zuppa di farro* (barleylike emmer soup), Wednesday *trippa,* Thursday *gnocchi,* and Friday *baccalà* and/or *pasta e ceci*.

Grappolo d'Oro ROMAN Andrea and son Paolo still oversee this upscale osteria in the heart of Rome, but quality has slipped somewhat and prices have risen steadily since their restaurant became the star of an 11-page *New Yorker* story, prompting every travel publication under the sun to review the joint. But if you stick to their famed specialties, you can still dine wonderfully. Some Roman dishes like *saltimbocca alla romana* or *rigatoni all'amatriciana* can be hit or miss, but still superb are the judiciously spicy *penne all'arrabbiata, fettuccine alla greca* (noodles with tomatoes and olives), *lasagna,* and *trippa alla romana.* Although the elbow-to-elbow tables in the rustic interior are agreeable, on sunny days reserve ahead for a table on the little piazza. At dinner it's taken over by tourists, but lunch is still a healthy mix of intellectuals, visitors, and the journalists who put this place on the map.

Piazza della Cancelleria 80 (across from Piazza S. Pantaleo). ⓒ 06-6864118. Primi 7.50€ ($8.60); secondi 11€–13€ ($13–$15). Mon–Sat noon–3pm and 7:15–11pm. AE, DC, MC, V. Closed Aug. Bus: 46, 62, 64 (to Piazza S. Pantaleo); 116 (to V. Baullari).

Hosteria Romanesca ⓡⓡ ROMAN CASARECCIA (HOME-STYLE) If you're looking to buck the tourists packing the famous but much-declined La Carbonara but still want a seat on the cobbles of lively Campo de' Fiori, head to Armando and Enzo's little 110-year-old osteria to line up for a table. It's the piazza atmosphere and well-tuned traditional dishes you come for, not the service, which some evenings seems nonexistent (there are just too many diners for two waiters and two cooks). Dishes include tried-and-true Roman faves like excellent *pasta all'amatriciana, saltimbocca alla romana,* and *cervello d'abbacchio* (fried lamb's brains; much better than boiled). In colder weather, the street-side tables disappear, and diners retreat under the wood beams of the tiny interior.

Campo de' Fiori 40. ⓒ 06-6864024. Reservations recommended. Primi 7€–8€ ($8.05–$9.20); secondi 8€–12€ ($9.20–$14). No credit cards. Tues–Sun noon–4pm and 7pm–midnight. Closed 20 days in Aug. Bus: 40, 46, 62, 64, 116.

L'Angolo Divino WINE BAR/LIGHT MEALS Massimo Crippa and his brothers successfully transformed their grandmother's wine shop into a fashionable wine bar just off Campo de' Fiori. Though old-fashioned in style, with wood ceilings and shelves of vino, the place is trendy in concept. That the menu is translated into English may be due to its location, for the crowd remains overwhelmingly Roman. Like most wine bars, it offers mixed platters of cheeses, salamis, smoked fish, and bruschetta, plus daily dishes like lasagna, *rustica ripiena* (a cousin to quiche), salads, and delectable vegetable terrines. There's a vast selection of wines by the glass, particularly strong in Italian vintages but with a good number of foreign labels as well.

Via dei Balestrari 12 (a block southeast of Campo de' Fiori). ⓒ 06-6864413. Reservations not accepted. Dishes 4€–12€ ($4.60–$14). MC, V. Tues–Sun 10am–3pm and 5:30pm–2am. Closed 15 days in Aug. Bus: 23, 40, 46, 62, 64, 116, 280.

Sora Margherita ⓡⓡ ROMAN JEWISH There's nothing to indicate the presence of this tiny little spot attached to the back of this neighborhood church, except during open hours, when people are lined up in the piazza waiting to get a table. Margherita Tomassini opened this nine-table osteria 40 years ago as an outlet for her uncle's Velletri wine. The vino still comes from the family farm (as does the olive oil), and it keeps getting better and better. Sadly, Margherita is no longer with us, but her spirit stays on in the kitchen with her classic Roman recipes of *agnolotti* (meat-stuffed ravioli in ragout), *fettuccine cacio e pepe* (with pecorino and pepper), and *gnocchi* (on Thurs). She began serving her legendary *polpette* (meatballs) almost 20 years ago so that her infant son would have some-thing soft to eat—patrons were soon clamoring for them to be added to the menu. Try the heavenly *parmigiana di melanzane*—in which eggplant slices are loaded down with mozzarella and baked long and slow in tomato sauce.

Piazza Cinque Scole 30 (east of V. Arenula). ℰ 06-6864002. Reservations not accepted. Primi 3€–7€ ($3.45–$8.05); secondi 7€–10€ ($8.05–$12). No credit cards. Sept–May Tues–Sat noon–3pm, Fri–Sat 8–11; lunch only July–Aug 1. Closed Aug. Bus: H, 8, 23, 63, 280, 780.

WORTH A SPLURGE

Ditirambo ℱℱ REGIONAL ITALIAN   In their spare time, a group of artists, actors, writers, and musicians planned this restaurant, and the results are out-standing. After only 4 years, it has established a coveted spot in the series of highly revered Italian and now American guidebooks. My best advice on order-ing is to trust your waiter, as the menu changes daily. You can always count on the freshest pastas, bread, and desserts (made by a Calabrian mother–daughter team) and on a wide variety of vegetable-based dishes like velvety zucchini mousse and savory endive strudel. I opted out of an entirely nonmeat meal by ordering the beef carpaccio, perfectly accompanied by fresh pea pods drizzled with balsamic vinegar. If you pop in without a reservation, your selection will be limited—to ensure the high quality of the ingredients, the management orders only what they plan on clearing out that day. If they're all sold out, cross the street for a more traditional Roman meal at its newer sibling Hosteria.

Piazza della Cancelleria 74–75 (at northern corner of Campo de' Fiori). ℰ 06-6871626. Reservations required. Primi 7€–8€ ($8.05–$9.20); secondi 10€–13€ ($12–$15). MC, V. Daily 8–11:30pm; Tues–Sun 1–3pm. Bus: 46, 62, 64, 116.

AROUND PIAZZA NAVONA & THE PANTHEON

If you're looking for a meal-size salad, try **Insalata Ricca 2,** Piazza Pasquino 72, southwest of Piazza Navona (ℰ 06-68307881; Bus: 46, 62, 64, 70, 80, 81, 87, 116, 186, 492, 628). It's open daily from noon to 5pm and 6:30pm to 12:30am. A perfectly placed and reliable spot is **Il Delfino,** Corso Vittorio Emanuele II 67, at the corner of Largo Argentina (ℰ 06-6861208; Tram: 8), an unremark-able *tavola calda* where you'll rub elbows with lunchtime professionals looking for a fast meal. It's open Tuesday through Sunday from 7am to 9pm. Otherwise, relax along with the rest of them at one of the places below.

With prices going through the roof, a picnic-style lunch is looking more and more appetizing. Many neighborhood *salumerie* offer ready-made prepared appetizers and entrees to go at lunchtime; try **Arci Food,** Via della Scrofa 31–32 (ℰ 06-68806335).

Al Piedone ROMAN   The overwhelming draw to this true Roman-style eatery is the *amatriciana bianca* sauce, an original recipe that predates the 16th-century advent of tomatoes from the New World. In wood-paneled rooms filled with businesspeople and a few British expatriates, you can discover the joy of this powerful sauce made from pancetta fried with garlic in pepperoncino-spiked olive oil, tossed with fresh ribbons of pasta, and dusted with Parmesan. Other worthy dishes are *tortelloni ricotta e spinaci* (leaves of white and green pasta wrapped around ricotta and spinach in a light tomato sauce), *fettuccine al porcino* (noodles with porcini mushrooms), and *involtini alla romana*.

Via Piè di Marmo 28 (southeast of the Pantheon). ℰ 06-6798628. Reservations recommended. Primi 6.50€–7.50€ ($7.45–$8.60); secondi 8€–14€ ($9.20–$16). No credit cards. Mon–Sat noon–3pm and 7–11pm. Closed 2 weeks in Aug. Bus: 46, 56, 60, 62, 64, 70, 81, 85, 87, 95, 115, 117, 160, 175, 186, 492, 628, 640, 850.

Antica Taverna ROMAN   At this taverna on a picturesque back street, you'll find a warm family welcome, intimate surroundings, and great food. My taste buds were stimulated by the marinated antipasti and blown away by the *mozzarella di bufala* (ultrafresh buffalo-milk cheese). By the arrival of the *rigatoni melanzane e zucchini* (pasta with eggplant and zucchini), my dining companions and I were nearing capacity, but I had quite a time keeping their forks out of my *spaghetti alla carbonara*. Less impressive were the secondi—specifically, the *trippa* (tripe, boiled) and the *osso bucco alla romana*, but I'll attribute this to personal taste and not to the execution of the dishes. The contorni are worth a mention: I don't generally like potatoes, but I quickly ate up an entire tasty plate of the *patate al forno* (thinly sliced and roasted).

Via Monte Giordano 12 (near Palazzo del Governo Vecchio). ℂ 06-8801053. Reservations suggested. Primi 7.50€ ($8.60); secondi 9€–13€ ($10–$15). AE, DC, MC, V. Daily noon–11pm. Bus: 40, 46, 62, 64, 70, 81, 87, 98, 116, 116T, 186, 204F, 280, 492, 870, 881.

Da Gino 🌟🌟 ROMAN   Relying on the menu that has brought it success for years, Da Gino remains a pure local trattoria to which few tourists venture. The lunch hour is hurried, attracting mostly politicos and journalists from Parliament across the street. Crowded under the *trompe-l'oeil* frescoed vaults, the zealous sink their forks into primi such as *ravioli al sugo* (cheese-stuffed pasta with a meat ragu), *spaghetti all'amatriciana*, or Gino's specialty, *tonnarelli alla ciociara* (pasta with peas and pancetta). One secondo not to miss: the *coniglio al vino* (rabbit cooked in white wine). Be sure to leave space for the best tiramisu you'll eat on your trip. Arrive before 1:15pm or forget about eating lunch here.

Vicolo Rosini 4 (an alley off Piazza del Parlamento). ℂ 06-6873434. Reservations not accepted. Primi 6.50€–7.50€ ($7.45–$8.60); secondi 8.50€–12€ ($9.75–$14). No credit cards. Mon–Sat 1–3pm and 8–10:30pm. Closed Aug. Bus: 81, 116, 117, 492, 628.

Enoteca Corsi 🌟🌟 ROMAN   Corsi has kept up with the times, but luckily not the prices, so while the enoteca inside the main entrance is every inch the *vini olii* shop of yesteryear (1937, to be specific), behind it and next door are large fan-cooled rooms to hold the lunchtime crowds at long tables. Your choices are limited to three primi and half a dozen secondi, so though the dishes are excellent in their simplicity, you may want a selection of tapas or a drink rather than a full meal. The chalkboard menu changes daily but may run from *penne all'arrabbiata, saltimbocca, trippa,* and *arrosto di vitello* to delectable dishes like tepid *pasta e patate* soup and *zucchine ripiene* (zucchini flowers stuffed with minced meats, then baked).

Via del Gesù 87–88 (off V. delle Plebescito). ℂ 06-6790821. Primi 7€ ($8.05); secondi 9€ ($10). AE, DC, MC, V. Mon–Sat noon–3:30pm. Closed Aug. Bus: H, 40, 46, 62, 63, 64, 70, 81, 87, 492, 628, 780.

Lilli ROMAN   It's hard to go wrong at this family-owned trattoria, and if you stick to the cheaper dishes, you can make this an affordable, authentic meal. The crowd is mainly locals who don't mind the long waits between courses while the staff huddles around the kitchen TV to catch a soccer match. When it's warm, the diners abandon the tiny room filled with mementos of owner Silvio Ceramicola's sporting past to sit out on the cobblestones of this dead-end alley. The time-tested primi include *tagliolini cacio e pepe, penne all'arrabbiata,* and *bucatini all'amatriciana*. The secondi include *trippa alla romana, pollo con peperoni,* and *polpettine in umida con fagioli* (tiny meatballs stewed with beans). However, the true specialty is delicious *fornata con patate al forno* (oven-roasted veal breast with potatoes).

Via Tor di Nonna 26 (at the base of steps down from Lungotevere Tor di Nonna). ℰ **06-6861916**. Reservations required. Primi 7.50€–8€ ($8.60–$9.20); secondi 8.50€–10€ ($9.75–$12). AE, MC, V. Mon–Sat 1–3pm and 8–11pm. Closed 15 days in Aug. Bus: 280.

Pizzeria Baffetto 🎲 *Kids* PIZZA   Reviews of Baffetto are mixed: Do people line up simply because it's Rome's most famous pizzeria or because the food is truly good? Whatever the answer, there's always a wait for a table at this institution, where the service is fast and furious. The tables are surrounded by photos of the directors, artists, and other international types who've shown up here over the past 40 years. The pizzas are the thin-crusted, wood-oven variety. The night's pizzas are chalked on a board, so when the waiter whisks past, be ready to order a *piccolo* (small), *media* (medium), or *grande* with the toppings of your choice; "plain" Margherita is the most popular. Get here early to avoid the adolescent crush.

Via del Governo Vecchio 114 (at the corner of V. Sora). ℰ **06-6861617**. Pizza 6€–8€ ($6.90–$9.20). No credit cards. Daily 6:30pm–1am (sometimes closed Sun in winter). Closed Aug 10–30. Bus: 40, 46, 62, 64, 70, 81, 87, 116, 492, 628.

Terra di Siena TUSCAN   The family that runs the capital's best Tuscan restaurant celebrates the cooking from their homeland south of Siena. You can dine amid rustic wood beams and softly lit goldenrod walls or, in nice weather, at a communal table on the lively piazza. The menu changes seasonally, but you can always start with *crostini misti* (toast rounds spread with liver pâté, spicy tomato sauce, or mushrooms), followed by *pici all'aglione* (hand-rolled fat spaghetti in garlicky tomato sauce) or *pappardelle al sugo di cinghiale* (wide noodles in wild boar sauce). In winter, dig into a hearty *ribollita* (stewlike vegetable-and-bread soup). Your secondo could be the pungent *cinghiale alla maremmana* (wild boar stewed with tomatoes) or the lighter *cacio toscano con le pere* (pears with ewe's-milk cheese). Stick with the good house wines—the bottled vintages are overpriced.

Piazza Pasquino 77–78 (southwest of Piazza Navona). ℰ **06-68307704**. Reservations highly recommended. Primi 9€–12€ ($10–$14); secondi 12€–18€ ($14–$21). AE, MC, V. Tues–Sun 1–3pm and 7:30–11pm. Closed 3 weeks in Aug. Bus: 46, 62, 64, 70, 81, 87, 115, 116, 116T, 186, 492, 628.

AROUND THE SPANISH STEPS & PIAZZA DEL POPOLO

Edy 🎲 *Finds* ROMAN/SEAFOOD   In an otherwise upscale area, Edmondo and Luciana offer genuine Roman cooking at downscale prices. You can sit under an old coffered and painted ceiling or at candlelit tables on the cobblestones to sample recipes that change seasonally. *Cartoccio con frutti di mare,* a spaghetti-and-seafood extravaganza baked and served in foil, is always on the menu; with any luck, you can try the *ravioli agli asparagi* (ravioli with asparagus) or the excellent *tagliatelle con ricotta e carciofi* (pasta in ricotta-and-artichoke sauce). For a secondo, try the *abbacchio Romanesco con patate* (spring lamb with potatoes), *bocconcini di vitello* (veal nuggets stewed with tomatoes, peas, and couscous), or *rombo alla griglia con patate* (grilled turbot with potatoes). Don't leave without ordering one of the homemade desserts.

Vicolo del Babuino 4 (off V. del Babuino, 3 blocks from Piazza del Popolo). ℰ **06-36001738**. Reservations highly recommended. Primi 7€–12€ ($8.05–$14); secondi 11€–18€ ($13–$21). DC, MC, V. Mon–Sat noon–3:30pm and 7pm–midnight. Closed 1 week in Aug. Metro: Spagna. Bus: 117, 119.

Fiaschetteria Beltramme (da Cesaretto) 🎲 ROMAN   This magnetically characteristic former hole-in-the-wall, here since 1886, got so popular that it was actually declared a national monument. Today the menu's a bit longer, the tablecloths are newer, and the prices are higher, at least for lunch. Still, local businesspeople line up daily for a seat under whirling fans. Dinner is just as crowded, but there are more families and visitors. Good primi choices are *antipasto misto, rigatoni al cesareto* (pasta with arugula, cherry tomatoes, mozzarella, olive oil, and herbs), and *tagliatelle ai funghi* (noodles with mushrooms). The secondi are traditional, like *bollito misto* (mix of boiled meats) and *abbacchio scottaditto*.

Via della Croce 39 (4 blocks from the Spanish Steps). No phone. Primi 8€ ($9.20); secondi 8€–12€ ($9.20–$14). No credit cards. Mon–Sat 12:15–2:45pm and 7:15–10:45pm. Metro: Spagna. Bus: 117, 119.

Il Brillo Parlante ⁂ OYSTER BAR/RESTAURANT/WINE BAR   It's standing room only at this tiny enoteca hidden in plain sight just steps from Piazza del Popolo, where the traditional working man's hangout is elevated to new levels of trendiness. Tables spill onto the narrow cobblestone street under an inviting awning in the warmer months, and you can choose from over 1,000 bottles of wine to complement the kitchen's menu of creative Italian cuisine. Tempting options include a *carpaccio di pere con parmigiano reggiano e aceto balsamico di Modena* (pear slices with parmigiano and balsamic vinegar), *verdura ripassata* (stir-fried chicory and spinach), and *filetto di bue danese* (grilled Danish beef filet), along with a variety of salads.

Via della Fontanella 12 (a block south of Piazza del Popolo). ☎ 06-3243334. Primi 8.50€ ($9.75); secondi 10€–25€ ($12–$29) AE, DISC, MC, V. Mon–Sat noon–2am. Metro: Flaminio or Spagna. Bus: 117, 119.

PizzaRé ⁂ (Kids) PIZZA   Another contender in the pizza wars, PizzaRé is the preeminent outpost for the increasingly popular *pizza alta*, the thick and chewy crust imported from Naples. Many die-hard purists order the Margherita, but exceptional as it is, you may want to try one of the other 40 varieties or the traditional calzone, oozing with tomatoes, mozzarella, and ham. Despite the inevitable backup at the door (unless you arrive when it opens), the service is cheerful and crisp, but with such competition for the ovens, you may want to split an appetizer of the *frittura mista* (fried starters) or one of the many abundant salads while you wait.

Via di Ripetta 14. ☎ 06-3211468. Reservations recommended. Pizza 6.50€–9.50€ ($7.45–$11). AE, DC, MC, V. Daily 12:45–3:30pm and 7:30pm–12:30am. Closed 1 week in Aug. Metro: Flaminio. Bus: 95, 117. Tram: 225, 490, 495, 628, 926.

NORTH OF STAZIONE TERMINI

Cantina Cantarini ⁂ MARCHIGIANA/ROMANA   In an upscale neighborhood, this 100-year-old trattoria mixes Roman faves with specialties from the Marches region. Courteous, fast service and reasonable prices ensure the arrival of a throng of locals accustomed to dining elbow to elbow at simple wooden tables or one of the sidewalk tables. *Spaghetti alla carbonara* and *alla matriciana* (very good) make their appearance alongside *fettuccine al salmone* or, in season, *ai funghi porcini*. The archetypal secondo is *fegato marchigiana* (breaded veal liver sautéed with sage), but you can also order *bollito misto* (mix of boiled meats) or *coniglio alla cacciatore* (hunter's style rabbit). For variety, stop by on Thursday evening through Saturday, when fresh fish selections like *spaghetti al nero di seppia* (squid ink) are added to the menu.

Piazza Sallustio 12 (east of V. Veneto; turn up V. Servio Tullio from V. XX Settembre and bear left). ☎ 06-485528. Reservations recommended. Primi 5€–9€ ($5.75–$10); secondi 6€–13€ ($6.90–$15). AE, DC, MC, V. Mon–Sat 12:30–3:30pm and 7:30–10:30pm. Closed 3 weeks in Aug, last week Dec/1st week Jan. Bus: 16, 37, 60, 61, 62, 136, 137, 910.

Magnosfera ROMAN/LIGHT MEALS   As the sliding doors of this cafeteria-style eatery part, the odor of fresh tomatoes takes away any doubt about where you will be dining. In a sea of rising prices and declining quality, Magnosfera features an ever-changing list of fresh and affordable pasta plates and salad dishes, including such light fair as caponata, *insalata caprese,* and sautéed vegetables. Other selections that jumped out at me on the day of my last visit were *pennette gamberi e rucola* (little penne with shrimp and arugula) and *seppie e ceci* (calamari and chickpeas).

Piazza Indipendenza 24. © **06-44703694.** Dishes 3.50€–6€ ($4–$6.90). No credit cards. Mon–Sat 7am–9:30pm. Metro: Termini. Bus: 75, 204, 310, 492, 649.

Trimani Il Wine Bar ✸✸ ITALIAN/WINE BAR/LIGHT MEALS   For a gourmet experience that won't break the bank, head to this postmodern wine bar, attached to the historic wine cellar of the same name. For Marco and Carla Trimani, serving fine foods to accompany wine chosen from their thousands of labels is merely an extension of the family's 170-plus years in the vino trade. The tiny rooms, long stylish bar, and outdoor gazebo are tinged with elegance. The daily changing menu may include Andalusian gazpacho or strongly flavored *trittico di crostini,* a trio of bread slices generously topped with Gorgonzola, Stilton, and Roquefort, then baked and drizzled with chestnut honey. In addition to wine accompaniments like cheeses and salamis, there are main dishes like *polenta con involtini di vitello alle erbe aromatiche e pancetta* (polenta with veal roll-ups flavored with herbs and pancetta) and aromatic *flan di carote con salsa agli spinaci* (carrot quiche with a spinach sauce).

Via Cernaia 37b (at V. Goito). © **06-4469630.** Primi, salads, and cheeses 7€–10€ ($8.05–$12); secondi 7€–20€ ($8.05–$23). AE, DC, MC, V. Mon–Sat 11:30am–3pm and 5:30pm–12:30am. Closed 2 weeks in Aug. Bus: 16, 37, 60, 61, 62 (to V. Cernaia); 116T, 175, 492, 910. Metro: Repubblica or Castro Pretorio.

IN SAN LORENZO

Arancia Blu ✸ INVENTIVE VEGETARIAN ITALIAN   This trendy spot serves Rome's best vegetarian cuisine, superior food even for the unconvinced. In the glow of soft lighting and wood ceilings, surrounded by wine racks and university intellectuals, the friendly waiters will help you compile a menu to fit any need, such as allergies or weight restrictions. The dishes are inspired by peasant cuisines from across Italy and beyond, and everything's made with organic and natural ingredients. Appetizers range from hummus and tabbouleh to zucchini-and-saffron quiche and *insalata verde con mele, Gorgonzola naturale e aceto balsamico* (salad with apples, Gorgonzola, and balsamic vinegar). The main courses change seasonally and may include couscous *con verdure* (vegetable couscous) or *ravioli ripieni di patate e menta* (ravioli stuffed with potatoes and mint, served under fresh tomatoes and Sardinian sheep's cheese). They offer almost 100 wines, cheese platters, and inventive desserts like *pere al vino* (pears cooked in wine, scented with juniper, and served with a semifreddo of orange honey).

Via dei Latini 65 (at V. Arunci). © **06-4454105.** Reservations highly recommended. Primi and secondi 7€–12€ ($8.05–$14). No credit cards. Daily 8pm–midnight. Bus: 71, 492.

Pommidoro ✸✸ *(Finds* ROMAN   The Bravi family—these days, Anna (cook), Aldo (hunter), and their brood—have for four generations been satisfying everyone from downtown cognoscenti and neighborhood cronies to intellectuals and celebrities like Pier Pasolini and Maria Callas. There's a glassed-in deck on the piazza, but the inside's more atmospheric, with a huge old fireplace grill. Or you can head downstairs to dine under low arches of hand-cast brick. Roman specialties reign supreme, from *amatriciana* and excellent *carbonara* to peppery *spaghetti cacio e pepe*, thanks to the finest, freshest ingredients. Wintry fare leans toward porcini mushrooms tossed with fettuccine, *pappardelle al sugo cinghiale* (wide noodles in boar sauce), and gamy dishes made with quail, woodcock, and duck. For those whose palate extends beyond the norm, there's *animelle alla cacciatore* (sweetbread stew) and chicken livers.

Piazza Sanniti 44 (turn off V. Tiburtina onto V. degli Ansoni). ℭ 06-4452692. Reservations highly recommended. Primi 8€ ($9.20); secondi 7€–12€ ($8.05–$14). AE, DC, MC, V. Mon–Sat noon–3pm and 7:30pm–midnight. Closed Aug. Bus: 71, 492.

Tram Tram ℛ *Finds* SOUTHERN ITALIAN/ROMAN　This crowded trattoria is run by the di Vittorio sisters, under the invaluable tutelage of their mother, Rosanna, who has infused some of her native Apulia into the menu. The dishes are well balanced between meat and fish, with a *lasagna vegetale* halfway between. Primi include *trofie alla siciliana* (pasta with swordfish and eggplant), handmade *orecchiette al ortolana* (ear-shape pasta with seasonal vegetables) or *alla norma* (with tomato, eggplant, and hard ricotta), and *rigatoni alla paiata*. The decibel levels are pretty high, in part due to the nearby tram rumbling by, causing the silverware and glasses to tinkle every few minutes and voices to rise to steady levels. The trams have inspired not only the steady chatter, but also the decor: old trolley signs and photos, even tram benches as seats.

Via dei Reti 44–46 (at the corner of V. dei Piceni). ℭ 06-490416. Reservations highly recommended. Primi 7€–8€ ($8.05–$9.20); secondi 8€–13€ ($9.20–$15). DC, MC, V. Tues–Sun 12:30–3pm and 7:30pm–12:30am. Closed 2–3 weeks in Aug. Bus: 71, 492.Tram 3, 19.

IN TESTACCIO

Da Felice ℛ ROMAN　There's no sign or menu, but every seat fills up for the plentiful cheap food at da Felice, where a dining experience is a ridiculous foray into the Twilight Zone at best and a complete washout at worst. RISERVATO signs occupy every empty table, even on traditionally slow Monday nights, so Felice can give the once-over to all potential guests and either lead you inside or say, "*Siamo completo*" (no vacancy) to anyone who rubs him the wrong way. But getting a seat is only half the battle. Felice ambles around the high-ceilinged room in his waiter's jacket (which is why the service is so slow) while his son mans the kitchen and his grandson helps serve. The dishes change with the days of the week and are made from the freshest market ingredients, but diners generally flock here for the chance at Felice's *abbacchio scottadito*. Rumor has it that if you don't order a primo, Felice won't serve you the *abbacchio*, but I'm sure there are plenty of other reasons for him to hold out. Other outstanding standards are the minestrone and the remarkable *tonarelli cacio e pepe* or *al sugo*. The most popular secondi—after the *abbacchio*—are the *involtino al sugo* and *spezzatino di vitello con peperoni* (veal smothered with bell peppers).

Via Maestro Giorgio 29 (at the corner of V. A. Volta). ℭ 06-5746800. Reservations highly recommended. Primi 4.50€–6€ ($5.15–$6.90); secondi 7€–11€ ($8.05–$13). No credit cards. Mon–Sat 12:30–2:30pm and 8–10:30pm. Closed Aug. Bus: 13, 23, 27, 75, 673, 715, 716, 719. Metro: Piramide.

La Torricella ℛ ROMAN　La Torricella may have gotten a face-lift, but the kitchen remains true to its ultratraditional *osteria* roots. The restaurant is set in the echoing rooms of what appears to be an old dock warehouse, with tall arches and a die-hard crowd of neighborhood regulars. The menu lists basic favorites like *spaghetti ai frutti di mare* (spaghetti with seafood), homemade *gnocchi* (on Thurs), *rigatoni con pagliata*, tasty *bucatini all'amatriciana*, *saltimbocca alla romana*, *abbacchio à scottadito*, *bistecca di manzo ai pepi verdi* (steak in cream sauce with green peppercorns), and fresh *sogliole* (sole), *spigola* (sea bass), *rombo* (turbot), and other fish.

Via E. Torricelli 2–12 (at V. G. B. Bodoni, just off the Lungotevere a few blocks up from Ponte Testaccio). ℂ **06-5746311.** Primi 6.50€–12€ ($7.45–$14); secondi 7.50€–12€ ($8.60–$14). MC, V. Tues–Sun 12:30–3:30pm and 7:30–11:30pm. Closed a few days in Aug. Metro: Piramide. Bus: 170, 719, 781.

WORTH A SPLURGE

Checchino dal 1887 ✹✹✹ ULTRAROMAN   Rome's greatest splurge is the mecca for people who classify eating as an art. The Mariani family started this temple of traditional cuisine six generations ago as a blue-collar wine shop patronized by workers from the slaughterhouse across the street. These men received the undesirable refuse of the day's butchering (offal, tails, feet, and so on), and Checchino turned these into culinary masterpieces—it even made oxtail a staple by inventing and perfecting *coda alla vaccinara* (stewed with tomatoes, celery, white wine, bittersweet chocolate, pine nuts, and raisins). Only for the adventurous is the *insalata di zampe* (salad with jellied trotters); otherwise, stick with the house specialty, *abbacchio alla cacciatore* (spring lamb browned in olive oil and flavored with anchovies, vinegar, and pepperoncini). Be sure to try some of the two dozen cheeses or a homemade dessert, each accompanied by the perfect glass of wine from among the 500 labels in the extensive wine cellar.

Via di Monte Testaccio 30 (at the southerly end of Testaccio). ℂ **06-5746318.** www.checchino-dal-1887.com. Reservations required. Fixed menus at 31€, 40€, 45€, and 60€ ($36, $46, $52, and $69). AE, DC, MC, V. Tues–Sat 12:30–3pm and 8–11pm. Closed Aug and 1 week at Christmas. Metro: Piramide. Bus: 95, 673, 719.

IN TRASTEVERE

Da Augusto ✹ ROMAN   This modest place has found its way into virtually every guidebook as a poster child for the Trastevere *osteria*. But even with all the press, the bulk of patronage remains neighborhood cronies. Maybe visitors just can't find the place, tucked into a forgotten corner of the area on a tiny square used as a parking lot. The lucky few, sitting elbow to elbow in the pair of rooms or at a handful of tables squeezed into the triangular piazza, get to dig into standbys like *rigatoni all'amatriciana, fettuccine cacio e pepe, trippa alla romana, involtini,* and succulent *abbacchio.* It gets rather busy, so don't expect solicitous service—just excellent home cooking.

Piazza de' Renzi 15 (between Vicolo delle Cinque and V. del Moro). ℂ **06-5803798.** Primi 2.85€–5€ ($3.25–$5.75); secondi 2.60€–7.50€ ($3–$8.60). No credit cards. Mon–Fri noon–3pm and 7pm–midnight; Sat noon–3pm. Bus: H, 8, 23, 280, 780.

Dar Poeta ✹ PIZZA   The pizza wars have called a truce here, where uncompromising thin-crust eaters sit side by side with those who prefer their pizza "high." Using the slow-rise method introduced in recent years by nouvelle pizza guru Angelo Iezzi, Dar Poeta's offerings have crispy or fluffy bases and creative toppings, including *taglialegna* (mixed vegetables, mushrooms, sausage, and mozzarella) and *bodrilla* (apples and Grand Marnier). The varied bruschette are first rate, and you can eat till late.

Vicola del Bologna 45 (off Piazza Santa Maria della Scala, not to be confused with V. del Bologna, off which it branches). ℂ **06-5880516.** Reservations recommended. Pizza 4.50€–8€ ($5.15–$9.20). AE, DC, MC, V. Tues–Sun 8pm–midnight. Bus: 280.

Il Ciak ✹✹ TUSCAN/GAME   When locals occasionally tire of Roman food, they head out for a variation on a theme. Il Ciak offers hearty Tuscan fare in a cozy rustic space, featuring wooden benches and a big bottle of pay-what-you-drink Chianti on each table. Movie stills from owner Paolo Celli's former life as an actor cover the walls, but the proof is in the pudding that no true Tuscan ever leaves his culinary roots. Celli hails from Lucca, a Tuscan city (see chapter 5) renowned for its olive oil, wines, and hearty barley soup. Typical primi are *papardelle al sugo di cinghiale* (wide noodles in wild boar sauce), *minestra di farro con fagioli* (barley soup with beans), and *ribollita* (vegetable soup made thick with bread). For a secondo, try the mighty *Fiorentina originale* (a steak barely grilled rare; if you can't handle this 800g/28-oz. slab, you can order the 400g/14-oz. *mezza*), *braciole di maiale* (pork chop), *cinghiale alla boscaiola* (woodsman's-style wild boar), or *starna al crostone* (partridge on toasted bread).

Vicola del Cinque 21 (just south of Piazza Trilussa, north of Piazza Santa Maria in Trastevere). ℂ 06-5894774. Reservations highly recommended. Primi 7.50€–10€ ($8.60–$12); secondi 13€ ($15). AE, DC, MC, V. Tues–Sun 8–11:30pm. Closed end of July to beginning of Aug. Bus: 23, 280.

Il Duca ⚔⚔ ROMAN/PIZZA   The noisy banter of Trasteverino and Roman dialects echoes through the brick arches and wood-ceiling interior of this institution—always a good sign. The walls, fantastically muraled with scenes of Rome, are as much of an attraction as the excellent cooking. But no matter how good the quality of the food or how extensive the choice, everyone comes for the lasagna, so wonderful it has made it off the occasional daily special menu and into the permanent annals of Il Duca. If you're unlucky enough to arrive after the last serving is gone, try the *spaghetti alla carbonara, spaghetti alla gricia,* or *gnocchi alla Gorgonzola.* For a secondo, the *saltimbocca alla romana, pollo arrosto con patate,* and *abbacchio à scottaditto* are divine.

Vicolo delle Cinque 52–56 (just around the corner from Piazza San Egidio, behind Piazza Santa Maria in Trastevere). ℂ 06-5817706. Reservations recommended. Primi 6.50€–9€ ($7.45–$10); secondi 8.50€–17€ ($9.75–$20); pizza 5.50€–7€ ($5.75–$10). AE, DC, MC, V. Tues–Sat 7pm–midnight; Sun noon–3pm and 7pm–midnight. Bus: H, 8, 23, 280, 780.

Ivo a Trastevere ⚔⚔ *Kids* PIZZA/ROMAN   Trastevere's huge, bustling pizza parlor is always thronged with locals and foreigners (is there any guidebook that doesn't list it?), but the hordes haven't led it to compromise taste or prices. The tables outside are hard to come by, but the street's fairly trafficked, so I always choose the crowded, closely spaced tables inside. The service is swift and brusque, but Ivo is an excellent place to introduce yourself to Roman-style wood-oven pizza. The "plain" Margherita is the favorite, but also good are *al prosciutto* and *capricciosa* (likely to include anchovies, prosciutto, olives, and a fried egg). There are plenty of pastas to choose from as well.

Via San Francesco a Ripa 158 (from Vle. di Trastevere, take a right onto V. Fratte di Trastevere, then left on V. San Francesco a Ripa). ℂ 06-5817082. Reservations not usually necessary. Primi 8€ ($9.20); secondi 8€–11€ ($9.20–$13) and up to 16€ ($18) for fish; pizza 7€–8€ ($8.05–$9.20). AE, DC, MC, V. Wed–Mon 12:30–3pm and 7:30–11:30pm. Bus: H. Tram: 8, 44, 75.

La Tana dei Noiantri ROMAN/ITALIAN/PIZZA   La Tana dei Noiantri has a vast menu of quite good food, but everybody really comes for the romance of dining out on the cobblestone piazza, under the illuminated eye of Santa Maria in Trastevere. The interior is a bit more formal, with wood ceilings and painted coats of arms above baronial fireplaces, staffed by waiters who have been around forever. There are no surprises among the primi, while the best secondi are the *abacchio arrosto con patate* and the *fritto cervello di abbacchio* (fried lamb's brains and zucchini). The sizable selection of fresh fish and seafood includes *cozze alla marinara* (mussels in tomato sauce).

Via della Paglia 1–3 (the street leading west out of Piazza Santa Maria in Trastevere). ℂ 06-5806404. Reservations highly recommended. Primi 5.50€–8€ ($6.30–$9.20); secondi 8€–13€ ($9.20–$15); pizza

You Get What You Pay For

At Rome bars, cafes, and gelaterie, don't just saunter up to the bar and order two fingers of vino. Go first to the cashier, order what you want, pay for it, and take the receipt to the counter, where you can order your cappuccino or your *coppa* (cup) or *cono* (cone) of gelato, putting the receipt down with a 20 or 50 *centesimi* (like our cents) piece as a tip. Remember also that a seat on the terrace will triple the price of that coffee you could have had standing at the bar.

6€–9€ ($6.90–$10). AE, MC, V. Wed–Mon noon–3pm and 7:30–11:30pm. Closed Jan 8–Feb 2. Bus: H, 8, 23, 280, 780.

Taverna della Scala ROMAN/PIZZA   This ever-popular basic trattoria offers a few tables set on the out-of-the-way piazza, but most diners end up in the small ground-floor dining room or in the stuccoed basement room surrounded by odd modern art. All the Roman staples are here: *bucatini all'amatriciana, penne all'arrabbiata, spaghetti alla puttanesca* (spicy "whore's pasta," with black olives, capers, garlic, and anchovies), and *farfalle alle mutandine rose* (bow-tie pasta "pink panties," in a rosé tomato-and-cream sauce). For a secondo, try the *ossobuco romano* (veal shank cooked with tomatoes; the marrow is considered a delicacy), *scaloppina al vino* (veal scallop in wine), or fresh fish like *spigola* (sea bass) or *orata* (sea bream) grilled.

Piazza della Scala 19. ℂ 06-5814100. Reservations recommended. Primi 6€–7€ ($6.90–$8.05); secondi 8€–13€ ($9.20–$15); pizza 5€–6€ ($5.75–$6.90). AE, MC, V. Wed–Sun 12:30–3pm and 7pm–midnight. Bus: 23, 280.

WORTH A SPLURGE

Sora Lella 🏵🏵🏵 ROMAN/INVENTIVE ITALIAN   This classic is refined rustic, with rough-hewn beams, elegant place settings, good service, and a great wine list. Aldo Trabalza and his sons honor the memory of his mother, Sora Lella Fabbrizi—cook, unlikely star of Italian TV, and Roman character—by serving traditional essentials alongside innovative lighter fare and half-forgotten Roman dishes with centuries of pedigree. The specialty primo is *tonnarelli alla cuccagna* (pasta with sausage, eggs, walnuts, cream, and a dozen other ingredients), but also good are *bombolotti alla ciafruiona* (pasta with tomatoes, artichokes, peas, and tuna) and *rigatoni con pagliata*. For a secondo, try the *abbacchio brodettato* (lamb in a sauté of eggs, lemon, Parmesan, and parsley) or *maialino al forno "antica romana"* (sweet-and-sour suckling pig with prunes, raisins, pine nuts, almonds, and baby onions).

Via Ponte Quattro Capi 16 (on Tiber Island, at the foot of Ponte Fabricio). ℂ 06-6861601. Reservations highly recommended. Primi 14€ ($16); secondi 18€–25€ ($21–$29). AE, DC, MC, V. Mon–Sat 12:45–2:30pm and 8–11pm. Bus: H, 23, 63, 280.

AROUND THE VATICAN

The no. 6 branch of the wildly popular Roman chain of salad-and-light-meals restaurants, **Insalata Ricca,** is across from the Vatican walls at Piazza del Risorgimento 5–6 (ℂ **06-39730387;** Bus: 23, 32, 49, 51, 81, 492, 982, 990, or 991). It's open daily from noon to 3:30pm and 7 to 11:30pm. If you're looking for an Italian pub with food, head to **Armando's Cafe,** Via Paolo Emilio 17, at Via Cola di Rienzo (ℂ **06-3243111;** Bus: 81), open Thursday through Tuesday from noon to 3pm and 7 to 11pm.

The Best Gelaterie & Cafes

Though Rome boasts no true gelato tradition of its own, Romans are demanding and remain loyal to only the cream-of-the-crop purveyors, so to speak. **Giolitti,** Via Uffici del Vicario 40, a few long blocks north of the Pantheon (✆ 06-6991243; www.giolitti.it), was the unchallenged leader in the *centro storico* until **San Crispino** opened a branch at Via Panetteria 32 near the Trevi Fountain (✆ 06-6793924). Using the "northern" recipe (made from a cream-based custard; Tuscan gelato uses a milk-based custard, and the Sicilian recipe uses the milk but ditches the egg yolks), San Crispino, with its pioneer location at Via Acaia 56/56A, near the Baths of Caracalla (✆ 06-70450412), is the winner. Its signature flavor is a subtle pistachio—get it in a cup, as cones are verboten here—expanding on the preservative- and additive-free principle of using only the finest ingredients (like honey from its own apiary or 20-year-old reserve Marsala wine).

Known for its yummy tartufo (see the beginning of this section for a description), **Tre Scalini,** Piazza Navona 28–32 (✆ 06-68801996), is a popular but unsightly bar that continues to draw crowds. Here are some other historic cafes you may want to pop into: Near the *tempietto* (small temple) of Santa Maria della Pace is the **Antico Caffè della Pace,** Via della Pace 4–7 (✆ 06-6861216), an early-1900s cafe abuzz with Romans drinking outrageously priced coffee until 3am. The **Antico Caffè del Greco,** Via Condotti 96 (✆ 06-6791700), opened in 1760, just in time for Casanova to while away the hours waiting to meet in secret with his lovers and for German author Goethe to become a regular during his prolonged stay in Rome. Nearby, just to the left of the Spanish Steps, is one of Rome's bastions of the Anglo-American expat scene, **Babington's Tea Rooms,** Piazza

Il Matriciano ROMAN   For more than 80 years, this classy classic *ristorante* has been beloved by Rome cognoscenti, Prati residents, and film directors for business lunches. Obviously, *they* know what they want because you may have to ask a few times to see a menu or wine list. At these prices, the portions could be larger and sauces more ample, but better quality than quantity, no? Antipasti include *mozzarella di bufala* (made from buffalo milk) and a *fritto misto* of zucchini flowers and broccoli. For a primo, try the superb namesake *bucatini alla matriciana, fettuccine casarecce* (with tomatoes and basil), or *tagliolini alla gricia.* The pride of the secondi are the *abbacchio al forno con patate* (lamb with tasty oven-roasted potatoes), *ossobuco cremoso con funghi* (osso buco with mushroom-cream sauce), and *filetto di bue* (ox steak).

Via dei Gracchi 55 (at the corner of V. Silla). ✆ 06-3213040. Reservations highly recommended. Primi 8€–9 ($9.20–$10); secondi 11€–14€ ($13–$16). AE, DC, MC, V. May–Oct Sun–Fri 12:30–3pm and 8–11:30pm; Nov–Apr Thurs–Tues 12:30–3pm and 8–11:30pm. Closed Aug 6–21 and Dec 24–Jan 2. Metro: Ottaviano. Bus: 19, 32.

Il Mozzicone ⚘ OSTERIA/PIZZERIA   From this covered cobbled corner on Piazza dei Catalone—with its brick fountain and post-Vatican visitors refilling their water bottles in the heat of the summer—the picture of the pilgrimage is complete. The food here at Il Mozzicone is no-nonsense home-style cooking, offering light di Spagna 23 (© 06-6786027), started by two little old ladies in 1893 and little changed since. Stop in to raise your pinkies to a very proper afternoon tea in this staunchly (and slightly uncomfortable, with hard wooden chairs) British reminder of the genteel 19th century. A pot of tea runs 7€ (8.05) on up, but excellent British cakes, sandwiches, and dishes are also available.

Near the Pantheon lies **Sant'Eustachio,** Piazza Sant'Eustachio 82 (© **06-6861309**), a traditional Italian stand-up bar serving since 1938 what's widely held to be Rome's best caffè, made with water carried into the city in an ancient aqueduct and with enough froth to disguise the minuscule amount of liquid at the bottom of the cup. The **Pasticceria Strabbioni,** Via Servio Tullio 2 (© **06-4873965**), is a cafe/pastry shop with fancifully decorated vaults, a courteous staff, and excellent pastries.

Piazza del Popolo is *the* place to see and be seen, drawing a nightly parade of Ferrari- and Maserati-driving couples to pose in the **Cafe Rosati,** Piazza del Popolo 4–5 (© **06-3225859**). The cafe still retains its 1922 Art Nouveau decor, but the Rosati's real draw is the nostalgia for the directors and producers of yesteryear that prompted countless budding *artistes* to stake out a table in wait for their big break. The cafe rests on its laurels, though its outdoor tables are preferable to those of its more down-to-earth rival Canova across the square. If you want to capture some of that lingering *Dolce Vita* spirit on Via Veneto, head to its old queen of Roman bars, the **Cafe Doney,** Via Veneto 145 (© **06-4821788**), which in its heyday was the epicenter of the glamour crowd (Marcello Mastroianni, Ava Gardner, Anita Ekberg).

starters such as *fiori di zucca* (fried zucchini flowers) or *filetto di baccalà* (fried sticks of cod) and simply mouth-watering spaghetti ragù. The *pollo arrosto* (roast chicken) is a great value, or opt instead for the heartier *braciole di maiale* (pork chop) or *fegato alla veneta* (liver, Venetian style, with onions). Il Mozzicone's lack of pretension and good value will have you feeling smug as you watch die-hard guidebook followers flocking to the more expensive Tre Pupazzi next door.

Borgo Pio 180. © 06-6861500. Primi 6.50€–8€ ($7.45–$9.20); secondi 6.50€–12€ ($7.48–$14). MC, V. Mon–Sat noon–3pm and 7–11pm. Bus: 23, 32, 34, 46, 51, 62, 64, 81, 98, 492, 881, 982, 990.

5 Sights to See

In recent years, some of Rome's most popular monuments, archaeological sites, and museums have begun staying open to 7, 8, or even 11:30pm during summer and offering "Art and Monuments Under the Stars" at least several nights a week. Some even throw in guided tours or a concert. Keep your eyes peeled in the events guides from mid-June to September. A more recently instituted annual event is the Settimana dei Beni Culturali (Cultural Heritage Week), in which entrance to all state-owned museums, buildings or sites of interest is free, free, free. If you're traveling to Rome (or anywhere in Italy, for that matter) at the end of May, check with the tourist office to see if the event is on.

A note on hours: The opening times given in the entries below will most certainly be outdated by the time you get to Rome. In general, hours are shorter in winter and prolonged on weekend evenings in summer. Also, keep in mind that ticket offices close between a half-hour to an hour before final closing. To circumvent most of the idiosyncrasies of Italian planning, call ℭ **800-991199** (in Rome toll-free) or pick up a free **Official City Map** at the tourist office or nearest kiosk (the back has the most up-to-date hours for all the sights around town). To be absolutely safe, check directly with the museum ahead of time.

ST. PETER'S & THE VATICAN

Did you know that Rome's greatest church and greatest museum are technically not even in Italy? The **Vatican** is the world's second-smallest sovereign state, a theocracy ruled by the pope with about 1,000 residents (some 550 of whom are Vatican citizens) living on 44 hectares (109 acres) of land. The Vatican is protected (theoretically) by its own militia, the curiously uniformed (some say by Michelangelo) Swiss Guards. It's been that way ever since the 1929 Lateran Pact with Italy's government. But don't worry: Your euros are still good here, though the efficient Vatican post office does use different stamps.

Basilica di San Pietro (St. Peter's Basilica) 𝄞𝄞𝄞   St. Peter's is one of the holiest basilicas in the Catholic faith, the pulpit for a parish priest we call the pope, one of the grandest creations of Rome's Renaissance and baroque eras, and the largest church in Europe. It was the biggest in the world, but the basilica has since been surpassed in size several times over. St. John the Divine in New York City will hold the title for largest church—if they ever finish it.

St. Peter's is unimaginably huge, longer than two football fields and 44m (144 ft.) high inside, but since every part of it is oversized (even the cherubs would dwarf a 6-ft. man), it doesn't appear nearly that large—until you look 184m (604 ft.) down to the opposite end and see the specks of people in the distance. Mocking bronze plaques set in the floor of the central nave mark just how short the world's other great cathedrals come up. The basilica itself takes at least an hour to see—not because there are many specific sights; it just takes that long to walk down to one end of it and back. A more complete visit will take 2 to 3 hours, including climbing Michelangelo's dome and descending to the papal crypt.

THE PIAZZA   You approach the church through the embracing arms of Bernini's oval colonnade, which encompasses **Piazza San Pietro (St. Peter's Square).** Actually, this "oval" is a perfect ellipse described by the twin arms of 284 Doric columns, arranged in four rows and topped by 96 statues of saints. Straight ahead is the facade of the basilica (Sts. Peter and Paul are represented by statues in front, Peter carrying the keys to the kingdom), and to the right, above the colonnade, are the dark brown buildings of the **papal apartments** and the **Vatican Museums.** In the center of the piazza is an **Egyptian obelisk,** brought from

---

⟨Tips⟩ St. Peter's Dress Code

St. Peter's (and all churches, for that matter) has a strict dress code: no shorts, no skirts above the knee, and no bare shoulders. *You will not be allowed in if you don't come dressed appropriately.* In a pinch, both men and women can buy a big cheap scarf from a nearby souvenir stand and wrap it around your legs as a long skirt or throw it over your shoulders as a shawl.

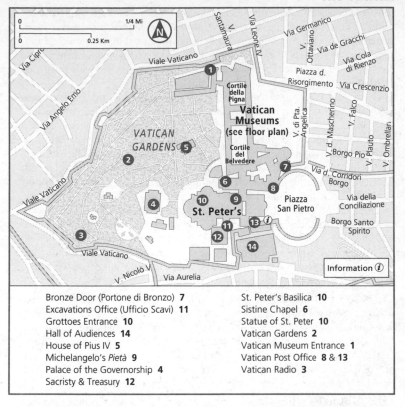

0 1/4 Mi
0 0.25 Km

Via Cipro
Viale Vaticano
V. Santamaura
Via Leone IV
Via Germanico
V. Ottaviano
Via de Gracchi
Via Cola di Rienzo
Piazza d. Risorgimento
Via Crescenzio
Via Angelo Emo
Cortile della Pigna
Vatican Museums (see floor plan)
V. di Pta. Angelica
V. Mascherino
V. Falco
V. Plauto
V. Ombrellari
VATICAN GARDENS
Cortile del Belvedere
Borgo Pio
Via d. Corridori Borgo
Viale Vaticano
St. Peter's
Piazza San Pietro
Via della Conciliazione
Borgo Santo Spirito
Viale Vaticano
V. Nicolò V
Via Aurelia

Information ⓘ

Bronze Door (Portone di Bronzo) **7**	St. Peter's Basilica **10**
Excavations Office (Ufficio Scavi) **11**	Sistine Chapel **6**
Grottoes Entrance **10**	Statue of St. Peter **10**
Hall of Audiences **14**	Vatican Gardens **2**
House of Pius IV **5**	Vatican Museum Entrance **1**
Michelangelo's *Pietà* **9**	Vatican Post Office **8** & **13**
Palace of the Governorship **4**	Vatican Radio **3**
Sacristy & Treasury **12**	

the ancient city of Heliopolis on the Nile delta. Flanking the obelisks are two 17th-century **fountains:** the one on the right (as you face the basilica) by Carlo Maderno, who designed the facade of St. Peter's, and the other by Carlo Fontana. Note that the ellipse creates a neat special effect: Between either of the fountains and the obelisk is a marble disk in the ground. Stand here to see the rows of the colonnade closest to you line up, appearing to be only one column deep.

THE BASILICA The **Basilica di San Pietro,** which replaced a crumbling 4th-century version, has gone through many architects, each attempting to realize his own personal vision. It was started by Bramante in 1506 (on a Greek cross floor plan) and was continued by Raphael (who adapted it to a Latin cross plan), then by Peruzzi (back to Greek cross), Antonio Sangallo the Younger (Latin cross again), Michelangelo (Greek cross again, though his major contribution was raising the dome), and Giacomo della Porta and Carlo Fontana (who completed it in 1590 more or less in line with Michelangelo's designs). Then, in 1605, they tore down the facade and brought in Carlo Maderno, who—tell me you didn't see this coming—lengthened the nave so as to finish it off in a Latin cross plan by 1626. For a baroque flourish, Bernini, in addition to creating the piazza out front, took care of much of the interior decor from 1629 through the 1650s.

To the right as you enter the basilica is the greatest single sight, Michelangelo's *Pietà* (1500). The beauty and unearthly grace of sweet-faced Mary and her dead son, Jesus, with details that seem exactingly perfect and yet are exaggerated for effect—the Virgin's lap is mountainously large in order to support the body of a full-grown man without seeming unbelievable—led some critics of the day to circulate a rumor that the 25-year-old Florentine sculptor could never have carved such a work. An indignant Michelangelo returned to the statue and did something he never did before or after: He signed it, chiseling his name right across the Virgin's sash. The *Pietà* has been behind protective glass since the 1970s, when a hammer-wielding lunatic attacked it.

Under the fabulous dome is Bernini's twisting-columned **baldacchino** (1524), a 29m (95-ft.) ridiculously fancy canopy for the papal altar constructed with bronze purloined from the Pantheon (this altar is placed over St. Peter's tomb). Of the four great piers supporting the dome, the first on your right is a backdrop for Arnolfo di Cambio's late-13th-century bronze of *St. Peter.* Cambio, architect of Florence's Gothic palazzi, was also an underrated sculptor, and his greatest work in Rome does double duty as a piece of art and a holy good-luck talisman for the faithful—you'll often see a line of people sidling up to touch or kiss his outstretched foot, by now worn to a shiny nub.

Alongside the usual collection of embroidered vestments, gilded chalices, and other bejeweled accouterments of the faith in the **treasury** (entrance just before the left transept) is the enormous bronze slab tomb of Pope Sixtus IV, cast by early Renaissance master Antonio del Pollaiuolo in 1493 and edged with bas-relief panels personifying the scholarly disciplines.

THE CRYPT   Recessed into that pier with the statue of St. Peter are the steps down to the **papal crypt** (aka **Vatican grottoes**); sometimes the entry is moved to another of the central piers. Along with the **tomb chapels** of lots of dead popes (plus Queen Christina of Sweden), you get to see 15th-century **bronze plaques** on the lives of Sts. Peter and Paul by Antonio del Pollaiuolo and remaining bits of Constantine's original basilica. See the crypt last, as they usually route you right from this up to the dome, then out onto the piazza, ending your visit.

THE SUBCRYPT   If the papal crypt isn't enough, you can also tour the **subcrypt around St. Peter's tomb,** with tombs and a necropolis dating all the way back to the origins of Christianity. St. Peter was probably martyred in the Circus of Nero, which lies under part of the current basilica, but the actual site of his grave was argued over for centuries. Then excavations in the 1940s uncovered here what many thought was merely a medieval myth: the Red Wall, behind which St. Peter was known to be buried and on which early Christian pilgrims scratched prayers, invocations, thanks, and many a "Killroyus was here" in Latin. Sure enough, behind this wall was found a small pocket of a tomb in which doctrine now holds the first pope was buried (however, there's no evidence other than circumstantial that the set of human bones found here actually belonged to Heaven's Gatekeeper). The only way to visit the subcrypt and necropolis is by reservation. You must apply at least 20 days in advance at the **Ufficio Scavi** (✆/fax **06-69885518; www.vatican.va**), through the arch to the left of the stairs up the basilica. You specify your name, the number in your party, your language, and the date you'd like to visit; they'll notify you by phone of your admission date and time. Guided tours are 10€ ($12).

THE DOME   The last great thing to do at the Vatican is climb **Michelangelo's dome,** 135m (443 ft.) from the ground at its top and 42m (138 ft.) in diameter (Michelangelo made his dome 1.5m/5 ft. shorter across than the Pantheon's, which he studied before beginning this one). If you don't want to climb all the way (once you start, you can't turn back), you can ride an elevator for parts of the ascent (you'll still have 320 steps to go), but you'll likely have to wait in a long line—buy your elevator ticket when you pay admission. Once at the

Attending a Papal Audience

If the pope is at home (and has time), he holds a public audience every Wednesday at 10am (sometimes as early as 9am in summer). This basically means you get to attend a short service performed by the pope, either in the Vatican's large Paolo IV Hall or, when it's really crowded, out on the piazza. You need a ticket for this (see below), but not for the brief Sunday noon blessing the pope tosses out his office window to the people thronging Piazza San Pietro below.

Audience tickets are free, but you must get them ahead of time (available Mon or Tues 9am–1pm). Apply in person at the **Prefecture of the Papal Household** (© **06-69883273**), located through the bronze door where the curving colonnade to the right of the church begins on Piazza San Pietro. You can also obtain tickets by writing at least 2 weeks beforehand to **Prefettura della Casa Pontifica**, Città del Vaticano, 00120 ITALIA. Specify your nationality, the number of tickets you need, and the date you'd like (Wed only). From mid-July to mid-September, His Holiness often cools his heels at his estate in nearby Castel Gandolfo, so there are few audiences then.

dome base, you wander through a little village of souvenir shops to the backside of the facade for a view over Piazza San Pietro. More stairs lead up to Carlo Maderno's lantern for a fantastic and dizzying **panorama of Rome** laid out at your feet. On a clear day, from this perch you can see far beyond the city to the low mountains and countryside beyond.

Note: Professors and scholars from Rome's North American College offer free tours of the basilica Monday through Friday at 2:15 and 3pm, Saturday at 10:15 and 2:15pm, and Sunday at 2:30pm. Meet in front of the Vatican info office to the left of St. Peter's main steps.

Piazza San Pietro (there's an information office/bookshop on the south/left side of the basilica steps). © 06-69881662 or 06-69884466. Free admission to church, sacristy, and crypt, 5€ ($5.75) for elevator most of the way up (4€/$4.60 on foot). Church: Apr–Sept daily 7am–7pm; Oct–Mar daily 7am–6pm. Dome: Apr–Sept daily 8am–5:45pm; Oct–Mar daily 8am–4:45pm. Crypt: Apr–Sept daily 7am–6pm; Oct–Mar daily 7am–5pm. Treasury: Apr–Sept daily 9am–6:45pm; Oct–Mar daily 9am–5:15pm. Metro: Ottaviano–San Pietro. Bus: 23, 32, 34, 46, 51, 62, 64, 81, 98, 492, 881, 982, 990.

Musei Vaticani (Vatican Museums) & Cappella Sistina (Sistine Chapel)
The Vatican harbors one of the world's greatest museum complexes, a series of some 12 collections and apartments whose highlights include Michelangelo's incomparable Sistine Chapel and the Raphael Rooms. It would be impossible to try to see it all in 1 day—a complete tour, including every nook and cranny in the collection, would cover a whopping 14km (8⅔ miles)! It's a good idea to get up extra early and be at the monumental museum entrance before it opens—30 minutes before in summer—or be prepared to wait behind a dozen busloads of tourists.

There are **four color-coded itineraries** you can follow, depending on your interests and time constraints. Plan A takes about 90 minutes—it shuttles you through the Raphael Rooms to the Sistine—and plan D takes upward of 5 hours and hits most of the highlights. To any tour, add 30 to 45 minutes for waiting in lines.

Note: My suggestion for the best *short* visit (2½ hr. total) is that before you hop on the plan A route, head to the right when you get to the end of the awning-covered corridor to run quickly (20–30 min.) through the *pinacoteca* (picture gallery), which isn't included on the short itinerary but really should be.

PINACOTECA (PICTURE GALLERY) 🎨🎨🎨   One of the top painting galleries in Rome shelters Giotto's *Stefaneschi Triptych* (1320), Perugino's *Madonna and Child with Saints* (1496), Leonardo da Vinci's unfinished *St. Jerome* (1482), Guido Reni's *Crucifixion of St. Peter* (1605), and Caravaggio's *Deposition from the Cross* (1604), alongside works from Simone Martini, Pietro Lorenzetti, Fra Angelico, Filippo Lippi, Melozzo da Forlì, Pinturicchio, Bellini, Titian, Veronese, and Il Guercino.

But the most famous name here is Raphael, the subject of room VIII, where you'll find his *Coronation of the Virgin* (1503) and *Madonna of Foligno* (1511) surrounded by the Flemish-woven tapestries executed to the master's designs. In the center of the room hangs Raphael's last and greatest masterpiece, *Transfiguration* 🎨 (1520). This 4m (13-ft.) study in color and light was discovered almost finished in the artist's studio when he died suddenly at age 37, and mourners carried it through the streets of Rome during his funeral procession.

STANZE DI RAFFAELLO (RAPHAEL ROOMS) 🎨🎨🎨   Pope Julius II didn't like his predecessor's digs (the Borgia Apartments, see below), so in 1508— a few months after commissioning Michelangelo to paint the ceiling of the Sistine Chapel—Julius hired Raphael to decorate these new chambers. As Raphael's fame and commissions grew, he turned more of his attention away from this job and let his assistants handle much of the painting in the first and last rooms you visit. But in the restored Stanza della Segnatura and Stanza di Eliodoro (the first two actually painted), the master's brush was busy. Note that the order in which you visit the rooms is also occasionally rearranged.

The first room, the **Stanza dell'Incendio,** was actually the third one painted (1514–17); it was done during the reign of Pope Leo X (also a Raphael fan), which explains why the frescoes detail exploits of previous popes named Leo. The best is the *Borgo Fire,* which swept the Vatican neighborhood in A.D. 847 and was extinguished only when Pope Leo IV hurled a blessing at it from his window in the background. The setting, though, is classical, showing Aeneas carrying his jaundiced father, Anchises, and leading his son, Ascanius, as they escape the fall of Troy (eventually, according to Virgil in *The Aeneid,* Aeneas will make it to the village started by Romulus and found the city of Rome). Though pupils like Giulio Romano painted most of the fresco, some experts see the master's hand at work in the surprised woman carrying a jug on her head and possibly in the Aeneas group.

The second room is perhaps the highlight, the **Stanza della Segnatura** 🎨🎨 (1508–11), containing Raphael's famous *School of Athens.* This mythical gathering of the philosophers from across the ages is also a catalog of the Renaissance, with many philosophers actually bearing portraits of Raphael's greatest fellow artists, including his mentor, the architect Bramante (on the right as balding Euclid, bent over while drawing on a chalkboard), Leonardo da Vinci (as Plato, the bearded patriarch in the center pointing heavenward), and Raphael himself (looking out from the lower-right corner next to his white-robed buddy Il Sodoma). In the midst of painting this masterpiece, Raphael took a sneak peek at what his rival Michelangelo was painting on the ceiling down the hall and was so impressed he returned to the *School of Athens* and added a sulking portrait of

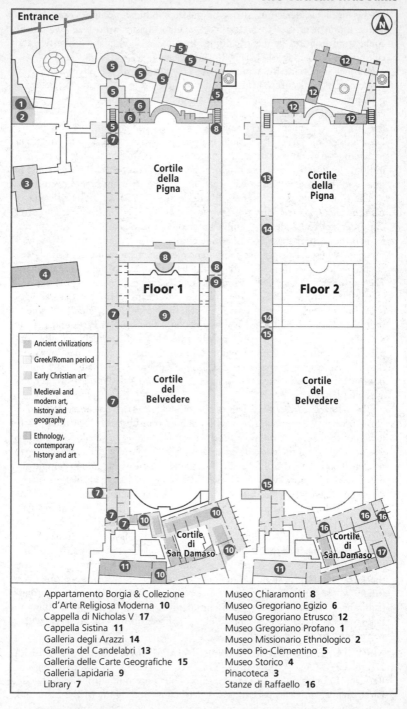

Entrance

Cortile della Pigna

Cortile della Pigna

Floor 1

Floor 2

Cortile del Belvedere

Cortile del Belvedere

Cortile di San Damaso

Cortile di San Damaso

Ancient civilizations

Greek/Roman period

Early Christian art

Medieval and modern art, history and geography

Ethnology, contemporary history and art

Michelangelo (as Heraclitus) sitting on the steps in his stonecutter's boots. It was a true moment of growth for the cocky young master, who realized even he could learn from the genius of another (in fact, he soon adapted his style and color palate, reflecting Michelangelo's influence).

Another important fresco here is the **Disputation of the Sacrament**, with three more portraits. Toward the middle of the right side, half hidden behind a golden-robed church dignitary, stands a dour man in red with a laurel-leaf crown—the poet Dante, whose *Inferno* revolutionized Italian literature by using the Tuscan vernacular rather than Latin (though Sicilians dispute this point). Look also on the far left for a pious man in black with just a wisp of white hair remaining—it's a portrait of the monastic painter Fra Angelico, whose great work in Rome lies just beyond these rooms. Bramante (again) bends over the railing in front and thumps a book (probably arguing some finer point of architecture).

The third room is the **Stanza di Eliodoro** ✿ (1510–14). The title fresco, **Heliodorous Expelled from the Temple**, shows the king's lackey trying to carry out orders to steal a Hebrew temple's sacred objects; a heavenly knight appears to help the faithful chase him off while a time-traveling Pope Julius II—a warrior pope whose battle against church enemies this fresco is metaphorically celebrating—looks on from his litter to the left. There's also the darkly dramatic **Freeing of St. Peter from Prison**, a Renaissance example of using "special effects" (the angel's brilliant glow would be enhanced by the natural light streaming through the window below). Another scene shows Pope Leo I (bearing Julius II's face) calling forth the armed and floating Sts. Peter and Paul in A.D. 452 to scare off a marauding Attila the Hun—the miracle actually happened at Mantua, but Raphael painted a Roman aqueduct and the Colosseum into the background! Pudgy-faced Cardinal Giovanni de' Medici, a Raphael patron and soon-to-be successor to Julius as Pope Leo X, looks on from his horse at the far left.

The Miracle of Bolsena depicts the origin (1264) of the feast of Corpus Christi, when a Bohemian priest who doubted transubstantiation (the miraculous transformation of the wafer and wine into the body and blood of Christ) was saying Mass in the town of Bolsena and the Eucharist wafer suddenly began to drip blood onto the altar cloth. Attending the scene at the lower right are members of the papal Swiss Guards; this detail provided some of the historic evidence on which the guards' current retro-Renaissance outfits are based.

The fourth room, the **Sala di Constantino** (1517–24), is the least satisfying, having largely been painted after Raphael's death, according to his hastily sketched designs. Giulio Romano and Rafaellino del Colle adapted some of their master's cartoons into the newly fashionable Mannerist style of painting. They probably did most of the **Battle at the Milvian Bridge** (Emperor Constantine the Great fights his would-be deposer, Maxentius), the **Vision of the Cross** (under whose miraculous sign the emperor wins), and the **Donation of Rome** (the now-converted Emperor Constantine gives princely power over Rome to Pope Silvester I), while a less apt pupil of Raphael's finished off the cycle with a weak **Baptism of Constantine.**

APPARTAMENTO BORGIA (BORGIA APARTMENTS) & CAPPELLA DE NICHOLAS V (CHAPEL OF NICHOLAS V)   After visiting the Raphael Rooms' Sala di Constantino, you pop out into the **Sala dei Chiaroscuro,** with a 16th-century wooden ceiling bearing the Medici arms and, in the corner, a little doorway many people miss and most tour groups skip.

Their loss. Through this doorway is the Vatican's most gorgeous hidden corner, the closet-size **Chapel of Nicholas V** ⍟ (1447–49), colorfully frescoed floor-to-ceiling with early Renaissance Tuscan genius by that devout little monk of a painter, Fra Angelico.

The **Borgia Apartments** downstairs from the Raphael Rooms were occupied by the infamous Spanish Borgia Pope Alexander VI and are now hung with bland pieces of modern art. But the walls and ceilings retain their rich frescoes, painted by Pinturicchio with early Renaissance Umbrian fantasy. A co-pupil of Raphael's under master Perugino, Pinturicchio had a penchant for embedding fake jewels and things like metal saddle studs in his frescoes rather than painting these details in. And while his art is not necessarily at its top form in these rooms, it's worth a look. From here you can climb back up and head straight to the Sistine Chapel or continue downstairs to visit the Modern Art Museum first.

MUSEO PIO CLEMENTINO (PIO-CLEMENTINO MUSEUM) ⍟   This is the best of the Vatican's ancient Greek and Roman sculpture collections. In the octagonal Belvedere Courtyard (Cortile del Belvedere)—the original core of the Vatican museums—you'll find the famed Laocoön group, a 1st-century B.C. tangle of a man and his two sons losing a struggle with giant snakes (their fate for warning the Trojans about the Greeks' tricky wooden horse), and the Apollo Belvedere, an ancient Roman copy of a 4th-century B.C. Greek original that for centuries continued to define the ideal male body (as late as the baroque era, a young Bernini was basing his own Apollo in the Galleria Borghese on this one). In the long Room of the Muses, you'll find the muscular Belvedere Torso, a 1st-century B.C. fragment of another Hercules statue that Renaissance artists like Michelangelo studied to learn how the ancients captured the human physique.

CAPPELLA SISTINA (SISTINE CHAPEL) ⍟⍟⍟   The pinnacle of Renaissance painting and Michelangelo's masterpiece covers the ceiling and altar wall of the **Sistine Chapel,** the grand hall where the College of Cardinals meets to elect a new pope. Photography and talking are not allowed (which is why tour groups clog the long Hall of Maps and Hall of Tapestries leading here as their guides discuss what they're about to see).

Pope Sixtus IV had the Sistine's walls frescoed with scenes from the lives of Moses (left wall) and Jesus (right wall) by the greatest early Renaissance masters: Botticelli, Perugino, Ghirlandaio, Pinturicchio, Roselli, and Signorelli. Each of these works would be considered a masterpiece in its own right if they weren't literally overshadowed by the ceiling. Pope Julius II had hired Michelangelo to craft a grand tomb for him (see the listing for St. Peter in Chains, later in this chapter), but then pulled the sculptor off the job and asked him instead to decorate the chapel ceiling—which at that time was done in the standard Heavens motif, dark blue with large gold stars. Michelangelo complained that he was a sculptor and not a painter of frescoes, but a papal commission can't be rebuffed.

Luckily for the world, Michelangelo was too much of a perfectionist not to put his all into his work, even at tasks he didn't much care for. He proposed to Julius that he devise a whole fresco cycle for the ceiling rather than just paint "decorations" as the contract called for. At first, Michelangelo worked with assistants, as was the custom, but soon he found that he wasn't a good team player and fired them all. So, grumbling and irritable and working solo, he spent 1508 to 1512 daubing at the ceiling, laying on his back atop a mountain of scaffolding, craning his neck, straining his arms, wiping droplets of paint out of his eyes—and all the while with an impatient pope glaring up from below.

When the frescoes were finally unveiled, it was clear they had been well worth the wait. Michelangelo had turned the barrel-vaulted ceiling into a veritable blueprint for the further development of Renaissance art, inventing new ways to depict the human body, new designs for arranging scenes, and new uses of light, form, and color that would be embraced by several generations of painters.

The scenes along the middle of the ceiling are taken from the Book of Genesis and tell the stories of Creation (the first six panels) and of Noah (the last three panels, which were actually painted first and with the help of assistants). In thematic order, they are: **Separation of Light from Darkness; Creation of the Sun, Moon, and Planets** (scandalous for showing God's butt and the dirty soles of his feet); **Separation of the Waters from the Land;** the fingers-almost-touching artistic icon of the **Creation of Adam** ⊛; **Creation of Eve; Temptation and Expulsion from the Garden** (notice how the idealized Adam and Eve in paradise become hideous and haggard as they're booted out of Eden); **Sacrifice of Noah; Flood;** and **Drunkenness of Noah.**

These scenes are bracketed by a painted false architecture to create a sense of deep space (the ceiling is actually nearly flat), festooned with chubby cherubs and 20 *ignudi,* nude male figures reaching and stretching, twisting and turning their bodies to show off their straining muscles and male physiques—Michelangelo's favorite theme. Where the slight curve of the ceiling meets the walls, interrupted by pointed lunettes, Michelangelo ringed the ceiling with Old Testament prophets and ancient Sibyls (sacred fortunetellers of the classical age in whose cryptic prophecies medieval and Renaissance theologians liked to believe they found foretellings of the coming of Christ). The triangular lunettes contain less impressive frescoes of the ancestors of Christ, and the wider spandrels in each corner depict Old Testament scenes of salvation.

In 1535, at age 60, Michelangelo was called back in to paint the entire end wall with a **Last Judgment** ⊛⊛⊛, a masterwork of color, despair, and psychology completed in 1541. The aging master carried on the medieval tradition of representing saints holding the instruments of their martyrdom—St. Catherine carries a section of the spiked wheel with which she was tortured and executed, and St. Sebastian clutches some arrows. Look for St. Bartholomew holding his own skin and the knife used to flay it off. St. Bart's face (actually a portrait of poet Pietro Aretino) doesn't match that of the one on the skin that he holds in his hand—which is supposed to, of course, be the same as his own face. Many hold that the almost terminally morose face shown on the skin he holds in his hand is a psychological self-portrait of sorts by Michelangelo, known to be a sulky, difficult character (and most likely a severe manic-depressive). The master was getting old, barbarians had sacked Rome a few years earlier, and both he and the city were undergoing religious crises—not to mention that Michelangelo was weary after years of dealing with the whims of the church and the various popes who were his patrons.

In the lower-right corner is a political practical joke—a figure portrayed as Minos, Master of Hell, but in reality a portrait of Biagio di Cesena, Master of Ceremonies to the pope and a Vatican bigwig who protested violently against Michelangelo's painting all the shameless nudes here (though some of the figures were partially clothed, the majority of the masses were originally naked). As the earlier Tuscan genius Dante had done to his political enemies in his poetic masterpiece *Inferno,* Michelangelo put Cesena into his own vision of Hell, giving him jackass ears and painting in a serpent eternally biting off his testicles. Furious, Cesena demanded that the pope order the artist to paint his face out, to which Pope Paul III reportedly said, "I might have released you from Purgatory, but over Hell I have no power."

Twenty-three years and several popes later, the voices of prudence (in the form of Pope Pius IV) got their way, and one of Michelangelo's protégés, Daniele da Volterra, was brought in—under protest—to paint bits of cloth draped over the objectionable bits of the nude figures. These loincloths stayed modestly in place until many were removed during the politically charged cleaning from 1980 to 1994, which also removed centuries of dirt and smoke stains from the frescoes. Some critics claim that Michelangelo himself painted some of the cloths on after he was done and that too many were removed; others wanted all the added draperies stripped from the work. It seems that the compromise, with the majority of figures staying clothed but a few bare bottoms uncovered, pleased nobody. In addition, the techniques used and the amount of grime—and possibly paint—taken off are bones of contention among art historians.

One thing is for certain. Since the restorations of both the ceiling and the *Last Judgment,* Michelangelo's colors just pop off the wall in warm yellows, bright oranges, soft flesh tones, and rich greens set against stark white or brilliant azure backgrounds. Many still prefer the dramatic, broodingly somber and muddled tones of the precleaning period. For all the controversy, the revelations provided by the cleanings have forced artists and art historians to reevaluate everything they thought they knew about Michelangelo's palette, his technique, his painterly skills, and his art.

OTHER VATICAN COLLECTIONS   The Vatican has many more museums; it would take months to go through them all. Among them are good collections of **Egyptian, Etruscan, paleo-Christian,** and **ancient Roman artifacts,** including the **Museo Gregoriano Profano (Gregorian Museum of Pagan Antiquities),** with a fantastic floor mosaic from an ancient Roman dining room "littered" with banquet leftovers.

The **Collezione d'Arte Religiosa Moderna (Collection of Modern Religious Art)** features papal robes designed by Matisse, while the **Pontificio Museo Missionario-Etnologico (Ethnological Museum)** covers 3,000 years of history across all continents (the Chinese section is particularly good). There's also a 2-hour foot-and-bus tour of the 16th-century **Giardini Vaticani (Vatican Gardens).** Book this a day or two in advance at the Vatican Information Office to the left of St. Peter's entrance (℃ **06-69884466** or 06-69884866). Visits generally run Monday, Tuesday, and Thursday through Saturday at 10am; tickets are 12€ ($14).

Viale Vaticano (on the north side of the Vatican City walls, between where V. Santamaura and the V. Tunisi staircase hit Vle. Vaticano; about a 5- to 10-min. walk around the walls from St. Peter's). ℃ **06-69883333.** www.vatican.va or www.christusrex.org/www1/vaticano/0-Musei.html. Admission 12€ ($14) adults, 8€ ($9.20) students under 26 and kids under 14. Free (but maddeningly crowded) last Sun of each month. Mar–Oct Mon–Fri 8:45am–2:20pm; Nov–Feb Mon–Sat and last Sun of month 8:45–12:20pm. Last admission 75 min. before closing. Closed Jan 1, Feb 11, Mar 19, Easter Monday, May 1, June 29, Aug 15–16, Nov 1, Dec 25–26, and many other religious holidays. Bus: 49 (or tram 19, 23, 32, 49, 51, 64, 81, 492, 907, 982, 990, 991). Metro: Ottaviano–San Pietro.

Ancient Rome Then and Now

To appreciate the Roman Forum, the Colosseum, and other ruins more fully, buy a copy of the small red book called *Rome Past and Present* (Vision Publications), sold in bookstores or on stands near the Forum. Its plastic overleaves show you how things looked 2,000 years ago.

And the Ship Sails On

New York has the Circle Line and Paris its boat rides on the Seine, and Istanbul is famous for its cruises up the Bosphorus. So it just didn't seem right for Rome's Tiber to go unnavigated. In 2003, Rome began hour-long guided **trips along the Tiber River** (© **06-6789361**; www.battel lidiroma.it), as well as day trips by boat to Ostia Antica. The short tours do get you off your feet for a spell, but the imposing levee walls block most of the riverfront property, so it's better to save up for a cruise during the romantic, flood-lit evening hours. One-hour cruises leave from Ponte Sant'Angelo and travel the section of the Tiber between the Tiber Island and Ponte Rinascimento (10€/$12; boats leave at 10am, 11:30am, 3:30pm, and 5pm); summer evening cruises depart from Ponte Sant'Angelo at 9pm. The day trip to Ostia Antica (11€/$13) leaves Ponte Marconi at 9:15am for the 2-hour cruise; the return boat leaves Ostia at 1:30pm.

Castel Sant'Angelo *Kids*   Hadrian's massive brick cylindrical tomb was transformed in the Middle Ages into Rome's greatest castle, serving triple duty as a papal military stronghold, a prison, and a place of torture (it's still connected to the Vatican by a raised brick viaduct that allowed the pope movement between the two). The castle takes its name from a miracle that occurred during the plague of 590: According to legend, the apparition of an angel in a symbolic stance of grace atop the mausoleum resulted in the end of the pestilence. In honor of the angel, the name of the castle was changed and the crowning statue was placed atop the structure.

Today, beyond Hadrian's burial chamber and the original 2nd-century brick-walled spiraling ramp, the castle is a museum with a hodgepodge of exhibits. The collections range from 16th-century ceiling frescoes to a small arms and armor museum covering everything from a 6th-century B.C. Etruscan gladiator's helmet to an officer's uniform from 1900, with some deadly swords, daggers, spears, guns, pikes, halberds, and the likes in between. The castle is slowly being transformed into a space for temporary exhibits, but it's worth a peek for the wonderful views of the Tiber and the statue-lined Ponte Sant'Angelo from the ramparts.

Lungotevere Castello. © 06-6819111. Admission 5€ ($5.75) adults, free for those under 18 and over 60. Tues–Fri and Sun 9am–7pm; Sat 9am–8pm (check for extended hours). Closed 2nd and 4th Tues of each month. Bus: 34, 49, 80, 87, 280, 492, 990. Metro: Lepanto.

THE FORUM, COLOSSEUM & BEST OF ANCIENT ROME

Foro Romano (Roman Forum) *Kids*   Slung between the Palatine and Capitoline hills, the Forum was the cradle of the Roman Republic, a low spot whose buildings and streets became the epicenter of the ancient world. It takes a healthy imagination to turn what are now dusty chunks of architrave jumbled on the ground, crumbling arches, and a few shakily re-erected columns into the glory of ancient Rome, but this archaeological zone is amazing nonetheless. You could wander through in an hour or two, but many people spend 4 or 5 hours and pack a picnic lunch to eat on the Palatine. It gets hot and dusty in August, so visit in the cool morning, wear a brimmed hat and sunscreen, and bring bottled water.

The Roman Forum & Environs

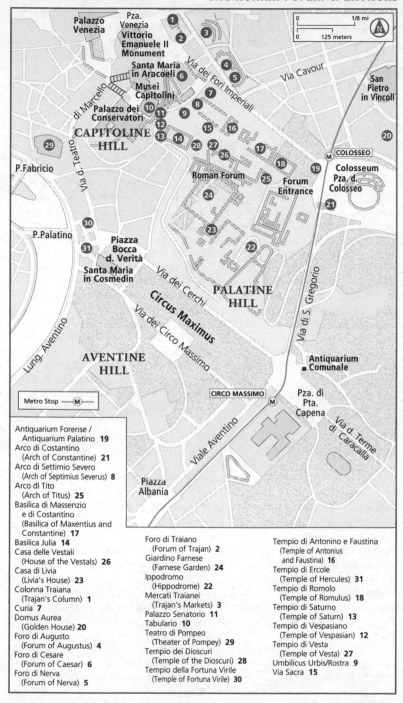

0 _____ 1/8 mi
0 _____ 125 meters

Palazzo Venezia
Pza. Venezia
Vittorio Emanuele II Monument
Santa Maria in Aracoeli
Musei Capitolini
Palazzo dei Conservatori
CAPITOLINE HILL
P.Fabricio
Via d. Teatro di Marcello
Via dei Fori Imperiali
Via Cavour
San Pietro in Vincoli
COLOSSEO
Roman Forum
Forum Entrance
Colosseum
Pza. d. Colosseo
P.Palatino
Piazza Bocca d. Verità
Santa Maria in Cosmedin
Via dei Cerchi
Circus Maximus
Via dei Circo Massimo
PALATINE HILL
Via di S. Gregorio
Lung. Aventino
AVENTINE HILL
Metro Stop —— M
CIRCO MASSIMO
Pza. di Pta. Capena
Antiquarium Comunale
Via d. Terme di Caracalla
Piazza Albania
Viale Aventino

The early Etruscan kings drained this swampy lowland, and under Republican rule it became the heart of the city, a public "forum" of temples, administrative halls, orators' podiums, markets, and law courts. Standing ranks of columns here and there mark the sites of once-important temples and buildings. Much of it means little to those of us who aren't fresh from a class in ancient history, so I'll highlight a few of the more visually spectacular sights.

At the entrance to Via Sacra ("Holy Way," down which triumphal military parades and imperial processions marched) at Piazza del Colosseo is the **Arco di Costantino (Arch of Constantine),** one of the largest of Rome's ancient triumphal arches, celebrating Emperor Constantine the Great's A.D. 312 victory over Maxentius at the Milvian Bridge. Though the arch's reliefs were primarily pirated from earlier sites and make no mention of the battle itself, it was perhaps one of the most significant of all ancient Rome's wars. It was during this battle that the emperor asked for a sign from the gods and in reply had a vision of a cross. After winning, Constantine dutifully converted himself—and then the entire Roman Empire—to Christianity.

At the top of Via Sacra is the second great surviving triumphal arch, the A.D. 81 **Arco di Tito (Arch of Titus)** 𝕽𝕽, on which one relief depicts the carrying off of treasures from Jerusalem's temple—look closely to see a menorah among the booty. This arch glorifies the war that ended with the expulsion of Jews from the colonized Judea, signaling the beginning of the Jewish Diaspora throughout Europe. From here, you can enter and climb the only part of the Forum archaeological zone that still charges admission, the **Palatine Hill** (see below). To continue in the free area, turn right at the arch, climbing between some overgrown ruins and medieval additions under the shade trees, then head left to enter the massive brick remains and coffered ceilings of the 4th-century **Basilica di Costantino e di Massenzio (Basilica of Constantine and Maxentius)** 𝕽. These were Rome's public law courts, and their architectural style was adopted by early Christians for their houses of worship (the reason so many ancient churches are called basilicas).

At the time of this writing, the area of the basilica was fenced in, so you may have to backtrack a bit, heading down the dirt ramp straight into the main artery of the Forum. Just beyond on your left is the partially reconstructed 3rd- to 4th-century **Casa delle Vestali (House of the Vestals)** 𝕽, against the south side of the grounds. This was home to the consecrated young women, selected between ages 6 and 10 from patrician families to serve as priestesses for 30 years, who tended the sacred flame in the Temple of Vesta. During their tenure, the Vestal Virgins were among Rome's most venerated citizens, with unique powers like the ability to pardon condemned criminals. The cult of the goddess Vesta was quite serious about the "virgin" part of the job description: If any of Vesta's servants were found to have "misplaced" their virginity, the miscreant was summarily buried alive. (Her amorous accomplice was merely flogged to death.) A similar fate awaited her if the sacred eternal flame went out on her watch. The overgrown rectangle of their gardens has lilied goldfish ponds and is lined with heavily worn broken statues of senior Vestals on pedestals (and, at any given time when the guards aren't looking, two to six visitors posing as Vestal Virgins on the empty pedestals). Just beyond is a bit of curving wall that marks the site of the little round **Tempio di Vesta (Temple of Vesta),** rebuilt several times after fires started by the sacred flame housed within.

Opposite (don't worry, we'll circle back) is a medieval church grafted onto and above the **Tempio di Antonino e Faustina (Temple of Antonius and**

Faustina), the eight columns still standing free of the church fabric at the top of some steps (it was built in A.D. 141 by Antonius Pius in honor of his late wife, Faustina). Continue toward the arch. Just before it on your right is Julius Caesar's large brick **Curia** ⚘, the main seat of the Roman Senate and remarkably well preserved (partly from being transformed in the Middle Ages into a church; if it's unlocked, pop inside to see the marble-inlaid floor, a 3rd-century original).

The A.D. 203 triumphal **Arco di Settimio Severo (Arch of Septimius Severus)** ⚘⚘ displays time-bitten reliefs of the emperor's victories in what are today Iran and Iraq. During the Middle Ages, when Rome was forced to cede to its wealthier rival, Constantinople, the city became a provincial backwater, and frequent flooding of the nearby river helped rapidly bury most of the Forum. This former center of the empire became, of all things, a cow pasture. Some bits of it did still stick out aboveground, including the top half of this arch, which was used to shelter a barbershop! It wasn't until the 19th century that people became interested in excavating these ancient ruins to see what Rome in its glory must once have been like.

Just to the left of the arch are the remains of a cylindrical lump of rock with some marble steps curving off it. That round stone was the **Umbilicus Urbus,** considered the center of Rome and of the entire empire, and the curving steps were the **Imperial Rostra,** where great orators and legislators stood to speak and the people gathered to listen. Against the back of the Capitoline Hill—the modern building of which is raised on a foundation of the ancient **Tabularium,** where the ancients stored their State Archives—you'll see the much-photographed trio of fluted columns with Corinthian capitals supporting a bit of architrave to form the corner of the **Tempio di Vespasiano (Temple of Vespasian).**

Start heading to your left toward the eight standing Ionic columns comprising the front and corners to the 42 B.C. **Tempio di Saturno (Temple of Saturn),** which housed the first treasury of Republican Rome. It was also where one of the city's biggest annual blowout festivals took place—the December 17 feast of Saturnalia. After a bit of tweaking, we now celebrate this as Christmas. Here you turn left to start heading back east, walking along the Forum's southern side past the worn steps and stumps of brick pillars (19th-c. reconstructions) that outline the enormous **Basilica Julia,** built by Julius Caesar. Past it are three standing Corinthian columns of the **Tempio dei Dioscuri (Temple of the Dioscuri),** dedicated to the original Gemini twins, Castor and Pollux. Actually, these identical twin gods were part of a fraternal triplet, all born out of the divine egg laid by Leda after Zeus disguised himself as a swan and impregnated her. Who was the other triplet? Helen of Troy, a woman so beautiful the ancient Greeks went to war with the Trojans over her.

Via dei Fori Imperiali (across from the end of V. Cavour), or Via delle Foro Romano (just south of the Campidoglio). ℂ **06-6990110.** Free admission (only for Forum area; see Palatine listing below). Daily 9am to 1 hr. before sunset. Metro: Colosseo. Bus: 60, 63, 75, 81, 84, 85, 87, 117, 160, 175, 186, 628, 673, 810, 850.

Palatino (Palatine Hill) & Museo Palatino (Palatine Museum) ⚘   The

Palatine Hill was where Rome began as a tiny Latin village (supposedly founded by Romulus) in the 8th century B.C. Later it was covered with the palaces of patrician families and early emperors. Today it's a tree-shaded hilltop of gardens and fragments of ancient villas that few visitors bothered to climb even before there was an admission charge. So it can make for a romantic, scenic escape from the crowds, a place where you can wander across the grassy floors of ancient palaces and peer down the gated passageways that were once the homes of Rome's rich and famous.

Tips Saving Money

Several money-saving combination tickets are available for visiting the major sights around Rome. The **7-day museum card** for 9€ ($10) offers admission to all National Museum sites: the Palazzo Altemps, Palazzo Massimo alle Terme, Crypta Balbi, and Terme di Diocleziano (including the Octagonal Hall). The 7-day archaeological card, which costs 20€ ($23), is good for admission to all of the above, plus the Colosseum, the Palatine Hill, the Baths of Caracalla, and three sites not covered in this guide (Villa dei Quintili, Tomb of Cecilia Metella, and Crypta Balbi). The two cards are also good for discounts of 1€ ($1.15) on guided visits to the sites and 1.50€ ($1.70) on the rental of cassette audioguides. Tickets can be purchased at any of the sites listed on each card. Also keep your eyes peeled for permutations.

In 1998, the **Museo Palatino** (at the back of the gardens; follow the main cobbled ramp straight up the hill) finally reopened after 13 years, displaying an excellent collection of Roman sculpture and finds from the ongoing digs in the Palatine villas. In summer, there are daily guided tours in English (see above); call in winter to see if they're still running. If you ask the museum's custodian, he may take you to one of the nearby locked villas and let you in for a peek at surviving frescoes and stuccoes.

From the Palatine's southern flank, you can look out over the long grassy oval that was the **Circo Massimo (Circus Maximus),** where Ben-Hur types used to race chariots (now mainly used by joggers and dog walkers).

Main entrance inside the Roman Forum (above); 2nd entrance at Via di San Gregorio 30. ℭ **06-6990110.** Admission to the Palatine 8€ ($9.20), includes entry into the Colosseum. Hours same as Forum's (see above); museum closes 80 min. earlier. Metro: Colosseo. Bus: Same as for Forum.

Colosseo (Colosseum) 𝄐𝄐𝄐 This wide, majestic oval is the world's most famous sports arena, even though it's been well over 1,500 years since gladiators fought each other to the death and condemned prisoners were thrown to the lions. Since then, the most impressive aspect of the Colosseum has been viewing it from afar, admiring that unmistakable silhouette, symbol of Rome itself, as you walk up Via dei Fori Imperiali (see the front cover of this guide). The Colosseum fell into disuse as the empire waned, earthquakes caused considerable damage, and later generations used its stones and marble as a quarry rich in precut building materials. The scavenging came to an end during the tenure of Pope Benedict XIV, whose conservationist streak led him to consecrate the Colosseum to the passion of Jesus, honoring it as a site of Christian martyrdom.

Started in A.D. 70 on the filled-in site of one of Nero's artificial fish ponds (see the entry for the Golden House below), this grand amphitheater was the "bread and circus" of the Roman Empire. Architecturally, the Colosseum is a poster child for classical order, built of three levels of arcades whose niches were once filled with statues and whose columns became more ornate with each level, following the Greek order of Doric, Ionic, and Corinthian, respectively. A plainer fourth level supported an apparatus of pulleys, beams, and canvas that created a retractable roof, winched out by a specially trained troupe of sailors to shade the seats from sun and rain (Astrodome, eat your heart out). This arena of blood and gore could amuse 50,000 at a time—the inaugural contest in A.D. 80 lasted 100 days and killed off 5,000 beasts and countless gladiators. These contests eventually drove to extinction several creatures, including the Middle Eastern lion and North African elephant.

As for man-to-man (or woman) combat, professional gladiators were young men who, either poor or ruined, slaves or criminals, were lured by the promise of prize riches to sell themselves into a kind of slavery to the trainers and lead brutish, dangerous lives. If a gladiator was seriously but not mortally wounded, he stretched out on the ground and raised his left arm for mercy. The victor then decided his opponent's fate; however, whenever the emperor was around, he made the call, giving us gestures that we still use today—the thumbs-up (spare the man) and thumbs-down (finish him off). The only release from gladiatorial life was death in the ring or the granting by the emperor of the *rudis,* a wooden sword that signaled a dignified, well-earned retirement from the games.

The Colosseum has now become the turnstile for Rome's largest traffic circle, around which thousands of cars whip daily, spewing exhaust all over this venerable monument. Preparation for the 2000 Papal Jubilee set an international team of archaeologists to work to reconstruct a portion of the wood floor, a section that once covered the long-exposed skeleton of underground passages that served as the green room for a cast of characters. A 2-year restoration of the Colosseum completed in 2003 opened up an additional 65% of the monument to visitors, including a subterranean corridor that served as a passageway for gladiators and animals. The excavation of a second corridor known as Commodus's Passage reveals newly exposed plaster carvings and mosaics. In addition, classical Greek tragedies have brought the drama back to the arena. The stage will remain so future events, barring rock concerts, can keep the aged monument alive.

Piazza del Colosseo. © 06-7004261. Admission 8€ ($9.20), includes entrance to the Palatine. Daily 9am to 1 hr. before sunset. Metro: Colosseo. Bus: 30, 75, 85, 87, 117, 175, 186, 673, 810, 850.

Domus Aurea (Nero's Golden House) ★★

After 20 years of excavations, one of the most monumental discoveries of ancient Rome is open. The Domus Aurea, built on Nero's orders in A.D. 64, following the famous fire that leveled Rome, displayed a megalomania and an excessiveness that bordered on the grotesque. The opulent palace (most notable for its preponderance of gold) and grounds comprised an area of almost 80 hectares (198 acres) that included the Palatine, Celio, Oppio, and Esquiline hills, an area of woods, pastures, vineyards, and even a lake. But Nero's clock was ticking and so was that of the palace: A year after his death, Vespasian, to reverse the injustices done during the previous "year of three emperors," began to restore the grounds to the people. The lake was drained to support the foundations of the Flavian Amphitheater, known today as the Colosseum. The palace survived only until A.D. 104, when its rooms were stripped of all their ornamentation and filled in with tons of dirt, providing a solid foundation for the Baths of Trajan. It was probably this act that permitted the palace to survive somewhat intact. The site was rediscovered in the 15th century, when passersby fell through the ceiling of the pavilion (this opening is seen on the tour). The discovery of such a wealth of frescoes resulted in the diffusion of the style called "the art of the grotesque," and 200 years later, the most famous names in Renaissance art (Pinturicchio, Raphael, Ghirlandaio, and so on) found their way here to check out the works.

The 45-minute tours depart every 15 minutes (it's best to reserve at the number below). Bring a sweater, as the site, now submerged and more like a cave, maintains a constantly chilly temperature (53°F/12°C in summer; 39°F/4°C in winter). The tour includes only 32 chambers, with most of the 150 identified rooms still buried, unreachable, or being restored. Lacking the gold, ivory, marble, and jewels that once adorned it, the structure is a shadow of what it once was, with bare arches, fragments of mosaics, and faded frescoes, but the visit nevertheless is an eye-opener. Highlights include the **Case Repubblicane (Republican House Rooms)**, with its tract of mosaic flooring in an unusual but regular rhomboidal design; the **Ninfeo di Ulisse e Polifemo (Nimphaeum of Ulysses and Polyphemus)**, named for the partially damaged mosaic on the ceiling; and the **Sala di Achille a Skyros (Hall of Achilles and Skyros)**, one of two symmetrical rooms flanking the Sala Ottagona (see below) and containing the only completely conserved painting in the pavilion. The tour ends at the **Sala Ottagona (Octagonal Hall)**, remarkable not only for its architectural uniqueness (in those days, rooms were generally rectangular), but also for its dome, which becomes hemispheric near the oculus in deference to the room's measurements.

Via della Domus Aurea, on the Esquiline Hill. ✆ 06-39967700 (advanced booking necessary). Admission 5€ ($5.75). Audio tour 3€ ($3.45), guided tour by appointment 6€ ($6.90). Tues–Sun 9am–7:45pm. Ticket sales end 1 hr. earlier. Metro: Colosseo. Bus: 30, 85, 87, 117, 186, 810, 850.

Fori Imperiali (Imperial Forums) ⚅ With the growth of late Republican Rome into the great metropolis of the empire, the burgeoning population began to crowd the Roman Forum's public buildings and temples. A succession of leaders and emperors, starting with Julius Caesar, began building new forums and markets east of the original Forum in ambitious bouts of urban expansion that provided for the populace, curried favor with the elite, and improved the city infrastructure all at the same time. Demolitions and concrete reconstructions of these Imperial Forums began in full force during the reign of the House of Savoie, but the Fascists had other ideas, bulldozing Via dei Fori Imperiali right down the center of the most significant, if not the largest, open-air museum in the world. Today visitors, accompanied by guides (who do little more than operate the sound system), make their way through the labyrinth of excavations, past archaeologists who'll be kept busy for years to come. The tour lasts about an hour.

The **Foro di Cesare (Forum of Caesar)** is the only one on the west side of Via dei Fori Imperiali, tucked between the huge Vittorio Emanuele Monument, the Capitoline, and the Roman Forum. It was the first of these new *fori,* begun by Julius Caesar in 54 B.C. and completed by Augustus after Julius's death. The popular general (with his eye on the dictatorship) used the money he'd made during his successful Gaulish wars to buy up all the private property flanking the Roman Forum, tear down the houses, and build public temples and markets in their stead. The three standing Corinthian columns were part of his Temple to Venus Genetrix, a goddess from whom Caesar claimed direct descent through Rome's legendary founder, Aeneas.

The first major forum on your right is the **Foro di Augusto (Forum of Augusto)**. The stairs and column stumps in the center once belonged to the 2nd-century B.C. Temple of Mars Ultor. Richly decorated, this square temple was lined with statues of *summi veri,* the imperial figures of Roman history, and ongoing excavations have uncovered depictions of the families of Caesar and Augustus. The only thing left of the public square and formal gardens of the **Foro di Vespasiano (Forum of Vespasian)**, begun by the emperor after the capture of Jerusalem in A.D. 71 and dedicated 4 years later after the fall of Masada, are the remains of the **Tempio della Pace (Temple of Peace)**. Pliny considered this temple, built by Vespasian to inaugurate an era of protracted peace, one of Rome's three most beautiful buildings. It contained treasures stripped from the

Temple of Jerusalem and art from the Domus Aurea (see above), gathered by Nero from all over the empire.

Not much more than the ancient two-story houses are left of the **Foro di Nerva (Forum of Nerva)**, begun by Domitian and inaugurated by Nerva in A.D. 97. The **Tempio di Minerva (Temple of Minerva)** was demolished in the 16th century (some decorative items survived) under the orders of Pope Paul V, who used the stones to build the Acqua Paola fountain on the Janiculum and the Borghese Chapel in Santa Maria Maggiore.

More dramatic is the last set of ruins, **Mercato di Traiano (Trajan's Market)** and **Foro di Traiano (Trajan's Forum)**. Of the five imperial *fori* unearthed here, Trajan's is the grandest and most remarkable because of the massive covered market he had built at its flank in the 2nd century. It consisted of over 100 shops built on three levels, a grand bazaar lined with stalls boasting marble porticos and barrel-vaulted ceilings. What's left are some fragments and sculptural bits, but a few have remarkably sharp and well-preserved detailing. Climb up to the top terrace for a bird's-eye panorama and explore the four stories of 150 empty *tabernae* (shops) that made up the world's first multilevel shopping mall. This site is also marked by several rows of re-erected columns that comprised the central part of the huge Basilica Ulpia, Rome's largest basilican law courts.

Behind them rises the area's most stunning sight, the 29m (95-ft.) **Colonna Traiana (Trajan's Column)** ✸, topped by a 16th-century statue of St. Peter. Around the column wraps a cartoon strip of deep bas-relief carvings that would measure 198m (649 ft.) if stretched out; it uses a cast of 2,500 to tell the story of Trajan's victorious A.D. 101 to 106 campaigns to subdue the Dacians. A spiral staircase inside leads to the top (closed), and the emperor's ashes were kept in a golden urn entombed at the base. Recent excavations have uncovered countless pieces of ornamented porticos and two colossal white marble **statues of Dacian prisoners** in a good state of preservation (casts of the carvings are kept at the Museo della Civiltà Romana).

Via IV Novembre 94. Ⓒ **06-6790048.** Admission 6.20€ ($7.15) adults, 3.10€ ($3.55) students, free for those under 18 and over 60. Summer Tues–Sun 9am–6:30pm; winter Mon–Sun 9am–4:30pm. Bus: H, 60, 63, 64, 70, 117, 170, 640.

Pantheon ✸✸   "Simple, erect, severe, austere, sublime." That's the poet Lord Byron groping for words to capture the magic of Rome's best-preserved ancient building, a "pantheon," or temple to all the gods. An architectural achievement like no other, the temple was built by Emperor Hadrian (an accomplished architect) in the early 2nd century, drawing on his advanced engineering skills to create a mathematically exacting and gravity-defying space inside. (Hadrian constructed the Pantheon over a temple erected by Marcus Agrippa but modestly kept the dedicatory inscription from Agrippa on the architrave of the porch's pediment.)

The **bronze entrance doors**—1,800-year-old originals—weigh 20 tons each. The rotunda is circular and the **coffered ceiling** a perfect half-sphere of a dome, with a 5.4m (17-ft.) **oculus** (eye) in the center (this is the only source of light, and it lets in rain in inclement weather). The dome is 43m (141 ft.) across and the building 43m (141 ft.) high—if you could find a soccer ball big enough, it would fit perfectly in this space. An engineering marvel such as this remained unduplicated until the Renaissance, and it was only relatively recently that Hadrian's secret was revealed. The roof is made of poured concrete (a Roman invention) composed of light pumice stone, and the weight of it doesn't bear down but is distributed by brick arches embedded sideways into the walls and channeled into a ring of tension around the lip of the oculus. It also helps that the walls are 7.5m (25 ft.) thick. The decoration is spare (its niches once contained white marble statues of Roman gods) but includes the **tombs** of Italy's short-lived 19th-century monarchical dynasty (three kings total, though only two are here, Vittorio Emanuele II and Umberto I) and the tomb of the great painter Raphael.

The Pantheon has survived the ages because it was left alone by the barbarians, who recognized its beauty, and by overzealous temple-destroying Christians, who reconsecrated it as a church in 609. Later Christians weren't as charitable. When Pope Urban VIII, a prince of the Barberini family, removed the bronze tiles from the portico and melted them down to make 80 cannons and St. Peter's baldacchino, it prompted one wit to quip, "What even the barbarians wouldn't do, Barberini did." The Pantheon is now a church dedicated to Santa Maria ad Martyres (St. Mary of the Martyrs)—every year on Pentecost, the 50th day after Easter, hundreds of thousands of red rose petals are dropped through the oculus, commemorating the descent of the Holy Spirit in the form of tongues of fire.

Piazza della Rotonda. Ⓒ **06-68300230.** Free admission. Mon–Sat 8:30am–7:30pm; Sun 8:30am–6:30pm. Bus: 8, 46, 62, 63, 64, 70, 81, 87, 116, 116T, 186, 492, 628, 640, 810.

ATTRACTIONS NEAR ANCIENT ROME
Musei Capitolini (Capitoline Museums) & Capitolino (Capitoline Hill) 🏛🏛
The **Capitoline Hill,** behind Piazza Venezia's Vittorio Emanuele Monument, has been the administrative seat of Rome's civic government since the 11th century and was a venerated spot used for the highest state occasions in Republican Rome. The trapezoidal **Piazza del Campidoglio** at its top, reached by a long set of low, sloping steps meant to accommodate carriages, was laid out by an elderly Michelangelo, who also designed the palace facades on its three sides. It's one of Rome's most unified open spaces and a prime example of High Renaissance ideals in aesthetics, architecture, and spatial geometry. At the square's center is a 2nd-century bronze equestrian statue of Marcus Aurelius, his outstretched hand seeming to bless the city (this is a copy; the original is in the Palazzo Nuovo). During restoration of a 1920 addition built by Mussolini, excavators uncovered the most famous temple of ancient Rome, the **Tempio di Giove (Temple of Jupiter).** The discovery of this 6th-century B.C. temple opened up a can of worms, exposing artifacts (like tombs of children) dating from the 16th century B.C. and shedding light on the origins of the Capitoline Hill.

The central **Palazzo Senatorio** houses the mayor's office, and the side palaces house the **Capitoline Museums,** the world's oldest collection of public art, occupying two buildings. On the left is the **Palazzo Nuovo,** filled with ancient sculpture like the *Dying Gaul,* busts of ancient philosophers, the *Mosaic of the Doves,* and the original statue of Marcus Aurelius (the regilded bronze had been tossed into the Tiber, and when Christians later fished it out, they thought it was Constantine the Great, the first Christian emperor, a misinterpretation that saved it from being hacked to pieces). On the right is the **Palazzo dei Conservatori,** whose entrance is to the left of a courtyard filled with the oversize marble head, hands, foot, arm, and kneecap of what was once a 12m (39-ft.) statue of Constantine II. The collections have their share of antique statuary, including the *Resting Faun,* a Roman sculpture that inspired Nathaniel Hawthorne's 19th-century novel *The Marble Faun;* in the gallery for temporary exhibits is the celebrated 6th-century B.C. Etruscan bronze *She-Wolf,* with the suckling **Romulus and Remus,** added in the 16th century, displayed in the adjoining room. The picture gallery is impressive, with works by Guercino, Veronese, Titian, Rubens, Cortona, and Caravaggio—standouts are the *Gypsy Fortune Teller*

A Tip to a View

Standing on Piazza del Campidoglio, walk around the right side of the Palazzo Senatorio to a terrace overlooking the city's best panorama of the Roman Forum, with the Palatine Hill and the Colosseum as a backdrop. Return to the square and walk around the left side of the Palazzo Senatorio to where you'll find a stair winding down past the Forum wall, passing close by the upper half of the Arch of Septimius Severus—a nifty little back door.

and the scandalously erotic *St. John the Baptist,* where the nubile young saint twists to embrace a ram and looks out at us coquettishly.

The Palazzo dei Conservatori and the Palazzo Nuovo are connected via the **Tabularium,** a subterranean gallery that as early as the 1st century B.C. was used as a warehouse for the archiving of hundreds of thousands of public records (tablets). Notice the partially excavated Temple of Venus, and don't miss the spectacular sweeping views over the Forum to the Palatine and Colosseum.

Piazza del Campidoglio (behind Piazza Venezia's Vittorio Emanuele Monument). ℂ **06-67102071** or 06-39746221. Admission 6.20€ ($7.15), or 7.80€ ($8.95) during special exhibitions. Tues–Sun 9:30am–8pm (in summer may stay open to 9pm; call ahead). Bus: H, 44, 46, 60, 62, 63, 64, 70, 81, 84, 87, 95, 160, 170, 186, 628, 640, 716, 780, 781, 810.

Santa Maria in Aracoeli 😿   Santa Maria in Aracoeli was old when it was first mentioned in the 7th century, but its current incarnation dates from the Franciscans in A.D. 1250. Legend holds that the Tiburtine Sibyl told Emperor Augustus that on this lofty spot would be an "altar to the first among gods," whereupon he had a vision of the heavens opening up and a woman bearing a child in her arms on the hilltop. Augustus dutifully built an *aracoeli* (Altar in the Sky) up here, but Christians later interpreted the prophecy as a reference to their God and replaced it with a church.

Past the unfinished brick facade is a slightly baroque Romanesque interior hung with chandeliers but retaining a Cosmatesque pavement and 22 mismatched columns recycled from pagan buildings. The elegant wood ceiling is carved with naval emblems and motifs to commemorate the great victory at Lepanto (1571). Donatello cast the worn tomb of Giovanni Crivelli to the right of the door, and the **first chapel** on the right was frescoed by Umbrian Renaissance master Pinturicchio. It is considered one of Pinturicchio's greatest.

To the left of the altar, with a 10th-century *Madonna d'Aracoeli* painting, is the chapel that once housed a highly venerated statue of the baby Jesus called the *Santo Bambino,* supposedly carved from an olive tree in the Garden of Gethsemane and imbued with miraculous powers to heal the sick and answer the prayers of children (the bambino spent half his time making the rounds of Rome's hospitals to visit the sickbeds of the terminally ill). The bambino received thousands of letters from around the world every year (most addressed simply "Santo Bambino, Roma"); they were left in his chapel, unopened, until they were burned so the prayers in them could waft heavenward. Roman children came to recite little speeches or sing poetry in front of the little holy statue, especially at Christmastime. Alas, the *Santo Bambino* was stolen in 1994.

Via Teatro di Marcello (up many steps, between Piazza Venezia's Vittorio Emanuele Monument and Piazza dei Campidoglio). ℂ **06-6798155.** Free admission. Daily 7am–noon and 3:30–5:30pm. Bus: 44, 46, 60, 62, 63, 64, 70, 81, 84, 87, 95, 160, 170, 186, 204F, 628, 640, 716, 780, 781, 810.

Rome Attractions

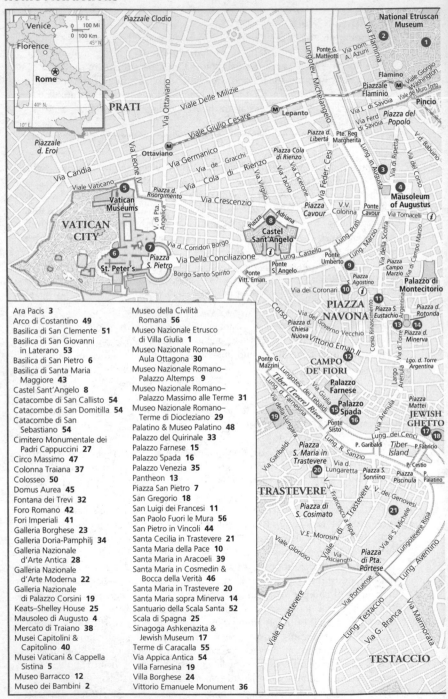

Ara Pacis **3**
Arco di Costantino **49**
Basilica di San Clemente **51**
Basilica di San Giovanni
   in Laterano **53**
Basilica di San Pietro **6**
Basilica di Santa Maria
   Maggiore **43**
Castel Sant'Angelo **8**
Catacombe di San Callisto **54**
Catacombe di San Domitilla **54**
Catacombe di San
   Sebastiano **54**
Cimitero Monumentale dei
   Padri Cappuccini **27**
Circo Massimo **47**
Colonna Traiana **37**
Colosseo **50**
Domus Aurea **45**
Fontana dei Trevi **32**
Foro Romano **42**
Fori Imperiali **41**
Galleria Borghese **23**
Galleria Doria-Pamphilj **34**
Galleria Nazionale
   d'Arte Antica **28**
Galleria Nazionale
   d'Arte Moderna **22**
Galleria Nazionale
   di Palazzo Corsini **19**
Keats–Shelley House **25**
Mausoleo di Augusto **4**
Mercato di Traiano **38**
Musei Capitolini &
   Capitolino **40**
Musei Vaticani & Cappella
   Sistina **5**
Museo Barracco **12**
Museo dei Bambini **2**

Museo della Civiltà
   Romana **56**
Museo Nazionale Etrusco
   di Villa Giulia **1**
Museo Nazionale Romano–
   Aula Ottagona **30**
Museo Nazionale Romano–
   Palazzo Altemps **9**
Museo Nazionale Romano–
   Palazzo Massimo alle Terme **31**
Museo Nazionale Romano–
   Terme di Diocleziano **29**
Palatino & Museo Palatino **48**
Palazzo del Quirinale **33**
Palazzo Farnese **15**
Palazzo Spada **16**
Palazzo Venezia **35**
Pantheon **13**
Piazza San Pietro **7**
San Gregorio **18**
San Luigi dei Francesi **11**
San Paolo Fuori le Mura **56**
San Pietro in Vincoli **44**
Santa Cecilia in Trastevere **21**
Santa Maria della Pace **10**
Santa Maria in Aracoeli **39**
Santa Maria in Cosmedin &
   Bocca della Verità **46**
Santa Maria in Trastevere **20**
Santa Maria sopra Minerva **14**
Santuario della Scala Santa **52**
Scala di Spagna **25**
Sinagoga Ashkenazita &
   Jewish Museum **17**
Terme di Caracalla **55**
Via Appica Antica **54**
Villa Farnesina **19**
Villa Borghese **24**
Vittorio Emanuele Monument **36**

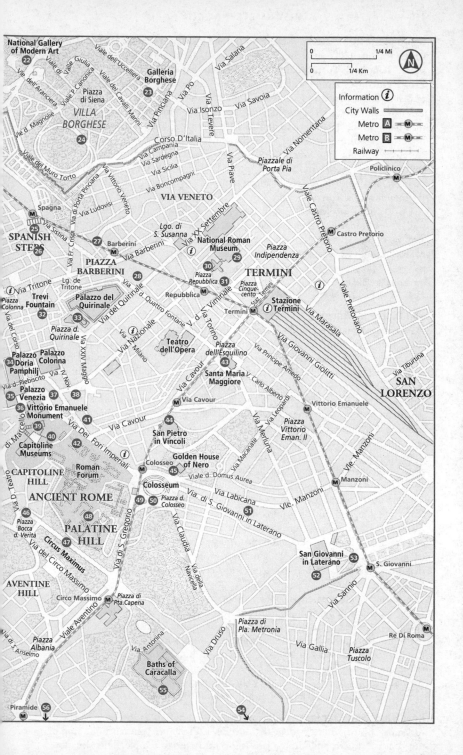

National Gallery
of Modern Art
22

Viale dell'Uccelliera

Galleria
Borghese
23

Via Salaria

Via Po

Via Isonzo

Via Savoia

Viale di Villa Giulia

Vle. dell'Aranciera

Via P. Canonica

Viale dei Cavalli Marini

Piazza
di Siena

Via Pinciana

Via Tevere

VILLA
BORGHESE

Vle di Magnolie

24

Corso D'Italia

Via Campania

Via Sardegna

Via Sicilia

Via Boncompagni

Via Nomentana

Viale del Muro Torto

Via Vittorio Veneto

Via di Porta Pinciana

Piazzale di
Porta Pia

Via Piave

Policlinico

Spagna

Via Ludovisi

VIA VENETO

Viale Castro Pretorio

Via Pretoriano

Castro Pretorio

SPANISH
STEPS
26

Via Sistina

Via Fr. Crispi

Lgo. di
S. Susanna

Via XX Settembre

National Roman
Museum
29

Piazza
Indipendenza

Castro Pretorio

Barberini
27

Via Barberini

PIAZZA
BARBERINI

28

Piazza
Repubblica
30

31

TERMINI

Via del Quirinale

Lg. de
Tritone

Palazzo del
Quirinale

Via IV Fontane

Piazza
Cinque-
cento

Via Marsala

SAN
LORENZO

Via Tritone

Trevi
Fountain
32

Piazza
Colonna

Repubblica

Via V. d. Viminale

Stazione
Termini

Via Giovanni Giolitti

Via del Corso

33

Piazza d.
Quirinale

Via Nazionale

Via Milano

Termini

Teatro
dell'Opera

Piazza
dell'Esquilino

Via Principe Amedeo

Via Tiburtina

Palazzo
Doria
Pamphilj
34

Palazzo
Colonna

Via XXIV Maggio

Via Cavour

43

Santa Maria
Maggiore

V. Carlo Alberto di

Palazzo
Venezia
35

37

38

Via IV Nov.

Via Cavour

Via Cavour

Vittorio Emanuele

Via d. Plebiscito

36

Vittorio Emanuele
Monument

41

Via Dei Fori Imperiali

44

Via Merulana

Piazza
Vittorio
Eman. II

Vle. Manzoni

Manzoni

di Marcello

39

40

42

San Pietro
in Vincoli

Viale d. Domus Aurea

Via Macanae

Via Labicana

Vle. Manzoni

Capitoline
Museums

Roman
Forum

Golden House
of Nero
45

Colosseo

Via di S. Giovanni in Laterano

CAPITOLINE
HILL

V. d. Teatro

ANCIENT ROME

49

50

Colosseum

Piazza d.
Colosseo

51

46

48

Piazza
Bocca
d. Verità

PALATINE
HILL
47

Via di S. Gregorio

Via Claudia

Via della Navicella

San Giovanni
in Laterano

53

S. Giovanni

AVENTINE
HILL

Circo Massimo

Circus Maximus

Piazza di
Pta.Capena

52

Via Sannio

Via di S. Anselmo

Piazza
Albania

Viale Aventino

Via del Circo Massimo

Via Antonina

Via Druso

Piazza di
Pla. Metronia

Via Gallia

Re Di Roma

Piazza
Tuscolo

Baths of
Caracalla
55

Piramide
56

54

Santa Maria in Cosmedin & the Bocca della Verità (Mouth of Truth) 🎯 Kids

At the Palatine Hill's western foot sit two small 2nd-century-B.C. temples—the square **Tempio di Portunus (Temple of Portunus)** and the round **Tempio di Ercole Vincitore (Temple of Hercules Victor)**, Rome's oldest marble structure—as well as **Santa Maria in Cosmedin,** with its early-12th-century bell tower and Cosmatesque floors. The church's front porch draws crowds who want to stick their hands inside the **Mouth of Truth,** a 4th-century B.C. sewer cover carved as a bearded face with a dark slot for a mouth (remember the scene with Gregory Peck and Audrey Hepburn in *Roman Holiday?*). Medieval legend holds that if you stick your hand in its mouth and tell a lie, it will clamp down on your fingers and bite them off (apparently, a priest once added some sting to this belief by hiding behind the mouth with a scorpion, dispensing justice as he saw fit).

Up Via di Teatro Marcello from the piazza out front, you can see the outer wall of what looks like a midget Colosseum with a 16th-century palace grafted atop its curve. This was actually the model for the Colosseum, the **Teatro di Marcello,** built by Augustus in 11 B.C. and dedicated to his nephew Marcellus.

Piazza Bocca della Verità 18. 𝄐 06-6781419. Free admission. Church daily 9am–1pm and 3–6pm; portico (containing Mouth of Truth) daily 9am–5pm (in summer, portico gates sometimes open as late as 8pm). Bus: 23, 44, 80, 81, 95, 160, 170, 280, 628, 715, 716, 780, 781.

San Pietro in Vincoli (St. Peter in Chains) 🎯

Besides housing the **chains** that supposedly once bound St. Peter in prison (now on display under the altar), this 5th-century church with the Renaissance portico facade is famous for containing one of Michelangelo's greatest masterpieces—and one of his most bitter failures. In 1505, Pope Julius II commissioned Michelangelo to create for him a tomb, and the master came up with a grandiose mausoleum to be festooned with 40 statues. The pope sent the sculptor off to the mountains of Carrara to search for marble, but when Michelangelo returned, Julius set him to work painting the Sistine Chapel ceiling instead. Julius died in 1512, a few months after Michelangelo completed the ceiling.

As he doggedly tried to continue work on the tomb over the next several decades, Michelangelo kept reducing his plans as other projects took up his time and Julius's descendants squabbled over how much they'd invest in the project. The master managed to finish two *Slaves,* which now reside in the Louvre in Paris, and roughed out five more, now in Florence's Accademia alongside his *David* (see chapter 4). He also crafted one of the figures destined for the upper corners of the tomb, a muscle-bound *Moses* 🎯 with satyr horns on his head (symbolizing the holy rays of light from medieval iconography), the Commandments tablets clutched in a hand and a portrait of Michelangelo hiding in his flowing beard.

And that's pretty much all poor old Pope Julius got in the end. This (relatively) modest wall monument, with a few other niched statues, was mostly executed by Michelangelo's assistants (though the master probably had a hand in the more delicate Rachel and Leah figures flanking Moses). In a final twist of fate, this is a monument only, not a tomb. Julius himself lies buried and forgotten in an unassuming grave in a corner of the Vatican.

Piazza San Pietro in Vincoli 4 (just off the south side of V. Cavour, sort of hidden up a set of stairs and through a tunnel). 𝄐 06-4882865. Free admission. Daily 7am–12:30pm and 3:30–6pm. Metro: Cavour. Bus: 75, 84, 117.

Basilica di San Clemente 🎯

Nowhere else in this city is the layering effect of Rome's history more evident than in this 12th-century church built atop a 4th-century church built atop a late-2nd-century pagan temple. This situation is far from unique in Rome—almost the entire city is built directly on top of the ancient one—but what's special about San Clemente is that you can actually climb down into those lower levels to explore Rome's sandwich of history.

The **upper church**—built in 1108 and run by the convent of Irish Dominican monks who rediscovered the lower levels in the 19th century—is beautiful enough to stand out on its own. It features a **pre-Cosmatesque pavement,** an ornate **marble choir** (a 6th- to 9th-century piece from the lower church), recently restored frescoes of the *Life of St. Catherine* (1228) by Masolino and his young disciple Masaccio in the first chapel on your right, and a 12th-century *Triumph of the Cross* mosaic in the apse. This last work shows a crucified Christ in the center, with the Tree of Life growing in twisting vine tendrils all around, loaded with medieval symbolism (Christ and the apostles pose as sheep along the bottom; the rivers of paradise flow from the base of the cross from which the faithful, represented by stags, drink; doves flutter about; and the hand of God reaches down from the canopy of the heavens).

Off the right aisle is a postcard-lined passage and the entrance to the **lower church,** built in the 4th century and largely demolished by barbarian sackings in 1084. It preserves a few crude frescoes, including the *Life of St. Clement* on the wall before you enter the nave, and the *Story of St. Alexis* on the left wall of the nave. When you've had your fill of this Dark Ages church, descend another flight of stairs to the ancient pagan **Mithraic temple** and the adjacent 1st-century **Roman palazzo.** Both later churches' altars are placed directly above this pagan one to Mithras, which depicts the god sacrificing a bull. As you wander in and out of the brick vaulted rooms of the grand palazzo, you'll hear the sound of rushing water; in one room you can even take a drink from the sweet spring water gushing out of an ancient pipeline to be routed along a small aqueduct set into the wall.

Via San Giovanni in Laterano/Via Labicana 95. ℂ 06-70451018. Free admission to church, excavations 3€ ($3.45). Mon–Sat 9am–12:30pm and 3:30–6pm; Sun 10am–noon and 3:30–6pm. Bus: 85, 87, 117, 186, 204F, 810, 850. Metro: Colosseo.

Basilica di San Giovanni in Laterano (St. John Lateran) ⍟

The cathedral of Rome (St. Peter's is merely a holy basilica on Vatican property) is oddly one of the least interesting of the city's grand churches. San Giovanni in Laterano has an illustrious history. It was founded by Constantine as Rome's first Christian basilica in A.D. 314 and was the model for all Christian basilicas. In the wake of seven cycles of destruction and rebuilding (due to fires, earthquakes, barbarian invasions, or wholesale remodeling), today's basilica is primarily a Borromini construction from the 1640s (and even parts of that were destroyed and are being restored after a 1993 bombing).

The massive Alessandro Galilei facade boasts stacked porticoes with a line of colossal saints, apostles, and Christ standing along the top. The gargantuan interior (69m/226 ft. long) has a unified decorative scheme designed by Borromini and a fine medieval Cosmatesque floor. On the aisle side of the first pillar on the right is a fresco by the proto-Renaissance genius Giotto (all that survives of a series of frescoes the master painted here in the early 14th century). The scene shows Boniface VIII proclaiming the first Jubilee Holy Year on this spot in 1300. The cloisters off the left transept are a peaceful oasis amid the bustle of Rome, a quadrangle of twisting columns inlaid with Cosmati stoneworks and walls lined with fragments from earlier incarnations of this cathedral.

Piazza San Giovanni in Laterano 4. ℂ 06-69886433. Free admission to church and baptistery; cloisters and museum 2.60€ ($3). Church daily 7am–7pm; baptistery daily 9am–1pm; cloisters and museum daily 9am–6pm. Bus: 16. Tram: 30, 81, 85, 87, 117, 186, 218, 590, 650, 714, 810, 850. Metro: San Giovanni.

ATTRACTIONS NEAR PIAZZA NAVONA & THE PANTHEON

Note that this neighborhood's greatest sight, the **Pantheon,** is covered under "The Forum, Colosseum & Best of Ancient Rome," above.

Piazza Navona 𝕒𝕒𝕒   Closed to traffic, studded with fountains, lined with cafes, and filled with tourists, street performers, artists, kids playing soccer, and couples cuddling on benches, Piazza Navona is one of Rome's archetypal open spaces. It's also one of the best places to kick back and relax in the heart of the city. The piazza owes its long, skinny, round-ended shape to the **Stadium of Domitian,** which lies partially excavated underneath; one travertine entrance arch from the north curve of the stadium is visible under a bank on Piazza di Tor Sanguigna, to the north of Piazza Navona. For visits underground, contact the office for the Stadio di Domiziano, Via del Porto d'Ottavia 29 (© **06-07103819**).

The **Fontana del Moro (Fountain of the Moor),** on the piazza's south end, was designed by Giacomo della Porta (1576); the **Fontana di Nettuno (Fountain of Neptune),** at the north end, by Antonio della Bitta and Gregorio Zappalà (1878); and the soaring **Fontana dei Quattro Fiumi (Fountain of Four Rivers)** 𝕒𝕒, in the center, by Gianlorenzo Bernini (1651). This last is a roiling masterpiece of rearing mer-horses, sea serpents, and muscle-bound figures topped by an obelisk; the giant figures at the corners represent the world's four great rivers (or at least those known in the 1650s): the Danube (Europe), the bearded Ganges (Asia), the bald Plate (Americas), and the Nile (Africa, with his head shrouded since the source of the Nile was unknown at the time). Borromini's curvaceous facade of **Sant'Agnese in Agone** rises next to the fountain, and tour guides love to tell the legend that Bernini designed a slight to Borromini in the fountain's figure of Plate, rearing back and throwing his arm up in a gesture of protection against the church facade falling on him. It's true that the two architects were archrivals, but the facade was started in 1653—2 years after Bernini finished the fountain.

The stadium's tradition as a place for chariot races and games was kept alive throughout the ages with medieval jousts, Renaissance festivals, and the 17th- to 19th-century practice of flooding it on August weekends for the populace to wade in and the nobles to parade around in the shallow pools in their carriages. It was a market from 1477 to 1869, and for quite some time has hosted a Christmastime fair selling traditional crèche figurines and statues along with toys and dolls of the Christmas Witch La Befana, who traditionally brings Italian children presents on January 6.

North of Corso Vittorio Emanuele II. Bus: 46, 62, 64, 70, 81, 87, 116, 116T, 186, 204F, 492, 628.

Santa Maria sopra Minerva 𝕒𝕒   Rome's only Gothic church was built in 1280 over the site of a Temple to Minerva (hence the name "St. Mary over Minerva"). The piazza out front sports a **whimsical statue** by Bernini of a baby elephant carrying a miniature Egyptian obelisk on its back (1667). The interior was heavily restored in the 19th century and contains some masterpieces by Tuscan Renaissance artists and the bodies of important Tuscan Renaissance personalities.

The last chapel on the right retains a sumptuous cycle of **frescoes** 𝕒 by Filippino Lippi (you insert coins in a light box, and the works are briefly illuminated). In the scene of *St. Thomas Condemning the Heretics,* on the lower half of the right wall, the two boys in the group on the right are Giovanni and Giulio de' Medici. These two grew up to become Pope Leo X and Pope Clement VII, respectively, and are buried in the apse in tombs by Antonio Sangallo the Younger. St. Catherine of Siena (1347–80), a skilled theologian and diplomat whose letters and visits were instrumental in returning the papacy from Avignon to Rome, is allegedly buried under the altar (a claim also made by the monks of St. Catherine's monastery at Mount Sinai), but since the saint's martyrdom resulted in a gruesome decapitation, I can say with certainty that her head is enshrined at her home in Siena.

To the left of the altar steps is Michelangelo's *Risen Christ* ⊛ (1514–21), leaning nonchalantly on a diminutive cross (such a strong, virile, and quite naked Christ wasn't to everyone's taste, and the church later added bronze drapery to cover the Lord's loins). In a corridor to the left of the choir, behind a small fence, is the **tomb slab of Fra Angelico,** the early Renaissance master and devout monk who died in the attached convent in 1455. Pope Nicholas V, who had commissioned a Vatican chapel from the painter 10 years earlier and was touched by the little monk's piety, modesty, and skill, wrote the epitaph.

Piazza della Minerva (southeast of the Pantheon). ℂ **06-6793926.** Free admission. Daily 7am–noon and 4–7pm. Bus: 8, 46, 62, 63, 64, 70, 81, 87, 116, 116T, 186, 492, 628, 640, 810.

Galleria Doria-Pamphilj ⊛   This formerly private art collection is now open to the public, with the layout preserved and paintings displayed more or less as they were in the 19th century. Since the works are jumbled like a giant jigsaw puzzle on the dimly lit walls, you need to use the list of artists and titles handed out at the entrance to match to the numbers on the works themselves. Among masterworks by Tintoretto, Correggio, Annibale and Lodovico Carracci, Bellini, Parmigianino, Jan and Pieter Brueghel the elder, and Rubens, you'll find two stellar paintings by Caravaggio, *Mary Magdalen* and the *Rest on the Flight into Egypt,* as well as a copy he made of his *Young St. John the Baptist,* now in the Capitoline Museums. Also here are Titian's *Salome with the Head of St. John the Baptist* and Bernini's *Bust of Innocent X,* the pope whose sister-in-law started this collection.

Piazza del Collegio Romano 1A (off V. del Corso near Piazza Venezia). ℂ **06-6797323.** www.doria pamphilj.it. Admission 8€ ($9.20) adults. Gallery Fri–Wed 10am–5pm; apts Fri–Wed 10:30am–12:30pm. Closed Aug 15–31. Bus: 46, 62, 64, 70, 80, 81, 85, 87, 95, 117, 119, 160, 175, 186, 492, 628, 640, 810, 850.

Museo Nazionale Romano (National Roman Museum)—Palazzo Altemps ⊛⊛   The home of the famed Ludovisi ancient sculpture collection, this is an example of Italy's ability to craft a 21st-century museum respecting the gorgeous architecture and frescoes of the Renaissance space in which it's installed and the aesthetic and historic value of the classical collection it contains. What was once a single National Roman Museum—which languished for decades inside the Baths of Diocletian—has split up across the city in four collections: the Ludovisi, Mattei, and Altemps collections of classical statuary here; more statuary and exquisite ancient Roman mosaics, bronzes, frescoes, coins, and jewelry at the Palazzo Massimo alle Terme (later in this chapter); bathhouse art and colossal statuary in the Aula Ottagona (see later in this chapter); and artifacts relating to the foundation of Rome at the recently restored Baths of Diocletian (later in this chapter).

The 16th- to 18th-century Palazzo Altemps is gorgeous, with a grand central courtyard and many surviving frescoes and original painted wood ceilings, especially upstairs, where you can wander onto a bust-lined loggia frescoed as a "Garden of Delights" in the 1590s. Statues aren't crammed into every nook and cranny—a few choice pieces have been set in each room, encouraging you to examine each statue carefully, walk around it, and read the placard (in English and Italian) explaining its significance and showing which bits are original and which were restored in the 17th century. Seek out the 2nd-century giant *Dionysus with Satyr;* a 1st-century B.C. copy of master Greek sculptor Phidias's most famous statue (now lost), the 5th-cenutry B.C. *Athena* that once held the place of honor in Athens's Parthenon; 2nd-century B.C. Ptolemaic **Egyptian statuary;** a pair of lute-playing *Apollos;* plenty of **imperial busts;** and a 3rd-century **sarcophagus** carved from a single block of marble and depicting in incredible detail the Roman legions fighting off invading Ostrogoth Barbarians.

Piazza Sant'Apollinare 44 (2 blocks north of Piazza Navona). ℂ 06-6833759. Admission 5€ ($5.75) adults, free for those under 18 or over 60. Tues–Sat 9am–2pm; Sun 9–1pm. Bus: 70, 81, 87, 116, 116T, 186, 492, 628.

San Luigi dei Francesi 𝄢   France's national church in Rome is a must-see for Caravaggio fans: In the last chapel on the left (insert coins to operate the lights for a short time) is his famous St. Matthew cycle of paintings. These huge canvases depict *The Calling of St. Matthew* 𝄢, on the left, the best of the three and amply illustrating Caravaggio's mastery of light and shadow to create mood and drama; *The Martyrdom of St. Matthew,* on the right; and *St. Matthew and the Angel,* over the altar. Interestingly, that scene with the angel inspiring St. Matthew to write his Gospel is not the one Caravaggio originally painted for the chapel. The church objected to that version, which showed the saint as a rough, illiterate peasant, the angel directly guiding his hand as he wrote. A wise collector not affiliated with the church bought that version (now destroyed), but its legacy appears here—Matthew's stool tips over the edge of the painting, as though about to tumble onto the altar. Before you leave, check out the **Domenichino frescoes** in the second chapel on the right aisle.

Piazza San Luigi dei Francesi 5 (just east of Piazza Navona). ℂ 06-688271. Free admission. Fri–Wed 7:30am–12:30pm and 3:30–7pm; also some Thurs mornings. Bus: 70, 81, 87, 116, 186, 492, 628.

San Agostino 𝄢   Around the corner from San Luigi dei Francesi is another stop on the Caravaggio tour, the early Renaissance San Agostino. The first altar on the left contains Caravaggio's almost Mannerist *Madonna del Loreto* 𝄢, with a pair of dirty-footed pilgrims kneeling before the velvet-robed Virgin, who's carrying a ridiculously oversize (if marvelously lifelike) Christ child. The picture's beautiful but a bit weird. Against the entrance wall is a shrine to the *Madonna del Parto,* a pregnant Virgin Mary (carved by Jacopo Sansovino in 1521) surrounded by thousands of votive offerings sent in supplication, especially by women who want to ensure a safe childbirth. The third pillar on the right side has a fresco by Raphael of *Isaiah* showing the influence of Michelangelo on the young painter.

Piazza San Agostino (northeast of Piazza Navona). ℂ 06-68801962. Free admission. Mon–Sat 8am–noon and 4:30–7:30pm. Bus: 70, 81, 87, 116, 116T, 186, 204F, 492, 628.

THE SPANISH STEPS, PIAZZA DEL POPOLO & NEARBY ATTRACTIONS

Fontana dei Trevi (Trevi Fountain) 𝄢   This huge baroque confection of thrashing mer-horses, splashing water, and striding Tritons all presided over by a muscular Neptune is one of Rome's most famous sights. It was sculpted in 1762 by Nicolà Salvi to serve as an outlet for the waters carried into Rome by the 21km (13-mile) Acqua Vergine aqueduct, built in 19 B.C. and still running (it also supplies the fountains in Piazza Navona and Piazza di Spagna). Tourists and young folk just hanging out on the curving steps throng the cramped little piazza from early morning till after midnight, making it one of the most densely crowded but scenic spots to squeeze into a marble seat and people-watch.

Legend and movies like *Three Coins in the Fountain* hold that if you toss a coin into this fountain, you're guaranteed to return to the Eternal City. General weathering and the chemical damage from all those rusting coins forced the fountain's restoration in 1990, and now the monies are collected regularly and donated to the Red Cross. Some say you must lob the coin with your right hand backward over your left shoulder. Others insist you must use three coins. Historians point out the original tradition was to drink the fountain's water, but unless you like chlorine, I'd stick to tossing euros.

Piazza di Trevi, a block south of Via Tritone. Bus: 52, 53, 60, 61, 62, 71, 95, 116, 116T, 175, 492.

Scala di Spagna (Spanish Steps) ⟡⟡   The off-center yet graceful curves of the **Spanish Steps** rising from the hourglass-shape Piazza di Spagna are decorated with bright azaleas in spring and teeming with visitors, Roman teens, and poseurs year-round. This monumental baroque staircase was built by Francesco de Sanctis in the 18th century and funded almost entirely by the French to lead up to their twin-towered **Trinitá dei Monti** church—with paintings by Michelangelo protégé Daniele da Volterra and frescoes by Raphael's pupil Giulio Romano inside. (The steps are officially called the Scalinata di Trinitá dei Monti, and the piazza at the bottom is called the Spanish Square after the Spanish Embassy, which once was located nearby.) At the bottom is the beloved **Barcaccia** ("Ugly Boat") fountain, sculpted by a teenage Bernini and his father, Pietro, who together managed to solve the dilemma of low water pressure at this point in the Acqua Vergine aqueduct system by forgoing the usual dramatic sprays and jets and instead crafting a sinking boat overflowing with water.

Historically, Piazza di Spagna has been Rome's Anglo-American center. British and American artists lived or had studios (many still do) on Via Margutta (parallel to V. del Babuino), the Anglican church is just down the road, the Grand Tour's poshest hotels still huddle at the top of the steps, Italy's first McDonald's and the American Express office are just a few yards up the piazza, and flanking the steps are the British 19th-century bastions of Babington's Tea Rooms and the house where John Keats spent his final months with Joseph Severn by his side. Inside the young Romantic poet's apartment at Piazza di Spagna 26 is the **Keats-Shelley House** (② 06-6784235). It was here in 1821, with a view over the steps, that Keats died of consumption (tuberculosis) at age 25. The rooms are stuffed with mementos, letters, Keats's death mask, portraits, and around 10,000 books by Shelley, Byron, Leight Hunt, and, of course, Keats. It's open Monday through Friday from 9am to 1pm and 3 to 6pm, and Saturday from 11am to 2pm. Admission is 2.60€ ($3).

From Piazza di Spagna to Piazza Trinità dei Monti. Metro: Spagna. Bus: 116, 116T, 117.

Ara Pacis (Altar of Peace)   Augustus had this "altar" built from 13 to 9 B.C. to celebrate the peace his campaigns to unify the new Empire had brought to Europe, northern Africa, and the Near East. Since the 16th century, bits of decorative frieze have been recovered from beneath buildings lining the Corso, most making their way to collections in the Louvre, the Vatican, and the Uffizi. The bulk of the altar, however, lay under the water table, serving as the foundation for several palazzi. Mussolini, always looking for ways to link the concept of his new Fascist empire with that of ancient Rome, ordered the rest of the altar excavated in 1937. His archaeologists came up with the brilliant plan of freezing the water in the soil, building new supports for the palaces above, and extracting the chunks of marble altar before the ground thawed again.

A project to enclose the altar inside a streamlined structure designed by the architect Richard Meier is in the works, and the Ara Pacis will remain sequestered behind a construction fence until a new enclosure is erected. Completion of the project is targeted for 2006. Nearby is Augustus's Mausoleum (see below).

Via di Ripetta at Lungotevere in Augusta/Piazza Augusto Imperatore. ℂ 06-68806848 or 06-67103819. Closed for restoration at press time. Bus: 13, 81, 204F, 590, 628, 913, 926.

Mausoleo di Augusto (Augustus's Mausoleum)   Completing the Ara Pacis "complex" is Augustus's Mausoleum, a neglected brick rotunda that once housed the remains of Rome's first emperor; his family; his general, Agrippa; and every Roman emperor up to Nerva (died A.D. 98). This awesome ring of brick 86m (282 ft.) in diameter was once crowned with a dirt mound and cypress trees but has been so abused throughout the centuries—it was a fortress in the Middle Ages, then an amphitheater in the baroque era (used for cockfights and bear baiting), and finally a concert hall until 1936—we're lucky the body survives with a few plaques of the old marble still in place. The mausoleum fills up one of Rome's long-abandoned Fascist-designed piazze, although, with the opening of some chic storefronts (Armani, the Gusto enoteca and restaurant), it's clearly undergoing a Renaissance.

Piazza Augusto Imperatore. ℂ 06-67103819. Admission 2€ ($2.30). Sat–Sun 10am–1pm or by appointment. Bus: 32, 81, 628, 913, 926.

Santa Maria del Popolo 🕭   Although the first church on this site was built in 1099 to exorcise Nero's ghost from local walnut trees, the current Renaissance/baroque structure dates from the 1470s. You'll have to search out the light switches and light boxes (bring lots of coins) in the shadowy Santa Maria del Popolo, but it's worth the trouble. Many of Rome's architectural celebrities had a hand in the church's reconstruction, namely Bregno, Pinturicchio, and Pontelli, with later additions by Bramante and Bernini.

The much-restored **frescoes** in the first chapel on the right are by the Umbrian early Renaissance master Pinturicchio (who also did the vault frescoes in the apse). Duck behind the altar to see the coffered shell-motif **apse**—one of Bramante's earliest works in Rome (flip on the lights at the box to your left). Sansovino carved the **Tomb of Sforza** and **Tomb of Girolamo Basso** (1505–07) here, combining classical triumphal arches with surprising sarcophagal depictions of the deceased; these Renaissance cardinals recline comfortably on cushions, only half asleep, without the lying-in-state look of medieval tombs. Set higher in the walls are Rome's first **stained-glass windows,** commissioned in 1509 from the supreme French master Guillaume de Marcillat.

In the first transept chapel to the left of the altar is a juxtaposition of rival baroque masters Annibale Carracci and Caravaggio. Crowd-pleasing Annibale was more popular in his day, as the highly modeled colorful ballet of his *Assumption of the Virgin* in the center suggests, but posterity has paid more attention to the moody chiaroscuro of Caravaggio's tensely dramatic original style. He used overly strong and patently artificial light sources to enhance the psychological drama of *The Conversion of St. Paul* and *The Crucifixion of St. Peter* and to draw you right into the straining muscles, wrinkled foreheads, dirty feet, and intense emotions of his figures.

When banking mogul Agostino Chigi commissioned his favorite artist, Raphael, to design a memorial chapel tomb for him, he had no idea he'd need it so soon. Both patron and artist died in 1520, by which time Raphael had barely begun construction on the pyramid-shape tombs of Agostino and his brother for the second-on-the-left **Cappella Chigi (Chigi Chapel).** Pope Alexander VII later hired others to complete the ceiling mosaics to Raphael's designs, with God in the center of the dome seeming to bless Agostino's personal horoscope symbols, surrounding him. Lorenzetto carved the smoother-bodied statues of Jonah and Elijah to match Raphael's sketches, but Bernini stuck to his own detailed style to depict Habakkuk with the angel and Daniel getting his foot licked by a bemused-looking lion. (Actually, Bernini is telling a Bible story; the angel is about to carry Habakkuk and his picnic basket across the chapel to feed Daniel, starving in the lion's den.) The altarpiece is by Sebastiano del Piombo and the macabre flying skeleton in the floor by Bernini.

Piazza del Popolo 12 (at the Porta del Popolo). ℭ **06-3610836.** Free admission. Mon–Sat 7am–noon and 4–7pm; Sun 8am–2pm and 4:30–7:30pm. Metro: Flaminio. Bus: 88, 95, 117, 119, 225, 490, 495, 628, 926.

Galleria Borghese *⚜⚜⚜*   Reopened in 1997 after a 14-year restoration, this small museum packs a punch and is an absolute must-see. The ticket reservation policy is annoying, but in summer the museum can be sold out for days, so try to book at least a day before (earlier, if possible). You'll spend 45 to 90 minutes wandering around this frescoed 1613 villa admiring the classical statues and mosaics, Renaissance paintings, and fabulous marble sculptures of the baroque, with frequent stops to return your lower jaw to its rightful position. Most of these compelling pieces were acquired by the villa's original owner, Cardinal Scipione Borghese, who bought Caravaggio's works when no one else wanted them.

The entrance to the **Pinacoteca (Picture Gallery)** is inside the villa (to the left of the exterior grand staircase) on an upper floor, accessible via two flights of a circular stairs. The 30-minute limit puts the pressure on, but if you rent the audio-cassette guide, you'll breeze through with no trouble. Here you'll find most of the painting collection, featuring a humbling lineup of Italian Renaissance masters like Andrea del Sarto, Perugino, Ghirlandaio, Fra Bartolomeo, Lorenzo di Credi, Antonella Messina, Pinturicchio, and Corregio. Just when you think the lineup will end, a masterful 1507 *Deposition* by the young Raphael or a *Madonna col Bambino e San Giovannino* by Botticelli appears. The foreign schools have their representation as well, and it's not difficult to spot a Titian, Dürer, or Rubens.

Exit the gallery and villa, circle the building (you may want to stop in the new cafe near the baggage check), and head up the grand staircase to gain access to the **sculpture gallery** *⚜*. The main room is a temple to ancient Rome—indeed, looking around, you'll understand why all the great archaeological sites are empty. The best stuff is here. Roman mosaics cover the floor, with depictions of gladiators and scenes of the hunt, while several alarmingly large busts stand watch. Beginning counterclockwise, enter the room to the left, where you'll find five Caravaggios, including the powerful *Madonna of the Serpent,* aka *Madonna dei Palafrenieri* (1605); the *Young Bacchus, Ill* (1653), the earliest surviving Caravaggio, said to be a self-portrait from when the painter had malaria; and *David with the Head of Goliath* (1610), in which Goliath may be another self-portrait. The Egyptian room contains objects brought back by Napoleon; notice the pyramids in the ceiling fresco and the female figure—representative of the gift of life and of the Nile, whose water sustains all life in Egypt.

Four rooms are each devoted to an early masterpiece by the baroque's greatest genius, Gianlorenzo Bernini. His *Aeneas and Anchises* (1613) was done at age 15 with the help of his father, Pietro; and the *Rape of Persephone* (1621) is a powerful narration in marble. Also here is *Apollo and Daphne* *⚜* (1624), in which the 26-year-old sculptor captures the moment the nymph's toes take root and her fingers and hair sprout leaves as her river god father transforms her into a laurel tree to help her escape from a Cupid-struck Apollo. Bernini's vibrant *David* ✦ (1623–24) is a baroque answer to Michelangelo's Renaissance take on the subject in Florence's Accademia. Michelangelo's *David* is pensive, all about proportion and philosophy. Bernini's *David* is a man of action, his body twisted as he's about to let fly the stone from his sling. Bernini modeled the furrowed brow and bitten lip of *David's* face on his own.

The grand finale is in the last room: a deceptive masterpiece in gleaming white marble. Neoclassical master Canova's sculpted portrait of Napoleon's notorious sister **Pauline Bonaparte as Venus** ✦ (1805) reclining on a couch was quite the scandal in its time. When asked whether she wasn't uncomfortable posing half-naked like that, Pauline reportedly responded, "Oh, no—the studio was quite warm." (It's ironic that this sculpture is one of the gallery's stars— Pauline Bonaparte married Prince Camillo Borghese in 1807 and sold many of the pieces of the original collection.)

Northeast corner of Villa Borghese park, off Via Pinciana. ✆ 06-328101 or www.ticketeria.it for mandatory ticket reservations, 06-8417645 for main desk. Admission 6.50€ ($7.45), free for those under 18 or over 65. 2€ ($2.30) mandatory booking fee. Summer Tues–Sat 9am–10pm, Sun 9am–8pm; winter Tues–Sun 9am–7pm. Metro: Spagna. Bus: 52, 53, 116, 910.

Museo Nazionale Etrusco di Villa Giulia (Etruscan Museum) ✦

Housed in a 16th-century Mannerist villa built for Pope Julius III by Ammanati, Vasari, and Vignola, this museum is dedicated to the Etruscans, who may have immigrated to Italy from Turkey in the 9th century B.C. They were the peninsula's first great culture, concentrated in what are today the provinces of Tuscany, Umbria, and the north half of Lazio (Rome's province). The height of their power as an association of loosely organized city-states was from the 7th to 5th centuries B.C., when their Tarquin dynasty even ruled Rome as its first kings. Etruscan society is a mystery to us since what little we know of it comes down mainly through vases and funerary art (it's hard to reconstruct an entire culture based solely on its cemeteries). But from what we can gather, they enjoyed a highly developed society, had a great deal of equality between the sexes, and appreciated the finer things in life, like banqueting, theater, and art.

This museum houses the most important Etruscan collection in Italy, unrivaled by anything even in Tuscany. The greatest piece is the touching and remarkably skilled 6th-century B.C. terra-cotta **Sarcophagus of Newlyweds** ✦ from nearby Cerveteri, whose lid carries full-size likenesses of a husband and wife sitting down to their eternal banquet. Also look for the 4th-century B.C. **Ficoroni Cist,** a bronze marriage coffer richly engraved with tales of the Argonauts; and a large painted terra-cotta statue of *Apollo* ✦ (ca. 500 B.C.), which once topped a temple to Minerva at Veio. The Castellani collection of ancient jewelry spans Minoan civilization through the Hellenistic and Roman eras, and includes some Asian pieces as well. But what strikes most visitors about the Villa Giulia are the kilometers upon kilometers of **pots,** from native pre-Etruscan styles through the Etruscan and Greek eras to the Roman one, many beautifully painted. Be sure to seek out the **Faliscan Krater,** with a scene of Dawn riding her chariot across the sky, and the early 7th-century B.C. **Chigi Vase,** showing hunting scenes and the Judgment of Paris.

Piazzale di Villa Giulia (on Vle. delle Belle Arti, in the northern reaches of Villa Borghese park). ✆ 06-3226571. Admission 4€ ($4.60) adults, 2€ ($2.30) ages 18–26, free for those under 18 or over 65. Tues–Sun 8:30am–7:30pm. Metro: Flaminio. Bus: 19, 30, 225, 628, 926.

Galleria Nazionale d'Arte Moderna (National Gallery of Modern Art) ⋆

In the heart of Villa Borghese, Rome's main modern art gallery concentrates on late-19th- and early-20th-century European and Italian art. There's Art Nouveau by Galileo Chini, futurism by Gino Severini, and *macchaioli* (a Tuscan variant on Impressionism) by Giovanni Fattori and Silvestro Lega. Assorted foreign schools are represented by Klimt, Duchamp, Mondrian, Cézanne, Degas, van Gogh, Modigliani, Goya, Ingres, Gauguin, Whistler, and Münch.

Viale delle Belle Arti 131 (in the Villa Borghese park). ℭ 06-322981. Admission 6.50€ ($7.45) adults. Tues–Sat 8:30am–7:30pm; Sun and holidays 8:30am–8pm (sometimes closes 2pm in winter). Bus: 225, 628, 926. Tram: 3, 19.Metro: Flaminio.

THE CATACOMBS OF THE APPIAN WAY

The arrow-straight **Via Appia Antica** was the first of Rome's great consular roads, completed as far as Capua by 312 B.C. and soon after extended the full 370km (229 miles) all the way to Brindisi in Apulia, the heel of Italy's boot. Its initial stretch in Rome is lined with ancient tombs of Roman families—burials were forbidden within the city walls as early as the 5th century B.C.—and, beneath the surface, kilometers of tunnels hewn out of the soft tufa stone.

These tunnels, or **catacombs,** were where early Christians buried their dead and, during the worst times of persecution, held church services discreetly out of the public eye. A few are open to the public, so you can wander through kilometer after kilometer of musty-smelling tunnels whose soft walls are gouged out with tens of thousands of burial niches—long shelves made for two to three bodies each. The requisite guided tours, hosted by priests and monks, feature a smidgen of extremely biased history and a large helping of sermonizing.

Via Appia Antica has been a popular **Sunday picnic site** for Roman families following the half-forgotten pagan tradition of dining in the presence of one's ancestors on holy days. This practice was rapidly dying out in the face of the traffic fumes that were choking the venerable road, but a 1990s initiative closed Via Appia Antica to cars on Sundays, bringing back the picnickers and bicyclists—along with in-line skaters and a new Sunday-only bus route to get out there.

You can take bus no. 218 from the San Giovanni Metro stop, which follows Via Appia Antica for a bit, then veers right onto Via Ardeatina at the Domine Quo Vadis church. After another long block, the no. 218 stops at Largo M. F. Ardeatine, near the gate to the San Callisto catacombs. From there, you can walk right on Via delle Sette Chiese to the San Domitilla catacombs or left down Via delle Sette Chiese to the San Sebastiano catacombs. Another option is to ride the Metro to the Colli Albani stop and catch bus no. 660, which wraps up Via Appia Antica from the south, veering off at the San Sebastiano catacombs. (If you're visiting all three, you can take the no. 218 to the first two, walk to the San Sebastiano, and then catch the no. 660 back to the Metro stop at Colli Albani.) On Sundays, bus no. 760F works its way from the Circo Massimo Metro stop down Via Appia Antica, turning around after it passes the Tomb of Cecilia Metella.

Alternatively, **Archeobus** (ℭ 06-46952252; **www.trambus.com/ ArcheoBus.htm**) will get you there and back for 7.75€ ($8.90) as part of its hop-on/hop-off service, which leaves from Piazza dei Cinquecento outside Termini, sidewalk C, hourly from 9:45am–4:45pm (extended hours in summer), and stops at various places of interest along the way, including Piazza Bocca della Verità, Circo Massimo, Viale Terme di Caracalla, and the catacombs. Return buses run back to Piazza Venezia beginning at 10:04pm until the last bus back at 8:04pm. Tickets are valid for the entire day and can be purchased on board the bus.

Catacombe di San Sebastiano (Catacombs of St. Sebastian) *Kids*

Though the tunnels run for 10km (6¼ miles) and the venerable bones of Sts. Peter and Paul were once hidden here for safekeeping, the St. Sebastian tour is one of the shortest and least satisfying of all the catacombs visits. The highlight is a chance to see a few well-preserved Roman (not Christian) tombs from what used to be an aboveground necropolis adjacent to the catacombs. Since this pagan graveyard was buried for centuries, the stucco decorations on the ceilings and frescoes inside were almost perfectly preserved.

Via Appia Antica 136. © 06-7850350 or 06-7887035. Admission 5€ ($5.75) adults. Mon–Sat 8:30am–noon and 2:30–5pm (until 5:30pm in summer). Closed Nov 10–Dec 10. Bus: See above.

Catacombe di San Callisto (Catacombs of St. Callixtus) *Kids*

These catacombs have the biggest parking lot and thus the largest crowds of tour bus groups—as well as the cheesiest, most Disneyesque tour, full of canned commentary and stilted jokes. Some of the tunnels, however, are phenomenal, 21m (69 ft.) high and less than 1.8m (6 ft.) wide, with elongated tomb niches pigeonholed all the way up to the top. Of all the catacombs, these are among the oldest and certainly the largest (19km/12 miles of tunnels covering more than 13 hectares/32 acres and five levels housing the remains of half a million Christians) and were the final resting place of 16 early popes. You also get to ogle some of the earliest Christian art—frescoes, carvings, and drawings scratched into the rock depicting ancient Christian symbols like the fish, anchor, and dove and images telling some of the earliest popular Bible stories.

Via Appia Antica 110. © 06-51301580 or 06-5136725. www.catacombe.roma.it. Admission 5€ ($5.75) adults. Thurs–Tues 8:30am–noon and 2:30–5pm (until 5:30pm in summer). Closed Feb. Bus: 660 from Colli Albani Metro stop to Via Appia Antica, or 218 from San Giovanni Metro stop to Largo M. F. Ardeatine, then walk.

Catacombe di San Domitilla (Catacombs of St. Domitilla) *Kids*

This oldest of the catacombs is the winner for the most enjoyable experience. The groups are small, most guides are entertaining and personable, and (depending on your group and guide) the visit may last 20 minutes or over an hour. You enter through a sunken 4th-century church. There are fewer "sights" here than in the other catacombs—though the 2nd-century fresco of *The Last Supper* is impressive—but some guides actually hand you bones out of a tomb niche so you can rearticulate an ancient Christian hip. (Incidentally, this is the only catacomb where you'll get to see bones; the tombs in the rest of the catacombs have been emptied and the remains reburied on the inaccessible lower levels.)

Via delle Sette Chiese 283. © 06-5110342. www.catacombe.roma.it. Admission 5€ ($5.75) adults. Wed–Mon 8:30am–noon and 2:30–5pm (until 5:30 in summer). Closed Jan. Bus: 218 from San Giovanni Metro stop to Largo M. F. Ardeatine, then walk.

MORE ATTRACTIONS
AROUND VIA VENETO & PIAZZA BARBERINI

Cimitero Monumentale dei Padri Cappuccini (Capuchin Crypt) *Kids*

The Capuchins are monks with a death wish—or, depending on how you look at it, with a healthy attitude toward their own mortality. They're a weird lot, very polite but with a penchant for making mosaics out of the bones of their brethren. That's what happened in the crypt of this church, where five chambers were filled between 1528 and 1870 with mosaics made from over 4,000 dearly departed Cappuccini (first dried out by temporary burial in the floors filled with dirt from Jerusalem). These fantastic displays form morbid patterns and baroque decorative details, from rings of knucklebones and garlands of pelvises to walls made from stacked skulls and scapulae used to create butterflies or hourglasses in an all-too-fitting *memento mori* motif. A few bodies lean against the walls in varying states of desiccated decay, and the full skeletons of two Barberini princelings adorn the last chamber, near a placard that drives home the ashes-to-ashes point in several languages, "WHAT YOU ARE, WE USED TO BE. WHAT WE ARE, YOU WILL BECOME."

Note: At press time, the Capuchin Crypt was closed for restorations and was not scheduled to reopen until March 2005. Call ahead before you go.

In Santa Maria Immacolata Concezione, Via Veneto 27. ℭ 06-4871185. Donation of 1€ ($1.15) expected. Fri–Wed 9am–noon and 3–6pm. Metro: Barberini. Bus: 52, 53, 60, 61, 62, 95, 116, 116T.

Galleria Nazionale d'Arte Antica (National Gallery of Ancient Art)

When a Barberini was finally made pope (Urban VIII) in 1624, the fabulously wealthy family celebrated by hiring Carlo Maderno to build them a huge palace, which Borromini and Bernini later embellished with window frames and doorways. Since 1949, Palazzo Barberini has housed half of Rome's National Gallery of paintings, works that span the 13th to the 17th centuries (the other half is in Trastevere's Palazzo Corsini; see later in this chapter).

The masterpieces are numerous, but while you're admiring the paintings hung on the walls, don't fail to look up at the ceilings, many of which were decorated by one of the masters of Roman baroque frescoes, Pietro da Cortona. Keep an eye out especially for the Great Hall, where Pietro frescoed his masterpiece, the allegorical *Triumph of Divine Providence* ⊛ (1633–39). It celebrates the Barberini dynasty in a sumptuously busy but masterful *trompe-l'oeil* space open to the heavens, with the Barberini bees swarming up to greet Divine Providence herself, who's being crowned by Immortality (most baroque pontiffs weren't known for their modesty).

As for the works on the walls, you'll pass icons of art like Filippo Lippi's *Annunciation* and *Madonna and Child;* Andrea del Sarto's *Holy Family;* Peruzzi's *Ceres;* Bronzino's *Portrait of Stefano Colonna;* Guido Reni's *Portrait of a Lady* believed to be Beatrice Cenci (condemned for murdering her father); and three Caravaggios, *Narcissus,* an action-packed gory *Judith Beheading Holofernes,* and an attributed *St. Francis in Meditation.* But the star painting has to be Raphael's bare-breasted *Fornarina* ⊛, a racy portrait of the artist's girlfriend, a baker's daughter named Margherita. Some critics claim it's actually a painting of a courtesan by Raphael's pupil Giulio Romano, but this wouldn't explain why the lass wears an armband bearing Raphael's name. Other great artists here are Filippino Lippi, Sodoma, Beccafumi, El Greco, Tintoretto, Titian, Paul Brill, and Luca Giordano.

Via Barberini 18. ℭ 06-4824184. Admission 5€ ($5.75) adults. Tues–Sat 9am–7pm; Sun 9am–1pm. Metro: Barberini. Bus: 52, 53, 60, 61, 62, 95, 116, 116T, 175, 492.

NEAR STAZIONE TERMINI

Basilica di Santa Maria Maggiore ⊛   This is the greatest and by far the best preserved of Rome's four basilicas, marking the city skyline with Rome's tallest bell tower, a graceful 14th-century addition. The main facade is a baroque mask that uses arcades and loggias to partially hide the fantastic mosaic of the earlier facade (1294–1308). Often you can climb stairs to view these mosaics up close, like scenes recounting the legend that this basilica was founded in the 350s by Pope Liberius, who, one night in August, had a vision of the Madonna telling him to raise the church on the spot and rebuild along an outline that would be demarcated by a miraculous snowfall the next morning. Every August 5, a special Mass takes place, with the snowfall beautifully reenacted using pale flower petals.

The basilica's basic design and decor have been preserved from the 6th century. The gargantuan space is some 85m (278 ft.) long, a dark, echoing environment suited to religious pilgrimages. The glowing coffered ceiling was the work of Giuliano da Sangallo, said to be gold-leafed using the very first gold brought back from the Americas by Columbus (a gift from Ferdinand and Isabella to the pope). The floor was inlaid with marble chips in geometric patterns by the Cosmati around 1150, while the mosaics lining the nave and covering the triumphal arch before the altar are glittering testaments to the skill of 5th-century craftsmen (the apse's *Coronation of the Virgin* mosaics were designed by Iacopo Torriti in the 1290s). The most striking later additions are the two magnificent and enormous late Renaissance and baroque chapels flanking the altar to form a transept (the Cappella Sistina on the left is particularly sumptuous).

Piazza Santa Maria Maggiore. Ⓒ 06-483195. Free admission to church, loggia 1.25€ ($1.45) or 2.50€ ($2.85) with guide. Church daily 9:30am–6:30pm; loggia daily 9:30am–5pm. Metro: Termini or Cavour. Bus: 16, 70, 71, 75 84, 360, 590, 649, 714.

Museo Nazionale Romano (National Roman Museum)—Palazzo Massimo alle Terme ⋆ Opened in 1998, this museum (paired with its sibling collection in the Palazzo Altemps, earlier in this chapter) blows away anything else you'll find in Rome when it comes to classical statues, frescoes, and mosaics. The 19th-century Palazzo Massimo alle Terme boasts a modernized museum of advanced lighting systems, explanatory placards in English, and a curatorial attention to detail heretofore unseen on the dusty old Roman museum scene.

There are no boring ranks of broken marble busts here—portrait busts are aplenty, but most are masterworks of expression and character, giving you an opportunity to put marble faces to the names of all those emperors and other ancient bigwigs. Among them is a **statue of Caesar Augustus** wearing his toga pulled over his head like a shawl, a sign he'd assumed the role of a priest (actually, of the head priest, which in Latin is Pontifex Maximus, a title that the Christian popes later adopted). Also on the ground floor are an **altar** from Ostia Antica whose reliefs bear a striking resemblance to 15th-century frescoes of the Nativity, and a hauntingly beautiful 440 B.C. **statue of a wounded Niobid,** collapsing as she reaches for her back, where one of Apollo and Artemis's arrows struck. Among the masterpieces on the first floor are a **discus thrower,** a bronze **Dionysus** fished out of the Tiber, bronze bits from **ancient shipwrecks** on Lake Nemi, and an incredibly well-preserved **sarcophagus** featuring a tumultuous battle scene between Romans and Germanic barbarians (all from the 2nd c.).

On the second floor are **Roman frescoes, stuccoes,** and **mosaics** spanning the 1st century B.C. to the 5th century A.D., most never seen by the public since they were discovered in the 19th century. You can visit only on a 45-minute guided tour, which is included in the price of your admission (your museum ticket will have a time printed on it, so be on the second floor at that time for the tour; you can visit the rest of the museum afterward). The frescoes and stuccoes are mainly countryside scenes, decorative strips, and a few naval battles, all carefully restored and reattached into spaces that are faithful to the original dimensions of the rooms from which they came. Also up here are halls and rooms lined with incredible mosaic scenes, among them the famous *Four Charioteers* ⋆ standing with their horses in the four traditional team colors (red, blue, green, and white) that ran the races around the Circus Maximus. There are also several rare 4th-century *opus sectile* (marble inlay) scenes from the Basilica di Giunio Bassa.

The basement has two sections. The first contains **ancient jewelry, gold hair nets, ivory dolls,** and the **mummy of an 8-year-old girl.** The second is an oversize vault containing Rome's greatest **numismatic collection.** It traces Italian coinage from ancient Roman Republic monies through the pocket change of Imperial Rome, medieval Italian empires, and Renaissance principalities, to the Italian lira, the euro, and a computer live feed of the Italian stock exchange.

Largo di Villa Peretti 1 (where Piazza dei Cinquecento meets V. Viminale). ℭ **06-48903500** or 06-4815576 to book. Admission 6€ ($6.90). Tues–Sun 9am–7:45pm (might close Sun at 2pm in winter). Metro: Termini or Repubblica. Bus: C, H, 16, 38, 64, 75, 86, 90, 92, 105, 157, 170, 175, 217, 310, 360, 492, 590, 640, 649, 714, 910.

Museo Nazionale Romano (National Roman Museum)—Terme di Diocleziano (Baths of Diocletian) ℛ

In mid-2000, the Baths of Diocletian finally opened. This massive complex was the largest of all the bath complexes in Rome—twice the size of the Baths of Caracalla and capable of accommodating 3,000 people at any given time. A rectangular area of 376×361m (1,233×1,184 ft., an entire residential block) was razed for its construction, taking advantage of the abundance of water converging here from three of the city's aqueducts. After over a year of sporadic and interminable closings, the Baths of Diocletian inaugurated the National Antiquities arm of the National Museum, a coherent exhibit on the foundations of Rome. Many new rooms have been unveiled, including those displaying artifacts never before seen by the public, with medals, funerary items, mosaics, and paintings.

Viale Enrico E. Nicola 78. ℭ **06-39967700.** Admission 5€ ($5.75). Tues–Sun 9am–7:45pm. Last ticket sold 1 hr. before closing. Bus: 60, 61, 62, 136, 137. Metro: Repubblica.

Museo Nazionale Romano (National Roman Museum)—Aula Ottagona

Flanking the Baths of Diocletian is the Octagonal Hall, whose rectangular exterior camouflages the domed geometric interior—perfect for the planetarium installed here in the 1920s. The hall probably connected the complex's gardens and open-air gymnasium with the caldarium and is now ringed with statues that came from various bath complexes around the empire. Look for the 2nd-century *Lyceum Apollo,* found near the Baths of Trajan here in Rome; the 1st-century *Aphrodite of Cyrene,* a Hellenistic work from Libya; and two magnificent bronze figures, *The Boxer,* signed by Appollonius from Athens, and *The Prince,* whose pose is identical to Lysippos's *Alexander the Great.*

Via G. Romita 3 (entrance between Piazza della Repubblica and the tourist office on V. Parigi). ℭ **06-4880530.** Free admission. Tues–Sat 9am–2pm; Sun 9am–1pm. Bus: 60, 61, 62, 136, 137; Metro: Repubblica.

THE AVENTINE & SOUTH

Terme di Caracalla (Baths of Caracalla) ℛ

Public bath complexes were meant to exercise the minds and the bodies of ancient Roman citizens. These built by Emperor Caracalla in A.D. 212 could hold up to 1,600 bathers at a time and are among the largest to survive from the Imperial age. Sections close regularly for restoration, but you will likely start your tour where the ancient bathers did, in the *palestra* (gym). After their exercises, the bathers proceeded to the *laconicum* (Turkish bath) to scrape their sweaty bodies clean, then moved on to the boiling hot *caldarium,* followed it with a spell soaking in the lukewarm *tepidarium,* and finally took a pore-closing dip in the cold waters of the *frigidarium.* After this they could get a rub-down and continue to the open-air *natatio* (swimming pool) or visit the on-site library or art gallery.

Via delle Terme di Caracalla 52. ℭ **06-5758626.** Admission 5€ ($5.75). May 2–Oct Tues–Sun 9am–7:30pm; Nov–Jan 15 Tues–Sun 9am–4:30pm; Jan 16–Feb 15 Tues–Sun 9am–5pm; Feb 16–Mar 15 9am–5:30pm. Year-round Mon 9am–2pm. Bus: 628, 760. Metro: Circo Massimo.

San Paolo Fuori le Mura (St. Paul Outside the Walls) 🟊   Another of Rome's four grand pilgrimage basilicas, St. Paul Outside the Walls burned down in 1873, but it has been faithfully reconstructed using as many elements as possible from the original. The **Byzantine doors,** with 11th-century incised bronze panels, were badly damaged in the fire but survived to be preserved on the inside of the west wall, between the central and south portals. The altar is said to mark the spot of St. Paul's burial (a 1st-c. tomb discovered beneath seems to support this tradition), and sheltering the altar is a late-13th-century *ciborium* by Arnolfo di Cambio. Nearby is a weird, giant **marble candlestick** carved in the 12th century with a whirl of medieval scenes. Venetian craftsmen executed the restored apse mosaics in the 1220s. The one part of the church to survive the fire almost intact is still its greatest draw, the lovely early-13th-century **cloisters** 🟊, whose columns are a cornucopia of variety, many twisted or paired and inlaid with gems, mosaics, or colored marble chips in glittering patterns.

Viale di San Paolo/Via Ostiense. ℂ **06-5410341.** Free admission. Daily 7:30am–6pm (cloisters close 1–3pm). Metro: San Paolo.

TRASTEVERE
Santa Maria in Trastevere 🟊   Rome's oldest church dedicated to the Virgin was established before A.D. 337 on the site of an inn where a well of olive oil sprang from the floor at the precise moment Christ was born (look for this detail in the mosaics of the apse inside). The current structure was raised in 1140, with a Romanesque bell tower and a 12th- to 13th-century facade mosaic (lit at night) of the Madonna and 10 women. The interior preserves a gorgeous Cosmatesque-like *opus sectile* floor, 21 columns pilfered from nearby ancient buildings, and a 1617 wood ceiling by Domenichino.

Filling the apse are some of Rome's most beautiful mosaics, the half-dome picturing *Christ and the Madonna* (1140) and, below that, six scenes from the *Life of the Virgin* by Pietro Cavallini (1291). These show the artist's remarkable use of color tones and foreshortening to create depth and to express character psychology and story line. (Cavallini was really the only artist in Rome who, as a slightly earlier contemporary of Florence's Giotto, was helping break art from its static Byzantine traditions to plunge it into a vibrant proto-Renaissance mode.)

Piazza Santa Maria in Trastevere. ℂ **06-5819443.** Free admission. Daily 8am–12:30pm and 4–7pm. Bus: H. Tram: 8, 280.

Santa Cecilia in Trastevere 🟊   The bland 18th-century interior of this convent church hides the fact that it dates from 824 and contains not only one of the greatest frescoes from late medieval Rome, but also the ruins of a Roman patrician house beneath. It was ostensibly the home of St. Cecilia, killed in A.D. 230 for political reasons and—since the Roman prosecutors used her practice of the illegal cult of Christianity as the chief accusation against her—an early martyr.

The mosaic **apse** dates from the 9th century, when Pope Paschal I rebuilt the church and brought Cecilia's body from the catacombs to rebury her beneath the altar. Under the present **altar,** with its Guido Reni painting and beautiful Arnolfo di Cambio *baldacchino* (1283), lies Stefano Maderno's touching 17th-century statue of *St. Cecilia.* Maderno was on hand to make sketches when Cardinal Sfondrati opened the saint's tomb in 1599, and they found Cecilia perfectly preserved under a gold funeral shroud. The cut across her neck tells of her famous martyrdom: After locking her in her own steam room for 3 days failed to do her in—indeed, Cecilia came out singing, for which she later was declared the patron saint of music—the executioners tried decapitating her. The three allowed strokes of the axe failed to finish the job, however, and Cecilia held on for another 3 days, slowly bleeding to death and converting hundreds with her show of piety (and this obvious evidence of the power of God protecting her).

You can descend to those **Roman ruins** beneath the church; try to coincide your visit to the crypt with the opening hours for the *affreschi di Cavallini*. The 18th-century interior redecorators slapped plaster over most of the bottom half of Cavallini's masterful *Last Judgment* ⚜ on the entrance wall but had to leave room for a large built-in balcony so the cloistered nuns could attend Mass unseen. In doing so, they unintentionally preserved the fresco's top half, and what remains here of Christ, the angels, and the apostles is stunning. Cavallini painted this in 1293 in a magnificent break from formulaic Byzantine painting. For the first time, each character has a unique face and personality, and all are highly modeled with careful shading and color gradients.

Piazza di Santa Cecilia 22. ⓒ **06-5899289.** Free admission to church, excavations and crypt 2€ ($2.30). Sun–Tues and Thurs–Fri 8am–6pm; Wed and Sat 4–6pm; Cavallini fresco Sun 11am–noon, Tues and Thurs 10am–noon. Bus: H. Tram: 8, 44, 280.

Villa Farnesina ⚜ Baldassare Peruzzi built this modestly sized but sumptuously decorated villa for banking mogul Agostino Chigi from 1508 to 1511. Chigi loved to show off his vast wealth and had good taste in artists, so he hired Raphael, Sodoma, and Peruzzi to decorate the interior of his new villa. The room off the ground-floor loggia has a ceiling painted by Peruzzi with Chigi's horoscope symbols, lunettes by Sebastiano del Piombo with scenes from Ovid's *Metamorphosis,* and the *Trionfo di Galatea (Triumph of Galatea)* ⚜ by Raphael (a perfectly composed Renaissance fresco depicting the nymph and her friends attempting to flee on the backs of pug-nosed dolphins from their mermen admirers). The ceiling in the **Loggia di Psiche (Loggia of Psyche)** is frescoed as an open pergola of flowers and fruit framing scenes from the myth of Psyche, a woman so beautiful Cupid himself fell in love with her. The fresco cycle was executed between 1510 and 1517 (restored in the 1990s) by Raphael's students Giulio Romano, Raffaellino del Colle, and Francesco Penni.

In the grand **Sala delle Prospettive (Hall of Perspectives)** upstairs, Peruzzi frescoed every inch of the walls to masterfully carry *trompe l'oeil* to its extremes and allow Chigi to glimpse an imagined world of Roman countryside and cityscapes between the painted marble columns of a (fake) open loggia. Even with the frescoes faded by time, Peruzzi's painterly and architectural tricks create a pretty convincing optical illusion. Notice how, from the correct angles, the room's real flooring and coffered ceiling are continued into the painted space with perfect perspective. The imperial army of Charles V, sacking the city in 1527, didn't seem to have much respect for this talent, scratching into the frescoes' plaster antipapal epithets in Gothic German script and signing their names and in one place the date (at the time, it was vandalism or graffiti; time has turned it into a precious historic record to be preserved behind Plexiglas shields). The small **bedchamber** off this room was frescoed with a delightful scene of the *Wedding Night of Alexander the Great,* by Sodoma.

Via della Lungara 230. ⓒ **06-68801767** or 06-6838831. Admission 4.15€ ($4.75) adults. Mon–Sat 9am–1pm. Bus: 280.

Galleria Nazionale di Palazzo Corsini (National Gallery of Palazzo Corsini) This 15th-century palace houses the original half of Rome's National Gallery of paintings (the other half is in the Palazzo Barberini, above). The paintings are hung for space rather than composition, but search out especially

Murillo's *Madonna and Child,* Caravaggio's *St. John the Baptist,* a **triptych** by Fra Angelico, and Guido Reni's *Salome with the Head of St. John the Baptist.* Also be on the lookout for fine works by Andrea del Sarto, Rubens, Van Dyck, Joos van Cleve, Guercino, and Luca Giordano.

Via della Lungara 10. © 06-68802323. Admission 5€ ($5.75) adults. Daily 9am–1pm. Bus: 280.

ROME'S PARKS & GARDENS

Rome's greatest central slice of nature is the **Villa Borghese** ☆☆ park, 90 hectares (222 acres) of gardens, statue- and bust-lined paths, fountains, and artificial lakes containing a biopark zoo, three top museums (reviewed above), and the 19th-century Pincio Gardens rising above Piazza del Popolo. The grand park is truly a breath of fresh air in an otherwise polluted city, especially now that the transverse roads have been closed to motor traffic. You can rent bikes, paddleboat on the small lake (there's a tiny 19th-century Greek-style temple on a mini-island), and take the kids to the revamped zoological biopark (see "Especially for Kids," below).

Rising above Trastevere, south of the Vatican, is a long ridge paralleling the Tiber called the **Gianicolo (Janiculum),** famously *not* one of the Seven Hills of Rome. There are a few sights up here, but the most attractive feature is simply the sweeping **view of Rome across the river** ☆, taking in everything from the Pincio Gardens on the left past the domes of the city center beyond the curve of the Colosseum on the right. This panorama is thrilling by day and beautiful by night, when the Gianicolo doubles as Rome's Lover's Lane (lots of steamy Fiat windows and lip-locked lovers stationed every 3m/10 ft. along the walls).

Toward the Gianicolo's southerly end is the **Acqua Paolo fountain,** a gargantuan 17th-century basin and fountain made from marble taken from the Forum that serves as both the outlet for Trajan's aqueduct and the requisite backdrop for all Roman newlyweds' wedding photos.

ESPECIALLY FOR KIDS

Kids are bound to tire out well before you, becoming ornery and just plain bored. Pace yourselves and keep up the kids' interest with breaks, picnics, a few sights just for them (more on that in a minute), and generous amounts of yummy gelato.

The **Time Elevator Roma,** Via di Santissimi Apostoli 20 (© **06-6990053;** www.time-elevator.it), the newest addition to a group of historical theme park rides that include those in Jerusalem, Philadelphia, Baltimore, and Atlantic City and at Walt Disney's Orlando Florida Epcot Center, is a great way to introduce kids to the cultural wealth of Rome. The 45-minute "ride" takes its audience back in time, with brief stops at the major junctures in Roman history. Its light-hearted approach makes the film both fun and educational, and provides a great baseline for kids before embarking on a more hands-on visit to the city. The show runs every 15 minutes daily from 9am to midnight, and headphones are provided in one of six available languages (not appropriate for children 5 and under).

Several sights seem to fire children's enthusiasm and imagination more than others. Some favorites (see above for details) are the arms and armor collection in **Castel Sant'Angelo** (okay, it's a boy thing); the gruesome bone montages of the **Capuchin Crypt;** the kilometers of subterranean passages of the **catacombs;** the **Mouth of Truth;** the **mummies** in the Egyptian wing of the Vatican; some of the **fountains** and **statues,** like Bernini's baby elephant obelisk; and **Trajan's Markets.** And few people, regardless of age, aren't seriously impressed by the **Colosseum** and the **Sistine Chapel.**

The **Museo dei Bambini** (**Children's Museum;** ✆ **06/3613776;**
www.mdbr.it), Via Flaminio 82, part of an international initiative that began
with the 1899 foundation of the Children's Museum of Brooklyn, is a stimulat-
ing hands-on learning environment geared to kids 3 to 12. The complex is even
constructed of recycled and recyclable materials. Each visit lasts 1 hour and 45
minutes. It's open to visitors Monday 9:30am and 11:30am; Tuesday through
Friday 9:30am, 11:30am, 3pm, and 5pm; and Saturday and Sunday 10am,
noon, 3pm, and 5pm. Admission is 6€ ($6.90) for adults and 7€ ($8.05) for
kids (5€/$5.75 for everybody on Thurs); children 3 and under get in free.

Several museums have separate spaces or programs for kids, with audiocas-
sette guides for them and pamphlets so they can follow along. The **Museo Barracco,** Corso Vittorio Emanuele II 158, highlights the sculpture collection in
the Egyptian, Mesopotamian, and Greek rooms for 6- and 7-year-old historians;
the **Museo della Civiltà Romana** prepares tours for 8- and 9-year-olds; and the
Pinacoteca Capitoline gears its tours to kids 10 to 12. For information, contact
the **Colleo del Museo,** at ✆ 06-39080730. For a more hands-on experience,
the **Villa Giulia** runs a didactic kids' program that includes a simulation of an
archaeological dig and a ceramic laboratory. Visits are by reservation, so contact
the **Organizzazione Cooperativo Arte in Gioco** at ✆ 06-44239949. Other
kid-oriented events are run independently or in conjunction with one of the
organizations above (sometimes at the **Galleria Borghese** or the **Museii Capitolini**); the **Comune di Roma** puts out a periodic brochure with a calendar of
events, available at any tourist information kiosk.

The **Villa Borghese** park is good for kids of all ages. There are facilities for
renting bikes, a merry-go-round on the Pincio, and paddle-boats on the Giardino del Lago. Also here is the renovated **Bioparco,** Piazzale del Giardino Zoo-
logico 1 (✆ **06-3608211**), which has been retooled from a zoo of cages to a
biological garden of natural-habitat enclosures that primarily house endangered
species and injured animals that are being rehabilitated to return to the wild. It
has become a teaching zoo, with placards at each enclosure that show via pic-
tograms what threats the animal faces in the wild (climate changes, pollution,
habitat destruction, hunting); the bears, wolves, lions, and apes are especially
popular. Admission is 8.50€ ($9.75) for adults and 6.50€ ($7.45) for children
ages 4 to 12. It's open daily from 9:30am to 7pm (to 5pm Nov–Feb).

The **Gianicolo (Janiculum Hill)** offers great city panoramas, a merry-go-
round, and, on Piazzale del Gianicolo, the **Teatrino di Pulcinella al Gianicolo** 🎭 (✆ 06-5827767 or 0349-1706874), an open-air puppet theater showing
the Neapolitan hand-puppet Pulcinella (Punch, of Punch and Judy fame).
Shows of this traditional Italian entertainment are currently run only on request
(or whenever enough kids show up; *always* call ahead for times). It's free, but
you're welcome to leave a donation. Get there any day at noon for the sounding
of the Janiculum cannon.

ORGANIZED TOURS
Enjoy Rome, Via Margherita 8/a (✆ **06-49382724;** fax 06-4450734;
www.enjoyrome.com; Metro: Termini), has a young staff from various English-
speaking countries, some who are specialists in archaeology, who run both 3-
hour **walking tours** (maximum 15–20 people; those of Ancient Rome and
Rome at Night run daily, those of the Vatican about three times weekly) and
daily 4-hour **bike tours** (bike and helmet included; maximum 10 people).
Walking tours cost 21€ ($24) for adults and 20€ ($23) for those under 26; bike
tours (including the bike) cost 25€ ($29).

The city-run **ATAC sightseeing bus no. 110** (© 06-46952252; www.metre
bus.it) runs a continuous circuit of the major sights that doubles as a hop-
on/hop-off service. The nonstop formula lasts 1¾ hours and costs 7.75€
($8.90), while the stop-and-go formula costs 13€ ($15). Buses depart every
half-hour from 10am to 6pm (9am–8pm Apr–Sept) from Termini; tickets can
be purchased on the bus or at the Romavision stand in Piazza dei Cinquecento
in front of Termini Station.

A number of other organizations offer hop on/hop off tours, the most economical being **Stop 'n' go City Tours** (© 06-3217054), with nine departures
daily and 14 selected stops. The hostesses are multilingual, and the cost for a day
is 12€ ($14; discounts available for multiple days). Buses leave from Stazione
Termini. The **Ciao Roma Trolley Tour** (© 06-4743795) charges 18€ ($21),
with a 3€ ($3.45) discount per person if you begin your tour after 1:30pm.
There are five departures daily to 11 points of interest around the city, including the Galleria Borghese, and you get a headset with recorded explanations of
the sites.

If you want live commentary, you'll have to pony up from 30€ to 40€
($35–$46) to **American Express,** Piazza di Spagna 38 (© 06-67642413), for
one of its 3- or 4-hour tours, which depart at 8:30am, 9:30am, and/or 2:30pm
daily, depending on the season. One tour gives a general overview of all Rome
and the Vatican, another focuses mainly on ancient Rome, a third hones in on
the tourist heart of the city, and the fourth is a nighttime tour.

6 Shopping

THE SHOPPING SCENE

Rome's **best buys** (not to be confused with bargains) are in antiquities, high
fashion, wine, ecclesiastical knickknacks, designer housewares, and flea-market
bargains.

The capital's tiniest boutique zone radiates out from the **Spanish Steps,** centered on the matriarch of high-fashion streets, **Via dei Condotti.** Condotti
runs arrow-straight from the base of the steps and has become rather too
famous for its own good, sprouting such downscale abominations as a Foot-
locker and other international chain outlets. This zone is bounded by **Via del
Corso,** ground zero for Rome's most fashionable see-and-be-seen *passeggiata*
(evening stroll). It, too, is lined with generally expensive bigger stores—great
for window-shopping, but if you're looking for bargain prices, head to **Via
Nazionale** and **Via del Tritone.**

Via dei Coronari, running west off the north end of Piazza Navona, has
always been the heart of Rome's antiques district. Almost every address here is a
dealer or restorer, and many of their wares or works-in-progress spill out onto
the narrow cobbled street. For art, the highest concentration of dealers and studios lies along **Via Margutta,** a side street parallel to Via del Babuino.

But while the locals do turn out to *passeggiata* on the Corso and window-shop
on Via dei Condotti, the actual shopping in these parts is pretty touristy. To
Romans, the true shopping nexus of the city is the upper-middle-class residential zone of **Prati,** just northeast of the Vatican, with the economic activity centered on wide **Via Cola di Rienzo.** Here you'll find generally lower prices, more
down-to-earth stores, and a much better opportunity to see how the citizens of
Rome really live and shop.

SHOPPING A TO Z

ANTIQUITIES   How much is a Grecian urn? Well, if you have to ask, you can't afford it. Pieces cost anywhere from 100€ to 4,810€ ($115–$5,532) at **M. Simotti Rocchi,** Largo Fontanella Borghese 76 (© **06-6876656**), a dealer in Etruscan, Greek, and Roman antiquities. That cheapest painted vase would be a 4-inch piece from the ancient equivalent of a child's tea set. Here you can pick up Roman coins, tiny terra-cotta ex-voto heads, or oil lamps starting at around 75€ ($86). Marble statues can cost up to 7,500€ ($8,625)—still, it's about one-third the price you'd find at Sotheby's in New York or London.

For lower prices, visit **Gea Arte Antica,** Via dei Coronari 233A (© **06-68801369**), where small oil lamps go for as little as 50€ to 100€ ($58–$115)—though the more nicely decorated ones, not to mention larger vases, start at around 500€ ($575). If you'd prefer to wear your classical acquisitions, check out **Massimo Maria Melis,** under "Jewelry," below.

BOOKS   Among the better English-language bookstores are the venerable **Lion Bookshop and Cafe,** Via dei Greci 33–36 (© **06-32654007**); the large **Anglo-American,** beyond the Spanish Steps at Via della Vite 102 (© **06-6795222**); and the even larger **Economy Bookshop,** Via Torino 136 (© **06-4746877**), which also offers a wide selection of cheap, used paperbacks and a free "Rome Travel Pack" with map and guides to the city's services.

Italy's version of Barnes & Noble is the Feltrinelli chain, and you'll find a wide selection of books in English at the huge **Feltrinelli International,** Via V. E. Orlando 84–86, off Piazza della Repubblica (© **06-4870999;** www. feltrinelli.it). Other branches are at Largo di Torre Argentina 5A (© **06-68803248**), Via del Babuino 49–40 (© **06-36001873**), and next door to the "International" one at Via V. E. Orlando 78–81 (© **06-4870171**).

Remainders, Piazza San Silvestro 27–28 (© **06-6792824**), is what the name says—a shop selling overstock books up to 50% off, including lots of glossy art and coffee-table books. **La Grotta del Libro,** Via del Pellegrino 172 (© **06-6877567**), and **Libreria Vecchia Roma,** Via del Pellegrino 94, both look like garages piled to the ceiling with books, advertising even cheaper coffee-table books at 50% to 80% off, but not as consistent a selection. **Le Pleiadi Librerie,** Via del Giubbaonari 76–77 (© **06-68807981**), is classier, with a wider selection of recently printed books on art and the city of Rome up to 50% off. Also don't miss the **antiquarian book and print market** on Piazza Borghese, with good deals on dated art books as well as spiffy Roman prints. And the **Libreria Babele,** Via dei Bianchi Vecchi 116 (© **06-6876628;** Bus: 46, 62, 64, 80, 116, 116T), is Rome's most central all-gay/lesbian bookstore.

DEPARTMENT STORES   Italy's top two chains are a bit pricey. In Rome, the designer label–driven **La Rinascente,** Via del Corso/Piazza San Silvestro (© **06-6797691**), is set apart by its cover-all-bases selection, English-language information and tax-free shopping desk, and central location in its own 19th-century high-rise. **Coin,** Piazzale Appio 7 (© **06-7080020;** Metro: San Giovanni), has recently been muscling in on La Rinascente territory by going more upscale in look and attitude, with stylish displays of upper-middle-class fashions—a chic Macy's.

For more everyday shopping, head to **Standa,** at Viale Trastevere 62–64 (© **06-5895342**), and Via Cola di Rienzo 173 (© **06-324-3319**), where Italians buy their socks and underwear. It runs back-to-school specials and carries bulk dish detergent, frying pans, lamps, cake mix, and other everyday items and clothes—an upscale Kmart with a supermarket in the basement. **Upim,** Piazza di Santa Maria Maggiore (© **06-4465579**), is another national chain that's just slightly above Standa.

DESIGN & HOUSEWARES   Italians are masters of industrial design, making the most utilitarian items into memorable art pieces. Rather than a percolator, they create the Pavoni espresso machine, and a lowly teapot becomes a whimsical Alessi masterpiece the MoMA is proud to display.

In a teeny storefront in Trastevere is **Azi,** Via San Francesco a Ripa 170 (© **06-5883303**), selling household items with more emphasis on form than function. If you're willing to fork over lots of euros or just want to browse among the bounty, check out **Spazio Sette,** Via dei Barbieri 7 off Largo di Torre Argentina (© **06-6869747**), Rome's slickest housewares emporium. It goes way beyond the requisite Alessi tea kettles to fill three huge stories with the greatest names and latest word in Italian and international design. Even if you aren't in the market for the living-room furnishings on the top floor, climb up to gawk at the frescoed ceilings. Another good bet is **Bagagli,** Via Cam. Marzio 42 (© **06-6871406**), with a discount section in back. You'll find a good selection of Alessi, Rose and Tulipani, and Villeroy & Boch china in a pleasantly kitschy old Rome setting (cobblestone floors and so on).

Bargain hunters should head to one of **Stock Market**'s two branches: Via dei Banchi Vecchi 51–52 (© **06-6864238**) and Via Tacito 60, near the Vatican (© **06-36002343**). You'll find mouthwatering prices on last year's models, overstock, slight irregulars, and artistic misadventures that the pricier boutiques haven't been able to move. Most is moderately funky household stuff, but you never know when you'll find a gem of design hidden on the shelves. If the big names don't do it for you, you may prefer **c.u.c.i.n.a.,** Via dei Babuino 118A (no phone), a stainless-steel shrine to everything you need for a proper Italian kitchen, sporting designs that are as beautiful in their simplicity as they are utilitarian.

DISCOUNT FASHION   Rome has several stock houses selling last year's fashions, irregulars, and overstock at cut-rate prices. One of the best is **Il Discount dell'Alta Moda,** with branches at Via di Gesù e Maria 16A near the Spanish Steps (© **06-3613796**) and Via Viminale 35 near Stazione Termini (© **06-4823917**). The selection of such labels as Versace, Donna Karan, Armani, Dolce & Gabbana, Venturi, Krizia, and Ferré shifts constantly, with prices that are still inflated at up to 50% off. Both men's and women's clothing are sold, plus accessories and outerwear.

Firmastock, Via delle Carrozze 18 (© **06-69200371**), carries everything from Levi's and Hugo Boss to Valentino, Armani, and Max Mara at 50% to 70% off already outrageous prices. The small, eclectic, and ever-changing inventory includes dresses, overcoats, shoes, and men's and women's suits. **New Fashion,** Via Simone de Saint Bon 85–87 in Prati (© **06-37513947**), carries women's suits and skirts from top designers like Moschino, Valentino, Max Mara, and Dolce & Gabbana, as well as lesser-known "Made in Italy" labels. The prices are higher than at the other stock houses listed here, but the discounts are honest and the outfits tend to be more consistently fashionable.

FOOD   Rome's top food emporium—after the fresh **food markets** around town—is undoubtedly **Castroni,** a legend since 1932 with the main shop at Via Cola di Rienzo 196 in Prati (© **06-6874383**) and an offspring store at Via Flaminio 28–32 just north of Piazza del Popolo (© **06-3611029**). Castroni carries a stupefying collection of the best foods, both fine and common, from around the world, including such exotic concoctions as peanut butter and Vegemite. Next door to the main Castroni is **Franchi,** Via Cola di Rienzo 204 (© **06-6874651;** www.franchi.it), a more traditional Italian-style *alimentari.* The excellent prepared foods include *calzoni fritti* and *calzoni al forno* (fried and baked versions of pizza pockets wrapped around cheese and ham)—the best in town by a long shot, with the daily long lines awaiting their appearance at 5pm to prove it.

Romans come from all over town and the 'burbs to buy their cheeses and milk products from among the fantastic selection at **Latteria Micocci,** Via Collina 16 (© **06-4741784).** For some offbeat food shopping in Trastevere, hit **Drogheria Innocenzi,** Piazza San Cosimato 66 (© **06-5812725),** an old-fashioned bit-of-everything grocery store with a newfangled eclectic stock. Part natural health-food emporium, part gourmet international foods store, and part medieval spice shop, it's the only place I've ever been able to find all the odd ingredients called for by the recipes in Apicius's ancient Roman cookbook.

GIFTS I've always thought that the greatest Roman gifts come from the combination of kitschy and holier-than-thou **Vatican gift shops** and souvenir stands encircling St. Peter's and the Vatican. You'll find everything from a light-up plastic Michelangelo's *Pietà,* pictures showing a smiling Christ from one angle and a crucified one from another, and models of the Virgin Mary that weep on command to your-name-here papal indulgences. There's even a "pope-ener" (an anthropomorphic corkscrew—by twisting the medallion printed with the pope's head, you cause his "arms" to raise slowly in benediction).

For singular timepieces, visit **Guaytamelli,** Via del Moro 59 in Trastevere (© **06-5880704),** where Argentinean Adrian Rodriguez crafts beautiful hour candles, hourglasses, and sundials in the forms of rings, sticks, pendants, and flip-top boxes—all of quality workmanship at rather low prices (from 7.50€/$8.63 for a sundial ring). There's even a tiny flat pendant sextant; turn the sandwich of engraved disks until they align with the stars, and it'll tell you the time at night.

JEWELRY For traditional pieces, **Tresor,** Via della Croce 71B–72 (© **06-6877753),** crafts classically worked 18-karat gold jewelry at prices not much higher than the market value of the raw material. At **Massimo Maria Melis,** Via dell'Orso 57 (© **06-6869188),** 21-karat gold is hand-worked to encase genuine coins and pieces of glass or carved stone from the Etruscan, Roman, and medieval eras. A pair of earrings set with Imperial Roman coins will set you back about 250€ ($288).

MARKETS The mother lode of Roman bazaars is **Porta Portese,** a flea market off Piazza Ippolito Nievo that began at the close of World War II as a black and gray market but has grown to be one of Europe's premier garage sales. You'll find everything from antique credenzas to used carburetors, bootleg CDs, birds that squawk "Ciao," previously owned clothes, Italian comic books, and used Leicas, all in a carnival atmosphere of haggling and hollering, jostling and junk jockeying, with beggars, pickpockets, and shrewd stall owners swirling around auditory pockets of badly dubbed dance music and the scents of sweet roasting corn. It runs every Sunday from dawn to lunchtime. Hang on to your wallet.

Snuggled up along a stretch of the Aurelian Wall off Via Sannio are the half-covered stalls of the **San Giovanni clothing market,** the best place to pick up inexpensive new and cut-rate used clothing (or cheap army surplus, in case you need an extra pack, sleeping bag, or tent) and outfit yourself like a true Roman. It runs Monday through Friday from 10am to 1pm and Saturday from 10am to 5pm. Everybody shows up here, including Rome's finest pickpockets and thieves—if you get here early enough (5:30am), you can even witness the unloading of the previous evening's clandestine haul. Keep your eyes open and try to fit in.

Campo de' Fiori, once the site of medieval executions, is today one of Rome's most lively squares. This cobblestone expanse starts bustling in the pre-dawn hours as the florists arrange bouquets of flowers and fruit, and vegetable vendors set up their stalls, imbuing the piazza with a burst and swirl of color and scents. The lively workaday life winds down after lunch, but the piazza reani-mates later in the evening with adolescent Romans and tourists in a carnival of dining and nightlifing.

MUSIC   Italy's biggest chain of record stores is **Ricordi,** with major branches in Rome at Via del Corso 506 (© 06-3612370), at Via C. Battisti 120D (© 06-6798022), and on Piazza Indipendenza (© 06-4440706). All have a wide selection of Italian and international music and listening stations, as well as the definitive collection of books and classical scores. For a good selection of used and new CDs, tapes, and vinyl, visit **Millerecords** (© 06-4958242), with two shops on Via dei Mille at no. 29 (jazz, rock, and pop) and no. 41 (classical). For underground selections, all the Italian DJs head to **Goody Music,** Via Cesare Beccaria 2 (© 06-3610959). The latest British and American independ-ent releases are at **Disfunzioni Musicali,** Via degli Etruschi 4–14 (© 06-4461984), just a few steps from the university.

SHOES & ACCESSORIES   Unless you're shopping for plastic shoes, much of the good stuff gets exported or sold here at prices weighted down by more zeros than you'd care to write a check out for. For midrange footwear, the **Bati** chain keeps up with the trends but not inflation. Two of the more centrally located stores are at Via Nazionale 88A and Via due Macelli 45.

For classically inspired and beautifully crafted shoes, sandals, and half-boots starting at around 150€ ($173), check out the boutique of **Fausto Santini,** Via Frattina 120 (© 06-6784114). It also does purses and bags along clean mod-ernist lines. If you like Santini's style but not the prices, head to Via Cavour 106 (© 06-4880934), the designer's discount outlet for last year's models, at 50€ to 100€ ($58–$115), and remainders, as low as 10€ ($12).

Want a wider range of accessories at stock shop prices? **Il Discount delle Firme,** on the tiny road off Largo del Tritone called Via dei Serviti 27 (© 06-4827790), carries perfumes, purses, ties, scarves, shoes, wallets, and belts from all the top names (and a few lesser-known Italian designers) at 50% off. Near the Vatican, your best bet is **Grandi Firme,** Via Germanico 8 (© 06-39723169), with a rotating accessory stock of purses, ties, belts, scarves, and shoes also up to 50% off from names like Fendi, Dior, Missoni, and Ferré.

If you want to hook yourself up with one of those colorful **Invicta** backpacks that seem a required part of every school uniform for Italian students from kindergarten through grad school, visit their showroom at Via del Babuino 27–28 (© 06-36001737). The **Standa** and **Upim** chains also carry these knap-sacks, generally in the kids' section.

TOYS   Rome's best toy store is **La Città del Sole,** Via della Scrofa 65 (© 06-68803805). Since 1977, this owner-operated branch of the national chain has sold old-fashioned wooden brainteasers, construction kits, hand puppets, 3D puzzles, and science kits. There's even a tots' book section, in case you want to start Junior on his Italian early. These are the sorts of toys that, while being gobs of fun, also help youngsters (and some adults) push and stretch their minds, encouraging creativity and imagination.

For slightly more mass-market toys—but still fantastic and largely European made—visit one of the **Giorni** branches in Prati. At Via dei Gracchi 31–33 (© **06-3217145**), you'll find only models, from build-it-yourself to ready out of the box, including the Bburago series of cast-metal cars. The softer side is at Via M. Colonna 26 (© **06-3216929**), where you'll find dolls, stuffed animals, and music boxes. For a more general selection, visit the Via Pompeo Magno 86 shop (© **06-3213540**), where the playthings are appropriate for ages up to 10, or head next door to Via Pompeo Magno 84 (© **06-3214736**), the toy outlet "for ages 8 to 99."

WINE & LIQUOR   Rome's most peculiar inebriatory experience has to be **Ai Monasteri,** off the north corner of Piazza Navona at Piazza Cinque Lune 76 (© **06-68802783**). Here are gathered the liqueurs, elixirs, *digestivi,* extracts, aperitifs, and other alcoholic ingestibles that are concocted by industrious monks at various monasteries, abbeys, and convents across Italy. It's sort of a central outlet shop for the country's collective monastic liquor cabinet/organic shop (it deals in soaps and oils, too).

The granddaddy of Rome's wine stores is **Trimani,** Via Goito 20 (© **800-014625** toll-free or 06-4468351), a family business since 1821 with literally thousands of bottles in a huge shop and even more in the cellars. This place ain't cheap, but it isn't unreasonable either. You'll find plenty of quaffable stuff for under 5€ ($5.75)—you just have to search it out among lots of classy, aged, high-profile bottles that can easily run upwards to 100€ ($115).

La Vecchia Cantina, Via Viminale 7B (© **06-460737**), is a good spot to pick up a cheap but decent bottle of *vino* for that picnic. For more atmosphere and selection, try the **Enoteca al Parlamento,** Via Prefetti 15 (© **06-6873446**), a stylish and old-fashioned wood-lined wine emporium where you rub shoulders with politicians and other business suits as you sample wine by the glass at the counter and choose from the select stock, which also includes liqueurs, champagnes, honeys, and marmalades. Another historic wine shop is **Buccone,** Via di Ripetta 19–20 (© **06-3612154**), with a selection so enormous it covers cheap Valpolicella as well as wines costing upward of 500€ ($575). You can also grab a nibble at the bar at Buccone, schedule a wine tasting, or dine in their charming trattoria, adjacent to the shop.

7 Rome After Dark

True Roman nightlife consists of lingering over a full restaurant meal until after midnight, with lots of good wine and good conversation among friends. Summertime in Rome is especially lively, as much of the city's clubs, performances, and events head outdoors, often to the various archaeological sites for things like opera under the stars or *Oedipus Rex* on the recently built stage of the Colosseum. Venues are ever changing, so you'll have to check with the tourist information offices or local papers for hours and schedules. For a more culturally related evening or a late night of bar hopping, check out the listings below and the events guides described under "Newspapers & Magazines" in "Fast Facts: Rome," earlier in this chapter.

THE PERFORMING ARTS

CLASSICAL MUSIC   Always check the events listings for information about concerts being held in Rome's medieval and baroque churches and, in summer especially, outdoor evening performances in evocative, archaeological settings surrounded by ancient columns and ruins.

One of Italy's premier musical associations, the **Accademia Nazionale di Santa Cecilia,** finally has a permanent seat at the **Auditorio,** Via della Concilliazione 4 (℗ **06-68801044,** 06-3611064 for the Via Vittoria 6 office, or 063938-7297 for tickets). The season runs October to May, with symphonic concerts Saturday to Tuesday and soloist and ensemble chamber music Friday. In summer, there are outdoor concerts in the Villa Giulia's theatrical *nymphaeum.*

The **Accademia Filarmonica Romana,** which performs in the **Teatro Olimpico** north of the center at Piazza Gentile da Fabriano 17 (℗ **06-3234890,** or 06-3938-7297 for tickets), was founded in 1821 and puts on Thursday concerts October to June that range from chamber music and classical hits to folk and ethnic music. The Accademia also hosts international ballet and dance companies. The **Orchestra Regionale del Lazio** performs at the **Teatro Nazionale,** Via Viminale 51 (℗ **06-485494** or 06-4870614), January to June, with a program from baroque classics to contemporary composers directed by mainly up-and-coming young Italian and international conductors and musicians.

Classical concerts are part of Rome's year-round calendar, taking place regularly at various churches and auditoriums. The **Accademia Nazionale di Santa Cecilia** (www.santacecilia.it) orchestra and choir began performing in its brand-new concert venue, the **Auditorium Parco della Musica,** in 2003 (L.go Luciano Berio 3; ℗ **06-8024-2501**). The tourist information office maintains up-to-date information on these events; swing by and pick up the latest brochures.

OPERA & BALLET   After years of languishing without funding or respect, Rome's newly restored late-19th-century **Teatro dell'Opera,** Piazza Beniamino Gigli 1, at the intersection of Via Torino and Via Viminale (℗ **800-016665** toll-free, 06-481601 office, or 06-48160255 box office; www.operaroma.it or www.themix.it), continues to attract the finest musicians, conductors, and performers for their opera and ballet seasons. The preseason runs October to December and the official season January to June. Seats cost from 45€ to 145€ ($52–$167); tickets can go as low as 13€ ($15) for an outdoor event. Tickets can be purchased at the box office (closed Mon), at the theater's website, or at any Banca di Roma location.

DISCOS & NIGHTCLUBS

If you put all of Rome's nightclubs back to back, you could easily fill several football fields and definitely blow out an eardrum. Many have followed the dangerous road into hardcore techno music, so I've decided to cover only those slightly more mainstream. **Via della Pace** near Piazza Navona is a popular nighttime strip, attracting a healthy mix of trendoids from the neighborhood as well as tourists. Bar hoppers will find plenty of hunting grounds in the neighborhoods of **Trastevere** and **San Lorenzo,** and the **Testaccio** quarter gets pretty lively after dark, with everyone's first stop the increasingly Latin **Four XXXX Pub,** Via Galvani 29/29a (℗ 06-5757296), closed in August.

Rome's attempt at a major Manhattan- or London-style disco is **Alien,** Via Velletri 13–19 (℗ **06-8412212**), with a funky sci-fi decor in an underground garage setting, with (mainly 20-something) dancing bodies. The music is cutting edge, and on Tuesday, it about-faces to become a New Age club. September to May, it's open Tuesday through Sunday from 11pm to 4am (June–July Fri–Sat only). Admission is 10€ to 18€ ($12–$21).

With its huge central bar and ample sofa setup, **Goa,** Via Libetta 13 (**℃ 06-5748277**), is the choice of Rome's trendy and celebrity set. Leonardo DiCaprio and entourage dropped by while filming *Gangs of New York.* The music is mainly hip-hop, "jungle," and tribal, to go with the ethnic decor and exotic incense. The club is open Tuesday through Sunday 11pm to 4am, and the cover ranges from 10€ to 18€ ($12–$21), depending on the event.

In the heart of the center is the ever-popular **Gilda,** Via Mario de' Fiori 97 (**℃ 06-6784838**), a famous disco/nightclub patronized by a fair lot of politicians (hence the creepiness factor) but also by plenty of Romans of all ages and lots of visitors, who arrive in droves to this club to act excruciatingly trendy but seemingly with no clear idea why. The admission is a scandalous 20€ ($23) and includes a drink. September to June, it's open Tuesday through Sunday from 10:30pm to 4am.

LATIN MUSIC CLUBS

Romans go crazy for Latin music, and two of the best clubs where you can enjoy it are in Trastevere. **Berimbau,** Via dei Fienaroli 30B (**℃ 06-5813249**), is a flashy and colorful South American club with a strict menu of samba and South American rhythms. There are free Latin dance lessons and a DJ for dancing after the live concert. September to June, it's open Wednesday through Sunday from 10:30pm to 3am. Including a drink, admission is 15€ ($17). Contrary to its name, **Bossa Nova,** Via Orti di Trastevere 23 (**℃ 06-5816121**), a Brazilian joint with live music nightly, plays mostly samba. There's scant seating, but the club's largely Brazilian clientele is on the dance floor anyway. Head over on Tuesday, and you get a free dance lesson. Admission is free; it's open September to July Tuesday through Sunday from 10:30pm to 3am.

JAZZ & BLUES CLUBS

If you make time for only one jazz club, make it **Alexanderplatz,** Via Ostia 9 in Prati (**℃ 06-39742171**), open nightly from 9:30pm to 1:30am. It's Rome's only club with a heavy dose of respect on the international jazz circuit, drawing names like Winton Marsalis, Lionel Hampton, and George Coleman, along with top Italian players. Meals are served starting at 9pm (not included in membership pass, but reasonable), with concerts beginning at 10:30pm and lasting to 1:30am or later. In summer, it moves outside to the gardens of Villa Celimontana. A one-time admission is 6€ ($6.90); a 1-month pass is 20€ ($23). The club is closed on Sunday.

The Roman home of the blues is in Trastevere at **Big Mama,** Vicola San Francesco a Ripa 18 (**℃ 06-5812551**). Since 1984, it has been hosting some of the world's top blues musicians when they come to Rome, sprinkling the offerings with funk and jazz as well. A monthly pass is 12€ ($14); one-time admission is 6€ ($6.90), but the prices sometimes go up for certain shows. The music is strictly live, so the club is open only when someone's on the ticket (closed July–Aug; call ahead).

BARS, PUBS & ENOTECHE

AROUND CAMPO DE' FIORI   You'll find a full gamut of nightspots in this corner of town. The exceedingly popular but old-fashioned wine bar called **Vineria Reggio,** no. 15 (**℃ 06-68803268**), is still holding its own amid the nightly crowds on this piazza. This spot is also known affectionately as Da Giorgio, and everyone calls in here sooner or later for decent wine by the glass from 1€ ($1.15), though you can also avail yourself of the beers on tap. During the day and the early evening, it throngs with locals and historic expatriates; at night, it's a seriously hip hangout for bright young things. It's also a good place to pick up a bottle after hours.

Next door is the "casual but chic" **Taverna del Campo,** no. 16 (© 06-6874402), a crowded stop for a quick bite where it's easy to fill up unexpectedly on *crostini, panini,* or even oysters and champagne. A few more doors down, you can cool your heels to the live-DJ music (and air-conditioning) of American-style **The Drunken Ship,** nos. 20–21 (© 06-68300535). Off the campo itself is the trendy **Taverna del Diavolo,** Via dei Chiavari 4–5 (© 06-6861359), a smart and understated wine bar and *birreria* serving a tempting bar menu.

NEAR PIZZA NAVONA & THE PANTHEON Every Italian town has one bar that serves as the area's living room, and in Rome that place is the dubiously named (an unmentionable four-letter-word translation—a double entendre for the fig trees sprouting in the small *piazzetta*) **Bar del Fico,** Piazza del Fico 27–28 (© 06-6865205). As sure as night becomes day, by 11pm this hangout is bursting at the seams, when large groups converge, drinks in hand, to decide where the evening will take them. By day, this bar/cafeteria is a bit mellower, serving lunch around regulars glued to a game of checkers or chess. The bar also hosts a rotating schedule of art exhibitions. It's open 8am to 3am.

Steer your beer cravings toward the basement rooms of the **Black Duke,** Via della Maddalena 29B (© 06-68300381), an Irish pub serving pub grub just north of the Pantheon. Another lively Irish pub is the **Abbey Theatre,** Via del Governo Vecchio 51–53 (© 06-6861341), a "Guinness bar"—the Irish beer company sells prefab rustic-style pubs, complete from the woodsy decor down to the kitschy Brit paraphernalia and dartboard. Even more genuine is **St. Andrew's Pub,** Vicola della Cancelleria 36 (© 06-6832638), so Scottish it's got tartan on the walls. There's Tennent's on tap along with that excellent Edinburgh double-malt red ale Devil's Kiss and Caffrey's stout (that one's Irish, but it's still good).

The most bizarre nightspot in the area is without doubt **Jonathan's Angels** ✵, Via della Fossa 16 (© 06-6893426), a temple to weirdo kitsch down a side street strung with Christmas lights. The owner was a circus acrobat and restaurateur before opening this funky, dark, casual bar and turning his energies to painting and sculpting. The walls are completely covered with representations of his artistic vision; note that the faces on all the portraits (even the nun) are his. If nothing else, come to use the over-the-top bathroom (where there'll inevitably be a line), complete with its own full-size cherub fountain.

Henry's Pub, Via Tor Millinia 34a (© 06-6869904), is a pretty gross joint with outdoor seating in the heart of the action off Piazza Navona's northwest end. Beware of what you drink—there's a sangria punch bowl into which the barman dumps the leftovers from mixed drinks. Next door at no. 32 is the **Vineria La Botticella** (© 06-6861107), a little vineria cum American-style bar with Devil's Kiss on tap. Down on Piazza Sant'Andrea della Valle is the ever-popular **John Bull Pub,** Corso Vittorio Emanuele II 107 (© 06-6871537), serving John Bull ale and Strongbow cider to a mainly young crowd (lots of American students); a barroom brawl isn't an uncommon form of entertainment.

The pièce de résistance of all meat-market spots is **Trinity College,** Via del Collegio Romano, off Via del Corso near Piazza Venezia (© 06-6786472). At the very least, go there to watch stereotypically dressed American exchange students in ponytails congregating under the watchful gaze of the Mediterranean Male, while the more sexually liberated Italian girls try to intercept. They say nobody leaves here alone.

NEAR THE SPANISH STEPS & PIAZZA DEL POPOLO   A Brit expat landmark for years, the **Victoria House Pub,** Via Gesù e Maria 18 (© 06-3201698), is a genuine English pub—though most of the ale on tap is Scottish (Tennent's) or Irish (Caffrey's). Italians flock to this little corner of England, going so far as to tolerate pub grub like shepherd's pie and the nonsmoking bar/sitting room at the back. If you fancy a spot of pool in a contemporary pub on a busy road near the Trevi Fountain (just before the tunnel off Piazza Trionfale), head to **The Albert,** Via del Traforo 132 (© 06-4818795).

The **Birreria Viennese,** Via della Croce 21 (© 06-6795569), is a Bavariantinged *bierhaus* with a woodsy dark interior and pretzels hanging at each table. You can order Austrian grub and beer by the liter mug. Down the block, the **Enoteca Antica di Via della Croce,** Via della Croce 76b (© 06-6790896), is a friendly, relaxed spot, a perfect place to rest your weary shopping feet. Sort of a traditional *enoteca* gone trendy, it offers wine-bar fare like salads and sampler platters of cheeses, along with wine by the glass, beer, and harder drinks.

On the decidedly more civilized side is **Gusto,** Piazza Augusto Imperatore 7 (© 06-3236363), an enoteca, restaurant, bookstore, and candy shop. There's live music to go along with a wide selection of wines and beers. The wine bar (snacks available) is open daily from 11am to 2am; the restaurant/pizzeria side is open daily 12:30 to 3pm and 7:30pm to midnight, and Sunday from noon to 3:30pm.

IN TRASTEVERE   New bars and clubs open in Trastevere every month—and about half are closed by the next one. Fortunately, Trastevere seems to know no limit of critical mass when it comes to nightlife, so even the remaining half is still enough to keep you busy after hours. The following places seem here to stay. **Birreria La Scala,** Piazza della Scala 60 (© 06-5803763), is a raucous Italianstyle beer hall and disco/pub. It's open to 1am and has lots of good food, snacks, and desserts, plus a decent selection of beers and wines. There's live music Tuesday, Thursday, and Sunday (preceded on Thurs and Sun by a magic show). The ever-popular **Artú,** Largo Fumasoni Biondi 5 (no phone), is part pub, part wine bar, and part cafeteria/tea salon serving decadent homemade desserts; there's also an ample menu for heartier appetites (closed Mon).

One of Trastevere's greatest stops for traditionalists doesn't even have a name or a sign. Out front of Via della Scala 64 is the moniker **Vini Olii** (Wines and Oils), harkening to a simpler era with its "name" spray-painted on the concrete door lintel. Come for cheap glasses of vino while you stand at the minuscule counter with the neighborhood's old men. The **Bar San Callisto,** Piazza San Callisto 3–4 (no phone), is a run-of-the-mill bar (in the Italian sense of the word), a bit dingier than most, that somehow has become a requisite stop for everyone from trendoids to tourists. But it's just a first stop—it closes at 10pm.

GAY & LESBIAN CLUBS

Before you hit the clubs, stop off at one of Rome's two gay bookstores, **Babele,** Via dei Banchi Vecchi 116 (© 06-6876628), and **Queer,** Via del Boschetto 25 (© 06-4740691), both clearinghouses for the latest information on the gay scene. You may also want to become a member of Arcigay (**www.arcigay.it**), Italy's national gay organization, which gets you free or reduced admission to many gay locales in Italy.

The hottest gay event in Rome these days is La Mucca Assassina party on Fridays at **Alpheus,** Via del Commercio 36 (© **06-5747826;** Metro: Piramide), where even Rome's heterosexual club-kids go to see and be seen. The kitschy fountain and sculpture along with the pink bar make it all a bit cheesy and "rave" at the same time. Admission with your first drink is 3€ to 10€ ($3.45–$12), depending upon the event. The rest of the week (Sept–June Tues–Sun; July–Aug Fri–Sat only), the club goes straight.

Gay Rome created such a winner in **Alibi,** Via Monte Testaccio 40–44 (© **06-5743448**), that the club's appeal has crossed over into mainstream nightlife. It has a rotating schedule of DJs and three rooms blaring disco, garage music, underground tunes, a mix of pop and dance hits, or house music. The energy and surprise theme parties as well as the extraordinary terrace ensure big crowds. It's open Wednesday through Sunday 11pm to 4am; admission is 7.50€ to 15€ ($8.50–$17).

8 Side Trips: Ostia Antica & Tivoli

OSTIA ANTICA: ROME'S ANCIENT SEAPORT

The ruins of Rome's ancient seaport, 23km (14 miles) west of the city, are just as important and almost as fascinating as those of Pompeii, with the smell of saltwater in the air but without the crowds. Just a Metro ride from Rome's center, **Ostia Antica** 🐠🐠 (© **06-56358099**) is only partly excavated, much of it overgrown with tall grasses and umbrella pines that give the place a romantic touch missing from so many tourist-ridden archaeological sites these days. Bring a picnic and make a day of it.

Most of the buildings date from between the 1st and the 4th centuries A.D., though the city was founded in the 4th century B.C. The site map handed out at the gate is very good, and most of the structures inside the park are now placarded in English. Most visitors follow the **Decumanus Maximus** (Latin for Main St.) from beginning to end, but take the time to explore the side streets, where you'll find intact shops, black-and-white floor mosaics, a few frescoes clinging to walls, and millstones hiding in the weeds behind bakers' shops.

Be sure to stop at the well-preserved 1st- and 2nd-century **Theater,** which could seat 2,700 people. Several giant marble theater masks still survive on tufa columns at the stage. The **Casa di Diana (House of Diana)** is a typical three-story house with shops on the ground floor, some frescoes on the walls inside, and a courtyard fountain of the huntress goddess that gave the house its name. Don't miss Ostia's on-site **museum** (© **06-5635801**), which houses all the bits that unscrupulous types might try to carry off (as the Dark Ages barbarians and early baroque-era excavators did with wild abandon).

On the town's Forum you'll find the **Capitolum,** an important temple with an imposing flight of steps and most of the brick cellar still standing. Finally, search out the **Terme dei Sette Sapienti,** a well-preserved baths complex named for the seven "sages" painted on the wall and spouting bathhouse homilies. The central hall retains its magnificent floor mosaic of hunting scenes.

Admission to the site is 4€ ($4.60), and it's open Tuesday through Sunday from 9am to an hour before sunset (the museum is open 8:30am–6pm in summer and 8:30am–4pm in winter; it's closed Mon). Take Rome's Metro line B to the San Paolo stop, where you can catch a twice-hourly local train to the Ostia-Scavi stop (1€/$1.15). If you fancy a day at Rome's very crowded **beach,** you can also ride this Metro line to Ostia-Lido or continue to the last stop, Cristoforo Colombo. From there it's another 8km (5 miles) to the area's nude/gay (but innocuous) beach.

TIVOLI & ITS VILLAS

The little city of **Tivoli,** 32km (20 miles) from Rome, was already 4 centuries old when the Eternal City itself was founded, and it became a popular spot for countryside villas during both the Imperial period and the Renaissance. To get there, take Rome's Metro line B to the Ponte Mammolo stop, where you catch the COTRAL bus (1.55€/$1.80) to Tivoli–Villa d'Este (every 30 min.) or Tivoli–Villa Adriana (every hour).

In the center of town is the **Villa d'Este** ☆ (② **0774-312070**), started by Piero Ligorio for the fabulously wealthy Cardinal Ippolito II d'Este in 1550 (the construction outlived both of them, and the gardens were added to up until 1927). This site is renowned less for the (relatively) modest villa itself than for the spectacular **gardens** ☆, a baroque fantasy of some 500 fountains terraced down a hillside and surrounded by artificial grottoes and scads of umbrella pines, cypresses, ilexes, elms, and cedars. Call before making the trip out here, to be sure the fountains will be going at full blast, because the play of water against sunlight is what the Villa d'Este is all about (the best time is sunny weekends). Though what's here is spectacular (including the high jets of the Neptune Fountain and the long wall of One Hundred Fountains whose decorative frieze is overgrown with moss), imagine what it must have been like when the famous Water Organ fountain was still playing its songs and the Fontana della Civitta was creating bird song and owl screeches. The villa is open Tuesday through Sunday from 9am to an hour before sunset, and admission is 6.50€ ($7.45).

Five kilometers (3 miles) before the town on the road to Rome lie the ruins of the most fabulous palace built during the Empire, the **Villa Adriana** ☆☆ (② **0774-530203**). The emperor Hadrian was quite an accomplished architect, designing not only Rome's Pantheon, but also his own lavish palace in A.D. 118, a countryside retreat within easy reach of the capital and so architecturally advanced it even included central heating. The well-traveled Hadrian picked up so many architectural ideas from his voyages that he decided to re-create his own versions of famous buildings here. That's why today you can wander the long pool inspired by the Egyptian city of **Canopus,** a statue-lined canal with a beautiful curved colonnade at one end and a Temple of Serapis at the other. Recent reinterpretation of the statues suggests that the whole ensemble may be meant to represent the Mediterranean world, with the temple at the end portraying Egypt, the statues that imitate the caryatids from Athens's Acropolis in the middle symbolizing Greece, and the statues of Amazons at the other end standing for Asia Minor.

To honor the genius of the ancient Greeks, Hadrian built himself a peristyle— a giant cloister measuring 230×96m (754×315 ft.)—called the **Pecile,** loosely modeled after Athens's Stoa Poikile (Painted Porch), under which the great philosophical school of Stoicism was founded. The **Teatro Marittimo** was a retreat for the emperor, who could escape with his thoughts to this circular structure in the middle of a pond and pull the wooden bridges after him for seclusion. The **Imperial Palace** is grouped around four courtyards; in the staff wing are some fine mosaics, and good portions of both the **Small Baths** and the **Large Baths** still stand at the compound's west end. The grounds of this archaeological park are vast, and parts are still being excavated. Wander for as long as you can, looking for the **Greek Theater** and the ruins of the **Accademia,** and pausing in the two **small museums** to get a better grip on the original layout. Bring a picnic lunch and stay the whole day. The villa is open Tuesday through Sunday from 9am to an hour before sunset; admission is 6.50€ ($7.45).

4

Florence: Birthplace of the Renaissance

by Reid Bramblett

Five hundred years ago, the rich and beautiful city of **Florence (Firenze)** was the heart of European life. The Renaissance was born and developed here in the 15th century, giving rise to many of the most important developments in art, science, literature, and architecture through luminaries like Giotto, Donatello, Brunelleschi, da Vinci, Michelangelo, and Pisa-born Galileo. Florence may no longer be the axis around which the cultural world revolves, but the Renaissance's elegance and aesthetic sensibility are still alive and well. The city boasts Europe's greatest concentration of artistic wealth, much of which you can experience even without entering any of its world-class museums.

Europe's cultural revolution was financed largely by the Medicis (and those who flourished amid their commercial success), Florence's unrivaled ruling family throughout much of the Renaissance. They came to power as bankers and used their unprecedented acumen and wealth to foster artistic and intellectual genius. The city is filled with this heritage: Fully half a dozen of Italy's principal museums, as well as myriad churches and palazzi, house major paintings and sculpture of that golden period when Florence was, as D. H. Lawrence described it, "Man's perfect center of the Universe."

1 Arriving

BY PLANE

Several European airlines now service Florence's expanded **Amerigo Vespucci Airport** (© **055-30615** for the switchboard, or 055-373498 for flight updates, 055-306-1700 for national flight info, or 055-306-1702 for international flight info; www.aeroporto.firenze.it), also called **Peretola,** just 5km (3 miles) northwest of town. There are no direct flights to or from the United States, but you can make easy connections through London, Paris, Amsterdam, Frankfurt, and so on. ATAF's regularly scheduled **Vola in Bus** connects the airport with Piazza della Stazione downtown, taking about 30 minutes and costing 4€ ($4.60); buy your ticket onboard the bus. Just as expensive (4€/$4.60) but without the local stops is the half-hourly **SITA bus** to and from downtown's bus station at Via Santa Caterina 15r (© **055-219383** or 800-373760; www.sita-on-line.it), behind the train station. Metered **taxis** line up outside the airport's arrival terminal and charge about 13€ ($15) to most hotels in the city center.

The closest major international airport is Pisa's **Galileo Galilei Airport** (© **050-849111;** www.pisa-airport.com), 97km (60 miles) west of Florence. Two to three **trains** (www.trenitalia.it) per hour leave the airport for Florence

(70–100 min.; 4.95€–5.80€/$5.70–$6.65). If your flight leaves from this airport and you'll be going there by train from Florence, you can check in your baggage and receive your boarding pass at the Air Terminal on Track 5 in Florence's Stazione Santa Maria Novella; show up 30 minutes before your train departure. Early-morning flights might make train connections from Florence to the airport difficult: The solution is the regular train from Florence into downtown Pisa, with a 10-minute 4€ ($4.60) taxi from the Pisa train station to the nearby Pisa airport; the no. 3 bus (**800-012-773** in Italy; www.cpt.pisa.it) makes the same hop in twice the time for 1€ ($1.15). **Collective Taxi,** a van service, runs passengers from Pisa's airport to the train station for a flat 2.50€ ($2.85) per person (4€/$4.60 if you want to ride out to the Leaning Tower).

BY TRAIN

Most Florence-bound trains roll into the **Stazione Santa Maria Novella,** Piazza della Stazione (**𝄢 800-888088** toll free in Italy, or 055-288765; www.tren italia.it), which you'll often see abbreviated as **S.M.N.** The station is on the northwestern edge of the city's compact historic center, a 10-minute walk from the Duomo and a 15-minute walk from Piazza della Signoria and the Uffizi. The best budget hotels are immediately east of there around Via Faenza and Via Fiume.

With your back to the tracks, you'll find a tiny **tourist info office** with a hotel-booking service office (charging 2.30€–8€/$2.65–$9.20) toward the station's left exit next to a 24-hour pharmacy. It's open daily from 8:30am to 9pm. The **train information office** is near the opposite exit to your right. Walk straight through the central glass doors into the outer hall for tickets at the *biglietteria.* At the head of Track 16 is a 24-hour luggage depot where you can drop your bags (3€/$3.45 per piece for 12 hr.) while you search for a hotel.

Some trains stop at the outlying **Stazione Campo di Marte** or **Stazione Rifredi,** which are worth avoiding. Although there's 24-hour bus service between these satellite stations and S.M.N., departures aren't always frequent and taxi service is erratic and expensive.

BY BUS

Dozens of companies run frequent service to Florence from cities within Tuscany and Umbria to two bus hubs, one on each side of the Stazione Santa Maria Novella: **SITA,** Via Santa Caterina da Siena 17r (**𝄢 800-373760** toll-free in Italy, or **055-219383;** www.sita-on-line.it), is important for those busing to San Gimignano or Siena; **Lazzi,** Via Mercadante 2, Florence (**𝄢 055-363041;** www.lazzi.it), specializes in service to Lucca, Pisa, and the coast (Viareggio, Forte dei Marmi).

BY CAR

Driving to Florence is easy; the problems begin once you arrive. Almost all cars are banned from the historic center—only residents and merchants with special permits are allowed in. The traffic police, who'll assume from your rental plates you're a visitor heading to your hotel, will more than likely stop you at some point. Have the name and address of the hotel ready, and they'll wave you through. You can drop off baggage there (the hotel will give you a sign for your car advising traffic police you're unloading); then you must relocate to a parking lot. Ask your hotel which lot is most convenient: Special rates are available through most of the hotels and their nearest lot.

Standard rates for parking near the center are 1.15€ to 3€ ($1.30–$3.45) per hour; many lots offer a daily rate of 15€ to 30€ ($17–$35). Least expensive, at

15€ ($17) a day, is the vast underground public **Parterre** lot just north of Piazza della Liberta; you must show a hotel receipt to get that tourist rate when you retrieve your car. They'll also loan you a bike for free. Don't park your car overnight on the street; if you're towed and ticketed, it will set you back substantially—and the headaches to retrieve your car are beyond description.

2 Essentials

VISITOR INFORMATION

TOURIST OFFICES   The city's **largest tourist office** is at Via Cavour 1r (© 055-290832; fax 055-2760383; www.firenzeturismo.it), about 3 blocks north of the Duomo. Outrageously, they now charge for the basic, useful info: .50€ (55¢) for a city map (though there's still a free one lacking only inane brief descriptions of the museums and sights), 2€ ($2.30) for a little guide to museums, and 1€ ($1.15) each for pamphlets on the bridges and the piazze of Florence. The monthly *Informacittà* pamphlet on events, exhibits, and concerts is still free. The office is open Monday through Saturday from 8:30am to 6:30pm and Sunday from 8:30am to 1:30pm.

At the head of the tracks in Stazione Santa Maria Novella is a **tiny info office** with some maps and a hotel-booking service (see "Accommodations You Can Afford," later in this chapter), open Monday through Saturday from 9am to 9pm (to 8pm Nov–Mar). The **station's main tourist office** (© 055-212245) is outside at Piazza della Stazione 4. With your back to the tracks, take the left exit, cross onto the concrete median, and turn right; it's about 30m (98 ft.) ahead. The office is usually open Monday through Saturday from 8:30am to 7pm (often only to 1:30pm in winter) and Sunday from 8:30am to 1:30pm.

Another office sits on an obscure side street south of Piazza Santa Croce, Borgo Santa Croce 29r (© 055-2340444), open Monday through Saturday from 9am to 7pm and Sunday from 9am to 2pm.

PUBLICATIONS   At the tourist offices, pick up the free monthly *Informacittà.* The bilingual *Concierge Information* (www.florence-concierge.it) magazine, free from the front desks of top hotels, contains a monthly calendar of events and details on attractions. *Firenze Spettacolo* (www.firenzespettacolo.it), a 1.55€ ($1.75) Italian-language monthly sold at most newsstands, is the most detailed and up-to-date listing of nightlife, arts, and entertainment.

WEBSITES   The official Florence information site, **www.firenzeturismo.it**, contains a wealth of up-to-date information on Florence and its province, including a searchable hotels form that allows you to specify amenities, categories, and the like.

Firenze By Net (www.mega.it/florence), **Firenze.Net** (http://english.firenze.net), and **FlorenceOnLine** (www.fol.it) are all Italy-based websites with English translations and good general information on Florence; the first two sites also feature much information on entertainment in the city. The site for **Concierge Information** (www.florence-concierge.it) is an excellent little guide to this month's events, exhibits, concerts, and theater, as is **Informacittà,** although the English version is still pending on the latter. Other sites worth checking out are **Your Way to Florence** (www.arca.net/florence.htm), **Time Out** (www.timeout.com/florence), **Know It All: Know Tuscany** (www.knowital.com), and **The Heart of Tuscany** (www.nautilus-mp.com/tuscany).

FESTIVALS & EVENTS The **Maggio Musicale** (Musical May; ℂ **199-109910** at .12€/15¢ per minute, or 0935-564767 outside Italy; www.maggio fiorentino.com) is Italy's oldest and most important music festival and one of Europe's most prestigious. Events take place at various indoor and outdoor locations, sometimes including the courtyard of the Pitti Palace and the Piazza della Signoria (for the final night's grand concert). Following in the revered footsteps of creative director Riccardo Muti, Maestro Zubin Mehta has been the honorary director since 1985, often conducting Florence's Maggio Musicale Orchestra. World-class guest conductors and orchestras appear during the festival, which, despite its moniker, runs from late April to June (but never later than the first few days of July). For schedules and ticket information, inquire at the tourist office.

June to August, the Roman amphitheater in nearby Fiesole comes alive with dance, music, and theater for the **Estate Fiesolana** (Summer in Fiesole; ℂ **055-5979005;** www.estatefiesolana.it). City bus no. 7 travels to Fiesole from the train station and Piazza del Duomo. July brings the annual **Florence Dance Festival** (ℂ **055-289276;** www.florencedance.org), held in the beautiful amphitheater in the Cascine Park. A wide range of dance is performed, varying from classic to modern, with an emphasis on the latter. Again, check with the tourist office for details.

The highlight of June 24, the feast day of Florence's patron saint, **San Giovanni (St. John the Baptist),** is the **Calcio Storico,** a no-holds-barred cross between rugby, soccer, and wrestling with a major dose of ice-hockey attitude, played with a ball and few (if any) rules. Color-coded teams representing Florence's four original parishes/neighborhoods, clad in 16th-century costume, square off against one another in playoff games in dirt-covered Piazza Santa Croce, competing vigorously for that year's bragging rights and final prize: a golden-horned ox. The final *partita* is most worth seeing, often falling on or around June 24 (the feast day of San Giovanni). Fireworks light the sky that night, best viewed from along the north banks of the Arno east of the Ponte Vecchio. See the tourist office for ticket information for seats in the bleachers. No tickets are needed to view the equally dazzling procession in full historical regalia that wends its way through the cobblestone streets and piazzas before each match.

CITY LAYOUT

Florence is a compact city best negotiated on foot. No two sights are more than a 20- or 25-minute walk apart, and all the hotels and restaurants in this chapter are in the relatively small *centro storico* (historic center). The center is loosely bounded by the Stazione Santa Maria Novella (S.M.N.) to the northwest, Piazza della SS. Annunziata to the northeast, Piazza Santa Croce to the east, and the Arno River to the south. South of the river is the **Oltrarno** (on the other side of the Arno), a "Left Bank" adjunct to the *centro storico* and home to the Pitti Palace, the Boboli Gardens, and the Piazzale Michelangiolo lookout.

In the *centro storico*, Florence's magnificent tricolor-marble **cathedral,** freestanding **bell tower,** and **baptistery** dominate **Piazza del Duomo.** You'll inevitably walk along many of the streets radiating from this imposing square. **Borgo San Lorenzo,** a narrow street running north from the baptistery, is best known for the excellent outdoor market at its far end, the **Mercato San Lorenzo,** selling everything from marbleized paper-wrapped boxes and frames to leather bags and jackets. It borders the train station neighborhood, where you'll find a cluster of the city's cheapest hotels.

The Red & the Black

Unlike in other Italian cities, there are two systems of street numbering in Florence: black *(nero)* and red *(rosso)*. Black numbers are for residential and office buildings and hotels, while red numbers (indicated by an R following the number) are for commercial enterprises like restaurants and stores. The numbering systems operate independently of each other—so the doorways on a given street may run 1r, 2r, 3r, 1 (black), 4r, 2 (black). Florence plans to eventually eliminate this system and renumber everything, creating the major confusion they've resisted for centuries, but it'll be years before this is put into effect.

Via dei Calzaiuoli, Florence's most popular pedestrian thoroughfare and shopping street, runs south from the Duomo, connecting the church with the statue-filled **Piazza della Signoria,** off of which opens the Uffizi Gallery. West of and parallel to this is **Via Roma,** which becomes **Via Por Santa Maria** on its way to the famed **Ponte Vecchio,** a bridge over the Arno lined with tiny goldsmiths' shops. Midway between the two is **Piazza della Repubblica,** a busy cafe-ringed square surrounded by expensive-to-moderate shopping streets. Farther west is **Via dei Tornabuoni,** Florence's boutique-lined shopping drag, and its elegant offshoot, **Via della Vigna Nuova.**

From Piazza della Signoria, **Via D. Gondi** leads east, becoming **Borgo dei Greci** on its way to **Piazza Santa Croce** at the center's eastern edge.

NEIGHBORHOODS IN BRIEF

Florentines generally divide their city into the two banks of the Arno River—the northern bank around the Duomo and Piazza della Signoria, and the Oltrarno southern bank around the Palazzo Pitti. I've broken it down further, mostly into the visitor-oriented neighborhoods surrounding particular sites or churches, to facilitate the location of hotels, restaurants, and so on. It's an arbitrary designation to help you understand the flavor of each, decide where you want to stay, and plan your days.

Around the Duomo & Piazza Della Signoria This is as central as you can get and offers the greatest concentration of attractions (the Duomo, Uffizi, Bargello, Palazzo Vecchio), restaurants, hotels, and so on. Real estate is understandably the most expensive, and visitors help pay for this. For centuries, the **Duomo** has been Florence's religious hub and **Piazza della Signoria** its civic hub. Many streets still follow the ancient grid pattern laid down by the Romans, and the narrow back streets of truncated medieval towers and stalwart palazzi are some of the most picturesque and evocative. While shops along the neighborhood's western boundary of the boutique-lined **Via dei Tornabuoni** belong to the high priests of made-in-Italy glamour, the area generally offers something for everyone. The same is true of hotels and restaurants that can range from the refreshingly unpretentious to the over-the-top-priced tourist traps.

Near the Train Station, the Mercato San Lorenzo & Santa Maria Novella North and northwest of the Duomo area, but still easily accessible by foot, this neighborhood is one of the busiest due to train-station traffic and marketplace shoppers. Colorful, yes; peaceful, hardly. However, it doesn't

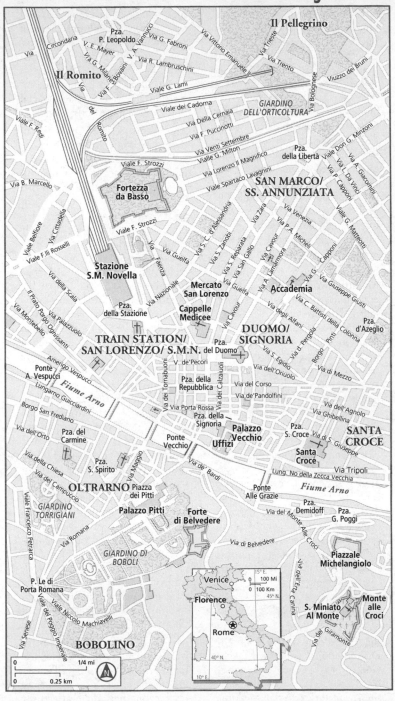

Florence Neighborhoods

Il Pellegrino

Il Romito

Pza. P. Leopoldo
V. E. Mayer
Via G. Milanesi
Via A. Vannucci
Via G. Fabroni
Via R. Lambruschini
Via F. Bovaini
Via del Romito
Circondaria
Via
Via Vittorio Emanuele II
Via Trieste
Via Trento
Viuzzo dei Bruni
Via Bolognese

Viale G. Lami

Viale dei Cadorna
GIARDINO DELL'ORTICOLTURA
Via Della Cernaia
Via F. Puccinotti
Via Venti Settembre
Vialle G. Milton
Via Lorenzo Il Magnifico
Viale Spartaco Lavagnini

Pza. della Libertà
Via Don G. Minzoni
Via A. Giacomini
Via L. Da Vinci
Via G. Matteotti
Via P. Capponi

Viale F. Strozzi

Via B. Marcello

Fortezza da Basso

SAN MARCO/ SS. ANNUNZIATA

Viale F. Strozzi

Viale Belfiore
Via Cittadella
Viale F.lli Rosselli

Via S. C. d'Alessandria
Via Venezia
Via P.A. Micheli
Via Zara
Via Cavour
Via G. Capponi
Via G. Giuseppe Giusti

Via della Scala
Il Prato
Via Palazzuolo
Porgo Ognissanti
Via Montebello

Stazione S.M. Novella

Via Guelfa
Via Faenza
Via Nazionale
Via S. Zanobi
Via S. Reparata
Via San Gallo
Via A. Lamarmora
Via Guelfa
Via Cavour

Mercato San Lorenzo

Accademia
Via degli Alfani
Via C. Battisti della Colonna

Pza. d'Azeglio

Pza. della Stazione

Cappelle Medicee

DUOMO/ SIGNORIA

Via d. Pergola
Borgo Pinti
Via di Mezzo

TRAIN STATION/ SAN LORENZO/ S.M.N.

Pza. del Duomo
V. de'Pecori
Via dell'Oriuolo
Via S. Egidio

Amerigo Vespucci
Ponte A. Vespucci
Lungarno Guicciardini
Borgo San Frediano
Via dell'Orto

Fiume Arno

Via dei Tornabuoni
Via de' Calzaiuoli
Pza. della Repubblica
Via Porta Rossa

Pza. della Signoria

Via del Corso
Via de'Pandolfini
Via dell'Agnolo
Via Ghibellina

Pza. S. Croce
Via di S. Giuseppe

SANTA CROCE

Pza. del Carmine
Via della Chiesa
Via del Campuccio

Pza. S. Spirito

Via Maggio

OLTRARNO Piazza dei Pitti

Ponte Vecchio
Uffizi
Palazzo Vecchio

Santa Croce

Via de' Bardi
Via Tripoli
Lung. No della Zecca Vecchia

Fiume Arno

Ponte Alle Grazie

Pza. Demidoff
Via del Monte Alle Croci

Pza. G. Poggi

GIARDINO TORRIGIANI

Palazzo Pitti
Forte di Belvedere

Via Romana
Via di Belvedere

Viale Francesco Petrarca

GIARDINO DI BOBOLI

Piazzale Michelangiolo

P. Le di Porta Romana

Viale del Poggio Imperiale
Viale Niccolò Machiavelli

Via del Giramonte
Via dell'Erta Canina

S. Miniato Al Monte

Monte alle Croci

BOBOLINO

0 — 1/4 mi
0 — 0.25 km

Venice
15° E
0 — 100 Mi
0 — 100 Km
45° N.

Florence

Rome

40° N.

10° E

carry the stigma of Rome's train station area (often seedy) or Venice's (inconvenient to most sites). The budget-hotel strips of Via Faenza and Via Fiume are nondescript but passable for those looking to cut costs; there's no danger, to speak of. The blocks surrounding the **Medici Chapels, Basilica di San Lorenzo,** and vast **Mercato San Lorenzo** are overwhelmed by hundreds of pushcart stalls, a potential plus for the shopping fiend; this is also where restaurant chefs and Florentines do their daily shopping. The 13th-century **Santa Maria Novella** church lends a note of quiet grace to the otherwise commercial and bustling area.

Near San Marco & Santissima Annunziata Defining the northern limits of the *centro storico,* Piazza San Marco is light-years away from the square of the same name in Venice. Traffic has taken over this square, and nearby high schools and university buildings keep it packed, too. It's home to the important **Museo San Marco,** dedicated to the work of Fra Angelico, and the expansive **Piazza SS. Annunziata,** said to be one of the Renaissance's most beautiful. However, make no mistake that the area's greatest magnet is Michelangelo's *David* in the **Accademia.** The relatively quiet side streets are removed enough from the Duomo crush to make this a preferred area for alternative hotel choices, though the walk to and from Duomo-area sites can be tiresome.

Near Santa Croce This large, neighborhood-like area east of the busy Via Proconsolo (and east of the Bargello and Uffizi in the Duomo area) is dominated by the Gothic **Santa Croce** church—by far the most visited of this area's sites. Nonetheless, it's an area that offers its fair share of genuine residential character in a city fast

succumbing to fast-food bars and tourist shops. An alluring choice of restaurants and quiet side streets, and a must-do visit to the Pantheon-like burials and frescoes for which Santa Croce is famous means you'll probably visit this eastern end of the *centro storico* at least once.

The Oltrarno The "Other Side of the Arno" is often referred to as the city's Left Bank. Escaping the prohibitive costs of the Duomo-dominated scenario north of here, it has been the alternative location for artists and artisans for centuries, but escalating costs today are slowly changing the neighborhood's dynamics—something not immediately obvious to visitors. The nightlife that revolves around the outdoor bars and restaurants of the tree-shaded **Piazza Santa Spirito** are still redolent of those bohemian days. Its historic sites are limited though important: The picture gallery at the **Palazzo Pitti** is second only to the Uffizi, and the frescoes of the Brancacci Chapel at **Santa Maria del Carmine** were some of the most seminal in the early years of the Renaissance. The Oltrarno was once the edge of the countryside, and it retains a sense of separateness and removal from the northern bank of the Arno, a 5-minute walk away. The side streets still accommodate the centuries-old workshops of wood carvers, furniture restorers, leather workers, and jewelry makers. Together with Santa Croce, this is one of the more residential neighborhoods, but with a spirited mix of restaurants, small shops, and wine bars.

In the Hills The oppressive weather of valley-trapped Florence has residents and visitors alike taking to the hills for a moment's respite from both the heat and the crowds. Although **Fiesole** (to the north) is considered a city in its own right, it's often seen as a suburb of Florence, and its views and restaurants make it a favorite escape. On the southern Oltrarno bank of the Arno and across from the area of Santa Croce is the lofty perch of **Piazzale Michelangiolo** and its postcard-perfect view of Florence and the Duomo (and Fiesole beyond). A visit to the lovely Romanesque **San Miniato** church, an easy stroll south of the piazzale, is recommended for a late-afternoon gelato break when Gregorian vespers are sung at the church and the sun sets on Florence's terra-cotta rooftops. Those in shape can walk here from the Ponte Vecchio by

taking **Via San Nicolo,** which initially runs parallel to the river and then turns south and passes through the ancient gate of the city, Porta San Nicolo, and heads up toward the piazzale, becoming a stepped pathway called the **Via del Monte alle Croci.** Alternatively, from the Ponte alle Grazie, east of the Ponte Vecchio on the Oltrarno side of the river, take **bus no. 13** for the 10-minute trip. A taxi from the center of town will probably cost around 8€ ($9.20), but you may risk being stuck without return transportation—they usually won't wait unless paid (but you can always take a bus or walk back).

GETTING AROUND

Florence—with almost all of its relatively small *centro storico* closed to commercial traffic—is one of the most delightful cities in Europe to explore on foot. The best city map is the pocket-size **LAC Firenze** with the yellow-and-blue jacket, available at most newsstands for 2.60€ ($3).

BY BUS   You'll rarely need to use Florence's efficient **ATAF bus system** (© 055-5650222 or 800-424500; www.ataf.net), since the city is so wonderfully compact. Many visitors accustomed to big cities like Rome step off their arriving train and onto a city bus out of habit, thinking to reach the center; within 5 minutes they find themselves in the suburbs. The cathedral is a mere 5- to 7-minute walk from the train station.

Bus **tickets** cost a ridiculous 1€ ($1.15) and are good for an hour. A **four-pack** *(biglietto multiplo)* is 3.90€ ($4.50) and a **24-hour pass** 4.50€ ($5.15). Tickets are sold at *tabacchi* (tobacconists), bars, and most newsstands. Once on board, validate your ticket in the box near the rear door to avoid a steep fine. If you intend to use the bus system, you should pick up a **bus map** at a tourist office. Since most of the historic center is limited to traffic, buses make runs on principal streets only, except for four tiny electric buses that trundle about the *centro storico.*

BY TAXI   You can't hail a cab, but you can find one at **taxi ranks** in or near major piazze or call one to your restaurant or hotel by dialing © **055-4242,** 055-4798, or 055-4390. Taxis charge .80€ (90¢) per kilometer, but there's a whopping minimum fare of 2.55€ ($2.95), rising to 5.50€ ($6.30) from 10pm to 6am and 4.30€ ($4.95) on Sunday and holidays, and a surcharge of 1.75€ ($2) just to pick you up; luggage costs .60€ (70¢) per piece. Don't forget to include a 10% tip. Taxis are really worth considering only for getting to and from the train station with luggage. For more info, check www.comune.firenze.it/tariffe/taxi.htm.

BY BICYCLE OR SCOOTER   Despite the relatively traffic-free historic center, biking has not really caught on here, but local authorities are trying to change that with **free bikes** (well, in past years there was a nominal .50€/55¢ fee). **Firenze Parcheggi,** the public garage authority (© **055-5000453;**

Country & City Codes

The **country code** for Italy is **39**. As in the rest of Italy, Florence no longer has a separate city code. (The old one, 055, is now incorporated into all numbers and must be dialed, zero and all, at all times.)

---

www.firenzeparcheggi.it), has set up temporary sites about town (look for stands at the train station, at Piazza Strozzi, at Via della Nina along the south side of Palazzo Vecchio, and in the large public parking lots) where bikes are furnished free from 8am to 7:30pm; you must return the bike to any of the sites.

If no bikes are left, you'll have to pay for them at a shop like **Alinari,** Via Guelfa 85r (© **055-280500;** www.alinarirental.com), which rents bikes (2.50€/$2.85 per hour; 12€/$14 per day) and mountain bikes (3€/$3.45 per hour; 18€/$21 per day). It also rents 50cc scooters (8€/$9.20 per hour; 28€/$32 per day) and 125cc mopeds (12€/$14 per hour; 55€/$63 per day).

BY RENTAL CAR   Don't rent a car to explore pedestrianized Florence itself. However, for day-tripping in the Chianti or exploring Tuscan hill towns, a car is vital. Arrange your rental from home for the best rates. If you need to do it on the spot, auto-rental agencies in Florence are centered on the Europa Garage on Borgo Ognissanti. **Avis** is at no. 128r (© **055-213629;** www.avis.com), and **Europcar** nearby at no. 53r–55r (© **055-290438;** www.europcar.com); **Hertz** is at Via Fininguerra 33r (© **055-2398205;** www.hertz.com). Most rental services have representatives at the Florence and Pisa airports, but you'll probably pay more to pick up a car there and drop it off in town.

FAST FACTS: Florence

American Express Amex is at Via Dante Alghieri 22r, 50122 Firenze (© **055-50981**), open Monday through Friday from 9am to 5:30pm and Saturday (banking services only) from 9am to 12:30pm. All traveler's checks (not just Amex ones) are changed without a fee.

Consulates The consulate of the **United States** is at Lungarno Amerigo Vespucci 38 (© **055-239951**), near its intersection with Via Palestro; it's open Monday through Friday from 9am to 12:30pm for drop-ins and 2 to 3:30pm by appointment only. The consulate of the **United Kingdom** is at Lungarno Corsini 2 (© **055-284133**), near Via Tornabuoni; it's open Monday through Friday from 9am to 12:30pm and 2:30 to 4:30pm. Citizens of **Australia, New Zealand,** and **Canada** should consult their embassies in Rome (see "Fast Facts: Rome," in chapter 3).

Doctors & Dentists A **Walk-in Clinic** (© **0330-774731**) is run by Dott. Giorgio Scappini. Tuesday and Thursday office hours are brief, from 5:30 to 6:30pm or by appointment at Via Bonifacio Lupi 32 (just south of the Tourist Medical Service; see "Hospitals" below). Monday, Wednesday, and Friday, go to Via Guasti 2 from 3 to 4pm (north of the Fortezza del Basso). British **Dr. Stephen Kerr** keeps an office at Via Porta Rossa 1 (© **055-288055;** www.dr-kerr.com), with office hours weekday mornings and drop-ins weekday afternoons from 3 to 5pm (home visits or clinic appointments are available 24 hr. daily).

For general dentistry, try **Dr. Camis de Fonseca,** Via Nino Bixio 9, northeast of the city center off Viale dei Mille (① 055-587632), open Monday through Friday from 3 to 7pm; he's also available for emergency weekend calls. The U.S. consulate can provide a list of other English-speaking doctors, dentists, and specialists. See also "Hospitals," below, for medical translator service.

Emergencies Dial ① 113 for an **emergency** of any kind. You can also call the **carabinieri** (the national police force, more useful than local branches) at ① 112, dial an **ambulance** at ① 118, and **report a fire** at ① 115. All these calls are free from any phone. For **car breakdowns,** call ① 116 (not free).

Hospitals The **ambulance telephone number** is ① 118. There's a special **Tourist Medical Service,** Via Lorenzo il Magnifico 59, north of the city center between the Fortezza del Basso and Piazza della Libertà (① 055-475411), open 24 hours; take bus nos. 8 or 80 to Viale Lavagnini or bus nos. 4, 12, or 20 to Via Poliziano.

Thanks to socialized medicine, you can walk into most any Italian hospital when ill (but not an emergency) and get taken care of speedily with no insurance questions asked, no forms to fill out, and no fee charged. They'll just give you a prescription and send you on your way. The most central are the **Arcispedale di Santa Maria Nuova,** a block northeast of the Duomo on Piazza Santa Maria Nuova (① 055-27581), and the **Misericordia Ambulance Service,** on Piazza del Duomo across from Giotto's bell tower (① 055-212222 for ambulance).

For a **free translator** to help you describe your symptoms, explain the doctor's instructions, and aid in medical issues in general, call the volunteers at the **Associazione Volontari Ospedalieri (AVO;** ① 055-2344567) Monday, Wednesday, and Friday from 4 to 6pm and Tuesday and Thursday from 10am to noon.

Laundry & Dry Cleaning Though there are several coin-op shops (mostly of the OndaBlu chain), you can get your wash done for you even more cheaply at a pay-by-weight *lavanderia*—and you don't have to waste a morning sitting there watching it go in circles. The cheapest are around the university (east of San Marco), and one of the best is a nameless joint at **Via Alfani 44r** (① 055-2479313), where they'll do an entire load for 6€ ($6.90), have it ready by afternoon, and even deliver it free to your hotel. It's closed Saturday afternoon. At other, non-self-service shops, check the price *before* leaving your clothes—some places charge by the item. Dry cleaning *(lavasecco)* is much more costly and available at *lavanderie* throughout the city (ask your hotel for the closest).

Mail & E-mail You can buy *francobolli* **(stamps)** from any *tabacchi* (tobacconists) or from the central post office. Florence's **main post office** (① 160 for general info, or 055-218156) is on Via Pellicceria 3, 50103 Firenze, off the southwest corner of Piazza della Repubblica. You can pick up letters sent *Fermo Posta* (Italian for *Poste Restante*) by showing ID. The post office is open Monday through Saturday from 8:15am to 7pm. All packages heavier than 2 kilograms (4½ lb.) must be properly wrapped and brought around to the parcel office at the back of the building (enter at V. dei Sassetti 4, also known as Piazza Davanzati). There is also a branch at the Uffizi, open Tuesday to Sunday from 8:15am to 6:45pm.

Drop **postcards and letters** into the boxes outside. To mail larger **packages,** drop them at *sportello* (window) 9/10, but first head across the room to window 21/22 for stamps. If that window is closed, as it often is, you buy your stamps at the next window, 23/24, which is also the pickup for *Fermo Posta* (*Poste Restante,* or held mail; see below).

You can also send packages via **DHL,** Via della Cupola 243 (© **055-308877** or 800-345345 in Italy for free pickup; www.dhl.it), or via **UPS,** Via Pratignone 56a in Calenzano (© **055-8825501** or 800-877877 in Italy; www.ups.com).

To **receive mail** at the central post office, have it sent to (your name)/Fermo Posta Centrale/50103 Firenze, Italia/ITALY. They'll charge you .15€ (17¢) per letter when you come to pick it up at window 23/24; bring your passport for ID. For people without an Amex card, this is a much better deal than American Express's similar service, which charges 1.50€ ($1.75) to receive and hold a noncardholder's mail. For Amex members, however, this service is free, so you can have your mail sent to (your name)/Client Mail/American Express/Via Dante Alghieri, 22r/50123 Firenze, Italia/ITALY.

To check or send e-mail, head to the **Internet Train** (www.internet train.it), with a dozen locations, including Via dell'Oriuolo 40r, just blocks from the Duomo (© **055-2345322**); Via Guelfa 54–56, near the train station (© **055-2645146**); Borgo San Jacopo 30r in the Oltrarno (© **055-2657935**); and in the underground tunnel from the train station toward town (© **055-2399720**). Access is 4€ ($4.60) per hour and 1€ ($1.15) for 10 minutes. (Internet Train also rents cellphones to visitors.) They also provide printing, scanning, Webcam, and fax services. Open hours vary but run at least daily from 10am to 10:30 or 11pm on weeknights, and noon to 7 or 8pm on weekends. **Netgate,** Via Sant'Egidio 14r (© **055-2347967**; www.thenetgate.it), charges 3.10€ ($3.55) per hour.

Newspapers & Magazines You can pick up the *International Herald Tribune* and *USA Today* from almost any newsstand. You'll find the *Wall Street Journal Europe* and the *London Times,* along with *Time* and *Newsweek,* at most larger kiosks. There's a 24-hour newsstand in the train station. For upcoming events, theater, and shows, see "Visitor Information," earlier in this chapter.

Pharmacies For pharmacy information, dial © **110**. Throughout Italy, pharmacies are marked by neon green crosses. There are **24-hour pharmacies** (also open Sun and state holidays) throughout Florence: in **Stazione Santa Maria Novella** (© **055-289435** or 055-216761; ring the bell 1–4am); **Molteni,** at Via dei Calzaiuoli 7r (© **055-289490** or 055-215472), just north of Piazza della Signoria; and **All'Insegna del Moro,** at Piazza San Giovanni 20r (© **055-211343**).

Police Dial © **113** for the **police** or, in an emergency, © **112** for the **carabinieri.** To report **lost property** or passport problems, call the *questura* (urban police headquarters) at © **055-49771**. Also see "Emergencies," above.

Safety Central Italy is an exceedingly safe area, with practically no random violent crime. There are, as in any city, plenty of **pickpockets** out to ruin your vacation, and Florence has the added joy of light-fingered Gypsy children (especially around the train station), but otherwise you're safe.

Do steer clear of the Cascine Park after dark, when it becomes somewhat seedy and you may run the risk of being mugged. And you probably won't want to hang out with the late-night heroin addicts shooting up on the Arno mud flats below the Lungarno embankments on the edges of town.

Telephone See "Fast Facts: Rome," in chapter 3.

Tipping See "Fast Facts: Rome," in chapter 3.

3 Accommodations You Can Afford

Many budget hotels are concentrated in the area around the Stazione Santa Maria Novella. You'll find most of the hotels in this convenient and relatively safe, if charmless, area on noisy Via Nazionale and its first two side streets, Via Fiume and Via Faenza; an adjunct is the area surrounding the Mercato San Lorenzo. The area between the Duomo and Piazza della Signoria, particularly along and near Via dei Calzaiuoli, is a good though invariably more expensive place to look.

Peak season is from mid-March to mid-July, September to early November, and December 23 to January 6. May and September are particularly popular, whether in the city or in the outlying Tuscan hills.

NEAR THE DUOMO & PIAZZA DELLA SIGNORIA

Albergo Firenze Renovations have transformed this former student hangout (still partly used as a study-abroad dorm) into a fine two-star hotel. Its location is divine, tucked away on its own little piazza at the heart of the *centro storico*'s pedestrian zone, but it's a bit too institutional to justify the midrange rates. The rooms are simple and brightly tiled but bland, although air-conditioning was recently added. This is a large operation without any of the warmth or ambience of a small family-run hotel, and the concierge and management are efficient but generally uninvolved.

Piazza Donati 4 (on V. del Corso, off V. dei Calzaiuoli), 50122 Firenze. ✆ **055-214203** or 055-268301. Fax 055-212370. www.albergofirenze.net. 57 units. 75€ ($86) single; 94€ ($108) double; 130€ ($150) triple; 160€ ($184) quad. Rates include continental breakfast. No credit cards. Parking 26€ ($30). Bus: A, 14, 23. **Amenities:** Bar; bike rental; tour desk. *In room:* A/C, TV, hair dryer.

Aldini There's little hyperbole in the Aldini's claim to being near the Duomo (it'll sound as if the bells are under your pillow). Within centimeters of the magnificent tricolor marble Duomo and its 14th-century campanile, the Aldini is in a 13th-century palazzo above the marginally less expensive Costantini. But the Aldini is more distinguished—a handsome, comfortable place with terra-cotta floors covered by Persian runners and large rooms whose floral bedspreads, matching drapes, and spacious bathrooms reflect a recent renovation. The front rooms have windows with partial views of the Duomo, though the clip-clop of horse-drawn carriages and the chatter of late-night strollers may disturb you.

Via dei Calzaiuoli 13 (3rd floor; south of Piazza del Duomo), 50122 Firenze. ✆ **055-214752.** Fax 055-291621. www.hotelaldini.it. 14 units. 85€ ($98) single; 135€ ($155) double; 170€ ($196) triple; 200€ ($230) quad. 15% discount if you pay cash. Rates include continental breakfast. Rates discounted 20% in low season. AE, DC, MC, V. Nearby garage parking 24€ ($28). Bus: A, 1, 6, 11, 14, 17, 22, 23, 36, 37. **Amenities:** Room service. *In room:* A/C, TV, minibar, hair dryer.

Florence Accommodations & Dining

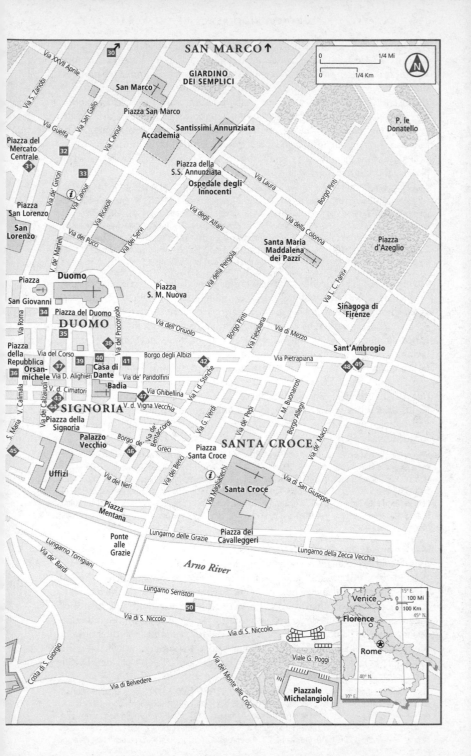

SAN MARCO ↑

GIARDINO
DEI SEMPLICI

30

Via XXVII Aprile

San Marco ✝

Piazza San Marco

Via S. Zanobi

Via Guelfa

Via San Gallo

Via Cavour

Santissimi Annunziata

Accademia

Piazza del
Mercato
Centrale

32

31

33

Via Ginori

Via Cavour

Piazza della
S.S. Annunziata

Ospedale degli
Innocenti

Via Laura

Via Ricasoli

Via degli Alfani

Via della Colonna

Borgo Pinti

P. le
Donatello

Piazza
San Lorenzo

San
Lorenzo

Via de' Martelli

Via dei Pucci

Via de' Servi

Via della Pergola

Santa Maria
Maddalena
dei Pazzi

Piazza
d'Azeglio

Via L. C. Farini

Piazza
Duomo
San Giovanni

34

Piazza del Duomo

DUOMO

35

Piazza
della
Repubblica

36

Orsan-
michele

37

Via del Corso

39

40

Via D. Alighieri

Casa di
Dante

41

38

Via de Procuinsolo

Via dell'Oriuolo

Piazza
S. M. Nuova

Borgo degli Albizi

42

Borgo Pinti

Via Fiesolana

Via di Mezzo

Via Pietrapiana

Sinagoga di
Firenze

Sant'Ambrogio

48 49

Via Roma

Via Calimala

S. Maria

V. Calimala

Via dei Calzaiuoli

43

44

V. d. Cimatori

SIGNORIA

Badia

47

Via de' Pandolfini

Via Ghibellina

V. d. Vigna Vecchia

Via I. d. Stinche

Via G. Verdi

Via de' Pepi

Via M. Buonarroti

Borgo Allegri

Via de' Macci

Piazza della
Signoria

Palazzo
Vecchio

45

46

Borgo de'

Via de' BentaccordI

Greci

Via de' Benci

Piazza
Santa Croce

SANTA CROCE

Via di San Giuseppe

Uffizi

Via del Neri

Via Magliabechi

Santa Croce

Piazza
Mentana

Piazza dei
Cavalleggeri

Ponte
alle
Grazie

Lungarno delle Grazie

Lungarno della Zecca Vecchia

Lungarno Torrigiani

Via de' Bardi

Arno River

Lungarno Serristori

Via di S. Niccolo

50

Costa di S. Giorgio

Via di S. Niccolo

Viale G. Poggi

Via di Belvedere

Via del Monte alle Croci

Piazzale
Michelangiolo

Venice

Florence

Rome

15° E
45° N.
40° N.
10° E

0   100 Mi
0   100 Km

0   1/4 Mi
0   1/4 Km

N

Alessandra ⟨★⟩   The etched-glass street doors hint of the architectural significance of the Alessandra's *palazzo nobile*, designed in 1507 by Baccio d'Angnolo,
a pupil of Michelangelo. This is a good spot to opt out of a private bathroom,
since only seven rooms share the four communal bathrooms, all large and freshly
redone; you'll never have to wait for a shared bathroom. The attentive housekeeping and spacious high-ceilinged rooms are most welcome, as is the free air-
conditioning (request it when reserving) and the new Internet workstation. The
hoteliers also rent out an apartment in a quiet section of the Oltrarno (across the
bridge from the Santa Croce neighborhood) for 775€ ($891) per week for two
people; check it out at www.florenceflat.com.

Borgo SS. Apostoli 17 (between V. dei Tornabuoni and V. Por Santa Maria), 50123 Firenze. ⓒ 055-283438.
Fax 055-210619. www.hotelalessandra.com. 27 units, 20 with bathroom. 95€ ($109) single without bath-
room, 115€ ($132) single with bathroom; 115€ ($132) double without bathroom, 160€ ($184) double with
bathroom; 160€ ($184) triple without bathroom, 200€ ($230) triple with bathroom. Rates include breakfast.
Ask about low-season rates. AE, MC, V. Parking in nearby garage 20€ ($23). Bus: B, 6, 11, 36, 37. **Amenities:**
Concierge; tour desk; limited room service (breakfast only); massage; babysitting; laundry service; same-day
dry cleaning; nonsmoking rooms. *In room:* A/C (in all but a few singles), TV, dataport, hair dryer, safe (in some).

Casci ⟨★⟩ ⟨*Kids*⟩   The friendly Lombardi family transformed this student pensione
into an attractive two-star hotel for older, more discerning guests several years
ago. Signora Lombardi and her son Paolo are sticklers for cleanliness (most bathrooms literally gleam). The central location means some rooms (with double-
paned windows) overlook busy Via Cavour, so for more quiet, ask for a room
facing the inner courtyard's magnolia tree. They serve an ample breakfast buffet
in a frescoed room and plan to add minibars to the rooms soon. Rossini, legendary composer of *The Barber of Seville* and *The William Tell Overture,* lived in
this palazzo from 1851 to 1855. In the off season (Nov–Dec and Feb), the Lom-
bardis offer a free museum ticket to everyone who stays at least 3 nights (and
with admissions running nearly $10 for most major museums, that's saying
something).

Via Cavour 13 (between V. dei Ginori and V. Guelfa), 50129 Firenze. ⓒ 055-211686. Fax 055-2396461.
www.hotelcasci.com. 25 units. 60€–105€ ($69–$121) single; 90€–145€ ($104–$167) double; 120€–185€
($138–$213) triple; 150€–225€ ($173–$259) quad. Rates include buffet breakfast. Off-season rates
20%–35% less; check website for special offers, especially Nov–Feb. AE, DC, MC, V. Valet parking 23€ ($26),
or in nearby garage (no valet) 15€ ($17). Bus: 1, 6, 11, 17. **Amenities:** Bar; concierge; tour desk; babysitting;
laundry service; dry cleaning; free Internet access; nonsmoking rooms. *In room:* A/C, TV, dataport, unstocked
fridge, hair dryer, safe.

Maria Luisa de' Medici ⟨★★★⟩ ⟨*Kids*⟩   Astoundingly comfy, wonderfully
quirky, and exceedingly friendly hotels like this don't exist anymore in Italy.
Around the corner from Dante's house, this pensione is named after the last
Medici princess, and the rooms are named after members of the Medici clan,
whose portraits grace their walls. The owner, Dr. Angelo Sordi, has furnished
them with 1960s avant-garde Italian furniture—contrasting with the museum-
quality baroque paintings and sculpture in the foyer and hall. With enormous
rooms sleeping up to five, the Maria Luisa is good for families, who'll also relish
the ample breakfast served in the rooms by Dr. Sordi's Welsh partner, Evelyn
Morris. One drawback: You have to walk up three flights.

Via del Corso 1 (2nd floor; between V. dei Calzaiuoli and V. del Proconsolo), 50122 Firenze. ⓒ 055-280048.
9 units, 2 with bathroom. Single rate on request. 70€–75€ ($81–$86) double without bathroom, 90€ ($104)
double with bathroom; 103€ ($118) triple without bathroom, 118€ ($136) triple with bathroom; 126€
($145) quad without bathroom, 146€ ($168) quad with bathroom. Rates include breakfast. No credit cards.
Nearby parking about 25€ ($29). Bus: A, 14, 23. **Amenities:** Concierge; tour desk. *In room:* Hair dryer, no
phone.

An Elevator Warning

Many *centro storico* hotels are housed in historic palazzi where elevators aren't always common. As one-, two-, and three-star hotels, many exist on just one or two floors in a palazzo, with a lobby rarely at street level— that means it's a one-floor walk up just to get to the front desk, and often another story or two to your room. If this is an issue, inquire when booking if there's an elevator, which floor the lobby is on, and which floor your room is on.

Orchidea 𝔉 The elegant English-speaking proprietor, Maria Rosa Cook, will gladly recount the history of this 13th-century palazzo where Dante's wife, Gemma Donati, was born (Dante's home and the Casa di Dante aren't far away). One of its floors houses an old-fashioned *locanda* (inn) whose large, high-ceilinged rooms are decorated with floral bedspreads and white lace touches. The furnishings are functional (with ceiling fans but still no air-conditioning) and the beds a little squishy. Room nos. 4 to 7 overlook a tiny junglelike garden rather than the sometimes noisy road. Plans to put phones in the rooms have yet to occur, but for now you can use the one in the common area (where there's also a TV).

Borgo degli Albizi 11 (1st floor; between the Duomo and Santa Croce), 50122 Firenze. ⓒ/fax 055-2480346. www.hotelorchideaflorence.it. 7 units, none with bathroom (1 quad has a shower). 55€ ($63) single; 75€ ($86) double; 100€ ($115) triple; 120€ ($138) quad. No credit cards. Parking nearby 15€–18€ ($17–$21). Bus: A, 14, 23. **Amenities:** Concierge; tour desk. *In room:* No phone.

WORTH A SPLURGE

Bigallo 𝔉 *Finds* I was quite cross to find that they'd decided to renovate this super-cheap standby with *the* best location (even closer to the Duomo than the Aldini, above) into three-star status (and double the prices). Its rooms are modular modern now—although two of these are wheelchair accessible—but in the location competition, it still wins for being above the Loggia del Bigallo on the corner of Piazza del Duomo. If you get one of the few rooms facing the Duomo, you'll have a view like no other, within poking distance of Giotto's bell tower. The traffic-free zone doesn't mean you won't have significant pedestrian noise that drifts up from the cobbled street below, as this is the city's most tourist-trammeled intersection.

They renovated this place to bring it in line with their other three hotels, including, a few blocks away on Via delle Oche and with side views of this living postcard, the **quieter Lanzi** (ⓒ/fax **055-288043;** www.hoteldelanzi.it). Should you choose to stay at the Lanzi, you'll find that prices for doubles and triples are the same as at the Bigallo, but singles run just 83€ to 129€ ($95–$148); amenities at the two hotels are similar.

Vicolo degli Adimari 2 (off the V. Calzaiuoli near the Piazza Duomo), 50122 Firenze. ⓒ 055-216086. Fax 055-214496. www.hotelbigallo.it. 17 units. 126€–183€ ($145–$210) single; 129€–186€ ($148–$214) double; 165€–251€ ($190–$289) triple. Rates include breakfast. AE, MC, V. Valet parking in garage 23€–30€ ($26–$35). Bus: A, 1, 6, 11, 14, 17, 22, 23, 36, 37. **Amenities:** Concierge; tour desk; car rental; room service; laundry service; dry cleaning; nonsmoking rooms. *In room:* A/C, TV, minibar, hair dryer, safe.

Hotel Torre Guelfa 𝔉𝔉 *Finds* Giancarlo and Sabina Avuri run one of the most atmospheric hotels in Florence. The first of many reasons to stay here is to drink in the breathtaking 360-degree view from the 13th-century tower, Florence's tallest privately owned tower. Although you're just steps from the Ponte

Vecchio, you'll want to put sightseeing on hold and linger in your canopied iron bed. So many people request room no. 15, with its huge private terrace and a view similar to the tower's, they've increased its price to 210€ to 230€ ($242–$265). Follow the strains of classical music to the salon, whose vaulted ceilings and lofty proportions hark back to the palazzo's 14th-century origins. In the late afternoon, you can climb the tower to enjoy a glass of wine, the brilliant panorama of the city spread out below.

The owners' newest hotel endeavor is the 18th-century **Palazzo Castiglione,** Via del Giglio 8 (© **055-214886;** fax 055-2740521), with four doubles (170€/$196) and two suites (200€/$230). Also ask them about their 15-room Tuscan hideaway, the **Villa Rosa di Boscorotondo** in Panzano (© **055-852577;** fax 055-8560835; www.resortvillarosa.com), a 35km (22-mile) drive from Florence in the heart of the Chianti, where the 15 doubles are 124€ ($143).

Borgo SS. Apostoli 8 (between V. dei Tornabuoni and V. Por Santa Maria), 50123 Firenze. © **055-2396338.** Fax 055-2398577. www.hoteltorreguelfa.com. 20 units. 80€–110€ ($92–$127) single; 150€–180€ ($173–$207) double; 180€–210€ ($207–$242) triple or jr. suite. Rates include continental breakfast. Parking in nearby garage 25€ ($29). AE, DC, MC, V. Bus: B, 6, 11, 36, 37. **Amenities:** Bar; concierge; tour desk; car-rental desk; courtesy car (for airport); limited room service; babysitting; laundry service; dry cleaning. *In room:* A/C, TV (in all but 6 1st-floor doubles), minibar, hair dryer.

Pendini (Ⓐ   The concept of the classic family-run pensione, quickly disappearing in Italy, is alive and well here: David and Emmanuele Abolaffio have kept intact the old-fashioned hominess of this century-old pensione. The rates have been kept intact as well; prices here haven't changed in two years, and that's really saying something in Florence. The nine spacious rooms overlooking Piazza della Repubblica are the most popular (guests don't seem to mind the late-night live music that comes from the square's cafes in summer); the rooms overlooking the inner courtyard are quieter. The family suites have two small bedrooms with a bathroom in common. The Pendini has been renovated but still exudes 19th-century elegance, for the owners rescued deserving original period pieces and supplemented them with convincing reproductions. A long corridor of parquet flooring covered with Persian runners leads to the inviting sitting room and the sunny breakfast room.

Via Strozzi 2 (Piazza della Repubblica), 50123 Firenze. © **055-211170.** Fax 055-281807. www.florenceitaly. net. 42 units. 80€–110€ ($92–$127) single; 110€–150€ ($127–$173) double; 150€–210€ ($173–$242) triple; 170€–250€ ($196–$288) quad; 170€–330€ ($196–$380) family suite. Rates include continental breakfast. AE, DC, MC, V. Valet garage parking 24€–31€ ($28–$36). Bus: A, 6, 22. **Amenities:** Concierge; tour desk; car rental; 24-hr. room service (breakfast and bar). *In room:* A/C, TV, dataport, hair dryer (ask at desk).

NEAR THE TRAIN STATION, MERCATO SAN LORENZO & SANTA MARIA NOVELLA

Inexpensive hotels proliferate in this area (generally safe but short on picturesque charm), particularly on **Via Faenza** and **Via Fiume,** where some buildings house as many as six pensioni. It makes most sense to walk to these hotels—all these are within a few blocks of the train station (which would be the bus stop anyway).

Abaco (Ⓐ★ (Value   Bruno runs a clean, efficient little hotel in a prime location and is one of the more helpful advice-filled hoteliers in town. The hotel has inherited a few nice touches from its 15th-century palazzo, including high wood ceilings, stone floors (some are parquet), and, in tiny no. 5, a carved *pietra serena* fireplace. Bruno's slowly replacing the mismatched furnishings with quirky antique-style pieces like gilded frame mirrors and rich half-testers over the beds. The hotel is at a busy intersection, but the double-paned windows help. He also provides free Internet access, and he'll wash and dry a load of laundry for you for just 7€ ($8.05).

Via dei Banchi 1 (halfway between the station and the Duomo, off V. de' Panzani), 50123 Firenze. ① 055-2381919. Fax 055-282289. www.abaco-hotel.it. 7 units, 3 with shower and sink, 3 with full bathroom. 51€ ($59) single without bathroom, 56€ ($64) single with bathroom; 65€ ($75) double without bathroom, 75€ ($86) double with shower only, 90€ ($104) double with bathroom; 110€ ($127) triple with bathroom. Breakfast 5€ ($6), free if pay cash. MC, V (but they prefer cash). Valet parking 24€ ($28) in hotel garage. Bus: A, 1, 6, 7, 10, 11, 14, 17, 22, 23, 36, 37. **Amenities:** Bar; bike rental; concierge; tour desk; car-rental desk; coin-op washer/dryer. In room: A/C, TV, dataport, hair dryer.

Albergo Azzi/Locanda degli Artisti   Musicians Sandro and Valentino, the young owners of this ex-pensione (also known as the Locanda degli Artisti), are creating here a haven for artists, artist manqués, and students. It exudes a relaxed bohemian feel—not all the doors hang straight and not all the bedspreads match, although strides are being made (and they've even discovered some old frescoes in room nos. 3 and 4). In 2003, they overhauled the hotel, going from a one-star (bottom end) to a two-star (inexpensive/moderate) hotel. This involved adding amenities to the rooms (TVs, phones, A/C, and such) and redoing the reception and public spaces, using as much as possible recycled and bio-friendly products. In June 2004, they added a sauna and Jacuzzi-style shower, plus four large suites with Jacuzzi tubs. You'll love the open terrace with a view where breakfast is served in warm weather, as well as the small library of art books and guidebooks. Four of the rooms without full bathroom have a shower and sink (but no toilet). In the same building, under the same management and with similar rates, are the **Anna** (eight units, four with bathroom; ① 055-2398322) and the **Paola** (seven units, four with shower/sink in room and some with frescoes; ① 055-213682).

Via Faenza 56 (1st floor), 50123 Firenze. ①/fax 055-213806. www.hotelazzi.it. 20 units, 13 with bathroom. 35€–48€ ($40–$55) single without bathroom, 50€–65€ ($58–$75) single with bathroom; 45€–65€ ($52–$75) double without bathroom, 65€–95€ ($75–$109) double with bathroom; 90€–150€ ($104–$173) suite with bathroom; 25€ ($29) bed in shared room. Breakfast 7€ ($8.05). AE, DC, MC, V. Parking in nearby garage 16€ ($18). Bus: A, 1, 4, 7, 10, 11, 12, 14, 25, 31, 32, 33, 36, 37. **Amenities:** Jacuzzi (shower-style); sauna; concierge; tour desk. In room: A/C (on request), TV (on request), hair dryer.

Armonia ⓥalue   Owned by Mario and Marzia, a young, English-speaking brother and sister, this pensione is a reliable no-frills choice when your budget keeps you near the train station. An occasional touch sets it apart: Some white-washed rooms have nice bedspreads, and breakfast is served in your room at no extra charge. The three rooms in the back are the quietest. You'll have the key to the front door, so you won't need to wake the night porter after hours. Prices here have remained fairly stable—highly unusual in Florence.

Via Faenza 56 (1st floor), 50123 Firenze. ① 055-211146. armonia1962@libero.it. 7 units, none with bathroom. 20€–42€ ($23–$48) single; 35€–66€ ($40–$76) double; 45€–90€ ($52–$104) triple; 70€–115€ ($81–$132) quad. No credit cards. Bus: A, 1, 7, 10, 11, 12, 14, 17, 25, 31, 32, 33, 36, 37. In room: No phone.

Bellettini ⓕ   A hotel has existed in this Renaissance palazzo since the 1600s. Gina and Marzia, sisters who are third-generation hoteliers, run this gem of terra-cotta tiles, wrought-iron or carved-wood beds, antiques, stained-glass windows, and hand-painted coffered ceilings. Room no. 44 offers a tiny balcony that, blooming with jasmine and geraniums by late spring, makes it second best only to room no. 45, with its view of the Medici Chapels and the Duomo's dome. The two bedrooms of no. 20 make it perfect for families. Breakfast is an impressive spread. In 2000, they added a lovely six-room annex with frescoes, marble bathrooms, minibars, and coffeemakers; rooms in the annex run a bit more: 110€ ($127) for a single, 170€ ($196) for a double, and 200€ ($230) for a triple.

The hotel shares management with the 26-room **Le Vigne,** Piazza Santa Maria Novella 24 (✆ **055-294449;** fax 055-2302263), which absorbs some of the overflow into large but simple renovated rooms. The rates are slightly lower than at the Bellettini. Duplex no. 119 is great for families.

Via dei Conti 7 (off V. dei Cerretani), 50123 Firenze. ✆ **055-213561** or 055-282980. Fax 055-283551. www.hotelbellettini.com. 28 units. 80€ ($92) single without bathroom, 100€ ($115) single with bathroom; 110€ ($127) double without bathroom, 140€ ($161) double with bathroom; 140€ ($161) triple without bathroom, 170€ ($196) triple with bathroom; 210€ ($242) quad with bathroom. Rates include buffet breakfast. AE, DC, MC, V. Nearby parking 21€ ($24). Bus: 1, 6, 7, 10, 11, 14, 17, 23, 36, 37. **Amenities:** Concierge; tour desk; room service; laundry service; dry cleaning. *In room:* A/C, TV, minibar (in annex), coffeemaker (in annex), hair dryer (ask at desk), safe.

Centro ✪

A block north of the Mercato San Lorenzo, this refurbished hotel occupies a palazzo that was home to Renaissance master painter Raphael in 1505 and 1506. There's precious little he'd recognize in its contemporary reincarnation, with amply sized rooms outfitted in colorful bedspreads and wood veneer furnishings; the bathrooms are tiled in white and brightly lit. New owners Andrea and Sandra Vendali continue to upgrade the place, slowly replacing the furnishing and fabrics with richer versions and laying springy carpet onto the tile floors. Second-floor rooms have air-conditioning (most of the rest get ceiling fans). No. 211 has a tiny balcony on the courtyard. In 2004 an elevator accessible from the ground floor was added, so it's no longer such a hike up to the first-floor reception. Even with that addition, however, prices have remained the same.

Via Ginori 17 (north of Piazza San Lorenzo), 50123 Firenze. ✆ **055-2302901.** Fax 055-212706. www.hotel centro.net. 16 units, 14 with bathroom. 42€–60€ ($48–$69) single without bathroom, 65€–95€ ($75–$109) single with bathroom; 95€–140€ ($109–$161) double with bathroom; 130€–190€ ($150–$219) triple with bathroom. Rates include buffet breakfast. AE, DC, MC, V. Valet parking in nearby garage 20€ ($23). Bus: 1, 6, 7, 10, 11, 17. **Amenities:** Concierge; tour desk; limited room service (breakfast); babysitting; laundry service; dry cleaning. *In room:* A/C (in 6 rooms), TV, hair dryer, safe.

Hotel Boston

The Boston is a peaceful, dignified place filled with original art and blessed with an outside shaded patio where breakfast becomes an idyllic way to start your day. The first two floors were built in the 17th century and have exposed wooden beams and plenty of charm (rooms on the newer third floor, equally recommended, are accessible by elevator). The Via Guelfa gets moderate traffic, so ask for a quiet room overlooking the back patio garden whose only noise is the clink of breakfast china that will serve as your wake-up call. When booking with the amenable Viti family, make sure you mention that you're a Frommer's reader to be eligible for their special discounted rates.

Via Guelfa 68 (west of V. Nazionale), 50129 Firenze. ✆ **055-496747.** Fax 055-470934. www.hotelboston firenze.it. 18 units, 14 with bathroom. 50€ ($58) single without bathroom, 75€ ($86) single with bathroom; 110€ ($127) double with bathroom; 150€ ($173) triple with bathroom; 170€ ($196) quad with bathroom. Rates include continental breakfast. These are special rates for Frommer's readers. Ask about low-season 15% discounts. MC, V. Parking 15€ ($17); valet parking 23€ ($26). Bus: 4, 7, 10, 12, 25, 31, 32, 33. **Amenities:** Laundry service; dry cleaning. *In room:* A/C, TV.

Merlini ✪ *Value*

Run by the Sicilian Gabriella family, this cozy third-floor walk-up boasts rooms appointed with wooden-carved antique headboards and furnishings (and a few modular pieces to fill in the gaps). It's one of only two hotels in all Florence with mosquito screens. The optional breakfast is served on a sunny glassed-in terrace decorated in the 1950s with frescoes by talented American art students and overlooking a large, leafy courtyard. Room nos. 1, 4 (with a balcony), and 6 to 8 all have views of the domes topping the Duomo and the Medici Chapels across the city's terra-cotta roofscape. A renovation tripled the number of private bathrooms and freshened up everything. This is a notch above your average one-star place, the best in a building full of tiny pensioni, but there's a 1am curfew.

Via Faenza 56 (3rd floor), 50123 Firenze. ⓒ **055-212848**. Fax 055-283939. www.hotelmerlini.it. 10 units, 6 with bathroom. 35€–45€ ($40–$52) single without bathroom; 60€–75€ ($69–$86) double without bathroom, 70€–90€ ($81–$104) double with bathroom; 85€–100€ ($92–$115) triple with bathroom; 75€–100€ ($86–$115) quad without bathroom. Breakfast 6€ ($6.90). Nearby parking 15€ ($17). AE, MC, V. Bus: A, 1, 4, 7, 10, 11, 12, 14, 25, 31, 32, 33, 36, 37. **Amenities:** Concierge; tour desk. *In room:* A/C (in 3 rooms), hair dryer (ask at desk), no phone.

Mia Cara *Value* The only way you'll pay less than at the Mia Cara is at the Noto family's hostel on the ground floor. At the hotel you'll find double-paned windows, spacious rooms, renovated plumbing, and attractive iron headboards. In fact, the hotel was recently refurbished in an effort to gain another star and is expected to reopen in 2005. When it does, you'll find that all rooms will have private bathrooms with hair dryers, as well as minibars, telephones, TVs, and air-conditioning—and even a few rooms outfitted for handicapped guests. As always, though, the rooms overlooking the small garden out back are more tranquil than those on the street side.

Angela, the English-speaking daughter, can be reached at the numbers below or at ⓒ **055-290804** (fax 055-2302601) for information on the downstairs **Archi Rossi Hostel** (www.hostelarchirossi.com). Its units sleep four to six for 18€ to 20€ ($21–$23) per person without a bathroom, and for 19€ to 22€ ($22–$25) with a bathroom, depending on number of beds in the room. (There are also private, bathroomless singles in the hostel for 29€/$33, including breakfast, and family rooms sleeping three to five for 24€/$27 each, including breakfast.) The hotel is closed from 11am to 2:30pm, with a 2am curfew. Both the hotel and the hostel have their own TV room and public phone. At the hostel, the rates include breakfast and Internet access.

Via Faenza 58 (2nd floor), 50123 Firenze. ⓒ **055-216053**. Fax 055-2302601. 22 units. Prices not set at press time, but are not expected to top 100€ ($115) per double. Ask about off-season discounts. No credit cards. No breakfast offered in hotel (only in hostel). 4 parking spots, sometimes free, sometimes up to 8€. Bus: A, 1, 4, 7, 10, 11, 12, 14, 25, 31, 32, 33, 36, 37. **Amenities:** Concierge; tour desk; nonsmoking rooms. *In room:* A/C, TV, minibar, hair dryer.

Monica *Finds* Gracious polyglot Rhuna Cecchini has supervised the face-lift of this hotel, resulting in a bright, airy ambience and refinished bathrooms. The prices have increased, but so have the amenities. Highlights are the terrazzo floors, wrought-iron bedsteads, exposed-brick archways, and wonderful terrace, which begins hosting breakfast the minute the weather turns warm. Most rooms are in the back of the building over the terrace, ensuring a quiet stay and pleasant rooftop views.

Via Faenza 66 (1st floor; at V. Cennini), 50123 Firenze. ⓒ **055-281706**. Fax 055-283804. www.hotelmonica firenze.it. 15 units, 10 with full bathroom, 2 with shower/sink but no toilet. 60€ ($69) single without bathroom, 70€ ($81) single with bathroom; 60€ ($69) double without bathroom or with shower, 100€ ($115) double with bathroom. 30€ ($35) each person extra in room. Rates include buffet breakfast. Parking in nearby garage 25€ ($29). AE, DC, MC, V. Bus: 4, 7, 10, 12, 25, 31, 32, 33. **Amenities:** Concierge; tour desk; limited room service (breakfast); laundry service; dry cleaning. *In room:* A/C, TV.

Nuova Italia *Finds* This top-notch hotel is watched over by affable English-speaking Luciano and Canadian-born Eileen Viti and their daughter, Daniela. Eileen met Luciano more than 30 years ago when she stayed at his family's hotel on the recommendation of an old *Frommer's Europe on $5 a Day.* Their hotel is a work in progress: One season, triple-paned windows and rare mosquito screens were installed; the next, bathrooms were retiled and air-conditioning and new carpeting appeared. This past year, they redid all the showers—amazingly, prices here haven't risen in 2 years! The family's love of art is manifested in framed posters and paintings, and Eileen is a great source of information about local exhibits. The staff here really puts itself to task for guests, recommending restaurants, shops, day trips—they've given me tips even the tourist office didn't know about.

Via Faenza 26 (off V. Nazionale), 50123 Firenze. ℂ 055-268430 or 055-287508. Fax 055-210941. 20 units. *For Frommer's readers:* 90€ ($104) single; 119€ ($137) double; 145€ ($167) triple. Rates include continental breakfast. AE, MC, V (but 8% discount if you pay in cash or traveler's checks). Valet garage parking about 20€ ($23). Bus: 1, 4, 7, 10, 11, 12, 25, 31, 32, 33. Closed Dec 1–26. **Amenities:** Concierge; tour desk; car-rental desk; limited room service (breakfast); babysitting; laundry service; dry cleaning. *In room:* A/C, TV, hair dryer.

Serena 𝄞   Run with pride by the Bigazzi family, this unpretentious but dignified place offers pleasant surprises: nicely tiled bathrooms, patterned stone floor tiles, molded ceilings, and early-1900s stained-glass French doors. The rooms are airy and bright, and kept clean as a whistle by the owner's wife.

If the Serena is full, try the charming two-star **Fiorita** (ℂ **055-283189;** fax 055-2728153; www.hotelfiorita.net), where the 13 rooms with air-conditioning, minibar, TV, and phone go for 85€ to 99€ ($98–$114) for a double (the price spikes up to 124€/$143 during holidays).

Via Fiume 20 (2nd floor), 50123 Firenze. ℂ 055-213643. Fax 055-280447. www.albergoserena.it. 8 units. 60€ ($69) single; 90€ ($104) double. Extra person 30€ ($35). Ask about off-season discounts. Continental breakfast 5€ ($5.75). AE, DC, MC, V. Public parking 20€ ($23). Bus: A, 4, 7, 10, 12, 13, 14, 25, 28, 31, 32, 33. **Amenities:** Bar; concierge; tour desk; nonsmoking rooms. *In room:* TV, hair dryer (ask at desk), safe.

WORTH A SPLURGE

Burchianti 𝄞𝄞 *Finds*   In 2002, rising rents forced the kindly owner of this venerable inn (established in the 19th c.) to move up the block into the *piano nobile* of a neighboring 15th-century palazzo. She definitely traded up. Incredible frescoes dating from 17th century and later decorate every ceiling but one tiny single, and many of the walls—actually, virtually all the walls are painted, but the yahoos of a previous age whitewashed over them and the hotel could afford to uncover only a few of them for the time being. When I visited, the workers were painting the trim, wiping off the terra-cotta tile floors, and finishing up installation of the inlaid marble bathrooms and period-style furnishings. This promises to become one of the most sought-after little hotels in Florence.

Via del Giglio 8 (off V. Panzani), 50123 Firenze. ℂ 055-212796. Fax 055-2729727. www.hotelburchianti. com. 10 units. 100€ ($115) single; 130€–170€ ($150–$196) double; 210€ ($242) suite. Rates include breakfast. AE, MC, V. No credit cards. Parking in garage next door 25€ ($29). Bus: A, 1, 6, 7, 10, 11, 14, 17, 22, 23, 36, 37. **Amenities:** Bar; concierge; tour desk; car-rental desk; limited room service (breakfast); babysitting; laundry service; dry cleaning. *In room:* A/C, TV (on request), dataport, minibar (in suite), hair dryer, safe.

Mario's 𝄞𝄞   In a traditional Old Florence atmosphere, Mario Noce and his enthusiastic staff run a first-rate ship. Your room might have a wrought-iron headboard and massive reproduction antique armoire, and look out onto a peaceful garden; the amenities include fresh flowers and fruit. The beamed ceilings in the common areas date from the 17th century, although the building became a hotel only in 1872. I'd award Mario's two stars, if not for its location—it's a bit far from the Duomo nerve center. Hefty discounts during off-season months (as low as the lowest rates listed below) de-splurge this lovely choice. The only room without a private bathroom has access to hall facilities not used by other guests.

Via Faenza 89 (1st floor; near V. Cennini), 50123 Firenze. ℂ **055-216801.** Fax 055-212039. www.hotel marios.com. 16 units, 15 with private bathroom. 110€ ($127) single without bathroom; 122€ ($140) single with bathroom; 165€ ($190) double; 212€ ($244) triple. Rates include buffet breakfast. AE, DC, MC, V. Valet parking 20€–25€ ($23–$29). Bus: 4, 7, 10, 11, 12, 25, 31, 32, 33. **Amenities:** Bar; concierge; tour desk; limited room service (breakfast); babysitting; laundry service; dry cleaning; nonsmoking rooms. *In room:* A/C, TV, dataport, hair dryer, safe.

NEAR PIAZZA SAN MARCO

Cimabue   Looking for a hotel with lots of charm and character, and a spirited multilingual couple who runs it all with pride? The small Cimabue may have only two stars, but they're two shining stars, from the firm orthopedic mattresses to the best freshly ground breakfast cappuccino. When Igino Possi and his Belgian wife, Daniele Dinau, renovated their acquisition in 1993, they saved what they loved best in this 1904 palazzo and renovated around it: the original terra-cotta pavement, ceiling frescoes in six rooms, suites of Art Nouveau headboards, and mirrored armoires. In 2005, the couple plans to add air-conditioning to all the guest rooms. During a recent visit, the guests were an interesting mix of two retired British professors, an American priest, a young Canadian couple on their honeymoon, and a stylish German art historian.

Via Benifacio Lupi 7 (west of V. San Gallo), 50129 Firenze. © 055-471989. Fax 055-4630906. www.hotel cimabue.com. 16 units. 60€–98€ ($69–$113) single; 78€–140€ ($90–$161) double; 90€–175€ ($104–$201) triple; 115€–195€ ($132–$224) quad. Rates include buffet breakfast. AE, DC, MC, V. Parking in nearby garage 18€ ($21). Bus: 1, 6, 7, 10, 11, 12, 17, 25, 31, 32, 33. *In room:* TV, hair dryer, safe.

IN THE OLTRARNO

Much more convenient than the remote though beautiful IYHF **youth hostel** in the hills of Fiesole (Ostello Villa Canerata, Vle. Augusto Righi 2/4, 50137 Firenze; © **055-601451;** fax 055-610300; www.ostellionline.org), the privately run **Ostello Santa Monaca,** Via Santa Monaca 6, 50124 Firenze (© **055-268338** or 055-2396704; fax 055-280185; www.ostello.it), is a lively gathering spot for the collegiate and newly graduated crowd in a 15th-century monastery, as well as a great place to trade budget tips and meet travel companions. Beds cost 17€ ($19), the lockout is 9:30am to 2pm, and curfew is 1am.

La Scaletta ⌂   Head for the umbrella-shaded roof terrace at sunset to marvel at the stunning 360-degree panorama overlooking the Pitti Palace. In one of only two historic palazzi on the street to survive World War II, this top-floor pensione was run for decades by the Barbieri family, but they bowed out in the fall of 2004. The hotel will go on, though what changes the new owners may bring is anybody's guess. For now, the spacious rooms boast terra-cotta floors, whitewashed walls, sturdy furnishings, and waffle towels in the modest bathrooms. Rooms downstairs are older in fashion, with *pietra serena* doorjambs, and there's even a huge family-style room with a fireplace. The rooms fronting Via Guicciardini have double-paned windows, while the quieter ones in back overlook the Boboli Gardens.

Via Guicciardini 13 (2nd floor; near Piazza de Pitti), 50125 Firenze. © **055-283028** or 055-214255. Fax 055-289562. www.lascaletta.com. 13 units, 11 with bathroom. 50€ ($58) single without bathroom, 95€ ($109) single with bathroom; 115€ ($132) double without bathroom, 140€ ($161) double with bathroom; 130€ ($150) triple without bathroom, 175€ ($201) triple with bathroom; 150€ ($173) quad without bathroom, 190€ ($219) quad with bathroom. Rates include continental breakfast. Ask about off-season discounts. MC, V. Nearby parking 10€–28€ ($12–$32). Bus: D, 6, 11, 36, 37. **Amenities:** Concierge; tour desk; limited room service (breakfast); babysitting; laundry service; dry cleaning. *In room:* A/C (in 8 rooms), TV (in 5, or on request), hair dryer.

Sorelle Bandini   This pensione occupies a landmark Renaissance palazzo on one of the city's great squares. You can live like the nobles of yore in rooms with 5m (16-ft.) ceilings whose 3m (9-ft.) windows and oversize antique furniture are proportionately appropriate. Room no. 9 sleeps five and offers a Duomo view from its bathroom window; room B is a double with a fantastic cityscape out the window. On closer inspection, you'll see the resident cats have left their mark on common-area sofas, and everything seems a bit ramshackle and musty. But that seems to be the point. The highlight is the monumental roofed veranda where Mimmo, the English-speaking manager, oversees breakfast and encourages brown-bag lunches and the chance to relax and drink in the views. Franco Zef-firelli used the pensione for some scenes in *Tea with Mussolini.* Quite frankly, their fame as a "typical old-fashioned" pensione went a bit to their heads—and to the prices, which slowly crept rather higher than they should be for a budget-class hotel. Perhaps they've figured this out—the prices listed below are a smidge lower than they were in the last edition.

Piazza Santo Spirito 9, 50125 Firenze. ⓒ 055-215308. Fax 055-282761. 12 units, 5 with bathroom. Single rate on request. 95€ ($109) double without bathroom, 115€ ($132) double with bathroom; extra person 35% more. Rates include continental breakfast. Bus: D, 11, 36, 37. **Amenities:** Concierge; tour desk; car-rental desk; limited room service (breakfast); babysitting. *In room:* No phone.

WORTH A SPLURGE

Silla ⓐ   On a shaded riverside piazza, this 15th-century palazzo's second-floor patio terrace is one of the city's nicest breakfast settings (in winter, there's a breakfast salon with chandeliers and oil paintings). The Silla's most recent reno-vation was in 2001, and the hoteliers continue to make minor modifications. Many rooms overlook the Arno and, when winter strips the leaves off the front trees, the spire of Santa Croce on the opposite bank. Every room is unique—some with beamed ceilings and parquet floors, others with floral wallpaper and stylish furnishings. The attention to detail and the friendly, skilled staff should make this hotel better known; word-of-mouth keeps it regularly full in pricey Florence, despite its refreshingly low profile.

Via dei Renai 5 (on Piazza Demidoff, east of Ponte delle Grazie), 50125 Firenze. ⓒ **055-2342888.** Fax 055-2341437. www.hotelsilla.it. 35 units. 125€ ($144) single; 175€ ($201) double; 220€ ($253) triple. Rates include buffet breakfast. Ask about off-season discounts. AE, DC, MC, V. Parking in hotel garage 16€ ($18). Often closes late Nov to late Dec. Bus: C, D, 12, 23. **Amenities:** Concierge; tour desk; room service; non-smoking rooms. *In room:* A/C, TV, minibar, hair dryer, safe.

4 Great Deals on Dining

Italian **meals** consist of three primary courses: the *antipasto* (appetizer), the *primo* (first course, usually a pasta or soup), and the *secondo* (the main course of meat or fish)—to which you must usually add a separate *contorno* if you want a side of veggies. You're expected to order at least two courses, if not all three.

Almost all the places below specialize in *cucina povera* or *cucina rustica,* based on the region's rustic and hearty cuisine. Despite its simplicity, Florentine cooking remains one of the most renowned in Italy for its well-balanced flavors and high-caliber ingredients.

Slabs of crusty bread are used for *crostini,* spread with chicken-liver pâté as the favorite Florentine antipasto. Hearty Tuscan peasant soups often take the place of pasta, especially *ribollita* (a stewlike minestra of twice-boiled cabbage, beans, and bread) or *pappa al pomodoro* (a similarly thick bread soup made from tomatoes and drizzled with olive oil). Look for *pasta fatta in casa* (the homemade pasta of the day), such as Tuscan pappardelle, thick flat noodles, often served *al cinghiale* (with a wild boar sauce) or with a simple tomato sauce. Your *contorno* will likely be the classic *fagioli all'uccelletto* (cannellini beans smothered in a sauce of tomatoes and rosemary or sage); sometimes *fagioli* are served plain, dressed only with extra-virgin olive oil.

Closed for Vacation

Despite Florence's importance as a modern-day Grand Tour destination, almost all restaurants (and stores and offices) close *per ferie* (for vacation) at some point in July or August from 2 to 6 weeks. The date may vary from year to year, so call any of the following establishments during this period before showing up. Your hotel will always know of a reliable choice in the neighborhood. In August, no one ever goes hungry, but your choices are considerably diminished.

Grilled meats are a specialty, the jewel being *bistecca alla fiorentina* ★★, an inch-thick charcoal-broiled steak on the bone: It's usually the most expensive item on the menu but is often meant to be shared by two (if you're not a sharer, tell the waiter it's *per una persona sola*). A wonderful splurge! Florentines also sing the praises of *trippa alla fiorentina,* but cow's stomach cut into strips and served with onions and tomatoes isn't for everyone.

Tuscany's most famous red **wines** are from the area designated as **Chianti** between Florence and Siena. You may be pleasantly surprised with the far less expensive *vino della casa* (house wine). Either a full bottle is brought to the table—you'll be charged *al consumo,* according to the amount you consume—or you'll be served by the quarter or half-carafe as you request.

Note: You can locate the restaurants below on the "Florence Accommodations & Dining" map on p. 192.

NEAR THE DUOMO & PIAZZA DELLA SIGNORIA

Alimentari Orizi SANDWICH BAR   Surprisingly few spots will make sandwiches to your specifications, and even fewer will give you the chance to pull up a seat and enjoy your food with a glass of wine at no extra cost. At this small *alimentari* (grocery store), Signor Orizi offers a choice of crusty rolls and breads and quality meats and cheeses to be sliced and arranged as you like (now with ketchup, mayonnaise, and mustard, too). There's a bar and half a dozen stools, but if the sun is shining, you can ask for your creation *da portare via* (to take away) and find a piazza bench with a view (Piazza della Repubblica to the east or Piazza Santa Maria Novella to the west). The coffee machine and fresh pastries make this a good breakfast option.

Via Parione 19r (off V. dei Tornabuoni). ℭ 055-214067. Sandwiches 3€–4€ ($3.45–$4.60); platters of cheeses or cold cuts 9€ ($10), including a glass of wine. AE, MC, V. Mon–Fri 8am–3pm and 5–8pm; Sat 8am–3pm. Closed Aug 1–15. Bus: A, B, 6, 11, 22, 36, 37.

Caffè Caruso *Kids* CAFE   On a quiet side street between Via Por Santa Maria and the Uffizi, a block from the Ponte Vecchio, this family-run cafe serves a variety of inexpensive hot dishes in what amounts to an expanded bar/*tavola calda* (small hot-table cafeteria). It's busy with locals at lunch, but the continuous hours promise less commotion if your appetite is flexible (however, the variety diminishes after the lunch crush). Choose from the display of four or five pastas, a few roasted meats (chicken, pork, roast beef), a dozen pizzas, and lots of vegetable side dishes (making this place great for light eaters and vegetarians). It isn't fancy, but the prices are rock bottom for this area. The cafe also hosts frequent concerts; call for schedules.

Via Lambertesca 16r (off V. Por Santa Maria). ℭ 055-281940. Primi 4.50€–5.50€ ($5.15–$6.30); secondi 5€–7€ ($5.75–$8.05); pizza and soda 8€ ($9.20). AE, MC, V. Mon–Sat 8am–6pm. Bus: B, 23.

Caffè Italiano ⚡ CAFE   Umberto Montano, the young owner of this handsome cafe, has created an early-1900s ambience in the second-floor dining room and offers a delicious lunch to standing-room-only crowds (come early). The delicate but full-flavored soups, mixed platter of salamis and cheeses, and unusual variety of vegetable *sformati* (terrines) top the list of choices, or you can order one of a dozen oversize salads. Stop by in the afternoon for dessert: Made on the premises by a talented pastry chef, they go perfectly with the exclusive blend of African coffees. You may hear that Montano owns two other restaurants, the **Osteria del Caffè Italiano** and **Alle Murate,** but I don't recommend them (both are overpriced and serve tiny portions—especially at pretentious Alle Murate—and the food at the Osteria is only so-so). Stick with Caffè Italiano.

Via Condotta 56r (off V. dei Calzaiuoli). © **055-291082.** www.caffeitaliano.it. Reservations recommended. Primi 5.50€ ($6.30); secondi and salads 7€–8.50€ ($8.05–$9.75). MC, V. Daily 8:15am–8:15pm (closed Sun in summer). Closed 2 weeks in Aug. Bus: A.

Cantinetta del Verrazzano ⚡ (Value WINE BAR   Owned by the Castello di Verrazzano, one of Chianti's best-known wine-producing estates, this woodpaneled *cantinetta* with a full-service bar/*pasticceria* and seating area helped spawn a revival of stylish wine bars as convenient spots for fast-food breaks. It promises a delicious self-service lunch or snack of focaccia, plain or studded with peas, rosemary, onions, or olives; buy it hot by the slice or as *farcite* (sandwiches filled with prosciutto, arugula, cheese, or tuna). Try a glass of their full-bodied Chianti to make this the perfect respite. Platters of Tuscan cold cuts and aged cheeses are also available.

Via dei Tavolini 18–20r (off V. dei Calzaiuoli). © **055-268590.** Focaccia sandwiches .95€–2.85€ ($1.10–$3.25); glass of wine 1.30€–8€ ($1.50–$9.20). AE, DC, MC, V. Mon–Sat 8am–9pm. Bus: A, 14, 23.

Ristorante Casa di Dante (da Pennello) ⚡ TUSCAN/ITALIAN   This is one of Florence's oldest restaurants, housed since the late 1400s in a palazzo that once belonged to Renaissance artist Albertinelli (Cellini, Pontormo, and Andrea del Sarto used to dine here). Its claim to fame is the antipasto table, groaning under the day's changing array of two dozen appetizers. Prices vary, but expect to spend 5€ to 8€ ($5.75–$9.20) for a good sampling. The best of the primi are under the handwritten *lo chef consigla* (the chef recommends) and *pasta fresa* (handmade pasta) sections of the menu. They do a perfectly grilled pork chop and, if the antipasti and pasta have done you in, several light omelets for a secondo.

Via Dante Alghieri 4r (between V. dei Calzaiuoli and V. del Proconsolo). © **055-294848.** Reservations recommended. Primi 5.50€–7.50€ ($6.30–$8.60); secondi 5.50€–13€ ($6.30$15); *menu turistico* 20€ ($23) without wine. AE, DC, MC, V. Tues–Sat noon–3pm and 7–10pm. Closed Aug. Bus: A, 14, 23.

Trattoria le Mossacce ⚡⚡ (Value FLORENTINE   This is a straightforward place for *cucina toscana,* deftly prepared and served in a lively and pleasant atmosphere. Favorites on the menu are the thick *ribollita* or any of the daily changing pastas. If the thought of a thick slab of steak is your idea of heaven, indulge in the regional specialty, the *bistecca alla fiorentina,* a splurge worth 14€ ($16).

Via del Proconsolo 55r (a block south of the Duomo). © **055-294361.** Reservations suggested for dinner. Primi 4.50€–5€ ($5.15–$5.75); secondi 5€–14€ ($5.75–$16). AE, DC, MC, V. Mon–Fri noon–2:30pm and 7–9:30pm. Closed Aug. Bus A, 14, 23.

NEAR THE TRAIN STATION, THE MERCATO SAN LORENZO & SANTA MARIA NOVELLA

Il Latini ⚡⚡⚡ (Moments TUSCAN   Octogenarian Narcisso Latini and his sons, Giovanni and Torello, operate one of the busiest tavernlike trattorias in town. There's always a line waiting for a cramped seat at one of the long wooden tables.

Taking a Gelato Break

Florence is a good spot for *gelato* (ice cream), with a number of great sources around town. The following are not only the best, but they also have the largest selections and are the most central. Ask for a *cono* (cone) or *coppa* (cup) from 1€ to 5€ ($1.15–$5.75)—point and ask for as many flavors as can be squeezed in.

Of all the centrally located gelaterie, **Festival del Gelato,** Via del Corso 75r, just off Via dei Calzaiuoli (© 055-2394386), has been the only serious contender to the premier Vivoli (below), offering about 50 flavors along with pounding pop music and colorful neon. It's open Tuesday through Sunday summer from 8am to 1am and winter from 11am to 1am.

Vivoli, Via Isole delle Stinche 7r, a block west of Piazza Santa Croce (© 055-239334), is still the city's institution. Exactly how renowned is this bright gelateria? Taped to the wall is a postcard bearing only "Vivoli, Europa" for the address, yet it was successfully delivered to this world capital of ice cream. It's open Tuesday through Sunday from 9am to 1am (closed Aug and Jan to early Feb).

One of the major advantages of the always crowded **Gelateria delle Carrozze,** Piazza del Pesce 3–5r (© 055-2396810), is its location at the foot of the Ponte Vecchio—if you're coming off the bridge and about to head on to the Duomo, this gelateria is immediately off to your right in a small alley that forks off the main street. In summer, it's open daily from 11am to 1am; in winter, hours are Thursday through Tuesday from 11am to 8pm.

A block south of the Accademia (pick up a cone after you've gazed upon *David*'s glory) is what local purists insist is Vivoli's only deserving contender to the throne as gelato king: **Carabé,** Via Ricasoli 60r (© 055-289476). It offers genuine homemade Sicilian gelato in the heart of Florence, with ingredients shipped in from Sicily by the hardworking Sicilian owners. Taste for yourself and see if Florentines can hope to ever surpass such scrumptiousness direct from the island that first brought the concept of ice cream to Europe. From May 16 to September, it's open daily from 10am to midnight; from February 15 to May 15 and October to November 15, hours are Tuesday through Sunday from 10am to 8pm.

But the delicious adventure is worth the wait, with most of the wines and many of the menu choices coming from the Latini estate in Chianti. There's a written menu, but you probably won't see it, since one of the brothers will explain the selection in a working version of English. Gargantuan eaters can indulge in the unofficial *menu completo*—a meaty feast that's not listed anywhere but will run you 35€ to 40€ ($40–$46), including all the wine and mineral water you can drink. More restrained appetites and wallets should order a la carte.

Via Palchetti 6r (off V. della Vigna Nuova). © 055-210916. Reservations required. Primi 5€–7€ ($5.75–$8.05); secondi 7€–11€ ($8.05–$13); unofficial fixed-price meal 35€–40€ ($40–$46), which includes absolutely everything, from appetizer to espresso and after-dinner drink. AE, DC, MC, V. Tues–Sun 12:30–2:30pm and 7:30–10:30pm. Closed Dec 23–Jan 4 and 15 days July–Aug. Bus: A, B, 6, 11, 36, 37.

Nerbone *(Moments* FLORENTINE   One of the city's best basic eateries, this red-and-green food stand is inside the covered meat-and-produce marketplace. Packed with marketgoers, vendors, and working-class types, it offers four small tables next to a meat counter. Daily specials include a limited choice of pastas, soups, huge plates of cooked vegetables, sausages, and fresh sandwiches, but the mainstay here is *panino con bollito,* a boiled beef sandwich that's *bagnato* (dipped in the meat juices). The service is swift, and wine and beer are sold by the glass. If at first you can't find Nerbone, just ask. It's worth the hunt and promises lots of local color and good eats.

In the Mercato Centrale, entrance on Via dell'Ariento, stand no. 292 (ground floor). © 055-219949. All dishes 3.50€–7€ ($4–$8.05). No credit cards. Mon–Sat 7am–3pm. Bus: 1, 6, 7,10, 11, 17.

Palle d'Oro ITALIAN   Everyone seems to prefer this trattoria's front bar area, usually packed with the market's vendors and shoppers enjoying a quick lunch of pasta, soup, and vegetable side dishes. The prices aren't much higher for table service in the less-crowded back room, but the front area's advantage is you don't have to order a full meal and you can eat and run. Look for the house specialty pasta, *penne della casa* (with porcini mushrooms, prosciutto, and veal). For a cholesterol boost with a kick, try the homemade *gnocchi alla Gorgonzola.*

Via Sant'Antonio 43–45r (near the Mercato Centrale). © 055-288383. Reservations suggested for dinner. Primi 3.10€–6€ ($3.55–$6.90); secondi 5.20€–10€ ($6–$12); fixed-price menu 13€ ($15). AE, DC, MC, V. Mon–Sat noon–2:30pm and 6:30–10pm. Closed Aug. Bus: 1, 6, 7,10, 11, 17.

Trattoria Antellesi *(★★* ITALIAN   This is an attractive spot in a converted Renaissance palazzo. As their restaurant empire expands, the young Florence/Arizona combination of chef Enrico and manager/sommelier Janice Verrecchia is around less these days, but their skilled staff guarantees a lovely Tuscan dining experience. Never without a smile, they'll talk you through a memorable dinner that should start with their signature antipasto of pecorino cheese and pears. Follow with *crespelle alla fiorentina* (crepes stuffed with ricotta and spinach and baked) or *spaghetti alla chiantigiana* (pasta with Chianti-marinated beef cooked in tomato sauce). This is the spot to try *bistecca alla fiorentina*—and one of the excellent moderately priced red wines.

Via Faenza 9r (near the Medici Chapels). © 055-216990. Reservations required. Primi 6.50€–7.50€ ($7.45–$8.60); secondi 10€–13€ ($12–$15). AE, DC, MC, V. Mon–Sat noon–2:30pm and 7–10:30pm. Bus: A, 1, 4, 10, 11, 12, 25, 31, 32, 33, 36, 37.

Trattoria Le Fonticine *(★* TUSCAN/BOLOGNESE   Gianna, the naturally talented Bologna-born chef and co-owner of this art-filled restaurant on the very edge of the Mercato San Lorenzo (look for the outdoor 16th-century wall fountain next door by Luca della Robbia, from which the restaurant takes its name), serves as an unofficial guarantee that you will leave your table with a smile. Silvano Bruci, Gianna's Florentine-born husband (and the collector of the restaurant's modern art), sees that his hometown's cuisine doesn't get short shrift: Diners enjoy the best of both worlds. Tortellini are the traditional pasta of Bologna, and they are handmade and stuffed here daily, with a hearty *ragu* sauce that overshadows the menu's admirable roster of competing primi (ask about the pasta sampler). Their gelato *dolci,* by the way, come from Vivoli (see "Taking a Gelato Break," above). If you're seated in the back room, you'll pass the open kitchen and be rewarded with a glimpse of the action. In 2004, Silvano and Gianna completed a major renovation of the restaurant.

Via Nazionale 79r (at V. dell'Ariento, north end of the Mercato San Lorenzo). © 055-282106. www.lefonticine.com. Reservations recommended. Primi 6€–11€ ($6.90–$13); secondi 9€–15€ ($10–$17). AE, DC, MC, V. Tues–Sat noon–3pm and 7–10pm. Closed Aug. Bus: 4, 12, 25, 31, 32, 33.

Trattoria Sostanza (aka Il Troia) *☆* FLORENTINE Sostanza is popularly called Il Troia (the trough) because people have been lining up at the long communal tables since 1869 to enjoy huge amounts of some of the best traditional food in the city. The menu changes often, but the primi are generally very simple: pasta in sauce, *tortellini* in *brodo* (meat-stuffed pasta in chicken broth), and *zuppa paesana* (peasant soup ribollita). The secondi don't steer far from Florentine traditions, either, with *trippa alla Fiorentina* or their mighty specialty *petti di pollo al burro* (thick chicken breasts lightly fried in butter). It's an extremely unassuming place. The Florentine attitude is so laid-back, you may not realize you're meant to be ordering when the waiter wanders over to chat. They also frown on anybody trying to cheat his or her own taste buds out of a full Tuscan meal.

Via Porcellana 25r (near the Borgo Ognissanti end). *©* 055-212691. Reservations strongly recommended. Primi 7€–8€ ($8.05–$9.20); secondi 7€–18€ ($8.05–$21). No credit cards. Mon–Fri 12:30–2:10pm and 7:30–9:45pm. Closed Aug. Bus: A, B, 6, 11, 36, 37.

Trattoria Zà-Zà *☆* TUSCAN The walls are lined with Chianti bottles and photos of old movie stars and not-so-famous patrons, the long wooden tables crowded with visitors and locals. Serving Tuscan favorites at reasonable prices amid a cheerful clatter, this trattoria is a good spot to try the fabled *bistecca alla fiorentina* without losing your shirt. Or if you'd rather savor many different tastes, the *antipasto caldo alla Zà-Zà* has a bit of everything. Things don't change much here, except for the tables set up on an unremarkable piazza. Zà-Zà has a serious competitor in the bare-bones **Da Mario,** around the corner at Via Rosina 2; it's open for lunch only (closed Sun) and absorbs the overflow.

Piazza Mercato Centrale 26r. *©* 055-215411. www.trattoriazaza.it. Reservations recommended. Primi 5.30€–10€ ($6–$12); secondi 10€–18€ ($12–$21); *menu turistico* without wine 13€ ($15). AE, DC, MC, V. Mon–Sat noon–3pm and 7–11pm. Closed Aug. Bus: 1, 6, 7, 10, 11, 17.

NEAR SANTA CROCE

I' Che C'è, C'è *☆☆* TUSCAN First of all, the name: It's a local expression that approximately translates to "What you see is what you get." You won't have to hope for more and certainly won't be settling for less because everything is excellently prepared. The irreverent name is compatible with the casual, family-run atmosphere, but the quality of the menu that's Tuscan in spirit hints of the chef/owner's formal training in the kitchens of London. Everything is kept simple, but the ingredients are obviously the best and the results full flavored. Unlike on many full-throttle Tuscan menus, fish is given its share of the limelight here. The set-price menu is one of the best deals in town.

Via Magalotti 11r (just east of V. Proconsolo, 2 blocks from the Arno). *©* 055-216589. Reservations recommended (not available for lunch set-price menu). Primi 4€–9€ ($4.60–$10); secondi 9€–15€ ($10–$17); fixed-price menu without wine 11€ ($13). AE, MC, V. Tues–Sun 12:30–2:30pm and 7:30–10:30pm. Closed Aug 10–17. Bus: B, 23.

Il Pizzaiolo *☆☆* *(Kids)* PIZZERIA/NEAPOLITAN The crowd milling about on the sidewalk (and they have reservations!) is confirmation this place serves the best pizza in town. Italy remains proudly regionalist about its food: Southerners contend they're the best pizza makers on the peninsula. And so Florence was elated to welcome Carmine, who headed north after 30 years in Naples, bringing along his family, his expertise, and integral ingredients like garlic and oregano. The simple pizza Margherita (fresh tomatoes, mozzarella, and basil) is perfection, as is the more endowed pizza *pazza* (fresh tomatoes, artichokes, olives, mushrooms, and oregano).

Via de' Macci 113r (at the corner of V. Pietrapiana). *©* 055-241171. Reservations required for dinner. Primi 4.65€–9.50€ ($5.35–$11); secondi 6€–13€ ($6.90–$15); pizza 4.50€–10€ ($5.15–$12). No credit cards. Mon–Sat 12:30–3pm and 7:30pm–midnight. Closed Aug. Bus: A, C, 14.

A Moveable Feast

In Florence, there are few supermarkets. Cold cuts are sold at a *salumeria*, which also sells cheese, though for a wide selection of cheese or for yogurt, you'll have to find a *latteria*. Vegetables and fruit can be found at a produce stand and store called a *fruttivendolo* or *orto e verdura*, and often at a small *alimentari*, the closest thing to a neighborhood grocery store. For bread to put all that between, visit a *forno*, which, along with a *pasticceria*, can supply you with dessert. And for a bottle of wine, search out a shop selling *vino e olio*. **Via dei Neri**, beginning at Via de' Benci near Piazza Santa Croce and stretching over toward Piazza della Signoria, has a handful of small specialty food shops and is a good area for picnic pickings.

If you prefer to find all you need under one roof, visit the colorful late-19th-century **Mercato Centrale**, a block-long, two-story marketplace that's a must-see and not just for food shoppers. Open Monday through Friday from 7am to 2pm and Saturday from 7am to 2pm (and 4–8pm in winter), it's at Via dell'Ariento 12, looming in the midst of the open-air Mercato San Lorenzo, on the block between Via San Antonino and Via Panicale.

If you're just as happy to have someone else make your sandwiches, seek out **Forno Sartoni**, Via dei Cerchi 34r, with fresh rolls and breads in front; the crowd in back waits for pizza bubbling from the oven, sold by the slice and weighed by the ounce—the average slice is 1.50€ ($1.75). It also makes a limited but delicious selection of fresh sandwiches (with prosciutto, mozzarella, and arugula, for example, at about 2€/$2.30) on freshly baked focaccia. Sartoni is predominantly a baker, so for a greater variety of quality cold cuts, stop by **Alimentari Orizi** (see above) and have the combination panino of your choice made up as you wait.

The **Boboli Gardens**, on the opposite side of the Arno behind the Palazzo Pitti (see "Sights to See," later in this chapter), is without a doubt the best green picnic spot in town. A grand amphitheater behind the palazzo provides historic seating, but it's worth the hike to the top, where the grounds join with those of the Fortezza Belvedere for the breathtaking view and green grass. If you'd just as soon pull up a park bench in the *centro storico*, a number of the city's most beautiful piazzas have stone benches and open spaces: **Piazza Santa Croce** comes to mind as much for its church's three-toned marble facade as for its proximity to Vivoli's for a post-lunch gelato. **Piazza Santa Maria Novella** offers stone benches and the only plots of grass in any of the city's squares. And if summer has set in, there are just two shady piazzas with benches: **Piazza Massimo d'Azeglio**, east of the Accademia, and lovely **Piazza Santo Spirito**, in the Oltrarno near the Palazzo Pitti.

Pizzeria I Ghibellini PIZZERIA/ITALIAN   With exposed brick walls and ceilings and curved archways inside, and umbrella-shaded tables on the picturesque piazzetta, I Ghibellini is a good bet year-round. Pizza is the draw, and there's a long list to make your choice difficult: Try the house specialty, pizza *alla*

Ghibellini (with prosciutto, mascarpone, and pork sausage). The many pastas include *penne alla boccalona,* whose tomato sauce with garlic and a pinch of hot pepper is just spicy enough.

Piazza San Pier Maggiore 8–10r (at the end of Borgo degli Albizi east from V. del Proconsolo). ⓒ 055-214424. Reservations suggested for dinner. Primi and pizza 4€–8€ ($4.60–$9.20); secondi 7€–16€ ($8.05–$18). AE, DC, MC, V. Thurs–Tues noon–4pm and 7pm–12:30am. Bus: A, 14, 23.

Ristorante Acqua al Due 🌟🌟 TUSCAN/ITALIAN   This is the perfect place to sample as much as you can at one sitting without breaking the bank or bursting your seams. The specialty is the *assaggio di primi,* a sampling of five types of pasta (with the occasional risotto thrown in) in various shapes and sauces. These aren't five full-size portions, but don't expect to have room for an entree after. There are also *assaggi* of *insalate* (salads) and *dolci* (sweets). Low prices and late hours make this comfortable place popular with a young international crowd.

Via della Vigna Vecchia 40r (at V. dell'Acqua). ⓒ 055-284170. www.acquaal2.it. Reservations required. Primi 7€–8€ ($8.05–$9.20); secondi 8€–17€ ($9.20–$20); *assaggio* 8€ ($9.20) for pasta, 4.65€ ($5.35) for dessert. AE, DC, MC, V. Daily 7:30pm–1am. Bus: A, 14, 23, 28.

Trattoria Cibreo 🌟🌟 TUSCAN   This is the casual trattoria of celebrated chef-owner Fabio Picchi. Its limited menu comes from the same creative kitchen that put on the map his premier—and three times as expensive—*ristorante* around the corner. The trattoria moved from its back-alley location to the main street in 1999, and this higher visibility has only made the lines longer, since they don't take reservations. Picchi takes his inspiration from traditional Tuscan recipes, and the first thing you'll note is the absence of pasta. After you taste the velvety *passata di pepperoni gialli* (yellow bell-pepper soup), you won't care much. The stuffed roast rabbit is fabulous as well, and—unusually for Italy—all second courses come with a side dish included in the price. My only complaint: They rush you through your meal in an un-Italian fashion in order to free up tables. Enjoy your after-dinner espresso at the **Caffè Cibreo** across the way.

Via de' Macci 122r. ⓒ 055-2341100. www.cibreo.com. Reservations not accepted. Primi 5€ ($5.75); secondi 13€ ($15). AE, DC, MC, V. Tues–Sat 1–2:30pm and 7:30–11pm. Bus: A, C, 14.

Trattoria Pallottino FLORENTINE   One long room with a few long tables on the cobblestone floor and a second room on the side are all there is to this local favorite, so reserve early or you won't get a seat. The cook makes a mean *bruschetta al pomodoro* (toasted bread topped with tomatoes over which you are invited to drizzle the olive oil liberally). For a first course, I look no further than the *spaghetti alla fiaccheraia,* with a tomato sauce mildly spiked with hot peppers. You might follow it with the *peposo* (beef stew loaded with black pepper). Skip dessert and pop in next door for a Vivoli gelato (see the box earlier in this section).

Via Isola delle Stinche 1r. ⓒ 055-289573. Reservations required for dinner. Primi 5€–8€ ($5.75–$9.20); secondi 7€–14€ ($8.05–$16); lunch menu with wine 12€ ($14; Tues–Fri only). AE, DC, MC, V. Tues–Sun 12:30–2:30pm and 7:30–10:30pm. Closed Aug 5–21. Bus: A, 14, 23.

IN THE OLTRARNO

Borgo Antico 🅺🆒 PIZZERIA/ITALIAN   In the spirit of the Oltrarno's Left Bank atmosphere, the Borgo Antico is a relaxed spot where you can order as little or as much as you want and enjoy it among a mix of visitors and Florentines. The scene inside is always buzzing, but from April to September, tables are set out where the million-dollar view of Brunelleschi's church is free. There are a dozen great pizzas and a number of combination super salads. Specialties of the day get equally creative (and expensive!). It's almost always hectic—if you get the hint they'd like your table, you'd do well not to linger.

Piazza Santo Spirito 6r. ℂ 055-210437. Reservations suggested for dinner. Primi 6€–15€ ($6.90–$17); secondi 10€–22€ ($12–$25); pizza 6€ ($6.90). AE, MC, V. Daily 12:45–2:30pm and 7:45pm–midnight. Bus: D, 6, 11, 36, 37.

Il Cantinone *Kids Kids* TUSCAN/ENOTECA   In the brick-vaulted wine cellar of a 16th-century palazzo, this candlelit wine bar can seem more jovial than romantic on nights when the wine gets flowing—and you'll find a fine selection of Chianti's best. Five or six reds are available by the glass, but don't overlook a liter of the good house wine. Order a number of appetizers and first courses, and you'll understand why they call Tuscany's peasant fare the food of kings. *Crostoni* are large slabs of home-baked bread slathered with prosciutto, *funghi* (mushrooms), tomatoes, mozzarella, or *salsiccia* (sausage). Primi choices might be a hearty *pappa al pomodoro* or *ribollita* soup or pasta of the day.

Via Santo Spirito 6r (off Piazza Santa Trinita). ℂ 055-218898. www.ilcantinonedifirenze.it. Reservations recommended. Primi 5€–8€ ($5.75–$9.20); secondi 6€–24€ ($6.90–$28); *crostoni* 5€ ($5.75); fixed-price menu at lunch 9€ ($10), at dinner 15€ ($17). AE, DC, MC, V. Tues–Sun 12:30–2:30pm and 7–10:30pm. Bus: D, 6, 11, 36, 37.

Osteria del Cinghiale Bianco *Kids* TUSCAN   In a medieval tower, with exposed stone walls setting the ambience, this friendly trattoria is dedicated to the *cinghiale*, the wild boar so ubiquitous in the Tuscan hills and traditional cuisine. Its presence is felt strongly during the fall game season, but you'll usually see year-round dishes like pappardelle pasta with cinghiale sauce and wild boar sausage *(salsiccia)* antipasto. But most of the menu is cinghiale free, such as the delicious *strozzapreti* (literally "priest stranglers"—don't ask), baked pasta with a ricotta-and-spinach mix, served with melted butter. Things are relaxed here during lunch, to which the owners have added an *insalata dello chef* (chef's salad). A few niches have been created for the romantically inclined, and it's a comfortable place to linger over dinner.

Borgo Sant' Jacopo 43r. ℂ 055-215706. www.cinghialebianco.it. Reservations required on weekends. Primi 5€–9€ ($5.75–$10); secondi 12€–15€ ($14–$17). No credit cards. Thurs–Mon 6:30–10:30pm, Sat–Sun 2:30–6:30pm. Closed July. Bus: C, 6, 11, 36, 37, 68.

Ricchi ITALIAN/SEAFOOD   Don't miss Ricchi when spring arrives and tables appear on one of Florence's best piazzas. A cafe by day and a restaurant by night, Ricchi's great inexpensive lunch menu is available year-round—if only they'd repeat the performance at dinner. Four or five pastas are made to order. As an alternative to the usual entrees, try one of the super salads. A shady piazza table is ringside, but take a look indoors at the 350 framed designs from a 1980 contest to complete the unfinished facade of Brunelleschi's Santo Spirito church. In the evening, the bar transforms itself into a proper restaurant specializing in seafood and Tuscan dishes.

Piazza Santo Spirito 8–9r. ℂ 055-215864. www.ristorantericchi.it. At lunch: primi 4.15€ ($4.75), secondi 7.75€ ($8.90). At dinner: primi 10€–16€ ($12–$18), secondi 13€–17€ ($15–$20). DC, MC, V. Mon–Sat: bar 7am–1am; lunch noon–2:30pm; restaurant 7:30–11pm. The bar sometimes opens on the 2nd Sun of the month, when the antiques market is on. Closed 15 days in Feb and 15 days in Aug. Bus: D, 6, 11, 36, 37.

Trattoria Casalinga FLORENTINE   *Casalinga* refers to the home cooking that keeps this unpretentious place always full. Sadly, though, an expansion a few years ago removed the last hints of the Renaissance aura from the place, replacing it with a cafeteria-like feel. Also along with the expansion came the frayed nerves of the help and a sometimes erratic performance from the kitchen. So maybe they won't win any culinary awards, but the menu is straightforward Tuscan: Try the hearty *ribollita* or the *ravioli al sugo di coniglio* in rabbit-flavored sauce. Save dessert or an after-dinner caffè for one of the cafes on nearby Piazza Santo Spirito.

Via Michelozzi 9r (between V. Maggio and Piazza Santo Spirito). © 055-2679243. Primi 3.50€–4€ ($4–$4.60); secondi 5€–10€ ($5.75–$12). Mon–Sat noon–2:30pm and 7–10pm. AE, DC, MC, V. Bus: D, 6, 11, 36, 37.

5 Sights to See

Seeing all of Florence in a short time requires organization. It's not just that there's so much to see in this great city; it's also that establishments (stores, churches, and so on) close for long lunch breaks, and some museums close for the day at 2pm or sooner (remember that the last entrance is at least 30 min., sometimes 45–60 min., before closing). Many museums are closed on Monday. The first thing you should do: Stop by a tourist office (see "Essentials," earlier in this chapter) for an up-to-the-minute listing of museum hours, or ask at your hotel.

ON & AROUND PIAZZA DEL DUOMO

Duomo (Cathedral of Santa Maria del Fiore) 𝕮𝕮𝕮   The red-tiled **dome** of Florence's magnificent Duomo dominates the skyline in the early 21st century just as it did when it was built more than 5 centuries ago. At the time it was completed in 1434, it was the world's largest unsupported dome, meant to dwarf the structures of ancient Greece and Rome. In Renaissance style, it's a major architectural feat and was the high point of architect Filippo Brunelleschi's illustrious career. Brunelleschi had to invent many new winch-and-pulley systems to raise his dome, an ingenious piece of engineering constructed of two shells, both of which thin as they approach each other and the top. You can climb **463 spiraling steps** 𝕮𝕮 (no elevator) and clamber up between these two layers to the lantern at the summit for a spectacular panorama. (You can enjoy a similar view, with fewer steps to climb, from the campanile, below.) Entrance to the stairs is from outside the church, on the south (bell tower) side, through the door marked CUPOLA DI BRUNELLESCHI.

The bands of marble (white, red, and green—the colors of the Italian flag) on the cathedral's **exterior** were taken from Tuscan quarries and added in the late 19th century, when Florence briefly became the capital of a united Italy. This tricolor marble mosaic, repeated on the baptistery and campanile, is an interesting contrast to the sienna-colored medieval fortresslike palazzi throughout the city. Though much of the **interior** decoration has been moved to the Museo dell'-Opera del Duomo (below), the cathedral still boasts on the entrance wall three **stained-glass windows** by Lorenzo Ghiberti (sculptor of the bronze bas-reliefs on the baptistery doors) next to Paolo Uccello's **giant clock** decorated with portraits of four prophets. In 1996, an extensive restoration was completed on the colorful 16th-century frescoes covering the inside of the cupola and depicting the *Last Judgment.* They were begun by Giorgio Vasari and finished by his less talented student Federico Zuccari. When the restorers began their work, they discovered a surprise: A good portion of the work was executed not in true fresco, but in tempera, which is much more delicate.

Beneath the Duomo's floor is the **Scavi della Cripta di Santa Reparata (crypt),** the ruins of the Romanesque Santa Reparata Cathedral, believed to have been founded in the 5th century on this site. It was continuously enlarged until it was done away with in 1296 to accommodate the present structure. Brunelleschi's tomb, discovered in 1972, is here. The entrance to the excavations is through a stairway near the front of the cathedral, to the right as you enter.

Florence Attractions

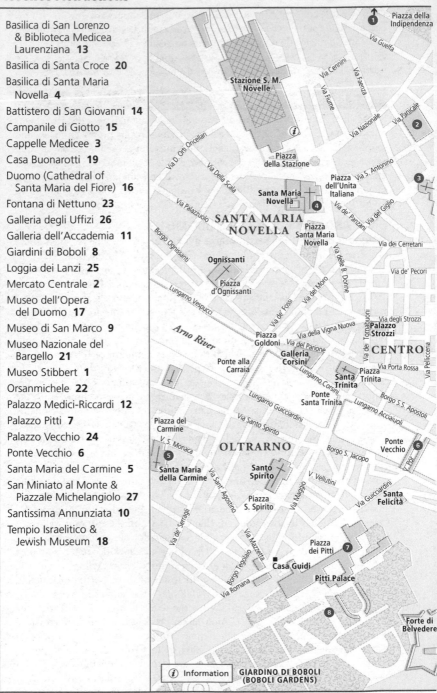

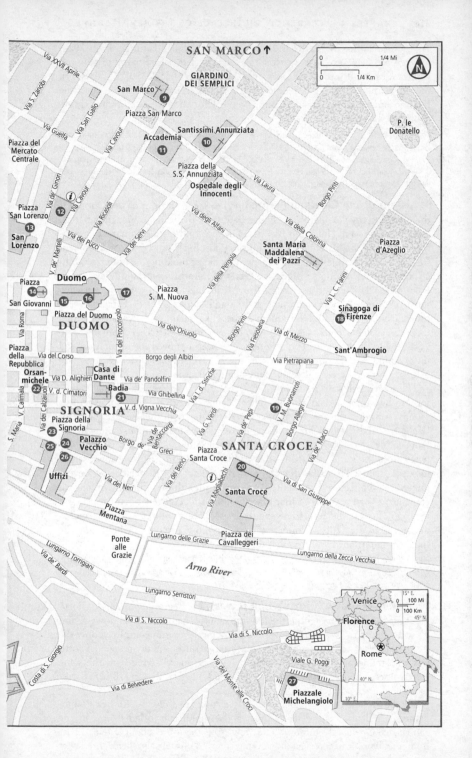

Volunteers offer **free cathedral tours** Monday through Saturday from 10am to 12:30pm and 3 to 5pm. Most speak English. If there are many of you and you want to confirm the volunteers' availability, call © **055-2710757** (Tues–Fri, mornings only). They sit at a table along the right (south) wall as you enter the Duomo and expect no payment, but a nominal donation to the church is always appreciated.

Piazza del Duomo. © **055-2302885**. www.operaduomo.firenze.it. Cathedral free admission, cupola 6€ ($6.90), Santa Reparata excavations 3€ ($3.45). Cathedral Mon–Wed 10am–5pm; Thurs 10am–3:30pm; Sat 10am–4:45pm; Sun 1:30–5pm (Sun morning for services only). Cupola Mon–Fri 8:30am–7pm; Sat 8:30am–5:40pm. Both close 3:30pm 1st Sat of every month; cathedral may stay open to 7pm in winter. Last entrance to ascend cupola 40 min. before close. Bus: A, 1, 6, 7, 10, 11, 14, 17, 22, 23, 36, 37.

Battistero di San Giovanni (Baptistery) ✦✦✦

In front of the Duomo is the matching tricolor-marble octagonal baptistery, dedicated to the city's patron saint, San Giovanni (John the Baptist). The highlight of the Romanesque baptistery, built in the 11th and 12th centuries (most likely on the site of an ancient Roman villa or temple) and one of Florence's oldest buildings, is Lorenzo Ghiberti's bronze exterior doors called the **Gates of Paradise,** on the side facing the Duomo (east). They were so dubbed by Michelangelo, who, when he first saw them, declared, "These doors are fit to stand at the gates of Paradise." Ten bronze panels depict Old Testament scenes, like Adam and Eve, in stunning three-dimensional relief. Ghiberti labored over his masterpiece from 1425 to 1452, dying 3 years later. The originals have been removed for restoration and those completed are now displayed in the Museo dell'Opera del Duomo (see below); all those exposed here are convincing replicas.

The **north side's doors** were Ghiberti's warm-up to the east doors, a commission he won at age 23 as the result of a contest held in 1401. Some art historians consider this to be the event that launched the Renaissance, for Ghiberti's submission (a bronze panel of *Abraham Sacrificing Isaac,* now in the Bargello, below) was chosen based on its dynamism and naturalism—very different from the static, stylized Gothic panels submitted by better-known sculptors, like Donatello, della Quercia, and Brunelleschi (who decided to devote himself to architecture as a result). The **south side's doors,** through which you enter, are a good example of that older Gothic style, courtesy of Andrea Pisano in 1336. Inside, the **baptistery vault** is decorated with magnificent gilded mosaics from the 1200s, dominated by an 8m (26-ft.) figure of Christ—they're the most important Byzantine mosaics in Florence.

Piazza di San Giovanni (adjacent to Piazza del Duomo). © **055-2302885**. www.operaduomo.firenze.it. Admission 3€ ($3.45), free for children under 6. Mon–Sat noon–7pm; Sun 8:30am–2pm. Last admission 30 min. before close. Bus: A, 1, 6, 7, 10, 11, 14, 17, 22, 23, 36, 37.

Campanile di Giotto (Giotto's Bell Tower) ✦

Beginning in 1334, Giotto spent his last 3 years designing the Duomo's Gothic campanile (bell tower), and it's still referred to as Giotto's Tower even though the master completed only the first two levels (and the next architect had to overhaul the faulty design—Giotto was an astoundingly great painter but a lousy engineer). Banded in the same three colors of marble as the cathedral and the baptistery, it's 6m (20 ft.) shorter than the dome.

The **bas-reliefs** on its slender exterior are copies of works by Andrea Pisano, Francesco Talenti, Luca della Robbia, and Arnoldi (the originals are in the Museo dell'Opera del Duomo). The view from the top is about equal to that from the Duomo; there are, however, a mere 414 steps up here and fewer crowds, but you won't get the chance to get close to Brunelleschi's masterpiece.

Both the dome and the bell tower offer remarkable cityscapes over a preserved historic center that was never permitted to build higher than the cathedral's dome.

Piazza del Duomo. ℭ 055-2302885. www.operaduomo.firenze.it. Admission 6€ ($6.90). Daily 8:30am–7:30pm. Last admission 30 min. before close. Bus: A, 1, 6, 7, 10, 11, 14, 17, 22, 23, 36, 37.

Museo dell'Opera del Duomo (Museum of the Dome) ✯✯

Opened in 1891, this museum behind the cathedral contains much of the art and furnishings that once embellished the Duomo and reopened in 2000 after a 2-year renovation. A **bust of Brunelleschi** at the entrance is a nod to the architect of the magnificent cupola (some of his original equipment and a death mask are housed in the first small room), and over the door hang two glazed **della Robbia terra cottas.** In the second inner room to your left are **sculptures** from the old Gothic facade (destroyed in 1587 to make way for today's neo-Gothic facade, which wasn't completed until the late 1800s), including work by the original architect, Arnolfo di Cambio, who was also responsible for the Palazzo Vecchio. Of the various statues, the most noteworthy are Donatello's weatherworn but noble *St. John* and Nanni di Banco's intriguing *San Luca.*

The highlights of the center room upstairs are the enchanting twin white marble *cantorie* (choirs) from the 1430s by Donatello and Luca della Robbia. But don't miss the two Donatello statues: his haggard figure of *Mary Magdalene* (a late work in polychrome wood originally in the baptistery) and *Lo Zuccone (Pumpkin Head)* from Giotto's bell tower. In the next room are the original **bas-reliefs** that decorated the first two stories of the exterior of Giotto's campanile.

One of the museum's most important displays is four of the original bronze panels from Ghiberti's **Gates of Paradise** ✯ door for the baptistery (the other six will appear after restoration). There's also a priceless 14th- to 15th-century silver-gilt **altarpiece** with scenes from the life of St. John, as well as one of Michelangelo's last *Pietà* sculptures, carved when the master was in his 80s and originally intended for his own tomb until he became so unsatisfied with it he attacked it with a hammer. He later let his students carry it away and finish off a few of the characters—they left the figure of Nicodemus untouched, it's said, because it was a self-portrait of Michelangelo.

Piazza del Duomo 9 (behind the dome end of the cathedral). ℭ 055-2302885. www.operaduomo.firenze.it. Admission 6€ ($6.90), free for children under 6. Mon–Sat 9am–7:30pm; Sun 9am–1:40pm. Last admission 40 min. before close. Bus: A, 1, 6, 7, 10, 11, 14, 17, 22, 23, 36, 37.

A Note About Museum & Church Hours

Remember that most stores close for a long lunch break, many of the museums close for the day at 2pm or earlier (the last entrance is at least 30 min. before closing), and many are closed Monday. First thing, stop by the tourist office for an up-to-date listing of museum hours and possible extended hours (in 2002, some museums stayed open—and empty—to 11:30pm). Also note that museum bookshops often close 15 to 30 minutes before the collections, an annoying practice that has cheated many tourists of their postcards or museum books if they wait until the guards are shooing them out of the Uffizi to leave. Some churches stay open through *riposo,* so save them for after lunch. And there are always the stalls of the open-air San Lorenzo market Monday through Saturday from 9am to 7pm.

ON & AROUND PIAZZA DELLA SIGNORIA

In Florence, all roads lead to elegant **Piazza della Signoria**—the cultural, political, and social heart of the city since the 14th century. Named after the *signoria*, the oligarchy that ruled medieval Florence, it serves as a picture-perfect outdoor sculpture gallery replete with pigeons, horse-and-buggies, tons of tourists, and outdoor cafes. It's one of Italy's most beautiful public squares.

The enormous **Fontana di Nettuno (Neptune Fountain;** Ammanati, 1576) was purportedly derided by Michelangelo as a waste of good marble. A small disk in the ground in front of it marks the spot where religious fundamentalist **Savonarola** was burned at the stake for heresy in 1498—a few years after inciting the original "bonfires of the vanities" while ruling the city during the Medici's temporary exile from Florence (even Botticelli got caught up in the fervor and is said to have tossed in a painting to fuel the flames). Flanking the life-size copy of Michelangelo's ***David*** (the original is in the Accademia) are copies of Donatello's ***Judith and Holofernes*** (original in the museum inside) and the ***Marzocco*** (original in the Bargello), the heraldic lion of Florence. Unfortunately placed next to David's anatomical perfection (across the stone steps) is Baccio Bandelli's ***Heracles*** (1534), which comes across looking like the "sack of melons" Cellini described it to be.

On the south side of Piazza della Signoria is the 14th-century **Loggia dei Lanzi** (also called Loggia della Signoria or, after its designer, Loggia di Orcagna), Florence's captivating outdoor sculpture gallery. It has finally been freed of its scaffolding, and the loggia is open for the first time in decades. Benvenuto Cellini's bronze ***Perseus*** ✿ (1545) was cleaned and restored in the 1990s and replaced in the prime corner spot in 2000. Giambologna's important ***Rape of the Sabine*** is also an original, a three-dimensional study in Mannerism, alongside his ***Hercules Slaying the Centaur*** and ***Duke Cosimo de' Medici.*** The wall-flower statues standing against the back are ancient Roman originals.

Galleria degli Uffizi (Uffizi Gallery) ✿✿✿

The Uffizi is one of the world's most important art museums and should be the first stop in Florence for anyone interested in the rich heritage of the Renaissance (be sure to make a reservation—see details in the box below). Six centuries of artistic development are housed in this impressive Renaissance palazzo, built by Giorgio Vasari (also a painter and Europe's first art historian) for Grand Duke Cosimo I de' Medici in 1560 to house the Tuscan duchy's administrative offices (*uffizi* means "offices" in local dialect). The collection, whose strong point is Florentine Renaissance art but includes major works by Flemish and Venetian masters, was amassed by the Medicis and bequeathed to the city in 1737 in perpetuity by Anna Maria Ludovica, the last of the Medici line, who stipulated that the unmatched collection of masterworks could never leave Florence.

The gallery consists of 45 rooms where paintings are grouped into schools in chronological order, from the 13th to the 18th centuries—but as you wander, don't overlook the rich details of the building itself, including frescoed ceilings, inlaid marble floors, and tapestried corridors. The superb collection begins in room no. 2 with Giotto's ***Maestà*** (1310), one of the first paintings to make the transition from the Byzantine to the Renaissance style. Look for the differences between Giotto's work and his teacher Cimabue's ***Maestà*** (1280) nearby. Some of the best-known rooms are dedicated to 15th-century Florentine painting, the eve of the Renaissance. In room no. 7 are major works by Paolo Uccello, Masaccio, and Fra Angelico, as well as the only works by Piero della Francesca in Florence.

Reserving Tickets for the Uffizi & Other Museums

As tourism to Italy increases, so do the lines at major museums. Much of the problem behind the often alarming wait at the Uffizi is the security policy regulating the number of visitors inside at any one time. Now you can buy tickets in advance for a designated time and day, eliminating a potential 3-hour wait. Call **Firenze Musei** at © 055-294883 or visit www.firenzemusei.it a minimum of 24 hours in advance (or weeks, if possible). Each reservation request adds 1.55€ ($1.80) to the museum admission—but this is more than worth it to save the wait. Advance tickets are possible for the Uffizi, Accademia, Palazzo Pitti, Cappelle Medicee, Museo di San Marco, Museo Nazionale del Bargello, and a handful of lesser museums, but I find it usually necessary (and highly recommended) only for the Uffizi and Accademia.

As you proceed, look for the elegant *Madonnas* of Filippo Lippi and Pollaiolo's delightful little panels that influenced Botticelli, whose masterworks are next.

For many, the Botticelli rooms (nos. 10–14) are the undisputed highlight. Arguably the most stunning are the recently restored *Primavera (The Allegory of Spring)*, whose three graces form the principal focus, and *The Birth of Venus* (commonly referred to as "Venus on the Half-Shell"). Botticelli's *Adoration of the Magi* is interesting for the portraits of his Medici sponsors incorporated into the scene, as well as a self-portrait of the artist on the far right in yellow.

Other notable works are Leonardo da Vinci's unfinished *Adoration of the Magi* and his famous *Annunciation* in room no. 15, Lukas Cranach's *Adam and Eve* in room no. 20, Michelangelo's circular *Doni Tondo* or *Sacra Famiglia (Holy Family)* in room no. 25, Raphael's *Madonna with the Goldfinch* in room no. 26, Titian's *Flora* and *Venere di Urbino (Venus of Urbino)* in room no. 28, Tintoretto's *Leda* in room no. 35, Caravaggio's *Medusa and Bacchus* in room no. 43, two **Rembrandt self-portraits** in room no. 44, and Canaletto's *Veduta del Palazzo Ducale di Venezia (View of the Doge's Palace in Venice)* in room no. 45.

Since the May 1993 bombing that damaged 200 works (37 seriously) and killed five (including the museum's director), the Uffizi has staged an amazing recovery. Only four of the works damaged were superior examples from the Italian Renaissance; two were destroyed beyond repair. Restorers worked around the clock to repair the substantial damage to the fabric of the building itself. In December 1998, Italy unveiled the "New Uffizi," a $15-million renovation that repaired all damaged rooms, added more than 1,858 sq. m (20,000 sq. ft.) of museum space, and displayed more than 100 works that had never been seen before. A handsome ground-floor book/gift store and the reopening of the elegant terrace cafe (at the end of the west wing) were part of the welcomed renovation.

In the spring of 2004, Italy's minister of culture announced additional plans to renovate the first floor of the Uffizi for exhibition space, doubling the museum's size and allowing for the display of as many as 800 works of art. At press time, reports suggested that the renovation, which was slated to begin in the summer of 2004, could be completed in 2006. The expansion is intended to make the Uffizi one of Europe's premier art museums, on a par with museums the size of Paris's Louvre or Madrid's Prado (although in terms of quality of art,

The Uffizi

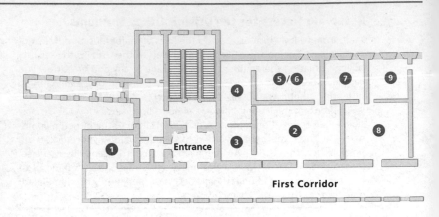

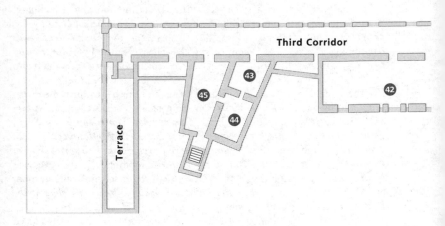

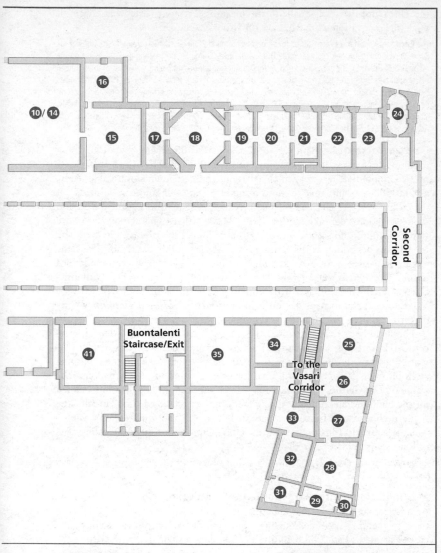

the Uffizi already is an equal). In the meantime, it's not clear what effect—if any—the renovation work will have on visitors to the Uffizi.

The **Corridoio Vasariano (Vasari Corridor)** is an aboveground "tunnel" running along the rooftops of the Ponte Vecchio buildings and connecting the Uffizi with Duke Cosimo I's residence in the Pitti Palace on the other side of the Arno. The corridor is lined with portraits and self-portraits by a stellar list of international masters, such as Bronzino, Reubens, Rembrandt, and Ingres. The damage incurred from the 1993 bombing has been repaired and the corridor has officially reopened, but it still requires special admission and an accompanying guide; inquire at the ticket window. Piazzale degli Uffizi 6 (south of Palazzo Vecchio and Piazza della Signoria). ⓒ 055-2388651. www.uffizi.firenze.it. Reservations: ⓒ 055-294883 or www.firenzemusei.it. Admission 8€ ($9.20), free for those under 18 or over 60. Tues–Sun 8:15am–7pm. Bus: A, B, 23, 71.

Palazzo Vecchio 𝄪 Florence's central square is dominated by an imposing rough-hewn fortress, the late-13th-century Palazzo Vecchio (Old Palace). Its severe Gothic style, replete with crenellations and battlements, is highlighted by a 92m (302-ft.) campanile that was a supreme feat of engineering in its day. It served as Florence's city hall for many years (a role it fulfills again today) and then was home to Duke Cosimo I de' Medici (that's Giambologna's bronze statue of him on horseback anchoring the middle of the piazza). He lived here for 10 years beginning in 1540, when much of the interior was remodeled to the elegant Renaissance style you see today, before moving to new accommodations in the Palazzo Pitti. You enter through the stunning **main courtyard,** with intricately carved columns and extraordinarily colorful 16th-century frescos by Vasari; the central focus is the fountain of a *Putto Holding a Dolphin,* a copy of Verrocchio's original (displayed upstairs).

The highlight of the interior is the massive first-floor **Salone dei Cinquecento (Hall of the Five Hundred),** whose rich frescoes by Vassari depict Florence's history. Formerly the city's council chambers where the 500-man assembly once gathered, it's still used for government and civic functions. The statue of *The Genius of Victory* is by Michelangelo (1533–34); commissioned for the tomb of Pope Julius II, it was later acquired by the Medici. Upstairs, the richly decorated and frescoed salons, such as the private quarters of Cosimo's wife, Eleanora de Toledo, offer an intriguing glimpse into how the ruling class of Renaissance Florence lived.

Piazza della Signoria. ⓒ 055-2768325. www.comune.fi.it. Admission 6€ ($6.90). Fri–Wed 9am–7pm; Thurs 9am–2pm. Bus: A, B, 23, 71.

Museo Nazionale del Bargello (Bargello Museum) 𝄪𝄪 If a visit to the Accademia has whetted your appetite for fine Renaissance sculpture, set aside time to see this national museum's outstanding collection—amazingly, the crowds are never bad. This daunting 1255 building originated as the seat of the city's *podestà* (chief magistrate) and served as the city's jail in Renaissance times. In the middle of the majestic courtyard plastered with the coats of arms of the *podestà* is a tank where prisoners used to be tortured and executed; some public hangings took place out the windows facing Via del Proconsolo. Today the Bargello, named for the 16th-century police chief *(bargello)* who ruled from here, houses three stories of treasures by Florentine Renaissance sculptors and a collection of Mannerist bronzes.

On the ground floor, the first room kicks off with some Michelangelos, including his "other" *David* (aka *Apollo,* sculpted 30 years after the original), *Brutus,* and the *Pitti Tondo,* depicting the Madonna teaching Jesus and St. John the Baptist to read. Take a look at his *Bacchus* (1497): It was done at age 22 and was the artist's first major work, effortlessly capturing the Roman god's drunken posture. Among the other important sculptures are Ammanati's *Leda and the Swan;* his student Giambologna's significant *Winged Mercury;* and several Donatellos, including his *St. George, St. John the Baptist,* and sexually ambiguous *David,* the first nude statue to be done by an Italian artist since classical times. In another room are the two **bronze plaques** by Brunelleschi and Donatello's master, Ghiberti, made for the competition in 1401 to decide who'd sculpt the baptistery's second set of doors—Ghiberti's won.

Via del Proconsolo 4 (at V. Ghibellina). ⓒ 055-2388606. www.sbas.firenze.it. Reservations: 055-294-883 or www.firenzemusei.it. Admission 4€ ($4.60). Tues–Sat 8:15am–1:50pm. Also open the 1st, 3rd, and 5th Mon of every month; closed the 2nd and 4th Sun of each month. Bus: A, 14, 23.

Ponte Vecchio ★★★ *Moments* Linking the north and south banks of the Arno River at its narrowest point, the Ponte Vecchio (Old Bridge) has long been a landmark symbol of the city. It was destroyed and rebuilt many times before the construction of the 1345 bridge you see today, designed by Taddeo Gaddi, and has stood lined with these same goldsmiths' shops for centuries. Many of the exclusive gold and jewelry stores are owned by descendants of the 41 artisans set up on the bridge in the 16th century by Cosimo I de' Medici. No longer able to tolerate the smell from the bridge's old butchers and skin tanners on his trips to and from the new Medici residence in the Palazzo Pitti on the other side of the river, Cosimo booted them out and moved in the classier goldsmiths (and upped the rent).

Florentines tirelessly recount the story of how, in 1944, Hitler's retreating troops destroyed all the bridges crossing the Arno (all since reconstructed, often with the original material or at least according to archival designs) with the exception of the Ponte Vecchio. To compensate, the Germans bombed both bridgeheads to block Allied access to it, resulting in the 1950s look of those buildings in the otherwise medieval areas of Via Por Santa Maria and Via Guicciardini.

At Via Por Santa Maria, north bank, and Via Guicciardini, south bank.

Orsanmichele ★ This 14th-century boxlike church is Florence's last remnant of ornate Gothic architecture and was originally built as a covered market with an upstairs granary. The downstairs was eventually converted into an oratory— the open archways were bricked up and the outside's **tabernacles** decorated with donations from the city's powerful *arti* (guilds), such as the tanners, silk weavers, bankers, furriers, and goldsmiths; their patron saints fill the 14 niches surrounding the exterior. Masters like Ghiberti, Donatello, and Giambologna were commissioned to cast the saints' images. They virtually comprise a history of Florentine sculpture from the 14th to the 16th centuries, though almost all have been relocated to the second-floor museum (below) and replaced by copies. In the candlelit interior—among the vaulted arches, stained-glass windows, and 500-year-old frescoes—is the colorful encrusted 14th-century **Gothic tabernacle** by Andrea Orcagna. It supports and protects the 1348 *Madonna and Child* painted by Giotto's student Bernardo Daddi.

Across Via dell'Arte della Lana from the Orsanmichele's main entrance is the 1308 **Palazzo dell'Arte della Lana.** Up the stairs inside, you can cross the hanging walkway to the first floor of the Orsanmichele. These are the old granary ròoms, now housing a **museum** containing statues that once surrounded the exterior. A few are still undergoing restoration, but eight of the original sculptures are here, well labeled, including Donatello's marble *St. Mark* (1411–13); Ghiberti's bronze *St. John the Baptist* (1413–16), the first life-size bronze of the Renaissance; and Verrocchio's *Incredulity of St. Thomas* (1473–83).

Value Cheap Thrills: What to See & Do in Florence for Free (or Almost)

- **Wander the Florentine markets.** Little in Italy compares to the sprawling outdoor **Mercato San Lorenzo** surrounding the San Lorenzo church and the covered early-1900s **Mercato Centrale.** The latter is a vast marketplace whose street-level stalls are occupied by butchers, fish vendors, and cheesemongers and saturated with local color galore; the upstairs is mostly given over to the fertile region's heady bounty of produce, fruit, and flowers—you'll never again see so many varieties of salad greens, pyramids of artichokes and plump tomatoes, porcini mushrooms as wide as Frisbees, and pearl-size wild strawberries. The outdoor market is comprised of hundreds of canvas-awninged stalls hawking tourist stuff, a lot of which is worth a walk-through for the guaranteed (and not infrequent) finds. Shop here for souvenirs first before hitting the city's countless tourist retail stores whose overhead hikes up their prices.
- **Take free tours.** Church volunteers await you in the **Duomo** for free English-language guided tours of this early Renaissance wonder (see "On & Around Piazza del Duomo," earlier in this chapter). Free guided tours are also offered in some of the museums and churches, such as the **Palazzo Vecchio, Santa Maria Novella,** and the **Brancacci Chapel** in Santa Maria del Carmine, during specially extended evening hours. Check with the tourist office to see if these tours are continuing. (**Note:** You may have to pay a small admission price to enter the churches.)
- **Catch the daily vespers.** Florence's most beautiful Romanesque church (and one of its oldest), **San Miniato** is the only venue for

---

For lack of staff, the Orsanmichele no longer keeps regular hours (the hours below aren't concrete)—odd, since it sits smack-dab on the main tourist thoroughfare of the city, halfway between the Duomo and the Uffizi; you'd figure it would get tons and tons of visitors. If your time in Florence is too tight for you simply to wander by, call before you visit to see if the church will be open.

Via Arte della Lana 1/Via dei Calzaiuoli. ℂ 055-284944. Free admission. Church daily 9am–noon and 4–6pm. Museum daily 9–9:45am, 10–10:45am, 11–11:45am (plus Sat–Sun 1–1:45pm). Both closed the 1st and last Mon of the month. Bus: A.

NEAR PIAZZA SAN MARCO & PIAZZA SANTISSIMA ANNUNZIATA

Galleria dell'Accademia (Accademia Gallery) 𝒜𝒜𝒜   The Accademia is home to Michelangelo's **_David_** (1501–04), his (and perhaps the world's) greatest sculpture. Michelangelo was just 29 and only recently recognized for his promising talents following the creation of the _Pietà_ in Rome's St. Peter's Basilica. Many are unaware of the roundabout origin of this famous statue. It started out as a 5m (16-ft.) column of white Carrara marble that had been quarried for another sculptor's commission and then abandoned after it was deemed "unworkable." Obviously, that decision was premature. Now _David_ looms in stark masculine perfection atop a 2m (6½-ft.) marble stand beneath the rotunda late-afternoon vespers. A handful of monks sing their timeless Gregorian chant, transporting you back to the nascent days of the hilltop church's 11th-century origin.

• **Watch a postcard-perfect sunset.** To see the Technicolor sunset over the Duomo amid the *centro storico's* terra-cotta rooftops (plastered on a million postcards), hike on up to the Oltrarno's **Piazzale Michelangiolo.** Here you'll find Michelangelo's second larger-than-life copy of the fabled *David* (the other is in Piazza della Signoria), standing vigil over Florence. Daytime sees the piazza transformed into a parking lot for tour-group buses; nighttime feels like a locals' lovers'-lane-meets-the-looking-for-excitement-after-hours crowd. Dusk is no less popular, with a truly magnificent *spettacolo* over the Arno trellised by its many bridges and offset by the hills of Fiesole rising behind.

• **Listen to music in Piazza della Repubblica.** The historic **Café Paszkowski** has been the site of alfresco evening music in this central square for generations. Its recent transformation from parking lot to dignified piazza of old was a welcome return to the way things were, as was the addition of the occasional planters-cum-seats from which to enjoy the crowd-gathering live music until the wee hours without having to pay the steep cover charges imposed by the cafes. Paszkowski's elegant next-door neighbor, **Gilli's,** is the traditional favorite cafe of choice, where you can nurse a Campari for hours for less than 6€ (**$6.90**) while listening to the classical, pop, and light jazz tunes that fill the piazza.

of the main room built exclusively for its display in 1873, when it was moved here from Piazza della Signoria. At the Piazza, a life-size copy stands in its place. A second replica also lords over Piazzale Michelangiolo.

In 2004, *David* underwent a months-long cleaning designed to bring the luminescence back to the sculpture. The unveiling that year was also a celebration of the sculpture's 500th anniversary. (We should all look so good at 500!)

The museum houses several other Michelangelos, including four never-finished *Prisoners* or **Slaves** struggling to free themselves, commissioned for the tomb of Julius II; Michelangelo believed he could sense their very presence captured within the stone and worked to release their forms. They offer a fascinating insight of how he approached each block of marble that would yield his many masterpieces. The *Palestrina Pietà* here was long attributed to Michelangelo, but most scholars now believe it's the work of his students. The statue of *St. Matthew* (begun in 1504) is by the master. A number of 15th- and 16th-century Florentine painters are also represented here; search out the *Madonna del Mare (Madonna of the Sea),* attributed to Botticelli or his student Filippino Lippi.

Via Ricasoli 58–60 (between Piazza del Duomo and Piazza San Marco). (✆ **055-2388609.** www.polomuse ale.firenze.it/musei/accademia. Reservations: (✆ **055-294883** or www.firenzemusei.it for a 1.55€ (**$1.80**) fee. Admission 6.50€ (**$7.45**). Tues–Sun 8:30am–7pm (to 10pm Sat). Bus: 1, 17.

Museo di San Marco 🦊🦊   Built in the 13th century and enlarged and rebuilt by Michelozzo as a Dominican monastery in 1437, this small museum is a monument to the devotional work of friar/painter Fra Angelico, an early master of the 15th-century Renaissance. To your right upon entering is a room containing Florence's largest collection of his **painted panels** and **altarpieces.** The Chapter House nearby is home to Fra Angelico's powerful large *Crucifixion* fresco. The ground-floor refectory was decorated by Domenico Ghirlandaio (under whom a young Michelangelo apprenticed) with a realistic *Cenacolo (Last Supper),* one of the most important of Florence's nine such *Last Suppers* found in ancient refectories (the tourist office has a list of the others).

At the top of the stairs to the second-floor monks' cells is Fra Angelico's masterpiece, the *Annunciation.* Each of the 44 small dorm cells is decorated with frescoes from the life of Christ painted by Fra Angelico or one of his assistants under the master's direction from 1439 to 1445 and intended to aid in contemplation and prayer. The frescoes in cell nos. 1, 3, 6, and 9 are the most beautiful. Larger and more luxurious, cell nos. 38 and 39 were designated for the occasional use of Cosimo il Vecchio, originator of the Medici dynasty who financed the enlargement of the monastery, and were frescoed with the aid of Angelico's student Benozzo Gozzoli.

At the end of the corridor is the **cell of Girolamo Savonarola,** which includes a stark portrait of the monastery's former prior by his convert and student, Fra Bartolomeo, as well as his sleeping chamber, his notebook, his rosary, and remnants of the clothes he wore at his execution. Savonarola was a religious fundamentalist who ruled Florence briefly at the head of a mob-rule theocracy, inspiring the people to burn priceless artwork and precious hand-illuminated books. After the pope threatened to excommunicate the entire city for following the mad preacher, Savonarola was found guilty of heresy, hanged, and burned at the stake on Piazza della Signoria in 1498, as depicted here in an anonymous 16th-century painting.

Piazza San Marco 3 (north of the Duomo on V. Cavour). (℃ **055-2388608.** Admission 4€ ($4.60). Mon–Fri 8:30am–1:50pm; Sat–Sun 8:15am–7pm. Closed 1st, 3rd, and 5th Sun and 2nd and 4th Mon of each month. Bus: 1, 6, 7, 10, 11, 17, 20, 25, 31, 32, 33, 67, 68, 70.

Santissima Annunziata 🦊   On your way to or from your visit to Michelangelo's *David* at the Accademia, stop by **Piazza SS. Annunziata** for a moment's respite in what has been called the most perfectly proportioned Renaissance square. It's surrounded on three sides by loggias, but at its center stands the **equestrian statue** of Grand Duke Ferdinando I de' Medici, the last work of Giambologna, cast after his death by Tacca (who's also responsible for the fountains on either side). Facing south is the 13th-century **Santissima Annunziata** church (reconstructed during the Renaissance by Michelozzo) with a number of major works by Andrea del Sarto (who's also buried here, along with Cellini and Il Pontormo). In Florence, brides don't toss their bouquets: For good luck, they bring them here and place them in front of a **tabernacle** designed by Michelozzo (to the left as you enter). It houses an allegedly miraculous portrait of the *Annunciation* (after whom the church was named), whose Madonna's face was said to have been painted by an angel. On the right as you enter the church is del Sarto's important *Birth of the Virgin* (1513); his *Madonna del Sacco* in an area off the cloisters is not always available for viewing.

As you exit the church, you'll see on your left the **Ospedale degli Innocenti (Hospital of the Innocents),** Europe's oldest foundling hospital. Its portico was designed by Brunelleschi and the area between its arches adorned with glazed terra-cotta reliefs of swaddled babies by Andrea della Robbia. It still functions as an orphanage in a limited capacity, but the small opening where Florentines could leave their unwanted infants in the dark of night, ring the bell, and run, is no longer in use. The **museum** (© 055-2491708) upstairs houses some fine Renaissance paintings by the likes of Ghirlandaio, Pontormo, and a young Botticelli. Admission is 2.60€ ($3), and it's open Thursday through Tuesday from 8:30am to 2pm.

Piazza SS. Annunziata. © 055-266181. Free admission. Daily 7:30am–12:30pm and 4–6:30pm. Bus: 6, 31, 32.

NEAR THE TRAIN STATION, THE MERCATO SAN LORENZO & SANTA MARIA NOVELLA

Basilica di San Lorenzo & Biblioteca Medicea-Laurenziana *(R)* San Lorenzo, whose barren, unfinished facade looms semihidden behind market stalls hawking soccer banners and synthetic-silk scarves, was the Medicis' parish church, as well as the resting place for most of the clan's early bigwigs, including Cosimo il Vecchio, founder of the family fortune and patron to Donatello (memorialized in front of the high altar with a plaque proclaiming him *pater patriae,* "father of his country"). Donatello's two **pulpits,** his final works, are worth a look, as is the second chapel on the right, with Rosso Fiorentino's *Marriage of the Virgin.* Designed by Brunelleschi and decorated by Donatello, the **Old Sacristy,** off the left transept, contains several important works. Outrageously, in 2002 the church began charging admission (so did Santa Maria Novella, but at least that one underwent an extensive renovation first and has some Titans of art to look at).

The key feature of the main part of the church is the **Biblioteca Medicea-Laurenziana** (1524), a stunning bit of architecture by Michelangelo housing one of the world's largest and most valuable collections of manuscripts and codices, a few of which are on display. An elaborate Michelangelo **stone staircase** leads to it from the quiet cloister (off the left aisle), the one real reason to peek in here after a visit to the church next door. Though the Laurentian Library is closed at press time, it's scheduled to reopen by the time you get here, possibly with new hours. San Lorenzo is best known, however, for the **Cappelle Medicee (Medici Chapels),** but you can't reach them from the church: You enter by going around through the Mercato San Lorenzo to the back of the church (see below).

Piazza San Lorenzo. © 055-216634. Admission 2.50€ ($2.85). Basilica Mon–Sat 10am–5pm. Biblioteca Medicea-Laurenziana Mon–Sat 9am–1pm. Bus: 1, 6, 7, 11, 14, 17, 23, 67, 68, 70, 71.

Cappelle Medicee (Medici Chapels) *(R)* On entering, you first pass through the massively overwrought marble wonderland of the **Cappella dei Principi (Chapel of the Princes),** added in 1604 but not finished until 1962. Your goal is the far more serene **Nuova Sacrestia (New Sacristy)** *(R)*, containing the Michelangelo-designed tombs for Lorenzo II de' Medici, Duke of Urbino and grandson of Lorenzo il Magnifico (with the sculptor's famous statues of female *Dawn* and male *Dusk*) on the left as you enter. On the opposite wall is the tomb of Giuliano de' Medici, Duke of Nemours (with the more famous female *Night* and male *Day*). These two pairs are some of Michelangelo's greatest works (1521–34). Never overlooked by guides is that *Dawn* and *Night* make obvious the virility with which Michelangelo sculpted females—only marginally less masculine and muscular than males, with breasts tacked on almost as an afterthought.

Piazza Madonna degli Aldobrandini (at the end of Borgo San Lorenzo, around the back side of San Lorenzo). © 055-2388602; 055-294888 or www.firenzemusei.it for reservations. Admission 6€ ($6.90). Daily 8:15am–5pm. Closed 1st, 3rd, and 5th Mon and 2nd and 4th Sun of each month. Bus: 1, 6, 7, 11, 14, 17, 23, 67, 68, 70, 71.

The Master's Famous Scribbles

A large number of charcoal sketches, confirmed to be by Michelangelo himself, were discovered by sheer chance in the 1980s in a room beneath the sacristy at the Medici Chapels. They're now available to the public for viewing for no additional admission, but only on special request: Ask at the ticket booth on your arrival.

Palazzo Medici-Riccardi & Cappella dei Magi (Chapel of the Magi) ✦✦
Finds Built by Brunelleschi's student Michelozzo for Cosimo il Vecchio (the Elder), founder of the Medici dynasty and grandfather of Lorenzo il Magnifico, this austere palazzo was the private home of the Medici clan from 1460 to 1540 (before Cosimo I moved with his new Spanish wife, Eleanora de Toledo, to the Palazzo Vecchio and eventually the Palazzo Pitti on the other side of the Arno) and was held as the prototype for subsequent residences of the nobility. Only two rooms are open to the public, but they make your trip worthwhile.

A staircase to the right off the entrance courtyard leads to the **Cappella dei Magi (Chapel of the Magi)** ✦. The jewel-box chapel takes its name from the gorgeously dense frescoes by Benozzo Gozzoli (completed in 1463), who worked into his depictions of the Wise Men's journey through the Tuscan countryside several members of the Medici family (the last Magi with the golden locks is a highly idealized version of a young Lorenzo il Magnifico) as well as his master, Fra Angelico. He even added himself on the right wall as you enter (look on the far left for a young man wearing a red hat inscribed "Opus Benotii," beneath the man wearing a light-blue hat). Upstairs is an elaborate 17th-century **baroque gallery** commissioned by the subsequent owners, the Riccardi; amid the gilt and stuccoes are masterful Luca Giordano frescoes, illustrating the Apotheosis of the Medicis. The palazzo now houses government offices, though parts of it are frequently used for temporary and traveling exhibits.

Entrance to the chapel is restricted to seven visitors for a 7-minute visit; as a result, you may have to wait in line. You can call ahead to reserve a time to come.

Via Cavour 3 (north of Piazza del Duomo). © 055-2760340. www.palazzo-medici.it. Palazzo and Cappella dei Magi 4€ ($4.60). Thurs–Tues 9am–7pm. Number of visitors limited; arrive early or call to book a time to visit. Bus 1, 6, 7, 11, 14, 17, 23, 67, 68, 70, 71.

Basilica di Santa Maria Novella ✦✦   Begun in 1246 and completed in 1360 (with a green-and-white marble facade, the top portion of which wasn't added until the 15th c.), this cavernous Gothic church was built to accommodate the masses who'd come to hear the word of God as delivered by the Dominicans. To educate the illiterate, the church was filled with cycles of frescoes that are some of the most important in Florence—a claim not to be taken lightly.

In the **Cappella Maggiore (Main Chapel)** behind the main altar, with a bronze crucifix by Giambologna, Domenico Ghirlandaio created a fresco cycle supposedly depicting the *Lives of the Virgin and St. John the Baptist,* when, in fact, what we see is a dazzling illustration of daily life in the golden days of Renaissance Florence. It's sprinkled with local personalities and snapshot vignettes, and a number of the faces belong to the Tornabuoni family, who commissioned the work. In the **Cappella Filippo Strozzi,** to the right of this, are frescoes by Filippino Lippi (son of Filippo Lippi). To the extreme right is the **Cappella dei Bardi,** covered with 14th-century frescoes; its lunette frescoes of the *Madonna* are believed to be by Cimabue (ca. 1285). To the left of the Cappella Maggiore is the **Cappella Gondi** and a 15th-century crucifix by Brunelleschi, his only work in wood. And to the extreme left is the **Cappella Gaddi,** with frescoes by Nardo di Cione (1357); the altarpiece is by Nardo's brother, Orcagna. The chapel awaits the return of Giotto's 13th-century crucifix, now with the restorer. Adjacent is the **sacristy,** worth a peek for the delicate glazed terra-cotta *lavabo* (sink where priests would wash their hands) by Giovanni della Robbia.

In the left aisle near the main entrance is Masaccio's 1428 *Trinità* **fresco,** the first painting in history to use perfect linear mathematical perspective. Nearby is Brunelleschi's 15th-century **pulpit** from which Galileo was denounced for his heretical theory that Earth revolved around the Sun.

If you're not yet frescoed out, exit the church and turn right to visit the museum (entered from outside the church through the gate to the left of the facade), comprised of the **Chiostro Verde (Green Cloister),** sporting Paolo Uccello's 15th-century fresco cycle of *Noah and the Flood* (ironically, it was heavily damaged in the 1966 Arno flood), and the **Cappellone degli Spagnoli (Spanish Chapel),** whose captivating series of Andrea de Bonaiuto's early Renaissance frescoes (recently restored) glorify the history of the Dominican church. The chapel got its name from the nostalgic Eleanora de Toledo, wife of Cosimo de' Medici, who permitted her fellow Spaniards to be buried here.

Piazza Santa Maria Novella (just south of train station). © 055-215918, or 055-282187 for museum. Basilica 2.50€ ($2.85), 1.50€ ($1.75) ages 12–18. Museo 2.60€ ($3). Basilica Mon–Thurs and Sat 9:30am–5pm; Fri and Sun 1–5pm. Museo Mon–Thurs and Sat 9am–2pm; Sun 8am–1pm. Bus: A, 6, 11, 12, 36, 37, 68.

Museo Stibbert *(Kids* Anyone even remotely interested in armor and the historic days of chivalry should spend some time in the musty, formerly private home of wealthy Scotch-Italian collector Frederick Stibbert. Opened to the public since shortly after his death in 1906 and considered one of the most important private collections in the world, Stibbert's house/museum is filled to the brim with—among countless other objects and antiques from the 16th to the 19th centuries—thousands of pieces of armor from East and West (with Europe's largest collection of Japanese armor) and all the bellicose trappings: maces, pole-axes, crossbows, blunderbusses, and the like.

The **Sala della Cavalcata (Hall of the Cavalcade)** is the high point of the house, with a dozen life-size models of knights on war horses dressed in full-body battle armor. In the **Salone della Cupola,** 50 men-at-arms wearing glistening suits of plate armor represent all parts of the world. Some of the historic armor is as striking as body sculpture, as decorative as body jewelry. The last few years (and the arrival of a new female European curator) have seen radical improvements in the museum's evolution, garnering the more appropriate attention it has long deserved.

Via Stibbert 26. © 055-475520. Admission 5€ ($5.75). Mon–Wed 10am–2pm; Fri–Sat 10am–6pm. Bus: 4.

AROUND SANTA CROCE

Basilica di Santa Croce & Cappella Pazzi (Pazzi Chapel) 𝕊𝕊𝕊 Begun
in 1294 by Arnolfo di Cambio, the original architect of the Duomo, the cavernous Santa Croce is the world's largest Franciscan church. The humble presence of St. Francis is best felt in the **two chapels** to the right of the main altar: Entirely covered with faded but important early-14th-century frescoes by Giotto, they depict the life of the Assisi-born saint and scenes from the Bible.

The Bardi is the more famous of the two, if only as a setting for a scene in the Merchant-Ivory film *A Room with a View;* its deathbed scene of St. Francis is one of the church's most important frescoes. To the left of the main altar is a wooden **crucifix** by Donatello, whose portrayal of Christ was thought too provincial by early-15th-century standards (his buddy Brunelleschi once commented, "Why, Donatello, you've put a peasant on the Cross!").

Santa Croce is the final resting place for many of the Renaissance's most renowned figures. Over 270 **tombstones** pave the floor of the church, but attention deservedly goes to **monumental tombs** like that of Michelangelo, designed by Vasari, the first on the right as you enter; the three allegorical figures represent Painting, Architecture, and Sculpture. Dante's empty tomb is right next to him (he was exiled from Florence in 1302 for political reasons and was buried in Ravenna in 1321; there's also a statue dedicated to him on the left side of the steps leading into the church), while Machiavelli rests in the fourth. Galileo and Rossini, among others, were also laid to rest here. Off the right transept and through the sacristy and gift shop is one of Florence's most renowned **leather shops,** where you can watch the artisans at work (great quality; not cheap).

The entrance to the tranquil **Cappella Pazzi (Museo dell'Opera di Santa Croce)** is currently outside the church, to the right of the main doors (though this may change in 2005, when a new visitor center is inaugurated—presumably paid for by all the obscenely high entry fees this formerly free house of God now charges). Commissioned in 1443 by Andrea de' Pazzi, a key rival of the Medici family, and designed by Filippo Brunelleschi, the chapel is a masterful example of early Renaissance architecture. The 12 glazed terra-cotta roundels of the *Apostles* are by Luca della Robbia, finished in 1452. Next door, the 13th-century **refectory** serves as the church's museum, housing many works from the 13th to the 17th centuries, highlighted by one of Cimabue's finest works, the *Crucifixion,* which suffered serious damage in the 1966 flood of the Arno. Completely submerged when floodwaters rose to 1m (3 ft.) in the church and 1.5m (5 ft.) in the museum, it has now been restored and is displayed on an electric cable that will lift it out of reach of future harm.

Piazza Santa Croce. Ⓒ 055-2466105. www.operadisantacroce.it. 4€ ($4.60) adults, 2€ ($2.30) ages 11–18. Basilica summer Mon–Sat 9:30am–5:30pm, Sun 1–5:30pm; winter Mon–Sat 9:30am–12:30pm and 3–5:30pm, Sun 3–5:30pm. Pazzi Chapel Mar–Oct Thurs–Tues 10am–6pm; Nov–Feb Thurs–Tues 10am–5pm. Bus: A, B, C, 12, 13, 14, 23.

Casa Buonarroti   This graceful and modest house, which Michelangelo bought late in life for his nephew, was turned into a museum by his heirs. Today it houses two of the master's most important early works: *Madonna alla Scala (Madonna on the Stairs)* and *Battaglia dei Centauri (Battle of the Centaurs),* both sculpted in his teenage years, when he was still working in bas-relief and before he created the Rome *Pietà.* The museum also houses a sizable collection of his drawings and scale models, particularly the one for the facade of San Lorenzo that was never realized.

Via Ghibellina 70 (5 blocks east of the Bargello). Ⓒ 055-241752. www.casabuonarroti.it. Admission 6.50€ ($7.45). Wed–Mon 9:30am–2pm. Bus: A, 14, 23.

Tempio Isrelitico & Jewish Museum   The 19th-century green copper–domed *Tempio Isrealitico* (Synagogue) warrants a visit by those interested in architecture or the heritage of Florence's Jewish community. It's a 15-minute walk east of the Duomo (but closer to Santa Croce) in an area of Florence that sees little tourism. The neo-Moorish temple dates from the 1860s, when the

Mercato Vecchio (Old Market) and its bordering Jewish Ghetto were cleared away to make way for Piazza della Repubblica. This Asian-inspired synagogue was begun in 1874, when its first stone arrived from Jerusalem. It was heavily damaged by the Nazis in 1944 (and completely restored soon after). A small museum houses a selection of Judaica dating back to the 17th century and includes a number of photos of the ghetto before it was razed.

Via Farina 4. © 055-2346654. www.firenzebraica.net. Admission 4€ ($4.60). June–Aug Sun–Thurs 10am–6pm; Apr–May and Sept–Oct Sun–Thurs 10am–5pm; Nov–Mar Sun–Thurs 10am–3pm; obligatory 45-min. guided tours every 25 min. Bus: 6, 31, 32, C.

IN THE OLTRARNO & BEYOND

Palazzo Pitti (Pitti Palace) ★★★   It's ironic that this rugged golden palazzo, begun in 1458 (presumably by Brunelleschi) for wealthy textile merchant/banker Luca Pitti, in an attempt to keep up with the Medicis, was bought by Medici descendants in 1549 when Pitti's heirs spiraled into bank-ruptcy. They used it as their official residence as rulers of Florence. The Medicis, beginning with Cosimo I and his wife, Eleanora di Toledo, who moved here from the Palazzo Vecchio, tripled its size, elaborately embellished it, and graced it with the Boboli Gardens (see below) that still fan up the hill behind it, once the quarry from which the palazzo's *pietra dura* was taken. Today it's home to seven museums, the largest collection of galleries in Florence under one roof.

GALLERIA PALATINA (PALATINE GALLERY) ★★★   These 26 art-filled rooms on the first floor are the stars of the palazzo. Home to one of the finest collections of Italian Renaissance and baroque masters in Europe, this gallery is the most important collection in Florence after the Uffizi's. The art of the 16th century is the forte of the Palatina, in particular that of Raphael and Titian. Of the outstanding Raphaels displayed here, look for the prized **Madonna of the Chair** (the best known of his many interpretations of the Madonna). His sec-ond most famous, **La Fornarina,** also known as **La Velata (The Veiled Woman),** is a portrait of his baker's daughter and young mistress; if she looks particularly Madonna-like, it's because she most likely posed for most of his Madonna commissions.

The gallery's treasures include a large collection of works by Andrea del Sarto; Fra Bartolomeo's **San Marco** and his beautiful last work, **Descent from the Cross;** some superb works by Rubens, including **The Four Philosophers;** and canvases by Tintoretto and Veronese. There are stunning portraits by Titian, includ-ing **Pope Julius II, The Man with the Gray Eyes,** and **The Music Concert**—his collection is regarded as some of the museum's most important, a hard call to make from such a cavalcade of superstars. Also represented are Caravaggio (namely, **The Sleeping Cupid,** 1608), Pontormo, Van Dyck, and Botticelli.

After wandering past the jigsaw-puzzle walls of the painting-lined Galleria Palatina, you may want to rest your eyes with a stroll through the green Boboli Gardens (see below) or allow for a brief visit in the second-most-visited museum in the palazzo, the Appartamenti Monumentali, no less extravagant than what you've just seen, but with a far less attention-riveting art collection.

APPARTAMENTI MONUMENTALI (MONUMENTAL APARTMENTS) ★★   These restored apartments, gilded and chandeliered, contain paintings (look for Caravaggio's **Portrait of a Knight of Malta**), tapestries, and over-the-top furnishings from the resplendent days of the Medici and later the dukes of Lorraine.

GALLERIA D'ARTE MODERNA (MODERN ART GALLERY)   You may not have come to Florence to view modern art, but those with any concentration left should head upstairs to this gallery. It houses an interesting array of 19th-century Italian Impressionists (known as the *Macchiaioli* school after the *macchie* or "spots" used in their Impressionist style). The leader of the movement, Giovanni Fattori, is well represented here, as are Lega, Signorini, and early-20th-century predecessors.

OTHER MUSEUMS OF INTEREST   Among the least visited of the Pitti's panoply of small museums is the **Museo degli Argenti (Silver Museum)**, on the ground floor, 16 rooms filled with the priceless private treasure of the Medici family. Other small museums that follow their own drums when it comes to hours and closures include the **Museo della Porcellana (Porcelain Museum)**, currently open; the **Museo delle Carozze (Coach Museum)**, closed indefinitely; and the **Galleria del Costume (Costume Gallery)**. The latter concentrates on costumes from the 18th to the 20th centuries, with some earlier exceptions.

Piazza Pitti. ✆ **055-294883** for all or individual numbers listed below. www.sbas.firenze.it. For reservations: ✆ **055-294883** or www.firenzemusei.it (3€/$3.45 fee). **Galleria Palatina:** ✆ **055-2388614.** Admission 6.50€ ($7.45). Tues–Sun 8:15am–6:50pm (may stay open later daily in summer). **Galleria d'Arte Moderna:** ✆ **055-2388601.** Admission 5€ ($5.75) on cumulative ticket with Galleria del Costume. **Galleria del Costume:** ✆ **055-2388713.** Admission 5€ ($5.75) on cumulative ticket with Galleria d'Arte Moderna. **Museo degli Argenti:** ✆ **055-2388709.** Admission 4€ ($4.60) on cumulative ticket with Museo della Porcellana. **Museo della Porcellana:** ✆ **055-2388605.** Admission 4€ ($4.60) on cumulative ticket with Museo degli Argenti. All 4 daily 8:30am–1:50pm; closed 1st, 3rd, and 5th Mon and 2nd and 4th Sun of each month. Bus: D, 11, 36, 37.

Giardini di Boboli (Boboli Gardens) 𝕒

The expansive Giardini Boboli begin behind the Pitti Palace and fan up to the star-shape Fortezza Belvedere crowning the hill. Enter the gardens via the rear exit of the Pitti Palace if you're visiting the museum, or the entrance to the left facing the palace if you're bypassing the museum. The green gardens, particularly beautiful in spring, were laid out in the 16th century by the great landscape artist Tribolo. They're filled with an amphitheater, graveled walks, grottoes, and antique and Renaissance statuary, and are the best spot in Florence for a picnic lunch. The view from the fortress (1590–95) is stunning, but there's not much to see inside unless there's a special exhibit; ask at the tourist office or look for posters around town.

Directly behind the Pitti Palace. ✆ **055-2651816.** Admission to gardens 4€ ($4.60) adults, free for those under 18 or over 60; free admission to fortress grounds, but exhibit admission varies. Nov–Feb daily 8:15am–5pm; Mar and Oct daily 8:15am–6pm; Apr–May and Sept daily 8:15am–7pm; June–Aug daily 8:15am–8pm. Closed the 1st and last Mon of every month. Fortress hours vary with exhibits. Bus: D, 11, 36, 37.

Santa Maria del Carmine & Cappella Brancacci 𝕒𝕒

This baroque church dates from the 18th century, when a fire ravaged the 13th-century structure built for the Carmelite nuns; the smoke damage was major, but the fire left the Brancacci Chapel miraculously intact. This was a miracle indeed, as the frescoes begun in 1425 by Masolino and continued by his brilliant student Masaccio were a watershed in art history, crucial to the development of the Renaissance. They were painstakingly restored in the 1980s, removing not only the dirt and grime, but also the prudish fig leaves trailing across Adam and Eve's privates. Now more clearly evident is the painters' unprecedented expression of emotion as well as their pioneering use of perspective and chiaroscuro.

Masaccio's ***Expulsion of Adam and Eve*** (extreme upper-left corner) best illustrates anguish and shame hitherto unknown in painting, while ***The Tribute Money*** (just to its right) is a study in unprecedented perspective. The bulk of the frescoes depict the *Life of St. Peter* (who appears in a golden orange mantle). The lower panels were finished by Filippino Lippi (son of the great Filippo Lippi) in 1480, 50 years after the premature death of Masaccio at 27; he faithfully imitated the young master's style and technique. Even later masters like Leonardo da Vinci and Michelangelo came to see what they could learn from this mastery of perspective, light, colors, and realism.

Piazza Santa Maria della Carmine (west of Piazza Santo Spirito in the Oltrarno). © 055-2382195. Church free admission. Cappella Brancacci 4€ ($4.60). Mon–Sat 10am–5pm; Sun 1–5pm. Bus: D, 6, 11, 36, 37, 68.

San Miniato al Monte & Piazzale Michelangiolo ✯✯   No trip up to the green lofty heights of Piazzale Michelangiolo for sunset is complete without a visit first to **San Miniato,** an outstanding example of Florentine Romanesque architecture and the oldest religious building in Florence after the baptistery. From the Ponte Vecchio and points below, you can marvel at its multicolor facade and glimmering 13th-century fresco, but it's worth the trip up if only for the breathtaking view of the city from the church steps. Construction of the present building began in 1013 (with the geometrical-design marble facade added later that century) on the site where St. Minias, a 3rd-century martyr, was said to have carried his severed head from the city below before collapsing dead at this precise spot.

The dark interior appears more mystical because of its undulating 13th-century Oriental carpet–like **pavement mosaic** with signs of the zodiac. In the center of the nave is a **chapel** by Michelozzo (1447) whose glazed terra-cotta ceiling is by Luca della Robbia. A visit to the 11th-century **crypt** with frescoes by Taddeo Gaddi (architect of the Ponte Vecchio) and with fine columns and original capitals is evocative of the church's early days. Stay for the daily vespers sung in Gregorian chant at 4:30pm (followed by Mass) by the handful of monks who live here. It's easy to see why Florentine nobility prefer to attend Christmas Mass here and why future brides dream of being married here. The adjacent **cemetery** is worth a stroll in search of the gravestone of Tuscan-born Carlo Lorenzini, also known as Carlo Colladi, author of *Pinocchio.*

Now stroll on over to the **Piazzale Michelangiolo** to catch sunset over Florence, take a photo of the second copy of Michelangelo's *David,* and enjoy the view you've seen on a thousand postcards.

Via del Monte alle Croci/Viale Galileo Galilei (behind Piazzale Michelangiolo). San Miniato: © 055-2342731. Free admission. Easter to early Oct daily 8am–7:30pm; winter daily 8am–1pm and 2:30–6pm. Bus: 12, 13.

ESPECIALLY FOR KIDS

While children may feel like this museum-rich city is filled with stuff way too old for them to relate to, Florence's biggest plus for parents is the city's accessibility and compact layout in relatively traffic-free streets. Much of your visit will be spent strolling the ancient streets of a city that's one big open-air museum. Young legs that can sustain a 400-plus step workout should head up to **Brunelleschi's cupola** (see the Duomo, earlier in this chapter) and/or the top of **Giotto's campanile** for an awesome view of the city and swarms of ant-size tourists. Your kids (and you) can recharge batteries during **picnic lunches** in the green Boboli Gardens or, higher yet, on the grounds of the Forte Belvedere.

If you're visiting in June, try to catch one of the four processions and games of the **Calcio Storico** (see the "Italy Calendar of Events," in chapter 2), with their historic costumes and armored knights on steeds. And your kids won't let you miss tasting your way through the many excellent **gelaterie,** whose variety (they can squeeze four or five flavors into some of those cups) and quality make Baskin-Robbins look ho-hum.

As Florentine authorities encourage residents to take up bike riding while the historic center's pedestrian zone grows, **bicycle stands** become more predominant. If your child can handle a two-wheeler well, you have the blessing of tooling around a flat city (Florence is no hill town) in a generally traffic-free zone (but the cobblestones can do you in).

The **Stibbert Museum**'s unusually extensive collection of armor (see earlier in this chapter) is also a guaranteed pleaser. And don't even think about leaving town without rubbing the nose of the famous bronze statue of the *porcellino* **(wild boar)** on the south side of the Straw Market (aka the Mercato Nuovo or New Market), ensuring good luck and a return to Florence.

ORGANIZED TOURS

American Express (see "Fast Facts: Florence," earlier in this chapter) has teamed up with **CAF Tours,** Via Roma 4 (© **055-283200;** www.caftours.com), to offer two half-day bus tours of town (39€/$45), including visits to the Uffizi, the Medici Chapels, and Piazzale Michelangiolo. They also offer day trips to Pisa, Siena/San Gimignano, the Chianti, Lucca, or Medici villas for 33€ to 49€ ($38–$56); and farther afield to Venice and Perugia/Assisi for 85€ to 110€ ($98–$127). You can book similar tours through most other travel agencies around town.

Florence's new **hop-on/hop-off bus tour,** which swings by many of the city's tourist destinations, is being heavily marketed by the city bus company, **ATAF** (www.ataf.net), and by the tourist office, but the city is easily managed on foot, and the tour isn't worth the ridiculous 20€ ($23) fee.

Walking Tours of Florence (© **055-2645033;** www.artviva.com) offers a basic 3-hour tour daily at 9:45am for 25€ ($29) for adults, 20€ ($23) for students under 26, and 10€ ($12) for children ages 6 to 12. Meet at their office on the mezzanine level of Piazza Santa Stefano 2 (a pocket-size piazza hidden off Via Por Santa Maria between V. Lambertesca and the Ponte Vecchio). They provide other thematic tours as well as private guides, and even offer walking tours of Pisa and the Cinque Terre from 49€ ($56).

Call **I Bike Italy** (© **055-2342371;** www.ibikeitaly.com) to sign up for 1-day rides in the surrounding countryside: Fiesole year-round for 80€ ($92), or the Chianti April 15 through October for 98€ ($113). A shuttle bus picks you up at 9am at the Ponte delle Grazie and drives you to the outskirts of town, and an enjoyable lunch in a local trattoria is included. You're back in town by 5pm. It might stretch your budget, but you should get out of this tourist-trodden stone city for a glimpse of the incomparable Tuscan countryside. They also offer a summertime 2-day trip (Tues–Wed) to Siena for 322€ ($370), which includes a walking tour up to Fiesole.

6 Shopping

In terms of good-value shopping, Florence is easy to categorize: It's paradise. This one-time capitalist capital, where modern banking and commerce first flourished, has something for every taste and price range. Whether you can afford little more than a bargain-priced wool sweater in the open-air market or are interested in investing in a butter-soft leather jacket that'll burst your budget, Florence is for you. Florentine merchants are not the born histrionic negotiators of the south or yesteryear, and few will encourage bargaining. Only if you're buying with traveler's checks and buying a number of items should you even broach the subject, and only in the most civilized manner. Good luck.

THE SHOPPING SCENE

BEST BUYS *Alta moda* fashion is alive and well and living on **Via dei Tornabuoni** and its elegant offshoot, **Via della Vigna Nuova,** where some of the high priests of Italian and international design and fashion share space with the occasional bank (which you may have to rob in order to afford any of the goods). But it makes for great window-shopping.

Between the Duomo and the river are the pedestrian-only **Via Roma** (which becomes **Via Por Santa Maria** before reaching the Ponte Vecchio) and the parallel **Via dei Calzaiuoli;** lined with fashionable jewelry and clothing stores (and the city's two largest department stores, **La Rinascente** and **Coin**), they're the city's main shopping streets. Stores here were traditionally only slightly less high fashion and less high priced than those on the gilded Via dei Tornabuoni—but there has been a recent trend to head down market. A stop at any of the area's **gelaterie** is a guaranteed spirit-lifter for the nonshoppers among you. **Via del Corso** and its extension east of Via del Proconsolo, **Borgo degli Albizi,** is another recommended shopping street, boasting historic palazzi as well as less pretentious and more approachable boutiques (though they're fewer in number).

Unless you have a Medici-size fortune and hope to leave with a Renaissance trinket, window-shop (only) the stores with museum-quality antiques on **Borgo Ognissanti** near the Arno and the perpendicular **Via dei Fossi. Lungarno Corsini** and **Lungarno Acciaiuoli** run along the river, where you'll find merchants offering fine paintings and sculpture, objets d'art, and antiques and miscellany. But perhaps the most impressive antiques row is **Via Maggio** in the Oltrarno and, to a far lesser degree, its perpendicular offshoot, **Via Santo Spirito.**

Florence is probably most famous for its **leather**⋆. Many travelers are happily, albeit mistakenly, convinced they can buy a leather coat for a song. No European city can hold a candle to Florentine quality and selection, but prices are higher than those rumors you may have heard. Expect to spend $150 to $300 for a leather jacket with moderate workmanship, detail, and quality. The shops around **Piazza Santa Croce** are the best places for leather and aren't much more expensive than the pushcarts at the San Lorenzo Market. Leather apparel may be beyond your budget, but consider the possibilities of small leather goods, from wallets and eyeglass cases to fashion accessories like shoes, belts, and bags.

Florence has been known for its gold for centuries, and jewelry shops of all price levels still abound. Dozens of exclusive gold stores line both sides of the pedestrian **Ponte Vecchio.** Gold is almost always 18 karat (ask them to point out the teensy stamp), beautifully crafted, and, though not a bargain, reasonably priced—think instant heirlooms.

MARKETS There's nothing in Italy, and indeed perhaps nothing in Europe, to compare with Florence's bustling, sprawling, open-air **Mercato San Lorenzo**⋆. Hundreds of awninged pushcarts crowd along the streets around the Basilica di San Lorenzo and the Mercato Centrale, offering countless varieties of hand-knit wool and mohair sweaters, leather jackets, handbags, wallets, and gloves—not to mention the standard array of souvenir T-shirts and sweatshirts, wool and silk scarves, and other souvenirs. (If you remember the place being filled with Gucci and Fendi knockoffs, you'll be disappointed that the police have done away with them almost entirely. The follow-up act is the easy availability of Prada and Moschino bags sold by Senegalese sidewalk vendors around town and on the Ponte Vecchio after store hours.)

The market stretches for blocks between Piazza San Lorenzo behind the Medici Chapels to Via Nazionale, along Via Canto de' Nelli and Via dell' Ariento, with stalls also along various side streets in between. From mid-March to October, the market operates daily from 9am to 7pm (closed Sun–Mon the rest of the year), though extremely slow periods (or heat waves and inclement weather) may result in many or all of the vendors staying home. Many vendors accept credit cards. These hundreds of tchotchke vendors buzz around the early-1900 **Mercato Centrale** food market (entrance on V. dell'Ariento), a riotous two-floor feast for all senses; whether you breeze through looking for picnic goodies or photo ops, it'll leave you breathless and hungry.

Much smaller, but still worth a look, is the outdoor **Mercato del Porcellino,** once known as the Straw Market and today commonly known as the **Mercato Nuovo (New Market),** where a couple of dozen stalls crowd beneath an open-sided arcade 2 blocks south of Piazza della Repubblica. Vendors offer mostly handbags, scarves, embroidered tablecloths, and miscellaneous souvenirs. The market is named for the bronze boar *(porcellino)* on the river side of the arcade, whose snout has been worn smooth by the countless Florentines who've touched it for good luck. Hours are generally from 9am to 6pm daily from mid-March to November 3 and Tuesday through Saturday the rest of the year.

The **Mercato delle Pulci** on small Piazza Ciompi (follow V. Oriuolo east out of Piazza del Duomo) is a rather unimpressive flea market open Tuesday through Saturday from 8:30am to 7pm; it doubles in size the last Sunday of every month. The **Mercato delle Cascine** takes place every Tuesday from 8am to 2pm in the grassy riverside park west of the Teatro Comunale. This is where the locals shop, so don't expect tourist merchandise; do expect more contained prices on household goods and everyday clothes. You may also want to check out Tuscany's major flea market in **Arezzo** (accessible by bus or direct train in an hour) the first weekend of every month.

SHOPPING A TO Z

BOOKSTORES   Even the smaller bookshops in Florence these days have at least a few shelves devoted to English-language books. **Feltrinelli International,** Via Cavour 12–20 (℃ **055-219524;** www.lafeltrinelli.it), is one of the few of any size. **G. Vitello,** Via dei Servi 94–96r (℃ **055-292445**), sells coffee-table books on art and all things Italian at up to half off the price you'd pay in a regular bookstore. There are other branches at Via Verdi 40r (℃ **055-2346894**) and Via Pietrapiana 1r (℃ **055-241063**).

For English-only shops, hit **Paperback Exchange,** Via Fiesolana 31r (℃ **055-2478154;** www.papex.it)—not the most central, but the best for books in English, specializing in titles relating in some way to Florence and Italy. Much of their stock is used, and you can't beat the prices—dog-eared volumes and all. Penguin books go for only 2€ to 3€ ($2.30–$3.45). You can also trade in that novel you've finished for another. **BM Bookshop,** Borgo Ognissanti 4r (℃ **055-294575**), is a bit smaller but more central and carries only new volumes. They also have a more well-rounded selection—from novels and art books to cookbooks and travel guides.

CERAMICS   La Botteghina, Via Guelfa 5r, north of the Mercato San Lorenzo (℃ **055-287367;** www.labotteghina.it), specializes in a more discerning selection from the ceramics capitals of Deruta and Montelupo. This is better quality, but you'll find small items for 15€ to 30€ ($17–$35). **Sbigoli,** Via Sant'Egidio 4r, east of the Duomo (℃ **055-2479713**), has a large selection of hand-painted Tuscan ceramics, particularly 16th- and 17th-century reproductions. Products of skilled craftsmanship are never cheap (and shipping, which this store offers, is bound to double your expense), but here, you'll find colorful terra-cotta mugs, ashtrays, and other small items that are reasonable. Short-term classes are available in the store's studio.

DEPARTMENT STORES   Coin, Via dei Calzaiuoli 56r (☎ **055-280531;** www.coin.it), is as close to Macy's as you'll get in Florence: four floors of made-in-Italy apparel and accessories for men, women, and children. Moderately priced items are mixed in with the high-end merchandise, and it all makes for enjoyable browsing even for those not buying. Check out the sales amid the January and July crowds. The newest arrival is the six-story branch of the national chain **La Rinascente,** Piazza della Repubblica 1 (☎ **055-219113;** www.rinascente.it). Often compared to Bloomingdale's, it's the nicest (and largest) store to represent the best of made-in-Italy merchandising.

DESIGN & HOUSEHOLD ITEMS   On your way to or from a visit to the Accademia to see *David,* check out the collection at **Viceversa,** Via Ricasoli 53r (☎ **055-696392;** www.viceversashop.com), showcasing the most interesting items from the creative studios of Milan. Much of this looks like it belongs in the Museum of Modern Art, with a number of small items that embody the latest in Italian design and make great souvenirs. You can spend a fortune or concentrate on bottle openers, key rings, ashtrays, pens, and hot plates, all for under 15€ ($17). For a balanced mix of the cutting-edge and traditional, time-tested kitchenware and household goods Italian style, head to **La Menagere,** Via dei Ginori 8r, near the Mercato San Lorenzo (☎ **055-213875**).

DISCOUNT FASHION   To get your high fashion at bargain-basement prices, head to one of the branches of **Guardaroba/Stock House Grandi Firme.** The Borgo degli Albizi 87r store (☎ **055-2340271**) carries mainly the past season's models, the Via dei Castellani 26r branch (☎ **055-294853**) carries spring/summer remaindered collections, and the Via Verdi 28r (☎ **055-2478250**) and Via Nazionale 38r (☎ **055-215482**) stores sell outfits from the past winter. **Stock House Il Giglio,** Via Borgo Ognissanti 86 (no phone) also carries big-name labels at 50% to 60% off.

HERBS & SPICES   Just a palazzo or two removed from Piazza della Signoria is the **Erboristeria Palazzo Vecchio,** Via Vacchereccia 9r (☎ **055-2396055**), an old-world herbal store whose traditions and origins (and some of its recipes and formulas) go back centuries. There are natural pomades and elixirs for everything from dandruff to the blues, but you'll be most interested in the nicely packaged scented soaps, room scents, essences, candles, and sachets. Packaged seasonings and spices used in the *cucina italiana* make nice gifts for Italophile friends. While this erboristeria is affordable, the theatrical landmark **Farmacia Santa Maria Novella,** Via della Scala 16r (☎ **055-216276;** www.smnovella.it), is not. It is still some place to see, though browsing is limited and the help notoriously unhelpful. The 16th-century setting alone is worth the trip, and you may be able to scrape up enough euros for some of the famous potpourri or beautifully packaged soaps and room scents.

JEWELRY   If you have the financial solvency of a small country, the place to buy your baubles is the **Ponte Vecchio,** famous for its goldsmiths and silversmiths since the 16th century. The craftsmanship at all the stalls is usually of a very high quality, and so they seem to compete instead over who can charge the highest prices. A more moderately priced boutique is Milan-based **Mario Buccellati,** Via dei Tornabuoni 71r (☎ **055-2396579**), which since 1919 has been making thick, heavy jewelry of high quality. In the back room is the silver.

Florence is also a good place to root around for the fake stuff. The audacious bijoux at **Angela Caputi,** Borgo San Jacopo 82r (© **055-212972;** www.angela caputi.com), aren't for the timid. Much of Angela's costume jewelry—from earrings and necklaces to brooches and even a small clothing line—is oversize and bold and often ultraflamboyant . . . and low priced.

LEATHER   The city is awash in leather stores of all quality ranges. The low end of the gamut is a departure point worth considering: the **Mercato San Lorenzo** (see above). A good 80% of the leather jackets are too cheaply made, but a fair number are passable to decent and sometimes even very good. The problem is finding them—you'll have to wade through a ton of mediocre stuff. Check seams, lining, and suppleness of leather. Don't bank on alterations once you get home: Few tailors do leather, and those that do charge dearly.

If you're not of the market mentality, try the respectable **Leather School** in the Basilica di Santa Croce, Piazza Santa Croce 16 (© **055-244533** or 055-234534; www.leatherschool.it). The fine quality of the varied selection of leather goods from wallets and key chains to bags and attaché cases isn't cheap, but it's not overpriced either. The same goes for the selection at **Madova Gloves,** Via Guicciardini 1r, on the south side of the Ponte Vecchio (© **055-2396526;** www.madova.com). A reasonable alternative to the pricey designer labels of Via dei Tornabuoni is **Anna,** Piazza Pitti 38–41r (© **055-283787**), which provides fine quality and a professional staff who know their stuff. The apparel is classic to fashionable, and the prices are high but reasonable, considering the goods. Seasoned tailors can do alterations in 24 hours.

PAPER GOODS   Marbleized paper and the myriad items it covers (agendas, albums, boxes, diaries, pencils, and pencil holders) is a centuries-old craft that has experienced a resurgence. For the unknowing, little-deserving, or innocent child awaiting their souvenirs back home, the low-quality photocopy quality of what is sold at the **Mercato San Lorenzo** will suffice. But for all else, the best value is at **Il Torchio,** Via de' Bardi 17 (© **055-2342862**), whose artisans take great pride in the quality of their hand-printed papers and the carefully crafted items they cover (they'll also consider custom work). Its easy-to-reach Oltrarno location east of the Ponte Vecchio keeps prices lower than those in the high-rent Duomo neighborhood. More central, with five locations in Florence, is **Il Papiro,** whose largest branch is at Via Tavolini 13r (© **055-213823;** www.madeinfirenze.it/papiro_e.htm).

SHOES   Quality shoe stores abound, from the exquisite Florentine institutions of Via dei Tornabuoni to the fun and ultracheap. For the latter, try **Peppe Peluso,** Via del Corso 1, at Via Proconsolo (© **055-268283**), the cheapest shoe store in town, its large rooms chockablock with medium-quality knockoffs of yesterday's, and some of tomorrow's, runway fashions. Men's and women's shoes are arranged according to size, with styles from the out-of-date to the up-to-date, priced as low as 30€ ($35).

7 Florence After Dark

Florence doesn't have the musical cachet or grand opera houses of Milan, Venice, or Rome, but there are two symphony orchestras and a fine music school in Fiesole. The city's public theaters are certainly respectable, and most major touring companies stop in town on their way through Italy.

One-stop shopping for most of the important venues in town is the ticket agency **Box Office,** Via Alamanni 39 (© **055-210804;** www.boxol.it), which tacks on a 10% commission. Your hotel can help you place the order by phone, although the agency does have some English-speaking staff. In addition to tickets for year-round events of all genres, they handle the summertime Calcio Storico folkloric soccer game and the Maggio Musicale and Estate Fiesolana (see the section on "Festivals & Events," earlier in this chapter).

Many concerts and recitals staged in major halls and private spaces are sponsored by the **Amici della Musica** (© 055-607440 or 055-608420; www. amicimusica.fi.it), so contact them to see what concerts may be on while you're in town. When Florentines really want a fine night out at the theater, they skip town and head to nearby Prato for the **Teatro Metastasio,** one of Italy's finest.

THE PERFORMING ARTS

CONCERT HALLS & OPERA   One of Italy's busiest stages, Florence's contemporary **Teatro Comunale,** Corso Italia 12 (© 055-213535 or 055-211158; www.maggiofiorentino.com), offers everything from symphonies to ballet to plays, opera, and concerts. The large main theater seats 2,000, with orchestra rows topped by horseshoe-shape first and second galleries. Its smaller Piccolo Teatro seating 500 is rectangular, offering good sightlines from most any seat. Tickets are 15€ to 100€ ($17–$115), with prices soaring to 150€ ($173) and beyond for prime seats at special or opening-night performances. The Teatro Comunale is the seat of the annual prestigious Maggio Musicale.

The excellent recently renovated **Teatro Verdi,** Via Ghibellina 99 (© 055-212320 or 055-2396242; www.teatroverdifirenze.it), schedules regular dance and classical music events, often with top foreign performers, troupes, and orchestras and the occasional European pop star. Ticket prices vary greatly—expect to pay 10€ to 30€ ($12–$35).

CHURCH CONCERTS   Many Florentine churches fill the autumn with organ, choir, and chamber orchestra concerts, mainly of classical music. A number of concerts and recitals staged in major halls and private spaces across town are sponsored by the **Amici della Musica** (© 055-607440 or 055-608420; www.amicimusica.fi.it), so contact them to see what "hidden" concert might be on while you're in town. The tiny **Santa Maria de' Ricci** (© 055-215044) on Via del Corso always seems to have music wafting from it; slipping inside to occupy a pew is occasionally free and sometimes a modest 3€ to 10€ ($3.45–$12). Around the corner at Santa Margherita 7, the **Chiesa di Dante** (© 055-289367) puts on quality concerts of music for, and often played by, youths and children (tickets required). The **Florentine Chamber Orchestra,** Via E. Poggi 6 (© 055-783374), also runs an autumn season in the **Orsanmichele;** tickets are available at the Box Office ticket agency (see above) or at the door an hour before the 9pm show.

LIVE-MUSIC CLUBS

For live bands to dance to in the center, head to **Dolce Zucchero,** Via dei Pandolfini 38r (© 055-2477894). "Sweet Sugar" is one of the better recent efforts to spice up Florence's nightlife and is popular with all ages. Under high ceilings are a long bar and a small dance floor with a stage for the nightly live musicians, usually a fairly talented cover act cranking out American and Italian dance songs for the packed crowd.

Caffè Caruso, Via Lambertesca 16r (off V. Por Santa Maria; © 055-281940; see "Great Deals on Dining," earlier in this chapter), is primarily a restaurant, but it also hosts occasional concerts.

DISCOS & NIGHTCLUBS

Universale, Via Pisana 77r (© **055-221122;** www.universalefirenze.it), is housed in a converted 1940s cinema and has successfully managed to draw everyone from folks in their early twenties to those pushing 50 (how they manage to keep collegians cutting loose from running into their young-at-heart parents here is a miracle). From 8pm, it's a popular restaurant on the balcony and a pizzeria on the main floor. Around 11pm, a live band takes the main floor stage for an hour or so, after which a DJ conducts the disco until 3am.

In the city center near Santa Croce, **Full-Up,** Via della Vigna Vecchia 25r (© **055-293006**), is a long-enduring disco/piano bar that's one of the top (and more restrained) dance spaces in Florence for the postcollegiate set. There are plenty of theme evenings (revival, samba, punk), so call to find out what's on.

Forever known as Yab Yum but reincarnated with a new attitude is **Yab,** Via Sassetti 5r (© **055-215160**), just behind the main post office on Piazza della Repubblica. This dance club for 20-somethings is a perennial favorite, a relic of a 1980s disco complete with rope line and surly bouncers.

A balanced combination of visitors and Italians—teenagers, students, and an under-30 crowd—fill the two-floor **Space Electronic,** Via Palazzuolo 37 (© **055-293082**). On the first floor are a video karaoke bar, a pub, an American-style bar, and a conversation area. Head upstairs for the dance floor with laser lights and a flying space capsule hovering above.

PUBS & BARS

There's an unsurprising degree of similarity among Florence's half-dozen **Irish-style pubs:** dark, woody interiors usually with several back rooms and plenty of smoke, and a crowd (stuffed to the gills on weekends) of students and 20- and 30-something Americans and Brits along with their Italian counterparts. The better pubs are the Florence branch of the successful Italian chain **Fiddler's Elbow,** Piazza Santa Maria Novella 7r (© **055-215056**); **The Old Stove,** Via Pellicceria 4r (© **055-284640**), just down from Piazza della Repubblica; and, under the same management, **The Lion's Fountain,** Borgo Albizi 34r (© **055-2344412**), on the tiny but lively Piazza San Pier Maggiore near Santa Croce. You'll find plenty of others around town—they pop up like mushrooms these days but often disappear just as quickly.

Red Garter, Via de' Benci 33r (© **055-2344904**), is a speakeasy that attracts a twenties-to-thirties crowd of Italians and some Americans, Australians, and English. A small bi-level theater room in the back has live music some nights—the last time I was here, it was a one-man band playing American and Italian rock hits mixed with some blues.

GAY & LESBIAN BARS

Florence has one of Italy's largest gay communities, with a tradition of gay tolerance that goes back to the early days of the Renaissance and some of the Medicis' homosexual proclivities (Michelangelo didn't specialize in male nudes for nothing). The Florentine fondness for *buon gusto* and inherent discretion remain all-important, however—except for the remarkable transvestites who populate the somewhat seedy Cascine Park after dark.

The **Arcigay/Arcilesbica** office is at Via Manara 12 (© **055-671298** or 055-555618; www.gaytoscana.it, www.gay.it, and www.azionegayelesbica.it), offering advice, psychological counseling, HIV testing, and information on the gay community and sponsoring gay-related events. It's open Monday through Saturday from 4 to 8pm, with Monday theme nights and Wednesday evenings devoted to lesbians, and Saturday afternoons to the younger set. It also publishes the free gay guide *Il Giglio Fuscia.*

Tabasco, Piazza Santa Cecilia 3r, near Piazza della Signoria (✆ 055-213000; www.tabascogay.it), is Florence's (and Italy's) oldest gay dance club. The crowd is mostly men in their twenties and thirties. The dance floor is downstairs, while a small video room and piano bar are up top. There are occasional cabaret shows and karaoke.

Florence's leading gay bar, **Crisco,** Via San Egidio 43r, east of the Duomo (✆ 055-2480580; www.crisco.it), is for men only. Its 18th-century building contains a bar and a dance floor.

The crowd is international at the **Flamingo Bar** (formerly Santanassa), Via del Pandolfini 26, near Piazza Santa Croce (✆ 055-243356). Thursday through Saturday, it's a mixed gay/lesbian party; the rest of the week, it's men only. On the street level is a crowded bar, sometimes with a live piano player. September to June on Friday and Saturday nights, the cellar becomes a disco.

CAFES

These cafes are more enjoyable and less ear-taxing than the bars above, and you can while away a nocturnal hour or two. For more conventional cafes, check out the staid and historic bars lining Piazza della Repubblica, particularly **Gilli's** (✆ 055-213896), open Wednesday through Monday from 7:30am to 1am; or the early-1900s **Caffè Rivoire** (✆ 055-214412), on Piazza della Signoria, open Tuesday through Sunday from 8:30am to midnight. Both have indoor/outdoor seating (there's usually live music in Piazza della Repubblica in summer).

Piazza Santo Spirito, hidden behind a tangle of back streets just blocks from the Pitti Palace, is the local youths' beloved piazza. Once a haven for drug users, the square has cleaned up its act but still claims enough edginess to be an authentic hangout for the alternative crowd. At the of-the-moment **Cabiria Caffè,** Piazza Santo Spirito 4r (✆ 055-215732), there's some seating inside, but the outdoor tables overlook the somber facade of the Santo Spirito church. There's a variety of reasonably priced fresh dishes (from 3.10€/$3.55), but this place bustles with young trendies who come to hang out before and after dinner. It's open Monday and Wednesday through Saturday from 8am to 1:30am.

From the clever Midas who gave Florence the internationally famous restaurant/trattoria Cibreocomes the handsome **Caffè Cibreo,** across the street at Via Andrea del Verrochio 5r (✆ 055-2345853). The cafe first became known for its informal and inexpensive lunch and dinner menus, many with dishes from the acclaimed kitchen across the way (dinner 7:30pm–midnight) or from nearby Il Pizzaiolo (see "Great Deals on Dining," earlier in this chapter). But this is also a lovely spot for an attractive older crowd who take their hot chocolate, tea blends, or coffee roasts seriously, or want to people-watch before or after dining. It's open from 7am to "after midnight."

WINE BARS

The most traditional wine bars are called *fiaschetterie,* after the word for a flask of chianti. They tend to be hole-in-the-wall joints serving sandwiches or simple food along with glasses filled to the brim—usually with a house wine, though finer vintages are often available. The best are **I Fratellini,** Via dei Cimatori 38r (✆ 055-2396096); **Antico Noè,** off Piazza S. Pier Maggiore (✆ 055-2340838); and **La Mescita,** Via degli Alfani 70r (✆ 055-2391604). There's also a traditional wine shop in the Oltrarno called simply **La Fiaschetteria,** Via de' Serragli 47r (✆ 055-287420), which, like many, doubles as a small locals' wine bar.

A more high-toned spot is the **Cantinetta Antinori,** Piazza Antinori 3 (© **055-292234**). It's housed in the palace headquarters of the Antinori wine empire at the top of Florence's main fashion drag, Via Tornabuoni. For a trendier wine bar focusing on handpicked labels offered with plates of cheese and other snacks, head to the Oltrarno and a real oenophile's hangout, **Il Volpe e L'Uva,** Piazza de' Rossi, behind Piazza Santa Felícita off Via Guicciardini (© **055-2398132**).

The Avuris, who run the Hotel Torre Guelfa (see "Accommodations You Can Afford," earlier in this chapter), have recently opened a great little wine bar right across from the Pitti Palace called **Pitti Gola e Cantina,** Piazza Pitti 16 (© **055-212704**), with glasses of wine from 4€ to 10€ ($4.60–$12) to help unwind from a day of museums. They also have light dishes, meat and cheese platters, and cakes for 7€ to 15€ ($8.05–$17).

Tuscany & Umbria

by Reid Bramblett

Tuscany (**Toscana**) and **Umbria** share much of the same cultural and artistic heritage, a history dating from the pre-Roman Etruscans, a cuisine, and, to some degree, a similarity in landscape. However, it'll behoove you never to mention these two regions in the same breath to a Tuscan or an Umbrian. Like two first cousins, Tuscany and Umbria are just as often fiercely individualistic in the characteristics and traditions they've preserved and nurtured over the centuries.

Italians are rarely modest about their unabashed love for the region they call home. But nowhere is this emotion-packed loyalty of *provincia* so deservedly heartfelt as in Tuscany, one of the country's most visited rural destinations. Richly endowed with a wide variety of topography, from the Apennine Mountains in the northwestern corner to the open rolling plains of the Maremma area in the south, Tuscany is also endowed with a coastal riviera (admittedly, less alluring than Liguria's, but with the benefit of wide, sandy beaches) and a number of idyllic islands in the Ligurian Sea, of which Elba, Napoleon's exile retreat, is the largest and most renowned.

The Umbrian cities featured in this chapter haven't changed much since the Middle Ages, but you'll never mistake them for museum cities: They're very much alive, fueled by their cultural interests and thriving economies only partially sustained by tourism. Two of Italy's most important summer festivals take place here, the Umbrian Jazz Festival in Perugia and the Spoleto Festival in Spoleto.

Most of the tourist offices in the towns and cities can supply you with lists of *affittacamere*, bed-and-breakfast accommodations that often offer the best deal in town. In many places, there's also the possibility of *agriturismo* accommodations in the countryside, ranging from the very basic to working farms with swimming and horseback riding. Lists are available, though they do little to describe or recommend one over the next.

1 Pisa & Its Tipping Tower

77km (48 miles) W of Florence, 21km (13 miles) W of Lucca, 335km (208 miles) N of Rome, 98km (61 miles) NW of San Gimignano

Legions descend on **Pisa** to see the famous tower that just won't stand up straight. Few other buildings have captured the world's imagination. Most surprising is the realization that the Leaning Tower—finally reopened to visitors in 2001—is but one of three principal structures occupying the vividly green piazza called Campo dei Miracoli and is the Duomo's free-standing (well, barely) campanile (bell tower). Also surprising may be the fact that Pisa is a large

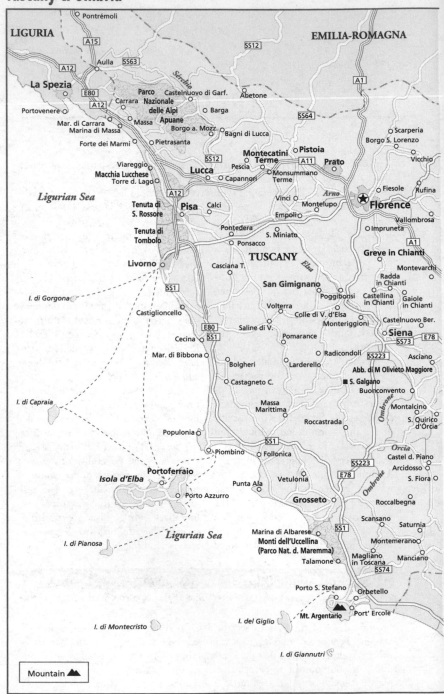

LIGURIA

EMILIA-ROMAGNA

Pontrémoli

A15

SS12

A1

Aulla   SS63

A12

A80

La Spezia

Parco   Castelnuovo di Garf.

Carrara   Nazionale   Abetone

Portovenere

A12   Massa   delle Alpi   Barga

Mar. di Carrara   Apuane   SS64

Marina di Massa   Borgo a. Mozz.

Forte dei Marmi   Pietrasanta   Bagni di Lucca   Scarperia

Borgo S. Lorenzo

Viareggio   Montecatini   Pistoia   Vicchio

Macchia Lucchese   SS12   Terme   A11   Prato

Torre d. Lago   Lucca   Pescia   Monsummano   Fiesole   Rufina

Capannori   Terme   Arno

Ligurian Sea   A12   Vinci   Montelupo   Florence

Pisa   Calci   Empoli   Vallombrosa

Tenuta di   Impruneta

S. Rossore   Pontedera   S. Miniato

Tenuta di   Ponsacco   A1

Tombolo   **TUSCANY**   Greve in Chianti

Casciana T.   Montevarchi

Livorno   Radda   Gaiole

San Gimignano   in Chianti   in Chianti

SS1   Poggibonsi   Castellina

I. di Gorgona   Volterra   in Chianti   Castelnuovo Ber.

Castiglioncello   Colle di V. d'Elsa   Siena

E80   Saline di V.   Monteriggioni   SS73   E78

Cecina   SS1   Pomarance   Asciano

Mar. di Bibbona   Radicondoli   SS223

I. di Capraia   Bolgheri   Larderello   Abb. di M Olivieto Maggiore

Castagneto C.   ■ S. Galgano   Buonconvento

Massa   Montalcino

Marittima   Roccastrada   S. Quirico

Populonia   d'Órcia

Orcia

Piombino   Follonica   SS1   Castel d. Piano

I. di Capraia   Arcidosso

Isola d'Elba   Portoferraio   SS223   S. Fiora

Vetulonia   E78

Porto Azzurro   Punta Ala   Roccalbegna

Grosseto

I. di Pianosa   **Ligurian Sea**   Scansano   Saturnia

Marina di Albarese   SS1   Montemerano

Monti dell'Uccellina   Magliano   Manciano

(Parco Nat. d. Maremma)   in Toscana

Talamone   SS74

Porto S. Stefano   Orbetello

I. di Montecristo   I. del Giglio   Mt. Argentario   Port' Ercole

I. di Giannutri

Mountain ▲▲

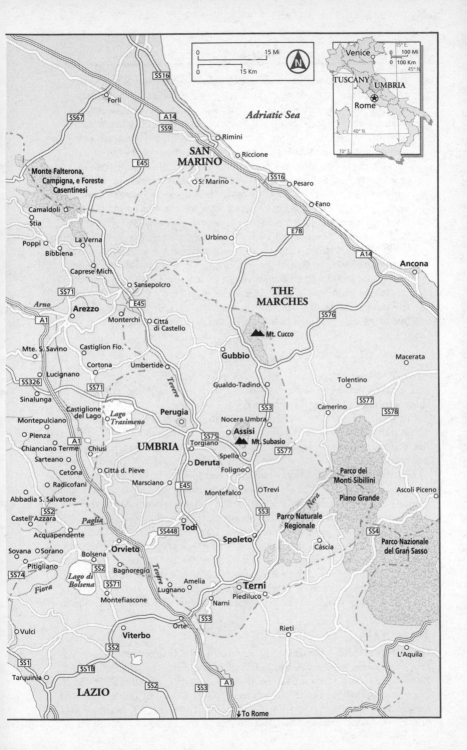

A Taste of Tuscany & Umbria

The Tuscan and Umbrian *cucina* draws heavily from the grains, beans, and ingredients of the farmer's simple pantry and the woods and forests covering its hills. Nouvelle cuisine it's not. Rustic *salsicce* (sausage) antipasti, *cacciagione* (game), and tender quality meats roasted or *alla griglia* are the highlight of every meal—the mighty **bistecca alla fiorentina** being the fabled (and bill-boosting) entree you'll want to try at least once. The unquestioned prominence of **olive oil** makes an appearance from the acclaimed groves of Lucca and Spoleto, the Tuscan and Umbrian suppliers of Europe's best *olio di oliva*. Renowned **Chianti wines** from the scenic pocket between Florence and Siena and distinctive **Orvieto whites** make this area an oenophile's dream—and you most likely won't be disappointed with the humble *vino della casa* (house wine). Umbria's touted claim to gastronomic fame is the underground *tartufo* (truffle) from Norcia, Spoleto, or San Miniato. Preciously grated over pastas and pizzas, it's expensive but its acquired taste is considered sublime by gourmand palates. This is the place to try it—not only for the local expertise and abundance, but also for the moderate prices (moderate when compared to over-the-top American prices).

riverside city with a population of 100,000—vibrant, contemporary, bustling, and relatively indifferent to its icon—something that may or may not appeal to those who expect a quaint Tuscan town.

Pisa is one of Italy's great ancient cities, its Roman roots going back more than 1,000 years before the building of the campanile. The mouth of the Arno River has long since silted up, placing Pisa inland 8km (5 miles) from the coast, but it was once a vital port and naval base for imperial Rome and for centuries fought to keep the Tyrrhenian coast free of invading Saracens. From the 11th to the 13th centuries, it grew to rival the three other maritime powers—Genoa, Amalfi, and Venice—and gloried in its military supremacy in the western Mediterranean. This was the city's Golden Age, when its artistic splendor flourished.

But internal rivalries and external strife from nearby Lucca and Florence chipped away at its political stability, and in 1406, it was defeated by the Florentines. There was a brief period of well-being under the Medicis and the flourishing of its prestigious university (established in 1343) and an even briefer period of independence from 1494 to 1509. But for the most part, Pisa's history melded with that of Florence's from the early 1500s until Italian unification in the 1860s.

ESSENTIALS

GETTING THERE   By Train   More than 20 trains (www.trenitalia.com) run daily from **Rome** (regional: 4 hr., 16€/$18; high-speed: 3 hr., 26€/$30). From **Florence,** 35 daily trains make the trip (80–90 min.; 5€–10€/$5.75–$12). There are trains about hourly from **Siena** (100–110 min.; 6.50€/$7.45). And **Lucca** zips 24 runs here every day (20–30 min.; 2.05€/$2.35). On the Lucca line, get off at the **Stazione San Rossore,** just a few blocks west of Piazza del

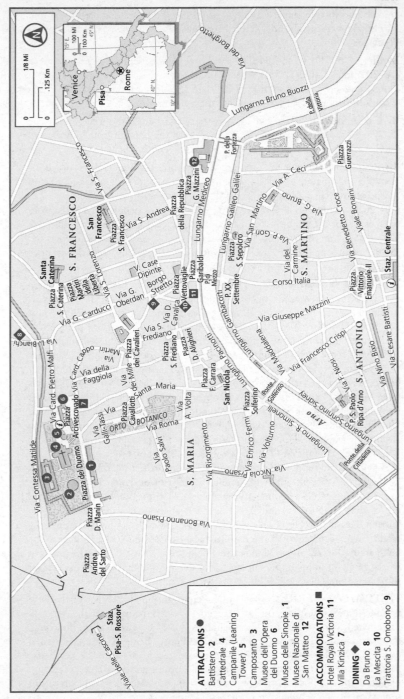

Pisa

ATTRACTIONS ●
Battistero **2**
Cattedrale **4**
Campanile (Leaning
 Tower) **5**
Camposanto **3**
Museo dell'Opera
 del Duomo **6**
Museo delle Sinopie **1**
Museo Nazionale di
 San Matteo **12**

ACCOMMODATIONS ■
Hotel Royal Victoria **11**
Villa Kinzica **7**

DINING ◆
Da Bruno **8**
La Mescita **10**
Trattoria S. Omobono **9**

Duomo and its campanile. All other trains, and the Lucca one eventually, pull into **Stazione Pisa Centrale.** From here, bus nos. A, B, or 3 will take you to Piazza del Duomo.

By Bus   Lazzi (© 0583-584876; www.lazzi.it) runs hourly buses from **Lucca** (20–30 min.; 2.20€/$2.55), where you can connect for hourly runs from **Florence** (2–2½ hr. total from Pisa; 6.90€/$7.95). Pisa's bus station is at Piazza Vittorio Emanuele II, just north of the main train station.

By Car   There's a Florence–Pisa autostrada along the Arno Valley. Take the SS12 or S12r from Lucca; the A12 comes down the coast from the north, and the SS1 runs north and south along the coast.

By Plane   Tuscany's main international airport, **Galileo Galilei** (© 050-500707; www.pisa-airport.com), is 3km (1¾ miles) south of Pisa. Trains zip you downtown to the train station in 5 minutes (1€/$1.15). A taxi to town takes only about 5 minutes (5€–8€/$5.75–$9.20)—some people even walk from town in about 20 minutes. You can also take a **Taxi Collettivo** (a "collective taxi" that leaves when it fills with passengers) at a slightly reduced rate: 4€ ($4.60) per person for a ride to Piazza Duomo, 2.50€ ($2.85) for a ride to Pisa's train station.

VISITOR INFORMATION   The main **tourist office** has moved yet again (the third time in 4 years), but this time the move made a lot of sense: Now it sits on Piazza della Torre Pendente, next door to the Leaning Tower (© **050-560464** or 050-830-253; www.pisa.turismo.toscana.it, though the tourism section of the city's municipal website, www.comune.pisa.it/turismo, is actually far more useful). From May to October, it's open Monday to Saturday from 9am to 6pm and Sunday 10:30am to 4:30pm. Another office is a few short blocks north of the train station on Piazza V. Emanule II (© **050-42291**). It's open Monday to Friday from 9am to 7pm and Saturday 9am to 1:30pm. Either has maps and pamphlets, but the staff is oddly uninformed on the city of Pisa. Usually, considerably more knowledgeable "Custodians of the Duomo" hang around the Museo dell'Opera del Duomo desk. The administrative **APT** office is at Via Pietro Nenni 24 (© **050-929777**; fax 050-929764).

A helpful state-supported **private tourism consortium** (© **050-830253**; fax 050-830243; www.pisae.it) will, among other services, book hotel rooms for free. Unfortunately, it's no longer located in the tourist office. Instead, head west out of the Campo dei Miracoli through the archway and turn right up Via Gioann Battista Niccolini. Walk north a few blocks, under an overpass, until the road changes its name to Via Pietrasantinta; the consortium office is next to the bus parking lot. It's open Monday to Friday from 9am to 7pm. To find out what's going on in town, pick up a copy of the free weekly *Indizi e Servizi* (at some newsstands and hotels).

FESTIVALS & MARKETS   The most important holiday is that of the local patron saint, **San Ranieri,** on June 16 and 17, when the banks of the Arno are illuminated with torches (the Luminaria), followed by a regatta the following day. It also means the arrival of the **Gioco del Ponte (Bridge Game),** celebrated on the last Sunday of June. On the Ponte di Mezzo, teams from the north and south banks of the Arno dress in Renaissance costume and reenact a reverse tug-of-war, trying to run each other over with a 7-ton decorated cart. An extravagant procession of 600 people in historic costume precedes the "battle."

Pisa's old-fashioned **food market** (Mon–Sat 8am–1:30pm) is centered on the picturesque 16th-century Piazza delle Vettovaglie, west of the arcaded shopping street of Borgo Stretto on the north side of the Arno. On the second weekend of every month (except July–Aug), an **antiques fair** fills the side streets on both sides of the Ponte di Mezzo. Many stores in the area stay open on Sunday as well.

SEEING THE LEANING TOWER & MORE

The **Campo dei Miracoli (Field of Dreams),** aptly named by Italian poet Gabriel D'Annunzio but more parochially known as **Piazza del Duomo,** sits within the northwestern stretch of the ancient city walls. The trio of elegant buildings on the piazza bears testimony to the importance of the Pisan Republic during the first 2 centuries of the last millennium: This would be forever Pisa's legacy and the first such grandiose undertaking since the time of ancient Rome. Once surrounded by farmlands, it still sits within its own lawn, a paean to spatial geometry and visual brilliance—the vivid emerald of the grass, the white marble icons against an intense blue sky. This is undoubtedly one of the world's most memorable squares.

Battistero (Baptistery) ⭐⭐   West of the Duomo, the lovely Gothic Baptistery is best known for the **hexagonal pulpit** ⭐ beautifully carved by Nicola Pisano in 1260, half a century before the one in the Duomo created by his son Giovanni. The largest of its kind in Italy (104m/341 ft. in circumference), the Baptistery was begun in 1152 but not finished until the end of the 14th century. The vast interior is noted for its plainness and its remarkable acoustics; tour guides usually illustrate the quality of echoes for their groups from the center of the building. If not, track down the custodian and ask him to do the same (and reward him for his trouble).

Piazza del Duomo. Ⓒ 050-560547. Admission: See "Campo dei Miracoli Admissions," above. Apr–Sept daily 8am–7:30pm; Mar and Oct daily 9am–5:30pm; Nov–Feb daily 9am–4:30pm. Bus: 1, 3, 11.

Cattedrale ⭐⭐   Begun in 1064 and finished in the late 1200s, the Duomo was the first construction to borrow from the Moorish architecture of Spain's Andalusia, with horizontal stripes (banding) of black and white marble, a facade of inlaid colored-marble design *(intarsia),* and four graceful open-air galleries of mismatched columns diminishing in size as they ascend. This became the archetype of Pisan Romanesque architecture and went on to be much imitated (as your visits to Lucca, Siena, and elsewhere will attest). The three sets of massive bronze doors facing the Baptistery are from the 16th century, replacing originals lost in a fire, but the highly stylized **Romanesque door of San Ranieri** (patron saint of Pisa) facing the tower is by Bonanno Pisano and dates from 1180, completed 7 years after he'd begun work on the bell tower. The cathedral's interior is cavernous, close to 120m (394 ft.) long and interrupted by 68 columns.

Campo dei Miracoli Admissions

Admission charges for the group of monuments and museums on the campo (except the Leaning Tower) are tied together in a needlessly complicated way. The Cattedrale alone costs 2€ ($2.30). Any other single sight is 5€ ($5.75). Any two sights are 6€ ($6.90). The Cattedrale plus any two other sights is 8€ ($9.20). An 8.50€ ($9.75) ticket gets you into the Baptistery, Camposanto, Museo dell'Opera del Duomo, and Museo delle Sinopie, while an 11€ ($12) version throws in the Cattedrale as well. Children under 10 enter free. For more information, visit the group's collective website at www.opapisa.it.

Giovanni Pisano's intricately carved **pulpit** (1301–11) is the church's greatest treasure, destroyed in the fire, warehoused for centuries, and rebuilt with pieces of the original when it was rediscovered in 1926. It's similar (and, some believe, superior) to an earlier one in the Baptistery by Giovanni's father, Nicola. Opposite the pulpit hangs the 16th-century bronze **Galileo Lamp.** Pisa's most illustrious son, Galileo Galilei (1564–1642), allegedly came up with his theory of pendulum movement by studying the swinging of the lamp set in motion by a sacristan—however, historians say the astronomer/physicist came up with the theory years before the lamp was cast. A survivor of the great fire, the apse's magnificent 13th-century mosaic *Christ Pantocrator,* was finished in 1302 by Cimabue.

Piazza del Duomo. ⓒ **050-560547.** Admission: See "Campo dei Miracoli Admissions," above. Apr–Sept Mon–Sat 10am–7:30pm, Sun 1–7:30pm; Mar and Oct Mon–Sat 10am–5:30pm, Sun 1–5:30pm; Nov–Feb Mon–Sat 10am–12:45pm and 3–4:30pm, Sun 3–4:30pm. Bus: 1, 3, 11.

Campanile (Leaning Tower) ★★★   This eight-story cylindrical campanile, in the same Pisan Romanesque style as the Duomo, was begun in 1174. As the architects completed the third floor in 1185, the tower began to list (at that point, only 3.8cm/15 in.) and construction was suspended for a century. Building was resumed in 1275 and eventually completed in 1372.

Countless millions had climbed its 294 steps to enjoy the view from the top when the tourism authorities finally closed it in a solemn ceremony on January 7, 1990, for both the safety of the public and the well being of their beloved Torre Pendente. In 1993, even its seven bells were silenced to avoid vibrations that could aggravate its condition. The drastic engineering reclamation that has been going on for over a decade has finally paid off in righting some of the dangerous lean and shoring up the tower's foundations, and it reopened in 2001.

Few give any credence to the romantic notion that the architect purposely intended it to lean to demonstrate his clever talents: The general consensus has always been that a shifting subsoil foundation caused it to slowly list over the centuries—it's now close to 4 to 5m (13–16 ft.; accounts vary) off the perpendicular. Galileo exploited its overhang in one of his famous experiments by dropping balls of different weights from the top floor to illustrate his theory of the constancy of gravity. From certain angles, you'll wonder what all the hubbub is about; from other angles, the visible gravity of the listing is alarming. The same sandy subsoil is said to have resulted in less dramatic shifts in the Baptistery and Duomo as well, though you may go cross-eyed looking too hard for imaginary tilts. If it stood straight, the tower would be approximately 56m (184 ft.) tall.

The number of visitors is now strictly controlled via compulsory 35- to 40-minute guided tours—and a massive admission charge. Visit **www.opapisa.it/boxoffice** to book tickets well ahead of your visit. The earliest available tickets start 16 days out. If you just show up in Pisa without reservations, you will *not* be able to get into the tower.

Piazza del Duomo. ⓒ **050-560547.** www.opapisa.it. Admission by reservation only 15€ ($17) plus 2€ ($2.30) booking fee (you can reserve only—at the number or website above—at most 15 days in advance, but be sure to do so as soon as possible, because it gets packed). Children under 8 not admitted. Show printed proof of receipt at the ticket offices of Opera della Primaziale Pisa 1 hr. prior to scheduled visit. Mon–Fri 8am–1:30pm. Bus: 1, 3, 11.

Camposanto (Cemetery)   The vast walled Camposanto, the most beautiful cemetery in the world, is on the northern side of the piazza. It was begun in 1278, legend goes, to hold the earth brought back from the Holy Land (said to be the sacred dirt from Calvary, where Jesus Christ was crucified) in 1203 by the Fourth Crusade so important Pisans could be buried in it. The magnificent 14th- and 15th-century frescoes that once covered the Camposanto were destroyed by a 1944 Allied air attack when Pisa was in the hands of the Nazis. When what remained of the frescoes was removed to be restored, workers discovered the artists' preparatory sketches, called *sinopie*, beneath (they're now housed in the Museo delle Sinopie, below). Of the few frescoes that escaped damage are *The Drunkenness of Noah*, by Benozzo Gozzoli; and the earlier, more important 14th-century trio *Triumph of Death, Last Judgment*, and *The Inferno*, whose authorship is disputed.

Piazza del Duomo. 🕐 050-560547. Admission: See "Campo dei Miracoli Admissions," above. Hours same as Baptistery's. Bus: 1, 3, 11.

Museo dell'Opera del Duomo (Duomo Museum)   This is the city's most important collection, housed in a recently restored 13th-century palazzo. Used as the Duomo's Chapter House and later as a Capuchin monastery, it's now divided into 19 rooms that are home to a wealth of artworks from the campo's buildings. Sculptures by the various members of the Pisano family and their students are the high points of the museum. From Giovanni Pisano, whose pulpit is the focal point of the Duomo, is his important statuette of *Madonna and Child* (1300), whose figures lean in to the natural curve of the ivory tusk from which the work is carved; it was found on the Duomo's main altar.

Another high point is the precious **Pisan cross** that led the local contingent off to the First Crusade in 1099. A 12th-century **bronze griffin**, a masterpiece of Islamic art, was picked up as war booty from the Saracens and placed in the Duomo before being relocated here. The Islamic influence felt in many of the pieces is testimony to Pisa's history as a powerful maritime republic in the Mediterranean; see the examples of the **inlaid marble intarsia** of Moorish-influenced designs that once decorated the Duomo's facade. The last few rooms house a small Roman and Etruscan **archaeological collection** from the Camposanto. Most important are the 19th-century **etchings** of its Renaissance frescoes (being restored at that time) that are the only record of the artwork destroyed when the cemetery was bombed in 1944.

Piazza Arcivescovado 6. 🕐 050-560547. Admission: See "Campo dei Miracoli Admissions," above. Hours same as Baptistery's. Bus: 1, 3, 11.

Museo delle Sinopie   Of limited interest except to those particularly intrigued by the story of the Camposanto and its frescoes, this well-arranged museum is the newest of the Campo dei Miracoli's additions. Created exclusively in a 13th-century hospice to display the preliminary fresco sketches found beneath those destroyed in 1944 by a bomb attack (see the Camposanto entry, above), the museum is dedicated to the *sinopie*, or reddish-brown sketches made from Sinope clay. They're all that remain of the majority of the Camposanto's frescoes by leading early Renaissance masters. There's also an explanation of how frescoes were created in those days.

Piazza del Duomo. 🕐 050-560547. Admission: See "Campo dei Miracoli Admissions," above. Hours same as Baptistery's. Bus: 1, 3, 11.

Museo Nazionale di San Matteo (National Museum) ✸   Most of the major paintings from Pisa's churches are now displayed here around the 15th-century cloister of the convent of San Matteo. Fourteenth-century religious works, from Pisa's final period of prosperity, make up the bulk of the collection that spans the 12th to the 17th centuries and includes mostly minor works by Simone Martini, Masaccio, Gentile da Fabriano, Donatello, Fra Angelico, Gozzoli, and Ghirlandaio, plus Nino Pisano's beautifully sculpted *Madonna del Latte.*

Lungarno Mediceo (near Ponte Fortezza). © 050-541865. Admission 4€ ($4.60). Tues–Sat 9am–7pm; Sun 8:30am–1pm. Bus: 5, 7, 13.

ACCOMMODATIONS YOU CAN AFFORD

Pisa is the quintessential day trip from Florence, and the selection of hotels is limited, with very reasonable prices. All the buses disgorging their passengers at the Leaning Tower will return them to their hotels in Florence at the end of the day. Should you have a problem with availability, call the **Consorzio Turistico** (see "Visitor Information," above) and ask them to reserve a hotel for you at no cost.

If the Royal Victoria (see below) is full, try the family-run **Villa Kinzica,** just off Piazza del Duomo at Piazza Arcivescovado 2 (© **050-560419;** fax 050-551204; www.hotelvillakinzica.it), where doubles with a view of the tower cost 108€ ($124), breakfast included.

Hotel Royal Victoria ⚤   "I fully endorse the above," wrote Teddy Roosevelt of this place in one of the antique guest books. It opened in 1839 as Pisa's first hotel, uniting several medieval towers and houses, and is Pisa's only inn of any real character. The rooms on the Arno tend to be larger, as do the quieter (and cooler) ones installed in the remains of a tower dating from the 980s. There are many frescoed ceilings, and one room is a triumph of *trompe l'oeil,* including fake curtains painted on the walls surrounding the bed. Several rooms with common doors can be turned into family suites for four (with two separate bathrooms), and there are plans to convert some of the larger Arno-side rooms into regular suites. The new small plant-filled terrace is a lovely place to take drinks or sun surrounded by roof tiles. Some rooms are very small and plain. However, in all, you'll probably find yourself, as Ruskin did in terse simplicity, "always very comfortable in this inn."

Lungarno Pacinotti 12, 56126 Pisa (near Ponte di Mezzo). © **050-940111.** Fax 050-940180. www.royal victoria.it. 48 units, 40 with bathroom. 65€ ($75) single without bathroom, 105€ ($121) single with bathroom; 75€ ($86) double without bathroom, 125€ ($144) double with bathroom; 135€ ($155) triple with bathroom; 222€ ($255) family suite. Discounts in slow periods, for booking more than 1 month in advance, or for a stay of 5 nights or more. Rates include continental breakfast. AE, DC, MC, V. Parking 18€ ($21) in hotel garage, 9€ ($10) if the room is at a discounted rate. Bus: 1, 3, 4, 7. **Amenities:** Bar; bike rental; concierge; tour desk; car rental (they have their own Smartcar); 24-hr. room service; babysitting; laundry service; dry cleaning (same-day); nonsmoking rooms. *In room:* A/C (in 25 units), TV, VCR (on request), modem hookup, hair dryer (on request).

GREAT DEALS ON DINING

Even if you're one of Pisa's countless day-trippers, try to arrange your day around a nice lunch at any of the following. Pisa has become a city for food lovers, and the new wave of young restaurateurs has brought it up a gastronomic notch in the last few years. One of Pisa's favorite trattorias, **Da Bruno,** Via Luigi Bianchi 12, north of the Campo dei Miracoli outside the Porta Lucca (© **050-560818**), is a bastion of tried-and-true Pisan specialties and one of the few restaurants open on Sunday. Du Bruno is open Wednesday through Sunday from noon to 3pm and 7 to 10:30pm; reservations are recommended.

La Mescita PISAN/ENOTECA   The marketplace location and simple decor of this popular tiny spot belie its reputation for fine cuisine. The menu changes with each meal but includes the delicious likes of a *sformatino di melanzane* (eggplant soufflé in tomato sauce), to be followed by *ravioli di ceci con salsa di gamberetti e pomodoro fresco* (ravioli stuffed with a garbanzo bean pâté and served in shrimp-and-tomato sauce) or *strozzapreti al trevisano e Gorgonzola* (a slightly bitter dish of pasta curlicues in a cheesy sauce topped with shredded red cabbage). You can stick to tradition with your secondo by ordering the *baccalà con patate e ceci* (salt cod with potatoes and garbanzo beans). Since the place operates as an enoteca after hours, the wine list is long and detailed.

Via D. Cavalca 2 (just off the market square of Piazza Vettovaglie). © 050-544294. Reservations recommended. Primi 9€–11€ ($10–$13); secondi 15€–16€ ($17–$18). AE, DC, MC, V. Tues–Sun 8–11pm, Sat–Sun 1–2:30pm. Closed 20 days in Aug. Bus: 1, 2, 4.

Trattoria S. Omobono ⋇ CASALINGA PISANA   Around a column surviving from the medieval church that once stood here, locals gather to enjoy authentic Pisan home cooking. You can get away with a full meal, including wine, for under 20€ ($23), opening with something like *brachette alla renaiaola* (an antique Pisan dish consisting of large pasta squares in a purée of turnip greens and smoked fish) or *tagliatelle alla scarpara* (pasta in a sausage ragù). The secondi are simple and straightforward: *baccalà alla livornese* (salt cod with tomatoes) or *maiale arrosto* (thinly sliced roast pork), with which you can order fried polenta slices or ultra-Pisan *ceci* (garbanzo) beans.

Piazza S. Omobono 6 (the piazza next to the market square Piazza Vettovaglie). © 050-540847. Reservations recommended. Primi 6€ ($6.90); secondi 8€ ($9.20). DC, MC, V. Mon–Sat 12:30–2:30pm and 7:30–10pm. Closed Aug 8–20. Bus: 1, 2, or 4.

2 Lucca & Its Renaissance Walls

72km (45 miles) W of Florence, 21km (13 miles) E of Pisa, 336km (208 miles) N of Rome, 96km (60 miles) NW of San Gimignano

You'll always remember the great walls of this unspoiled (albeit no longer undiscovered) Tuscan town: Brick ramparts rebuilt most recently in the 16th and 17th centuries encircle this graceful city in their Renaissance swath. Although **Lucca** boasts a population of 90,000, only a marginal percentage lives within the ancient walls, where a thriving small-town atmosphere prevails. The city preserves much of its tangible past: A flourishing colony of Rome in 180 B.C., its ancient legacy is still evident in the grid pattern of its streets.

A sophisticated silk and textile trade reinterpreting the luxurious silks from the Orient made this small town famous around Europe in the Middle Ages and early Renaissance. The streets are still lined with handsomely preserved medieval towered palazzi reflecting Lucca's heyday. However, the town's power slowly dissipated—it tenaciously kept its independence from neighboring Pisa and Florence for many centuries but finally fell to Napoleon, who in 1805 handed it over to his sister Elisa Baciocchi as a principality; in 1815, it was absorbed into the Tuscan Grand Duchy. The quiet streets—where 25,000 workers once operated 3,000 handlooms—open onto small, picturesque squares, each anchored by a marble-faced church. Lucca's medieval highlights are the Duomo and the elaborate San Michele, both exquisite examples of Pisan-Lucchese architecture.

Proximity to Pisa's Galileo Galilei Airport makes Lucca an excellent first or last stop in Tuscany, recommended over the larger city of Pisa despite its legendary Leaning Tower (stay in Lucca and make a day trip to Pisa). The lack of traffic enhances Lucca's unhurried air, where moneyed matriarchs, whose noble family histories have survived the centuries, do their daily shopping around town on battered bicycles. The hotel situation doesn't bode well for budget travelers, but once you find a place to settle down, you'll discover that the general lack of mass tourism is the city's, and your, greatest blessing.

ESSENTIALS

GETTING THERE   By Train   Lucca is on the Florence–Viareggio train line (www.trenitalia.com), with 21 trains daily from **Florence** (70–90 min.; 4.55€/$5.25). **Pisa** zips 24 runs here every day (20–30 min.; 2.05€/$2.35). Lucca's **train station** is a short walk south of the Porta San Pietro, or you can take *navetta* minibus no. 16 into town.

By Car   The A11 runs from Florence through Prato, Pistoia, and Montecatini before hitting Lucca. The SS12 runs straight up here from Pisa.

By Bus   Lazzi buses (© 0583-584876; www.lazzi.it) run hourly from both **Florence** (70 min.; 4.70€/$5.40) and **Pisa** (40–50 min.; 2.20€/$2.55) to Lucca's Piazzale Verdi.

VISITOR INFORMATION   The main **tourist office** is just inside the city walls at Piazza Santa Maria 35 (© **0583-919931;** fax 0583-469964; www. luccaturismo.it), open daily from 9am to 7pm (Nov–Mar daily 9am–1pm and 3–6pm). It provides an excellent free pocket map and good pamphlets on Lucca and the Garfagnana. For events and theater information, pick up the English-language monthly *Grapevine* for 1.50€ ($1.70) at most newsstands. Another great resource online is **luccapro.cribecu.sns.it**; yet another is the privately run (but currently Italian language only) **www.in-lucca.it.**

FESTIVALS & MARKETS   Musical festivals celebrate the town's melodious history. From April to June, the churches take part in a **Festa della Musica Sacra (Festival of Sacred Music).** All September long, the **Settembre Lucchese** brings concerts and Puccini operas performed in the theater where many premiered, the Teatro Comunale on Piazza del Giglio. On September 13, an 8pm candlelit procession from San Frediano to the Duomo honors Lucca's most prized holy relic, the **Volto Santo** statue of Christ that tradition holds was carved by Nicodemus himself. Contact the tourist office for details.

A huge **antiques market,** one of Italy's most important, is held the third Sunday (and preceding Sat) of every month on Piazza Antelminelli and the streets around the Duomo. It's great fun but also leaves rooms hard to find and restaurants booked, especially at lunch (even those normally closed Sun reopen for this one). It's spawned a local **art market** on Piazza del Arancio on the same dates, and the final Sunday of the month sees an **artisans' market** on Piazza San Giusto. There's a cute little **Christmas market** on Piazza dell'Anfiteatro from December 8 to December 26, and September 13 to September 29 brings an **agricultural market** to Piazza San Michele, featuring Lucca's wines, honeys, and D.O.C. olive oils.

GETTING AROUND   A set of *navette* (electric minibuses) whiz dangerously down the city's peripheral streets, but the flat town is easily traversable on foot.

To really get around like a Lucchese, though, you need to **rent a bike.** There are four main rental outfits. The **city-sponsored stand** is on Piazzale Verdi (© **0583-442937;** closed Nov to mid-Mar). **Cicli Barbetti,** near the Roman amphitheater at Via Anfiteatro 23 (© **0583-954444**), is open Monday through Friday from 9am to 12:30pm and 2:30 to 6pm, and Saturday from 2:30 to 6pm; it's also open Saturday morning and Sunday if the weather is nice. Only one bicycle shop in town is open all day: **Antonio Poli,** Piazza Santa Maria 42

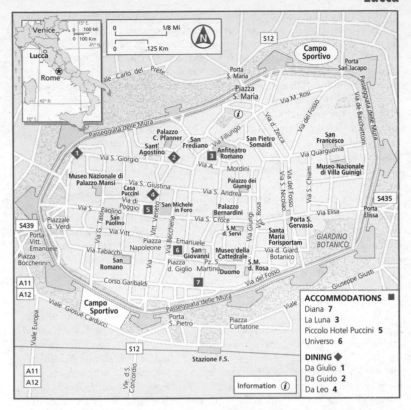

ACCOMMODATIONS ■
Diana **7**
La Luna **3**
Piccolo Hotel Puccini **5**
Universo **6**

DINING ◆
Da Giulio **1**
Da Guido **2**
Da Leo **4**

(© **0583-493787;** www.biciclettepoli.com); its hours are from 8:30am to 7:30pm, but it's closed Sunday from mid-November to February and Monday mornings year-round. You can also try **Cicli Bizzarri,** next door at Piazza S. Maria 32 (© **0583-496031;** www.ciclibizzarri.com), open Monday through Saturday from 8:30am to 1pm and 2:30 to 7:30pm, and Sunday from March to mid-September. Rates are the same at all four rental places: Bicycles are 2.10€ ($2.40) per hour or 11€ ($13) per day; mountain bikes are 3.10€ ($3.55) per hour or 16€ ($18) per day.

Taxis rank at the train station (© **0583-494989**), at Piazza Napoleone (© **0583-492691**), and at Piazzale Verdi (© **0583-581305**).

SIGHTS TO SEE

The aerial photograph of Lucca's **Anfiteatro Romano (Roman Amphitheater),** between Via Fillungo and Via Mordini, on local postcards is remarkable, showing the perfect elliptical shape of the theater built here in the 2nd century. The buildings from varying eras you see today were erected on its ancient foundations, and many incorporated its arches into their walls. The most recent structures date from the 19th century, when Napoleon's sister Elisa, as city governor, attempted to clean up the medieval jumble. The amphitheater, which once could seat 10,000, testifies to Lucca's importance as a Roman city; the city's neat grid pattern of streets further reflects its origin as a Roman outpost.

Succumb to the leisurely pace of this city and stroll or bike the shady 4km (2½-mile) path atop its perfectly intact **Renaissance walls** ⊕. Here, you can enjoy a view of the city's architecture within the walls and the lovely countryside that unfolds without. These are the city's third set of walls, an enormous feat of engineering and Europe's best-preserved Renaissance defense ramparts. They were begun in the 16th century long after centuries of feuds and strife, apparently from the belief that good fences make good neighbors. They measure 35m (115 ft.) at the base and 12m (39 ft.) high, with a double avenue of 19th-century trees lining their 18m (59-ft.) width. The emerald lawns stretching beyond them weren't planted until the last century. You can access the tree-lined promenade at any of the 11 bastions (there are six gates), such as the one behind the tourist office on Piazzale Verdi (which is where, during summer, you can rent a bike; see "Getting Around," above). A full circuit of the walls takes about an hour by foot and 20 minutes by bike.

Cattedrale di San Martino ⊕⊕⊕   Started in 1060 and completed 2 centuries later, the Duomo has an admirable asymmetrical **facade** ⊕⊕ (to accommodate the bell tower from a former building on this site) with three galleries of slender mismatched twisting columns and early-13th-century bas-reliefs. It's one of the finest examples of the exuberant Pisan-Romanesque architecture for which this area of Tuscany is known (Pisa's Duomo is usually held as the supreme archetype).

The star of the church's interior and Lucca's most precious relic is the robed figure of Jesus on the cross: The hauntingly beautiful wooden **Volto Santo (Holy Visage)** ⊕ is enshrined in its own elaborate 15th-century Tempietto (marble chapel) by Lucchese sculptor Matteo Civitali. The darkened crucifix is said to have been carved by Nicodemus, a fervent follower of Christ who helped lower him from the cross, and is believed to show a true image of Jesus (art historians attribute the work to 12th-century Eastern origin). Set adrift at sea, it was miraculously transported from the Holy Land across the Mediterranean and washed up on Tuscany's shores near La Spezia; the bishop of Lucca transported it here in 782. Local merchants spread the word throughout Europe, and Lucca gained fame for its portrait of Christ throughout the Middle Ages and became a point of pilgrimage for those on their way to Rome. Every September 13 and 14, the town turns out in a special evocative procession to carry the venerated statue dressed up in kingly jewel-encrusted robes through streets illuminated by candlelight.

Competing for historic importance is the recently restored **Tomb of Ilaria del Carretto Guinigi** ⊕⊕, now in the former sacristy along with the superb **Madonna and Saints altarpiece** by Domenico Ghirlandaio (1494), the young Michelangelo's fresco master. Sculpted with her beloved dog at her feet (representing fidelity) by Sienese master Jacopo della Quercia (1408), who breathed softness into the silklike folds of her dress, Ilaria was the young wife of a prominent lord of Lucca, in a politically arranged marriage that became a true union of love. She died at 26 after giving birth to their daughter and is a much beloved figure in local history—the marble tomb is the Duomo's masterpiece. Look into the second chapel on the left for a 1598 painting by Bronzino, the *Presentation of Mary at the Temple,* and the third chapel on the right for the *Last Supper* (1590–91), by Tintoretto and his students.

The nearby small **Museo della Cattedrale (Cathedral Museum)** ⊕ displays choice pieces of art such as paintings, silver chalices and reliquaries, and wooden and marble statuary from the Duomo's original collection. The restoration was severe, but there's still much left to admire in the space created by joining a 13th-century tower, a 14th-century palazzo, and an adjacent 16th-century church. Future plans are to relocate the Tomb of Ilaria to the museum, though there's no projected date. In the meantime, don't miss the early-15th-century statue of *St. John the Baptist* (once gracing the Duomo's facade) by the tomb's sculptor, Jacopo della Quercia, and the bejeweled regalia the *Volto Santo* wears on the days it's carried through town. The museum is open from March through October daily from 10am to 6pm; from November through February, Monday through Friday from 10am to 3pm, and Saturday and Sunday from 10am to 6pm. Admission is 3.50€ ($4) for adults and 2€ ($2.30) for children ages 6 to 12.

Also nearby, **San Giovanni** and its baptistery (open the same hours as the museum) recently reopened after years of work unearthing stratum on stratum of archaeological foundations. It provides a one-stop look into the cathedral's and city's distant past. The deepest and lowest level you can visit is the original Roman foundation from the 1st century B.C.; the latest is the foundation of the church's most recent reincarnation from the late Middle Ages.

Piazza San Martino. ℂ 0583-957068. Free admission to church; Ilaria tomb (in sacristy) 2€ ($2.30) adults, 1.50€ ($1.75) children 6–14. Cumulative ticket for tomb, Museo, and San Giovanni 5.50€ ($6.30) adults, 3€ ($3.45) children 6–14. Daily 9:30am–5:45pm (to 6:45pm Sat).

San Michele in Foro ☆

San Michele is the social and geographic, if not the religious, center of town, built on the original site of the Roman Forum (hence its name). Understandably mistaken as the Duomo by visitors, San Michele, begun in 1143, is second in importance only to the Duomo and dedicated to the winged archangel Michael, who crowns its facade. It's a wonderful example of the Pisan-Lucchese architecture influenced by Pisa's Duomo. The **remarkable facade** begins with ground-level arches, above which four tiers of twisted, patterned columns of every variety, size, and thickness are displayed; the facade soars considerably higher than the church itself. A number of national patriots, such as Cavour and Garibaldi, were added during a heavy 19th-century restoration. The impressive campanile is the city's highest.

Take a minute to stroll past the buildings lining the piazza. Some date back to the 13th century, while others are as recent as the 15th and 16th centuries. **Giacomo Puccini** was born in 1858 just a block from here on Via di Poggio 30. Both his father and his grandfather were organists here, and young Giacomo sang in the choir.

Piazza San Michele. ℂ 0583-48459. Free admission. Daily 7:30am–noon and 3–6pm.

San Frediano ☆

A colorful 13th-century *Christ in Majesty* mosaic on the stark-white facade of San Frediano sets it apart from the city's countless other churches, one reason it figures on the short list (with the Duomo and San Michele) of Lucca's most visited. Also typical of the local Pisan-Lucchese style, but minus the open loggias full of ornate columns, it's dedicated to the 6th-century Irish bishop St. Frigidian, who is said to have brought Christianity to Lucca (the first town in Tuscany to embrace it) and is buried under its high altar. Upon entering, you'll see one of the church's highlights, an elaborately carved huge 13th-century **baptismal font.** Beyond the font and high on the wall is the glazed terra cotta *Annunciation,* by Andrea della Robbia. Behind the font is the chapel of St. Zita, the patron saint of domestics and ladies-in-waiting. Her feast day is April 26, when the Piazza San Frediano is carpeted with flowers and her lace-enwrapped body is carried out to be glorified by the locals.

If you've already visited the Duomo (see above), you'll have seen the Tomb of Ilaria Caretto by master Sienese sculptor Jacopo della Quercia, whose marble reliefs on an altar and a pair of tombstones (1422) is here in the **Cappella Trenta,** the fourth chapel on the left. Nearby, in the second chapel you can find the 16th-century frescoes of *The Life of San Frediano* and *Arrival of the Volto Santo,* by Amico Aspertini (the yearly procession of the holy relic begins at the Duomo and ends here).

As you leave the church, head around the left side to Via Battisti, to the 17th-century **Palazzo Pfanner** (© 0583-491243), whose sumptuous walled gardens were used as location shots for the 1996 film *The Portrait of a Lady.* From March to November 15, it's open daily from 10am to 6pm; admission is 2.50€ ($2.85) each to the gardens or the palazzo, or 5€ ($5.75) for both. (If you tool around the city's ramparts, you can look down into the gardens for free.)

Piazza San Frediano. © 0583-493627. Free admission. Mon–Sat 7:30am–noon and 3–5pm; Sun 10:30am–5pm.

Museo Nazionale di Palazzo Mansi (National Museum) 𝕽   This small-scale museum is both impressive and appropriate for a city of this size and historic background. This was the town dwelling of the Mansi, a wealthy local family that still lives in the family country villa outside town. The 16th- to 19th-century palazzo is now used as a picture gallery for works by Guido Reni, Bronzino, Pontormo, and others, though not for their most important pieces. Don't leave without seeing the **Camera degli Sposi (Bridal Chamber),** an elaborate 17th-century Versailles-like alcove of decorative gold leaf, putti, and columns, where trembling Mansi brides awaited their conjugal duties amid the sumptuous Luccan silks and heavy brocades.

Via Galli Tassi 43. © 0583-55570. Admission 4€ ($4.60), free for those under 18 or over 65. Tues–Sat 9am–7pm; Sun 9am–2pm.

ACCOMMODATIONS YOU CAN AFFORD

The hotel situation in Lucca continues to be disheartening. Most of the one- and two-star hotels are in the newer, less interesting section of town outside the walls. In high season, be sure to make a hotel reservation in advance, or you may have to stay in Florence, nearby Pisa, or (if you have a car) one of the seaside resorts.

I hesitate to recommend the cheapest thing going within the walls: the **Diana,** Via Molinetto 11 (© 0583-492202; fax 0583-467795; www.albergodiana. com), which has passable-enough plain doubles with phones and TVs for around 52€ to 67€ ($60–$77) and is just half a block from the Duomo. In the *dipendence* around the corner are six rather nicer doubles for 84€ to 114€ ($97–$131). The staff, however, can turn from seemingly friendly to downright nasty at the drop of a hat.

La Luna 𝕽   Located in a small courtyard a block from the amphitheater and near San Frediano for more than 2 centuries, this choice may have a little less charm than the Piccolo Puccini but offers better availability in high season. The rooms are well thought out and decorated in a fresh contemporary vein—though those who splurge on the suites (sleeping two to four) will find more space, with early 1900s ceiling frescoes, original fireplaces, and large sitting areas. Fourteen of La Luna's rooms were redone within the past year. Late risers with big appetites can tuck into the ample breakfast buffet and skip lunch—though that would be a shame, given Lucca's choice of eateries. An alternative to the pricey breakfast is the lobby bar, where coffee and a croissant will keep costs down.

Corte Compagni 12, 55100 Lucca (off V. Fillungo near the amphitheater). © **0583-493634.** Fax 0583-490021. www.hotellaluna.com. 30 units. 80€ ($92) single; 110€ ($127) double; 175€ ($201) suite. AE, DC, MC, V. Breakfast 11€ ($12). Parking 11€ ($12) in garage. Closed Jan 6–Feb 6. **Amenities:** Concierge. *In room:* A/C, TV, dataport, minibar, hair dryer, safe (in 14 rooms).

Piccolo Hotel Puccini 🏨🏨   This charming three-star hotel occupies a 15th-century palazzo in front of the building where Puccini was born, and some of the rooms overlook the small piazza and its bronze statue of Puccini. Paolo and Raffaella, the enthusiastic young couple who have recently taken over, have brightened up the place with a marble-tiled lobby, flower arrangements in the public areas, and an extremely friendly attitude. In 2005, all of the bathrooms will be remodeled. The hotel is a perfect choice for those who appreciate tasteful attention and discreet professionalism. Breakfast is optional, so head for any of the cafes on Piazza San Michele, one of Lucca's loveliest squares. Book early to make sure you find room at this inn: Word is out.

Via di Poggio 9, 55100 Lucca (just off Piazza San Michele). © **0583-55421.** Fax 0583-53487. www .hotelpuccini.com. 14 units. 58€ ($67) single; 83€ ($95) double. Breakfast 3.50€ ($4.05). AE, DC, MC, V. Free street parking nearby, or 9€–15€ ($10–$17) in nearby garage. **Amenities:** Bike rental; concierge; tour desk; car rental; shuttle to airport and train station; 24-hr. room service; massage (in room); babysitting; laundry service; same-day dry cleaning; all nonsmoking rooms. *In room:* TV, dataport, hair dryer, safe.

Universo   This hotel-with-an-attitude aspires to be the grandest of Lucca's limited roster, and an ongoing renovation is resuscitating the rooms to their former 19th-century charm (although it's standardizing their appearance a bit as well). Ask for one of the refurbished rooms overlooking small Piazza del Giglio and its Teatro Comunale (others overlook expansive Piazza Napoleone, recently pedestrianized). They vary greatly in decor from contemporary to period, with the occasional added treats of molded ceilings, antiques, and hand-painted tiles in the bathrooms. Only a few rooms also have air-conditioning and minibars (specify when booking).

Piazza del Giglio 1, 55100 Lucca (off Piazza Napoleone). © **0583-493678.** Fax 0583-954854. www.hotel universolucca.it. 58 units. 85€–120€ ($98–$138) single; 150€ ($173) double. Breakfast included. MC, V. 10 free parking spaces or nearby lots for about 1€ ($1.15) per hour 8am–8pm. **Amenities:** Restaurant; bar; concierge; tour desk; car rental; room service; babysitting; nonsmoking rooms. *In room:* A/C (in about 20), TV, hair dryer (on request).

GREAT DEALS ON DINING

Da Giulio 🍴🍴 LUCCHESE/TUSCAN HOME COOKING   Delighted foreigners and locals agree that this big, airy, and forever busy trattoria is one of Tuscany's undisputed stars. Though casual, Da Giulio isn't the place to occupy a much-coveted table for just pasta and a salad. Save your appetite and come for a full-blown Tuscan feast, trying all the rustic specialties. Begin with the thick *farro* soup made with a local barleylike grain or the fresh *maccheroni tortellati* pasta stuffed with fresh ricotta and spinach, both perfection. Perfect also are the grilled and roasted meats, like the *arrosti misti* of beef and turkey and the *pollo al mattone,* chicken breast flattened and roasted under the weight of heated bricks. The waiters know not to recommend certain local favorites to non-Italians, unless you look like the tripe, *tartara di cavallo* (horse meat tartare), or veal snout type. Fixed-price menus are sometimes available for about 15€ ($17).

Via Conce 45, Piazza San Donato (nestled in the very northwest corner of the walls). © **0583-55948.** Reservations recommended. Primi 4.15€–5.15€ ($4.75–$5.90); secondi 7€–25€ ($8.05–$29). AE, DC, MC, V. Tues–Sat and 3rd Sun of month noon–3pm and 7:30–10:15pm. Closed 10 days in Aug and 10 days around Christmas.

Da Guido *Value* LUCCHESE/TUSCAN   The amiable proprietor, Guido, welcomes local cronies and hungry out-of-towners with the same warm smile and filling meals that keep 'em all happy. The bar in the front and the TV locked into a sports channel create a laid-back atmosphere that'll make you want to linger. The fresh tortellini made on the premises and the simplicity of the roast *coniglio* (rabbit) or *vitello* (veal) will wipe out any thoughts you may have of ordering anything else. This is a cut below the price and quality level of Giulio's (see above), but you're guaranteed a good home-cooked meal in a no-frills, family-run trattoria.

Via Cesare Battisti 28 (near Piazza Sant'Agostino and San Frediano, west of the Roman amphitheater). ℂ 0583-476219. Primi 2.60€–4€ ($3–$4.60); secondi 4.15€–5€ ($4.75–$5.75); *menu turistico* with wine 11€ ($13). AE, MC, V. Mon–Sat noon–2:30pm and 7:30–10pm. Closed 3–4 weeks in Aug.

Da Leo TUSCAN/LUCCHESE   It isn't often that a homespun trattoria dramatically improves its cooking while retaining its low prices and the devoted following of local shopkeeps, groups of students, and solitary art professors sketching on the butcher-paper place mats between bites. This place is now good enough to recommend for the best cheap meals in the center. There's usually an English menu floating around somewhere—the good-natured waiters are used to dealing with foreigners who've discovered one of the most authentic Lucchese dining spots in town, run by the amiable Buralli family. This isn't as barebones as Guido's, nor quite as polished as the well-regarded Giulio's, but it's just as beloved by a devoted local following nonetheless. Its location, two steps from the central Piazza San Michele, draws tourists who happen by, lured into the peach-colored rooms by the aroma of roasting meats and the scent of rosemary. The ubiquitous *farro* soup made from emmer (a kind of barley), followed by the simple but delicious *pollo fritto con patate arroste* (fried chicken with roast potatoes) with the good house wine, is my stock order.

Via Tegrimi 1 (just north of Piazza San Michele). ℂ 0583-492236. www.trattoriadaleo.it. Reservations recommended. Primi 4.70€ ($5.40); secondi 8.80€–16€ ($10–$18). No credit cards. Mon–Sat noon–2:30pm and 7:30–10:30pm.

SIDE TRIPS FROM LUCCA

A number of villas of historic importance are within biking distance of Lucca's center. The **Villa Reale** in Marlia (ℂ **0583-30108**) was once home to Napoleon's sister Elisa Baciocchi; March to November, you can take a 6€ ($6.90) guided tour of its grounds daily on the hour from 10am to noon and 3 to 6pm. From March to November 12, the **Villa Torrigiani** in Camigliano (ℂ **0583-928008** or 0583-928041) is open Wednesday through Monday from 10am to noon and 3 to 5pm (in summer 10am–1pm and 3–7pm). Admission is 9€ ($10) to the villa and grounds, or 7€ ($8.05) for just the park. Visit Lucca's tourist board for a map and a listing of occasional summer concerts that take place in their gardens.

3 San Gimignano & Its Medieval Towers

57km (35 miles) SW of Florence, 90km (56 miles) SE of Pisa, 42km (26 miles) NW of Siena, 100km (62 miles) SE of Lucca

For centuries, **San Gimignano** has arrested the traveler's imagination as the quintessential Tuscan hill town. Its stunning skyline bristles with medieval towers (there remain 14 of an estimated 70) whose construction dates from the 12th and 13th centuries, when they were built as much for defensive purposes as for the prestige of outdoing the neighbors. San Gimignano is on the ancient

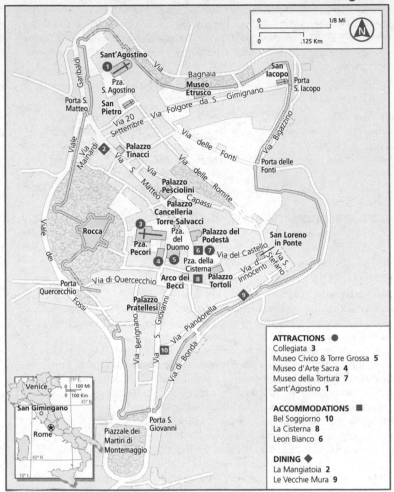

San Gimignano

Francigena road that transported medieval trade and pilgrims from northern Europe to Rome (imagine the impressive sight it was to those approaching from afar, with its 70-odd towers heralding the town's prominence)—it was quite the wealthy agricultural town in its 14th-century heyday and could afford to build handsome palazzi and impressively frescoed churches. It has held on to its rugged good looks and gained the sobriquet of "Medieval Manhattan." Much is written about its distinctive profile and its towers being the archetypes for today's skyscrapers (some of the remaining towers are over 45m/148 ft. high). San Gimignano boasts the perfect combination of a rural small-town atmosphere, stunning views, a crop of great restaurants, and enough history and museums to occupy the curious and impress the discerning.

ESSENTIALS
GETTING THERE   By Train   Twenty or so daily trains (www.trenitalia.com) run on the line between **Siena** (20–30 min.; 2.05€/$2.35) and Empoli, where you can also connect from **Florence** (65–75 min.; 4.55€/$5.25). The train doesn't

actually stop anywhere near San Gimignano itself, but rather at a town called Poggibonsi in the valley below. From Poggibonsi, nearly 20 **Tra-in** buses (© **0577-937207;** www.trainspa.it) make the run to San Gimignano Monday through Saturday (20–25 min.; 1.60€/$1.85), but only two run on Sunday (7:20am and 12:55pm).

By Car   Take the Poggibonsi exit off the **Florence-Siena** autostrada or the SS2. San Gimignano is 12km (7½ miles) from Poggibonsi.

By Bus   **SITA** (© **055-47821;** www.sita-on-line.it) runs four dozen buses daily from **Florence** to Poggibonsi (70–90 min.; 4.30€–5.50€/$4.95–$6.30), about one-quarter of which meet right up with the connection on to San Gimignano (see "By Train," above). **Tra-in** (© **0577-204111** or 0577-937207; www.trainspa.it) runs about three dozen daily buses from **Siena** to Poggibonsi (35–45 min.; 4.50€/$5.15). In San Gimignano, buy bus tickets at the tourist office.

VISITOR INFORMATION   The **tourist office** is at Piazza del Duomo 1 (© **0577-940008;** fax 0577-940903; www.sangimignano.com). It's open daily March through October from 9am to 1pm and 3 to 7pm, and November through February from 9am to 1pm and 2 to 6pm.

SPECIAL EVENTS & MARKETS   San Gimignano has two patron saints: **San Gimignano** himself (a 4th-c. bishop from Modena), whose feast day is celebrated January 31; and **Santa Fina** (who died in 1253, at age 15), whose feast day is on March 12. Both are celebrated with a High Mass in the Duomo and an all-day outdoor fair in the main square.

San Gimignano also boasts one of Tuscany's more animated **Carnevale,** held each of the 4 Sundays before Ash Wednesday. The third weekend of June is the **Fiera delle Messi,** when the town effortlessly resuscitates its medieval character during a weekend of outdoor markets, musical and theatrical events, and a jousting tournament of knights on horseback, all in medieval costume. Since 1924, mid-June to August has been dedicated to dance and music performances for the **Estate Sangimignese** festival, when you can look for art exhibits, outdoor classical concerts, alfresco opera, or ballet in Piazza della Cisterna. See the tourist office for a schedule. Santa Fina shows up again for the first Sunday of August's **Festa di Ringraziamento;** the next day, a small fair takes place in the main square. The only market in town worth a look is the bustling **biweekly produce market** on Piazza del Duomo Thursday and Saturday mornings.

SIGHTS TO SEE

The **Museo d'Arte Sacra (Museum of Sacred Art)** has finally emerged from its massive reorganization. Pop in for a few minutes to see its medieval tombstones and wooden sculptures—enter from Piazza Pecori, under the arch to the left of the Duomo's facade. April through October the museum is open weekdays from 9:30am to 7:30pm, Saturday from 9:30am to 5pm, and Sunday from 1 to 5pm. November through March it's open Monday to Saturday from 9:30am to 5pm and Sunday from 1 to 5pm. The museum is closed from January 21 to February 28. Admission is 3€ ($3.45) for adults and 1.50 ($1.70) for children ages 6 to 18.

Collegiata ☆☆   Because there's no longer a bishop of San Gimignano, the Duomo (cathedral) has been demoted to a Collegiata (though it'll forever be a Duomo in the locals' eyes) and is a prime example of not judging a 12th-century church by its facade. It was never finished outside, but its interior is heavily frescoed with Bible scenes, testimony to the city's past prosperity and one of

> **_Tips_ Saving Money**
>
> The **cumulative ticket** covers the Torre Grosso, the little Pinacoteca paint-
> ing gallery in the Palazzo Pubblico, the tiny Museo Archeologico detail-
> ing the region's Etruscan era, the Spezeria Santa Fina (a preserved
> Renaissance pharmacy), the new Galleria d'Arte Moderna, and the weird
> little Museo Ornitologico (a couple of glass cases holding stuffed birds in
> the dimly lit confines of a tiny deconsecrated church). The ticket costs
> 7.50€ ($8.60) for adults and 5.50€ ($6.30) for those under age 18 or over
> 65; it's free to children under 6. The prices listed below are for individual
> entrance to each attraction.

Tuscany's, perhaps Italy's, most lavishly decorated churches. On the north wall
are three levels with 26 scenes from the Old Testament by Bartolo dei Fredi
(1367); on the south wall are 22 scenes from the life of Christ by Lippo Memmi
(1333–41); the entrance end of the interior nave wall is decorated with scenes
from the _Last Judgment,_ attributed to Taddeo di Bartolo (1410); and against the
west wall Benozzo Gozzoli painted a _Martyrdom of St. Sebastian_ (1464)—brilliant colors set off by the black-and-white-striped marble arches of Pisan-
Romanesque architecture.   Don't miss the tiny **Cappella di Santa Fina** ✦ in
the southwest corner for the frescoes by Florentine Renaissance master
Domenico Ghirlandaio (1475) recounting the life of a young girl named Fina
born in San Gimignano in 1238. The town's towers appear in the background
of the scene depicting her funeral. Fina spent most of her 15 years in prayer and
is the patron saint (though never officially canonized, but don't bring this up
with the locals), together with St. Gimignano, of the town. Be sure to find
another of Ghirlandaio's superb works, _The Annunciation_ ✦ (1482), gracing a
loggiaed courtyard adjacent to the Baptistery.

Piazza del Duomo. © 0577-940316. Admission on cumulative ticket or 3.50€ ($4) adults, 1.50€ ($1.75)
ages 6–18. Mar Sun 1–5pm, Mon–Sat 9:30am–5pm; Apr–Oct Sun1–5pm, Mon–Fri 9:30am–7:30pm, Sat
9:30am–5pm; Nov–Jan 26 Mon–Sat 9:30am–5pm, Sun 1–5pm. Closed Jan 27–Feb 28.

Museo Civico (Civic Museum) & Torre Grossa (Big Tower) ✦✦   Labor to
the top of the 14th-century Palazzo del Popolo's 35m (115-ft.) **Torre Grossa**
(1311), the highest of San Gimignano's towers and the only one in town you can
climb. You'll feel as if you're on top of a flagpole with heart-stopping views of
the town, its towers, and the bucolic sweep of country beyond. It may just be
the best tower-top view of its kind in Tuscany—and that's saying something.
Once you've gotten that out of your system, backtrack to see the **Civic
Museum**'s collections. The first public room, the **Sala di Dante,** is frescoed with
hunting scenes and is the spot where the poet Dante, as ambassador from pro-
Pope (Guelph) Florence, came to pro-emperor (Ghibelline) San Gimignano in
1300 to plead for unity. Here you'll find the museum's—and the town's—masterpiece, a _Maestà_ by Sienese Lippo Mimmi (1317). The second-floor _pina-
coteca_ **(picture gallery)** is composed mostly of 12th- to 15th-century paintings
from the Sienese school, with highlights by Benozzo Gozzoli, Pinturicchio, and
Filippino Lippi, as well as a late-14th-century Taddeo di Bartolo painting of San
Gimignano himself holding the town in his lap.

Piazza del Duomo. © 0577-940312 (ask for museo). Admission on cumulative ticket (see "Saving Money,"
above), or 5€ ($5.75) adults, 4€ ($4.60) under 18 or over 65, free for children under 6. Mar–Oct daily
9:30am–7pm; Nov–Feb daily 10am–5:30pm (to 1:30pm Dec 24–31).

Museo della Tortura (Torture Museum) ⚡ *Kids*   Is it karmic happenstance or a quirk of history that this museum of medieval torture is housed in the 13th-century Palazzo del Diavolo (Devil's Palace)? One of Tuscany's more unusual attractions, this surprisingly expansive chamber of horrors contains over 100 instruments of torture. Most are original pieces, and all are thoughtfully and impressively displayed and explained in Italian and English. This is good because items like knuckle- and skull-crushers and iron gags to stifle screams aren't always immediately recognizable to the innocent. Though for little 'uns it might be too much, boys from adolescence on should have a gruesome blast. It's worth the admission just to see the cast-iron chastity belts.

Via del Castello 1 (just off Piazza della Cisterna). © 0577-942243. Admission 8€ ($9.20) adults, 5.50€ ($6.30) students. Mar 16–July 18 daily 10am–7pm; July 19–Sept 17 daily 10am–midnight; Sept 18–Nov 1 daily 10am–8pm; Nov 2–Mar 15 Mon–Fri 10am–6pm, Sat–Sun 10am–7pm.

Sant'Agostino ⚡   If you're not all frescoed out after a visit to the Collegiata, visit the large, 13th-century Sant'Agostino in the north end of town by following the flagstone Via San Matteo through one of San Gimignano's less commercial corners. The church's simple Romanesque exterior contrasts with its rococo interior completed in the mid-1700s. The interior's highlight is the cycle of frescoes covering the choir behind the main altar and showing 17 scenes from *The Life of St. Augustine* ⚡ by Benozzo Gozzoli, a 15th-century Florentine painter. Hired after yet another plague passed through town in 1464, Gozzoli was commissioned to cover the walls floor to ceiling.

Piazza Sant'Agostino. © 0577-907012. Free admission. Daily 7am–noon and 3–7pm (Oct–Apr closes at 6:30pm).

ACCOMMODATIONS YOU CAN AFFORD

The hotels in this most popular hill town aren't cheap. If you arrive without a reservation, **Siena Hotels Promotion,** Via San Giovanni 125 (© **0577-940809;** fax 0577-390940113; www.hotelsiena.com), will help you find a room. Those watching their euros may want to stay in the more modern satellite community of Santa Chiara, a few minutes' walk from the Porta San Giovanni. You can check out pictures of all the hotels below (and others) at **www.sangimignano.com.** Ask the tourist office for a list of B&B or farm accommodations in the countryside.

Bel Soggiorno   Close to the San Giovanni city gate and a 5-minute walk uphill toward the main square, this well-known hostelry of simply decorated rooms gets mentioned despite the sometimes cranky management for two reasons. The dozen or so rooms (three of which share a large patio) command awesome views of the hills of Tuscany's Val d'Elsa (but these rooms cost more), and the restaurant, where guests are encouraged though not obliged to have their meals, is quite decent.

If you have access to wheels and long for a more rural environment, ask at the desk about their country property, the 50-room **Le Pescille** (© **0577-940186;** fax 0577-943165), a converted farmhouse/hotel boasting a lovely setting 4km (2½ miles) out of town, with a pool, a tennis court, and reasonable rates comparable to those below. It's open from mid-March to October.

Via San Giovanni 91, 53037 San Gimignano (near Porta San Giovanni). © 0577-940375. Fax 0577-907521. www.hotelbelsoggiorno.it. 22 units. Ask for single rates; 98€ ($113) double; 120€ ($138) elite double with view; 130€–140€€ ($150–$161) double suite; 150€ ($173) triple suite. Rates include breakfast. AE, DC, MC, V. Parking 13€ ($15) in garage outside walls. Closed Jan–Feb; restaurant closed Jan 7–Feb 28. **Amenities:** Restaurant; pool (at Pescille); tennis (at Pescille); Jacuzzi (at Pescille); concierge; car rental; laundry service; same-day dry cleaning. *In room:* A/C, TV, VCR (in suites), minibar (in 9), hair dryer (on request).

La Cisterna ☆   The town's nicest hotel in this price category is housed in a series of truncated towers flanking central Piazza della Cisterna and run by the Salvestrini family since 1919. Like the Bel Soggiorno, it includes one of the town's better restaurants, Le Terrazze (open Fri–Tues for lunch and dinner, Wed for dinner only). Upstairs you'll find some large rooms, many of which have balconies offering spellbinding panoramas. However, the rest are small and have no view, making them seem even smaller. Air-conditioning was recently added to all the rooms. The hotel has been used as the setting for films, from *Where Angels Fear to Tread* to *Tea with Mussolini*.

Piazza della Cisterna 23–24, 53037 San Gimignano. (℃ **0577-940328**. Fax 0577-942080. www.hotel cisterna.it. 49 units. 58€–75€ ($67–$86) single; 82€–95€ ($94–$109) standard double, 102€–110€ ($117–$127) superior double, 102€–120€ ($117–$138) deluxe double; 112€–133€ ($129–$153) junior suite. Half- and full-pension plans available. 8% discount for stays of 3 nights or more. Rates include buffet breakfast. AE, DC, MC, V. Parking 12€ ($14) in lot. Closed Jan 8–Mar 7; restaurant closed Jan 8–Mar 7. **Amenities:** Restaurant (closed Tues and lunch Wed); concierge; room service (bar only); laundry service. *In room:* A/C, TV, minibar (in suites), hair dryer, safe.

Leon Bianco   Across from La Cisterna, this smaller hotel occupies a beautifully restored palazzo. The central part is in a 12th-century patrician home that was expanded in the next century with a medieval tower on either side, parts of which are incorporated into the hotel. The modernized rooms are historically offset with exposed brick walls, vaulted ceilings, archways, and terra-cotta floors, and priced according to size and view: Five overlook the piazza, nine have countryside views, and all others overlook an enclosed courtyard. The superior rooms are, for the most part, merely larger and have minibars. From May to September, the brick courtyard is the lovely setting for breakfast, and the sunny roof terrace is perfect for postcard writing. There's no restaurant, but try La Cisterna's or Bel Soggiorno's down the street.

Piazza della Cisterna 8, 53037 San Gimignano. (℃ **0577-941294**. Fax 0577-942123. www.leonbianco.com. 26 units. 75€ ($86) single without view; 85€ ($98) standard double without view, 100€ ($115) standard double with view, 125€ ($144) superior double with view; 145€ ($167) triple. Rates include buffet breakfast. AE, DC, MC, V. Closed 20 days before Christmas and Jan 7 to early Feb. **Amenities:** Bar; bike rental; concierge; room service (7am–11pm); laundry service; nonsmoking rooms. *In room:* A/C, TV, dataport, minibar (in superior rooms), hair dryer, safe.

GREAT DEALS ON DINING

La Mangiatoia ☆☆ TUSCAN   "The Eatin' Trough" is a quirky mix of largish but still cozy rooms boasting heavily stuccoed stone walls inset with backlit stained-glass cabinet doors. This place is fond of Latin quips and dramatic classical music, and the staff is friendly. Alas, the food's a mix, too—stick to the more unusual dishes, intriguing and excellently prepared choices where the cooks seem to try harder. The *gnocchi deliziose* (spinach gnocchi in Gorgonzola sauce) is great, as is the *tagliatelle dell'amore* (with prosciutto, cream, tomatoes, and a little hot spice). After that, you can try the *coniglio in salsa di carciofi* (rabbit with artichokes), but I'd choose the more adventurous *cervo in dolce et forte* (an old recipe of venison cooked with pine nuts and a strong sauce of pinoli, raisins, vinegar, and chocolate—traditionally used to cut the gaminess of several-day-old venison). The desserts are excellent.

Via Mainardi 5 (near Porta San Matteo). (℃ 0577-941528. Reservations recommended. Primi 8€–12€ ($9.20–$14); secondi 13€–15€ ($15–$17). MC, V. Wed–Mon 12:30–2:30pm and 7:30–10pm. Closed Nov–Dec.

Le Vecchie Mura *Value* TUSCAN/ITALIAN   The first thing you must do is see if either of the two comfortable bedrooms with bathrooms is available (50€/$58 double). If not, console yourself with a marvelous meal downstairs in the cool, brick-vaulted trattoria in what served as a patrician family's stables in the 1700s. The thick *ribollita* (cabbage-based bread soup) and homemade *tagliatelle al cinghiale* (pasta with wild-boar sauce) are deservedly the house specialties. The regional specialty of wild boar shows up as a favorite entree, marinated in the local Vernaccia white wine and then grilled. Across the narrow graveled road is a small alfresco terrace whose gorgeous views out over the ancient city walls and valley beyond may make concentrating on your meal difficult.

Via Piandornella 15 (a twisting walk down the 1st right off V. San Giovanni as you walk up from Porta San Giovanni). ℂ 0577-940270. www.vecchiemura.it. Reservations recommended. Primi 6.80€–8€ ($7.80–$9.20); secondi 9€–11€ ($10–$12). AE, DC, MC, V. Wed–Mon 6–10:30pm. Closed Jan–Feb.

4 The Chianti Road

The fabled **Chianti** 🅰 region stretches between Florence and Siena along **La Chiantigiana (the Chianti Road)**, known as the **SP 222.** This 105-sq.-km (40-sq.-mile) stretch of land is many people's idea of paradise on Earth—tall hills topped by medieval castles and valleys dotted with small market towns. Ten thousand acres of these rolling hills are blanketed with grapevines producing the Chianti wines that have long made this region famous.

The name *Chianti,* probably derived from the name of a local noble Etruscan family, the Clantes, has been used to describe the hills between Florence and Siena for centuries, but it wasn't until the mid–13th century that Florence created the *Lega del Chianti* to unite the region's three most important centers—Castellina, Radda, and Gaiole—who chose the black rooster as their symbol. In 1716, the boundaries of the Chianti were officially established, making it the world's first officially designated wine-producing area.

Along the way, look for the sign DEGUSTAZIONE or VENDITÀ DIRETTA, advertising wine operations that offer tastings and sales direct to the public. The signs AZIENDA AGRICOLA, TENUTA, and FATTORIA indicate the wine-producing operations—some multimillion-dollar affairs, others unsung and family run. Each offers its own unique experience.

ESSENTIALS

GETTING AROUND   The only way to explore the Chianti effectively is to **drive.** But know that many of the roads off the major SP 222 (La Chiantigiana) are unpaved and sometimes heavily potholed. **Biking** through the Chianti can be one of Tuscany's most rewarding and scenic strenuous workouts. See chapter 2 for tour companies, or go on your own by renting a bike in Greve at **Marco Ramuzzi,** Viale Falsettacci 6 (ℂ 055-853037). The cost is 13€ to 16€ ($15–$18) per day (scooters 16€/$18 to 23€/$26 per half-day, or 26€/$30 to 39€/$45 per full day), though the daily price goes down the longer you keep it. The region's low mountains and stands of ancient forest are also excellent for **hiking.** For exploring by any means, you'll need a good map; both the huge Edizione Multigrafic (EMG) 1:50,000 map and the smaller free 1:70,000 sheet called "Il Chianti" put out by the Florentine tourist board are excellent for backroads exploring. (*Drivers be warned:* These maps do, on occasion, mark dry streambeds as "unpaved roads.")

You can visit the major towns by **bus,** but be prepared to stay a while until the next ride comes along. **SITA** (ℂ 055-214721; www.sita-on-line.it) from Florence services Strada (40 min. from Florence), Greve (65 min.), Panzano (75 min.), Radda or Castellina (95 min.), and Gaiole (2 hr.); it leaves at least hourly

The Chianti Road

Florence

Arno River

A1

Bagno a Ripoli

San Piero a Ema

Grassina

Venice

Florence

Area of Detail

Rome

Ugolino

Impruneta

La Chiantigiana
SP222

S. Stefano a Tizzano

A1

Castello di Tizzano

San Polo in Chianti

San Casciano in Val di Pesa

Strada in Chianti

Spedaluzzo

SS2

Castello di Vicchiomaggio

Le Bolle

Dudda

Castello di Verrazzano

Badia a Passignano

San Cresci

Castello di Querceto

Lucolena di Sotto

Tavernelle in Val di Pesa

Montefioralle

Greve in Chianti

Lucolena

Sambuca

Fontodi

Barberino Val di Pesa

Rignana

Castello Vignamaggio

Panzano in Chianti

Lámole

San Donato in Poggio

Piazza

Castello di Volpaia

Monsanto

Pietrafitta

Badia a Coltibuono

Villa

←To San Gimignano

SS429

Villa Strozzi-Sonnino

Radda in Chianti

Gaiole in Chianti

Poggibonsi

Castellina in Chianti

Vertine

Barbischio

San Giusto

Meleto

Castagnoli

Colle di Val d'Elsa

Fonterutoli

Castello di Ama

SS408

Lecchi

Castello di Brolio

SS2

SP222

San Sano

Monti

SS484

Quercegrossa

Monteriggioni

Fattoria dei Pagliaresi

0   2 Mi

0   2 Km

N

Fattoria della Aiola

Siena

Vineyard

Information

for stops up through Greve and Panzano, and at least one to three times a day all the way through to Gaiole. About eight (Mon–Sat) **Tra-in** buses (© 0577-204111; www.trainspa.it) from Siena hit Radda, Gaiole, and Castellina. You can get to Impruneta by a **CAP** bus (© 055-214637; www.capautolinee. it) from Florence.

VISITOR INFORMATION   You can pick up information at the **Florence tourist office** (see chapter 4) or the **Siena tourist office** (see next section). The unofficial capital of the area is **Greve in Chianti,** and its **tourist office** (© 055-8546287; fax 055-8544149) is in a modern little shack on the right just as you arrive in Greve coming from the north. It makes an effort to provide Chianti-wide info. From Easter to October, it's open Monday through Friday 10am to 1pm and 3 to 7pm, and Saturday 10am to 1pm. In winter, it may keep shorter hours.

You can also try **www.chianti.it/turismo,** a website with links to many hotels and restaurants in the area.

WINE FESTIVALS   The second weekend in September, Greve in Chianti hosts the main annual **Rassegna del Chianti Classico,** a bacchanalian festival of food and dancing that showcases wine from all the region's producers. **Radda** sponsors its own **wine festival** on the last weekend in May, where buying the 5€ ($5.75) commemorative glass lets you sample 50 to 60 wines for free. There's also a free concert, evening snacks, and a communal grappa tasting at 10pm.

THE FLORENTINE CHIANTI

EN ROUTE TO GREVE   Cross Florence's eastern Ponte San Niccolò and follow the signs from Piazza Ferrucci on the other side toward Grassina and the SP 222. The SP 222 takes you through **Strada in Chianti,** where a Donatello-school crucifix rests in the church of San Cristofano.

At the bend in the road called Le Bolle is a right turnoff for **Vicchiomaggio** (© 055-854079; fax 055-853911; www.vicchiomaggio.it), a Lombard fortress modified in the 15th century and today one of the best preserved of the Chianti castles. Its estate, under British ownership, produces well-regarded wines, which you can taste for free at the roadside Cantinetta San Jacopo shop daily from 9am to 12:30pm and 2:30 to 6:30pm (as late as 7:30pm in summer). You can visit the cellars with 1 day's notice. They also offer cooking courses (anywhere from an hour or 2 to several days) and rent rooms.

A bit farther along on the right is the turnoff for the **Castello di Verrazzano** (© 055-854243; fax 055-854241; www.verrazzano.com), the 12th-century seat of the Verrazzano family (Giovanni Verrazzano, born here in 1485, discovered New York City). The estate has been making wine since at least 1170, and you can sample it on tours of the cellars Monday through Friday from 11am to 3pm (best to arrive early). On weekends, you can buy the wine at the small stand on SP 222 (© 055-853211).

GREVE IN CHIANTI   Greve (*Grey*-vey) is the Chianti's main market town, dating back to the 13th century and today serving as the region's center of the wine trade and unofficial capital. The central **Piazza Matteotti** is a rough triangle of mismatched arcades centered on a statue of **Giovanni Verrazzano.** At the narrow end of the piazza sits the pretty little church of **Santa Croce,** with an *Annunciation* by Bicci di Lorenzo and a 13th-century triptych.

Greve is the host of Chianti's annual September wine fair, and there are, naturally, dozens of wine shops in town. The better ones are the **Bottega del Chianti Classico,** Via Cesare Battisti 2–4 (© 055-853631; www.chianticlassicoshop.com), and the **Enoteca del Chianti Classico,** Piazzetta Santa Croce 8 (✆ 055-853297). At Piazza Matteotti 69–71 is one of Italy's most famous butchers, **Macelleria Falorni** (✆ 055-852029; www.falorni.it), a wonderland of prosciutto and salami established in 1700. **Tourist information** (✆/fax 055-8545243) is available in the dollhouse 1960s "castle" on Via Luca Cini at the corner of a large car park.

NEAR GREVE   One kilometer (about a half-mile) east of Greve perches the medieval hamlet of **(Castello di) Montefioralle,** an evocative stone village of one circular street, with the pretty 10th-century Pieve di San Cresci just outside the walls.

The road beyond Montefioralle continues over several kilometers of dirt roads to the **Badia a Passignano** ★ (✆ 055-8071622), dramatically situated amid a cypress grove atop vineyards. The monastery was established in 1049 by the Vallombrosan order. Its small Romanesque church of San Michele got a baroque overhaul in the late 1500s courtesy of local artist Il Passignano. Sunday at 3pm, meet at the church for a free tour of the monastery; the highlight is the Ghirlandaio brothers' (Davide and Domenico) fresco of *The Last Supper* (1476) in the refectory. Monday through Friday the monastery's closed, but you can visit the **osteria** (✆ 055-8071278) to buy the Antinori wines produced in the Badia's vineyards and to tour the cellars.

South of Greve, the SP 222 takes you past the left turn for **Villa Vignamaggio** (✆ 055-854661; fax 055-8544468; www.vignamaggio.com), whose elegant gardens served as the set for Kenneth Branagh's *Much Ado About Nothing* (1993). The 14th- or 15th-century villa was once home to the *Mona Lisa,* born here in 1479. Vignamaggio wines are counted among the region's top bottles. Book ahead, and you can tour the cellar and ornate gardens and sample three wines with simple snacks or more elaborate wines and snacks (plus vin santo). They also rent rooms.

The Chiantigiana next cuts through **Panzano in Chianti;** the tourist office is **InfoChaniti,** Via Chiantigiana 6 (✆ 055-852933; www.infochianti.com). The town is known for its embroidery and for another famed butcher, **Antica Macelleria Cecchini,** Via XX Luglio 11 (✆ 055-852020). Panzano also sports an excellent wine shop: the **Enoteca Baldi,** Piazza Bucciarelli 25, on the main traffic triangle at the Chiantigiana (✆ 055-852843).

The SP 222 continues south toward Castellina in Chianti (see below).

THE SIENESE CHIANTI

EN ROUTE TO RADDA   **Castellina in Chianti,** an Etruscan town and Florentine bastion against Siena, is one of the more medieval-feeling hill towns of the region. The tourist office is the **Colline Verdi** travel agency, Via della Rocca 12 (✆/fax 0577-740620). Castellina's medieval walls survive almost intact, and the central piazza is dominated by an imposing crenellated **Rocca** fortress. The nearby soldier's walk, **Via delle Volte,** is an evocative street tunnel with open windows facing out to the valley below. The best local wine tasting is at **La Castellina,** Via Ferrucio 26 (✆ 0577-740454). The **Bottega del Vino,** Via della Rocca 13 (✆ 0577-741110; www.enobottega.it), is a good wine shop. Outside town on the road to Radda is a 6th-century-B.C. Etruscan tomb, the **Ipogeo Etrusco di Montecalvario.**

From here you can shoot 18km (11¼ miles) down the Chiantigiana to Siena, past the medieval village and winery of **Fonterutoli** (✆ 0577-740212; www.fonterutoli.com), in the same family since 1435. The direct sales office in town is usually locked; the *ristorante* across the way has a bar (open daily

10am–10:30pm) where you can sample wines (the person behind the bar will open the sales office if you want to buy a case). Fonterutoli olive oil is particularly fine.

The road continues on to Siena, passing through **Quercegrossa,** the birthplace of Siena's great sculptor Jacopo della Quercia. But if you want to explore what many consider the best of the Chianti, it's time to cut east into the rugged, mountainous heart of the old Lega del Chianti along the SS429 toward Radda.

Just before you hit Radda, a signposted right turn will take you a winding 7km (4⅓ miles) past the **Castello di Ama,** a top-rated vineyard whose Frenchified wine-making methods you can experience at the **Rinaldi Palmira** direct sales office (℡ **0577-746021;** open year-round, though tastings are available only Easter to Sept) down the road in the hamlet of **Lecchi.** From here, the road continues to **San Sano** (see "Accommodations You Can Afford," below).

RADDA IN CHIANTI & ENVIRONS   **Radda in Chianti** has retained its importance as a wine center along with its medieval street plan and a bit of the walls. The center of town is the 15th-century **Palazzo del Podestà,** studded with the mayoral coats of arms of past mayors; it contains the **tourist office** (℡/fax **0577-738494;** www.chiantinet.it), open Monday through Saturday from 10am to 1pm and 3 to 7pm. Again there is a local butcher, in Radda's case **Luciano Prociatti,** who runs an alimentari on Piazza IV Novembre 1 at the gate into town (℡ **0577-738055**).

Seven kilometers (4⅓ miles) north of Radda on a secondary road is the perfectly stony-medieval **Castello di Volpaia** (℡ **0577-738066;** fax 0577-738619; www.volpaia.com), a first-rank wine estate. The central tower has an enoteca for drop-in tastings of one of the wines that helped found the Chianti Consorzio in 1924, with direct sales from 10am to 6pm (closed Feb and Tues Nov–Mar) of their wines, award-winning olive oils, and vinegars. You can tour the winery, installed in a series of buildings throughout the little village, by calling ahead, preferably a week in advance. They also rent apartments and two small villas and lease out a small hotel on a neighboring hill.

Three kilometers (1¾ miles) east of Radda, get on the left byroad for a 19km (12-mile) trip to the beautifully isolated **Badia a Coltibuono** (℡ **0577-749498;** fax 0577-749235; www.coltibuono.com). The abbey was expanded by the Vallombrosan monks from 770 to the early 1800s, when it became an agricultural estate. Today the estate is owned by the Stucci-Prinetti family, whose current matriarch—married into the Medici line—is the internationally renowned cookbook author Lorenza de' Medici. Her staff hosts the famed (and outrageously expensive) The Villa Table culinary school here in summer, and her son Paolo runs the fine **restaurant** (℡ **0577-749424;** closed Mon and Nov–Feb). A direct sales office for their products is at the **osteria** (℡ **0577-749479**) down at the main road.

EN ROUTE TO SIENA   Follow the scenic road leading south out of Radda toward Siena, and you'll see, on the left side, the **ceramic workshop** 𝍊 and showroom of master **Giuseppe Rampini** (℡ **577-738043;** www.rampini ceramics.com).

Heading south directly from Badia a Coltibuono on the SS408 will take you through **Gaiole in Chianti,** the third member of the Lega del Chianti. The tourist office is at Via Ricasoli 50 (℡ **0577-749411;** gaiole@chiantinet.it; open Mon, Wed, and Fri 9:30am–1pm and 3–6:30pm). This is an ancient market town like Greve but is basically modernized without much to see, aside from the wine shops the **Cantina Enoteca Montagnani,** Via B. Bandinelli

13–17 (© **0577-749517**), and the **Cantinetta del Chianti,** Via F. Ferruci 20 (© **0577-749125**).

Farther south of Gaiole, the SS484 branches east toward Castelnuovo Berardenga and the famous 15th-century **Castello di Brolio** (© **0577-749066;** www.ricasoli.it), in the Ricasoli family since 1141 (except for a brief, near disastrous 1980s interlude as part of the Seagram's empire). The first official formula for Chianti Classico wine was concocted here in the mid–19th century by "Iron Baron" Bettino Ricasoli—nobleman, experimental agriculturalist, and the second prime minister of Italy. The Iron Baron's Chianti recipe balanced Sangiovese, Canaiolo, Trebbiano, and Malvasia grapes, and was used when Italy's wine-governing D.O.C. and D.O.C.G. laws were written up in the 1960s. Today Chianti laws have been much relaxed, and many estates (including Brolio) are making Chianti out of pure Sangiovese grapes, but this vineyard remains at the forefront of Tuscan viticulture. Monday through Saturday from 9am to noon and 3 to 7pm (to 6pm Sun), you can pull the bell at the main door to visit some of the castle grounds, including the small chapel where Bettino is buried. You can also step into the gardens to walk along the wall for nice Chianti views. Admission is 3€ ($3.45). In summer, the gardens are open daily 9am to noon and 3 to 6pm; in winter, they're open from 9am to noon and 2 to 5pm.

To buy their award-winning wines, visit the modern bottling rooms/cantina, the **Barone Ricasoli Cantina di Brolio** (© **0577-7301;** turnoff a few hundred feet from the long driveway to the castle). They offer cantina tours, with free tastings at the end, Monday to Saturday 10 to 11am or 2 to 3:30pm; call at least a few days in advance. The store itself, the **Enoteca del Castello di Brolio,** is open year-round Monday to Saturday 9am to 6pm (in summer Sun 11am– 7pm). There are plans to move this wine shop, tasting room, and cantina tour away from the modern bottling center and up to a building at the foot of the road to the *castello,* near the quite good **Osteria del Castello** restaurant (© **0577-747277**).

The westerly byroad out of here is the quickest to join the SS408 as it heads south, out of the land of the black rooster and into Siena (see the next section).

ACCOMMODATIONS YOU CAN AFFORD

Borgo Argenina ★★   From the flagstoned terrace of Elena Nappa's new hilltop B&B (she bought the whole medieval hamlet), you can see the farmhouse where Bertolucci filmed *Stealing Beauty* in 1996. Against remarkable odds (she'll regale you with the anecdotes), she has created the rural retreat of her and your dreams. When you arrive, you'll likely find Elena upstairs next to a roaring fire in the kitchen, sewing. Elena's design talents (she was a fashion stylist in Milan) are amazing, and the guest rooms boast antique wrought-iron beds, deluxe mattresses, handmade quilts, hand-stitched lace curtains, and timeworn terra-cotta tiles. The bathrooms are made to look old-fashioned, though the plumbing is modern. Since the place isn't easy to find, English-speaking Elena will fax you directions when you reserve. When faced with all the questions foreign guests often inundate her with when booking (Do you have air-conditioning? Is there parking? How much deposit do I need to make?), Elena replies, "Don't worry. Just come!" Good advice.

Loc. Argenina (near San Marcellino Monti), 53013 Gaiole in Chianti. © **0577-747117**. Fax 0577-747228. borgoargenina@libero.it. (She prefers e-mail and will respond within the day.) www.borgoargenina.it. 6 units, 2 houses, 1 villa. 130€–150€ ($150–$173) double; 160€–200€ ($184–$230) apt suite; 450€ ($518) villa for 4. 3-night minimum stay. Rates include country breakfast. MC, V. Free parking. Ask for directions when reserving. **Amenities:** Outdoor swimming pool; bike rental; concierge; tour desk; room service (breakfast); laundry service; nonsmoking rooms. *In room:* Dataport, kitchenette (in villa), minibar, hair dryer.

Hotel Il Colombaio ⚘ This excellently priced modest hotel is housed in a 16th-century stone house at the edge of Castellina (near the Etruscan tomb and a 5-min. walk into town for restaurants) and once sheltered shepherds who spent the night after selling their sheep at market. The good-size rooms with their sloping beam-and-tile ceilings, terra-cotta floors, and iron bed frames seem to belong to a well-to-do 19th-century farming family. Upstairs accommodations are lighter and more airy than the ground-floor rooms (formerly stalls) and enjoy better views over the vineyards (a few overlook the road). Six of the rooms are in an annex across the road. The house's old kitchen has been converted into a comfy rustic reading room. You breakfast in winter under stone vaults and in summer on a terrace sharing its countryside vistas with the pool.

Via Chiantigiana 29, 53011 Castellina in Chianti (SI). ℭ 0577-740444. Fax 0577-740402. www.albergoil colombaio.it. 21 units. 82€ ($94) single; 87€–103€ ($100–$118) double. Rates include breakfast. AE, MC, V. **Amenities:** Restaurant (1 block away); outdoor pool (June–Sept); concierge; tour desk; car-rental desk; limited room service (breakfast only); massage; babysitting; laundry service. In room: TV, hair dryer.

San Sano Giancarlo Matarazzo and his German wife, Heidi, traded in their jobs as schoolteachers in Germany for this idyllic niche of Chianti and opened a special rural hideaway. The lack of TVs in the rooms is meant to enhance the tranquillity, and the medieval jumble of 13th-century stone buildings boasts a beautifully sited pool nestled amid the vineyards. The decor is rustic, simple, and perfect—and so are the views. The Matarazzos will help you map out day trips over scenic back roads to wine estates and hill towns (Radda and Gaiole are both about 10km/6¼ miles away) that will give you the chance to sample local trattorie—but most guests wind up gravitating back here to the cozy country kitchen for optional dinners of *cucina toscana* and animated dinner talk. And Siena is a lovely 20km (12-mile) drive away.

Località San Sano, 53010 Lecchi in Chianti. ℭ 0577-746130. Fax 0577-746156. www.sansanohotel.it. 14 units. 70€–125€ ($81–$144) single; 125€–139€ ($144–$160) double; 160€ ($184) triple. Rates include buffet breakfast. AE, DC, MC, V. **Amenities:** Restaurant; outdoor pool; car-rental desk. In room: A/C, TV, minibar, hair dryer, safe.

5 Siena & the Palio delle Contrade

34km (21 miles) S of Florence, 100km (62 miles) SE of Pisa, 42km (26 miles) SE of San Gimignano, 230km (143 miles) NE of Rome, 107km (66 miles) NW of Perugia

Siena is often bypassed by the mad rush of visitors traveling the Rome–Florence autostrada. Others allot it minimum time to revel in its perfectly preserved medieval charm. You'll see almost nothing of the baroque so prevalent in Rome or the Renaissance character of nearby Florence. Founded as Sena by the Etruscans and colonized by ancient Rome as Saena Julia, Siena flourished as a republic in the Middle Ages from the wool and textile trade and pre-Medici banking. It was one of the major cities of Europe in its day and became a principal center of art and culture as well. Piazza del Campo, the imposing palazzi, the Duomo, and the churches you see today were the result of a building boom that flourished during those years. Its noted university dates from that period, founded in 1240. But beginning in 1348, prosperity was aborted after devastating and recurring bouts with the bubonic plague that diminished the city's population from 100,000 to 30,000. Today's population, just over 60,000, is one still proud of its rich medieval heritage.

Locking horns over the centuries with its powerful neighbor Florence and never having fully stabilized after its brush with the Black Death, Siena finally succumbed to Florence after an 18-month siege in 1554 to 1555, became part of the Grand Duchy of Tuscany under Medici rule, and was reduced to a small provincial town. Florence's disinterest in Siena during the golden years of the Renaissance is your great fortune: Seemingly frozen in time, it's one of the country's best-preserved medieval cities. Because of the days when coffers overflowed, it boasts some of the most beautiful Gothic cathedrals, town halls, and main squares (Piazza del Campo) in all of Italy.

The Monte dei Paschi Bank in the postcard-perfect Piazza Salimbeni was founded in 1472; it's Europe's (many say the world's) oldest bank and still one of Italy's most solvent. It has long played a large role in sponsoring much of the city's cultural life. But while Siena's architectural expansion may have never progressed beyond the early Renaissance, Siena is still a very vital city, as you can witness during the early-evening *passeggiata* hour when the city's folk take to strolling Via di Città, Via Banchi di Sotto, and Via Banchi di Sopra. Proud, handsome, fashionably turned out, and more welcoming than the ultrareserved Florentines, the Sienese still stand by the famous inscription at the ancient Porta Camolia: "Siena opens up its heart to you more than any other."

Siena is an ideal gateway for central and southern Tuscany for those with and without cars. From here, you can meander off to experience the various hill towns and hamlets in the Siena orbit of patchwork farmland and vine-draped estates. While the rest of Tuscany sleeps, return here for its artistic riches and marginal dash of cosmopolitan cultural life and a number of dining choices. Best of all, finish your day with that after-dinner gelato in any of the cafes ringing beautiful Piazza del Campo, the best place around to sit and take in your extreme good luck.

ESSENTIALS

GETTING THERE   By Train   The bus is often more convenient, since Siena's train station is outside town. Some 13 trains (www.trenitalia.com) daily connect Siena with **Florence** (1½–2¼ hr.; 5.40€/$6.30). Siena's **train station** (© 0577-280115) is at Piazza Fratelli Roselli, about 3km (1¾ miles) north of town. Take the C minibus to Piazza Gramsci in Terza di Camollia, or a taxi (© 0577-49222).

By Car   There's an autostrada highway direct from **Florence** (it has no route number; follow the green autostrada signs toward Siena), or you can take the more scenic routes: down old Via Cassia SS2 or the Chiantigiana SP 222 through the Chianti (see above). From **Rome,** get off the A1 north at the Val di Chiana exit and follow the SS326 west for 50km (31 miles). The SS223 runs 70km (43 miles) here from **Grosetto** in the Maremma. From **Pisa,** take the highway toward Florence and exit onto the SS429 south at Empoli (100km/62 miles total).

Trying to drive into the one-way pedestrian-zoned center isn't worth the headache. Siena **parking** (© 0577-22871; www.sienaparcheggi.com) is now coordinated, and all the lots charge 1.50€ ($1.75) per hour or 36€ ($41) per day—though almost every hotel has a discount deal with the one nearest them for anywhere from 40% to 100% off. The lots are well signposted, with locations just inside city gates Porta Tufi (the huge and popular "Il Campo" lot, though it's a 20-min. walk from the Campo!), Porta San Marco, and Porta Romana; under the Fortezza (another large lot) and around La Lizza park (the latter closed on market Wed and soccer Sun); and at Piazza Amendola (just outside the northern Porta Camollia). You can **park for free** a bit farther away around the unguarded back (northwest) side of the Fortezza all week long. There's also free parking outside the southeast end of town at Due Ponti (beyond the Porta Pispini) and Coroncina (beyond the Porta Romana); from both, you can get a *pollicino* minibus into the center (see "Getting Around," below).

Siena

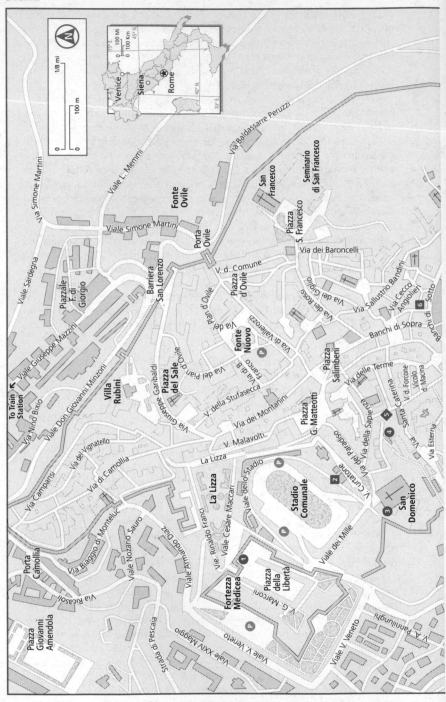

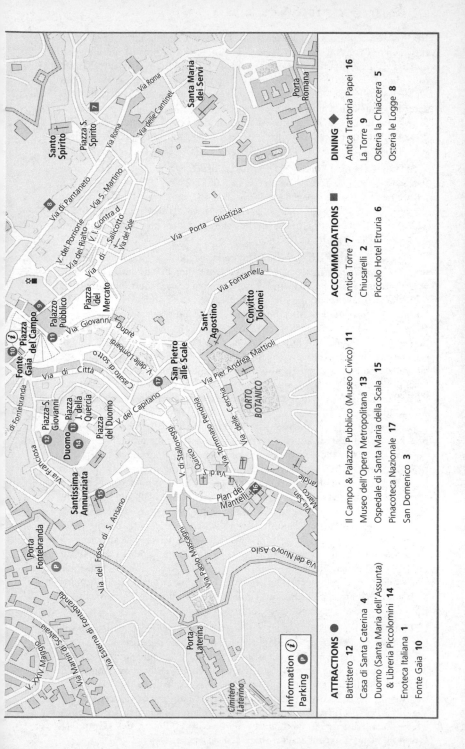

ATTRACTIONS ●

Battistero **12**
Casa di Santa Caterina **4**
Duomo (Santa Maria dell'Assunta)
 & Libreria Piccolomini **14**
Enoteca Italiana **1**
Fonte Gaia **10**

Il Campo & Palazzo Pubblico (Museo Civico) **11**
Museo dell'Opera Metropolitana **13**
Ospedale di Santa Maria della Scala **15**
Pinacoteca Nazionale **17**
San Domenico **3**

ACCOMMODATIONS ■

Antica Torre **7**
Chiusarelli **2**
Piccolo Hotel Etruria **6**

DINING ◆

Antica Trattoria Papei **16**
La Torre **9**
Osteria la Chiàccera **5**
Osteria le Logge **8**

Information ⓘ
Parking Ⓟ

By Bus   Since buses from **Florence** are faster and let you off right in town, they're more convenient than trains. **Tra-in** (www.trainspa.it) runs express coaches (19 daily; 75 min.; 8€/$9.20) and slower local buses (18 daily; 90 min. to 2 hr.; 6€/$6.90) from **Florence**'s SITA station to Siena's Piazza San Domenico or Piazza Gramsci. Siena is also connected hourly Monday through Saturday with **San Gimignano** (see that section for the confusing details). Siena's Tra-in **bus ticket office** is underneath Piazza Gramsci (℃ 0577-204246), and there's a **small office** at Piazza San Domenico, under the right side of the church exterior (℃ 0577-247909 or 0577-204111).

VISITOR INFORMATION   The **tourist office**, where you can get a great free map, is at Piazza del Campo 56 (℃ 0577-280551; fax 0577-270676; www.terresiena.it). It's open daily from 9am to 7pm (winter hours may be shorter). The main administrative APT office is at Via di Città 43 (℃ 0577-42209). For help finding a hotel, see the agencies under "Accommodations You Can Afford," later in this chapter.

FESTIVALS & MARKETS   Travel material would have you believe otherwise, but there's more to see here than the twice-annual Palio horse race. A 2-week **Antiques Fair** takes place in February of even years. A **Settimana dei Vini (Wine Week)** takes place the first week of June at the Enoteca Nazionale. The **Settimana Musicale Sienese,** a noteworthy weeklong classical musical festival, takes place in July or August, attracting world-class names and usually culminating at the beginning of August. Contact the tourist office for a schedule or call the Accademia Musicale Chigiana (℃ 0577-22091; www.chigiana.it), the city's prestigious music conservatory. The **weekly market** is a large affair that takes place on Wednesday (8am–1pm) near the Fortezza Medicea and La Lizza Park. Vendors hawk everything from tube socks to CDs and fresh-cut flowers to tripe sandwiches.

Foremost of the year's events is the legendary **Palio delle Contrade** 𝒜𝒜𝒜, held July 2 (7:30pm) and August 16 (7pm); the latter is the more important of the two. Tickets in the bleachers are exorbitant, usually costing at least 100€ ($115). They can be purchased only directly from the piazza's 30-some-odd stores and cafes; some have faxes, and you can get a list of names and contacts at the tourist office. Tickets for either of the two Palios usually are sold out by January (and hotels by Feb); a last-minute appeal directly to a store or cafe owner may turn up a cancellation. The whole scenario is pretty much a frustrating and often useless venture unless you know the mayor. The alternative is to join the crowd, anywhere from 50,000 to 100,000 strong, that stands in the inner piazza (the later in the day you show up, the farther from the outer rail you'll find free space). Remember that this all happens during peak summer heat, vision is limited, and emotions run high. But hey, it's free. For more on the Palio, see the box "The Palio delle Contrade," below.

CITY LAYOUT   Siena is splayed out like a *Y* along three ridges with deep valleys in between, effectively dividing the city into thirds, called *terze.* The *terze* are each drawn out along three main streets following the spines of those ridges. The southern arm, the **Terza di San Martino,** slopes gently down around **Via Banchi di Sotto** (and the various other names it picks up along the way). To the west lies the **Terza di Città** (home to the Duomo and Pinacoteca), centered on **Via di Città.** The **Terza di Camollia** runs north around **Via Banchi di Sopra.** These three main streets meet at the north edge of **Piazza del Campo (Il Campo),** Siena's gorgeous scallop-shape central square.

> ### *Tips* Saving Money
>
> Siena has several **reduced-price cumulative ticket** combos you can pick up at any of the participating museums or sights.
>
> The two-day, 10€ ($12) **Biglietto Musei Comunali** covers civic museums—**Museo Civico, Santa Maria della Scala,** and the new contemporary art gallery in the **Palazzo delle Papesse** on Via di Città (where admission is 5€/$5.75). The **Biglietto Cumulative SIA** is valid for 7 days but costs 13€ ($15) in winter and 16€ ($18) in summer. It covers the attractions listed above, as well as the **Baptistery,** the **Museo dell'Opera Metropolitana,** and the **Libreria Piccolomini.**
>
> Also available is the **Biglietto Museo e Torre,** a cumulative ticket that gets you in to both the Museo Civico and the Torre del Mangia for 10€ ($12).

Tip: Each *terza*'s main ridge-topped street is relatively flat—for Siena—while, off to either side, medieval alleys drop precipitously. If you hate climbing hills, the shortest (or at least less strenuous) distance between two points in Siena isn't a straight line, but a curve that follows the three main drags as much as possible.

GETTING AROUND   Although it looks and feels like a small Tuscan hill town, Siena truly is a city (albeit a small one), and its sights are widely spread. There's no efficient public transport system in the center, so it's up to your feet to cover the territory. There are plenty of steep ups and downs, and no shortcuts from one *terza* to another without a serious workout.

The city does run **minibuses** called *pollicini* (© 0577-204246), which dip into the city center from 6am to 9pm. The B services the Terza di San Martino and out the Porta Pispini gate, as does bus no. 5 (there's also an N night bus on this route 9pm–1am). Confusingly, there are four A buses, differentiated by color. A **pink** goes around Terza di San Martino (and out the Porta Romana gate), as does bus no. 26; A **green** and A **yellow** cover Terza di Città (green from Porta Tufi to the Duomo, yellow from Porta San Marco to the Duomo); and A **red** takes care of the southerly part of Terza di Camollia (from Piazza della Indipendenza out Porta Fontebranda).

You can call for a radio **taxi** at © 0577-49222 (7am–10:50pm only). They also queue at the train station and in town at Piazza Matteotti.

EXPLORING SIENA

Il Campo ✫✫✫   You'll see posters and postcards with aerial shots of the unusual fan-shape piazza, though they don't prepare you for its sheer breadth or monumental beauty. All roads and events, all visitors and residents, gravitate toward it; you can catch a glimpse of its sunlit expanse from a dozen narrow alleys that lead down and empty into it. Built at the point where the city's three hills converge and the Roman forum once rose, Il Campo is divided into nine marble-trimmed strips representing the city's Government of Nine, established in 1290, but is also said to imitate the folds in the cloak of the Virgin Mary, protector of the city since time immemorial. The piazza has always been center stage—the one-time place of executions, bullfights, and demonstrations—and is today lined with handsomely restored 13th- and 14th-century palazzi and their ground-floor cafes and stores.

The piazza is still a great place to hang out, like the Ramblas in Barcelona and the Spanish Steps in Rome. Locals meet, gossip, shop, and cross it at every angle;

university-goers loiter about; and seniors congregate against this backdrop of matchless harmony. At its highest point is the piazza's famous **Fonte Gaia,** dedicated to the ancient mythological goddess of the seas (though many sources say its name translates as "gay and carefree"). It's a poor 19th-century copy of the early-15th-century fountain by local master Jacopo della Quercia (you can find some of the much-decayed original marble reliefs in the Palazzo Pubblico's Museo Civico) and is fed by a 24km (15-mile) aqueduct that has supplied the city with fresh water since the 14th century.

The **Palazzo Pubblico,** also known as the **Palazzo Comunale,** is a stunning symbol of civic pride. Still the site of the Town Hall, it takes up nearly all of Piazza del Campo's south side. Its elegant Gothic facade, completed in 1310 and expanded in the 17th century, is slightly curved, in keeping with the piazza's unusual parameter. The interior is open to the public as a Museo Civico (see below).

The palazzo's 96m (315-ft.) brick bell tower, the marble-crowned **Torre del Mangia** (entered via the palazzo's courtyard), is the highest medieval tower in Italy after Cremona's and was named after its first bell ringer, nicknamed *mangiagaudagni* (literally, "profit-eater") because of his notorious idleness. Its bells were used to announce the opening and closing of the city gates, threat of attack, and special events like the arrival of a pope. Its 505 steps will provide you with vertigo-inducing views over Il Campo, Siena's *centro storico,* and the Tuscan countryside that picks up where the modern city sprawl beyond the city walls diminishes. (The other heart-stopping view in town is from atop the Facciatione, adjacent to the Duomo; see below.)

At the base of the tower is the **Cappella di Piazza** (1352–76), erected by the grateful Sienese people in thanksgiving for the passing of the Black Death in 1348. It's not open to the public.

Piazza del Campo. Piazza free, always open. Torre del Mangia: Admission 6€ ($6.90); 5€/$5.75 with reservation) or on cumulative ticket (see "Saving Money," above). Nov–Mar 15 10am–4pm; Mar 16–June and Sept–Oct 10am–7pm; July–Aug 10am–11pm. Last admission 45 min. before close.

Palazzo Pubblico—Museo Civico ✸✸✸   Within the Palazzo Pubblico, this museum houses some of the Sienese school of art's most significant works. One of the two important rooms is the **Sala del Mappamondo (Globe Room),** named after a long-lost map of the world and frescoed in 1315 with two important works by the prominent local artist Simone Martini, a student of Duccio. On the left is his splendidly restored *Maestà* ✸ (1315), and on the opposite wall is *Guidoriccio da Folignano* ✸ (1328), depicting a captain of the Sienese army in full battle regalia. Both were meant to protect the city from harm and pestilence (the latter fresco had always been attributed to Martini until recent controversy that keeps historians divided).

The next room, the **Sala di Pace (Hall of Peace),** was the meeting place for the medieval Government of Nine and today contains the two famous allegorical frescoes by local master Ambrogio Lorenzetti: *Allegory of Good and Bad Government and Their Effects on Town and Countryside* ✸ (1337–39). You won't have a hard time determining which is which. They're some of the earliest and most important secular artworks to survive from medieval Europe. Lorenzetti is believed to have died from the plague not long after completing the fresco cycle.

In the Palazzo Pubblico, Piazza del Campo. ✆ 0577-292226. www.comune.siena.it/museocivico. Admission on cumulative ticket (see "Saving Money," above), or 7€ ($8.05) adults (6€/$6.90 with reservation), 4.50€ ($5.15), free for kids under 11. Nov–Mar 15 daily 10am–6:30pm; Mar 16–Oct daily 10am–7pm. Last admission 45 min. before close.

The Palio delle Contrade

Twice a year, Siena packs Piazza del Campo with dirt, and the city's traditional *contrade*—the neighborhood wards that still govern many aspects of Sienese life—hold a fast-paced, bareback horse race called the Palio. It is the highlight of a week of trial runs, feasts, parades, spectacles of skill, and solemn ceremonies, a tradition that goes back, in one form or another, to at least 1310.

Ten *contrade* are chosen by lot each year to ride in the **July 2** Palio. The other seven, plus three from the July race, run the even bigger Palio on **August 16.** Lest you think the Palio is a race of skill: Your chance to ride, your horse, and the order in which you're lined up are each chosen by separate lots—even your jockey (always a hired outsider) is a wild card, since you may not pay him more than a rival is bribing him to throw the race. The jockey exists mainly to lash at other riders with his short whip; in the end, it's the horse that wins (if no rivals have drugged it), whether there's a rider still on it or not. The prize for all this mayhem? The *palio* is merely a banner painted with the image of the Virgin Mary. Well, you also win the honor of your *contrada* for the coming year. The Palios really start on June 29 and August 13, when the lots are drawn to select the racers and when the trial runs begin for the next 2 days. Each Palio holds *contrade,* a pre-Palio feast that lasts until the Palio day's 7:45am Jockey's Mass in the Campo's Cappella della Piazza. There's a final heat at 9am, but the highlight is the 3pm (3:30pm in July) Blessing of the Horse in each *contrada's* church. Unless invited by a *contrada,* you're not going to get into any of the packed churches for this, so your best strategy is to stick around the Campo all day. Standing in the piazza's center is free; the grandstands require tickets. Stake out a piazza spot close to the start/finish line before 2pm. Just before 5pm, the pageantry begins, with processions including the *palio* banner carried in a war chariot drawn by two white oxen. *Contrada* youths in Renaissance costume juggle huge, colorful banners in a *sbandierata* flag-throwing display.

At 7:30pm (7pm in July), nine of the horses start lining up between two ropes, waiting for the 10th horse to come galloping up from behind and start the race—three laps, a minute and a half. Then it's time for the winning *contrada* to burst into song, the losers to cry, and those suspecting their jockeys of taking bribes to chase the riders through the streets. Except for the winners, the banquets that night, at long tables laid out on the streets of each *contrada,* are more solemn than the feasts of the night before.

Duomo (Santa Maria dell'Assunta) ★★★ Begun in 1196, this black-and-white-striped marble Duomo dedicated to Our Lady of the Assumption tops Siena's highest hill and is one of Italy's most beautiful Gothic churches. If you arrive by bus in Piazza San Domenico, look for its perfect view from afar. Much of what you see was completed in the 13th century. The unfinished free-standing construction to the right of the cathedral is what the Sienese call the

Facciatone (Big Facade). In 1339 (when Siena was reaching its medieval zenith and felt the need to keep up with its old-time rival Florence, which had just built an enormous Duomo), plans were launched to build an even greater Duomo that would incorporate the extant structure as the transept and become Christendom's largest church outside Rome. Work was abandoned forever when money ran short, the bubonic plague of 1348 altered local history, and the economy fell apart.

The exterior's extravagant marble bands (borrowed from Pisan-Lucchese architecture) are reflected in the interior. Your entry can be visually startling, with your focus soon drawn to the priceless **pavement of masterful mosaics** 𝄞𝄞, 56 etched and inlaid marble panels created by more than 40 artisans between the mid–14th and 16th centuries, with some finished in the 19th century. They're partially roped off and many are covered by protective cardboard, but all are uncovered in September and October (when admission to the cathedral is charged).

Beneath the central vault is the octagonal **pulpit** 𝄞, whose famous upper panels depicting the life of Christ were carved by master Tuscan sculptor Nicola Pisano in 1265, assisted by his son Giovanni (who designed the Duomo's lower facade in 1284) and Arnolfo di Cambio. It's his masterpiece, even greater and more elaborate than his then-recent work in Pisa's baptistery, and is one of the Duomo's (and the city's) most important artistic treasures. Within the Duomo at an entrance in the north (left) aisle is the lavish **Libreria Piccolomini** 𝄞𝄞, built in the late 15th century by Cardinal Francesco Piccolomini (the future Pius III—for all of 18 days in office before he died) to house the important illuminated book collection of his uncle, Pope Pius II, the quintessential Renaissance man/humanist. The elder pontiff's life is the subject of 10 brilliantly colored giant frescoes, the masterpiece of Umbrian artist Pinturicchio (1509); he was assisted by his students, including a young Raphael. One of the most famous frescoes depicts the canonization of Siena-born St. Catherine, the third fresco on the left as you enter. An ancient Roman copy of a Greek-inspired statue of the *Three Graces* stands in the center. As you leave the library, on your right you'll see the late-15th-century **Piccolomini altar,** adorned with four statues attributed to a young Michelangelo; though commissioned to do 15, he left early for Florence to create his *David.*

Piazza del Duomo. 🅒 **0577-283048.** www.operaduomo.siena.it. Admission to church and Libreria Piccolomini 3€ ($3.45), 6€ ($6.90) when the floor is uncovered, or on cumulative ticket (see "Saving Money," above). Mar–Oct Mon–Fri 10:30am–7:30pm and Sat 1:30–6:30pm; Nov–Feb Mon–Fri 10:30am–6:30pm and Sat 1:30–5:30pm. Last admission 30 min. before close.

Museo dell'Opera Metropolitana (Duomo Museum) 𝄞𝄞   Located in the

"new" part of the Duomo that was never finished, with the adjoining Facciatone, this museum houses much of the sculpture and artwork that formerly graced the cathedral inside and out. Most interesting is the first floor's collection of weatherworn Gothic facade statuary by Giovanni Pisano, with an important contribution by Donatello, a marble tondo of the *Madonna and Child.* Upstairs in a room by itself is the *Maestà* 𝄞 (1311), the museum's most celebrated work, once the Duomo's altarpiece. It's a complex work by Duccio di Buoninsegna, a student of Cimabue and a native son of Siena, and has long been considered one of the most important late medieval paintings in Europe. Follow signs for access to the top of the Facciatone (no elevator) for an **inspiring view** 𝄞 over Siena, arguably better than the view from the Torre del Mangia. During peak months when hours allow, try to make it here for sunset.

Piazza del Duomo 8. ☎ 0577-283048. www.operaduomo.siena.it. Admission 6€ ($6.90) or on cumulative ticket (see "Saving Money," above). Mar 15–Sept daily 9am–7:30pm; Oct daily 9am–6pm; Nov–Mar 14 daily 9am–1:30pm.

Battistero (Baptistery) ✦

Due to its separate entrance and obscure placement down the stairs and around the back-right flank of the Duomo, few people visit this baptistery. Look for the 15th-century hexagonal **baptismal font** by local son Jacopo della Quercia, adorned with gilded bronze bas-relief panels by Donatello and Ghiberti. If you've already visited Lucca, you'll have seen his important Tomb of Ilaria in the sacristy of the local Duomo.

Piazza San Giovanni (down the stairs around the back right flank of the Duomo). ☎ 0577-283048. Admission 3€ ($3.45) or on cumulative ticket (see "Saving Money," above). Mar 15–Sept daily 9am–7:30pm; Oct daily 9am–6pm; Nov–Mar 14 daily 10am–1pm and 2–5pm.

Ospedale di Santa Maria della Scala ✦

The hospital across from the Duomo entrance cared for the infirm from the 800s up until the 1990s, when it began to restructure as a museum and exhibition space. At press time, temporary shows were being held, but there are plans to perhaps move here the Pinacoteca's paintings as well as the city's archaeological collections. The original decorations inside merit a visit themselves, and if the round stained-glass window from the cathedral's apse is still under restoration here, by all means check it out—it's your only chance to see up close the oldest stained glass of Italian manufacture, designed by Duccio in 1288.

The first fresco you see, just after the ticket booth, is Domenico Beccafumi's luridly colored *Meeting at Porta Andrea* (after 1512). Off the next long hall to the right are spaces for temporary exhibits, and off to the left, just past the bookshop, is the entrance to the **Sala del Pellegrinaio** ✦, which held hospital beds until just a few years ago. The walls were frescoed in the 1440s with scenes from the history of the hospital and its good works (all labeled). Most are vivid masterpieces by Domenico di Bartolo, richly colored and full of amusing details. However, Vecchietta did the upwardly mobile orphans over the exit door; Jacopo della Quercia's less talented and little-known brother, Priamo, did a cartoonish scene on the left wall; and a pair of Mannerist hacks filled in the spaces at the room's end.

Vecchietta also painted the **Old Sacristy,** or **Cappella del Sacro Chiodo,** from 1446 to 1449. One of his few frescoes here that hasn't gone to pieces is a double-take *Last Judgment,* with Christ's final say on the Saved and the Damned oddly represented two times, in split-level. Serving as an altarpiece is di Bartolo's *Madonna del Manto* (1444) fresco with its sinopia.

Downstairs are rooms documenting the restoration of Jacopo della Quercia's Fonte Gaia with plaster casts, and the **Oratorio di Santa Caterina della Notte.** This latter was decorated mainly in the 17th century by Rustici and Rutilio Manetti but also contains a rich *Madonna and Child with Saints, Angels, and Musicians,* by Taddeo di Bartolo (ca. 1400), in the back room. You exit through the church of **Santissima Annunziata,** with a bronze *Risen Christ* by Vecchietta over the high altar and an apse-covering fresco by Sebastiano Conca (1732).

Piazza del Duomo 2. ☎ 0577-224811. www.santamaria.comune.siena.it. Admission on cumulative ticket (see "Saving Money," above), or 6€ ($6.90) adults without reservations, 5.50€ ($6.30) adults with reservations; 3.50€ ($4) students/seniors over 65 without reservations, 3€ ($3.45) students/seniors over 65 with reservations; free for kids under 11. Nov–Dec 24 and Jan 7–Mar 15 daily 10:30am–4:30pm; Dec 25–Jan 6 and Mar 16–Oct daily 10am–6pm.

Pinacoteca Nazionale (National Picture Gallery) ⟨✦⟩   If you've already visited the Duomo Museum or the Museo Civico, you'll recognize some of the names and styles of the Sienese school of painters whose works are displayed here in the 14th-century Gothic Palazzo Buonsignori. Though it can't hold a candle to what was transpiring simultaneously in Florence, this sliver of local art history is fascinating. Visitors usually bypass the ground floor and head to the second floor's treasures, highlighted by the works of Duccio, antiquity's last great painter and the most acclaimed of Siena's movement; in his works you can follow artistic advancements in composition, perspective, and expression. His student Simone Martini is also represented, as are brothers Pietro and Ambrogio Lorenzetti. The use of gold hung on longer in the Sienese school than in the Florentine, perhaps because the patrons who commissioned the works wanted to have them shine in gloomy chapels. Florence moved on to more advanced developments, while Siena was slow to break with its religious compositions.

Via San Pietro 29. ⟨𝒞⟩ **0577-281161.** Admission 4€ ($4.60). Mon 8:30am–1:30pm; Tues–Sat 8:15am–7:15pm; Sun 8:15am–1:15pm.

Enoteca Italiana (Italian Wine Cellar) ⟨*Moments*⟩   There could be no better setting to showcase Italy's timeless wine culture, making this a unique destination for serious connoisseurs and casual oenophiles alike. Set within the massive military fortress built by Cosimo de' Medici in 1560 after Siena had fallen to Florence, this wine-tasting bar provides a wide selection of vintages to be enjoyed inside and out, where tables are set on a terrace. It's most popular in the late afternoon or early evening, when local wine devotees and a young crowd drop in for an *aperitivo,* choosing from dozens of wines sold by the glass (or by the bottle). The emphasis is on Tuscan wines—many made around Siena—but this enoteca is a national concern owned and operated by the government to support the Italian wine tradition. Its 750-label collection is representative of the various regions and is one of the most prodigious selections of its kind in Italy.

Fortezza Medicea. ⟨𝒞⟩ **0577-227187.** www.enoteca-italiana.it. Reservations recommended. Free admission; glass of wine 2€ ($2.30), 3€ ($3.45), or 5.50€ ($6.30). Mon noon–8pm; Tues–Sat noon–1am. Closed Jan 1–15.

Casa di Santa Caterina   This is the 14th-century birthplace and home of St. Catherine of Siena, patron saint of Italy (together with St. Francis of Assisi) and one of the first women ever elevated to Doctor of the Church. If you've arrived at a time when a tour group or other crowd is present, wait until they leave so you can fully absorb the serenity of this simple and reflective place. After you cross a brick-lined courtyard, the points of interest are the **small chapel** on your right, where a painted 13th-century **crucifix** is said to be the one in front of which she received the stigmata in 1375, and an **oratory** to the left built on the spot of the family home, with wide steps leading down to her cell. St. Catherine died at 33 in 1380, the year that St. Bernard of Siena was born (d. 1444). Their mysticism exerted a deeply felt grip on the age, a time of heightened spirituality during an onslaught of droughts, bubonic plagues, and declining economies. The eloquent St. Catherine is perhaps most remembered for her instrumental involvement in persuading Pope Gregory XI to return the seat of the papacy to Rome from Avignon in France after a 67-year exile. She was canonized in 1464, and her home was transformed into this pilgrimage site not long thereafter.

Costa di San Antonio (between V. della Sapienza and V. Santa Caterina). ⟨𝒞⟩ **0577-247393.** www.caterinati. org. Free admission. Easter to Oct daily 9am–12:30pm and 3–6pm; winter daily 9am–12:30pm and 3:30–6pm. Bus: A (red), 2, 5.

San Domenico ✹   This monastic church has always been closely linked with St. Catherine, who had taken the Dominican veil in 1355 after her first vision of Christ. The barnlike 13th-century church juts above a high position affording beautiful views of the Duomo and the rooftops. But it's most visited for the **Cappella di Santa Caterina (Chapel of St. Catherine)** ✹, halfway along the nave on the right wall, added in 1460 to house the saint's severed head in a gilded tabernacle. In 1526, Il Sodoma frescoed all but the right wall with scenes from the saint's life. Catherine experienced most of her trances and visions of Christ in this church and received her stigmata in the raised **Cappella delle Volte (Chapel of the Vaults)** in the west end of the church (on your right as you enter). Over the chapel's altar, a contemporary portrait of her by one of her friends, Andrea Vanni (ca. 1380), is said to be the only authentic depiction of her.

Piazza San Domenico. No phone. Free admission. Apr–Oct 7am–12:55pm and 3–6:30pm; Nov–Mar 9am–12:55pm and 3–6pm. Bus: 1, 3, 6, 10, 18, 30, 31, 37, 106.

SHOPPING

Siena puts up a noble effort to keep up with its centuries-old rival Florence as a shopping destination but pales in comparison. It is, however, far better in variety and quantity than any of the other cities in this chapter, with the only close contenders being Perugia and Deruta (a side trip from Perugia for those interested in ceramics alone).

The elegance of the Sienese is obvious in the cluster of stores along the principal streets covered in "City Layout," earlier in this section. There are the predictable designer and accessories boutiques of top names, but you may be more interested in the ceramics stores and shops selling artisanal crafts *(prodotti toscani)*. The ceramics store **Ceramiche Artistiche Santa Caterina,** with showrooms at Via di Città 51, 74, and 76 (✆ 0577-283098) and a workshop outside town at Via P.A. Mattioli 12 (✆ 0577-45006), is of a very high quality. On this same block of Via di Città are at least five other ceramics shops selling everything from spoon rests to turkey-size platters, simply decorated (less expensive) or elaborately covered (very expensive). Also nearby is **Il Papiro,** Via di Città 37 (✆ 0577-284241), whose attractive paper goods you may have seen in its hometown of Florence, but in this retail outpost you'll also find a handsome series of postcards and note cards of watercolor vignettes depicting Siena's loveliest medieval palazzi.

If you've meandered around, you may have happened on any of the five **Nannini** bars or pasticcerie, sacred local institutions. The Nannini name is known beyond the confines of Siena, if not for its famous packaged sweets than for the pop singer Gianna Nannini (a cross between Madonna and a Streisand wannabe). Their largest and oldest bar/cafe is on Via Banchi di Sopra near Piazza del Campo (✆ 0577-41591). Although the fruit-and-nut cake *panforte* and the cookielike *ricciarelli* sweets made of almond paste are associated with Siena and Nannini's, food connoisseurs will guide you to the city's best one-stop shop for gourmet products, the **Enoteca San Domenico,** Via del Paradiso 56, just off Piazza San Domenico (✆ 0577-271181; www.enotecasandomenico.it). Here the just-sweet-enough *ricciarelli* are marvelous, and the selection of regional wines, oils, dried herbs, and other handsomely packaged gourmet goods will cover every hard-to-shop-for person on your list, yourself included.

ACCOMMODATIONS YOU CAN AFFORD

There are no youth hostels in town; ask at the tourist office about the two a few kilometers outside town (one in a lovely corner of Chianti). Both are under the same management as the hostel in San Gimignano (see earlier in this chapter).

If all the hotels below are full, try the English-speaking **Prenotazioni Alberghiere** (hotel reservations) stand on Piazza San Domenico (© 0577-288084; fax 0577-280290; www.hotelsiena.com), where you'll pay 1.50€ to 4€ ($1.70–$4.60) per reservation, according to the category of hotel. In summer, the office is open Monday through Saturday from 9am to 8pm (to 7pm in winter).

For **long stays**, Siena's fabled Piccolomini family has opened one of its Renaissance palazzi as furnished rentals by the week or month. Close to Piazza del Campo, top-floor apartments with a view sleeping two or three rent for $1,400 per week; the larger one that sleeps four or five runs $1,900. To those rates you must add utilities; prices get progressively lower for longer stays. In New York, contact Manfredi Piccolomini (© **212-932-3480;** fax 212-932-9039; www.palazzoantellesi.com). In Italy, call his mother's Florence number (© **055-244456;** fax 055-2345552).

Antica Torre 𝒜𝒜   Installed in a 16th-century tower (one of Siena's more recent constructions) with a timeworn travertine stairwell, this unusual and charming hotel offers cozy—some might call them small—rooms. The rooms on the higher floors are slightly larger and feature lovely views over the rooftops and green hills. Most rooms have cool terra-cotta pavements, exposed-beamed ceilings, white-lace curtains, and beds with wrought-iron headboards; the bathrooms are compact and updated. TVs are available on request. Though the hotel is on a quiet side street in a relatively residential niche of town, it's only a 10-minute walk to Piazza del Campo. You can even breakfast in one of the piazza's inexpensive outdoor cafes for less than what you'd pay at the hotel. The breakfast room, a 14th-century potter's *bottega* on top of which the tower was built, is charming but not for claustrophobics—especially before morning coffee.

You may also be interested in the **Palazzo di Valli,** Via Enea Silvio Piccolomini 135 (© **0577-226102**), the Landolfo's new 12-room countryside hotel converted from a 17th-century villa set amid olive trees and flower gardens. It lies .8km (½ mile) from the Porta Romana gate (a bus carries you to the Campo in 5 min.). Doubles there go for about 124€ to 135€ ($145–$155), including breakfast, bathroom, TV (on request), phone, and minibar. It's open from April to October.

Via di Fieravacchia 7, 53100 Siena. ©/fax **0577-222255.** www.anticatorresiena.it. 8 units. 90€ ($104) single; 110€ ($127) double; 120€ ($138) triple. Prices lower in slow periods. Breakfast 7€ ($8.05). AE, DC, MC, V. Parking in streets around hotel or in public lot nearby for 12€ ($14). **Amenities:** Gym available 9m (30 ft.) down the street; concierge. *In room:* A/C, TV (on request), hair dryer.

Chiusarelli   Two regal palms stand guard before the columned facade of this neoclassical 19th-century villa turned hotel. It's an easy 1-block walk from the bus station for those with light luggage and also an easy walk uphill to the central piazza once you're ready to sightsee. Availability is slightly better in prime months if you book in advance. The modernized rooms have all been redone in 2004—light sleepers should request a room overlooking the green stadium behind, not terribly picturesque but quieter (except during Sun matches) than those on Via Curatone. This is a "proper" hotel, with a bar, a breakfast terrace, a restaurant (avoid it and go to one of my suggestions below), and tour groups.

Viale Curtatone 15, 53100 Siena (near San Domenico). © **0577-280562.** Fax 0577-271177. www. chiusarelli.com. 49 units, 48 with bathroom. 62€ ($71) single without bathroom, 78€ ($90) single with bathroom; 117€ ($135) double with bathroom; 158€ ($182) triple with bathroom; 194€ ($223) quad with bathroom. Rates include breakfast. AE, MC, V. Parking 18€–20€ ($21–$23) in garage. **Amenities:** Bar; restaurant; concierge; tour desk; Internet point; room service (limited); massage. *In room:* A/C, TV, dataport, hair dryer, safe.

Piccolo Hotel Etruria ★★ *Finds*   This hotel is lovely enough to be your base in Tuscany—it's too great a find to be used as a one-night stop. The proud Fattorini family oversaw every painstaking detail in its last renovation, and the taste and quality level are something you usually find in hotels at thrice the cost. The rooms are simple but thoughtfully decorated and charming; the use of terracotta pavements and blond wood is ubiquitous. They're divided between the main building and a *dipendenza* across the street; some guests prefer the privacy of the latter, and others the friendly presence of the Fattorini in the former. The many appreciated touches include floral bedspreads, sheer white curtains, and hair dryers in the new bathrooms. The Fattorinis' in-house restaurant specializes in home-style cuisine. The one drawback is the 12:30am curfew. In high season, book well in advance—this secret is out.

Via Donzelle 3, 53100 Siena (off V. Banchi di Sotto). © 0577-288088. Fax 0577-288461. www. hoteletruria.com. 13 units, 12 with bathroom. 45€ ($52) single without bathroom, 50€ ($58) single with bathroom; 80€ ($92) double with bathroom; 105€ ($121) triple with bathroom. Extra bed 25€ ($29). Breakfast 5€ ($5.75). AE, DC, MC, V. Free parking. Closed around Dec 10–27. **Amenities:** Restaurant; room service (breakfast only). *In room:* A/C, TV, hair dryer, safe.

GREAT DEALS ON DINING

Antica Trattoria Papei ★ SIENESE   It's rather ambitious, in a city whose origins date from the Roman Empire, for a restaurant to call itself the "Ancient Trattoria" when it's been around for a mere 55 years. But three generations of the proud Papei family have put this wonderful restaurant on the map from day one. You'll understand why its future is secure when the homemade *papparedelle alla cinghiale* (flat noodles in a wild-boar tomato sauce) arrive at your outdoor table on one of the city's oldest piazze. The theme continues with *coniglio all'arrabiata* (rabbit marinated in white wine and simmered with sage and a pinch of hot pepperoncino). One of the myriad possibilities for nonhunters is the homemade *pici*, a hand-rolled egg pasta that looks like fat spaghetti and is served with a full-flavored fresh tomato sauce. Though foreigners have discovered the place, locals rigorously hang on (they avoid the modern room to the right as you enter, and so should you).

Piazza del Mercato 6 (behind the Palazzo Pubblico). © 0577-280894. Reservations suggested. Primi 6.20€ ($7.15); secondi 6.50€–10€ ($7.45–$12). AE, MC, V. Tues–Sun noon–3pm and 7–10:30pm.

La Torre ★ *Value* TUSCAN   You can usually trust a place that doesn't hide its kitchen. La Torre's is in plain view, next to a dozen tightly packed tables under an undulating brick ceiling. It's a popular place, so reserve ahead or show up early. All the pasta is homemade, none more deliciously than the *pici* and the plump tortellini, and is served with the sauce of your choice topped with a generous heap of Parmesan cheese. Afterward, try the *vitello arrosto* (slices of roast veal) or *piccione al forno* (oven-baked pigeon).

Via Salicotto 7–9 (9m/30 ft. off Il Campo to the left of the Palazzo Pubblico). © 0577-287548. Reservations recommended. Primi 6€–8€ ($6.90–$9.20); secondi 9€–10€ ($10–$12); *menu turistico* with wine 18€ ($21). No credit cards. Fri–Wed noon–3pm and 7–10pm. Closed Aug 17–Sept 1.

Osteria La Chiacchera SIENESE CUCINA POVERA   This is a tiny joint with worn wooden tables, terra-cotta floors, and barrel ends embedded everywhere. "The Chatterbox" proudly serves Sienese poor-people's food. Plenty of couples come here to make moon eyes at each other and save money on the date (not only is it cheap, but there's no cover charge or service fee—tips are greatly appreciated). A choice first course is the *pici boscaiola* (long strands of fat handrolled pasta in tomato-and-mushroom sauce), though the *penne arrabbiata* (in piquant tomato sauce) goes pretty quickly, too. Secondi are simple peasant dishes like *salsicce e fagioli* (grilled sausages with beans) and *stracotto* (beef and boiled potatoes in piquant tomato sauce). They also do a mean chocolate pie.

Costa di Sant'Antionio 4 (near San Domenico, off V. della Sapienza under the Hotel Bernini). ℭ 0577-280631. Reservations recommended. Primi 3.60€–6€ ($4.15–$6.90); secondi 4.50€–7€ ($5.15–$8.05). No credit cards. Daily noon–3pm and 7pm–midnight.

WORTH A SPLURGE

Osteria le Logge ✶✶✶ SIENESE/TUSCAN   Owner Gianni Brunelli is passionate about what he does, and so is his legion of devotees. This is one of those rare Sienese eateries for which you should reserve a table before arriving in town rather than risk settling for one of Gianni's cookbooks when the standing-room-only scenario turns you away. There's always a fresh homemade pasta to launch a memorable meal, followed by entrees that are all about the simple perfection of grilled meats, though I've seen vegetarians looking mighty content, too. The excellent choice of extra-virgin olive oil is enough to confirm the owner's seriousness, seconded by a small but discerning wine list that's topped by his own limited production of Rosso and Brunello di Montepulciano. You won't understand how exceptional this atmospheric locale is (a cabinet-lined former pharmacy) until you've eaten elsewhere in Siena.

Via del Porrione 33 (just off the Campo). ℭ 0577-48013. Reservations required. Primi 7.50€–11€ ($8.60–$13); secondi 15€–22€ ($17–$25); fixed-price menu 45€ ($52). AE, DC, MC, V. Mon–Sat noon–2:45pm and 7–10:30pm. Closed Jan 7–Feb 2.

SIDE TRIPS FROM SIENA

The wine-producing towns of southern Tuscany are still relatively unknown compared to those found along the Chianti Road (see earlier in this chapter), being just a few kilometers too far for Florence-based day-trippers. They're more easily accessible from Siena and can generally be reached by public transportation, though a rental car will facilitate enormously the logistics and flexibility of a day trip.

MONTALCINO   Located 43km (27 miles) south of Siena, sleepy and small but well-to-do Montalcino is the home of the powerhouse D.O.C.G. **Brunello di Montalcino wine** ✶✶ and its lighter-weight cousin Rosso di Montalcino. The town has remained unchanged since the 16th century, and you'll find an especially lovely vista from the 14th-century **Fortezza** (ℭ **0577-849211;** www.enotecalafortezza.it), which moonlights as its enoteca. The enoteca came under new management in 2003, but rest assured: The new staff is as adept as the old at helping you become better acquainted with the wines. From April to October, it's open daily from 9am to 8pm; from November to March, hours are Tuesday through Sunday from 9am to 1pm and 2 to 6pm. By-the-glass wines begin at 1.50€ ($1.70), but head right for the Brunello, at 4€ ($4.60), and a savory plate of the local cheeses or salami for Montalcino's perfect meal. Admission to the fortress's ramparts is 3.50€ ($4) for adults and 1.50€ ($1.75) for students, or you can buy a 6€ ($6.90) cumulative ticket that also gets you into the Museo Civico (see below). Another wonderful place for wine tasting is the **Caffè/Fiaschetteria Italiana,** Piazza del Popolo 6 (ℭ **0577-849043**), open Friday through Wednesday from 7:30am to midnight. In a 19th-century ambience or at a few choice tables outside, you can revel in a self-styled Brunello tasting, with three or four varieties by the glass for 4€ to 12€ ($4.60–$14). You can buy a bottle to bring home with you, if you want to part with 40€ ($46).

In the handsomely restored former St. Augustine monastery, Montalcino's small **Museo Civico (Civic Museum),** Via Ricasoli 31 (© **0577-846014**), is a collection of Sienese paintings dating from the 1400s to the Renaissance. It's open Tuesday through Sunday from 10am to 1pm and 2 to 5:40pm January through March. April through December, it's open Tuesday to Sunday from 10am to 5:50pm (although it sometimes closes at 1 or 2pm if they're short of staff). Admission is 4.50€ ($5.15) for adults and 3€ ($3.45) for children under 12, or you can buy the 6€ ($6.90) cumulative ticket that also gets you into the fortress (see above). Two of the area's most alluring experiences, however, are outside the town walls. The 12th-century Cistercian abbey of **Sant'Antimo** (© **0577-835659;** www.antimo.it) rests in its own pocket-size vale amid olive trees and cypresses 10km (6½ miles) south of Montalcino. One of Tuscany's most perfectly intact Romanesque churches, it's especially worth visiting during the several times daily when the handful of monks who still live here perform Gregorian chants. Although the church is open daily from 6am to 9pm, tourists are welcome to visit Monday through Saturday from 10:15am to 12:30pm and 3 to 6:30pm, and Sunday from 9:15 to 10:45am and 3 to 6pm. Admission is free. Outside these times, the monks are worshipping, and visitors' access is limited. If, however, you'd like to listen to the chant *and* gawk at the architecture, attend Mass on weekdays at 9:15am or Sunday at 11am.

While at Sant'Antimo, follow the signs for the nearby **Fattoria Barbi** (© **0577-841111;** www.fattoriadeibarbi.it), one of the most respected producers of Brunello, in the same family since the 16th century. Tours with free wine tastings are available Monday through Saturday hourly from 10am to noon and 3 to 5pm. The *taverna* restaurant (© **0577-841200**) serves up excellent country meals, with most products direct from the estate's farm (closed Wed–Thurs). Rustic accommodations at the inn will tempt you to stay on indefinitely.

From Siena, there are a dozen or so **Tra-in buses** to Montalcino (60–90 min., 3€/$3.45). Montalcino's **tourist office** is at Via Costa dei Municipio 8 (©/fax **0577-849331**), open Tuesday through Sunday from 10am to 1pm and 2 to 6pm.

PIENZA   This Renaissance jewel (24km/15 miles from Montalcino and 52km/32 miles from Siena) is easy to reach from Montalcino by public bus. But with just two or three bus departures from Siena and no trains, a rental car will make your life easier. Director Franco Zeffirelli found the perfect backdrop awaiting him here to film *Romeo and Juliet* in 1968, bypassing "fair Verona" as the obvious choice. Pienza was also used in the Oscar-winning epic *The English Patient.*

Pienza is most noteworthy as testament to the ego of a quintessential Renaissance man. Pope Pius II (of Siena's illustrious Piccolomini family) was born here in 1405 when it was called Corsignano. In 1459 (a year after becoming pope), he commissioned Florentine architect Bernardo Rossellino to level the medieval core of town and create the first stage of what would become the model High Renaissance city (he renamed it Pienza, in his own honor). The grand scheme didn't get very far (the pope died in 1464), but what was done remains now perfectly preserved (and protected by UNESCO)—just look at the graceful **Piazza Pio II**. Visit the piazza's **Palazzo Piccolomini** (the pope's private residence, lived in by descendents of the Piccolominis until 1968) and the **Duomo;** walk behind the Duomo for sweeping **views** of the dormant Mount Amiata and the wide Val d'Orcia. The piazza is also the location of the **tourist office** (©/fax **0578-749071**). Ask about the free guided tours of the town during summer. You can find more about the city online at **www.pienza.info**.

You can see most of the town, with a population of 2,500, in just half a day. It will take only 5 minutes to cover Pienza's main drag, **Corso Rossellino,** whose food stores specialize in the gourmet products from this bountiful corner of Tuscany, namely wines, honey, and its famous **pecorino cheese** ⊛ (also known as *cacio*). Cheese tasting is more popular than wine tasting here, and stores offer their varieties of *fresco* (fresh), *semistagionato* (partially aged), *pepperocinato* (dusted with hot peppers), or *tartufato* (embedded with truffles). Taste as much cheese as you will, but by all means save room for lunch at the town's well-known and reasonably priced **Dal Falco,** Piazza Dante Alghieri 7 (𝄢 0578-749856; fax 0578-748551; www.nautilus-mp.com/tuscany/affitti/falco), open Saturday through Thursday from noon to 2:45pm and 7 to 10pm (closed 10 days each in Feb, July, and Nov). A meal of homemade *pici* pasta and a delicious grilled meat will cost around 20€ ($23). Six simple doubles upstairs with private bathrooms and TVs (but no phones) are just 62€ ($71) per double, or 78€ ($90) for the family room that sleeps four.

AREZZO   Only 74km (46 miles) east of Siena and an easy 1-hour train trip from Florence (81km/50 miles), Arezzo boasts a lovely medieval demeanor that was introduced to the world as the backdrop for the first part of Tuscan native Roberto Benigni's Oscar-winning film *La Vita è Bella (Life Is Beautiful).* It's worth a day's stay for a meander through its medieval *centro storico* and a visit to Piero della Francesca's stunning fresco cycle, the **Legend of the True Cross** ⊛ (1452–66), in the 14th-century **San Francesco** church (𝄢 0575-20630) on Piazza San Francesco. In 2000, a hugely successful 15-year restoration to bring the frescoes back to colorful glory was completed—but now you've got to pony up 6€ ($6.90) to get in. Call 𝄢 0575-302001 for required reservations for the Piero cycle, or visit www.pierodellafrancesca.it. Twenty-five visitors are admitted at a time for 30-minute visits; you must collect your tickets 30 minutes prior to your entry.

Nearby is the wonderfully charming lopsided **Piazza Grande** ⊛, lined on one side by a loggia designed by local boy Giorgio Vasari, though all you get of the 12th-century **Santa Maria della Pieve** church is the apse end; for the stacked Lombard-Romanesque facade, you'll have to walk around to the Corso Italia side.

Arezzo is transported back to the Dark Ages with its much-felt historic **Giostra del Saracino (Saracen Joust)** ⊛, held in the off-kilter **Piazza Grande** the last Sunday in August and the first Sunday in September; for tickets, contact the tourist office (see below). If you can't get tickets for the joust itself, go for the elaborate *corteo* (procession) wending through the narrow cobblestone streets beforehand—the rich costumes and authentic armor (on knights and horses alike) are the result of meticulous archival research and the theatrical know-how of Tuscan-born Franco Zeffirelli. If you can time it right, Italy's best and largest **antiques fair** the first weekend of every month fills the main piazza.

Should you arrive in town and nothing much is happening, go for lunch or dinner at everyone's favorite trattoria in town, the **Antica Osteria L'Agania,** Via Mazzini 10, 2 blocks from San Francesco church (𝄢 0575-295381; www. osteriagania.it). It's open Tuesday through Sunday from noon to 3pm and 7 to 10:30pm. If it's full, you'll be happy next door at the **Trattoria del Saraceno,** no. 6 (𝄢 0575-27644), for a similarly casual ambience. It's open Thursday through Tuesday from noon to 4pm and 7 to 10pm. Arezzo's finest restaurant, the **Buca di San Francesco,** Via San Francesco 1 (𝄢 0575-23271; www. bucadisanfrancesco.it), is housed in the frescoed cellar of a 14th-century palazzo next door to the San Francesco church. It's a bit more expensive (average dinner is 20€–30€/$23–$35 without wine) and a lot more dramatic, and the traditional Tuscan menu is delicious. It's open Wednesday through Monday from noon to 3pm and Wednesday to Sunday from 7 to 10pm. The **tourist office** is at Piazza della Repubblica 22, just outside the train station (© **575-377678;** fax 575-20839; www.apt.arezzo.it). You can get to Arezzo **from Florence by train,** dozens daily, in 60 to 90 minutes. Coming **from Florence by bus** isn't as convenient: CAT buses take 80 minutes to 2 hours. A few LFI **buses leave Siena** daily (trip time: 1 hr. 30 min.—because it makes local stops).

6 Perugia: Capital of Umbria

80km (50 miles) SE of Arezzo, 188km (117 miles) NE of Rome, 154km (95 miles) SE of Florence, 26km (16 miles) NW of Assisi, 75km (47 miles) NE of Orvieto, 110km (68 miles) SE of Siena

Umbria is the "green heart of Italy" and **Perugia** its commercial and economic capital. Close your eyes to the charmless modern-day sprawl you pass through on your way into the elegant heart of the ancient city. Principally known today for its celebrated university and as home to Biuttoni and Perugina chocolate (now part of Nestlé), Perugia is a prosperous city dressed in medieval hill town clothing. It's a good base for travelers with and without cars who'd like to visit Umbria's many characteristic hill towns, like Assisi, Gubbio, and Spoleto and the ceramics town Deruta. Even Orvieto is a feasible day trip (about 81km/50 miles) for those with wheels. Perugia's historic center's cosmopolitan and urban bustle is a vibrant contrast to the rustic sleepiness of Umbria's hinterland for those inclined to venture afield.

If everyone you see seems to be 21 (and playing hooky), it's because, in addition to the ancient state university, one of Italy's largest, there's also a Università per Stranieri, the country's most prestigious school teaching the Italian language and culture to foreigners. Set up by Mussolini to improve the image of Italy abroad, it now enrolls more than 5,000 students representing more than 110 countries. This explains the proliferation of concerts, pizzerie, and music stores, as well as the air of energy and vitality that crescendos during the annual Umbria Jazz Festival, since 1973 one of Europe's foremost music events.

ESSENTIALS

GETTING THERE   By Train   Coming from **Rome,** there are five direct trains (www.trenitalia.com; 2½ hr.; 10€/$12) and about eight more requiring a transfer at either Foligno or Terontola. From **Florence,** seven trains go directly to Perugia, or you can take one of the dozen daily trains to Terontola/Cortona that meet up with a connecting train to Perugia (2–2¼ hr. total; 7.90€/$9.10). From **Assisi,** some 24 trains run direct daily (20 min.; 1.65€/$1.90). These lines are part of the FS state-run rail system and stop at the **Fontiveggie Station** on Piazza Vittorio Veneto, a 15-minute ride on bus nos. 15, 26, 27, 29, or 32 to 36 from Piazza Italia in the center of Perugia.

Perugia also sits on the privately run FCU (© **075-575401;** www.fcu.it) train line serving Umbria. Sixteen daily trains run north from Terni through **Todi** (35–45 min.; 4.40€/$5.05), pulling into the outlying Ponte San Giovanni Station (© **075-393615**), then chugging 8 minutes up a capillary line to the Santa Anna Station in town (© **075-5723947**), under the curve of Viale Roma under the Piazza Italia end of town. All outgoing trains depart first from the Santa Anna Station.

By Car   From Florence, take the A1 south to the Valdichiana exit and the SS75bis to Perugia. The SS326 also leads to this interchange from Siena. From Rome, exit the A1 north at Orte to take the SS204 to the SS3bis north. The SS3 and SS3bis cross at Perugia to connect with northern and southern Umbria. The center is closed to traffic, though you may drop off your baggage at your hotel.

Parking (© 075-5721938; www.sipaonline.it) is fairly abundant, with the most convenient being the underground pay lot at Piazza Partigiani, at .80€ (90¢) for the first hour and 1.05€ ($1.20) each subsequent hour; or you can *pay when you first arrive* at the special "tourist rate" 7.75€ ($8.90) per day for the first 2 days, then 5.20€ ($6) per each additional day (you get a temporary parking pass ticket that lets you come and go as you please). The lot is south of the city, but there's an underground escalator through the buried medieval city up to Piazza Italia. Two other pay lots are under the Mercato Coperto (elevator up to Piazza Matteotti) and at Pellini (escalator up to V. dei Priori). Below the latter is free parking on Piazza della Cupa, with an escalator up to Pellini.

By Bus   Only one daily SITA bus makes the trip from Florence (1¾ hr.; 10€/$12), and you must reserve a seat (© **800-373-760** in Italy, or 055-214721; www.sita-on-line.it). SULGA lines (© **800-099-661** in Italy, or 075-5009641; www.sulga.it) also has one bus daily from **Florence,** and four to five a day from **Rome** (2½ hr.; 9.80€/$11), some continuing on to Rome's airport (3¼ hr.; 17€/$20). APM (© **800-512-141** or 075-506781; www.apm perugia.it) buses connect Perugia with **Assisi** (six daily; 50 min.; 2.80€/$3.20) and **Gubbio** (8–11 daily; 80 min.; 3.60€/$4.15). The **bus depot** in Perugia is on Piazza Partigiani, an escalator ride below Piazza Italia. The stand there sells tickets for all lines.

VISITOR INFORMATION   The **tourist office** is at Piazza IV Novembre 3, to the right of the Palazzo dei Priori steps (© **075-5736458;** fax 075-5739386), open Monday through Saturday from 8:30am to 1:30pm and 3:30 to 6:30pm, and Sunday from 9am to 1pm. The website for all of Umbria is **www. umbria2000.it.** Pick up a copy of *Viva Perugia* (.50€/55¢) to find out what's going on around town (www.perugiaonline.com).

FESTIVALS & MARKETS   Perugia is something of a musical nucleus for central Italy. The fun starts with the rather tame **Rockin' Umbria** festival at the end of June. For information, contact ARCI-Perugia, Via della Viola 1 (© **075-5731074;** fax 075-5730616). It's followed by one of Europe's most important jazz festivals, **Umbria Jazz** ⚘⚘, which usually runs from mid-July to the beginning of August. The festival draws top international names to town for concerts, and instructors from Boston's prestigious Berklee School of Music hold seminars and workshops. It's so popular that a smaller version, **Umbria Jazz Winter,** takes place from December 29 to January 5. It includes a traditional New Year's Eve banquet and all-night jazz parties. For information, contact the Associazione Umbria Jazz–Perugia, Piazza Danti 28, Casella Postale 228 (© **075-5732432;** fax 075-5722656; www.umbriajazz.com).

During the second and third weeks of September, Perugini celebrate music of a different sort in the **Sagra Musicale Umbra,** an international festival of sacred music that has, since 1937, become one of the top musical events of its kind in Italy. For more information, contact the Associazione Sagra Musicale Umbra–Perugia, Via Podianai 11 (© **075-5721374;** fax 075-5727614; www.sagramusicaleumbra.com). The summer-long gig is rounded out the last week of September with **Perugia Classico,** a classical music festival that includes

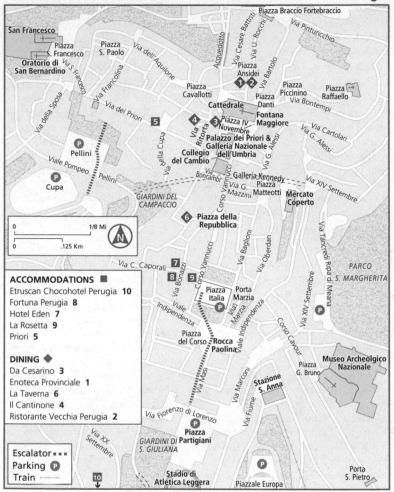

Piazza Braccio Fortebraccio

San Francesco

Piazza S. Francesco

Oratorio di San Bernardino

Via Cesare Battisti

Via Pinturicchio

Piazza Ansidei ❶ ❷

Piazza S. Paolo

Via dell'Aquilone

Acquedotto

Via U. Rocchi

Via Bartolo

Piazza Cavallotti

Piazza Piccinino

Piazza Raffaello

Via Bontempi

Via Francolina

Piazza Danti

Cattedrale

Fontana Maggiore

Piazza IV Novembre ❸

Via Cartolari

Via G. Alessi

Via dei Priori

Via della Sposa

❺

Della Cupa

Pellini

❹

Via Ritorta

Palazzo dei Priori & Galleria Nazionale dell'Umbria

Collegio del Cambio

Via G. Alessi

Viale Pompeo Pellini

Via Boncambi

Galleria Kennedy

Via G. Mazzini

Piazza Matteotti

Via XIV Settembre

Cupa

GIARDINI DEL CAMPACCIO

Corso Vannucci

Mercato Coperto

❻ Piazza della Repubblica

0   1/8 Mi
0   .125 Km
N

Via C. Caporali

Via Baglioni

Via Oberdan

PARCO S. MARGHERITA

❼
❽ Via Bonazzi ❾
Piazza Italia

Porta Marzia

Via Marzia

Via XIV Settembre

Via Tancredi Ripa di Meana

Viale Indipendenza

Corso Cavour

ACCOMMODATIONS ■
Etruscan Chocohotel Perugia **10**
Fortuna Perugia **8**
Hotel Eden **7**
La Rosetta **9**
Priori **5**

DINING ◆
Da Cesarino **3**
Enoteca Provinciale **1**
La Taverna **6**
Il Cantinone **4**
Ristorante Vecchia Perugia **2**

Piazza del Corso

Rocca Paolina

Via Masi

Via Marconi

Via Fiume

Stazione S. Anna

Piazza G. Bruno

Museo Archeolgico Nazionale

Escalator ••••
Parking Ⓟ
Train

Via XX Settembre

Via Fiorenzo di Lorenzo

GIARDINI DI S. GIULIANA

Piazza Partigiani

❿

Stadio di Atletica Leggera

Piazzale Europa

Porta S. Pietro

an antique-instrument market, concerts, shows, musical workshops, and chamber-music performances throughout town. Contact the Comitatio Promotore Perugia Classico, c/o Comune di Perugia, Ripartizione XVI Economia e Lavoro, Via Eburnea 9 (ⓒ **075-5772253;** fax 075-5772255; www.perugiaclassico.it).

The weeklong **Eurochocolate Festival** is held annually from mid- to late October in Perugia. Pick up a list of hour-by-hour festivities held throughout town, staged by chocolate manufacturers from all over the world. You can witness a chocolate-carving contest, when the scraps of 1,000-kilogram (2,205-lb.) blocks are yours for the sampling, and entire multiple-course menus are created around the chocolate theme. Half-day lessons from visiting chefs are also available. For details, contact the **Eurochocolate Organization,** Via D'Andreotto 19, 06124 Perugia (ⓒ **075-5732670;** fax 075-5731100; www.chocolate.perugia.it).

On July 29 and 30, the cathedral shows off the **marriage ring of the Virgin,** which 15th-century Perugini swiped from rival Chiusi. You might drop by town the last week of October for the **antiques market** held in the Rocca Paolina.

November 1 to November 5, the town holds secular celebrations for the **Fiera dei Morti** in honor of All Saints' Day (contact the *comune* at © 075-5773898). **Market days** are Tuesday and Saturday on Via Ercolane and Saturday at Pian di Massiano. There's also a daily covered market off Piazza Matteotti.

CITY LAYOUT   The main pedestrian thoroughfare is **Corso Vannucci,** lined with historic cafes, bars, the city's best stores, and palazzi, with narrow vaulted streets branching off west and east and invariably leading down, often with steps built into them. The corso is anchored on the north end by **Piazza IV Novembre** and the Fontana Maggiore, the city's social hub, with the Duomo just beyond it; and on the south end (after widening briefly into **Piazza della Repubblica**) by **Piazza Italia,** home to the shaded Giardini Carducci, with benches and a super view over the Tiber Valley. Beneath the gardens are the foundations of the 16th-century Rocca Paolina and the *scala mobile* network of escalators that bring you down through the ruins of the fortress to the town's lower level, main public parking lot, and long-distance bus station at Piazza Partigiani.

SIGHTS TO SEE

If ever there was a venue on which to see and be seen, it's Perugia's **Corso Vannucci,** the city's north-south pedestrian nerve center. Small clumps of the young and beautiful; people at tables collecting signatures supporting human rights, local politicians, or the cause of the moment; matrons with their dogs; pensioners with their cronies discussing soccer and union dues increases; cafe tables capturing the sun (or shade)—you'll find that and much more. Siena's major strip was named after Pietro Vannucci, better known as Perugino (1445–1523), Perugia's most celebrated local painter, whose works you can see in the National Gallery.

The **Fontana Maggiore (Great Fountain)** 𝕽𝕽 is the elaborately decorated two-tiered centerpiece of picturesque **Piazza IV Novembre.** The fountain resurfaced in 1999 from the glass-domed bubble that protected it during a 5-year renovation and once again gleams as the city's greatest artistic treasure. It was designed in 1278 by a local monk/architect, Fra Bevignate (known in his time for his involvement in the construction of Orvieto's Duomo), to commemorate the completion of the town's aqueduct. It was decorated with a lower tier of 50 bas-relief panels by Gothic master sculptor Nicola Pisano, already known for the pulpits commissioned for Siena's Duomo and his hometown of Pisa's baptistery; this was his last major work. The panels of the Fontana Maggiore depict everything from Aesop's fables and signs of the zodiac to episodes from Genesis and the origin of ancient Rome. The upper tier of 24 statuettes and panels is attributed to Nicola's son, Giovanni.

The plain-faced **Cattedrale (Cathedral)** to the north of the fountain was built after the fountain's completion. It was begun in 1347, and its external walls have been left in their uncompleted state. A number of 15th- and 16th-century paintings decorate the baroque interior, but the most curious item is the alleged wedding band of the Virgin Mary, displayed (though hidden within 15 boxes that graduate in size, each locked by a key kept under safekeeping with a different church official) in the **Cappella del Sant'Anello (Chapel of the Holy Ring),** the first chapel on the left.

Palazzo dei Priori & Galleria Nazionale dell'Umbria (National Gallery)

𝕽𝕽𝕽   The bulk of the impressive **Palazzo dei Priori (Priors' Palace)** lines the west side of Corso Vannucci, but its oldest facade presides over Piazza IV Novembre. From the 13th century, the pink-tinged facade is distinguished by a grand staircase (used by tired visitors and by students enjoying a social moment between classes) and bronze copies of the 13th-century griffin (the city symbol) and the Guelph (papal) lion holding the massive chains that were once used to close the city gates of Siena, taken from the town after a Perugian victory in 1358. It's crowned by a row of bristling crenellations above rows of Gothic windows. Used as the town hall for hundreds of years, the Palazzo dei Priori is one of the greatest extant examples of secular architecture from its period.

On the Corso Vannucci side is an entrance to the **Collegio del Cambio** (see below) and an entrance for the stairs to the fourth-floor **Galleria Nazionale,** which has just undergone an extensive renovation and reorganization. This showcase of Umbrian art traces the school's chronology from the 13th to the 18th centuries, as well as the schools that influenced it. The rooms dedicated to Tuscan masters like Duccio, Fra Angelico, and Piero della Francesca just about steal the show. But a dozen or so paintings by local celebrity Pietro Vannucci, alias Perugino, are the treasures, particularly his *Pietà* and late-15th-century *Adoration of the Magi.* Known for his gentle landscapes and as being the teacher of both Pinturicchio and Raphael, Perugino is one of the principal figures of the Italian Renaissance, certainly the most illustrious of the Umbrian school of painting. Others may contend that the deep colors of Pinturicchio— the one responsible for the Piccolomini Library in Siena's Duomo—demand their fair share of attention.

Other than very minor damage done to the Duomo, the Palazzo dei Priori absorbed the brunt of the 1997 serial earthquakes that shook Umbria and were felt marginally in Perugia (see the Assisi section following). The scaffolding is down, but the fissures in the palazzo's ancient facade remain, with massive steel bolts securing things, visible from both the outside and the inside.

Palazzo dei Priori, Corso Vannucci 19. (℗ **075-5741247.** www.gallerianazionaleumbria.it. Admission 6.50€ ($7.45). Daily 9am–7:30pm. Closed 1st Mon of every month. Bus: 4, 6, 7, 9, 10, 11, 12, 13s, 13d, 15, 81, 82, 83, 87.

Collegio del Cambio (Exchange Guild) & Collegio della Mercanzia (Merchants' Guild) ☆☆ The work of Perugino is the highlight of the small 15th-century **Collegio del Cambio,** the precursor of Perugia's commodities exchange. This was the seat of the Exchange Guild, whose affluent members chose Perugino, the finest artist of the time, to fresco their offices (1496–1500). These vibrant frescoes are his masterpieces—including scenes from the Bible, the prophets, and female figures representing the virtues—and a vivid depiction of late-15th-century fashion. Perugino didn't overlook his own self-portrait on a trompe-l'oeil column on the left wall as you enter. Pinturicchio and 17-year-old apprentice Raphael were said to have collaborated with him. The Exchange Guild's neighbors in the Merchant's Guild had their headquarters, the **Collegio della Mercanzia** (℗ **075-5730366**), decorated in the 15th century with carved woodwork on the walls and ceiling.

Palazzo dei Priori, Corso Vannucci 25. (℗ **075-5728599.** Admission to either 2.60€ ($3) adults, 1.60€ ($1.85) for those over 65, free for those under 12. Combined ticket for both: 3.10€ ($3.55) adults, 2.10€ ($2.40) for those over 65. Dec 20–Jan 6 Tues–Sat 9am–12:30pm and 2:30–5:30pm, Sun 9am–1pm; Mar 1–Oct 31 Mon–Sat 9am–12:30pm and 2:30–5:30pm, Sun 9am–1pm; Nov 1–Dec 19 and Jan 7–Feb 28 Tues–Sat 8am–2pm, Sun 9am–12:30pm. Bus: 4, 6, 7, 9, 10, 11, 12, 13s, 13d, 15, 81, 82, 83, 87.

Museo Storico di Perugina (Perugina Museum) *Kids* The Perugina chocolate industry is a Perugia success story. Founded in 1907 by two local families, it grew from strength to strength, heightened by the creation of the *bacio*

(kiss) candy in 1922. Then, of course, heartless chocogiant Nestlé came and bought the concern right out from under the Italians. It currently produces 200 million *baci* per year, to be found in stores worldwide (though the exported ones often lack the fortune cookie–style love-oriented quotes inside the wrapper). A popular runner-up in popularity is the gaily wrapped Easter eggs that are as much a tradition as the holiday itself. Opened in 1997 for the 90th anniversary of the manufacturer, the Perugina Museum explores the long history of the trademark. Sadly, visits to the factory floor are for school groups only, but if you visit you get to see a yummy video on chocolate making and (the entire reason to schlep out here, really) receive free samples. You can buy Perugina goodies in just about any bar/cafe, though there's no Perugina outlet per se. A well-stocked choice is always the Caffè del Cambio (see "Great Deals on Dining," below), any of the other bar/cafes on Corso Vannucci, or the Perugina store on the east side of Piazza Italia.

Località San Sisto, Nestlé Italiana. ℂ 075-5276796. Free admission. Mon–Fri 9am–12:30pm and 2:30–5:30pm; Sat by appointment.

ACCOMMODATIONS YOU CAN AFFORD

Promhotel Umbria is a local travel agency that can book you into one of more than 80 hotels in Perugia and throughout Umbria (ℂ 0678-62033 toll free in Italy, or 075-5002788; fax 075-5002789; promhotelumbria@krenet.it).

Also note that the **Hotel Eden,** Via Cesare Caporali 9, west off Piazza Italia, 06123 Perugia (ℂ 075-5728102; fax 075-5720342), offers 20 contemporary rooms with TVs and phones for 36€ ($41) single and 57€ ($66) double (breakfast 5€/$5.75 extra per person). And at the **Etruscan Chocohotel Perugia,** Via Campo di Marte 134, 06123 Perugia (ℂ/fax 075-5837314; www.chocohotel.it), all 94 air-conditioned rooms have modern Italian-style furniture and large bathrooms. The real draw, though, is staying in a "chocohotel": Each floor is dedicated to a type of chocolate (milk, dark, gianduia), and each room has a "chocodesk." The restaurant features a cocoa-based menu, and in the chocostore you can sample many concoctions. Nonchocolate amenities include a large roof deck with a panoramic view and a good-size pool. Rates are 54€ to 80€ ($62–$92) single and 88€ to 140€ ($101–$161) double, and there's free parking.

Fortuna Perugia　The charming Fortuna offers four-star accommodations at three-star rates. Beveled- and leaded-glass doors welcome you to this hotel, where thoughtful service and details like silk- and dried-flower arrangements and white-lace doilies hint at a provincial inn. The coziness continues in most of the rooms, where a contemporary character prevails despite the floral bedspreads and upholstery and blond-wood headboards and tables. New management took over in 1998, and work is being done here and there—during which time they discovered 18th-century frescoes on the third floor, making room no. 309 highly requested. For the guests who don't snag it, there's always the frescoed salon with a Murano chandelier—or room nos. 408, 501, and 502, which require climbing a short flight of stairs but reward you with great countryside panoramas. Other rooms have views over the rooftops or the Umbrian valley, and 14 new rooms were recently added. In warm weather, breakfast is served on the roof garden/terrace with stunning vistas; your cappuccino will never taste this good again.

Via Bonazzi 19 (west of Piazza Italia), 06123 Perugia. ℂ 075-5722845. Fax 075-5735040. www.umbria hotels.com. 45 units. 67€–86€ ($77–$99) single; 97€–124€ ($112–$145) double; 140€–160€ ($161–$184) executive suite. Rates include buffet breakfast. DC, MC, V. Parking free on the street (ask for a permit) or 20€ ($23) per day in nearby garage. **Amenities:** Bar; golf nearby; concierge; room service (breakfast); babysitting (on request); laundry service. *In room:* A/C, TV, dataport (in some), minibar, hair dryer, safe.

La Rosetta ⟨ This favorite of the international music crowd that descends for the Umbria Jazz Festival began as a small inn in 1927 and has gradually expanded, explaining its almost labyrinthine layout and the variety in the quality and decor of the rooms, which were renovated in 2003. Some are done in a late-18th-century style, quite grand with parquet floors and frescoed ceilings; others are carpeted and more modest, the contemporary furnishings' Deco touches harking back to the hotel's 1920s origins. All rooms are peaceful and well maintained, and the rates are actually rather low for a four-star hotel. An accommodating staff and perfect location augment its appeal, with an excellent (though slightly expensive) restaurant (open daily for lunch and dinner). Huge room no. 55, with a spectacular trompe-l'oeil frescoed ceiling vault and view into the medieval courtyard (beware noisy guests returning late), carries a special splurge price tag of 182€ ($209).

Piazza Italia 19, 06121 Perugia. ⟨/fax **075-5720841**. www.perugiaonline.com/larosetta. 90 units. 79€ ($91) single; 120€–168€ ($138–$193) double. Ask for discounts for longer stays. Rates include buffet breakfast. AE, DC, MC, V. Parking 15€ ($17) in garage. **Amenities:** Restaurant; concierge; tour desk; car-rental desk; limited room service; babysitting; laundry service; dry cleaning. *In room:* A/C (on top floor), TV, dataport, minibar, coffee maker, hair dryer, safe.

Priori ⟨ (Value Three short blocks down Via dei Priori and behind the Palazzo dei Priori, this modernized hotel still enjoys the fruits of a 1995 renovation. Half the spacious rooms with terra-cotta floors overlook San Filippo Neri; the lucky ones overlook the hotel terrace and the valley beyond. The terrace is surprisingly spacious, given the typical hill-town problems of limited space. When weather permits, breakfast here beneath the white canvas umbrellas. A new annex in an adjoining historic palazzo means three new apartments are also available (call for rates).

Via Vermiglioli 3 (at V. dei Priori), 06123 Perugia. ⟨ **075-5729155**. Fax 075-5723213. www.hotelpriori.it. 57 units. 48€–66€ ($55–$76) single; 68€–91€ ($78–$105) double; 100€–140€ ($115–$161) suite. Ask about discounts during slow periods. Rates include buffet breakfast. MC, V. Parking 10€–15€ ($13–$17) in garage. **Amenities:** Bar; concierge; tour desk; car-rental desk; room service (breakfast only); babysitting; laundry service; dry cleaning. *In room:* A/C, TV, hair dryer (on request).

GREAT DEALS ON DINING

In addition to the restaurants below, stop by some of the lovely local cafes, such as the **Caffè Sandri,** Corso Vannucci 32; **Caffè Ferrari,** Corso Vannucci 43; and **Caffè del Cambio,** Corso Vannucci 29. They're all reasonably priced central spots for a light lunch, offering sandwiches and even primi for 3€ to 10€ ($3.45–$12) at the bar or at tables indoors and out. Caffè Sandri is the local favorite, small but rich with atmosphere, its wood-paneled 19th-century interior cramped but cozy. It quadruples in seating capacity when warm weather permits it to set up outdoor tables in the middle of the corso's pedestrian catwalk. The hot meeting spot in town, the **Caffè di Perugia,** Via Mazzini 10–14, off the Corso Vannucci, is elegantly housed in a medieval palazzo, comfortably looking like it has always been there. Fixed-price lunches include a primo plus vegetable side dish (9€/$10), or spend half that for a sandwich and drink at the busy bar.

Food fans should make sure to have at least one casual meal at the **Enoteca Provinciale,** Via Ulisse Rocchi 18 (⟨ **075-5724824**), where substantial bruschette and platters of salads or regional cheeses and salami are just a savory side; the draw here is the 5 to 10 red and white regional wines available by the glass in a beautifully restored 13th-century palazzo. It's open Monday through Saturday from 10am to 9:30pm, and Sunday from 10am to 3pm.

Da Cesarino ⭐ UMBRIAN   Cesarino's location is easy to find on the piazza anchored by the Fontana Maggiore, with the preferred outdoor tables offering a view of this most characteristic corner of time-locked Perugia. The cooking is a hats-off salute to the bounty and wonder of simple home-style cooking—traditional *cucina umbra* at its best. Whatever today's special pasta is, order it. If you eat indoors, you'll be privy to free cooking lessons if you're seated near the open kitchen where white-capped signoras roll out fresh pasta while a white-aproned man tends to the open hearth and its crackling and sizzling meats on a spit.

Piazza IV Novembre 4–5 (west of the Fontana Maggiore). © 075-5728974. Reservations recommended. Primi 7€–11€ ($8.05–$13); secondi 9€–20€ ($10–$23). AE, DC, MC, V. Thurs–Tues 12:30–3pm and 7:30–11pm.

Il Cantinone *(Value* UMBRIAN   If you're in search of something casual and inexpensive in the area of Corso Vannucci or Piazza IV Novembre, wander down the narrow street west of the Fontana Maggiore and, where the pedestrian traffic flows right, look to the left, where you'll find this popular pizzeria in a cool brick-vaulted medieval setting. Despite its central location, the prices are kept moderate while the lure of their pizzas (evenings only) keeps the place full. There's a full menu of local specialties as well, though the steady patrons are pizza devotees who return for the *pizza alla Gorgonzola e porcini* (made with Gorgonzola and mushrooms) or any one of the dozens of others. There's even a nonsmoking room.

Via Ritorta 4–8 (near the Duomo). © 075-5734430. Reservations recommended. Primi 6€–8€ ($6.90–$9.20); secondi 6€–15€ ($6.90–$17); pizza 4€–6.50€ ($4.60–$7.45). AE, DC, MC, V. Wed–Mon 12:30–2:30pm and 7:30–11pm. Closed Dec 22–Jan 5.

La Taverna ⭐⭐ CREATIVE UMBRIAN   The location of this eatery in the cantina of a 14th-century palazzo, reached via a dark-stepped alley curiously called the Street of the Witches, is too much to resist. Surprisingly, the space is bright and welcoming, even elegant, with waiters in jackets and white ankle-length aprons hovering over candlelit tables beneath high barrel-vaulted brick ceilings. The menu is as traditional as it is innovative, the latter half hinting at the Umbrian chef's experience abroad—in Florida, no less. The trappings of La Taverna (and the owner did just upgrade his porcelain and crystal) may strike you as a splurge choice, but unless you let loose with any of the discerning wine list's better options and overindulge in the justifiably well-known dessert cart, the cost of a lovely and romantic dinner here needn't set you back.

Via delle Streghe 8 (near Corso Vannucci's Piazza Repubblica). © 075-5724128. Reservations recommended. Primi 5.25€–12€ ($6–$14); secondi 10€–15€ ($12–$17). AE, DC, MC, V. Tues–Sun 12:30–2:30pm and 7:30–11:30pm.

Ristorante Vecchia Perusia UMBRIAN   There are just 10 tables in this homey trattoria where the aroma from the open kitchen is enough to make you order one of everything. If you don't have an Umbrian grandmother, come here for the genuine *cucina umbra* you've been missing (though not Grandma's smile; the service leaves *much* to be desired). Every day a new *pasta fresca* appears (look for the *tagliatelle con porcini freschi,* made with fresh mushrooms), but happy habitués seem to go with the *crepe alla perusia* (crepes spread with four cheeses and ham, rolled, smothered with mushroom-cream sauce, and baked). The menu also offers traditional Umbrian game (*faraona*/pheasant, *coniglio*/rabbit) and the simplicity of a grilled pork or veal chop.

Via Ulisse Rocchi 9 (north of Piazza IV Novembre), Perugia. © 075-5725900. Reservations suggested. Primi 6€–8€ ($6.90–$9.20); secondi 9€–12€ ($10–$14). MC, V. Mon–Sat 12:30–2:30pm and 7–11pm.

A SIDE TRIP FOR CERAMICS

Known since the Middle Ages as a ceramic center, the tiny town of **Deruta** lies 20km (12 miles) south of Perugia by car (or take the S3 bus; there are a few daily 30-min. buses but no train service—check at Perugia's tourist office for the schedule, and be sure not to miss the last bus back). Deruta's embarrassment of choices can be mind boggling, for you'll find store after store, particularly along Via Tiberina.

My favorites are the traditionalists **Deruta Placens,** with shops at Via B. Michelotti 25 (① **075-972277**) and Via Umberto I 16 (① **075-9724027**); and **Ceramiche Miriam,** where at Marcella Favaroni's Via Umberto I 15 shop (① **075-9711452**) she paints vividly colorful and intricate patterns at half the prices most shops charge. Her husband's shop at Piazza dei Consoli 26 (① **075-9711210**) carries more traditional pieces and quality Renaissance reproductions.

The **Museo Regionale della Ceramica (Regional Museum of Ceramics),** Largo San Francesco (① **075-9711000;** www.museoceramicaderuta.it), houses a precious collection of Deruta ceramics from the Middle Ages to the 1930s. It's open daily from 10am to 1pm and 3:30 to 7pm (check for shorter hours off season). Admission varies—a near-constant string of temporary exhibits alter the price—and can range from 2.60€ to 6€ ($3–$6.90).

7 Assisi & the Basilica di San Francesco

190km (118 miles) SE of Florence, 26km (16 miles) SE of Perugia, 177km (110 miles) NE of Rome, 48km (30 miles) N of Spoleto

More than 700 years—and countless billions of pilgrims and tourists—have passed since St. Francis lived and died in the small hill town of **Assisi,** with its muted pink-and-white stone, sitting on the wooded slopes of Mount Subasio. It's Umbria's most visited city and yet, despite the mania of shops selling St. Francis everything—from ashtrays and pot holders to embroidered tea towels and glow-in-the-dark rosary beads—the spirit of the young barefoot monk who forsook these very material goods to preach poverty, chastity, and obedience lives on. His spirit may seem diminished at times when unparalleled crowds and heat reach their peak, but it's easy to find again, in a quiet moment at the saint's crypt below the Lower Basilica or during a delightful walk to the shaded serenity of the unspoiled hermitage outside the city's medieval walls. The universality of his humanity and love for nature and the animal kingdom transcends all nationalities and religions, and Francis is often held as a medieval flower child, an environmentalist of the Middle Ages who wrote the first poems in the Italian language. If the church had to create a figure who would endure the last millennium and go forward bravely into the next and be embraced by so many, it couldn't have outdone this disarmingly simple character who lived to love God and all those who inhabited this planet—a welcome departure from the doom-and-gloom strictures of the Dark Ages.

Born in 1182 to a local well-to-do family of textile merchants, Francis renounced his social status and youthful carousing only after a number of apparitions and visions. He traveled on foot through Italy, Spain, and Egypt, a revolutionary spirit who took the Roman Catholic church back to the basics when the papacy was rotten with corruption. Dante compared him to John the Baptist; his fame grew quickly beyond the confines of Umbria and even Italy. In 1210, he founded an order of mendicant monks that became known thereafter as the Franciscans. Within 15 years, a growing community of 5,000 followed the

barefoot asceticism of *Il Poverello* (the Poor One), and he enjoyed great venera-
tion and acceptance in his lifetime. In 1224, he was the first ever to receive the
"stigmata" wounds in his hands, feet, and side at a hilltop retreat in Tuscany
called La Verna—mirroring the same wounds inflicted on Jesus Christ during
his Crucifixion. His friendship with the lovely Chiara (Clare), a local girl of a
minor noble family who followed him, would soon be followed by her founding of the Second Order of St. Francis, the nuns known as the Sorelle Clarisse,
the Poor Sisters of St. Clare (more simply known as the Poor Clares). This happened in 1212 when Clare was just 17. Together Francis and Clare pushed this
sleepy Umbrian town onto the church's center stage, where it has remained ever
since. Today the Franciscans form the largest of all Catholic monastic orders.

St. Francis's spirit somehow survives the unashamed commercialization of the
town. Young groups of Italian and European students who come for seminars;
art lovers who descend on the Basilica of St. Francis for its glorious frescoes by
Giotto, Cimabue, Simone Martini, and the Lorenzetti; and pilgrims from the
Earth's four corners who come to pay homage to one of the holiest men to have
walked this planet find in these narrow back streets something of the town as it
was in the saint's own time. As a former Roman stronghold, Assisi reached its
medieval zenith in the years surrounding the lives of Francis and Clare. Much of
what you see today is true to its 13th-century origins, and the city, with its patrician palazzi made of a local pink-tinged stone, is handsomely preserved.

Atheists, agnostics, and devotees alike continue to visit Assisi as a site of pilgrimage, artistic appreciation, and cultural curiosity; during peak months, numbers are legion. Moderately priced accommodations are very good (and the
restaurants serving Umbrian specialties even better) and numerous, but booking
ahead during busy months is almost obligatory. Things quiet down in the
evening—the majority of pilgrims and religious groups usually lodge outside
town in the larger roadside hotels—but you may want to move on after a day or
two spent seeing the sites.

ESSENTIALS

GETTING THERE   By Train   From **Perugia** there are about 20 trains
(www.trenitalia.com) daily (20–30 min.; 1.65€/$1.90). From **Florence** there
are five daily Rome-bound trains, from which you transfer at Terontola/Cortona
for Assisi (2–3 hr. traveling time, often with long layovers; 9€/$10). There are
also seven direct trains from Florence (2 hr.; 17€/$19). Coming from **Rome,**
three trains go to Assisi directly and eight daily trains make the connection
through Foligno (1¾–3 hr. total; 9€–14€/$10–$17).

The **station** (① 075-8040272) is in the modern valley town of Santa Maria
degli Angeli, about 5km (3 miles) from Assisi, with bus connections (bus C) to
Assisi every 20 minutes (.80€/90¢); or you can take a **taxi** (① 075-8040275)
for about 10€ to 12€ ($12–$14).

By Bus   Eight **APM/Sit** buses (① **800-512-141** in Italy, or 075-506781;
www.apmperugia.it) run daily from **Perugia** (1 hr.; 2.80€/$3.20); about five
buses run from **Gubbio** (1 hr.; 4.80€/$5.50). **Sulga** (① **075-5009641;**
www.sulga.it) runs two buses daily from **Rome**'s Tiburtina Station (3 hr.;
11€/$13), and one daily from Piazza Adua in **Florence** (2½ hr.;
9.80€–11€/$11–$13). In Assisi, you can get tickets at any *tabacchi* or at the
tourist office. Most buses leave Assisi from Piazza Matteotti, northeast of Piazza
del Comune, though most also pass by the lower half of Piazza San Pietro (at the
bottom of the big traffic curve) at the other end of town.

Assisi

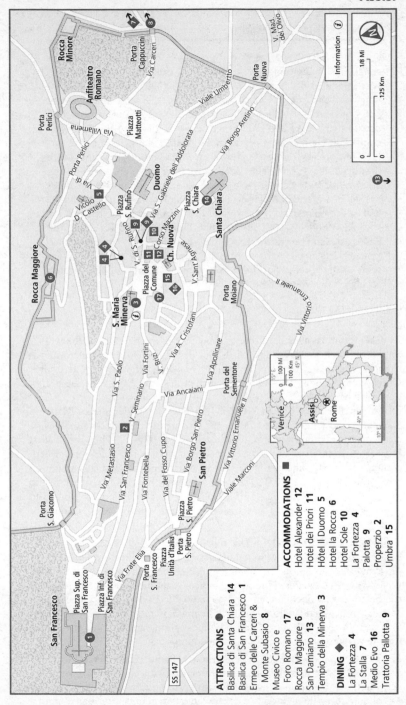

SS 147

ATTRACTIONS ●
Basilica di Santa Chiara **14**
Basilica di San Francesco **1**
Ermeo delle Carceri &
  Monte Subasio **8**
Museo Civico e
  Foro Romano **17**
Rocca Maggiore **6**
San Damiano **13**
Tempio della Minerva **3**

DINING ◆
La Fortezza **4**
La Stalla **7**
Medio Evo **16**
Trattoria Pallotta **9**

ACCOMMODATIONS ■
Hotel Alexander **12**
Hotel dei Priori **11**
Hôtel Il Duomo **5**
Hotel la Rocca **6**
Hotel Sole **10**
La Fortezza **4**
Palotta **9**
Properzio **2**
Umbra **15**

Umbria's Quake Damage

On September 26, 1997, serial earthquakes (5.7 and 5.6 on the Richter scale) with the epicenter just outside Assisi violently shook this otherwise serene corner of Umbria. More than 13,000 Umbrians were left homeless, and the structure that sustained the most damage was Assisi's crown jewel, the Basilica di San Francesco. During a second quake, two monks and two inspectors were killed by the 2 tons of debris that crashed from the basilica's vaulted ceiling, and entire sections of priceless frescoes—some of the world's most important—were destroyed. Pope John Paul visited in January 1998, encouraging the area's residents to bear up "in a Franciscan spirit" and heal the wounds of their hearts and of their homeland. Repair work began immediately and was completed fairly quickly, although you'll continue to see some scaffolded buildings throughout Umbria in the years to come. The Basilica di San Francesco actually managed to reopen for the Jubilee Year 2000 (a minor miracle in itself), with the only major "victims" some of the lesser ceiling frescoes by Cimabue—almost all of Giotto's fabulous work was saved.

By Car   From Perugia, head southeast on SS3; at the junction of Route 147, follow signs east for Assisi. It's a half-hour drive. The entire historic center is closed to traffic, but traffic police will let you drop off your bags at a hotel. Check with the hotel for special agreements they may have with the nearest municipal parking lot.

You can **park** (✆ **075-813707**) in the huge lot under Piazza Matteotti ("Parcheggio C"; ✆ **075-815164**) on the town's eastern edge; on Piazza Unità d'Italia outside Porta San Pietro ("Parcheggio A"; ✆ **075-815311**), the smallest but nearest to the Basilica di San Francesco; or outside the walls' southeastern corner at Porta Moianbo and Porta Nuova ("Parcheggio B," with an elevator up into town; ✆ **075-813707**). These are all pay-by-the-hour lots that fill up quickly in summer. Rates are 1.15€ ($1.30) per hour, but if you're staying in an Assisi hotel, they'll give you an **Assisicard** that lets you park for 24 hours for 12€ ($14).

VISITOR INFORMATION   The **tourist office** (✆ **075-812534** or 075-812450; fax 075-813727; www.umbria2000.it) has been hopscotched around to different offices on Piazza del Comune ever since the quake. Ask about its list of *Case Religiose di Ospitalità,* 17 local religious convents, monasteries, and religious-run hostelries that offer doubles for 25€ to 60€ ($29–$69). The office is open Monday through Friday from 8am to 2pm and 3:30 to 6:30pm, Saturday from 9am to 1pm and 3:30 to 6:30pm, and Sunday from 9am to 1pm. The private website **www.assisionline.com** also has good information.

FESTIVALS & MARKETS   The **Settimana Santa (Holy Week)** that precedes Easter is understandably commemorated with numerous processions between churches, including evocative night processions by torchlight. The feast day of the **Calendimaggio** ✿ is the year's largest event and is celebrated during a 3-day period the first week of May (starting the first Thurs after May 1). The entire town turns out in elaborate medieval costume to reenact the rivalry between two upper and lower factions of town that can be traced back to the 1300s; there are competitions of concerts, crossbows, and flag throwing, to name a few. Call the tourist office for more information.

Oddly, **San Rufino** (after whom the Duomo is named) and not St. Francis is the patron saint of Assisi, and his feast day is celebrated on August 11 with a procession and crossbow contest in medieval costume. It's followed by the feast day of **Santa Chiara (St. Clare)** on August 12. On October 3 and 4, the **Festa di San Francesco** commemorates the saint's death; as patron saint of Italy, St. Francis is duly honored with great pageantry.

The yearly **Assisi Antiquariato antiques fair** is held for 2 weeks at the end of April and the beginning of May in the suburb of Bastia. A **weekly market** fills Piazza Matteotti every Saturday morning.

EXPLORING ASSISI

Mount Subasio is a protected regional park offering an extensive network of footpaths that attracts do-it-yourself trekkers and mountain bikers. A map called *Sentieri di Mt. Subasio* (Footpaths of Mount Subasio) is sometimes available at the tourist office. If it's out of stock, look for two alternatives usually on sale in local shops: the map put out by **C.A.I.** (Club Alpino Italiano) or the map put out by **Kompass.** Half-hearted walkers who are happy with a brisk amble but nothing more taxing should consider the Ermeo delle Carceri (see below).

Piazza del Comune is the heart of Assisi, and much of what you see dates from the 12th to the 14th centuries and the very days of economic prosperity eschewed by Francis and Clare. Its most ancient component is the white **Tempio della Minerva (Temple of Minerva)** ☆☆, the majestic Corinthian-columned temple on its north side that dates as far back as the 1st century B.C. It is considered so perfect in classical design and proportion, "one could never stop looking at its facade," wrote an enthralled Goethe during his 18th-century Italian journey. Its most recent reincarnation is as a baroque church that provides, at most, a pew and a cool moment for reflection.

Beneath the flagstoned piazza, and unbeknownst to the flocks of tourists that fill it, sit the remains of the ancient Roman Forum. Glimpses of its ongoing renovation are part of the draw of the generally overlooked **Museo Civico e Foro Romano (Civic Museum and Roman Forum),** entrance on Via Portica off the western edge of Piazza del Comune (✆ **075-813053;** www.sistemamuseo.it), and its collection of Etruscan and Roman artifacts; admission is 2.50€ ($2.85) for adults and 2€ ($2.30) for children under 18 and seniors over 65. Year-round, the museum is open in the mornings daily from 10am to 1pm; afternoon hours, though daily, vary according to the season. From March 16 through June and from September through October 15, it's open from 2 to 6pm; from July through August, the museum is open from 2:30 to 7pm; and from October 16 through March 15, it's open from 2 to 5pm.

A Church Warning

With the exception of the Basilica di San Francesco, all **churches** in Assisi are open from 7am to noon and 2pm to sunset. The basilicas of San Francesco and Santa Chiara have a strict **dress code;** entrance is forbidden to those showing bare knees, shoulders, or midriffs (so no shorts, miniskirts, or sleeveless shirts).

Basilica di San Francesco (Basilica of St. Francis)   Shored up and extending from the western end of town, the Basilica of St. Francis is the first thing you see on approaching this pink-hued hill town. It was a massive architectural feat and is still one of the engineering marvels and most outstanding monuments to art and faith of the medieval period in the Western world. If you haven't pinpointed what bothers you about it, it most likely is what has bothered the Franciscan religious community for centuries: The commanding figure cut by the two-tiered basilica has little, if nothing, to do with the vows of utter poverty and humility and stark asceticism that were the tenets of St. Francis's back-to-basics life. This may hardly be the Vatican's lavish display of extravagance, but it's nevertheless disheartening to know that Brother Elias of Cortona, one of Francis's earliest disciples and the controversial monk who firmly took control in the years following Francis's death in 1226 (he was canonized almost immediately in 1228), cashed in on the saint's popularity by selling indulgences across Europe. (Brother Leone, who sympathized with Il Poverello's beliefs, futilely argued that Francis would be horrified.) Elias's fund-raising resulted in the building of this impious monument to wealth and importance, a point of international Catholic pilgrimage seconded by Rome and Bethlehem alone. It was therefore especially devastating that the basilica (particularly the Upper Basilica) was the structure that suffered the most damage during the 1997 earthquakes and that it was within the church that the region's only deaths occurred (two friars accompanying two local officials who had come to survey the damage). During the unexpected second earthquake, the Upper Basilica's vaulted ceilings collapsed and more than 2 tons of debris rained down, priceless 700-year-old frescoes included. You may have seen it on television during coverage of the earthquakes; the video equipment used by the officials actually captured the ceiling's collapse—and their deaths.

LOWER BASILICA   The Lower (and slightly older) Basilica was speedily reopened after the earthquakes, its damage only marginal by comparison. Reached by the entrance in Piazza Inferiore di San Francesco on the south side of the church, the Lower Basilica is low, dark, and mystical—if you're lucky enough to find a moment of calm in between the arrival of fender-to-fender tour buses—and almost entirely covered with frescoes by the greatest pre-Renaissance painters of the 13th and 14th centuries. The **Cappella di San Martino** *✿* (first chapel on the left), dedicated to St. Martin of Tours, the father of monasticism in 4th-century France, is covered with early-14th-century frescoes by the important Simone Martini of Siena. The earliest and one of the most prominent artists to work in the church was Cimabue (1240–1302), whose frescoes in the transept are some of the most important here. To the right of the main altar, his faded but masterful *Madonna, Child and Angels* *✿* (also known as the *Maestà*) includes St. Francis looking on, the popular depiction of him you'll see duplicated endless times around town. Below Cimabue's paintings are the tombs of five of Francis's original followers.

Across the transept to the left of the altar is a cycle of frescoes surrounding the *Deposition of the Cross,* one of the masterpieces of Tuscan painter Pietro Lorenzetti, a contemporary of Simone Martini from Siena. But the frescoes creating one of art history's greatest controversies are those attributed to Cimabue's most famous student, Giotto (1226–1337)—both Cimabue and Giotto worked extensively in the Upper Basilica as well. In the early 1900s, most art historians had decided it was nameless followers or fellow apprentices of Giotto, and not the master himself, who had covered much of both basilicas with cycles of frescoes. His work, they believed, was far too mature for the 20-something student who hadn't yet proven himself in his epochal work covering Perugia's Arena Chapel; these frescoes depicted an expression and emotion that broke with the static icons of the rigid Byzantine school and heralded the onset of the Renaissance. The 1995 completion of the restoration of the **Cappella della Maddalena (Chapel of St. Mary Magdalen)**, the third and final chapel to the right of the nave close to the altar, confirmed Giotto's authorship (1307) in the eyes of many Italian scholars. To keep everyone happy, authorship is still attributed to "Giotto and workshop." The friars sing vespers in the Lower Basilica Monday through Saturday, at 5pm in summer and 6pm in winter.

CRYPT   From the Lower Basilica halfway up the nave, you can reach the crypt (free admission), where the saint's body wasn't discovered until 1818. A new and typically simple stone tomb was built in the early 1900s. Four of his closest followers are buried with St. Francis.

TESORO (TREASURY) & COLLEZIONE PERKINS (PERKINS COLLECTION)   From another entrance in the Lower Basilica (behind the main altar to the right), you can reach this collection, where glass cases display the likes of chalices and silver objects, but of most note are the saint's original gray patchwork sackcloth (the brown tunic was adopted by the order much later), the white tunic worn by him during the last year of his life, a knotted rope belt, and worn slippers. On a more somber note is the stone upon which he rested his head in his coffin and the suede cloth used to cover his stigmata. The Perkins Collection is a small but rich collection bequeathed by an American philanthropist with some surprisingly important Tuscan Renaissance artworks.

UPPER BASILICA   From the south transept of the Lower Basilica, stairs lead to the Upper Basilica (1230–53), built on the Romanesque framework of the lower church. Where the lower spaces encouraged awe, contemplation, and meditation, the upper reaches of the airy Gothic basilica are another experience entirely. Tall, bathed in light, it was meant to be, it would seem, the blank canvas on which Giotto was to create the masterpiece frescoes depicting *The Life of St. Francis* ✪ (1296–1304). These highlights of the basilica generally escaped the earthquakes' wrath intact. Twenty-eight scenes (the last four not attributed to Giotto) unfold left to right beginning in the transept. One of the most famous and charming of panels is the *Sermon to the Birds* found on the entrance wall, underlining the saint's tenet that all nature is the reflection of God. In many of the narrations, you'll see medieval Assisi illustrated much as you see it now, starting with the first panel's *Homage in Piazza del Comune*.

Giotto was believed to be just 29 when he began this cycle of frescoes, already a longtime lay follower of St. Francis. He seemed to particularly embrace the message of St. Francis, whose love of man and warmth of expression is reflected in Giotto's radical break from the lifeless images of the Byzantines' icons. The single undivided nave was meant to accommodate the masses, and Giotto's extensive pictorial narrations were meant to educate them about Assisi's native son while attempting to express his love for nature and humanity. Francis broke with the traditional excesses of the medieval papacy as Giotto revolutionized the art world with his break from the lifeless Byzantine order. Other highlights are the 15th-century **choir,** made of 105 inlaid stalls. The choir's central "throne" was reserved for the pope, the only papal throne outside St. Peter's. Located behind and above the throne in the left transept are time- (and not earthquake-) damaged cycles by Cimabue dominated by his dramatic *Crucifixion* ⚜, the pigments oxidized by time into a sort of photonegative fresco.

Piazza Superiore di San Francesco/Piazza Inferiore di San Francesco. ℂ 075-819001. www.sanfrancesco assisi.org. Admission: Basilica free; treasury and Perkins Collection 1.55€ ($1.80), free for under 18. Lower church daily 6:30am–7pm; upper church daily 8:30am–7pm; treasury and Perkins Collection Easter to Oct Mon–Sat 9:30am–noon and 2:30–6pm. You may visit church for Mass on Sun morning (before 2pm), but tourist visits at this time are frowned on.

Ermeo delle Carceri & Monte Subasio ⚜ *Moments*   St. Francis and his followers spiritually "imprisoned" themselves in prayer at this isolated retreat on the ilex- and oak-wooded slope of Monte Subasio. They lived in tiny *carceri* (cells) naturally carved out of the stone centuries before the extant friary was built. A timeworn holm oak, thought to be at least 1,000 years old, still stands supported by metal crutches near the saint's cave where he meditated and prayed. The gnarled tree is said to have shaded Francis and the birds that gathered to listen to his sermons; they once flew off in the four cardinal directions, symbolizing how the Franciscans would one day leave Assisi to bring the word of Francis to all corners of the world.

Leave behind the crowds in the basilica and the town's tourist shops; it's an easy 1-hour walk from the town's eastern gate, the Porta Cappuccini (leaving from the Rocca Minore north of the Porta isn't recommended, as the pathway isn't as clearly marked), on a signposted paved road past cypresses and with wide-open views used by pedestrians and cars. A handful of friars still live at the retreat established by St. Bernard of Siena (who lived here after Francis, 1438–40) and act as guides; a donation is appreciated, as the friars live by alms alone. A visit here better conveys the spirit and serenity of St. Francis than the cavernous basilica built by his followers.

Via Ermeo delle Carceri (4km/2½ miles from Porta Cappuccini). ℂ 075-812301. Free admission. Ermeo delle Carceri daily 6:30am–7pm. Walk or take a taxi from Piazza Santa Chiara for 9€–11€.

Basilica di Santa Chiara ⚜   St. Clare died surrounded by her nascent following of nuns in the Convent of San Damiano down below on August 12, 1253; just 12 years later, this pink-and-white basilica made from local marble was dedicated to her and became the home of the Poor Clares (the small community is currently living in Perugia until earthquake repairs are finished). The interior is spartan, due to the 17th-century whitewashing of elaborate frescoes by orders of a German bishop who attempted to discourage tourism and the temptations it would supply the nuns. The **Oratorio del Crocifisso (Oratory of the Crucifix)** houses a few relics of the saint and the 12th-century **Crucifix of San Damiano** that spoke to a young St. Francis in 1209, informing him of his calling. It's indefinitely closed to the public while earthquake repairs continue. The crypt containing the remains of St. Clare is open. An anonymous crucifix older than the church itself hangs over the main altar. The adjacent small **San Giorgio** church predates the basilica; it was the site of Francis's early schooling and where his remains awaited the completion of the basilica upon his death. On the basilica's terracelike piazza, lovely views of the surrounding Umbrian countryside draw locals and visitors at any hour of the day, particularly during sunset hours.

Piazza Santa Chiara. ℂ 075-812282. Free admission. Dress code same as for the Basilica di San Francesco (see above). Daily 7am–noon and 2pm–sunset.

San Damiano   If you stand alone amid the olive groves and wildflowers, in the serenity of the Spoleto Valley, this quiet spot will easily evoke the time and atmosphere of a young Francis who came here (the church dates from the 11th c.) to escape the wrath of his father. It was in this church in 1209 that a wooden crucifix told a restless, world-weary, 27-year-old Francis to "Go and repair the Church," referring to the decadent papacy and corrupt monastic orders (the crucifix is now housed in Santa Chiara, above). Francis took the orders literally, however, and sold his father's textile stock and offered the money to St. Damian's priest, who threw the money pouch back at him. In 1210, he found the approval of Pope Innocent III to create his own order of mendicant monks and, in 1212, a second order for women. St. Clare later lived here at San Damiano as abbess, her Order of Poor Clares moving up to the newly constructed Basilica di Santa Chiara after her death. You can visit the simple 13th-century convent's dormitory where a cross marks the spot of the saint's death in 1226.

The cloisters and refectory still have the original tables and benches where the nuns shared their meager meals. St. Francis visited just once during Clare's stay here and is said to have composed his famous *Canticle of the Creatures* here. To get here: From Piazza Santa Chiara or the Basilica di Santa Chiara, take Via Borgo Aretino, and at the Porta Nuova (the eastern gate to the city), take a right and head south down a steep road to San Damiano following the signs. It's 20 to 30 minutes downhill; a road for vehicle traffic runs parallel to a pedestrian road. Taxis that have dropped passengers off usually linger to take you back uphill for 10€ to 15€ ($12–$17) one-way.

Via San Damiano (1.5km/1 mile from Porta Nuova). 𝄞 **075-812273.** Free admission. Daily 10am–12:30pm and 2–6pm.

ACCOMMODATIONS YOU CAN AFFORD

Advance hotel reservations are a must. Never show up in Assisi, especially from Easter to fall, without a reservation. If you do, you'll spend half your morning at the tourist office calling hotels, only to find yourself stuck overnight in one of the hideous behemoths 5 miles away in Santa Maria degli Angeli.

If the following places are full and you need help finding a room, contact the **Consorzio Alberghi ed Operatori Turistiche,** Via A. Cristofani 22a (𝄞 **075-816566;** fax 075-812315; www.visitassisi.com), a kind of clearinghouse for local hotels that'll help you stick to your budget by booking a hotel category you request, with no fee involved.

Unless you have no choice or it's all the same to you, make sure you insist on being in the historic center of town and not the satellite town of Santa Maria degli Angeli (which always tries to pass itself off as *Assisi centro* to unwitting tourists) down near the train station or, worse yet, the town of Bastia, where tour buses usually put up their groups 4km (2½ miles) outside town. If the town is full (or closed—a number of hotels and restaurants close up in Jan–Feb), don't overlook the option of using Perugia as your base.

With an average of seven rooms at about 45€ to 70€ ($52–$81) per double, a number of small hotels in the center fill up fast and are often closed in winter. Among them, try **La Fortezza,** Vicolo dei Fortezza 19b (𝄞 **075-812418;** www.lafortezzahotel.com); **Hotel Il Duomo,** Vicolo San Lorenzo 2 (𝄞 **075-812742;** fax 075-812803); **Hotel La Rocca,** Via Porta Perlici 27 (𝄞/fax **075-812284;** www.hotelarocca.it); **Palotta,** Via San Rufino 6 (𝄞/fax **075-812307;** www.pallottaassisi.it); or **Properzio,** Via San Francesco 38 (𝄞 **075-813188;** fax 075-815201).

Hotel Alexander ☆ *Value*   Though now owned by a hotel just around the corner, the Alexander still feels a bit as if you're visiting your Umbrian parents' house for the weekend. The good-size accommodations in this medieval building across the street from where St. Francis was born are carpeted and scattered with rugs and Savonarola chairs for atmosphere. They have clean white walls, comfy beds, and fairly new bathrooms. Most of the rooms have multiple beds, which, together with the homelike atmosphere, makes the place great for families. The separately owned Pizzeria Otello underneath will even make pizza to go, so you can bring it back and really feel at home.

Piazza Chiesa Nuova 6 (just down from Piazza del Comune), 06081 Assisi (PG). ℂ/fax **075-816190** or 075-812-237 (its parent Hotel Priori). www.assisi-hotel.com. 8 units. Ask for single rates; 60€–100€ ($69–$115) double. Discounts in low season. Rates include breakfast in Hotel Priori. MC, V. Parking 8€–11€ ($9.20–$13) in nearby garage. **Amenities** (all via the Hotel Priori): Concierge; tour desk; car-rental desk; courtesy car (pay); room service (breakfast only); massage (in-room); babysitting; laundry service; dry cleaning. *In room:* TV.

Hotel dei Priori ☆   A stay in this 16th-century palazzo with stained-glass windows will take you back in time to when local families made their fortunes in trade and textiles and lived like royalty. Royal rates are something this book avoids, but I find the lovely rooms in this hotel housed in a landmark building to be more than reasonable. Spend the extra euros and book one of the 10 superior *camere dei Priori*, replete with 19th-century frescoed ceilings. Persian runners, valuable antiques, and handsome prints decorate the public rooms and guest rooms, all of which were refreshed in a 1998 renovation. This is the type of character and history you'd never be able to afford in a similar hotel in Rome or Florence.

Corso Mazzini 15 (1 block east of the Piazza del Comune), 06081 Assisi. ℂ **075-812237.** Fax 075-816804. www.assisi-hotel.com. 34 units. 69€–73€ ($79–$84) single; 98€–119€ ($113–$137) standard double; 134€–156€ ($154–$179) superior double; triple and quad rates on request. Rates include buffet breakfast. Ask about off-season discounts. AE, DC, MC, V. Parking nearby 7€–11€ ($8.05–$13). May close Jan–Feb. **Amenities:** Restaurant; bar; concierge; room service; massage (in-room); babysitting; laundry service; dry cleaning; nonsmoking rooms. *In room:* A/C, TV, dataport, minibar (in superior doubles), hair dryer, safe (in superior doubles).

Hotel Sole   This is one of the loveliest family-run hotels for these prices I've seen in Umbria. Its excellent location is enhanced by the charm of the freshly redone rooms and those across the street in the annex. There's an elevator in the annex, though not in the principal building, yet I prefer the latter, whose spacious rooms have generally been done with more charm. Furnishings range from contemporary to antique (and antique-inspired) wrought-iron painted beds and thoughtfully chosen framed prints. The family's restaurant, the Hostaria Ceppo della Catena, is set in theatrically stone-vaulted rooms in a 15th-century palazzo above the hotel, where half board can be arranged; open from March to October.

Corso Mazzini 35 (between Piazza del Comune and Santa Chiara), 06081 Assisi (PG). ℂ **075-812373.** Fax 075-813706. www.assisihotelsole.com. 37 units. 42€ ($48) single; 62€ ($71) double; 83€ ($95) triple; 95€ ($109) quad. Pension plan available. Breakfast 6€ ($6.90). AE, DC, MC, V. Parking 12€ ($14) in nearby lot. **Amenities:** Restaurant; bar; concierge; tour desk; car-rental desk; room service (breakfast and bar); babysitting. *In room:* A/C (request when booking; costs 10€/$12 extra per day), TV, hair dryer (in half), safe.

Umbra ☆☆   The bulk of this three-star hotel dates from the 15th century, but the basement's laundry and kitchen area boast ancient Roman foundations. Three generations of a local family have proudly run this hotel, known for its well-respected alfresco restaurant (fixed price 23€/$26; closed all day Sun and Wed at lunch). Patrons dine in a shaded garden patio where bird songs easily remind you that St. Francis was born just blocks away, and lamp-lit dinners are no less romantic. Most rooms are highlighted with well-worn 18th- and 19th-century antiques. When booking, ask for one of the rooms overlooking the Umbrian Valley; a few are doubles blessed with balconies. The main square is just paces away, but it's easy to feel removed from the pilgrimage jostle.

Via dei Archi 6 (15 paces off the west end of Piazza del Comune), 06081 Assisi (PG). © 075-812240. Fax 075-813653. www.hotelumbra.it. 25 units. 75€ ($86) single; 98€ ($113) standard double; 103€–113€ ($118–$130) superior double. Rates include breakfast. AE, DC, MC, V. Parking 12€ ($14) in nearby garage. Closed mid-Jan to Easter. **Amenities:** Restaurant; bike rental; concierge; tour desk; car-rental desk; room service (breakfast and bar); babysitting; laundry service; dry cleaning. *In room:* A/C, TV, minibar, hair dryer.

GREAT DEALS ON DINING

La Fortezza ★★ *Finds* UMBRIAN/CREATIVE   Up a stepped alley from Piazza del Comune, this lovely restaurant has been run by generations of the Chiocchetti family for more than 40 years and is prized for its high quality and reasonable prices. An exposed ancient Roman wall to the right of the entrance establishes the antiquity of this handsomely refurbished palazzo with brick-vaulted ceilings (the rest dates from the 13th c.). The delicious homemade pastas are prepared with sauces that follow the season's fresh offerings, while the roster of meats skewered or roasted on the grill *(alla brace)* ranges from veal and lamb to duck. The ubiquitous *tartufo nero* (black truffle) is available here. La Fortezza also rents seven rooms upstairs (see "Accommodations You Can Afford," above).

Vicolo della Fortezza/Piazza del Comune (up the stairs near the V. San Rufino end). © 075-812418. www.lafortezzahotel.com. Reservations recommended. Primi 5€–9€ ($5.75–$10); secondi 8€–12€ ($9.20–$14); fixed-price menu 21€–34€ ($24–$39) without wine. AE, MC, V. Fri–Wed 7:30–9:30pm; Sat–Sun 12:30–3pm and 7:30–9:30pm.

La Stalla ★★★ *Finds* RUSTIC UMBRIAN   Now *this* is what a countryside trattoria is all about. It's a series of former livestock stalls made of stone walls and low-beamed ceilings thoroughly blackened by and still filled with smoke. The smoke rises tantalizingly from the open wood-fire grill and will have your mouth watering long before you secure a seat at one of the wobbly long communal tables. It's noisy, it's chaotic, it's not for the fainthearted, and it offers what just may be one of your most memorable Umbrian meals, especially if you squeeze in with the traditional Sunday lunch crowds. Start with the *assaggini di torta al testo,* small samplers of Assisian flatbread split and stuffed with prosciutto and cheese or spinach and sausage. Next up: the *trittico,* a scooped-out wooden platter laden with a trio of the house specialty primi, usually *strangozzi, gnocchi* (both in tomato sauce), and *bigoli* (a ricotta-and-spinach log dusted with Parmesan). For secondi, you have a wide range of choices: *bistecca di vitello* (grilled veal), *spiedino di cacciagione* (grilled game), or *spiedino di maiale* (grilled pork). Their *salsicce* (sausages) are out of this world. The conversation, generous imbibing, and general good mood can carry on for hours after official closing time.

Via Ermeo delle Carceri 8 (1.6km/1¾ miles east of town). © 075-812317. Reservations strongly recommended (not always accepted). Primi 3.50€–5€ ($4–$5.75); secondi 4€–9€ ($4.60–$10). No credit cards. Tues–Sun noon–2:30pm and 7–10:30pm. Head out Porta Cappuccini; the turnoff is about 1km/½ mile along on the right (follow the signs for the Fontemaggio campground/hostel complex).

Medio Evo ★ UMBRIAN/ITALIAN   Down a steep S-curve from the center of town, Medio Evo offers well-spaced tables under magnificent stone-vaulted medieval ceilings. For antipasto, treat yourself to simple but exquisite aged *prosciutto di Parma*. There are concessions to local ingredients in dishes like *conchiglie alla Norcina* (shell pasta with black truffles and sausage), but also creations that smack of northern Europe, like *pennette alla moscavita* (with salmon, vodka, and tomatoes). For your second course, the Valdichiana beefsteak reigns supreme, and you can order it *alla Fiorentina* (grilled with a bit of olive oil and pepper), as an *entrecôte "Madagascar"* with green peppers, or as a flambéed filet *alla moda dello chef.* Pork, mutton, and veal are available for lighter appetites, or try the superb *fritto misto* with fried meats and vegetables, cheese, olives, and salami.

Via dell'Arco dei Priori 4B (a dogleg down from Piazza del Comune). ✆ 075-813068. Reservations strongly recommended. Primi 6€–11€ ($6.90–$13); secondi 7€–13€ ($8.05–$15); fixed-price menu without wine 18€ ($21). AE, DC, MC, V. Thurs–Tues 12:15–2:30pm and 7–10pm. Closed July.

Trattoria Pallotta UMBRIAN Pallotta's pair of brightly lit stone-and-plaster rooms sees its share of tourists siphoned off from nearby Piazza del Comune, but it hasn't wavered from serving good Umbrian food at fair prices. The *antipasto misto* is a meal in itself, with Assisi's *torta al testa,* crostini, sliced meats, and more. The *strangozzi alla Pallotta* are served with a pesto of olives, mushrooms, and some pepperoncino for kick, and the *ravioloni al burro e salvia* come in a butter-and-sage sauce. Move on to *coniglio alla cacciatore* (rabbit in tomato sauce with a side of plain *torta al testo*) or a *pollo arrosto* (roast chicken). Although the *menu turistico* includes wine, the tasting menu offers better food choices. Ask about the comfortable rooms for rent upstairs (see "Accommodations You Can Afford," above).

Vicolo della Volta Pinta 3 (just through the Palazzo del Comune's large main arch on Piazza del Comune). ✆ 075-812649. www.pallottaassisi.it. Reservations recommended. Primi 4.50€–8.50€ ($5.15–$9.75); secondi 6€–15€ ($6.90–$17); *menu turistico* with wine 16€ ($18). AE, DC, MC, V. Wed–Mon noon–2:30pm and 7:15–9:30pm. Closed 1 week in late Feb. Bus: A, B.

8 Gubbio

39km (24 miles) NE of Perugia, 170km (105 miles) SE of Florence, 200km (124 miles) N of Rome, 90km (56 miles) SE of Arezzo, 54km (33 miles) N of Assisi

An austere, proud mountain outpost, the tiny, no-nonsense stone town of **Gubbio** hangs on to its medieval charm and wonderful flavor of authenticity, despite its growing popularity with off-the-beaten-trackers looking for a picturesque hill town minus the tourists. Untrammeled it is not, but compared to, say, San Gimignano, you can consider Gubbio downright quiet, undiscovered, and cocooned in the middle of nowhere. The last few years have shown a commendable growth in the accommodations scene, with renovations and a handsome new hotel in an enviably located historic palazzo.

Set into the rugged steep slope of forest-clad Mount Ingino, Gubbio was a modestly prosperous Roman settlement, Iguvium, whose Roman amphitheater from the time of Augustus still sits at the foot of today's town. Like its Umbrian neighbor Spoleto, south of here, it flourished from its strategic location on the heavily trafficked Via Flaminia, linking ancient Rome and the imperial capital of Ravenna on the Adriatic. Today's visitor can easily evoke the Eugubium of the Dark Ages, a busy little market center, when its most important local personality, the sage Bishop Ubaldo Baldassini (now Gubbio's beloved patron saint) sidestepped destruction by the fierce hand of Barbarossa (Red Beard) in 1155. Its second-most celebrated resident was the ferocious Wolf of St. Francis fame. The 13th-century saint, from the nearby town of Assisi, strove to save the life of the hungry animal, which had been attacking flocks and terrorizing residents. After an alleged heart-to-heart, the saint convinced the wolf to change its ways and accepted its paw in peace. The townsfolk agreed to feed it regularly and a pact was sealed. This simple tale of *The Taming of the Wolf of Gubbio* has survived more than 7 centuries, though the part about the repenting wolf bursting into tears after striking the deal with St. Francis may be discounted as historic embellishment.

Much of the Gubbio that welcomes visitors today was built in the early 14th century, when local master architect Matteo Gattapone, responsible for the famous arched bridge of Spoleto, constructed the Palazzo dei Consoli on the much-photographed central Piazza Grande. From 1387 to 1508, the Montefeltro counts of Urbino oversaw a long, if not brilliant, period of rule. It was during this time, as happened with its Umbrian neighbor Deruta, that Gubbio became widely known as a center for the high-quality glazed ceramics and majolica that came from its workshops; many are still operating, but don't expect the quantity of choice you'll find in Deruta. Maestro Giorgio Andreoli (1465–1552), one of the world's greatest masters of the craft, developed a particularly intense ruby-red glaze that was never discovered by neighboring towns. He is the city's most famous resident after St. Ubaldo and that pesky wolf.

ESSENTIALS

GETTING THERE **By Train** The closest **station** is at Fossato di Vico (✆ **075-919230**), 19km (12 miles) away on the Rome–Anacona line. Eight trains (www.trenitalia.com) run daily from **Rome** (2¼ hr.; 10€/$12) and eight daily from **Spoleto** (45–60 min.; 3.50€/$4). Nine daily buses (six on Sun) connect the train station with Gubbio in 30 minutes.

By Car The SS298 leads north from Perugia through rugged scenery. The most convenient **parking** lot is off Piazza 40 Martiri (.50€/55¢ per hr.; pay at the Easy Gubbio office). There's also free parking off Via del Teatro Romano on the south edge of town and at the base station for the funivia, outside the east walls.

By Bus **ASP** (✆ **075-9220918**) has 11 buses Monday through Saturday (four on Sun) from **Perugia**'s Piazza Partigiani (70 min.; 3.60€/$4.15). If you're coming from the north, you'll probably have to change in **Umbertide,** from where there are three daily ASP runs to Gubbio (45 min.). From **Florence,** take the daily 5pm **SULGA** bus (✆ **075-5009641;** www.sulga.it) to Perugia, where within 40 to 70 minutes (no connection on Sun) there's the ASP connection to Gubbio described above. The total traveling time is about 3 hours. Monday through Saturday, there's a 4pm SULGA bus from **Rome**'s Tiburtina Station (3½ hr.; 16€/$18). Buses to Gubbio arrive at/leave from Piazza 40 Martiri. Tickets are available at the newsstand on the piazza or at Easy Gubbio.

VISITOR INFORMATION The **tourist office** is at Piazza Oderisi 6, a wide spot on Corso Garibaldi (✆ **075-9220693** or 075-9220790; fax 075-9273409; www.umbria2000.it or www.comune.gubbio.pg.it; open Mon–Fri 8:30am–1:45pm and 3:30–6:30pm, Sat 9am–1pm and 3:30–6:30pm, Sun 9:30am–12:30pm and 3:30–6:30pm; Oct–Mar, afternoon hours are 3–6pm). The private websites **www.ciaogubbio.it** and **www.easygubbio.it** also have lots of good information.

FESTIVALS & MARKETS The end-all festival in town is the **Corso dei Ceri** ★★★, on May 15, the eve of the Festa di Sant'Ubaldo, Gubbio's patron saint. Three 5m-tall (16-ft.) wooden "candles" *(ceri)* weighing 400 kilos (882 lb.)

each, crowned with small statues of Sts. Ubaldo, George, and Anthony, are vertically raced through town to the hilltop Basilica di San Ubaldo. Oddly, St. Ubaldo always wins, but that doesn't diminish the excitement level—or the number of folks who show up to follow all the events that take place before, during, and after the race.

To keep May a merry month, the last Sunday is dedicated to the **Palio della Balestra** *☆*, a crossbow competition against its ancient rival Sansepolcro in medieval costume (the rematch in Sansepolcro takes place in mid-Sept). An internal competition among four local teams is held on August 14.

The **Gubbio Festival** brings performers of international status to town for 3 weeks of mainly classical instrumental music in late July. Also during this period, the city sponsors **classical music concerts** in the grassy ruins of the **Roman theater.** During the **Torneo dei Quartieri** on August 14, the city's crossbow sharpshooters duke it out, and there's flag tossing and a historic procession—a warm-up for the competition against Sansepolcro 3 weeks later. Gubbio shows off its revered albino tuber at the **White Truffle and Agricultural Fair** from October 29 to November 2.

On the last Sunday of every month, there's an **antiques market** on Piazza 40 Martiri, where the regular **weekly market** is also held on Tuesday.

SEEING GUBBIO

The wide-open expanse of the brick-paved **Piazza Grande** *☆* is the center stage of the **Città Alta (High City).** A good chunk of the old medieval town was razed and leveled to make way for this square and the crenellated **Palazzo dei Consoli** *☆☆* (© 075-9274298) and the slender campanile that dominates it. Meant to represent the power and pride of a small medieval commune in the golden age of its 14th-century political and economic might, it does just that. Behind the nondescript facade is the palazzo's cavernous municipal council chamber, the **Salone dell'Arengo;** the **Pinacoteca (Picture Gallery);** and the **Museo Civico** (© 075-9274298), whose **Tavole Eugubine (Eugubine Tablets)** are by far the museum's highlight. The seven bronze tablets discovered by a shepherd in 1444 are held to be Umbria's most important archaeological find, the oldest known documents detailing religious practices in Europe (the best the scholars can figure, these tablets instruct priests how to interpret omens). The only extant example of the ancient written Umbrian language, they may date back as far as the 3rd to 1st centuries B.C. The museum also houses the city's only work of ceramics (1527) by Gubbio's master artisan Mastro Giorgio (d. 1552); with none to its name, the city bought it at Sotheby's for an undisclosed sum in 1992. Admission to the Palazzo dei Consoli, Pinacoteca, and Museo is 5€ ($5.75); they're open daily from 10am to 1pm and 3 to 6pm (until 5pm Oct–Mar).

From here, head up Via Ducale following signs for the Palazzo Ducale and the Duomo. The **Palazzo Ducale,** Via Federico da Montefeltro, at Via Ducale and Via della Cattedrale (© 075-9275872), was built in the 1470s as a scaled-down version of the ruling Duke Federico di Montefeltro's more lavish palace in Urbino. Most of the lordly trappings and furnishings are gone, but it's worth a visit for some of the original frescoes, a smattering of baroque paintings, and the hanging gardens with a view that are open in summer. Admission is 2€ ($2.30); it's open Monday through Saturday from 9am to 1:30pm and 2:30 to 7pm, and Sunday from 9am to 1:30pm.

If you weren't blown away by the Palazzo Ducale, you may want to save yourself a visit to the 12th-century **Duomo** across the way, a Gothic pile that pales when compared with some of those in the region you've likely seen in Spoleto, Orvieto, or Assisi (© **075-9220904;** free admission; open daily 10am–1pm and 3–7pm).

From behind the Duomo, follow the signs for one of Gubbio's two popular treks for the sturdy of knee. The least taxing is the paved road to the **Basilica di Sant Ubaldo,** halfway up the side of Monte Ingino above town at 807m (2,647 ft.). The walk up steep Via Sant Ubaldo is 2km (1¼ miles) along a consistent incline—most Eugubians drive it, reaching the basilica for their Sunday-afternoon stroll. An open *funivia* (cable car; © **075-9273881**) departs from the Porta Romana (a remaining 13th-c. tower that permitted access to town), east of Piazza Grande (open daily 9am–sunset, with a 1:15–2:30pm break Oct–June; tickets for the funivia are 4€ ($4.60) for adults and 3€ ($3.45) for those ages 4 to 13 one-way, or 5€ ($5.75) for adults and 4€ ($4.60) for children round-trip). The quiet 16th-century basilica holds the remains of the city's 12th-century patron saint in a glass casket and the three massive wooden *ceri* that turn the town upside down every May 15 when they're raced in a folkloric feast second only to Siena's Palio in terms of local hysteria (see "Festivals & Markets," above).

Got your second wind? You can continue by foot (the way is signposted) from the Basilica another 15 minutes or so to the remains of the 12th-century military fortress **La Rocca,** on the 900m (2,952-ft.) pinnacle of Monte Igino, for one-of-a-kind views of the wild Apennine Mountains and the Umbrian plains.

SHOPPING

You can't miss the fact that Gubbio is still famous for **ceramics** after all these years. The two main shopping strips are **Via dei Consoli,** heading west out of Piazza Grande, and **Via XX Settembre,** heading east from the piazza, though you can find small shops selling the town's artisanal crafts along its secondary streets, too. You'll find everything from items of amateur quality to those appropriate for serious collectors, the latter represented by the well-situated **La Mastro Giorgio di Valentino Biagioli,** Piazza Grande 3 (© **075-9271574**). Another excellent retail outlet/workshop is **Rampini Ceramiche d'Arte,** Via Leonardo da Vinci 94 (© **075-9272963**), where traditional patterns influence modern designs.

Copies of medieval *balestre* (crossbows) are but a sampling of the exquisite *ferro battuto* (wrought-iron) craftsmanship handed down through the centuries. The best store/laboratory in town is **Artigianato Ferro Artistico,** Via Baldassini 22 (© **075-9273079**). Handsomely crafted leather goods are the reason to search out the store/workshop of **Mastri Librai,** Via dei Consoli 48 (© **075-9277425;** www.gubbio.com/mastri-librai).

ACCOMMODATIONS YOU CAN AFFORD

Off-season rates are also offered by some hotels in winter, as well as during the slow months of June and July (considered high season in other towns).

Bosone Palace 🏰🏰   Until the Relais Ducale opened, the Bosone was the city's most atmospheric hotel. Built in the 1300s and enlarged during the Renaissance, it's steps from Piazza Grande and allows you to enjoy a return to lifestyles of the rich and famous of other centuries. Owned by the local patrician Raffaelli clan, this formerly private residence once hosted an exiled Dante Alighieri (persona non grata in his hometown of Florence for trumped-up political charges). Its lobby's monumental marble staircase leads to standard rooms that are comfortable, simple, and spacious, and whose bathrooms are mostly new (so much for time travel). Ask for one of the three with small terraces and big views. For the remarkable, book one of the two dramatic Renaissance suites with stuccoed ceilings elaborately frescoed in the 17th century and with reproduction period furnishings.

Via XX Settembre 22 (near Piazza Grande), 06024 Gubbio (PG). ☎ 075-9220688. Fax 075-9220552. www.mencarelligroup.com. 30 units. 62€–73€ ($71–$84) single; 83€–99€ ($95–$114) double; 145€–181€ ($167–$208) 4-person suite. Rates include buffet breakfast. AE, DC, MC, V. Free parking nearby. **Amenities:** Concierge; tour desk; car-rental desk (ask at least a day in advance, as it has to be brought from Perugia); courtesy car (from bus stop; request when booking); room service (24-hr.); laundry service; dry cleaning. *In room:* TV, minibar, hair dryer.

Gattapone   After reopening in 1999 following a complete refurbishment, the long-loved Gattapone deservedly graduated to three-star status, but with prices that are more than reasonable given the quality and style. It's housed in a medieval building on a stepped alley down from Piazza Grande; many rooms overlook the Romanesque church and bell tower of San Giovanni. The redesigned rooms, however, reflect little of the hotel's ancient roots, with the exception of an occasional wood-beamed ceiling left intact. The tiles in the updated bathrooms pick up the color scheme of each room. If you call on arrival, the hotel will send its van to collect you and your luggage. This is a sibling hotel of the Bosone, a more imposing palazzo but not yet slated for a face-lift.

Via Beni 6. ☎ 075-9272489. Fax 075-9272417. www.mencarelligroup.com. 18 units. 65€–75€ ($75–$86) single; 90€–105€ ($104–$121) double; 125€–140€ ($144–$161) suite. Rates include buffet breakfast. AE, DC, MC, V. Parking 8€ ($9.20) in Piazza 40 Martiri nearby. Closed Jan 8–Feb 1. **Amenities:** Concierge; room service. *In room:* TV, minibar, hair dryer, safe.

WORTH A SPLURGE

Relais Ducale 🏕🏕   Housed in the aristocratic guest quarters of the ruling dukes of Urbino, nestled between their Palazzo Ducale (see above) and Piazza Grande (see above), this relatively new hotel offers a combination of historic importance and unrivaled panoramic location, with hanging gardens shaded by regal palms and scented by jasmine. The timeless view that must have bedazzled the guests of the ruling Montefeltro dukes is the same one enjoyed by today's guests lingering over breakfast in the gardens or gazing out from many of the elegantly appointed rooms. Parquet floors, damask bedspreads and matching curtains, and the occasional historic touch (stone vaulted ceilings) or modern luxury (Jacuzzi baths) make this Gubbio's unrivaled premier hotel. If you're not staying here, stop by the Caffè Ducale at Piazza Grande 5 (the hotel rises above the cafe, carved into many levels and medieval structures), the most refined of the city's watering holes.

Via Galeotti 19/Viale Ducale 2 (can also enter from the cafe in the center of Piazza Grande). ☎ 075-9220157. Fax 075-9220159. www.mencarelligroup.com. 30 units. 98€–103€ ($113–$118) standard single, 114€ ($131) superior single; 135€–163€ ($155–$187) standard double, 175€–212€ ($201–$244) deluxe double; 210€–253€ ($242–$291) junior suite. Rates include buffet breakfast. AE, DC, MC, V. Parking 8€ ($9.20) in private garage. **Amenities:** Restaurants (family owns 3 nearby, including Taverna del Lupo recommended below, for which pensione plans are available); bar; access to nearby gym; bike rental; concierge; tour desk; car-rental desk; courtesy car (from bus stop or train station); secretarial services; room service; massage (in-room); babysitting; laundry service; dry cleaning; nonsmoking rooms. *In room:* A/C, TV, VCR (on request), fax, minibar, hair dryer, safe.

GREAT DEALS ON DINING

One of my favorite neighborhood trattorie in town, **Taverna del Buchetto**, in an atmospheric 13th-century warehouse near Porta Romana at Via Dante 30 (☎ 075-9277034), had been "closed for restorations" for about a year at the time this book went to press. There's no word on if, or when, it'll ever reopen. It never hurts to check, though (and will be well worth a meal if they do start up again).

Taverna del Lupo ☆☆ UMBRIAN The Mencarelli empire that today includes the hotels described above started here more than 3 decades ago in what continues to be Gubbio's culinary landmark. The family-run restaurant is large but divided into vaulted and brick-walled rooms that are handsomely appointed with Umbrian ceramics and prints. The atmosphere is one of elegant coziness, with a professional kitchen that rarely goes wrong with the regional specialties. In 2004, the finishing touches were put on a much-expanded wine cellar, which offers an array of fine vintages. Flexible hours accommodate those trying to see the sites and sample local gastronomy on a limited day trip. The fixed-price menu is an interesting splurge, but I opt for anything *tartufo* (truffle) enhanced (beginning with the full-flavored sauce used for the special homemade tagliatelle). It's well worth the extra euros.

Via Ansidei 21 (on the corner of V. Repubblica, a few blocks uphill from Piazza 40 Martiri). ℂ 075-9274368. www.mencarelligroup.com. Reservations strongly recommended. Primi 9.50€–22€ ($11–$25); secondi 13€–24€ ($14–$27); tasting menu without wine 39€ ($44). AE, DC, MC, V. Tues–Sun noon–4pm and 7–11pm.

9 Spoleto & the Spoleto Festival

129km (80 miles) N of Rome, 209km (130 miles) S of Florence, 48km (30 miles) SE of Assisi, 64km (40 miles) SE of Perugia

The world-famous **Spoleto Festival** (until recently known as the Festival dei Due Mundi/Festival of Two Worlds) has put Spoleto back on the map after centuries of historical obscurity. However, it was that obscurity that was responsible for the town's untouched medieval preservation, which still makes it worth visiting, even when the world-class arts festival isn't turning it on its ear. Established by Italian-American composer/maestro Gian Carlo Menotti in 1957, the celebrated arts festival brings together performers from all over the world for 3 weeks of dance, concerts, art, and drama known for their diversity and quality.

Much is made of the city's Roman past. As Spoletium, it was one of the empire's most important outposts. Strategically situated on the well-trafficked Via Flaminia linking Rome and the late imperial capital of Ravenna, it flourished for centuries and proudly held out when fiercely attacked by Hannibal in the 3rd century. It became the capital of the important Lombard Duchy of Spoleto from the 6th to the 8th centuries. The arrival of the emperor Barbarossa in 1155 saw widespread destruction of the region, after which the city only partially recovered before falling into the hands of the church and the stifling Papal States. The 15th-century Pope Alexander VI presented the town to his teenage daughter, Lucrezia Borgia, and appointed her governor. And that was pretty much the cap on excitement until Maestro Menotti arrived in 1957. Spoleto was far enough away from the epicenter of Umbria's 1997 earthquakes to have escaped with little damage.

There's no traipsing through countless museums and dimly lit churches in Spoleto. The much-used adjectives *quaint* and *charming* are put to excellent use here. After a visit to the Duomo—whose lovely, sloping piazza passes for one of the country's most evocative outdoor venues during the festival's closing-night concert—your time will be spent wandering the vaulted back streets and poking around small antiques shops and gourmet-stocked stores, always winding up in ancient Piazza del Mercato, a perfect reminder of the city's ancient roots as a market town during its day in the Dark Ages.

ESSENTIALS

GETTING THERE   By Train   Spoleto is a main station on the Rome-Ancona line, and all 16 daily trains (www.trenitalia.com) from **Rome** stop here (about 1½ hr.; 6.80€/$7.80). From **Perugia**, 10 trains make the 60-minute trip (3.50€/$4 total). The C bus heads from the **station** (© 0743-48516) up to Piazza Libertà in the upper town (bus D stops at Piazza Garibaldi in the lower town). Make sure you ask the driver if the bus is going toward the *centro storico*.

By Bus   Spoleto's bus company, **SSIT** (© 0743-212211; www.spoletina.com), runs buses into Piazza della Vittoria (connected to Piazza Garibaldi) from **Perugia** (two afternoon runs, weekdays only; 1 hr.; 5€/$6) and **Rome** (an early morning and midafternoon run to Terni, where you can switch to many Spoleto-bound coaches, 2½ hr. total; 5€/$5.75). If you can reach Foligno by other means, there are lots of buses from there.

By Car   Spoleto is literally on the SS3 (the road tunnels under the city), the old Roman Via Flaminia running north from Rome and connecting in Foligno with the SS75 from Perugia. Parking in the old town is free only along Via Don Bonilli next to the soccer stadium and off Viale dei Cappuccini (turn left off the SS3 onto Vle. G. Matteotti, then left again). There's also a parking lot off Piazza della Vittoria at the north end of lower Spoleto. Parking in the metered *zona blu* spaces in the center generally costs .60€ (70¢) per hour.

VISITOR INFORMATION   The large **information center** at Piazza della Libertà 7 (© **0743-220773** for hotels, 0743-238920 for sightseeing and events; fax 0743-46241; www.umbria2000.it), hands out scads of info and an excellent, if oversize, map. It's open daily from 10am to 1pm and 2 to 7pm (3:30–6:30pm Nov–Mar), and Saturday and Sunday from 10am to 1pm and 4 to 7pm (closed Sun afternoon in winter). The area's website, **www.comune.spoleto.pg.it**, although in Italian only, is also useful.

FESTIVALS & MARKETS   For 3 weeks beginning the last week of June, Spoleto turns its attention to the **Festival di Spoleto (Spoleto Festival;** www.spoletofestival.it) 𝕬𝕬, the American-Italian arts-and-music festival. World-class symphonies and music ensembles as well as dance and drama troupes come from all over the world, culminating in the final evening's standing-room-only symphonic performance on Piazza del Duomo. There are often 5 to 10 events happening daily at different indoor/outdoor venues. Tickets usually go on sale mid-April. Edinburgh-type fringe and alternative performances are finding their way into the program to resuscitate some of the cutting-edge energy of the festival's early years, and tickets can often be found at the last moment. For general program information and instructions for ticket purchase after mid-April, contact the **Associazione Festival dei Due Mondi** (© **800-565-600** toll free in Italy, or 0743-220032; fax 0743-220321, or 0743-44700 from outside Italy; www.spoletofestival.it). Also try the **Teatro Nuovo** (© **0743-40265**).

To keep the cultural activity level at a consistent high, the relatively new **Spoletoestate (Spoleto Summer)** arts festival picks up where its big-sister festival leaves off, organizing performances around town from July to September. See the tourist office for listings.

A daily morning **produce-and-flower market** (except Sun) takes over ancient Piazza del Mercato, originally the site of the Roman Forum, in fragrant and organized chaos. The second Sunday of every month, a **Mercato delle Briciole** takes place here and in neighboring piazzas (pick up information at the tourist office), where merchants hawk collectibles and choice antiques, together with junky stuff.

Spoleto

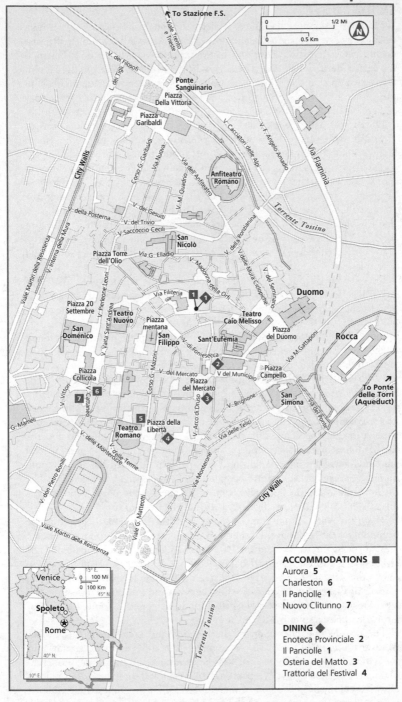

0   1/2 Mi
0   0.5 Km

To Stazione F.S.

Viale Trento e Trieste
V. dei Filosofi
L. dei Tigli
Ponte Sanguinario
Piazza Della Vittoria
Piazza Garibaldi
Corso G. Garibaldi
Via Nuova
Via dell'Anfiteatro
V. Cacciatori delle Alpi
V. F. Angelo Amadio
Via Flaminia
Anfiteatro Romano
City Walls
Viale Martiri della Resistenza
V. Interna della Mura
V. della Posterna
V. dei Gesuiti
V. del Trivio
V. Saccoccio Cecili
V. M. Quadrio
San Nicolò
Via G. Elladio
Piazza Torre dell'Olio
V. Madonna della Orti
V. della Ponzanina
V. delle Mura Ciclopiche
V. del Seminario
Torrente Tossino
Duomo
Via Filiteria
Piazza 20 Settembre
San Doménico
V. Pierleone Leoni
V. Sant'Andrea
V. Sant'Andrea
Teatro Nuovo
Piazza mentana
San Filippo
Teatro Caio Melisso
Sant'Eufemia
V. di Fontesecca
Piazza del Duomo
Via M. Gattaponi
Rocca
Piazza Collicola
Corso G. Mazzini
V. del Mercato
V. del Municipio
Piazza Campello
To Ponte delle Torri (Aqueduct)
V. Vittori
V. Cattaneo
D
Piazza del Mercato
V. Brignone
San Simona
Via del Ponte
G. Mameli
Teatro Romano
Piazza della Libertà
V. Arco di Druso
Via delle Terme
V. delle Tellci
V. don Pietro Bonilli
Via delle Monterone
Via Montevone
City Walls
Viale Martiri della Resistenza
Viale G. Matteotti
Torrente Tossino

15° E.
0   100 Mi
0   100 Km
45° N.
Venice
Spoleto
Rome
40° N.
10° E.

SIGHTS TO SEE

With the exception of the Duomo, there isn't much to see here. But a walk through town will illustrate the antiquity of a city that's still very much alive and doesn't live for tourism's sake alone. Just west of the main Piazza della Libertà is the **Teatro Romano (Roman Theater)** ⚔ (© 0743-223277), from the 1st century, when Spoleto was a thriving Roman city. It has been restored and is a popular venue for festival performances, with an attached museum of archaeology and antiquities (admission 2€/$2.30; Mon–Sat 9am–7pm, Sun 9am–1pm).

From Piazza della Libertà, take a right on Via Brignone and a left on Via Arco di Druso, which leads into **Piazza del Mercato,** a window to centuries past. Stores around its periphery sell the gourmet products of Umbria, including the prized black truffles from nearby Norcia. Outdoor cafes like the **Bar Primavera** (no. 8; excellent gelato) set up tables outside as alfresco command posts for taking in the piazza life. Explore the vaulted alleys and hidden corners just off the piazza, or follow the characteristic **Via dei Duchi** north out of Piazza del Mercato to window-shop on one of the city's most pleasant streets. At its end, turn left onto Via del Mercato or right onto Via Fontesecca for more streets evocative of the city's medieval past, now inhabited by tasteful shops, antiques stores, and boutiques.

It's a short walk east to Piazza del Duomo and the **Duomo** ⚔⚔ (© 0743-44307), a 12th-century building (on the site of a 7th-c. church) whose simple but elegant facade is graced by five rose windows and crowned with a mosaic by Solsterno (1207). The most illustrious (recently restored and mercifully untouched by the 1997 earthquakes) pictorial masterpiece of the city is found in the domed apse—the last works done by Florentine painter Filippo Lippo (1467–69). From left to right, they're the *Annunciation,* the *Passage of the Virgin Mary,* and the *Nativity;* the *Coronation* fills the space above. In the scene of the Virgin's death, you'll find self-portraits of the painter and his son Filippino to the right. His premature death, rumor goes, came from poisoning when he was found to have seduced the nubile daughter of a noble family. It was bad enough that, as a monk, he'd taken up with Lucrezia Buti, a nun who posed as the Madonna in many of his works. Filippino, the son of Filippo and Lucrezia (and student of his father's old protégé Botticelli), designed his father's tomb found in a chapel in the right transept, funded by Florence's Lorenzo de' Medici, the master's patron; the body mysteriously disappeared for a brief period 2 centuries later, stolen, they say, by descendants of the compromised girl.

The other work of note is the fresco cycle in the **Cappella di Erioli,** at the beginning of the right nave. The author was a 17-year-old Pinturicchio, not yet famous for his future work in the Piccolomini Library in Siena's Duomo. The Duomo is open from 8am to 12:30pm and 3 to 5:30pm (to 7pm Mar–Oct). Down the steps on the west side of Piazza del Duomo are the shaded hanging gardens of **Piazza della Signoria,** whose benches and postcard views of the valley make this the city's most idyllic picnic spot (buy your provisions at the open-air market before vendors pack up at 1pm).

The decade-long renovation of the towered and crenellated papal **Rocca Albornoz** ⚔ (© 0743-223055) was completed in 2000, and you can now tour some of its frescoed halls and peer into the archaeological excavation pits; eventually, it may house the city's painting collection and an exhibit on Spoleto's glory days as the head of a Lombard and medieval Duchy. Built by the Gubbio-born architect Gattapone from 1359 to 1363 for the tireless papal envoy Cardinal Albornoz (also responsible for the Rocca above Assisi), it was temporary home to Lucrezia Borgia, the teenage daughter of 15th-century Pope Alexander VI. It was also used as a prison, most recently having housed Pope John Paul II's would-be assassin, Ali Agha, for a brief period. Admission is 4.65€ ($5.35) for adults, and 3.60€ ($4.15) for ages 7 to 14 and those over 60. It's open (though these hours may change) from March 15 to June 10 and September 16 to October 31 Monday through Friday from 10am to 1pm and 3 to 7pm, and Saturday and Sunday from 10am to 7pm; from June 11 to September 15 daily from 10am to 8pm; and from November 1 to March 14 Monday through Friday from 2:30 to 5pm, and Saturday and Sunday from 10am to 5pm.

Take a walk, if only for the town's best picture-perfect views, around the right side of the Rocca to the 14th-century **Ponte delle Torri (Bridge of the Towers)** 𝄞𝄞. Gattapone built it on the foundation of an ancient Roman aqueduct. Its 10 Gothic arches span a 228m-wide (748-ft.) chasm 72m (236 ft.) above a torrent; to this day, it's held as an awe-inspiring engineering endeavor for that period. A favorite summertime hike is to the rural **monastery of Monteluco,** once favored by St. Francis and St. Bernardino of Siena (open daily 9am–noon and 3–6pm). The tourist office can supply you with maps of walking paths to Monteluco and other sites of interest in the immediate countryside.

ACCOMMODATIONS YOU CAN AFFORD

Rates are usually discounted from November to March (low season). If you plan to visit during the festival, book 2 to 3 months in advance (last-minute cancellations are rare). You may also consider commuting by car or bus from Perugia or the neighboring towns during the festival when the town is at zero vacancy. Note that prices during the 3-week festival may be higher than those quoted below: Hoteliers charge whatever they believe the demand will support.

Aurora 𝄞 This hotel is rather stylish for these rates, and although it sits just a few steps off Piazza della Libertà, it's in a small courtyard, so you get both a central location and a very quiet stay. By 2004, all the rooms had been completely refurbished in a coordinated decor of wall-to-wall carpeting, discreetly patterned wallpaper, and deep-mauve curtains, putting this popular spot even more in demand; book early. In the hotel but independently managed is the acclaimed Ristorante Apollinare, one of the city's more upscale dining spots; its menu offers regional Umbrian specialties prepared with a light and, at times creative, hand (half- and full-pensione plans are available).

Via Apollinare 3 (near Piazza Libertà), 06049 Spoleto (PG). ⓒ **0743-220315.** Fax 0743-221885. www.hotel auroraspoleto.it. 23 units. 30€–51€ ($35–$59) single; 52€–80€ ($60–$92) double. Rates include buffet breakfast. AE, DC, MC, V. Free parking on streets nearby. **Amenities:** Restaurant; bar; concierge; tour desk; car-rental desk; courtesy car (pay); room service. *In room:* A/C (in all by 2005), TV, minibar, hair dryer (in most).

Charleston 𝄞𝄞 *Finds* This friendly hotel is nestled in a medieval district next to the new modern art museum. Many of the rooms are quite large and have a 1970s artist's loft feel, with good use of available space and mismatched but tasteful furnishings—though new owners are replacing most with antique-style pieces. Rough-hewn chestnut-beamed ceilings mirror the wood-plank floors (some are carpeted), and the walls are hung with modern art prints and original works. The firm beds are spread with Black Watch plaid coverlets. If you're feeling particularly hedonistic, you can cough up 10€ ($12) for a trip to the basement sauna, or just cozy up on a cushy sofa before the wintertime fire that crackles between the TV and sitting lounges. The room TVs come with VCRs, and the front desk always has a movie or two in English. They also organize all sorts of specialized tours (cooking classes, horseback rides, truffle hunts, and so on).

Piazza Collicola 10 (near San Domenico), 06049 Spoleto (PG). ℭ **0743-220052** or 0743-223235. Fax 0743-221244. www.hotelcharleston.it. 21 units. 40€–72€ ($46–$83) single; 52€–130€ ($60–$150) double; 99€–150€ ($114–$173) triple. Rates include breakfast. AE, DC, MC, V. Parking 8€–10€ ($9.20–$12) in private garage. **Amenities:** Restaurant; 2 bars; sauna (see review); bike rental; concierge; tour desk; car-rental desk; 24-hr. room service (breakfast and bar); babysitting; laundry service; dry cleaning (same day); nonsmoking. *In room:* A/C, TV, VCR in most (videos 3€/$3.45), dataport, minibar, hair dryer.

Il Panciolle *(Value)*   You can't beat this inexpensive family-run place for new and nicely decorated rooms so close to the Duomo. The freshly painted white walls offset the rooms' matching sets of oak headboard, armoire, and bedside table; the bathrooms are smallish but were recently redone and are as nice as you could hope for at these rates. In warm weather, you can breakfast on the restaurant's flagstone terrace, which is also a wonderful setting for a home-style dinner (see "Great Deals on Dining," below).

Via del Duomo 3–5 (2 blocks west of Piazza della Signoria), 06049 Spoleto. ℭ/fax **0743-45677.** 7 units. 30€–40€ ($35–$46) single; 40€–55€ ($46–$63) double. Continental breakfast 5€ ($5.75). No credit cards. **Amenities:** Restaurant (under separate ownership); bar. *In room:* TV, minibar, hairdryer.

Nuovo Clitunno   Little is left from the time when this 19th-century palazzo was a firehouse. But the Tomassoni family's welcome augments the comfort and warmth of the public area's fireplace, beamed ceilings, and gold-plastered walls. Public areas, the restaurant, and the terrace were renovated in 2003. To accommodate disparate tastes, the rooms have recently been refitted in two styles. Request an *in stile* ("old style") room, and you'll have reserved one of 18 lovely rooms with terra-cotta floors, antique iron beds, armoires, and rough-hewn ceiling beams. The majority of rooms are decorated in "standard" style (less expensive than the old-style rooms), with stylish contemporary furnishings in warm pastel colors. All have new bathrooms, but only 15 of the standard rooms offer a handsome view over the Vale Spoletino. Not all rooms have air-conditioning; it is available at no extra cost but should be requested when booking.

Piazza Sordini 6 (just west of Piazza della Libertà), 06049 Spoleto. ℭ **0743-223340.** Fax 0743-222663. www.hotelclitunno.com. 45 units. 45€–80€ ($52–$92) single; 70€–100€ ($81–$115) standard double, 80€–110€ ($92–$127) *in stile* double; 90€–130€ ($104–$150) suite. Rates include buffet breakfast. AE, DC, MC, V. Free parking. Closed Feb. Bus from station: A, B, C. **Amenities:** Restaurant; tennis court (200m/655 ft. away); bike rental; children's playground (100m/330 ft. away); concierge; tour desk; car-rental desk; courtesy car (from train station); room service (24-hr. for bar service); massage (in-room); babysitting; laundry service; same-day dry cleaning; nonsmoking rooms. *In room:* A/C (in some; ask when booking), TV, VCR (on request), modem hookup, minibar, hair dryer, safe.

GREAT DEALS ON DINING

Enoteca Provinciale *(↔)* UMBRIAN/SPOLETINA   Have at least one of your lunches, light dinners, or snacks in the converted livestock stalls of this medieval tower, where casual meals are accompanied by wine tastings. Meals consist of the region's simplest and, in this case, most delicious offerings. The toasted *bruschetta all'olio di Spoleto* showcases the local olive oil; homemade *strangozzi al tartufo* pasta is just an excuse to revel in its unrivaled truffle sauce; *polenta alla spoletina* is made with a barleylike flour (not the usual cornmeal) and heaped with sausage and lentils. You can sample a cross-section of more than 30 red and white Umbrian wines by the glass—and take a bottle home with you, if you like—but be sure to toast the night with the very unusual *amaro di tartufo*, a bitter liqueur made from the ubiquitous truffle. The atmosphere is relaxed and jovial, and you'll be welcomed into the fold the longer you stay and the more you imbibe.

Via Aurelio Saffi 7. ℂ **0743-220484.** Primi 5€–10€ ($5.75–$12); secondi 6€–13€ ($6.90–$15); wine from 1.50€–6€ ($1.75–$6.90) per glass; menu turistico with wine 15€ ($17). AE, DC, MC, V. Wed–Mon 11am–3pm and 7–11pm (to midnight in summer).

Il Panciolle 👓👓 SPOLETINA   This family-run restaurant, popular with performers during the festival, offers two wonderfully distinctive eating experiences: a wintertime evening in the cantina's stone-walled room with beamed ceilings and an open fireplace, where the aroma of roasting meat teases your appetite before you're even seated; and, in warm weather, a dinner on the open flagstoned terrace, shaded by a huge pine and with an open view of the Spoleto Valley. What remains invariable is the *cucina umbra casalinga,* the home cooking that's the kitchen's specialty. Homemade *strangozzi* pasta can be enjoyed simply prepared with *aglio e olio* (garlic and olive oil) or dressed up royally with *funghi e tartufi* (truffles and mushrooms). The meats *alla brace* (grilled over an open fire) are delicious, but also sample the grilled mozzarella or the smoke-cured cheese *scamorza alla brace,* a peasant's dish you could serve to a king. For the charming rooms above the restaurant (but separately managed), see "Accommodations You Can Afford," above.

Via del Duomo 3–5/Vicolo degli Eroli 1. ℂ **0743-45598.** www.ristoranteilpanciollespoleto.com. Reservations recommended. Primi 7€–16€ ($8.05–$18); secondi 7€–25€ ($8.05–$29). AE, DC, MC, V. Thurs–Mon 12:30–2:30pm and 7:45–10:45pm; Tues 12:30–2:30pm. Closed Aug 1–12.

Osteria del Matto 👓👓 (Finds UMBRIAN OSTERIA   It might have opened in December 2000, but this is truly an osteria of the old school, with simple, solid food and good wines. The stocky, shared wood tables cluster under tall rough beamed ceilings, crude 14th-century brick arches, and goldenrod plaster walls scattered with wine bottle–laden shelves. There's no menu to choose from, just a blackboard telling you what you're going to eat. Various *salumi* hang in the little kitchen area alongside a prosciutto slung in its holder, ready to be carved by hand by the gregarious Filippo Matto (a former butler to Gian Carlo Menotti at his Scottish estate) for your antipasto—a mix of meats, onion frittata wedges, artichokes, and crostini. Afterward, there's just a single pasta dish (if you're lucky, the farro stew made with sausage, wine, pepperoncino, and soup veggies), followed by the *dolce* of the day—I got a berry marmalade *crostata.*

Vicolo del Mercato 5 (under the big arch on the south side of Piazza del Mercato). ℂ **0743-225506.** Full meal without wine 14€–16€ ($16–$18). MC, V. Wed–Mon 11am–3pm and 5pm–2am.

Trattoria del Festival (Kids UMBRIAN   The cavernous pair of brick vaulted rooms here are large enough to host the festival hordes yet still leave room for die-hard locals who come for the best fixed-priced menus in town. The two most expensive of these (at 25€ and 35€/$29 and $40) are the ones to order, since they let you sample a pair of primi (chef's surprise, but one is sure to involve truffles) and include all the incidentals, save wine. Start with a foot-long *bruschetta al pomodoro* with a couple of cream-stuffed veal rolls before sinking your fork into the *tagiatelle tartufate* (a particularly successful use of the elusive black mushroom) or the *penne all'erbe* (in a hot-and-spicy tomato sauce laden with chopped herbs). The secondi also tend to be very simple but good. If you don't care for the excellent *frittata al tartufo* (mixed meat fry with truffles), try the *salsicce alle brace* or the *pollo arrosto.*

Via Brignone 8. ℂ **0743-220993.** www.trattoriadelfestival.com. Reservations suggested. Primi 6€–13€ ($6.90–$15); secondi 7€–13€ ($8/05–$15); most fixed-price menus without wine 16€–22€ ($18–$25). AE, DC, MC, V. Fri–Wed noon–3pm and 6:30pm–late.

10 Orvieto

87km (54 miles) W of Spoleto, 86km (53 miles) SW of Perugia, 152km (94 miles) S of Florence, 121km (75 miles) N of Rome

One of the most dramatically sited hill towns in Italy, **Orvieto** is perfectly situated between Florence and Rome, atop a volcanic plateau over 300m (984 ft.) above a wide valley. It's an amazing sight, one visible from kilometers away, when the setting sun is reflected off the glittering mosaic facade of the Duomo—which, by the way, is one of Italy's most outstanding cathedrals.

Orvieto was of Etruscan origin—one of the original league of 12 important satellite cities and possibly its religious center—and was later destroyed in 264 B.C. by the Romans, who transformed it into their own stronghold. As with the Etruscans before them, they sculpted the porous tufa butte into a labyrinth of tunnels, storage caves, cisterns, wells, and living spaces. (You can visit parts of the **"Orvieto Underground"** daily with an English-speaking guide for 5.50€/ $6.30, usually at 11am, 12:15pm, 4pm, and 5:15pm, but more frequently in summer; contact the tourist office or call ℂ **0763-344891;** www.orvietounder ground.it.) The Middle Ages saw the city thriving as an influential *commune,* enjoying its golden days in the 13th and 14th centuries, when many palazzi and churches were built. Orvieto was also a prominent papal seat: As many as 33 pontiffs had their summer residence here. The proximity to the Vatican was a plus, as was the high-altitude tabletop setting that made it a natural fortress while guaranteeing cool weather during Rome's infernal summers.

Those intending to stay overnight and longer may have to fend off not only the day-trippers, but also the possible disappointment of its limited sites. Those with cars, however, will enjoy using Orvieto as a base for visiting the area's prominent vineyards and other charming hill towns, such as Todi and Spoleto.

ESSENTIALS

GETTING THERE   By Train   Several trains (www.trenitalia.com) on the main **Rome-Florence** line stop at Orvieto daily (1¾–2¼ hr. from Florence, 12 daily, 9.90€/$11; 1–1½ hr. from Rome, 14 daily, 6.80€/$7.80). From **Perugia,** take the train to Terontola (16 daily) for this line heading south toward Rome (2–2½ hr. total; 6.10€/$7).

Orvieto's **train station** is in the boring new town of Orvieto Scalo in the valley. To reach the city, cross the street and take the **funicular,** a modern version of the steep cog railway that ran on hydraulic power in the 19th century. You can buy a funicular-only ticket for .70€/80¢ or a combined funicular-and-bus ticket for .80€/90¢ that lets you hop on a minibus at the top of the funicular run (Piazza Cahen) and ride into the center of town: The "A" bus heads to Piazza del Duomo, and the "B" bus to central Piazza della Repubblica via Piazza XXIX

ⓘ Tips Saving Money

The useful **Carta Unica cumulative ticket** for 13€ ($14) adults and 11€ ($12) students/over 60 gets you into the Duomo's Cappella San Brizio, the Museo Claudio Faina, the Torre del Moro, and the Orvieto Underground tour—plus either one funicular plus one bus ride *or* 5 hours in the ex-Campo della Fiera parking lot. It's available at the tourist office, all the above sights, and the funicular depots.

Marzo (it then doubles back to the Duomo). Or you may wish to get the "Carta Unica" combination ticket that covers the funicular, bus, and museums (see below). From in front of the train station, you can also grab bus no. 1 that runs to Piazza XXIX Marzo in the city (get two tickets—one for the return trip—at the bar inside the station, as they're hard to come by in town).

By Bus   Train transportation to any of the above destinations is generally preferred to the extremely limited bus service to and from Orvieto. For bus information, call ✆ **0763-301234** or visit the tourist office.

By Car   If you're coming from **Todi,** the SS448 is the fastest route, but the twisting SS79bis is more scenic; from **Perugia,** shoot down the SS3bis through Deruta to Todi and branch off from there. The SS71 runs here from just east of **Chiusi** in southern Tuscany, and the A1 autostrada between **Florence** and **Rome** has an exit at the valley town Orvieto Scalo.

The most convenient **free parking** is in Orvieto Scalo outside the train station (take the funicular to town; see "By Train," above); at the top of the funicular run on Piazza Cahen (with both free and pay spaces); and, if you can find room, at the free lot off Via Roma. There's a new large pay lot (.55€/65¢ per hr.; 6.20€/$7[¼] for 24 hr.) at the ex-Campo della Fiera in the valley below the south end of town, with elevators to take you up to Orvieto level.

VISITOR INFORMATION   The **tourist office** is opposite the Duomo at Piazza Duomo 24 (✆ **0763-341772;** fax 0763-344433; www.comune.orvieto.tr.it or www.umbria2000.it), open Monday through Friday from 8:10am to 1:50pm and 4 to 7pm, Saturday and Sunday from 10am to 1pm and 3 to 6pm.

FESTIVALS & MARKETS   Seven weeks after Easter, **Pentecost Sunday** (usually falling in June) is festively celebrated in Orvieto. On this day, **La Palombella** commemorates the descent of the Holy Spirit on the Apostles amid much fanfare. Nine weeks after Easter, **Corpus Christi** (usually the first half of June) reenacts an event in 1264 in the time of Pope Urban IV (see the Duomo listing, below). Since 1950, the precious, ancient relic (the Holy Corporal) kept in the Duomo is carried through the streets, accompanied by a *corteo* of 400 people in costume, evoking the period when Orvieto was a prominent papal seat. For 5 days surrounding New Year's Eve (and ending Jan 3), **Umbria Jazz Winter,** the relatively new mini jazz festival, has been catching on. Call ✆ **075-5733363** or visit **www.umbriajazz.com** for information.

Every Thursday and Saturday, a morning market fills **Piazza del Popolo** with fresh produce and fruits, as well as an interesting smattering of stalls hawking clothing, ceramics, and miscellaneous items.

ORVIETO'S DUOMO

Duomo ✪✪✪   This city's singular draw is its spacious Piazza del Duomo and 13th-century **Duomo,** one of Italy's treasures. The Duomo is noted for its breathtaking facade influenced by dozens of architects and artists; inside, the Duomo contains one of the greatest fresco cycles of the Renaissance in the **Cappella di San Brizio (Chapel of San Brizio)** ✪✪, recently reopened after a lengthy period of restoration. The cycle, begun by Fra Angelico and completed by Luca Signorelli, depicts in vivid detail the Last Judgment, one that was said to have influenced Michelangelo and his own interpretation in the Sistine Chapel. Leonardo da Vinci wouldn't give it the time of day.

The Duomo was built to shelter the relic of the Miracle of Bolsena, an incident that happened in 1263 just a few kilometers south of Orvieto and has since been celebrated by the Catholic church as the feast of the Corpus Christi. A doubting priest who questioned the sacrament of the Transfiguration (one of the church's most sacred mysteries: that the consecrated communion Host contains the incarnation—the actual body and blood—of Christ), witnessed that the bleeding host had stained the linen altar cloth. This precious relic is now protected in a gold-and-enamel reliquary (1339) that mimics the facade of the cathedral in the **Cappella del Corporale,** a chapel to the left of the main altar, and it's paraded through town once a year to major fanfare (see "Festivals & Markets," above). It spawned what would become the construction of Orvieto's cathedral, one of the most important in Italy (and that's saying something).

Much attention is given to the glittering **mosaics** of the elaborate facade, but in fact, they weren't added until the 17th and 18th centuries and aren't major works. Work continued as recently as this century: The Duomo's controversial (mainly because they're contemporary) central **bronze doors** were made in 1964 by Sicilian sculptor Emilio Greco. Some of the earliest work are the **bas-reliefs** on the lower parts of the pillars (protected by Plexiglas due to threats of vandalism in the 1960s)—the work of Sienese master Lorenzo Maittani, one of the original architects involved in the cathedral's early years until his death in 1330. The facade's delicate **rose window** was the work of Florentine Andrea Orcagna from the mid–14th century. If you're still in town at sunset, join the small knot of savvy visitors who know to be nowhere else when the moment occurs; the lighting of the window is unforgettable.

Piazza del Duomo. (✆ **0763-341167.** www.opsm.it. Free admission to church; admission to Cappella San Brizio ((✆ **0763-342477)** 3€ ($3.45), free for under 10 (or on cumulative ticket; see "Saving Money," above). Tickets available at tourist office across the piazza. Daily 7:30am–12:45pm and 2:30–5:15pm; to 6:15pm Mar–Oct; to 7:15pm Apr and Sept; Cappella San Brizio opens at 8am, and is closed Sun morning.

CRAFTS & WINE

The shopping scene is limited but varied, representing Orvieto's tradition of centuries-old crafts: lace and embroidery work, woodwork (carved objects, inlays, and veneers), ceramics, and wine (with the local D.O.C. white wine Orvieto Classico holding out as everyone's favorite purchase). Shops are concentrated around the area of the Duomo and along the pedestrian shopping strips west of the Duomo, namely **Via del Duomo** and **Via Cavour.**

Visit **Michelangeli,** Via Gualtiero Michelangeli 3 (✆ **0763-342660;** www.michelangeli.it), for the most creative woodwork and inlays in town. One of the very few lace workers left in town is the gracious **Maria Moretti,** Via Maurizio 1 (✆ **0763-341714).** Ceramics are easy to come by, with a number of artisan shops along the pedestrian strips mentioned above. Wine lovers should give some time and attention to the city's many *cantine* and *enoteche* open to the public:

Cantina Foresi, Piazza del Duomo 2 (✆ **0763-341611),** represents a number of local wine producers, as does **La Bottega del Buon Vino,** Via del. Cava 26 (✆ **0763-342373;** www.pozzodellacava.it/visita/servizi/bottega.htm), which sits above ancient Etruscan excavations (ask the friendly shopkeeper if you can take a peek; consider hanging around for lunch as well, at the enoteca's popular trattoria).

The tourist office has a brochure and map called *Andar per Vigne (Visiting the Vineyards),* with information about a dozen major producers in the region within a 5- to 20km (3- to 13-mile) radius of Orvieto and their visiting hours. The **Castello di Sala** of the storied Antinori family probably wins out as the most picturesque, replete with a medieval castle, an ideal setting, and important vintages.

ACCOMMODATIONS YOU CAN AFFORD

Corsorzio Orvieto Promotion, Via Loggia de' Mercanti 12 (℃ **0763-344666;** fax 0763-343943; www.orvietoturismo.it), will help with hotel reservations free of charge if the following hotels are full. Specify the category or price range you're interested in.

Strict budgeteers may want to contact the **Hotel Virgilio,** Piazza del Duomo 5–6 (℃ **0763-341882;** fax 0763-343797; www.hotelvirgilio.com). It has 13 very basic modern rooms with some of the ugliest lamps I've ever seen, but it's smack on Piazza Duomo. Doubles run 70€ to 85€ ($81–$98), including breakfast, and the hotel is closed from mid-January to mid-February.

Palazzo Piccolomini ✫✫✫   Looking very pretty in pink, this 16th-century palazzo was the Orvieto home of the illustrious Tuscan family that gave us two popes. It reopened as a hotel in 1998 following a complete refurbishment that has kept the historic shell and its grand dimensions, plus vaulted ceilings and wide halls, while creating an uncluttered ambience that's quasiminimalist, with terra-cotta floors and white slip-covered furniture.

Piazza Ranieri 36 (2 blocks down from Piazza della Repubblica), 05018 Orvieto (TR). ℃ 0763-341743. Fax 0763-391046. www.hotelpiccolomini.it. 31 units. 96€ ($110) single; 138€ ($156) double; 175€ ($201) triple; 227€ ($261) suite. AE, DC, MC, V. Valet parking 10€ ($12), or do-it-yourself for 6€ ($6.90) in main public lot next door. **Amenities:** Restaurant; bar; concierge; tour desk; car-rental desk; courtesy car (from station); 24-hr. room service; massage (in-room); babysitting; laundry service; dry cleaning; nonsmoking rooms. *In room:* A/C, TV, VCR (on request), dataport, minibar, hair dryer safe.

WORTH A SPLURGE

La Badia ✫✫   This 12th-century abbey has been a hotel since 1968 and is one of Orvieto's best accommodations, albeit a location out of the town proper (and the prices have risen alarmingly lately). The harmonious blend of wood and solid tufa-block walls helps the place retain a strong medieval air. The furnishings are a mix of modern and antiques that came from the Badia itself or the houses on its property, including some beautiful inlaid wood pieces. Although the decor varies widely, it's singularly tasteful, with amusing touches like TVs fitted into old stone niches. Some rooms are palatial while others are cramped; a few are lofted and can sleep families without crowding. The suites are roomy, and those in the outbuilding connected to the church have Jacuzzis and a view of Orvieto up on its rocky perch. Bathrooms on the first floor have been renovated, but the older ones elsewhere throughout La Badia carry their age well. Be sure to duck into the Romanesque church to see the frescoes and gorgeous cosmatesque-style floor.

Loc. La Badia 8 (about 3km/1¾ miles south of town off the road to Bagnoreggio), 05019 Orvieto (TR). ℃ 0763-301959 or 0763-301876. Fax 0763-305396. www.labadiahotel.it. 28 units. Ask for single rates; 150€–250€ ($173–$288) double; 230€–330€ ($265–$380) suite. Breakfast 12€ ($14). AE, MC, V. Free parking. Closed Jan–Feb. **Amenities:** Restaurant; bar; outdoor pool (June–Sept); tennis court; concierge; room service (bar only); laundry service (48 hr.). *In room:* A/C, TV, minibar, hair dryer.

GREAT DEALS ON DINING

If you're between meals or just looking for a nibble, consider the **Enoteca Barberani** (see "Crafts & Wine," above) or the **Bar/Caffè Montanucci,** Via Cavour 21, for the best coffee in town. You can shop for delicious picnic ingredients at either of the two best delicatessens: **Dai Fratelli,** Via del Duomo 10, or **Antonia Carraro,** Via Cavour 101. Piazza del Duomo is ground zero for tourist spots but also the location of the **Cantina Foresi,** no. 2, perfect for a tasty sandwich and a glass of local wine, and the **Gelateria del Duomo,** no. 14, for the best ice cream in town.

Osteria dell'Orso 🤼🤼 UMBRIAN/ABRUZZESE   Chef Gabriele di Gian-domenico uses the freshest local ingredients and traditions (mixed with those of his native Abruzzi) to create memorable dishes that change daily, which is why his Neapolitan partner, Ciro Cristiano, prefers to recite them to you in delectable detail rather than break out the printed menu. In the tiny rooms surrounded by Michelangeli wood sculptures—including a remarkably realistic "lacy" curtain—you can sample fresh homemade tagliatelle served perhaps with mushrooms and truffles, with broccoli, or with Neapolitan baby tomatoes, basil, and shredded Scamorza cheese. The local specialty secondo is chicken with olives, or you can try Gabriele's *faraona* (game hen) stuffed with truffles.

Via della Misericordia 18–20. ℂ **0763-341642**. Reservations recommended. Primi 6€–10€ ($6.90–$12); secondi 10€–15€ ($12–$17); fixed-price menu 24€ ($28). AE, DC, MC. Wed–Sun 12:30–2:30pm and 7:30–10pm. Closed Feb and July.

Tipica Trattoria Etrusca 🤼🤼 ORVIETANA   Precede or cap off a visit to Orvieto's Duomo with a meal here, and you'll have orchestrated the perfect day at moderate cost and immense personal pleasure. The Etrusca offers a cool respite during a hot Umbrian afternoon, on the ground level of a 15th-century palazzo whose roots (like much of Orvieto) are lost in Etruscan times. A much requested primo is the regional homemade pasta *umbrichelli,* an almost chewy flour-and-water spaghetti served here *alla orvietana* (a slightly spicy tomato sauce with bacon). To complete a meal typical of this game-rich region, sample the tried-and-true Umbrian specialty of rabbit, *coniglio all'Etrusca* in a savory sauce of herbs and spices. Stay close to home with fresh ricotta cheese from a local supplier, dusted with sugar and covered with fresh berries for a light dessert. A thoughtful selection of Umbrian and Tuscan wines fills the restaurant's wine cellars, carved into the ancient Etruscan foundations below.

Via Lorenzo Maitani 10 (1 block from the Duomo). ℂ **0763-344016**. www.argoweb.it/trattoria_etrusca. Reservations recommended. Primi 6€–13€ ($6.90–$15); secondi 9€–15€ ($10–$17); fixed-price menu without wine 20€ ($23). AE, DC, MC, V. Tues–Sun 12:15–3pm and 7:15–10pm. Closed Jan.

6

Bologna & Emilia-Romagna

by Reid Bramblett

Emilia-Romagna comprises two ancient lands: Emilia, named for Via Emilia, the ancient Roman road that bisects its plains and art cities; and Romagna, named for its prominence in the Roman Empire. History has left its mark here on some of Italy's most beautiful, yet lesser-known cities— **Ravenna,** last capital of the empire and later the stronghold of the Byzantines and the Visigoths; **Ferrara,** a center of art and culture during the Renaissance; **Modena,** famous for vinegar and opera stars; and **Bologna,** a university center since the Middle Ages and Italy's most youthful and exuberant city.

Many travelers whiz through Emilia-Romagna on high-speed trains and autostradas en route to and from Florence, Milan, Venice, or Rome. They're not only bypassing some of Italy's finest art and architecture, but they are missing the opportunity to experience a way of life that has been largely unaffected by those two great demons of the 20th century: mass tourism and massive industrialization.

1 Bologna: Home of Europe's Oldest University

105km (65 miles) N of Florence, 210km (130 miles) SE of Milan, 210km (130 miles) S of Venice, 380km (236 miles) N of Rome

Bologna is known the world over as the home of the oldest university in Europe, and this venerable institution accounts for much of what you'll see of the city's past and present. By the 13th century, scholars had begun descending upon the city in droves, and the city took shape to accommodate them. Bologna's famous loggias, 40km (25 miles) of them total, are covered sidewalks that have given students and locals the opportunity to stroll and discourse in any kind of weather. The burgeoning community built *palazzi* (palaces) and churches, and artists came from throughout Italy to decorate them. These treasures remain amid a handsome cityscape of ocher-colored buildings, red-tile rooftops, and the occasional tower constructed by powerful medieval families to display their wealth and power. The students remain a vibrant presence in Bologna, giving the city a youthful exuberance.

ESSENTIALS

GETTING THERE   By Plane   European flights land at **Aeroporto G. Marconi** (✆ **051-6479615;** www.bologna-airport.it), 8km (5 miles) north of the city and connected to the train station by **Aerobus** (✆ **051-290290;** www. atc.bo.it), which runs every 15 minutes. The Aerobus trip takes 15 minutes, and service runs from 6:05am to 11:45pm at a cost of 4.50€ ($5.20).

By Train   Trains arrive from and depart for the following major Italian cities almost hourly: **Florence** (60–90 min.; 4.65€–14€/$5.35–$16), **Rome** (2¾–4 hr.; 19€–38€/$22–$44), **Milan** (1½–2½ hr.; 10€–23€/$12–$26), and **Venice**

Emilia-Romagna

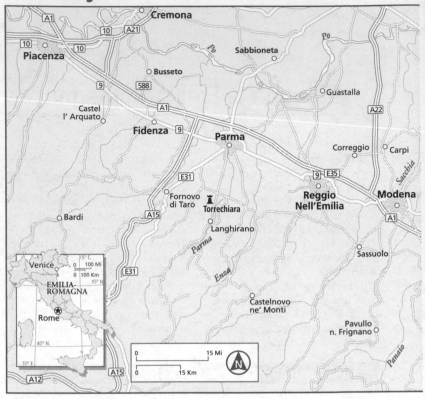

(1¾–2¼ hr.; 7.90€–12€/$9.10–$14). Bus nos. 25 and 30 make the run from the station to Piazza Maggiore in the center of the city, which is within a comfortable walking distance of about 15 minutes down Via Indipendenza, Bologna's major avenue.

By Bus   Bologna relies more on trains than it does on buses for service to other cities. But **ATC buses** serve suburban towns from a terminal just outside the train station (© **051-290290;** www.atc.bo.it). Of interest to travelers is the hourly bus to **Ferrara** (65 min.; 3.30€/$3.80).

By Car   Bologna lies directly on the A1 autostrada, which runs up the center of the peninsula and connects Rome and Milan. Using this high-speed corridor, Bologna is only an hour from Florence and 2 hours from Milan. Bologna is also linked by the A13 autostrada to Venice (about 2 hr.) and by the A14 to Rimini (a little over an hour) and the other Adriatic cities.

VISITOR INFORMATION   The **main tourist office** is in the Palazzo Comunale on Piazza Maggiore (© **051-246541;** fax 051-6393171; www.comune. bologna.it), open daily from 9am to 8pm. The **branch office** in the train station will book rooms Monday through Saturday from 8:30am to 7:30pm. The **airport office** is open Monday through Saturday from 8am to 8pm and Sunday from 9am to 3pm. For tourism information on the region, visit **www.emilia romagnaturismo.it**.

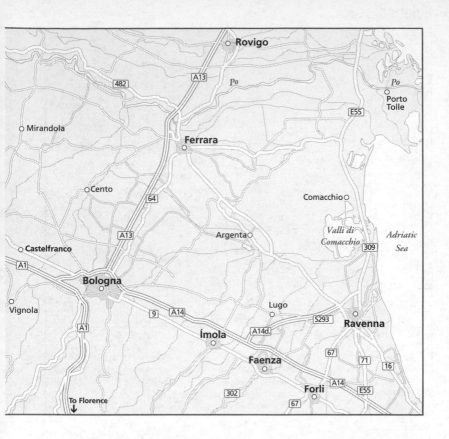

FESTIVALS & MARKETS If you're in Bologna April to October, you can spend your evenings at the classical and jazz concerts and other events that are part of the **Bologna Festival.** The performances are held in church cloisters and other scenic settings throughout the city center. Performances can range from Mozart *(Don Giovanni)* to the Academy of St. Martin in the Fields, from the Dee Dee Bridgewater & Trio to the Tokyo Quartet. Tickets start at 15€ ($17). For details, call © **051-6493397** or check out **www.bolognafestival.it.**

A much less tame event is the **Made in Bo** festival (© **051-533880;** www. madeinbo.it), a series of late-night outdoor rock concerts held in summer (June–July or July–Aug) in Parco Nord (bus no. 25 serves the area from the train station; free buses from Piazza Maggiore are provided for some events). Ask the tourist office for details on both these festivals, as well as the many concerts, dance and theater performances, and other events the city stages throughout the year.

CITY LAYOUT The center of Bologna is **Piazza Maggiore,** about a 10-minute walk down **Via dell'Indipendenza** from the train station. All sights are more or less on a short radius from this central square, where the Neptune Fountain, the Basilica di San Petronio, the Palazzo Comunale, and other sights of monumental Bologna are located.

Since old Bologna is densely concentrated within the ring roads that follow the lines of its old walls, most everything of interest is only a 10- to 15-minute walk from the Piazza Maggiore. For instance: Following **Via Rizzoli,** which

Bologna

ACCOMMODATIONS ■
Accademia **2**
Centrale **12**
Dei Commercianti **8**
Orologio **11**
Panorama **13**
Roma **9**

Rossini **5**
Touring **7**

DINING ◆
L'Osteria del Montesino **15**
Olindo Faccioli **6**
Ristorante al Montegrappa
   da Nello **10**

Trattoria Anna Maria **4**
Trattoria Belfiore **1**
Trattoria Da Danio **14**
Trattoria Fantoni **15**
Trattoria-Pizzeria Belle
   Arte **3**

skirts the north end of the piazza, you come to Bologna's famous leaning towers, and from there **Via Zamboni** leads northeast toward the university and the
Pinacoteca Nazionale; **Via Ugo Bassi** runs west from the piazza to **Via del
Pratello** and the surrounding area, with its antiques shops and osterie; and **Via
degli Orefici** takes you southeast into the midst of Bologna's colorful food markets and toward the San Stefano church complex.

FAST FACTS: Bologna

Bookstore National chain **Feltrinelli International**, Via Zamboni 7b (℃ **051-
268070**; www.lafeltrinelli.it), sells a large selection of English-language
titles. **Libreria Il Portico**, Via Rizzoli 9 (℃ **051-231074**), is a discount bookstore with a couple of bookcases of English-language books (maybe two-
thirds classics and literature) at the same cut rates as the rest of their
merchandise.

Crime Bologna reportedly has a low incidence of purse snatching and other
crimes against tourists; however, beware of pickpockets in and around
the train station. In recent years, there has been an alarming and highly visible increase in the number of heroin addicts, especially in the streets off Via
dell'Indipendenza.

Drugstores The Farmacia Comunale at Piazza Maggiore 6 (© 051-239690) is open 24 hours.

Emergencies As in all of Italy, the general emergency number is © 113. The military carabinieri at © 112 are the most useful police force. To report a fire, call © 115; for medical emergencies, call © 118.

Hospitals Hospitals in and near the city center are **Ospedale Santa Orsola,** Via Massarenti 9 (© 051-342416), and **Ospedale Maggiore,** Largo Nigrisoli 2 (© 051-6478214).

Mail The **main post office** is on Piazza Minghetti, a few blocks southeast of Piazza Maggiore, off Via Farini (© 051-230699; www.poste.it). It's open Monday through Friday from 8am to 6:30pm and Saturday from 8:15am to 12:20pm. All other offices are open Monday through Saturday from 8am to 12:30pm. The postal code for central Bologna is 40124.

Taxis **Radio Taxi COTABO** (© 051-372727; www.cotabo.it) provides 24-hour radio taxi service. You can find taxis at taxi stands throughout the city, often in major piazzas. In the city center, you will find taxi stands on Via dell'Indipendenza and on Via Rizzoli near Piazza Maggiore.

SIGHTS TO SEE

Bologna's central square and heart of the city, **Piazza Maggiore,** is flanked by the city's finest buildings: the medieval **Palazzo di Rei Enzo,** named for Enzo, king of Sardinia, who died here in 1272 after languishing in captivity for 23 years; the Romanesque **Palazzo del Podesta;** and the **Palazzo Comunale,** seat of the local government. The square is dominated, though, by a relative newcomer: an immodestly virile 16th-century bronze statue of Neptune, who presides over the ornate **Fontana del Nettuno,** inhabited by sensual sirens.

Bologna's **university** is Europe's oldest, rooted in a Roman law school from A.D. 425 and officially founded in the 10th century. By the 13th century, more than 10,000 students from all over Europe were descending on this center of learning. Their scholarly numbers have included Thomas à Becket, Copernicus, Dante, Petrarch, and, much more recently, Federico Fellini. Always forward-thinking, even in the unenlightened Middle Ages, the university employed female professors, and the political leanings of today's student body are displayed in leftist slogans that emblazon the 15th- to 19th-century buildings. You may visit one of the old buildings, the **Palazzo di Archiginnasio** (© 051-276811; www.archiginnasio.it), near the university district, south of Piazza Maggiore, just behind the Duomo at Piazza Galvani 1. This large baroque palazzo houses a Teatro Anatomico (anatomical theater), where ancient wooden benches surround a much-used marble slab and skinless carved human pillars support the lectern. The anatomical theater is open Monday to Friday 9am to 6:45pm and Saturday 9am to 1:45pm; the rest of the palazzo is open Monday through Saturday from 9am to 1pm. Admission is free.

Basilica di San Petronio Massive as this church is, it's not nearly as big as its 14th-century architects intended it to be. Rome got wind of the Bolognese scheme to build a church bigger than St. Peter's and cut off funding. Even so, the structure that was erected over the next 3 centuries is impressively grand. It is fronted by a facade partially striped in white and red (the city's heraldic colors) and punctuated by one of the great works of the Italian Renaissance: a **marble**

doorway surrounded by bas-reliefs depicting the Madonna and Child and scenes from the Bible, carved by Jacopo della Quercia and now sadly weather worn.

The cavernous interior beyond (where Charles V was crowned Holy Roman Emperor in 1530) is richly decorated with frescoes, the best of which are in the chapels to the left as you enter. One contains Lorenzo Costa's *Madonna and Child,* and the other (fourth on the left) is enlivened with colorful depictions of *Heaven and Hell,* the *Life of St. Petronius,* and *Stories of the Magi* by Giovanni da Modena (who also did the frescoes in and around the left aisle's first chapel). All chapels are equipped with light boxes.

Embedded in the floor of the left aisle is an enchanting curiosity—Italy's largest **sundial,** a 66m (216-ft.) astronomical clock installed by the astronomer Cassini in 1655. The two-room "museum" at the end of the left aisle contains drawings and wooden models of the church and various plans for its facade, some fine illuminated choir books, and the usual gilt and silver reliquaries, robes, and chalices.

Piazza Maggiore. ℭ **051-225442.** Free admission. Mon–Sat 7:30am–1pm and 2:30–6pm. Museum Mon–Sat 9:30am–12:30pm and 2:30–5:30pm; Sun 2:30–5:30pm. Bus: 10, 11, 17, 20, 25, 27, 30, 37.

Basilica di Santo Stefano   This remarkable assemblage of hallowed buildings incorporates four churches from the 5th to the 13th centuries. A walk through the complex provides a remarkable overview of the history of Bologna. The first church you enter is the **Crocifisso,** begun in the 11th century (as you enter, notice the pulpit built into the facade). San Petronio, Bologna's patron saint, lies in the church to the left, the most charming in the group, the 12th-century **San Sepolcro,** a polygon modeled after the church of the Holy Sepulchre in Jerusalem. According to legend, the basin in the courtyard is the one in which Pontius Pilate absolved himself after condemning Christ to death (in truth, it's an 8th-c. Lombard piece). The oldest church is the 5th-century **Santi Vitale e Agricola,** incorporating fragments of a Roman temple to Isis; Charlemagne allegedly worshiped here in the 8th century. Just beyond is the 13th-century **Trìnita** and the complex's 11th-century **cloisters,** where plaques honor Bologna's war dead. A small museum/gift shop opens off the back, containing some unmemorable paintings and frescoes spanning the 13th to the 18th centuries. Here is yet another church: the tiny **Cappella della Benda.**

Via Santo Stefano 24. ℭ **051-223256.** Free admission. Daily 9am–1pm and 3:30–5:30pm. Bus: 11, 18, 25, 27.

San Domenico   Here, in the sixth chapel on the right, is one of the great treasures of Bologna, the beautifully crafted **tomb of San Domenico (St. Dominic)** ⨀, founder of the teaching order that bears his name, who died in Bologna in 1221 (and whose venerated X-ray decorates the chapel wall). These saints and angels are a joint effort of Michelangelo, Pisano, and, most notably, Nicolo di Bari, who was so proud of his work on the cover of the tomb *(arca)* that he dropped his last name and is better known as Nicolo dell'Arca. Postcards near the entrance to the chapel show you who carved what. A 20-year-old Michelangelo did the candle-bearing angel at the lower right and the statue of San Petronius bearing a tiny model of Bologna up on the tomb toward the left. He also carved San Proculus, with his cloak slung over one shoulder, on the tomb's backside, but you can no longer walk around to see it, thanks to a new fence and gate. The chapel's apse fresco is by Guido Reni, who's buried in the baroque chapel across the nave. The two striking stilt-tombs on the piazza out front date from 1298 and 1300.

Piazza San Domenico 13. ℭ **051-6400411** or 051-237017. Free admission. Mon–Sat 9:30am–12:30pm and 3:30–6:30pm; Sun 3:30–5:30pm. Bus: 17, 30.

San Giacomo Maggiore & Oratorio di Santa Cecilia   The masterpiece in this 13th-century church, which took on its Gothic appearance in subsequent centuries, is the chapel/burial chamber of the Bentivoglio family, who ruled Bologna through the 15th century. Among the masterpieces here are a *Madonna and Child* by Francesco Francia, along with the **frescoes** the Bentivoglios commissioned from Ferrarese master Lorenzo Costa to depict life in a Renaissance court, an apt decoration for Bologna's most influential (and tyrannical) clan. An underground passage connects the chapel to the spot, now occupied by the Teatro Comunale, where the family's palazzo stood until it was razed by an angry mob in the 16th century.

Entered from Via Zanobi 15 (toward the back of the left flank of the church), the **Oratorio di Santa Cecilia** was frescoed with scenes from the lives of St. Catherine and her husband, St. Valerian, by the best artists working in Bologna in the 16th century. These included Il Francia (the two scenes closest to the altar on either side), Lorenzo Costa (the two panels abutting Il Francia's), and Amico Aspertini (the two scenes closest to the entry door on either side; he may have had a hand in the four middle panels as well).

Piazza Rossini. (© 051-225970, or Oratorio 051-6487580. Free admission. Church daily 6:45am–1pm and 4–6pm; Oratorio daily 10am–6pm. Bus: 25, 27, 30, 37, 50.

Torre Garisenda & Torre degli Asinelli (Of the more than 200 towers that once rose above Bologna—built by noble families as symbols of their wealth and prestige—only these and a scattering of others still stand, but barely—the 50m (164-ft.) **Torre Garisenda** tilts a precarious 3m (9¾ ft.) off the perpendicular, and the 96m (315-ft.) **Torre degli Asinelli** leans 2.3m (7½ ft.). A climb up the 500 steps of the Torre degli Asinelli rewards you with a stunning view of Bologna's red-tile rooftops and the surrounding hills. At the base of the towers, the seven main streets of medieval Bologna spread out from Piazza Porta Ravegna.

Piazza Porte Ravegna. Torre degli Asinelli. Admission 3€ ($3.45). May–Sept daily 9am–6pm; Oct–Apr daily 9am–5pm. Bus: 13, 14, 19, 25, 27.

Museo Civico Archeologico (Archaeological Museum)   The Etruscan and Roman finds from the surrounding region and many fine Egyptian antiquities make this museum one of Italy's best collections of antiquities. The Egyptian holdings have been reorganized and are now housed in well-lit quarters on the lower level; they include a portion of the *Book of the Dead* and **bas-reliefs** from the tomb of Horemheb. As you move up through the building, you walk through another relatively new ground-floor exhibit, a wing housing replicas of well-known Greek and Roman statues, to the peaceful central courtyard, which is littered with ancient milestones from Via Emilia. The next floor is filled with the museum's impressive Etruscan col-

> **Tips Saving Money**
>
> A **cumulative ticket** for all the city's civic museums (including the archaeology and medieval ones reviewed here) is available for 6€ ($6.90) for 1 day or 8€ ($9.20) for 3 days.

lection (crowded into glass cases a la the 19th c.), which includes many remnants from Bologna's own beginnings as the Etruscan outpost Felsina. Among the burial items and other artifacts is a bronze urn from the 5th century B.C., the **Situla di Certosa,** decorated with a depiction of a ceremonial procession.

Via dell'Archiginnasio 2. (© 051-2757211. www.comune.bologna.it/museoarcheologico. Admission 4€ ($4.60) adults; 2€ ($2.30) ages 15–18, students, and those over 60; free for those under 15. Tues–Sat 9am–6:30pm; Sun 10am–6:30pm. Bus: 11, 13, 14, 19, 20, 25, 27, 29, 30, A, B.

Museo Civico Medioevale (Medieval Museum)   Though a Roman wall runs through the courtyard, the collection here is determinedly devoted to depicting life in medieval Bologna. It also has a healthy handful of medieval objects from cultures around the world (collections left over from previous incarnations of the museum). During the Middle Ages, the city revolved around its university, and the most enchanting treasures are the sepulchers of professors, surrounded for eternity by carvings of dozing and mocking students. Also on view are fascinating cooking utensils from daily life in medieval Bologna, illuminated manuscripts, and a sizeable collection of arms and armor. The museum's name hasn't kept it from squirreling away a few small Renaissance and baroque bronzes by the likes of Giambologna, Bernini, and Algardi.

Via Manzoni 4. (€) 051-203930. www.comune.bologna.it/iperbole/MuseiCivici. Admission 4€ ($4.60) adults; 2€ ($2.30) ages 15–18, students, and those over 60; free for those under 15. Tues–Sat 9am–6:30pm; Sun 10am–6:30pm. Bus: 11, 20, 27, 28, C.

Pinacoteca Nazionale (National Picture Gallery)   Many of these second-floor galleries, which are badly in need of better lighting and signage, are devoted to Bolognese painters or painters from elsewhere who worked in Bologna. The galleries house, for instance, Italy's largest repository of paintings by Bologna's most illustrious artist, Guido Reni (1575–1642). Perhaps his best-known work, *Ritratto della Madre,* a portrait of his mother, is here, and in the same room hang many of his other works, including *Samson the Victorious.* More striking, however, is a work by an earlier Bolognese artist, Vitale da Bologna: the 14th-century *St. George and the Dragon.* The museum's most sought-out work is not by a native son, but by Raphael, whose *Ecstasy of St. Cecilia* is one of the great achievements of Renaissance painting.

Via delle Belle Arti 56. (€) 051-4209411. www.pinacotecabologna.it. Admission 4€ ($4.60) adults, 2€ ($2.30) students ages 18–25, free for those under 18 or over 65. Tues–Sun 9am–7pm. Bus: 18, 20, 32, 33, 36, 37.

ACCOMMODATIONS YOU CAN AFFORD

High season in Bologna is any time the city is hosting one of its trade fairs; low season is during much of the summer—especially in August, when the Bolognese tend to flee the city for cooler realms. Don't be shy about bargaining for a better rate during slow periods; hotel-keepers eager to fill empty rooms will often offer them at rates that are substantially lower than the ones they publish.

Accademia   If you're looking for a high level of comfort and service, don't even consider staying here. On the other hand, the location on a lively street near the university is superb, and the surroundings are full of character. The rooms are spread across several floors of a centuries-old palazzo, and the lobby and entrance, with well-worn stone flooring and vaulted ceilings, are deceivingly grand, as is the staircase (no elevator). Several years ago, at least, the bright, no-frills, comfortable rooms were refurbished with bland contemporary armoires, desks, and headboards. Alas, I can't say more than that, as the generally dis-agreeable management refuses to let me in to see any of the rooms each year I update this book (I got in the first time only because I happened to be spending the night). Last I saw, the bathrooms didn't seem to have been updated for a couple of decades, so the fixtures and tiles were worn, and the half-size bathtubs can pose a bit of a challenge.

Via delle Belle Arti 6, 40124 Bologna. (€) 051-232318. Fax 051-263590. www.hotelaccademia.com. 28 units, 24 with bathroom. 45€–70€ ($52–$81) single without bathroom, 60€–90€ ($69–$104) single with bathroom; 65€–100€ ($75–$115) double without bathroom, 80€–125€ ($92–$144) double with bathroom. Rates include breakfast. No credit cards. Parking 6€ ($6.90). Bus: C. **Amenities:** Bar. *In room:* TV.

Centrale ⋆ This attractive pensione offers one of Bologna's best values: It's cheap, central, and clean; it has all the amenities you need; and the hoteliers are often making improvements. An ancient cage elevator deposits you at the door on the third floor of an old apartment house a few blocks off Piazza Maggiore. Once inside you'll find yourself in the amiable company of the English-speaking owner and an interesting mix of travelers from all over the world. A nicely appointed bar, a breakfast room, a sitting room, and several of the guest rooms are on this floor, while others are reached via an internal staircase to the floor above. Oriental runners and crystal chandeliers lend an air of elegance to the halls, and the charm extends to the white-tile-floored rooms. All have been redone with crisp modern furnishings and pleasant pastel fabrics. The bathrooms can be small but are newly tiled and nicely fitted out with large sinks and commodious stall showers. Most rooms are unusually spacious for Italy, and several have three and four beds, making this an especially affordable stopover for families. (I like no. 18, with a big window overlooking a brick tower and church dome.) All the rooms have air-conditioning, except the three singles with no bathrooms (even the doubles without bathrooms have it).

Via delle Zecca 2 (off V. Ugo Bassi, 2 blocks west of Piazza Maggiore), 40121 Bologna. ℂ 051-225114. Fax 051-235162. werterg@tin.it. 25 units, 20 with bathroom. 50€ ($58) single without bathroom, 65€–70€ ($75–$81) single with bathroom; 70€–78€ ($81–$90) double without bathroom, 85€–95€ ($98–$109) double with bathroom; 110€–120€ ($127–$138) triple with bathroom. Breakfast 8€ ($9.20). AE, DC, MC, V. Limited parking 7€ ($8.05). Closed Christmas week and 1 week in mid-Aug. Bus: 25. In room: A/C, TV, safe.

Panorama ⋆ (Value) I'm delighted whenever I discover another charming, old-fashioned pensione like this one still in business. In fact, if you don't mind rooms without bathrooms or air-conditioning (but with fans), you may want to consider staying here even if your budget allows for more luxurious accommodations. The location near Piazza Maggiore is excellent, and the women who own/manage the hotel, which occupies the top floor of an old apartment house, make guests feel like family. The rooms are very large and high-ceilinged, and most look through large windows over a pleasant courtyard to the hills above the city (avoid nos. 6–10, whose double-paned windows can't keep out the traffic noise). The furnishings are functional but modern and include enough wooden armoires and other homey touches to render them cozy. Some rooms sleep four or five.

Via Livraghi 1 (off V. Ugo Bassi, 3 blocks west of Piazza Maggiore), 40121 Bologna. ℂ 051-221802. Fax 051-266360. panorama.hotel@libero.it. 13 units, none with private bathroom. 55€ ($63) single; 70€ ($81) double. No breakfast. No credit cards. Bus: 10, 25. In room: TV.

Roma ⋆ This gracious hotel enjoys a marvelous location only steps away from Piazza Maggiore and offers many of the amenities you'd expect in larger hotels—including a cozy bar off the lobby, an adequate though not outstanding in-house restaurant, an efficient English-speaking staff at the front desk, porters to carry your bags, and a garage. What really makes this hotel worth seeking out, though, are its unusually comfortable rooms. Most have foyers between the bathrooms and bedrooms that have closets at one end, so they double as dressing rooms. The rooms are large and bright, with brass beds that are often king-size, roomy armchairs, and long tables where you can spread out belongings without being messy. (For those who prefer neutral decor, one drawback may be the profusion of tastefully matching floral patterns that dominates the wallpaper, draperies, and comforters.) The green-tiled bathrooms were redone several years ago and tend to be huge, with bidets and luxuriously deep tubs (though you'll have to hold the shower nozzle yourself, and there's rarely a curtain). Ask for one of the rooms on the top floor with a terrace (nos. 301–303 and 306–309).

Via d'Azeglio 9, 40123 Bologna. ℂ 051-226322. Fax 051-239909. www.hotelroma.biz. 86 units. 91€ ($105) single; 150€ ($173) double. Rates include buffet breakfast. AE, DC, MC, V. Garage parking 16€ ($18). **Amenities:** Restaurant (Italian); bar; concierge; limited room service; laundry service. *In room:* A/C, TV, pay movies, minibar, safe.

Rossini   Its location in the heart of the university district is what draws many guests to this plain but comfortable hotel, often filled with visiting academics. If you prefer basic comfort at a good price to luxury and fancy amenities, the Rossini will fit the bill, if not thrill. The rooms aren't much more than functional, right down to the no-nonsense small bathrooms. The rooms tend to be large, however, with very firm beds, and the bland modern furnishings include well-lit desks and even reading lights over the beds. A 2000 renovation nearly doubled the hotel's size and included installation of an elevator, addition of TVs to the rooms with bathrooms, and installation of air-conditioning to the eight top-floor rooms. The lobby bar is a fun place to sip wine and listen to intellectual chatter.

Via Bibiena 11, 40126 Bologna. ℂ 051-237716. Fax 051-268035. 21 units, 18 with bathroom. 35€–48€ ($40–$55) single without bathroom, 45€–75€ ($52–$86) single with bathroom; 45€–75€ ($52–$86) double without bathroom, 80€–110€ ($92–$127) double with bathroom; 114€ ($131) triple with bathroom. Breakfast 3€ ($3.45). AE, DC, MC, V. Nearby parking 7€ ($8.05). *In room:* A/C (some units), TV. Bus: C.

Touring   This quiet hotel on the edge of the *centro storico* near San Domenico completed renovations in 2002. The stylish rooms are nicely fitted out with shiny hardwood or faux-marble ceramic floors, sleek contemporary furnishings, and (in almost all) air-conditioning (a few have ceiling fans). The bathrooms are striking, many with gilt-framed mirrors on the white tile walls, deep sinks (double sinks in a few units), roomy stall showers, and hair dryers and scales. Some rooms are quite large indeed, and many on the third and fourth floors have large balconies. The eight nonsmoking rooms come with minibars. The roof terrace affords wonderful views, and in 2004 a small Jacuzzi was added up here so guests can better enjoy them.

Via de' Mattuiani 1–2 (off Via Garibaldi), 40124 Bologna. ℂ 051-584305. Fax 051-334763. www.hotel touring.it. 36 units. 70€–125€ ($81–$144) single; 99€–235€ ($114–$270) double; 165€–335€ ($190–$385) junior suite for 2–5. Rates include breakfast. AE, MC, V. Limited street parking 7€ ($8.05), garage parking 21€ ($24; book ahead). Bus: 30 to Piazza Tribunale. **Amenities:** Jacuzzi; bike rental; car rental; limited room service; babysitting; laundry service; nonsmoking rooms. *In room:* A/C, TV, pay movies, hair dryer, safe.

WORTH A SPLURGE

Dei Commercianti ✦✦   This lovely building faces the flanks of San Petronius and was built in the 12th century as the city's first seat of government. A recent renovation took full advantage of this provenance, to the point of showing off some of the original beams and flooring in cutaway views through protective glass and occasionally even a bit of fresco. There are lovely antique pieces and Oriental carpets in the lobby, and vaulting and columns in the breakfast room. The polished woodwork and rustic touches extend down the twisting halls into the stunning rooms, which have been carved out of the centuries-old structure and vary widely in size and shape. Even the smallest, though, are welcoming. Most of the beds are canopied or have iron frames; the fabrics are rich red, gold, and blue; many of the ceilings are beamed; and lots of rooms have inlaid marble tables. The bathrooms are modern and come with hair dryers and glass-enclosed showers. Some rooms have nicely planted small terraces (a few overlooking San Petronius). Internet access is offered for no more than the cost of the local phone call to connect.

Via Pignattari 11, 40124 Bologna. ℂ 051-233052. Fax 051-224733. http://commercianti.hotel-bologna.net. 132€–300€ ($152–$345) single; 190€–341€ ($219–$392) double. Rates include buffet breakfast. AE, DC, DISC, MC, V. Parking 22€ ($25). **Amenities:** Bike rental; concierge; room service; laundry service; dry cleaning. *In room:* A/C, TV, fax, minibar, hair dryer, iron, safe.

Orologio ⍟   A loyal cadre of travelers have come to love this renovated small hotel, which looks across a small pedestrian street adjacent to Piazza Maggiore, on the clock-tower side of the town hall (hence the name). Aside from this wonderful location, two of the attractions are the lounge, with its comfy couches and Internet terminal (you pay for the local phone call), and the adjacent breakfast room, where a generous buffet is served. Another plus is the welcome afforded by the English-speaking staff and members of the Orsi family, who own this and other hotels in central Bologna and whose welcome extends to the loan of a bike for a spin around town. The rooms are small but nicely done, with sponge-washed wall coverings and old photos of Bologna, wrought-iron bed frames and handsome contemporary furnishings, and well-equipped modern bathrooms with hair dryers. The suites, while not very large, have two rooms with extra touches like ceiling stuccoes in the bathrooms or marble column capitals serving as end tables. All told, the recent price hike wasn't justified, but the location can't be beat.

Via IV Novembre 10, 40123 Bologna. ℂ 051-231253. Fax 051-260552. http://orologio.hotel-bologna.net. 34 units. 120€–300€ ($138–$345) single; 173€–341€ ($199–$392) double. Rates include buffet breakfast. AE, DC, MC, V. Parking about 20€ ($23). *In room:* A/C, TV, minibar.

GREAT DEALS ON DINING

There's good reason it's called "Bologna the Fat." Chubby tortellini are filled with cheese and meat and topped with cream sauces. Heaping platters of grilled meats are served without a care for cholesterol. Not surprisingly, you can eat very well in Bologna—what is surprising is that you need not spend a fortune doing so.

L'Osteria del Montesino *(Value* SARDEGNAN/WINE BAR   Of the many osterie lining Via del Pratello, this would be my choice for a light meal. It has a huge selection of crostini, and you can taste them all when you order a heaping platter of *crostini misti* for 6.20€ ($7.15). A daily trio of pastas costs 5.20€ ($6) for one, 5.70€ ($6.60) to sample two, or 6.20€ ($7.15) for all three or for the ricotta-and-spinach *tortellacci* (weekends only). These primi—along with most wines and the various mixed meat and cheese platters—ignore the famed local cuisine and are proudly Sardegnan. The salads are excellent, and many are heaped high with such substantial ingredients as roast chicken and shrimp. The interior rooms are typical Italian tavern, but most regulars queue up for a table on the covered front terrace, usually open except in the chilliest midwinter months.

Via del Pratello 74b. ℂ 051-523426. Primi and crostini 2.20€–6.20€ ($2.55–$7.15); salads 6.70€–7.20€ ($7.70–$8.30). MC, V. Tues–Sun 8am–1:15am.

Olindo Faccioli ⍟⍟ BOLOGNESE   Wander into this inconspicuous little place for a glass of wine, and you may end up spending the entire evening. Just a few tables are wedged into two tiny handsome rooms lined high with the more than 400 vintages served by the proprietor, and one of these rooms has been designated nonsmoking (highly unusual in Italy). While this selection and the ambience are reason enough to linger, you'll probably want to stay to sample the limited but delicious offerings from the kitchen. There's no menu, but the daily fare is posted on a chalkboard—or, when they forget to do that, recited orally. If you want to eat, try to arrive before 9pm to ensure that you'll get a table before the rooms fill with patrons who linger over wine into the late evening. A carpaccio of tuna or a selection of bruschette or *crostini misti* (toasted breads with various toppings) is the perfect opener, followed by one of the few specials that change each evening but lean toward lighter vegetarian fare—zucchini flowers stuffed with mozzarella, *crespellini* (cheese-filled little crepes), and *tagliatelle con pesto* (flat noodles topped with homemade pesto). While 2am is the official closing time, Carlo, the owner, often chooses to stay open later, and he keeps the restaurant open in August if he doesn't want to take a vacation.

Via Altabella 15/B. (©) **051-223171.** Primi 8€ ($9.20); secondi 8€–16€ ($9.20–$18). DC, MC, V. Mon–Sat 6pm–2am. Closed 15 days in Aug.

Trattoria Anna Maria *⚡* EMILIA-ROMAGNOLA   Anna Maria, the friendly proprietor, always seems to be on hand at this animated spot. She and her staff serve some of the finest trattoria food in Bologna in a big room adorned with old photos of opera stars who've performed at the Teatro Comunale. All the pasta is freshly made and appears in some unusual variations, such as *quadrettini* (four shapes of ricotta-stuffed pasta floating in chicken broth) and a wonderful *tortellini al Gorgonzola.* While any of these pasta dishes constitutes a meal in itself, you may be tempted to try one of the substantial second courses, most of which are simple, deliciously prepared dishes from the region and include the likes of *trippa con fagioli* (tripe and beans) and *fegato con cipolli* (liver and onions).

Via Belle Arti 17a. (©) **051-266894.** Reservations recommended. Primi 9€–11€ ($10–$13); secondi 8.50€–12€ ($9.80–$14). AE, MC, V. Tues 7:30pm–midnight; Wed–Sun 12:30–3pm and 7:30pm–midnight. Closed July 27–Aug 27.

Trattoria Belfiore *(Value* BOLOGNESE   This series of narrow, high-ceilinged rooms is on one of the old streets that run between Via dell'Indipendenza and the university area, and as a result, it attracts an incongruous group of students and businesspeople who chatter noisily as friendly waiters run back and forth from the kitchen. This is not the place for a romantic conversation or a foray into haute cuisine—simple is the rule. Dishes don't get much more elaborate than tortellini, risotti, or a platter of *salsiccia al ferri* (grilled sausages) or *pollo arrosto* (roast chicken), but like much of the fare, including the pizzas, they're prepared over an open fire and are delicious and very fairly priced.

Via Marsala 11a. (©) **051-226641.** Primi 5€–7€ ($5.75–$8.05); secondi 6€–13€ ($6.90–$15); pizza 2.60€–5.20€ ($3–$6). AE, DC, MC, V. Wed–Mon 12:30–2:30pm and 7:30–11:30pm.

Trattoria Da Danio *(Value* BOLOGNESE   This simple restaurant, which consists of one brightly lit tiled room, is family run and usually filled with the clamor of families who live in this old neighborhood just east of Piazza Maggiore (follow V. Ugo Bassi its length to V. San Felice). The kitchen sends out good, substantial servings of traditional Bolognese fare: heaping bowls of tortellini topped with Bolognese sauce, delicious gnocchi stuffed with spinach and ricotta, homey chicken and pork dishes, and the like. The 12€ ($13) *menu à prezzo fisso* (pasta, main course, side dish, wine, water, and cover) is a great deal.

Via San Felice 50. (©) **051-555202.** Reservations not necessary. Primi 4€–11€ ($4.60–$13); secondi 4€–13€ ($4.60–$15); *menu turistico* 7.50€ ($8.65) for 1 course with wine; fixed-price menu 12€ ($13) for full meal with wine and water. AE, DC, MC, V. Daily noon–3pm and 7–11:30pm. Bus: 13.

Trattoria Fantoni *⚡ (Value* BOLOGNESE   Of all the casual eateries along Via del Pratello, this down-to-earth restaurant is probably my favorite. The two simple dining rooms are almost always jammed with people who work in the neighborhood (which is why the management closes on weekends), and the menu reflects their culinary tastes. You can sample horse meat, which appears on many traditional Bolognese menus, prepared here several ways, including *bistecca cavallo* and *cavallo alla tartara* (horse steak and horse-meat tartare). Or you can opt for nicely prepared versions of more familiar fare, such as *salsiccia* (grilled sausage) or *tacchino alla griglia* (turkey breast). The vegetable dishes are especially good— the *melanzane al forno* (baked eggplant) and *finocchi lessi* (boiled fennel) constitute meals in themselves. The food is so good and the prices so low—especially at lunch—that you can expect to wait for a table just about any evening.

Via del Pratello 11/A. ℃ 051-236358. Reservations recommended. Primi 3.50€–4€ ($4.05–$4.60) at lunch, 2€–4€ ($2.30–$4.60) at dinner; secondi 5€–7€ ($5.75–$8.05) at lunch, 6.50€–11€ ($7.50–$13) at dinner. No credit cards. Tues–Sat noon–2:30pm and 8–10pm; Mon noon–2:30pm. Closed Aug (some years July), 10 days in Dec and Jan.

Trattoria-Pizzeria Belle Arte PIZZERIA/ITALIAN/SEAFOOD Why do theatergoers flock here after performances at the nearby Teatro Comunale? Because the food is excellent and the kitchen keeps later hours than most Bologna restaurants. Even on weeknights you may have to wait to get a table in the handsome brick- and panel-walled dining room, but once the *tortellini alla panna* (homemade tortellini in cream sauce) or *tagliatelli con funghi porcini* (flat noodles with porcini mushrooms) starts arriving at the table, you'll be glad you waited. Lately, they've been making a go of a fish-and-paella-oriented half of the menu. Or choose from a stupendous selection of pizzas that emerge from a wood-burning oven. There's also a nice selection of oversize salads.

Via Belle Arti 14. ℃ 051-225581. www.belleartitrattoriapizzeria.com. Primi 7€–13€ ($8.05–$15); secondi 7€–17€ ($8.05–$20), pizza 4€–9€ ($4.60–$10); set-price menus 25€–34€ ($29–$39). AE, MC, V. Thurs–Tues noon–3pm and 7–11:30pm. Closed Aug.

WORTH A SPLURGE

Ristorante al Montegrappa da Nello ⋆⋆ BOLOGNESE Just watching the whirl in the clamorous, cavernous dining rooms is part of the experience at this venerable Bologna institution. You can get by with a simple and relatively inexpensive meal here, but you'll probably want to spend the extra euros and sample the excellently prepared fare, which relies on the fresh ingredients of the season, without fiscal constraint. Truffles and porcini, the hallmarks of the house, appear in salads, atop rich pastas, and accompanying grilled meats, which range into wild boar and venison in season. There's a menu, but because the chef prepares only what's fresh at the market that day, it's best just to let the waiters tell you what they're serving. In fact, you can get a preview of the daily offerings in appetizing displays near the entrance.

Via Montegrappa 2. ℃ 051-236331. Reservations recommended. Primi 6€–9€ ($6.90–$10); secondi 9.50€–26€ ($11–$30). AE, DC, MC, V. Tues–Sun noon–3pm and 7–11:30pm. Closed Aug.

BOLOGNA AFTER DARK

A good way to keep up with performances in Bologna—whether a poetry reading in the back of a bar or a pop concert at the Stadio Comunale—is to scan the posters plastered on walls around the university. The tourist office also distributes updates on cultural events. *Il Bo,* a weekly that covers local events, has many listings; it's in Italian but is sprinkled liberally with English and distributed for free around the city.

THE PERFORMING ARTS The **Teatro Comunale,** Via Largo Respighi 1 (℃ 051-529999; www.comunalebologna.it), hosts Bologna's lively opera, orchestra, and ballet seasons, as well as intriguing shows such as homages to Frank

A Moveable Feast

At the **Enoteca Italiana,** Via Marsala 2b (© **051-235989;** www.enoteca italiana.it), an inviting and aromatic shop-cum-wine bar on a side street just north of Piazza Maggiore, you can stand at the bar and sip on a local wine while enjoying a sandwich. For a moveable feast, you can also stock up on a wide selection of ham, salamis, and cheese at the deli counter and enjoy a picnic near the gurgles of the Neptune Fountain. The shop is open daily from 10:30am to 3pm and 6 to 9:30pm.

On a stroll through the **Pescherie Vecchie,** the city's market area, you can also assemble a meal. Along the **Via Drapperie** and adjoining streets, salumerie, cheese shops, bakeries, and vegetable markets are heaped high with attractive displays. The stalls of Bologna's other food market, the **Mercato Clavature,** Via Clavature 12, are open Monday through Saturday from 7am to 1pm (and 4–6pm in summer except Thursday.

Zappa or Charlie Chaplin. The box office is open Monday through Friday from 3:30 to 7pm, and Saturday from 9:30am to 12:30pm and 3:30 to 7pm.

BARS   Given its young and restless student population, Bologna stays up later than most Italian cities. The main night-owl haunts are **Via del Pratello** and, near the university, **Via Zamboni** and **Via delle Belle Arte.** You can usually find a place for a drink, a shot of espresso, or a light meal as late as 2am.

Head to the **Cabala American Bar,** Strada Maggiore 10 (© **051-265445**), to hear a pianist who plays nightly and favors American classics and show tunes (open at 7:30pm; music 10pm–4am). You'll want to retire at 10:30pm to the cellars of a 16th-century palazzo near the university at **Cantina Bentivoglio,** Via Mascarella 4b (© **051-265416;** www.cantinabentivoglio.it). That's when you'll hear some of the best jazz in Bologna. It's also a popular spot for filmgoers, who stop in for some food (most dishes 6€–12€/$7–$14) and tunes after catching one of the first-run movies at the Odeon 2 across the street. The cantina is open Tuesday through Sunday from 8pm to 2am.

There's Guinness and Harp on tap and an attendant Anglophone following at the **Irish Times Pub,** Via Paradiso 1 (© **051-261648**), though a well-dressed but not always so well-behaved young Italian crowd predominates in the noisy, smoky, publike rooms. It's open daily from 7:30pm to 2am (2:30am Fri–Sat), with 3.50€ ($4.05) pints during happy hour until 9pm (10:30pm Tues). More popular these days is the **Cluricaune Irish Pub,** Via Zamboni 18b (© **051-263419;** www.cluricaune.com), a raucous joint near the university with quite good live music some nights (no cover) and seating out under the street's arcade. Happy hour lasts until 8:30pm (10:30pm Wed) and knocks 1€ ($1.15) off most drinks.

The **Osteria de Poeti,** Via Poeti 1 (© **051-236166;** www.osteriadepoeti.com), is Bologna's oldest osteria and has been in operation since the 16th century—the brick-vaulted ceilings, stone walls, and ancient wine barrels provide just the sort of ambience you would expect in such a historic establishment. Stop in to enjoy the live jazz and folk music on tap Tuesday through Sunday from 9:30pm to 3am (also open for lunch Tues–Fri 12:30–2:30pm).

GAY BARS   Bologna is the seat of Italy's Arcigay movement, and that plus the large student population makes it rather more open to same-sex couples. **Cassero/Salara,** in its new seat at Via Don Minzoni 18 (✆ **051-6494416,** or "phone friend" help line 051-555-661; www.cassero.it), is a combination of the main gay/lesbian organization's offices, help center, and meeting point that happens to turn into the hottest gay/lesbian disco Saturday nights. The downstairs disco also hosts a variety of shows, cabaret, movies, and concerts throughout the week. During the day (weekdays 2–7pm and 9–11pm), they offer gay-friendly services, including a library and a help line. Though Italians need to be members of Arcigay to use the facilities, the bar is more than happy to welcome foreign tourists free of charge.

2 Ferrara: Where the Estes Ruled

45km (28 miles) N of Bologna, 110km (68 miles) S of Venice, 250km (155 miles) SE of Milan, 425km (264 miles) N of Rome

One family, the Estes, accounts for much of what you'll find in this enchanting city on the plains of Romagna. From 1200 to 1600, the Estes ruled and ranted from their imposing palazzo/fortress that's still the centerpiece of **Ferrara.** They endowed the city with palaces, gardens, and avenues, as well as intrigues, including those of their most famous duchess, Lucrezia Borgia. After the Estes left (when Rome refused to recognize the last heir of the clan as duke), Ferrara fell victim to neglect and, finally, during World War II, to bombs. Despite the bombing, much of the Renaissance town remains and has been restored. In fact, this city of rose-colored brick is one of the most beautiful in Italy and, shrouded in a gentle mist from the surrounding plains as it often is, one of the most romantic.

ESSENTIALS

GETTING THERE   By Train   Half-hourly trains arrive from and depart for **Bologna** (25 60 min.; 2.80€–9.90€/$3.20–$11) and **Venice** (1¼–2 hr.; 3.80€–15€/$4.40–$17). There are one to two trains per hour to **Ravenna** (1–1¼ hr.; 4.15€/$4.80). One to three trains hourly connect with **Padua** (45–85 min.; 4.25€–11€/$4.90–$13).

Tips Saving Money

A cost-efficient way to tour Ferrara's many museums is to purchase one of the two *biglietto cumulativo* for 6.50€ ($7.50), or 4.50€ ($5.20) for students and those over 65. The "Arte Antica" version covers the Palazzo Schifanoia, Museo della Cattedrale, and Museo Civico Lapidario. The less useful (only because its museums are generally less interesting to a wide audience) "Arte Moderna" version covers the modern art collections contained together in the Palazzo Massari: Museo Giovanni Boldini e dell'Ottocento, Museo Filippo De Pisi, Museo M. Antonioni, and Arte Contemporanea pavilion. You can purchase either at the ticket offices of any of the participating museums. You might also consider the **Card Musei (Museums Card),** which will get you reduced admission at several of Ferrara's communal museums, including Palazzo Schifanoia, the Palazzo dei Diamanti, and the Museo d'Arte Moderna. It costs 13€ ($14) for adults and 7.50€ ($8.65) for those under 18 or over 65.

The **train station** is a 15-minute walk from the center; just follow Viale Costituzione through the small park in front of the station to Viale Cavour, which leads directly into the center of town. City bus nos. 1, 2, and 9 stop in front of the station and go to the center.

By Bus   Ferrara's **main bus terminal** (© 0532-599418; www.acft.it) is south of the center near the city walls on Rampari San Paolo. However, most buses also stop in front of the more conveniently located train station (© 0532-599490). Buses link Ferrara hourly with both **Bologna** (65 min.; 3.30€/$3.80) and **Modena** (1 hr. 50 min.; 4.65€/$5.35).

By Car   Ferrara is about half an hour north of Bologna on A13 and about a little more than an hour south of Venice, which is reached via A13 to Padua and, from there, via A4.

VISITOR INFORMATION   The extremely helpful **tourist office** is in the Castello Estense (© 0532-299303; fax 0532-212266; www.ferraraterraeacqua.it or www.comune.fe.it). It's open daily from 9am to 1pm and 2 to 6pm.

FESTIVALS & MARKETS   Though not quite as dramatic as its counterpart in Siena, Ferrara's **Palio di San Giorgio** is a much-attended event held in the Piazza Ariostea the last Sunday of May. Two-legged creatures run first, in separate races for young men and young women. They're followed by donkeys and, in the main event, barebacked horses mounted by jockeys representing Ferrara's eight traditional districts.

During summer, the streets of Ferrara seem like one great theater. Excellent jazz and classical concerts are the main events of **Estate à Ferrara,** an outdoor festival that begins in early July (including 9:30pm outdoor concerts on Piazza Municipale) and runs until late August (most official concerts indoors), when the festivities are augmented by street musicians, mimes, and orators who partake in the **Busker's Festival** (© 0532-249337; www.ferrarabuskers.com). You can pick up a copy of the events pamphlet *Ferrara in Tasca* at the tourist office or download it from their website, www.ferraraterraeacqua.it.

EXPLORING FERRARA

Casa Romei   The most famous visitor to this airy villa, built from 1440 to 1450 by local merchant Giovanni Romei, was Lucrezia Borgia, who retreated here from the rigors and intrigues of court life at the *castello.* (She was the wife of Duke Alfonso I d'Este, and her reputation for murders, poisonings, and other intrigues has been shown by history to be largely unwarranted.) The lovely rooms, connected by loggias that wrap around two peaceful courtyards, are partially filled with frescoes and statues rescued from Ferrara's deconsecrated churches and convents, but it's the elegant architecture of the house that will win you over.

Via Savonarola 30 (at Via Praisolo). © 0532-240341. Admission 2€ ($2.30) adults, 1€ ($1.15) ages 18–25, free for those under 18 or over 65. Tues–Sun 8:30am–7:30pm.

Castello Estense (Este Castle)   This imposing, moat-encircled castle dominates the city center and much of Ferrara's Renaissance history. It was built in 1385, and it was here in 1435 that Nicolo III d'Este, with a contrivance of window mirrors, caught his young wife Parisina Maletesta *in flagrante delicto* with his son Ugo and had them beheaded in the dank dungeons below. Robert Browning recounted the deed in his poem "My Last Duchess," and today's visitors clamber down a dark staircase to visit the damp cells where the lovers and others who fell out of favor with the Este clan once languished. Not to be overlooked is the fact

Pedaling Around

To get around like a true Ferrarese, you can **rent a bike** from the lot just to the left of the train station as you leave the main entrance (✆ 0532-772190); it's open Monday through Saturday from 5am to 8pm. A few blocks east of the bus station along the city wall is another rental outfit at Piazzale Kennedy 4 (✆ 0532-202003), open daily from 9:30am to 1pm and 3 to 7pm. In the center, there's a rental shop at Via della Luna 10 (✆ 0532-206017), open daily from 9am to 12:30pm and 3:30 to 7:30pm. Rates at all tend to run around 2€ ($2.30) per hour, 9€ to 10€ ($10–$12) for a half-day, and 8€ to 11€ ($9–$13) for a full day.

that the Estes also made Ferrara a center of art and learning, and the infamous (and unjustly maligned) Lucrezia Borgia entertained poets and artists beneath the fragrant bowers of the orangerie.

Most of the palace is now used as offices for the province, but you can still catch a glimpse of the Estes' enlightenment in what remains of their grand salons—the **Sala dell'Aurora** and **Sala dei Giochi (Game Room),** both ornately festooned with frescoes. Another remnant of court life is the marble chapel built for Renta di Francia, the daughter of Louis XII. Those fond of views and stout of heart can climb the 122 steps to the top of the **Torre dei Leoni** (which predates the castle) Tuesday through Sunday from 9:30am to 4:45pm; admission is an extra 1€ ($1.15).

Via Cavour and Corso Ercole I d'Este. ✆ 0532-299233 or 02-43355322. Admission 10€ ($12) adults, 8.50€ ($9.80) students. Mon–Thurs 9am–2pm; Fri–Sun 9am–10pm.

Cimitero di Certosa & Cimitero Erbacio (Jewish Cemetery)   The centerpiece of the Certosa is **San Cristoforo,** a long, graceful sweep of a church by architect Biagio Rossetti. The **Jewish Cemetery,** with its ancient tumble of overgrown tombstones, is the most haunting place in Ferrara. A monument to the Ferrarese murdered at Auschwitz is a reminder of the fate of the city's once sizable Jewish community, whose last days are recounted in the book and film *The Garden of the Finzi-Continis,* evocatively set in the gardens and palaces of Ferrara and required viewing for anyone planning to visit the city. To learn more about Jewish Ferrara, take a guided tour (in Italian, at 10am, 11am, or noon) at the **Museo Ebraico di Ferrara,** Via Mazzini 95 (✆ 0532-210228), open Sunday through Thursday for the guided tours only. Admission is 4€ ($4.60) for adults, 3€ ($3.45) for those under 18 or over 65, and 1.50€ ($1.75) for students.

Both near the walls off Corso Porta Mare. 0532-230-175. Free admission. Certosa: daily 7:30am–7:30pm (to 6pm in winter). Cimitero Erbacio: Mon–Thurs 9am–4:30pm (to 6pm in summer).

Duomo   With its pink-marble facade highlighted by layers of arches, this handsome 12th-century cathedral reflects a heady mix of the Gothic and the Romanesque. The glory of the otherwise austere structure is its marble porch, where carvings by an unknown artist depict a fearsome *Last Judgment.* An 18th-century renovation relegated many of the paintings, sculptures, and other works that noble families commissioned for the cathedral over the centuries to the **Museo della Cattedrale,** installed in the ex-Church of San Romano around the right side of the Duomo at the corner with Via San Romano.

The pride of the collection is a painting depicting **St. George slaying the dragon,** by Cosmè Tura, Ferrara's 15th-century master. Another masterpiece here is Jacopo della Quercia's *Madonna of the Pomegranate,* in which Mary seems to balance the fruit in one hand and the Christ Child in the other. A nearby relief showing the 12 months of the year once graced the cathedral's exterior, where it served prosaically as a calendar for the largely illiterate citizenry.

The **Loggia dei Mercanti (Loggia of the Merchants),** flanking one side of the church, is still the scene of active secular trade, as it has been since the 18th century, and the surrounding streets and piazzas are filled with lively cafes.

Corso Liberta and Piazza Cattedrale. © 0532-207449. Church: Mon–Sat 7:30am–noon and 3–6:30pm; Sun 7:30am–12:30pm and 3:30–7:30pm. Museum: © 0532-209988. Admission 4.50€ ($5.20) adults, 2€ ($2.30) students and those over 65, free for those under 18. Tues–Sun 9am–1pm and 3–6pm.

Palazzo dei Diamanti (Palace of Diamonds) & Pinacoteca Nazionale (National Picture Gallery)   You'll have no problem figuring out where this palazzo gets its name: 9,000 pointed marble blocks cover the facade. Less interesting are the collections in the museums clustered within. The most deserving of a visit is the Pinacoteca Nazionale, containing some notable works by Cosmè Tura, Il Garofalo, and other painters of the Ferrara school, as well as Carpaccio's *Death of the Virgin.* By and large, though, the holdings aren't spectacular. The ground-floor galleries often house temporary exhibits and charge separate admission; check with the ticket office here or with the tourist office to see what's on view.

Corso Ercole I d'Este 21. © 0532-205844 or 0532-209988. Admission 4€ ($4.60) adults, 2€ ($2.30) students ages 18–25, free for those under 18 or over 65. Tues–Wed and Fri–Sat 9am–2pm; Thurs 9am–7pm; Sun 9am–1pm.

Palazzo Ludovico il Moro   Ludovico il Moro, famed duke of Milan who married Beatrice d'Este, commissioned this lovely little palazzo as a place to retire from his courtly duties. Unfortunately, Beatrice died young, and the duke spent his last years as a prisoner of the French. The couple's 15th-century palace, built around a lovely rose garden, contains their furniture and paintings and provides a lovely view of life in Ferrara during its Renaissance heyday. Part of the palazzo houses the small but fascinating collections of the **Museo Archeologico.** The bulk of the treasures are Etruscan and Greek finds unearthed near Ferrara at Spina.

Via XX Settembre 124. © 0532-66299. Admission 4€ ($4.60) adults, 2€ ($2.30) ages 18–25, free for those under 18 or over 65. Tues–Sun 9am–2pm (may stay open to 8pm in summer).

Palazzina Marfisa d'Este   A recent restoration has returned the 16th-century home of this ardent patron of the arts to its former splendor. Period furniture and ceiling frescoes (most retouched in the early 1900s) bespeak the heyday of the Este dynasty, and the little theater in the garden is a reminder that drama, on stage as well as off, was one of the family's great passions.

Corso Giovecca 170. © 0532-209988. Admission 2€ ($2.30) adults, 1.50€ ($1.75) students and those over 65, free for those under 18. Tues–Sun 9am–1pm and 3–6pm.

Palazzo Massari   The museums housed in this exquisite palace contain Ferrara's modern art holdings, including the Museo Giovanni Boldini, with works by the 19th-century Italian painter, and the Museo d'Arte Contemporanea (Museum of Modern Art), largely devoted to the output of Filippo De Pisis—who studied the *metafisica* school of Giorgio de Chirico—plus works by contemporary regional artists. There's also a Padiglione di Arte Contemporanea, open only for special exhibits.

Corso Porto Mare 9. © 0532-209988. www.comune.fe.it. Admission: Museo Giovanni Boldini 4.20€ ($4.85) adults, 2€ ($2.30) over 65. Museo d'Arte Contemporanea 2€ ($2.30) adults, 1.60€ ($1.85) for those over 65. Both free for those under 18. Both daily 9am–1pm and 3–6pm.

Palazzo Schifanoia & Museo Civico d'Arte Antica (Civic Museum of Ancient Art)   Borso d'Este, who made Ferrara one of the Renaissance's leading centers of art, commissioned the frescoes you'll find here in the **Salone dei Mesi (Salon of the Months).** It's a fascinating cycle of the months that's both a Renaissance wall calendar and a rich portrayal of life and leisure in the 15th-century Este court. Each of the 12 sections shows Ferrara's aristocrats going about their daily business; looming above them in each, though, is a different god from classical mythology. The work is a composite of the genius of Ferarra's heyday— Francesco del Cossa painted the *March, April,* and *May* scenes; Ercole de'Roberti and other court painters executed the rest; and Cosmè Tura, the official painter of the Este court, oversaw the project. Also here is a small collection of coins, bronzes, and other artifacts unearthed from the plains around Ferrara, 14th- and 15th-century ivories, and some medieval and Renaissance ceramics (including a pair of Andrea della Robbia saints).

Via Scandiana 23. ⓒ 0532-209988. Admission 4.50€ ($5.20) adults, 2€ ($2.30) students and those over 65, free for those under 18. Tues–Sun 9am–6pm.

ACCOMMODATIONS YOU CAN AFFORD

Unless otherwise specified, rates at the high end of the ranges below apply in summer.

Borgonuovo Bed & Breakfast 🌟🌟 *(finds)*   This elegant B&B is the most charming hostelry in Ferrara. The gracious owner, Signora Adele Orlandini, has spruced up an apartment that once housed her father's law offices and that is located in a medieval palazzo on a pedestrian street around the corner from the Castello Estense. She accommodates her guests in stylish large rooms with a tasteful mix of country-style and Art Deco antiques and posh new bathrooms (one large double also has a kitchenette). She also provides a hearty breakfast (served in the lovely garden, weather permitting), bicycles, discount coupons for museums and nearby shops, and plenty of advice on how to enjoy her native Ferrara. Book well in advance, since Signora's rooms and hospitality are much in demand. Fortunately, she has recently added two elegant new apartments with antique furnishings in the building next door. One is a mansard apartment with rooftop views and kitchenette; the other has higher ceilings and a large living room. Both come with two double bedrooms and a kitchenette, and can comfortably sleep up to five (but—and this is fantastic—cost no more than a regular double for two). Services in the apartments are the same as in the main locanda itself (you take your breakfast there), but get your own key to a separate entrance. The signora also offers an 8-day Italian language course for adults (in conjunction with a nearby language school), consisting of 3-hour lessons each day in the hotel's little garden.

Via Cairoli 29, 44100 Ferrara. ⓒ 0532-211100 or 0532-248000. Fax 0532-246328. www.borgonuovo.com. 4 rooms, 2 apartments. 55€ ($63) single; 85€–95€ ($98–$109) double; mansard apt 85€ ($98) per couple; other apt 95€ ($109) per couple (both up to 5). Add a bed to any room for 26€ ($30). All rates include breakfast. Parking 3€–5€ ($3.45–$5.75). AE, MC, V. Bus: 1, 2, 9, 11. **Amenities:** Free bikes for guests; room service; babysitting; laundry service; dry cleaning. *In room:* A/C, TV, dataport, kitchenette (in 1 double and apts), minibar, hair dryer, safe.

Casa degli Artisti   Though the surroundings are utilitarian, this basic old budget hotel is very reasonably priced, excellently located in the atmospheric medieval Jewish quarter mere blocks from the Duomo, and not without charm. The simple rooms are big, bright, and clean; the heavy 1950s-era pieces are a nice change from the banal furnishings you find in most hotels in this price range; and the shared bathroom facilities are plentiful and clean. Rooms have orthopedic mattresses, sinks, and bidets. Plus, there are some pleasant and unusual amenities here—guests have use of kitchen facilities at the end of the hall on each floor, and there's a nice terrace on the roof.

Via Vittoria 66, 44100 Ferrara. ℂ 0532-761038. 20 units, 3 with bathroom. 25€ ($29) single without bathroom; 43€ ($49) double without bathroom, 60€ ($69) double with bathroom. Limited parking with their permit or 2€ ($2.30) nearby. No credit cards.

Europa   Built in 1700, this elegant palazzo a block from the Castello Estense has served as a hotel since 1880. Many subsequent renovations have left it with a somewhat contemporary look, though enough of the original architecture remains to render the premises atmospheric. The ground-floor sitting rooms and bar area are furnished in 19th-century antiques, as are several enormous guest rooms on the floor above that have been converted from grand salons and have frescoed ceilings, the original checkerboard terra-cotta tile floors, Art Nouveau furnishings, and Murano chandeliers (including most along the main street). While the other rooms (same price) are less grand, they are gracious and large, with a nice mix of contemporary furnishings and reproduction Venetian antiques. You can at least enjoy the modest ceiling frescoes of the breakfast room. All units have gleaming new bathrooms.

Corso Giovecca 49 (between V. Palestro and V. Teatini), 44100 Ferrara. ℂ **0532-205456.** Fax 0532-212120. www.hoteleuropaferrara.com. 46 units. 60€–72€ ($69–$83) single; 90€–112€ ($104–$129) double; 112€–136€ ($129–$156) triple; 136€–160€ ($156–$184) quad; 112€–142€ ($129–$163) suite. Rates include buffet breakfast. Parking 8€ ($9.20). AE, DC, MC, V. **Amenities:** Bar; bike rental; limited room service; laundry service; nonsmoking rooms. *In room:* A/C, TV, dataport, minibar, hair dryer.

San Paolo 🗶 *Value*   My favorite budget choice in Ferrara is on the edge of the old Jewish ghetto, with its warren of lanes and small shops, and faces the old city walls. Add to this atmospheric location the attentive service of the proprietors, who rent bikes (5€/$6 per day), dispense advice on sightseeing and restaurants, and serve coffee from the little lobby bar. The rooms, on the other hand, are pretty bland, but they're comfortable and decorated in inoffensive contemporary blond furnishings, with small but functional bathrooms. The hotel expanded in 2000 with some dozen new rooms (orthopedic beds, heated towel racks—but waffle towels—and box showers), and the rest of the premises were redone in the same style by 2003. The management is always taking small steps to invigorate the place, and in 2004, air-conditioning was added to all the rooms.

Via Baluardi 9, 44100 Ferrara. ℂ **0532-762040.** Fax 0532-768333. www.hotelsanpaolo.it. 31 units. 55€ ($63) single; 85€ ($98) double; 100€ ($115) triple. AE, DC, MC, V. Free parking on street or in nearby lot. Bus: 2 from train station. **Amenities:** Bike rental; concierge. *In room:* A/C, TV, hair dryer.

WORTH A SPLURGE

Ripagrande 🗶   Occupying a converted Renaissance palazzo near the center of town, this enchanting hotel provides the perfect atmosphere. The cavernous entrance foyer and public rooms are walled in rose-colored brick, have tall vaulted ceilings, and are built around two cloisterlike courtyards and a garden. Upstairs, the rooms are large and distinctive, furnished in a carefully chosen mix of reproductions and contemporary furnishings. About half the rooms are junior suites, most long and narrow but with very high ceilings, and are split into three levels: a bathroom and dressing room connected by a short staircase to a sitting room, with a loftlike bedroom above. Several top-floor rooms (some of which were being fitted with Jacuzzi tubs when I last visited) open onto large terraces overlooking red-tile rooftops. The price of a room includes the use of bicycles.

Via Ripagrande 21, 44100 Ferrara. © **0532-765250.** Fax 0532-764377. www.ripagrandehotel.it. 40 units. Mar–June and Sept–Nov 140€ ($161) single, 175€ ($201) double, 195€ ($224) triple, 185€–205€ ($213–$236) junior suite; Dec–Feb and July–Aug 125€ ($144) single, 155€ ($178) double, 175€ ($201) triple, 160€–185€ ($184–$213) junior suite. Rates include buffet breakfast. AE, DC, MC, V. Limited free parking on street or 15€ ($17) in nearby lot. **Amenities:** Restaurant; golf nearby; bike rental; concierge; car-rental desk; limited room service; same-day laundry service; dry cleaning. *In room:* A/C, TV, minibar, hair dryer.

GREAT DEALS ON DINING

The walls and Ferrara's other green spaces are ideal for a **picnic.** Buy what you need on narrow brick Via Cortevecchia, near the cathedral. It's lined with salumerie, cheese shops, and bakeries. The nearby **Mercato Comunale,** at the corner of Via Santo Stefano and Via del Mercato, is crowded with food stalls and is open Monday through Saturday from around 7:30am (when stalls begin to be set up) to 1pm and Friday from 3:30 to 7:30pm. At **Negozio Moccia,** Via degli Spadari 9, you can indulge in a chunk of *panpeteto,* Ferrara's hallmark chocolate-covered fruitcake.

Al Brindisi WINE BAR/OSTERIA   What claims to be the oldest wine bar in the world (since 1435) serves a staggering selection of wines by the glass (from 1.50€/$1.75) and a wonderful selection of panini and other light fare. In fact, you may want to come here to sample the offerings of the kitchen as well as those of the cellar. The *torta rustica,* a selection of little pies filled with an assortment of vegetables, is perfect as a starter or a light meal. The *tortelli di zucca* (pumpkin ravioli) is sublime here, as is a substantial combination of sausage and potatoes. This excellent food and drink is served in the convivial confines of two timbered rooms stacked to the ceiling with wine bottles. When the weather is nice, you can sit at boothlike tables on a little lane facing a flank of the Duomo. The tourist menu is quite a bargain and includes a feast of appetizers, a special main course of the day, dessert, and a carafe of wine.

Via Adelardi 11. © **0532-209142.** www.albrindisi.com. Dishes 5€–8€ ($5.75–$9.20); tasting menus 10€–41€ ($12–$48). DC, MC, V. Tues–Sun 9am–1am. Closed July 10–Aug 20.

Antica Osteria Al Postiglione *Value* WINE BAR   Dozens of beers and an extensive selection of local wines are available at this cozy wine bar/osteria on a narrow lane near the Teatro Comunale and Piazza Castello. You can also eat very well. The family members who cook and wait tables make the pastas fresh each day and pride themselves on such simple home-cooked dishes as grilled *salsiccia* (sweet sausages), *mozzarella al forno* (baked mozzarella), and *pasta e fagioli* (a substantial soup of beans and pasta). The desserts, including a delicious *zuppa inglese* (the Italian version of English trifle, a decadent concoction of pound cake soaked in rum and smothered in sweet custard cream), are made fresh daily.

Snacks & Gelato

The outdoor terrace and large interior room of the **Duca d'Este,** Piazza Castello 22 (© **0532-207688**), one of several cafes surrounding the Castello, are almost always full of locals who stop by at all times of the day and evening for coffee or stronger libations and snacks. A nice selection of sandwiches and salads is served, as is a daily selection of pasta dishes. The main draws here, though, seem to be the gelato, available in 40 flavors, and the fresh pastries that can be accompanied by excellent coffee, making this a mandatory stop in the morning.

Via dei Teatro 4. ℭ 0532-241509. Sandwiches 3.50€–6€ ($4.05–$6.90); primi 4€–8€ ($4.60–$9.20); secondi 7€–10€ ($8.05–$12); *menu turistico* 15€ ($17; all courses, with water and wine). AE, MC, V. Daily 9:30am–3:30pm and 5pm–1am.

Antica Trattoria Volano ⭐⭐ FERRARESE   Just south of the city walls, a block from the traditional market square, this roadside trattoria has been satisfying hungry travelers since the 1700s. The decor is unassuming (and a tad staid), and the traffic noise detracts, but the cooking is superb. The menu is a veritable study in traditional Ferrara specialties. To sample the best of them all, order a *tris di primi:* a trio of *cappellaci di zucca* (squash-stuffed ravioli), *taglioline al prosciutto,* and *tortelloni di ricotta;* or warm yourself up with their delicious *cappelletti in brodo* (pasta soup). Stay in the sampler category with the *misto bolliti* (a selection of boiled meats), or try the ultra-traditional *salama da sugo* (local salami diced, cooked in red wine and cognac, and dolloped over mashed potatoes), or *trippa alla parmigiana* (tripe with Parmesan). For dessert, try the excellent *zuppa inglese* (trifle) or the *Mandulin dal Pont* (dry cookies served with sweet Moscato wine).

Viale Volano 20. ℭ 0532-761421. Primi 7€–8€ ($8.05–$9.20); secondi 7€–12€ ($8.05–$14). AE, DC, MC, V. Sat–Thurs noon–2:30pm and 7–10pm. Closed 15 days in Aug. Bus: 3c, 4c, 7, 11.

Buca San Domenico PIZZA/PASTA   This local institution, on a charming square just a couple of blocks from the *castello,* reopened under new ownership mere days before I first stopped in for a pizza. But the new management doesn't plan to change much of what kept this informal spot booked solid on Saturday and Sunday evenings. The main dining room is cozy and rustic, with wooden booths and the fragrant odor of baking pizzas and wood smoke wafting from the large rear ovens. (Alas, the adjoining room is modern and garishly lit.) You can dine very well and inexpensively on what many locals consider to be the best pizza in town, or you can venture into the simple menu. The best choices are the homemade pastas—I hope the excellent *tortelli di zucca* (pumpkin ravioli) of old makes a comeback, but if it doesn't, there's always *tagliolini freschi alla ferrarese* (the house's pasta special, with prosciutto crudo).

Piazza Sacrati 22b. ℭ 0532-200018. Reservations suggested. Primi 6€–17€ ($6.90–$20); secondi 10€–25€ ($12–$29); pizza 4€–7€ ($4.60–$8.05); fixed-price menu without wine 21€ ($24). AE, DC, MC, V. Daily noon–2:30pm and 7–11pm. Closed 2 weeks in Aug.

La Provvidenza ⭐ FERRARESE/SEAFOOD   One of the pleasures of dining at this charming restaurant a few steps from the town walls is to walk here along a stone-paved road leading past the Palazzo dei Diamanti and many of the city's loveliest old mansions and brick-walled gardens. Once inside the dining room, with its cream-colored walls and attractively rustic furnishings, you'll feel you're in the country; there's even an arbor-shaded, partially enclosed garden for outdoor dining in good weather. If you want to eat a full meal, begin with grilled vegetables, salamis, and other selections from the irresistible antipasto buffet. The pastas are excellent and include *cappellaci* (pasta pillows stuffed with squash), *straccetti al granchio* (pasta with crab), *bavette con bottarga* (pasta with dried roe), and tortellini stuffed with Gorgonzola and walnuts. The *salama da sugo* (giant sausage stewed in tomato sauce) comes with mashed potatoes, or order a grilled fish like *rombo* (turbot), *tonno* (tuna), or *anguilla* (eel), or a *misto pesce brace* (mixed seafood grill). The dessert of choice (all pastries are made in house) is a Ferrarese specialty, *torta di tagliatelle.*

Corso Ercole I d'Este 92 (at Vicolo Parchetto). ℭ 0532-205187. Reservations recommended. Primi 8€–10€ ($9.20–$12); secondi 13€–18€ ($15–$21). AE, DC, MC, V. Tues–Sat noon–2:30pm and 8–10:30pm; Sun noon–3pm.

3 Ravenna & Its Amazing Mosaics

75km (45 miles) SE of Bologna, 75km (47 miles) SE of Ferrara, 135km (84 miles) NE of Florence

Few cities in Europe are so firmly entrenched in so distant a past. The last days of ancient Western civilization waned in this flat little city on the edge of the marshes that creep inland from the Adriatic. Though **Ravenna** has been an off-the-beaten-track backwater since the 6th century, it continues to dazzle visitors with its mosaics and other artistic vestiges of the Romans, the Byzantines, and the Visigoths. Aside from its horde of treasures, Ravenna is a fine place to pass the time in sun-drenched piazzas and pleasant cafes.

ESSENTIALS

GETTING THERE   By Train   Twelve trains travel daily from **Ferrara** to Ravenna (1–1¼ hr.; 4.15€/$4.80). Ferrara is the connection point for trains to **Venice** (2 hr.). There are at least hourly direct runs from **Bologna** (70–90 min.; 4.60€/$5.30) and from the Adriatic coastal resort **Rimini** (1 hr.; 2.80€/$3.20). The **train station** is only about a 10-minute walk down Viale Farini (which becomes V. Diaz) from Piazza del Popolo.

By Bus   While trains link Ravenna with many other cities in Emilia-Romagna, local **ATM** buses (✆ **0544-689900;** www.racine.ra.it/atm) connect Ravenna with a number of nearby towns, including some nearby beach resorts. Buses leave from the front of the train station, where you'll also find a ticket office that's open Monday through Saturday from 6:30am to 8:30pm (7:30pm in winter) and Sunday from 7am to 8pm (7:30am–7:30pm in winter). At other times, you can buy tickets from a newsstand inside the station.

By Car   Ravenna is about an hour southeast of Bologna on A14 and A13, and a little more than an hour southeast of Ferrara on the slower S309.

VISITOR INFORMATION   The **tourist office** is just off Piazza del Popolo at Via Salara 8 (✆ **0544-35404;** fax 0544-35094; www.turismo.ravenna.it and www.racine.ra.it/ravennaintorno). It's open Monday through Saturday from 8:30am to 7pm (to 6pm Oct–Apr) and Sunday from 10am to 4pm. The office now gives visitors free bikes to use for the day. You might also want to check out the private website **www.ravennablu.it** for more info on the city.

FESTIVALS & MARKETS   Ravenna takes advantage of its lovely piazzas to stage concerts and other performances throughout the summer. The **Ravenna Festival International** (✆ **0544-249244;** www.ravennafestival.org)—lasting 6 or 7 weeks between June and August—has become world renowned, drawing a top list of classical musicians and opera stars; tickets begin at 10€ ($12). The church of San Francescso runs a **Centro Dantesco (Dante Center),** honoring Ravenna's adopted son with readings and exhibits throughout the year; check with the tourist office or visit **www.centrodantesco.it**.

A walk through Ravenna's lively food market, the **Mercato Coperto,** will introduce you to the bounty of the land. It's near the center on Piazza Andrea Costa, and is open Monday through Saturday from 7am to 2pm and Friday from 4:30 to 7:30pm.

EXPLORING RAVENNA

Most of Ravenna's stunning mosaics adorn buildings that are in and near the city center, most within a 5-minute walk from Piazza del Popolo. The exception is Sant'Apollinare in Classe, 10 minutes away by bus nos. 4 or 44 from the train station or, closer to the center, Piazza Caduti.

Ravenna's Cumulative Ticket & Open Hours

They keep changing the way this works, but currently the **cumulative ticket** covers the Basilica di San Vitale, Basilica di Sant'Apollinare Nuovo, Mausoleum of Galla Placidia, Battistero Neoniano, and Cappella di Sant' Andrea/Museo Arcivescovile. It costs 6.50€ ($7.50) for adults and 5.50€ ($6.35) for students during the school year. From March through mid-June, there is a 2€ ($2.30) supplement.

The open hours (all daily) for all are as follows: November through February 28 9:30am to 4:30pm; March 9:30am to 5:30pm; April to September 9am to 7pm; and October 9:30am to 5pm. The last admission to each is 15 minutes before closing.

For more information, check **www.turismo.ravenna.it** and **www.ravenna mosaici.it**.

Basilica di Sant'Apollinare Nuovo   The famous mosaics in this 6th-century church, punctuated by Greek columns taken from a temple, are clearly delineated by gender. On one side of the church, the side traditionally reserved for women, a procession of 22 crown-carrying virgins makes its way toward the Madonna; on the other side, the men's side, 26 male martyrs march toward Christ. The mosaics near the door provide a fascinating look at the 6th-century city and its environs—one on the right shows the monuments of the city, including Emperor Theodoric's royal palace, and one on the left shows the port city of Classe.

Via di Roma. ℭ 0544-541688. www.ravennamosaici.it. Admission and hours: See box above.

Basilica di San Vitale 🜊   Ravenna's most dazzling display of mosaics adorns the dome of this 6th-century octagonal basilica that's not by accident exotically Byzantine in its design—Emperor Justinian commissioned the church to impose the power of Byzantine Christianity over Ravenna. The emperor and his court appear in splendidly detailed mosaics of deep greens and golds on one side of the church; Theodora, his empress (a courtesan born into the circus whose ambition, intelligence, and beauty brought her to these lofty heights), and her ladies-in-waiting appear on the other; and above and between them looms Christ, clean-shaven in this early representation.

Via San Vitale 17. ℭ 0544-541688. www.ravennamosaici.it. Admission and hours: See box above.

Battistero Neoniano (Baptistery)   This enchanting 4th-century octagon was built as the baptistery of a cathedral that no longer stands; it's now behind Ravenna's banal present-day Duomo, built in the 19th century. Fittingly for the structure's purpose, the blue and gold mosaics on the dome depict the baptism of Christ by St. John the Baptist, surrounded by the Twelve Apostles. Entrance to the baptistery includes, and is included in, admission to the nearby Museo Arcivescovile.

Via Battistero. ℭ 0544-219938. Admission and hours: See box above.

Museo Arcivescovile (Archbishop's Museum) & Cappella di San Andrea   The highlight of this small museum, housed in the 6th-century Archbishop's Palace and in itself a remarkable monument, is another 6th-century treasure—the ivory throne of Emperor Maximilian. Adjoining the museum is a small chapel built in the shape of a cross and dedicated to St. Andrea, every inch

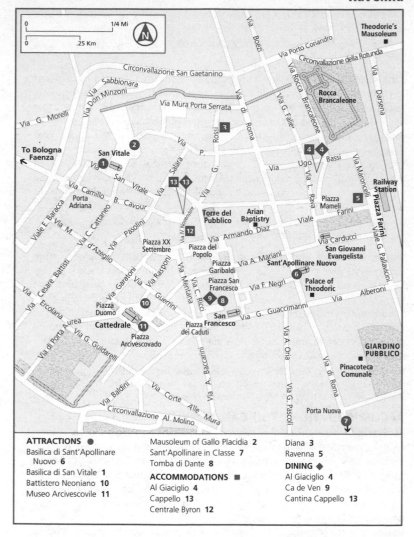

ATTRACTIONS ●
Basilica di Sant'Apollinare Nuovo **6**
Basilica di San Vitale **1**
Battistero Neoniano **10**
Museo Arcivescovile **11**

Mausoleum of Gallo Placidia **2**
Sant'Apollinare in Classe **7**
Tomba di Dante **8**

ACCOMMODATIONS ■
Al Giaciglio **4**
Cappello **13**
Centrale Byron **12**

Diana **3**
Ravenna **5**

DINING ◆
Al Giaciglio **4**
Ca de Ven **9**
Cantina Cappello **13**

of which is emblazoned with dazzling mosaics. Of the early Christian imagery that confronts you here, the most remarkable scene is of a warlike Christ, wearing armor and stepping on a serpent.

Piazza Arcivescovado. ℭ 0544-541688. www.ravennamosaici.it. Admission and hours: See box above.

Mausoleum of Galla Placidia Perhaps the most striking of all Ravenna's monuments is this small and simple tomb of Galla Placidia, lit only by small alabaster windows. The life of this early Christian was not without drama. She was the sister of Honorius, last emperor of Rome and wife of Ataulf, king of the Visigoths. Upon his death, she became regent to her 6-year-old son, Valentinian III, and, in effect, ruler of the Western world. The three sarcophagi beneath a canopy of blue and gold mosaics—a firmament of deep blue lit by hundreds of bright gold stars—are meant to contain Galla Placidia's remains and those of her son and husband, but it is more likely that she lies unadorned in Rome, where she died in A.D. 450.

Via San Vitale, behind the Basilica di San Vitale. © 0544-541688. www.ravennamosaici.it. Admission and hours: See box above.

Sant'Apollinare in Classe
This long and high early Christian basilica and its campanile have loomed amid the pine woods near the old Roman port, long ago silted up, since the 6th century. The plain exterior belies the splendor that lies within. At the end of the long, sparse nave, punctuated by Greek columns, you come to the apse, the dome of which is covered with lustrous gold mosaics—made so by the application of gold leaf that suggests a heavenly light. Imagine how transporting the effect was when the floor, too, was tiled in gold mosaic. The dominating figure depicted here, flanked by 12 lambs representing the apostles, is St. Apollinare, the bishop of Ravenna to whom the basilica is dedicated.

Via Romeo Sud 224, Classe. © 0544-473661. Admission 2€ ($2.30). Tues–Sat 8:30am–7:30pm; Sun 1–7pm. Bus: 4 or 44 from Piazza Farini in front of the train station (every 20 min.).

Museo Dantesco and Tomba di Dante (Dante's Tomb)
In exile from Florence, the poet Dante Alighieri made Ravenna his home, and it was here that he finished his *Divine Comedy*, of which the *Inferno* is but the first third, and where he died in 1321. Despite efforts by the Florentines to reclaim their famous son's remains, he resides here for eternity, next to the Basilica di San Franceso, beneath an inscription, "Here in this corner lies Dante, exiled from his native land, born to Florence, an unloving mother." The adjoining Museo Dantesco contains a small collection of Dante memorabilia.

Via Dante Alighieri 4. © 0544-30252 or 0544-33067. www.centrodantesco.it. Museum admission 2€ ($2.30), tomb free admission. Museum: Apr–Oct Tues–Sun 9am–noon and 3:30–6pm; Nov–Mar Tues–Sun 9am–noon. Tomb: Apr–Oct daily 9am–7pm; Nov–Mar 9am–noon and 3–5pm.

ACCOMMODATIONS YOU CAN AFFORD

Al Giaciglio *Value* If your needs don't extend beyond having the basic comforts, look no further than this family-run hotel/restaurant—you're not going to find better lodgings for the price in Ravenna. The rooms are no-frills but bright, clean, and quite comfortable, with a homey array of mismatched furniture. The cot springs sag a bit, but not direly. Almost half of the units have functional bathrooms; shared facilities are plentiful and spotless. There's a good restaurant downstairs (Al Giaciglio; see below), and the location, 5 minutes from the center and near the train station and Ravenna's medieval castle and its surrounding park, is excellent. Given the prices and these appealing features, you'd be wise to reserve.

Via R Brancaleone 42, 48100 Ravenna. ©/fax 0544-39403. mmambo@racine.ra.it. 16 units, 9 with bathroom. 25€–38€ ($29–$44) single without bathroom, 28€–43€ ($32–$49) single with bathroom; 35€–50€ ($40–$58) double without bathroom, 40€–65€ ($46–$75) double with bathroom. Breakfast 5€ ($5.75). MC, V. *In room:* TV.

Cappello *★★* Ravenna now has a hotel that's truly exciting—and remarkably affordable, given the luxuries and amenities it provides. Opened in 1998, the Cappello occupies a beautifully restored 14th-century palazzo in the city center. The four suite-category rooms (the lower prices in the ranges above are for one person in the suite, the higher rates for two) have been carved out of the grand salons and are enormous, while other rooms are smaller and occupy less grand but no less stylish quarters of the old palazzo. Fifteenth-century frescoes grace the two junior suites, while throughout the rest of the hotel, terra-cotta floors, painted beamed ceilings, and other architectural features have been restored when possible. The furnishings are either reproduction or classic contemporary designs—the funky sculptural lamps and lighting fixtures were selected and installed by a Bergamo designer. The sumptuous bathrooms are fitted with stall showers and tubs. Some suites have pullout couches to accommodate extra guests. Since the Cappello is operated as an annex of the Diana (see below), services are minimal—the front desk is staffed only during the day—but there are two restaurants on the premises (for the cheaper, cozier Cantina Cappello osteria, see below). The hotel is up two short flights of stairs from a hallway often used to exhibit a local artist. Reserve well in advance.

Via IV Novembre 41, 48100 Ravenna. (C) 0544-219813. Fax 0544-219814. www.albergocappello.it. 7 units. 93€ ($107) single; 110€ ($127) double; 110€–150€ ($127–$173) junior suite; 135€–180€ ($155–$207) suite. Rates include buffet breakfast. Parking available. AE, DC, MC, V. **Amenities:** Room service. In room: A/C, TV, minibar, hair dryer, safe (some rooms).

Centrale Byron   True to its name, this hotel couldn't be more central, right off Piazza del Popolo. The second part of the name is a tribute to Lord Byron, who shared a nearby palazzo with his mistress and her husband. Despite these colorful associations (and an elegant marble lobby and chandeliered bar), this hotel is no-nonsense and serviceable. Upstairs, the narrow halls are harshly lit, but the modern-style furnishings in the immaculate rooms, while fairly run-of-the-mill, are pleasant, and most were replaced in 1999 or 2002. Lone travelers make out well with unusually large and sunny single accommodations, many of which are equipped with "French beds" (wider than a single bed but a little narrower than a double). A handful of rooms are smaller than the rest and weigh in at the lower rates quoted below. Internet access is available at reception.

Via IV Novembre 14, 48100 Ravenna. (C) 0544-33479 or 0544-212225. Fax 0544-34114. www.hotelbyron. com. 53 units. 55€–64€ ($63–$74) single; 90€–107€ ($104–$123) double. Rates include buffet breakfast. AE, DC, MC, V. Parking 13€–15€ ($15–$17) in supervised lot or garage. Closed 20 days in Jan or Feb. **Amenities:** Concierge; room service; laundry service; dry cleaning. In room: A/C, TV, minibar, hair dryer (on request), safe.

Diana ⭐ (Value)   Though this stylish hotel occupies an old palazzo just north of the city center, it has the feel of a pleasant country hotel. The surrounding streets are residential and quiet, and the bright lobby, breakfast room, and bar open onto a lovely garden. The rooms, no two of which are the same, are handsomely decorated with an innovative flair—with pretty striped wallpapers and mahogany headboards and armoires. Those on the top floor are the most charming, with sloping ceilings and large skylights. All bathrooms have recently been redone with care and have glass-enclosed tub/shower arrangements, heated towel racks, and hair dryers. The range in rates below applies to three categories of rooms: standard (slightly smaller, with blander but new furnishings), superior (larger with nicer stuff), and deluxe (superior plus minibar). By late 2004/early 2005, some of the superior rooms will be converted into "executive" ones with the addition of DSL lines, massage tables, and trouser presses.

Via G. Rossi 47, 48100 Ravenna. (C) 0544-39164. Fax 0544-30001. www.hoteldiana.ra.it. 33 units. 57€–78€ ($66–$90) single; 83€–115€ ($95–$132) double; 110€–125€ ($127–$144) triple. Rates include breakfast. AE, DC, MC, V. Parking in garage. In room: A/C, TV, pay movies.

Ravenna   Across from the train station, this pleasant hotel is handy for late arrivals and early departures but is also only a 10-minute walk to the sights in the town center. You'll find many more amenities than you'd expect from a hotel in this price range. An elevator has recently been installed, and, for a welcoming touch, the halls and public spaces are attractively enlivened with paintings and prints. The tile-floored rooms, fitted out with standard hotel-issue modern furnishings, feature orthopedic mattresses and are large and immaculately kept (some very large rooms have been equipped with extra beds for families). Most are far enough from the street to be extremely quiet, and all but the few rooms without bathrooms have TVs. The bathrooms are up-to-date but tiny, and since many of the showers aren't enclosed (a nozzle, a drain, and no curtain), you'll have to keep your wits about you if you want to keep towels and toiletries dry during your ablutions.

Via Maroncelli 12, 48100 Ravenna. ℭ **0544-212204.** Fax 0544-212077. 26 units, 22 with bathroom. 35€–40€ ($40–$46) single without bathroom, 40€–48€ ($46–$55) single with bathroom; 40€–55€ ($46–$63) double without bathroom, 45€–70€ ($52–$81) double with bathroom. Breakfast not offered. MC, V. Free parking.

GREAT DEALS ON DINING

The slick-looking **Sorbetteria degli Esarchi,** Via IV Novembre 11, off Piazza del Popolo (ℭ **0544-36315**), seems to supply its offerings to every visitor who sets foot in Ravenna. Esarchi is popular with locals, too, because it uses only the freshest ingredients and follows secret recipes that unfailingly deliver delicious results. The eponymous sorbets are especially notable and come in a dozen or so flavors, depending on what fresh fruit is available. Creamier gelati are also available and, like the sorbets, are made on the premises several times a day. Esarchi is open daily from 11am to 10 or 11pm (closed Mon in winter).

Al Giaciglio RAVENNESE   This comfortable, friendly restaurant comprises a few large paneled rooms on the ground floor of the pensione of the same name (see above). The no-nonsense food is delicious, with a nice selection of basics such as tortellini, spaghetti Bolognese, and *scaloppini alla Gorgonzola.* All the pasta is homemade, and on Friday, fish is added to the menu, but without raising prices, as is often the case elsewhere.

Via Rocca Brancaleone 42. ℭ **0544-39403.** Primi 5.50€ ($6.35); secondi 10€ ($12), *menu turistico* 15€ ($17). AE, DC, MC, V. Mon–Fri 7–10pm.

Ca de Ven ⊛ RAVENNESE   The most atmospheric osteria in Ravenna is tucked away under massive brick vaults on the ground floor of a 16th-century building next to Dante's tomb. In fact, Dante is said to have lived here when the premises served as a lodging house. The ornate shelves that line most of the walls come from a later reincarnation and were installed to outfit a 19th-century spice shop; they now display hundreds of varieties of Emilia-Romagna wines, many of which are available by the glass to accompany a light meal (from 1.50€/$1.75 a glass). *Piadine,* the delicious local flatbread, is a specialty here, topped with cheeses, meat, or vegetables—or served plain as a perfect accompaniment to cheese and assorted salamis. The osteria offers three to four pasta and meat courses daily. If there are two of you, you can share a *bis di primi* (pick two) for 8€ ($9.20) each, or a *tris di primi* (sample three) for 9€ ($10).

Via C. Ricci 24. ℭ **0544-30163.** Sandwiches and light dishes 3.50€–6€ ($4.05–$6.90); primi 6€–9€ ($6.90–$10); secondi 7€–14€ ($8.05–$16). AE, DC, MC, V. Tues–Sun 11am–2pm and 5:30–10:15pm.

Cantina Cappello WINE BAR   The high-shuttered windows, timbered ceiling, and ocher-colored walls render this room on the ground floor of the stylish *albergo* of the same name (see above) both chic and inviting. In fact, with the attractive surroundings, friendly service, excellent choices of drink and food, and handy location just off Piazza del Popolo, this is my first choice for a light meal in Ravenna. And now that seating has been extended to the garden courtyard at lunch, it makes for an even more pleasant atmosphere. You can order just about any wine from Emilia-Romagna, and the house choices are available by the glass (from 1.50€/$1.75) or carafe (from 6€/$6.90). The food, however, isn't to be overlooked. You can order a *tavolozza* (mixed platter of cheeses, crostini, salami, and salad) or choose from the daily pasta and meat specials. From 6 to 8:30pm is *aperitivo* hour, when loads of tiny snacks and tea sandwiches are free for anyone who bellies up to the bar for a glass of wine. Don't leave without ordering one of the delicious coffees.

Via IV Novembre 41. ℂ 0544-219876. Reservations suggested. Primi 5€–9€ ($5.75–$10); secondi 6€–19€ ($6.90–$22). AE, DC, MC, V. Tues–Sat 12:30–2:30pm and 7:30–10:30pm; Sun 12:30–2:30pm.

FAENZA: A DAY TRIP FROM RAVENNA

In the 16th century, the local artisans brought fame to this little city by applying new firing techniques to the production of majolica-style pottery and creating faience ware that became the international rage. The tradition, which involves giving a ceramic piece a white glaze and then applying designs in yellow and blue tones, lives on.

GETTING THERE   Faenza is only half an hour **from Ravenna** by train (2.40€/$2.75), but you will have to time your trip carefully. The six daily trains from Ravenna to Faenza run sporadically and at odd hours with large gaps. **From Bologna,** trains run at least hourly and make the trip in 25 to 40 minutes; the one-way fare runs from 2.80€ to 4.85€ ($3.20–$5.60). By car, it is a quick trip of less than half an hour via S253 from Ravenna to Faenza. From Bologna, the trip down A14 takes about 45 minutes.

VISITOR INFORMATION   Faenza's **tourist office** is in the heart of town at Piazza del Popolo 1 (ℂ **0546-25231;** www.prolocofaenza.it and proxy.racine.ra.it). November to March, it's open Tuesday through Saturday from 9am to 12:30pm and 3:30 to 5:30pm (closed Thurs afternoons); April to October, hours are daily from 9:30am to 12:30pm and 3:30 to 6:30pm (closed Sun afternoons).

SEEKING OUT CERAMICS   Almost as soon as you set foot in town, you should visit the **Museo Internazionale delle Ceramiche,** Viale Baccarini 19 (ℂ **0546-697311;** www.micfaenza.org). You'll get an overview of the town's famous craft, a taste of styles from all of Italy's other traditional ceramics centers, and a firm grounding in ceramics from the Etruscans and pre-Columbian Peruvians to Chinese masters and contemporary artists, artisans, and designers. The most popular works are those by modern masters not usually associated with ceramics—a platter by Picasso incorporates his famous dove of peace design, and there are works by Matisse, Chagall, and Léger as well. April to October, the museum is open Tuesday through Saturday from 9am to 7pm and Sunday from 9:30am to 6:30pm; November to March, hours are Tuesday through Friday from 9am to 1:30pm, and Saturday and Sunday from 9am to 5:30pm. Admission is 6€ ($6.90) for adults and 3€ ($3.45) for those over 65, students, and children.

Faenza is still very much an artisan's center, with a major institute for ceramics study, **Instituto d'Arte per la Ceramica,** and many workshops where you can buy the wares of artisans. To save some hoofing from shop to shop, from late June to late October, you can get a good overview of the best several dozen artisans and workshops in town by visiting the **Summer Ceramics Show** in the Palazzo delle Esposizioni, Corso Mazzini 92 (ℂ **0546-211145;** www.estateceramica.com), open daily 10am to 7pm; admission is free. Each workshop has a selection of pieces on display, so you can take notes on the ones you like and, using the handy map keyed to a number system, go visit the producers that most catch your fancy. (You can buy the display pieces at the show, too, but with a 10% markup.) In even-numbered years, this regular exhibit is joined by an antique ceramics fair during the third week of September. The tourist office can also provide you with that list and map of workshops, or just look for any *bottega* displaying the official oval sign of a handshake.

4 Modena

40km (25 miles) NW of Bologna, 56km (35 miles) SE of Parma, 400km (250 miles) N of Rome

Via Emilia has run through the center of **Modena** since the city was founded as a Roman colony in 183 B.C., and this prominent location seems to have brought nothing but prosperity. Modena is, after all, known the world over for producing the finest balsamic vinegar, Ferrari and Maserati automobiles, prosciutto, and Lambrusco wine (a thick, fizzy red), as well as for the culinary achievements of its chefs and the operatic voices of citizens Luciano Pavarotti and Mirella Freni.

Modena is a treat for the eye, too. Visitors will be delighted to find an elegant city of palaces, churches, piazze, and artworks, most of which can be attributed to the Este family. Forced to leave Ferrara at the end of the 16th century, the Estes came to Modena and soon began building suitable quarters—the Palazzo Ducale, which now houses the military academy—and clearing away cramped medieval lanes to create elegant avenues and piazze. You can easily visit Modena on a day trip from Bologna or Parma, but there is enough to see and do to warrant a stopover of at least a night. In fact, given Bologna's proximity and tendency to fill up during its trade fairs, Modena makes a pleasant alternative.

ESSENTIALS

GETTING THERE   By Train   Trains arrive from and leave two to three times an hour for **Bologna** (25–35 min.; 4.75€/$5.50) and **Parma** (30–40 min.; 5€–10€/$5.75–$12).

The **train station** is a 10-minute walk from the center; follow Corso Vittorio Emanuele and Via Farini to Piazza Grande. Bus no. 7 also runs from the station to the piazza (.80€/90¢). You can **borrow a bike** from the city for free, so long as you bring a form of ID and a 10€ ($12) deposit. There are bikes on Via Scudari at the tourist office or in front of the train station from 7:30am to 7:30pm (if you keep it overnight, there's an 8€/$9.20 charge).

By Bus   Buses, leaving from the station just to the right of the train station off Viale Monte Kosica, serve the surrounding region. Hourly buses also link Modena with **Ferrara** (1 hr. 50 min.; 5€/$5.75).

By Car   Modena is conveniently located on A1, halfway between Bologna to the south and Parma to the north, and only about half an hour from either.

VISITOR INFORMATION   The **tourist office** is in the historic center at Via Scudari 12 (© **059-206660;** fax 059-206659; www.comune.modena.it/infoturismo and www.provincia.modena.it). It's open Monday from 3 to 6pm, Tuesday through Saturday from 9am to 1pm and 3 to 6pm, and Sunday from 9am to 1pm.

FESTIVALS & MARKETS   All of Modena seems to be a stage during 1 week each year at the end of June or beginning of July, when vendors, artists, mimes, and other performers take to the streets for the **Settimana Estense.** Festivities culminate in a parade in which the town turns out in Renaissance attire.

Fiera d'Antiquariato, the fourth weekend of every month, invites vendors selling antiques, junk, crafts, and ordinary household supplies; there are musical performances and food stalls as well. The fair is held just outside the city center at Ex Ippodromo exhibition park (take bus no. 7). The tourist office can provide further details.

SIGHTS TO SEE

Duomo   Built in the 12th century, this cathedral, with its arched and carved facade, is one of the glories of the European Romanesque. Many of these intricate reliefs are the work of the sculptor Wiligemus and depict scenes from the Old Testament; others—including the lions surrounding the main portal and the scenes from the life of Modena's patron saint, late-4th-century Bishop Geminiano, decorating the south entrance—are by Viligelmo. Rising from the rear of the edifice is the **Ghirlandina,** a 12th- to 14th-century bell tower. You may want to retire to one of the cafes facing Piazza Grande to admire this remarkable assemblage before venturing inside the Duomo, where **polychrome reliefs** depicting the New Testament on the rood screen (an ornamental screen), a huge painted **Crucifix,** and more **sculpted lions** lend a Byzantine air to the vast space. St. Geminiano's stone coffin lies in the crypt under the choir (which has nice inlaid stalls)—though his arm is encased in silver on the altar—and the coffin is carried through the streets on his feast day, January 31.

Piazza Grande. ℂ 059-216078. www.duomodimodena.it. Free admission. Daily 7am–12:30pm (to noon July–Aug) and 3:30–7pm.

Biblioteca Estense (Estense Library)   One of Europe's most extensive historic libraries contains more than half a million books and some 15,000 incunabula, codices, and other rare manuscripts. While most of the collection is open only to scholars, the gems are displayed in one large room, the Sala Mostra. Among the medieval maps and letters is the most treasured illustrated manuscript of Renaissance Italy: the *Bibbia di Borso d'Este,* a magnificently illustrated 1,200-page Bible.

Palazzo dei Musei, Largo Sant'Agostino 337 (at the northwestern end of V. Emilia). ℂ 059-222248. www. cedoc.mo.it/estense. Admission 2.60€ ($3). Mon–Sat 9am–1pm.

Galleria Estense   A 5-minute walk up Via Emilia from Piazza Grande brings you to another treasure of Modena, the sizeable art collection that the Este family brought with it from Ferrara and continued to add to during its tenure here. Shown off to their best advantage in newly renovated galleries, the works are staggering in their magnitude and array—a *Portrait of Duke Francesco I* by Velazquez next to a bust of him by Bernini, along with canvases by Tintoretto, Correggio, Andrea del Sarto, Guido Reni, Cima da Conegliano, Il Guercino, Ludovico Carracci, and Emilian artist Cosimo Tura. It's a sign of the Estes' wide-ranging tastes that the collection also includes an El Greco and canvases by Flemish masters such as Joos van Cleve, Jan Gossaert, and Pieter Brueghel the Younger.

Palazzo dei Musei, Largo. Sant'Agostino 337 (at the northwestern end of V. Emilia). ℂ 059-4395711. www.galleriaestense.it. Admission 6€ ($6.90)—it's actually a cumulative ticket that lasts for 2 days and covers 4 other minor museums: Museo Civico Archeologico Etnologico, Musei del Duomo, Museo Civico d'Arte, and Museo Lapidario Estense. Tues–Sun 8:30am–7:30pm.

Galleria Ferrari (Car Museum)   For those whose taste extends beyond vinegar to Modena's other famous product, a visit to the Ferrari showroom and museum, part of the famed automaker's factory, is a must. Racing enthusiasts will find the many trophies that the Ferrari team has won in international competitions over the years—including, after a long dry spell, a major victory in 2000—but pride of place belongs to the gorgeous automobiles the company has produced over the years.

Via Dino Ferrari 43, in the town of Maranello (about 10 min. south of the center via bus no. 2 from the bus station, near the train station off Vle. Monte Kosica). © 0536-949713. www.galleria.ferrari.com. Admission 12€ ($14) adults, 9€ ($10) students and over 65, 7€ ($8.05) children under 10. Tues–Sun 9:30am–6pm.

ACCOMMODATIONS YOU CAN AFFORD

Centrale   The Centrale is indeed in the center of things, wonderfully situated on a charming old street a block from the Duomo. Besides the great location, there's an inviting breakfast room and bar area downstairs and unusually large rooms upstairs. The furnishings are contemporary and bland; the bathrooms are tiny and come with stall showers, though some of these have recently been redone. Most rooms have nice views over the surrounding palazzi of old Modena. Three of the accommodations include a short corridor leading to a small extra room with a single bed, making them ideal for families.

Via Rismondo 55, 41100 Modena. © 059-218808. Fax 059-238201. www.hotelcentrale.com. 40 units, 38 with bathroom. 29€–40€ ($33–$46) single without bathroom, 51€–80€ ($59–$92) single with bathroom; 52€–80€ ($60–$92) double without bathroom, 83€–130€ ($95–$150) double with bathroom; 103€–175€ ($118–$201) triple with bathroom. Buffet breakfast 10€ ($12). AE, DC, MC, V. Parking 10€ ($12) in garage or free on street (ask for permit). Closed Aug 13–22. Bus: 4, 6, 7, 11. **Amenities:** Room service (breakfast); laundry service; nonsmoking rooms. *In room:* A/C, TV, DVD, dataport, hair dryer, safe.

WORTH A SPLURGE

Canalgrande ⊛   Chances are, you won't regret exceeding your budget on this exquisite hotel, which provides just the sort of ambience you'd expect in a city as atmospheric and elegant as Modena. The ground-floor public areas and breakfast rooms of this 17th-century villa retain splendid terra-cotta floors and elaborate plasterwork and frescoes, and are decorated in a pleasing blend of Victorian and traditional furnishings. French doors open to a beautifully planted garden (ask for a room facing this side of the building). Upstairs, ongoing renovations are bringing the guest rooms up-to-date in perfect style—the silk pastel-colored draperies and bed coverings, linen sheets, and Venetian-style or 19th-century reproductions provide handsome surroundings. The new bathrooms are sumptuous and come with amenities like massaging shower heads, hair dryers, and heated towel racks. Service is both efficient and friendly. There's an osteria-style restaurant in the cellars, La Secchia Rapita.

Corso Canalgrande 6, 41100 Modena. © 059-217160. Fax 059-221674. www.canalgrandehotel.it. 70 units. 118€ ($136) single; 169€ ($194) double; 260€ ($299) suite. Rates include buffet breakfast. AE, DC, MC, V. Parking 10€ ($12) in garage or free on street (ask for permit). **Amenities:** Restaurant; concierge. *In room:* A/C, TV, minibar, hair dryer.

GREAT DEALS ON DINING

Giusti ⊛⊛ MODENESE   I hesitate to mention this five-table eatery only because it can be so hard to procure a table—often you must reserve at least a month before you plan to be in Modena—but the experience of lunching here is well worth the effort. You enter through a shop fragrant with balsamic vinegars and parmigiano, and put yourself in the hands of Nano Morandi and Laura Galli, the husband-and-wife proprietors. You'll want to try the capon in two forms—a capon broth with tortellini (which, like all the pastas, is made on the premises) and a crunchy capon salad dribbled with aged balsamic vinegar. A *stinco* (roasted joint) of veal or pork is the perfect dish with which to proceed, and, even if you feel you can't, do indulge in one of the delicious homemade cakes.

Vicolo Squallore 46. (C) 059-222533. Reservations required. Primi 13€ ($15); secondi 17€–29€ ($20–$33). AE, MC, V. Tues–Sat 12:30–2pm. Closed July 20–Aug 31 and Dec 1–Jan 16.

Ristorante Oreste (R (Value **MODENESE**   Oreste was last redecorated in 1959, and the glass globe lamps, blond paneling, and Danish-modern furnishings suggest a timelessness that is reflected in the flawless service and an excellent menu of traditional Modenese favorites. You can sample a wonderful assortment of antipasti (including prosciutto supplied directly from a nearby producer and vegetables delivered fresh daily to the kitchen door) at the self-service buffet for 5€ to 15€ ($5.75–$17), depending on how high you heap the platter and what choices you make (veggies are cheaper than high-quality meats). Many vegetarian pastas are available (including a risotto with wild mushrooms and tortellini stuffed with ricotta and spinach), but Oreste is justifiably well known for its flawlessly prepared meat dishes. You would be hard pressed to find a richer *osso buco* or more succulent roast of veal or pork (served with heavenly rosemary-infused potatoes)—and because their egg-based homemade pastas are so rich, you'd better skip either the primo or the antipasto if you want to have room for a secondo. The attentive staff is happy to help you with the extensive wine list, which includes many local vintages.

Piazza Roma 31a. (C) **059-243324.** Reservations recommended. Primi 8€–12€ ($9.20–$14); secondi 10€–15€ ($12–$17). AE, DC, MC, V. Thurs–Tues noon–3pm and 7:30–10:30pm. Closed Sun evening and July 10–31.

WORTH A SPLURGE
Fini (R(R **MODENESE**   Fini was founded as an annex to a salumeria in 1912 and since then has become one of Italy's most noted restaurants—and it lives up to its far-flung reputation without fail. The surroundings are vaguely Art Deco and surprisingly relaxed, service is impeccable without being stuffy, and the kitchen sends out meals that are sure to be memorable. An unusual and delectable starter is the pâté of chicken and prosciutto. Carnivores should move on to

---

Living Off the Fat of the Land

Modena's well-deserved reputation for culinary excellence is not confined to the city's elegant restaurants. To equip yourself for a picnic, pick your way through the food stalls of the 1931 **covered market** on Via Albinelli, open weekdays from 6:30am to 2pm and Saturday from 5 to 7:30pm in summer. Purists may want to procure local hams during tastings at the **Consorzio del Prosciutto di Modena,** Viale Corassori 72 ((C) **059-343464**), and accompany them with wines from the **Consorzio Tutela del Lambrusco di Modena,** Via Schedoni 41 ((C) **059-235005;** www.lambrusco.net).

More readily available are the balsamic vinegars, prosciutto, and other foodstuffs sold at several gourmet shops throughout the city. Two of these emporia are connected with well-known restaurants: the 400-year-old **Salumeria Giuseppe Giusti,** Viale Trento Trieste 25 ((C) **059-2100712;** www.giusti1605.com), and **Fini,** Piazza San Francesco ((C) **059-223314**).

the house's famous *carrello dei setti tagli di bollito* (a cart with seven kinds of boiled meats to carve, accompanied by sauces like *mostarda de Cremona*—fruits preserved in mustard sauce). The fare doesn't get too much lighter than fried sweetbreads or kidneys topped with truffle shavings. However, vegetarians will be satisfied with many of the pasta dishes, which change daily and are nicely infused with *funghi porcini* and other fresh ingredients in season. The 75€ ($86) *menu degustatione* (tasting menu) is a culinary tour de force—and practically unfinishable, seeing as how it includes an antipasto, two first courses, *and* two second courses, along with a cheese course and dessert. The wine list includes many Lambruscos from Fini's own vineyards.

Rua Frati Minori 54. ℭ 059-223314. www.hrf.it. Reservations required. Primi 15€–38€ ($17–$44); secondi 25€–40€ ($29–$46); *menu degustatione* 75€ ($86). AE, DC, MC, V. Wed–Sun 12:30–3pm and 8–11pm. Closed June 1–Sept 3 and Dec 22–Jan 1.

7

Venice: La Serenissima

by Reid Bramblett

Yes, the tourist hordes have become so relentless there doesn't seem to be a low season anymore. And, yes, the prices here can be double what they are elsewhere in Italy. But, after all, this is the fabled city of canals: This is Venice, *La Serenissima* (the Serene Republic), what Lord Byron described as "a fairy city of the heart." People flock here for a very good reason: Venice is extraordinary, magical, and worth every euro. It shouldn't exist and yet it does, and it's a living, breathing, singular city that seems almost too exquisite to be genuine.

Venice was at the crossroads of the Byzantine and Roman worlds for centuries, a fact that lends to its unique heritage of art, architecture, and culture. And although traders and merchants no longer pass through "La Repubblica Serena" as they once did, it nonetheless continues to find itself at a crossroads: an intersection in time between the uncontested period of maritime power that built it and the modern world that keeps it ever-so-gingerly afloat.

Sometimes the entire city seems like a museum—and with the crush of visitors eager to experience *La Serenissima,* it is often congested with tourists who forget that delicate Venice is still very much a living city. In 2003, Venice's mayor acknowledged that although tourism accounts for 70 percent of the city's economy, tourists can be a headache. He drew up six commandments for visitors: Thou shalt not: litter, undress in public, walk around in a bathing suit, swim in the canals, ride bicycles, or eat in the streets.

Enjoy all that Venice offers, old and new, but know that the most fun you have might be in getting lost away from the tourist hordes.

1 Arriving

BY PLANE

You can fly into Venice from North America via Rome or Milan with Alitalia or a number of other airlines, or by connecting through a major European city with European carriers. No-frills carriers Ryanair (www.ryanair.com) and EasyJet (www.easyjet.com) fly direct from London much, much more cheaply than the major airlines.

Flights land at the **Aeroporto Marco Polo,** 7km (4⅓ miles) north of the city on the mainland (© **041-2609260** for flight info, or 041-2609240 for general information; www.veniceairport.it).

There are two **bus** alternatives for getting to Venice: The special **ATVO airport shuttle bus** (© **041-5205530;** www.atvo.it) connects with Piazzale Roma not far from Venice's Santa Lucia train station, and the closest point to Venice's attractions accessible by land. Buses leave for and from the airport about every 20 minutes, cost 3€ ($3.45), and make the trip in about 30 minutes. The slightly less expensive, twice-hourly **local public ACTV bus** no. 5 (© **041-5287886;**

www.actv.it) costs 1.50€ ($1.75) and takes 30 to 45 minutes. Buy tickets for either at the newsstand just inside the terminal from the bus stop. With either bus, you'll have to walk to and from the final stop at Piazzale Roma to the nearby vaporetto stop for the final connection to your hotel. It's rare to see porters around who'll help with luggage, so pack light.

A **land taxi** from the airport to the Piazzale Roma, where you can pick up your vaporetto will run about 30€ ($35).

The most fashionable and traditional way to arrive in Piazza San Marco is by sea. For 10€ ($12), the **Cooperative San Marco/Alilaguna** (℡ 041-5235775; www.alilaguna.it) operates a large *motoscafo* **(shuttle boat)** service from the airport with two stops at Murano and the Lido before arriving after about 1 hour in Piazza San Marco. Call for the daily schedule of a dozen or so trips from about 6am to midnight, which changes with the season and is coordinated with the principal arrival/departure of the major airlines (most hotels have the schedule). If your hotel isn't in the Piazza San Marco area, you'll have to make a connection at the vaporetto launches (your hotel can help you with the specifics if you've booked before leaving home).

A **private water taxi** *(taxi acquei;* 20–30 min. to/from the airport) is convenient but costly—a legal minimum of 55€ ($63), but usually more around 75€ ($86) for two or three passengers with few bags. However, it's worth considering if you're pressed for time, have an early flight, have a lot of luggage (a Venice no-no), or can split the cost with a friend or two. The water taxi may be able to drop you off at the front (or side) door of your hotel or as close as it can maneuver, given your hotel's location (check with the hotel before arriving). Your taxi captain should be able to tell you before boarding just how close he can get you. Call **Corsorzio Motoscafi Venezia** (℡ 041-5222303; www.motoscafi venezia.it).

BY TRAIN

Trains (www.trenitalia.com) from **Rome** (4½–5 hr.; 36€–45€/$41–$52), **Milan** (2½–3½ hr.; 12€–21€/$14–$24), **Florence** (3–4 hr.; 18€–27€/$21–$31), and all over Europe arrive at the **Stazione Santa Lucia** (℡ 800-888-088 toll-free in Italy). To get there, all must pass through (but not necessarily stop at) a station marked VENEZIA–MESTRE. Don't be confused: Mestre is a charmless industrial city that's the last stop on the mainland. Occasionally trains end in Mestre, in which case you have to catch one of the frequent 10-minute shuttles connecting with Venice; if so, take a moment to look around, as the Mestre station was designed by famed architect Rienzo Piano, who did Paris's Centre Pompidou and the new *New York Times* building in Manhattan. Still, it's inconvenient, so when booking your ticket, confirm that the final destination is Venezia–Stazione Santa Lucia.

Between the station's large front doors is a small, understaffed **tourist office** (℡ 041-5298727), with lines that can be discouraging and a strict "one person allowed in at a time" policy. It's open daily from 8am to 6:30pm (closed Sun in winter). The **train info office,** marked with a lowercase *i,* is also in the station's main hall and is staffed daily from 8am to 8pm.

On exiting, you'll find the Canal Grande (Grand Canal) in front of you, making a heart-stopping first impression. You'll find the docks for a number of **vaporetto** lines (the city's public ferries or "water buses") to your left and right. Head to the booths to your left, near the bridge, to catch either of the two lines plying the Canal Grande: the **no. 82 express,** which stops only at the station, San Marcula, Rialto Bridge, San Tomà, San Samuele, and Accademia before hitting San Marco (26 min. total); and the misnamed **no. 1** *accellerato,* which is actually the local, making 14 stops between the station and San Marco (a 31-min. trip). Both leave every 10 minutes or so, but every other no. 82 stops short at Rialto, meaning you'll have to disembark and hop on the next no. 1 or no. 82 that comes along to continue to San Marco.

Note: The no. 82 goes in two directions from the train station: left down the Canal Grande toward San Marco—which is the (relatively) fast and scenic way—and right, which also gets you to San Marco (at the San Zaccaria stop) but takes twice as long because it goes the relatively boring way around Dorsoduro. Make sure the no. 82 you get on is headed to San Marco.

BY BUS Although rail travel is more convenient and commonplace, Venice is serviced by long-distance buses from all over mainland Italy and some foreign cities. The final destination is Piazzale Roma, where you'll need to pick up vaporetto nos. 1 or 82 (see "By Train," above) to connect you with stops in the heart of Venice and along the Grand Canal.

BY CAR The only wheels you'll see in Venice are those attached to luggage. Venice is a city of canals and narrow alleys. No cars allowed—even the police and ambulance services use boats. Arriving in Venice by car is problematic and expensive—and downright exasperating if it's high season and the parking facilities are full (they usually are). You can drive across the Ponte della Libertà from Mestre to Venice itself but can go no farther than Piazzale Roma at the Venice end, where many garages eagerly await your money. Do some research before choosing a **garage**—the rates vary widely, from 19€ ($22) per day for an average-size car at the communal **ASM garage** (© 041-2727211; www.asmvenezia.it) to 26€ ($30) per day at private outfits like **Garage San Marco** (© 041-5232213; www.garagesanmarco.it). If you have reservations at a hotel, check before arriving: Most of them offer guests coupons for some of the parking facilities; just submit them on departure when payment is due (ask the hotel at which garage you need to park).

Vaporetto line nos. 1 and 82, described under "By Train" above, stop at both Piazzale Roma before continuing down the Canal Grande to the train station and, eventually, Piazza San Marco.

2 Essentials

VISITOR INFORMATION

TOURIST OFFICES There's a small office in the train station (see above), but the new main office is located right where you get off the vaporetto at the San Marco stop, in a stone pavilion wedged between the small green park on the Grand Canal called the Giardinetti Reali and the famous Harry's Bar. The office is called the **Venice Pavilion/Palazzina dei Santi** (© 041-5225150 or 041-5298711; www.turismovenezia.it; Vaporetto: San Marco) and is, frankly, more interested in running its gift shop than in helping tourists. It's open daily from 10am to 6pm. They've kept open the old (but just as indifferent) office under the arcade at the west end of **Piazza San Marco** at no. 71F, on the left of the tunnel-like street leading to Calle dell'Ascensione (© 041-5208964; fax 041-5290399; Vaporetto: San Marco). It's open Monday through Friday from 9am to 3:30pm. During peak season, a small info booth with erratic hours operates in the arrivals hall at the Marco Polo Airport.

The tourist office's *LEO Bussola* brochure is useful for museum hours and events, but their map helps you find only vaporetto lines and stops (a street map is well worth buying at a news kiosk; see below). More useful is info-packed

> **Tips Saving Money**
>
> Anyone between 16 and 29 is eligible for the terrific **Rolling Venice Card,** which gives discounts in museums, restaurants, stores, language courses, hotels, and bars across the city. It's valid for a year and costs 3€ ($3.45). From July to September, you can stop by the special Rolling Venice office in the train station daily from 8am to 8pm; in winter, you can get the pass at the Transalpino travel agency just outside the station's front doors and to the right, at the top of the steps, open Monday through Friday from 8:30am to 12:30pm and 3 to 7pm, and Saturday from 8:30am to 12:30pm. Year-round, you can pick one up at the Informagiovani Assessorato alla Gioventù, Corte Contarina 1529, off the Frezzeria west of St. Mark's Square (© 041-2747650), open Monday through Friday from 8:30am to 12:30pm and 3 to 7pm, and Saturday from 8:30am to 12:30pm.

monthly *Un Ospite di Venezia* (www.unospitedivenezia.it); most hotels have a handful of copies. Also keep an eye out for the ubiquitous posters around town with **exhibit and concert schedules.** The classical concerts held mostly in churches are touristy but fun and are advertised by an army of costumed touts handing out leaflets on highly trafficked streets. The official site of the city government (also full of good resources) is **www.comune.venezia.it.**

WEBSITES   The city's **official tourist board** website is www.turismovenezia.it. Several good privately maintained sites are **Meeting Venice** (www.meeting venice.it), *Un Ospite di Venezia* (www.unospitedivenezia.it), and **Doge of Venice** (www.doge.it).

FESTIVALS & EVENTS   Venice's most special event is the yearly pre-Lenten **Carnevale** (© 041-2410570; www.venice-carnival.com), described fully in the box on p. 405. Stupendous fireworks light the night sky during the **Festa del Redentore,** on the third Saturday and Sunday in July. This celebration marking the July 1576 lifting of a plague that had gripped the city is centered on the Palladio-designed Chiesa del Redentore (Church of the Redeemer) on the island of Giudecca. A bridge of boats across the Giudecca Canal links the church with the banks of Le Zattere in Dorsoduro, and hundreds of boats of all shapes and sizes fill the Giudecca. It's one big floating *festa* until night descends and an awesome half-hour *spettacolo* of fireworks fills the sky.

The **Venice International Film Festival,** in late August and early September, is the most respected celebration of celluloid in Europe after Cannes. Films from all over the world are shown in the Palazzo del Cinema on the Lido as well as at various venues—and, occasionally, in some of the *campi.* Ticket prices vary, but those for the less sought-after films are usually modest. Check with the tourist office for listings.

Venice hosts the latest in modern and contemporary painting and sculpture from dozens of countries during the prestigious **Biennale d'Arte** (© 041-5218846 or 041-2719005; www.labiennale.org), one of the world's top international modern art shows. It fills the pavilions of the public gardens at the east end of Castello from late May to October every odd-numbered year. Many great modern artists have been discovered at this world-famous show. Tickets (10€/$12) can be reserved online or by calling © 199-199100 in Italy. The **Regata Storica** that takes place on the Grand Canal on the first Sunday in September is an extravagant seagoing parade in historic costume as well as a genuine regatta. Just about every seaworthy gondola, richly decorated for the occasion and piloted by gondolieri in colorful livery, participates in the opening cavalcade. The aquatic parade is followed by three regattas that proceed along the Grand Canal. You can buy grandstand tickets through the tourist office, or come early and pull up a piece of embankment near the Rialto Bridge for the best seats in town.

April 25 is a local holiday, the **feast day of St. Mark,** beloved patron saint of Venice and of the ancient Serene Republic. A special high Mass is celebrated in the Basilica di San Marco, roses are exchanged between loved ones, and a quiet air of *festa* permeates the town, where everything pretty much shuts down for the day.

CITY LAYOUT

Keep in mind as you wander seemingly hopelessly among the *calli* (streets) and *campi* (squares) that the city wasn't built to make sense to those on foot but rather to those plying its canals. No matter how good your map and sense of direction, time after time you'll get lost. Just view it as an opportunity to stumble across Venice's most intriguing corners and vignettes.

Venice lies 4km (2½ miles) from terra firma, connected to the mainland burg of **Mestre** by the **Ponte della Libertà,** which leads to **Piazzale Roma.** Snaking through the city like an inverted S is the **Canal Grande (Grand Canal),** the wide main artery of aquatic Venice. The "streets filled with water" are 177 narrow *rio* (canals) cutting through the interior of the two halves of the city, flowing gently by the doorsteps of centuries-old *palazzi* (palaces). They'd be endlessly frustrating to the landlubbing visitors trying to navigate the city on foot if not for the 400 footbridges crossing them, connecting Venice's 118 islands.

Only three bridges cross the Grand Canal: the **Ponte degli Scalzi,** just outside the train station; the elegant white marble **Ponte Rialto,** connecting the districts of San Marco and San Polo and by far the most recognizable; and the wooden **Ponte Accademia,** connecting the Campo Santo Stefano area of the San Marco neighborhood with the Accademia museum across the way in Dorsoduro.

The **free street map** offered by the tourist office and most hotels has good intentions, but it doesn't even show, much less name or index, all the *calli* and pathways of Venice. For that, pick up a more detailed map (ask for a *pianta della città*) for sale in any of a number of bookstores or newsstands. The best (and most expensive) available is the easy-to-read, spiral-bound, highly detailed **Touring Club edition.** The recognizable red, white, and black map put out by **Nicola Vincitorio Pub** is just as handy, with a street index. Surprisingly complete enough for even heavy tourist use, it's available at just about every newsstand

---

Tips A Note on Addresses

Within each *sestiere* (district) is a most original system of numbering the palazzi, using one continuous string of 6,000 or so numbers. The format used for addresses in this chapter is the official mailing address: the *sestiere* name followed by the building number in that district, followed by the name of the street or campo on which you'll find that address—for example, San Marco 1471 (on Salizzada San Moisè) means the mailing address is San Marco 1471, and you'll find it in the San Marco district on Salizzada San Moisè. Be aware that San Marco 1471 may not necessarily be found close to San Marco 1475 and that many buildings aren't numbered at all.

(though prices vary). The newspaper and magazine stand at the train station carries a number of alternatives to the poorly detailed tourist-office freebie. Apparently, word got out centuries ago that maps in Venice are useless things. If you're lost, you're better off asking a local Venetian to point you in the right direction.

NEIGHBORHOODS IN BRIEF

Beginning in the 12th century and made official in 1711, the city has been divided, for tax-related purposes, into six *sestieri* ("sixths" or districts). The Canalazzo, or Grand Canal, neatly divides them into three on each bank.

San Marco The most visited (and, thus, most expensive) of the *sestieri*, this central district is anchored by the magnificent **Piazza San Marco** and the **Basilica di San Marco** to the south and the **Ponte Rialto** (bridge) to the north. It's the city's commercial, religious, and political heart and has been for more than a millennium (it was also its musical heart until a fire destroyed **La Fenice** opera house in 1996; La Fenice now stands a hollow shell, waiting to be rebuilt). Though you'll find glimpses of the real Venice here, ever-rising rents have nudged resident Venetians to look for housing in the outer neighborhoods: You'll be hard-pressed to find a grocery store or dry cleaners in San Marco. But if you're looking for Murano glass trinkets and mediocre restaurants, you'll find an embarrassment of choices. This area is a mecca for first-class hotels—with direction from Frommer's, however, you can stay here in the heart of Venice without going broke.

Cannaregio Sharing the same side of the Grand Canal with the San Marco district, Cannaregio stretches north and east from the **Santa Lucia train station** to include the **Jewish Ghetto** and into the canal-hugging vicinity of the **Ca' d'Oro** and the **Ponte Rialto.** Its outer reaches are unspoiled and residential (what tourist crowds? you'll wonder); one-third of Venice's ever-shrinking population of 20,000 is said to live here. Venice's majority of one-star hotels are clustered about the train station—not a dangerous neighborhood, but not one known for its charm, either. The gloss and dross of the tourist-shop-lined **Lista di Spagna** strip continues as it morphs into the **Strada Nuova** in the direction of the Rialto Bridge.

Castello This district, whose tony "boulevard," **Riva degli Schiavoni,** follows the **Bacino di San Marco (St. Mark's Basin),** is lined with first-class and deluxe hotels. It begins just east of Piazza San Marco, skirting Venice's most congested area to absorb some of the crowds and better hotels and restaurants. But head farther east in the direction of the **Arsenale** or inland away from the Bacino, and the people traffic thins out, despite major sites like **Campo SS. Giovanni e Paolo** and the **Scuola di San Giorgio.**

San Polo This mixed-bag *sestiere* of residential corners and tourist sites stretches northwest of the **Ponte Rialto** to the principal **Santa Maria dei Frari** church and the **Scuola Grande di San Rocco.** The hub of activity at the foot of the bridge is greatly due to the Rialto market, which has taken place here for centuries—some of the city's best restaurants have flourished here for generations, alongside some of its worst tourist traps. The spacious **Campo San Polo** is the main piazza of Venice's smallest *sestiere*.

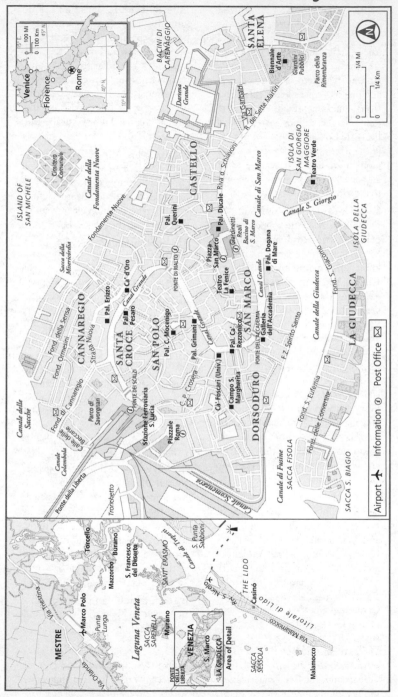

Venice Neighborhoods

ISLAND OF SAN MICHELE

Cimitero Comunale

Canale della Fundamenta Nuove

Canale della Misericordia

BACINI DI CAREMAGGIO

Darsena Grande

Darsena Grande

SANTA ELENA

Biennale d'Arte ⊠

Giardini Pubblici

Parco della Rimembranza

R. dei Sette Martiri

Via Garibaldi

CASTELLO

Pal. Querini ■

Sacca della Misericordia

Fond. della Sensa

Fond. Ormesini

Canale delle Sacche

Fond. di Cannaregio

Calle delle Beccarie

Canale Colombola

CANNAREGIO

Strada Nuova

Pal. Erizzo ■

■ Ca' d'Oro

Pal. Pesaro ■

Canal Grande

SANTA CROCE

Pal. C. Mocenigo ■

SAN POLO

■ Pal. Grimani

C. P. Crosera

Ca'-Foscari (Univ.) ■

Campo S. Margherita ⊠

Canal Grande

DORSODURO

Pal. Ca' Rezzonico ■

Galleria dell'Accademia

PONTE DELL'ACCADEMIA

F.Z.-Spirito Santo

PONTE DI RIALTO ①

Pal. Ducale Riva d. Schiavoni

Piazza San Marco ①

Teatro La Fenice ■

SAN MARCO

Giardinetti Reali

Bacino di S. Marco

Pal. Dogana di Mare

Canale di San Marco

ISOLA DI SAN GIORGIO MAGGIORE

■ Teatro Verde

Canale S. Giorgio

ISOLA DELLA GIUDECCA

Fond. S. Giacomo

LA GIUDECCA

Canale della Giudecca

Fond. S. Eufemia

Fond. delle Convertite

Canale di Fusine

SACCA FISOLA

Canale Scomenzera

Canal Scomenzera

Stazione Ferroviaria S. Lucia ①

PONTE DEI SCALZI

Parco di Savorgnan

Piazzale Roma

Ponte della Libertà

Tronchetto

SACCA S. BIAGIO

MESTRE

Via Triestina

Via Olanda

Punta Lunga

SACCA SERENELLA

Murano

SACCA SESSOLA

Torcello

Mazzorbo

Burano

S. Francesco del Deserto

SANT' ERASMO

Marco Polo

Laguna Veneta

Av. Punta Sabbioni

Canale di Treporti

Punta Sabbioni

AV. S. NICOLÒ

THE LIDO

Casinò ■

Litorale di Lido

Via Malamocco

Malamocco

VENEZIA

S. Marco

LA GIUDECCA

PONTE DELLA LIBERTÀ

Area of Detail

Airport ✈   Information ①   Post Office ⊠

Venice

Florence

Rome

0 100 Mi
0 100 Km

1/4 Mi
1/4 Km

Santa Croce North and northwest of the San Polo district and across the Grand Canal from the Santa Lucia train station, Santa Croce stretches all the way to **Piazzale Roma.** Its eastern section is generally one of Venice's least visited sections—making it all the more desirable for curious visitors. Less lively than San Polo, it's just as authentic, seemingly light-years away from San Marco. The quiet and lovely **Campo San Giacomo dell'Orio** is considered its heart.

Dorsoduro The residential area of Dorsoduro is on the opposite side of the **Ponte Accademia** from the San Marco district. Known for containing the **Accademia** and **Peggy Guggenheim** museums, it's the largest of the *sestieri* and has been something of an artists' haven (hence the tireless comparison with New York's Greenwich Village—a far cry) until recent rent escalations forced much of the community to relocate. Good neighborhood restaurants, a charming gondola boatyard, the lively **Campo Santa Margherita,** and the sunny quay called **Le Zattere** (a favorite promenade and gelato stop) all add to the character and color that make this one of the city's most visited areas.

La Giudecca Venice shares its lagoon with several other islands. Located opposite Piazza San Marco and Dorsoduro, La Giudecca is a tranquil working-class residential area where you'll find the youth hostel and a handful of hotels (including the deluxe Cipriani, one of Europe's finest).

Lido Di Venezia This slim 11km-long (6¾-mile) area is the city's **beach.** Separating the lagoon from the open sea and permitting car traffic, it's a popular summer destination because of its concentration of seasonal hotels (these landmark hotels serve as home base for the annual Venice Film Festival), but the Lido is also quite residential.

Mestre This dreary gateway to Venice is located on the mainland and has nothing to explore. In a pinch, its host of inexpensive hotels is worth consideration when Venice's hotels are full, but that's about it.

Murano, Burano & Torcello These three islands, northeast of the city and easily accessible by public transportation, are popular tourist destinations. Since the 13th century, **Murano** has exported its glass products worldwide; it's an interesting day trip if you have the time (or the desire to visit a furnace or glass-blowing factory or the noteworthy glass museum), but shoppers can do just as well in Venice's myriad glass stores. The intensely colorful (and I mean that quite literally) fishing village of **Burano** was and still is famous for its lace, an art now practiced by so few that prices are generally unaffordable. **Torcello** is the most remote and least populated, and the 40-minute boat ride is worthwhile for history and art buffs, who'll be awestruck by the cathedral's incredible Byzantine mosaics, some of the finest outside Ravenna.

San Michele This cemetery island is the final resting place of celebrities such as Igor Stravinsky and Sergei Diaghilev.

GETTING AROUND

Aside from boats, the only way to explore Venice is by **walking**—and getting lost repeatedly. You'll navigate many twisting streets whose names change constantly and don't appear on any map, streets that may very well simply end in a blind alley or spill abruptly into a canal. And you'll cross dozens of footbridges.

Moments Cruising the Canals

A leisurely cruise along the **Canal Grande (Grand Canal)** ✦✦✦ from Piazza San Marco to the Ferrovia—or the reverse—is one of Venice's must-dos. Hop on the **no. 1 vaporetto** in the late afternoon (it's open in the prow; grab one of the outdoor seats), when the weather-worn colors of the former homes of Venice's merchant elite are warmed by the soft light and reflected in the canal's rippling waters and when the traffic has eased somewhat. Some 200 palazzi, churches, and imposing Republican buildings from the 14th to the 18th centuries (many of the largest now converted into banks, museums, and galleries) line this 3.2km (2-mile) ribbon of water looping through the city like an inverted s, crossed by only three bridges (the Rialto spans it at midpoint).

It's the world's grandest Main Street, many of whose waterfront palazzi have been converted into condos. Lower, water-lapped floors are now deserted, but the higher floors are still coveted by the city's titled families, who've inhabited these glorious residences for centuries. Other palazzi have become the summertime dream-homes-with-a-view of privileged expats, drawn here as irresistibly as the romantic Venetians-by-adoption who preceded them—Richard Wagner, Robert Browning, Lord Byron, and (more recently) Woody Allen.

As much a symbol of Venice as the winged lion, the **gondola** ✦✦✦ is one of Europe's great traditions, truly as romantic as it looks (detractors who write it off as too touristy have most likely never tried it). Although it's often quoted in print at differing official rates, expect to pay 62€ ($71) for up to 40 minutes, with up to six passengers, and 31€ ($36) for an extra 25 minutes. There's a 16€ ($18) surcharge after dark (with 39€/$45 for each 25 min. beyond the first 50), but aim for late afternoon before sundown when the light does its magic on the canal reflections (and bring a bottle of *prosecco* bubbly). If the price is too high, ask visitors at your hotel or others lingering at the gondola stations if they'd like to share it. Establish the cost, time, and route explanation (any of the back canals are preferable to the trafficked and often choppy Grand Canal) with the gondolier before setting off. They're regulated by the **Ente Gondola** (✆ **041-5285075;** www.gondola venezia.it), so call if you have any questions or complaints.

And what of the serenading gondolier immortalized in film? An ensemble of accordion player and tenor is so expensive it's shared among several gondolas traveling together. A number of travel agents around town book the evening serenades for 26€ ($30) per person. The number of gondolieri willing to brave the winter cold and rain is minimal, although some come out of their wintertime hibernation for the Carnevale period.

There are 12 **gondola stations** around Venice, including Piazzale Roma, the train station, the Rialto Bridge, and Piazza San Marco. There are also a number of smaller stations, with gondoliers standing alongside their sleek 11m (36-ft.) black wonders looking for passengers. They all speak enough English to communicate the necessary details.

Treat getting bewilderingly lost in Venice as part of the fun, and budget more time than you'd ever think necessary to get to wherever you're going.

As you wander, look for the ubiquitous **yellow signs** whose destinations and arrows direct you toward five major landmarks: **Ferrovia** (the train station), **Piazzale Roma,** the **Rialto** (Bridge), **Piazza San Marco,** and the **Accademia** (Bridge). If you're in a hurry, follow them. If you're not, turn left when they indicate right to quickly leave the tourist hordes behind and enjoy Venice's local flavor.

BY VAPORETTO   The various *sestieri* are linked by a comprehensive **vaporetto (water bus/ferry)** system of about a dozen lines operated by the **Azienda del Consorzio Trasporti Veneziano (ACTV),** Calle Fuseri 1810, off the Frezzeria in San Marco (✆ **041-5287886;** www.actv.it). Transit maps are available at the tourist office and most ACTV stations. It's easier to get around on foot; the vaporetti principally serve the Grand Canal (and can be crowded in summer), the outskirts, and the outer islands. The crisscross network of small canals is the province of delivery vessels, gondolas, and private boats.

The **one-way ticket** is a steep 3.50€ ($4.05). A **round-trip ticket** is 6€ ($6.90) valid until the end of the day, but the **24-hour ticket** at 11€ ($12) is a good buy if you'll be making more than three trips in a day. Also available is the **3-day ticket** (22€/$25). However, in 2004 Venice decided that even those usurious rates weren't high enough for tourists if they dare to sail the Grand Canal on popular routes no. 82 and no. 1. The city now actually forces you to fork over 6€ ($6.90) on the Grand Canal to ride what is essentially the public bus—albeit one that takes you down a stunning and incredible "main drag." Shameful.

Most lines run every 10 to 15 minutes from 7am to midnight, then hourly until morning; most vaporetto docks (the only place you can buy tickets) have timetables posted. Note that not all stations sell tickets after dark; if you didn't buy a pass or extra tickets beforehand, you'll have to settle up with the conductor on board (you'll have to find him—he won't come looking for you) for an extra .50€ (55¢) per ticket or gamble on a 21€ ($24) fine, no excuses accepted.

Just three bridges span the Grand Canal. To fill in the gaps, *traghetti* **skiffs** (oversize gondolas rowed by two standing gondolieri) cross the Grand Canal at eight intermediate points. You'll find a station at the end of any street named Calle del Traghetto on your map and indicated by a yellow sign with the black gondola symbol. Since the last edition, **the fare has *nearly tripled*** to 1.80€ ($2.05), which you hand to the gondolier when boarding. Most Venetians cross standing up. For the experience, try the "S. Sofia" crossing that connects the Ca' d'Oro and the Pescheria fish market, opposite each other on the Grand Canal

---

Beware the *Acqua Alta*

During the notorious tidal *acqua alta* ("high water") floods, the lagoon backwashes into the city, leaving up to 1.5–1.8m (5–6 ft.) of water in the lowest-lying streets (Piazza San Marco, as the lowest point in the city, goes first). The floods can start as early as late September or October, usually taking place from November to March. As many as 50 per year have been recorded since they first started in the late 1700s. The waters usually recede after just a few hours and are often virtually gone by noon. Walkways are set up around town, but wet feet are a given, and the complex system of hydraulic dams being constructed out in the lagoon to cut off these high tides won't be in operation until the end of this decade.

Venetian Dialect: What Would Dante Say?

Even non-Venetian Italians look befuddled when trying to decipher this city's street names and signs (if you can find any). Venice's colorful thousand-year history as a once-powerful maritime republic has everything to do with its local dialect, which absorbed nuances and vocabulary from far-flung outposts in the East and from the flourishing communities of foreign merchants who lived and traded in Venice. A linguist could gleefully spend a lifetime trying to make some sense of it all. But for the Venice-bound traveler just trying to make sense of Venetian addresses, the following should give you the basics. (And don't even try to follow a conversation between two gondolieri!)

ca': The abbreviation of the word *casa* is used for the noble *palazzi*, once private residences and now museums, lining the Grand Canal: Ca' d'Oro, Ca' Pesaro, and Ca' Rezzonico. There's only one *palazzo* in Venice—the Palazzo Ducale, the former doge's residence. However, as time went on some great houses gradually began to be called *palazzi*, so today you'll encounter the Palazzo Grassi or the Palazzo Labia.

calle: Taken from the Spanish (though pronounced as if Italian: *cal*-lay), this is the most commonplace word for "street," known as *via* or *strada* elsewhere in Italy. There are numerous variations. *Ruga,* from the French word *rue,* once meant a calle flanked with stores, a designation no longer valid. A *ramo* (literally "branch") is the offshoot of a street and is often used interchangeably with *calle. Salizzada* once meant a paved street, implying that all other less important calles were once just dirt-packed alleys. A *stretto* is a narrow passageway.

campo: Elsewhere in Italy, a square is a *piazza.* In Venice, the only piazza is the Piazza San Marco (and its two bordering *piazzette*), plus Piazzale Roma. All other squares are *campi* or the diminutive, *campielli.* Translated as "field" or "meadow," these were once small unpaved grazing spots for chickens or cows. Almost every one of Venice's campi carries the name of the church that dominates it (or once did). Most have wells, no longer used, in the center.

canale: There are three principal wide canals: the Canal Grande (affectionately called Il Canalazzo, the Canal), the Canale della Giudecca, and the Canale di Cannaregio. Each of the other 160-odd smaller canals is called a *rio.*

fondamenta: Referring to the foundations of the houses lining a canal, this is a walkway along the side of a rio. Promenades along the Grand Canal near Piazza San Marco and the Rialto are called *riva,* as in Riva del Vin or Riva del Carbon, where cargo such as wine and coal were once unloaded.

rio: Any canal other than one of the biggies.

rio terra: This was once a canal; now it's a *calle.* A *piscina* is a filled-in basin, now acting as a campo or piazza.

Country & City Codes

The **country code** for Italy is **39**. Like the rest of Italy, Venice no longer has a separate city code. (It used to be the 041 that is now merely the start of all Venice numbers.) Now, unlike in the past, you must always dial the zero. As they run out of new numbers, other codes will be used.

just north of the Rialto Bridge—the gondoliers expertly dodge water traffic at this point of the canal where it's the busiest and most heart-stopping.

BY WATER TAXI   *Taxi acquei* **(water taxis)** charge high prices and aren't for visitors watching their money. For (unlikely) journeys up to 7 minutes, the rate is 14€ ($16), and .25€ (30¢) for every 15 seconds thereafter. Each bag over 50cm (20 in.) long costs 1.15€ ($1.30), plus there's a 4.40€ ($5.05) supplement for service from 10pm to 7am and a 4.65€ ($5.35) surcharge on Sunday and holidays (these last two can't be applied simultaneously). If they have to come get you, tack on another 4.15€ ($4.75). Those rates cover up to four people; if any more squeeze in, it's another 1.60€ ($1.85) per extra passenger.

Six water-taxi stations serve key points in the city: the **Ferrovia** (© 041-716286), **Piazzale Roma** (© 041-716922), the **Rialto Bridge** (© 041-5230575), **Piazza San Marco** (© 041-5229750), the **Lido** (© 041-5260059), and **Marco Polo Airport** (© 041-5415084). **Radio Taxi** (© 041-5222303 or 041-723112) will come pick you up anywhere in the city.

BY GONDOLA   To come all the way to Venice and not indulge in a gondola ride could be one of your biggest regrets. Yes, it's touristy and, yes, it's expensive (see "Cruising the Canals," above), but only those with a heart of stone will be unmoved by this quintessential Venetian experience. Don't initiate your trip, however, until you've agreed on a price and synchronized watches. Oh, and don't ask them to sing—if only for your own sake.

FAST FACTS: Venice

American Express   American Express is at San Marco 1471, 30124 Venezia, on Salizzada San Moisè just west of Piazza San Marco (© 041-5200844). May through October, banking hours are Monday through Saturday from 8am to 8pm. (All other services are available 9am to 5:30pm.) From November through April, hours are Monday through Friday from 9am to 5:30pm and Saturday from 9am to 12:30pm.

Bookstores   **Libreria Studium,** San Marco 337 (© 041-5222382), carries lots of travel guidebooks and maps as well as books in English. Another good choice is **Libreria al Ponte,** Calle della Mandola, 3717D (© 041-5224030), which stocks travel guidebooks and English-language books. Two other centrally located bookstores that carry a line of softcover and hardcover books in English are the **Libreria Sansovino,** in the Bacino Orseolo 84, immediately north of the Piazza San Marco (© 041-5222623), and the **Libreria San Giorgio,** Calle Larga XXII Marzo 2087 (© 041-5238451), beyond the American Express Office toward Campo Santo Stefano. Both carry a selection of books about Venetian art, history, and literature.

For art books and other colorful hardbacks on history and Italian sights with which to hold down your coffee table, at 40% to 50% off, head to **Libreria Beronti Mario,** San Marco 3637B (Rio Terra dei Assassini; ✆ 041-5229583), or **Libreria Beronti Alberto,** San Marco 4718 (Calle dei Fabbri; ✆ 041-5224615).

Business Hours Standard hours for **shops** are Monday through Saturday from 9am to 12:30pm and 3 to 7:30pm. In winter, shops are closed Monday morning, while in summer they're closed Saturday afternoon. Most **grocers** are closed Wednesday afternoon throughout the year. **Banks** are usually open Monday through Friday from 8:30am to 1:30pm and 2:35 to 3:35pm or 3 to 4pm. In Venice and throughout Italy, just about everything is closed **Sunday,** but tourist shops in the San Marco area are permitted to stay open in high season. **Restaurants** are required to close at least 1 day per week *(il giorno di riposo),* but the particular day varies. Many are open for Sunday lunch but close for Sunday dinner and close Monday when the fish market is closed. Restaurants typically close 1 to 2 weeks for holidays *(chiuso per ferie)* sometime in July or August, frequently over Christmas, and sometimes in January or February before the Carnevale rush.

Consulates The nearest **U.S. Consulate** is in Milan, at Largo Donegani 1 (✆ 02-290351), open Monday through Friday from 9am to noon for visas only; from Monday to Friday, it's also open for telephone service info from 2 to 4pm. The **U.K. Consulate** in Venice is at Dorsoduro 1051 (✆ 041-5227207), at the foot of the Accademia Bridge just west of the museum in the Palazzo Querini; it's open Monday through Friday from 9am to noon and 2 to 4pm. The **United States, Canada,** and **Australia** have consulates in Milan, about 3 hours away by train. Along with **New Zealand,** they all maintain embassies in Rome (see "Fast Facts: Rome," in chapter 3).

Crime Be aware of petty crime like pickpocketing on the crowded vaporetti, particularly the tourist routes where passengers' attention is on the passing scenery rather than on their bags. Venice's deserted back streets were once virtually crime free; occasional tales of theft are circulating only recently. Generally speaking, it's one of Italy's safest cities.

Dentists & Doctors For a shortlist, check with the U.S. or U.K. consulate or the American Express office. Or, ask your hotel to set up an appointment for you. If you need immediate care, first aid is available 24 hours a day in the emergency room *(pronto soccorso)* of major hospitals. Try the **Ospedale Civile di Venezia** (✆ 041-5294111), Campo SS. Giovanni e Paolo, or **Fatebenefratelli di Venezia** (✆ 041-783111), Cannaregio 3458.

Drugstores Venice's pharmacies take turns staying open late. To find out which one is open in your area, ask at your hotel, check the rotational duty signs posted outside all drugstores, or dial ✆ 192 or 041-5230573. **International Pharmacy,** Via XXII Marzo 2067 (✆ 041-5294111; Vaporetto: San Marco), is well recommended and centrally located.

Emergencies In Venice and throughout Italy, dial ✆ 113 to reach the **police.** Some Italians recommend that you forgo the police and try the military-trained **carabinieri** (✆ 112). For an **ambulance,** phone ✆ 118 or 05-5100. To report a **fire,** dial ✆ 115. For any **tourism-related complaint** (rip-offs, exceedingly shoddy service, and so on), dial the special agency Venezia No Problem toll-free at ℂ **800-355920**.

Holidays Venice's patron saint, San Marco or St. Mark, is honored on April 25.

Laundry The self-service laundry most convenient to the train station is the **Lavaget,** Cannaregio 1269, to the left as you cross Ponte alle Guglie from Lista di Spagna; the rate is about 10€ ($12) for up to 4.5 kilograms (10 lb.). The most convenient to San Marco is **Gabriella,** San Marco 985, on Rio Terrà Colonne (off Calle dei Fabbri), where they wash and dry clothes for you within an hour or two for 15€ ($17). They are open Monday to Friday 10am to 12:30pm and 2:30 to 7pm.

Mail & E-mail Venice's **Posta Centrale** is at San Marco 5554, 30124 Venezia, on the San Marco side of the Rialto Bridge at Rialto Fontego dei Tedeschi (ℂ **041-2717111** or 041-5285813; Vaporetto: Rialto). This office sells stamps at Window 12 Monday through Saturday from 8:30am to 6:30pm (for parcels, 8:10am–1:30pm). If you're at Piazza San Marco and need postal services, walk through Sottoportego San Geminian, the center portal at the opposite end of the piazza from the basilica on Calle Larga dell'Ascensione. Its usual hours are Monday through Friday from 8:30am to 2pm and Saturday from 8:30am to 1pm. You can buy *francobolli* **(stamps)** at any *tabacchi* (tobacconists). The limited mailboxes seen around town are red.

   To check e-mail, log on at **Venetian Navigator,** Castello 5269 on Calle delle Bande, between San Marco and Campo Santa Maria Formosa (ℂ **041-5226084**; Vaporetto: San Marco, Zaccaria, Rialto), open daily from 10am to 10pm (Nov–Apr 10am–1pm and 2:30–8:30pm). **Internet Cafe,** San Marco 2976–2958 on Campo San Stefano (ℂ **041-5208128**; www.nethousecafes.com; Vaporetto: San Samuele, Giglio), is open 24 hours. All the cafes charge about 6€ ($6.90) per hour.

Police In an emergency, dial ℂ **113** or 112.

Tax & Tipping See "Fast Facts: Rome," in chapter 3.

Telephone See Fast "Facts: Rome," in chapter 3.

3 Accommodations You Can Afford

Few cities boast as long a high season as Venice, beginning with the Easter period. May, June, and September are the best weather-wise and so are the most crowded. July and August are hot—at times, unbearably so (few one- and two-star hotels offer air-conditioning; when they do, it usually costs extra). Like everything else, hotels are more expensive here than in any other Italian city and with no apparent upgrade in amenities. The least special of those below are clean and functional; at best, they're charming and thoroughly enjoyable. Some may even provide you with your best stay in Europe.

   Most hotels usually observe high- and low-season rates, though they're slowly adopting a single year-round rate. Even where it's not indicated in the listings, be sure to ask when you book or arrive at a hotel whether off-season rates are in effect. High season here is from about March 15 to November 5, with a lull in July and August (when discounts are often offered). Some small hotels close (sometimes without notice or to renovate) from November or December until Carnevale, opening about 2 weeks around Christmas and New Year's at high-season rates.

From November to Carnevale (except Christmas Eve to Jan 6) also constitutes low season in the hotels that stay open.

I strongly suggest you reserve in advance, even off season. If you haven't booked, arrive as early as you can, definitely before noon. The **Hotel Reservations booth** in the train station will book rooms for you, but the lines are long and (understandably) the staff's patience is often thin. For 1€ ($1.15) they'll try to find you a hotel in the price range of your choice. Upon confirmation from the hotel, they'll accept the deposit from you by credit card and issue you a voucher, and you pay the balance on your arrival at the hotel.

Another alternative for reserving the same day as your arrival is the **A.V.A. (Venetian Hoteliers Association;** ⓒ **800-843006** in Italy, or 041-5222264; www.veneziasi.it). Simply state your price range, and they'll confirm a hotel while you wait. There's no fee for the service, and there are offices at the train station, in Piazzale Roma garages, and at the airport. Sometimes A.V.A. offers specials that include free transfer from the airport to your hotel.

Hotel preparations for the Jubilee Year 2000 included renovations and upgrades, and those improvements were reflected in a sharp increase in room rates. Unfortunately, those rates didn't ease back, and the introduction of the euro resulted in even higher prices. The good news is that now, at least, you'll have accommodations of a better quality (or at least with more amenities of questionable necessity), but the bad news is that yesteryear's finds are disappearing. The rates below were compiled in summer 2004, with the hoteliers estimating what they'll charge in 2005. You can expect the usual increase of 4% to 8%, but you may be hit with an increase of as much as 20% if the hotel you pick is one that has been redone recently.

A few peculiarities about Venice hotels have everything to do with the fact that this city built on water doesn't consistently offer what you may take for granted: elevators, light, and space. Hotels here often have tiny bathrooms. The rooms are generally smaller than elsewhere and can be dark, and canal views aren't half as frequent as we'd like them to be. This doesn't mean a welcoming family-run hotel in an atmospheric neighborhood can't offer a memorable stay. Just don't expect the amenities of the Danieli or Grand Canal vistas.

Note: Unless otherwise specified, all units come with private bathrooms.

IN SAN MARCO

Ai do Mori ⭐⭐ *Value* Antonella, the young hands-on owner/manager, creates an efficient yet comfortable ambience, with special care given to Frommer's readers. The more accessible lower-floor rooms (there's no elevator and the hotel begins on the 2nd floor) are slightly larger and offer rooftop views, but the top-floor rooms boast views of San Marco's cupolas and the Torre dell'Orologio, whose two bronze Moors ring the bells every hour (the large double-paned windows help ensure quiet). A 1998 face-lift brought new tiled bathrooms (with hair dryers and heated towel racks), TVs, firm mattresses, and air-conditioning; another renovation in 2001 gave every room but one a private bathroom and revealed the rest of the wood beams on the ceilings above brightly painted walls and comfy new furnishings. Room nos. 4 (a small double) and 5 (a triple) share a bathroom and a small hallway and can be turned into a family suite. Additionally, Antonella has now opened a four-room annex nearby; call for rates.

San Marco 658 (on Calle Larga San Marco, 658), 30124 Venezia. ⓒ **041-5204817** or 041-5289293. Fax 041-5205328. www.hotelaidomori.com. 14 units, 13 with bathroom. 30€–90€ ($35–$104) single or double

Venice Accommodations & Dining

ACCOMMODATIONS ■

Adua **8**
Ai do Mori **33**
Albergo Guerrato **23**
Albergo Santa Lucia **6**
Al Gambero **35**
Al Piave **29**
Foresteria Valdese (Palazzo Cavagnis) **28**
Hotel Ai Due Fanali **1**
Hotel American **13**
Hotel Bernardi-Semenzato **24**
Hotel Campiello **45**
Hotel Dolomiti **5**
Hotel Falier **4**
Hotel Flora **39**

Hotel Fontana **43**
Hotel Galleria **15**
Hotel Gallini **37**
Hotel Locanda Remedio **30**
Hotel Messner **40**
Hotel San Geremia **9**
Locanda Casa Verardo **32**
Locanda Fiorita **17**
Locanda Sturion **19**
Pensione Accademia **10**
Pensione Alla Salute (Da Cici) **41**
Pensione La Calcina **12**
Residenza d'Epoca Ca'Favretto San Cassiano **3**

DINING ◆

Ai Tre Spiedi **25**
Al Covo **47**
A Le Do Spade **21**
Bistrot de Venise **34**
Brek **7**
Cantina do Mori **22**
Da Aciugheta **31**
Da Sandro **18**
Osteria alle Botteghe **16**
Osteria alle Testiere **27**
Pizzeria alle Oche **2**

Pizzeria/Trattoria al Vecio Canton **42**
Rosticceria San Bartolomeo **26**
Rosticceria Teatro Goldoni **36**
Trattoria Ai Cugnai **14**
Trattoria Alla Madonna **20**
Trattoria alla Rivetta **44**
Trattoria da Fiore **16**
Trattoria da Remigio **46**
Taverna San Trovaso **11**
Vino Vino **38**

Near the Stazione FS. S. Lucia

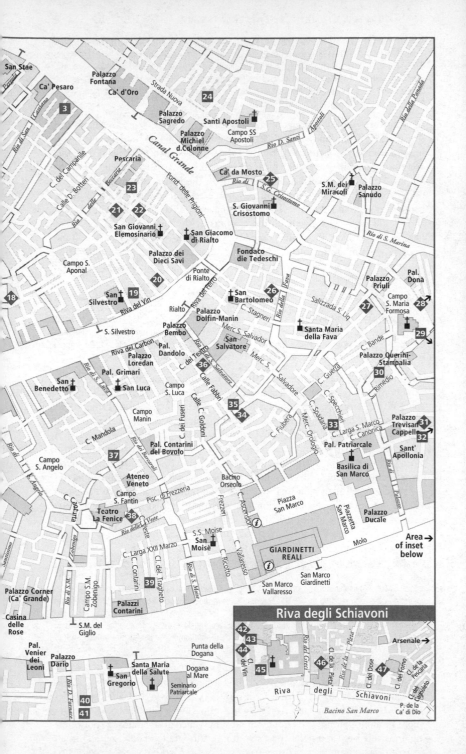

San Stae

Ca' Pesaro

3

Palazzo
Fontana
Ca' d'Oro

Strada Nuova

24

Palazzo
Sagredo

Santi Apostoli

Palazzo
Michiel
d.Colonne

Campo SS
Apostoli

Rio D. Santi

Canal Grande

Pescaria

Ca' da Mosto

Rio di

25

S.G. Crisostomo

S.M. dei
Miracoli

Palazzo
Sanudo

C. del Campanile

C. del Botteri

Calle D. Botteri

23

Beccarie

Rio I. delle

S. Giovanni
Crisostomo

21 **22**

San Giovanni †
Elemosinario

† San Giacomo
di Rialto

Rio di S. Marina

Palazzo dei
Dieci Savi

Fondaco
die Tedeschi

Palazzo
Priuli

Pal.
Donà

Campo S.
Aponal

Ponte
di Rialto

20

Campo
S. Maria
Formosa

28

18

San
Silvestro

19

Riva del Vin

Rialto

Riva del Ferro

† San
Bartolomeo

26

C. Stagneri

Rio della Fava

Salizzada S. Lio

27

29

S. Silvestro

Palazzo
Dolfin-Manin

Merc S. Salvador

Santa Maria
della Fava

C. Bande

Palazzo Querini-
Stampalia

Palazzo
Bembo

Riva del Carbon

Pal.
Dandolo

San
Salvatore

Merc. S.

30

C. del Teatro

Rio di S. Luca

Palazzo
Loredan

Salvatore

Rimedio

Pal. Grimari

36

Calle Fabbri

C. Guerra

San †
Benedetto

† San Luca

Campo
S. Luca

Calle C. Fuseri

35

34

C. Fiubera

C. Specchieri

C. Larga S. Marco
C. Canonica

Palazzo
Trevisan
Cappello

31

32

Campo
Manin

Campo
S. Angelo

C. Mandola

Rio del Barcaroli

37

Pal. Contarini
del Bovolo

Calle C. Goldoni

33

Merc. Spadaria

Pal. Patriarcale

Sant'
Apollonia

Ateneo
Veneto

Bacino
Orseolo

Basilica di
San Marco

Campo
S. Fantin

Pisc. di Frezzeria

Frezzeria

Piazza
San Marco

C. Ascension

Piazzetta
San Marco

Palazzo
Ducale

Teatro
La Fenice

38

Rio delle Veste

S.S. Moisè

San
Moisè

C. Vallaresso

C. Larga XXII Marzo

GIARDINETTI
REALI

Molo

Area →
of inset
below

Palazzo Corner
(Ca' Grande)

C. Contarini

39

Cl. del Traghetto

Rio di S. Moisè

San Marco
Vallaresso

San Marco
Giardinetti

Casina
delle
Rose

Campo S.M.
Zobenigo

Palazzi
Contarini

S.M. del
Giglio

Pal.
Venier
dei
Leoni

Palazzo
Darip

Punta della
Dogana

Santa Maria
della Salute

San
Gregorio

Dogana
al Mare

Seminario
Patriarcale

40

41

Riva degli Schiavoni

42

43

44

Cl. del Vin

45

Rio del Greci

Cl. de la Pietà

Arsenale →

46

Cl. de la Pietà

Cl. del Dose

47

Cl. del Forno

Cl. de la Pescaria

Riva   degli   Schiavoni

P. de la
Ca' di Dio

Bacino San Marco

373

without bathroom, 50€–130€ ($58–$150) single with bathroom; 60€–130€ ($69–$150) double with bathroom; 60€–150€ ($69–$173) triple with bathroom; 80€–180€ ($92–$207) quad with bathroom; 120€–220€ ($138–$253) family suite for 4 or 5. Ask about off-season rates. No breakfast. MC, V. Vaporetto: San Marco. Exit Piazza San Marco beneath Torre dell'Orologio; turn right onto Calle Larga San Marco, and the hotel is on the left, just before McDonald's. **Amenities:** Bar; concierge; nonsmoking rooms. *In room:* A/C, TV, hair dryer, safe.

Al Gambero 👁👁 Midway on a main strip connecting Piazza San Marco and the Rialto Bridge, one of Venice's former budget hotels underwent a full makeover in 1998. Surrounded by striped damasklike bedspreads and curtains, you can slumber in one of the 14 canalside rooms (five with bathrooms, including no. 203 with a small balcony). Rooms on the first two floors have higher ceilings, though upstairs rooms are the most freshly renovated (in 2002, when bathrooms were added to all). The owners have acquired an adjacent apartment and should have added five or so more rooms by the time you visit. The entire hotel is nonsmoking. By Venice standards, the budget-level Gambero has all the trappings of a midscale hotel at still moderate prices. Guests receive a 10% discount in the lively ground-floor Bistrot de Venise (see "Great Deals on Dining," later in this chapter).

San Marco 4687 (on Calle dei Fabbri), 30124 Venezia. © 041-5224384 or 041-5201420. Fax 041-5200431. www.locandaalgambero.com. 27 units. 50€–130€ ($58–$150) single; 90€–210€ ($104–$242) double; 150€–260€ ($173–$288) triple; 180€–300€ ($207–$345) quad. Rates include buffet breakfast. MC, V. Vaporetto: Rialto. Turn right along the canal, cross the small footbridge over Rio San Salvador, turn left onto Calle Bembo, which becomes Calle dei Fabbri; the hotel is about 5 blocks ahead on the left. **Amenities:** Restaurant; bar; concierge; tour desk. *In room:* A/C, TV, dataport, minibar, hair dryer, safe.

Hotel Gallini Though the 1997 fire at La Fenice opera house doused this neighborhood's spark, it's now back to business as usual at the Gallini. The amiable Ceciliati brothers, Adriano and Gabriele, have been at the helm since 1952 and offer four floors (no elevator) of bright, spacious rooms and big modern bathrooms (all rooms should have bathrooms by the time you get here). Ten rooms overlook narrow Rio della Verona, and 15 have air-conditioning (an extra 5€/$5.75 daily); rooms without air-conditioning are cooled with fans. Though there's nothing wrong with it in particular; the place is charmless, but since it's the largest place I suggest in this area, it's a good moderately priced choice when smaller options are full. In addition, it's worth noting that their prices haven't risen for this edition. The housekeeping staff seems to be forever cleaning. Rich-looking marble floors in green, red, or speckled black alternate with intricate parquet to lend an old-world air.

San Marco 3673 (on Calle della Verona), 30124 Venezia. © 041-5204515. Fax 041-5209103. www.hotel gallini.it. 40 units, 35 with bathroom. 70€ ($81) single without bathroom, 100€ ($115) single with bathroom; 100€ ($115) double without bathroom, 140€ ($161) double with bathroom; 180€ ($207) triple with bathroom. Off-season rates up to 15€ ($17) lower. Rates include continental breakfast and a year-round Frommer's discount of 10€ ($12); show this book. AE, MC, V. Closed Nov 15 to Carnevale. Vaporetto: Sant' Angelo. Follow the zigzagging road south toward Campo Sant'Angelo; exit the campo at the northeast end by taking Calle della Mandola; turn right at the Ottica (optometrist) onto Calle dei Assasini, which becomes Calle della Verona. **Amenities:** Bar; concierge; tour desk; room service; babysitting. *In room:* A/C (in 15 rooms), TV (some rooms), minibar (in 20 rooms), hair dryer.

Hotel Locanda Remedio 👁👁 *(Finds* In 2003, the Remedio became the three-star annex of the four-star **Hotel Colombina** (Castello 4416, Calle del Reme-dio; © 041-2770525; fax 041-2776044; info@hotelcolombina), so changes might be afoot. For now, the hotel remains, by Venetian standards, a spot offering unusually large and quiet rooms with fine antiques (and good repros) in an ancient palazzo around the corner from one of St. Mark's busiest streets. Most rooms are on the second floor (no. 27 has lovely ceiling frescoes) off a ballroom-size corridor. The small bathrooms have been modernized, and VCRs are attached to the TVs (movies in English are available at the desk).

San Marco 4412 (on Calle del Remedio), 30122 Venezia. ℂ 041-5206232. Fax 041-5210485. www.hotel colombina.com/remedio. 10 units. For Frommer's readers: 93€ ($107) single; 155€ ($178) double; 202€ ($232) triple; 248€ ($285) quad. Rates include buffet breakfast. AE, MC, V. Vaporetto: San Marco. Exit Piazza San Marco under Torre dell'Orologio and turn right at the Max Mara store onto Calle Larga San Marco; at Ristorante All'Angelo, turn left onto Calle va al Ponte dell'Angelo and take the 1st right onto Ramo del Anzolo; cross the small footbridge onto Calle del Remedio. **Amenities:** Concierge; tour desk; in-room massage; nonsmoking rooms. *In room:* A/C, TV, minibar, hair dryer.

Locanda Fiorita ☆ (*Value* New owners have created a pretty little hotel in this Venetian red palazzo, parts of which date from the 1400s. In 1999, they renovated everything in 18th-century Venetian style. The wisteria vine partially covering its facade is at its glorious best in May or June, but the Fiorita is excellent year-round for its simply furnished rooms boasting new bathrooms (now with hair dryers) and its location on a campiello off the grand Campo Santo Stefano. Room nos. 1 and 10 have little terraces beneath the wisteria pergola and overlook the campiello: They can't be guaranteed on reserving, so ask when you get there. The only room without a bathroom has its own private facilities down the hall. Just a few meters away at Calle San Stefano 3465 is **Ca' Morosini-Dependance** (ℂ **041-2413800;** fax 041-5228043; www.camorosini.com), the Fiorita's three-star annex. There you'll find even more rooms with views of the campo.

San Marco 3457 (on Campiello Novo), 30124 Venezia. ℂ **041-5234754.** Fax 041-5228043. www.locanda fiorita.com. 10 units, 8 with bathroom, in main house; 6 units in annex. Main house: 60€–78€ ($69–$90) single without bathroom; 85€–110€ ($98–$127) double without bathroom, 95€–130€ ($109–$150) double with bathroom. Annex: 100€–130€ ($115–$150) single with bathroom; 140€–180€ ($161–$207) double with bathroom. Extra person 30% more at either. Rates include continental breakfast. AE, MC, V. Vaporetto: S. Angelo. Walk to the tall brick building, then turn right around its side; cross a small bridge and turn left down Calle del Pestrin; a bit farther down on your left is a small square 3 stairs above street level; the hotel is against its back. **Amenities:** Concierge; tour desk; room service; babysitting; nonsmoking rooms. *In room:* A/C, TV, dataport (in 6 rooms), minibar, hair dryer (in 15 rooms), safe (in 6 rooms).

WORTH A SPLURGE

Hotel Flora ☆ The simple name of this small, charming hotel refers to its greatest attribute: a jewel-like patio garden immediately beyond the welcoming lobby. A delightful place to have breakfast, afternoon tea, or an aperitif, it is enclosed by climbing vines and ivy-covered walls, with an antique well, potted flowers, and blooming plants that create a cool green enclave, one of the hotel's many pleasant places to retreat to with your thoughts or a companion. Seamlessly run by two generations of the highly professional Romanelli family and their friendly staff, the Flora has long been one of Venice's favorite spots and is ideally located just west of the American Express office on a tony shopping street. Despite rooms that can vary greatly (from small to standard in size, and from rather plain to the nicest period-style ones overlooking the garden), and small bathrooms that could do with a face-lift, it is forever full of loyal devotees and romance-seekers. On the top floor, room no. 47 looks onto the alleged Desdemona's palazzo (of Shakespeare's tragedy *Othello*), with the dome of La Salute church beyond. The owners of Hotel Flora recently opened a new hotel in the same area. **Locanda Novecento** (San Marco 2683–2684; ℂ **041-2413765;** fax 041-5212145; www.locandanovecento.it) is a boutique hotel offering luxury accommodation in nine rooms, each decorated along the theme of *1900*. Rooms have the same amenities as those found at the Flora.

San Marco 2283 (off Calle Larga/V. XXII Marzo, near Campo San Moisè), 30124 Venezia. ℭ 041-5205844. Fax 041-5228217. www.hotelflora.it. 44 units. 180€ ($207) single; 230€ ($265) double; 280€ ($322) triple. Rates include continental breakfast. AE, DC, MC, V. Slow period discounts of approximately 15%. Vaporetto: San Marco-Vallaresso. Walk down Calle Vallaresso and turn left onto the Via XXII Marzo. After crossing the San Moisè Bridge and passing the Deutsche Bank, you'll see a sign on the left side of the street for the hotel, located down a narrow passageway off the Via XXII Marzo. Amenities: Bar; concierge; tour desk; 24-hr. room service; babysitting; laundry service; dry cleaning. In room: A/C, TV, dataport, hair dryer, safe.

IN CANNAREGIO

Expect most (but not all) of these suggestions to be in or near the Santa Lucia train station neighborhood, one full of trinket shops and budget hotels. This area is comparatively charmless (though safe), and in the high season it's wall-to-wall with tourists who window-shop their way to Piazza San Marco, an easy half-hour to 45-minute stroll away. Vaporetto connections from the train station are convenient.

Adua   It ain't too pretty, but it's cheap (for Venice), conveniently located near the station, clean, and run very well. The Adua family, in the low-end hotel business more than 30 years, completed a welcome renovation in 1999, giving the largish rooms a unified summery look with contemporary wood furnishings painted pale green. An independent palazzo across the street with six refurbished rooms (without bathroom, TV, or air-conditioning) costs about 20% less.

Cannaregio 233A (on Lista di Spagna), 30121 Venezia. ℭ 041-716184. Fax 041-2440162. www.aduahotel. com. 13 units, 9 with bathroom. 47€–80€ ($54–$92) single without bathroom, 60€–110€ ($69–$127) single with bathroom; 50€–80€ ($58–$92) double without bathroom, 70€–120€ ($81–$138) double with bathroom. Extra bed 50% more. Low-season rates 10%–15% less. Breakfast 6€ ($6.90). AE, MC, V. Vaporetto: Ferrovia. Exit the train station and turn left onto Lista di Spagna. Amenities: Concierge; 24-hr. room service; nonsmoking rooms. In room: A/C, TV, hair dryer.

Albergo Santa Lucia   The flagstone patio/terrace of this contemporary building is bordered by roses, oleander, and ivy, a lovely place to enjoy breakfast, with coffee and tea brought in sterling silver pots. The kindly owner, Emilia Gonzato; her son, Gianangelo; and his wife, Alessandra, oversee everything with pride, and it shows: The large rooms are simple but bright and clean, with modular furnishings and a print or pastel to brighten things up.

Cannaregio 358 (on Calle della Misericordia), 30121 Venezia. ℭ 041-715180. Fax 041-710610. www.hotels lucia.com. 18 units, 12 with bathroom. 60€ ($69) single without bathroom; 85€ ($98) double without bathroom, 110€ ($127) double with bathroom; 140€ ($161) triple with bathroom; 170€ ($196) quad with bathroom. Continental breakfast 5€ ($5.75). AE, DC, MC, V. Generally closed Dec–Jan. Vaporetto: Ferrovia. Exit the train station, turn left onto Lista di Spagna, and take the 2nd left onto Calle della Misericordia. Amenities: Concierge; tour desk; room service (breakfast). In room: A/C, TV, hair dryer.

Hotel Bernardi-Semenzato 𝕽𝕽 (Value   The exterior of this weatherworn palazzo hidden on a side street just off wide Strada Nuova doesn't hint of its fabulous 1995 renovation. The overhaul left hand-hewn ceiling beams exposed, air-conditioned rooms with antique-styled headboard/spread sets, and bathrooms modernized and brightly retiled. The enthusiastic English-speaking owners, Maria Teresa and Leonardo Pepoli, offer three-star style and amenities, but they're content to offer one-star rates (prices get even better off season). Upstairs rooms enjoy higher ceilings and more light. The *dipendenza* (annex) 3 blocks away offers you the chance to feel as if you've rented an aristocratic apartment, with parquet floors and Murano chandeliers—room no. 5 is on a corner with a beamed ceiling and fireplace, no. 6 (a family-perfect two-room suite) overlooks the confluence of two canals, and no. 2 overlooks the lovely garden of a palazzo next door.

In 2003, the hoteliers opened yet another **annex** nearby consisting of just four rooms, all done in a Venetian style, including one large family suite (150€/$172; two guest rooms, one of which can sleep four, sharing a common bathroom). Several of these rooms have canopied beds.

Cannaregio 4366 (on Calle de l'Oca), 30121 Venezia. ℂ 041-5227257. Fax 041-5222424. www.hotel bernardi.com. Hotel: 18 units, 10 with bathroom. Annex: 12 units. *For Frommer's readers:* 33€ ($38) single without bathroom, 60€ ($69) single with bathroom; 60€ ($69) double without bathroom, 90€ ($104) double with bathroom; 80€ ($92) triple without bathroom, 100€ ($115) triple with bathroom; 85€ ($98) quad without bathroom, 120€ ($138) quad with bathroom. Continental breakfast 5€ ($5.75). Ask about off-season rates, usually 15% lower. AE, DC, MC, V. Closed Jan 20–30. Vaporetto: Ca' d'Oro. Walk straight ahead to Strada Nova, turn right toward Campo SS. Apostoli, and look for Cannaregio 4309, a stationery/toy store on your left; turn left on Calle Duca, then take the 1st right onto Calle de l'Oca. **Amenities:** Concierge; tour desk; room service. *In room:* A/C, TV, dataport, minibar, hair dryer, safe.

Hotel Dolomiti For those who prefer to stay near the train station, this is an old-fashioned, reliable choice. Because it has large, clean, but ordinary rooms spread over four floors (but no elevator), your chances of finding availability are better at this hotel, one of the larger places I suggest. It's been in the Basaldella family for generations—the current head manager, Graziella, was even born in a second-floor room—and they and their efficient polyglot staff supply dining suggestions; umbrellas, when necessary; and a big smile after a long day's sightseeing. Rooms without bathrooms always come with sinks. The Basardellis are slowly renovating the guest rooms; those that don't have air-conditioning will soon.

Cannaregio 72–74 (on Calle Priuli ai Cavalletti), 30121 Venezia. ℂ 041-715113 or 041-719983. Fax 041-716635. www.hoteldolomiti-ve.it. 32 units, 22 with bathroom. 50€–70€ ($58–$81) single without bathroom, 70€–95€ ($81–$109) single with bathroom; 60€–90€ ($69–$104) double without bathroom, 80€–140€ ($92–$161) double with bathroom; 84€–111€ ($97–$128) triple without bathroom, 120€–180€ ($138–$207) triple with bathroom. Inquire about low-season discounts. Rates include breakfast. MC, V. Closed Nov 15–Jan 31. Vaporetto: Ferrovia. Exit the train station, turn left onto Lista di Spagna, and take the 1st left onto Calle Priuli. **Amenities:** Bar; concierge; tour desk; babysitting. *In room:* A/C (in newest rooms), hair dryer (some rooms).

Hotel San Geremia 𝕽𝕽 *Finds* Mention Frommer's when booking and show this guidebook when checking in, and you'll get the rates below. If this gem of a two-star hotel had an elevator and was in San Marco, it would cost twice as much and still be worth it. The tastefully renovated rooms are freshened up almost every year. Consider yourself lucky to snag one of the seven overlooking the campo (or, better yet, one of three top-floor rooms with small terraces). The rooms have blond-wood paneling with built-in headboards and closets or whitewashed walls with deep-green or burnished rattan headboards and matching chairs. The small bathrooms offer hair dryers and heated towel racks. Everything is overseen by an English-speaking staff and owner/manager Claudio, who'll give you helpful tips and free passes to the winter Casino. In 2003, air-conditioning was added to 10 of the rooms.

Cannaregio 290A (on Campo San Geremia), 30121 Venezia. ℂ 041-716245. Fax 041-5242342. www.san geremia.com. 21 units, 14 with bathroom. 85€ ($98) double without bathroom, 130€ ($150) double with bathroom. Frommer's readers get a discount of 10% in high season, or 20% in winter. Ask about rates/availability for singles, triples, and quads. Rates include continental breakfast. AE, DC, MC, V. Vaporetto: Ferrovia. Exit the train station, turn left onto Lista di Spagna, and continue to Campo San Geremia. **Amenities:** Concierge; tour desk; Internet point; room service (breakfast); babysitting; nonsmoking rooms. *In room:* TV, hair dryers, safe.

IN CASTELLO

Al Piave 𝕽 *Kids* The Puppin family's tasteful hotel is a steal: This level of attention coupled with the sophisticated *buon gusto* in decor and spirit is rare in this price category. You'll find orthopedic mattresses under ribbon candy–print or floral spreads, immaculate white lace curtains, stained-glass windows, new bathrooms, and even (in a few rooms) tiny terraces. The family suites—with two bedrooms, minibars, and shared bathrooms—are particularly good deals, as are the small but stylishly rustic apartments with kitchenettes and washing machines (in the two smaller ones). Renovations are planned to turn some of the doubles into "superior" rooms in the coming year. A savvy international crowd has discovered this classy spot, so you'll need to reserve far in advance.

Castello 4838–4840 (on Ruga Giuffa), 30122 Venezia. ⓒ 041-5285174. Fax 041-5238512. www.hotelalpiave. com. 25 units. *For Frommer's readers:* 90€–125€ ($104–$144) single; 110€–180€ ($127–$207) double; 150€–210€ ($173–$242) triple; 150€–230€ ($173–$265) family suite for 3; 200€–260€ ($230–$288) family suite for 4; 220€–300€ ($253–$345) family suite for 5. Often heavy discounts off season. Rates include continental breakfast. AE, DC, MC, V. Closed Jan 7 to Carnevale. Vaporetto: San Zaccaria. Walk straight ahead on Calle delle Rasse to small Campo SS. Filippo e Giacomo, take a right on Calle San Provolo, and cross the canal to Campo San Provolo; take a left, cross the 1st small footbridge, and follow zigzagging Calle that becomes Ruga Giuffa. **Amenities:** Concierge; tour desk; babysitting; nonsmoking rooms. *In room:* A/C, TV, minibar, fridge (family suite), hair dryer, safe.

Foresteria Valdese (Palazzo Cavagnis) 🎇 (Value

Those lucky enough to get a place at this weathered, albeit elegant, 16th-century palazzo will find simple accommodations in a charming *foresteria,* the name given to religious institutions that traditionally provided lodging for pilgrims and guests. Affiliated with Italy's Waldesian and Methodist Church, the large, dormitory-style rooms are often booked with visiting church groups, though everyone is warmly welcomed and you'll find an international and inter-religious mix here. Each of the plainly furnished rooms in this once-noble residence opens onto a balcony overlooking a quiet canal. The 18th-century frescoes that grace the high ceilings in some are by the same artist who decorated the Correr Museum—and will cost you a bit extra. The two apartments complete with kitchen facilities are the best budget choice in town for traveling families of four or five. (Be aware that guests staying in private rooms or apartments are required to stay 2 nights; those staying in dormitories can stay just 1.) A sweeping renovation begun in 1995 has *finally* been completed. The reception is open Monday through Saturday from 9am to 1pm and 6 to 8pm, and Sunday from 9am to 1pm. The entire hotel is nonsmoking.

Castello 5170 (at the end of Calle Lunga Santa Maria Formosa), 30122 Venezia. ⓒ **041-5286797.** Fax 041-2416238. www.diaconiavaldese.org/venezia. 6 units (2–4 beds) often requiring 2-night stay; 3 dorms (with 8, 11, or 12 beds), none with bathroom. 2 miniapts (sleeping 4 and 5; minimum stay often required) with kitchen and bathroom. 21€ ($24) dorm bed (22€/$25 if you stay just 1 night); 57€ ($66) double without bathroom, 75€ ($86) double with bathroom; 104€ ($120) quad with bathroom; 104€ ($120) apt for 4; 116€ ($132) apt for 5. Rates include breakfast, except in apts. MC, V (but pay 3.5% more to use credit cards). Closed 2 weeks in Nov. Vaporetto: Rialto. Head southeast to the Campo Santa Maria Formosa; look for the Bar all'Orologio, just where Calle Lunga Santa Maria Formosa begins. The campo is just about equidistant from Piazza San Marco and the Rialto Bridge. **Amenities:** Internet point; nonsmoking rooms. *In room:* TV (except in dorms), dataport, kitchenette (in apts), no phone.

Hotel Fontana 🎇

Three generations of Stainers have been behind the front desk since 1968 (for centuries prior to that, the Fontana was a convent for Austrian nuns), and their warmth seems to pour from the lobby's leaded-glass windows. The four-story hotel offers a pensione-like family atmosphere coupled with a crisp, professional operation and rooms with lovely antique furnishings but a decided lack of wattage in the overhead lights. The choice two units on the upper floor have private terraces. There's no elevator, but those who brave the climb to the top floors are compensated by views of San Zaccaria's 15th-century facade.

Castello 4701 (on Campo San Provolo), 30122 Venezia. ℂ **041-5220579.** Fax 041-5231040. www.hotel fontana.it. 16 units. 110€ ($127) single; 170€ ($196) double; 200€ ($230) triple; 230€ ($265) quad. Rates include buffet breakfast. Rates lower in low season, up to 50% off in deepest winter. AE, DC, MC, V. Vaporetto: San Zaccaria. From Riva Schiavoni, take any narrow street north to Campiello SS. Filippo e Giacomo; exit this small campo from the east side, in the direction of Campo San Zaccaria, until you reach Campo San Provolo. **Amenities:** Concierge; tour desk; room service. *In room:* TV, dataport, hair dryer (on request).

Locanda Casa Verardo 🖈   In 2000, Daniela and Francesco took over this one-star pensione and transformed it into a fine three-star hotel (and more than doubled its size), while still maintaining the feel of a Venetian palazzo romantically faded by time. A second renovation in late 2001 installed "deluxe" rooms with air-conditioning, minibars, and cushier furnishings, plus two rooms for travelers with disabilities. The hoteliers also finished a massive restructuring of the hotel, which includes the addition of two new terraces (one of which is on the roof). The wood-paneled lobby is anchored by an ancient stone well. The rooms are done in chipped-stone floors, Murano chandeliers, and eclectic furnishings from imposing armoires and repro 17th century to pseudo Deco and modern functional. Three rooms have small terraces. The best accommodations come with scraps of old ceiling frescoes—and tops are the six overlooking a little canal. The airy main hall doubles as a breakfast room.

Castello 4765 (at the foot of the Ponte Storto), 30122 Venezia. ℂ **041-5286127.** Fax 041-5232765. www.casaverardo.it. 26 units. 60€–120€ ($69–$138) deluxe single; 90€–186€ ($104–$214) classic double, 110€–220€ ($127–$253) deluxe double; 130€–275€ ($150–$316) deluxe junior suite. Rates include breakfast (buffet in high season, continental in low season). AE, DC, MC, V. Vaporetto: San Zaccaria. Walk straight ahead on Calle delle Rasse to Campo SS. Filippo e Giacomo; continue straight through the small campo to take Calle Chiesa and cross the 1st small bridge, Ponte Storto; the hotel is on the left. **Amenities:** Bar; concierge; tour desk; room service (breakfast, drinks); babysitting. *In room:* A/C (in deluxe), TV, dataport, minibar (in deluxe), hair dryer, safe (only in 2).

WORTH A SPLURGE

Hotel Campiello 🖈🖈   This gem is on a tiny campiello just off prestigious Riva degli Schiavoni. The atmosphere is airy and bright, its relaxed hospitality and quality service due to the Bianchini sisters, Monica and Nicoletta. A 1998 renovation transformed much of the rooms' contemporary style into a more traditional decor; most are now done in authentic 18th-century and Art Nouveau antiques—inlaid dressers and bas-reliefs on the headboards. The building's original 15th-century marble-mosaic pavement is still evident, a vestige of the days when it was a convent under the patronage of the nearby San Zaccaria; you'll catch a glimpse of the pavement in the lounge area opening onto a pleasant breakfast room.

Castello 4647 (on Campiello del Vin), 30122 Venezia. ℂ **041-5205764.** Fax 041-5205798. www. hcampiello.it. 16 units. 72€–120€ ($83–$138) single; 88€–150€ ($101–$173) small double, 103€–180€ ($118–$207) double. 8% discount if pay cash. Ask about discounts in low season. Rates include continental breakfast. AE, DC, MC, V. **Amenities:** Bar; concierge; 24-hr. room service; babysitting; nonsmoking rooms. *In room:* A/C, TV, dataport, minibar (12 rooms), hair dryer, safe.

IN DORSODURO

Hotel Falier 🖈   Owned by the same fellow who put the lovely Hotel American (see below) on Venice's moderately priced map, the Falier is his savvy interpretation of less expensive lodging, particularly worth booking when half-price low-season rates apply. Renovated in the early 1990s, it is a reliably good value at this price range, with standard-size rooms (and modern bathrooms) attractively decorated with white lace curtains and flowered bedspreads; some rooms have wood-beamed ceilings. The old-world lobby sets your first impression, with potted ferns, Doric columns, and triangular marble floors. The neighborhood needs mentioning, as detractors may feel the need to be closer to Piazza San Marco, when the truth is that the Falier is much closer to the real Venice, in a lively area lined with stores and bars. It is situated between the large Campo Santa Margherita, one of the city's most dynamic piazzas, and the much visited Frari Church.

Dorsoduro 130 (Salizada San Pantalon), 30135 Venezia. © 041-710882 or 041-711005. Fax 041-5206554. www.hotelfalier.com. 19 units. 60€–170€ ($69–$196) single use of double room; 75€–180€ ($86–$207) double. Rates include continental breakfast. AE, MC, V. Vaporetto: Ferrovia. If you've packed lightly, the walk from the train station is easy, easier yet from the Piazzale Roma. From the train station, cross the Scalzi Bridge, turn right along the Grand Canal for 45m (150 ft.), then turn left toward the Tolentini Church. Continue along the Salizzada San Pantalon in the general direction of Campo Santa Margherita. **Amenities:** Concierge; tour desk. *In room:* A/C, TV, hair dryer, safe.

Hotel Galleria 🖈🖈 If you've always dreamed of flinging open your hotel window to find the Grand Canal in front of you, choose this 17th-century palazzo. But reserve way in advance—these are the cheapest rooms on the canal and the most charming at these rates, thanks to new owners Luciano Benedetti and Stefano Franceschini. All are done in a modestly sumptuous 17th and 18th century style, a rich look that didn't change in late 2003/early 2004 when Luciano and Stefano overhauled the entire hotel, keeping the old-fashioned feel alive but replacing everything from the floors and bathrooms to the wallpaper and windows. Don't be surprised if 2005 sees some slight increases. Six rooms overlook the canal; others have partial views that include the Ponte Accademia over an open-air bar/cafe (which can be annoying to anyone hoping to sleep before the bar closes). The bathrooms are small, but they came out quite nicely from the renovation. Breakfast, with oven-fresh bread, is served in your room.

Dorsoduro 878A (at the foot of the Ponte Accademia), 30123 Venezia. © 041-5232489. Fax 041-5204172. 10 units, 6 with bathroom. 70€ ($81) single without bathroom, 115€ ($132) single with bathroom; 95€–105€ ($109–$121) double without bathroom, 110€–150€ ($127–$173) double with bathroom. Extra bed 30% more. Rates include continental breakfast. AE, DC, MC, V. Vaporetto: Accademia. With the Accademia Bridge behind you, the hotel is just to your left, next to Totem Il Canale gallery. **Amenities:** Concierge; tour desk; room service; babysitting. *In room:* Hair dryer.

Hotel Messner 🖈 The Messner and the Alla Salute (see below) are the best choices in the Guggenheim area (the choice of those in-the-know looking for a quiet alternative to St. Mark's), at budget-embracing rates. The Messner is a two-part hotel: In the *Casa Principale* (Main House) are the handsome beamed-ceiling lobby and public rooms of a 14th-century palazzo and modernized guest rooms with comfortable modular furnishings and Murano chandeliers (three overlook picturesque Rio della Fornace). The 15th-century, one-star *dipendenza* (annex) 2m (6⅔ ft.) away doesn't show quite as much attention to detail in the decor but is perfectly nice. In summer, you get to take breakfast in a small garden. In 2002, they opened a new annex just 3m (10ft.) away, with just six large rooms done in an antique Venetian style.

Dorsoduro 216–217 (on Fondamenta Ca' Balà), 30123 Venezia. © 041-5227443. Fax 041-5227266. www. hotelmessner.it. Main house 11 units; main annex 20 units; 2nd annex 6 units. Main house and 2nd annex: 100€ ($115) single; 145€ ($167) double, 160€ ($184) double suite; 165€ ($190) triple, 180€ ($207) triple suite; 190€ ($219) quad, 200€ ($230) quad suite. Main annex: 90€ ($104) single; 115€ ($132) double; 145€ ($167) triple; 160€ ($184) quad. Rates include continental breakfast. AE, DC, MC, V. Closed Dec 1–27. Vaporetto: Salute. Follow the small canal immediately to the right of La Salute; turn right onto the 3rd bridge and walk straight until you see white awning, just before you reach Rio della Fornace. **Amenities:** Restaurant; bar; concierge; 24-hr. room service; babysitting; nonsmoking rooms. *In room:* A/C, TV, dataport, hair dryer, safe.

Pensione Alla Salute (Da Cici) 🖈 *Kids* An airy lobby with beamed ceilings and cool marble floors, a small but lovely terrace garden, and a cozy cocktail bar occupy the ground level of this converted 17th-century palazzo on Rio della Fornace. Upstairs, the comfortable guest rooms have high ceilings and huge windows (10 with canal views and 4 facing the garden), many of them large enough to accommodate families of four or even five. Breakfast is served in the garden in warm weather. The entire hotel is now nonsmoking.

Dorsoduro 222 (on Fondamenta Ca' Balà), 30123 Venezia. ⓒ 041-5235404. Fax 041-5222271. www.hotel salute.com. 56 units, 37 with full bathroom, 12 with shower only. 80€ ($92) single without bathroom, 115€ ($132) single with bathroom; 100€ ($115) double without bathroom, 140€ ($161) double with bathroom; 135€ ($155) triple without bathroom, 180€ ($207) triple with bathroom. Ask about rooms sleeping 4–5. Discounts given Mar and July–Aug. Rates include continental breakfast. MC, V. Often closes in Jan or Feb for upkeep; call ahead. Vaporetto: Salute. Facing La Salute, turn right and head to the 1st small bridge; cross it and walk ahead as straight as possible to the next narrow canal; turn left, before crossing the bridge, onto Fondamenta Ca' Balà. **Amenities:** Bar. *In room:* A/C (5 rooms), hair dryer, no phone.

Pensione La Calcina ⚓ British author John Ruskin holed up here in 1876 when penning *The Stones of Venice* (you can request his room, no. 2, but good luck), and this hotel on the sunny Zattere in the southern Dorsoduro has remained a quasisacred preference of writers, artists, and assorted bohemians. You can imagine their horror when a recent overhaul was announced—but it was executed so sensitively the third-generation owners refused to add TVs. However, the rates have recently started creeping up. Half of the unfussy but luminous rooms overlook the Giudecca Canal in the direction of Palladio's 16th-century Redentore. The outdoor floating terrace and the rooftop terrace are glorious places to begin or end any day. The three suites and two apartments were completed in 2002.

Dorsoduro 780 (on Zattere al Gesuati), 30123 Venezia. ⓒ 041-5206466. Fax 041-5227045. www.lacalcina. com. 33 units. 55€–75€ ($63–$86) single without bathroom, 75€–96€ ($86–$110) single with bathroom, 86€–106€ ($99–$122) single with bathroom and canal view; 99€–148€ ($114–$170) double with bathroom, 130€–186€ ($150–$214) double with bathroom and canal view; 187€–239€ ($215–$275) suites or apts. Rates include buffet breakfast. AE, DC, MC, V. Vaporetto: Zattere. Follow le Zattere east; hotel is on the water before the 1st bridge. **Amenities:** Bar; concierge; limited room service; laundry service. *In room:* A/C, TV, dataport, hair dryer, safe.

WORTH A SPLURGE

Hotel American ⚓⚓ Despite its potentially unromantic name (did you travel transatlantic for this?), the Hotel American is recommended for both its style and its substance; it's one of the nicest of Venice's moderate hotels. The perfect combination of old-fashioned charm and utility, this three-story hotel located near the Peggy Guggenheim Collection offers a dignified lobby and breakfast room liberally dressed with lovely Oriental carpets and marble flooring, polished woods, and leaded-glass windows and French doors. The best choices here are the larger corner rooms and the nine overlooking a quiet canal; some even have small terraces. Every room is outfitted with traditional Venetian-style furnishings that usually include hand-painted furniture and Murano glass chandeliers. If it's late spring, don't miss a drink on the second-floor terrace beneath a wisteria arbor dripping with plump violet blossoms. They also offer a 10% discount on meals at Bistrot de Venise (see "Great Deals on Dining," below).

Dorsoduro 628 (on Fond. Bragadin), 30123 Venezia. ⓒ 041-5204733. Fax 041-5204048. www.hotelamerican. com. 30 units. 210€ ($242) single; 270€ ($310) double; 320€ ($368) double with canal view. Rates include buffet breakfast. Extra person 60€ ($69). AE, MC, V. Vaporetto: Accademia. Veer left around the Galleria dell'Accademia museum, taking the 1st left turn; walk straight ahead until you cross the 1st small footbridge. Turn right to follow the Fondamenta Bragadin that runs alongside the Rio di San Vio canal. The hotel is on your left. **Amenities:** Bar; concierge; tour desk; Internet point; limited room service; nonsmoking rooms. *In room:* A/C, TV, dataport, minibar, hair dryer, safe.

Pensione Accademia ✶✶ This pension is beloved by Venice regulars. You'll have to reserve far in advance to get any room here, let alone one overlooking the breakfast garden, which is snuggled into the confluence of two canals. The 17th-century villa is fitted with period antiques in first-floor suites, and the atmosphere is decidedly old-fashioned and elegant (Katharine Hepburn's character lived here in the 1955 classic *Summertime*). Formally and appropriately Called the *Villa Maravege* (Villa of Wonders), it was built as a patrician villa in the 1600s and used as the Russian Consulate until the 1930s. Its outdoor landscaping (the Venetian rarities of a flowering patio on the small Rio San Trovaso that spills into the Grand Canal and the grassy formal rose garden behind) and interior details (original pavement, wood-beamed and decoratively painted ceilings) create the impression that you're a privileged guest in an aristocratic Venetian home from another era.

Dorsoduro 1058 (Fondamenta Bollani, west of the Accademia Bridge), 30123 Venezia. ℂ **041-5237846.** Fax 041-5239152. www.pensioneaccademia.it. 27 units. 80€–125€ ($92–$144) single; 130€–183€ double ($150–$210), 170€–275€ ($196–$316) superior double. Rates include breakfast. Off-season discounts available. AE, DC, MC, V. Vaporetto: Accademia. Step off the vaporetto and turn right down Calle Gambara, which doglegs first left and then right. It becomes Calle Corfu, which ends at a side canal; walk left for a few feet to cross the bridge, then head to the right back up toward the Grand Canal and the hotel. **Amenities:** Bar; concierge; tour desk; room service; massage; babysitting; laundry service; dry cleaning. *In room:* A/C, TV, dataport, minibar, hair dryer, safe.

IN SAN POLO

Albergo Guerrato ✶✶ *(Value)* The Guerrato is as reliable and clean a budget hotel as you're likely to find at these rates. Brothers-in-law Roberto and Piero own this former pensione in a 13th-century convent and manage to keep it almost always booked (mostly with Americans). The firm mattresses, nicely modernish bathrooms, and flea-market finds (hand-carved antique or Deco headboards and armoires) show their determination to run a budget hotel in pricey Venice. They don't exaggerate when calling their breakfast, accompanied by classical music, *buonissimo*. The Guerrato is in the Rialto's heart, so think of 7am noise before requesting a room overlooking the marketplace (with a peek down the block to the Grand Canal and Ca' d'Oro). Piero and Roberto have recently acquired the building's top floor (no elevator, 70 steps) and installed five nice new double rooms with air-conditioning, three with great views, which cost 140€ ($161) as doubles, 160€ ($184) as triples, and 180€ ($207) as quads. Note that the maximum prices below are only for official purposes; they actually never charge the highest rates (usually 6€/$6.90 or so less).

Roberto also rents (2-night minimum) two lovely, fully equipped apartments between San Marco and the Rialto. The one-bedroom is 120€ to 130€ ($138–$150) for two, or 180€ to 200€ ($207–$230) for four (though it would be cramped), while the much larger two-bedroom (on three levels) goes for 180€ to 200€ ($207–$230) for four.

San Polo 240A (on Calle Drio or Dietro la Scimia, near the Rialto Market), 30125 Venezia. ℂ **041-5227131.** Fax 041-2411408. web.tiscalinet.it/pensioneguerrato. 20 units, 14 with bathroom. 80€–100€ ($92–$115) double without bathroom, 100€–120€ ($115–$138) double with bathroom; 98€–115€ ($109–$132) triple without bathroom, 129€–145€ ($148–$167) triple with bathroom; 150€–170€ ($173–$196) quad with bathroom. Pay in cash, get 5€–6€ ($5.75–$6.90) off. Rates include buffet breakfast. MC, V. Closed Dec 22–26 and Jan 10–31. Vaporetto: Rialto. From the north side of the Ponte Rialto, walk straight ahead through the stalls and market vendors; at the corner of Banca di Roma, go 1 more short block and turn right; the hotel is halfway down the narrow street. **Amenities:** Concierge; tour desk; babysitting; nonsmoking rooms. *In room:* A/C, hair dryer.

WORTH A SPLURGE

Locanda Sturion *★★ Finds*   Though there's been a pensione on this site since 1290, a recent gutting and rebuilding has tastefully reincarnated the Sturion into a moderate hotel managed by the charming Scottish-born Helen and co-owner Flavia. The hotel's reception area is perched four flights (and 69 challenging steps) above the Grand Canal (and, depending on the location of your room, there could be even more stairs involved). Unfortunately, only two in-demand rooms offer canal views of the Rialto Bridge (as does the delightful breakfast room—is there a better way to start your day?) and command higher rates; they are spacious enough to accommodate families or groups of three, even four. The other rooms have charming views over the Rialto area rooftops. Throughout, the hotel is tastefully decorated with 18th-century-inspired Venetian furniture, parquet floors, red carpeting, and rich damasklike wallpaper. The hoteliers recently renovated two nearby apartments with kitchens. The two-person apartment runs 100€ to 200€ ($115–$230); the four-person apartment is 150€ to 300€ ($172–$345). Both include breakfast at the hotel. The entire hotel is nonsmoking.

San Polo 679 (on Calle dello Sturion), 30125 Venezia. ℭ 041-5236243. Fax 041-5228378. www.locanda sturion.com. 11 units. 70€–150€ ($81–$173) single; 120€–220€ ($138–$253) double without Grand Canal view, 210€–260€ ($242–$299) double with Grand Canal view; 170€–280€ ($196–$322) triple without Grand Canal view, 235€–320€ ($270–$368) triple with Grand Canal view. Quads available. Special rates for families. Rates include buffet breakfast. MC, V. Vaporetto: Rialto. From the Rialto stop, cross the bridge, turn left at the other side, and walk along the Grand Canal; Calle dello Sturion will be the 4th narrow alleyway on the right, just before San Polo 740. **Amenities:** Bar; concierge; tour desk; limited room service; babysitting. *In room:* A/C, TV, dataport, minibar, coffeemaker, hair dryer, safe.

IN SANTA CROCE

Hotel Ai Due Fanali *★★ Finds*   Ai Due Fanali's 16th-century altar-turned-reception-desk is the first clue that this is the hotel of choice for lovers of aesthetics and impeccable taste with restricted budgets. The hotel is located on a quiet square in the residential Santa Croce area, a 10-minute walk across the Grand Canal from the train station but a good 20-minute stroll from the Rialto Bridge. Signora Marina Stea and her daughter Stefania have beautifully restored a part of the 14th-century Scuola of the Church of San Simeon Grando with their innate *buon gusto*. It is evident from the lobby furnished with period pieces to the third-floor breakfast terrace with a glimpse of the Grand Canal. Guest rooms boast headboards painted by local artisans, high-quality bed linens, chrome and gold bathroom fixtures, and good, fluffy towels. Prices drop considerably from November 8 to March 30, with the exception of Christmas week and Carnevale. Ask about the four equally classy waterfront apartments with a view (and kitchenette) near Vivaldi's Church (La Pietà) east of Piazza San Marco; the units sleep four to five people at similar rates per person.

Santa Croce 946 (Campo San Simeone Profeta), 30125 Venezia. ℭ 041-718490. Fax 041-718344. www.aidue fanali.com. 16 units. 78€–165€ ($90–$190) single; 93€–205€ ($107–$236) double; 181€–388€ ($208–$446) apt. Extra person 25% more. Rates include continental breakfast. Off-season discounts of 40%. AE, MC, V. Closed most of Jan. Vaporetto: When arriving in town, don't bother with a ferry, as the hotel's just a 10-min. walk from the train station or Piazzale Roma parking lots; when coming back to the hotel via vaporetto at the end of a long day, get off at the Riva di Biasio stop. **Amenities:** Bar; concierge; tour desk; 24-hr. room service; laundry service; same-day dry cleaning. *In room:* A/C, TV, dataport, minibar, hair dryer, safe.

WORTH A SPLURGE

Residenza d'Epoca Ca'Favretto San Cassiano *★★*   Call this place a moderate splurge, which gets two stars for its location and views. About half the rooms here look across the Grand Canal to the gorgeous Ca' d'Oro (accounting for the highest rates below) and tend to be larger than the others, most of which open onto a side canal. The hotel is built into a 16th-century palace and steeped in dusty old-world elegance, with Murano chandeliers (but no elevator). The rooms are outfitted in modest, dark-wood '70s-style faux antiques. The breakfast room is done in 18th century–style pastels and stuccoes—get down to breakfast early to snag one of the two tiny tables on the wide balcony overlooking the Grand Canal. There's also a wood-beamed bar and TV lounge with a canal-view window and a few small tables on the private boat launch; there you can sip an *aperativo* of an evening, gaze at the Ca' d'Oro, and generally make other tourists on the passing vaporetti intensely jealous because they're booked elsewhere.

Santa Croce 2232 (Calle della Rosa), 30135 Venezia. ℂ **041-5241768.** Fax 041-721033. www.sancassiano.it. 35 units. 55€–240€ ($63–$276) single; 70€–342€ ($81–$393) double; 91€–445€ ($105–$512) triple. Rates include buffet breakfast. AE, DC, MC, V. Vaporetto: San Stae. Turn left to cross in front of the church, take the bridge over the side canal, and turn right. Then turn left, cross another canal, and turn right, then left again. Cross yet another canal and turn right, then immediately left and then left again toward the Grand Canal and the hotel. **Amenities:** Bar; concierge; tour desk; car-rental desk; room service; massage (in-room); babysitting; laundry service; dry cleaning. *In room:* A/C, TV, dataport, minibar, hair dryer, safe.

4 Great Deals on Dining

Eating cheaply in Venice isn't easy, though it's by no means impossible. So plan well and don't rely on the serendipity that may serve you in other cities. If you've qualified for a Rolling Venice card, ask for the guide listing dozens of restaurants offering discounts. Bear in mind that Venice is a city of early meals compared to Rome and other points south: You should be seated by 7:30 to 8:30pm. Most kitchens close at 10 or 10:30pm, even though the restaurant may stay open to 11:30pm or midnight.

Venetian *cichetti* are tapaslike finger foods such as calamari rings, speared fried olives, potato croquettes, and grilled polenta squares, traditionally washed down with an *ombra* (shadow), a small glass of wine. Venice has countless cafes and neighborhood bars called *bacari* where you can order a selection of *cichetti*, a *panino* (sandwich on a roll), or a *toast* (grilled ham-and-cheese sandwich). All of the above will cost about .75€ to 1.30€ (85¢–$1.50) if you stand at the bar, or as much as double that if you sit at a table. You'll find a concentration of well-stocked bars along the Mercerie shopping strip connecting Piazza San Marco with the Ponte Rialto, the always lively Campo San Luca (look for Bar Torino, Bar Black Jack, or Leon Bianco), and Campo Santa Margherita. Avoid the tired-looking pizza (reheated by microwave) sold in most bars—informal sit-down neighborhood pizzerias offer savory and far fresher renditions for a minimum of 3€ ($3.45), plus your drink and cover charge.

Fishy Business

If you order fresh fish or seafood, know that it'll hike up the price of an average meal. And don't forget that the menu price commonly refers to *l'etto* (100g), a fraction of the full cost (have the waiter estimate the full cost before ordering); larger fish are intended to feed two. Eating a meal based on the day's catch (restaurants are legally bound to print on the menu whether the fish is frozen) will be enjoyable but never inexpensive, so avoid splurging on fish or seafood on Monday, when the Fish Market (and most self-respecting fish-serving restaurants) is closed.

On Venetian menus you'll see things you won't see elsewhere, plus local versions of time-tested Italian favorites. For primi, both pasta and risotto (more liquidy in the Veneto than usual) are commonly prepared with fish or seafood: *Risotto alla sepie* or *alla seppioline* (tinted black by cuttlefish ink and also called *risotto nero,* or black risotto), and *spaghetti alle vongole* or *alle vorace* (with clams; clams without their shells aren't a good sign!) are two common specialties. Both also appear with *frutti di mare* ("fruits of the sea"), which can be a little bit of whatever looked good at that morning's fish market. *Bigoli,* homemade whole-wheat pasta, isn't commonly found elsewhere, while creamy *polenta,* often served with *gamberetti* (small shrimp) or *schie* (tiny shrimp) or as an accompaniment to *fegato alla veneziana* (calves' liver with onions Venetian style), is a staple of the Veneto and perhaps Venice's only nonfish specialty. Fish and seafood to look out for are *branzino* (sea bass), *rombo* (turbot or brill), *moeche* (small soft-shell crab), *granseola* (crab), and *sarde in saor* (sardines in a sauce of onion, vinegar, pine nuts, and raisins).

From a host of good local **wines,** try the dry white tocai and pinot from the Friuli region and the light, champagne-like *prosecco* Venetians consume almost like a soft drink (it's the base of Venice's famous Bellini drink made with white peach purée). Popular reds include merlot, cabernet, raboso, and refosco. The quintessentially Italian Bardolino, Valpolicella, and Soave are from the nearby Veneto area. **Grappa,** the local firewater, is an acquired taste often offered in a dozen variations. Neighborhood *bacari* (wine bars) provide the chance to taste the fruits of leading wine producers in the grape-rich regions of the Veneto and neighboring Friuli.

Note: You can locate the restaurants below on the "Venice Accommodations & Dining" map on p. 372.

IN SAN MARCO

Bistrot de Venise 🛪🛪 VENETIAN   This relaxed spot offers outdoor and indoor seating (even a nonsmoking section), young English-speaking waiters, and an eclectic menu. It's a popular meeting spot for Venetians and young artists, and you're made to feel welcome to write postcards over a cappuccino, enjoy a simple lunch like risotto and salad, or dine when most of Venice is shutting down. Linger over an elaborate meal that might include local favorites like *figa' de vedelo a la venexiana* (Venetian calves' liver) and the odd *morete a la caorlotta* (tagliolini made with cocoa, topped by a festival of crustaceans) or dishes from 15th-century Venetian recipes. Peek in the back room (or check the website) to see what's going on in the evening—art exhibits, cabarets, live music, or poetry readings.

San Marco 4687 (on Calle dei Fabbri), below the Albergo al Gambero. 🌀 041-5236651. www.bistrotde venise.com. Primi 9€–18€ ($10–$21); secondi 18€–24€ ($21–$28). Tasting menus: light lunch 20€–25€ ($23–$29); classico 35€ ($40); storico 45€ ($52). MC, V. Daily noon–1am. Closed 1 week before Christmas. Vaporetto: Rialto. Turn right along the canal, cross the small footbridge over Rio San Salvador, turn left onto Calle Bembo, which becomes Calle dei Fabbri; the Bistrot is about 5 blocks ahead in the direction of Piazza San Marco.

Osteria alle Botteghe 🛪 Kids PIZZERIA/ITALIAN   Easy on the palate, easy on the wallet, and even easy to find (if you've made it to Campo Santo Stefano), this is a great casual choice for pizza, a light snack, or a full meal. You can have stand-up *cichetti* and fresh sandwiches at the bar or windowside counter, while more serious diners can head to the tables in back to enjoy the dozen pizzas, the pastas, or the *tavola calda,* a glass counter filled with prepared dishes like eggplant parmigiana, lasagna, and fresh-cooked vegetables in season, reheated when you order.

San Marco 3454 (on Calle delle Botteghe, off Campo Santo Stefano). © 041-5228181. Primi 4.15€ ($4.75); secondi 7€–8€ ($8.05–$9.20); *menu turistico* 8.80€ ($10). DC, MC, V. Mon–Sat 11am–4pm and 7–10pm. Vaporetto: Accademia or Sant'Angelo. Find your way to Campo Santo Stefano by following the stream of people or by asking; take narrow Calle delle Botteghe at the Gelateria Paolin across from Santo Stefano.

Rosticceria San Bartolomeo *(Value* ITALIAN/TAVOLA CALDA   With long hours and a central location, this refurbished old-timer is Venice's most popular *rosticceria* (and for good reason), so the continuous turnover guarantees fresh food. With a dozen pasta dishes and as many fish, seafood, or meat entrees, San Bartolomeo can satisfy any combination of culinary desires. Since the ready-made food is displayed under a glass counter, you don't have to worry about mistranslation—you'll know exactly what you're ordering. There's no cover charge if you take your meal standing up or seated at the stools in the aroma-filled ground-floor area. For those who prefer to linger, head to the dining hall upstairs—but it costs more and you could do much better than this institutional setting.

San Marco 5424 (on Calle della Bissa). © 041-5223569. Primi and pizza 5.90€–6.90€ ($6.80–$7.95); secondi 7€–13€ ($8.05–$14); *menu turistico* 10€–18€ ($12–$20). Prices about 20%–30% higher upstairs. AE, DC, MC, V. Summer daily 9am–9:30pm; winter Tues–Sun 9:30am–9:30pm. Vaporetto: Rialto. With the bridge at your back on the San Marco side of the canal, walk straight ahead to Campo San Bartolomeo; take the underpass slightly to your left marked SOTTOPORTEGO DELLA BISSA; you'll come across the *rosticceria* at the first corner on your right; look for GISLON (its old name) above the entrance.

Rosticceria Teatro Goldoni ITALIAN/INTERNATIONAL/FAST FOOD   Bright and modern (although it has been here for more than 50 years), this showcase of Venetian-style fast food tries to be a bar, cafe, *rosticceria,* and *tavola calda* on the ground floor and a pizzeria upstairs. A variety of sandwiches and pastries beckon from a downstairs display counter, and another offers prepared foods (eggplant parmigiana, roast chicken, *pasta e fagioli,* lasagna) that will be reheated when ordered; there are also a dozen pasta choices. The combination salads are freshest and most varied for lunch and a welcome concession to Americans. This won't be your most memorable meal in Venice, but you won't walk away hungry or broke.

San Marco 4747 (at the corner of Calle dei Fabbri). © 041-5222446. Primi and pizza 6€–15€ ($6.90–$17); secondi 8€–20€ ($9.20–$23); *menu turistico* 14€ ($16) with wine. AE, DC, MC, V. Daily 9:30am–9:30pm. Vaporetto: Rialto. Walk from the San Marco side of the bridge to Campo San Bartolomeo and exit it to your right in the direction of Campo San Luca.

Trattoria da Fiore *(Finds* VENETIAN   Don't confuse this laid-back trattoria with the expensive Osteria da Fiore. You might not eat better here, but it'll seem that way when your relatively modest bill arrives. Start with the house specialty, the *pennette alla Fiore* for two (with olive oil, garlic, and seven in-season vegetables), and you might be happy to call it a night. Or try the *frittura mista* (over a dozen varieties of fresh fish and seafood). The bouillabaisse-like *zuppa di pesce alla chef* is stocked with mussels, crab, clams, shrimp, and tuna—at only 13€ ($15), it doesn't get any better and is a meal in itself. This is a great place to snack or make a light lunch out of *cichetti* at the Bar Fiore next door (10:30am–10:30pm).

San Marco 3561 (on Calle delle Botteghe). © 041-5235310. www.trattoriadafiore.com. Reservations suggested. Primi 8.50€–18€ ($9.75–$21); secondi 15€–25€ ($17–$29). MC, V. Wed–Mon noon–3pm and 7–10pm. Closed Jan 10–20 and Aug 1–15. Vaporetto: Accademia. Cross the bridge to the San Marco side and walk straight ahead to Campo Santo Stefano; exit the campo at the northern end, and take a left at the Bar/Gelateria Paolin onto Calle delle Botteghe.

Vino Vino 😊😊 *Value* WINE BAR/ITALIAN   Vino Vino is an informal wine bar serving well-prepared simple food, but its biggest pull is the impressive selection of local and European wines sold by the bottle or glass (check out the website), with great *cichetti* to accompany them. The Venetian specialties are written on a chalkboard but also usually displayed at the glass counter. After placing your order, settle into one of about a dozen wooden tables squeezed into the two storefront-style rooms. Credit the high quality of the food to the fact that Vino Vino shares a kitchen (and an owner) with the eminent and expensive Antico Martini restaurant a few doors down. It's a great spot for a leisurely self-styled wine tasting (1€–3€/$1.15–$3.45 per glass), with great *cichetti* bar food. At dinner, the food often runs out around 10:30pm, so don't come too late.

San Marco 2007 (on the Ponte delle Veste near La Fenice). ℭ 041-5237027. www.vinovino.co.it. Primi 5.50€–9€ ($6.30–$10); secondi 9€–12€ ($10–$14). AE, DC, MC, V. Wed–Mon 10:30am–11:30pm (to 12:30am Sat). Vaporetto: San Marco. With your back to the basilica, exit Piazza San Marco through the arcade on the far left side; keep walking straight, pass American Express, cross the canal and, before the street jogs left, turn right onto Calle delle Veste.

IN CASTELLO

Da Aciugheta 😊 *Value* VENETIAN/WINE BAR/PIZZERIA   A long block north of the chic Riva degli Schiavoni hotels lies one of Venice's best wine bars, expanded to include an elbow-to-elbow trattoria/pizzeria in back. Its name refers to the toothpick-speared marinated anchovies that join other *cichetti* lining the popular front bar, where you can enjoy an excellent selection of Veneto and Italian wines by the glass. The staff is relaxed about those not ordering full multiple-course meals—a pasta and glass of wine or pizza and beer will keep anyone happy. There's an unusually long list of half-bottles of wine and an even more unusual nonsmoking room. Tables move out onto the small piazza when the warm weather moves in.

Castello 4357 (in Campo SS. Filippo e Giacomo, east of Piazza San Marco). ℭ 041-5224292. Primi 6€–17€ ($6.90–$20); secondi 10€–15€ ($12–$17); pizza 6€–10€ ($7–$12); *menu turistico* 14€ ($16). AE, MC, V. Daily 8am–midnight (closed Wed Nov–Mar). Vaporetto: San Zaccaria. Walk north on Calle delle Rasse to Campo SS. Filippo e Giacomo.

Pizzeria/Trattoria al Vecio Canton *Kids* ITALIAN/PIZZA   Good pizza is hard to find in Venice, and I mean that in the literal sense. Tucked away in a northeast corner behind Piazza San Marco on a well-trafficked route connecting it with Campo Santa Maria Formosa, the Canton's wood-paneled, taverna-like atmosphere and great pizzas are worth the time you'll spend looking for the place. There is a full trattoria menu as well, with a number of pastas and side dishes *(contorni)* of vegetables providing a palatable alternative.

Castello 4738a (at the corner of Ruga Giuffa). ℭ 041-5285176. www.alveciocanton.com. Reservations not accepted. Primi and pizza 6€–9€ ($6.90–$10); secondi 11€–18€ ($13–$21). AE, DC, MC, V. Wed 7–10:30pm; Thurs–Mon noon–2:30pm and 7–10:30pm. Vaporetto: San Zaccaria. From the Riva degli Schiavoni waterfront, walk straight ahead to Campo SS. Filippo e Giacomo; turn right and continue east to the small Campo San Provolo. Take a left heading north on the Salizzada San Provolo, cross the 1st footbridge, and you'll find the pizzeria on the 1st corner on the left.

Trattoria alla Rivetta 😊 SEAFOOD/VENETIAN   Lively and frequented by gondoliers (always a clue of quality dining for the right price), merchants, and visitors drawn to its bonhomie and bustling popularity, this is one of the safer bets for genuine Venetian cuisine and company in the touristy San Marco area, a 10-minute walk east of the piazza. All sorts of fish—the specialty—decorate the window of this brightly lit place. Another good indicator: There's usually a bit of a wait, even off season.

Castello 4625 (on Salizzada San Provolo). © 041-5287302. Primi 7€–11€ ($8.05–$13); secondi 11€–15€ ($13–$17). AE, MC, V. Tues–Sun noon–2:30pm and 7–10pm. Vaporetto: San Zaccaria. With your back to the water and facing the Hotel Savoia e Jolanda, walk straight ahead to Campo SS. Filippo e Giacomo; the trattoria is tucked away next to a bridge off the right side of the campo.

Trattoria da Remigio 🏮🏮 ITALIAN/VENETIAN   Famous for its straightforward renditions of classics, Remigio is the kind of place where you can order simple *gnocchi alla pescatora* (homemade gnocchi in tomato-seafood sauce) and *frittura mista* (a cornucopia of fried seafood that makes a flavorful but light secondo) and know it'll be memorable. It bucks the current Venetian trend by offering excellent food and service at reasonable prices. The English-speaking headwaiter, Pino, will talk you through the day's perfectly prepared fish dishes (John Dory, sole, monkfish, cuttlefish). You'll even find a dozen meat choices. There are two pleasant but smallish dining rooms. Remigio's—less abuzz and more sedate than Trattoria Alla Madonna (see below)—is well known though not as easy to find, but just ask any local.

Castello 3416 (on Calle Bosello near the Scuola San Giorgio dei Greci). © 041-5230089. Reservations required. Primi 6€–10€ ($6.90–$12); secondi 9€–20€ ($10–$23). AE, DC, MC, V. Mon 1–3pm; Wed–Sun 1–3pm and 7–11pm. Vaporetto: San Zaccaria. Follow Riva degli Schiavoni east until you come to the white Chiesa della Pietà; turn left onto Calle della Pietà, which jogs left into Calle Bosello.

WORTH A SPLURGE

Al Covo 🏮🏮 VENETIAN/SEAFOOD   For years this lovely restaurant has been consistently (and deservingly) popular with American food writers, putting it on the shortlist of every food-loving American tourist. There are nights when it seems you hear nothing but English spoken. But this has never compromised the incredible dining at this warm and welcoming spot, where the preparation of superfresh fish and an excellent selection of moderately priced wines is as commendable today—perhaps more so—as in its nascent days of pretrendiness. Much of its tourist-friendly atmosphere is due to the naturally hospitable Diane Rankin, the co-owner and dessert whiz who hails from Texas. She will eagerly talk you through a wondrous fish-studded menu that can otherwise seem Greek to non-Venetians. Her husband, Cesare Benelli, is known for his infallible talent in the kitchen. Together they share an admirable dedication to their charming gem of a restaurant—the quality of an evening at Al Covo is tough to top in this town. The restaurant will begin accepting credit cards in 2005.

Castello 3968 (Campiello della Pescheria, east of Chiesa della Pietà in the Arsenale neighborhood). © 041-5223812. www.ristorantealcovo.com. Reservations required. Primi 12€–19€ ($14–$22); secondi 25€–33€ ($29–$38); 3-course fixed-price lunch 38€ ($44); fixed-price dinner 63€–79€ ($72–$91). AE, MC, V (in 2005). Fri–Tues 12:45–2:15pm and 7:30–10pm. Closed Dec 15–Jan 15 and 2 weeks in Aug. Vaporetto: Arsenale. Walk a short way back in the direction of Piazza San Marco, turning right at the bar/cafe il Gabbiano. The restaurant is on your left. Otherwise, it is an enjoyable 20-min. stroll along the waterfront Riva degli Schiavoni from Piazza San Marco, past the Chiesa della Pietà and the Metropole Hotel.

Osteria alle Testiere 🏮🏮 VENETIAN/ITALIAN   The limited seating for just 24 savvy (and lucky) patrons at butcher-paper-covered tables, the relaxed young staff, and the upbeat taverna-like atmosphere belie the seriousness of this informal newcomer. Already proving it will persist far beyond the usual 15 minutes of culinary fame, this is your guaranteed choice if you are of the foodie genre, curious to experience the increasingly interesting Venetian culinary scene without going broke. Start with the carefully chosen wine list; many of the 90 labels can be ordered by the half-bottle. The delicious homemade *gnocchetti ai calamaretti* (pasta with baby squid) makes a frequent appearance, as does the traditional secondo specialty, *scampi alla busara*. Its "secret" recipe includes identifiable ingredients such as tomato, cinnamon, and a dash of hot pepper. Cheese is a rarity in these parts, except for Alle Testiere's exceptional cheese platter.

Castello 5801 (on Calle del Mondo Novo off Salizzada San Lio). (C) **041-5227220.** Reservations required for each of 2 seatings. Primi 14€–15€ ($16–$17); secondi 22€–30€ ($25–$35). MC, V. Tues–Sat lunch noon–2:30pm; dinner has 2 seatings: 7 and 9:30pm. Vaporetto: Equidistant from the Rialto and San Marco stops. Find the store-lined Salizzada San Lio (west of the Campo Santa Maria Formosa), and from there ask where to turn off onto Calle del Mondo Novo.

IN DORSODURO

Taverna San Trovaso 🍴 VENETIAN   Wine bottles line the wood-paneled walls, and low vaulted brick ceilings augment the sense of character in this canal-side tavern. The *menu turistico* includes wine, an ample *frittura mista* (assortment of fried seafood), and a dessert. The gnocchi is homemade, the local specialty of calves' liver and onions is great, and the simply grilled fish is the taverna's claim to fame. There's also a variety of pizzas. For a special occasion that'll test your budget but not bankrupt you, consider the four-course menu: It starts with a fresh antipasto of seafood followed by pasta and a fish entree (changing with the day's catch), and includes side dishes, a dessert, and wine. While in the neighborhood, stroll along Rio San Trovaso toward the Giudecca Canal: On your right will be the Squero di San Trovaso, one of the few boatyards that still makes and repairs gondolas.

Dorsoduro 1016 (on Fondamenta Priuli). (C) **041-5203703.** Reservations recommended. Primi and pizza 5€–12€ ($5.75–$14); secondi 8€–17€ ($9.20–$20); *menu turistico* 18€ ($21). AE, DC, MC, V. Tues–Sun noon–2:45pm and 7–9:45pm. Vaporetto: Rialto. Walk to the right around the Accademia and take a right onto Calle Gambara; when this street ends at the small Rio di San Trovaso, turn left onto Fondamenta Priuli.

Trattoria Ai Cugnai 🍴🍴 *Value* VENETIAN   The unassuming storefront of this longtime favorite does little to announce that herein lies some of the neighborhood's best dining. The name refers to the brothers-in-law of the three women chefs, all sisters, who serve classic *cucina venexiana*, like the reliably good spaghetti *alle vongole verace* (with clams) or *fegato alla veneziana*. The homemade gnocchi and lasagna would meet any Italian grandmother's approval (you won't go wrong with any of the menu's *fatta in casa* choices of daily homemade specialties). Equidistant from the Accademia and the Guggenheim, Ai Cugnai is the perfect place to recharge after an art overload.

Dorsoduro 857 (on Calle Nuova Sant'Agnese). (C) **041-5289238.** Primi 5€–9€ ($5.75–$10); secondi 5€–17€ ($5.75–$19). AE, MC, V. Tues–Sun 12:30–3pm and 7–10:30pm. Vaporetto: Accademia. Head east of the bridge and the Accademia in the direction of the Guggenheim Collection; on the straight street connecting the 2 museums, the restaurant is on your right.

IN SAN POLO

A Le Do Spade 🍴 WINE BAR/VENETIAN   Since 1415, workers, fishmongers, and shoppers from the nearby Mercato della Pescheria have flocked to this wine bar. There's bonhomie galore amid the locals here for their daily *ombra*—a large number of excellent Veneto and Friuli wines available by the glass. A counter is filled with various *cichetti* (potato croquettes, fried calamari, polenta squares, cheeses) and a special *picante panino* whose secret mix of superhot spices will sear your taste buds. Unlike at most *bacari*, this quintessentially Venetian cantina has added a number of tables and introduced a sit-down menu; competitor Cantina do Mori (see below) is a better choice for stand-up bar food. The main room is more atmospheric, but the recently reopened—and, sadly, modern-paneled—back room was where Casanova once engaged in amorous assignations (there was a back door so he could make his escape if any enraged husbands should show up).

San Polo 860 (on Sottoportego do Spade). ℂ **041-5210574.** www.dospadevenezia.it. Primi 7€–10€ ($8.05–$12); secondi 8€–13€ ($9.20–$15); *menu fisso* 14€–15€ ($16–$17). AE, MC, V. Mon–Wed and Fri–Sat 9am–3pm and 5–11pm; Thurs 9am–3pm. Vaporetto: Rialto or San Silvestro. At the San Polo side of the Ponte Rialto, walk away from the bridge and through the open-air market until you see the covered fish market on your right; take a left and then take the 2nd right onto Sottoportego do Spade.

Cantina do Mori 𝓡𝓡 *(Finds* WINE BAR/SANDWICHES Since 1462, this has been the watering hole of choice in the market area; legend even pegs Casanova as a habitué. Here's the best place to try *tramezzini*—you're guaranteed fresh combinations of thinly sliced meats, tuna, cheeses, and vegetables, along with tapaslike *cichetti*. They're traditionally washed down with an *ombra*. Venetians stop to snack and socialize before and after meals; if you don't mind standing (there are no tables), do as they do. And now with a limited number of primi, like *melanzane alla parmigiana* (eggplant parmigiana) and *fondi di carciofi saltati* (lightly fried artichoke hearts), my obligatory stop here is more fulfilling than ever before.

San Polo 429 (entrances on Calle Galiazza and Calle Do Mori). ℂ **041-5225401.** Sandwiches and *cichetti* bar food 1€–3€ ($1.15–$3.45); wine from 2.10€ ($2.40) a glass. No credit cards. Mon–Sat 8:30am–9:30pm. Vaporetto: Rialto. Cross the Ponte Rialto to the San Polo side, walk to the end of the market stalls, turn left, then turn immediately right and look for the small wooden cantina sign on the left.

Da Sandro 𝓡 *(Kids* ITALIAN/PIZZERIA Like most pizzerie/trattorie, Sandro offers a dozen varieties of pizza (his specialty) as well as a full trattoria menu of pastas and entrees. But if you're looking for a 6.20€ ($7.15) pizza-and-beer meal, this is a reliably good spot on the main drag linking the Rialto to Campo San Polo. You won't raise any eyebrows if you order just a pasta or a pizza and pass on the meat or fish. There's communal seating at a few wooden picnic tables placed outdoors, with eight small tables stuffed inside. The restaurant is oddly split between properties on either side of the street; definitely try to get seated in the cozier half, with its time-blackened beamed ceilings and wood-paneled walls.

San Polo 1473 (on Campiello dei Meloni). ℂ **041-5234894.** Primi and pizza 6.30€–8.50€ ($7.25–$10); secondi 9.30€–17€ ($11–$20); fixed-price menus 15€–19€ ($17–$22). AE, MC, V. Sat–Thurs 11:30am–11:30pm. Vaporetto: San Silvestro. With your back to the Grand Canal, walk straight to store-lined Ruga Vecchia San Giovanni and take a left; head toward Campo San Polo until you come to Campiello dei Meloni.

Trattoria Alla Madonna ITALIAN/VENETIAN Packing them in for more than 50 years, this Venetian institution has it all: a convenient location, a mix of locals and foreigners, a decor of high-beamed ceilings and walls frame-to-frame with local artists' work, and a professional kitchen that prepares a menu of fresh fish and seafood to perfection. With all of this and (by Venetian standards) moderate prices, it's no surprise this place is always jumping. So don't expect the waiter to smile if you linger over dessert. Most of the first courses are served with seafood, like the spaghetti or risotto with *frutti di mare* or the pasta with *sepie* (cuttlefish), blackened with its own natural ink. Most of the day's special fish selections are best simply and deliciously prepared *alla griglia* (grilled).

San Polo 594 (on Calle della Madonna). ℂ **041-5223824.** www.ristoranteallamadonna.com. Reservations not accepted for tables of fewer than 8. Primi 9€–11€ ($10–$13); secondi 9€–15€ ($10–$17). AE, DC, MC, V. Thurs–Tues noon–3pm and 7–10pm. Closed 2 weeks in Aug and all of Jan. Vaporetto: Rialto. From the foot of the Ponte Rialto on the San Polo side of the Grand Canal, turn left and follow Riva del Vin along the Grand Canal; Calle della Madonna (also called Sottoportego della Madonna) will be the 2nd calle on your right (look for the big yellow sign); the restaurant is on your left.

IN SANTA CROCE

Pizzeria alle Oche 𝓡 *(Kids* PIZZERIA When I just want to hole up with a pizza in a relaxed setting, I head for the Baskin-Robbins of Venice's pizzerias, an

American-style tavern restaurant of wood beams and booths decorated with classic signs (you know, 1950s Coca-Cola signs and the like). Italians are zealously unapologetic about tucking into a good-size pizza and a pint of beer (with more than 20 here from which to choose); the walk to and from this slightly peripherally located hangout (with outside eating during warm weather) allays thoughts of calorie counts. Count 'em: 85 varieties of imaginative pizza fill the menu, including a dozen of the tomato-sauce-free "white" variety *(pizza bianca)*. The clientele is a mixed bag of young and old, students and not, Venetian and visitors.

Santa Croce 1552 (on Calle del Tintor south of Campo San Giacomo dell'Orio). ℂ 041-5241161. Reservations recommended for weekends. Primi 5.20€–6.30€ ($6–$7.25); secondi 5.80€–7.50€ ($6.65–$8.60); pizza 4.30€–7.40€ ($4.95–$8.50). MC, V. Daily noon–3pm and 7pm–midnight. Vaporetto: Equidistant from Rio San Biasio and San Stae. You can walk here in 10 min. from the nearby train station; otherwise, from the vaporetto station, find your way to the Campo San Giacomo dell'Orio and exit it south onto the well-trammeled Calle del Tintor.

IN CANNAREGIO

Brek, Lista di Spagna 124 (ℂ 041-2440158; Vaporetto: Ferrovia), that Northern Italian chain of upscale cafeterias, has recently opened a popular Venice branch near the train station; it's open daily 11:30am to 10:30pm.

Ai Tre Spiedi ✮ VENETIAN   Venetians bring their visiting friends here to make a *bella figura* (good impression) without breaking the bank, then swear them to secrecy. Rarely will you find as pleasant a setting and appetizing a meal as in this casually elegant small trattoria with some of the most reasonably priced fresh fish that'll keep meat-eaters happy as well. Their spaghetti O.P.A. (with parsley, pepperoncino, garlic, and olive oil) is excellent and their spaghetti al pesto the best this side of Liguria. This and Trattoria da Fiore (see above) are the most reasonable choices for an authentic Venetian dinner of fresh fish. Careful ordering needn't mean much of a splurge, either—though, inexplicably, prices have risen dramatically in the last two years.

Cannaregio 5906 (on Salizzada San Cazian). ℂ 041-5208035. Primi 4.50€–7.50€ ($5.15–$8.60); secondi 11€–17€ ($12–$19); *menu turistico* 15€–20€ ($17–$22) without wine. AE, MC, V. Tues–Sat noon–2:30pm and 7–10pm; Sun noon–2:30pm. Vaporetto: Rialto. On the San Marco side of the bridge, walk straight ahead to Campo San Bartolomeo and take a left, passing the post office, Coin department store, and San Crisostomo; cross the 1st bridge after the church and turn right at the toy store onto Salizzada San Cazian.

PICNICKING

You don't have to eat in a fancy restaurant to have a good time in Venice. Prepare a picnic and, while you eat alfresco, observe the life of the city's few open piazzas or the aquatic parade on its main thoroughfare, the Grand Canal. And you can still indulge in a late dinner *alla veneziana*. Plus, doing your own shopping for food can be an interesting experience because there are very few supermarkets as we know them, and small *alimentari* (food shops) in the highly visited neighborhoods (where few Venetians live) are scarce.

MERCATO RIALTO   Venice's principal open-air market is a sight to see, even for nonshoppers. It has two parts, beginning with the **produce section,** whose many stalls, alternating with souvenir vendors, unfold north on the San Polo side of the Ponte Rialto (behind these stalls are a few permanent food stores whose delicious cheese, cold cuts, and bread selections make the perfect lunch). The vendors are here Monday through Saturday from 7am to 1pm, with a number who stay on in the afternoon.

At the market's farthest point, you'll find the covered **fresh-fish market,** with its carnival atmosphere, on the Grand Canal opposite the magnificent Ca' d'Oro. The area is filled with a number of small *bacari* frequented by market vendors and shoppers where you can join in and ask for your morning's first glass of *prosecco* with a *cichetto* pick-me-up. The fish merchants take Monday off and work mornings only.

CAMPO SANTA MARGHERITA   Tuesday through Saturday from 8:30am to 1 or 2pm, open-air stalls selling fresh fruit and vegetables set up shop here. You should have no trouble filling out your picnic spread with the fixings available at the various shops around the campo, including an exceptional *panetteria* (bakery), Rizzo Pane, at no. 2772; a fine *salumeria* (deli) at no. 2844; and a good shop for wine, sweets, and other picnic accessories next door. There's even a conventional supermarket, **Merlini,** just off the campo in the direction of the quasiadjacent Campo San Barnabà at no. 3019. This is also the area where you'll find Venice's heavily photographed **floating market** operating from a boat moored just off Campo San Barnabà at the Ponte dei Pugni. This market is open daily from 8am to 1pm and 3:30 to 7:30pm, except Wednesday afternoon and Sunday. You're almost better off just buying a few freshly prepared sandwiches (*panini* when made with rolls, *tramezzini* when made with white bread).

THE BEST PICNIC SPOTS   Alas, picnicking in Venice means you won't have much in the way of green space (it's not worth the boat ride to the Giardini Publici past the Arsenale, Venice's only green park). An enjoyable alternative is to find some of the larger piazze or campi that have park benches, and in some cases even a tree or two to shade them, such as **Campo San Giacomo dell'Orio** (in Santa Croce). The two most central are **Campo Santa Margherita** (in Dorsoduro) and **Campo San Polo** (in San Polo). Personally, I like staking out a sliver of canal-front *fondamenta* and picnicking simply, dangling my feet off the marble embankment over the water.

For a picnic with a view, scout out the **Punta della Dogana (Customs House)** area near La Salute for a prime viewing site at the mouth of the Grand Canal. It's directly across from Piazza San Marco and the Palazzo Ducale—pull up a piece of the embankment here and watch the water activity against a canvaslike backdrop deserving of the Accademia. In this same area, the small **Campo San Vio** near the Guggenheim is on the Grand Canal and even boasts a bench or two. If you want to create a real Venice picnic, you'll have to take the no. 12 boat out to the near-deserted island of **Torcello,** with a hamper full of bread, cheese, and wine, and reenact the romantic scene of Katharine Hepburn and Rossano Brazzi in *Summertime.*

5 Sights to See

Venice is notorious for changing and extending the opening hours of its museums and, to a lesser degree, its churches. Before you begin your sightseeing, ask at the tourist office for the season's list of museum and church hours. During the peak months, you can enjoy extended museum hours—some places stay open to 7 or even 10pm. Alas, these hours aren't released until about Easter of every year. Even then, little is done to publicize the information, so you'll have to do your own research.

THE VENICE CARD

Venice, so delicate it cannot handle the hordes of visitors it receives every year, has been toying with the idea of charging admission to get into the city itself. Instead, the mayor's office has begun experimenting with a **Venice Card** (© **899-909090** in Italy, or 041-2714747 or 041-2424 outside of Italy; www.

venicecard.it), which allows holders discounts on a wide range of services and sights throughout the city. The "blu" version will get you free passage on buses and vaporetti, usage of public toilets, and a discount at the public ASM parking garage. The "orange" version adds to these services admission to all the sights covered under the expanded version of the Musei di Piazza San Marco cumulative ticket (see below), plus the Ca' Rezzonico and the museums on Murano and Burano—and the card lets you bypass the often long lines.

For adults over 30, the "blu" card costs 14€ ($16) for 1 day, 29€ ($33) for 3 days, and 51€ ($59) for 7 days; for ages 4 to 29, the "blu" card costs 9€ ($10) for 1 day, 22€ ($25) for 3 days, and 49€ ($56) for 7 days. For adults, the "orange" card costs 28€ ($32) for 1 day, 47€ ($54) for 3 days, and 68€ ($78) for 7 days; for ages 4 to 29, the "orange" card costs 18€ ($21) for 1 day, 35€ ($40) for 3 days, and 61€ ($70) for 7 days. You can order a card in advance by phone or online, and they'll tell you where to pick it up. There are also versions of the Venice Card that include a ride into town from the airport, but it doesn't save you any money in the long run, so just skip it.

IN SAN MARCO

Basilica di San Marco (St. Mark's Basilica) ★★★   For centuries, Venice was Europe's principal gateway between the Orient and the West, so it shouldn't be surprising that the architectural style for this sumptuously Byzantine basilica, with five mosquelike bulbed domes, was borrowed from Constantinople. Legend has it that, in 828, two enterprising Venetian merchants smuggled St. Mark the Evangelist's remains from Alexandria in Egypt by packing them in pickled pork to bypass the scrutiny of Muslim guards. And so St. Mark replaced the Greek St. Theodore as Venice's patron saint, and a small chapel was built on this spot in his honor. Through the subsequent centuries (much of what you see was built in the 11th c.), wealthy Venetians vied with one another in donating gifts to expand and embellish this church, the saint's final resting place and, with the Palazzo Ducale, a symbol of Venetian wealth and power. Exotic and mysterious, it's unlike any other Roman Catholic church you'll visit.

And so it is that the Basilica di San Marco earned its name as the **Chiesa d'Oro (Golden Church),** every inch of its cavernous interior exquisitely gilded with Byzantine mosaics added over some 7 centuries (the earliest from the 11th c.). For a close look at many of the most remarkable ceiling mosaics and for a better view of the Oriental carpet–like patterns of the intricate undulating pavement mosaics below, pay the museum admission to go upstairs to the **Galleria and Museo Marciano** (www.museosanmarco.it; the entrance to these is in the atrium at the principal entrance). This was originally the *matroneum* (women's gallery). One room showcases the restored *Triumphal Quadriga* of four gilded-bronze horses (2nd or 3rd c.) brought in 1204 to Venice from Constantinople (though probably cast in Imperial Rome) together with the Lion of St. Mark (the patron saint's icon and Venice's mascot) and other booty from the Crusades. The statue group was a symbol of the unrivaled Serene Republic and is the only *quadriga* (four horses tethered together) to have survived from the classical era.

From the Galleria, you can also climb onto the outdoor **Loggia dei Cavalli,** an unexpected highlight providing an excellent view of the piazza and what Napoleon called "the most beautiful salon in the world" upon his arrival in Venice in 1797. The emperor later carted the *quadriga* (a replica of which now stands on the loggia) off to Paris, but it was returned after the fall of the French Empire. The 500-year-old Torre dell'Orologio (Clock Tower) stands to your

Venice Attractions

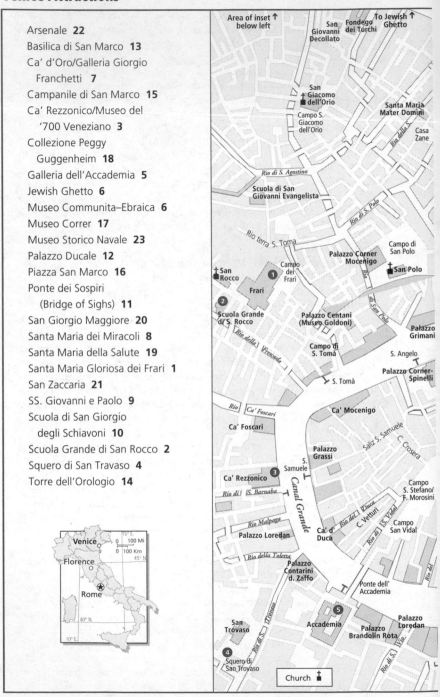

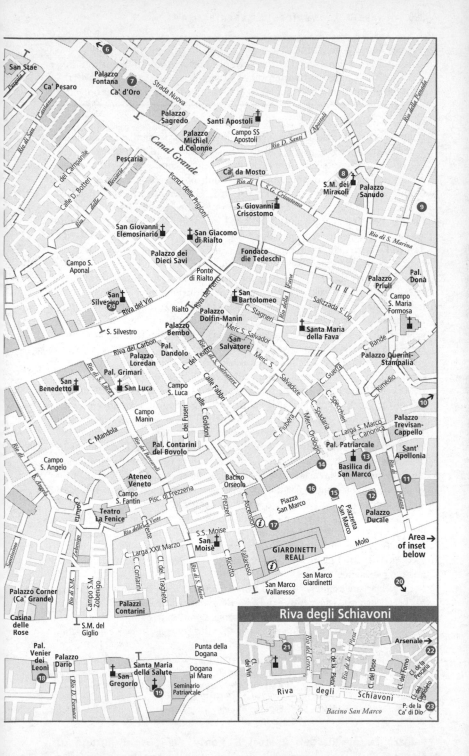

San Stae

Ca' Pesaro

Pescara

Palazzo Fontana

Ca' d'Oro

Strada Nuova

Palazzo Sagredo

Palazzo Michiel d.Colonne

Santi Apostoli

Campo SS Apostoli

Rio D. Santi

C. del Campanile

Calle D. Botteri

Pescaria

Canal Grande

Fond. delle Prigioni

Ca' da Mosto

Rio di

Rio S.G. Crisostomo

S.M. dei Miracoli

Palazzo Sanudo

S. Giovanni Crisostomo

Rio di S. Marina

San Giovanni Elemosinario

San Giacomo di Rialto

Palazzo dei Dieci Savi

Fondaco die Tedeschi

Pal. Donà

Palazzo Priuli

Campo S. Maria Formosa

Campo S. Aponal

Ponte di Rialto

San Bartolomeo

Salizzada S. Liò

C. Bande

Palazzo Querini-Stampalia

San Silvestro

Riva del Vin

Rialto

Riva del Ferro

Palazzo Dolfin-Manin

C. Stagneri

Palazzo Bembo

Merc S. Salvador

San Salvatore

Santa Maria della Fava

Rimedio

S. Silvestro

Riva del Carbon

Palazzo Loredan

Pal. Dandolo

C. del Teatro

Merc S. Salvatore

Merc. S.

C. Guerra

C. Specchieri

Palazzo Trevisan-Cappello

Pal. Grimari

San Benedetto

San Luca

Campo S. Luca

Calle Fabbri

Salvadore

Sant' Apollonia

Campo Manin

C. dei Fuseri

Calle C. Goldoni

C. Flubera

Merc. Spadaria

C. Larga S. Marco

C. Canonica

Pal. Patriarcale

Basilica di San Marco

Palazzo Ducale

C. Mandola

Pal. Contarini del Bovolo

Rio di S. Benardo

Bacino Orseolo

Merc. Orologio

Campo S. Angelo

Ateneo Veneto

Campo S. Fantin

Pisc. di Frezzeria

Piazza San Marco

Piazzetta San Marco

C. Caotorta

Teatro La Fenice

Rio della Verste

Campo S. Angelo

Frezzeri

Ascension

Molo

Area of inset below

S.S. Moise

San Moise

C. Vallaresso

GIARDINETTI REALI

C. Larga XXII Marzo

C. del Traghetto

Rio di S. Moise

C. Ricotto

San Marco Vallaresso

San Marco Giardinetti

Palazzo Corner (Ca' Grande)

Campo S.M. Zobenigo

Palazzi Contarini

Casina delle Rose

S.M. del Giglio

Pal. Venier dei Leoni

Palazzo Dario

Punta della Dogana

Santa Maria della Salute

San Gregorio

Dogana al Mare

Seminario Patriarcale

Riva degli Schiavoni

Cl. del Vin

Rio del Greci

Cl. de la Pietà

Riva de la Pietà

Cl. del Dose

Cl. del Forno

Arsenale

Cl. de la Pescaria

Cl. del Cappeleto

Riva degli Schiavoni

P. de la Ca' di Dio

Bacino San Marco

A St. Mark's Warning

At all times, guards stand at the entrance and are serious about forbidding entry to anyone in inappropriate attire, including shorts, short skirts, and anything baring the shoulders. Bring a shawl or two to cover up.

---

right; to your left is the Campanile (Bell Tower), and beyond lie the glistening waters of the open lagoon and Palladio's San Giorgio on its own island.

The church's greatest treasure is behind the main altar, whose green marble canopy on alabaster columns covers the tomb of St. Mark: the magnificent Gothic altarpiece known as the **Pala d'Oro (Golden Altarpiece),** encrusted with close to 2,000 precious gems and 255 enameled panels. It was created as early as the 10th century and embellished by master Venetian and Byzantine artisans between the 12th and the 14th centuries. Also worth a visit is the **Tesoro (Treasury),** to the far right of the main altar, housing a collection of the Crusaders' plunder from Constantinople and other icons and relics amassed by the church over the years. Much of the Venetian booty has been incorporated into the interior and exterior of the basilica in the form of marble, columns, capitals, and statuary. Second to the Pala d'Oro in importance is the 10th-century *Madonna di Nicopeia,* a bejeweled icon absconded from Constantinople and exhibited in its own chapel to the left of the main altar. She's held as one of present-day Venice's most protective patrons.

Admission to the basilica is free but restricted, and there's often a line in high season—don't leave Venice without visiting its candlelit glittering interior, still redolent of Eastern cultures. In July and August (with much less certainty the rest of the year), church-affiliated volunteers give **free tours** Monday through Saturday, leaving four or five times daily (not all are in English), beginning at 11am; groups gather in the atrium, where you'll find posters with schedules. The basilica is open for those wishing to attend **Sunday morning Mass;** all others are strongly discouraged from entering during services (see hours below). There's also a **6:45pm Sunday Mass** during which the mosaics are floodlit (it's not for "tourists"—if you want to see the spectacle, you have to stay for the full Mass and sit quietly in a pew with the rest of the congregation).

You can book an entry to the basilica (the line to get in can last an hour or more at peak times in the high season) at www.alata.it; just show your voucher (you select a 10-min. window of entry time on the website) at the Porta di San Pietro to the left of the main entrance, and you can bypass that awful line. Best of all, it's absolutely free.

Large bags are no longer allowed inside the basilica, and a left luggage office has been established at Ateneo San Basso (Piazzetta dei Leoncini, in front of the Gate of Flowers on the north facade). It's open Monday to Saturday from 10am to 4pm and Sunday from 2 to 4pm. Note that the hours of the office differ from those of the basilica and museum.

San Marco, Piazza San Marco. (C) 041-5225205 or 041-5236597. www.basilicasanmarco.it. Basilica free admission. Museo Marciano (www.museosanmarco.it; St. Mark's Museum, also called La Galleria, includes Loggia dei Cavalli) 3€ ($3.45) adults, 1.50€ ($1.75) students. Tesoro (Treasury) 2€ ($2.30) adults, 1€ ($1.15) students. Pala d'Oro (altar screen) 1.50€ ($1.75) adults, 1€ ($1.15) students. Basilica, Tesoro, and Pala d'Oro: Apr–Sept Mon–Sat 9:45am–5pm, Sun 2–5pm; Oct–Mar Mon–Sat 9:45am–4pm, Sun 1–4pm. Museo Marciano: Apr–Sept daily 9:45am–5pm; Oct–Mar daily 9:45am–4pm. Vaporetto: San Marco.

Palazzo Ducale (Doge's Palace) & Ponte dei Sospiri (Bridge of Sighs) 𝒜𝒜𝒜   The pink-and-white marble Gothic **Palazzo Ducale,** residence/

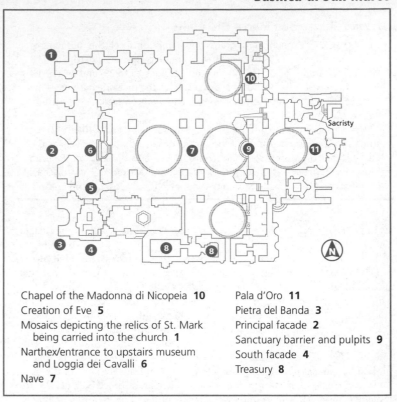

Sacristy

Chapel of the Madonna di Nicopeia **10**
Creation of Eve **5**
Mosaics depicting the relics of St. Mark being carried into the church **1**
Narthex/entrance to upstairs museum and Loggia dei Cavalli **6**
Nave **7**

Pala d'Oro **11**
Pietra del Banda **3**
Principal facade **2**
Sanctuary barrier and pulpits **9**
South facade **4**
Treasury **8**

government center of the officials and doges ("dukes," elected for life) who ruled Venice for more than 1,000 years, stands between the Basilica di San Marco and the Bacino San Marco (St. Mark's Basin). A symbol of prosperity and power, it was destroyed in a succession of fires and built and rebuilt in 1340 and 1424 in its present form, escaping the Renaissance fever that was in the air at the time. Forever being expanded, it slowly grew to be one of Italy's greatest civic structures.

Adjacent to the basilica is the 15th-century **Porta della Carta (Paper Gate),** where the doges' official proclamations and decrees were posted. This entrance opens onto a splendid inner courtyard with a double row of Renaissance arches, but until interminable restoration work on the facade is finished, you enter on the lagoon side. Inside the courtyard, you'll see Jacopo Sansovino's enormous **Scala dei Giganti (Stairway of the Giants),** scene of the doges' lavish inaugurations and never used by mere mortals, leading to the interior's wood-paneled courts and elaborate meeting rooms. Venetian masters including Veronese, Titian, Carpaccio, and Tintoretto richly decorated the walls and ceilings of the principal rooms to illustrate the history of the puissant Venetian Republic and impress diplomats and emissaries from the far-flung corners of the Maritime Republic with the uncontested prosperity and power it had attained.

If you want to understand something of this magnificent palace, the fascinating history of the 1,000-year-old Maritime Republic, and the intrigue of the government that ruled it, rent an **audio** guide at the entrance or, even better,

---

Value **Piazza San Marco Discounts**

One ticket, the **Museum Card,** grants you admission to all the museums of **Piazza San Marco** (✆ 041-5209070; www.museiciviciveneziani.it). For 11€ ($12.65) for adults, 5.50€ ($6.30) for students ages 15 to 29, and 3€ ($3.45) for children ages 6 to 14, you'll have access to all the piazza's museums—the Palazzo Ducale, Museo Correr, Museo Archeologico Nazionale, and Biblioteca Nazionale Marciana.

The **Museum Pass,** which costs 16€ ($18) for adults and 10€ ($12) for students, gives you access to all the attractions listed above as well as the Ca' Rezzonico, Museo del Settecento Veneziano, Museo di Palazzo Mocenigo (Costume Museum), Casa di Goldoni, Museo del Vetro (Glass Museum) on Murano, and Museo del Merletto (Lace Museum) on Burano.

---

sign up for the fantastic "Secret Itineraries" tour (see "The Secrets of the Palazzo Ducale," below).

The first room you'll come to is the **Sala delle Quattro Porte (Hall of the Four Doors),** whose ceiling is by Tintoretto. The next main room, the **Sala del Anti-Collegio** (adjacent to the **Sala del Collegio,** whose ceiling is by Tintoretto), is where foreign ambassadors waited to be received (hence the embellishment of its canvases, serving as self-aggrandizement) by the Collegio committee's 25 members: It's decorated with Tintorettos and Veronese's *Rape of Europe,* one of the palazzo's finest. It steals some of the thunder from Tintoretto's *Three Graces* and *Bacchus and Ariadne*—the latter considered one of his best by some critics. A right turn from this room leads into one of the most impressive of the spectacular interior rooms, the richly adorned **Sala del Senato (Senate Chamber),** with Tintoretto's ceiling painting, *The Triumph of Venice.* Here laws were passed by the Senate, a select group of 200 chosen from the Great Council. The latter was originally an elected body, but from the 13th century on, it was an aristocratic stronghold that could number as many as 1,700.

After passing again through the Sala delle Quattro Porte, you'll come to the Veronese-decorated **Stanza del Consiglio dei Dieci (Room of the Council of Ten),** of particular historic interest as it's where justice was dispensed and decapitations ordered. Formed in the 14th century to deal with emergencies, the Council of Ten was considered more powerful than the Senate and feared by all. Just outside the adjacent chamber, the **Sala della Bussola (Compass Chamber),** notice the **Bocca dei Leoni (Lion's Mouth),** a slit in the wall into which anyone could slip a signed and witnessed denunciation or accusation of alleged enemies of the state for quick action by the much feared Ten (signed and witnessed to avoid back-stabbing; if the accused was found innocent, the accuser himself would have to face the Ten!).

The main sight on the next level down—indeed the main sight of the entire palace—is the **Sala del Maggior Consiglio (Great Council Hall).** This enormous space is made special by Tintoretto's huge *Paradiso* at the far end of the hall above the doge's seat (he was in his seventies when he undertook the project with the help of his son and died 6 years later). Measuring 7×23m (23×75 ft.), it is the world's largest oil painting; together with Veronese's gorgeous *Il Trionfo di Venezia (The Triumph of Venice)* in the oval panel on the ceiling, it affirms the power emanating from the Council sessions held here. Tintoretto also did the **portraits of the 76 doges** encircling the top of this chamber; note

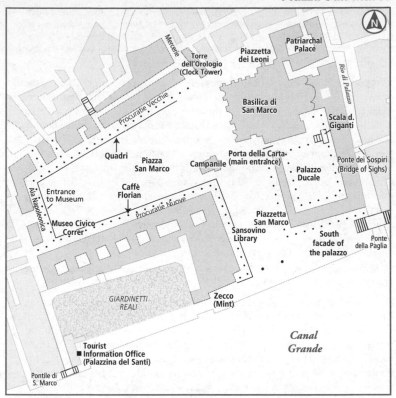

that the picture of the Doge Marin Falier, the only doge to be convicted of treason (beheaded in 1355), has been blacked out. Venice has never forgiven him. Although elected for life since sometime in the 7th century, over time *il doge* (*doe*-jay) became nothing but a figurehead (they were never allowed to meet with foreign ambassadors alone); the power rested in the Great Council.

Exit the Great Council Hall via the tiny doorway on the opposite side of Tintoretto's *Paradiso* to find the enclosed **Ponte dei Sospiri (Bridge of Sighs),** which connects the Doge's Palace with the grim **Palazzo delle Prigioni (Prisons).** The bridge took its current name only in the 19th century, when visiting northern European poets romantically envisioned the prisoners' final breath of resignation upon viewing the outside world one last time from its little window before being locked in their fetid cells awaiting the justice of the Terrible Ten. Some of the stone cells still have the original graffiti of past prisoners, many of them locked up interminably for petty crimes. But Venice's most famous prisoner had to have been 18th-century lothario Giacomo Casanova, who, following his arrest in 1755 (he was accused of being a Freemason and spreading antireligious propaganda), was locked away in "The Leads," low cells tucked into the attic of the Doge's Palace itself. He was one of the rare few to escape 15 months after his imprisonment, alive, returning to Venice 20 years later. ("Secret Itineraries" tours—especially those in English—play up this story for dramatic effect and give you all the harrowing details, should you not have time to read the man's memoirs.)

San Marco, Piazza San Marco. ✆ 041-2715911. www.museiciviciveneziani.it. Reservations ✆ 041-5209070. Admission on San Marco cumulative ticket (see "Piazza San Marco Discounts," above) or 11€ ($13) adults, 5.50€ ($6.30) students ages 15–29, 3€ ($3.45) ages 6–14, free for children under 6. "Itinerari Segreti" guided tour 10:30am Thurs–Tues by reservation only. Apr–Oct daily 9am–7pm; Nov–Mar daily 9am–5pm (ticket office closes 60 min. earlier). Vaporetto: San Marco.

Campanile di San Marco (Bell Tower) 𝒜   It's an easy elevator ride up to the top of this 97m (318-ft.) bell tower for a breathtaking view of the cupolas of St. Mark's. It's the highest structure in the city, offering a pigeon's-eye view that includes the lagoon and its neighboring islands; the red rooftops, church domes, and bell towers of Venice; and, oddly, not a single canal. On a clear day, you may even see the outline of the distant snowcapped Dolomite Mountains. The tower was built in the 9th century and then rebuilt in the 12th, 14th, and 16th centuries, when Jacopo Sansovino added the marble loggia at its base. It collapsed unexpectedly in 1902, miraculously hurting no one except a cat. It was rebuilt exactly as before, using most of the same materials, only shorter (solving the structural problem). They even rescued one of the five historic bells still used today (each bell was rung for a different purpose, such as war, the death of a doge, religious holidays, and so on).

San Marco, Piazza San Marco. ✆ 041-5224064. Admission 6€ ($6.90) adults, 3€ ($3.45) students. Apr–June daily 9:30am–5pm; July–Sept daily 9:45am–8pm; Oct–Mar daily 9:45am–4pm. Vaporetto: San Marco.

Torre dell'Orologio (Clock Tower)   As you enter the magnificent Piazza San Marco, the Clock Tower is one of the first things you see, standing on the north side, next to and towering above the Procuratie Vecchie (the ancient administration buildings for the republic). The Renaissance tower was built in 1496, and the clock mechanism of that same period still keeps perfect time but has gotten a cleaning by Piaget, the sponsor of a renovation that has kept it closed for years now. (Officials have been saying, "It will reopen next year at the latest," since 1998; by 2002, they were allowing themselves 2 more years, so the "estimate" became 2004. As I write this, it *is* 2004, and officials are now saying the tower will reopen in 2005. Don't hold your breath.) The two bronze figures up top, known as Moors because of the dark color of the bronze, pivot to strike the hour. The base of the tower has always been a favorite *punto di incontro* for Venetians ("Meet me at the tower") and is the entrance to the ancient Mercerie (from the word for merchandise), the principal souklike retail street of both high-end boutiques and trinket shops that zigzags its way to the Ponte Rialto. Visits to the top will resume on the tower's reopening.

Finds **The Secrets of the Palazzo Ducale**

I can't recommend the **Itinerari Segreti (Secret Itineraries) guided tours** highly enough. It offers an unparalleled look into the world of Venetian politics over the centuries and is the only way to access the otherwise restricted quarters and hidden passages of this enormous palace, such as the doge's private chambers and the torture chambers where prisoners were interrogated. The story of Casanova's imprisonment and escape is the tour highlight. Reserve in advance by phone (tours are often sold out a day or two in advance at least) or in person at the ticket desk. The tour is 13€ ($14) for adults, 7€ ($8.05) for students, and 4€ ($4.60) for children ages 6 to 14.

San Marco, Piazza San Marco. (C) **041-2715911.** www.museicivicivenezieni.it. Clock Tower is under restoration, with reopening set for 2005. Admission and hours weren't set at press time, but it's likely that admission will be by timed visits in small groups only. Vaporetto: San Marco.

Museo Correr ✦   This museum is no match for the Accademia but does include some interesting paintings of Venetian life, plus a fine collection of artifacts (like coins, costumes, the doges' ceremonial robes and hats, and an incredible pair of 15-in. platform shoes) that gives an interesting feel for aspects of daily life in the city's heyday. Bequeathed to Venice by the aristocratic Correr family in 1830, the museum is divided into three sections: the **Painting Section,** the **History Section,** and the **Museum of the Risorgimento** (Italy's 1797–1866 unification movement). The latter two aren't worth much mention. Of the painting collection from the 13th to the 18th centuries, Vittorio Carpaccio's *Le Cortigiane (The Courtesans),* in room no. 15 on the upper floor, is one of the museum's most famous works (though there's a question as to whether the subjects are actually courtesans or respectable noble ladies), as are the star-attraction paintings by the Bellini family, father Jacopo and sons Gentile and Giovanni. For a lesson in just how little this city has changed in the last several hundred years, head to room no. 22 and its anonymous 17th-century **bird's-eye view of Venice.** Most of the rooms have a sign with a few paragraphs in English explaining the significance of the contents.

San Marco 52, west end of Piazza San Marco. (C) **041-2405211.** www.museicivicivenezieni.it. Admission on San Marco cumulative ticket (see "Piazza San Marco Discounts," above) or 11€ ($13) adults, 5.50€ ($6.30) students ages 15–29, 3€ ($3.45) ages 6–14, free for children under 6. Apr–Oct daily 9am–7pm; Nov–Mar daily 9am–5pm (ticket office closes 60 min. earlier). Vaporetto: San Marco.

IN DORSODURO

Galleria dell'Accademia (Accademia Gallery) ✦✦✦   The glory that was La Serenissima lives on at the Accademia, the definitive treasure house of Venetian painting and one of Europe's great museums, contained in a deconsecrated church and its adjoining *scuola* (confraternity hall). The collection is exhibited chronologically from the 13th to the 18th centuries, and there's no one hallmark masterpiece; rather, this is an outstanding and comprehensive showcase of works by all the great masters of Venice. It includes Paolo and Lorenzo Veneziano from the 14th century; Gentile and Giovanni Bellini (and Giovanni's brother-in-law Andrea Mantegna from Padua) and Vittore Carpaccio from the 15th century; Giorgione (whose *Tempest* is one of the gallery's top highlights), Tintoretto, Veronese, and Titian from the 16th century (works by Tintoretto and Veronese are found frequently in Venice's churches and scuolas, but the bulk of Titian's work is here; exceptions are those found in La Salute and the Frari); and, from the 17th and 18th centuries, Canaletto, Piazzetta, Longhi, and Tiepolo, among others.

Most of all, the works open a window onto the Venice of 500 years ago—you'll see in the canvases how little Venice has changed over the centuries. Admission is limited, due to fire regulations, and lines can be daunting (check for extended evening hours in the peak months), but put up with the wait and don't miss it. **Guided tours** in English (5.50€/$6.50) are given at 10am, 11am, and noon (book at (C) **041-5200345,** or 199-199100 in Italy). **Audio tours** cost 4€ ($4.60) for one person and 6€ ($6.90) for two people. They now even have a **videoguide** on a palm-top computer (with audio commentary and headphones) for 6€ ($6.90).

Dorsoduro, at foot of Accademia Bridge. (C) **041-5222247.** www.gallerieaccademia.org. Reservations: (C) 041-5200345 (1€/$1.15 fee). Admission 6.50€ ($7.45) adults, free for under 12, cumulative ticket with Ca' d'Oro and Museo d'Arte Orientale/Ca' Pesaro 11€ ($13). Tues–Sun 8:15am–7:15pm; Mon 8:15am–2pm (summer hours might be longer). Last admission 30 min. before close. Vaporetto: Accademia.

Moments **A Dorsoduro Photo-Op**

Just north of the Zattere (the wide walkway running along the Giudecca Canal), the **Squero San Trovaso** is next to the church of San Trovaso on the narrow Rio San Trovaso (near the Ponte Accademia). One of Venice's most photographed sights, this small boatyard from the 17th century is surrounded by Tyrolian-looking wooden structures (a rarity in this stone city built on water) that are home to the multigenerational owners and original workshops for the traditional Venetian boat, the sleek black gondola. The workers don't mind if you watch them at work from across the narrow Rio di San Trovaso, but don't try to invite yourself in. It's the perfect midway photo-op after a visit to the Accademia and a trip to the gelateria Da Nico, Zattere 922, whose chocolate gianduiotto is not to be missed.

Collezione Peggy Guggenheim 🔍🔍   One of the most comprehensive and important collections of modern art in the world and one of the most visited attractions in Venice, this collection of painting and sculpture was assembled by eccentric and eclectic American expatriate Peggy Guggenheim. She did an excellent job of it, with particular strengths in cubism, European abstraction, surrealism, and abstract expressionism since about 1910. Max Ernst was one of her early favorites (she even married him), as was Jackson Pollock. Among the major works are Magritte's *Empire of Light,* Picasso's *La Baignade,* Kandinsky's *Landscape with Church (with Red Spot),* Metzinger's *The Racing Cyclist,* and Pollock's *Alchemy.* The museum is also home to several haunting canvases by Ernst, Giacometti's unique figures, Brancusi's fluid sculptures, and numerous works by Braque, Dalí, Léger, Mondrian, Chagall, and Miró.

On the Grand Canal, the elegant 18th-century Palazzo Venier dei Leoni, never finished (the reason for its unusual one-story structure), was purchased by Peggy Guggenheim in 1949 and became her home in Venice until her death in 1979. The graves of her canine companions share the lovely interior garden with several works of the **Nasher Sculpture Garden,** while the canalside patio watched over by Marino Marini's *Angel of the Citadel* is one of the best spots to linger and watch the canal life. A new book/gift shop and cafe/bistro (expensive) have opened in a separate wing across the inside courtyard where temporary exhibits are often housed.

Check the tourist office for an update on hours; the museum is often open when many others are closed, and sometimes it offers a few hours a week of free admission. Don't be shy about speaking English with the young staff working on internship; most are American, and they run **free educational talks** on specific works daily, plus a **free guided tour** of the collections. Call ② **041-2405401** for tour times and to reserve a space. If you can't make the tour, 5€ ($5.75) audioguides are available.

Dorsoduro 701 (on Calle San Cristoforo). ② **041-2405411.** www.guggenheim-venice.it. Admission 10€ ($12) adults, 8€ ($9.20) seniors over 65, 5€ ($5.75) students, free for children under 12 and holders of the Rolling Venice card (see "Saving Money," earlier in the chapter). Wed–Mon 10am–6pm. Vaporetto: Accademia. Walk around left side of Accademia, take the 1st left, and walk straight ahead following signs—you'll cross a canal, then walk alongside another, until you turn left when necessary.

Ca' Rezzonico (Museo del '700 Veneziano; Museum of 18th-Century Venice)   This handsome 17th-century canalside *palazzo* reopened in 2001 after major renovations. Reflecting its early days, it offers an intriguing look into what living in a grand Venetian home was like in the last days of the Republic. Begun by Baldassare Longhena, the 17th-century architect of La Salute, the Rezzonico home is a splendid backdrop for this collection of period paintings (especially works by Tiepolo, Guardi, and Longhi), furniture, tapestries, and artifacts. This museum is one of the best windows into the sometimes frivolous life of the Venice of 200 years ago, as seen through the tastes and fashions of the wealthy Rezzonico merchant family—the lavishly frescoed ballroom alone will evoke the lifestyle of the idle Venetian rich. English poet Robert Browning, after the death of his wife, Elizabeth Barrett Browning, made this his last home; he died here in 1889.

Dorsoduro 3136 (on Fondamenta Rezzonico). (②) 041-2410100. Admission on San Marco cumulative ticket (see "Piazza San Marco Discounts," above) or 6.50€ ($7.45) adults, 4.50€–($5.15) students ages 15–29, 2.50€ ($2.85) children 6–14, free for children under 6. Apr–Oct Wed–Mon 10am–6pm; Nov–Mar Wed–Mon 10am–5pm. Vaporetto: Ca' Rezzonico. Go right, cross a footbridge, and look for the museum entrance on the left.

Santa Maria della Salute (La Salute) ⊛   Usually referred to simply as La Salute, this 17th-century baroque jewel proudly reigns at this commercially and aesthetically important point, almost directly across from Piazza San Marco, where the Grand Canal empties into the lagoon. The first stone was laid in 1631 after the Senate decided to honor the Virgin Mary of Good Health (La Salute) for delivering Venice from a plague. They accepted the revolutionary plans of a relatively unknown young architect, Baldassare Longhena (he went on to design, among other projects in Venice, the Ca' Rezzonico). He dedicated the next 50 years to overseeing the Salute's progress and died a year after its inauguration but 5 years before its completion. The octagonal Salute is recognized as a baroque masterpiece for its exuberant exterior of volutes, scrolls, and more than 125 statues, and for its rather sober interior highlighted by **Luca Giordano altarpieces.** There's a small gallery of important works in the sacristy (enter through a small door to the left of the main altar). A number of ceiling paintings and portraits of the Evangelists and church doctors are all by Titian. On the right wall is Tintoretto's *Marriage at Cana,* one of his best.

Dorsoduro (on Campo della Salute). (②) 041-2743928. www.marcianum.it. Church free admission. Sacristy 1.50€ ($1.75). Daily 9am–noon and 3:30–6pm. Vaporetto: Salute.

IN SAN POLO

Scuola Grande di San Rocco (Confraternity of St. Roch) ⊛⊛⊛   This Renaissance men's clubhouse is a dazzling monument to **Tintoretto**—the largest collection of his work anywhere. The series of more than 50 dark and dramatic works took more than 20 years to complete, making this the richest of the many *scuole* (confraternity guilds) that once flourished in Venice. Jacopo Robusti (1518–94), called Tintoretto because his father was a dyer, was a devout, unworldly man who traveled beyond Venice only once. His epic canvases are filled with phantasmagoric light and mystical spirituality.

Begin upstairs in the side chamber called the **Sala dell'Albergo,** where the most notable of the enormous canvases is the moving *La Crocifissione (The Crucifixion).* In the center of the gilt ceiling of the **Great Hall,** also upstairs, is *Il Serpente di Bronzo (The Bronze Snake).* Among the eight paintings downstairs, each depicting a scene from the New Testament, the most noteworthy is *La Strage degli Innocenti (The Slaughter of the Innocents),* so full of dramatic urgency and energy the figures seem almost to tumble from the frame.

Although dark by nature of the painter's brush, the works were restored in the 1970s. A useful guide to the paintings inside is posted on the wall just before the museum entrance. There are a few Tiepolos among the paintings, as well as a solitary work by Titian. Note that the works on or near the staircase aren't by Tintoretto. The **Accademia di San Rocco** (℘ 041-962999; www.musicinvenice. com) sponsors highly recommended chamber orchestra concerts in these evocative environs.

San Polo (on Campo San Rocco adjacent to Campo dei Frari). ℘ 041-5234864. www.scuolagrandesanrocco.it. Admission 5.50€ ($6.30) adults, 4€ ($4.60) for under 26, free for under 18. Mar 28–Nov 2 daily 9am–5:30pm; Nov 3–Mar 27 daily 10am–4pm. Vaporetto: San Tomà. Walk straight ahead on Calle del Traghetto, turn right, and then turn immediately left across Campo San Tomà; walk as straight ahead as you can, on Ramo Mandoler, Calle Larga Prima, and Salizzada San Rocco, which leads into a campo of the same name—look for the crimson sign behind Frari Church.

Santa Maria Gloriosa dei Frari (Church of the Frari) ﷯﷯   Known simply as "I Frari," this immense 13th- and 14th-century Gothic church is around the corner from the Scuola Grande di San Rocco. Built by the Franciscans (*frari* is a dialectal distortion of *frati,* meaning "brothers"), it's something of a memorial to the ancient glories of Venice. Since St. Francis and the order he founded emphasized prayer and poverty, it's not surprising the church is austere inside and out. It does, however, house two **Titian masterpieces** (you might have noticed the scarcity of Titian's works in Venice outside the Accademia and La Salute), the most striking being the *Assumption of the Virgin* ﷯﷯ over the main altar, painted when the artist was only in his late twenties. In his *Virgin of the Pesaro Family* ﷯, in the left nave, Titian's wife posed for the figure of Mary, then died soon afterward in childbirth. The church's other masterwork is Bellini's *Madonna and Child* ﷯﷯, a triptych displayed in the sacristy (take the door on the right as you face the altar); it's one of his finest portraits of Mary. There's also Donatello's *St. John the Baptist,* an almost primitive-looking woodcarving. The **grandiose tombs** of two famous Venetians are also here: Canova (d. 1822), the Italian sculptor who led the revival of classicism, and Titian, who died in 1576 during a deadly plague.

San Polo 3072 (on Campo dei Frari). ℘ 041-2728618. www.basilicadeifrari.it or www.chorusvenezia.org. Admission 2.50€ ($2.85), or 8€ ($9.20) with cumulative Chorus Pass (see "For Church Fans," above). Mon–Sat 9am–6pm; Sun 1–6pm. Vaporetto: San Tomà. Walk straight ahead on Calle del Traghetto, then turn right and then immediately left across Campo San Tomà; walk as straight ahead as you can, on Ramo Mandoler, then on Calle Larga Prima, and turn right when you reach the beginning of Salizzada San Rocco.

IN CASTELLO

SS. Giovanni e Paolo (Sts. John and Paul)   This massive Gothic church was built by the Dominican order between the 13th and the early 15th centuries. An unofficial Pantheon where 25 doges are buried (a number of tombs are part of the unfinished facade), it's also home to a number of artistic treasures. Visit the **Cappella della Rosario** off the left transept to see the three

---

For Church Fans

The **Associazione Chiesa di Venezia** (℘ 041-2750462; www.chorusvenezia. org) now curates most of Venice's top churches. Admission to each of the association's churches is 2.50€ ($2.85), but if you're a real church aficionado, buy the 8€ ($9.20) 3-day Chorus Pass, which allows you to visit all of the following: Santa Maria del Giglio, Santo Stefano, Santa Maria Formosa, Santa Maria dei Miracoli (reviewed below), San Giovanni Elemosinario, San Polo, Santa Maria Gloriosa dei Frari (reviewed below), San Giacomo dall'Orio, San Stae, Sant'Alvise, Madonna dell'Orto, San Pietro di Castello, Santissimo Rendentore, Santa Maria del Rosario (Gesuati), and San Sebastiano.

Carnevale a Venezia

Venice's top event is **Carnevale** ✦ (© 041-2410570), a theatrical resuscitation of the bacchanalia Napoleon outlawed upon his arrival. The festival marks the unbridled celebration preceding Lent, the period of penitence and abstinence prior to Easter, and its name is derived from the Latin *carnem levare* ("to take meat away"), since many people gave up meat for the duration of Lent. Today's Carnevale events, masked balls, and costumes usually evoke that 18th-century swan song. Many of the concerts around town are free, when baroque to samba to gospel to Dixieland jazz fill the piazze and byways; check with the tourist office for a list of events.

Although Carnevale lasts no more than 5 to 10 days today (culminating the Fri–Tues before Ash Wednesday), 18th-century revelers came from all over Europe to take part in festivities that began months ahead, gaining crescendo until their raucous culmination at midnight on Shrove Tuesday. As the Venetian economy declined and its colonies and trading posts fell to other powers, the Republic in its swan song turned to fantasy and escapism. The faster its decline was, the longer and more unlicensed became its anything-goes merrymaking. Masks became ubiquitous, affording anonymity and pardoning a thousand sins. They permitted the fishmonger to attend the ball and dance with the baroness, the properly married to carry on as if they were not. The doges condemned it and the popes denounced it, but nothing could dampen Carnevale spirit until Napoleon arrived in 1797.

Resuscitated in 1980 by local powers to fill the empty winter months, Carnevale is calmer nowadays, though just barely. The born-again festival got off to a shaky start, met at first with indifference and skepticism, but in the years since, it has grown from strength to strength. The new Carnevale is at its dazzling best now with 2 decades under its belt, a harlequin patchwork of musical and cultural events, many of them free. At any given moment, musical events are staged in any of the city's dozens of piazze—from reggae and zydeco to jazz and baroque and chamber music—and special art exhibits are mounted at museums and galleries. The recent involvement of international corporate commercial sponsors has met with a mixed reception, though it seems to be the direction of the future.

Carnevale isn't for those who dislike crowds—the crowds are what it's all about. Truly enjoying Carnevale means giving in to the spontaneity of magic and surprise around every corner, the mystery behind every mask. Period masks and costumes are everywhere. Groups travel in coordinated getups ranging from a contemporary passel of Felliniesque clowns to the court of the Sun King in all its wigged-out drag-queen best. The places to be seen in costume (only appropriate costumes need apply) are the historic cafes lining Piazza San Marco, the Florian being the unquestioned Command Post. Don't expect to be seated in full view at a window seat unless your costume is straight off the stage of the local opera house.

restored ceiling canvases by Veronese. In the right aisle is the recently restored and brilliantly colored *Polyptych of St. Vincent Ferrer* (ca. 1465), attributed to a young Giovanni Bellini. You'll also see the foot of St. Catherine of Siena encased in glass.

Adjacent to the church is the **Scuola di San Marco,** an old confraternity-like association now run as a civic hospital, most noteworthy for its beautiful 15th-century Renaissance facade. Anchoring the large **campo,** a popular crossroads for this area of Castello, is a **statue of Bartolomeo Colleoni,** a Renaissance *con-dottiere,* by Florentine master Andrea Verrocchio; it's one of the world's great equestrian monuments and Verrocchio's best.

Castello 6363 (on Campo Santi Giovanni e Paolo). ℰ **041-2416014.** Admission 2.50€ ($2.85). Mon–Sat 7am–7pm. Vaporetto: Rialto.

San Zaccaria (St. Zacchary) ℛ

Behind (east of) St. Mark's Basilica is a 9th-century Gothic church with its original 13th-century campanile and a splendid Renaissance facade designed by Venetian architect Mario Codussi in the late 15th century. Of the interior's many artworks is the important *Madonna Enthroned with Four Saints* by Giovanni Bellini in 1505. Recently restored, it hangs above the second altar in the left aisle; art historians have long held this as one of his finer Madonnas. Apply to the sacristan to see the **Sisters' Choir,** with works by Tintoretto, Titian, Il Vecchio, Anthony Van Dyck, and Bassano. The paintings aren't labeled, but the sacristan will point out the names of the artists. In the fan vaults of the Chapel of San Tarasio are the faded ceiling frescoes of the Florentine-born artist Andrea del Castagno, who was the first to bring the spirit of the Renaissance to Venice.

Castello, Campo San Zaccaria. ℰ **041-5221257.** Free admission. Mon–Sat 10am–noon and 4–6pm. Vaporetto: San Zaccaria.

Museo Storico Navale (Naval History Museum) & Arsenale (Arsenal) ℛℛ

The Naval History Museum's most fascinating exhibit is its collection of model ships. It was once common practice for vessels to be built not from blueprints, but from the precise scale models that you see here. The prize of the collection is a model of the legendary **Bucintoro,** the lavish ceremonial barge of the doges. Another section of the museum contains an array of historic vessels. Walk along the canal as it branches off from the museum to the **Ships' Pavilion,** where the historic vessels are displayed.

To reach the Arsenal from the museum, walk up the Arsenale Canal and cross the wooden bridge to the Campo del'Arsenale. You will soon reach the land gate of the **Arsenale,** not open to the public. Occupying one-fifth of the city's total acreage, the Arsenal was once the very source of the republic's maritime power. It is now used as a military zone and is as closed as Fort Knox to the curious. The marble-columned Renaissance gate with the republic's winged lion above is flanked by four ancient lions, each of which was booty, brought at various times from Greece and points further east. The Arsenal was founded in 1104, and at the height of Venice's power in the 15th century, it employed 16,000 workers who turned out merchant and wartime galley after galley in an early version of massive assembly lines at speeds and in volume unknown until modern times.

Castello 2148 (Campo San Biasio). ℰ **041-5200276.** Admission 1.55€ ($1.80). Mon–Sat 8:45am–1:30pm. Vaporetto: Arsenale.

Scuola di San Giorgio degli Schiavoni ℛ

At the St. Antonino Bridge (Fondamenta dei Furlani) is the second most important guild house to visit in Venice. The Schiavoni were an important and wealthy trading colony of Dalmatian

merchants who built their own scuola or confraternity (the coast of Dalmatia—
the former Yugoslavia—was once ruled by the Greeks, hence the scuola's alternative name of San Giorgio dei Greci).

Between 1502 and 1509, Vittore Carpaccio (himself of Dalmatian descent)
painted a pictorial cycle of nine masterpieces illustrating episodes from the lives
of St. George (patron saint of the scuola) and St. Jerome, the Dalmatian patron
saints. These appealing pictures freeze in time moments in the lives of the saints:
St. George charges his ferocious dragon on a field littered with half-eaten bodies
and skulls (a horror story with a happy ending); St. Jerome leads his lion into a
monastery, frightening the friars; St. Augustine has just taken up his pen to reply
to a letter from St. Jerome when he and his little dog are transfixed by a miraculous light and a voice telling them of St. Jerome's death.

Castello 3259, Calle Furlani. ℂ **041-5228828**. Admission 3€ ($3.45). Tues–Sat 10am–12:30pm and
3:30–6pm; Sun 9:30am–12:30pm. Vaporetto: San Zaccaria.

IN GUIDECCA & SAN GIORGIO

San Giorgio Maggiore *Moments* This church sits on the little island of
San Giorgio Maggiore in the Bacino San Marco basin just off St. Mark's Square.
It is one of the masterpieces of Andrea Palladio, the great Renaissance architect
from nearby Vicenza. Most known for his country villas built for Venice's
wealthy merchant families, Palladio was commissioned to build two churches
(the other is the Redentore on the neighboring island of Giudecca), beginning
with San Giorgio, designed in 1565 and completed in 1610. To impose a classical facade on the traditional church structure, Palladio designed two interlocking facades, with repeating triangles, rectangles, and columns that are carefully
and harmoniously proportioned. Founded as early as the 10th century, the
church was reinterpreted by Palladio with whitewashed surfaces, stark but
majestic, and with unadorned but harmonious space. The main altar is flanked
by two epic paintings by an elderly Tintoretto, *The Fall of Manna* to the left and
the more noteworthy *Last Supper* to the right, famous for its chiaroscuro.
Through the doorway to the right of the choir leading to the **Cappella dei
Morti (Chapel of the Dead)** you will find Tintoretto's *Deposition.*

To the left of the choir is an elevator that you can take to the top of the campanile to experience an unforgettable view of the island itself, the lagoon, and
the Palazzo Ducale and Piazza San Marco across the way.

A handful of remaining Benedictine monks gather for Sunday Mass at 11am,
sung in Gregorian chant.

On the island of San Giorgio Maggiore, across St. Mark's Basin from Piazzetta San Marco. ℂ **041-5227827**.
Church free admission. Campanile (bell tower) 3€ ($3.45). Mon–Sat 9:30am–12:30pm and 2:30–5:30pm;
Sun 2:30–5:30pm. Take the Giudecca-bound vaporetto (no. 82) on Riva degli Schiavoni and get off at the 1st
stop, the island of San Giorgio Maggiore.

IN CANNAREGIO

Ca' d'Oro (Galleria Giorgio Franchetti)   The 15th-century Ca' d'Oro is
one of the best preserved and most impressive of the hundreds of patrician
palazzi lining the Grand Canal. After the Palazzo Ducale, it's the city's finest
example of Venetian Gothic architecture. A restoration of its delicate pink-and-
white facade (its name, the Golden Palace, refers to the gilt-covered facade that
faded long ago) was completed in 1995. Inside, the ornate beamed ceilings and
palatial trappings provide an attention-grabbing backdrop for the private collection of former owner Baron Franchetti, who bequeathed his *palazzo* and artwork
to the city during World War I. The core collection, expanded over the years,

now includes sculptures, furniture, 16th-century Flemish tapestries, an impressive collection of bronzes (12th–16th c.), and a gallery whose most important canvases are Andrea Mantegna's *San Sebastiano* and Titian's *Venus at the Mirror,* as well as lesser paintings by **Tintoretto, Carpaccio, Van Dyck, Giorgione,** and **Jan Steen.** For a delightful break, step out onto the palazzo's loggia, overlooking the Grand Canal, for a view up and down the aquatic waterway and across to the Pescheria, a timeless vignette of an unchanged city. Off the loggia is a small but worthy ceramics collection open from 10am to noon.

Audioguides are available for rent: 4€ ($4.60) for one, 6€ ($6.90) for two.

Cannaregio between 3931 and 3932 (on Calle Ca' d'Oro north of Rialto Bridge). ⓒ 041-5238790. www. cadoro.org. Reservations ⓒ 041-5200345 (1€/$1.15 fee). Admission 5€ ($5.75) adults, free for those under 12, cumulative ticket with Accademia and Museo d'Arte Orientale/Ca' Pesaro 11€ ($13). Mon 8:15am–2pm; Tues–Sun 8:15am–7:15pm. Vaporetto: Ca' d'Oro.

Santa Maria dei Miracoli   At a charming canal crossing hidden in a quiet corner of the residential section of Cannaregio northeast of the Rialto Bridge, the small 15th-century "Miracoli" is once again open to the public after a laborious 10-year renovation. It is one of the most attractive religious buildings in Europe, with one side of the precious polychrome-marbled facade running alongside a canal, creating colorful and shimmering reflections. The architect, Pietro Lombardo (a local artisan whose background in monuments and tombs is obvious) would go on to become one of the founding fathers of the Venetian Renaissance.

The less romantic are inclined to compare the Miracoli to a large tomb with a dome, but the untold couples who have made this perfectly proportioned jewel-like church their choice for weddings will dispel such insensitivity. The small square in front is the perfect place for gondolas to drop off and pick up the newly betrothed. The inside is intricately decorated with early Renaissance marble reliefs, its pastel palette of pink, gray, and white marbles making an appropriately elegant venue for all those weddings. In the 1470s, an image of the Virgin Mary was responsible for a series of miracles (including bringing back to life someone who spent half an hour at the bottom of Giudecca Canal) that led pilgrims to leave gifts and, eventually, enough donations to build this church. Look for the icon now displayed over the main altar.

Cannaregio, Rio dei Miracoli. No phone. www.chorusvenezia.org. Admission 2.50€ ($2.85) or 8€ ($9.20) with cumulative Chorus Pass (see "For Church Fans," above). Mon–Sat 10am–5pm; Sun 1–5pm. Vaporetto: Rialto. Located midway between the Rialto Bridge and the Campo SS. Giovanni e Paolo.

Museo Communità Ebraica and Il Ghetto (Jewish Ghetto) ⍟   Venice's relationship with its Jewish community has fluctuated over time from acceptance to borderline tolerance. In 1516, 700 Jews were forced to move to this then-remote northwestern corner of Venice, to an abandoned site of a 14th-century foundry (*ghetto* is old Venetian dialect for "foundry"). As was commonplace with most of the hundreds of islands making up Venice, the area was surrounded by water. Its two access points were controlled at night and early morning by heavy gates manned by Christian guards (paid for by the Jews), both protecting and segregating its inhabitants. Within 1 century, the community grew to more than 5,000, representing many languages and cultures. Although the original **Ghetto Nuovo (New Ghetto)** was expanded to include the **Ghetto Vecchio** and later the **Ghetto Nuovissimo (Newest Ghetto),** land was limited and quarters always cramped. A very small, ever-diminishing community of Jewish families continues to live here: Some 2,000 are said to live in all Venice and Mestre.

The only way to visit any of the area's five 16th-century synagogues is through a **tour** given in English by the Museo Communità Ebraica (museum admission is included). Your guide will elaborate on the commercial and political climate of those times, the unique skyscraper architecture (overcrowding resulted in many buildings having as many as seven low-ceilinged stories), and the daily lifestyle of the community until the 1797 arrival of Napoleon, who declared the Jews free citizens.

Cannaregio 2902 (on Campo del Ghetto Nuovo). © 041-715359. Museum admission 3€ ($3.45) adults, 2€ ($2.30) children; museum and synagogue tour 8€ ($9.20) adults, 6.50€ ($7.45) children. Museum: June–Sept Sun–Fri 10am–7pm; Oct–May Sun–Fri 10am–6pm (early closings possible on Fri). Synagogue tours leave hourly 10:30am–4:30pm. Vaporetto: Guglie.

ESPECIALLY FOR KIDS

It goes without saying that a **gondola ride** will be a thrill for any child or adult. If that's too expensive, consider the convenient and far less expensive alternative: **vaporetto no. 1.** They offer two entirely different experiences: that of seeing Venice through the back door (and taking a ride past Marco Polo's house) and a tool down its aquatic Main Street, the Grand Canal, respectively. Look for the ambulance boat, the garbage boat, the firefighters boat, the funeral boat, even the Coca-Cola and McDonald's delivery boats. Best sightings are the special gondolas filled with flowers and rowed by gondolieri in livery taking the happy bride and groom to the church.

Judging from the squeals of delight, **feeding the pigeons in Piazza San Marco** (purchase a bag of corn and you'll be draped in pigeons in a nanosecond; these birds have radar) could be the epitome of your child's visit to Venice, and it's the optimal photo op. Be sure your child won't be startled by all the fluttering and flapping (or the scrabbling feet; that's what I remember from age 11 when my parents did this to me). A jaunt to the neighboring island of **Murano** can be as educational as recreational—follow the signs to any *fornace,* where a glass-blowing performance of the island's 1,000-year-old art is free entertainment. But be ready for the almost guaranteed sales pitch that follows.

Before you leave town, take the elevator to the top of the **Campanile di San Marco** (the city's highest structure) for a pigeon's-eye view of Venice's rooftops and church cupolas, or get up close and personal to the *Triumphal Quadriga* on the facade of the Basilica San Marco. Its outdoor loggia with a view holds the copies of the famous *quadriga* (you can see the real ones in the Basilica's Museo Marciano), but the view from here is something you or your children won't forget.

Many children enjoy the **Museo Navale** and the **Arsenale,** with its ship models and old vessels, and the many historic artifacts in the **Museo Correr** that are a vestige of when Venice was a world unto itself.

ORGANIZED TOURS

Most of the central travel agencies have posters in their windows advertising half- and full-day walking tours of the city's sights. Most of these tours are piggybacked onto those organized by **American Express** (see "Fast Facts: Venice," earlier in this chapter) and should cost the same: about 21€ ($24) for a 2-hour tour and 34€ ($39) for a full day, per person.

Free organized tours of the Basilica di San Marco and some of the other churches can be erratic, as they're given by volunteers.

Organized 3- to 4-hour visits to **"The Islands of the Venetian Lagoon"** include brief stops on Murano, Burano, and Torcello (see "Exploring Venice's Islands," at the end of this chapter).

6 Shopping

THE SHOPPING SCENE

A mix of low-end trinket stores and middle-market to upscale boutiques lines the narrow zigzagging **Mercerie** running north between Piazza San Marco and the Ponte Rialto. More expensive clothing and gift boutiques make for great window-shopping on **Calle Larga XXII Marzo,** beginning west of Piazza San Marco and wending its way to the expansive Campo Santo Stefano near the Accademia. The narrow **Frezzeria,** also west of the piazza and not far from Piazza San Marco, offers a grab bag of bars, souvenir shops, and tony clothing stores.

In a city that for centuries has thrived almost exclusively on tourism, remember this: Where you buy cheap, you get cheap. You'll find few bargains, and there's nothing to compare with Florence's San Lorenzo Market; the nonproduce part of the Rialto Market is as good as it gets, where you'll find cheap T-shirts, glow-in-the-dark plastic gondolas, and tawdry glass trinkets. Venetians aren't known for bargaining. You'll stand a better chance when paying in cash or buying more than one of an item.

Venice is uniquely famous for several local crafts that have been produced here for centuries and are hard to get elsewhere: the **glassware** from the island of Murano, the delicate **lace** from Burano, and the *cartapesta* (papier-mâché) **Carnevale** masks you'll find in endless *botteghe* (workshops), where you can watch artisans paint amid their wares.

Now here's the bad news: There's such an overwhelming sea of cheap glass gewgaws it becomes something of a turn-off (shipping and insurance make most things unaffordable; the alternative is to hand-carry something so fragile). There are so few women left on Burano willing to spend countless hours keeping alive the art of lacemaking that the few pieces you'll see not produced by machine in Hong Kong are sold at stratospheric prices; ditto on the truly high-quality glass (though trinkets can be cheap and fun). Still, you can find exceptions in all of the above, and when you find them, you'll know.

SHOPPING A TO Z

ANTIQUES The interesting **Mercatino dell'Antiquariato (Antiques Fair)** takes place three times yearly in the charming Campo San Maurizio between Piazza San Marco and Campo Santo Stefano. Dates change yearly for the 3-day weekend market but generally are the first weekend of April, mid-September, and the weekend before Christmas. More than 100 vendors sell everything from sublime Murano glass to quirky dust collectors. Early birds may find reasonably priced finds like Murano candy dishes from the 1950s, "Venetian pearl" glass beads older still, old Italian posters advertising Campari-sponsored regattas, or postcards of Venice that could be from the 1930s or the 1830s—things change so little. Those for whom price is less of an issue might pick up antique lace by the yard or a singular museum-quality piece of hand-blown glass from a local master.

CRAFTS The small **Murano Art Shop,** San Marco 1232, on the store-lined Frezzeria, parallel to the western border of and close to Piazza San Marco (© **041-5233851;** Vaporetto: San Marco), is a cultural experience. At this precious shop, every inch of wall space is draped with the whimsical crafts of the city's most creative artisans. Fusing the timeless with the contemporary and whimsical—with a nod to the magic and romance of Venice past—the results are a dramatic and ever-evolving collection of masks, puppets, music boxes, marionettes, costume jewelry, and the like. It's all expensive, but this rivals a visit to the Doge's Palace.

When it seems as if every gift-store window is awash with collectible bisque-faced dolls in elaborate pinafores and headdresses, go to **Trilly Venice,** Castello 4974, on Fondamenta dell'Osmarin, off Campo San Provolo on your way east out of Piazza San Marco toward San Zaccaria (℅ **041-5212579;** www.trilly venice.com; Vaporetto: San Marco). There, the hand-sewn wardrobes of rich Venetian fabrics and painstakingly painted faces are particularly exquisite. The perfect souvenir starts at 30€ ($35) in this well-stocked workspace.

EMBROIDERED LINENS A doge's ransom will buy you an elaborately worked tablecloth at **Jesurum,** San Marco 4856, on the busy Mercerie shopping strip zigzagging from Piazza San Marco to the Ponte Rialto (℅ **041-5242540;** www.jesurum.it; Vaporetto: San Marco). However, some of the small items make gorgeous affordable gifts for discerning friends for under 15€ ($17): drawstring pouches for your baubles, hand-embroidered linen cocktail napkins in different colors, or hand-finished doilies and linen coasters.

FOOD Food lovers will find charmingly packaged food products for themselves or friends at **Giacamo Rizzo,** Cannaregio 5778, on Calle San Giovanni Grisostomo, northeast of the Ponte Rialto (℅ **041-5222824;** Vaporetto: Rialto). Pasta is fashioned in the shape of gondolas, colorful Carnevale hats, and dozens of other imaginatively shaped possibilities (colored and flavored with squash, beet, or spinach). Those with a sweet tooth should head in the opposite direction, to **Pasticceria Marchini,** San Marco 2769, at the Ponte San Maurizio, just before Campo Santo Stefano (℅ **041-5229109;** www.golosessi.com; Vaporetto: San Samuele or Giglio). A selection of traditional cookies is beautifully prepackaged for traveling—the delicate *baicoli,* cornmeal raisin *zaleti,* and S-shape *buranelli.* Packages of cookies start at 6.20€ ($7.15).

GLASS If you're going to go all out, look no further than **Venini,** Piazzetta dei Leoni 314 (℅ **041-5224045**), since 1921 one of the most respected and innovative glassmakers in all of Venice. Their products are more works of art than merely blown glass. So renowned are they for their quality, Versace's own line of glass objets d'art is done by Venini. The **workshop** on Murano is at Fondamenta Vetrai 50 (℅ **041-2737211**). Cheap they are not, but no one else has such lovely or original representations of hand-blown Murano glassware.

You should also visit the spacious emporium of quality glass items at **Marco Polo** (San Marco 1644; ℅ **041-5229295**), just west of the Piazza San Marco. The front half of the first floor offers a variety of small gift ideas (candy dishes, glass-topped medicine boxes, paperweights).

Glass beads are called "Venetian Pearls," and an abundance of exquisite antique and reproduced baubles are the draw at **Anticlea,** at Castello 4719 (on the Campo San Provolo in the direction of the Church of San Zaccaria; ℅ **041-5286946**). Once used for trading in Venice's far-flung colonies, they now fill the coffers of this small shop east of Piazza San Marco, sold singly or already strung. The open-air stall of **Susie and Andrea** (Riva degli Schiavoni, near Pensione Wildner; just ask) has handcrafted beads that are new, well made and strung, and moderately priced. The stall operates from February through November.

LEATHER One usually thinks of Florence when thinking of Italian leather goods. But the plethora of mediocre-to-refined shoe stores in Venice is testimony to the tradition of the small shoe factories along the nearby Brenta canal that supply most of Italy and much of the world with its made-in-Italy footwear. Venice has plenty of fine shoe stores—including **Bruno Magli,** San Marco 1302 (Calle dell'Ascensione; ℅ **041-5227210**), and **Mori e Bozzi,** Cannaregio 2367

(Rio Terrà della Madonna; © 041-715261)—but one store deserves singling out for sheer oddness. Even if you're not in the market for shoes, stop by **Rolando Segalin,** San Marco 4365 (Calle dei Fuseri; © 041-5222115), for fantastical footwear in an acid trip of colors and shapes, including curly-toed creations; many are intended for Carnevale costumes.

MASKS A shortage of mask *botteghe* (workshops) in Venice isn't your problem; the challenge is ferreting out the few exceptionally talented artists producing one-of-a-kind theatrical pieces. Only the quality-conscious should shop at **La Bottega dei Mascareri,** San Polo 80, at the northern end of the Ponte Rialto (© 041-5223857; Vaporetto: Rialto), where the charming Boldrin brothers' least elaborate masks begin under 15€ ($17). Anyone who thinks a mask is a mask is a mask should come here first for a look-see.

7 Venice After Dark

Visit one of the tourist offices for current English-language schedules of the month's special events. The monthly *Ospite di Venezia,* distributed free, is extremely helpful but usually available only in the more expensive hotels. If you're looking for nocturnal action, you're in the wrong town. Your best bet is to sit in the moonlit Piazza San Marco and listen to the cafes' outdoor orchestras, with the illuminated basilica before you—the perfect opera set.

THE PERFORMING ARTS

Venice has a long and rich tradition of classical music, and there's always a concert going on somewhere. Several **churches,** such as **San Stefano, San Stae,** the **Scuola di San Giovanni Evangelista,** and the **Scuola di San Rocco,** regularly host classical music concerts (with an emphasis on the baroque) by local and international artists. Venice, after all, the home of Vivaldi, and the **Chiesa di Vivaldi** (officially the **Chiesa Santa Maria della Pietà**) is the most popular venue for the music of the composer and his contemporaries. It was here that the red priest (Vivaldi, so called because of his red hair) was the choral director, and it is here that you'll find perhaps the highest-quality ensembles (with tickets slightly more expensive). If you're lucky, they'll be performing *Le Quattro Staggioni (The Four Seasons).* Tickets are sold at the church's box office (© 041-5208767; www.vivaldi.it) on Riva degli Schiavoni, at the front desk of the Metropole Hotel next door, or at many of the hotels around town; they're usually 25€ ($29) for adults or 15€ ($17) for students. Information and schedules are available from the tourist office. Tickets for most concerts should be bought in advance, but the frequency of concerts means they rarely sell out. *Note:* Performances have been temporarily moved to the Il Palazzo Papafava, a 15th-century palace in Cannaregio (Calle Racheta 3764), near the Ca' d'oro vaporetto stop.

After years of construction, the famous **Teatro La Fenice** (San Marco 1965, on Campo San Fantin; © 041-786562 or 041-786580; www.teatrolafenice.it) has finally reopened. In January 1996, the city stood still in shock as Venice's principal stage for world-class opera, music, theater, and ballet went up in flames. Carpenters and artisans were on standby to begin working around the clock to re-create the teatro (built in 1836) according to archival designs. Inaugural performances in December 2003 included appearances by Riccardo Muti, musical director of La Scala, and Elton John. However, that was just the inaugural. The theater actually began hosting a regular schedule in late 2004. Tickets cost around 20€ ($23); tickets online can be obtained at www.charta.it or at the Teatro website.

CAFES

Venice is a quiet town in the evening and offers very little in the way of nightlife. For tourists and locals alike, Venetian nightlife revolves around the city's many bar/cafes on Piazza San Marco, one of the world's most remarkable piazzas. The epicenter of life in Venice, it's also the most expensive and touristed place to linger over a Campari or cappuccino. The nostalgic 18th-century **Caffè Florian,** San Marco 56A–59A (✆ **041-5205641;** www.caffeflorian.com), on the south side of the piazza, is the most famous (closed Wed in winter) and most theatrical inside; have a Bellini (*prosecco* and fresh peach nectar) at the back bar and spend half what you'd pay at an indoor table. Alfresco seating here is even more expensive when the band plays on but is worth every euro for the million-dollar scenario. It's said that when Casanova escaped from the prisons in the Doge's Palace, he stopped here for a coffee before fleeing Venice.

On the opposite side of the square at San Marco 133–134 is the old-world **Caffè Lavena** (✆ **041-5224070;** closed Tues in winter). At no. 120 is **Caffè Quadri** (✆ **041-5289299;** www.quadrivenice.com; closed Mon in winter), with a (pricey) romantic restaurant upstairs where two much-requested tables overlook the piazza. At all spots, a cappuccino, tea, or Coca-Cola at a table will set you back about 6€ ($6.90). But no one will rush you, and if the sun is warm and the orchestras are playing, I can think of no more beautiful public open-air salon in the world. Around the corner (no. 11) and in front of the pink-and-white marble Palazzo Ducale with the lagoon on your right is the best deal, **Caffè Chioggia** (✆ **041-5285011;** closed Sun). Come here at midnight and watch the Moors strike the hour atop the Clock Tower from your outside table, while the quartet or pianist plays everything from quality jazz to pop (they also take requests) until the wee hours (and without taking a break every 6 min.).

CLUBS, BARS & GELATERIE

Although Venice boasts an old and prominent university, clubs and discos barely enjoy their 15 minutes of popularity before changing hands or closing down (some are open only in summer). Young Venetians tend to go to the Lido or mainland Mestre.

For just plain hanging out in the late afternoon and early evening, popular squares that serve as meeting points are **Campo San Bartolomeo,** at the foot of the Ponte Rialto, and nearby **Campo San Luca;** you'll see Venetians of all ages milling about engaged in animated conversation, particularly from 5pm to dinnertime. In late-night hours, for low prices and a low level of pretension, there's huge open **Campo Santa Margherita,** about halfway between the train station and Ca' Rezzonico. Look for the popular **Green Pub** (no. 3053), **Bareto Rosso** (no. 2963), and **Bar Salus** (no. 3112). **Campo Santo Stefano** is also worth a visit, namely to sit and sample the goods at the **Bar/Gelateria Paolin** (no. 2962), one of the city's best ice-cream sources. Its runner-up, **Gelateria Nico,** is at Dorsoduro 922, on the Zattere, south of the Accademia. For occasional evenings of live music or cabaret, or for just a relaxed late-night hangout for a drink and a bite, consider the ever-popular **Bistrot de Venise** (see "Great Deals on Dining," earlier in this chapter).

Note: Most bars are open Monday through Saturday from 8pm to midnight.

The **Devil's Forest Pub,** San Marco 5185, on Calle Stagneri (✆ **041-5200623;** Vaporetto: San Marco), offers the outsider an authentic chance to take in the convivial atmosphere and find out where Venetians do hang out. It's popular for lunch with the neighborhood merchants and shop owners, and ideal for relaxed socializing over a beer and a host of games like backgammon, chess, and Trivial Pursuit.

A variety of simple pasta dishes and fresh sandwiches runs 4€ to 7€ ($4.60–$8.05). It's open daily from 10am to 1am.

Bácaro Jazz (℃ **041-5285249;** www.bacarojazz.com; Vaporetto: Rialto) is a happening cocktail bar (Bellinis are great) with restaurant seating in the back (tasty Venetian cuisine from 7€/$8.05). It's across from the Rialto post office at San Marco 5546, just north of Campo San Bartolomeo (the San Marco side of Rialto Bridge). It's a mix of jazzy music (a bit too loud), rough plank walls, industrial steel tables, and a corrugated aluminum ceiling. The bar is open Thursday through Tuesday from 11am to 2am (happy hour 2–7:30pm).

With a half-dozen beers on tap, **El Moro Pub,** at Castello 4531 (Calle delle Rasse; ℃ **041-5282573**), is the biggest draw in town. The crowd can be a bit older here, where post-university types congregate at the bar. TVs sometimes transmit national soccer or tennis matches, and the management welcomes those who linger, but sensitive nonsmokers won't want to.

Good food at reasonable prices would be enough to regularly pack **Paradiso Perduto,** Cannaregio 2540, on Fondamenta della Misericordia (℃ **041-720581;** Vaporetto: Ferrovie), but its biggest draw is the live jazz performed on a small stage several nights a week. Popular with Americans and other foreigners living in Venice, this bar was once largely devoid of tourists, primarily because of its hard-to-find location, but it looks as if the word is out. The good selection of well-prepared pizzas and pastas goes for under 6€ ($6.90); arrive early for a table. It's open Thursday through Tuesday from 7pm to 1 and sometimes 2am.

DANCE CLUBS

Venice is a quiet town at night and offers little in the line of dance clubs. Evenings are best spent lingering over a late dinner, having a pint in a *birrerie,* nursing a glass of *prosecco* in one of Piazza San Marco's tiny outdoor cafes, or enjoying popular after-hours places like **Paradiso Perduto** (see above). Dance clubs barely enjoy their 15 minutes of popularity before changing hands or closing; some of those that have survived are open only in summer.

University-age Venetians tend to frequent the Lido or mainland Mestre, but if you really need that disco fix, you're best off at **Piccolo Mondo,** Dorsoduro 1056, near the Accademia (℃ **041-5200371;** Vaporetto: Accademia). Billed as a disco/pub, it serves sandwiches during lunch to the tune of America's latest dance music and offers a happy hour in the late afternoon in winter. But the only reason you'd want to come is if you want a disco night (summer only). Mostly curious foreigners and the young to not-so-young Venetians who seek them out frequent the club; often there's live music. It's open daily from 10pm to 4am in summer, and 10am to 4pm and 5 to 8pm in winter.

Another club that seems to be surviving is **Casanova** (℃ **041-988465** or 041-4171727), near the train station on Lista di Spagna 158a. The bar and restaurant open at 6pm, but at 10pm the bar becomes a disco open until 4am (the restaurant stays open until around midnight). Admission is often free (if you arrive before midnight), but sometimes there's a 5€ ($5.75) or more cover that includes the first drink. Tuesday is "spritz night" (the Venetian Campari-and-soda, which adds white wine); Wednesday they play smash hits; Thursday is rock, pop, alternative, and indie favorites; Friday is salsa and Latino; and Saturday brings house and hip-hop.

GAY & LESBIAN BARS

There are no gay bars in Venice, but you'll find some in nearby Padua, a lovely old city about 35 minutes from Venice by train. However, Venice does have a local division of a government-affiliated agency, **Arcigay Arcilesbica,** V.A. Costa 38A in Mestre (© **347-1559436;** www.arcigay.it). It serves as a home base for the gay community, with info on AIDS services, gay-friendly accommodations, and such. The best hours to call (it's in Mestre and hard to find) are Monday from 7 to 9pm, and Tuesday and Thursday from 9 to 11pm.

THE CASINO

From May to October, **Casino Municipale di Venezia,** located at Palazzo Vendramin Calergi, Cannaregio 2400 (Fondamenta Vendramin; Vaporetto: Marcuola; © **041-5297111;** www.casinovenezia.it), moves to its nondescript summer location on the Lido, where a visit is not as strongly recommended as during the winter months, when it is housed in this handsome 15th-century palazzo on the Grand Canal. Venice's tradition of gambling goes back to its glory days of the republic, and they live on here in this august Renaissance palace built by Mauro Codussi. Though not of the caliber of Monte Carlo (and occasionally slow on a midweek winter's night), this is one of only four casinos on Italian territory—and what a remarkable stage setting it is! Richard Wagner lived and died in a wing of this palazzo in 1883.

Check with your hotel before setting forth; some offer free passes for their guests. Otherwise, if you're not a gambler or curiosity seeker, it may not be worth the admission cost of 10€ ($12; though frequent promotions sometimes toss the admission fee right back at you in chips to help prime your spending). *Note:* A passport and jacket are required. The casino is open daily from 3pm (11am for the slots) to 3am.

8 Exploring Venice's Islands

Venice shares its lagoon with three other principal islands: **Murano, Burano,** and **Torcello.** Guided tours of the three are operated by a dozen agencies with docks on Riva degli Schiavoni/Piazzetta San Marco (all interchangeable). The 3- and 4-hour tours run 13€ to 21€ ($15–$24), usually include a visit to a Murano glass factory (you can easily do that on your own, with less of a hard sell), and leave daily around 9:30am and 2:30pm (times change; check in advance).

You can also visit the islands on your own conveniently and easily using the vaporetto. Line nos. 12, 13, 41, and 42 make the journey to Murano from Fondamente Nove (on the north side of Castello), and line no. 12 continues on to Burano and Torcello. The islands are small and easy to navigate, but check the schedule for the next island-to-island departure (usually hourly) and eventually for your return so you don't spend most of your day waiting for connections.

MURANO & ITS GLASS ⊕

The island of **Murano** has long been famous throughout the world for the products of its glass factories, but there's little to find in variety or prices you won't find in Venice. A visit to the **Museo Vetrario (Museum of Glass Art),** Fondamenta Giustinian 8 (© **041-739586**), will put the island's centuries-old legacy into perspective and is recommended for those considering major buys. April through October it's open Thursday through Tuesday from 10am to 4pm; November to March it's open from 10am to 5pm. Admission is free on the cumulative San Marco ticket (see "Piazza San Marco Discounts," above) or 4€ ($4.60) for adults and 2.50€ ($2.85) for ages 6 to 14. Dozens of *fornaci* (**furnaces**) offer free shows of mouth-blown glassmaking almost invariably hitched to a hard-sell ("No obligation! Really!") tour of the factory outlet. These retail showrooms of delicate glassware can be enlightening or boring, depending on your frame of mind. Almost all the places ship, often doubling the price. On the other hand, these pieces are instant heirlooms.

Murano also has two worthy churches: **San Pietro Martire** (no phone), with its altarpieces by Tintoretto, Veronese, and Giovanni Bellini; and the ancient **Santa Maria e Donato** (𝄢 **041-739704**), with an intricate Byzantine exterior apse and a 6th-century pulpit and columns inside resting on a fantastic 12th-century inlaid floor. Both are open daily from 9:15am to noon and 4 to 7pm.

BURANO & ITS LACE 𝄜𝄜

Lace is the claim to fame of tiny, colorful **Burano,** a craft kept alive for centuries by the wives of fishermen waiting for their husbands to return from sea. It's still worth a trip if you have time to stroll in the island's opera set of back streets, whose canals are lined with the brightly colored simple homes of the *Buranesi* fishermen. The local government continues its attempt to keep its centuries-old lace legacy alive with subsidized classes. Visit the **Museo del Merletto (Museum of Lace Making),** Piazza Galoppi (𝄢 **041-730034**), to understand why anything so exquisite shouldn't be left to fade into extinction. April through October, it's open Thursday through Tuesday from 10am to 4pm; November to March it's open from 10am to 5pm. Admission is free on the cumulative San Marco ticket (see "Piazza San Marco Discounts," earlier in this chapter) or 4€ ($4.60) for adults and 2.50€ ($2.90) for ages 6 to 14.

TORCELLO & ITS MOSAICS 𝄜𝄜

Nearby **Torcello** is perhaps the most charming of the islands. It was the first of the lagoon islands to be called home by the mainland population fleeing persecution (from here they moved to the area around the Rialto Bridge), but today it consists of little more than one long canal leading from the vaporetto landing past sad-sack vineyards to a clump of buildings at its center.

Torcello boasts the oldest Venetian monument, the **Cattedrale di Torcello (Santa Maria Assunta),** whose foundation dates from the 7th century (𝄢 **041-2702464** or 041-2702458). It's famous for its outstanding 11th- to 12th-century Byzantine mosaics—a *Madonna and Child* in the apse and a *Last Judgment* on the west wall—rivaling those of Ravenna and St. Mark's Basilica. The cathedral is open daily from 10am to 6pm (to 5pm in winter), and admission is 3€ ($3.45). Also of interest is the adjacent 11th-century church dedicated to **St. Fosca** and a small **provincial archaeological museum;** the church's hours are the same as the cathedral's, and the museum is open Tuesday through Sunday from 10am to 12:30pm and 2 to 4pm. Museum admission is 2€ ($2.30); the museum plus the basilica together is just 4€ ($4.60); all three cost 6€ ($6.90). The nearby *campanile* **(bell tower)** costs an additional 2€ ($2.30) to climb.

Peaceful Torcello is uninhabited except for a handful of land-working families. It's a favorite picnic spot, though you'll have to bring your food from Venice, since on the island there are no stores. There's only one bar/trattoria here and one rather expensive restaurant—the Cipriani, of Hemingway fame. Once the tour groups have left, the island offers a very special moment of solitude and escape when St. Mark's bottleneck becomes oppressive.

THE LIDO & ITS BEACHES

Although only a 15-minute vaporetto ride away, Venice's **Lido beaches** aren't much to write home about. The Adriatic waters have had pollution problems and, for bathing and sun worshiping, there are much nicer beaches in Italy. But the parade of local families with children, wealthy Italian visitors, foreigners, and (during the famed film festival) celebrities who frequent this *litorale* throughout summer is an interesting sight. You'll find the celebrities at the elitist beaches affiliated with the deluxe hotels, like the legendary Excelsior or the Grand Hotel des Bains, where Thomas Mann set his story *Death in Venice.*

There are a number of beach areas: The ***spiaggia libera* (public beach)** is called the **Bucintoro,** a 10-minute walk to the opposite end of Gran Viale Santa Maria Elisabetta (referred to as the Gran Vle.) from the vaporetto station Santa Elisabetta; to the left of this is the **Veneziana Spiaggia,** with umbrella and cabin rentals. At **San Nicolò,** 1.6km (1 mile) away, also reached by bus B, you'll have to pay 10€ ($12) per person (standard at Italy's beaches) for use of the amenities and umbrella rental. Alternatively, you can patronize the more crowded and noisier public beach, **Zona A** at the end of Gran Viale. If you stay at any of the Lido hotels, you'll find that most of them have some kind of agreement with the different beach establishments or *bagni.* Vaporetto lines cross the lagoon to the Lido from the San Zaccaria–Danieli stop near San Marco.

The Lido's wide, shaded boulevards are your best bet for jogging while you're visiting Venice. The Lido's big plus is wheels: those of cars and bicycles. Cars are permitted, but since it's flat country, biking is far more fun. You can rent bikes at a number of places along the Gran Viale Santa Maria Elisabetta for 3€ to 6€ ($3.45–$6.90) per hour.

The Veneto & South Tyrol

by Reid Bramblett

For centuries, the Venetian Republic ruled most of the northeastern region called the **Veneto,** turning its attentions inland once its maritime power was well established throughout the Mediterranean and eastward. Many of the inland cities of the Veneto, though, had been around for centuries when the city of Venice was officially founded with the election of its first doge in A.D. 726. As ancient Roman strongholds, these cities had already lived through their own period of glory. This rich heritage makes a tour through the Veneto a rewarding and often fascinating trip. Verona's wealth of Roman sites and magnificent ancient amphitheater have garnered it the nickname "Little Rome." Still standing in the main squares of Padua, Vicenza, and Verona are columns topped by the winged-lion mascot of St. Mark—a symbol of the distant and often glorious days of the Most Serene Republic of Venice. Venetian Renaissance *palazzi* (palaces), frescoed churches, and basilicas proudly line the cities' main drags. Shakespeare may have never stepped foot in these parts, but he was sufficiently fascinated that he chose to place many of his best works in "fair Verona" and the surrounding area.

Until the arrival of Napoleon in 1797, the Veneto, sharing the bounty of the Serene Republic, was built up and embellished. Many of the Palladian villas dotting the hills were the extravagant summer legacy of wealthy Venetian merchants whose urban palazzi lined Venice's Grand Canal. The Byzantine-Oriental influence so prominent in Venice's Gothic architecture can be seen in the region's churches and municipal buildings—the earlier structures adorned by the frescoes of Giotto and his ilk; the later ones decorated by the Venetian masters Veronese, Titian, Tintoretto, and Tiepolo.

The Veneto is a region of great physical diversity. The northeastern boundaries of the region reach up to the pink-tinged mountain range of the regal Dolomites, which separate Italy from the Tyrol. Farther south, the alluvial plains surrounding the mighty Po River are relentlessly flat, though punctuated by the Berici Mountains south of Vicenza and the Euganean Hills near Padua. The region's rivers—the Po, Adige, Brenta, Piave, and others—provide a fertile breeding ground for the surrounding hills, where vineyards, fruit orchards, and lucrative small-scale farms thrive.

A very different landscape dominates the **Dolomites.** Two mountain ranges, the Alps and the Dolomites, cut into this region, which stretches north from Lombardy and the Veneto. Here you'll discover an Italy that often doesn't seem very Italian at all. Most of the Dolomites and **South Tyrol**—which encompasses the Trentino and Alto Adige regions—belonged to Austria until it was handed over to Italy at the end of World War I, and many residents (especially in and around Bolzano and Bressanone) still prefer the ways of the north to those of the south. They speak German (to them, these towns are Bozen and Brixen), eat

Austrian food, and go about life with Teutonic crispness. And they live amid mountain landscapes that are more suggestive of Austria than of Italy.

The region's two mountain ranges are physical opposites: The eastern Alps are gentle and beautiful; the dramatically craggy peaks of the Dolomites, a little farther to, the east, are actually coral formations that only relatively recently reared up from ancient seabeds. Throughout Trentino–Alto Adige, soaring peaks, highland meadows, and lush valleys provide a paradise for hikers, skiers, and rock climbers; set amid these natural spectacles are pretty and interesting towns to explore.

1 Padua & Giotto's Fabulous Frescoes

42km (26 miles) W of Venice, 81km (50 miles) E of Verona, 32km (20 miles) E of Vicenza, 234km (145 miles) E of Milan

The University of Bologna had already grown to 10,000 students by the time **Padua** (Padova in Italian) founded its university in 1222. Padua was an ancient Roman stronghold that became the academic heartbeat of the powerful Venetian Republic. For this reason, it is one of the most important medieval and Renaissance cities in Italy. Dante and Copernicus studied here; Petrarch and Galileo taught here. When you wander the narrow, cobbled, arcaded side streets in the timeless neighborhoods surrounding the "Bo" (named after a 15th-c. inn that once stood on the present-day site of the university), you will be transported back to those earlier times.

Padua is a vital city, with a young university population that gets about on bicycles and keeps the city's piazzas and cafes humming. The historic hub of town is still evocative of the days when the city and its university flourished in the late Middle Ages and the Renaissance as a center of learning and art.

Pilgrims have also secured Padua's place on the map: For more than 700 years, the enormous Basilica di Sant'Antonio has drawn millions from around the world. A mendicant Franciscan monk born in Lisbon, Antonio spent his last years in Padova. He died here in 1231 and was canonized almost immediately; the basilica—a fantastic mingling of Romanesque, Byzantine, and Gothic architecture—was begun within a year. St. Anthony is one of the Roman Catholic Church's most beloved saints, known best, perhaps, for his powers to locate the lost. Countless handwritten messages left on his tomb inside the great domed church call upon this power to help find everything from lost love to lost limbs. Both the church and the miracle worker are simply referred to as "il Santo." The church warrants a visit as much for its artistic treasures and architectural importance as for its religious significance; it remains one of Europe's principal destinations of pilgrimage.

Pilgrims of another ilk have long made the journey here to admire Giotto's magnificent frescoes in the Scrovegni Chapel—to some, even more brilliant than his more famous cycle in Assisi, fully restored from 1999 to 2001.

ESSENTIALS

GETTING THERE   By Train   The main train station is at Piazza delle Stazione (© **049-8751800;** www.trenitalia.com), in the northern part of town, just outside the 16th-century walls. Padova is well connected by frequent train service to points directly west and east: Verona (50–70 min.; 4.55€–6.90€/$2.25–$7.95), Venice (20–40 min.; 2.45€–8.90€/$2.80–$10), Vicenza (15–30 min.; 2.45€–8.25€/$2.80–$9.50), and Milano (2½–3 hr.; 11€–19€/$13–$22).

The Veneto & South Tyrol

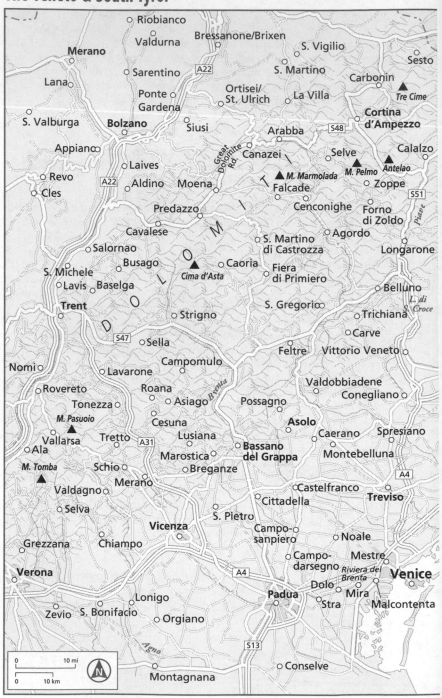

Riobianco
Valdurna
Bressanone/Brixen
S. Vigilio
Sesto
Merano
Sarentino
A22
S. Martino
Carbonin
Lana
Ortisei/
St. Ulrich
La Villa
Tre Cime
Ponte
Gardena
S. Valburga
Bolzano
Siusi
Arabba
S48
Cortina
d'Ampezzo
Appiano
Great Dolomite Rd.
Canazei
Selve
Calalzo
Revo
Laives
M. Pelmo
Antelao
Cles
Aldino
Moena
M. Marmolada
Zoppe
Falcade
Forno
di Zoldo
S51
Predazzo
Cenconighe
Piave
Cavalese
S. Martino
di Castrozza
Agordo
Longarone
Salornao
Busago
Caoria
Fiera
di Primiero
S. Michele
Cima d'Asta
Belluno
Lavis
Baselga
S. Gregorio
L. di
S. Croce
Trent
Strigno
Trichiana
S47
Sella
Carve
Nomi
Lavarone
Campomulo
Feltre
Vittorio Veneto
Rovereto
Roana
Brenta
Valdobbiadene
Tonezza
Asiago
Possagno
Conegliano
M. Pasuoio
Cesuna
Asolo
Spresiano
Vallarsa
Tretto
A31
Lusiana
Caerano
Ala
Marostica
Bassano
del Grappa
Montebelluna
M. Tomba
Schio
Breganze
A4
Valdagno
Merano
Castelfranco
Treviso
Selva
Cittadella
Vicenza
S. Pietro
Grezzana
Chiampo
Campo-
sanpiero
Noale
Verona
Campo-
darsegno
Mestre
Riviera del
Brenta
Venice
Lonigo
Padua
Dolo
Mira
Zevio
S. Bonifacio
Orgiano
Stra
Malcontenta
0   10 mi
N
0   10 km
Agno
S13
Montagnana
Conselve

Mittewald

Drau

Liesing

AUSTRIA

Millstatter
See

Weissensee

Gail

S. Stefano
di Cad.

Forni
Avoltri

Sappada

Paluzza

Pontebba

Vigo

Forni
di Sopra

Ampezzo

Dogna

Tolmezzo

▲ M. Pramaggiore

Villa
Santina

Resiutta

Stolvizza

SLOVENIA

A23

Venzone

S. Francesco

Gemona
d. Friuli

Bohinjsko Jazero

Chievolis

Mecuno

Claut

Tarcento

Kobarid

Maniago

Pinzano

Spilimbergo

Cividale
d. Friuli

Avrano

S. Martino
di C.

Digliano

Udine

Kanal

Fontana-
fredda

S. Giorgio

Paparotti

Tagliamento

Pordenone

S13

Pozzuolo

Manzano

Nova Gorica

Casarsa

Flambro

A23

Gorizia

Palmanova

Brugnera

Villalta

Torsa

Cervignano
di Friuli

Annone

Marano

Ausa-
corno

Monfalcone

Oderzo

A4

Portogruaro

Aquileia

Grignano

Ponte
di Piave

Ceggia

Brussa

Lignano
Sabbiadoro

Grado

Golfo di
Trieste

Trieste

Livenza

S. Dona
di Piave

Bibione

Caposile

Caorle

Lido di Jesolo

SLOVENIA

Golfo di Venezia

VENETO

SOUTH
TYROL

15° E.

45° N.

Rome

0   100 Mi
0   100 Km

40° N.

10° E.

CROATIA

Adriatic Sea

A Taste of the Veneto

The foods of the Veneto are as diverse as its geography. From the mountains and the foothills comes a proliferation of mushrooms and game. Much of the cuisine is based on the rice and corn grown here; **polenta** makes frequent appearances on most menus, served with a hearty game stew with hints of Austrian influences. Rice is commonly prepared as **risotto,** a first course served along with the season's vegetables or, more characteristically, offerings from the Adriatic on the east. The olive oil of Tuscan cuisine is used here only minimally—it's not unusual to sense the use of butter, more commonly associated with Emilian food. But above all, it's the Adriatic that dictates the regional cuisine, even here in the landlocked environs of the Veneto, where fish and shellfish feature heavily in the local diet. Outside influences are also behind the proliferation of desserts, a throwback to the two times in history when the Veneto was ceded to Austria—sweet remnants of the occupation are still evident in many pastry shops. The now universal favorite **tiramisu** is said to have originated in the Veneto.

Wine is an integral element in any meal; it's no compromise to limit yourself to the local wines, which are some of Europe's finest. The Veneto—and, in particular, Verona—plays an all-important role in the production and exportation of such world-renowned wines as Soave, Bordolino, and Valpolicella. No other region in Italy produces as many D.O.C. (Denominazione di Origine Controllata, zones of controlled name and origin) red wines as the Veneto. The rich volcanic earth of the Colli Euganei yields a good number of these reds, while a light and *frizzante prosecco* hails from the hills around Asolo.

From the train station, bus nos. A, M, T, 3, 4, 8, 12, and 18 head toward **downtown.**

By Bus   The main **ACAP bus station** is located behind (east of) the Scrovegni Chapel and Arena Gardens area on Via Trieste 40 near Piazza Boschetti (© 049-8241111; www.aps-online.it). Frequent bus service to Venice and Verona costs approximately the same as train tickets, though tourists and locals alike seem to use this station principally for the smaller outlying cities such as Bassano del Grappa (75 min.; 3.50€/$4).

By Car   Padua is on the A4 autostrada that links Venice with Milan. All the points of interest listed below are located within the city's historical center, which is closed to traffic. When booking at your hotel, ask about the closest parking lot. Hotels usually have an agreement with their neighborhood parking lot and pass those savings along to hotel guests.

VISITOR INFORMATION   The **tourist office** is in the train station (© 049-8752077; fax 049-8755008; www.apt.padova.it). It's open Monday through Saturday from 9am to 7pm and Sunday from 9am to noon. Another office is at the cathedral on Piazza del Santo (© 049-8753087). It's open daily April through October. A more central office is located in Galleria Pedrocchi (© 049-8767927). It is open Monday to Saturday from 9am to 12:30pm and 3 to 7pm. Southwest of Padua is a small but renowned wine area, and at the tourist office you can get a **"Strada dei Vini"** wine route map (when in stock!). It also leads you to the small city of Terme di Abano, famous as a center for radioactive springs and mud treatments unique to this volcanic range.

GETTING AROUND   Hotels, restaurants, and major points of interest are all inside the historical center and can be easily reached on foot. Public ACAP buses service much of the center's streets, which are otherwise limited to traffic (pick up a bus map from the tourist office). **Single tickets** (valid for 60 min.) cost .85€ (95¢); a 90-min. **round-trip ticket** is 1.50€ ($1.70).

FESTIVALS & MARKETS   The beloved **Sant'Antonio** celebrates his feast day June 13, when his relics are carried about town in an elaborate procession by thousands of pilgrims from all over the world.

The **outdoor markets** (Mon–Sat) in the twin Piazza delle Erbe **(fresh produce)** and Piazza della Frutta **(clothing and dry goods)** flanking the enormous Palazzo della Ragione are some of Italy's best. The third Sunday of every month sees the area of the Prato delle Valle inundated by more than 220 **antiques and collectibles dealers,** one of the largest antiques fairs in the region (© 049-8205856). Only early birds will beat the large number of local dealers to the good stuff.

Antiques lovers with a car might want to visit Italy's second-largest **Mercato dell'Antiquariato** the last Sunday of every month at the 18th-century Villa Contarini, in Piazzola sul Brenta (© 0329-2372475). The lovely 30-minute drive can be combined with a visit to some of the other Palladian and Palladian-inspired country villas along the Brenta Canal (see "A Day Trip from Padua: The Forgotten Riviera," later in this chapter). An estimated 320 vendors hawk their wares.

Less important, but far more frequent, is the weekly **Saturday outdoor flea market** of nonantique goods (clothes, pet food, household goods—nothing fascinating, but an interesting peek into local life and a good place to pick up kitchen items to re-create the *cucina Italiana* back home), also held in the Prato della Valle. The market's large number of inexpensive shoe stands is testament to the many shoe factories for which the nearby Brenta Canal area is famous. Even if you don't buy anything, visiting either market will give you a chance to see the 18th-century Prato delle Valle, one of the largest piazzas in Europe. Just southwest of the Basilica di Sant'Antonio, it's ringed by a canal and populated by more than 80 statues.

SIGHTS TO SEE

Cappella degli Scrovegni (Scrovegni Chapel or Arena Chapel) ☆☆☆

This is the one uncontested must-see during your stay in Padua. Inside the chapel, art lovers armed with binoculars behold the scene in awe—the recently renovated cycle of **vibrant frescoes** by Giotto that revolutionized 14th-century painting is still considered among the most important early Renaissance art. A brilliant cobalt blue is the dominant color of the illustrations, which are easy to understand and painted in typical medieval comic-strip format; here they take on an unprecedented degree of realism and emotion.

This cycle is even larger, more complete, and better preserved than the famed St. Francis frescoes Giotto later painted in Assisi. Giotto worked from 1303 to 1306 to completely cover the ceiling and walls with 38 scenes illustrating the lives of Mary and Christ from floor to ceiling. With your back to the front door, the three bands that cover the walls are: top right, Life of Joachim; top left, Life of the Virgin; right center, The Childhood of Christ; left center, Christ's Public

Life; right bottom, The Passion of Christ (the third panel of Judas kissing Christ is perhaps the best known of the entire cycle); left bottom, Christ's Death and Resurrection. Above the entrance is the fresco of the Last Judgment: Christ, as judge, sits in the center, surrounded by the angels and apostles. Below him, to the right, are the blessed, while to the left, Giotto created a terrible hell in which devils and humans are condemned to eternal punishment.

The area around the ancient Roman Arena where the chapel now stands (and hence the chapel's alternative name) was purchased in 1300 by a wealthy Paduan, Enrico Scrovegni. He built an extravagant palazzo (destroyed in 1820) and a family chapel, which stands next to it, whose exterior remains simple and unadorned. The chapel was dedicated to Scorvegni's father an unethical usurer so notorious in his time that he was refused a Christian burial. The son hoped to atone for his father's ways and commissioned Tuscan-born Giotto, whose work he had seen in the Basilica di Sant'Antonio. Giotto felt obligated to include the father in the portrait of the Last Judgment's blessed souls. Dante felt otherwise, immortalizing him by placing him amid the usurers condemned to hell in his epic *Inferno.*

Note: Be prepared for high-season lines, a wait made even longer by the small numbers of controlled groups (25 people max) allowed to enter the chapel at any one time. Your visit is limited to a scandalously brief 15 minutes. If that's too short for you, consider visiting the chapel between 7 and 9:30pm on the 12€ ($14) "Double Turn" ticket (reservation fee included); it allows you 30 minutes in the chapel. For a slightly reduced rate, buy the 8€ ($9.20) "Evening Ticket," for admission between 7 and 9:30pm. *You must book timed-entry tickets at least 24 hours in advance.* Each online reservation—even for holders of the Padvoa Card, which allows for free admission—incurs a 1€ ($1.15) reservation fee. You must pick up your tickets at least 1 hour prior to your assigned entry time.

Piazza Eremitani 8 (off Corso Garibaldi). © 049-2010020 or www.cappelladegliscrovegni.it for required reservations (call center lines Mon–Fri 9am–7pm, Sat 9am–1pm). Admission, including 1€ ($1.15) reservation fee, 12€ ($14) adults, 5€ ($5.75) ages 6–17, free for those under 6 or with purchase of PadovaCard (see "A Money-Saving Tip," below), although a reservation is still required and you will be charged the reservation fee. MC, V (online reservations only). Daily 9am–7pm; until 10pm in summer. Entrance through the Museo Eremitani. Bus: 3, 8, 10, 12, 32, 42.

Museo Civico Eremitani (Civic Museum of the Hermits) ⭐

The centuries-old cloisters that were once home to the monks (*eremitani* means hermits) who officiated in the adjacent Scrovegni Chapel (officially part of the museum complex) have been handsomely renovated to provide an airy display space as the city's new civic museum. Its prodigious collection begins on the ground floor with the Archeological Museum's division of Egyptian, Roman, and Etruscan artifacts and antiquities. The upstairs collection represents an impressive panorama of minor Venetian works from major Venetian artists from the early 15th to 19th centuries. You'll find works by Titian, Tiepolo, and Tintoretto, whose *Crucifixion* is the museum's finest work. Special mention is given to Giotto's unusual wooden *Crucifix* and Bellini's *Portrait of a Young Senator.*

Piazza Eremitani 8 (off Corso Garibaldi and adjacent to the Cappella Scrovegni). © **049-8204550. Reservations** (if buying cumulative ticket with Capella Scrovegni): © **049-2010020** or www.cappella degliscrovegni.it. Admission to **Musei Civico Eremitani** only: 10€ ($12) adults, 8€ ($9.20) 6–17, free for children under 6 and seniors over 65. **Joint ticket** with the Cappella Scrovegni (includes a 1€/$1.15 reservation fee) 12€ ($14) adults, 5€ ($5.75) ages 6–17, free for those under 6 (although admission still requires a reservation and you will be charged the reservation fee); free with purchase of PadovaCard (see "A Money-Saving Tip," below). MC, V (online reservations only). Feb–Oct daily 9am–7pm; Nov–Jan 9am–6pm. Bus: 3, 8, 10, 12, 32, 42.

Padua

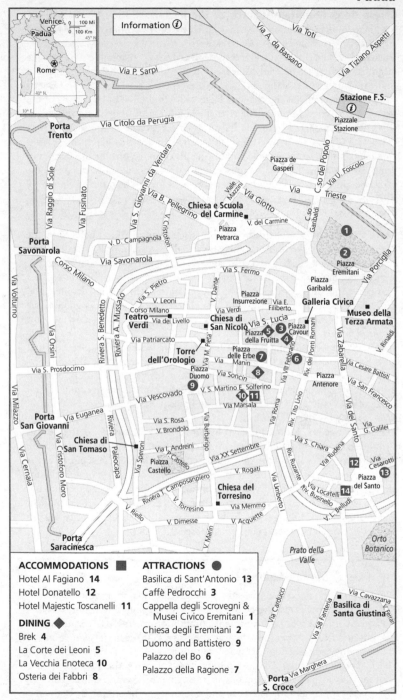

Venice
Padua
Rome

15° E.
0   100 Mi
0   100 Km
45° N.
40° N.
10° E.

Information ⓘ

Via Toti
Via A. da Bassano
Via P. Sarpi
Via Tiziano Aspetti

Stazione F.S.
ⓘ
Piazzale Stazione

Via Citolo da Perugia

Porta Trento

Piazza de Gasperi

C.so del Popolo
Via U. Foscolo
Via Trieste

C.so Garibaldi

Via Giotto
Viale Mazzini

Chiesa e Scuola del Carmine
V. del Carmine

Piazza Petrarca

1

V. D. Campagnola

Porta Savonarola

Via Savonarola

Corso Milano

Via S. Fermo

Piazza Eremitani
2

Via Porciglia

Via Raggio di Sole
Via Fusinato
Via S. Giovanni da Verdara
Via B. Pellegrino
V. Cristofori

Piazza Insurrezione
Via E. Filiberto

Piazza Garibaldi

Galleria Civica

Via S. Pietro
V. Leoni

Corso Milano
Via dei Livello

Teatro Verdi

Chiesa di San Nicolo

Piazza Verdi

Via S. Lucia

Piazza Cavour

Museo della Terza Armata

Via Benedetto
Riviera S. Benedetto
Riviera A. Mussato

Via Patriarcato

Piazza della Fruìtta
5 **3**
4

Riv. dei Ponti Romani

Via Zabarela

Via Rinaldi

Via Orsini

Torre dell'Orologio

Piazza delle Erbe
Via M. Pieta
Manin
7
6

Via VIII Febbraio

Via Cesare Battisti

Via S. Prosdocimo

Piazza Duomo
9

Via Soncin
8

Piazza Antenore

Via San Francesco

Via Volturno
Via Milazzo

Via Vescovado

V. S. Martino E. Solferino
10 **11**
Via Marsala

Via Roma
Riv. Tito Livio

Via del Santo

Via G. Galilei

Porta San Giovanni

Via Euganea
Riviera Paleocapa

Via S. Rosa
V. Brondolo

Via Barbarigo

Via XX Settembre

Riv. Ruzante

Via S. Chiara

Via Rudena

12
Via Cesarotti
13

Via Cernaia
Via Cristoforo Moro
Via Speroni

Chiesa di San Tomaso

Via I. Andreini
P. Castello

Piazza Castello

V. Rogati

Via Umberto I

Via S. Chiara

Via Locatelli
Riv. Businello
14

Piazza del Santo

Porta Saracinesca

Riviera T. Camposanpiero
V. Torresino

Chiesa del Torresino
Via Memmo

V. Acquette

Riv. V. L. Belludi

V. Riello
V. Dimesse
V. Marin

Orto Botanico

Prato della Valle

Via Carducci
Via 58 Fanteria
Via Cavazzana

Basilica di Santa Giustina

Via Tofani

Porta S. Croce

Via Marghera

Chiesa degli Eremitani (Church of the Hermits)   Padua's worst tragedy was the complete destruction of this church by Nazi bombings in 1944; some art historians consider it the country's worst artistic wartime loss. It has been remarkably restored to its original early-13th-century Romanesque style, but the magnificent cycle of frescoes painted from 1454 to 1457 by the 23-year-old Andrea Mantegna could not be salvaged, except for a corner of the **Ovetari Chapel** on the right of the chancel. Here you'll find enough fragments of the frescoes (discovered in the rubble after the bombing) to understand the loss of what was considered one of Italy's great artistic treasures. Mantegna (1431–1506) was born in Padua and studied under the Florentine master Donatello, who lived here while completing his commissions for the Basilica di Sant'Antonio as well as the famous equestrian statue that now stands in the piazza before it. Classical music concerts are occasionally held in the church.

Piazza Eremitani (off Corso Garibaldi). © **049-8756410.** Free admission. Daily 8:15am–6:15pm (until 6:45pm in summer). Bus: 3, 8, 18, 22, 32, 42.

Caffè Pedrocchi ⊛   The Pedrocchi is a historic landmark, as beloved by the Paduans as "their" own St. Anthony (who actually hailed from Portugal). When it first opened in 1831, it was the largest cafe in Europe—whom were they expecting? Famous are the literary and political characters and local luminaries who made this their command post—French-born Henri Beyle, aka Stendhal, had it in mind when he wrote "The best Italian cafe is almost as good as the Parisian ones." Countless others were less reserved, calling it arguably the most beautiful coffeehouse in the world.

Heavily damaged during World War II, the caffè has been completely rebuilt in its original neoclassical 19th-century stage-set splendor. After a laborious renovation and a heralded 1998 reopening that was, for Padua, the social event of the year, it's again the social heartbeat of the city for both university students and ladies of a certain age. On a more prosaic note: It has the nicest restrooms in town, for the use of caffè patrons.

In warm weather, Pedrocchi opens its doors (hence its curious description as a "doorless cafe") onto the pedestrian piazza; sit here for a while to absorb the Paduan spirit. As is always the case, drinks cost less when you're standing at the bar, but then you will have missed the *dolce far niente* (sweetness of doing nothing) experience for which Pedrocchi has always been known. A cappuccino, tea, beer, or glass of white *prosecco* will cost from 2.30€ ($2.65) at your table (half that at the bar), and hunger can be held at bay with a plate of dainty teatime pastries or a grilled ham-and-cheese toast, each 3.10€ ($3.55).

Value **A Money-Saving Tip**

If you plan on taking in all the sites of Padova during a short visit—or even if you plan on visiting the Scrovegni Chapel and only one other site—a **PadovaCard** is a worthy investment. In addition to free use of the city's buses and free parking in some areas, the 13€ ($15) card gets you admission to the Cappella degli Scrovegni (although you still must call to make a reservation), Musei Civici Eremitani, the Palazzo della Ragione, and other sites in Padova and the province, as well as a seat in Caffé Pedrocchi. The card is valid for 48 hours, and one card can be shared by both an adult and a child younger than 12. The card is for sale at tourist offices and at sites and attractions where you use the card.

Pedrocchi often hosts live music in the evenings; check their website for dates, or just stop by during your visit to drink in the atmosphere.

Via VIII Febbraio 15 (at Piazza Cavour). © 049-8205007 or 049-8781231. www.caffepedrocchi.it. Tues–Sun 9:30am–12:30pm and 3:30–6pm (for historical salons upstairs, admission 3€/$3.45 or free with Padova Card). Bar daily 7am–midnight.

Bo (Università Palazzo Centrale)   Galileo taught here from 1592 to 1610, and his battered desk and podium are still on display in Italy's second-oldest university (after Bologna). His name joins a legendary honor roll of students and professors—Petrarch, Dante, the poet Tasso, Copernicus—who came here from all over Europe. The University of Padua was founded in 1222 and grew to become one of the most famous and ambitious learning centers in Europe, reaching its zenith in the 16th and 17th centuries.

Today a number of buildings are spread about town, but the **Palazzo del Bo** (named after the long-gone "Bo," or Ox Inn, a favorite student hangout in the 15th c.) is the university's main seat. Ongoing restoration keeps most of it off-limits, but the perfectly preserved **Teatro Anatomico (Anatomical Theater)** 🏛 is one of the few sites open for a visit. Built in 1594, it was here that William Harvey most probably developed his theory of the circulation of blood when getting his degree in 1602.

Via VIII Febbraio (south of Piazza Cavour). © 049-8275111. Admission 3.60€ ($4.15). By guided tour, some in English. Ask at tourist office for status of renovation. Bus: 3, 8, 11, 12, 13, 16, 18, 22, 42.

Palazzo della Ragione (Law Courts), Piazza delle Erbe & Piazza della Frutta   Just south of Caffè Perocchi and an inevitable destination for those meandering about the historic center of town, the picturesque open-air markets of **Piazza delle Erbe (Square of the Herbs)** and **Piazza della Frutta (Square of Fruit)** frame the massive 13th-century palazzo at their center. Together they have stood as the town's political and commercial nucleus for centuries. Before being distracted by the color, smells, and cacophony of the sprawling outdoor fruit and vegetable market stalls, turn your attention to the magnificent **Palazzo della Ragione,** whose interior is as impressive as its exterior.

Food shops by the dozen fill its ground floor, and stand-up bars and outdoor cafes make this "lunch central." The two-story, loggia-lined "Palace of Reason" is topped with a distinctive sloped roof that resembles the inverted hull of a ship, the largest of its kind in the world. It was built in 1219 as the seat of Padua's parliament and was used as an assembly hall, courthouse, and administrative center to celebrate Padua's newly won independence as a republican city. The palazzo was considered a masterpiece of civil medieval architecture. However, in 1420, an extremely damaging fire destroyed, among other things, an elaborate cycle of frescoes by Giotto and his students that adorned **il Salone (the Great Hall).** The Hall, 81m (266 ft.) long, was almost immediately rebuilt and is today the prime draw, for both its floor-to-ceiling 15th-century frescoes immediately commissioned after the fire—similar in style and astrological theme to those that had been painted by Giotto (and one of the very few complete zodiac cycles to survive into modern times)—and a large wooden sculpture of a horse that some art historians have attributed to Donatello. Museum-quality exhibits are often held at this impressive venue, giving you twice the reason to visit.

On the far (west) side of the adjoining piazza's canvas-topped stalls, flanking the Palazzo della Ragione, is the **Piazza dei Signori,** most noteworthy for the 15th-century clock tower that dominates it, the first of its kind in Italy.

Tips When Venice Overflows

Padua is convenient to both Venice and Verona. It doesn't offer a wide choice of desirable hotels in the *centro storico*, but you'll pay close to half the rates of comparable accommodations in Venice. Plus, you'll find the commute, just 31km (19 miles), an easy and inexpensive one (and often a necessary one when Venice is booked full).

Piazza delle Erbe/Piazza della Frutta. ℰ **049-8205006.** www.padovanet.it/museicivici. Admission to palazzo 8€ ($9.20) adults, 4€ ($4.60) children. Tues–Sun 9am–6pm (to 7pm Feb–Oct). Bus: 3, 8, 11, 12, 13, 16, 18, 22, 42.

Basilica di Sant'Antonio ℰℰ   This enormous basilica's imposing interior is richly frescoed and decorated, and is filled with a number of tombs, works of art, and inlaid checkerboard marble flooring. It's all there to honor one man, Padua's patron St. Anthony (Sant'Antonio). Simply and commonly referred to as "il Santo," Anthony was born in Lisbon in 1195 and died just outside of Padua in 1231. Work began on the church almost immediately but was not completed until 1307. Its eight domes bring to mind the Byzantine influence also found in Venice's St. Mark's Basilica, which predates Padua's Romanesque-Gothic construction by more than 2 centuries. A pair of octagonal, minaret-like bell towers enhances its Eastern appearance.

The faithful could not care less about the architecture; they flock here year-round to caress the **tomb** holding the saint's body (off the left aisle) and to pray for his help in finding what they've lost. The tomb is always covered with flowers, photographs, and handwritten personal petitions left by devout pilgrims from every corner of the globe whose numbers have remained constant over the centuries. The saint is the patron of lost or mislaid objects, and the faithful who flock here come to find everything from lost love to lost health. The series of nine bronze bas-reliefs of scenes from the saint's life are some of the finest works by 16th-century Northern Italian sculptors. The seven bronze statues and towering central *Crucifixion* that adorn the main altar are by Donatello (1444–48) and are the basilica's artistic highlight.

In his lifetime, St. Anthony was known for his eloquent preaching, so interpret as you will the saint's perfectly (some say miraculously) preserved tongue, vocal chords, and jawbone on display in the **Cappella del Tesoro** in the back of the church directly behind the main altar. These treasured relics are carried through town in a traditional procession every June 13 to celebrate the feast day of il Santo. You'll also see one of the original tattered tunics belonging to il Santo dating from 1231.

Standing out amid the smattering of stalls across the large piazza, in front of the basilica selling St. Anthony–emblazoned everything, is Donatello's famous *Gattamelata* equestrian statue. The first of its size to be cast in Italy since Roman antiquity, it is important for its detail, proportion, and powerful contrast between rider (the inconsequential Venetian condottiere Erasmo da Narni, nicknamed the "Spotted Cat") and horse. It would have a seminal effect on Renaissance sculpture and casting and restored the lost art of the equestrian statue.

Piazza del Santo (east of Prato delle Valle). ℰ **049-8789722.** www.basilicadelsanto.org. Free admission. Summer daily 6:20am–7:45pm; winter daily 6:20am–7pm. Bus: 3, 8, 11, 12, 13, 16, 18, 22; Minibus: Navette Antenore.

ACCOMMODATIONS YOU CAN AFFORD

When making reservations, note that low season is usually considered December and January, and July and August. Inquire about discounts if you'll be in Padua at this time of year.

Hotel al Fagiano ℛ Although small and family run, this newly renovated and well-located hotel is a great value-for-your-money deal for the budget-minded. It doesn't exactly ooze coziness and charm, but given the less than encouraging hotel situation in town, the Fagiano's bright, modern, and clean rooms are still a standout choice. Bathrooms have been freshly redone and include niceties such as hair dryers and bright lighting. Also, you rarely find air-conditioning and TV at these rates; the hotel offers both. Located just a few steps off the expansive Piazza del Santo (its most appealing asset), don't confuse this Fagiano with the recently renamed Hotel Buenos Aires, formerly known as the Fagiano and just a block away.

Via Locatelli 45 (west of Piazza del Santo), 35123 Padova. ℂ 049-8750073. Fax 049-8753396. www.al fagiano.it. 29 units. 54€–58€ ($62–$67) single; 75€–81€ ($86–$93) double; 85€–92€ ($98–$106) triple. Breakfast 6.50€ ($7.45). Rates slightly discounted off season and for rooms without private bathroom. Parking 10€ ($12). AE, DC, MC, V. Bus: 3, 8, 11, 12, 13, 16, 18. **Amenities:** Bar; bike rental. *In room:* A/C, TV, dataport, hair dryer.

WORTH A SPLURGE

Hotel Donatello ℛ This is a modern hotel in an old building, flush with amenities and enjoying a great location right at the Basilica di Sant'Antonio. Over half the rooms overlook the basilica, though those on the inner courtyard (some with hardwood flooring rather than carpets) are quieter. Guest quarters vary as the management slowly refreshes and updates a few each year. Some feature plush modular furnishings, some retro-Empire style. Some of the older bathrooms have tubs with hand-held shower nozzles, but most are modernized. Apartments sleeping three to four come with two bedrooms and a common bathroom.

Via del Santo 102–104, 35123 Padova. ℂ 049-8750634. Fax 049-8750829. www.hoteldonatello.net. 45 units. 107€ ($123) single; 147€–168€ ($169–$193) double; 195€ ($224) triple; 262€ ($301) apt for 3 or 4. Breakfast 13€ ($14). AE, DC, MC, V. Parking 16€ ($18) in hotel garage. Bus: 3, 8, 11, 12, 13, 16, 18, 22; Minibus: Navette Antenore. **Amenities:** Restaurant (international); bar; concierge; tour desk; room service; laundry service; dry cleaning. *In room:* A/C, TV w/pay movies, dataport, minibar, hair dryer, safe.

Hotel Majestic Toscanelli ℛℛ A four-star hotel this nice would cost a great deal more in nearby Venice, which is why the Toscanelli often finds itself with guests who make this their home base while visiting neighboring cities and the surrounding area. A 1992 redo has kept the hotel's old-world charm fresh and handsome. Rooms are tastefully done in classic decor with coordinated pastel themes, burnished cherrywood furniture, and large bathrooms bright with white ceramic and marble tiles. Work in 1999 freshened up the lobby, transforming it with highlights of gold leaf that hint of the Venetian rococo era, and the recent addition of three new suites is just part of the continuing improvements. Off the lobby, a bright and attractive breakfast room serves a good buffet breakfast. This quiet, historic neighborhood is entirely closed to traffic, with porticoed alleyways lined with antiques shops and wine bars. From here, it's an easy walk to the Via Roma and the Piazza delle Erbe.

Via dell'Arco 2 (2 blocks west of V. Roma and south of the Piazza delle Erbe), 35122 Padova. ℂ 049-663244. Fax 049-8760025. www.toscanelli.com. 34 units. 95€ ($109) single; 153€–169€ ($176–$194) double; 197€ ($227) junior suite; 215€ ($247) suite; 36€ ($41) extra bed. Rates include buffet breakfast. Rates discounted mid-July to Aug. AE, DC, MC, V. Valet garage parking 19€ ($22). Bus: 3, 8, 11, 12, 13, 16,

18, 22, 42. **Amenities:** Bar; concierge; tour desk; car-rental desk; courtesy car; room service; babysitting; laundry service; dry cleaning; nonsmoking rooms. *In room:* A/C, TV w/pay movies, fax (on request), dataport, minibar, coffee maker (in suites), hair dryer, safe (in doubles).

GREAT DEALS ON DINING

Brek *Value* ITALIAN CAFETERIA   Brek is self-service *all'italiana,* a homegrown Northern Italian chain of upscale cafeterias that make concessions to the time-pressed modern world without sacrificing old-world quality. Put your language problems and calorie counting aside as you help yourself to pastas that are made up fresh while you wait and point to the sauce of your choice. There's an express counter just for omelets, another for entrees and pizza. The dessert cart groans under a copious array of cheeses, fresh fruits, fruit salads, and fruit-topped tarts and cobblers. Join the thoroughly local eat-on-the-run lunch crowd from the university and surrounding shops, and save your day's budget for a dinner splurge.

Piazza Cavour 20. © 049-8753788. www.brek.com. No reservations accepted. Primi and pizza 2.80€–6€ ($3.20–$6.90); secondi 4€–10€ ($4.60–$12). AE, DC, MC, V. Sat–Thurs 11:30am–3pm and 6–10pm.

La Corte dei Leoni ★ *Finds* WINE BAR/PADOVANA   After a heady wander through the sights, sounds, and smells of Padova's open-air marketplace, one of Italy's most colorful and authentic, head for a moment's respite at this restaurant/enoteca. Your head need spin no longer, despite the 800 labels with which it stocks its well-respected wine cellar. Each week, 20 different bottles are available *al calice* (by the glass) at 1.80€ to 5€ ($2.05–$5.75), so you can sample many. A stylishly minimal decor in the cool white and moss-green interior is attractive, but the outdoor courtyard where centuries-old horse stables have been converted for modern-day grazers is the warm-weather draw, as is the summer-evening jazz. The interesting antipasti are as sophisticated as the setting: Look for the *mousse di fegato grasso d'oca tartufato,* a lighter-than-air foie gras heightened by the hint of truffles, or a platter of Italian cheeses or salami, each a perfect complement to Leonardi's very impressive selection of wines, with some interlopers from the Napa Valley. Only a handful of dishes is offered, but each is excellently prepared, such as *mezzelune* (a kind of ravioli) stuffed with ricotta and eggplant in a sauce of fresh mushrooms and mountain cheese, and *petto d'anatra in salsa d'uva* (duck breast cooked with grapes that somehow escaped their fate as wine).

Via Pietro d'Abano 1 (on a side street just north of the Piazza della Frutta). © 049-8750083. www.corte deileoni.com. Reservations suggested. Primi 7€–10€ ($8.20–$12); secondi 14€–17€ ($16–$20). AE, DC, MC, V. Sun 12:30–2:30pm; Mon 6:30pm–12:30am; Tues–Sat 12:30–2:30pm and 6:30pm–12:30am. Closed 1 week in Aug.

Osteria Dei Fabbri ★ PADOVANA   Simple, well-prepared food is the great equalizer. This rustic, old-fashioned tavern or osteria is a lively spot where intellectual types share tables with Zegna-suited bankers, and students stop by for a tipple or to find a quiet corner in which to pore over the newspaper (a pastime not encouraged during hours when meals are served). Some of the day's specials are displayed on the heavy oak bar—antipasti of grilled vegetables, rosemary potatoes, seafood salads—while hot dishes pour out of the kitchen. There's always at least one homemade pasta choice to start with, and *osso buco,* the specialty of the house, is especially memorable when accompanied by any of the local (and excellent) Venetian wines available by the bottle or glass. Stop by for at least the *dopo cena* (after-dinner drink) to top off your day in Padova. If this restaurant is full—or if its recent, and really unjustified, doubling of prices put you off—head two blocks over to the reliable **Osteria L'Anfora** at Via del Soncin 13 (east of Piazza Duomo; ℭ **049-656629**), for inexpensive wine and good food.

Via dei Fabbri 13 (on a side street south of Piazza delle Erbe). ℭ 049-650336. www.osteriadefabbri.it. Reservations suggested. Primi 7.50€–8.50€ ($8.60–$9.75); secondi 11€–17€ ($13–$20). AE, DC, MC, V. Mon–Sat noon–3pm and 7:30–11pm.

WORTH A SPLURGE

La Vecchia Enoteca ⁄★★ PADOVANA   The sophistication of the Veneto's prodigious viticulture is shown off here in an appropriately refined venue that could easily fit into a less expensive category. Cozy, in a rustic and elegant kind of way, La Vecchia Enoteca is for that special evening of white linen and smooth service when you'd like the full-blown experience of Padovan cuisine and award-deserving wines (hence its placement in our splurge department). Prices are unintimidating enough to encourage diners to leave caution at the door and indulge in a delicious menu and commendable selection of regional and Italian wines. The menu showcases the bounty-rich Veneto: The traditional polenta and risotto change with the season, as does the light, homemade gnocchi. Meat possibilities are numerous and tempting, while the influence of the Adriatic appears in entrees such as the favored *branzino in crosta di patate,* sea bass roasted in a light crust of potatoes. This enoteca is another rarity in Italy: a nonsmoking restaurant.

Via S. Martino e Solferino 32 (just south of Piazza delle Erbe). ℭ 049-8752856. Reservations recommended. Primi 6€–10€ ($6.90–$13); secondi 15€–18€ ($17–$21). MC, V. Mon 7–10pm; Tues–Sat 12:45–2pm and 7:30–10pm. Closed 3 weeks in Aug.

PADUA AFTER DARK

The classical-music season usually runs October to April at different venues around town. Among them, the historic **Teatro Verdi** at Via dei Livello 32 (ℭ **049-8777011**) is the most impressive. Padua's **orchestra** (www.pvorchestra. org) frequently performs there. Programs are available at the tourist office. Look for posters advertising performances by the world-class **Solisti Veneti,** who are Paduans but spend most of the year, alas, traveling abroad. Tickets to hear the orchestra start at 15€ ($17).

As a university city, Padua's student population makes its presence known at all times—everyone looks 22 and in search of themselves. You can network with the student crowd at any of the popular **cafes along Via Cavour,** or at the osterie, wine bars, and beer dives in the porticoed medieval side streets encircling the Palazzo della Ragione (the area around the Bo) and its bookends Piazza delle Erbe and Piazza della Frutta.

A DAY TRIP FROM PADUA: THE FORGOTTEN RIVIERA

The navigable **Brenta Canal** links Padua with Venice in the east and gave its name to the **Riviera del Brenta.** This area is ambitiously called the "Forgotten Riviera" because of the dozens of historic summer villas built here by Venice's aristocracy and wealthy merchants; you visit by car or boat. Some of the villas are far more outstanding than others. Only one was designed by the 16th-century master architect Palladio (Villa Foscari), but many are Palladian-inspired (see "Vicenza: City of Palladio," below, for background on Palladio and how to visit his villas). The best way to see them all is on a cruise down the Brenta. Call the Brenta Canal **tourist office** for more information (ℭ **041-424973;** www. riviera-brenta.it).

You can view more than 30 villas from the boats (some only partially or at a great distance) but visit only 3. The important 18th-century **Villa Pisani** ✦✦ (© 049-502074) in Stra was commissioned by the family of a Venetian doge and is famous for its ballroom frescoes by Tiepolo and the hedge maze in its gardens. From March to October, it's open Tuesday to Sunday 9am to 7pm; October to March, it's open Tuesday to Sunday 9am to 4pm. Admission is 5€ ($5.75) for the villa and 2.50€ ($2.85) for just the park and gardens. It's free for seniors over 60 and children under 18.

The other two biggies are in Mira. Fair warning: Both keep erratic hours. The 18th-century **Barchessa Valmarana** ✦✦ (© 041-4266387 or 041-5609350) is dramatically set amid weeping willows, open Tuesday through Sunday from April to October 9:30am to noon and 2:30 to 6pm. Admission is 6€ ($6.90; free for those under 14). Tours leave every half-hour 9:30 to 11:30am and 2:30 to 5:30pm. (Note that sometimes they decide to open Sun only, and many years, Nov–Mar, you can visit only as part of a large group, such as with the cruises detailed below.) The **Villa Foscari** (aka **Villa Malcontenta**, "The Unhappy Woman"; © 014-5470012 May–Oct, or 041-5203966 Nov–Apr; www.lamalcontenta.com) is one of Palladio's finest examples. It's open from May to October Tuesday and Saturday from 9am to noon, and other days by appointment. Requisite 7€ ($8.05) guided tours require advance reservation.

The most popular **Brenta cruise** is **Il Burchiello**, run by Siamic Express, Via Trieste 42 (© 049-8206910; fax 049-8206923; www.ilburchiello.it). It can be disorganized, however. (In the past, they have lost reservations, changed hours without advising clients, and sometimes forgotten passengers at stops along the way—yes, I speak from experience. However, new management installed just after I took my latest trip with them may have cleared all that up by now.) A similar outfit, with which I have no experience, is **I Batelli del Brenta,** Via Porciglia 34 (© 049-8760233; fax 049-8763410; www.antoniana.it—click on the cartoonish map of the canal).

For more information on plying the rivers, canals, and other watery byways of the region, check out the local rivercraft consortium's website at **www.padovanavigazione.it.**

Il Burchiello leaves Padua at 9am Wednesday, Friday, and Sunday and takes you by bus from their office in Padua (on public bus terminus Piazzale Boschetti just northeast of the Ermetani) to the first stop, Stra and its Villa Pisani. After a tour of the villa, you board the boat, stop at the other two big villas and once for lunch, and arrive in Venice at 6:20pm. If you're doing the Brenta in the other direction, they leave from Venice's Pietà dock on Riva degli Schiavoni at 9am Tuesday, Thursday, and Saturday, arriving in Padova at 6:40pm. I Batelli del Brenta embarks in Padova from the Scalinata del Portello at 8:30am Saturday and Sunday, arriving in Venice at 7:30pm; from Venice's Riva degli Schiavoni dock in front of Caserma Cornolid, they leave Saturday at 8:50am, finishing in Padova at 7:30pm.

Both charge 62€ ($71) for adults and 36€ ($41) for ages 6 to 17 for the trip, which includes admission to the Villa Malcontenta/Foscari and the Villa Widmann, but not the Villa Pisani (see above). The optional seafood lunch is another 24€ ($28). In summer, Il Burchiello may offer a reduced rate. The return trip is not included, so either catch one of the cheap, frequent trains back or ask about taking your luggage on board so that you can simply continue your trip from the end point.

If you want to **do the tour yourself,** the largest concentration of country villas can be found between Stra and Mira. The secondary road S11 runs alongside some of the canal; at certain points it departs from the canal but remains the best of any extant roadways for viewing the villas. Don't try this without wheels: Erratic public bus connections make this tour close to impossible if you don't have a car. Still, a car tour requires some planning, as visiting hours and days differ from villa to villa and season to season. See the tourist office about a map.

2 Vicenza: City of Palladio

32km (20 miles) W of Padua, 74km (46 miles) W of Venice, 51km (32 miles) E of Verona, 204km (126 miles) E of Milan

Vicenza pays heartfelt homage to Andrea di Pietro della Gondola (born in Padua in 1508, died in Maser in 1580). He came to Vicenza at age 16 and lived out his life and dreams here under the name Palladio at a time when Vicenza was under the sway of Venice's still-powerful Republic. Although not highly innovative, he was the most important architect of the High Renaissance, one whose living monuments inspired and influenced architecture in the Western world over the centuries to this very day. Vicenza and its surroundings are a mecca for the architecture lover, a living museum of Palladian and Palladian-inspired architectural monuments and consequently designated a protected UNESCO World Heritage Site in 1994. Even if you've never heard of Palladio, you'll appreciate an evening stroll through the town's illuminated piazzas and along boutique-lined streets—and you may just become a rookie architecture buff: A day in Vicenza is worth a semester back in school.

Today Vicenza is one of the wealthiest cities in Italy, thanks in part to the burgeoning local computer-component industry (Federico Faggin, inventor of the silicon chip, was born here). It is also the traditional center of the country's gold-manufacturing industry (one-third of Italy's gold is made here, and each year three prestigious international gold fairs make finding a hotel in these parts impossible) and one of Europe's largest producers of textiles. The average Vicentino is well off, and it shows; join the entire town for the daily *passeggiata* and pick up on the palpable attitude.

ESSENTIALS

GETTING THERE   By Train   The train station is in Piazza Stazione, also called Campo Marzio (© **0444-325046;** www.ftv.vi.it for station or www.trenitalia.com for tickets), at the southern end of Viale Roma. Frequent service (two to three per hour) connects Vicenza with Venice (52–67 min.; 3.80€–8.90€/$4.35–$10), Padua (20 min.; 2.45€–4.45€/$2.80–$5.10), and Verona (30 min.; 3.35€–8.85€/$3.85–$10).

By Bus   The FTV bus station (© **0444-223115** or 0444-223111; www.ftv.vi.it) is on Viale Milano, just to the west (left) of the train station. Buses leave frequently for all the major cities in the Veneto and to Milano; prices are comparable to those for train travel.

By Car   Vicenza is on the A4 autostrada that links Venice to the east with Milano to the west. Coming from Venice (about 1 hr.), you'll bypass Padua before arriving in Vicenza.

VISITOR INFORMATION   The tourist information office is at Piazza Matteotti 12 (© **0444-320854;** fax 0444-327072; www.ascom.vi.it/aptvicenza or www.comune.vicenza.it), next to the Teatro Olimpico. The office is open daily from 9am to 1pm and 2 to 6pm. From mid-October to mid-March, closing time is 5:30pm. During summer, an office at the train station is open Monday through Saturday from 9am to 2pm and Sunday from 1 to 6pm. A third office (© **0444-544122;** fax 0444-325001) is in Piazza dei Signori, near the basilica. It's open daily 9am to 1pm and 2 to 6pm.

FESTIVALS The well-established summertime series of **Concerti in Villa** ⋒ (© **0444-399104**) takes place from the last week of June to the last week of July. A few concerts are held outdoors at Vicenza's famed Villa la Rotonda; for others you will need a car. The tourist office will have the schedule and info on seat availability. Tickets usually cost around 15€ to 20€ ($17–$23). The stage of the delightful **Teatro Olimpico** (© 044-302425 or 0444-222154; www.olimpico. vicenza.it) now hosts shows again from September to October, mainly classical plays (this year was the *Oedipus* cycle) or Shakespeare (*Henry V* and *Hamlet* are sort of strange in Italian). Tickets start at 10€ ($12).

EXPLORING THE PALLADIAN HERITAGE

Vicenza's primary sights are now all grouped onto a cumulative admission ticket called the **Card Musei.** It's good for 3 days; includes admission to the Teatro Olimpico, Museo Civico, and Museo Naturalistico Archeologico; and costs 7€ ($8.05) for adults and 4€ ($4.60) for students. Another, more inclusive, Card Musei adds the Museo del Risorgimento e della Resistenza and costs 8€ ($9.20) for adults and 4.50€ ($5.15) for students. Children under 14 get into these museums for free.

PIAZZA DEI SIGNORI

South of Corso Palladio on the site of the ancient Roman Forum and still the town hub, this central square should be your first introduction to the city and Palladio, its local boy wonder.

The magnificent, bigger-than-life **Basilica Palladiana** ⋒⋒ (© **0444-323681;** www.basilicapalladiana.it) is not a church at all and was only partially designed by Palladio. Beneath it stood a Gothic-style Palazzo della Ragione (Law Courts and Assembly Hall) that Palladio was commissioned to convert to a High Renaissance style befitting a flourishing late-16th-century city under Venice's benevolent patronage. It was his first public work and secured his favor and reputation with the local authorities. He created two superimposed galleries, the lower with Doric pillars, the upper with Ionic. The roof was destroyed by World War II bombing but has since been rebuilt in its original style. The Basilica is open from April to September Tuesday through Saturday from 9:30am to 12:30pm and 2:15 to 5pm, and Sunday from 9am to 12:30pm and 2 to 7pm. Off season, it's closed Sunday afternoon; admission is free (although a small fee may be charged during special exhibitions).

The towering 12th-century **Torre Bissara** (or Torre di Piazza) bell tower belonged to the original church and stands near two columns at the piazza's east end (the Piazza Blade), one topped by the winged lion of Venice's Serene Republic, the other by the *Redentore* (Redeemer). Of note elsewhere in the piazza are the **Loggia del Capitaniato** (1570), begun but never finished according to plans by Palladio except for the four massive redbrick columns (on the north side of the piazza alongside the well-known Gran Caffè Garibaldi). Behind the Basilica (to the south) is the **Piazza delle Erbe** ⋒, site of the daily produce market.

CORSO ANDREA PALLADIO

This is Vicenza's main street, and what a grand one it is, lined with the magnificent palazzi of Palladio and his students (and their students who, centuries later, were still influenced by the mastery of Palladio's work), today converted into cafes, swank shops, and imposing banks. The first one of note, starting from its southwest cap near the Piazza Castello, is the **Piazza Valamarana** at no. 16, begun by Palladio in 1566. On the right (behind which stands the Piazza dei Signori and the Basilica Palladiana) is the **Palazzo del Comunale**, the Town Hall built in 1592 by Scamozzi (1552–1616), a native of Vicenza and Palladio's protégé and star pupil. This is said to be Scamozzi's greatest work.

From the Corso Palladio and heading northeast, take a left onto the **Contrà Porti**, the second most important street for its Palladian and Gothic palazzi. The two designed by Palladio are the **Palazzo Barbarano Porto**, at no. 11, and (opposite) **Palazzo Thiene**, at no. 12 (now the headquarters of a bank). Gothic palazzi of particular note can be found at nos. 6 to 10, 14, 16, 17, and 19. Parallel, on Corso Fogazzaro, look for no. 16, **Palazzo Valmarana**, perhaps the most eccentric of Palladio's works.

Returning to Corso Palladio, look for no. 145/147, the pre-Palladian **Ca d'Oro (Golden Palace),** named for the gold leaf used in the frescoes that once covered its facade. It was bombed in 1944 and rebuilt in 1950. The simple 16th-century palazzo at no. 163 was Palladio's home.

Before reaching the Piazza Matteotti and the end of the Corso Palladio, you'll see signs for the **Church of Santa Corona** 𝕽, set back on the left on the Via Santa Corona 2 (open daily 8:30am–noon and 2:30–6pm). An unremarkable 13th-century Gothic church, it shelters two masterpieces (and Vicenza's most important church paintings) that make this worth a visit: Giovanni Bellini's *Baptism of Christ* (fifth altar on the left) and Veronese's *Adoration of the Magi* (third chapel on the right). This is Vicenza's most interesting church, far more so than the cavernous Duomo southwest of the Piazza dei Signori, but worth seeking out only if you've got the extra time. At the end of the Corso Palladio at its northeastern end is Palladio's world-renowned Teatro Olimpico and, across the street, the Museo Civico in the Palazzo Chiericati.

Teatro Olimpico & Museo Civico 𝕽𝕽𝕽   The splendid **Teatro Olimpico** was

Palladio's greatest urban work and one of his last. He began the project in 1580, the year of his death at the age of 72; it would be completed 5 years later by his student Vicenzo Scamozzi. It was the first covered theater in Europe, inspired by the theaters of antiquity. The seating area, in the shape of a half-moon as in the old arenas, seats 1,000. The stage seems profoundly deeper than its actual 4m (13 ft.), thanks to the permanent stage "curtain" and Scamozzi's clever use of *trompe l'oeil* added after Palladio's death. The stage scene represents the ancient streets of Thebes, while the faux clouds and sky covering the dome further the impression of being in an outdoor Roman amphitheater. Drama, music, and dance performances are still held here year-round; check with the tourist office.

Across the Piazza Matteotti is another Palladian opus, the **Palazzo Chiericati,** which houses the **Museo Civico (Municipal Museum).** Looking more like one of the country villas for which Palladio was equally famous, this major work is considered one of his finest and is visited as much for its two-tiered, statue-topped facade as for the collection of Venetian paintings it houses on the first floor. Venetian masters you'll recognize include Tiepolo, Tintoretto, and Veronese, while the lesser known include works from the Vicenzan (founded by Bartolomeo Montagna) and Bassano schools of painting.

Piazza Matteotti (at Corso Palladio). ℰ **0444-222101** or 0444-222154. www.olimpico.vicenza.it. Admission (to Teatro, Museo Civico, Museo Archeologico) 7€ ($8.05). Sept–June Tues–Sun 9am–5pm; July–Aug Tues–Sun 9am–6pm. Bus: 1, 2, 5, 7.

VILLAS & A BASILICA NEARBY

To reach the two important villas in the immediate environs of Vicenza, southeast of the train station, you can walk, bike, or take the no. 8 bus. First stop by the tourist office for a map and check on visiting hours, which tend to change from year to year. The following two villas are generally open from mid-March to early November.

The **Villa Rotonda** 𝒜𝒜𝒜 (© 0444-321793; fax 0444-8791380), alternatively referred to as Villa Capra Valmarana after its owners, is considered one of the most perfect buildings ever constructed and has been added to the World Heritage List by UNESCO. It is a particularly important must-do excursion for students and lovers of architecture. Most authorities refer to it as Palladio's finest. Obviously inspired by ancient Greek and Roman designs, Palladio began this perfectly proportioned square building topped by a dome in 1567; it was completed by Scamozzi after Palladio's death, between 1580 and 1592. It is worth a visit if only to view it from the outside (in fact, you can really see much of it from the gate). Admission for outside viewing is 3€ ($3.45); admission for visits to the lavishly decorated interior is 6€ ($6.90). The grounds are open from March 15 to November 4 Tuesday through Sunday from 10am to noon and 3 to 6pm; the interior is open only Wednesday and Saturday during the same hours.

From here it is only a 10-minute walk to the **Villa Valmarana** 𝒜𝒜 (© 0444-543976), also called *ai Nani* (dwarves) after the statues that line the garden wall. Built in the 17th century by Mattoni, an admirer and follower of Palladio, it is an almost commonplace villa whose reason to visit is an interior covered with remarkable 18th-century frescoes by Giambattista Tiepolo and his son Giandomenico. Admission is 6€ ($6.90); open hours are complicated. The villa is open mornings as follows: from March 15 to November 5 Wednesday, Thursday, Saturday, and Sunday from 10am to noon. It's open afternoons Tuesday through Sunday as follows: from March 15 to April from 2:30 to 5:30pm, May through September from 3 to 6pm, and from October to November 5 from 2 to 5pm. (Note that, at the whim of the owners, you can sometimes visit outside regular hours; they prefer doing so only for groups of 20 or more, but in my experience, they'll let you in if you happen by—though admission may cost a few euro more.)

Also in this area is the Basilica or **Santuario di Monte Berico** 𝒜 (© 0444-320999), built in 1668 by a Bolognese architect. If you've already visited the Villa Rotonda, you will understand where he got his inspiration. The interior's most important work is in a chapel to the right of the main altar, a *Lamentation* by Bortolomeo Montagna (1500), founder of the local school of painting and one of the Veneto's most famous. The terrace in front of the church affords beautiful views of Vicenza, the Monti Berici, and the distinct outline of the nearby Alps. The basilica is open in summer months Monday through Saturday from 6am to 12:30pm and 2:30 to 7:30pm, and Sunday from 6am to 8pm; it closes earlier in winter months. Admission is free.

ACCOMMODATIONS YOU CAN AFFORD

Unlike Padua, which gets the overflow when Venice is full, or the tourism-magnet Verona, Vicenza can be very quiet in high season, August, or winter months when trade fairs are not in town; some hotels close without notice for a few weeks if the demand is low. Make sure you call in advance because the city's number of hotels is limited.

Due Mori 𝒜   A full renovation in 1996 has resulted in this fresh, bright, inexpensive hotel choice. Add that to the Due Mori's family-run hotel's history as the oldest in Vicenza and its convenient location on a quiet side street just west of the sprawling Piazza dei Signori, and you have the deservedly most popular spot in town for the budget-minded. All to say: Book early. In a modernized shell of a centuries-old palazzo, tasteful and authentic 19th-century pieces distinguish otherwise plain rooms whose amenities are kept at a minimum, but so are the prices. This is as good as it gets in the very center of Palladio's home town.

Via Do Rode 26 (1 block west of Piazza dei Signori), 36100 Vicenza. ℂ **0444-321886.** Fax 0444-326127. www.hotelduemori.com. 30 units, 27 with bathroom. 42€ ($48) single with bathroom; 50€ ($58) double without bathroom, 75€ ($86) double with bathroom; add 9€ ($10) for a 3rd bed. Breakfast 5€ ($5.75). MC, V. **Amenities:** Bar. *In room:* Dataport, hair dryer (ask at desk).

Hotel Cristina Located west of the Piazza Castello and the green Giardino Salvi, this recently refurbished hotel is within easy walking distance of the historic center's principal sites. It's a good choice for those with wheels and a few extra dollars. A contemporary approach with occasional exposed beams and marble and parquet flooring results in handsome, well-maintained lodging and makes this one of Vicenza's preferred three-star properties. An internal courtyard provides welcome parking space. Guests have access to bicycles for touring the traffic-free center of town, as well as the nearby villas just southeast of the train station. After all that cycling, coast back to the hotel and into its recently added Finnish sauna.

Corso San Felice 32 (west of Salvi Gardens), 36100 Vicenza. ℂ **0444-323751.** Fax 0444-543656. www.paginegialle.it/hotelcristinavicenza. 33 units. 80€–92€ ($92–$106) single; 100€–120€ ($115–$138) double. Rates include buffet breakfast. Discounts possible in low season. AE, DC, MC, V. Parking 8€ ($9). **Amenities:** Bar; sauna; free bikes; concierge; tour desk; room service; laundry service. *In room:* A/C, TV, dataport, minibar, hair dryer, safe.

Palladio *Value* A popular two-star choice spread over three floors (no elevator), the Palladio is the friendliest of the city's few hotels worth mentioning. Just a 2-minute walk from the Piazza dei Signori (and equidistant from the Piazza Matteotti and the Teatro Olimpico), this family-run hotel offers small, no-frills but efficient rooms in a quiet neighborhood. The beds may be cots, but they are underpinned by a board to ensure a good night's sleep. Most rooms on the back and along a side courtyard have balconies; top floor no. 32 even has a small terrace.

Via Oratorio dei Servi 25 (east of the Piazza dei Signori), 36100 Vicenza ℂ **0444-321072.** Fax 0444-547328. hotelpalladio@libero.it. 24 units, 15 with bathroom. 28€–45€ ($32–$52) single without bathroom, 45€–70€ ($52–$81) single with bathroom; 52€–78€ ($60–$90) double without bathroom, 60€–90€ ($69–$104) double with bathroom. Rates include breakfast. AE, DC, MC, V. Bus from station: 1, 5, 7, 2. **Amenities:** Bar; laundry service. *In room:* TV, dataport, hair dryer.

GREAT DEALS ON DINING

Antica Casa della Malvasia *Ⓕ* VICENTINO This ever-lively, taverna-like osteria sits on a quiet, characteristic side street that links the principal Corso Palladio with the Piazza dei Signori. Service is with a smile and informal, the cooking homemade and regional. The food is reliably good, but it's just an excuse to accompany the selection of wines (80), whiskies (100), grappas (150), and teas (more than 150). No wonder this place always buzzes. Even if you don't eat here, stop in for a late-night toddy, Vicentino style. It's a favorite spot for locals and visitors alike, and there's often live music on Tuesday and Thursday evenings.

Contrà delle Morette 5 (off Corso Palladio). ℂ **0444-543704.** Reservations suggested during high season and on weekends. Primi 4.70€–6€ ($5.40–$6.90); secondi 6.50€–11€ ($7.45–$13) at lunch and 6€–10€ ($6.90–$12) at dinner. AE, DC, MC, V. Tues–Sun noon–2:30pm and 7pm–midnight (sometimes later). Closed Aug.

Gran Caffè Garibaldi CAFE   If it's a lovely day, set up camp here in the shade of a table with an umbrella that overlooks Vicenza's grand piazza. The most historically significant cafe in Palladio's city is as stage-set impressive inside as you would imagine. The upstairs restaurant is too expensive for what it offers, but the outside terrace gives you the chance to sit and gaze upon the wonders of the whale-size Basilica, yet another Palladian masterpiece. A chef's salad like Insalata Garibaldi makes a great lunch, as do any of the sandwiches and panini. Or just nurse a cappuccino or aperitivo for the same euros at your outside table; prices are slightly less at the bar, but go for the front-row seats and the theater-in-the-round offered by the city's beautiful Piazza dei Signori.

Piazza dei Signori 5. ℂ **0444-544147.** Panini from 3€ ($3.45), salads from 6€ ($6.90). MC, V. Thurs–Tues 8am–1am.

Righetti *Value* VICENTINO/ITALIAN   For a self-service operation, this place is a triple surprise: The diners are all local (and loyal); the food is reliably good—of the home-cooked generous portions kind; and indoors is rustic, welcoming, and pleasant, considering its inexpensive profile. But it's the opportunity to sit outdoors in the quiet, traffic-free Piazza Duomo that's the biggest draw. First stake out a table by setting your place, then order your food at the counter (prepared fresh on the spot), and when you're finished eating, just tell the cashier what you had and he'll add up the bill. There are three or four first courses to choose from (Tues and Fri are risotto days) and as many entrees. Evenings offer the option of grilled meats (which makes eating indoors in the cold winter months more enjoyable), though this is the perfect relaxed place to revel in a simple lunch of pasta and a side vegetable.

Piazza Duomo 3/4. ℂ **0444-543135.** Primi 2.60€–5.20€ ($3–$6); secondi 4.15€–8.30€ ($4.75–$9.55). No credit cards. Mon–Fri noon–3pm and 7–10:30pm. Closed first 3 weeks of Aug.

WORTH A SPLURGE

Trattoria Tre Visi *🐦🐦* VICENTINO/ITALIAN   Operating since the early 1600s around the corner until a 1997 change of address, this Vicentino institution is now located on this important palazzo-studded street in a setting somewhat less dramatic than the previous 15th-century palazzo (though here there is an alfresco courtyard). The menu has stayed unchanged, however, and this is good: Ignore items that concede to foreign requests and concentrate on the regional dishes they know how to prepare best. Almost all the pasta is made fresh daily, including the house specialty, *bigoli con anitra,* a fat, spaghetti-like pasta served with duck ragout. The region's signature dish, *baccalà alla vicentina* (a poor man's dish that, when prepared properly, is delicious), is a tender salt codfish simmered in a stew of onions, herbs, anchovies, garlic, and parmigiano for 8 hours before arriving at your table in perfection. Ask your kind waiter for help in selecting from Veneto's wide spectrum of very fine wines: It will enhance your bill but also the memories you'll bring home.

Corso Palladio 25 (near Piazza Castello). ℂ **0444-324868.** www.trevisi.vicenza.com. Reservations suggested. Primi 6€–10€ ($6.90–$12); secondi 12€–16€ ($14–$18). AE, DC, MC, V. Tues–Sat 12:30–2:30pm and 7:30–10pm; Sun 12:30–2:30pm.

DAY TRIPS FROM VICENZA

In addition to visiting the two villas located in the immediate outskirts of Vicenza, a tour of the dozens of country **ville venete** farther afield is the most compelling outing from Vicenza. Check at the tourist office for availability of organized tours, something that has been on again and, more frequently, off again for the last few years. You most probably will have to do it yourself, which means having access to wheels. The tourist office will arm you with reams of information to help you sort out the problem of erratic visiting hours (many of the villas are still privately owned and inhabited, and not all can be toured; others permit visits to the grounds but not the interiors). The tourist office also has maps and a host of varied itineraries outlining the most important villas; many are UNESCO protected sites. Public transportation to these villas is close to nonexistent. If you do have access to a car, ask about the summer concert series in June and July, Concerti in Villa (see "Festivals," earlier in this section), which has drawn first-class talent in the classical music world.

Bassano del Grappa, about 37km (23 miles) north of Vicenza, can be incorporated into a tour of the villas. Renowned for its centuries-old production of ceramics and of grappa, it is a picturesque town located on the Brenta River. A covered wooden bridge built by Palladio in 1568 is a highlight of the small *centro storico*. The facades of the city's arcaded homes are painted in the traditional manner, and small squares make this a lovely break from the art-laden larger towns discussed in this chapter. Bassano's yearly **Opera Estate Festival** takes place from early July through August, with alfresco performances of opera, concerts, and dance. For information, call the **tourist office,** Largo Corona d'Italia 35 (© **0424-524351;** fax 0424-525301). It's open Monday through Friday from 9am to 12:30pm and 2 to 5pm, and Saturday from 9am to 12:30pm. To get here from Vicenza, you can take one of two dozen daily **FTV** buses (© **0444-223115** or 0444-223111; www.ftv.vi.it) that make the 1-hour trip. Frequent buses from Padua to Bassano take half the time, making fewer stops. One-way tickets from either Vicenza or Padua cost about 3.50€ ($4).

The delightful medieval walled village of **Marostica,** about 28km (17 miles) north of Vicenza (and 7km/4⅓ miles west of Bassano), comes alive a la *Brigadoon* every other summer, in even years only. The entire town dresses up to commemorate a true centuries-old chess game between two enamored knights for the hand of Lionora. (Are you surprised? This is the region that gave us Romeo and Juliet.) The chivalric *Partita a Scacchi* is re-enacted on the main piazza with real people as the pieces, dressed in full elaborate Renaissance costume, preceded by a flag-throwing procession with everyone in town taking part. The evocative torch-lit nighttime setting is gorgeous. A few of the worst seats are usually available each day of performance, but it's best to purchase tickets months in advance. Tourist information, **Pro Marostica,** is at Piazza Castello 1 (© **0424-72127;** fax 0424-72800). Marostica's engaging **Sagra del Ciliege (Cherry Festival)** takes place in June. You can get here on one of two dozen daily buses from Vicenza (40 min.; 2.50€/$2.85). Dozens of local buses daily do the short run from Bassano to Marostica (it's only 7km/4⅓ miles away). By car, head west on S248.

3 Verona: Home to Juliet & Her Romeo

114km (71 miles) W of Venice, 80km (50 miles) W of Padua, 61km (38 miles) W of Vicenza, 157km (97 miles) E of Milan

Suspend all disbelief regarding the real-life existence of Romeo and Juliet, and your stay in **Verona** will be magical. After Venice, this is the Veneto's most visited city. Verona reached a cultural and artistic peak during the 13th and 14th centuries under the powerful, often cruel, and sometimes quirky Della Scala, or Scaligeri, dynasty that took up rule in the late 1200s. In 1405, it surrendered to Venice, which remained in charge until the invasion of Napoleon in 1797.

During the time of Venetian rule, Verona became a prestigious urban capital and controlled much of the Veneto and as far south as Tuscany. You'll see the emblem of the *scala* (ladder) around town, heraldic symbol of the Scaligeri dynasty. The city retains its locked-in-time character that recalls its medieval and Renaissance heyday, and the magnificent medieval palazzi, towers, churches, and stagelike piazzas you see today are picture-perfect testimony to its centuries-old influence and wealth.

And what about Romeo and Juliet? Did they really exist? Originally a Sienese legend, first put into novella form in 1476, this story was subsequently retold in 1524 by Veneto-born Luigi da Porto. He chose Verona in the years 1302 to 1304, during the reign of the Scaligeri, and renamed the young couple Romeo and Giulietta. The popular *storia d'amore* was translated into English and became the source of and inspiration for Shakespeare's tale (no one ever said it was original, though the 1998 film *Shakespeare in Love,* a highly enjoyable fictionalized tale, will have you believing it's the Bard's own). Translated into dozens of languages and performed around the world (just look at the number of Asian and Eastern European tourists who flock to Juliet's House), this is a tale of pure love in the tempestuous times of a medieval city whose streets were stained with the blood of feuding families. It's universal and timeless in its content—and no other city setting is so authentically stagelike (though Zeffirelli chose to film his classic 1968 interpretation in the tiny Tuscan town of Pienza, south of Siena—see chapter 5).

Remarkably, visitors spend precious little time in this beautiful medieval city. Statistics clock most tourists stopping for a mere overnight stay (or less). I recommend a stay of at least 2 nights. While it offers a short list of attractions, Verona is a handsome town to take in and enjoy at a leisurely pace.

ESSENTIALS

GETTING THERE   By Train   Verona is easily accessed on the west-east Milan-Venice line as well as the north-south Brennero-Rome line. At least 30 trains (www.trenitalia.com) daily run west from **Venice** (regional: 2 hr., 6€/$6.90; high speed: 87 min., 13€/$15). Even more arrive from Milan (regional: 2 hr., 6.80€/$7.80; high speed: 85 min., 12€/$13).

Trains also connect Verona with Vicenza (30–50 min., 3.35€/$3.85; high speed: 30 min., 8.85€/$10), Padua (regional: 55 min., 4.55€/$5.25; high speed: 50 min., 9.90€/$11), and Bologna (regional: 90 min. to 2 hr. 40 min., 5.75€/$6.60; high speed: 80 min., 14€/$17).

The Stazione Porta Nuova **train station** (✆ 045-590688) is located rather far south of the Piazza Brà (and Arena) area and is serviced by at least half a dozen local bus lines. The bus network in the historic center is limited, so if you have luggage, you'll probably want a taxi to get to your hotel. To get downtown from the train station, walk straight out to the bus island marked MARCIAPIEDE F (parallel to the station) to catch minibus nos. 72 or 73 (.95€/$1.10 tickets at the newsstand in the station or the AMT booth on Marciapiede A). Get off on Via Stella at Via Cappello for the center. Alternatively, over half the buses from the station stop at Piazza Brà, so just peruse the posted route signs.

By Bus   The bus station, **AMT** (Azienda Mobilità Trasporti; ✆ 045-8871111; www.amt.it), is at Piazza XXV Aprile directly across from the train station. Buses leave from here for all regional destinations, including Largo di Garda (see chapter 9). Although there is bus service to Vicenza, Padua, and Venice (only the summertime departures for Venice are direct; in other months, there's a change), it is easier and cheaper to travel by train.

By Car   The A4 autostrada links Venice and Milan; the exit for downtown Verona is Verona Sud. Coming from the north or south, use the A22 autostrada, taking exit Verona Nord.

VISITOR INFORMATION   A **central tourist office** is at Piazza Chiesa 34 (©/fax **045-7050088;** www.tourism.verona.it or www.verona-apt.net), where summer hours are Monday to Saturday 9am to 8pm, and Sunday 10am to 1pm and 4 to 7pm (winter hours are usually shorter, and it's closed Sun). Another office is at Via degli Alpini 9, adjacent to the Arena off Piazza Brà (© **045-8068680;** fax 045-8010682), open Monday through Saturday from 9am to 6pm. A **small office** at the train station (© **045-8000861**) is open Tuesday through Saturday from 8am to 7:30pm, and Sunday and Monday from 10am to 4pm.

FESTIVALS & MARKETS   The Teatro Romano is known for its *Festival Shakespeariano* (**Shakespeare Festival**) ⭐ from mid-June to the beginning of September, which celebrated its 50th anniversary in 1998 with a week of English-language performances by the Royal Shakespeare Company. Festival performances begin in late May and June with jazz concerts. In July and August, there are a number of ballets (such as Prokofiev's *Romeo and Juliet*) and modern dance performances. Check for a schedule (© **045-8077500** or 045-8066485, or try the tourist office; www.estateteatraleveronese.it). Last-minute tickets go

---

Will the Fat Lady Sing?

The well-known **opera season** ⭐⭐⭐ begins in late June and extends through August in **Verona's Arena,** the ancient amphitheater, begun in 1913 with a staging of *Aïda* to commemorate the 100th anniversary of Verdi's birth. *Aïda* in all of its extravagant glory has been performed yearly ever since; when I last attended, in 2000, they incorporated modern dance and minimalist scenery to great effect. Expect to see other Verdi works, such as *Un Ballo in Maschera, Nabucco, La Traviata,* and *Rigoletto.*

Those seated on the least expensive, unreserved stone steps costing 20€ ($22) Friday and Saturday, 22€ ($25) otherwise, enjoy fresh air, excellent acoustics, and a view over the Arena's top to the city and surrounding hills beyond. The rub is that Jose Carreras will appear to be only 1 inch high. Numbered seats below cost from 70€ to 154€ ($81–$177). Try, if possible, to book ahead; otherwise, you'll have to tough it out by lining up at 4 or 5pm for the 6pm opening of the gates for unreserved seating (and the show doesn't start until 9pm!).

The **box office** is located on Via Dietro Anfiteatro 6b. Credit card purchase is accepted by phone or online (© 045-8005151; fax 045-8013287; www.arena.it). You pick up tickets the night of the performance. If you hope to find tickets upon arrival, remember that *Aïda* is everyone's most requested performance; weekend performances are usually sold out. As a last-minute resort, be nice to your hotel manager or concierge—everyone has a connection, or a relative with a connection. And even on the most coveted nights (weekend performances by top names), scalpers abound.

on sale at the Teatro Romano box office on Piazza Brà at 8:15pm (most performances start at 9pm). Tickets range from 13€ to 26€ ($15–$30), plus booking charges.

During Verona's summer-long **festival of the arts,** see what's happening in the Piazza dei Signori, Where frequent free concerts (jazz, tango, classical) keep everyone out until the wee hours. And for something truly unique, check out *Sognando Shakespeare* **(Dreaming Shakespeare):** Follow this *teatro itinerante* (traveling theater) of young, talented actors in costume as they wander about the medieval corners of Verona from site to site, reciting *Romeo e Giulietta* (in Italian only) in situ, as Shakespeare would have loved it to be. For information, contact the tourist office. For information about performances July through September, call the tourist office at 🕿 **045-8000065.**

Other important events are the famous 4-day **horse fair, Fieracavalli,** in early November, and the important 5-day **VinItaly wine fair** (that overlaps with the equally important **Olive Oil Fair**) mid-April. (Verona's schedule of fairs is long and varied; while not many are of interest to those outside the trades involved, their frequency can create problems for tourists in regard to hotel availability.) The Piazza San Zeno hosts a traveling **antiques market** the third Saturday of every month; come early.

GUIDED TOURS   An air-conditioned *bus turistîco* departs thrice daily (10:30am, noon, and 3:30pm) for a 1½-hour *Giro Turistico* tour of the city's historical center every day except Monday from June 1 to September 28. The cost is 15€ ($17) for a recorded spiel in four languages, and you can buy your ticket on the bus. The bus leaves from the Gran Guardia in the Piazza Brà, across from Palazzo Barbieri. The Saturday afternoon tour leaves at 3:30pm with a real live tour guide that ups the cost to 20€ ($23).

SIGHTS TO SEE

The city lies alongside the banks of the S-shape Adige River. The impressive ancient Roman amphitheater, the **Arena,** sits at the southern end of the city's hub in cafe-ringed **Piazza Brà.** The piazza is linked by the popular pedestrian **Via Mazzini** to **Piazza delle Erbe** and its adjacent **Piazza dei Signori.** The grid of pedestrian-only streets in between is lined with handsome shops and cafes, and makes up the principal strolling and window-shopping destination in town.

On the first Sunday of any month, entry is free for the following sites: Castelvecchio Museum, the Roman Theater, and Juliet's Tomb.

THE TOP ATTRACTIONS

Arena di Verona 🎭🎭🎭   The best-preserved Roman amphitheater in the world and the best known in Italy after Rome's Colosseum, the elliptical Arena was built in a slightly pinkish marble around the year A.D. 100 and stands in the very middle of town, with the Piazza Brà on its southern flank. Built to accommodate more than 20,000 people (outdone by Rome's contender that could seat more than twice that), it is in remarkable shape today (despite a 12th-c. earthquake that left only four arches of the outer ring standing), beloved testimony to the pride and wealth of Verona and its populace.

Its acoustics (astoundingly good for an open-air venue) have survived the millennia and make it one of the wonders of the ancient world and one of the most fascinating venues for live performances today, conducted without microphones. If you're in town during the summer opera performances in July and August, do everything possible to procure a ticket (see "Will the Fat Lady Sing?" above) for

Verona

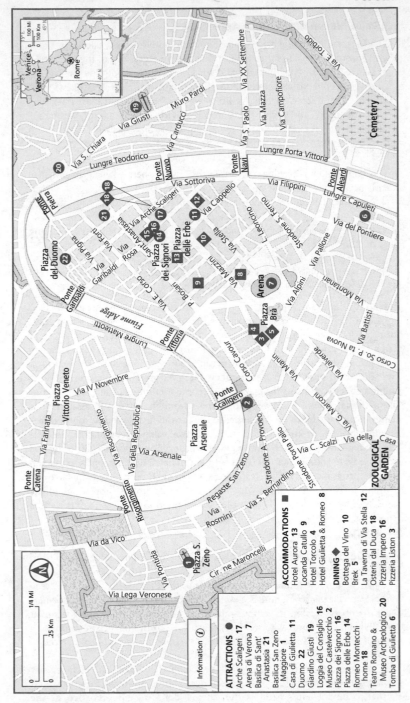

ATTRACTIONS ●
Arche Scaligeri **17**
Arena di Verona **7**
Basilica di Sant'
    Anastasia **21**
Basilica San Zeno
    Maggiore **1**
Casa di Giulietta **11**
Duomo **22**
Giardino Giusti **19**
Loggia del Consiglio **16**
Museo Castelvecchio **2**
Piazza dei Signori **16**
Piazza delle Erbe **14**
Romeo Montecchi
    home **18**
Teatro Romano &
    Museo Archeologico **20**
Tomba di Giulietta **6**

ACCOMMODATIONS ■
Hotel Aurora **13**
Locanda Catullo **9**
Hotel Torcolo **4**
Hotel Giulietta & Romeo **8**

DINING ◆
Bottega del Vino **10**
Brek **5**
La Taverna di Via Stella **12**
Osteria dal Duca **18**
Pizzeria Impero **16**
Pizzeria Liston **3**

Information ℹ

443

Value Verona by Cumulative Ticket

The **VeronaCard**, a *biglietto cumulativo* (cumulative ticket), allows you to visit several of the city's sites for just one fee. Two versions of the card are available. The 8€ ($9.20) card, valid for just 1 day, lets you ride the city's buses and enter its museums, monuments, and churches. The 12€ ($14) card offers the same attractions but gives you 3 days rather than 1 day in which to do it. You'll find the VeronaCard for sale at any of Verona's attractions or at *tabacchi* in the town center, or call ℭ 045-8077503.

---

any of the outdoor evening performances. Even opera-challenged audience members will take home the memory of a lifetime.

The cluster of outdoor cafes and trattorias/pizzerias on the western side of the Piazza Brà line a wide marble esplanade called Il Liston. They stay open long after the opera performances end, and some serious after-opera people-watching goes on here.

Piazza Brà. ℭ 045-8003204. Admission 3.10€ ($3.55) or free with VeronaCard (see "Verona by Cumulative Ticket," above). Tues–Sun 8:30am–6:30pm; Mon 1:45–7:30pm. During the July–Aug summer opera season 9am–3:30pm. Last admission 45 min. before close.

Piazza delle Erbe This bustling marketplace—the palazzi-flanked Square of the Herbs—sits on the former site of the Roman Forum where chariot races once took place. The herbs, spices, coffee beans, and bolts of silks and damasks that came through Verona after landing in Venice from faraway Cathay have given way to the fresh and aromatic produce of one of Italy's wealthiest agricultural regions—offset by the inevitable, ever-growing presence of T-shirt and french fry vendors, as the piazza has become something of a tourist trap. But the perfume of fennel and vegetables fresh from the earth still assaults your senses in the early morning, mixing with the cacophony of vendors touting their plump tomatoes, dozens of different variations of salad greens, and picture-perfect fruits that can't possibly taste as good as they look, but do. Add to this the canary lady, the farmer's son who has brought in half a dozen puppies to unload, and the furtive pickpocket who can spot a tourist at 50 paces—and you have one of Italy's loveliest little outdoor markets. A ground-zero rest stop is one of the steps leading up to the small, 14th-century fountain in the piazza's center and a Roman statue dubbed *The Virgin of Verona*.

Between Via Mazzini and Corso Porta Borsari. Open-air produce/flower market Mon–Sat 8am–7pm.

Piazza Dei Signori (Piazza Dante) To reach the Piazza dei Signori from the Piazza delle Erbe, exit under the Arco della Costa (the "Arch of the Rib"). The perfect antidote to the color and bustle of the Piazza delle Erbe, the serene and elegant Piazza dei Signori is a slightly sober square, one of Verona's innermost chambers of calm. Its center is anchored by a large 19th-century statue of the "divine poet" Dante, who found political exile from Florence in Verona as a guest of Cangrande I and his Scaligeri family. (In appreciation, Dante wrote of his patron in his poem "Paradiso.")

If you enter from the Arch, you'll be facing the **Scaligeris'** 13th-century crenellated **residence** before it was taken over by the governing Venetians. Left of that, behind Dante's back, is the **Loggia del Consiglio (Portico of the Counsel),** a 15th-century masterpiece of Venetian Renaissance style. Opposite that and facing Dante is the 12th-century Romanesque **Palazzo della Ragione,** whose courtyard and fine Gothic staircase should be visited. This piazza is Verona's finest microcosm, a balanced and refined assemblage of historical architecture. Secure an outdoor table at the square's legendary command post, the **Antico Caffè Dante,** and take it all in over a late-afternoon Campari and soda.

Piazza dei Signori, adjacent to Piazza delle Erbe.

Museo Castelvecchio 🕸🕸   A 5-minute walk west of the Arena amphitheater
on the Via Roma and nestled on the banks of the swift-flowing Adige River, the "Old Castle" is a crenellated fairy-tale pile of brick towers and turrets, protecting the bridge behind it. It was commissioned in 1354 by the Scaligeri warlord Cangrande II to serve the dual role of residential palace and military stronghold. It survived centuries of occupation by the Visconti family, the Serene Republic of Venice, and then Napoleon, only to be destroyed by the Germans during World War II bombing. Its painstaking restoration was initiated in 1958 by the acclaimed Venetian architect Carlos Scarpa, and the building reopened in 1964, now a fascinating home to some 400 works of art.

The ground-floor rooms, displaying statues and carvings of the Middle Ages, lead to alleyways, vaulted halls, multileveled floors, and stairs, all as architecturally arresting as the Venetian masterworks from the 14th to 18th centuries it offsets—notably those by Tintoretto, Tiepolo, Veronese, Bellini, and the Verona-born Pisanello—that you'll find throughout. Don't miss the large courtyard with the equestrian statue of the warlord Cangrande I (a copy can be seen at the family cemetery at the Arche Scaligeri) with a peculiar dragon's head affixed to his back (actually his armor's helmet, removed from his head and resting behind him).

A stroll across the pedestrian bridge behind the castle affords you a fine view of the castle, the **Ponte Scaligeri** (built in 1355 and also destroyed during World War II; it was reconstructed using the original materials), and the river's banks.

Corso Castelvecchio 2 (at V. Roma, on the Adige River). © 045-594734 or 045-8005817. www.comune. verona.it/Castelvecchio/cvsito. Admission 3.10€ ($3.55; 4.20€/$4.85 during special exhibitions); free 1st Sun of each month or with VeronaCard (see "Verona by Cumulative Ticket," above). Tues–Sun 8:30am–7:30pm; Mon 1:45–7:30pm. Last admission 45 min. before close.

Casa di Giulietta (Juliet's House) 🕸🕸   There is no proof that a Capuleti
(Capulet) family ever lived here (or if they did, that a young girl called Juliet ever existed), and it wasn't until 1905 that the city bought what was an abandoned, overgrown garden and decided its future. Rumor is, this was once actually a whorehouse.

So powerful is the legend of Juliet that over half a million tourists flock here every year to visit the simple courtyard and home that are considerably less affluent-looking than the sumptuous Franco Zeffirelli version you may remember (the movie was filmed in Tuscany). Myriad are those who leave behind layer upon layer of graffiti along the lines of "Laura, ti amo!," or who engage in the peculiar tradition (whose origin no one can seem to explain) of rubbing the right breast (now buffed to a bright gold) of the 20th-century bronze statue of a forever nubile Juliet.

The curious might want to fork over the entrance fee to see the spartan interior of the 13th-century home, restored in 1996. Ceramics and furniture on display are authentic of the era but did not belong to Juliet's family—if there was a Juliet at all. Stop by just before closing time, when the courtyard is relatively empty of tourists and it is easiest to imagine Romeo uttering, "But Soft! What light through yonder window breaks? It is the east, and Juliet is the sun!" No one is willing to confirm (or deny) that the balcony was added to the palazzo as recently as 1928. (Doesn't stop many a young tourist lass from posing on it, staring dreamily at the sky.)

La Tomba di Giulietta (Juliet's Tomb; ✆ **045-8000361)** is about a 15-minute walk south of here (near the Adige River on V. delle Pontiere 5). The would-be site of the star-crossed lovers' suicide is found within the graceful medieval cloisters of the Capuchin monastery of San Francesco al Corso. Diehard romantics may find this tomb with its surely posed "sarcophagus" rather more evocative than the crowded scene at Juliet's House and worth the trip. Others will find it overrated and shouldn't bother. Admission is 2.60€ ($3) for adults, 1.50€ ($1.75) for children, and free with VeronaCard (see "Verona by Cumulative Ticket," above). The adjacent church is where their secret marriage was said to have taken place. There is a small museum of frescoes (Museo degli Affreschi; ✆ **045-8000361)** adjacent.

Via Cappello 23 (southeast of Piazza delle Erbe). ✆ 45-8034303. Admission (to building only; courtyard is free) 3.10€ ($3.55) adults, 2.10€ ($2.40) students, 1€ ($1.15) ages 7–14 or free with VeronaCard (see "Verona by Cumulative Ticket," above). Tues–Sun 8:30am–7:30pm; Mon 1:30–7:30pm. Last admission 45 min. before close.

MORE ATTRACTIONS

Arche Scaligeri (Scaligeri Tombs) 𝄞   Exit the Piazza dei Signori opposite the Arch of the Rib. Immediately on your right, at the corner of Via delle Arche Scaligeri, are some of the most elaborate Gothic funerary monuments in Italy— the raised outdoor tombs of the Scaligeri family (seen behind the original decorative grillwork), powerful and often ruthless rulers of Verona. The most important are those by the peculiar names of Mastino I (founder of the dynasty, date of death unknown), Mastino II (Mastiff the Second, d. 1351), and Cansignorio (Head Dog, d. 1375). The most interesting is found over the side door of the family's private chapel Santa Maria Antica—the tomb of Cangrande I (Big Dog, d. 1329), with *cani* (dogs) holding up a *scala* (ladder), both elements that figure in the Scaligeri coat of arms. That's Cangrande I—patron of the arts and protector of Dante—and his steed you see above (the original can be seen in the Museo Castelvecchio). Recently restored, these tombs are considered one of the country's greatest medieval monuments. Entry is only to the neighboring Torre dei Lamberti; the tomb area itself is usually closed to visitors.

Around the corner on Via delle Arche Scaligeri 2 is the alleged 13th-century home of Juliet's significant other, **Romeo Monterchi** ("Montague," in Shakespearian), which incorporates the popular Osteria dal Duca (See "Great Deals on Dining," below).

Via Arche Scaligeri. ✆ 045-8032726. 2.60€ ($3) to go up the tower with an elevator, 2.10€ ($2.40) on foot. Tues–Sun 9:30am–7:30pm, Mon 1:45–7:30pm. Last admission 30 min before close.

Basilica San Zeno Maggiore 𝄞𝄞   This is one of the finest examples of Romanesque architecture in Northern Italy, built between the 9th and 12th centuries. Slightly out of the old city's hub but still easily reached by foot, San Zeno, dedicated to the city's patron saint, is Verona's most visited church. Spend a moment outside to appreciate the fine, sober facade, highlighted by the immense 12th-century **rose window,** the *Ruota della Fortuna* (Wheel of Fortune).

This pales in importance compared to the **facade** 𝄞𝄞 below—two pillars supported by marble lions and massive doors whose 48 bronze panels were sculpted from the 9th to the 11th centuries and are believed to have been some of the first castings in bronze since Roman antiquity. They are one of the city's most cherished artistic treasures and are worth the trip here even if the church is closed. Not yet as sophisticated as those that would adorn the Baptistery doors of Florence's Duomo in the centuries to come, these are like naive illustrations from a child's book and were meant to educate the illiterate masses with scenes from the Old and New Testaments and the life of San Zeno. They are complemented by the stone bas-reliefs found on either side of the doors, the 12th-century work of Niccolo who was also responsible for the Duomo's portal. The 14th-century tower on the left belonged to the former abbey, while the free-standing slender campanile on the right was begun in 1045.

The massive **interior** ⍟ is filled with 12th- to 14th-century frescoes and crowned by the nave's ceiling, designed as a wooden ship's keel. But the interior's singular highlight is the famous triptych of the *Madonna and Child Enthroned with Saints,* by Andrea Mantegna (1459), behind the main altar. Absconded by Napoleon, the beautiful centerpiece—a showcase for the Padova-born Mantegna's sophisticated sense of perspective and architectural detail—was eventually returned to Verona, although two side panels stayed behind in the Louvre and in Tours. Look in the small apse to the left of the altar for the colored marble statue of a smiling San Zeno, much loved by the local Veronesi, in an act of blessing.

Piazza San Zeno. ℂ 045-592813. www.chieseverona.it. Admission 2€ ($2.30), 1€ ($1.15) students and seniors over 65, free for children under 11 or on cumulative ticket (see "A Church Tip" below). Mar–Oct Mon–Sat 8:30am–6pm, Sun 1–6pm; Nov–Feb Tues–Sat 10am–4pm, Sun 1–5pm.

Basilica di Sant'Anastasia   Built between 1290 and 1481, this is Verona's largest church, considered the city's finest example of Gothic architecture, even though the facade remains unfinished. A lovely 14th-century campanile bell tower is adorned with frescoes and sculptures. The church's interior is typically Gothic in design, highlighted by two famous *gobbi* (hunchbacks) who support the holy-water fonts, an impressive patterned pavement, and 16 side chapels containing a number of noteworthy paintings and frescoes from the 15th to the 16th centuries.

Most important is Verona-born Pisanello's *St. George Freeing the Princess of Trebisonda* (1433), after several relocations now back in its original spot way up above the terra cotta–filled Cappella Pellegrini in the right transept. It is considered one of his best paintings and is of the armed-knight-and-damsel-in-distress genre—with the large white rump of St. George's steed as one of its focal points. Also worth scouting out are the earlier 14th-century frescoes by the Giotto-inspired Altichiero in the Cavalli Chapel next door.

Piazza Anastasia at Corso Anastasia. ℂ 045-592813. www.chieseverona.it. Admission 2€ ($2.30), 1€ ($1.15) students and seniors over 65, free for children under 11 or on cumulative ticket (see "A Church Tip" below). Mar–Oct Mon–Sat 9am–6pm, Sun 1–6pm; Nov–Feb Tues–Sat 10am–4pm, Sun 1–5pm.

Teatro Romano (Roman Theater) and the Museo Archeologico (Archaeological Museum) ⍟   The oldest extant Roman monument in Verona dates

---

⸤ *Tips* A Church Tip

Verona's churches have banded together as the **Associazione Chiese Vive** (ℂ **045-592813**; www.chieseverona.it). Admission to any one church is 2€ ($2.30) or free for children under 11. Or you can get a cumulative ticket for 5€ ($5.75) for adults and 4€ ($4.60) for students and those over 65, granting admission to Sant'Anastasia, San Zeno, San Lorenzo, San Fermo, and the Duomo complex (the last only noon–4pm on this cumulative ticket).

from the time of Augustus, when the Arena was built and Verona was a strong Roman outpost at the crossroads of the empire's ancient north/south, east/west highways. There is something almost surreal about attending an open-air performance of Shakespeare's *Two Gentlemen of Verona* or *Romeo and Juliet* here— even if you can't understand a word. (See "Festivals & Markets," earlier in this section.) Classical concerts and ballet and jazz performances are also given here, with evocative views of the city beyond. A small **Archaeological Museum** housed above in a lovely old monastery is included in the admission ticket.

Via Rigaste Redentore (over the Ponte Pietra bridge behind the Duomo, on the north banks of the river Adige). ℂ 045-8000360. Admission 2.60€ ($3), 1€ ($1.15) ages 7–14; free 1st Sun of each month or free with VeronaCard (see "Verona by Cumulative Ticket," above). Tues–Sun 8:30am–7:30pm; Mon 1:30–7:30pm. Bus: 23, 31.

Duomo ⚜ Begun in the 12th century and not finished until the 17th, the city's main church still boasts its original main doors and portal, magnificently covered with low reliefs in the Lombard Romanesque style that are attributed to Niccolo, whose work can be seen at the Basilica of San Zeno Maggiore. You enter, however, way around to the right. The church was built upon the ruins of an even more ancient paleo-Christian church dating to the late Roman Empire. Visit the Cappella Nichesola, the first chapel on the left, where Titian's serene but boldly colorful *Assumption of the Virgin* is the cathedral's principal treasure, with an architectural frame by Sansovino (who also designed the choir). Also of interest is the semicircular screen that separates the altar from the rest of the church, attributed to Sanmicheli. To its right rises the 14th-century tomb of Saint Agatha.

The excavations of **Sant Elena** church, also in the Duomo complex, reveal a bit of 6th-century mosaic floor. The Baptistery contains a Romanesque font carved with scenes from the nativity cycle.

Don't leave the area without walking behind the Duomo to the river: Here you'll find the 13th-century **Torre di Alberto della Scala** tower and nearby **Ponte della Pietra** bridge, the oldest Roman monument in Verona (1st c. B.C.; rebuilt in the 14th c.). There has been a crossing at this point of the river since Verona's days as a 1st-century Roman stronghold when the Teatro Romano was built on the river's northern banks and the Arena at its hub.

Piazza Duomo (at V. del Duomo). ℂ 045-592813. www.chieseverona.it. Admission 2€ ($2.30), 1€ ($1.15) students and seniors over 65, free for children under 11 or on cumulative ticket (see "A Church Tip" above). Mar–Oct Mon–Sat 9:30am–6pm, Sun 1–6pm. Nov–Feb Mon–Sat 10am–4pm, Sun 1:30–5pm.

SHOPPING

Unlike in Venice, all those people walking the boutique-lined pedestrian streets are locals, not tourists. Come to Verona to spend some time doing what the locals do, shopping and stopping in any of the myriad cafes and *pasticcerie*. Unlike Venice, Verona does not live for tourism alone, and it shows: Only the most predictable souvenirs are found in the tourist trinket market. Shopping is mostly for the Veronesi, and upscale clothing and accessories boutiques line the two most fashionable shopping streets, **Via Mazzini** (connecting the Arena and the Piazza delle Erbe) and **Via Cappello** (heading southeast from the piazza and past Juliet's House). Also check out **Corso Borsari** and **Corso Sant'Anastasia** (heading west and east, respectively, out of the Piazza delle Erbe); the latter has a concentration of interesting antiques stores.

ACCOMMODATIONS YOU CAN AFFORD

Although the following prices reflect peak-season rates, expect inflated prices during the July/August opera season (when Venice offers low-season discounts)

Moments Views & Gardens

The view of Verona from the **Roman Theater** is beautiful any time of day, but particularly during the evening performances—the ancient Romans knew a thing or two about dramatic settings. For other views, you can take a rickety elevator to the 10th-century **Church of Santa Libera** above the theater, or to the former monastery and cloisters of **San Girolamo,** which now houses a small archaeological museum. Above this is the **Castel San Pietro,** whose foundations go back to the times of the Romans and whose terraces offer the best view in town.

Nearby are the well-known, multitiered **Giardino Giusti** (*©* **045-8034029**) gardens, whose formal 16th-century layout and geometrical designs of terraces, fountains, statuary, and staircases inspired, among many, Mozart and Goethe. The gardens are open daily from 9am to dusk (to 8pm in summer); admission is 4.50€ ($5.15).

or when one of the major trade fairs is in town. With these exceptions, **low season** is from November to mid-March. The **C.A.V.** (Cooperativa Albergatori Veronesi), at Via Patuzzi 5, is an organization of dozens of hotels that will help you with bookings for a fee determined by your choice of hotel category (*©* **045-8009844;** fax 045-8009372; www.cav.vr.it).

Hotel Aurora 🛪   Until now, it was location, location, location that had loyal guests returning to the Aurora. As of a 1996 refurbishing of all guest rooms and en suite bathrooms, it's the updated decor as well. Six doubles are blessed with views of one of the world's great squares, the Piazza delle Erbe, and its white-umbrella stalls that make up the daily marketplace. Consider yourself blessed if you snag the top-floor double (there is an elevator!) with a small balcony. There's another terrace overlooking the *mercato* for the guests' use on the second floor, just above the breakfast room where the hotel's daily ample buffet is served.

Piazza delle Erbe 2 (southwest side of piazza), 37121 Verona. *©* 045-594717. Fax 045-8010860. www. hotelaurora.biz. 19 units, 16 with bathroom. 56€–68€ ($64–$78) single without bathroom, 90€–116€ ($104–$133) single with bathroom; 98€–130€ ($113–$150) double with bathroom. Rates include buffet breakfast. Prices discounted 10% off season. AE, DC, MC, V. Parking 10€ ($12) in lot. Bus: 72, 73. **Amenities:** Bar; concierge. *In room:* A/C, TV, hair dryer.

Hotel Torcolo 🛪   Lifelong friends Signoras Silvia and Diana are much of the reason behind the deserving success of this small, comfortable hotel just 1 peaceful block off the lively Piazza Brà. Bright and homey, it is inviting for its unfussy but tasteful decor. Each guest room is individually done, one lovely for its wrought-iron bed, another for the intricate parquet floor, another still for the 19th-century furnishings. No. 31 is a country-style, sunny top-floor room (the hotel has an elevator) with exposed ceiling beams, while nos. 16 (a triple), 18, 21, and 34 are done with original Liberty-style furnishings. Each year the hoteliers redo a few more rooms. They truly care about your comfort here, as shown in the orthopedic mattresses on stiff springs, double-paned windows (though it's quiet already), extra air conditioners on the top floor, and extra-wide single beds. They even consider the travelers' nationalities: They accept pets because of Swiss travel habits, have a few rooms with tubs for the Japanese, and offer some softer beds for the French. You can take the rather expensive breakfast outdoors on the small patio (if the weather is pleasant), in a breakfast nook, or in your room.

Vicolo Listone 3 (just 1 block off the Piazza Brà), 37121 Verona. ✆ **045-8007512** or 045-8003871. Fax 045-8004058. www.hoteltorcolo.it. 19 units. 75€ ($86) single; 108€ ($124) double. Breakfast 10€ ($12). These rates are in effect during the peak July–Aug opera season. Inquire about lower rates during regular and low seasons. AE, DC, MC, V. Parking free on street or 10€ ($12; cash only) in nearby garage. Closed Jan 20–Feb 15. From train station: any bus to Piazza Brà. **Amenities:** Concierge; tour desk; room service; nonsmoking rooms. *In room:* A/C, TV, dataport (3 rooms), minibar, hair dryer, safe.

Locanda Catullo *(Value)* It's a three-floor hike to this homey, pensione-like place that has been run by the affable Pollini family for more than 25 years. However, it's ultra-central and the rooms are spacious and clean, the bathrooms nice and bright. The prices attract the 20- and 30-something euro-counters who make up the majority of the hotel's clientele. With impressive details and touches such as decorative plaster molding, French doors, and marble or parquet floors, the superfluous hanging tapestries and dried flower arrangements become almost too much. Single rooms are large and come equipped with a sink; solo travelers feel comfortable in the family atmosphere that prevails. There's no breakfast service available, but the bar downstairs couldn't be more convenient.

Via Catullo 1 (just north of the V. Mazzini; entrance from the alleyway Vicolo Catullo), 37121 Verona. ✆ **045-8002786.** Fax 045-596987. Locandacatullo@tiscali.it. 21 units, 5 with bathroom. 40€ ($46) single without bathroom; 55€ ($63) double without bathroom, 65€ ($75) double with bathroom; 80€ ($92) triple without bathroom, 95€ ($109) triple with bathroom. No credit cards. Parking 10€ ($12). From train station: any bus to Piazza Brà. **Amenities:** Bar. *In room:* No phone.

WORTH A SPLURGE

Hotel Giulietta & Romeo *(★★)* A block from the Arena is this handsomely refurbished palazzo-hotel recommended for its upscale ambience, cordial can-do staff, and location in the heart of the *centro storico*. Brightly lit rooms are warmed by burnished cherrywood furnishings, and the large marble-tiled bathrooms are those you imagine finding in tiny first-class hotels at less reasonable rates. The hotel takes its name seriously; sure enough, there are two small marble balconies a la Juliet on the facade (and some more prosaic ones at the back), but their view is unremarkable. The hotel is located on a narrow side street that is quiet and convenient to everything.

Vicolo Tre Marchetti 3 (south of V. Mazzini, 1 block east of the Arena), 37121 Verona. ✆ **045-8003554.** Fax 045-8010862. www.giuliettaeromeo.com. 30 units. 80€–120€ ($92–$138) single; 130€–190€ ($150–$219) double. Rates include buffet breakfast. Mention Frommer's when booking and show book upon arrival for a 10% discount. AE, DC, MC, V. Free parking on street (ask for permit) or 17€ ($20) in nearby garage. From train station: any bus to Piazza Brà. **Amenities:** Bar; bike rental; concierge; Internet point; tour desk (summertime only); 24-hr. room service; babysitting; laundry service; dry cleaning; nonsmoking rooms. *In room:* A/C, TV, dataport, minibar, hair dryer, safe.

GREAT DEALS ON DINING

Bottega del Vino *(★)* VERONESE/WINE BAR Oenophiles can push an evening's meal here into the stratosphere if they succumb to the wine cellar's unmatched 80,000-bottle selection, the largest in Verona. This atmospheric *bottega* first opened in 1890, and the old-timers who spend hours in animated conversation seem to have been here since then. The atmosphere and conviviality are reason enough to come by for a tipple at the well-known bar, where 5 dozen good-to-excellent wines are for sale by the glass (1€–10€/$1.15–$12). There's no mistaking Verona's prominence in the wine industry here. At mealtimes the regulars head home, and the next shift arrives: Journalists and local merchants fill the few wooden tables, ordering simple but excellent dishes by which the

Veneto's wines have infiltrated the kitchen, such as the risotto al Amarone, sauced with Verona's most dignified red.

Via Scudo di Francia 3 (off V. Mazzini), Verona. © 045-8004535. www.bottegavini.it. Reservations necessary for dinner. Primi 6€–10€ ($6.90–$12); secondi 8€–22€ ($9.20–$25). Restaurant Wed–Mon noon–3pm (bar 10:30am–3pm) and 7pm–midnight (bar 6pm–midnight). AE, DC, MC, V.

Brek *Value* PIZZERIA/CAFETERIA   The Veronesi (and Italians in general; Brek is part of a Northern Italian restaurant chain) are forever dismissing this place as a mediocre tourist spot. But then, who are all these Italian-speaking, local-looking patrons with their trays piled high, cutting in front of me in line at the pizza station and clamoring for the best tables outside with brilliant views of the sun-kissed Arena? This strip of the Piazza Brà is lined with pleasant alfresco alternatives such as the more serious Olivo and Tre Corone, but Brek is an informal, inexpensive preference of mine for a casual lunch where you can splurge (a lot) and walk away satisfied and solvent. Yes, this is fast food alla Veronese—but do the Italians ever really go wrong in the culinary department? Inside it's a food fest, with various pastas and fresh vegetables made up as you wait, and some self-service with displays of fruit salads and mixed green salads.

Piazza Brà 20. © 045-8004561. www.brek.com. Reservations not accepted. Primi and pizza 2.80€–6€ ($3.20–$6.90); secondi 4€–9€ ($4.60–$10). AE, MC, V. Daily 11:30am–3pm and 6:30–10pm. Bus: Any bus to Piazza Brà.

La Taverna di Via Stella *Finds* OSTERIA VERONESE   Though it was opened only a few years ago by the Vantini brothers and their two friends, the Taverna already feels like it's been a popular neighborhood osteria for decades. There are faux medieval "fresco fragments" on the walls and small wooden tables to seat the locals (the whole fire squad stopped in last time I visited), who pack in for huge portions of Veronese cuisine. To go with the taverna's 250 labels in the wine cellar, try *gnocchi con pastise de' caval* (gnocchi pasta dumplings in the very Veronese horse ragù), *bigoli al torchio* with shredded duck, *coniglio alla veronese con pesto* (rabbit served in a crushed basil and garlic pesto), or *pastise de' caval con polenta* (horse goulash with polenta).

Via Stella 5c. © 045-8008008. Reservations recommended. Primi 6€–7.50€ ($6.90–$8.60); secondi 7.80€–18€ ($8.95–$21). DC, MC, V. Tues–Sun noon–3pm and 7:15–11pm. Bus: 11, 12, 13, 51.

Osteria dal Duca *Kids* VERONESE   There are no written records to confirm that this 13th-century palazzo was once owned by the Montecchi (Montagues) family and, thankfully, the discreet management never considered calling this place the Ristorante Romeo. But here you are, nonetheless, dining in what is believed to be Romeo's house, a characteristic medieval palazzo, and enjoying one of the nicest meals in town in a spirited and friendly neighborhood ambience. You might find *penne con pomodoro e melanzane* (fresh tomato sauce with eggplant) or a perfectly grilled chop or filet with rosemary-roasted potatoes. It will be simple, it will be delicious, you'll probably make friends with the people sitting next to you, and you will always remember your meal at Romeo's Restaurant. If you don't have an adventurous palate, avoid anything on the menu that has *cavallo* or *asino* in it, unless you want to sample horse meat, a local specialty.

Via Arche Scaligeri 2 (east of Piazza dei Signori). © 045-594474. Reservations suggested. Primi 6.50€ ($7.45); secondi 9.50€–15€ ($11–$17); *menu turistico* 13€–19€ ($15–$22). MC, V. Mon and Wed–Sat noon–3pm and 6:30pm–midnight; Tues noon–3pm. Closed Dec 24–Jan 7. Bus: 72.

Pizzeria Impero *Kids* PIZZERIA/TRATTORIA   Location is not everything, but to sit with a pleasant lunch or moonlit dinner in this most elegant of piazze will be one of those Verona memories that stays with you. Impero makes a perfectly respectable pizza (with a full trattoria menu, to boot), and any of the two dozen or so varieties will taste pretty heavenly if you're sharing an outdoor table with your Romeo or Juliet.

If Impero is full and the Arena area is more convenient to your day's itinerary, try the well-known and always busy **Pizzeria Liston,** a block off Piazza Brà at Via Dietro Listone 19 (℗ **045-8034003**). It also serves a full trattoria menu (all credit cards accepted; closed Wed). Its pizzas are said to be better, but its side-street setting—even with outdoor tables—doesn't quite match the Impero's.

Piazza dei Signori 8. ℗ 045-8030160. No reservations accepted. Primi and pizza 6€–9€ ($6.90–$10), secondi 7€–16€ ($8–$18). DC, MC, V. Summer daily noon–2am. Winter Thurs–Tues noon–3:30pm and 7pm–midnight.

CAFES, PASTRIES & WINE BARS

When all is said and done in Verona, one of the most important things to consider is where you'll stop to sip, recharge, socialize, nibble, and revel in this handsome and affluent town.

CAFES & PASTRIES   Verona's grande dame of the local cafe society is the **Antico Caffè Dante** ⟨ℛ⟩, in the beautiful Piazza dei Signori (no phone). Verona's oldest cafe, it is rather formal indoors (read: expensive), where meals are served. But it's most recommended for those who want to soak up the million-dollar view of one of Verona's loveliest ancient squares from the outdoor tables smack in the midst of it all. During the Arena summer season, this is the traditional après-opera spot to complete—and contemplate—the evening's experience. It's open from 9am to 4am.

The oldest of the cafe/bars lining Verona's market square is **Caffè Filippini,** at Piazza delle Erbe 26 (℗ **045-8004549**). Repeated renovations have left little of yesteryear's character or charm, but centuries-old habits die hard: It's still the command post of choice, whether indoors or out (preferably out), a lovely spot to take in the cacophony and colorful chaos of the market. It's open daily in summer months and Thursday through Tuesday in winter. Hours are always from 8am to 1am.

An old-world temple of caffeine, **Caffè Tubino** (Corso Porta Borsari 15/d, 1 block west of the Piazza delle Erbe; ℗ **045-8032296**) is stocked with packaged blends of Tubino-brand teas and coffees displayed on racks lining parallel walls in a small space made even smaller by the imposing crystal chandelier. The brand is well known, is nicely packaged, and makes a great gift. It's open daily from 7am to 11pm. On the same street is **Pasticceria Bar Flego** (Corso Porta Borsari 9; ℗ 045-8032471), a beloved institution with eight tiny tables for two. Accompany a frothy cappuccino with an unbridled sampling of their deservedly famous bite-size pastries by the piece at .65€ to 1€ (75¢–$1.15) each. A regional specialty is the *zaletti,* traditional cookies made with corn flour, raisins, and pine nuts—much better tried than described! The pasticceria is closed on Monday.

One of Verona's oldest and most patronized *pasticcerie* is **Cordioli,** a moment's stroll from Juliet's house on Via Cappello 39 (℗ **045-8003055**). There are no tables and it's often three deep at the bar, but with coffee this good and pastries this fresh (made on the premises), it's obvious why. Verona's perfect souvenir? How about homemade *baci di Giulietta* (vanilla meringues called Juliet's kisses) and *sospiri di Romeo* (Romeo's sighs, chocolate hazelnut cookies)? It's closed Sunday afternoon and Wednesday.

WINE BARS   Verona is the epicenter of the region's important viticulture (Veneto produces more D.O.C. wine than any other region in Italy), but the old-time wine bars are decreasing in number and atmosphere. Recapture the spirit of yesteryear at **Carro Armato,** in a 14th-century palazzo at Vicolo Gatto 2A/Vicolo San Piero Martire (1 block south of Piazza Sant'Anastasia; ✆ **045-8030175**), a great choice for after-hours or any hour when you want to sit and sample some of 30 or so regional wines by the glass (1€–4€/$1.15–$4.60) and make an informal meal out of fresh and inexpensive bar food. Oldsters linger during the day playing cards or reading the paper at long wooden tables, while a younger crowd fills the place in the evening. A small but good selection of cheeses and cold cuts or sausages might be enough to take the edge off, but there is always an entree or two and a fresh vegetable side dish. It's open Monday through Friday from 10am to 2pm and 5pm to 2am, and Saturday and Sunday nonstop hours.

The wonderfully characteristic old wine bar, **Enoteca dal Zovo,** on Vicolo San Marco in Foro 7/5 (off Corso Porta Borsari near the above-mentioned Caffè Tubino; ✆ **045-8034369**), is run by Oreste, who knows everyone in town. They all stop by for his excellent selection of Veneto wines averaging 1€ ($1.15) a glass, or you can go for broke and get top-flight wines starting at 2€ ($2.30). Oreste's *simpatica* American-born wife, Beverly, can give you a crash course. Salami, olives, and finger foods will help keep you vertical, since the few stools are always occupied by senior gentlemen who are as much a part of the fixtures as the hundreds of dusty bottles of wines and grappa that line the walls. It's open Tuesday through Sunday from 8am to 1pm and 2 to 8pm.

SIDE TRIPS FROM VERONA

The ancient Greeks called Italy *Enotria*—the land of wines. It produces more wine than any other country in the world, so the annual **VinItaly** ✷✷ (www.vinitaly.it) wine fair held every April in Verona is an understandably prestigious event. The Veneto produces more D.O.C. (Denominazione di Origine Controllata, zones of controlled name and origin) than anywhere else in Italy, particularly the Veronese trio of Bardolino and Valpolicello (reds) and soave (white).

The costly, dry Valpolicello wine known as Amarone comes from the vineyards outside of Verona. **Masi** ✷ is one of the most respected producers, one of many in the Verona hills whose cantine are open to the public for wine tasting. Visit Verona's tourist information office for a listing of wine estates open to the public. No organized tours are available and you'll need your own wheels, but oenologically minded visitors will want to taste some of Italy's finest wines at the point of their origin.

4 Trent

230km (143 miles) NW of Milan, 101km (63 miles) N of Verona, 57km (35 miles) S of Bolzano

Surrounded by mountains, this beautiful little city on the banks of the Adige River definitely has an Alpine flair. Yet unlike other towns here in the far north, which tend to lean heavily on their Austrian heritage, **Trent (Trento)** is still essentially Italian. The piazzas are broad and sunny, the palaces are ocher-colored and tile-roofed, Italian is the lingua franca, and pasta is still a staple on menus. With its pleasant streets and the remnants of its most famous event—the 16th-century Council of Trent, a strategy session by the Catholic Church on how to stem the tides of Protestantism being spread by those heretics Martin Luther and Calvin across the Alps, and also lay the groundwork for the Inquisition—Trent

Getting a Lift Out of Town

For a breezy view of Trento and a heart-thumping aerial ride as well, take the cable car (Funivia Trento) from Ponte di San Lorenzo near the train station up to **Sardagna,** a village on one of the mountainsides that enclose the city. You may want to provision yourself at the market and enjoy an Alpine picnic on one of the grassy meadows nearby. The cable car (© **0461-822075**) runs daily every 30 minutes from 7am to 6:30pm. The fare is .85€ (95¢) each way, or free with the Trento Card (see Trent's Cumulative Ticket," below).

is a nice place to stay for a night or to visit en route to Bolzano (see section 5 later in this chapter) and other places in the Trentino-Alto Adige.

ESSENTIALS

GETTING THERE   By Train   Strategically located on a main north-south rail line between Italy and Austria, Trento is served by some 30 trains (www.trenitalia. com) a day to and from **Verona** (regional: 67 min., 4.65€/$5.35; high speed 58 min., 7.65€/$8.80), a major transfer point for trains to Milan, Florence, Rome, Venice, Trieste, and all points south. There are about 40 trains a day from **Bolzano** (32 min.; 5€/$5.75).

By Bus   Atesina buses (© **0461-821000;** www.atesina.it), which leave from a terminal next to the train station, are the major links to outlying mountain towns. There's also hourly service to and from **Riva del Garda** on Lago di Garda (see chapter 9; 1 hr. 40 min.).

By Car   The A22 autostrada connects Trento with Verona in about an hour; from Verona, you can connect with the A4 for Milan (total trip time between Milan and Trento is about 2½ hr.) and with A22 to Modena, and from there A1 for Florence and Rome (Trento is a drive of about 3½ hr. from Florence and about 6½ hr. from Rome). A22 also runs north to Bolzano, a little over half an hour away. The slower S12 also connects Trento and Bolzano, and from it you can get on the scenic Strada di Vino.

VISITOR INFORMATION   The local **tourist office,** near the Duomo at Via Manci 2 (© **0461-983880;** fax 0461-984508; www.apt.trento.it), is open daily from 9am to 7pm.

FESTIVALS & MARKETS   In May and June, churches around the city are the evocative settings of performances of the **Festivale di Musica Sacra (Festival of Sacred Music).** Its final performances coincide with **Festive Vigiliane,** a medieval pageant for which townspeople turn up in the Piazza del Duomo appropriately decked out. An ambitious program aptly named **Superfestival** stages musical performances, historic dramas, and reenactments of medieval and Renaissance legends in castles surrounding Trento; it runs from late June through September. Call the tourist office (© **0461-839000**) for performance dates.

A small **daily food market** covers the paving stones of Piazza Alessandro Vittorio daily from 8am to 1pm. A larger **market,** this one with **clothing, crafts,** and **bric-a-brac,** is held Thursday from 8am to 1pm in Piazza Arogno near the Duomo. This same piazza hosts a **flea market** the third Sunday of every month.

WHAT TO SEE & DO

To reach the center of town from the train station, where you will also find parking, follow the Via Pozzo through several name changes until it reaches the

Piazza del Duomo as Via Cavour. As you amble around this lovely town, you'll soon learn that much of what's notable about Trento is in some way connected with the **Council of Trent,** called by the Vatican from 1545 to 1563 to counter the effects of the new wave of Protestantism that was sweeping down from the north.

The outcomes of the many council sessions were announced in the 13th- to 16th-century **Duomo** (✆ 0461-234419), which is delightfully situated on the wide expanse of cafe-filled Piazza del Duomo. This square, with a statue of Neptune at its center, is referred to as the city's *salotto* (sitting room), so popular is it as a place to pass the time. The enormous 15th-century cross in the Duomo's Chapel of the Crucifix presided over the Council's many sessions and was given this baroque home between 1682 and 1688. Under the altar of the main church is the Basilica Paleocristiana, a 6th-century church later used as a crypt for the city's powerful prince-bishops. A few scraps of mosaics and carvings remain. The Duomo is open Monday through Saturday from 9:30am to 12:30pm and 2:30 to 6pm; its crypt is open from 10am to noon and 2:30 to 5:30pm. Admission to the crypt is 1€ ($1.15), or free with the Museo Diocesano ticket (see below).

The Duomo's **Museo Diocesano Tridentino** (✆ 0461-234419; www. museodiocesanotridentino.it) is housed in the adjoining, heavily fortified 13th-century palace of these bishops. The museum displays some fascinating paintings of Council sessions that serve almost as news photos of the proceedings (one provides a seating plan for delegates), as well a collection of medieval and Renaissance paintings, 16th-century tapestries and statuary, and other objects from the Duomo's treasury. The Museo is open Wednesday through Monday from 9:30am to 12:30pm and 2 to 5:30pm; admission is 3€ ($3.45) for adults and .50€ (55¢) for ages 14 to 18, or free with the Trento Card (see "Trent's Cumulative Ticket," above). Included in the fee is the Duomo's crypt (see above).

Many Council sessions were held in the **Castello di Buonconsiglio** (✆ 0461-233770; www.buonconsiglio.it), which you can reach by walking north from the Duomo along Via Belenzani, then east on Via Roma. Both, especially the former, are lined with palaces, many with faded frescoes on their facades, built to house the church officials who came to Trento to attend the council sessions. The maze-like Castello incorporates the 13th-century Castelvecchio, surrounded by medieval fortifications, and the elegant Magno Palazzo, a palace built for a prince-bishop in the 15th century. Within the vast complex is the Museo Provincale d'Arte, where the pride of the collection is the 15th-century *Ciclo dei Mesi (Cycle of the Months)* ✦, housed in the **Torre dell'Aquila,** or Eagle's Tower. It's an enchanting fresco cycle that presents a detailed look at life at court and in the countryside, showing amusements among the lords and ladies and much hard work among the peasants.

You can also visit the cell where native son Cesare Battiste was held in 1916 for his part in the Irredentist movement, which sought to return Trento and other parts of the region to Italy. This indeed came to pass with the Treaty of

---

Value Trent's Cumulative Ticket

A new cumulative ticket, the **Trento Card,** allows visitors access to the city's museums, free rides on public transportation and the cable car to Sardagna, and discounts on parking and at stores, restaurants, and hotels throughout Trent. The card is 9€ ($10) for 24 hours, or 14€ ($16) for 48 hours.

Versailles in 1919, but not before Battiste was hanged in the moat that surrounds the Castelvecchio.

From April through September, the complex is open Tuesday through Sunday
from 9am to noon and 2 to 5:30pm; October through March, it's open 9am to
noon and 2 to 5pm. Admission to the castello is 5€ ($5.75) or free with the
Trento Card (see "Trent's Cumulative Ticket," above); to climb the Torre Aqu-
lia, it's 1€ ($1.15) more (reservation required).

ACCOMMODATIONS YOU CAN AFFORD

Accademia Hotel 🔆   This simple but nicely amenitied hotel is the best
choice in the center, though prices are a bit steep. It's set in a restored medieval
house on an alley about a block from the Duomo and Piazza Santa Maria Maggiore (whose bell tower some rooms overlook). The reception area's whitewashed
vaulted ceilings and stone door jambs don't really carry over into the rooms,
which are a bit spartan, if well equipped, with modular or rattan furnishings,
sometimes under nice sloping ceilings. Things would improve dramatically if the
friendly staff would only replace the thin, stained carpet that covers every floor.

Vicolo Colico 4, 38100 Trento (of V. Cavour). ✆ 0461-233600. Fax 0461-230174. www.accademiahotel.it.
42 units. 90€ ($104) single; 140€ ($161) double; 155€ ($178) triple. Stay 3 weeknights or 2 weekend nights
at a 20% discount. Rates include buffet breakfast. AE, DC, MC, V. **Amenities:** Restaurant; woodsy enoteca;
concierge; limited room service (for bar; meal service only during restaurant hours); laundry service; dry cleaning; nonsmoking rooms. *In room:* A/C, TV, dataport, minibar, hair dryer, safe.

Hotel Aquila D'Oro 🔆   A recent renovation of an older hotel that, in turn,
occupied a centuries-old palazzo has created some of the nicest rooms in Trento,
with a wonderful location right around the corner from the Piazza Duomo.
Decor throughout is stylishly contemporary, with a nice smattering of Oriental
carpets, vaulted ceilings, and other interesting and cozy architectural touches in
public rooms. The guest rooms are a little plainer but have glossy, streamlined
new furnishings and gleaming tile bathrooms.

Via Belezani 76, 38100 Trento. ✆/fax 0461-986282. www.aquiladoro.it. 19 units. 63€ ($72) single; 95€
($109) double; 115€ ($132) triple. Rates include buffet breakfast. AE, DC, MC, V. Parking 2€ ($2.30). **Ameni-
ties:** Concierge; tour desk; car-rental desk; limited room service; nonsmoking rooms. *In room:* A/C, TV, dataport, minibar, hair dryer.

Hotel Venezia   This old hotel is rather less charming than its next-door
neighbor, Aquila D'Oro, and its "amenities" consist entirely of toilet paper and
one towel, but it's certainly cheap. Marked by 1950s-style furnishings, the simple, high-ceiling rooms are a bit dowdy but offer solid, old-fashioned comfort.
(Unfortunately, some beds still bear the sags left by generations of travelers.) Its
selling point: Those in the front come with stunning views over the Piazza
Duomo. Some of the younger members of the family who run the hotel speak
English and are more than happy to dispense advice on what to see and do in
town and the surrounding area. Some of the older ones are quite surly. No one
staffs the desk at the actual hotel entrance; go to the one a few doors up on the
corner of Piazza Duomo.

Via Belenzani 70 at Piazza Duomo, 38100 Trento. ✆/fax 0461-234559. www.hotelveneziatn.it. 47 units, 34
with bathroom. 30€ ($35) single without bathroom, 43€ ($49) single with bathroom; 41€ ($47) double
without bathroom, 63€ ($72) double with bathroom. Breakfast 5€ ($5.75). MC, V. Parking 2€ ($2.30). *In
room:* Hair dryer, no phone.

GREAT DEALS ON DINING

It's almost a requirement to stroll down Trento's Renaissance streets with a gelato
from **Torre Verde–Gelateria Zanella,** on Via Suffragio 6 (✆ 0461-232039). Many

of the flavors are made from fresh, local fruits in season, while others make no such attempt at wholesomeness and incorporate the richest chocolate and cream.

Birreria Pedavena ⍟ BEER HALL/PIZZERIA   It seems as if this beer hall–style cafeteria can feed all of Trento, and it just might. Recently expanded, it draws a big crowd for coffee and pastries in the morning and keeps serving a huge mix of pastas, *wurstel*, *canederli*, and pizza all day. You can sit outside in the new garden, but if you're inside, you'll still have a view—the expansion was designed to showcase the workings of the Pedavena's new brewery, where the house label, Lag's, is made. You will probably be happiest if you order simply, maybe a plate of *wurstel* (essentially, hot dogs) or goulash or one of the excellent pizzas. Pedavena keeps some of the latest hours in town, making this something of a late evening spot in a town where nightlife is scarce.

Piazza Fiera 13 at Via Santa Croce. ℂ **0461-986255.** www.birreriapedavena.com. Primi 3.80€–5.05€ ($4.35–$5.80); secondi 4.70€–9.30€ ($5.40–$11); pizza 3.80€–6.95€ ($4.35–$8). MC, V. Wed–Mon 9am–12:30am (bar and light meals 8:30am–12:15am). Closed mid-July to mid-Aug.

La Cantinota ⍟ ITALIAN/TYROLEAN   With its white tablecloths, excellent service, and reasonably priced menu, La Cantinota could be the most popular restaurant in Trento. The indoors are done with vaulted ceilings set with oil paintings, like some sort of ersatz refectory; a goose wanders among the tables in the atrium garden. The fare includes Italian and Tyrolean dishes and is truly inspired, making use of fresh local ingredients: wonderful homemade gnocchi, *strangola preti* (spinach dumplings coated in melted butter), rich risottos with porcini mushrooms, grilled sausages with polenta, and *vitello barolo* (veal with a rich red-wine sauce). The adjoining piano bar is popular with local talent who tend to intersperse Frank Sinatra renditions with yodeling. From 10:30pm to 3am, La Cantinota transforms into a piano bar.

Via San Marco 22/24. ℂ **0461-238527.** Reservations recommended. Primi 6.50€–9€ ($7.45–$10); secondi 13€–17€ ($15–$20); pizza 5€–6.50€ ($5.75–$7.45). AE, DC, MC, V. Fri–Wed noon–3pm and 7–11pm (piano bar 10:30pm–3am).

Scrigno del Duomo ⍟⍟ *(Finds* WINE BAR/ITALIAN   This stylish wine bar and restaurant is a surprisingly good value, considering the quality of the creative cooking, immaculate service, and stellar location—from the front courtyard tables set under the frescoed facade, you can peek through the gate at the fountain splashing on Trento's main piazza. The interiors mix the antique with the post-modern: Renaissance painted beams or baroque stucco ceilings, designer CD changers, aluminum chairs and sconces. More than 35 wines are available by the glass (2.60€–7.50€/$3–$8.60). Dishes change constantly with the seasons and chef's whims. On my last visit, I sampled *lasagnette di asparagi con prosciutto corccante* (white asparagus lasagna in a béchamel sauce sprinkled with crunchy prosciutto bits) and a *trancio di salmone alle erbe con legume e salsa al jogurt* (salmon fillet in a yogurt sauce sided with steamed veggies).

Piazza Duomo 29. ℂ **0461-220030.** www.scrignodelduomo.com. Reservations required at restaurant, but not at wine bar. Primi 6€–8€ ($6.90–$9.20); secondi 12€–18€ ($14–$21). Fixed-price menus 35€–55€ ($40–$63) without wine. AE, DC, MC, V. Daily 11am–3pm and 6pm–12:30am.

EN ROUTE TO BOLZANO: THE STRADA DI VINO

Some of Italy's finest wines are produced on the vines that cloak the hillsides between Trento and Bolzano. (These local wines include many pinot grigios and pinot noirs, among whites, and Vernatsch, the most common red of the region.) If you are traveling by car between the two cities, you can make the trip on the well-marked Strada di Vino (Weinstrasse). Leave Trento on S12; 15km (9¼ miles)

Trentino–Alto Adige on the Web

In addition to the city websites listed under each town throughout this chapter, the Trentino province around Trento maintains its own site at **www.provincia.tn.it.** The South Tyrol is represented by a few private sites, such as **www.sudtirol.com, www.stol.it,** and **www.hallo.com.** The Dolomiti are represented at various sites, all claiming to be "the official" one (all are loaded with good information, at any rate), including **www.dolomiti.it** and **www.altoadige.com.**

---

north, you'll come to the main turnoff for the village of Lavis. Follow this turnoff, and from here, easy-to-follow yellow signs will lead you along a series of twisting roads through seemingly endless vineyards and around Lago di Caldaro to Bolzano. Many of the vineyards have tasting rooms open to the public and sometimes offer cheese, sandwiches, and other refreshments as well. If you don't have your own wheels, the tourist offices in Trento and Bolzano can provide lists of local tour companies that lead wine tours.

5 Bolzano (Bozen)

154km (95 miles) N of Verona, 118km (73 miles) S of Innsbruck, 57km (35 miles) NE of Trento

Without even crossing a border, you'll find yourself in a place that doesn't resemble Italy at all. During its long history, this pretty town at the confluence of the Talvera and Isarco rivers has been ruled by the bishops of Trent, the counts of Tirol, and the Hapsburgs, to name but a few of the empires to which it has belonged. **Bolzano** has been part of Italy since the end of World War I, but as you explore the narrow streets and broad piazzas and stroll through the parks that line the town's two rivers, you get the sense that the city is more Nordic than Italian—a notion underscored by the city's high-gabled, Tyrolean-style houses and preference for the German tongue.

ESSENTIALS

GETTING THERE   By Train   Bolzano is on the north-south rail line that links Verona with Innsbruck, Austria, via the Brenner Pass. Some 30 trains (www. trenitalia.com) run daily from **Verona** (regional: 1 hr. 45 min., 7€/$8.05; high speed: 90 min., 11€/$13); 40 trains a day from **Trento** (32 min.; 3€/$3.45). Hourly train service links Bolzano with **Merano** (38 min.; 3.25€/$3.75).

By Bus   Bolzano is the hub of the excellent **SAD bus network,** serving even the most remote mountain villages (© **0471-450111;** www.sii.bz.it). Hourly buses run to and from **Merano** (1 hr.; 3.40€/$3.90) and **Bressanone** (1 hr.; 4.60€/$5.30). Two daily morning buses (currently 9:15am and 11:10am) make the trip to **Cortina,** with a change in Dobbiaco (about 4 hr.; 11€/$13). The extremely helpful staff at the bus station, the round building 1 block up from the train station and on the left, will help you make sense of the routing.

By Car   The A22 autostrada connects Bolzano with Trento in a little over half an hour and with Verona (where you can connect with the A4 for Milan and Rome) in a little over an hour. Farther south, you will hit Modena, where you can connect with the A1 for Florence and Rome. A22 runs north to Innsbruck.

VISITOR INFORMATION   The city **tourist office,** near the Duomo at Piazza Walther 8 (© **0471-307000;** fax 0471-980128; www.bolzano-bozen.it), dispenses a wealth of information on Bozen and the South Tyrol. It's open Monday through Friday from 9am to 6:30pm and on Saturday from 9am to 12:30pm. The local **events calendar** "BoBo" can also be found online at www. bobo.it.

FESTIVALS & MARKETS   Bolzano celebrates spring with weekend **concerts** throughout April and May in Piazza Walther and adds a **flower show,** with more music, around the first of May. The city's most serious musical event is the **Concorso Internazionale Piantistico F. Busoni,** an international piano competition held the last 2 weeks of August. The **Festival del Teatro di Strada** draws wandering musicians, mimes, puppeteers, and other performers to the streets of the Old City in October. One of the more colorful events in the region is the **Bartolomeo Horse Fair,** which brings together the region's most beautiful equines on the Renon plateau, which can be reached by funicular (see "Funiculars," below).

One of the most enjoyable walks in the Old City takes you through the stalls of the **fruit and vegetable market** in Piazza delle Erbe, which operates Monday through Saturday from 8am to 7pm. From November 28 to December 23, the city hosts a well-attended **Mercatino di Natale (Christkindlmarkt),** in which handmade ornaments, wooden toys, and other seasonal crafts, along with Christmas pastries and mulled wine, are sold from booths in a festively decorated Piazza Walther.

A **flea market** *(mercatino delle pulci)* fills the Passeggiata del Talvera along the River Talvera (follow V. Museo from the center of town) the first Saturday of every month, opening at 8am and closing at 5pm.

WHAT TO SEE & DO

With its two rivers, surrounding hills, expansive greens, and medieval center, Bolzano is an extremely appealing city that melds urban sophistication with an appreciation for nature. The compact medieval Old City is still the heart of town, and at its center **Piazza Walther** honors a 12th-century wandering minstrel. The piazza seems to capture the mood of its lighthearted historical associations with a fringe of cafe tables to one side and the brightly tiled roof and lacy spire of the **Duomo** on the other. The interior of this 12th- to 14th-century church is far more plain than its exterior but is enlivened somewhat by much-faded frescoes and an intricately carved pulpit (℄ 0471-978676; open Mon–Fri 9:45am–noon and 2–5pm and Sat 9:45am–noon, Sun for services only).

A far more enticing church is the **Chiesa dei Domenicani** ⚡ (℄ 0471-973133), just a few steps west of the Duomo. Inside this 13th-century structure are two sets of frescoes that comprise the city's greatest artistic treasure. From the

---

Free Bikes!

The best way to get about town—certainly out to the castles and to Gries—is on one of the free bikes offered by the commune. There's a stand on the left side of Viale Stazione just before Piazza Walther, and another on Piazza Gries. Just leave a 5€ ($5.75) deposit, have a passport or driver's license handy (they write the number down), and bring the bike back by 7pm. Unfortunately, this initiative is guaranteed only from Easter to October; in winter, you may have to cough up a few euros to rent from **Velo Sport,** Via Grappoli 56 (℄ 0471-977719).

15th century, on the walls of the cloisters, one depicts court life. The other, in the Cappella di San Giovanni (under the arch behind the altar and to the right), is a 14th-century religious cycle attributed to the school of Giotto, including the **Triumph of Death.** In these rich frescoes, a heady dose of realism comes through, along with the beginnings of the use of such elements as perspective and foreshortening, which suggests the influence of the early Renaissance. It's open Monday through Saturday from 9:30am to 6pm, and Sunday for services only.

There is one more church to see in Bolzano, but before you reach it, you will be distracted by the considerable worldly pleasures this city has to offer. If you walk north from Piazza Walther, you will soon come to the lively clamor of **Piazza dell'Erbe,** actually one long, wide street that winds past a statue of *Neptune* through the old town and is so named because it has hosted Bolzano's fruit and produce market for centuries. The piazza is lined with shops selling bread, cheese, strudel, wine, and other comestibles, which spill into stalls along the pavement to create a cheerful, open-air supermarket. At the north end is Bolzano's atmospheric main shopping street, **Via dei Portici,** also closed to traffic. It's lined with 15th-century houses whose porticoes overhang the sidewalk to create a cozy effect that definitely feels more northern European than Italian.

The aforementioned church, **Chiesa dei Francescani** (© **0471-977293**), is across Via dei Portici on Via Francescani. Inside is a sumptuously carved altar from 1500, one of the Gothic masterpieces of the Trentino-Alto Adige. The 14th-century cloisters are charming—intimate, frescoed on one side, gracefully vaulted, and beautifully planted. The church is open Monday through Saturday from 10am to noon and 2:30 to 6pm, and Sunday for services only.

Bolzano's newest and, by far, most popular sight is the thoroughly modernized **Museo Archeologico dell'Alto Adige** ☆☆☆, Via Museo 43 at Via Cassa di Risparmio (© **0471-320100;** www.iceman.it), better known as "Oützi's House" since it was remodeled in 1998 to house the famed 5,300-year-old "Iceman." This mummy made headlines in 1991 when a pair of German hikers discovered him sticking out of a melting glacier high in the Tyrol mountains—though whether he was of Alpine origin or was merely trying to cross the Alps is still being debated (his equipment and one of his last meals seem to have come from lower-altitude valleys, nearer Verona). Along with the mummy were preserved remnants of clothing (including shoes and a bearskin hat), a flint dagger, a copper ax, and a quiver with flint-tipped arrows he was in the process of making. The museum is open May through September Tuesday through Sunday from 10am to 6pm (to 8pm Thurs), and October through April Tuesday through Sunday from 9am to 5pm (to 8pm Thurs). Admission is 8€ ($9.20) for adults, 5.50€ ($6.30) for students under 28 and seniors over 65, and 16€ ($18) for a family card (two adults plus any kids under 14); children under 6 are admitted free. The excellent audioguides are an extra 2€ ($2.30).

A walk across the River Talvera (follow V. Museo west across the Ponte Talvera) brings you into the newer **"Italian" section** of Bolzano, constructed in the 1920s when the Mussolini government encouraged workers from other parts of Italy to settle here in the newly won territory. Those who answered the call were either inspired or intimidated by the imposing Fascist-era structures put up along Corso Libertá (including the **Monumento della Vittoria,** a triumphal arch that is frequently the target of attacks by German-speaking groups who want the region to revert to Austrian rule).

In a few blocks, though, the Corso brings you into the pleasant confines of **Gries,** once an outlying village and now a quaint, leafy neighborhood built around the **Abbazia dei Benedettini di Gries,** a Benedictine abbey (not usually open to the public) prettily surrounded by vineyards and gardens. Just beyond is the **Vecchia Parrochiale di Gries,** the village's parish church, whose treasures include a 12th-century crucifix and an elaborately carved 15th-century altar (© 0471-283089; open Mon–Fri 10:30am–noon and 2:30–4pm; closed Nov–Mar). If you wish to continue walking, Gries is the terminus of the **Passeggiata del Guncina,** a beautifully maintained 8km (5-mile) trail that leads through parklike forests planted with many botanical specimens to a belvedere.

CASTLES   Of the many castles that surround Bozen, the closest to the center is the **Castel Mareccio,** just a short walk along the River Talvera. (From the Piazza delle Erbe, follow the V. Museo west to the Ponte Talvera and, from there, the Lungo Talvera Bozen north for less than .5km/⅓ mile.) Though it is now used as a convention center and its five towers rise from a residential neighborhood of recent vintage, this 13th-century fortress is a stunning sight, all the more so since it is surrounded by a generous swath of vineyards that have been saved from urban encroachment, and backed by forested hills. You can step inside for a glimpse at the stone-walled medieval interior and enjoy a beverage at the bar; the castle is open to the public Wednesday through Monday from 9am to 6pm (hours vary when conferences are in session; © 0471-976615).

A longer walk of about 2km (a little over a mile; or take the free bus from Piazza Walther) leads out of town north to the 13th-century **Castel Roncolo** 𝕱𝕱 (© 800-210003 in Italy, or 0471-329808; www.comune.bolzano.it/roncolo), beautifully ensconced high above the town and beneath a massive, foreboding cliff face. The interior is decorated with faded but fascinating frescoes from the 14th and 15th centuries that depict secular scenes from the story of *Tristan and Isolde* and other tales of romantic love and chivalry. These painted scenes are remarkably moving in their almost primitive craftsmanship that nonetheless reveals a certain worldliness. Admission is 8€ ($9.20) for adults, 5.50€ ($6.30) for students and those over 60, and 13€ ($15) for a family card for four; hourlong guided tours in English cost an extra 2.60€ ($3) per person (minimum six people). The castle is open Tuesday through Sunday October through June from 10am to 6pm and July through September from 10am to 8pm. To get here, follow the Via Castel Roncolo north from the Chiesa dei Francescani; you will pass one side of the Castel Mareccio, at which point signposts will lead you along Via Beatro Arrigo and Via San Antonio for a gradual uphill climb to Castel Roncolo.

FUNICULARS   Several cable cars will whisk you right from the center of Bozen into the surrounding mountains. The most dramatic ride takes you from a terminal near the train station 900m (2,952 ft.) up to the **Altopiano del Renon** (www.renon.com), a pasture-covered plateau that provides dizzying views down to Bozen and up to higher Dolomite peaks. The funicular deposits you in **Soprabolzano (Oberbozen),** where you can sip a beer and enjoy the view. Then venture farther by footpath or electric tram into a bizarre landscape of spindly rock spires worn needle-thin by erosion and each seeming to balance a boulder on its top; this scenery surrounds the village of **Collabo.** The cable car (© 0471-978479; www.sii.bz.it) makes the ascent in 15 minutes and operates daily from a terminus 500m (1,640 ft.) east of the train station on Via Renon. It operates hourly from 7am to 8pm. The round-trip, 15 minutes each way, costs 7€ ($8.05) and includes tram fare between Soprabolzano and Collabo (3.50€/$4 if you skip the tram).

The **Funivia di San Genesio** whisks you up a forested hillside to the pretty village of San Genesio Atesino, surrounded by woods and mountain peaks.

Cable cars (© **0471-978436;** www.jenesien.net or www.sii.bz.it) leave every half-hour from 9am to 12:30pm and 2:30 to 6pm from a terminus on Via Sarentino on the northern outskirts of Bozen (take bus no. 12). The trip takes 15 minutes, and the round-trip fare is 3.20€ ($3.70). San Genesio's little tourist office (© **0471-354196;** fax 0471-354085; www.jenesien.net) is open Monday through Friday from 9am to 1pm (July–Nov also 3–5pm). It can set you up with a horseback ride across the high Alpine meadows from 13€ ($15) per hour; it's best to call ahead.

ACCOMMODATIONS YOU CAN AFFORD

Hotel Feichter   This charming little inn is one of the few hotels in the Old City itself and, for the location and atmosphere it provides, is one of the city's better lodging values. On the main floor, there's a Tyrolean-style lobby and a bar and self-service restaurant that resemble a *weinstube*. The rooms may not be full of mountain ambience (and the bathrooms are cramped), but they have serviceable, modern furnishings that are comfortable. The extremely firm beds are equipped with that wonderful local luxury: thick down quilts. There's also a narrow courtyard set with picnic tables and shaded by a grape arbor.

Via Grappoli 15, 39100 Bolzano. © **0471-978768.** Fax 0471-974803. www.paginegialle.it/feichter. 30 units. 52€ ($60) single; 80€ ($92) double; 95€ ($109) triple. Rates include breakfast. Free parking. Closed 3 weeks in Feb. MC, V. **Amenities:** Restaurant; concierge; tour desk. *In room:* TV, hair dryer (ask at desk).

Hotel Regina   For pleasant and affordable lodgings in Bozen, you need look no farther than this modern hotel across the street from the train station—a decent location, as you're still only 3 blocks from the main square, but the rate disparity reflects the noisiness of the busy main street out front. Families, take note: The bright rooms are unusually large, and there are several quads and one mansard quint on hand. While accommodations are quite plain, they're very nicely decorated with streamlined Scandinavian furnishings, and all offer a level of comfort and have amenities you would expect in a much more expensive hotel—including large bathrooms nicely equipped with stall showers. Lower-ceiling mansard rooms are also offered for 5€ ($5.75) less than the lowest rates quoted below.

Via Renon 1, 39100 Bolzano. © **0471-972195.** Fax 0471-978944. www.hotelreginabz.it. 40 units. 60€–65€ ($69–$75) single; 83€–100€ ($95–$115) double; 108€–120€ ($124–$138) triple; 116€–132€ ($133–$152) quad. Rates include buffet breakfast. AE, DC, MC, V. Parking free on street. **Amenities:** Bar (24 hr.); concierge; tour desk; nonsmoking rooms. *In room:* TV, hair dryer (ask at desk).

Stadt Hotel Citta 🎔🎔   This modernized old hotel, with an attractive arcaded facade typical of this city's distinctive architecture, commands a sunny corner of Bozen's main piazza. It was massively overhauled in 2000–01. The large and bright guest rooms have been done in a contemporary style, with nice touches such as extra-wide beds in many twins and singles and, when they could keep them, hardwood floors. The family suites consist either of two rooms and a bathroom off a common hall, or two rooms, each with its own bathroom, that connect. There's a similar arrangement in a double-bedded studio suite (the couch in the second room can pull out). Top-floor rooms are cozier, with slope-edged singles. The bathrooms are spanking new. The best rooms overlook the square and the Duomo. Mussolini stayed in one of them (no. 303), a suite with a corner balcony. The ground-floor bar and cafe that opens to the square is a popular gathering spot. The handsome paneled and terra cotta–tiled lobby is also a much-used meeting place.

Piazza Walther 21, 39100 Bolzano. © **0471-975221.** Fax 0471-976688. www.hotelcitta.info. 102 units. 85€–96€ ($98–$110) single; 115€–150€ ($132–$173) double; 140€–185€ ($161–$213) triple; 170€–260€ ($196–$299) suite. Rates include breakfast. AE, MC, V. Parking 13€ ($15) in garage. **Amenities:**

A Taste of South Tyrol

The cuisine of the Alto Adige is more or less Austrian, with a few Italian touches. *Canederli* (dumplings) often replace pasta or polenta and are found floating in rich broths infused with liver, *speck* (smoked ham) replaces prosciutto, and *Wiener schnitzel grostl* (a combination of potatoes, onions, and veal—the local version of corned beef hash) and pork roasts are among preferred secondi. As you move east into Friuli–Venezia Giulia, the cuisine remains firmly of the mountain variety, with some exotic and hard-to-pronounce variations reflecting the region's mixed cultural heritage. Among these are *cvapcici,* Trieste's signature meatball dish, and *brovada,* a secondo that combines turnips, grape skins, and pork sausage—a farmer's supper, if ever there was one. San Daniele, probably the best **prosciutto** in all Italy (no small claim), comes from this region. The preferred spirit is heady **grappa,** made from grape skins and sure to take the chill out of the night air.

Restaurant; bar under the arcades of Piazza Walther; basement complex with Turkish baths, sauna, and huge whirlpool tub; concierge; tour desk; 24-hr. room service; laundry service; nonsmoking rooms. *In room:* A/C, TV, dataport, hair dryer.

GREAT DEALS ON DINING

Some of the least expensive meals in towns are supplied by the **vendors** who dispense a wide assortment of *wurstel* from carts in the Kornplatz and Piazza dell'Erbe.

Cavallino Bianco ⭐ TYROLEAN   This atmospheric *stube* (beer hall) is darkly paneled and decorated with carved wooden furniture to create a cozy, typically Tyrolean atmosphere. The restaurant opens early to operate as a cafe, dispensing coffee and pastry for breakfast, and remains open well into the night, sending out hearty lunches and dinners of local fare with only a slight Italian influence. Fried Camembert, herrings, and assorted salami are among the dozens of appetizers, while a pasta dish (and there are many to choose from) is likely to be followed by a main course of Wiener schnitzel or würstel.

Via dei Bottai/Bindergasse 6. ℂ 0471-973267. Primi 4.10€–6.20€ ($4.70–$7.15); secondi 7€–15€ ($8.05–$17). No credit cards. Mon–Fri 8am–1am; Sat 8am–3pm.

Ristorante Hostaria Argentieri SEAFOOD   You'll feel like you've come back to Italy when you step into this attractive, cream-colored, tile-floored room. There are several risottos and a grilled steak on the menu, but most of the offerings are fishy—unusual, and much in demand, up here in the Dolomiti. You can start with tasty *tagliolini al salmone* (salmon and pasta) or *bigoli alla veneta* (homemade pasta with anchovies and capers), followed by grilled *branzino, rombo,* or *trancio di spada* (swordfish steak). In good weather, there is dining on a tiny terrace in front of the restaurant, facing an attractive cobblestone street that is indeed Tyrolean in character.

Via Argentieri 14. ℂ 0471-981718. Reservations highly recommended. Primi 9€–16€ ($10–$18); secondi 20€–30€ ($23–$35). DC, MC, V. Mon–Sat noon–2:30pm and 7–10:30pm.

Vogele ⭐⭐ TYROLEAN   If you ask someone in Bozen where to eat, there's a very good chance you will be sent to this attractive, always busy *weinstube* and restaurant in the center of the old city just off Piazza Erbe. Like many such places in Bozen, it is open continuously all day and in the evening. Some of the patrons seem to stop by for every meal and for coffee or a beer in between. One of the two long, cross-vaulted rooms is set up as a cafe, and the other as a dining room (or you can eat under the arcade out front). Both have traditional, woody Tyrolean furnishings. Wherever you sit, you can order lightly (or relatively so, if you wish) from the long appetizer menu, maybe a platter of *speck* (ham) or *affumicato della casa* (smoked meats). First and second courses alike include many traditional favorites. A wonderful *zuppa di vino* (a soup with a white wine and cream base) or different kinds of *canederli* (dumplings that here are laced with liver, bacon, or ham) are the ways to begin. Follow it with a *stinco di maiale* (roast pork shank) or other roasted meat.

Via Goethe 3. (C) 0471-973938. Primi 6€–8.50€ ($6.90–$9.75); secondi 8€–17€ ($9.20–$19). Mon–Sat 9am–midnight (closed Sat for dinner in June–July).

BARS & CAFES

Nightlife in Bozen—and daytime wine tasting—centers on the long curve of **Pizza delle Erbe.** You'll find plenty more wine bars, pubs, stube, and tiny live-music venues in addition to the following.

To sample the local wines (from 1€/$1.15 a glass), step into this tiny little stand-up bar at **Etti's Thekki** at Piazza Erbe 11 (C) 0471-971705). **Hopfen & Co.,** Piazza Erbe 17 (C) 0471-300788), is a tiny Tyrolean pub serving their own brew to the wooden tables crowded inside and a few tiny round ones out on the sidewalk corner. They also serve up grub, mostly hearty local fare like *wurstel, bier goulash,* and *speck canederli,* for 5€ to 12€ ($5.75–$14).

The chic **Exil,** at Piazza del Grano/Kornplatz 2 (C) 0471-971814), is filled with a young crowd night and day, and for them it probably provides a welcome alternative to the many weinstubes around town. Exil has the ambience of a coffeehouse (excellent coffee, pastries, and sandwiches are served) and a bar as well, with many kinds of beers from Italy and north of the Alps on tap. On weekend evenings, the elegant **Laurin Bar,** in the Parkhotel Laurin (C) 0471-311000), turns its Art Nouveau lobby—a sumptuous room overlooking the hotel's private park—into a jazz club. An enthusiastic crowd turns out, making this one of the most popular places in town.

You won't find a more distinctive Bozen locale in which to bend your elbow than **Fishbanke,** at Via Dr. Streiter 26A (C) 0471-971714). In fact, a stop at this outdoor wine bar is mandatory if your visit coincides with one of its seasonal openings. Wine, beer and a few snacks (cheese and bruschetta) are served on the well-worn stone slabs of Bozen's centuries-old former fish market, an unusual experience that attracts a friendly crowd of regulars who, along with the animated proprietor, are always pleased to welcome strangers into their midst.

6 Bressanone

40km (25 miles) N of Bolzano, 68km (42 miles) E of Merano

Tucked neatly in the Val d'Isarco between the Eisack and Rienz rivers and surrounded by orchards and vineyards that climb the lower flanks of the surrounding peaks, **Bressanone (Brixen)** is a gem of a Tyrolean town with a hefty past belied by today's quaint, small-town atmosphere. From 1027 to 1803, Bressanone was the center of a large ecclesiastical principality, and its bishop-princes ruled over much of the South Tyrol. Their impressive monuments arise amid the town's heavily gabled, pastel-colored houses and narrow cobblestone streets.

ESSENTIALS

GETTING THERE   By Train   Bressanone lies on the same north-south rail line as Bolzano and Verona, making connections between those cities extremely easy. There are more than 30 trains (www.trenitalia.com) a day from **Bolzano** (35 min.; 3.25€–4.45€/$3.75–$5.90), where you can change for **Merano.** From **Trento,** trains run almost hourly (60–75 min.; 4.65€–7.65€/$5.35–$8.80).

By Bus   SAD buses (© 0471-450111; www.sii.bz.it) leave from the front of the train station and connect Bressanone and **Bolzano** (1 hr.; 4.60€/$5.30) and outlying villages. Several buses run daily (half-hourly in ski season) to **Sant'Andrea** (see "Hitting the Slopes," below), a good base for hiking and skiing (20 min.; 1.50€/$1.70); service is augmented by a ski bus that is free for pass holders. There are also two daily buses to **Cortina,** with a change at Dobbiaco (about 2¾ hr.; 9.75€/$11).

By Car   Bressanone is about a half-hour drive north of Bolzano on A22. It's easy to get around Bressanone by foot—it's compact, and many of its streets are closed to cars. If you arrive by car, you will probably use the large parking lot on the south of the city on Via Dante (you'll pass it as you drive into the city from the autostrada); the center is 5 minutes away up the Via Roma. From the train station, follow Viale Stazione for about 10 minutes to the center.

VISITOR INFORMATION   The **tourist office,** at the *centro storico* end of Via Stazione leading from the train station at no. 9 (© **0472-836401;** fax 0472-836067; www.brixen.org), is open Monday through Friday from 8:30am to 12:30pm and 2:30 to 6pm, and Saturday from 9am to 12:30pm. The provincial website, **www.provinz.bz.it,** has a section with tourism links.

FESTIVALS & MARKETS   With its cozy, twisting medieval lanes and snug Tyrolean-style houses, Bressanone is especially well suited to Christmas celebrations. The main holiday event is a **Christkindlmarkt (Christmas market)** from late November to Christmas Eve. Stalls on and around Piazza del Duomo sell hand-carved ornaments, crafts, holiday pastries, and other seasonal merchandise. A **fruit-and-vegetable market** enlivens Piazza Parrocchia near the Duomo Monday through Saturday from 8am to noon and 3 to about 6pm.

WHAT TO SEE & DO

The center of town is the **Piazza Duomo,** a long, rectangular, tree-shaded square with cafes on one side and the white facade of the Duomo on the other. A baroque renovation to the tall exterior, flanked by two bell towers, has masked much of the cathedral's original 13th-century architecture, of which you'll see more in the interior and in the crypt. The heavily frescoed cloisters (entered through a door to the right of the main one) are especially charming, even though their view of *Judgment Day* is gloomy. The Duomo is open daily from 6am to noon and 3 to 6pm; there are guided tours (in Italian and German) Monday through Saturday at 10:30am and 3pm.

Just south of the Piazza del Duomo, on the adjoining Piazza Vescovile, stands the palace of the prince-bishops, whose power over the region—and the fragility of that power—is made clear by the surrounding moat and fortifying walls. The massive 14th-century palace now houses the **Museo Diocesano,** where more than 70 rooms display wooden statuary, many somewhat unremarkable Renaissance paintings by local artists. Considered the museum's treasure and the sight most likely to capture your attention is an extensive and enchanting collection of antique nativity scenes, filling eight rooms; it's one of the largest such assemblages anywhere. Frequent exhibits often double the admission price below. The museum (© 0472-830505; www.dioezesanmuseum.bz.it) is open from March 15 to October 31 Tuesday through Sunday from 10am to 5pm. The nativity-scene galleries open again from December 1 to January 31 daily from 2 to 5pm. Admission to the complete museum collection is 3.50€ ($4); to the nativity scene exhibit only, it costs 2€ ($2.30).

ACCOMMODATIONS YOU CAN AFFORD

Goldene Krone Vital Stadthotel   Everything about this amiable hotel at the edge of the Old City suggests solid comfort, from the homey, wood-paneled lounge to the *weinstube*-style bar, to the breakfast room and restaurant, where boothlike tables are lit by pretty shaded lamps. There are several categories of guest rooms, hence the range of prices. Those in the lower range are pleasant enough, with streamlined modern furnishings, and many have terraces. The more expensive rooms are really quite special, though, and well worth the extra expense. They're actually suites, with separate sitting and sleeping areas, equipped respectively with roomy couches and armchairs and king-size beds. The bathrooms are grand, with double sinks and large tubs equipped with Jacuzzi jets. In 2003, the hoteliers reimagined the Goldene Krone as a spa hotel. At the new top-floor gym and sauna, you can indulge in beauty treatments or massages, or even a milk bath.

Via Fienili 4, 39042 Bressanone. © 0472-835154. Fax 0472-835014. www.goldenekrone.com. 48 units. 65€–85€ ($75–$98) single; 100€–140€ ($115–$161) double; 120€–200€ ($138–$230) suite. Rates include buffet breakfast. Half board 15€ ($17). AE, DC, MC, V. Free parking. Closed Jan 6–Feb 6. **Amenities:** Restaurant; bar; free bikes; concierge; tour desk; car-rental desk; limited room service; massage; babysitting; laundry service; dry cleaning; nonsmoking rooms. *In room:* TV, dataport, minibar, hair dryer (in some), safe.

WORTH A SPLURGE

Hotel Elefante   One of the Tyrol's oldest and most famous inns is named for a 16th-century guest—an elephant accompanying Archduke Maximilian of Austria on the long trek from Genoa to Vienna, where the beast was to become part of the royal menagerie. During its 2-week stay, the pachyderm attracted onlookers from kilometers around, and the innkeeper renamed his establishment and

---

Hitting the Slopes

Bressanone's major playground is **Monte Plose,** and the gateway to ski slopes and hiking trails alike is the outlying village of **Sant'Andrea** (see "By Bus," under "Getting There," above). Skiing here is not as glamorous as it is in better-known resorts like Cortina, but it is excellent and much less expensive. A ski pass is 26€ to 30€ ($30–$34) per day and can be purchased at one of the outlets near the Sant'Andrea funicular (© 0472-200433), which costs 10€ ($12) round-trip and runs July to October weekdays from 9am to noon and 1 to 6pm, Saturday and Sunday from 9am to 6pm, and December through May daily from 9am to 4:30pm. (Winter schedules vary considerably with snow conditions; a summer ascent will take you to a network of alpine trails near the stop at Valcroce.) The tourist board in Bressanone provides maps, information on skiing, mountain refuges, and other details you need to know to enjoy this mountain wilderness.

commissioned a delightful elephant-themed fresco that still graces the front of the building. Today's hotel matches its provenance with excellent service and extraordinary environs that include dark paneled hallways and grand staircases. The distinctive old rooms are full of nooks and crannies and furnished with heavy old Tyrolean antiques and some tasteful modern pieces, including wonderfully solid beds. A generous buffet breakfast emphasizes delicious Austrian pastries. Two of the hotel's nicest assets are a large garden and a pleasant swimming pool.

Via Rio Bianco 4, 39042 Bressanone. © **0472-832750.** Fax 0472-836579. www.hotelelephant.com. 44 units. 65€–83€ ($75–$95) single; 130€–166€ ($150–$191) standard double; 165€–186€ ($190–$214) deluxe double; 217€ ($250) suite. Half- and full pension available. Breakfast 5€–13€ ($5.75–$15). AE, DC, MC, V. Free parking. Closed Jan 10–Mar 5 and Nov 5–Dec 1. **Amenities:** Restaurant; bar; outdoor heated pool; tennis courts; exercise room; sauna; bike rental; concierge; tour desk; courtesy car; small business center; limited room service; massage (in-room); babysitting; laundry service; dry cleaning; individual safes. *In room:* TV, dataport, minibar, hair dryer.

GREAT DEALS ON DINING

Fink TYROLEAN   It only seems right that Bressanone's charmingly arcaded main street should have a restaurant like this, with paneling hung with antlers and oil paintings, and an excellent local cuisine. There are many mountain-style dishes that you are likely to encounter only within a close radius of Bressanone, including *piatto alla Val d'Isarco,* a platter of locally cured hams and salamis, and *zuppa di vino,* a traditional Tyrolean soup made with white wine that here includes crusty pieces of cinnamon toast. The *miale gratinato,* a pork roast topped with a cheese sauce, is surprisingly light and absolutely delicious, as are the local cheeses served for dessert. If in doubt about what to order, just ask— the English-speaking staff is extremely gracious. The upstairs dining room has a slightly more refined cuisine and atmosphere to go with the higher prices.

Via Portici Minori 4. © **0472-834883.** Primi 2.50€–8.50€ ($2.90–$10) downstairs, 8€–11€ ($9–$12) upstairs; secondi 9€–13€ ($10–$15) downstairs, 14€–19€ ($16–$22) upstairs. AE, DC, MC, V. Thurs–Mon noon–2:30pm and 7–10pm; Tues noon–2:30pm. Closed July 1–14.

Finsterwirt WINE BAR   Occupying the ground-floor rooms of Oste Scuro restaurant (see below) and run by the same family, this tavern near the cathedral has the same dark paneling and leaded-window ambience. The fare and service, however, are much more casual, though excellent. You are welcome to settle into one of the nooklike tables for as long as you'd like to enjoy a beer or a glass of local wine (from 1€/$1.15) and a plate of fresh goat cheese or a platter of *speck* and salami. A lovely rear garden, candlelit at night, is open throughout the summer and well into chillier days when people from more southerly climes wouldn't think of sitting outdoors.

Vicolo Duomo 3. © **0472-835343.** www.finsterwirt.com. Reservations recommended. Primi 7€–8€ ($8–$9.20); secondi 13€–15€ ($15–$17). AE, DC, MC, V. Tues–Sat noon–2pm and 7–9pm; Sun noon–2pm. Closed Jan 9–31 and June 20–July 4.

Oste Scuro TYROLEAN   What may be Bressanone's temple of gastronomy (Fink, above, is a close contender) occupies a welcoming series of intimate candlelit rooms above the Finsterwirt *weinstube* (see above). The first of these rooms contains a stand-up bar where patrons stop by just to order one of the excellent wines by the glass. It would be a shame not to dine here, though, because the kitchen excels at simple but innovative preparations of the freshest local ingredients. A *tartina di ricotta* is a concoction of creamy cheese atop a bed of lightly sautéed spinach. And even if you have been finding the region's steady diet of *canederli* (dumplings) heavy, try them here, where they are light and infused with fresh wild mushrooms. The kitchen excels at meat dishes, included an herb-infused veal roast. Fresh berries top off a meal in season, and the strudels are perfection.

Vicolo Duomo 3. (C) 0472-835343. www.finsterwirt.com. Reservations recommended. Primi 6€–10€ ($6,90–$12); secondi 13€–18€ ($15–$21). AE, DC, MC, V. Tues–Sat noon–2pm and 7–9pm; Sun noon–2pm. Closed Jan 10–Feb 2 and June 15–30.

7 Cortina d'Ampezzo

133km (82 miles) E of Bolzano, 166km (100 miles) N of Venice

Italy's best-known mountain resort, put on the international map when it hosted the 1956 Winter Olympics, has a glamorous, moneyed reputation. Long before the Olympics, though, **Cortina** was attracting European Alpine enthusiasts, who began coming here for stays in the town's first hotels as early as the 1860s. In 1902, Cortina hosted its first ski competitions, and in 1909, the completion of the first road in and out of the town, the magnificent Strada di Dolomiti (built by the Austro-Hungarian military), opened the slopes to more skiers.

Even without its 145km (90 miles) of ski runs and 50 cable cars and chairlifts that make the slopes easily accessible, Cortina would be one of Europe's most appealing Alpine towns. The surrounding Dolomite peaks are simply stunning. Eighteen of them rise more than 3,000m (9,840 ft.), ringing Cortina in an amphitheater of craggy stone. In full light, the peaks are a soft bluish-gray, and when they catch the rising and setting sun, they take on a welcoming rosy glow.

True to its reputation for glamour, Cortina can be expensive (especially in Aug and the high ski-season months of Jan–Mar). Many well-to-do Italians have houses here, and a sense of privilege prevails. What's often forgotten, though, is that for all the town's fame, strict zoning has put a damper on development. As a result, Cortina is still a mountain town of white timbered houses built beside a rushing stream and surrounded by forests, meadows and, of course, the stunning Dolomite peaks.

ESSENTIALS

GETTING THERE   By Bus   Frequent **SAD** bus service provides the only public transportation in and out of Cortina ((C) **800-846047**; www.sii.bz.it). There are two daily buses each from **Bolzano** (about 4 hr.; 14€/$16), stopping in **Bressanone** (about 2¾ hr.; 9.75€/$11) that head to Cortina, but with a change in Dobbiaco. There's also one daily bus to and from Venice ((C) **035-237641**; 4 hr. 20 min.; 17€/$20), and a daily bus to and from Milan ((C) **02-801161**; 6½ hr.; 40€/$46). The bus station in Cortina is located in the former train station on Via Marconi.

By Train   The closest train station to Cortina is the one at Calalzo di Cadore, 30km (19 miles) south. There are 10 trains (www.trenitalia.com) a day to Calalzo from **Venice**, but only two are direct (2 hr. 20 min.; 6.90€/$7.95); with connections, allow 3 to 4 hours (7.75€/$9). There are also six daily direct runs from **Padua** (3 hr.; 7.75€/$8.9). From Calalzo, 30 daily buses connect with Cortina (4€/$4.60).

By Car   The spectacularly scenic Strada di Dolomiti (see above) links Bolzano and Cortina, while S51 heads south toward Venice, connecting south of Belluno to Autostrada A27, for a total trip time of about 3 hours between Cortina and Venice.

VISITOR INFORMATION   The **APT tourist office,** Piazzetta San Francesco 8 ((C) **0436-3231;** fax 0436-3235; www.dolomiti.com, though I find the private www.dolomiti.org site much more useful), is open daily from 9am to 12:30pm and 4 to 7pm. In addition to a list of accommodations, the English-speaking staff will provide a wealth of information on ski slopes, hiking trails, and bus schedules.

FESTIVALS & MARKETS The Piazza Italia near the bus station doubles as Cortina's **marketplace.** Stalls sell produce, mountain cheeses, clothing, housewares, and other items on Tuesday and Friday mornings from 8:30am to 1pm. While chic Cortina concerns itself mostly with secular pursuits, the town turns out for a solemn religious procession down the main street, Corso Italia, on **Good Friday.**

WHAT TO SEE & DO

The main in-town activity in Cortina appears to be walking up and down the main street, the pedestrian-only **Corso Italia,** wearing the most fashionable ski-wear money can buy. Most of the buildings are new but pleasingly low-scale and Alpine in design, and at the town center is the pretty 18th-century church of **Santi Filippo e Giacomo,** with a charming bell tower eclipsed only by the surrounding majestic peaks. It is on the slopes of these peaks that most visitors set their sights, enjoying an amazing array of outdoor activities.

EXPLORING PEAKS Skiers and nonskiers alike will enjoy the eye-popping scenery on a trip up the surrounding mountainsides on the funicular systems that leave right from town. The most spectacular trip is the ascent on the **Freccia nel Cielo (Arrow in the Sky),** which departs from a terminus near the Stadio Olimpico del Ghiaccio (Olympic Ice Skating Stadium), about a 10-minute walk north and west of the town center. The top station is at Tafano di Mezzo, at 3,163m (10,375 ft.); the round-trip is 24€ ($28). It is less expensive (20€/$23) and almost as satisfying if mountain scenery and not high-Alpine skiing is your quest, to make the trip only as far as **Ra Valles,** the second stop, at 2,550m (8,364 ft.). The views over glaciers and the stony peaks are magnificent, and a bar serves sandwiches and other refreshments on an outdoor terrace. The funicular runs from mid-July to late September and mid-December to May 1, with departures every 20 minutes from 9am to 4 or 5pm, depending on sunset; call ✆ **0436-5052** for information.

The **Funivia Faloria** (✆ **0436-2517**) arrives and departs from a terminus on the other side of town, about a 10-minute walk southeast of the town center. The ride is a little less dramatic than the one on the longer Freccia nel Cielo. Even so, the ascent over forests and meadows, then up a sheer cliff to the 2,100m-high (6,888-ft.) ski station at Faloria, is not without thrills, and the view from the terrace bar at Faloria, down to Cortina and to the curtain of high peaks to the north, is one you won't soon forget. Like the Freccia nel Cielo, the Funivia Faloria runs from mid-July to late September and mid-December to May 1, with departures every 20 minutes from 9am to 4 or 5pm, depending on sunset. The round-trip fare is 8€ ($9.20).

Another trip for funivia enthusiasts is the one from the top of Passo Falzarego, 25km (16 miles) west of Cortina, to **Lagazoul,** a little skiing and hiking station at the 2,550m (8,364-ft.) level. In summer, you can follow a network of trails at the top and scamper for kilometers across the dramatic, rocky terrain. The ride is a nearly vertical ascent up the rocky face of the mountain. As an eerie alternative to the funicular, you can make the climb up or down through a series of tunnels dug into the cliff during World War I. Falzarego is the last pass through which you descend if you follow the Strada di Dolimiti into Cortina, so you may want to stop and board the funicular for a scenery-filled introduction to the region. If you are not driving, five buses a day make the 35-minute trip between Cortina and the funicular stop at the top of the Passo Falzarego; the fare is 1.65€ ($1.90) each way. The funivia runs from mid-July to late September and mid-December to May 1, with departures every 30 minutes. The round-trip fare is 11€ ($13). Call ✆ 0436-867301 for information.

DOWNHILL SKIING   Cortina is Italy's leading ski resort, and it lives up to this reputation with eight exceptional ski areas easily accessible from town. Two of the best, **Tofana-Promedes** and **Faloria-Tondi,** are accessible by funiculars that lift off from the edges of town (see "Exploring Peaks," above), as are the novice slopes at **Mietres.** You can enjoy these facilities fairly economically with one of the comprehensive **Dolomiti Superski passes** that provide unlimited skiing (including all chairlift and funicular fees, as well as free shuttle bus service to and from Cortina and the ski areas) at all eight of Cortina's ski areas and those at 10 outlying resorts. You can get passes for any number of days up to 21. A few sample prices: During high season, from December 24 to January 8 and January 30 to March 12, 1 day is 38€ ($44), 3 days is 108€ ($124), and 7 days is 201€ ($231). Shave off about 4€ ($4.60) per day for low season, from January 7 to February 3 and March 11 to 24. For more information, contact the tourist office or **Dolomiti Superski,** Via d. Castello 33, 32043 Cortina (✆ **0436-862171** or 0471-795397; www.dolomitisuperski.com).

For **lessons,** contact the **Scuola di Sci Cortina,** Corso Italia (✆ **0436-2911;** www.scuolascicortina.it), which offers six consecutive mornings of group lessons for 178€ to 185€ ($205–$213) in high season, 153€ ($176) in low season (add about 65€/$75, and they'll throw in ski rentals as well). Private lessons cost 40€ ($46) per hour for one person, plus 12€ ($14) for each additional person.

You can **rent** skis at many outlets throughout town, including stands at the lower and upper stations of the Freccia nel Cielo cable car and other funiculars. Rentals average 14€ to 27€ ($16–$31) per day for skis and poles (less for longer periods), plus 5€ to 10€ ($5.75–$12) for boots.

HIKING & ROCK CLIMBING   In this mountainous terrain, these two activities are often synonymous. The tourist office can provide maps of hiking trails throughout the surrounding region. For high-altitude hiking, canyoning, and rock climbing, you may want to join one of the excursions led by **Gruppo Guide Alpine Cortina,** Corso Italia 69A (✆ **0463-868505;** www.guidecortina.com), open from 8am to noon and 4 to 8pm.

HORSEBACK RIDING   **Fattoria Meneguto,** in outlying Fraina (✆ **0463-860441**), offers group and individual riding through the lovely valleys surrounding Cortina. The stables are open from late spring to late fall from 10am to noon and 3 to 7pm. Call ahead to arrange for a ride, and be prepared to show you know how to sit in the saddle (Italians actually get a sort of driver's license for horseback riding; since we Yanks lack this, we have to prove ourselves on the spot). Rides cost 10€ ($12) for 30 minutes and 20€ ($23) for an hour.

ICE-SKATING   At the **Stadio Olimpico del Ghiaccio,** just to the northwest of the town center on Via del Stadio (✆ **0436-4380**), you can practice turns on the two recently refurbished rinks where Olympians tried for the gold in the 1956 Winter Olympic Games. Admission plus skate rental should be around 9€ ($10).

MOUNTAIN BIKING   The roads and tracks leading into the peaks provide arduous biking terrain; many cyclists from all over the world come to Cortina to practice for events. If you want to test your mettle, you can rent a bike from the **Due & Due,** Via Roma 70 (© **0436-4121;** www.dueduecortina.com). Rentals are 25€ to 28€ ($29–$32) per day. The English-speaking staff will point you in the direction of routes that match your abilities.

RELAXING Unwind after any of these activities at the indoor **swimming pool** at the **Piscina Coperta Comunale** (© **0436-860581**), just north of town in outlying Guargne. It is open from early July though October daily from 3:30 to 8pm (until 9:30pm Tues and Thurs); admission is 6.50€ ($7.45). You can also kick back and soothe those sore muscles in its **sauna** for 19€ ($22), or 21€ ($24) for a private session.

ACCOMMODATIONS YOU CAN AFFORD

Cortina is booked solid during the high season: August, Christmas, and from late January to March. You should reserve well in advance. Rates are lowest in late spring and early fall. Keep in mind that many innkeepers prefer to give rooms to guests who will stay several days or longer and who will take meals at the hotel. Given the scarcity of reasonably priced restaurants in town, you will probably be happy settling for a half- or full-board plan. The tourist board provides a list of private homes that take in guests, a way to keep costs down while enjoying the local hospitality, which is considerable.

Hotel Bellaria The Majoni family, which owns this pleasant hotel a short walk from the center on the northern edge of town, did a complete refurbishing recently, but they chose to keep prices down for the benefit of the patrons who come here season after season. As a result, they still provide some of Cortina's most reasonably priced accommodations. They house their guests in handsome, sunny rooms that overlook the mountains and have fresh Alpine-style pine furnishings, firm new beds, and crisp fabrics. All of the bathrooms have been redone and fitted with heated towel racks. Downstairs, there's a lovely paneled lounge, a dining room, a pleasant terrace in front of the house, and a lawn out back.

Corso Italia 266, 32043 Cortina d'Ampezzo. © 0436-2505. Fax 0436-5755. www.hbellaria.it. 22 units. 42€–114€ ($48–$131) single; 70€–190€ ($81–$219) double. Rates include breakfast. Half pension available. DC, MC, V. Closed 1 month in fall or spring. **Amenities:** Restaurant; bar; concierge; tour desk; courtesy car; room service; babysitting; laundry service; dry cleaning; nonsmoking rooms. *In room:* TV, dataport, hair dryer.

Hotel Montana ⚔ Right in the center of town, this hotel occupies a tall, pretty, Alpine-style house and is run by the amiable Adriano and Roberta Lorenzi, who provide some of the resort's nicest lodgings for the price. Guest rooms are pleasant and cozy, with old-style armoires, hardwood floors, and down quilts on the beds. Many open to balconies overlooking the peaks. Most of the doubles are quite large, and many are beautifully paneled and have separate sitting areas. Half the rooms here are singles, making this an ideal spot for solo travelers. There is no restaurant, but breakfast is served in a pleasant room where guests tend to linger through much of the morning.

Corso Italia 94, 32043 Cortina d'Ampezzo. © 0436-862126. Fax 0436-868211. www.cortina-hotel.com. 30 units. 35€–64€ ($40–$74) single; 55€–126€ ($63–$145) double. Check website for deals and discounts. Rates include breakfast. AE, DC, MC, V. Closed Nov and June. **Amenities:** Bike rental; video arcade; concierge; tour desk; room service; babysitting; laundry service. *In room:* TV, dataport, hair dryer (ask at desk), safe.

WORTH A SPLURGE

Hotel Menardi ⚔ One of the oldest and most charming hostelries in Cortina successfully combines the luxury and service of a fine hotel with the homelike comfort of a mountain inn. The Menardi family, which converted its farmhouse into a guesthouse in the 1920s, has over the years beautifully appointed the public rooms with antiques and comfortable furnishings, and done up the high-ceilinged, wood-floored guest rooms simply but tastefully with painted or pine armoires and bedsteads, down quilts, and attractive floral fabrics. Rooms in the rear of the house are especially quiet and pleasant, looking across the hotel's spacious lawns to the forests and peaks. Some newer (but still panel-and-pine Alpine) rooms are located in an annex next door; many of them have large balconies with picnic tables. Most guests take half board to avail themselves of the excellent meals in a dining room converted from the former stalls (at the turn of the 20th c., they rented extra horses to carriages about to tackle the mountain roads). It is also possible to make bed-and-breakfast arrangements when the hotel is not fully booked. A rather pretty public foot trail leads from the back lawn into town in 15 minutes.

Via Majon 110, 32043 Cortina d'Ampezzo. ℂ 0436-2400. Fax 0436-862183. www.hotelmenardi.it. 49 units. 55€–115€ ($63–$132) single; 90€–210€ ($104–$242) double. Rates include buffet breakfast. Half pension 22€–25€ ($25–$29) more per person. DC, MC, V. Parking free. Closed Apr 3–June 1 and Sept 18–Dec 22. **Amenities:** Restaurant; bar; golf course (9 holes, 3km/1¾ miles away); bike rental; children's playground; concierge; tour desk; car-rental desk; 24-hr. room service; laundry service; dry cleaning. *In room:* TV, dataport, minibar, hair dryer, safe.

GREAT DEALS ON DINING

Inexpensive meals are hard to come by in Cortina—even pizzerias are few and far between. For a low-cost meal, you might want to equip yourself for a **picnic** at **La Piazzetta,** Corso Italia 53, with a mouthwatering assortment of salamis, cheeses, breads, and other fare. Another source of supplies is the department store **La Cooperativa,** Corso Italia 40 (ℂ **0436-861245**), the largest, best-stocked supermarket for kilometers around.

Al Camin ALPINE   If you follow the Via Alvera along the Ru Bigontina, a rushing mountain stream, about 10 minutes east from the center of town, you'll come to this charming, rustic restaurant. The tables in the wood-paneled dining room are grouped around a large stone fireplace. The menu offers many local favorites. Your meal may include what is known in this part of the region as *kenederli* (these dumplings flavored with liver are known as *canederli* outside of the immediate vicinity of Cortina). Some dishes, many of them seasonal, you may not encounter elsewhere—these include *radicchio di prato,* a mountain green that appears in early spring and is served dressed with hot lard; and, in winter, *formaggio fuso con funghi e polenta,* a lush combination of creamy melted mountain cheese and wild mushrooms served over polenta.

Via Alverà 99. ℂ 0436-862010. www.alcamin.it. Reservations recommended. Primi 6€–10€ ($6.90–$12); secondi 7€–18€ ($8.05–$21). MC, V. Tues–Sun noon–3pm and 7–11:30pm.

Caffè Royal   The Corso Italia, Cortina's pedestrians-only main street, is the center of the town's social life. This cafe is one of several that occupy the ground floor of large hotels along the street, and it is one of the more pleasant. As soon as it's even remotely possible to sit outdoors, tables are set out front on a sunny terrace. At other times, patrons are welcome to sit for hours over coffee, pastries, or sandwiches in a pleasant room off the lobby of the hotel of the same name.

Corso Italia. ℂ 0436-867045. Sandwiches and other snacks from about 2€ ($2.30). MC, V. Wed–Mon 8am–9pm.

La Tavernetta ALPINE   In December 2003, this beloved stylish-yet-reasonable restaurant moved a few blocks from its old home into a rustic space on Via del Castello. The menu, however, remained the same, relying on local ingredients and the typical, hearty dishes of the Alto Adige. You might want to begin with a dish of polenta delicately infused with *asparagi selvatici* (the tips of fresh wild asparagus) or *gnocchi di spinachi* (gnocchi filled with spinach and topped with a rich wild game sauce), then move on to a robust *stinco di vitello con patate* (veal shank served with creamy potato) or *cervo in salsa di mirtilli* (venison with a sauce of myrtle berries with polenta).

Via del Castello 53. (*) **0436-868102.** Reservations recommended. Primi 7€–12€ ($8.05–$14); secondi 13€–20€ ($15–$23). AE, MC, V. Thurs–Tues noon–2:30pm and 7:30–11pm.

9

Milan, Lombardy & the Lakes

by Reid Bramblett

There's a lot more to Italy's most prosperous province, **Lombardy (Lombardia),** than the factories that fuel its economy. Many of the attractions here are urban—in addition to Milan, a string of Renaissance cities dots the Lombardian plains, from Pavia to Mantua. To the north, the region bumps up against craggy mountains and romantic lakes, and to the south it spreads out in fertile farmlands fed by the Po and other rivers. The Lombardians, who over the centuries have been ruled by feudal dynasties (Spanish, Austrian, French), are a little more Continental than their neighbors to the south, faster talking, and a little faster paced as well. They even dine a little differently, tending to eschew olive oil for butter and often forgoing pasta for polenta and risotto.

Among the region's greatest treasures (aside from some notable works of art and architecture) are the Italian lakes, admired over the centuries by poets and writers from Catullus to Ernest Hemingway. Backed by the Alps and ringed by lush gardens and verdant forests, each has its own charms and, accordingly, its own enthusiasts. Not least among these charms is their easy accessibility to many Italian cities, making them ideal for short retreats: Lago Maggiore (Lake Maggiore) and Lago di Como (Lake Como) are both less than an hour's distance from Milan, and Lago di Garda (Lake Garda) is tantalizingly close to Venice, Verona, and Mantua.

1 Milan: More Than *The Last Supper*

552km (342 miles) NW of Rome, 288km (179 miles) NW of Florence, 257km (159 miles) W of Venice, 140km (87 miles) NE of Turin, 142km (88 miles) N of Genoa

Milan (Milano) is Italy's financial center, business hub, and fashion capital, as well as one of its most industrialized major cities. But it's crowded, noisy, hot in summer and damp and foggy in winter, less easygoing, and more expensive than most Italian cities—in short, not as appealing as Venice, Florence, or Rome. Milan, though, reveals its long history in a pride of monuments, museums, and churches—its cathedral is one of Europe's great Gothic monuments, and another church contains Leonardo's *The Last Supper*. It also sets one of Italy's finest tables and supports a cultural scene embracing La Scala (one of the world's top opera houses), high-fashion boutiques and shows, and throbbing nightlife. With its dazzling shop windows and sophisticated ways, Milan is a pleasure to get to know—and, despite all that's been said about the exorbitant prices, you needn't empty the bank account to do so.

ESSENTIALS
GETTING THERE   By Plane   Both of Milan's airports are operated by **SEA** (© **02-74852200;** www.sea-aeroportimilano.it).

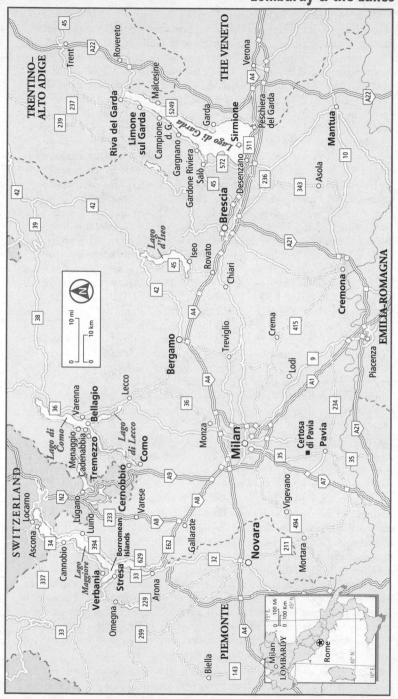

Milan Malpensa, 45km (28 miles) west of the center, is Milan's new international airport. It has been crowned worst major airport in Europe by the continent's official oversight committee in terms of flight delays and convenience (it's far from the city, and the rail link wasn't ready until 2 years after the airport opened). For general information, call ✆ 02-74852200 or 02-76800613.

A 50-minute Malpensa Express train (✆ 02-277763; www.ferrovienord.it/webmxp) costs 9€ ($10) and heads half-hourly to Cadorna train station in western Milan rather than the larger or more central Stazione Centrale from which most trains onward to other Northern Italian points leave (you'll have to take the Metro to get there). More convenient, perhaps, are the Malpensa shuttle buses, which will take you directly to that central downtown rail station; your choices are **Malpensa Bus Express** (✆ 02-96192301), which costs 5.50€ ($6.30), or the cheaper **Malpensa Shuttle** (✆ 02-58583185)—same exact service, lower price: 4.50€ ($5.15)—two to three times per hour for the 50-minute ride to the east side of Milan's Stazione Centrale. The trip into town by taxi costs a whopping 60€ to 75€ ($69–$86). If you're going to the airport to leave on a flight, make sure you call the airline beforehand to find out which terminal you need, as Malpensa's Terminal 1 and Terminal 2 are actually kilometers apart.

Milan Linate, only 7km (4⅓ miles) east of the center, handles some European flights (which are increasingly being moved to Malpensa) and domestic flights. For information, dial ✆ 02-74852200. **Starfly buses** (✆ 02-717106) run from Linate to Stazione Centrale every 20 minutes from 7am to 7pm and every half-hour from 7 to 9pm; allow 20 minutes for the trip. Purchase tickets (4€/$4.60) on the bus or from the Malpensa Shuttle terminal at the east end of Stazione Centrale. You can also take city bus no. 73 to and from Linate, from the southeast corner of Piazza San Babila, a few blocks east of the Duomo (1€/$1.15). A taxi trip into town costs about 12€ to 18€ ($14–$21).

Air Pullman buses (✆ 02-58583202) also connect Malpensa and Linate every 90 minutes from 6am to 8pm. The trip takes 1 hour and 15 minutes and costs 8€ ($9.20).

By Train   Milan is one of Europe's busier rail hubs, with connections to all major cities on the Continent. Trains arrive and depart about every half-hour to and from **Venice** (2½–3½ hr.; 12€–21€/$14–$24) and hourly to and from **Rome** (4½–6 hr.; 38€–47€/$44–$54) and **Florence** (2¾–4 hr.; 17€–29€/$20–$33).

The **Stazione Centrale,** a vast Fascist-era structure, is about a half-hour walk northeast of the center, with easy connections to Piazza del Duomo by Metro, tram, and bus. The station stop on the Metro is Centrale F. S.; it's only 10 minutes (and 1€/$1.15) away from the Duomo stop, in the city's heart. If you want to see something of the city en route, take bus no. 60 from the station to Piazza del Duomo. If you decide to walk, follow Via Pisani through the district of high-rise office buildings around the station to the equally cheerless Piazza della Repubblica, and from there continue south on Via Turati and Via Manzoni to Piazza del Duomo. Chances are, you'll arrive at Stazione Centrale, but some trains serve Milan's other train stations: **Stazione Nord** (with service to/from Como, among other cities), **Porta Genova** (with service to/from Alessandria and Asti), and **Porta Garibaldi** (with service to/from Lecco).

By Bus   Given Milan's excellent rail links with other cities in Lombardy and throughout Italy, it's usually unnecessary to travel by long-distance buses, which tend to take longer and cost more than the trains do. If you choose to travel by intercity bus, expect to arrive at and depart from **Autostradale,** in front of the Castello Sforzesco on Piazza Castello (Metro: Cairoli). The ticket

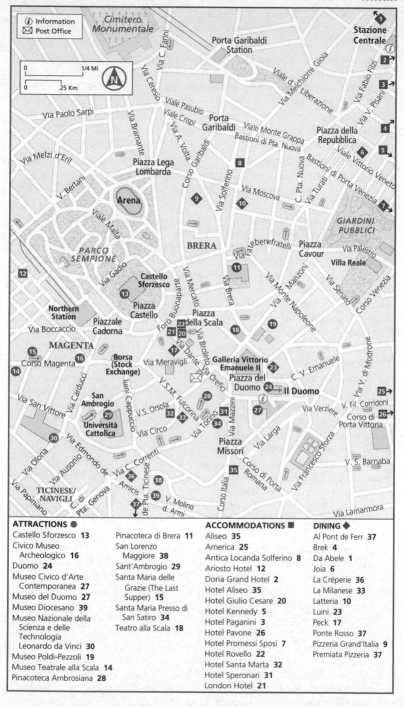

Milan

Cimitero
Monumentale

Porta Garibaldi
Station

Stazione
Centrale

Via C. Farini

Via Ceresio

Via Paolo Sarpi

Via Bramante

Viale Pasubio

Viale Crispi

Via A. Volta

Porta
Garibaldi

Viale Monte Grappa

Bastioni di Pta. Nuova

Viale d. Melchiorre Gioia

Via Melchiorre Gioia

Via Fabio Filzi

Via V. Pisani

Piazza della
Repubblica

Via Melzi d'Eril

V. Bertani

Corso Garibaldi

Via Solferino

Via Moscova

C. Pta. Nuova

Via Turati

Bastioni di Porta Venezia

Viale Vittorio Veneto

Piazza Lega
Lombarda

Arena

Viale Malta

Via Gadio

PARCO
SEMPIONE

BRERA

Via Mercato

Foro Buonaparte

GIARDINI
PUBBLICI

Fatebenefratelli

Piazza
Cavour

Villa Reale

Via Palestro

Via Senato

Corso Venezia

Castello
Sforzesco

Piazza
Castello

Via Brera

Via Monte Napoleone

Via Manzoni

Northern
Station

Piazzale
Cadorna

Via Boccaccio

Piazza
della Scala

MAGENTA

Corso Magenta

Borsa
(Stock
Exchange)

Via Meravigli

Via Dante

Via Broletto

Via Orefici

Galleria Vittorio
Emanuele II

Piazza del
Duomo

Il Duomo

C. V. Emanuele

Via V. di Modrone

V. Fil. Corridoni

Corso di
Porta Vittoria

San
Ambrogio

Via Carducci

Luini Cappuccio

V.S.M. Fulcorina

V.S. Orsola

Via Torino

Via Mazzini

Via Verziere

Università
Cattolica

Via Circo

Via Larga

Piazza
Missori

V. S. Barnaba

Via Olona

Via Edmondo de

Via C. Correnti

Corso Italia

Corso di Porta
Romana

Corso Francesco Sforza

Via San Vittore

Via Ausonio

Amicis

Via della Ponte. Genova

TICINESE/
NAVIGLI

Via Papiniano

C. di Pta. Ticinese

V. Molino
d. Armi

Via Lamarmora

ATTRACTIONS ●

Castello Sforzesco **13**
Civico Museo
  Archeologico **16**
Duomo **24**
Museo Civico d'Arte
  Contemporanea **27**
Museo del Duomo **27**
Museo Diocesano **39**
Museo Nazionale della
  Scienza e delle
  Technologia
  Leonardo da Vinci **30**
Museo Poldi-Pezzoli **19**
Museo Teatrale alla Scala **14**
Pinacoteca Ambrosiana **28**

Pinacoteca di Brera **11**
San Lorenzo
  Maggiore **38**
Sant'Ambrogio **29**
Santa Maria delle
  Grazie (The Last
  Supper) **15**
Santa Maria Presso di
  San Satiro **34**
Teatro alla Scala **18**

ACCOMMODATIONS ■

Aliseo **35**
America **25**
Antica Locanda Solferino **8**
Ariosto Hotel **12**
Doria Grand Hotel **2**
Hotel Aliseo **35**
Hotel Giulio Cesare **20**
Hotel Kennedy **5**
Hotel Paganini **3**
Hotel Pavone **26**
Hotel Promessi Sposi **7**
Hotel Rovello **22**
Hotel Santa Marta **32**
Hotel Speronari **31**
London Hotel **21**

DINING ◆

Al Pont de Ferr **37**
Brek **4**
Da Abele **1**
Joia **6**
La Créperie **36**
La Milanese **33**
Latteria **10**
Luini **23**
Peck **17**
Ponte Rosso **37**
Pizzeria Grand'Italia **9**
Premiata Pizzeria **37**

office ((C) **02-33910794;** www.autostradale.com) is open daily from 6:30am to 9:30pm. The most useful run is on one of 12 daily buses to and from **Turin** (2¼ hr.; 17€/$20).

By Car   Milan is well served by Italy's superhighway *(autostrada)* system. The A1 links Milan with Florence and Rome (Florence is a little over 3 hr. away by car, Rome is a little under 6 hr.), and the A4 connects Milan with Verona and Venice to the east and Turin to the west (Venice is about 2½ hr. from Milan by car, Turin a little over 1 hr.). Driving and parking in Milan are not experiences to be relished; in fact, much of the central city is closed to traffic. Many hotels make parking arrangements for guests; ask when you reserve a room.

VISITOR INFORMATION   The main **Azienda di Promozione Turistica del Milanese (APT) tourist office** is in the Palazzo del Turismo at Via Marconi 1 on the Piazza del Duomo ((C) **02-72524301;** www.milanoinfotourist.com). Hours are Monday to Friday from 8:30am to 8pm, Saturday from 9am to 1pm and 2 to 7pm, and Sunday from 9am to 1pm and 2 to 5pm. There is also an **office in Stazione Centrale** ((C) **02-72524360**), open Monday to Friday 8am to 7pm, Saturday 9am to 6pm, and Sunday 9am to 12:30pm and 1:30 to 6pm. The tourism section of the city's website (**www.turismo.comune.milano.it**) is also helpful, as is the museums site **www.museidelcentro.mi.it.**

These offices issue maps, museum guides, hotel and restaurant listings, and a wealth of other useful information, but since they're now privately run, they charge nominal fees for most of the more useful pamphlets, including 1€ ($1.15) for *Milano: Where, When, How.* Monthly events brochure *Milano Mese,* and *Hello Milano* (www.hellomilano.it), both with extensive listings of museum exhibitions, performances and other events, are still free.

FESTIVALS & MARKETS   Though it's overshadowed by the goings-on in Venice, Milan's pre-Lenten **Carnevale** is becoming increasingly popular, with costumed parades and an easygoing good time, much of it focusing on Piazza del Duomo beginning a week or so before Ash Wednesday. Just before the city shuts down in August, the city council stages a series of June and July **dance, theater, and music events** in theaters and open-air venues around the city.

In a city as well dressed as Milan, it only stands to reason that some great-looking castoffs are bound to turn up at **street markets.** Milan's largest street market is the one held on Via Papiniano in the Ticinese/Navigli district on Tuesday mornings from 8am to 1pm and on Saturday from 9am to 7:30pm; many of the stalls sell designer seconds as well as barely used high-fashion wear (Metro: Sant'Agostino).

There's an **antiques market** on Via Fiori Chiari in the Brera district the third Saturday of each month, from 9am to about 7:30pm, but not in August (Metro: Moscova), and another the last Sunday of each month on the quays along the Canale Grande in the Navigli district the last Sunday of each month, from 9am to about 7:30pm ((C) **02-89409971;** Metro: Sant'Agostino).

Every Sunday morning, there's a large **flea market,** with everything from books to clothing to appliances, at the San Donato metro stop. A fascinating array of handicrafts from different regions of Italy and around the world is on sale at the market around Viale Tunisia Tuesday through Sunday from 9:30am to 1pm and 3 to 7:30pm ((C) **02-29408057;** Metro: Porta Venezia).

The city's largest **food market** is the one at Piazza Wagner, just outside the city center due west of the church of Santa Maria delle Grazie (follow Corso

Magenta and its extension, Corso Vercelli to Piazza Piemonte; the market is 1 block north); it's held Tuesday through Saturday from 8am to 1pm and 4 to 7:30pm, and Monday from 8am to 1pm; the displays of mouthwatering foodstuffs fill an indoor market space and stalls that surround it (Metro: Piazza Wagner).

CITY LAYOUT　Think of Milan as a series of concentric circles radiating from Piazza del Duomo at the center. Within the inner circle, once enclosed by the city walls, are many of the churches, museums, and shops that'll consume your visiting hours. For a general overview of the lay of the land, obtain one of the serviceable maps, with indexes, the tourist offices provide for free.

The city's major neighborhoods encircle the hub, **Piazza del Duomo.** Looking east from the Duomo, you can see the imposing **Castello Sforzesco,** at one end of the well-heeled **Magenta neighborhood.** You can walk to the Castello in about 15 minutes by following **Via Orefici** to **Piazza Cordusio** and, from there, **Via Dante.** The other major draw in Magenta is **Santa Maria delle Grazie** *(The Last Supper);* to reach it, leave Via Dante at **Via Meravigli,** which becomes **Via Magenta** and leads to the church (total walking time from Piazza del Duomo to the church is about 20 min.).

Heading north from Piazza del Duomo, walk through the city's glass-enclosed shopping center (the world's first), the **Galleria Vittorio Emanuelle II.** Emerging from the northern end of the Galleria, you'll be steps away from **Piazza della Scala** and Milan's famous opera house, **La Scala.** A walk northeast of about 5 minutes along **Via Manzoni** takes you to **Via Montenapoleone** and the city's high-fashion shopping district, the epicenter of Italian design. A walk of about 10 minutes north of Piazza della Scala along **Via Brera** brings you into the atmospheric **Brera neighborhood,** where cobblestone streets and old *palazzi* (palaces) surround the city's major art collection, the **Pinacoteca di Brera.**

Another neighborhood to set your sights on is **Ticinese/Navigli,** often referred to just as the Navigli, which translates as "canals." Due south of Piazza del Duomo, the Navigli's old quays follow what remains of an elaborate canal system, designed in part by Leonardo da Vinci, that once laced the city. The moody charm of this area isn't lost on prosperous young Milanese, who are converting old lofts and moving into former quarters of the working classes. The attendant bars, shops, and restaurants on the ground floors have appeared to serve their needs; it's the only part of Milan open in August. You can walk to the Navigli in about 30 minutes from Piazza del Duomo by following **Via Torino** south to **Corso Porta Ticinese,** but a Metro ride to the Porta Genova will get you there more quickly.

GETTING AROUND　An extensive and efficient **subway system (Metropolitana Milanese), trams,** and **buses** make it very easy to move around Milan. The metro closes at midnight, though buses and trams run all night. Tickets good for one metro ride (or 75 min. of surface transportation) cost 1€ ($1.15). You can also purchase a ticket good for unlimited travel for 1 day (3€/$3.45) or 2 days (5.50€/$6.30). Tickets are available at metro stations and at newsstands. It's obligatory to stamp your ticket when you board a bus or tram—you can be slapped with a hefty fine if you don't. For information about Milan public transportation, visit the ATM information office in the Duomo metro stop, open Monday through Friday 8:30am to 8pm, and weekends 9am to 1pm and 2 to 7pm (to 5pm Sun; © **02-72524301** or 800-808181; www.atm-mi.it).

FAST FACTS: Milan

American Express The office is at Via Larga 4 (© 02-721041). It's open Monday through Friday from 9am to 5:30pm and Saturday from 9am to 5pm (Metro: Cairoli). Cardholders can arrange cash advances, receive mail (the postal code is 20122), and wire money.

Bookstores Milan has two English-language bookshops. The **American Bookstore,** between the Duomo and Castello Sforzesco at Via Camperio 16 at the corner with Via Dante (© 02-878920), is open Monday from 1 to 7pm and Tuesday through Saturday from 10am to 7pm (Metro: Cardusio). The **English Bookshop,** Via Ariosto at Via Mascheroni 12 (© 02-4694468; www.englishbookshop.it), is open Monday through Saturday from 9am to 8pm. **Rizzoli,** the glamorous outlet of one of Italy's leading publishers in the Galleria Vittorio Emanuele (© 02-8052277; www.libreriarizzoli.it), also has some English-language titles, as well as a sumptuous collection of art and photo books. It's open daily from 8am to 8pm. For English-language newspapers and magazines, check out the newsstands in Stazione Centrale and around Piazza del Duomo.

Consulates The **U.S. Consulate** is at Via Principe Amadeo 2/10 (© 02-290351); it's open Monday through Friday from 9 to 11am and 2 to 4pm (Metro: Turati). The **Canadian Consulate,** at Via Pisani 19 (© 02-67581), is open Monday to Thursday 8:30am to 12:30pm and 1:15 to 5:30pm (Metro: F.S. Centrale or Repubblica); the **British Consulate,** Via San Paolo 7 (© 02-23001), is open Monday to Friday from 9:15am to 12:15am and 2:30 to 4:30pm (Metro: Duomo); the **Australian Consulate,** at Via Borgogna 2 (© 02-777042), is open Monday to Thursday 9am to noon and 2 to 4pm (Metro: San Babila); and the **New Zealand Consulate,** at Via Arezzo 6 (© 02-48012544), is open Monday to Friday from 9am to 11am (Metro: Pagano).

Crime For police emergencies, dial © 113; you can reach the English-speaking staff of the tourist police at © 02-863701. There is a police station in Stazione Centrale, and the main station, the **Questura,** is just west of the Giardini Pubblici at Via Fatebenefratelli 11 (© 02-62261; Metro: Turati). Milan is generally safe, with some notable exceptions, especially at night, including the public gardens, Parco Sempione, and the area to the west of Stazione Centrale. The train station is notorious for pickpockets, whose favorite victims seems to be distracted passengers lining up for the airport buses at the east side of the building. You should likewise be vigilant for pickpockets on all public transportation and at street markets.

Drugstores Pharmacies rotate 24-hr. shifts; dial © 192 to find pharmacies that are open around the clock on a given day, or look for a sign posted in most pharmacies announcing which shop is keeping a 24-hr. schedule. The **Farmacia Stazione Centrale** (© 02-6690935), in the main train station, is open 24 hours daily and some of the staff speaks English.

Emergencies The general number for emergencies is © 113. For the police, call © 112; for first aid or an ambulance, dial © 118.

Hospitals The **Ospedale Maggiore Policlinico** (© 02-5503; www.policlinico.mi.it) is centrally located a 5-minute walk southeast of the Duomo at Via

Francesco Sforza 35 (Metro: Duomo or Missori). Some of the medical personnel speak English.

Lost Property The lost baggage number for **Aeroporto della Malpensa** is 📞 **02-74854215.** For **Aeroporto Linate,** the number is 📞 **02-70102094.** The English-speaking staff at these offices handle luggage that has gone astray on most airlines serving the airports, though a few airlines maintain their own lost baggage services. The **lost and found at Stazione Centrale** (located in the same office as the luggage storage) is open daily from 7am to 1pm and 2 to 8pm (📞 **02-6371-2667**). The **city-run lost-and-found office** is just south of Piazza del Duomo, at Via Friuli 30 (📞 **02-5516141**), and is open Monday to Friday 8:30am to 12:45pm and 2:15 to 5pm (Metro: Duomo or Missori).

Luggage Storage The luggage storage office in Stazione Central is open daily from 5am to 4am; the fee is 2.60€ ($3) per piece of baggage for each 12-hour period.

Post Office The main post office, **Poste e Telecommunicazioni,** is just west of Piazza del Duomo, at Via Cordusio 4 (📞 **02-72482126;** www.poste.it; Metro: Cardusio). Windows are open Monday to Friday 8:30am to 5:30pm and Saturday 8:30am to 1:50pm. Most branch offices are open Monday to Saturday 8:30am to 1:30pm. There is a post office in Stazione Centrale, open Monday through Friday 8:15am to 5:30pm and Saturday 8:15am to 3:30pm.

Taxis To find a taxi in Milan, walk to the nearest taxi stand, usually located near major piazzas and major Metro stops. In the center, there are taxi stands at Piazza Duomo and Piazza della Scala. Or, call a **radio taxi** at 📞 **02-4040, 02-6767, 02-8585, 02-5353, or 02-8383** (the desk staff at many hotels will be happy to do this for you, even if you are not a guest). Cab meters start at 3.10€ ($3.55) and add a nighttime surcharge of 3.10€ ($3.55) and a Sunday surcharge of 1.55€ ($1.80).

Telephones You'll find public telephones throughout Milan. Local calls cost .10€ (11¢), and the phones accept coins or phone cards *(carta telefonica),* which you can purchase at tobacco shops in denominations of 1€ ($1.15) up to 7.50€ ($8.60). You can also make calls from the SIP/Telecom office in Stazione Centrale, open daily from 8am to 9:30pm, and the one in the Galleria Vittorio Emanuele, open daily from 8am to 9:30pm. Some phones in these offices also accept major credit cards, and you can buy Italian phone cards on the premises. The area code for Milan is 📞 **02.**

SIGHTS TO SEE

Duomo ★★★ When Milanese think something is taking too long, they refer to it as *la fabricca del duomo*—the making of the Duomo, a reference to the 5 centuries it took to complete the magnificent Gothic cathedral that rises from the center of the city. The last of Italy's great Gothic structures—begun by the ruling Visconti family in 1386—is the fourth largest church in the world (after St. Peter's in Rome, Seville's cathedral, and a new one on the Ivory Coast), with 135 marble spires, a stunning triangular facade, and 3,400-some statues flanking the massive but airy, almost fanciful, exterior.

The cavernous **interior,** lit by brilliant stained-glass windows, seats 40,000 but is unusually spartan and serene, divided into five aisles by a sea of 52 columns. The poet Shelley used to sit and read Dante amid monuments that include a gruesomely graphic statue of *St. Bartholomew Flayed* and the tombs of Giacomo de Medici, two Visconti, and many cardinals and archbishops. Another British visitor, Alfred, Lord Tennyson, rhapsodized about the view of the Alps from the **roof** (elevators on the church's exterior northeast corner; stairs on the exterior north side), where you get to wander amid the Gothic pinnacles, saintly statues, and flying buttresses. You are joined high above Milan by the spire-top gold statue of *Madonnina* (the little Madonna), the city's beloved protectress.

Back on terra firma, the **crypt** contains the remains of San Carlo Borromeo, one of the early cardinals of Milan. A far more interesting descent is the one down the staircase to the right of the main entrance to the **Battistero Paleocristiano,** the ruins of a 4th-century baptistery believed to be where Saint Ambrose baptized Saint Augustine.

The Duomo houses many of its treasures across the piazza from the right transept in the **Museo del Duomo** section of Milan's Palazzo Reale. Among the legions of statuary saints is a gem of a painting by Jacopo Tintoretto, *Christ at the Temple,* and some riveting displays chronicling the construction of the cathedral. Adjoining this is the **Museo Civico d'Arte Contemporanea** (with works by living artists and such masters as De Chirico and Modigliani).

Piazza del Duomo. ✆ 02-86463456 or 02-72022656. www.duomomilano.com. Duomo free admission. Roof: 3.50€ ($4.05); 5€ ($5.75) with elevator. Crypt: 1.55€ ($1.75). Baptistery: 1.50€ ($1.75). Museum: 6€ ($6.90) adults, 3€ ($3.45) children under 18 and seniors over 65. Combination ticket for museum and elevator to roof 7€ ($8.05) Tues–Sun 9:30am–12:30pm and 3–6pm. Duomo: daily 6:50am–7pm. Roof: daily 7am–5:30pm. Crypt: daily 9am–noon and 2:30–6pm. Baptistery: Tues–Sun 10am–noon and 3–5pm. Metro: Duomo.

Santa Maria delle Grazie/The Last Supper   What draws so many visitors to Milan in the first place is the *Cenacolo Vinciano,* Leonardo da Vinci's *The Last Supper.* From 1495 to 1497 Leonardo painted this poignant portrayal of confusion and betrayal for the far wall of the refectory when this was a Dominican convent. Aldous Huxley called this fresco the "saddest work of art in the world," a comment in part on the deterioration that set in even before the paint had dried on the moisture-ridden walls. The fresco got a lot of well-intentioned but poorly executed "touching up" in the 18th and 19th centuries, though a recent lengthy restoration has done away with these centuries of overpainting, as well as tried to undo the damage wrought by the clumsy patching and damage inflicted when Napoleon's troops used the wall for target practice, and from when Allied bombing during World War II tore off the room's roof, leaving the fresco exposed to the elements for 3 years.

In short, *The Last Supper* is a mere shadow of the work the artist intended it to be, but the work, which captures the moment when Christ told his Apostles

---

Milan in a Day

For an excellent overview of the city, hop aboard vintage 1920s **tram no. 20,** distinguished by CIAO MILANO emblazoned on its sides, for a tour with commentary in English and five other languages. The 1¾-hour tours are hop-on/hop-off for a full day and run daily at 11am and 1pm (also 3pm in summer) from Piazza Castello (Metro: Cairoli). The cost is 20€ ($23). For more details, call ✆ 02-72524301.

Combo Ticket

A combination ticket for admission to the Pinacoteca di Brera, the *Last Supper*, and the Museo Teatrale alla Scala costs 10€ ($12)—a fantastic value.

that one of them would betray him, remains amazingly powerful and emotional nonetheless. Only 25 people are allowed to view the fresco at one time, and you must pass through a series of devices that remove pollutants from clothing. Accordingly, lines are long and tickets are usually sold out days in advance. I'm serious: If you don't book ahead, you'll likely be turned away at the door, even in the dead of winter when you'd expect the place to be empty (tour bus groups swallow up inordinately large batches of tickets, leaving precious few for us poor do-it-yourself travelers).

Often overlooked are the other great treasures of the late-15th-century church itself, foremost among them the fine dome and other architectural innovations by one of the great architects of the high Renaissance, Donato Bramante (one of the first architects of St. Peter's in Rome). To one side of the apse, decorated in marble and terra cotta, is a lovely cloister.

Piazza Santa Maria delle Grazie. *Last Supper:* ✆ 02-89421146. www.cenacolovinciano.it. Admission 6.50€ ($7.45) plus a ridiculously inflated booking fee of 1.50€ ($1.75). Tues–Sun 8am–7:30pm (may close at 1:45pm in winter). Church: ✆ 02-4676111. Free admission. Mon–Sat 7:30am–noon and 3–7pm; Sun 7:20am–12:15pm and 3:30–9pm (may close earlier in winter). Metro: Cardona or Conciliazione.

Galleria Vittorio Emanuele II 🏵🏵

Milan's late-19th-century version of a mall is this wonderful steel-and-glass-covered, cross-shape arcade. The elegant Galleria is the prototype of the enclosed shopping malls that were to become the hallmark of 20th-century consumerism. It's safe to say that none of the imitators has come close to matching the Galleria for style and flair. The designer of this urban marvel, Giuseppe Mengoni, didn't live to see the Milanese embrace his creation: He tripped and fell from a girder a few days before the Galleria opened in 1878. His shopping mall par excellence provides a lovely route between the Duomo and La Scala and is a fine locale for watching the flocks of well-dressed Milanese—you'll understand why the Galleria is called *Il Salotto di Milano* (the drawing room of Milan).

Just off Piazza del Duomo and Piazza della Scala. Metro: Duomo.

Pinacoteca di Brera 🏵🏵🏵

This 17th-century palazzo houses one of Italy's finest collections of medieval and Renaissance art; it's inarguably the world's finest collection of Northern Italian painting. The concentration of so many masterpieces here is the work of Napoleon, who used the palazzo as the repository for the art he confiscated from public and private holdings throughout northern Italy; fittingly, a bronze likeness of the emperor greets you as you enter the courtyard. Just as a sampling of what you'll encounter in these 40 or so rooms, three of Italy's greatest masterpieces hang here: Andrea Mantegna's amazingly foreshortened *Dead Christ* 🏵🏵🏵, Raphael's *Betrothal of the Virgin* 🏵🏵, and Piero della Francesa's *Madonna with Saints (the Montefeltro Altarpiece)* 🏵🏵. It is an indication of this museum's ability to overwhelm visitors that the last two absolute masterpieces hang near each other in a single room dedicated to works by Tuscan and Umbrian painters.

Paintings are continually being rearranged, but in the wake of a recently completed renovation, in the first rooms you will not encounter Napoleonic bounty, but the museum's sizeable collection of 20th-century paintings. From there, you

enter several galleries of sumptuous Venetian works, including Jacopo Tin-
teretto's *Finding of the Body of St. Mark* ⊕, in which the dead saint eerily confronts appropriately startled grave robbers who come upon his corpse.
Caravaggio (*Supper at Emmaus* ⊕⊕ is his masterpiece here) is surrounded by
works of his followers. Just beyond is a room devoted to works by foreigners,
among them Rembrandt's *Portrait of a Young Woman*. Given Napoleon's fondness for the Venetian schools, it is only just that the final rooms are again filled
with works from that city, including Canaletto's *View of the Grand Canal*.

You can rent an **audioguide** for 3.50€ ($4), or 5.50€ ($6.30) for two. Inexpensive guided tours in English have sometimes been available in the past on
weekends, so you might want to call ahead and ask if they're on this season.

Via Brera 28. ℂ 02-722631, or 02-89421146 (for reservations). www.brera.beniculturali.it. Admission 5€
($5.75). Tues–Sun 8:30am–7:15pm. Metro: Lanza or Montenapoleone. Tram: 1, 4, 8, 12, 14, 27. Bus: 61, 97.

Castello Sforzesco ⊕⊕ (Value)

Though it's been clumsily restored many
times, most recently at the end of the 19th century, this fortresslike castle continues to evoke Milan's two most powerful medieval and Renaissance families,
the Visconti and the Sforza. The Visconti built the castle in the 14th century,
and the Sforza, who married into the Visconti clan and eclipsed them in power,
reconstructed it in 1450. The most influential residents were Ludovico il Moro
and Beatrice d'Este (he of the Sforza and she of the famous Este family of Ferrara). After ill-advisedly calling the French into Italy at the end of the 15th century, Ludovico died in the dungeons of a château in the Loire valley—but not
before the couple made the Castello and Milan one of Italy's great centers of the
Renaissance. It was they who commissioned the works by Bramante and
Leonardo da Vinci, and these splendors can be viewed on a stroll through the
kilometers of salons that surround the Castello's enormous courtyard.

The salons house a series of small city-administered museums known collectively
as the Civici Musei Castello Sforzesco. They include a pinacoteca with works by
Bellini, Correggio, and Magenta, and the extensive holdings of the Museo d'Arte
Antica, filled with Egyptian funerary objects, prehistoric finds from Lombardy, several giant tapestries in a room filled with historical musical instruments, and the last
work of 89-year-old Michelangelo, his unfinished *Rondanini Pietà* ⊕⊕.

Piazza Castello. ℂ 02-62083940. www.milanocastello.it. Free admission. Tues–Sun 9am–5:30pm. Metro:
Cairoli, Cadorna, or Lanza.

Chiesa di San Lorenzo Maggiore ⊕

The oldest church in Milan attests to
the days when the city was the capital of the Western Roman Empire. The 4th-
century early Christian structure has been rebuilt and altered many times over
the centuries (its dome, the highest in Milan, is a 16th-c. embellishment), but it
retains the flavor of its roots in its octagonal floor plan and a few surviving remnants. These include 5th-century mosaics (one depicting a beardless Christ) in
the Cappella di Sant'Aquilino, which you enter from the atrium. A sarcophagus
in the chapel is said to enshrine the remains of Galla Placidia, sister of Honorius, last emperor of Rome and wife of Ataulf, king of the Visigoths. Ironically,
her mausoleum is one of the mosaic masterworks of Ravenna, and it is most
likely she is buried in Rome, where she died. You'll be rewarded with a glimpse
of even earlier history if you follow the stairs from behind the altar to a cryptlike room that contains what remains of a Roman amphitheater.

Corso di Porta Ticinese 39. ℂ 02-89404129. www.sanlorenzomaggiore.com. Admission 2€ ($2.30) adults,
1€ ($1.15) children. Mon–Sat 8am–12:30pm and 2–6:30pm; Sun 10:30–11:15am and 3–5:30pm. Metro:
Missori. Tram: 3. Bus: 94.

Chiesa di Sant'Ambrogio ⑆ From the basilica that he constructed on this site in the 4th century A.D.—when he was bishop of Milan and when the city, in turn, was briefly capital of the Western Roman Empire—Saint Ambrose had a profound effect on the development of the early church. Little remains of Ambrose's church, but the 11th-century structure built in its place and renovated many times since is remarkable. It has a striking atrium, lined with columned porticos and opening on one side to the brick facade, with two ranks of loggias and, on either side, a bell tower. Look carefully at the door on the left, where you'll see a relief of Saint Ambrose. Note the overall effect of this architectural assemblage because the church of Sant'Ambrogio set a standard for Lombard Romanesque architecture that you'll see imitated many times on your travels through Lombardy.

On your wanderings through the three-aisled nave, you'll come upon a gold altar from Charlemagne's days in Milan and, in the right aisle, the all-too-scant remains of a Tiepolo fresco cycle, most of it blown into oblivion by World War II bombs. The little that remains of the original church is the Sacello di San Vittore in Ciel d'Oro, a little chapel in which the cupola glows with 5th-century mosaics of saints (enter from the right aisle). The skeletal remains of Ambrose himself are on view in the crypt. One of the "later" additions as you leave the main church from the left aisle is another work of the great architect Bramante—his Portico dell Canonica, lined with elegant columns, some of which are sculpted to resemble tree trunks.

Piazza Sant'Ambrogio 15. ℂ **02-86450895.** www.santambrogio-basilica.it. Church: Free admission. Sacello di San Vittore: 2€ ($2.30). Mon–Sat 9:30am–noon and 2:30–6pm. Metro: Sant'Ambrogio. Bus 50, 58, 94.

Chiesa Santa Maria Presso di San Satiro What makes this beautiful church, just south of Piazza del Duomo, so exquisite is what it doesn't have— space. Stymied by not being able to expand the T-shape apse to classical Renaissance, cross-shape proportions, the architect Bramante created a marvelous relief behind the high altar. The effect of the *trompe-l'oeil* columns and arches is not entirely convincing but is nonetheless magical. Another gem lies to the rear of the left transept: the Cappella della Pietà, so called for the 15th-century terracotta *Pietà* it now houses but built in the 9th century to honor Saint Satiro, the brother of Saint Ambrose. The namesake statue is not the most alluring adornment in this charming little structure; it's the lovely Byzantine frescoes and Romanesque columns that will catch your eye. While this little-visited complex is now eclipsed by other, more famous Milan churches, it was an important pilgrimage site in the 13th and 14th centuries, after news spread through Christendom that an image of the Madonna here shed real blood when stabbed.

Via Torino (at Via Speronari). ℂ **02-874683.** Free admission. Daily 9am–noon and 2:30–6pm. Metro: Duomo or Missori.

Civico Museo Archeologico ⑆ *Value* The most fascinating finds in this sizable repository of civilizations past are the everyday items from Milan's Roman era— tools, eating utensils, jewelry, and some exquisite and remarkably well-preserved glassware. The exhibits, which seem to fill every corner of the 16th-century monastery in which the museum is housed, include Greek, Etruscan, and Roman pieces from throughout Italy; there's also a section devoted to ancient remains from Ghandara, India. You can get a glimpse of Roman architecture in the garden, where two Roman towers and a section of a road, part of the walls enclosing the settlement of Mediolanum, once capital of the Western Roman Empire, remain in situ.

Corso Magenta 15. ℂ **02-86450011.** Admission 2€ ($2.30). Tues–Sun 9:30am–5:30pm. Metro: Cadorna.

Museo Nazionale della Scienza e della Tecnologia Leonardo da Vinci ⊛

The heart and soul of this engaging museum are the **working-scale models** ⊛⊛ of Leonardo's submarines, airplanes, and other engineering feats that, for the most part, the master only ever invented on paper (each exhibit includes a reproduction of the master's drawings and a model of his creations). This former Benedictine monastery and its beautiful cloisters are also filled with planes, trains, carriages, sewing machines, typewriters, optical devices, and other exhibits, including some enchanting re-creations of workshops, that comprise one of the world's leading collections of mechanical and scientific wizardry.

Via San Vittore 21. ⓒ 02-48555331. www.museoscienza.org. Admission 7€ ($8.05) adults, 5€ ($5.75) for those under 18 or over 60. Tues–Fri 9:30am–5pm; Sat–Sun 9:30am–6:30pm. Metro: Sant'Ambrogio.

Museo Poldi-Pezzoli ⊛⊛

The pleasant effect of seeing the Bellinis, Botticellis, and Tiepolos amid these salons is reminiscent of a visit to other private collections, such as the Frick Collection in New York City and the Isabella Stewart Gardner Museum in Boston. This stunning treasure trove leans a bit toward Venetian painters (such as Francesco Guardi's elegantly moody *Grey Lagoon*) but also ventures widely throughout Italian painting and into the northern and Flemish schools. It was amassed by 19th-century collector Giacomo Poldi-Pezzoli, who donated his villa and its treasures to the city in 1881. Antonio Pollaiuolo's *Portrait of a Young Woman* is often likened to the *Mona Lisa*, in that it is a haunting image you will recognize immediately upon seeing it. The collections also include porcelain, watches, jewels, and many of the palazzo's original furnishings.

CD-ROM terminals let you explore bits of the collections not currently on display, especially arms and armor, the best of which is housed in an elaborate *pietra-serena* (the dark gray stone, typical to Tuscany) room designed by Pomodoro. For now they offer free audioguides (there may be a charge in the future). The admission ticket is actually a cumulative one that includes admission to the Museo Teatrale della Scala (in effect, you get the Scala one free).

Via Manzoni 12. ⓒ 02-794889. www.museopoldipezzoli.it. Admission 6€ ($6.90) adults, 4€ ($4.60) for those 11–18 or over 60. Tues–Sun 10am–6pm. Metro: Duomo or Montenapoleone. Tram: 2.

Pinacoteca Ambrosiana ⊛⊛

Much to the appreciation of art lovers who waited through the late 1990s for the museum to reopen, this exquisite collection is housed in newly restored galleries. The collection focuses on treasures from the 15th through 17th centuries: An *Adoration* by Titian, Raphael's cartoon for his *School of Athens* in the Vatican, Botticelli's *Madonna and Angels,* Caravaggio's *Basket of Fruit* (his only still life), and other stunning works hang in a series of intimate rooms. Notable (or infamous) among the paintings is *Portrait of a Musician,* attributed to Leonardo but, according to many scholars, of dubious provenance; if it is indeed a Leonardo, the haunting painting is the only portrait of his to hang in an Italian museum. The adjoining **Biblioteca Ambrosiana,** open to scholars only except for special exhibitions, houses a wealth of Renaissance literaria, including the letters of Lucrezia Borgia and a strand of her hair. The most notable holdings, though, are Leonardo's *Codice Atlantico,* 1,750 drawings and jottings the master did between

Combo Ticket

A combination ticket for admission to the Pinacoteca Ambrosiana, Museo del Duomo, and the new Museo Diocesano costs 12€ ($14).

'Til the Fat Lady Sings Again: The Restoration of La Scala

Arguably the single most important opera house in the world, Milan's **Teatro alla Scala** 🎭🎭 was built in the late 18th century on the site of a church of the same name in Piazza della Scala. La Scala is hallowed ground to lovers of Giuseppe Verdi (who was the house composer for decades), Maria Callas, Arturo Toscanini (conductor for much of the 20th c., a position held since 1970 by Riccardo Muti), and legions of other composers and singers who have hit the high notes of fame in the world's most revered opera house.

Although La Scala emerged from one renovation in 1999, the famed theater went under wraps yet again in 2001, not to return to its duties and the traditional December 7 gala opening night until 2005, at the earliest. In the meantime, the show does go on, as shows must, in custom-built digs called the **Teatro degli Arcimboldi** (📞 **02-72003744;** www.teatroallascala.org), way the heck up in the northern suburb of Bicocca.

The **Museo Teatrale alla Scala,** on the other hand, has simply moved to a building just beyond *The Last Supper,* at Corso Magenta 71 (📞 **02-4691528**), where you can get a whiff of operatic nostalgia for days gone by amid such mementoes as Toscanini's batons, a strand of Mozart's hair, a fine array of Callas postcards, original Verdi scores, a whole mess of historic gramophones and record players, and costumes designed by some of Milan's top fashion gurus and worn by the likes of Callas and Rudolf Nureyev on La Scala's stage. The museum is open Tuesday through Sunday from 9am to 6pm; admission is 5€ ($5.75).

1478 and 1519. These and the library's other volumes, including a rich collection of medieval manuscripts, are frequently put on view to the public; at these times, an entrance fee of 10€ ($12) allows entrance to both the library and the art gallery.

Piazza Pio XI, 2. 📞 **02-809921.** www.ambrosiana.it. Admission 7.50€ ($8.60) adults, 4.50€ ($5.15) children. Tues–Sun 10am–5pm. Metro: Cordusio, Duomo.

Museo Diocesano 🎭 *(Finds)* This museum, set just inside the Parco delle Basiliche—a collection of grass-fringed paths, playgrounds, and volleyball courts created just after World War II on the site of Milan's ancient execution grounds—opened in November 2001. It brings together the best works from small church museums and treasuries across Milan and Lombardy, from the Church of Sant'Ambrogio on down, alongside works of religious significance donated from various private collections. Among the works from the now-defunct Museo di Sant'Ambrogio is an important 10th-century carved wooden tondo of *S. Ambrogio.*

The Crespi collections include many 14th- and early-15th-century Gothic works by such Tuscan-school masters as Bernardo Daddi, Sano di Pietro, Agnolo Gaddi, Taddeo di Bartolo, Bicci di Lorenzo, and Nardo di Cione. The giant, excellently preserved 1510 altarpiece of saints by Marco d'Oggiono came from the church of Santo Stefano. Other paintings include works by the prolific

16th-century Campi clan of Cremona; a Tintoretto *Christ and the Adulterer;* a luminous *Crucifixion with Mary Magdalene,* by Francesco Hayez; many late-15th-century paintings by local boy Il Begognone; 17th- and 18th-century landscapes by Panini, Zuccarelli, and others; and Previati's important *Via Crucis* cycles from the 1880s. And what would a church museum be without a passel of 17th-century Flemish tapestries?

There are free audioguides in English and lots of helpful multimedia panels scattered throughout the museum.

Corso di Porta Ticinese 95. (✆) 02-89420019. www.museodiocesano.it. Admission 6€ ($6.90) adults, 4€ ($4.60) for those 6-18 or over 60. Tues–Sun 10am–6pm (to 10pm Thurs). Metro: Missori or Sant'Ambrogio.

SHOPPING

The best fashion gazing is to be done along four adjoining streets north of the Duomo known collectively as the **Quadrilatero d'Oro (Golden Quadrilateral): Via Montenapoleone, Via Spiga, Via Borgospesso,** and **Via Sant'Andrea,** lined with Milan's most expensive high-fashion emporia. (To enter this hallowed precinct, follow Via Manzoni a few blocks north from Piazza della Scala; San Babila is the closest metro stop.) The main artery of this shopping heartland is Via Montenapoleone, lined with the chi-chi'est boutiques and most elegant fashion outlets, with parallel Via della Spiga running a close second.

For more down-home shopping with the Milanese, cruise wide Corso Buenos Aires, home to a little bit of everything, from shops that hand-sew men's dress shirts to CD megastores. As it crosses Piazza Oberdan/Piazza Venezia heading south, it becomes Corso Venezia and the stores start moving up the scale.

HIGH FASHION AT LOW PRICES

Even if your wallet can't afford it, stop by to browse the flagship **Armani Megastore,** Via Manzoni 31, near La Scala (✆ **02-72318630;** www.armani-viamanzoni31.com; Metro: Montenapoleone). To celebrate 25 years in business in the summer of 2000, Giorgio opened this new flagship store/offices covering 743 sq. m (8,000 sq. ft.) with outlets for his high-fashion creations, the Emporio Armani and Armani Jeans lines, plus the new Armani Casa selection of home furnishings; flower, book, and art shops; a high-tech Sony electronics boutique/play center in the basement; and an Emporio Café and branch of New York's Nobu sushi bar.

If your fashion sense is greater than your credit line, don't despair: Even the most expensive clothing of the Armani line is usually less expensive in Italy than it is abroad, and citywide *saldi* (sales) run from early January into early February and again in late June and July.

Inspired by the window displays in the **Quadrilatero,** you can scour the racks of shops elsewhere for designer seconds, last year's fashions, imitations, and other bargains. The best place to begin is **Il Salvagente,** several blocks east of the Quadrilatero off Corso XXII Marzo at Via Fratelli Bronzetti 16 (✆ **02-76110328;** Metro: San Babila), where you can browse through an enormous collection of designer clothing for men, women, and children (mostly smaller sizes) at wholesale prices. **DMagazine,** Via Montenapoleone 26 (✆ **02-76006027;** Metro: Montenapoleone), may sit on the boutique-lined main chopping drag, but its merchandise is pure discount overstock from big labels such as Armani (I saw slacks for 99€/$114), Prada (how about a sweater for 72€/$83?), and Fendi (designer scarves for 44€/$46 anyone?).

Another haven for bargain hunters is the **Navigli.** Women can shop at **Eliogabaldo,** Piazza Sant'Eustorgio 2 (✆ **02-8378293;** Metro: San Agostino), where some of the offerings may be secondhand, but only in the sense that a model donned them briefly for a show or shoot. **Biffi,** Corso Genova 6 (© 02-8375170; Metro: San Agostino), attracts fashion-conscious hordes of both sexes in search of designer labels and the store's own designs. One more Navigli stop, and again well stocked with designer wear for men and women— but especially dresses (no changing rooms, so come prepared)—is nearby **Floretta Coen Musil,** Via San Calocero 3 (© 02-58111708; Metro: San Agostino), open Monday through Saturday afternoons only from 3:30 to 7:30pm, no credit cards.

The other hunting ground for discount fashions is **Corso Buenos Aires,** northeast of the center and just east of Stazione Centrale (follow Via Vitruvio from Piazza Duca d'Aosta in front of the station; Metro stops Lima and Loreto are the gateways to this bargain stretch).

Men will want to stop at **Darsena,** Corso Buenos Aires 16 (© 02-29521535), where you just might find an Armani suit or jacket at a rock-bottom price. **Il Drug Store,** Corso Buenos Aires 28 (© 02-29515592), keeps Milanese of both sexes attired, affordably so, in chic clothing best worn by the young and the thin. **Calzaturificio di Parabiago,** Corso Buenos Aires 52 (© 02-29406851), shods men and women fashionably at reasonable prices, with an enormous selection and a helpful staff. For designer shoes at a discount, look no further than **Rufus,** Via Vitruvio 35 (© 02-2049648), which carries men's and women's styles from lots of labels for under 80€ ($92; Metro: Centrale F.S. or Lima).

ITALIAN DESIGN

The top name in Italian homeware design since 1921 has been **Alessi,** which just since the late 1980s has hired the likes of Michael Graves, Philippe Starck, Frank Ghery, and Ettore Sottsass to design the latest in tea kettles, bottle openers, and other housewares. They maintain a main showroom at Corso Matteotti 9 (© 02-795726; Metro: San Babila) and a sales outlet at Via Montenapoleone 19 (© 02-76021199; www.alessi.com; Metro: Montenapoleone).

The 1980s was really part of a renaissance of Italian industrial design. This is the era when design team **Memphis** led by Ettore Sottsass virtually reinvented the art form, recruiting the best and brightest architects and designers to turn their talents to lighting fixtures, kitchen appliances, office supplies, and even furnishings. Italian style has stayed at the very top of the designer homewares market (well, sharing popularity space with Scandinavian furniture) ever since. Part of the Memphis credo was to create the new modern, then bow out before they became establishment, so they self-destructed in 1988. You can still find their influential designs in many homeware shops and in the showroom at Via della Moscova 27 (© 02-6554731; www.memphis-milano.it; Metro: Turati).

LINENS

For Milanese design with which to dress the bed and table and not the body, visit **Frette,** Via Visconti di Modrone (© 02-777091; www.frette.it; Metro: San Babila). This outlet branch of the high-fashion linen house offers the line of tablecloths, towels, robes, and bedding that it supplies to the world's top hotels at substantial discounts. They have other stores at Via Montenapoleone 21 (© 02-783950; Metro: Montenapoleone), Via Manzoni 11 (© 02-864433; Metro: Montenapoleone), Corso Buenos Aires 82 (© 02-29401072; Metro: Lima), Corso Vercelli 23/25 (© 02-4989756; Metro: Conciliazione), and Via Torino 42 (© 02-86452281; Metro: Duomo).

The elegant swirling paisleys of **Etro,** Via Montenapoleone 5 (© 02-76005049; www.etro.it; Metro: Montenapoleone), have been decorating the walls, furniture covers, and accessories in some of Italy's richest and aristocratic homes since 1969. They've since expanded into full lines of clothing and leather goods, as well as perfumes and accessories (those available at the branch on the corner of Via P. Verri and Via Bigli, © 02-76005450; Metro: Montenapoleone).

Spacci Bassetti, Via Procaccini 32 (© 02-3450125; Metro: Garibaldi F.S., but closer on tram 33 or 94), is a discount outlet of the august Bassetti line of high-quality linen, and the huge space offers the luxurious towels and sheets at excellent prices. They have regular (nondiscount) stores at Corso Buenos Aires 52 (© 02-29400048; Metro: Lima) and Via Botta 7A (© 02-55183191; Metro: Porta Romana).

BOOKS
For general books in English, see "Fast Facts: Milan," earlier in this chapter. If it's a bookish souvenir you're after, **Remainders',** in the Galleria Vittorio Emanuele II (© 02-86464008; Metro: Duomo), hawks glossy coffee-table tomes and art books at half-price and offers cut rates on English books on the second floor—just a few novels, plus lots of art and academic books.

ACCOMMODATIONS YOU CAN AFFORD
Most Milan hotels are oriented toward business types, with precious few left over for the relatively few tourists who don't high-tail it for more popular cities such as Venice or Florence. It's difficult to find rooms in any price category when fashion shows and trade fairs are in full swing (often Oct and Mar). Many hotels raise their prices at these times, too. August is low season, and hotels are often willing to bring prices down considerably (though you really don't want to be here), as they will sometimes on slow weekends. Unless otherwise indicated, price ranges below reflect a seasonal fluctuation. Always ask for the lowest possible rate when booking and be prepared to bargain.

Though they won't book a room for you, the tourist office (see under "Visitor Information," earlier in this chapter) will help you track down hotels within your budget (and, if you go to the main office in person, will even call around for you).

NEAR THE DUOMO
Hotel Aliseo   A 10-minute walk south of the Duomo, this attractive pensione offers a lot of comfort in addition to its good location. The management is friendly, and rooms are furnished with pleasant modern pieces and decent beds. Each has a tiny washroom with sink and bidet but no toilet; large, spanking-clean bathrooms are in the hallway. Rooms on the street side open to small balconies but are noisier than those overlooking the *cortile*. The Aliseo—which used to be called the Ullrich—books up quickly, so be sure to call ahead.

Corso Italia 6, 21023 Milano. © 02-86450156 or 02-804535. 12 units, 5 with bathroom. 45€–55€ ($52–$63) single without bathroom; 65€–75€ ($75–$86) double without bathroom; 90€–100€ ($104–$115) double with bathroom. Rates include breakfast. MC, V. Metro: Duomo. Tram: 15, 24, 65, 94. *In room:* TV, hair dryer.

Hotel Santa Marta 𝒜   The narrow Via Santa Marta is a slice of old Milan, cobblestoned and lined with charming old buildings, one of which houses the Santa Marta. It's also across the street from one of the city's most atmospheric restaurants (the Milanese), and a short walk from the Duomo and other sights. Recent modernizations have preserved the old-fashioned ambience while adding such modern comforts as air-conditioning. The tile-floored guest rooms are comfortable and decorated with a matter-of-fact fashion sense; some cramped others are quite large, and a renovation is scheduled for late 2004. Still, a recent drastic increase in prices seems to be unjustified. If they're full, they'll send you to their sister hotel, the Rovello (see below).

Via Santa Marta 4, 20123 Milano. © **02-804567** or 02-804621. Fax 02-86452661. www.hotel-santamarta.it. 15 units. 70€–110€ ($81–$127) single; 150€–190€ ($173–$219) double; 180€–260€ ($207–$299) triple. Rates include continental breakfast. AE, DC, MC, V. Parking in nearby garage 15€–20€ ($17–$23). Closed 15 days in Aug. Metro: Cordusio or Duomo. Tram: 1, 2, 3, 4, 12, 14, 15, 19, 20, 24, 27. **Amenities:** Bar; 24-hr. room service; laundry service; nonsmoking rooms. *In room:* A/C, TV, hair dryer.

Hotel Speronari ❋ *Finds*   This is a budget hotel in a deluxe location, tucked into a tiny pedestrian side street between Via Torino and Via Mazzini across from the church of Santa Maria Presso San Satiro. The staff is earnest, and the rooms are basic but done well: cool tile floors, functional furnishings, ceiling fans, brand-new cot springs, and fuzzy towels in the bathrooms. Even those without full bathroom have a sink and bidet, and all save a few of the rooms without bathrooms have TVs. Rooms on the third and fourth floors are brighter, and those on the courtyard a tad quieter than rooms facing the street (there are terribly convenient trolleys a half-block in either direction, but they come with a distant but noisy rumble for rooms on the street side).

Via Speronari 4, 20123 Milano. © **02-86461125.** Fax 02-72003178. hotelsperonari@inwind.it. 33 units, 17 with bathroom. 50€ ($58) single without bathroom, 62€ ($71) single with shower but no toilet; 76€ ($87) double without bathroom, 96€ ($110) double with bathroom; 130€ ($150) triple with bathroom; 155€ ($178) quad with bathroom. MC, V (but 3€/$3.45 discount if paying in cash). Metro: Duomo or Missori. Tram: 1, 2, 3, 4, 12, 14, 15, 19, 20, 24, 27. **Amenities:** Bar; concierge; tour desk. *In-room:* TV, dataport, hair dryer (ask at desk), safe.

IN MAGENTA & BRERA

Hotel Giulio Cesare ❋   A recent renovation has brought this old establishment thoroughly up-to-date, with a grandiose marble lobby and a handsome lounge and bar area with deep couches. Upstairs, the rooms are contemporary chic but reflect the building's centuries-old heritage with their tall windows and high ceilings. Some are quirkily shaped and a few singles are cramped, but the white tile floors and minimalist furnishings are starkly modern. The new bathrooms gleam and are equipped with stall showers and flat towels. Management can be a bit brusque. This is one of several similarly priced hotels on the block, a generally quiet street tucked away off Via Dante between the Duomo and La Scala in one direction and the Castello in the other. (See the London and Rovello listings below).

Via Rovello 10, 20121 Milano. © **02-72003915.** Fax 02-72002179. www.giuliocesarehotel.it. 25 units. 93€ ($107) single; 150€ ($173) double. Rates include breakfast. AE, MC, V. Metro: Cordusio. Tram/Bus: 1, 2, 3, 4, 12, 14, 18, 19, 20, 24, 27. **Amenities:** Bar; 24-hr. room service. *In room:* A/C, TV, hair dryer.

Hotel Rovello ❋   The Rovello is one of three hotels I recommend on this quiet street between the Duomo and the Castello. Like its neighbor, the Giulio Cesare, it was thoroughly renovated in 1999, with striking results. The unusually large guest rooms occupy the first and second floors of a centuries-old building and incorporate many of the original architectural details, including exposed timbers and beamed ceilings. Handsome contemporary Italian furnishings are set off by gleaming hardwood floors, the tall casement windows are covered with attractive fabrics, and walls are painted in soothing green and gold tones. The orthopedic mattresses are covered with thick quilts for a homey feel. Many of the rooms have dressing areas in addition to the large new bathrooms. A breakfast of rolls and coffee is served in a sunny room off the lobby.

Via Rovello 18, 20121 Milano. ℂ **02-86464654.** Fax 02-72023656. www.hotel-rovello.it. 10 units. 100€ ($115) single; 110€–195€ ($127–$224) double. Rates include breakfast. AE, DC, MC, V. Parking 30€ ($35). Metro: Cordusio. Tram/Bus: 1, 2, 3, 4, 12, 14, 18, 19, 20, 24, 27. **Amenities:** Bar; concierge; room service; laundry service. *In room:* A/C, TV, dataport, hair dryer.

London Hotel 🌟 Unlike its neighbor, the Giulio Cesare, the London sticks to its old-fashioned ways. The big fireplace and cozy green velvet furniture in the lobby say a lot about the comfort level and friendly atmosphere that bring many guests back time after time. Just beyond the lobby, there's a bar where beverages are available almost around the clock; guests can purchase cappuccino or a continental breakfast in the morning. Upstairs, the rooms look like they haven't been redecorated in a number of decades, but they're roomy and bright, and the heavy old furnishings lend a charm very much in keeping with the ambience of the hotel. Rooms on the first floor tend to be the largest, and they get smaller as you go up. Guests receive a 10% discount at the trattoria next door, the Opera Prima.

Via Rovello 3, 20121 Milano. ℂ **02-72020166.** Fax 02-8057037. www.hotellondonmilano.com. 29 units, 24 with bathroom. 60€–80€ ($69–$92) single without bathroom, 80€–100€ ($92–$115) single with bathroom; 100€–130€ ($115–$150) double without bathroom, 120€–150€ ($138–$173) double with bathroom; 160€–200€ ($184–$230) triple with bathroom. Continental breakfast 8€ ($9.20). MC, V. Parking 25€ ($29) in nearby garage. Closed Aug and Christmas. Metro: Cordusio. Tram/Bus: 1, 2, 3, 4, 12, 14, 18, 19, 20, 24, 27. **Amenities:** Bar; concierge; 24-hr. room service; laundry service; same-day dry cleaning. *In room:* A/C, TV, dataport, hair dryer.

Worth a Splurge

Antica Locanda Solferino 🌟🌟🌟 If this charming old hotel in the arty Brera neighborhood hadn't been discovered long ago by members of the fashion world and film stars (this was Marcello Mastroianni's preferred Milan hostelry), you would consider it a find. The rooms have more character than they do modern comforts, but, to the loyal guests, the eclectic smattering of country antiques and Art Nouveau pieces more than compensates for the absence of minibars. Nor do the repeat customers seem to mind that some of the bathrooms are miniscule (though modern) or that there is no lobby or breakfast room (coffee and rolls are delivered to your room). So be it—this is a delightful place to stay in one of Milan's most enticing neighborhoods, and reception manager Gerardo Vitolo is very friendly. New Jacuzzi baths and air-conditioning in some rooms only add to the experience. The rooms on the tiny courtyard are quieter, but those on the street have plant-filled balconies (the best is no. 10 on the corner, if you don't mind a tub rather than a shower).

Via Castelfidardo 2, 20121 Milano. ℂ **02-6570129** or 02-6592706. Fax 02-6571361. www.anticalocanda solferino.it. 11 units. 90€–140€ ($104–$161) single; 150€–190€ ($173–$219) double; 170€–240€ ($196–$276) apt. Rates include breakfast served in-room. AE, MC, V. Parking 20€–25€ ($23–$29) in nearby garage. Closed 2–3 weeks in mid-Aug. Metro: Moscova or Repubblica. Tram/Bus: 11, 29, 30, 33, 41, 43, 94. **Amenities:** Concierge; tour desk; car-rental desk; laundry service; dry cleaning. *In room:* A/C (2 rooms; 5 rooms by 2005), TV, hair dryer.

Ariosto Hotel 🌟🌟 Tucked away in a residential neighborhood of apartment houses and old villas near the Santa Maria della Grazie church, the Ariosto is a refreshingly quiet retreat—all the more so because many of the newly refurbished rooms face a private garden, and some open onto balconies overlooking it. All the rooms are decorated with wood-and-wicker furnishings, shiny parquet floors, and hand-painted wallpaper. Most of the rooms are decently sized, but singles tend to be skinny. Many of the doubles have separate dressing areas off the tile or stone bathrooms, which are equipped with hair dryers and a few with Jacuzzis. There's free Internet access in the lobby and satellite movie channels on the telly.

Via Ariosto 22, 20145 Milano. © 02-4817844. Fax 02-4980516. www.hotelariosto.com. 53 units. 145€ ($167) single; 205€ ($236) double; 219€ ($252) triple. Those are the highest rates, applied during trade fares, and may be discounted by as much as 45% during slower periods. Rates include breakfast. AE, DC, MC, V. Parking 20€–25€ ($23–$29) in garage. Closed 20 days in Aug. Metro: Conciliazione. Tram/Bus: 29, 30, 61, 67, 68. **Amenities:** Restaurant; bar; bike rental; concierge; car-rental desk; room service; laundry service; dry cleaning; nonsmoking rooms. *In room:* A/C, TV w/pay movies, dataport, minibar, hair dryer.

EAST OF THE DUOMO

America   Though this establishment is a bit off the beaten track in a middle-class neighborhood due east of Piazza del Duomo, the young owner and his family work overtime to make this pensione one of the best lower-priced lodgings in Milan. The newly refurbished rooms occupy the fourth floor of an apartment house. Several have private bathrooms, and all are bright and nicely decorated with streamlined, wood-veneer modern furnishings—many sporting a thematic stars-and-stripes color scheme. Guests are welcome to join the resident innkeepers in the living room and watch TV. All of the rooms without bathrooms have sinks, and two even have showers (but no toilet). The Rolling Stone music club, a venerable fixture on the Milan nightlife scene, is on the ground floor of the building, a good reason to ask for a room facing the quieter *giardino* courtyard (no. 10 even has a balcony). For more conventional sightseeing, the Duomo is about 20 minutes away by foot or 10 minutes by tram.

Corso XXII Marzo 32 (the block east of Piazza Emilia), 20135 Milano. © 02-7381865. Fax 02-7381490. www.milanohotelamerica.com. 10 units, 2 with bathroom. 36€ ($41) single without bathroom; 52€–62€ ($60–$71) double without bathroom, 68€ ($78) double with bathroom. AE, MC, V. Tram/Bus: 12, 27, 45, 60, 66, 73, 92. *In room:* TV.

Hotel Pavone ⭐   The family-run Pavone is just off the Corso di Porta Vittoria, around the corner from the Palace of Justice and about a 15-minute walk east of the Duomo. The surrounding neighborhood is more geared to business than to the tourist trade, but the friendly desk staff is eager to point out nearby restaurants and other conveniences, which are plentiful. Rooms are a bit sparse, with gray tile floors and no-nonsense Scandinavian-style furniture, but they were spruced up in 2003 with new linens and decor. Most are unusually large and cloaked in a silence unusual for big-city Milan, but for the quietest rest, check into nos. 12, 14, 16, or 18, all of which overlook a garden. The beds in most singles are extra wide. Many rooms are outfitted as triples and are large enough to accommodate an extra bed, making this a fine choice for families.

Via Dandolo 2 (off Corso di Porta Vittoria), 20122 Milano. © 02-55192133. Fax 02-55192421. www.hotel pavone.com. 24 units. 70€–130€ ($81–$150) single; 100€–185€ ($115–$213) double; 150€–250€ ($173–$288) triple. Continental breakfast 5€ ($5.75). AE, MC, V. Parking 10€ ($12). Tram: 12, 23, 27, 60, or 73. **Amenities:** Bar; concierge; 24-hr. room service; laundry service. *In room:* A/C, TV, dataport, hair dryer, safe.

NEAR STAZIONE CENTRALE & CORSO BUENOS AIRES

Hotel Kennedy *(Value*   The name reflects the English-speaking management's fondness for the late president, and the Bianchi family is genuinely welcoming to the many Americans who find their way to their pensione a block off the southern end of Corso Buenos Aires. Their homey establishment on the sixth floor of an office-and-apartment building (there's an elevator) is sparkling clean and offers basic accommodations in large, tile-floored rooms. Room no. 13 has a terrace, while no. 15 has a small balcony that even glimpses the spires of the Duomo in the distance. Amenities include a bar in the reception area, where coffee and soft drinks are available, as is a light breakfast of brioche and coffee that doesn't cost much more than it would in a cafe.

Viale Tunisia 6 (6th floor), 20124 Milano. © 02-29400934. Fax 02-29401253. www.kennedyhotel.it. 12 units, 3 with shower, 5 with bathroom. 40€–55€ ($46–$63) single without bathroom; 55€–75€ ($63–$86) double without bathroom, 70€–100€ ($81–$115) double with bathroom; 80€–120€ ($92–$138) triple with bathroom; 100€–140€ ($115–$161) quad with bathroom. Breakfast 4€ ($4.60). AE, DC, MC, V. Parking 10€–20€ ($12–$23) in nearby garage. Metro: Porta Venezia. Tram: 5 or 11. **Amenities:** Bar. *In room:* TV, dataport, hair dryer.

Hotel Paganini ⭐ (Value)   Occupying an old house on a quiet residential street off the north end of Corso Buenos Aires, the Paganini has minimal public areas (except for a reception area with a self-serve espresso machine), but the guest rooms are large, bright, and embellished with tile floors, high ceilings with elaborate moldings, solid beds, and banal modular furnishings of varying ages. The one room with a bathroom is just inside the entrance, with wood floors, a ceiling decorated with molded stuccoes, and plenty of elbow room. The shared facilities are modern enough and kept spanking clean by the owners (he lived in Brooklyn for a number of years), who are happy to point their guests to restaurants and sights. The best rooms are in the rear, overlooking a huge private garden. There is much to be said for this location: The station is only a 10-minute walk way down Via Pergolsi, and if shopping is on your agenda, the nearby Corso Buenos Aires is one of the city's bargain fashion meccas.

Via Paganini 6, 20131 Milano. © 02-2047443. www.paginegialle.it/hotelpaganini. 8 units, 1 with bathroom. 55€ ($63) single or double; 83€ ($95) triple. AE, DC, MC, V. Parking in garage across street 15€ ($17), or free on street. Metro: Loreto. Tram/Bus: 33, 55, 55/, 56, 56, 90, 91, 93. **Amenities:** Concierge; room service; laundry service. *In room:* TV, dataport, hair dryer.

Hotel Promessi Sposi ⭐⭐   Travelers often find their way to this rambling hotel on the recommendation of former guests, many of them in the fashion world, who tend to rave about the friendly service (Jerry at the desk lived in New York City until the age of 10), unusually pleasant accommodations, and excellent value. Downstairs there's a cheerful lobby and bar area furnished with multicolored couches and overlooking Piazza Oberdan and the public gardens through large windows. Upstairs the spacious rooms are outfitted with comfortable rattan furniture painted burgundy and/or cream. Bathrooms are spacious and nicely maintained. Rooms on the back, overlooking a drab narrow alley between buildings, are considerably quieter (but less well lit) than those on busy Corso Buenos Aires and Piazza Oberdan—double glazing helps but can't solve the noise. However, I'd still ask for nos. 222 or 332, which sit at the narrow end of the building and, as such, are quite large, with windows on three sides and small balconies. The name, which translates as "The Fiancées," is a reference to the 19th-century masterpiece by Lombardian novelist Alessandro Manzoni, a close second to Dante's *Inferno* on the required reading list in Italian high schools.

Piazza Oberdan 12, 20129 Milano. © 02-29513661. Fax 02-29404182. www.hotelpromessisposi.com. 40 units. 60€–88€ ($69–$101) single; 90€–134€ ($104–$154) double; 123€–170€ ($141–$196) triple. 5% discount for stays of longer than 3 days (but not during trade fairs). Rates include buffet breakfast. AE, DC, MC, V. Parking 15€–20€ ($17–$23) in nearby garage, or free on street. Metro: Porta Venezia. Tram: 9, 20, 29, 30. **Amenities:** Bar. *In room:* A/C, TV w/pay movies, dataport, coffeemaker, hair dryer.

Worth a Splurge

Doria Grand Hotel ⭐   This luxury hotel offers enormously discounted weekend prices (the lower rates below applied Fri–Sun nights) that makes it reasonable on weekends, most of August, and the Christmas/New Year holiday (check for exact dates before booking; never applied during trade fairs). The Doriagrand is one of the large newer hotels that cluster around the station and is far more comfortable and stylish than most hotels in its luxury class. The good-size guest rooms are exquisitely appointed with handsome wood and marble-topped furniture, rich fabric wall coverings and draperies, and amenities such as linen sheets, ISDN jacks, satellite channels and pay-per-view, and complimentary bedroom slippers and bathrobes. The beautiful marble bathrooms are equipped with generously sized tubs, vanities, hair dryers, and a large selection of toiletries. A sumptuous buffet breakfast is served in a stylishly decorated room on a level above the lobby, and on Thursday and Friday evenings the piano bar becomes a jazz club.

Viale Andrea Doria 22, 20124 Milano. ℂ 02-67411411. Fax 02-6696669. www.doriagrandhotel.it. 124 units. 108€–305€ ($124–$351) single; 138€–400€ ($159–$460) double; 253€–490€ ($291–$564) suite. Rates include buffet breakfast. AE, DC, MC, V. Parking 29€ ($33) in garage. Metro: Loreto or Caiazzo. Tram: 1, 90, 91, 92. **Amenities:** Restaurant; concierge; tour desk; car-rental desk; courtesy car; business center; limited room service; in-room massage; babysitting; laundry service; same-day dry cleaning; nonsmoking rooms. *In room:* A/C, TV w/pay movies, dataport, minibar, hair dryer, safe.

GREAT DEALS ON DINING

Geared to business as the city is, the Milanese are more willing than Italians elsewhere to break the sit-down-meal tradition and grab a sandwich or other light fare on the run. And with so many students and young professionals underfoot, Milan has no shortage of pizzerie and other low-cost eateries.

NEAR THE DUOMO

La Crêperie CREPERIE   About a 10-minute walk southeast of Piazza Duomo (Via C. Corenti is an extension of Via Torino, one of the major avenues fanning out from the square), this busy creperie is an ideal stop for a light lunch or a snack while visiting the nearby church of Sant'Ambrogio or Museo Nazionale di Scienza e di Tecnica. The far-ranging offerings include *prosciutto e formaggio* (ham and cheese) or the dessert variety (the Nutella, with the creamy chocolate spread, is highly recommended). They've recently expanded beyond crepes to serve other foreign and exotic hand-held foods, such as hot dogs *americani* and waffles. Before 3pm Monday to Friday, you can get the "lunch special": one nondessert crepe, plus one sweet one and a drink, for 5€ ($5.75).

Via C. Corenti 21. ℂ 02-8395913. www.la-creperie.it. Crepes 1.50€–4€ ($1.75–$4.60). Mon–Sat noon–1am; Sun 4pm–midnight (closed Sun in summer). Closed July 15–Aug 25. Metro: Sant'Ambrogio.

Luini 👁👁 SNACKS   A Milan institution since 1948, it's so good they've even opened a branch in London. At this stand-up counter near the Galleria, you'll have to elbow your way through a throng of well-dressed patrons to purchase the house specialty: *panzerotto,* a pocket of pizza crust stuffed with all sorts of ingredients, including the basic cheese and tomato. You'll also find many different kinds of panini here.

Via S. Radegonda 16. ℂ 02-86461917. www.luini.it. Panzerotto 2.20€ ($2.55). No credit cards. Mon 10am–3pm; Tues–Sat 10am–8pm. Closed Aug. Metro: Duomo.

IN MAGENTA & BRERA

Latteria 👁👁 MILANESE   The main business here at one time was dispensing milk and eggs to a press of neighborhood shoppers, but now the emphasis is on serving the La Brera neighborhood delicious, homemade fare in a room decorated with paintings and photographs of roses. The minestrone and other vegetable soups are delicious, as are the many variations of risotto, including some otherwise hard-to-find variations such as *riso al salto,* a delicious dish of leftover *risotto alla milanese* that is fried with butter. The menu changes daily, and the friendly staff, including owners Arturo and Maria, won't mind explaining the different dishes. The place is tiny and doesn't take bookings, so if you want to get one of the popular tables, arrive when it opens or wait until 8:30pm or later when a few free up as the early-dining tourist clientele clears out and the locals take over.

Via San Marco 24. ℃ 02-6597653. Reservations not accepted (and it fills up fast). Primi 8€–10€ ($9.20–$12); secondi 7€–14€ ($8.05–$16). No credit cards. Mon–Fri 12:30–2:30pm and 7:30–10pm. Closed Aug. Metro: Moscova.

Pizzeria Grand'Italia 𝆑𝆑 (Value) PIZZA/PASTA   One of Milan's most popular pizzerias—any time one of my Milanese friends says "Hey, let's go get pizza!" this is invariably where he or she takes me. Grand'Italia serves up a huge assortment of salads, pizzas, homemade pastas, and *focacce farcite* (focaccia bread stuffed with cheese, mushrooms, and other fillings), along with wine and oil from the Furfaro family's farm in Tuscany. Rather than get a whole pie, you get one thick-crusted megaslice topped however you like it. The late hours make this a prime night spot, and part of the fun is watching the chic, young Milanese stopping by for a snack as they make the rounds of the nearby Brera district bars and clubs.

Via Palermo 5. ℃ 02-877759. Pizza from 4€ ($4.60); salads from 6€ ($6.90). No credit cards. Daily noon–2:45pm and 7pm–1:30am. Metro: Moscova.

Worth a Splurge

La Milanese 𝆑𝆑𝆑 MILANESE   Giuseppe and Antonella Villa preside with a watchful eye over the centuries-old premises (a restaurant since 1933), tucked into a narrow lane in one of the oldest sections of Milan, just west of the Duomo. In the three-beamed dining room, Milanese families and other patrons share the long, crowded tables. Giuseppe, in the kitchen, prepares what many patrons consider to be some of the city's best traditional fare. The *risotto alla milanese* with saffron and beef marrow, not surprisingly, is excellent, as is a minestrone that's served hot in the winter and at room temperature in the summer. The *costolette alla milanese,* breaded and fried in butter, is all the better here because only the choicest veal chops are used and it's served with the bone in. The *osso buco* is cooked to perfection. If you want to try their twin specialties without pigging out, the dish listed as *risotto e osso buco* buys you a half-portion each of their *risotto alla milanese* and the *osso buco* for just 18€ ($21). Polenta, with rich Gorgonzola cheese, is one of the few nonmeat second courses. The attentive staff will help you choose an appropriate wine.

Via Santa Marta 11. ℃ 02-86451991. Reservations required. Primi 6€–8€ ($6.90–$9.20); secondi 11€–18€ ($13–$21); *menu turistico* 39€ ($45) without wine. AE, DC, MC, V. Wed–Mon noon–3pm and 7pm–1am. Closed Dec 25–Jan 8, Apr 24–May 2, and July 20–Aug 31. Metro: Cardusio.

Peck 𝆑𝆑 (Value) DELI   Milan's most famous food emporium offers a wonderful selection of roast veal, risottos, porchetta, salads, aspics, cheeses, pastries, and other fare from its exquisite larder in this natty snack bar around the corner from its shop. If you choose to eat here, you will do so at a stand-up bar where, especially around lunchtime, it can be hard to find elbow room. This shouldn't discourage you, though, because the pleasure of having access to such a cornucopia of delicacies at a reasonable price will be a gourmand's vision of paradise. By the way, their full-fledged restaurant around the corner at Via Victor Hugò 4 (℃ 02-876774), recently remodeled and now called **Cracco-Peck,** serves hightest traditional and creative cuisine but charges such heart-stopping prices—their fixed-price tasting menus cost 88€ to 105€ ($101–$121)—we decided not to include a full write-up.

Via Spadari 9. ℃ 02-8023161. www.peck.it. Primi 3.50€–12€ ($4–$14); secondi 9€–20€ ($10–$23). AE, DC, MC, V. Mon–Sat 7:30am–9pm. Closed Jan 1–10 and July 1–20. Metro: Duomo.

NEAR STAZIONE CENTRALE & CORSO BUENO

Brek *(Value* CAFETERIA   This outlet of Italy's popular cafet[...] be dismissed too quickly. Brek takes food, and its presentatio[...] and risotto are made fresh; pork, veal, and chicken are roaste[...] large selection of cheeses would put many a formal restaura[...] lent wines and many kinds of beer are available. Behind-the-count[...] friendly and helpful, and the country-style decor is quite attractive.

Via Lepetit 20. ℂ 02-6705149. www.brek.com. Primi and pizza 2.80€–4.10€ ($3.20–$4.70); secondi 4€–7.50€ ($4.60–$8.60). AE, MC, V. Mon–Sat 11:30am–3pm and 6:30–10:30pm; Sun 6:30–10:30pm. Metro: Stazione Centrale.

Da Abele MILANESE   Once you get away from the sights and shops of the city center, you'll find yourself in some middle-class neighborhoods. Da Abele is in one of them, a pleasant enclave of shops and apartment houses east of Stazione Centrale and north of Corso Buenos Aires shopping strip (a few blocks north of Piazzale Loreto). This plain trattoria caters to local residents (hence its evening-only hours—they take reservations only before 8:30pm; afterward, it's first come, first served) and serves a nice selection of soups (including a hearty seafood *zuppa di pesce*) and many kinds of risotto, including one with *frutti di mare* (a selection of fresh seafood) and others with fresh porcini in season. The amiable staff doesn't mind if you venture no further into the menu, but if you do, there is a nice selection of roast meats as well. Sadly, they joined that large percentage of shameful Italian businesses that used the arrival of the euro to drastically inflate their prices.

Via Temperanza 5. ℂ 02-2613855. Primi 7.50€ ($8.60); secondi 10€–12€ ($12–$14). AE, DC, MC, V. Tues–Sun 8–11:30pm. Closed July 20–Sept 1. Metro: Pasteur.

Worth a Splurge

Joia 𝄞𝄞 VEGETARIAN   Milanese, who tend to be carnivorous, have embraced this refined vegetarian restaurant just north of the public gardens with great enthusiasm. Travelers may welcome the respite from Northern Italy's orientation to red meat; those who have become accustomed to smoke-free environments back home will enjoy the *non fumatore* section of Joia's blond-wood, neutral-tone dining rooms. The innovative vegetarian creations of Swiss chef Pietro Lemman incorporate the freshest vegetables and herbs, which appear in many traditional pasta dishes, such as *lasagne con zucchine pomodoro* (layered with zucchini and fresh tomatoes and served at room temperature), *ravioli di melanzana* (stuffed with eggplant), or tagliolini with a simple tomato sauce. Any of these first courses can be ordered as a main course, and many of the main courses can be ordered as starters. These secondi include some excellent fish choices, as well as elaborate vegetables-only creations such as *melanzani viola al vapore con finferli* (steamed eggplant with chanterelle mushrooms). There's a wonderful assortment of cheeses and, likewise, a long wine list.

Via P. Castaldi 18. ℂ 02-2049244. www.joia.it. Reservations highly recommended. Primi 15€–22€ ($17–$25); secondi 20€–25€ ($23–$29); lunch menu 25€ ($29); tasting menus 50€–75€ ($58–$86). AE, DC, MC, V. Mon–Fri noon–2:30pm and 7:30–11:30pm. Closed Aug. Metro: Repubblica.

IN THE NAVIGLI

Al Pont de Ferr 𝄞𝄞 *(Finds* PAN-ITALIAN   This is one of the more respectable of the dozens of restaurants around the Navigli, with tables set out on the flagstones overlooking the canal (regulars know to bring tiny cans of bug spray to battle the mosquitoes in summer). The *paste e fagioli* is livened up with bits of sausage, and the ricotta-stuffed ravioli inventively sauced with a pesto of and veggies. For a second course, you can try the *tocchetti di coniglio* .n-roasted rabbit with potatoes), *porchetta* (pork stuffed with spices), or veg-.table *couscous alla Trapanesi*—or just sack the whole idea of a secondo and order up a *tavolozza* selection of excellent cheeses. There's a surprisingly good selection of half-bottles of wine, but most full bottles start at 15€ ($17) and go senselessly higher. On the whole, portions could be a whole lot larger, but you gotta love a place whose menu opens with the quip, "Good cooking is the friend of living well and the enemy of a hurried life."

Ripa di Porta Ticinese 55 (on the Naviglio Grande) © 02-89406277. Primi 5€–9€ ($5.75–$10); secondi 9€–16€ ($10–$18). Mon–Sat 12:30–2:30pm and 8–11pm. AE, MC, V. Tram: 3, 15, 29, 30, 59.

Ponte Rosso ௸ MILANESE/FRIULIANA   This is an old-fashioned trattoria on the canal, a long railroad room crowded with tiny tables and a short, simple menu of simple, hearty home cooking. The owner hails from Trieste originally (which explains the old Triestino photos on the walls), so kick a meal off with *salumi friuliani*, a mixed platter of cured meats from the region famous for pro-ducing the most delicate prosciutto in Italy. The *insalata di pasta* is a cold pasta salad with olives, capers, and mozzarella. They do a mean *minestrone* vegetable soup, Triestino *sarde in saor* (vinegar-kissed fried sardines), *manzo in salsa verde* (beef in an herb sauce), and *torta di verdure* (vegetable quiche).

Ripa di Porta Ticinese 23 (on the Naviglio Grande) © 02-8373132. Primi 8€–10€ ($9.20–$12); secondi 10€–14€ ($12–$16). AE, DC, MC, V. Tues–Sat noon–3pm and 7–11pm; Mon 7–11pm (also open last Sun of the month). Tram: 3, 15, 29, 30, 59.

Premiata Pizzeria ௸ *Value* PIZZA/PAN-ITALIAN   The most popular pizze-ria in the Navigli stays packed from early dinnertime until the barhopping crowd stops by for late-night munchies. The restaurant rambles back forever, exposed copper pipes tracing across the ceilings of rooms wrapped around shaded outdoor terraces set with long, raucous tables. Seating is communal and service hurried, but the wood oven pizzas are excellent. If you're hungrier, there's a long menu of pastas and meat courses, while lighter appetites can enjoy a selec-tion of salads, or cheese or salami platters made for two.

Via Alzaia Naviglio Grande 2. © 02-89400648. Reservations suggested. Primi 8€–10€ ($9.20–$12); sec-ondi 11€–18€ ($13–$21); pizza 6€–12€ ($6.90–$14). MC, V. Wed–Mon noon–2:30pm and 7:30–11:30pm; Tues 7:30–11:30pm. Tram: 3, 15, 29, 30, 59.

CAFES & GELATO

Bar Zucca/Caffè Miani, at the Duomo end of the Galleria Vittorio Emanuele II (© 02-86464435; www.caffemiani.it; Metro: Duomo), is best known by its original name, "the Camparino." It's the most attractive and popular of the Gal-leria's many bars and introduced Italy to Campari, the country's ubiquitous red cordial. You can linger at the tables set up in the Galleria or in one of the Art Nouveau rooms inside.

You can find organic gelato at the **Gelateria Ecologica,** Corso di Porta Tici-nese 40 (© 02-58101872; Metro: Sant'Ambrogio or Missori), in the Tici-nese/Navigli neighborhood. It's so popular, there's no need for a sign out front. Strollers in the atmospheric Brera neighborhood sooner or later stumble upon the **Gelateria Toldo,** Via Ponte Vetero 9 (© 02-86460863; Metro: Cordusio or Lanza), where the gelato is wonderfully creamy and many of the sorbetto selec-tions are so fruity and fresh they seem healthful.

The **Pasticceria Confetteria Cova,** Via Montenapoleone 8 (© 02-76000578; Metro: Montenapoleone), is nearing its 200th year in refined surroundings near the similarly atmospheric Museo Poldi-Pezzoli. It's usually filled with shoppers making the rounds in this high-fashion district. You can enjoy a quick coffee and a brioche at the long bar or take a seat in one of the elegant adjoining rooms.

The **Pasticceria Marchesi,** Via Santa Maria alla Porta 13 (© **02-862770;** Metro: Cardusio), is a distinguished pastry shop, with an adjoining wood-paneled tearoom. Since it's only steps from Santa Maria delle Grazie, you can enjoy the old-world ambience and a cup of excellent coffee (or one of the many teas and herbal infusions) as you dash off postcards of *The Last Supper.* Of course, you'll want to accompany your beverage with one of the elegant pastries, perhaps a slice of the panettone (cake laden with raisins and candied citron) that's a hallmark of Milan. No one prepares it better than they do at Marchesi. It's open Tuesday through Sunday from 8am to 8pm.

MILAN AFTER DARK

On Wednesday and Thursday, Milan's newspapers tend to devote a lot of ink to club schedules and cultural events. If you don't trust your command of Italian to plan your nightlife, check out the tourist office on Piazza del Duomo—there are usually piles of flyers announcing upcoming events. The tourist office also keeps visitors up-to-date with *Milano: Where, When, How,* a periodical it distributes (for /\$1€/\$1.15) with schedules of events, as well as listings of bars, clubs, and restaurants.

THE PERFORMING ARTS   For the lowdown on the long-term renovations of Milan's premier opera house, **Teatro alla Scala,** and the new "temporary" (until 2005) venue for performances up in the northern burbs, see the box earlier in this chapter under "Sights to See."

Milan's Giuseppe Verdi Symphony Orchestra conducted by Riccardo Chailly now plays at the **Auditorium di Milano,** a renovated 1930s movie house at Via S. Gottardo 42/Largo Gustav Mahler (© **02-83389222;** www.auditorium dimilano.org; Metro: Duomo, then tram no. 3 or 15). Concerts run from late September to May, usually on Thursday and Friday at 8:30pm and Sunday at 4pm. There's a Sunday morning (11am) early matinee program that mixes chamber music and other smaller-scale performances, while kids get their own series of musical programs Saturday at 3:30pm.

MOVIES   In Italy, English-language films are almost always dubbed into Italian, providing English speakers with an opportunity to bone up on their Italian but taking some of the fun out of a night at the movies. Fortunately, there are always a few theaters that screen English-language films in the original version 1 night a week: **Anteo,** Via Milazzo 9 (© **02-6597732**), on Monday (Metro: Moscova); **Arcoboleno,** Viale Tunisia 11 (© **02-29406054**), on Tuesday (Metro: Porta Venzia); and **Mexico,** Via Savona 57, (© **02-**48951802), on Thursday (Metro: Porta Genova). Admission is usually 4€ (\$4.60) for a matinee and 6€ to 7.20€ (\$6.90–\$8.30) after 6pm.

Nightlife Tip

The Navigli/Ticinese neighborhood is currently on the ascent as Milan's prime night turf, though the Brera retains its pull with night owls as well.

PUBS   A publike atmosphere, induced in part by Guinness on tap, prevails at Liberty-style **Bar Magenta,** Via Carducci 13 at Corso Magenta (© **02-8053808**), in the neighborhood for which it takes its name; it's open Tuesday through Sunday (Metro: Cadorna). One of the more popular La Brera hangouts, with a young following, is **El Tombon de San Marc,** Via San Marco 20 at Via Montebello (𝄽 **02-6599507**), which, despite its name, is an English pub–style bar and restaurant open Monday through Saturday (Metro: Moscova).

If you're not quite young and up to partying with those who are, a pleasant alternative to Milan's youth-oriented venues is **Bar Margherita,** where there's jazz on the sound system (and sometimes live on stage) and a nice selection of wines and grappa from about 2€ ($2.30). They lay out a good selection of munchies-on-toothpicks (crostini, frittata wedges, and other canapés) around dinnertime. It's in La Brera at Via Moscova 25 (𝄽 **02-6590833**), open Monday through Saturday from 7am to 2am (Metro: Moscova).

Among the Navigli nightspots (growing in number all the time) is **El Brellin,** an intimate, canalside piano bar with its own minicanal on Vicolo della Lavandaia, off Alzaia Naviglio Grande 14 (𝄽 **02-58101351**), open Monday through Saturday (Metro: Genova F. S.). **Birreria La Fontanella,** Alzaia Naviglio Pavese 6 (𝄽 **02-8372391**), has canalside tables outside and the oddest-shaped beer glasses around—that half-a-barbell kind everyone seems to order is called the "Cavalliere." It's open Tuesday through Sunday from 7pm to 3am (Metro: Genova F. S.).

JAZZ CLUBS   Since Capolinea got ousted (*warning:* The club's name is still there at Via Ludovico il Moro 119, but it's *not* the old jazz club where the greats came to play; rather, it's some pathetic mimic of it slapped together by the next-door neighbors who forced the original owners out of this space), the best venue on the jazz club scene is **Le Scimmie,** where cover ranges from free to 8€ ($9.20), plus it has its own bar-boat moored in the canal. It's in the Navigli at Via Ascanio Sforza 49 (𝄽 **02-89402874;** www.scimmie.it) and operates Wednesday through Monday (Metro: Porta Genova), with shows starting at 10:30pm.

MUSIC & DANCE CLUBS   The dance scene changes all the time in Milan, but at whatever club is popular (or in business) at the moment, expect to pay a cover of 10€ to 15€ ($12–$17). Models, actors, sports stars, and the attendant fashion set favor **Hollywood,** which is small, chic, and centrally located in La Brera at Corso Como 15 (𝄽 **02-6555574,** or 02-6555318 after 10:30pm). It closes Monday and from July 23 to September 7 (Metro: Moscova).

Grand Café Fashion, Corso di Porta Ticinese 60 at Via Vetere (𝄽 **02-89400709** or 0336-347333), is a multipurpose nightspot halfway to the Navigli, with a restaurant open from 9pm and a disco nightly from 11:30pm. It brings a beautiful crowd to the Ticinese neighborhood, where they dance the night away, sometimes to thematic evenings like Latino Mondays and, er, lap–dance Sundays (Metro: Porta Genova).

Milan's most venerable disco/live music club is **Rolling Stone,** Corso XXII Marzo 32 (𝄽 **02-733172**), in business since the 1950s. Most of the performers these days are of a rock bent, and the club is as immensely popular as ever. Cover runs about 12€ to 20€ ($14–$23), depending on who's performing; it's less expensive for women than for men, and more expensive on weekends than on weekdays. It's closed Sunday and Monday (Tram: 12, 27, 45, 60, 66, 73, 92).

GAY CLUBS   Milan's largest gay club is **Nuovo Idea,** Via de Castillia 30 (𝄽 **02-69007859;** www.dinet.it/nuovaidea). It attracts a mostly male crowd of all ages and offers everything from disco to polkas, in a huge techno room. The club is open Thursday through Sunday (Metro: Gioia). **Recycle,** Via Calabria 5 (𝄽 **02-3761531**), is a women-only club Friday through Sunday from 9pm to 2am, sometimes later (mixed crowd welcome Wed–Thurs nights).

Via Sammartini along the train station's left flank (Metro: Central F. S.) is a good street to hit, with **Next Groove** at no. 23 (℃ **02-66980450**), a mixed gay and lesbian disco bar of the phone-on-the-table sort and thematic evenings, open daily; and **After Line Disco Pub** at no. 25 (℃ **02-6692130**), a bar-restaurant where a giant-screen TV and strobe light switch on after dinner to turn it into a dance club with a game room for lesbians Tuesday through Sunday.

2 Bergamo
47km (29 miles) NE of Milan, 52km (32 miles) NW of Brescia

Bergamo is two cities. Bergamo Bassa, the lower, a mostly 19th- and 20th-century city, concerns itself with everyday business. Bergamo Alta, a beautiful medieval/Renaissance town perched on a green hill, concerns itself these days with entertaining the visitors who come to admire its piazze, palazzi, and churches; enjoy the lovely vistas from its belvederes; and soak in a hushed beauty that inspired Italian poet Gabriel d'Annunzio to call old Bergamo "a city of muteness." The distinct characters of the two parts of this city go back to its founding as a Roman settlement, when the *civitas* was on the hill and farms and suburban villas dotted the plains below.

ESSENTIALS
GETTING THERE   By Train   Trains arrive from and depart for **Milan** hourly (50–60 min.; 3.85€/$4.40). Given the frequency of train service, you can easily make a daylong sightseeing loop from Milan. If you're coming from or going on to nearby **Lake Como,** there's hourly service between Bergamo and Lecco, on the southeast end of the lake (40 min.; 2.50€/$2.85).

By Bus   An extensive bus network links Bergamo with many other towns in Lombardy. There are five to six buses a day to and from Como (2 hr.; 4.30/$5€) run by **SPT** (℃ **031-247247**). Service to and from Milan by **Autostradale** (℃ **02-33910794;** www.autostradale.com) runs every half-hour (1 hr.; 4.20€/$4.85). The bus station is next to the train station on Piazza Marconi.

By Car   Bergamo is linked directly to Milan via the A4, which continues east to Brescia, Verona, and Venice. The trip between Milan and Bergamo takes a little over half an hour. Parking in or near the Città Alta, most of which is closed to traffic, can be difficult. There is a parking lot on the northern end of the Città Alta near Porta Garibaldi (about 1€/$1.15 per hour) and street parking along Viale delle Mura, which loops around the outer flanks of the walls of the Città Alta.

VISITOR INFORMATION   The **Città Bassa tourist office,** Viale Vittorio Emanuele 20 (℃ **035-210204;** fax 035-230184; www.apt.bergamo.it), is 9 long blocks straight out from the train station; it's open Monday through Friday from 9am to 12:30pm and 2 to 5:30pm. The **Città Alta office,** Vicola Aquila Nera 2 (℃ **035-232730;** fax 035-242994), is just off Piazza Vecchia, open daily the same hours.

FESTIVALS & MARKETS   Bergamo is a cultured city, and its celebrations include the May-through-June **Festivale Piantistico,** one of the world's major piano competitions. In September, the city celebrates its native composer **Gaetano Donizetti** with performances of his works, most of them at the Teatro Donizetti in the Città Bassa (see below).

CITY LAYOUT   Piazza Vecchia, the Colleoni Chapel, and most of the other sights that bring visitors to Bergamo are in the **Città Alta**—the exception is the

Accademia Carrara, which is in the Città Bassa but on the flanks of the hillside, so it's within easy walking distance of the upper town sights. **Via Colleoni** cuts a swath through the medieval heart of the Città Alta, beginning at **Piazza Vecchia.** To reach this lovely square from the funicular station at **Piazza Mercato delle Scarpi,** walk along **Via Gombito** for about 5 minutes. Most of the Città Alta is closed to traffic, but it's compact and easy to navigate on foot. Down below, the main square known as the **Sentierone** is the center of the **Città Bassa.** It's about a 5-minute walk from the train station north along **Viale Papa Giovanni XXIII.**

GETTING AROUND Bergamo has an extensive **bus system** (✆ 02-67087474; www.atb.bergamo.it) that runs through the Città Bassa and to points outside the walls of the Città Alta; tickets are .95€ ($1.10) and are available from newsstands and tobacco shops. With the exception of the trip from the train or bus stations up to the Città Alta, you probably won't have much need of public transit, since most of the sights are within an easy walk of one another.

To reach the Città Alta from the train station, take buses no. 1 or 1A and make the free transfer to the **Funicolare Bergamo Alta,** connecting the upper and lower cities and running every 7 minutes 6:30am to 12:30am. You can make the walk to the funicular easily in about 15 minutes (and see something of the pleasant new city en route) by following Viale Papa Giovanni XXIII and its continuations Viale Roma and Viale Vittorio Emanuele II straight through town to the funicular station.

If you're feeling hearty, a footpath next to the funicular winds up to Città Alta; the steep climb up (made easier by intermittent staircases) takes about 20 minutes. Bus no. 1A also continues up and around the Città Alta walls to end just outside Porta San Vigilio, and hence more convenient to hotels San Lorenzo and Gourmet.

EXPLORING THE CITTA BASSA

Most visitors scurry through Bergamo's lower, newer town on their way to the Città Alta, but you may want to pause long enough to enjoy a coffee along the **Sentierone,** the elongated piazza/street at the center of town. This spacious square graciously combines a mishmash of architectural styles (including 16th-century porticos on one side, the Mussolini-era Palazzo di Giustizia and two imitation Doric temples on another). Locals sit in its gardens, lounge in its cafes, and attend classical concerts at the **Teatro Donizetti.** This 19th-century theater is the center of Bergamo's lively culture scene, with a fall opera season and a winter-to-spring season of dramatic performances; for details, check with the tourist office or call the theater at ✆ 035-4160602 (http://teatro.gaetano-donizetti.com).

The main draw for most visitors down here, though, is the **Galleria dell'Accademia Carrara** ✦✦, Piazza Carrara 82a (✆ 035-399640; www.accademiacarrara.bergamo.it). The city's exquisite art gallery is one of the finest in Northern Italy, founded in 1795 when Napoleon's troops were busy rounding up the art treasures of their newly occupied northern Italian states. Many of these works ended up in Bergamo under the stewardship of Count Giacomo Carrara. The collection came into its own after World War I, when a young Bernard Berenson, the 20th century's most noted art connoisseur, took stock of what was here and classified the immense holdings, making sure "every Lotto [was] a Lotto." Lorenzo Lotto (1480–1556) was a Venetian who fled the stupefying society of his native city and spent 1513 to 1525 in Bergamo perfecting his highly emotive portraits. Many of his works from the Accademia recently toured the United States, but they're now back in place in the salons of a neo-classical palace alongside a staggering inventory with paintings by Bellini, Canaletto, Carpaccio, Guardi, Mantegna, and Tiepolo. Most of these master-works are in the 17 third-floor galleries.

It's easy to become overwhelmed here, but among the paintings you may want to view first is Lotto's *Portrait of Lucina Brembrati,* in which you'll see the immense sensitivity with which the artist was able to imbue his subjects. Look carefully at the moon in the upper-left corner—it has the letters ci painted into it, a playful anagram of the sitter's first name; in Italian, *moon* is *luna,* and this one has a ci in the middle). Botticelli's much reproduced *Portrait of Giuliano de Medici* hangs nearby, as does Raphael's sensual *St. Sebastian.* You can visit the Accademia on foot from the Città Alta by following Via Porta Dipinta halfway down the hill to the Porto Sant'Agostino and then a terraced, ramplike staircase to the doors of the museum. From the Città Bassa, the museum is about a 10-minute walk from the Sentierone—from the east end of the square, take a left on Largo Belloti, then a right on Via Giuseppe Verdi and follow that for several blocks to Via Pignolo and turn left to Via Tomaso, which takes you to Piazza Carrara (the route is well signposted). Admission is 2.60€ ($3) for adults and free for those under 18 or over 60. It's open Tuesday to Sunday 9:30am to 1pm and 2:30 to 6:45pm (Oct–Mar, 10am–1pm and 2:30–5:45pm).

Across the street is the **Galleria d'Arte Moderna e Contemporanea** (© 035-399528), containing works by such 20th-century masters as Fattori, Boccioni, De Chirico, Morandi, and Kadinsky. Admission is free, and it's open Tuesday to Saturday 10am to 1pm and 3 to 7pm, and Sunday 10am to 7pm.

EXPLORING THE CITTA ALTA

The higher, older part of Bergamo owes its stone palazzos, proud monuments, and what remains of its extensive fortified walls to more than 3 centuries of Venetian rule, beginning in 1428, when soldiers of the Republic wrestled con-trol of the city out of the hands of the Milan-based Visconti. The Venetians left their mark elegantly in the town's theatrically adjoining squares, **Piazza Vecchia** and **Piazza del Duomo,** which together create one of the most beautiful out-door assemblages in Italy—actually, French writer Stendahl went so far as to call this heart of old Bergamo the "most beautiful place on earth."

On Piazza Vecchia, you'll see traces of the Venetian presence in the 12th-cen-tury **Palazzo della Ragione (Courts of Justice),** which has been embellished with a graceful ground-floor arcade and the Lion of San Mark's, symbol of the Venetian Republic, above a 16th-century balcony reached by a covered staircase (the bells atop its adjoining tower, the **Torre Civico,** sound the hours sonorously). The interiors will remain closed over the next few years for renovations. Across the piazza, the **Biblioteca Civica** was modeled after the Sansovino Library in Venice. Piazza del Duomo, reached through one of the archways of the Palazzo della Ragione, is filled with an overpowering collection of religious structures that include the **Duomo** and the much more enticing **Cappella Colleoni** (see below), the **Baptistery,** and the **Basilica di Santa Maria Maggiore** (see below).

Colleoni has lent his name to the upper town's delightful main street, cob-blestoned and so narrow you can just about touch the buildings on either side when standing in the center. If you follow it to its far western end, you'll emerge into **Largo Colle Aperto,** refreshingly green and open to the Città Bassa and valleys below. For better views and a short excursion into the countryside, board the **Funicolare San Vigilio** for the ascent up the San Vigilio hill; the funicular runs daily every 12 minutes or so between 7am and midnight and costs .95€ ($1.10). The strategic importance of these heights was not lost on Bergamo's medieval residents, who erected a summit-top **Castello** (© 035-236284), now mostly in ruin. Its keep, still surrounded by the old walls, is a park in which every bench affords a far-reaching view. It's open daily April to September 9am to 8pm, October and March 10am to 6pm, and November to February 10am to 4pm.

The Castello is a good place to begin a trek around the flanks of the Città Alta—first back down the San Vigilio hill (or take the funicular), then back into the Città Alta through the Porta San Alessandro. For a look at the old walls and some more good views, instead of following Via Colleoni back into the center of the town, turn left on Via della Mura and follow the 16th-century bastions for about half a mile to the Porta Sant'Agostino on the other side of the town.

Cappella Colleoni ⭑⭑⭑

Bartolomeo Colleoni was a Bergamese *condottiere* who fought to maintain the Venetian stronghold on the city. In return for his labors, the much-honored soldier was given Bergamo to rule for the republic. If you've already visited Venice, you may have seen Signore Colleoni astride the Verrocchio equestrian bronze in Campo Santi Giovanni e Paolo. He rests for eternity in this elaborate funerary chapel designed by Amadeo, the great sculptor from nearby Pavia (where he completed his most famous work, the Certosa). The pink-and-white marble exterior, laced with finely sculpted columns and loggias, is airy and almost whimsical. Inside, the soldier and his favorite daughter, Medea, lie beneath a ceiling frescoed by Tiepolo and surrounded by reliefs and statuary; Colleoni appears on horseback again atop his marble tomb.

Piazza del Duomo. © 035-210061. Free admission. Apr–Oct daily 9am–12:30pm and 2–6:30pm; Nov–Mar Tues–Sun 9am–12:30pm and 2–4:30pm.

Basilica di Santa Maria Maggiore ⭑

Behind the plain marble facade and a portico whose columns rise out of the backs of lions lies an overly baroque gilt-covered interior hung with Renaissance tapestries. Gaetano Donizetti, the wildly popular composer of frothy operas who was born in Bergamo in 1797 (see below) and returned here to die in 1848, is entombed in a **marble sarcophagus** that's as excessive as the rest of the church's decor. The finest works are the **choir stalls,** with rich wood inlays depicting landscapes and biblical scenes; they're the creation of Lorenzo Lotto, the Venetian who worked in Bergamo in the early 16th century and whose work you'll encounter at the Accademia and elsewhere around the city. The stalls are usually kept under cloth to protect the sensitive hardwoods from light and pollutants, but they're unveiled for Lent. The octagonal **Baptistery** in the piazza outside the church was originally inside but removed, reconstructed, and much embellished in the 19th century.

Piazza del Duomo. © 035-223327. Free admission. Mon–Sat 8am–noon and 3–7pm (to 6pm Oct–Apr); Sun 8–10:30am and 3–7pm.

Museo Donizettiano

This charming little museum commemorates Gaetano Donizetti, who was born in Bergamo in 1797 and—little wonder, given the romance of his boyhood surroundings—became one of Italy's most acclaimed composers of opera. Fans can swoon over his sheet music, piano, and other memorabilia and see the deathbed where he succumbed to syphilis in 1848. Thus inspired, you can make the pilgrimage to the humble house where he claimed to have been born in a cellar, the **Casa Nateledi Gaetano Donizetti,** Via B. Canale 14 (© 035-399432), a rural street that descends the hillside from the Porta Sant'Alessandro on the western edge of the city. It's open Saturday and Sunday only from 11am to 6:30pm (donations requested).

Via Arena 9. ℭ 035-247116. www.museostoricobg.org. Admission 3€ ($3.45). Apr–Sept daily 10am–1pm and 2:30–5pm; Oct–Mar Tues–Sun 10am–1pm. Bus 1, 1a.

ACCOMMODATIONS YOU CAN AFFORD

The charms of staying in the Città Alta are no secret. Rooms tend to fill up quickly, especially in summer and on weekends. Reserve well in advance.

Agnello d'Oro ★★ *Value*   In keeping with its location a few steps from Piazza Vecchia, the Agnello d'Oro looks like it's right out of an old tourist brochure extolling the quaint charms of Italy. The tall, narrow ocher-colored building, with flower boxes at each of its tall windows, overlooks a small piazzetta where a fountain splashes next to potted greenery. The wood-paneled lounge and intimate dining room add to the charm quotient, which declines somewhat as you ascend in a tiny elevator to the rooms. These lean more toward serviceable comfort than luxury, but warm color schemes and old prints help compensate for the lack of space and amenities; the bathrooms are roomy and have been modernized. Front rooms (the ones to request) have narrow balconies overlooking the piazza. This is the most popular hostelry in the Città Alta (even though the friendliness level of the desk staff can vary wildly), so reservations are mandatory.

Via Gombito 22, 24129 Bergamo Alta. ℭ 035-249883. Fax 035-235612. www.agnellodoro.it. 20 units. 52€ ($60) single; 92€ ($106) double. Continental breakfast 6€ ($6.90). Parking in public lot. AE, MC, V. **Amenities:** Concierge; tour desk; limited room service. *In room:* TV, dataport, hair dryer.

Gourmet ★   This pleasant hotel offers the best of both worlds—it's only steps away from the Città Alta (a few hundred ft. outside the Porta Sant'Agostino on the road leading up to the Castello) but on a rural hillside, giving it the air of a country retreat. The villa-style building is set behind walls in a lush garden and enjoys wonderful views. A wide terrace on two sides makes the most of these views and the songs of caged canaries. Many of the very large, bright rooms look across the hillside to the heavily developed valley, too. They're furnished in plain modern (or at least modern a few decades ago) fashion geared more to solid comfort than to style, with king-size beds. The apartment is large, on two floors with a sitting area and kitchen downstairs and upstairs two bedrooms, a double and a twin, each with bathroom. There's a highly reputed restaurant downstairs, hence the name, with indoor and outdoor tables and midrange prices on Bergamesco and Lombard cuisines.

Via San Vigilio 1, 24129 Bergamo. ℭ/fax 035-4373004. www.gourmet-bg.it. 11 units. 62€ ($71) single; 92€ ($106) double; 190€ ($219) apt for 4. Continental breakfast 10€ ($12). AE, DC, MC, V. Free parking at hotel. Closed Dec 27–Jan 7. **Amenities:** Restaurant; bar; 24-hr. room service. *In room:* A/C, TV, minibar, hair dryer.

San Lorenzo ★★   Bergamo Alta was blessed with some much-needed additional hotel rooms when this stylish place opened in 1998, in a former convent building of Santa Agata. The centuries-old setting is tailor-made for this unusually pleasant inn—most of the rooms face a courtyard and open through French doors to a balcony that wraps around it; though the hotel is right in town, just a few steps off Via Colleoni, its hillside location provides views over the green slopes flowing down to the valley below. The rooms are small but comfortable, with striped silk draperies and bed coverings and cane-backed lounge chairs; the marble bathrooms come with hand-held shower massagers and hair dryers. A sumptuous buffet breakfast is served in the breakfast room. The discovery of Roman ruins put the brakes on construction of an underground parking facility, though the hotel provides a permit allowing you to park for free in the adjoining square.

Piazza Mascheroni 9A, 24129 Bergamo. ℂ 035-237383. Fax 035-237958. www.hotelsanlorenzobg.it. 24 units. 91€ ($105) single; 130€ ($150) double; 145€ ($167) triple. Rates include continental breakfast. AE, DC, MC, V. Parking free. **Amenities:** Bar; limited room service; laundry service; same-day dry cleaning; non-smoking rooms. *In room:* A/C, TV, dataport, minibar, hair dryer, safe.

GREAT DEALS ON DINING

Your gambols through the Città Alta can be nicely interspersed with fortifying stops at the city's many pastry shops and stand-up eateries. **Forno Tresoldi,** Via Colleoni 13, sells excellent pizzas and focaccia breads topped with cheese, salami, and vegetables by the slice (from 2€/$2.30). It's open Tuesday through Sunday from 8am to 1:30pm and 4 to 10pm.

Antica Hosteria del Vino Buono 𝕜𝕜𝕜 NORTHERN ITALIAN   At this cozy trattoria tucked into smallish rooms in a corner house on Piazza Mercato delle Scarpe at the top of the funicular station, an enthusiastic young staff takes food and wine seriously. It's a pleasure to dine in the handsome surroundings of brick, tile work, and photos of old Bergamo. For an introduction to food from the region, try one of the several tasting menus. Polenta figures prominently and is served *alla bergamese* (with wild mushrooms) and sometimes with olive paste folded into it—you can even sample three with the *tris di polenta.* The main courses lean toward meat. A dish like roast quail or rabbit should be accompanied by a Valcalepio Rosso, a medium-strength red from local vineyards (avoid the house red, a harsh cabernet).

Via Donizetti 25. ℂ 035-247993. Reservations recommended. Primi 7€ ($8.05); secondi 9€–13€ ($10–$15). AE, DC, MC, V. Tues–Sun noon–2:30pm and 7–10:30pm.

Taverna del Colleoni & Dell'Angelo 𝕜 CREATIVE NORTHERN ITALIAN   Pierangelo Cornaro and chef Odorico Pinato run one of Bergamo's top restaurants, bang on the main square in a Renaissance palazzo—in summer the best tables are outside on the piazza; otherwise, you're in a refined medieval-looking space of high vaulted ceilings. The ingredients are fresh and the recipes are inspired by local tradition, but the menu has a more creative *cucina nuova* (nouvelle portions, nouvelle prices). The best part of the menu is the back page, where they list some of their more typical dishes, such as *fiorade bergamesche ai porcini e mirtilli* (wide noodles with porcini and blueberries), *cannoli di farro al ragù di cinghiale, salsa di zucca e patate* (pasta tubes made of emmer flour stuffed with wild boar and served under a pumpkin-potato sauce), *stoccafisso gratinato alla moda dell'Angelo* (cod casserole with cheese and polenta), and *cous cous siciliano di gamberi allo zafferano* (couscous tinged with saffron and studded with shrimp). Desserts are good, too.

Piazza Vecchia 7. ℂ 035-232596. www.colleonidellangelo.com. Reservations recommended. Primi 11€–16€ ($13–$18); secondi 12€–26€ ($14–$30); lunch menu 31€ ($36), dinner "gourmand" menu 60€ ($69), neither with wine. AE, DC, MC, V. Tues–Sun noon–2:30pm, 7:30–10:30pm.

Vineria Cozzi 𝕜𝕜 *Value* NORTHERN ITALIAN   Cozzi isn't just a wine bar, but a Bergamo institution. Its cane chairs are well worn with use by Bergamese and visitors who can't resist stopping in for a glass of wine while walking down Via Colleoni. Hundreds of bottles from throughout Italy line the walls and are served by the glass (from 1.55€/$1.80). It has dropped a bit of the old enoteca feeling (no more quick sandwiches and meat platters) and gone a bit more into full-fledged restaurant mode, but it's still a cozy and inexpensive place to eat well. The changing daily offerings usually include several pasta dishes and polenta with rich cheese folded into it, perhaps a torta stuffed with fresh vegetables, and a main course or two—if the duck breast stuffed with cabbage is available, order it.

Via Colleoni 22. © 035-238836. www.vineriacozzi.it. Primi 8€–11€ ($9.20–$13); secondi 8€–12€ ($9.20–$13). AE, MC, V. Daily 11am–2am. Closed Wed in winter and Fri in summer. Also closed 10 days in Jan and 12 days in Aug.

CAFES

Caffè del Tasso ✿, Piazza Vecchia 3, is a prime piece of real estate on the main square of the Città Alta. It began life as a tailor's shop more than 500 years ago, but it's been a bar since 1581. Legend has it that Garibaldi's Red Shirts used to gather here (Bergamo was a stronghold of Italian independence, which explains why an edict from 1845 on the wall of this cafe prohibits rebellion).

While the location of **Caffè della Funicolare** in the Piazza Mercato delle Scarpe, in the upper terminal of the funicular that climbs the hill from the Città Bassa to the Città Alta, doesn't suggest a memorable dining experience, the station dates from 1887 and has enough Belle Epoque flourishes and curlicues to make the surroundings interesting. Plus, the dining room and terrace look straight down the hill to the town and valley, providing some the best tables with a view (accompanied by low-cost fare) in the upper town. Stop in for a coffee, one of the 50 kinds of beer on tap or the more than 100 kinds of whiskeys and Scotches, and a sandwich or a salad.

3 Mantua: A Gem of Lombardy

158km (98 miles) E of Milan, 62km (38 miles) N of Parma, 150km (93 miles) SW of Venice

One of Lombardy's finest cities is in the farthest reaches of the region, making it a logical addition to a trip to Venice or Parma as well as to Milan. Like its neighboring cities in Emilia-Romagna, **Mantua (Mantova)** owes its past greatness and its beautiful Renaissance monuments to one family—in this case, the Gonzagas, who rose from peasant origins to conquer the city in 1328 and ruled benevolently until 1707. You'll encounter the Gonzagas—and, because they were avid collectors of art and ruled through the greatest centuries of Italian art, the treasures they collected—in the massive Palazzo Ducale that dominates much of the town center; in their refreshing suburban retreat, the Palazzo Te; and in the churches and piazzas that grew up around their court.

One of Mantua's greatest charms is its location—on a meandering river, the Mincio, which widens here to envelop the city in a necklace of moodily romantic lakes. Often shrouded in mist and surrounded by flat, lonely plains, Mantua can seem almost melancholy. Aldous Huxley wrote of the city, "I have seen great cities dead or in decay—but over none, it seemed to me, did there brood so profound a melancholy as over Mantua." Since his visit in the 1930s, though, the Palazzo Ducale and other monuments have been restored, and what will probably strike you more is what a remarkable gem of a city Mantua is.

ESSENTIALS

GETTING THERE   By Train   Ten trains daily arrive from **Milan** (2 hr.; 8.05€/$9.25). There are hourly runs from **Verona** (24–48 min.; 2.25€–4.45€/ $2.60–$5.10), with connections to Venice.

By Car   The speediest connections from Milan are via the autostradas, the A4 to Verona and the A22 from Verona to Mantua (the trip takes less than 2 hr.).

From Mantua, it's also an easy drive south to Parma and other cities in Emilia-Romagna, on S420.

VISITOR INFORMATION   The **tourist office** is at Piazza Mantegna 6 (© **0376-328253;** fax 0376-363292; www.aptmantova.it), open Monday through Saturday from 8:30am to 12:30pm and 3 to 6pm, and Sunday from 9:30am to 12:30pm (closed most Sun in Jan–Feb).

FESTIVALS & MARKETS   Mantua enlivens its steamy summer with a **jazz festival** the third weekend (Thurs–Sun) of July. Year-round, Piazza delle Erbe is the scene of a bustling **food market** Monday through Saturday from 8am to 1pm. On Thursday mornings, a bigger **market,** filled with clothing, housewares, and more food, spills through Piazza Magenta and adjoining streets.

CITY LAYOUT   Mantua is tucked onto a point of land surrounded on three sides by the **river Mincio,** which widens here into a series of lakes, named prosaically **Lago Superiore, Lago di Mezzo,** and **Lago Inferiore.** Most of the sights are within an easy walk of one another within the compact center, which is only a 10-minute walk from the lakeside train station. Follow **Via Solferino** to **Via Marangoni,** turn right, and follow that to **Piazza Cavallotti,** where a left turn on **Corso Umberto I** will bring you to **Piazza delle Erbe,** the first of the gracious piazzas that flow through the city center to the palace of the Gonzagas. You can also make the trip on the no. 2 bus, which leaves from the front of the station.

EXPLORING THE CITY

As you wander around, you'll notice that Mantua's squares are handsomely proportioned spaces surrounded by medieval and Renaissance churches and palazzi. The piazze open one into another, creating the wonderful illusion that walkers in the city are strolling through a series of opera sets.

The southernmost of these squares, and the place to begin your explorations, is **Piazza delle Erbe (Square of the Herbs)** ⚘, so named for the produce-and-food market that transpires in stalls to one side (see "Festivals & Markets," above). Mantua's civic might is clustered here in a series of late-medieval and early Renaissance structures that include the **Palazzo della Ragione (Courts of Justice)** and **Palazzo del Podestà (Mayor's Palace),** from the 12th and 13th centuries, and the **Torre dell'Orologio,** topped with a 14th-century astrological clock. Also on this square is Mantua's earliest religious structure, the **Rotonda di San Lorenzo** ⚘, a miniature round church from the 11th century (daily 10am–1pm and 2–6pm; may close afternoon in winter; free admission). The city's Renaissance masterpiece, **Sant'Andrea** (see below), is off to one side on Piazza Mantegna.

In the adjoining **Piazza Broletto** (just north as you work your way through the old city), the statue of Virgil commemorates the poet who was born near here in 70 B.C. and celebrated Mantua's river Mincio in his *Bucolics.* The next square, **Piazza Sordello,** is huge, rectangular and somberly medieval, lined with crenellated palazzi. Most notably, though, the massive hulk of the **Palazzo Ducale** (see below) forms one wall of the piazza. To enjoy Mantua's soulful lakeside vistas, follow Via Accademia through Piazza Arche and the **Lungolago Gonzaga.**

Sant'Andrea   A graceful Renaissance facade fronts this 15th-century church by Leon Battista Alberti, with an 18th-century dome by Juvarra. The simple arches seem to float beneath the classic pediment, and the unadorned elegance forms a sharp contrast to other Lombardy monuments, like the Duomo in

Milan, the Cappella Colleoni in Bergamo, and the Certosa in Pavia. Inside, the classically proportioned vast space is centered on a single aisle. The Gonzaga court painter Mantegna is buried in the first chapel on the left. The crypt houses a reliquary containing the blood of Christ (allegedly brought here by Longinus, the Roman soldier who thrust his spear into Jesus's side), which is carried through town on March 18, the feast of Mantua's patron, Sant'Anselmo.

Piazza Mantegna. (C) **0376-328504.** Free admission. Daily 7:30am–noon and 3–7pm.

Palazzo d'Arco   Mantua's aristocratic d'Arco family lived in this elegant Renaissance palazzo until 1973, when the last member of the family donated it to the city. Though most of the extant palazzo is neoclassical (1780s), the gardens shelter a wing from the 15th century. The highlight of the rooms is the **Sala dello Zodiaco,** brilliantly frescoed with astrological signs by Giovanni Falconetto in 1520.

Piazza d'Arco 4. (C) **0376-322242.** www.museodarco.it. Admission 3€ ($3.45). Mar–Oct Tues–Sun 10am–12pm and 2:30–6pm; Nov–Feb Sat–Sun 10am–12:30pm and 2–4:30pm.

Palazzo Ducale   Behind the walls of this massive fortress/palace lies the history of the Gonzagas, Mantua's most powerful family, and what remains of the treasure trove they amassed in a rule that began in 1328 and lasted into the early 18th century. Between their skills as warriors and their penchant for marrying into wealthier and more cultured houses, they managed to acquire power, money, and an artistic following that included Pisanello, Titian, and, most notably, Andrea Mantegna, their court painter, who spent most of his career working for his Mantua patrons.

The most fortunate of these unions was that of Francesco Gonzaga to Isabelle d'Este in 1490. This well-bred daughter of Ferrara's Este clan commissioned many of the art-filled frescoed apartments you see today, including the **Camera degli Sposi** in Isabella's apartments—the masterpiece, and only remaining fresco cycle, of Mantegna. It took the artist 9 years to complete the cycle, and in it, he included many of the visitors to the court; it's a fascinating account of late-15th-century court life.

Most of Mantegna's works for the palace, though, have been carted off to other collections; his famous *Parnassus,* which he painted for an intimate room known as the studiolo, is now in the Louvre, as are works that Perugino and Corregio painted for the same room (in one of the more compelling current stories from the art world, Mantua is demanding their return).

The Gonzagas expanded their palace by incorporating any structure that lay within reach, including the Duomo and the Castello di San Giorgio (1396–1406). As a result, it's now a small city of 500 rooms connected by a labyrinth of corridors, ramps, courtyards, and staircases, filled with Renaissance frescoes and ancient Roman sculpture. The **Sala del Pisanello** frescoes feature Arthurian legends (mostly Tristram and Isolde) painted by Pisanello between 1436 and 1444 and were discovered beneath layers of plaster only in 1969. The **Salle degli Arazzi (Tapestry Rooms)** are hung with copies—woven at the same time but by a different Flemish workshop—of the Vatican's tapestries designed by Raphael and his students (among them Giulio Romano). The **Camera degli Sposi** was frescoed by Mantegna (the *trompe-l'oeil* oculus in the center of the ceiling is an icon of Renaissance art and a masterpiece of foreshortening).

Other highlights include the **Galleria degli Specchi (Hall of Mirrors);** the low-ceilinged **Appartemento dei Nani (Apartments of the Dwarfs),** where a replica of the Holy Staircase in the Vatican is built to miniature scale (in keeping with noble custom of the time, dwarfs were part of Isabella's court); and the **Galleria dei Mesi (Hall of the Months).** Some of the mostly delightful chambers in the vast complex make up the **Appartimento Estivale (Summer Apartment),** which overlooks a courtyard where hanging gardens provide the greenery.

Piazza Sordello. ② 0376-352111. www.mantovaducale.it. Admission 6.50€ ($7.45). Tues–Sun 8:45am–7:15pm.

Palazzo Te Frederico Gonzaga, the pleasure-loving refined son of Isabella d'Este, built this splendid Mannerist palace as a retreat from court life. You'll see that the purpose of this palace was to amuse as soon as you enter the courtyard—the keystone of the monumental archway is designed to look like it's falling out of place. Throughout the lovely whimsical interior, sexually frank frescoes (by Giulio Romano, who left a scandal behind him in Rome that arose over his licentious engravings) depict Psyche and other erotically charged subject matter and make unsubtle reference to one of Frederico's favorite pastimes (horses and astrology, Frederico's other passions, also figure prominently).

The greatest and most playful achievement here, though, has to do with power: In the **Sala dei Giganti (Room of the Giants),** Titan is overthrown by the gods in a dizzying play of architectural proportion that gives the illusion that the ceiling is falling. The palazzo is a 20-minute walk from the center of town along Via Mazzini. En route, devotees of Mantua's most famous painter may choose to stop for a look at the **Casa di Mantegna,** Via Acerbi 47 (② **0376-360506**). Admission is free, and it's open Tuesday through Sunday from 10am to 12:30pm and 3 to 6pm (hours may vary).

Viale Te. ② 0376-323266. Admission 8€ ($9.20) adults, 2.50€ ($2.85) ages 12–18 and seniors over 65; free for under 12. Tues–Sun 9am–6pm; Mon 1–6pm. Box office closes a half-hour earlier.

ACCOMMODATIONS YOU CAN AFFORD

If you're interested in the lowest-priced accommodations, the tourist office can provide details and make reservations for rooms at five hostel-like farmhouses in the surrounding countryside. Rates are about 15€ ($17) per person. Since several of the properties are within a few kilometers of town, you can reach them without too much trouble by bike or combination bus ride and trek.

ABC Moderno The prices at this recently renovated hotel across from the train station are remarkably low, considering the pleasant surroundings and the amenities. A pleasant lounge area and breakfast room open onto a sunny terrace. Upstairs, the renovated rooms have bright tile floors, fresh plaster and paint, new modular furnishings, and modern bathrooms. Architectural details, such as stone walls and patches of old frescoes, have been uncovered to provide decorative touches. The management is extremely helpful, and their hospitality extends to lending out the three bikes they have on hand for free (first come, first served). If the Moderno is full, bypass the other nearby hotels, which tend to be dreary and overpriced.

Piazza Don Leoni 25, 46100 Mantova. ② 0376-323347. Fax 0376-322349. www.hotelabcmantova.it. 31 units. 55€–77€ ($63–$89) single; 66€–99€ ($76–$114) double. Rates include buffet breakfast. MC, V. Parking 6€–15€ ($6.90–$17). **Amenities:** Restaurant (cafe); bar; bike rental; concierge; tour desk. *In room:* A/C, TV, dataport, hair dryer.

Broletto This atmospheric old hotel is in the center of the old city, only a few steps from the lake and the castello, making it a fine base for a late-night stroll through the moonlit piazze. The rooms have contemporary furnishings that are vaguely rustic in design, with orthopedic bed frames. Bright corner room no. 16 has balconies and windows on two sides. The most alluring features of the decor, though, are massive beams on the ceilings and other architectural details from the palazzo's 16th-century origins.

Via Accademia 1, 46100 Mantova. © **0376-326784.** Fax 0376-221297. 16 units. 65€–70€ ($75–$81) single; 107€–115€ ($123–$132) double; 120€–130€ ($138–$150) triple. Continental breakfast 6.50€ ($7.45). MC, V. Closed Dec 22–Jan 4. **Amenities:** Concierge; tour desk; car-rental desk; babysitting; laundry service. *In room:* A/C, TV, dataport, minibar, hair dryer.

Mantegna On a quiet side street just a few steps south of the *centro storico*, the Mantegna offers solid comfort in surroundings that are thoroughly modern. The cozy narrow singles resemble ships' cabins, but the doubles are unusually roomy. All have been renovated within the past few years and have new bathrooms; many face a sunny and quiet courtyard.

Via Fabio Filzi 10, 46100 Mantova. © **0376-328019.** Fax 0376-368564. www.hotelmantegna.it. 42 units. 75€ ($86) single; 120€ ($138) double; 140€ ($161) triple. Buffet breakfast 8€ ($9.20). AE, MC, V. Parking free in courtyard. Closed Dec 24–Jan 7 and 2 weeks in Aug. **Amenities:** Bar; concierge. *In room:* A/C, TV, dataport, minibar, hair dryer.

WORTH A SPLURGE

San Lorenzo 𝍏𝍏 One of Italy's more gracious inns was fashioned out of a row of old houses just off Piazza delle Erbe. Oil paintings and Oriental carpets grace the marble-floored salons. The guest rooms, no two of which are alike, are furnished with exquisite reproductions of 18th- and 19th-century antiques— plus at least one original piece in each room—and come with elegant touches like a bit of stucco work on ceilings as well as all the conveniences you'd expect from a luxury hotel. A panoramic roof terrace overlooks the towers and rooftops of the *centro storico*, and the lavish buffet breakfast is served in an elegant room overlooking the rotunda, with a series of sitting salons around a bar nearby.

Piazza Concordia 14, 46100 Mantova. © **0376-220500.** Fax 0376-327194. www.hotelsanlorenzo.it. 32 units. 130€–150€ ($150–$173) single; 160€–175€ ($184–$201) double; 160€–190€ ($184–$219) junior suite. Rates include breakfast. Frequent promotions may lower the price up to 40% in slow periods (ask when you call). AE, DC, MC, V. Parking 20€ ($23) in garage. **Amenities:** Concierge; 24-hr. room service; babysitting; laundry service; same-day dry cleaning. *In room:* A/C, TV, VCR (on request), fax (on request), dataport, minibar, hair dryer, safe.

GREAT DEALS ON DINING

Mantovian cuisine is quite refined—exquisite risotto dishes, an array of pastas stuffed with pumpkin and squash and, given the proximity of lakes and rivers, a fine selection of fish appear on menus.

Leoncino Rosso 𝍏𝍏 MANTOVANA This fine old restaurant with an attractive rustic dining room, just off Piazza Broletto (on a parallel street) in the center of the old city, has been serving food since 1750. This is a good place to sample Mantua's distinctive cuisine. Topping the list is *tortelli di zucca,* a large ravioli pillow stuffed with pumpkin. If you want to continue to eat as the Mantovese do, move on to *stracotto mantovano* (stewed donkey; that store next door is a horsemeat butcher). For more familiar fare from the barnyard, try the delicious *cotechino e fagioli* (pork sausage and beans). You can tell it's a local place by the TV in the corner (a bit loud, actually) that always manages to have a soccer game playing.

Via Giustiziati 33. © **0376-323277.** Reservations recommended. Primi 5.50€–7€ ($6.30–$8.05); secondi 6.50€–8€ ($7.45–$9.20); fixed-price menu 20€ ($23). AE, DC, MC, V. Mon–Sat noon–3:30pm and 7–10:30pm; Sun noon–3:30pm. Closed 15 days in Aug and 1 week in Jan.

Ochina Bianca 𝍏𝍏 MANTOVANA Gilberto and Marcella Venturini serve distinctive variations on the local cuisine in these simple yet elegant dining rooms a few blocks north of the center. Many of the dishes rely on fresh fish from the Mincio, which finds it way into such creations as *peperoni ripieni di pesce di fiume* (peppers filled with smoked fish and topped with a fresh tomato sauce) and many of the risotti. Grilled or sautéed freshwater fish is also often on the menu, as are traditional meat specialties like *coniglio alla porchetta* (roasted rabbit with pork stuffing). The zucchini flowers stuffed with ricotta and parmigiano and kissed with anchovy paste are almost as good an antipasto as the tiny salmon rolls (wrapped around fat so it melts and flavors as the fish cooks), served on a potato purée as a main course. *Torta sabbiosa* is a local dessert, a raisined plum cake soaked in Guinness, and the homemade gelato is delicious. The carefully chosen wine list is extensive.

Via Finzi 2. ⓒ 0376-323700. Reservations required. Primi 7.50€–8€ ($8.60–$9.20); secondi 13€–13€ ($14–$15). MC, V. Tues–Sun 12:45–2pm and 7:45–10pm. Closed last 3 weeks in August.

Trattoria due Cavallini ⭐ *Value* MANTOVANA   Your reward for the 10-minute walk south of the center (follow Via Trieste and its continuation, Corso Garibaldi) is a meal at one of Mantua's favorite informal trattorias for more than 65 years, where you can eat in a shady courtyard in good weather. The menu is typically Mantovian, with excellent *tortelli di zucca* and an aromatic *stinco di miale* (roasted pork joint, infused with fresh herbs). The *torta sbrisolona,* a traditional Mantovese cake of cornmeal, almonds, and butter, is served fresh from the oven.

Via Salnitro 5. ⓒ 0376-322084. www.mangiareamantova.com. Primi 3.10€–8€ ($3.55–$9.20); secondi 6.20€–8€ ($7.15–$9.20). AE, MC, V. Wed–Mon 12:15–2pm and 8–10pm. Closed July 15–Aug 18.

4 Lake Garda: Largest of the Italian Lakes

Sirmione: 127km (79 miles) E of Milan, 149km (92 miles) W of Venice. Riva del Garda: 170km (105 miles) E of Milan, 199km (123 miles) NW of Venice, 43km (27 miles) S of Trent

Poets, composers, and mere mortals have been rhapsodizing about the Italian lakes for centuries—most vocally since the 18th century, when it became de rigueur for travelers on the Grand Tour to descend through the Alps and enjoy their first days on Italian soil on the shores of the lakes.

Lake Garda (Largo di Garda), the largest and easternmost of the lakes, laps against the flat plains of Lombardy and the Veneto at its southern extremes, and in the north becomes fjordlike and moody, its deep waters backed by Alpine peaks. All around the lake, Garda's shores are green and fragrant with flowery gardens, groves of olives and lemons, and forests of pines and cypress. This pleasing, vaguely exotic landscape has attracted the likes of poet Gabriele D'Annunzio, whose villa near Gardone is one of the major attractions, and Benito Mussolini, whose Republic of Salo was headquartered here. Long before them, the Romans discovered the hot springs that still gush forth at Sirmione, the famed resort on a spit of land at the lake's southern reaches. Today's visitors come to swim (Garda is the cleanest of the major lakes), windsurf (Riva del Garda, at the northern end of the lake, is Europe's windsurfing capital), and enjoy the easygoing ambience of Garda's many pleasant lakeside resorts.

SIRMIONE

Garda's most popular resort juts several kilometers into the southern waters of the lake on a narrow peninsula of cypress and olive groves. Despite an onslaught of visitors, Sirmione manages to retain its charm. Vehicular traffic is kept to a minimum (the few motorists allowed onto the marble streets of the old town are required to switch off their cars' engines at traffic lights). The emphasis is on strolling, swimming in waters that are warmed in places by underwater hot springs, and relaxing on the sunny terraces of pleasant lakeside hotels. One caveat: You may find Sirmione less than charming in July and August, when the crowds descend in full force.

ESSENTIALS

GETTING THERE **By Train** Connections are via nearby Desenzano (20 min. from Sirmione by half-hourly bus; 1.30€/$1.50), which is on the Milan–Venice rail lines, with trains almost every half-hour in either direction, stopping in **Verona** (25 min.; 2.25€–4.45€/$2.60–$5.10), **Venice** (1½–2½ hr.; 7.90€–12€/$9.08–$13), and **Milan** (1–1½ hr.; 6.35€–9.20€/$7.30–$11).

By Bus Hourly bus service links Sirmione with **Verona** (1 hr.; 2.90€/$3.35). For more information, contact **APT** in Verona (© 045-8004129). In summer, a special bus makes a 35-minute 7pm run from **Verona** Monday, Wednesday, Friday, and Saturday (13€/$15).

By Boat Hydrofoils and ferries operated by **Navigazione Lago di Garda** (© 800-551801 or 030-9149511; www.navigazionelaghi.it) ply the waters of the lake. One to two hourly ferries and four daily hydrofoils connect Sirmione with **Desenzano** (20 min., 2.60€/$3 by ferry; 10 min., 5.10€/$5.85 by hydrofoil). Two daily ferries and three daily hydrofoils connect Sirmione with **Gardone** (70–120 min., 5.50€/$6.30 by ferry; 55 min., 8€/$9.20 by hydrofoil), **Limone** (3 hr., 7.50€ by ferry; 1 hr. 40 min., 9.80€/$11 by hydrofoil), and **Riva** (almost 4 hr., 8€/$9.20 by ferry; 2 hr. 10 min., 11€/$12 by hydrofoil). Service is curtailed from October to April.

By Car Sirmione is just off the A4 between Milan and Venice. From Bologna, Florence, Rome, and other points south, take the A22 north from Modena to Verona and, from there, the A4 west to Sirmione. The trip from Venice takes about 1½ hours, and the trip from Milan a little over an hour. There's ample parking in the lakeside lots lining Viale Marconi, the broad avenue that runs down the peninsula to the entrance of the old town.

VISITOR INFORMATION The **tourist office** is outside the old town near the castle at Viale Marconi 2 (© 030-916245 or 030-916114; www.brescia holiday.com). Easter to October, hours are daily 9am to 12:30pm and 3 to 6pm (though the hotel reservations people actually keep it open all day long until 9pm); November to March, hours are Monday to Friday 9am to 12:30pm and 3 to 6pm, and Saturday 9am to 12:30pm. The helpful English-speaking staff dispenses a wealth of information about Sirmione and other sights on the lake and will reserve a room for you.

EXPLORING THE TOWN

In addition to its attractive though tourist-shop-ridden **old town,** Sirmione has lakeside promenades, pleasant beaches, and even some open countryside where olive trees sway in the breeze. Anything you'll want to see can be reached easily on foot, though an open-air tram makes the short run out to the Roman ruins from the northern edge of the old town (but not between 12:30 and 2:30pm).

The moated and turreted **Castello Scaligero** (© 030-916468) marks the only land-side entrance to the old town. Built in the 13th century by the della Scala family, who ruled Verona and many of the lands surrounding the lake, the castle warrants a visit mainly for the views from its towers. It's open Tuesday through Sunday from April to mid-October from 9am to 8pm and from mid-October to

March from 9am to 1pm. Admission is 4€ ($4.60) for adults, 2€ ($2.30) for ages 18 to 25, and free for those under 18 or over 65.

From the castle, Via Vittorio Emanuele leads through the center of the town and emerges after a few blocks into the greener, garden-lined lanes that wind through the tip of the peninsula to the **Grotte di Catullo** (© 030-916157). Whether or not these extensive ruins at the northern tip of the peninsula were really, as they're alleged to have been, the villa and baths of the pleasure-loving Roman poet Catullus is open to debate. Even so, their presence here, on a hilltop fragrant with wild rosemary and pines, demonstrates that Sirmione has been a deservedly popular retreat for millennia, and you can wander through the evocative remains while enjoying wonderful lake views. March to October 14 the ruins are open Tuesday to Saturday 8:30am to 7pm and Sunday 9am to 6pm; October 15 to February hours are Tuesday to Saturday 8:30am to 4:30pm and Sunday 9am to 4:30pm (the little museum remains open until 7pm daily); admission is 4€ ($4.60) for adults, 2€ ($2.30) for ages 18 to 25, and free for those under 18 or over 65.

If you want to enjoy the clean waters of the lake, the place to head is the small **Lido delle Bionde beach** near the castle off Via Dante. In summer, the beach concession rents lounge chairs with umbrellas for 5€ ($5.75) per day, as well as kayaks and pedal boats (8€/$9.20 per hour).

ACCOMMODATIONS YOU CAN AFFORD

Sirmione has many pleasant, moderately priced hotels, all of which book up quickly in July and August, when they also charge higher rates (reflected in the high end of the rates below). You aren't allowed to drive into the old town until a guard at the entrance near the castle confirms that you have a hotel reservation. The tourist office will help you find a room in your price range on the day you arrive, but they won't book ahead of time.

Eden ⏇ The American poet Ezra Pound once lived in this pink-stucco lakeside hotel, located on a quiet side street leading to the lake in the center of town. Despite its long history as a lakeside retreat, the Eden has recently been modernized with taste and an eye to comfort. You can see the lake from most of the attractive rooms, decorated in contemporary furnishings. The mirrored walls enhance the light and lake views. The large bathrooms are new, and many have big tubs. The marble lobby opens to a delightful shaded terrace and a swimming pier that juts into the lake.

Piazza Carducci 17/18, 25019 Sirmione (BS). © 030-916481. Fax 030-916483. www.hoteledenonline.it. 33 units. 88€–105€ ($101–$121) single; 120€–160€ ($138–$184) double. Breakfast 10€ ($12). AE, DC, MC, V. Free parking (400m/13 ft. from hotel) or 10€ ($12) in garage. Closed Nov to Easter. **Amenities:** Bar; concierge; tour desk; room service; babysitting; laundry service. *In room:* A/C, TV, minibar, hair dryer, safe.

Grifone ⏇⏇ *Value* One of Sirmione's best-value lodgings is also one of its most romantic—the vine-clad stone building next to the castle enjoys a prime piece of lake property. You can enjoy this setting from a shady patio off the lobby, from a small beach, or from any of the guest rooms with a view. Brother and sister Nicola and Christina Marcolini oversee the hotel and adjoining restaurant with a great deal of graciousness, carrying on several generations of a family business. The rooms are simple but pleasant, with tile floors and plain furnishings; top-floor rooms (nos. 36–42) have small balconies from which to survey the views. The tidy bathrooms have stall showers or curtainless tubs. The Grifone books up quickly, often with return guests, so reserve well in advance.

Via Bocchio 4, 25019 Sirmione (BS). ℂ **030-916014.** Fax 030-916548. www.sirmionehotel.com. 16 units. 30€ ($35) single; 55€ ($63) double. No credit cards. Free parking. Closed late Oct to Easter. **Amenities:** Restaurant; bar. *In room:* Hair dryer (ask at desk).

Olivi 🏨🏨   This pleasant modern hotel offers the chance to live the high life at reasonable rates. It's not directly on the lake, which you can see from most rooms and the sunny terrace, but instead commands a hilltop position near the Roman ruins amid pines and olive groves. The rooms are stunningly decorated in varying schemes of bold, handsome pastels, and earth tones. The rooms have separate dressing areas off the bathrooms, and most have balconies. There's a pool in the garden and, to bring a lakeside feeling to the grounds, an artificial river that streams past the terrace and glass windows of the lobby and breakfast room.

Via San Pietro 5, 25019 Sirmione (BS). ℂ **030-9905365.** Fax 030-916472. www.gardalake.it/hotel-olivi. 58 units. 85€–105€ ($98–$121) single; 126€–194€ ($145–$223) double. Rates include breakfast. AE, MC, V. Closed Jan. **Amenities:** 2 restaurants; 2 bars; pool; concierge; tour desk; car-rental desk; courtesy car; room service; massage; babysitting; laundry service; dry cleaning. *In room:* A/C, TV, minibar, hair dryer, in-room safe.

GREAT DEALS ON DINING

In addition to the choices below, you can get a quick pizza with a view of the lake from the terrace at **L'Archimboldo,** Via Vittorio Emanuele 71 (ℂ **030-916409**), closed Tuesday.

La Roccia ITALIAN/PIZZA   This trattoria/pizza parlor caters to the flocks of tourists who stream through Sirmione, but it does so with excellent food and unusually pleasant surroundings. In good weather, the best seating is in the large garden to one side of the restaurant. The menu includes more than 20 excellent pizzas made in a wood-burning oven, plus plenty of traditional pastas, including lasagna and excellent cheese tortellini in a cream-and-prosciutto sauce. The fish (try the trout roasted or fried in butter and sage) and meat are excellent, and the best dishes are grilled over an open fire.

Via Piana 2. ℂ **030-916392.** Primi 6.50€–9.50€ ($7.45–$11); secondi 9€–17€ ($10–$19); pizza 4.50€–9€ ($5.15–$10). AE, DC, MC, V. Fri–Wed 12:30–3pm and 7–10:30pm (daily in Aug). Closed Nov–Mar.

Ristorante Al Progresso SEAFOOD/ITALIAN   This fan-cooled room on the main street of the old town is appealingly plain but has a touch of style. The pastas include excellent tortellini variations, and some come with shellfish from the not-too-distant Adriatic. Fresh lake trout is often on the menu—grilled or *al Sirmionese* (boiled with a house sauce of garlic, oil, capers, and anchovies)— as are some simple veal preparations, including a *vitello al limone,* made with fresh lemons that grow on the shores of the lake.

Via Vittorio Emanuele 18–20. ℂ **030-916108.** Primi 6.50€–9€ ($7.45–$10); secondi 8.50€–16€ ($9.75–$18). AE, DC, MC, V. Fri–Wed (daily in summer) noon–2:30pm and 6:30–10:30pm. Closed either Nov–Dec or Dec–Jan (depending on flow of tourism).

RIVA DEL GARDA

The northernmost town on the lake is not just a resort, but a real town, too, with medieval towers, a nice smattering of Renaissance churches and palazzi, and narrow cobblestone streets where the everyday business of a prosperous Italian town proceeds on its alluring way.

ESSENTIALS

GETTING THERE   By Train   See "By Train," under Sirmione above, for connections to Desenzano, from which you must take a bus (see below).

By Bus   Six buses a day link Riva and **Desenzano** on the southern end of the lake, about a 2-hour trip (4.90€/$5.65). You can also travel between **Sirmione** and Riva by bus, though except for a 4:30pm direct run, you must transfer at Peschiera (2 hr.; 6€/$6.90). From **Limone,** there are 11 trips daily (18 min.; 1.30€/$1.50). Twenty-five daily buses connect Riva and **Trento** (1 hr. 40 min.; 3.10€/$3.55). From **Verona,** there are 16 a day (2 hr.; 4.90€/$5.65), and from **Brescia** five daily (2 hr.; 5.15€/5.95).

By Boat   Navigazione Lago di Garda (see Sirmione above for information) runs the boats. Fifteen ferries and three hydrofoils per day connect Riva with **Limone** (35–45 min., 5.50€/$6.30 by ferry; 30 min., 8€/$9.20 by hydrofoil). Two ferries and three hydrofoils per day connect Riva with **Gardone** (2 hr. 45 min., 6.80€/$7.80 by ferry; 1 hr. 20 min., 9.30€/$11 by hydrofoil), **Sirmione** (almost 4 hr., 8€/$9.20 by ferry; 2 hr. 10 min., 11€/$12 by hydrofoil), and **Desenzano** (4 hr. 15 min., 9.20€/$11 by ferry; 2½ hr., 12€/$13 by hydrofoil). Schedules vary with the season, with limited service in the winter.

By Car   The fastest link between Riva and points north and south is the A22, which shoots up the east side of the lake (exit at Mori, 13km/8 miles east of Riva). A far more scenic drive is along the western shore, on the beautiful corniche between Riva and Salo that hugs cliffs and passes through kilometer after kilometer of tunnel. Depending on the route, by car, Riva is about an hour from Verona and about 45 minutes from Sirmione.

VISITOR INFORMATION   The **tourist office,** which supplies information on hotels, restaurants, and activities in the area, is near the lakefront Giardini di Porta Orientale 8 (© **0464-554444;** fax 0464-520308; www.garda.com or www.gardatrentino.com). From June 16 to September 15, it's open Monday through Saturday from 9am to noon and 3 to 6:30pm, and Sunday from 10am to noon and 4 to 6:30pm; from April to June 15 and September 16 to October, hours are Monday through Saturday from 9am to noon and 3 to 6:15pm; from November to March, hours are Monday through Friday from 9am to noon and 2:30 to 5:15pm.

EXPLORING THE TOWN

Riva's old town is pleasant enough, though the only historic attractions of note are the 13th-century **Torre d'Apponale** and, nearby, the moated lakeside castle, **La Rocca.** Part of the castle interior now houses an unassuming collection of local art and crafts (© **0464-573869;** www.comune.rivadelgarda.tn.it/museo), open Tuesday through Saturday from 9:30am to 5pm (Mar 15–June 15 and Sept 17–Nov 3 it's closed for *riposo* 12:30–3pm) and Sunday 9:30am to noon and 2 to 5pm; admission is 3€ ($3.45).

The tourist office runs a few **free guided tours** (in many languages, including English). Weekends they do walking tours of the town itself, Tuesday and Friday tours of a few sights in the area. You must book by 5pm the previous day at © **0464-554444.**

The main attraction is the lake itself, which Riva takes advantage of with a **waterside promenade** stretching for several kilometers past parks and pebbly beaches. The water is warm enough for swimming from May to October, and air currents fanned by the mountains make Garda popular for windsurfing year-round.

WATER & LAND SPORTS   A convenient point of embarkation for a lake outing is the beach next to the castle, where you can rent **rowboats** or **pedal**

boats for about 6€ to 7€ ($6.90–$8.05) per hour (buy 2 hr., get a third free); from March to October, the concession is open daily from 8am to 8pm.

For a more adventurous outing, check out the **windsurfing** at the **Nautic Club Riva,** Via Roverto 44 (© **0464-552453;** www.nauticclubriva.com), where you can rent equipment for 15€ ($17) for 1 hour, or 2€ ($37) for 4 hours; a pass to use it for 10 total hours whenever you want costs 130€ ($150). Multiday and weekly packages, as well as lessons, are also available.

You can rent **mountain bikes** from **Superbike Girelli,** Viale Damiano Chiesa 15 (© **0464-556602**), for 10€ ($12) per day (4€/$4.60 per hour); or from **Fori e Bike,** Viale dei Tigli 24 (© **0464-551830**), for 8€ to 13€ ($9.20–$15) per day (the higher price for the better mountain bikes).

ACCOMMODATIONS YOU CAN AFFORD

Montanara   It ain't fancy, but it's cheap. The Montanara is squirreled away above its cheap trattoria in a quiet part of the *centro storico*. The wood-floored midsize rooms occupy three stories of an old palazzo and are exceedingly basic— not to say a bit down at the heels—but are kept immaculate, with a picture or two framed on the whitewashed walls to relieve some of the spartan-ness. Rooms without bathrooms have at least a sink. The two top-floor accommodations are the best for their general brightness and high ceilings.

Via Montanara 18–20, 38066 Riva del Garda (BS). © 0464-554857. Fax 0464-561552. 9 units, 5 with bathroom. 17€ ($20) single without bathroom; 32€ ($37) double without bathroom, 36€ ($41) double with bathroom. Breakfast 6€ ($6.90). MC, V. Free parking. Closed Nov to Easter. **Amenities:** Restaurant; bar. *In room:* No phone.

Portici   The management pays much more attention to their ground-floor restaurant/bar under a portico of the main square than they do to the hotel, but perhaps that's because it's mainly booked by tour groups—keeping this central and surprisingly reasonable choice off the radar of more independent travelers. Sadly, its location in the upper leg of the piazza's L shape deprives almost all rooms of a lake view—and the functional units are boringly modern, to boot, done up in a monotonous blue tone. Still, for these prices, you can easily walk to a cafe to enjoy the view.

Piazza III Novembre 19, 38066 Riva del Garda (BS). © 0464-555400. Fax 0464-555453. www.hotel portici.it. 45 units. 39€–54€ ($45–$62) single; 62€–92€ ($71–$106) double. Rates include breakfast. Half board available. MC, V. Closed Nov–Mar. **Amenities:** Restaurant; bar. *In room:* TV, hair dryer.

Sole ★★   One of the finest hotels in town enjoys a wonderful location right on the lake at the main square. The management lavishes a great deal of attention on the public rooms and guest rooms and charges very fairly. The lobby is filled with rare Persian carpets and abstract art. The rooms reached via a sweeping circular staircase are warm and luxurious, with tasteful furnishings and marble-trimmed bathrooms; the best rooms have balconies hanging out over the lake. Lake-view rooms are outfitted in antique style; those overlooking the square and town are done in modern functional. Amenities include a formal restaurant, a casual cafe/bar extending onto a lakeside terrace, a rooftop solarium with sauna, and a nearby gated parking lot.

Piazza III Novembre 35, 38066 Riva del Garda (TN). © 0464-552686. Fax 0464-552811. www.hotelsole.net. 81 units. 74€–106€ ($85–$122) single without lake view; 92€–116€ ($106–$133) single with lake view; 96€–160€ ($110–$184) double without lake view; 112€–180€ ($129–$207) double with lake view. Half board costs only about 8€ ($9.20) extra per person, full board 15€ ($17). AE, DC, MC, V. Parking on street 1€ ($1.15), in garage 6€ ($7). Closed Nov to mid-Mar (except at Christmastime and during frequent trade fares). **Amenities:** Restaurant; bar; small exercise room; sauna; free bikes; concierge; tour desk; room service; laundry service. *In room:* A/C, TV, dataport (in some rooms), minibar, hair dryer, safe.

GREAT DEALS ON DINING

Birreria Spaten ITALIAN/TYROLEAN This noisy indoor beer garden occupies the ground floor of an old palazzo and features a wide-ranging mix of food from the surrounding regions, so you can dine on the cuisine of Trent (Trento) or Lombardy or from the other side of the Alps. Many of the German and Austrian visitors who favor Riva opt for the schnitzel-sauerkraut-sauerbraten fare, but you can also enjoy a pasta like *strangolapreti* (spinach-and-ricotta dumplings in a butter sauce), one of 30 pizzas, or a simply grilled lake trout. If you can't decide, the *Piatto Spaten* is an ample 14€ ($16) sampler of their Tyrolean specialties: *cotechino* (spicy sausage), wurstel, *canederli* (a giant bread dumpling), a ham steak, and sauerkraut.

Via Maffei 7. (℃) 0464-553670. Primi 6€–10€ ($6.90–$12); secondi 10€–18€ ($12–$21); pizza 5€–9€ ($5.75–$10). MC, V. Thurs–Tues 11am–3pm and 5:30pm–midnight. Closed Nov–Feb.

5 Lake Como

78km (47 miles) NE of Milan. Mennagio: 35km (21 miles) NE of Como and 85km (51 miles) N of Milan. Varenna: 50km (30 miles) NE of Como and 80km (48 miles) NE of Milan

The first sight of the dramatic expanse of azure-hued **Lake Como** 🎯🎯🎯, ringed by gardens and forests and backed by the snowcapped Alps, is likely to evoke strong emotions. Romance, soulfulness, even gentle melancholy—these are the stirrings that over the centuries the lake has inspired in poets (Lord Byron), novelists (Stendhal), composers (Verdi and Rossini), and plenty of other visitors, too—be they deposed queens, such as Caroline of Brunswick, whom George IV of England exiled here for her adulterous ways, well-heeled modern travelers who glide up and down these waters in the ubiquitous lake steamers, or these days the rich and über-famous (George Clooney recently moved into the neighborhood; he bought a villa from Teresa Heinz and her hubby, John Kerry).

Aside from its emotional pull, Como is also just an enjoyable place to spend time. Less than an hour from Milan by train or car, its deep waters and verdant shores provide a wonderful respite from modern life. Tellingly, Lake Como served as a backdrop for the romantic scenes in *Star Wars II: Attack of the Clones*—one of the very few settings in the film that was *not* created entirely by CGI computer programs. I guess even George Lucas realized that Como was a place of such unearthly beauty as to need little digital touching up.

COMO

The largest and southernmost town on the lake isn't likely to charm you. Long a center of silk making, this city that traces its roots to the Gauls, and, after them, the Romans, bustles with commerce and industry. You'll probably want to stay in one of the more peaceful settings farther up the lake, but Como amply rewards a day's visit with some fine Renaissance churches and palaces and a lovely lakefront promenade.

ESSENTIALS

GETTING THERE By Train One to three trains hourly connect **Milan** and Como's Stazione San Giovanni on Piazzale San Gottardo (regional: from Milan's Piazza Garibaldi station, 55–65 min., 3.30€/$3.80; high speed: from Milan's Statione Centrale station, 35–40 min., 4.85€/$5.55).

VISITOR INFORMATION The **regional tourist office** dispenses a wealth of information on hotels, restaurants, and campgrounds around the lake from its offices at Piazza Cavour 17 ((℃) **031-269712** or 031-3300111; www.lakecomo.org).

It's open daily from 9am to 1pm and 2 to 5pm (sometimes closed Sun in winter). There is also a **city tourist office** in a little trailer that has moved around a bit since it opened in 2000 but that stays near Piazza del Duomo, currently on Via Maestri Comacini around the right side of the cathedral (© 031-3371063). The office is open Monday through Friday from 10am to 12:30pm and 2:30 to 6pm, and Saturday and Sunday from 10am to 6pm.

EXPLORING COMO

Part Gothic and part Renaissance, the **Duomo,** Piazza del Duomo in the center of town just off the lake (© 031-265244), is festooned with exuberant masonry and sculpture. Statues of two of the town's famous native sons, Pliny the Elder and Pliny the Younger, flank the main entrance. Inside, beneath an 18th-century dome by Juavara—the architect who designed much of Turin—is a lavish interior hung with mostly 16th-century paintings and tapestries, with lots of helpful leaflets in English to explain the major works of art. It's open daily from 7:30am to noon and 3 to 7pm. The black-and-white-striped 13th-century **Broletto (Town Hall)** abuts the Duomo's left flank, and adjoining it is the **Torre del Comune.** As a study in contrasts, the starkly modernist and aptly named **Casa del Fascio,** built in 1936 as the seat of the region's fascist government, rises just behind the Duomo.

Como's main street, **Corso Vittorio Emanuele II,** cuts through the medieval quarter, where wood-beamed houses line narrow streets. Just 2 blocks south of the Duomo, the five-sided, 12th-century **San Fedele** stands above a charming square of the same name; parts of the church, including the altar, date from the 6th century. It's open daily from 8am to noon and 3:30 to 7pm. To see Como's most alluring church, though, it's necessary to venture into the dull outlying neighborhood southwest of the center, where, just off Viale Roosevelt, you'll come to the five-aisle, heavily frescoed **Basilica of Sant'Abbondio** (© 631-3388111), a Romanesque masterpiece from the 11th century with great 14th-century frescoes (pay .50€/55¢ to illuminate them). It's open daily from 8am to 6pm (unless a wedding, popular here, is on).

Lakeside life revolves around **Piazza Cavour** and the adjoining **Giardini Publici,** where the circular **Tempio Voltano** (© 031-574705) houses memorabilia that'll enlighten you about the life and experiments of native son and electricity pioneer Alessandro Volta. It's open Tuesday through Sunday from 10am to noon and 3 to 6pm (2–4pm Oct–Mar); admission is 3€ ($3.45). For a quick retreat and some stunning views, take the **funicular** (© 031-303608) for a 7-minute ride up to the top of **Brunate,** the forested hill above the town (it leaves from the Lungo Lario Trieste every 15 min. or so in summer, every half-hour in winter). The tourist office has maps of several trail hikes from the top.

ACCOMMODATIONS YOU CAN AFFORD

The Suisse (see below) is actually a pretty good value—especially when you consider Como's sad, moderately priced hotel scene. But if you're really pinching pennies, you could do worse (not much worse, mind you) than the seven barebones rooms above the **Ristorante Sociale,** Via Maestri Comacini 8 (© 031-264042). Their big selling points are a prime location next door to the Duomo and that the double rooms go for just 38€ ($44) without private bathroom, 48€ ($55) with bathroom.

Hotel Metropole Suisse ⚔ This massive 1892 hotel closes one side of Como's main square overlooking the lake. Accommodations vary; some are carpeted with very nice contemporary furnishings and proper beds (not cots); others are older with wood floors, brass beds, and embroidered upholstery. Almost all rooms overlook the lake at least partially—some full-on (the best with small balconies), some askance over the cafes ringing the piazza, others beyond the tree-lined promenade leading to the city park. The corner bar/lounge has picture windows for lake views, and the restaurant (under separate management) has tables out on the piazza.

Piazza Cavour 19, 22100 Como. 𝒞 **031-269444.** Fax 031-300808. www.hotelmetropolesuisse.com. 71 units. 112€–139€ ($129–$160) single; 134€–196€ ($154–$225) double; 196€–216€ ($225–$248) triple; 189€–210€ ($217–$242) junior suite. Rates include buffet breakfast. AE, DC, MC, V. Parking 13€ ($15). **Amenities:** Restaurant; bar; golf (nearby); sauna; concierge; tour desk; car-rental desk; room service; babysitting; laundry service; same-day dry cleaning; nonsmoking rooms. *In room:* A/C, TV w/pay movies, minibar, hair dryer, safe.

GREAT DEALS ON DINING

Pasticceria Monti CAFE   Above all, the busy Monti on the main lakefront piazza is one of Como's favorite places to gather and watch passersby. You can enjoy some of the excellent gelato or a coffee or cocktail, plus excellent sandwiches and other light fare, including daily pasta dishes.

Piazza Cavour 21. 𝒞 **031-301165.** Gelato from 1€ ($1.15) for a single scoop; pastries from 1.50€ ($1.75); sandwiches from 2.50€ ($2.85). MC, V. Wed–Mon 7am–2am (to 1am in winter).

Ristorante Sociale *Value* NORTHERN ITALIAN   Simple dishes at low prices. This trattoria tucked under an arcade next to the Duomo's right flank is where Comashci go after a play or concert at Como's Teatro Sociale (the walls are plastered with unsung heroes of the Northern Italian stage and the yellowing posters of plays in which they appeared). It's where the local soccer team celebrates victories, where the equivalent of the ladies' auxiliary meets to have long, voluble conversations while enjoying one of the best-priced fixed menus on the lake. You get your choice of four primi, four secondi, a side dish, and water or wine (though they usually give you both at no extra charge). Just steer clear of the fish—it's frozen . . . rather scandalous for a place located just 2 blocks from the fishing boats bobbing in the lake harbor. They also rent rooms (see above).

Via Maestri Comacini 8. 𝒞 **031-264042.** Primi 4€–8€ ($4.60–$9.20); secondi 7€–14€ ($8.05–$16); fixed-price menu 16€ ($18) with wine. AE, DC, MC, V. Tues–Sun noon–2pm and 7:30–10:30pm.

BELLAGIO & THE CENTRAL LAKE REGION

By far the loveliest spot on the lake (and where travelers should definitely set their sights) is the section known as the Centro Lago. Three towns—Bellagio, Varenna, and Mennagio—sit across the water from one another on three different shorelines.

ESSENTIALS

GETTING THERE & GETTING AROUND   By Train The closest train station to Bellagio and the other Central Lake towns is in Como (see above); from there you can continue by bus or boat.

By Boat From Como, boats stop first at Bellagio (by ferry 2 hr.; by hydrofoil 35–45 min.). They continue on to Mennagio (by ferry another 15 min.; by hydrofoil another 5 min.). About half the boats then stop in Varenna as well (plus there are about 2 dozen short-haul ferries each from Bellagio and Mennagio to Varenna): by ferry another 10 minutes; by hydrofoil another 5 minutes. You can also get **day passes** good for just the central lake or for the whole lake.

Many of the ferries carry cars for an additional fee. Schedules vary with season, but from Easter to September, a ferry or hydrofoil makes the trip from

Como to Bellagio and other towns along the lake at least hourly. For more information, contact **Navigazione Lago di Como** (© 800-551801 or 031-579211); the office is on the lakefront in Como on Lungo Lario Trieste.

By Bus   There are one to three **SPT buses** (© 031-247111; www.sptcomo.it) per hour from Como to Bellagio (about 70 min.; 2.50€/$2.85). Buses leave Como from in front of the main train station; get tickets at the bar inside.

By Car   Bellagio is connected to Como by a picturesque lakeshore road, S583, which can be very crowded in summer. The A9 links Como with Milan in about an hour. To reach Mennagio from Como, follow Route S340 along the western shore of the lake. For Varenna, follow S342 to Nibionno, a speck of a town, where it intersects with S36, which runs north through industrialized Lecco and thence along the lake's eastern shore. These roads tend to be crowded, especially on weekends and in summer, so allow at least an hour of travel time.

VISITOR INFORMATION   The **Bellagio tourist office** is inside the little ferry terminal on Piazza Mazzini (©/fax **031-950204;** www.bellagiolakecomo. com). Its hours are Monday and Wednesday through Saturday from 9am to noon and 3 to 6pm, and Tuesday and Sunday from 10:30am to 12:30pm and 3:30 to 5:30pm.

BELLAGIO ＡＡＡ

Bellagio is at the tip of the peninsula at a point where the lake forks into three distinct basins: One long leg sweeps north into the Alps, Como is at the southern end of the western leg, and Lecco is at the southern end of the eastern leg. Boats from Bellagio make it easy to visit the nearby shores of the Centro Lago— not that you'll be in a great hurry to leave this pretty old town, with its steep narrow streets, lakeside piazza, and beautiful gardens.

EXPLORING THE TOWN

Bellagio is often called one of the most beautiful towns in Italy. Nestled amid cypress groves and verdant gardens, its earth-toned old buildings climb from the lakefront promenade along stepped cobbled lanes. While Bellagio is a popular retreat for everyone from Milanese out for a day of relaxation, to British and Americans who come to relax for a week or two, the town is, for the most part, unmarred by tourism.

One of Bellagio's famed gardens surrounds the **Villa Melzi** (© 031-951281), built by Franceso Melzi, a friend of Napoleon and an official of his Italian Republic. The villa was later the retreat of Franz Liszt and is now the home of a distinguished Lombardian family; they allow the public to stroll through their acres of manicured lawns and fountains and visit a pavilion where a collection of Egyptian sculpture is on display. It's open from March 18 to October, daily from 9am to 6:30pm; admission is 5€ ($5.75).

Bellagio's other famous gardens are those of the **Villa Serbelloni,** occupying land once owned by Pliny the Younger and now in the hands of the Rockefeller Foundation. You can visit the gardens on twice-daily guided tours (reserve ahead), about 1½ hours long, in Italian and English (tours require six people minimum, 20 people maximum). From April to October, tours are Tuesday through Sunday at 11am and 4pm and cost 6.50€ ($7.45); for more information and to book a spot on the tour, call © **031-951555** (www.villaserbelloni.it). You meet at the little tower on the back side of Piazza della Chiesa, a steep block and a half up from the port.

ACCOMMODATIONS YOU CAN AFFORD

For a wider selection of moderately priced hotels, you'd do best to head across the lake from Bellagio to Mennagio or Varenna (see below).

Giardinetto The best lodging deal is at this little hotel at the top of town, reached from the lakefront by Bellagio's narrow stepped streets. A snug lobby with a big fireplace opens to a gravelly grapevine-covered terrace, where you're welcome to bring your own food for an alfresco meal. Most of the rooms also overlook the terrace (a flight and a half with no elevator). Most are quite large and bright, with big windows (those on the upper floors provide nice views from balconies over the town and lake beyond, especially nos. 18–20) and furnishings like solid old armoires and, in the better rooms, box-spring-and-mattress beds rather than the usual cots. Some, though, are on the airshaft or even come with no window whatsoever. The place is basic but comfortable enough.

Piazza del Chiesa, 22021 Bellagio. ⓒ 031-950168. 13 units, 11 with bathroom. 30€ ($35) single without bathroom; 45€ ($52) double without bathroom. 52€ ($60) double with bathroom. Breakfast 6€ ($6.90). No credit cards. Closed Nov–Apr. *In room:* Hair dryer.

Suisse ⓖ The simple rooms above this restaurant in a 15th-century lakeside villa on the main square are currently at budget status in terms of decor (though the price has crept up), but they plan to renovate another level up soon. The parquet floors will remain, as will the stylish solid wood furnishings—with lovely details of inlay or carving. The bathrooms are plain, and there's no elevator, but you're right on the harbor, and the midprice restaurant is quite good. It offers Italian fare year-round, with an inventive fusion flair in summer; the downstairs room looks very plain (though you can also sit out front under the arcades), but the upstairs dining room is understatedly elegant, with a stuccoed ceiling and a lake-view terrace. March to November, the restaurant is open daily (closed Wed Oct–Feb).

Piazza Mazzini 23, 22021 Bellagio. ⓒ 031-950335. Fax 031-951755. www.bellagio.co.nz/suisse. 10 units. Ask for single rates; 100€–154€ ($115–$177) double. Rates include breakfast. Half- and full-pension plans available. AE, DC, MC, V. Closed Dec-Feb. **Amenities:** Restaurant; bar; concierge; tour desk; room service. *In room:* TV, hair dryer, no phone.

Worth a Splurge

Du Lac ⓖⓖ The Leoni family ensures that an air of graciousness and old-fashioned comfort pervades its 150-year-old hotel overlooking the lake from the main piazza. Downstairs, a bar spills onto the arcaded sidewalk in front and there are a series of pleasant sitting rooms. Meals are served in a nicely appointed dining room with panoramic views of the lake, and in the guest rooms, all of which are unique, cushy armchairs and a nice smattering of antiques and reproductions lend a great amount of charm. Many of the smallish rooms have balconies or terraces, and there's a rooftop sun terrace with sweeping lake views. In 2002, they opened a sports center nearby with a pool, tennis courts, and a children's center, free for guests.

Piazza Mazzini 32, 22021 Bellagio. ⓒ 031-950320. Fax 031-951624. www.bellagiohoteldulac.com. 44 units. 60€–100€ ($69–$115) single; 80€–130€ ($92–$150) double. Rates include buffet breakfast. Half- and full-board available. MC, V. Closed early Nov to Easter. **Amenities:** Restaurant; bar; concierge; tour desk; car-rental; babysitting; laundry service; same-day dry cleaning. *In room:* A/C, TV, minibar, hair dryer, safe (in suites and superior rooms).

GREAT DEALS ON DINING

Bar Café Rossi ⓖⓖ LIGHT FARE One of the nicest of Bellagio's pleasant lakefront cafes is tucked under the arcades of the town's main square. You can dine at one of the few outside tables or in the delightful Art Nouveau dining room, with its intricate tile work, carved wood cabinets, and stuccoed ceilings. Wine and the excellent house coffee are available all day, but a nice selection of pastries and sandwiches makes this a good stop for breakfast or lunch.

Piazza Mazzini 22/24. Ⓒ 031-950196. Sandwiches 2.50€–4€ ($2.85–$4.60). AE, DC, MC, V. Fri–Wed 7:30am–10pm (open daily, often to midnight, Apr–Sept).

Barchetta ✿✿ SEAFOOD/LOMBARDA   One of Bellagio's best restaurants specializes in fresh lake fish and other seafood. In all but the coldest weather, food is served on a bamboo-enclosed heated terrace. (A bar was recently added on the terrace.) Most of the pastas don't use seafood but are innovative variations on traditional recipes, such as *ravioli caprino* (with goat's cheese, topped with pear sauce) and savory risotto with hazelnuts and pistachios. For a main course, however, you should try one of the delicious preparations of local perch or angler fish; the meat entrees, including baby lamb chops with rosemary, are also excellent. You can enjoy a pasta dish, as well as a meat and a fish dish, on one of the set menus. In 2004, the restaurant's ground floor was converted into a faster, less expensive version of the eatery.

Salita Mella 13. Ⓒ 031-951389. www.acena.it/labarchettadibellagio. Reservations highly recommended. Primi 8€–15€ ($9.20–$17); secondi 16€–21€ ($18–$24); tasting menu 45€ ($52) with wine. AE, DC, MC, V. Wed–Mon noon–2:30pm and 7–10:30pm; Tues–Wed 7–10:30pm. Closed Nov–Mar.

La Grotta ✿ (Value) ITALIAN/PIZZERIA   Tucked away on a stepped street just off lakefront Piazza Manzini, this cozy, informal restaurant consists of a series of vaulted-ceiling dining rooms. The service is extremely friendly, and the wide-ranging menu includes many pasta and meat dishes. Most of the regulars, though, come for the fish specials, including lake trout, or the delectable pizzas that are the best for miles around (I've made sure of this by sampling them six of seven times).

Salita Cernaia 14. Ⓒ 031-951152. Primi 6€–9€ ($6.90–$10); secondi 7€–12€ ($8.05–$13); pizza 5€–10€ ($5.75–$12). AE, DC, MC, V (credit cards accepted only for bills totaling more than 21€/$24). Tues–Sun noon–2:30pm and 7pm–1am (open daily July–Sept).

VARENNA

You can happily spend some time clambering up and down the steep steps that substitute for streets in this charming village (on the eastern shore of the lake about 20 min. by ferry from Bellagio) that, until not too long ago, made its living by fishing. The main attractions, though, are outside of town.

The hilltop ruins of the **Castello di Vezio** (Ⓒ 0341-831000) are about a 20-minute walk above the town on a gradually ascending path. The main reason for a visit is to enjoy the stunning views of the lake, its shoreline villages, and the backdrop of mountains at the northern end. May through June, the castle is open daily from 10am to 6pm, and July through September, from 11am to 8pm; admission is 1€ ($1.15).

The **gardens of the Villa Monastero** (Ⓒ 0341-830129) are more easily accessible at the southern edge of town along Via 4 Novembre, and you can reach them by following the series of lakeside promenades through the old town from the ferry landing. This villa and the terraced gardens that rise from the lakeshore were once a not-so-spartan monastery—until it was dissolved in the late 17th century, when the nuns in residence began bearing living proof that they were on too friendly terms with the priests across the way. If you find it hard to tear yourself from the bowers of citrus trees and rhododendrons clinging to terraces, you'll find equally enchanting surroundings in the adjoining gardens of the **Villa Cipressi** (© 0341-830113).

Both gardens are open daily March to October: Villa Monastero 10am to 7pm and Villa Cipressi 9am to 7pm. Admission is 2€ ($2.30) for adults and 1.30€ ($1.50) for those under 10 or over 60 to just one garden, and 3.50€ ($4) for adults and 2.50€ ($2.90) for kids and seniors to visit both. Call © 0341-830113 for more details.

In season, **ferries** make the 20-minute run between Bellagio and Varenna about every half-hour (see above). There's a tiny **tourist office** at Piazza S. Giorgio/Via 4 Novembre (© 0341-830367), open Tuesday to Saturday 10am to 12:30pm and 3 to 6pm, and Sunday 10am to 12:30pm.

ACCOMMODATIONS YOU CAN AFFORD

Milano ★★ *Value*   You'd have to look hard to find a more pleasant retreat by the lake. This old house hanging over Varenna's lakefront was taken over in 2002 by Bettina and Egidio Mallone, a friendly young Italian-Swiss couple. Their plans are to renovate it into a boutique hotel but retain the family atmosphere, which has long been the Milano's hallmark, with the aid of two cats and their infant daughter, Carlotta. Sadly, prices have risen sharply as they slowly overhaul the entire hotel; prices have already jumped more than 30% over the past 2 years. They've redone the common area downstairs in a modern style, and installed a TV with satellite channels and a computer for free Internet access. The rooms were overhauled in 2003 with new beds and antique-style furnishings, and spanking-new bathrooms as of 2004. All have balconies and views—nos. 1 and 2 open onto a wide terrace, and nos. 5 and 6 all have full-on lake vistas; the other half overlook the neighbor's pretty garden with askance lake views. The furnishings are a pleasant mix of old and unobtrusive modern pieces, brightened up with small Persian rugs. In summer, breakfast is served on the outdoor terrace. They have started serving three-course dinners (except Sun and Tues) out on the terrace in nice weather for 20€ ($23). They also rent out an apartment nearby (no views, though), preferably to families or groups of four, for 55€ ($63) per person, including breakfast back at the hotel.

Via XX Settembre 29, 23829 Varenna. © 0341-830298. Fax 0341-830061. www.varenna.net. 8 units. 100€–105€ ($115–$121) single with lateral lake view, 105€–110€ ($121–$127) single with full lake view; 115€–125€ ($132–$144) double with lateral lake view, 125€–135€ ($144–$155) double with full lake view. Rates include buffet breakfast. Three-course dinner 20€ ($23) upon request. AE, MC, V. Closed late Mar–Feb. **Amenities:** Bar; concierge; tour desk; Internet terminal; room service; massage; laundry service; dry cleaning. *In room:* Safe.

Villa Cipressi ★★ *Finds*   If you enjoyed your tour of Varenna's lush gardens (see above), there's no need to leave. This 16th-century villa and several outbuildings were converted to a hotel in the early 1800s; it's now geared to conferences but takes other guests, space permitting. Though the rooms have been renovated without any attempt to retain historic character, they're extremely large and attractive. Suites take advantage of the high ceilings and contain loft bedrooms, with sitting areas below that can easily fit a couple of single beds for families. Although not every room gets a lake view, all save a few small ones on the road side enjoy marvelous views over the gardens, which you can also enjoy on the delightful terraces. There are plans to add air-conditioning at some point. In June 2002, 10 new rooms were opened on the top floor with lake views and high ceilings decorated with molded stuccoes—the best is the corner suite, with a coffered ceiling, alcove bed, four windows, and a (nonworking) fireplace. They're busily preparing five more accommodations in a 15th-century building on the property.

Via IV Novembre 18, 22050 Varenna. ℂ 0341-830113. Fax 0341-830401. www.hotelvillacipressi.it. 32 units. 78€–85€ ($90–$98) single; 95€–105€ ($109–$121) double without lake view, 110€–130€ ($127–$150) double with lake view; 120€–135€ ($138–$155) "superior" double or suite without lake view. 180€–198€ ($207–$228) superior suite with lake view. Rates include buffet breakfast. AE, DC, MC, V. Usually closes late Oct–Mar, but some years open year-round. **Amenities:** Restaurant; bar; concierge; car-rental desk; courtesy car; babysitting. *In room:* A/C (in ⅔ of rooms), TV, dataport, hair dryer.

GREAT DEALS ON DINING

Vecchia Varenna ⭐⭐ LOMBARD/SEAFOOD   One of your most memorable experiences in this region could be a meal at this romantic restaurant at the water's edge in Varenna's oldest section. Dining is in a beautiful stone-floored room with white stone walls or on a terrace on the water. The kitchen makes the most of local herbs and vegetables and, of course, the bounty of the lake—for starters, *quadrucci* (pasta pockets) are stuffed with trout, and one of the best of the many risottos combines wild mushrooms and *lavarello* (a white fish from the lake). Grilled lake trout stuffed with mountain herbs is a sublime main course, though many other kinds of lake fish are also available.

Via Scoscesa 10. ℂ 031-830793. www.vecchiavarenna.it. Reservations required. Primi 11€ ($13); secondi 15€ ($17). MC, V. Tues–Sun 12:30–2pm and 7:30–9:30pm. Closed Jan.

MENAGGIO

This lively resort town hugs the western shore of the lake, across from Bellagio on its peninsula and Varenna on the distant shore. Hikers should stop at the **tourist office** on Piazza Garibaldi 8 (ℂ/fax **0344-32924;** www.menaggio.com), open Monday through Saturday from 9am to noon and 3 to 6pm (July–Aug also Sun 7:30am–6:30pm). The very helpful staff distributes a booklet, *Hiking in the Area Around Menaggio,* with descriptions of more than a dozen walks, accompanied by maps and instructions on what buses to take to trail heads. The town's bus stop is at Piazza Garibaldi (Sun on V. Mazzini); tickets are sold at Bar Centrale or the newsstand on Via Calvi at the piazza.

The major nearby attraction is about 2.5km (1⅓ miles) south of town: The **Villa Carlotta** (ℂ **0344-40405;** www.villacarlotta.it) is the most famous villa on the lake and was begun in 1643 for the Marquis Giorgio Clerici, who made his fortune supplying Napoleon's troops with uniforms; he spent much of it on his neoclassical villa and gardens. After a succession of owners, including Prussian royalty who lavished their funds and attention on the gardens, the villa is now in the hands of the Italian government. It's filled with romantic paintings, statues by Canova and his imitators, and Empire furnishings, but the gardens are the main attraction, with azaleas, orchids, banana trees, cacti, palms, and forests of ferns spreading in all directions. You can take the C10 bus from Menaggio or walk along the lake. The nearest ferry landing is at Cadenabbia, just north of the gardens, though ferries to Menaggio are more frequent. The villa and gardens are open daily March 16 to 31 and October from 9 to 11:30am and 2 to 4:30pm, and April to September 9am to 6pm. Admission is 7€ ($8.05) for adults and 3.50€ ($4) for students and seniors over 65.

WATERSPORTS   The lido, at the north end of town, has an excellent **beach,** as well as a **pool,** and is open from late June to mid-September daily from 9am to 7pm. For information on water-skiing and other activities, contact **Centro Lago Service,** in the Grand Hotel Victoria along the lakeside Via Castelli (ℂ **0344-32003**). Also ask at the hostel (see below) about boat and bike rentals, which are available to nonguests during slow periods.

ACCOMMODATIONS & DINING YOU CAN AFFORD

Albergo-Ristorante Il Vapore ✿   This very pleasant small restaurant/hotel faces a quiet square just off the lakefront. The rooms are comfortable, with rather nice modern furnishings (plus antiques in a few) and fuzzy towels in the cramped bathrooms. Six rooms open onto partial lake views: nos. 21 and 22 from tall windows, 25 and 26 from small terraces, 28 and 29 (the biggest room, with windows on two sides for a breeze) from tiny balconies. They usually won't accept reservations for just 1 or 2 nights (but you can just stop by and ask). The downstairs restaurant serves meals of local specialties from the nearby mountain valleys beneath the wisteria-shaded arbor of the entranceway or in an attractive pale-blue dining room with paintings by local artists.

Piazza Grossi 3, 22017 Menaggio. ℂ **0344-32229.** Fax 0304-34850. www.italiaabc.com/a/ilvapore. 10 units. 28€ ($32) single without lake view; 45€ ($52) double without lake view; 50€ ($58) double with lake view. Breakfast 6.50€ ($7.45). No credit cards. Closed 20 days in Nov and late Feb/early Mar. **Amenities:** Bar. *In room:* No phone.

Ostello La Primula *Value*   I don't particularly like hostels (didn't even when I was a student), so when I list one, you know it's got something special. This delightful example is easily accessible from Bellagio and other towns on the *Centro Lago* by boat, and is frequented about evenly by frugal adults and backpacking students. The dorms are relatively cozy, with no more than six beds per room. Most of the rooms have a view of the lake—nos. 3, 4, and 5 on the first floor even share a balcony. Everyone enjoys the view from the large, sunny communal terrace. One drawback: no luggage lockers. It's run by a couple of ex-social workers, and they serve a 12€ ($14) dinner that's so good it even attracts locals (you're expected to set your own table on the terrace, retrieve each course as it's called, and wash your own dishes).

You can explore the surrounding countryside on one of the bikes that are available or get onto the lake in one of the kayaks (rental of either for a full day is 11€/$12). Internet access is 3.50€ ($4) per 15 minutes; laundry is 3.50€ ($4) per load. The hostel offers special programs, such as 1-week cooking courses and an organized week-long hike through the area. Curfew is 11:30pm.

Via IV Novembre 106, on the south edge of town. ℂ/fax **0344-32356.** www.menaggiohostel.com. 11 units, 4 with bathroom. 14€ ($16) per person in dorm; 14€ ($16) per person in family suite with private bathroom. Rates include breakfast. Closed Nov 6–Mar 14. Office open 8–10am and 5–11:30pm. **Amenities:** Restaurant; bar; watersports equipment; bike rental; laundry service. *In room:* No phone.

6 Lake Maggiore & the Borromean Islands

Stresa: 80km (50 miles) NW of Milan

Anyone who reads Hemingway will know this lake and its forested shores from *A Farewell to Arms*. That's just the sort of place **Lake Maggiore (Lago Maggiore)** is—a pleasure ground steeped in associations with famous figures (Flaubert, Wagner, Goethe, and Europe's other great minds seem to have been inspired by the deep, moody waters backed by the Alps) and not-so-famous wealthy visitors. Fortunately, you need not be famous or wealthy to enjoy Maggiore, which is on the Swiss border just a short dash east and north of Milan.

STRESA

The major town on the lake is a pretty, festive little place, with a long lakefront promenade, a lively and attractive commercial center, and a bevy of restaurants and hotels that range from the expensively splendid to the affordably comfortable.

ESSENTIALS

GETTING THERE   By Train   Stresa is linked with **Milan** by 20 trains a day (58–84 min.; 4.25€–6.90€/$4.85–$7.95).

By Boat   Boats arrive and depart from Piazza Marconi, connecting Stresa with the Isole Borromee and with many other lakeside spots. Most boats on the lake are operated by **Navigazione Sul Lago Maggiore** (© 800-551801 or 0322-233200; www.navlaghi.it).

By Car   A8 runs between Milan and Sesto, near the southern end of the lake; from there, Route S33 follows the western shore to Stresa. The trip takes a little over an hour.

VISITOR INFORMATION   The **tourist office** has moved to the ferry dock (©/fax **0323-31308**), open Monday through Saturday (daily Mar–Oct) from 10am to 12:30pm and 3 to 6:30pm. You can also get info from **www. lagomaggiore.it** and **www.stresa.it**. For hiking information, ask for the booklet *Percorsi Verdi.*

EXPLORING STRESA & THE ISLANDS
Stresa
Strolling and relaxing seem to be the main activities in Stresa. The action is at the **lakeside promenade,** running from the center of town north past the grand lakeside hotels, including the Iles des Borromees, where Hemingway set *A Farewell to Arms.* Sooner or later, though, most visitors climb into a boat for the short ride to the famed islands themselves, the Isole Borromee.

Borromean Islands
These three islands, named for the Borromeo family, which has owned them since the 12th century, float in the misty waters off Stresa and entice visitors with their stunning beauty. Note that Isola Bella and Isola Superiore have villages you can hang out in for free, but Isola Madre consists solely of the admission-charging gardens.

Public **ferries** leave for the islands every half-hour from Stresa's Piazza Marconi; an 8€ ($9.20) **day pass** is the most economical way to visit all three—and if you buy your admission tickets for the *isole* sights at the Stresa ferry office along with your ferry tickets, you'll save 1€ ($1.15) off each—though the generally grumpy ticket agents will not advise you of this; you have to ask. Buy tickets only from the public Navigazione Lago Maggiore (© **800-551801** or 0322-233200; www.navlaghi.it), in the big building with triple arches. Private boats also make the trip out to the island at obscene rates; you'll see other ticket booths, and hucksters dressed as sailors will try to lure you aboard (for large groups, the prices can be reasonable, but do your negotiating on the dock before you get on the boat). For more information, visit **www.borromeoturismo.it**.

ISOLA BELLA   Isola Bella (5 min. from Stresa) remains true to its name, with splendid 17th-century gardens that ascend from the shore in 10 luxuriantly planted terraces. The Borromeo palazzo provides a chance to explore opulently decorated rooms, including the one where Napoleon and Josephine once slept. It's open daily March 20 to November 2 from 9am to 5:30pm. Admission is 9€ ($10) for adults and 4€ ($4.60) for ages 6 to 15. You can get a cumulative ticket for Isola Bella and Isola Madre for 15€ ($17) for adults and 7€ ($8.05) for kids. Audio tours help make sense of it all for 3.50€ ($4) each or 5€ ($5.75) to rent two sets of headphones. For more details, call © **0323-30556.**

Tips Budgeting Your Time

To squeeze as much of Stresa's sights in as you can in a day, note that the ferry back from the Isole Borromei stops first at the Mottarone funivia area before chugging down the coast to the center of Stresa and the main docks. You can hop off here either to (a) ride the cable car up the mountain or (b) simply to walk back into Stresa along a pretty lakeside promenade, past crumbling villas and impromptu sculpture gardens, in about 20 minutes.

ISOLA SUPERIORE   Most of Isola Superiore, also known as Isola Pescatore (10 min. from Stresa), is occupied by a not-so-quaint old fishing village—every one of the tall houses on this tiny strip of land seems to harbor a souvenir shop or pizza stand, and hordes of visitors keep them busy.

ISOLA MADRE   The largest and most peaceful of the islands is Isola Madre (30 min. from Stresa), every inch of which is covered with the exquisite flora and exotic, colorful birds of the 3.2-hectare (8-acre) **Orto Botanico** (© 0323-31261). The map they hand out at the entrance/ticket booth details all the flora; you're on your own to ID the various peacocks, game fowl, exotic birds, funky chickens, and other avians that strut, flit, and roost amid the lawns around the central villa (1518–85), filled with Borromeo family memorabilia and some interesting old puppet show stages. The botanical garden is open the same hours as Isola Bella daily March 27 to October 24 from 9am to 5:30pm. Admission is 8.50€ ($10) for adults and 4€ ($4.60) for ages 6 to 15, or on the cumulative ticket with Isola Bella (see above).

HIKING & BIKING IN THE AREA

The forested slopes above Stresa are prime hiking and mountain-biking terrain. To reach a network of trails, take the funivia from near the lakefront at the north end of town up **Monte Mottarone;** the funivia (© 0323-30399 or 0323-30295) runs every 20 minutes from roughly 9 to 11:40am and 12:40 to 5:30pm. (hours vary with the season). It costs 7€ ($8.05) one-way (12€/$14 round-trip) to take the funivia, and that covers taking along a bike, which you can rent at the station for 21€ ($24) for a half-day or 26€ ($30) for a full day. The **Alpina garden** halfway up is open Tuesday to Saturday 9am to 6pm and Sunday (July–Aug) 9:30am to 6:30pm.

If you don't want to venture too far from the lake, there's a nice **beach** near the station.

ACCOMMODATIONS YOU CAN AFFORD

Meeting *Value*   The name comes from the proximity of Stresa's small conference center, where a much-attended music festival is held from July to early September. Although the lakefront is a 5-minute walk away, the setting is quiet and leafy, though light sleepers at the back may notice the trains passing in the distance. The rooms, in Scandinavian modern, are big and bright, and many have terraces. There's a cozy bar and lounge downstairs, as well as a casual (but slightly impersonal) dining room. In 2000, they overhauled the exterior, adding balconies to all rooms lacking them (they plan to add air-conditioning soon as well).

Via Bonghi 9, 28049 Stresa. © 0323-32741. Fax 0323-33458. www.stresa.it. 27 units. 65€–90€ ($75–$104) single; 75€–105€ ($86–$121) double. Rates include breakfast. AE, DC, MC, V. Parking 7.50€

($8.60). Closed Jan–Feb. **Amenities:** Restaurant; bar; bike rental; concierge; tour desk; car-rental desk; 24-hr. room service; laundry service; dry cleaning. *In room:* TV, dataport, hair dryer.

Mon Toc 👍   Just uphill from the train station, this family-run hotel surrounded by a big private garden and lawn is convenient to the lake and town (a 10–15-min. walk) but enough removed to provide an almost countrylike atmosphere. With functional furniture, the rooms are unusually pleasant for a hotel in this price range and have tidy bathrooms (though a few are of the miniscule, molded, airplane variety). The friendly owner refuses, out of honesty, to call the sliver of lake visible over the rooftops from the second-floor rooms (no elevator) a "lake view."

Via Duchessa di Genova 67–69, 28049 Stresa. ✆ **0323-30282.** Fax 0323-933860. www.hotelmontoc.com. 15 units, 12 with bathroom. 40€ ($46) single without bathroom, 45€ ($52) single with shower but no toilet; 78€ ($90) double with bathroom; 95€ ($109) triple with bathroom (the 3 that share a bathroom are all singles). Rates include buffet breakfast. AE, DC, MC, V. Closed Jan or Nov. **Amenities:** Home-cooking restaurant; bar; concierge; tour desk; room service (breakfast). *In room:* TV.

Primavera 👍👍   For much of the spring and summer, the street in front of this hotel is closed to traffic and filled with flowering plants and cafe tables. The relaxed air prevails throughout this bright little hotel, a block off the lake in the town center. A tiny lounge and bar are downstairs. Upstairs, the tile-floored rooms are furnished in functional walnut veneer; you can have a minifridge on request. Many rooms have balconies, just wide enough to accommodate a pair of chairs, with flower boxes overlooking the town. A few fourth-floor rooms get in a sliver of lake view around the apse and stone bell tower of the Duomo.

Via Cavour 30, 28049 Stresa. ✆ **0323-31286.** Fax 0323-33458. www.stresa.it. 34 units. 65€–90€ ($75–$104) single; 75€–105€ ($86–$121) double. Rates include breakfast. AE, DC, MC, V. Parking 7.50€ ($8.60) at Hotel Meeting. Closed mid-Nov to Dec 20, Jan 7–Feb. **Amenities:** Bar; bike rental; concierge; tour desk; car-rental desk; 24-hr. room service; laundry service; dry cleaning. *In room:* TV, dataport, minibar (on request), hair dryer, safe.

Worth a Splurge

La Palma 👍👍   The Palma is one of the nicest of Stresa's luxury hotels and, given the high-level comfort and the amenities, one of the most reasonably priced. Most of the large rooms, recently redone in rich floral fabrics and wood tones, open to balconies overlooking the lake, and 98% of the spacious marble bathrooms have Jacuzzis. There's a rooftop sun terrace and fitness center, with a hot tub sauna, but the most pleasant places to relax are the flowery garden in front of the hotel and the terrace surrounding the lakeside pool.

Lungolago Umberto I, 33, 28838 Stresa. ✆ **0323-933906** or 0323-32401. Fax 0323-933930. www.hla palma.it. 120 units. 100€–160€ ($115–$184) single; 150€–220€ ($173–$253) double; 235€–280€ ($270–$322) triple/junior suite. Rates include buffet breakfast. AE, DC, MC, V. Parking free. Closed mid-Nov to mid-Mar. **Amenities:** Restaurant; bar; pool; tennis courts; exercise room; Jacuzzi; sauna; bike rental; concierge; tour desk; car-rental desk; courtesy car; 24-hr. room service; babysitting; laundry service; dry cleaning; nonsmoking rooms. *In room:* A/C, TV, dataport, minibar, hair dryer, safe.

GREAT DEALS ON DINING

Hotel Ristorante Fiorentino *(Value* ITALIAN   It's hard to find friendlier service or homier trattoria-type food in Stresa, especially at these prices. Everything that comes out of the family-run kitchen is made fresh daily, including cannelloni and other pastas. You can dine in a big cozy room or on a patio out back in good weather.

Via Bolongaro 9–11. ✆ **0323-30254.** Primi 4.50€–8€ ($5.15–$9.20); secondi 7€–18€ ($8.05–$21); *menù turistico* 14€ ($16) without wine. AE, DC, MC, V. Mar–Oct daily 11am–3pm and 6–10pm. Closed Dec–Mar.

Ristorante Pescatore ✿ SEAFOOD   This small dining room in the center of town is where residents of Stresa come for a fish meal. The starters include a wonderful seafood salad, an appetizer of smoked salmon or tuna, and a number of pasta dishes served with clams or squid. The main courses include a paella worthy of southern Spain (the owners and some of the cooks and waiters are Spanish), as well as *zarzuela de pescada*, a rich fish stew. Lake and ocean fish are always fresh and served grilled and topped with the simplest sauces.

Vicolo del Poncivo. ✆ **0323-31986**. Reservations recommended. Primi 7.70€–18€ ($8.85–$21); secondi 10€–21€ ($12–$24); fixed-price menu 14€ ($16) without wine. DC, MC, V. Fri–Wed noon–2pm and 7–10pm. Closed Dec–Feb.

Taverna del Pappagallo ✿ ITALIAN/PIZZERIA   Most of Stresa seems to congregate in this pleasant restaurant for the most popular pizza in town. But just about all the fare that comes out of the family-run kitchen is delicious, including delectable homemade gnocchi and such dishes as grilled sausage. Weather permitting, try to dine at one of the tables in the pleasant garden.

Via Principessa Margherita 46. ✆ **0323-30411**. www.tavernapappagallo.com. Primi and pizza 4€–11€ ($4.60–$13); secondi 8€–12€ ($9.20–$14). No credit cards. Thurs–Mon 11:30am–2:30pm and 6:30–10:30pm (daily in summer).

Worth a Splurge

Verbano ✿✿ ITALIAN   This restaurant has a fairy-tale location on the point of the "Fisherman's Isle," taking up the jasmine-fringed gravelly terrace next to the hotel. The waters lap right up to the wall, and the views are over the back side of Isola Bella and the lake around you on three sides. The cooking needn't be anything special, given its location in a prime tourist spot, but surprisingly, it is almost as lovely as the setting. The *zuppa di verdure* (vegetable soup) is hearty, with barley and grains. *Paglia e fieno* ("hay and straw") is a mix of regular (yellow) and spinach (green) tagliatelle noodles in a ragù made of scorpion fish, carrots, and zucchini. The *crespelle con passato di melanzane e toma* are pasta sheets wrapped around a puree of eggplant and local cheese. For your secondi, definitely try grilled lake trout, or the *luccio percia* (lake perch) filet in a smoked salmon and poppy crust sided with rice stained black with squid ink. Landlubbers can dig into *faraona dissosata farcita con spinaci e ricotta* (guinea fowl done up like ravioli, stuffed with ricotta cheese and spinach). They also rent some beautiful **rooms** in the villa upstairs: 100€ ($115) for a single and 145€ ($167) for a double.

Isola Superiore dei Pescatori. ✆ **0323-32534**. Reservations recommended. Primi 5€–10€ ($5.75–$12); secondi 11€–18€ ($13–$21). AE, DC, MC, V. Daily noon–2:30pm and 7–10pm (sometimes closed Wed in winter). Closed Jan.

10

Piemonte & the Valle d'Aosta

by Reid Bramblett

Piemonte (Piedmont) means "at the foot of the mountains." The mountains, of course, are the Alps, which define the region and part of Italy's northern and western borders. These dramatic peaks are visible throughout the province, most of which rises and rolls over fertile foothills that produce a bounty as rich as the region is green. This is the land of cheeses, truffles, plump fruit, and, of course, wines, among them some of Italy's most delicious reds, including Barbaresco, Barbera, and Barolo—the latter considered (along with Tuscany's Brunello) one of Italy's top two beefy, structured reds. Rising from the vineyards are medieval and Renaissance towns and villages, many of which remain untrammeled by the modern world.

Not that all of Piemonte is rural, of course. **Turin,** an industrial capital and home to Fiat, Italy's main auto manufacturer, is the region's capital. Within the ring of sprawling suburbs lies an elegant city of mannerly squares, baroque palaces, and stunning art collections. The Turinese and their neighbors from other parts of Italy often retreat to the **Valle d'Aosta,** the smallest, northernmost, and most mountainous of the Italian provinces.

1 Turin & the Mysterious Shroud

669km (415 miles) NW of Rome, 140km (87 miles) E of Milan

It's often said that **Turin** is the most French city in Italy or the most Italian city in France. The reason is partly historic and partly architectural. From the late 13th century to Italy's unification in 1861 (when the city served very briefly as capital), Turin was the capital of the House of Savoy. The Savoys were as French as they were Italian, and their holdings extended well into the present-day French regions of Savoy and the Côte d'Azur. The city's Francophile 17th- and 18th-century architects, inspired by the tastes of the French court, laid out broad avenues and airy piazzas and lined them with low-slung neoclassical buildings.

Most visitors come to Turin with business in mind (often at the Fiat and Pirelli works in the sprawling industrial suburbs). Those who take the time to look around the historic center, though, will find an elegant and sophisticated city that has changed little since more gracious centuries, with some fine museum collections and the charm of a place that, for all its Francophile leanings, is quintessentially Italian and perhaps the most pleasant big city in Northern Italy.

Tapped to host the 2006 Winter Olympics, Turin is gearing up to accommodate the thousands of athletes, spectators, and media who will descend on the city for 2 weeks (the Games run Feb 10–26). As tourist attractions and various city operations are refurbished to impress the worldwide audience, expect to find changes—including price increases—throughout Turin. To learn more about preparations for the 2006 winter games, visit **www.torino2006.org**.

A Taste of Piemonte & the Valle d'Aosta

Given such vast geographic diversity, it's not surprising that the region's cuisine varies according to the topography. In the southern stretches of Piemonte, the palate turns primarily to those magnificent red **wines** from the wine villages around Asti and Alba. Barbaresco, Barbera, Barolo, Dolcetto, Nebbiolo—the names are legendary, and they often appear on the table to accompany meat dishes stewed in red wine; one of the most favored of these is *brasato al barolo* (beef or veal braised in Barolo). The best dish with which to kick off a meal here is usually available only in winter: *bagna cauda,* literally translated as "hot bath," a plate of raw vegetables that are dipped into a steaming sauce of olive oil, garlic, and anchovies. Two pastas you will encounter on menus are *agnolotti* (a thick tube often stuffed with an infusion of cheese and meat) and *tajarin* (a flat egg noodle that may be topped with porcini mushrooms, sauces made with walnuts, or the local delicacy that is perhaps the region's greatest contribution to Italian cuisine: **white truffles**). As the land climbs higher toward the Valle d'Aosta, mountain fare takes over—**polenta** (a cornmeal mush varying from soupy and sticky to almost cakelike) is a popular *primo* or side to a *secondo.* Stews are thick with beef and red wine (*carbonada* is the most common of these). Buttery **fontina** is the preferred cheese.

ESSENTIALS

GETTING THERE By Plane Domestic and international flights land at the **Caselle International Airport** (✆ 011-5676361; www.turin-airport.com), 16km (9 miles) north of Turin. SADEM Buses (✆ 011-3000611; www.sadem.it) run between the airport and the city's main bus terminal on Corso Inghilterra and Porto Nuova train station every half-hour to 45 minutes; the trip takes 40 minutes and costs 5€ ($5.75).

By Train Turin's main train station is **Stazione Porta Nuova,** just south of the center on Piazza Carlo Felice, which marks the intersection of Turin's two major thoroughfares, Corso Vittorio Emanuele and Via Roma. From this station, there are 20 trains (www.trenitalia.com) a day to and from **Milan** (1 hr. 50 min.; 7.90€–15€/$9.10–$17), 12 trains a day to and from **Venice** (via Milan in 5–5½ hr.; 27€/$31), 22 trains a day to and from **Genoa** (around 2 hr. 15 min.; 7.90€–14€/$9.10–$16), and 9 trains a day to and from **Rome** (7–9 hr.; 35€/$40). **Stazione di Porta Susa,** west of the center on Piazza XVIII Dicembre, connects Turin with many outlying Piemonte towns.

By Bus Turin's main bus terminal is **Autostazione Terminal Bus,** Corso Inghilterra 3, near Stazione di Porta Sousa (✆ 011-4332525). For regional bus info, call **SADEM** (✆ 011-3000611; www.sadem.it) about the buses that connect Turin and **Aosta** (only one or two direct in 2 hr.; most change in Ivrea in 3 hr.; 6.45€/$7.40), or Turin and **Milan** (2 hr. 15 min.; 6.15€/$7.10), as well as many smaller towns in Piemonte.

By Car Turin is at the hub of an extensive network of autostradas. A4 connects Turin with Milan, a little over an hour away; A6 connects Turin with the Ligurian coast (and, from there, with Genoa via A10, with a total travel time

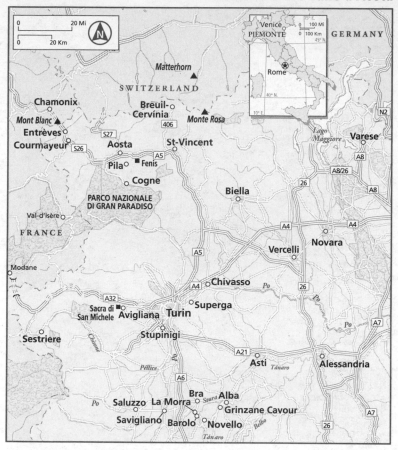

between the two cities of about 1½ hr.); A5 connects Turin with Aosta, about an hour away; and A21 connects Turin with Asti and Piacenza, where you can connect with the A1 for Florence (about 3½ hr. from Turin) and Rome (about 6½ hr. from Turin).

VISITOR INFORMATION   **Tourist offices** are in Piazza Solferino (© **011-535181;** fax 011-530070; www.turismotorino.org or www.comune.torino.it) and in the Porta Nuova train station (© **011-531327**). Both are open daily from 9:30am to 7pm (the office at the train station closes at 3pm Sun) and will book rooms for you up to 48 hours in advance. There's also an office in the airport (© **011-5678144**), open daily from 8:30am to 10:30pm. You'll find more information online at www.regione.piemonte.it.

FESTIVALS & MARKETS   Dance, opera, theater, and musical performances (mostly classical) are on the agenda in June and the first week of July, during the **Sere d'Estate** festival; companies come from around the world to perform. September is the month to enjoy classical music—more than 60 classical concerts are held on stages around the city during the month-long **Settembre Musica** festival (© **011-4424777;** www.comune.torino.it/settembremusica).

Turin

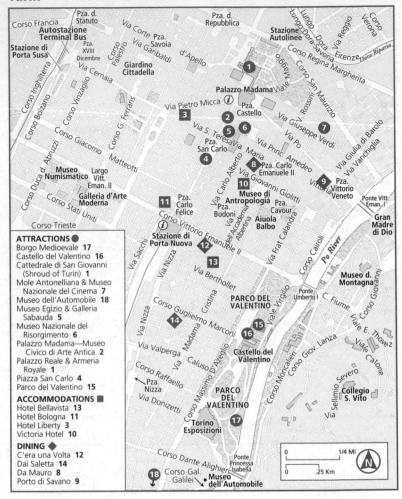

Turin map:

Corso Francia — Pza. d. Statuto — Autostazione Terminal Bus — Stazione di Porta Susa — Pza. d. Repubblica — Stazione Autolinee

Via Corte — Pza. Savoia — Via Garibaldi — d'Apello — Lungo Dora Reggio — Corso Verona — Corso Regina Margherita — Dora Riparia

Pza. XVIII Dicembre — Via Cernaia — Giardino Cittadella — Via Pietro Micca — **Palazzo Madama** — Pza. Castello

Corso Inghilterra — Corso Bolzano — Corso Vinzaglio — Via S. Teresa — Via Maria — Via Princ. Amedeo — Via Po — Via Giuseppe Verdi — Via Giulia di Barolo

Corso Giacomo Matteotti — Corso G. Ferraris — Pza. San Carlo — Via Carlo Alberto — Via Giovanni Giolitti — Pza. Carlo Emanuele II — Via Vanchiglia

Museo Numismatico — Largo Vitt. Eman. II — Galleria d'Arte Moderna — **Museo di Antropologia** — Pza. Vittorio Veneto — Ponte Vitt. Eman. I

Corso Duca d'Abruzzi — Corso Stati Uniti — Corso Trieste — Pza. Carlo Felice — Pza. Bodoni — Aiuola Balbo — Gran Madre di Dio

Stazione di Porta Nuova — Corso Vittorio Emanuele II — Via Sacchi — Via Nizza — Via Berthollet — Corso Guglielmo Marconi — **PARCO DEL VALENTINO** — Ponte Umberto I — Museo d. Montagna

Via Valperga — Via Madama Cristina — Via Caluso — Corso Massimo D'Azeglio — **Castello del Valentino** — Po River — Corso Giov. Lanza — Viale E. Thovez — Viale Catone

Corso Raffaello — Pza. Nizza — Via Donizetti — **PARCO DEL VALENTINO** — Torino Esposizioni — Corso Dante Alighieri — Ponte Princessa Isabella — Museo dell'Automobile — Collegio S. Vito

Corso Gal. Galilei

0 — 1/4 Mi — 0 — .25 Km — N

ATTRACTIONS ●
Borgo Medioevale **17**
Castello del Valentino **16**
Cattedrale di San Giovanni
  (Shroud of Turin) **1**
Mole Antonelliana & Museo
  Nazionale del Cinema **7**
Museo dell'Automobile **18**
Museo Egizio & Galleria
  Sabauda **5**
Museo Nazionale del
  Risorgimento **6**
Palazzo Madama—Museo
  Civico di Arte Antica **2**
Palazzo Reale & Armeria
  Royale **1**
Piazza San Carlo **4**
Parco del Valentino **15**

ACCOMMODATIONS ■
Hotel Bellavista **13**
Hotel Bologna **11**
Hotel Liberty **3**
Victoria Hotel **10**

DINING ◆
C'era una Volta **12**
Dai Saletta **14**
Da Mauro **8**
Porto di Savano **9**

Bric-a-brac of all kinds, be it household utensils, books, or used clothing, fills the stalls of the **Mercato del Baton,** held every Saturday at Piazza della Repubblica. **Gran Baton** fills the piazza the second Sunday of every month and is a larger affair, with some genuine antiques and artworks included in the mix. **Mercato della Crocetta** at Largo Cassini sells clothing at very low prices. For a look at the bounty of the surrounding farmlands, wander through the extensive outdoor **food market at Porta Palazzo,** Monday through Saturday from 6:30am to 1:30pm and Saturday from 3:30 to 7:30pm.

CITY LAYOUT You will get a sense of Turin's refined air as soon as you step off the train into the mannerly 19th-century **Stazione Porta Nuova.** The stately arcaded **Via Roma,** lined with shops and cafes, proceeds from the front of the station through a series of piazzas toward the **Piazza Castello** and the center of the city, about a 15-minute walk.

Directly in front of the station, the circular **Piazza Carlo Felice** is built around a garden surrounded by outdoor cafes that invite even business-minded

Turinese to linger. A few steps farther along the street will lead you into the **Piazza San Carlo,** which is flanked by the twin churches of San Carlo and Santa Christina. At the end of Via Roma, the Palazzo Madama, so named for its 17th-century inhabitant Marie-Christine, dominates the **Piazza Castello.** Just off the piazza is the Palazzo Reale, residence of the Savoys from 1646 to 1865, whose gardens now provide a pleasant respite from traffic and paving stones.

From here, a walk east toward the river along **Via Po** takes you through Turin's university district to one of Italy's largest squares, the much-elongated **Piazza Vittorio Veneto** and, at the end of this elegant expanse, the **Po River.**

GETTING AROUND   It's easy to get around central Turin on foot, but there's also a vast network of **GTTATM** (Gruppi Torinese Trasporti) trams and buses (© **800-019152;** www.comune.torino.it/gtt). Tickets are sold at newsstands: .90€ ($1.05) for 70 minutes, 2.60€ ($3) for 24 hours. The Torino Card (see "Sights to See," below) gets you free travel for 48 hours.

FAST FACTS: Turin

Bookstores **Libreria Internazionale Luxemborg,** between Piazza San Carlo and Piazza Castello at Via Accademia delle Scienze 3 (© **011-5613896),** has a large selection of English-language books and a helpful staff; it is open Monday through Saturday from 7am to 7:30pm. Another good bet for books in English is the chain **Libreria Feltrinelli,** Piazza Castello 19 (© **011-541627;** www.feltrinelli.it). Turin has many stores specializing in rare books and old prints, and many of these shops sell their wares from the secondhand bookstalls along Via Po, which runs between Piazza Castello and the river.

Consulates **British** subjects will find their consulate at Via Saluzzo 60 (© **011-6509202),** open Monday and Thursday from 9:15am to 12:15pm and 2:30 to 4:30pm. **Americans** will find their nearest consulate in Milan (see chapter 9).

Crime Turin is a relatively safe city, but use the same precautions you would exercise in any large city. Specifically, avoid the riverside streets along the Po at night, when they tend to be deserted. In an **emergency,** call © **113.** The **central police station** is near Stazione di Porta Susa at Corso Vinzaglio 10 (© **011-55881112).**

Drugstores A convenient late-night pharmacy is **Farmacia Boniscontro,** Corso Vittorio Emanuele 66 (© **011-541271).** It's open most of the day and night, closing only between 12:30 and 3pm.

Emergencies The general **emergency** number is © **113.** For an **ambulance,** dial © **118.**

Internet The **Internet Train** (© **011-543000;** www.internettrain.it), just down the street from the central Piazza Castello at Via Carlo Alberto 18, is open Monday to Friday 9:30am to 10pm, Saturday 9:30am to 8pm, and Sunday 3 to 7pm.

Laundry **Speedy Wash,** east of the station at Via Principe Tommaso 12 (© **338-1213622),** charges 7.80€ ($9) for a wash and dry (soap included) of a small load. Though it's technically do-it-yourself, the staff is always around to throw your load into the dryer for you, provided you pick up your things by the end of the day. It offers do-it-yourself dry cleaning as well. It's open daily from 9am to 8:30pm.

Post Office Turin's **main post office** is just west of Piazza San Carlo at Via Alfieri 10 (© **011-5060111**). It's open Monday through Friday from 8:15am to 5:30pm and Saturday from 8:30am to 1pm.

Taxis You can find taxis at cab stands. Especially convenient in the central city are the stands in front of the train stations, around Piazza San Carlo and Piazza Castello. Dial © **011-5737**, 011-5730, or 011-3399 for a radio taxi. The basic fare is 3.10€ ($3.55), plus 1.30€ ($1.50) for each kilometer. There is a 2.05€ ($2.40) night surcharge and a 1€ ($1.15) surcharge on Sundays and holidays.

SIGHTS TO SEE

A 14€ ($17) **Torino Card** (sold at the tourist office) will grant you plus one child under 12 discounts on concerts and the like, free admission to 82 museums, discounts on cultural events, and 48 hours of free public transport within Turin. For 17€ ($20), your card is valid for 72 hours.

Cattedrale di San Giovanni Battista   The controversial **Shroud of Turin (Santissima Sindone)** and the chapel in which it is sometimes enshrined, **Cappella della Santa Sindone,** hold pride of place in this otherwise uninteresting, pompous 15th-century church. Even without the presence of one of Christendom's most precious relics (and it's only rarely on view in the silver casket elevated on an altar in the center of the room), the chapel is well worth a visit. Recently restored after a 1997 fire (one of many the shroud has miraculously survived, with an occasional singeing, over the centuries), the chapel is somberly clad in black marble. But, as if to suggest that better things await us in the heavens, it ascends to an airy, light-flooded, six-tiered dome, one of the masterpieces of Italian baroque architecture.

The shroud, of course, is allegedly the one in which the body of Christ was wrapped when taken down from the cross—and to which his image was miraculously affixed. The image is of a man 5 feet 7 inches tall, with bloodstains consistent with a crown of thorns, a cut in the rib cage, cuts in the wrists and ankles, and scourge marks on the back from flagellation. Recent carbon dating suggests that the shroud was manufactured sometime around the 13th or 14th centuries, but the mystery remains, at least in part, because no one can explain how the haunting image appeared on the cloth. Also, additional radio carbon dating has suggested that, since the shroud has been exposed to fire (thus affecting carbon readings), it could indeed date from around the time of Christ's death. Despite scientific skepticism, the shroud continues to entice hordes of the faithful.

The shroud is usually tucked away out of sight at **Museo della Sindone (Holy Shroud Museum),** around the corner at Via San Domenico 28 (© **011-4365832;** www.sindone.org), open daily from 9am to noon and 3 to 7pm. Admission is 5.50€ ($6.35) for adults and 2.50€ ($2.90) for those under 14 or over 65. The shroud was last on view during Italy's Jubilee celebrations in 2000. Technically, it shouldn't be on display again until the next Jubilee, in 25 years, but it tends to pop up every 5 to 15 years for special occasions (and rumor has it that it may go on permanent display, either in the cathedral or in its own space). Otherwise, you'll have to content yourself with a series of dramatically backlit photos of the relic near the entrance to the Cappella della Santa Sindone, and a replica on display in the church.

In front of the cathedral stand two landmarks of ancient Turin—the remains of a Roman **theater** and the Roman-era city gate **Porta Palatina,** flanked by twin 16-sided towers.

Piazza San Giovanni. ℂ 011-5661540 or 011-4361540. Free admission. Daily 8am–12:30pm and 3–7pm. Bus: 6, 11, 12, 27, 56, 57.

Mole Antonelliana & Museo Nazionale del Cinema (National Film Museum)

Turin's most peculiar building—in fact, one of the strangest structures anywhere—is comprised of a squat brick base, a steep conelike roof supporting several layers of Greek temples piled one atop the other, and a needlelike spire, all of it rising 166m (544 ft.) above the rooftops of the city center (a height that at one time made the Mole the world's tallest building). Begun in 1863 and designed as a synagogue, the Mole is now a monument to Italian unification and architectural hubris and, as of fall 2000, home to Italy's **National Film Museum.** The museum's first section tracks the development of moving pictures from shadow puppets to kinescopes. The rest is more a tribute to film than a true museum, offering clips and stills to illustrate some of the major aspects of movie production, from *The Empire Strikes Back* storyboards to the creepy steadycam work in *The Shining.* Of the memorabilia on display masks from *Planet of the Apes, Satyricon,* and *Star Wars* hang together near *Lawrence of Arabia*'s robe, Chaplin's bowler, and a dress from *What Ever Happened to Baby Jane?.* Curiously, most of the clips (all in Italian dubbed versions), as well as posters and other memorabilia, are heavily weighted toward American movies, with exceptions mainly for the major players of European/international cinema like Fellini, Bertolucci, Truffaut, and Wim Wenders.

Even if you skip the museum, you can ascend to an **observation platform** at the top, an experience that affords two advantages—the view of Turin and the surrounding countryside, backed by the Alps, is stunning, and, as Guy de Maupassant once said of the Eiffel Tower, it's the only place in Turin where you won't have to look at the damned thing.

Via Montebello 20. ℂ 011-8125658. www.museonazionaledelcinema.org. Admission to museum 5.20€ ($6), observation platform 3.62€ ($4.15), both 6.80€ ($7.80). Tues–Fri and Sun 9am–8pm; Sat 9am–11pm. Bus: 55, 56, 61, 68.

Museo dell'Automobile (Automobile Museum)

As befits a city responsible for 80% of Italian car manufacturing, this shiny collection of mostly Italian automobiles, housed in a purpose-built, light-filled exhibition hall of classic 1960s design, draws car buffs from all over the world. Not too surprisingly, a century's worth of output from Fiat, which is headquartered in Turin, is well represented, and displays trace how the company influenced the 20th-century history of the city. The collection includes most of the cars that have done Italy proud over the years, including Lancias, Isotta Frashinis, and the Itala that came in first in the 1907 Peking-to-Paris rally. Oddities include a roadster emblazoned with the initials ND, which Gloria Swanson drove for her role as faded movie queen Norma Desmond in *Sunset Boulevard.*

Corso Unita d'Italia 40. ℂ 011-677666. www.museoauto.org. Admission 5.50€ ($6.35) adults, 4€ ($4.60) for those under 15 or over 65. Tues–Sat 10am–6:30pm; Sun 10am–8:30pm. Bus: 17, 34, 35; tram: 1.

Museo Egizio & Galleria Sabauda

Turin's magnificent **Egyptian collection** is one of the world's largest. This was, in fact, the world's first Egyptian museum, thanks to the fact that the Savoys ardently amassed artifacts through most of their reign, and the museum continued to mount collecting expeditions throughout the early 20th century. Of the 30,000 pieces on display, some of the more captivating exhibits are in the first rooms you enter on the ground floor. These include the **Rock Temple of Ellessiya,** from the 15th century B.C., which the Egyptian government presented to the museum in gratitude for Italian efforts to save monuments threatened by the Aswan Dam. The two statuary rooms nearby are staggering in the size and drama of the objects they house, most notably two **sphinxes** and a massive, richly painted **statue of Ramses II.** Smaller objects—mummies, funerary objects, and a papyrus *Book of the Dead*—fill the galleries on the next floor. The most enchanting exhibit here is the everyday paraphernalia, including eating utensils and shriveled foodstuffs, from the tomb of the 14th-century B.C. architect Khaie and his wife.

The Savoys' other treasure trove, a magnificent collection of **European paintings,** fills the salons of the Galleria Sabauda above the Egyptian collection. The Savoys' royal taste ran heavily to painters of the Flemish and Dutch schools, and the works by Van Dyck, van Eyck, Rembrandt, and Van der Weyden, among others, comprise one of Italy's largest collections of northern European paintings. In fact, two of Europe's most prized Flemish masterpieces are here, Jan van Eyck's *Stigmata of St. Francis* and Hans Memling's *Passion of Christ.* Italian artists, including those from the Piemonte, are also well represented; one of the first canvases you see upon entering the galleries is the work of a Tuscan, Fra Angelico's sublime *Virgin and Child.*

Via Accademia delle Scienze 6. Museo Egizio: 𝄢 011-5617776. www.museoegizio.org. Admission 6.50€ ($7.50) adults, free for those under 18 or over 65. Tues–Sun 8:30am–7:30pm. Galleria Sabauda: 𝄢 011440-6903 or 011-547-440. www.artito.arti.beniculturali.it. Admission 4€ ($4.60) adults, 2€ ($2.30) ages 18–25, free for those under 18 or over 65. Tues–Sun 8:30am–7:30pm (to 11pm Sat in summer). Cumulative ticket for both museums 8€ ($9.20). Bus: 61; tram: 18.

Museo Nazionale del Risorgimento (National Museum of the Risorgimento)

Much of modern Italian history has been played out in Turin, and much of it, fittingly, in this palazzo that was home to the first king of a unified Italy, Vittorio Emanuele II, and the seat of its first parliament, in 1861. While any self-respecting town in Italy has a museum of the Risorgimento, the movement that launched Italian unification, this one is the best. Documents, paintings, and other paraphernalia recount the heady days when Vittorio Emanuele banded with Garibaldi and his Red Shirts to oust the Bourbons from Sicily and the Austrians from the north to create a unified Italy. The plaques summing up each room are in English and will finally reveal to you just who those people are after whom half the major streets and piazzas in Italy are named—including Mazzini, Vittorio Emanuele II, Massimo d'Azeglio, Cavour, and Garibaldi. The last rooms house a fascinating collection that chronicles Italian Fascism and the resistance against it, which evolved into the Partisan movement during World War II.

Via Accademia delle Scienze 5. 𝄢 011-5621147. www.regione.piemonte.it/cultura/risorgimento. Admission 5€ ($5.75) adults, 3.50€ ($4) for those under 18 or over 65. Tues–Sun 9am–7pm. Bus: 55, 61, 72, 72; tram: 13, 15, 18.

Palazzo Madama—Museo Civico di Arte Antica (Civic Museum of Ancient Art)

Don't be misled by the baroque facade, added by architect Filippo Juvarra in the 18th century. If you walk around the exterior of the palazzo (named for its most popular resident, Madama Reale, aka Marie Christine of France), you'll discover that the massive structure incorporates a medieval castle, a Roman gate, and several Renaissance additions. Juvarra also added a monumental marble staircase to the interior, most of which is given over to the far-reaching collections of the Museo Civico di Arte Antica. At press time, the museum was undergoing a reorganization. Although the collections weren't on display, visitors were being admitted free for a look at the staircase. The holdings focus on the medieval and Renaissance periods, shown off against the castle's unaltered stony medieval interior. One of Italy's largest collections of ceramics is here, as well as some stunning canvases, including Anotello da Messina's *Portrait of a Man*. In 2004, the museum reopened following an extensive 15-year renovation.

In the Palazzo Madama, Piazza Castello. (C) 011-4429912. www.comune.torino.it/palazzomadama or www.fondazionetorinomusei.it. Admission 5€ ($6), but new prices had not been announced at press time. Tues–Fri and Sun 10am–8pm; Sat 10am–11pm. Bus: 6, 11, 12, 27, 56, 57.

Palazzo Reale (Royal Palace) & Armeria Royale (Royal Armory)   The residence of the House of Savoy, begun in 1645 and designed by the Francophile count of Castellamonte, reflects the ornately baroque tastes of European ruling families of the time—a fact that will not be lost on you as you pass from one opulently decorated, heavily gilded room to the next. (The Savoys had a keener eye for painting than for decor, and most of the canvases they collected are in the nearby Galleria Sabauda.) What's most notable here are some of the tapestries, including the Gobelins depicting the life of Don Quixote, in the Sala delle Virtu (Hall of Virtues), and the collection of Chinese and Japanese vases in the Sala dell'Alcova. One of the quirkier architectural innovations, an antidote to several monumental staircases, is a manually driven elevator from the 18th century.

One wing houses the **Armeria Reale,** one of the most important arms and armor collections in Europe, especially of weapons from the 16th and 17th centuries. (Most rooms in the museum reopened after extensive renovations in Oct 2003; the balance of the exhibition should reopen by late 2004.) Behind the palace, and offering a refreshing change from its frippery, are the **Giardini Reali (Royal Gardens),** laid out by Le Nôtre, more famous for the Tuileries and the gardens at Versailles.

Piazza Castello (Armeria entrance at no. 191). Palazzo: (C) 011-4361455. Admission 6.50€ ($7). Tues–Sun 8:30am–7pm (to 11pm Sat in summer). Armeria: (C) 011-543889. Admission 4€ ($4.60), free for those under 18 or over 60. Tues and Thurs–Sun 8:30am–7:30pm; Wed and Fri 8am–2pm. Bus: 6, 11, 12, 27, 56, 57.

PARKS & PIAZZAS

Piazza San Carlo, Turin's most beautiful square, is the city's outdoor living room, surrounded by arcaded sidewalks that house the terraces of the cafes for which Turin is famous (see below). In the center is an equestrian statue of Duke Emanuele Filiberto of Savoy, and facing each other at the northern end of the piazza are a pair of 17th-century churches, San Carlo and Santa Cristina. The overall effect is one of elegant harmony.

The **Parco del Valentino** (© 011-6699372), a lush sweep of greenery along the Po south of Corso Vittorio Emanuele II, provides a wonderful retreat from Turin's well-mannered streets and piazzas. It is open daily from 8am to 8pm. Aside from riverfront promenades and extensive lawns and gardens, inside the park there's a collection of enchanting buildings. The **Borgo Medioevale** (© 011-4431701), built for Turin's 1884 world exposition, is a faithful reconstruction of a medieval village based on those in rural Piemonte and the Val d'Aosta, with shops, taverns, houses, churches, and even a castle. It's open daily from 9am to 8pm.

The nearby **Castello del Valentino** is the real thing—a royal residence, begun in the 16th century but completed in the 17th century for Turin's beloved Marie Christine ("Madama Reale," wife of Savoy king Vittorio Amedeo) as a summer residence. It's a sign of Madama's Francophile leanings that, with its sloping roofs and forecourt, the castle resembles a French château. Since used as a school of veterinary medicine and a military barracks and currently as a university facility, the castello is continually undergoing renovations. Much of it, including many frescoed salons, is open to the public only on special occasions.

NEARBY ATTRACTIONS

Basilica di Superga   As thanksgiving to the Virgin Mary for Turin's deliverance from the French siege of 1706, Vittorio Amadeo II commissioned Juvarra, the Sicilian architect who did his greatest work in Turin, to build this baroque basilica on a hill high above the city. The exterior, with a beautiful neoclassic porch and lofty drum dome, is far more interesting than the gloomy interior, a vast circular chamber beneath the dome with six side chapels. The church more or less serves as a pantheon for the House of Savoy, whose tombs are scattered about, many in the so-called **Crypt of Kings** beneath the main chapel. There's a fine view of the Alps from the terrace in front. The trip up to the basilica on a narrow railway through verdant parkland is a favorite Turinese outing.

About 6.4km (4 miles) northeast of the town center in Parco Naturale della Collina di Superga. ℂ 011-8980083. Basilica or crypt: Admission 3€ ($3.45) adults, 2€ ($2.30) seniors over 65, free for children under 12. Basilica: Apr–Oct daily 9:30am–noon and 1:30–6pm; Nov–Mar daily 9:30am–noon and 1:30–5pm. Crypt: Apr–Oct daily 9:30am–1:30pm and 2:30–7:30pm; Nov–Mar daily 9:30am–6:30pm. Reached by rack railway (2.05€/$2.35), with a terminus at Stazione Sassi on Piazza Gustavo Modena (follow Corso Casale on east side of the River Po). Tram: 15 from Via XX Settembre to Stazione Sassi.

Palazzina di Caccia di Stupinigi   The other great work of the architect Juvarra (see the Basilica di Superga, above) is this sumptuous, lavishly decorated hunting lodge commissioned by the Savoys in 1729. The main part of the lodge, to which the members of the House of Savoy retired for hunts in the royal forests that still surround it, is shaped like a Saint Andrew's cross (the lower arms extended and curved back inwards like giant pincers), fanning out from a circular, domed pavilion topped with a large bronze stag. The lavish interior is filled with furniture, paintings, and bric-a-brac assembled from the many Savoy residences, technically comprising a **Museo d'Arte e Ammobiliamento (Museum of Art and Furniture).** Stroll through the acres of excessively decorated apartments to understand why Napoleon chose this for his brief residency in the region. Outstanding among the many, many frescoes are the scenes of a deer hunt in the King's Apartment and the *Triumph of Diana* in the grand salon. The elegant gardens and surrounding forests provide lovely terrain for a jaunt.

Stupinigi, 8.5km (5¼ miles) southwest of the city center. ℂ 011-3581220. Admission 6.20€ ($7.15) adults, 4.15€ ($4.80) ages 6–14, 2.05€ ($2.35) for those over 65, 15€ ($17) family ticket with 1 child under 18, 20€ ($23) family ticket with 2 children. Tues–Sun 10am–6pm (to 5pm late Oct to late Mar). Bus: 63 from Porta Nuova train station to Piazza Caio Mario; change to bus 41.

ACCOMMODATIONS YOU CAN AFFORD

Unlike the areas around train stations in most large cities, the **Porta Nuova** neighborhood is semi-stylish and perfectly safe, and many of the city's hotels are here, just a 10-minute stroll from the center.

Hotel Bellavista   The neighborhood between the Porta Nuova railway station and Parco del Valentino is pleasant and residential, and this pensione occupies the sixth floor of an apartment house on a quiet street. What is likely to strike you immediately is just how pleasant the surroundings are—step off the elevator, and you will find yourself in a sun-filled corridor that's a garden of houseplants and opens onto a wide terrace. There's also a pleasant bar area, where guests can buy rolls and coffee at breakfast. Rooms are airy and comfortable but a little less inspiring in decor, with banal, functional modern furnishings. Most, though, afford pleasant views over the surrounding rooftops—the best outlooks in the house are across the river toward the hills. What most rooms don't have is a private bathroom, though the several communal ones are well placed, so most rooms are only a few steps away from a facility.

Via Galliari 15, 10125 Turin. ℂ 011-6698139. Fax 011-6687989. 18 units, 7 with bathroom. 36€ ($40) single without bathroom, 45€ ($52) single with bathroom; 55€ ($63) double without bathroom, 65€ ($75) double with bathroom. Breakfast 5€ ($5.75). AE, MC, V. **Amenities:** Bar; nonsmoking rooms. *In room:* TV.

Hotel Bologna 🏆 *Value*   This family-run hotel just across the street from the Porta Nuova train station offers location, affordable comfort, and a very attentive, English-speaking staff. Each of the 50 rooms, spread over several floors of a gracious 18th-century apartment house, is different. Some are quite grand, incorporating frescoes, fireplaces, and other original details (of these, room nos. 52 and 64 are the largest and most elegant). Other rooms have been renovated in sleek modern style, with laminated, built-in cabinetry and neutral carpeting. Still others fall in between, with well-maintained 1970s-style furnishings and linoleum flooring. Whatever the vintage, all of the rooms are spotlessly clean and nicely maintained. In 2001, two small suites with a separate sitting room were added and are available for the same rates as the regular rooms.

Corso Vittorio Emanuele II 60, 10121 Turin. ℂ **011-5620290** or 011-5620193. Fax 011-5620193. www.hotelbolognasrl.it. 45 units. 52€–54€ ($60–$62) single; 72€–74€ ($83–$85) double. Rates include breakfast AE, MC, V. **Amenities:** Bar; Jacuzzi (3 rooms); concierge; tour desk; car-rental desk; room service. *In room:* A/C, TV, minibar (in some rooms), hair dryer, safe.

Hotel Liberty 🏆🏆 *Finds*   An excellent location a few blocks southwest of Piazza Castello puts the Liberty within easy walking distance of most of Turin's museums, other monuments and shops, and restaurants. What's most remarkable about this hotel, though, is its ambience. It occupies an early-20th-century mansion built in the Art Deco style, which in Italian is known as Liberty. Many of the original features, such as ornately carved doorways and etched windows, remain, and the public rooms especially retain a great deal of grandeur with turn-of-the-20th-century furnishings and polished parquet floors; there's a small bar and restaurant off the lobby. The guest rooms are large and nonfussily stylish, with some period pieces augmented by comfortable newer furnishings, including firm beds; the smallish bathrooms have been brought nicely up-to-date. (Things may look a bit different during your stay, however; the hotel was undergoing renovations in 2004.) These surroundings seem all the more pleasant with the attentive presence of the Anfossi family, which has run this charming hotel for decades and heads a consortium of small, family-run hotels in Italy.

Via P. Micca 15 (between Via Mercanti and Via San Francesco d'Assisi), 10121 Turin. ℂ **011-5628801.** Fax 011-5628163. www.hotelliberty-torino.it. 35 units. 90€ ($104) single; 125€ ($144) double; 25€ ($28) extra bed. Rates include continental breakfast. AE, DC, MC, V. Parking 16€ ($18) in a few spots in courtyard (ask when booking) or 18€ ($21) in nearby garage. Bus: 4, 11, 12, 13, 56, 63. **Amenities:** Restaurant (Italian); bar; concierge; tour desk; limited room service; laundry service; nonsmoking rooms. *In room:* A/C (in 12 rooms), TV w/pay movies, dataport, hair dryer.

WORTH A SPLURGE

Victoria Hotel 🏆🏆   Step through the doors of this somewhat plain-looking building between the Via Roma and the river, and you'll think you're in an

English country house. That's the whole idea, and the Anglophile decor works splendidly. The lobby looks like a country-house drawing room, with floral sofas, deep armchairs, and a view onto a garden; the room doubles as a bar and is an extremely pleasant place to enjoy a drink before setting out for one of the nearby restaurants. The glass-enclosed breakfast room, where a sumptuous buffet is served, resembles a conservatory. Accommodations are classified as deluxe or standard, depending on size and decor. "Standard" guest rooms are handsomely furnished in a chic style that soothingly combines contemporary and traditional styles, with mahogany bedsteads and writing desks, and rich fabric wall coverings and draperies. "Deluxe" accommodations, each with its own distinctive look, are oversize and furnished in carefully chosen antiques, with such flourishes as canopied beds and richly covered divans; plus, they're the only ones with air-conditioning. A major renovation (expected to be completed in 2005) will add a new breakfast room, garden, garage, and swimming pool to the Victoria.

Via Nino Costa 4 (a tiny street, unlabeled on most maps, off Via Giuseppe Pomba between Via Giolitti and Via Cavour), 10123 Turin. ℂ 011-5611909. Fax 011-5611806. www.hotelvictoria-torino.com. 106 units. 107€ ($123) standard single, 130€ ($150) deluxe single; 154€ ($177) standard double, 173€ ($199) deluxe double; 200€ ($230) junior suite. Rates include breakfast. Parking 15€ ($17). AE, DC, MC, V. **Amenities:** Bike rental; concierge; limited room service; laundry service; same-day dry cleaning. *In room:* A/C (in 75%, those termed "Deluxe"), TV, minibar, hair dryer, safe.

GREAT DEALS ON DINING

Dai Saletta 🔞 PIEMONTESE   One of the few kitchens in Turin that remains open into the wee hours turns out a nice selection of homey trattoria fare, served in a tiny, cramped dining room several long blocks south of the train station. Homemade pasta dishes are delicious; try the hearty *tortelloni alla salsiccia* (a large pasta shell stuffed with sausage) or *peposelle* (a thick pasta tossed with Gorgonzola and walnuts) as an appetizer or a main course. For those who want to venture on, the kitchen offers such traditional favorites as tripe.

Via Belfiore 37 (just south of Via Oddino Morgari). ℂ 011-6687867. Primi 7€ ($8.05); secondi 8€ ($9.20). AE, DC, MC, V. Mon–Sat 12:30–2:30pm and 8–10:30pm. Closed Aug. Bus: 1, 16.

Da Mauro ITALIAN/TUSCAN   These simple tile-floored rooms are more relaxed than many Turinese restaurants, and if the informal ambience and the menu remind you of regions farther south, your instincts are right. The family that owns and runs the restaurant emphasizes Tuscan dishes, though the menu seems to run the gamut of Italian cooking. There are several spicy pasta dishes, including a deftly prepared cannelloni, and the meat courses are indeed similar to those you would find in Tuscany—steak, lamb, sausages, and game birds are simply grilled or roasted.

Via Maria Vittoria 21 (between Via Bogino and Via San Francesco da Paola). ℂ 011-8170604. Primi 4€–6.50€ ($4.60–$6.90); secondi 5€–10€ ($5.75–$12). No credit cards. Tues–Sun 12:30–3pm and 7–10pm. Closed July.

Porto di Savano 🔞🔞 *Value* PIEMONTESE   What is probably the most popular trattoria in Turin is tucked under the arcades along the city's largest piazza. Seating is family style, at long tables that crowd a series of rooms beneath old photos and mementos, and the typically Piemontese fare never fails to please (all the more so on Sun, when many other restaurants in central Turin are closed). Several variations of gnocchi are usually made fresh daily, as is the Piemontese flat noodle, *tajarin,* and *agnolotti al sugo d'arrosto* (cheese-stuffed pasta in a roast pork ragù). Another way to start a meal is with a *risotto ai porcini.* Follow these primi with one of the grilled meat (or trout or salmon) dishes, which are the house specialties.

Piazza Vittorio Veneto 2. ℭ 011-8173500. www.portodisavona.com. Reservations recommended. Primi 5.50€–8€ ($6.35–$9.20); secondi 7.50€–15€ ($8.65–$17). MC, V. Tues 7:30–10:30pm; Wed–Sun 12:30–2:30pm and 7:30–10:30pm. Closed Jan 1–7. Bus: 30, 53, 55, 56, 61, 70.

WORTH A SPLURGE

C'era Una Volta ✿✿✿ TURINESE   To enter "Once Upon a Time," you must ring a bell at street level, then climb the stairs or take the elevator to a large, old-fashioned dining room filled with heavy old tables and chairs and dark credenzas. Until recently, it offered only the set-price tasting menu—and for most of us that was plenty (in fact, that was often *more* than plenty, in that we didn't have to make plans to eat anything for the next 24 hr.). However, due to popular demand by eager diners who just couldn't handle the massive meals, the restaurant has now introduced a la carte dishes—while rigorously refusing to change anything else about this classic Torinese establishment. The food, delivered by a highly professional waitstaff that has been here for years, is authentically Torinese and never seems to stop coming. A typical menu, which changes daily, might include crepes with ham and cheese, risotto with artichokes, a carrot flan, rabbit stew, a slice of beef with polenta, and any number of other wonderfully prepared dishes. A meal like this deserves a fine Barolo or other regional wine.

Corso Vittorio Emanuele II 42. ℭ 011-6504589. Reservations recommended. Primi 7€–8.50€ ($8.05–$10); secondi 14€–16€ ($16–$18); tasting menu 24€ ($28) without wine. AE, MC, V. Mon–Sat 7–10:30pm. Closed Sun and Aug.

CAFES & DELICACY SHOPS

Cafe sitting is a centuries-old tradition in sophisticated Turin. Via Roma and the piazzas it widens into are lined with gracious salons that have been serving coffee to Torinese for decades, even centuries. Below are some of the city's classic cafes. While espresso and pastries are the mainstays of the menu at all of them, most also serve chocolates—including the mix of chocolate and hazelnuts known as *gianduiotti*—that are among the city's major contributions to culinary culture.

Turin has a sizable sweet tooth, satisfied by any number of pastry and candy shops. Perhaps the best chocolatier north of Perugia is **Pfatisch/Peyrano** ✿, Corso Vittorio Emanuele II 76 (ℭ **011-538765;** www.peyrano.com), open Monday through Saturday from 9am to 12:45pm and 4 to 7:30pm, and Sunday from 9am to 1pm. A wide variety of chocolates and other sweets, including sumptuous meringues, has been dispensed since 1836 at **Fratelli Stratta,** Piazza San Carlo 191 (ℭ **011-547920;** www.stratta1836.it), open Tuesday through Sunday from 9:30am to 1pm and 3 to 7:30pm, and Monday from 3 to 7:30pm.

The surrounding region is known not only for its wines, but also for vermouth—the famed **Cinzano,** for instance, is produced south of the city in the town of Santa Vittoria d'Alba. Come evening, a glass of vermouth is the preferred drink at many of the city's cafes. **Paissa,** at Piazza San Carlo 196 (ℭ **011-5628462**), open Monday through Saturday from 9am to 1pm and 3:30 to 7:30pm (closed Wed afternoons), is an excellent place to purchase local vermouths by the bottle.

Caffè Confetteria al Bicerin ✿ CAFE   What claims to be Turin's oldest cafe in continuous operation (since 1763) is famous for its illustrious clientele, which has included Nietszche, Dumas, and Puccini, as well as its signature drink—the Bicerin (local dialect for "something delicious"). It's a heady combination of coffee, hot chocolate, and cream—to be accompanied by one of the house's exquisite pastries.

Piazza della Consolata 5. ℰ 011-4369325. www.bicerin.it. Sandwiches and pastries from 2€ ($2.30). MC, V. Mon–Tues and Thurs–Fri 8:30am–9:30pm; Sat–Sun 8:30am–12:30pm and 3:30–7:30pm. Closed Aug.

Caffè-Pasticceria Baratti e Milano CAFE   No small part of the pleasure of sitting for a time in this stylish cafe, opened in 1875, is watching a clientele that includes auto executives, students from the nearby university, elegantly clad shoppers, and visitors to the nearby museums, all sipping espressos and munching on the delicious house pastries.

Piazza Castello 27. ℰ 011-4407138 or 011-752903. Sandwiches and pastries 1.50€–3€ ($1.75–$3.45). AE, DC, MC, V. Tues–Sun 8am–1am.

Caffè San Carlo ⭐ CAFE   One of the essential stops on any tour of Turin is this classic cafe. The San Carlo opened its doors in 1837 and ever since has been accommodating patrons beneath a huge chandelier of Murano glass in a salon that is a remarkable assemblage of gilt, mirrors, and marble. An adjoining, frescoed tearoom is quieter and only a little less grand.

Piazza San Carlo 156. ℰ 011-532586 or 011-8122090. Sandwiches, pastries, and dishes 2€–11€ ($2.30–$13). AE, DC, MC, V. Tues–Sun 7am–1am; Mon 7am–8pm.

TURIN AFTER DARK

Turin has a lively classical-music and opera scene, and you can get info on these and other cultural events at the **Vetrina Infocultura** office at Piazza San Carlo 159 (ℰ **800-015475** or 011-443-9040), open Monday to Saturday 11am to 7pm. Aside from the city's much-attended summer festivals (see "Festivals & Markets," earlier in this section), there are regular classical concerts by the National Symphonic Orchestra at the **Auditorium della RAI,** Via Rossini 15 (ℰ **011-8104653;** www.orchestrasinfonica.rai.it). Other concerts, dance performances, and operas are staged at the city's venerable **Teatro Regio** (ℰ **011-8815241;** www.teatroregio.torino.it), in the center of the city on Piazza Castello.

A DAY TRIP FROM TURIN

Sacra di San Michele ⭐⭐⭐   Perched high atop Monte Pirchiriano—part of it projecting over the precipice on an elaborate support system that was one of the engineering feats of the Middle Ages—this dramatically situated abbey dedicated to St. Michael provides views and an astonishing look at medieval religious life. It may well remind you of Mont-St-Michel in France (both are laced with endless flights of stairs) or, with its dizzying views and scary drops, of the abbey in the novel and film *The Name of the Rose* (probably because author Umberto Eco based his fictional abbey on this one). Actually, Mont-St-Michel was one of the 176 religious institutions that once fell under the jurisdiction of San Michele. It was started in 983, but the extant church dates to the abbey's 12th-century heyday. A vast staircase hewn out of rock and clinging to the abbey's buttresses (known as Scalone dei Morti, Stairs of Death, because corpses were once laid out here) leads to the massive carved doorway depicting the signs of the zodiac and the drafty Gothic and Romanesque church, decorated only with scraps of 16th-century frescoes by Secondo del Bosco. Another stairway leads down to three tiny chapels carved into the rock and containing tombs of some of the earliest members of the House of Savoy.

On Saturday (and some Fri) evenings April to July and August to September, the atmospheric church hosts free concerts of everything from chant and liturgical music to Renaissance chamber pieces, gospel, and traditional Celtic airs; check the website for schedules.

Outside Aviglina, 15km (9½ miles) west of Turin's ring road. (© 011-939130. www.sacradisanmichele.com. Admission 3.50€ ($4.05) adults, 2.50€ ($2.90) ages 6–14 and those over 65 (Sun afternoon it's 4.50€/$5 adults, 3€/$3.45 youths and seniors because they give tours leaving every 20 min. that cover even more of the complex). Mar 16–Oct 15 Tues–Sat 9:30am–12:30pm and 3–6pm, Sun 9:30am–noon and 2:40–6pm; Oct 16–Mar 17 closes 5pm Tues–Sun.

GETTING THERE   Take one of 15 trains a day from Turin to Sant'Ambrogio Torinese (30–60 min.; 2.20€/$2.55). From there, it's a stiff 1½-hour trek up to the abbey. In summer only, call ahead to see about the once-daily bus that in past years has met trains from Torino at the Avigliana station (usually around 9am) to carry pilgrims up here. By car, follow the A32 from Turin's western ring highway toward Bardonecchia/Frejus. Get off at the Avigliana exit and follow brown signs to the Sacra. The trip takes about an hour.

2 The Piemonte Wine Country

Asti: 60km (37 miles) SE of Turin, 127km (79 miles) SW of Milan. Alba: 60km (37 miles) S of Turin, 155km (96 miles) SW of Milan

South of Turin, the **Po Valley** rises into the rolling Langhe and Roero hills, flanked by orchards and vineyards. You'll recognize the region's place names from the labels of its excellent wines, among them Asti Spumanti, Barbaresco, and Barolo. Tasting these vintages at their source is one reason to visit the wine country, of course; another is to stroll through the medieval and Renaissance towns that rise from the vineyards and the picturesque villages that crown many a hilltop. Vines are not all that flourish in the fertile soil—truffles top the list of the region's gastronomic delights, which also include down-home country fare like rabbit and game dishes, excellent cheeses, and plump fruit.

ASTI

The **Asti** of sparkling-wine fame is a bustling city more concerned with everyday business than entertaining visitors, but many treasures can be found in the history-drenched old town—medieval towers (120 of them still stand), Renaissance palaces, and broad piazzas provide the perfect setting in which to sample the town's famous product.

ESSENTIALS

GETTING THERE   By Train   One to four trains an hour link Asti with **Turin** (30–60 min.; 3.50€–6.20€/$4.05–$7.15). Six trains run hourly between Asti and Alba (30–50 min.; 2.50€/$2.90).

By Bus   From Turin, **Arfea** (© **0144-322023** or 0131-445433; www.arfea.it) runs two buses per day, one in the morning and one midafternoon, for the hourlong ride to Asti (4€/$4.60).

By Car   Asti, 73km (45 miles) east of Turin, can be reached from Turin in less than an hour via the A21 autostrada.

VISITOR INFORMATION   The **APT tourist office** is near the train station at Piazza Alfieri 29 (© **0141-530357;** fax 0141-538300; www.terredasti.it). May to September, hours are Monday through Saturday from 9am to 6:30pm and Sunday from 10am to 1pm; October to April, hours are Monday through Saturday from 9am to 1pm and 2:30 to 6:30pm, and Sunday from 10am to 1pm. Among the office's offerings is a **Carta Terre e Vini d'Asti,** an annotated map that will point you to surrounding vineyards that offer wine tastings.

FESTIVALS & MARKETS   In late June and early July, Asti stages **AstiTeatro** (© **0141-399111** or 0141-399032), a theater festival with performances that

Horses & Donkeys

Asti and Alba, bitter rivals through much of the Middle Ages, each celebrate the autumnal harvest with equine celebrations that are horses of very different colors.

The **Palio** (© 0141-399482), Asti's annual horse race, is run the third Sunday of September. Like the similar but more famous horse race mounted by the Tuscan city of Siena, Asti's palio begins with a medieval pageant through the town and ends with a wild bareback ride around the Campo del Palio. The race coincides with Asti's other great revel, the **Douja d'Or,** a weeklong fair-cum-bacchanal celebrating the grape.

On the first Sunday of October, Alba pulls a spoof on Asti with the **Palio degli Asini (Race of the Asses;** © 0173-362806). The event, which coincides with Alba's annual truffle fair, is not as speedy as Asti's slicker, horseback palio, but it's a lot more fun. Good-natured as the event is, though, it is rooted in some of the darkest days of Alba's history. In the 13th century, Asti, then one of the most powerful republics of Northern Italy, besieged Alba and burned the surrounding vineyards. Then, adding insult to injury, the victors held their palio in Alba, just to put the humbled citizenry further in its place. Alba then staged a palio with asses, a not-so-subtle hint of what they thought of their victors and their pompous pageantry.

incorporate dance and music as well. In 2003, AstiTeatro celebrated its 25th anniversary. September, though, is the town's busy cultural month, with townsfolk and horses alike donning medieval garb for its famous **Palio** on the third Sunday (see "Horses & Donkeys," above). Local wine producers converge on the town the 2 weeks before the Palio for the **Douja d'Or** (www.doujador.it), an exhibition of local vintages accompanied by tastings; this is an excellent way to sample the products of the many wineries in the hills surrounding Asti and nearby Alba. On the second Sunday of September, surrounding villages mount feasts (almost always accompanied by a communal meal) known collectively as the **Pjasan.**

Agricultural center that it is, Asti has two **food markets.** The largest is held Wednesday and Saturday from 7:30am to 1pm in the **Campo del Palio,** with stalls selling every foodstuff imaginable—seeds, herbs, flowers, farm implements, and no end of other merchandise spilling over to two adjoining piazzas, the Piazza della Liberta and Piazza Alfieri. Meanwhile, Asti's covered food market, the **Mercato Coperto,** is also located in this vicinity, on Piazza della Liberta, and is open Monday through Wednesday and Friday from 8am to 1pm and 3:30 to 7:30pm, Thursday from 8:30am to 1pm, and Saturday from 8am to 7:30pm. There's also a small **antiques fair** on the fourth Sunday of each month except August.

EXPLORING THE TOWN

If you take the train to Asti, you will step right into the heart of the action—the town's lively clothing-and-food **markets** occupy three adjoining piazzas just to the north of the station (Campo del Palio, Piazza Liberta, and **Piazza Alfieri**). If you're driving into Asti, you're most likely to find parking in one of the lots in this area as well.

Walk through the piazzas to **Corso Alfieri;** the town's Renaissance palaces are located on or just off this major thoroughfare, usually closed to traffic. This street and Asti's grandest piazza are named for the town's most famous native son, the 18th-century poet Vittorio Alfieri. His home, on the Corso at no. 375, houses a small, memento-filled museum.

Second to none in Asti is San Secondo, the town's patron saint. He was imprisoned at the western end of Corso Alfieri in the **Torre Rossa**—much of which dates to the 1st century (probably part of a Roman gate), with two levels tacked on in the 11th century—then beheaded on the spot just south of Corso Alfieri where the church erected in his honor, the **Collegiata di San Secondo** (☎ 0141-530066), now stands. Not only does this Romanesque-Gothic structure have the honor of housing the saint's remains in its eerie crypt, but it is also the permanent home of the coveted Palio Astigiano, the banner awarded to the horseman who wins the town's annual Palio (see "Horses & Donkeys," above; Secondo is the patron saint of this event). The church is open daily from 10:45am to noon and 3:30 to 5:30pm (Sun morning for Mass only).

Asti's "other" church is its 14th-century, redbrick **Cattedrale** (☎ 0141-592924), which you can reach by walking through Piazza Cairoli, at the western end of Corso Alfieri, into the nearby Piazza Cattedrale. Every inch of this brick church's cavernous interior is festooned with frescoes by late-18th-century artists, including Gandolfino d'Asti; *trompe l'oeil* vines climb many of the columns. The cathedral is open daily from 8:30am to noon and 3 to 5:30pm.

The most notable feature of the church of **San Pietro in Consavia** (☎ 0141-353072), at the eastern end of Corso Alfieri, is its 10th-century round baptistery; the 15th-century interior and adjoining cloisters house a one-room paleontology collection (open Tues–Sun 10am–12:30pm and 3–7pm).

ACCOMMODATIONS YOU CAN AFFORD

Rainero ⊱ Occupying a centuries-old house, the Rainero enjoys a wonderful location near the Campo del Palio and San Secondo. Not only is this setting convenient, but since many of the surrounding streets are closed to traffic, the neighborhood is quiet. Room nos. 301 to 303 have terraces (views only of surrounding modern buildings), and nos. 153 and 155 have balconies looking onto a cobbled street; there's also a large roof terrace. Despite the provenance of the structure, renovations are tasteful but lean toward a clean, modern look. As a result, the rooms are perfectly comfortable, though a little bland. The modular furnishings vary and seem to represent each decade since the 1960s; the best have bent-tube bedsteads and granite-topped sinks with brass-plated fixtures. Room nos. 157 and 158 (which families can connect) open off a hanging walkway over a pretty pair of tiny courtyards and red-tile roofs; no. 158 is large enough to be a quad and has a table and chairs on the walkway out front. Large room no. 161 gets one of those plant-filled courtyards all to itself. Renovations in 2004 included the addition of an elevator and extensive work to make half the rooms nonsmoking.

Via Cavour 85, 14100 Asti. ☎ 0141-353866. Fax 0141-594985. www.hotelrainero.com. 53 units. 52€ ($60) single; 100€ ($115) double; 155€ ($178) suite. Continental breakfast 2.20€ ($2.55), breakfast buffet 8€ ($9.20). AE, DC, DISC, MC, V. Closed 1st week of Jan. **Amenities:** Bar; 24-hr. room service; laundry service; same-day dry cleaning; nonsmoking rooms. *In room:* A/C, TV, dataport, minibar, hair dryer.

GREAT DEALS ON DINING

There has been an inn in the Natta family's medieval palazzo at Via Q Sella 2 since 1777. **L'Altra Campana** (☎ 0141-437083; www.altracampana.it) is known for serving delicious yet moderately priced Piemontese food. But the inn shut its doors in early 2004 for renovations, and no one—not even the tourist office—knows when (or even if) they'll reopen. Here's hopin' they will be back in business by the time you visit.

Il Convivio 🙊🙊 PIEMONTESE The decor of this double-height pastel-colored dining room is straightforward, with a clean, contemporary look. These no-nonsense surroundings reflect that the main business here is to serve excellently prepared food and accompany it with the region's best, but not necessarily most expensive, wines. (Wines are dispensed from an extensive cave you're welcome to visit, and you can also buy wine by the bottle or case on the premises.) Only a few starters, pasta dishes, and main courses are prepared daily, and these vary. However, they always include wonderful fresh-made pastas, such as the lightest gnocchi in a sweet pepper sauce; a soup incorporating vegetables bought that morning from Asti's markets; and some serious meat dishes, such as a masterful *ossobucco di vitello,* or *coniglio* (rabbit that here is often sautéed with olives and white wine). Desserts, including a heavenly *panna cotta al cioccolato,* are as memorable as the rest of the dining experience.

Via G. B. Giuliani 4–6. ℭ 0141-594188. Reservations recommended. Primi 5.50€–6.50€ ($6–$7); secondi 8€–10€ ($9.20–$12). AE, DC, MC, V. Mon–Sat noon–2:30pm and 8–9:30pm. Closed Dec 24–Jan 6 and 15 days in summer.

ALBA

Lovely old **Alba** retains a medieval flavor that's as mellow as the wines it produces. It's a pleasure to walk along the Via Vittorio Emanuele and the narrow streets of the old town, visit the 14th-century Duomo, and peer into shop windows with lavish displays of Alba's wines; its other famous product, truffles; and its less noble but enticing *nocciola,* a decadent concoction of nuts and chocolate.

ESSENTIALS

GETTING THERE By Train Only one direct train (in the evening, after 6pm) runs between Turin and Alba (80 min.; 3.90€/$4.50); otherwise, there's one per hour requiring a change in Asti, Brà, or Cavallermaggiore (80–90 min.; 3.90€–9.30€/$4.50–$11). An hourly train runs between Asti and Alba (30–50 min.; 2.45€/$2.80).

By Bus Alba's Autostazione bus terminal (ℭ 0173-362949; www.atibus.it) is on Piazza Medford. Hourly Satti (ℭ 800-990097 or 011-5764790; www.satti.it) buses make the trip between Alba and Turin in about 1½ hours.

By Car The most direct way to reach Alba from Turin is to follow the A6 autostrada for 35km (22 miles) south to the exit near Brà, and from the autostrada exit S231 east for 24km (15 miles) to Alba. If you want to work Alba into a trip to Asti, take A21 to Asti and, from there, follow S231 southwest for 30km (19 miles) to Alba.

VISITOR INFORMATION Alba has two **tourist offices.** The downtown branch is halfway along Corso Vittorio Emanuele, at no. 19 (ℭ/fax 0173-362562; www.comune.alba.cn.it), open daily from 9am to 1pm and 2 to 6pm (may close Sun in winter). A **regional info office** is at Piazza Medford 3, across from the bus station (ℭ 0173-35833 or 0173-362807; fax 0173-363878; www.langheroero.it), open Monday through Friday from 9am to 12:30pm and 2:30 to 6:30pm, and Saturday from 9am to 12:30pm (afternoons, too, in Oct).

FESTIVALS & MARKETS October is Alba's big month. Its annual **truffle festival** is held the first week, and this, in turn, climaxes in the **Palio degli Asini**

(**Race of the Asses;** ℂ 0173-362806), a humble version of neighboring Asti's equine palio (see "Horses & Donkeys," above). On Saturday and Sunday mornings from the second weekend in October through December, Alba hosts a **truffle market,** where you may well be tempted to part with your hard-earned cash for one of the fragrant specimens (which could cost as much as $1,000 a pound).

EXPLORING THE TOWN

Alba's two major sights face the brick expanse of **Piazza Risogimento,** at the northern end of its major thoroughfare, **Corso Vittorio Emanuele.** The 14th-century brick **Duomo** is flanked by a 13th-century bell tower. Most of the interior and paintings hail from the late 19th century, save the two late baroque lateral chapels and the **elaborately carved and inlaid choir stalls** ✦ from 1512.

The town's two art treasures hang in the council chamber of the **Palazzo Comunale** across the square (go through the door on the right and up to the top of the stairs)—an early-16th-century portrait of the *Virgin* by Alba's greatest painter, Macrino d'Alba, and *Concertino,* by Mattia Preti, a follower of Caravaggio. It's open only during city office hours, Tuesday through Friday from 8:15am to 12:15pm and Saturday from 8:15am to noon.

From here, stroll the shopping promenade **Corso Vittorio** a few blocks to enjoy the low-key pace in the traffic-free heart of the town.

ACCOMMODATIONS YOU CAN AFFORD

Savona   Renovations have added a slick, modern look to this old hotel facing a shady little piazza at the south edge of the old town. In fact, the premises have more or less been denuded of character, but the hotel offers solid comfort and many more amenities than you would expect for the price. Downstairs are a slick breakfast room and a bar that is also popular with patrons from the town. Upstairs, the guest rooms are pleasantly decorated in pastel shades and have contemporary furnishings and shiny new bathrooms, most with bathtubs and many with Jacuzzis, especially in the modest split-level junior suites preferred by bigwigs like Pavarotti when they stay. Many open onto small terraces; the quietest face an interior courtyard. The TVs are interactive, allowing you to call up reams of information on Alba, its wines, and the surrounding area (or watch satellite channels and pay-per-view movies). The housekeeping staff seems to work overtime to keep the premises clean and running like clockwork.

Via Roma 1 (a block from Piazza Savona), 12051 Alba (CN). ℂ 0173-440440. Fax 0173-364312. www.hotelsavona.com. 99 units. 64€ ($74) single; 96€ ($110) double; 130€ ($150) junior suite. Rates include breakfast. AE, DC, MC, V. Parking 6€ ($6.90) in courtyard. **Amenities:** Restaurant; bar; concierge; room service; in-room massage; laundry service; same-day dry cleaning. *In room:* A/C, TV w/pay movies, dataport, minibar, hair dryer.

Villa La Meridiana/Az. Agrituristica Reine ✦   On a hillside outside Alba (about 1.6km/1 mile from the center of town), this sprawling, ivy-covered villa, the home of the Pionzo family, is a pleasant and convenient retreat. Public areas include a flower-filled patio, a covered terrace overlooking the town and countryside, a room with a billiard table and gym equipment, a patio with a barbecue and wood oven you can use, and (in summer) a pool. The family will arrange for you to go truffle hunting with trained dogs. A breakfast of homemade cakes and jams, accompanied by cheeses from local farms, is served in a brick-vaulted dining room. You'll find an array of accommodations in the main villa and its extension, formerly the stalls and peasant quarters. Some (nos. 3 and 4 or nos. 5 and 6) can be combined to create family suites, and the four miniapartments come with kitchenettes (no. 1 has two rooms and a large terrace). All are decorated in a pleasant mix of old country furnishings that have been passed down through the family. No. 6 even has a working fireplace. All except two cozy doubles (nos. 4 and 5, which have shady groves out the windows) provide airy views over the city and the surrounding hill towns with a snowy Alpine backdrop or of the family's Barbera vineyards, apricot orchard, and pine grove; some rooms have terraces.

To get here, from the Piazza Grassi in Alba, follow signs to Barbareso, which will take you into the hills on Via Nizza-Acqui. A sign to the villa is about 1.6km (1 mile) outside of Alba; turn left and follow the unpaved road to its end, where there is a gated drive onto the property.

Loc. Altavilla 9, 12051 Alba. ℂ/fax 0173-440112. cascinareine@libero.it. 9 units. 65€ single ($75); 75€ ($86) double; 85€ ($98) suite; 90€ ($104) miniapts. Rates include continental breakfast. No credit cards. Free parking. **Amenities:** Outdoor pool; golf nearby; tennis nearby; billiards; small exercise room; bike rental; concierge; tour desk; room service (breakfast only); nonsmoking rooms. *In room:* TV, kitchenette (apts only), fridge (apts only), coffeemaker (apts only), hair dryer, no phone.

GREAT DEALS ON DINING

Enoclub ⚘ PIEMONTESE   The evocatively chic brick-vaulted basement is devoted to fine wine coupled with solid, slightly refined Piemontese cooking. The variety of rich pasta dishes includes *tarajin* (Piemonte's answer to tagliatelle) topped with a rich lamb sauce, and *fettuccine di farro* (noodles made from the barleylike grain emmer rather than wheat) tossed with pesto and served with potatoes and beans. The secondi are meaty: veal steak with aromatic herbs, rabbit cooked in red wine, and duck breast in a black olive paste.

Up on the ground floor is the busy **Umberto Notte** bar (open evenings only), one of Alba's few late-night scenes, dispensing wines by the glass from 1€ ($1.15). This is a fine place to sample the produce of the local vineyards as well as wines from all over the world.

Piazza Savona 4. ℂ 0173-33984994. Reservations recommended. Primi 8€ ($9); secondi 12€–14€ ($14–$16); tasting menu 30€ ($35) without wine. AE, DC, MC, V. Tues–Sun noon–2:30pm and 7:30pm–midnight; Sun noon–2:30pm. Closed Aug.

Lalibera ⚘⚘ PIEMONTESE   A careful eye to design permeates this stylish osteria in the center of town. The marble floors, blond contemporary furnishings, and pale green walls provide a restful environment in which to enjoy the variations on traditional cuisine. An *antipasto misto* is a nice way to sample the daily specialties, which are often lighter than most of the regional cuisine—they might include *insaltina de tacchino* (a salad of fresh greens and roast turkey breast), *vitello tonato* (the traditionally warm-weather Venetian dish of veal and tuna sauce), *fiori di zucca* (zucchini flowers stuffed with a trout mousse), or another truffle season specialty, the *raviolone* (one giant ricotta-and-spinach ravioli cupped around an egg yolk and showered with *parmigiano* and truffle shavings). Pasta dishes are equally innovative, and many of them, such as *agnolotti* (a large tubular pasta stuffed with cabbage and rice), often combine fresh vegetables.

Via E. Pertinace 24a. ℂ 0173-293155. Reservations recommended. Primi 8€ ($9.20); secondi 10€–14€ ($12–$16). AE, DC, MC, V. Tues–Sat noon–2pm and 8–10pm; Mon 8–10pm. Closed 3 weeks in late Feb/early Mar and 1st 2 weeks of Sept.

VISITING THE WINE VILLAGES

Just to the south of Alba lie some of the region's, and Italy's, most enchanting wine villages. As you set out to explore the wine country, consider three words: **Rent a car.** While it's quite easy to reach some of the major towns by train or bus from Turin, setting out from those centers for smaller places can be difficult (there are some buses, but they tend to be very few and far between). In Turin, contact **Avis,** Corso Turati 15 (© **011-501107;** www.avis.com), or **Hertz,** Via Magellano 12 (© **011-502080;** www.hertz.it). Before you head out on the labyrinth of small country roads, outfit yourself with a good map and list of vineyards from the tourist office in Alba or Asti.

THE WINES   While the wines of Chianti and other Tuscan regions are on the top of the list for many oenologically minded travelers, the wines of Piemonte are often less heralded among non-Italians, and unjustifiably so. Most are of exceptional quality and usually made with grapes grown only in the Piemonte and often on tiny family plots, making the region a lovely patchwork of vineyards and small farms. Here are some wines you are likely to encounter again and again as you explore the area.

Barbesco is refined, dry, and, with Barolo, one of the region's most exalted wines. **Barbera d'Alba** is smooth and rich, the product of many of the delightful villages south of Alba. **Barolo** is called the king of reds (and is considered one of Italy's top two wines), the richest and heartiest of the Piemonte wines, and the one most likely to accompany game or meat. **Dolcetto** is dry, fruity, and mellow (not sweet, as its name leads many to assume). **Nebbiolo d'Alba** is rich, full, and dry (the best Nebbiolo grapes are used to make Barbaresco and Barolo).

Spumanti is the sparkling wine that has put Asti on the map for many travelers, and **Moscato d'Asti** is a floral dessert wine. You can taste and purchase these wines at cantinas and enotecas in almost all towns and villages throughout the region; several are noted below.

THE REGION   The central road through the region and running between Alba and Asti is S231, a heavily trafficked and unattractive highway that links many of the region's towns and cities. Turn off this road whenever possible to explore the region's more rustic backwaters.

One of the loveliest drives takes you south of Alba to a string of wine villages in what are known as the **Langhe hills** (from Corso Europa, a ring road that encircles the Old City in Alba, follow signs out of town for Barolo). After 5 miles (8km), you'll come to the turnoff for **Grinzane di Cavour,** a hilltop village built around a castle housing an enoteca (© **0173-262159**), open February to December Wednesday to Monday 9am to noon and 2 to 6pm (2:30–6:30pm in summer), where you can enjoy a fine sampling of local wines from their over 300 labels.

Continuing south another 4km (2½ miles), you'll come to the turnoff to **La Morra,** another hilltop village that affords stunning views over the rolling, vineyard-clad countryside from its central Piazza Castello (with parking). It has places to eat (see below) and taste the local wines. The **Cantina Comunale di La Morra** (© **0173-509204**), on the Piazza del Municipo, operates both as the local tourist office and as a representative for local growers, selling and offering tastings of Barolo, Nebbiolo, Barbara, and Dolcetto (.50€–2.50€/60¢–$2.90 per glass). You can also procure a map of hikes in the local countryside, many of which take you through the vineyards to the doors of local growers. The office is open Wednesday through Monday from 10am to 12:30pm and 2:30 to 6:30pm.

Directly across the valley from La Morra (about 5km/3 miles away), the romantic-looking, dominating 12th-century castle of **Barolo** (about 2km/1½ miles from La Morra), is enticingly visible from miles around. Here, too, are a number of restaurants (see below) and shops selling the village's rich red wines. Among these outlets is the **Castello di Barolo** ⚜ itself (© **0173-36403056277;** www.turismoinlanga.it), which houses a wine museum, enoteca, and tourist office in its cavernous cellars. A tasting flight of three Barolo wines (all from the same year, but different zones, so you can more accurately compare labels) costs 5€ ($5.75). It's open Friday to Wednesday 10am to 12:30 and 3 to 6pm (closed Jan). Admission to the museum is 3.50€ ($4).

Tiny **Novello** is a hilltop village about 15km (9⅓ miles) south of Alba located about 3km (1¾ miles) away from Barolo on well-signposted roads. It crowns the adjoining hilltop, offering some pleasant accommodations and yet more stunning views.

ACCOMMODATIONS YOU CAN AFFORD

See "Visiting the Wine Villages," above, for information on how to get to the towns where the following hotels and restaurants are located.

Barbabuc ⚜   This charming and intimate hotel, which wraps around a garden, lies behind the centuries-old facade of a house near the village square and is managed by the same private tourism consortium that owns nearby Barolo castle. Walls of glass brick and open terraces fill the premises with air and light. The rooms are placed on different levels of a central staircase, ensuring privacy, and are simply furnished in a tasteful mix of contemporary Italian pieces and country antiques on terrazzo floors. A few even have third beds or hide-a-beds for families. The well-equipped bathrooms have corner stall showers. A roof terrace offers countryside views over the surrounding houses. Downstairs, you'll find a handsome bar area and sitting room that opens to the pretty garden, an enoteca where you can taste local wines, and an intimate dining room where a lavish buffet breakfast is served. The entire hotel is nonsmoking.

Via Giordano 35, 12060 Novello. © 0173-731298. Fax 0173-731490. www.barbabuc.it. 9 units. 40€–60€ ($46–$69) single; 60€–80€ ($69–$92) double. Rates include buffet breakfast. AE, DC, MC, V. Free parking in front of hotel. Closed Jan. **Amenities:** Bar; scooter rental; concierge; tour desk; room service; laundry service; dry cleaning. *In room:* Hair dryer.

La Cascina del Monastero ⚜⚜ *Finds*   The main businesses at this delightful farm complex just minutes away from La Morra toward Barolo (4km/2½ miles) are bottling wine and harvesting fruit. But Giuseppe and Velda di Grasso have converted part of the oldest and most character-filled building into a bed-and-breakfast. Guests can relax on a large covered terrace, furnished with wicker couches and armchairs, or on the grassy shores of a pond. A sumptuous breakfast of fresh cakes, yogurt, cheese, and salami is served in a vast brick-walled reception hall. The guest rooms, reached by a series of exterior brick staircases, have been smartly done with exposed timbers, golden-hued tile floors, brass beds, and attractive antique bureaus and armoires. Bathrooms are sparkling new and quite luxurious, with state-of-the-art stall showers and luxuriously deep basins. The higher rate is for larger rooms, including the miniapartments with kitchenette. Room renovations in 2004 included the conversion of several doubles into suites. A trattoria, long planned, is still in the works but should be completed in 2005.

Fraz. Annunziata. 12064 La Morra. © **0173-509245.** Fax 0173-500861. www.cascinadelmonastero.it. 10 units. 70€ ($81) single; 80€–85€ ($92–$98) double. Rates include continental breakfast. MC, V. Closed Jan–Feb. **Amenities:** Outdoor pool; golf nearby; bike rental; small children's playground; 24-hr. room service; babysitting; laundry service. *In room:* TV, dataport, kitchenette (in miniapartments) minibar, coffeemaker, hair dryer, iron.

GREAT DEALS ON DINING

La Cantinetta de Maurilio e Paolo ⚔ PIEMONTESE Two brothers, Maurilo and Paolo Chiappetto, do a fine job of introducing guests to the pleasures of the Piemontese table in their cozy dining room around an open hearth (in nice weather, book ahead for a table out on the tiny back terrace). A seemingly endless stream of servings, which change daily, emerge from the kitchen: a wonderful country pâté; *bagna cauda* (translated as "hot bath"), in which raw vegetables are dipped into a heated preparation of oil, anchovies, and garlic; ravioli in a truffle sauce; risotto with wild mushrooms; that funky giant egg-stuffed *raviolo* also found at Lalibera in Alba (see above); a thick slab of roast veal; a tender cut of beef; and salad made with wild herbs. If you can't make up your mind, try the 15€ ($17) *pasta misto*. The wonderful house wines come from the vines that run right up to the back door of this delightful restaurant (a bar/enoteca is up front if all you want is a glass or two).

Via Roma 33, Barolo. ✆ 0173-56198. Reservations recommended. Primi 8€ ($9.20); secondi 10€–15€ ($12–$17); tasting menu 26€ or 31€ ($30 or $36). AE, DC, MC, V. Fri–Tues noon–2:30pm and 8–10:30pm; Wed noon–2:30pm. Closed Jan and 15 days in July.

L'Osteria del Vignaiolo ⚔⚔ PIEMONTESE Halfway up the road to hilltop La Morra in the village of Santa Maria, this stylish countryside restaurant draws a clientele from many of the surrounding villages as well as from Alba, about 13km (8 miles) away. Pale gold walls, richly hued tiled floors, and handsome furnishings achieve a sophisticated rustic ambience, and the kitchen adds flair to local favorites. Duck breast appears in a salad of fresh-picked greens; *porcini* (wild mushrooms) are served in many variations, perhaps lightly fried or grilled and served with polenta. The *tortelli di zucca* (pumpkin-stuffed pasta pillows in a sauce of toasted hazelnuts) is flavorful and light. Veal appears thinly sliced in tagliatelle or, more traditionally, infused with herbs and simply grilled. Wines, of course, are local, many from Barolo, the lights of which you can see twinkling across the valley (especially if you snag one of the wrought-iron tables out on the flagstone terrace next to a hillside of grapevines).

Santa Maria 12, La Morra. ✆ 0173-50335. Reservations recommended. Primi 7€ ($8.05); secondi 10€ ($12); tasting menu 30€ ($35). AE, MC, V. Fri–Tues 12:30–1:45pm and 7:45–9:15pm. Closed Feb and July.

Ristorante Belvedere PIEMONTESE The view from the baronial main room, built around a large brick hearth and perched high above vineyards that roll away in all directions, is in itself a pleasure and draws many diners here. When tour buses arrive to fill the back rooms and downstairs, service can turn brusque. But while the Belvedere is no longer the welcoming rustic retreat it once was, its moves toward refinement (classy table settings, complimentary Spumanti and crostini while you consider the menu) have been pulled off well, and the kitchen maintains the high standards that have made it one of the region's most popular restaurants. A wonderful salad of truffles and Parmesan cheese, and homemade ravioli in a mushroom sauce are among the house specialties, which include many other pastas and risottos. Main courses lean heavily toward meat, including a rich *petto di anatra* (duck breast), *coniglio farcito alle erbe aromatiche* (deboned rabbit stuffed with herbs), and *straccotto di vitello al Barolo*, a shank of veal braised with the local wine. The wine list is 83 pages long and has a table of contents. The wine prices are surprisingly decent (keep in mind that this area's wines are among Italy's most expensive).

Piazza Castello 5, La Morra. ✆ 0173-50190. Reservations recommended. Primi 8€–9€ ($9.20–$10); secondi 13€–15€ ($15–$17); fixed-price menu without wine 38€ ($44). AE, DC, MC, V. Tues–Sat 12:30–2pm and 7:30–9pm; Sun 12:30–2pm. Closed Jan–Feb.

Vineria San Giorgio WINE BAR Not only is this friendly wine bar in the center of La Morra, at the corner of Piazza Castello, but it also serves as the village social center, and the series of attractive rooms is filled with amiable chatter throughout the day and evening. Rough stone walls and vaulted brick ceilings provide just the right ambience in which to linger and enjoy the local wines (sold by the glass from 1€/$1.15) and such regional fare as salamis and cheeses, accompanied by homemade bread. Sandwiches are also available, as are three or four daily specials, usually including a delicious lasagna or other pasta dish.

Via Umberto I 1, La Morra. ℂ 0173-509594. Light meals 1.55€–8€ ($1.80–$9.20). AE, MC, V. Tues–Sun 11am–2am (daily in Oct).

3 Aosta & the Valle d'Aosta

Aosta: 113km (70 miles) NW of Turin, 184km (114 miles) NW of Milan. Courmayeur-Entrèves: 35km (22 miles) W of Aosta, 148km (92 miles) NW of Turin

Skiers, hikers, and fresh-air and scenery enthusiasts flock to this tiny mountainous region less than 2 hours by train or car north of Turin, eager to enjoy one of Italy's favorite Alpine playgrounds. At its best, the **Valle d'Aosta** fulfills its promise. Snowcapped peaks, among them the Matterhorn and Mont Blanc, rise above the valley's verdant pastures and forests; waterfalls cascade into mountain streams; romantic castles cling to wooded hillsides.

Also plentiful in the Valle d'Aosta are crowds—especially in August, when the region welcomes hordes of vacationing Italians, and January to March, the height of the winter ski season—and one too many overdeveloped tourist centers to accommodate them. You would be best off coming at one of the nonpeak times, when you can enjoy the valley's beauty in relative peace and quiet.

Whenever you happen to find yourself in the Valle d'Aosta, two must-sees are the town of **Aosta** itself, with its Roman and medieval monuments set dramatically against the backdrop of the Alps (and a fine place to begin a tour of the surrounding mountains and valleys), and the natural wonders of **Parco Nazionale del Gran Paradiso.** If you are looking for drama, add to the itinerary the thrill of a cable car ride over the shoulder of Mont Blanc to France. While much of the Valle d'Aosta is accessible by train or bus, you'll probably want a car to explore the quieter reaches of the region.

Of course, recreation, not sightseeing, is what draws many people to the Valle d'Aosta. Some of the best **downhill skiing,** accompanied by the best facilities, is on the runs at Courmayeur and Breuvil-Cervíinia. The Valle D'Aosta is also excellent for **cross-country skiing** and **hiking** (see the box "Into the Great Outdoors," below).

AOSTA

GETTING THERE By Train Aosta is served by 12 trains a day to and from **Turin** (2–3 hr.; 6.80€/$7.80). There are 10 trains a day to and from **Milan** (3–4 hr., with a change in Chivasso; 10€/$12).

By Bus Aosta's bus station, across the piazza and a bit to the right from the train station, handles about eight buses (only one or two direct; most change in Ivrea) to and from **Turin** daily; the 3-hour trip (2 hr. on the direct) costs 6.40€ ($7.35). Four to five daily buses connect Aosta and **Milan** (2½–3½ hr.; 11€/$13). Buses also connect Aosta with other popular spots in the valley, among them **Courmayeur,** where you can connect with a shuttle bus to the Palud cable car (see later in this chapter); and **Cogne,** a major gateway to the Parco Nazionale del Gran Paradiso (see below). For information, call ℂ 0165-262027.

By Car The A5 autostrada from Turin shoots up the length of the Valle d'Aosta en route to France and Switzerland via the Mont Blanc tunnel; there are numerous exits in the valley. The trip from Turin to Aosta normally takes about 1½ hours, but traffic can be heavy in the busy tourist months—especially in August and January to March, the height of the ski season.

VISITOR INFORMATION The **tourist office** in Aosta, Piazza Chanoux 8 (© **0165-236627**; www.regione.vda.it/turismo), dispenses a wealth of info on hotels, restaurants, and sights throughout the region, along with listings of campgrounds, maps of hiking trails, information about ski-lift tickets and special discounted ski packages, outlets for bike rentals, and rafting trips. It's open Monday through Saturday from 9am to 1pm and 3 to 8pm (closed Sun afternoons Oct–May).

FESTIVALS & MARKETS Aosta celebrates its patron saint and warm winter days and nights with the **Fiera Sant'Orso** on the last 2 days of January. The festival fills the streets and involves dancing, drinking vast quantities of mulled wine, and perusing the local crafts pieces, such as lovely woodcarvings and woven blankets, offered for sale by vendors from throughout the Valle d'Aosta. Aosta's other major event is the **Battaille des Reines,** the Battle of the Cows, in which these mainstays of the local economy lock horns—the main event is held the third Sunday in October, and preliminary heats take place throughout the year. Aosta's **weekly market** day is Tuesday, when stalls selling food, clothes, crafts, and household items fill the Piazza Cavalieri di Vittorio Veneto.

EXPLORING THE AREA

This mountain town, surrounded by snowcapped peaks, not only is pleasant, but has soul—the product of a history that goes back to Roman times. While you're not going to find much pristine Alpine quaintness here in the Valle d'Aosta's busy tourist and economic center, you can spend some enjoyable time strolling past Roman ruins and medieval bell towers while checking out the chic shops that sell everything from Armani suits to locally made Fontina cheese.

The "Rome of the Alps" sits majestically within its preserved walls, and the monuments of the Empire make it easy to envision the days when Aosta was one of Rome's most important trading and military outposts. Two Roman gates arch gracefully across the Via Anselmo, Aosta's main thoroughfare: the **Porta Pretoria,** the western entrance to the Roman town, and the **Arco di Augusto** (sometimes called Arco Romano), the eastern entrance built in A.D. 25 to commemorate a Roman victory over the Celts. A **Roman bridge** spans the river Buthier. Just a few steps north of the Porta Pretoria you'll find the facade of the **Teatro Romano (Roman Theater)** and the ruins of the **amphitheater,** which once accommodated 20,000 spectators; the ruins of the **forum** are in an adjacent park. The theater and forum are open daily, in summer from 9:30am to noon and 2:30 to 6:30pm, and in winter from 9:30am to noon and 2 to 4:30pm; admission is free. Architectural fragments from these monuments and a sizable collection of vessels and other objects unearthed during excavations are displayed in Aosta's **Archaeological Museum** on Piazza Roncas (© **0165-238680**). It's open daily from 9am to 7pm, and admission is free.

Behind the banal 19th-century facade of Aosta's **Duomo,** Piazza Giovanni XXIII (© **0165-40251**), lie two remarkable treasures: an ivory diptych from A.D. 406 that depicts the Roman emperor Honorius and is housed along with other precious objects in the treasury, and 12th-century mosaics on the floor of the choir and in front of the altar. Heavy-handed restorations cloud the fact that the church actually dates from the 10th century. It's open Monday through Saturday from 8am to 12:30pm and 2:30 to 5:30pm (though they often just stay open all day), and Sunday from 12:30 to 5:30pm. The treasury is open April to September Monday through Saturday from 8 to 11:30am and 3 to 5:30pm, and Sunday from 8 to 9:30am, 10:30 to 11:30am, and 3 to 5:30pm; October to March, it's open Sunday from 8 to 9:30am, 10:30 to 11:30am, and 3 to 5:30pm. Admission to the treasury is 2.10€ ($2.40) for adults and .75€ (85¢) for children under age 10.

The **Collegiata dei Santi Pietro e Orso,** at the eastern edge of the old city off Via San Anselmo 9 (✆ **0165-262026**), is a hodgepodge from the 6th through the 18th centuries. An 11th-century church was built over the original 6th-century church, and that, in turn, has been periodically enhanced with architectural embellishments representing every stylistic period from the Gothic through the baroque. In a room above the nave (the door on the left aisle marked AFFRESCHI OTTONIANI; search out the sacristan or ring the bell), the remains of an 11th-century fresco cycle recount the life of Christ and the Apostles on the bits of medieval church wall above the 15th-century vaults. The frescoes are open daily April to September from 9am to 7pm and October to March from 10am to 5pm. The 12th-century cloisters are a fascinating display of Romanesque storytelling—40 columns are capped with carved capitals depicting scenes from the Bible and the life of Aosta's own Saint Orso.

SIDE TRIPS FROM AOSTA

CASTLE OF FENIS   Built by the Challants, viscounts of Aosta throughout much of the Middle Ages, this castle (✆ **0165-764263;** www.aostavalley.com) near the town of Fenis is the most impressive and best preserved of the many castles perched on the hillsides above the Valle d'Aosta. You can enjoy fine views of the Alps and the valley below. One of the most appealing parts of a visit to Fenis is catching a glimpse into everyday life in a medieval castle—you can climb up to wooden loggias overlooking the courtyard and visit the cavernous kitchens. Alas, you can't scamper among the ramparts, turrets, towers, and dungeons, thanks to a new Italian safety law requiring that steps be short and wide, corridors wide enough, and emergency exits plentiful.

March to June and September, the castle is open daily from 9am to 7:30pm; July and August hours are daily from 9am to 8pm; and October to February hours are Wednesday through Monday from 10am to 12:30pm and 1:30 to 4:30pm (to 6pm Sun). Requisite half-hour guided tours (in Italian only) leave every 30 minutes. Come early; tours tend to fill up quickly in summer, and you can't book. Admission is 5€ ($5.75) for adults and 3.50€ ($4.05) for students. The castle is 30km (19 miles) east of Aosta on Route S26. There are 13 buses a day (only one, at 6:20am, on Sun) from Aosta (1.60€/$1.85; 30 min.).

BREUIL-CERVINIA-BREUIL & THE MATTERHORN   You don't come to Cervinia-Breuil to see the town, a banal collection of tourist facilities—the sight to see, and you can't miss it, is the **Matterhorn** ⚘, called **Monte Cervino** in Italian (www.cervinia.it). Its distinctive profile looms majestically above the valley, beckoning year-round skiers and those who simply want to savor a refreshing Alpine experience by ascending to its glaciers via cable car to the Plateau Rosa (26€/$30 round-trip) from 8:30am to 4:30pm; it's closed September 10 to mid-October. An excellent trail also ascends from Breuil-**Cervinia-Breuil** up the flank of the mountain. After a moderately strenuous uphill trek of 90 minutes, you come to gorgeous **Lac du Goillet** ⚘, and from there it's another 90 minutes to the **Colle Superiore delle Cime Bianche** ⚘, a plateau with heart-stopping views.

Into the Great Outdoors

Recreation, of course, is what draws many people to the Valle d'Aosta. You'll find some of the best **downhill skiing** and facilities on the runs at **Courmayeur,** at **Breuvil-Cervíinia,** and in the **Valle di Cogne.** At the first two, you can expect to pay 29€ to 34€ ($33–$39) and up for daily lift passes. Cogne is rather less expensive, with daily passes running around 15€ to 18€ ($17–$21). Multiday passes, providing access to lifts and slopes of the entire valley, run about 94€ ($108) for 3 days and 122€ ($140) for 4 days, with per-day rates sliding down a scale to end up at 14 days for 330€ ($380). For more info, call ℂ **0165-238871** or go to www.skivallee.it. Ski season starts in October and runs through April, if the snow holds out.

A money-saving option is to take one of the *Settimane Bianche* (White Week) **packages** that include room and board and unlimited skiing, and are available at resorts throughout the Valle d'Aosta. You can expect to pay at least 270€ to 300€ ($310–$345) at Courmayeur, and from 200€ to 225€ ($230–$260) at Cogne or one of the other less fashionable resorts. Contact the tourist board in Aosta for more information.

Cross-country skiing is superb around Cogne in the Parco Nazionale del Gran Paradiso, where there are more than 48km (30 miles) of trails. The Valle d'Aosta is also excellent **hiking** terrain, especially in July and August. For information about hiking in Parco Nazionale del Gran Paradiso, ask at the tourist offices of Aosta and especially Cogne.

The **tourist office,** Via Carrel 29 (ℂ **0166-949136;** www.montecervino.it), can provide information on other hikes, ski packages, and serious ascents to the top of the Matterhorn. Breuil-Cervinia is 54km (33 miles) northwest of Aosta via routes A5 and S406. **From Aosta,** you can take one of the Turin-bound trains and get off at Chatillon (20 min.; 1.80€/$2.05), and continue from there on one of the seven daily buses to Breuil-Cervinia (1 hr.; 2€/$2.30).

PARCO NAZIONALE DEL GRAN PARADISO   The little town of Cogne is the most convenient gateway to one of Europe's finest parcels of unspoiled nature, the former hunting grounds of King Vittorio Emanuele that now comprise this vast and lovely national park. The park encompasses five valleys and a total of 3,626 sq. km (1,414 sq. miles) of forests and pastureland where many Alpine beasts roam wild, including the ibex (a long-horned goat) and the chamois (a small antelope), both of which have hovered near extinction in recent years.

Humans can roam these wilds via a vast network of well-marked trails. Among the few places where the hand of man intrudes ever so gently on nature is in scattered hamlets within the park borders and in the **Giardino Alpino Paradisiao** (ℂ **0165-74147**), a stunning collection of rare Alpine fauna near the village of Valnontey, just 1.6km (1 mile) south of Cogne. It's open from June 12 to September 12 daily from 10am to 6:30pm (5:30pm June and Sept); admission is 2.50€ ($2.90) for adults and 1.10€ ($1.15) for children ages 12 to 18 and those over 65.

Visitor Information   Cogne also offers some downhill skiing, but it is better regarded for its many cross-country-skiing trails. The **tourist office** in Cogne,

Piazza Chanoux 34–36 (© **0165-74040;** www.cogne.org), provides a wealth of information on hiking and skiing trails and other outdoor activities in the park and elsewhere in the region; it's open daily from 9am to 12:30pm and 3 to 6pm. You can also get info at **www.pngp.it.** Cogne is about 29km (18 miles) south of Aosta via S35 and S507. There are seven buses a day to and from Aosta; the 50-minute trip costs 2.05€ ($2.35).

ACCOMMODATIONS YOU CAN AFFORD

Many hotels in the Valle d'Aosta require that guests take their meals on the premises and stay 3 nights or more. However, outside of busy tourist times, hotels often have rooms to spare and are willing to be a little more liberal in their policies. Rates vary almost month by month; in general, expect the highest room rates in August and at Christmas and Easter, and the lowest in the fall. For the best rates, check with the local tourist boards for information on *Settimane Bianche* (White Week) packages, all-inclusive deals that include room, board, and ski passes.

Belle Epoque *Value*   The stuccoed exterior of this old building in a quiet corner of the historic center has a cozy Alpine look to it, but the same can't be said of the somewhat stark interior. What's appealing about this hotel is the family-run atmosphere and the price, appreciated all the more in this often-expensive resort region. Rooms are large enough but spartan, with the bare minimum of modern pieces scattered about. Some have balconies and updated, tidy little bathrooms. An equally serviceable trattoria occupies most of the ground floor; you can arrange half pension for about 44€ ($51) per person. There's no elevator.

Via d'Avise 18, 11100 Aosta. ©/fax 0165-262276. 14 units, 11 with bathroom. 20€–26€ ($23–$30) single without bathroom, 22€-30€ ($25–$35) single with bathroom; 40€–48€ ($46–$55) double without bathroom, 50€–60€ ($58–$69) double with bathroom. Breakfast 5.50€ ($6.25). AE, MC, V. **Amenities:** Restaurant; bar; room service; babysitting. *In room:* No phone.

Bus *☆*   One of the nicest things about this newer hotel is its location on a pleasant side street just a short walk from the center of Aosta. The Roman ruins and other sights are within a 5-minute walk, yet this quiet neighborhood has an almost rural feel to it. Downstairs you'll find a contemporary-style bar, restaurant, and breakfast area. Upstairs, the smallish guest rooms are comfortably furnished in a somewhat somber modern style that includes many wood-veneer touches and thin, worn carpeting. The bathrooms are serviceable but suffer from the dreaded waffle towels. Since the hotel is taller than the surrounding houses, rooms on the upper floors overlook meadows and the surrounding mountains. Except at peak times, rooms are usually available without board. Fifteen rooms have air-conditioning; if you prefer the opposite sensation, a sauna is downstairs.

Via Malherbes 18, 11100 Aosta. © **0165-236958** or 0165-43645. Fax 0165-236962. www.netvallee.it/ hotelbus. 39 units. 50€–65€ ($58–$75) single; 75€–90€ ($86–$104) double; half board 50€–70€ ($58–$81) per person. Rates include breakfast. AE, DC, MC, V. **Amenities:** Valdostana restaurant; bar; tiny exercise room; sauna; 24-hr. room service; laundry service. *In room:* A/C (in 15), TV, minibar, hair dryer.

Milleluci *☆☆☆ Finds*   From its noticeably cooler perch on a hillside just above the town, this chaletlike hotel in a breezy garden offers pleasant views. Cristina's great-grandmother converted the family farm into a hotel 40 years ago, and it's been handed down from mother to daughter ever since. Downstairs, a large wood-beamed sitting area is grouped around an attractive hearth (always ablaze in winter) and woodsy bar. The spacious rooms (larger on the second floor, cozy on the first) sport some nice touches like traditional wood furnishings, beamed ceilings, canopied beds (in suites and in one double), rich fabrics, terrazzo floors, and handsome prints. All have spacious bathrooms with heated towel racks. Two suites are tucked under the eaves; another pair is going in on the second floor. The stupendous buffet breakfast alone would be reason to stay: all homemade cakes, freshly whipped cream, *frittata* wedges (eggs from their own chickens, veggies from the garden), Alpine cheeses, and more. In nice weather, you can take breakfast on the wraparound terrace overlooking the town. By the end of 2004, the hotel should have a small fitness room installed.

In Roppoz, off Via Porossan 1km (½ mile) northeast of Arco di Augusto, 11100 Aosta. © **0165-235278.** Fax 0165-235284. www.hotelmilleluci.com. 31 units. 80€–100€ ($92–$115) single; 100€–120€ ($115–$138) double; 120€–150€ ($138–$173) double with a canopy bed; 200€ ($230) suite; 190€–240€ ($219–$276) adjoining rooms for 4. Rates include breakfast. AE, DC, MC, V. Free parking. **Amenities:** Outdoor pool (heated); Jacuzzi; sauna; playground; concierge; tour desk; courtesy car; room service (breakfast only); in-room massage; babysitting; nonsmoking rooms. *In room:* TV, VCR, fax (on request), dataport, minibar, hair dryer, safe

GREAT DEALS ON DINING

This is the land of mountain food—hams and salamis are laced with herbs from Alpine meadows; creamy cornmeal polenta accompanies meals; a rich beef stew, *carbonada*, warms winter nights; and buttery Fontina is the cheese of choice.

Grotta Azzurra PIZZA/SOUTHERN ITALIAN   The best pizzeria in town also serves, as its name suggests, a bounty of fare from southern climes, along the lines of spaghetti with clam sauce. There is a wide selection of fresh fish, which makes this somewhat worn-looking trattoria popular with locals. The pizzas emerge from a wood-burning oven and are often topped with Fontina and other rich local cheeses and salamis.

Via Croix de Ville 97. © **0165-262474.** Primi 4.50€–9€ ($5.20–$10); secondi 5.50€–15€ ($6.30–$17); pizza 4€–8€ ($4.60–$9.20). MC, V. Thurs–Tues noon–2:30pm and 6–10:30pm. Closed July 10–27.

Taverna da Nando PIZZA/VALDOSTAN   On Aosta's main thoroughfare in the center of town, this popular basement eatery achieves a rustic ambience with stuccoed vaulted ceilings, traditional mountain furnishings, and warm (if excruciatingly slow) service. The kitchen, too, sticks to local traditions, serving such dishes as *fonduta* (a creamy fondue of Fontina, milk, and eggs served atop polenta), *crepes à la Valdostana* (filled and topped with melted cheese), and *carbonada con polenta* (beef stew dished over polenta). There is also an excellent selection of grilled meats, pizzas, salads, and bruschette, as well as a wine list that includes many choices from the Valle d'Aosta's limited but productive vineyards and from the Piemonte.

Via de Tillier 41. © **0165-44455.** Primi 5.15€–9€ ($5.90–$10); secondi 7€–13€ ($8.05–$15); pizza 4€–7€ ($4.60–$8); fixed-price menus 12€–28€ ($14–$32). AE, DC, MC, V. Tues–Sun noon–3pm and 7:15–10pm. Closed 15 days in late June/early July.

Trattoria Praetoria VALDOSTAN   This small, woody trattoria, one of the friendliest and best priced in Aosta, takes its name from the nearby Roman gate and its menu from the surrounding countryside. This is the place to throw concerns about cholesterol to the wind and introduce your palate to Valdostan cuisine. Begin with *fonduta* (fondue) and follow it with *boudin* (spicy sausages served with potatoes) or *carbonada* (a hearty beef stew).

Via San Anselmo 9. © **0165-44356.** Primi 6.50€–9€ ($7.50–$10); secondi 7€–18€ ($8.05–$21). MC, V. Fri–Tues 12:15–2:30pm and 7:15–9:30pm; Wed 12:15–2:30pm.

COURMAYEUR-ENTREVES

The one-time mountain hamlet of **Courmayeur** is now the Valle d'Aosta's resort extraordinaire, a collection of traditional stone buildings, pseudo-Alpine chalets, and large hotels catering to a well-heeled international crowd of skiers. Even if you don't ski, you can happily while away the time sipping a grog while regarding the craggy bulk of Mont Blanc (Monte Bianco, this side of the border), which looms over this end of the Valle d'Aosta and forms the snowy barrier between Italy and France. The Mont Blanc tunnel—which normally makes it possible to zip into France in just 20 minutes—reopened in March 2002, 3 years after a devastating fire.

Entrèves, 3km (1¾ miles) north of Courmayeur, is the sort of place that the latter probably once was: a pleasant collection of stone houses and farm buildings surrounded by pastureland. Quaint as the village is in appearance, at its soul it is a worldly enclave with some nice hotels and restaurants catering to skiers and outdoor enthusiasts who prefer to spend time in the mountains in surroundings that are a little quieter than Courmayeur.

ESSENTIALS
GETTING THERE   By Bus   Thirteen daily buses connect Courmayeur with Aosta (1 hr.; 2.50€/$2.90). At least hourly, buses (more in summer; ✆ **0165-841305**) run between Courmayeur's Piazzale Monte Bianco and Entrèves and La Palud (10 min.; .75€/85¢).

By Car   The A5 autostrada from Turin to the Mont Blanc tunnel passes Courmayeur. The trip from Aosta to Courmayeur on this much-used route takes less than half an hour (lots of time in tunnels; for scenery, take the parallel S26 in about 1 hr.), and total travel time from Turin is less than 2 hours.

VISITOR INFORMATION   The **tourist office** in Courmayeur, Piazzale Monte Bianco 8 (✆ **0165-842060** or 0165-842072; www.courmayeur.net or www.regione.vda.it/turismo), provides information on hiking, skiing, and other outdoor activities in the region, as well as hotel and restaurant listings. It's open late July to late August and Christmas to January 6 daily 9am to 1pm and 2:30 to 7pm; late April to late July and late August through November Monday to Saturday 9am to 12:30pm and 3 to 6:30pm, Sunday 9:30am to 12:30pm and 3 to 6pm; December 1 to December 24 and January 7 to late April Saturday and Sunday only 9am to 1pm and 2:30 to 7pm.

ACCOMMODATIONS YOU CAN AFFORD
Edelweiss   In winter, the pine-paneled salons and cozy rooms of this chalet-style hotel near the center of town attract a friendly international set of skiers, and in summer, many Italian families spend a month or two here at a time. The Roveyaz family extends a hearty welcome to all and provides modern mountain-style accommodations. (You wonder, however, why the contemporary bathrooms have heated towel racks but only flat towels.) Many rooms open onto terraces overlooking the mountains, and the nicest rooms are those on the top floor, tucked under the eaves. Hoteliers have added a small fitness center. Basic, nonfussy meals are served in the cheerful main-floor dining room. You can arrange a half-board deal for 40€ to 65€ ($46–$75) per person, depending on the season.

Via Marconi 42, 11013 Courmayeur. ✆ **0165-841590.** Fax 0165-841618. www.albergoedelweiss.it. 30 units. 40€–70€ ($46–$81) single; 70€–120€ ($81–$138) double. Rates include buffet breakfast. AE, MC, V. Free parking. Closed May–June and Oct–Nov. **Amenities:** Aostan restaurant; bar; small gym; a few bikes for free; babysitting; laundry service; nonsmoking rooms. *In room:* TV, hair dryer.

La Grange 𝄡𝄡   What may well be the most charming hotel in the Valle d'Aosta occupies a converted barn in the bucolic village of Entrèves and is ably

Across Mont Blanc by Cable Car

One of the Valle d'Aosta's best experiences is to ride the series of cable cars from La Palud, just above Entrèves, across Mont Blanc to several ski stations in Italy and France and down into Chamonix, France. You make the trip in stages—first past two intermediate stops to the last aerie on Italian soil, **Punta Helbronner** (20 min. each way). At 3,300m (10,824 ft.), this ice-clad lookout provides stunning views of the Mont Blanc glaciers and the Matterhorn and other peaks looming in the distance. (In summer, you may want to hop off before you get to Punta Helbronner at **Pavillion Frety** and tour a pleasant botanic garden, Giardino Alpino Saussurea; open daily June 24–Sept 30.)

For sheer drama, continue from Punta Helbronner to **Aiguille du Midi** in France in a tiny gondola to experience the dramatic sensation of dangling more than 2,300m (7,544 ft.) in midair as you cruise above the Géant Glacier and the Vallée Blanche (30 min. each way). From Aiguille du Midi, you can descend over more glaciers and dramatic valleys on the French flank of Mont Blanc to the resort town of **Chamonix** (50 min. each way).

In **low season** (June 1–28 and Sept 9–Nov 3), the ride to Punta Helbronner costs 31€ ($36) round-trip, or 86€ ($99) for the family pass that covers two adults and two kids. From Helbronner to Aiguille du Midi, you must buy tickets at Helbronner for an additional 18€ ($20); to continue all the way from Helbronner to Chamonix in France is 39€ ($45). In **high season** (June 26–Sept 5; precise dates vary each year), the "Trans Mont Blanc" tickets, good for the round-trip from Courmayeur to Chamonix, cost 67€ ($77); just to Helbronner and back costs 34€ ($39; including admission to the Alpine Garden); the family ticket runs 96€ ($110). The trip on to Aiguille du Midi or Chamonix costs the same year-round. On all tickets, at all times of year, children ages 4 to 11 get 50% off, ages 12–15 get 25% off, and adults over 60 get a 10% discount.

Hours for these cable cars vary wildly, and service can be sporadic depending on weather conditions (winds often close the gondola between Hellbronner and Aiguille du Midi), but in general they run every 20 minutes from 7:20am (8:20am in fall and spring) to 12:30pm and 2 to 5:30pm (all day long July 22–Aug 27; closed Nov 2–Dec 10) The last downward run is 5:30pm in summer and 4:30pm in winter. The Hellbronner–Aiguille du Midi gondola is open only May through September. Hourly buses make the 10-minute run from Courmayeur to the cable car terminus at La Palud. For more info, call ℭ **0165-89925** (or go to www.montebianco.com); for a report of weather at the top and on the other side, dial ℭ **0165-89961**.

managed by Bruna Berthold. No two of the rooms are the same, though all are decorated with a pleasing smattering of antiques and rustic furnishings; some have balconies looking out onto Mont Blanc, which quite literally hovers over the property. The stucco-walled, stone-floored lobby is a fine place to relax, with couches built around a corner hearth and a small bar area. A lavish buffet

---

(Moments **Drinking with the Best of Them**

The **Caffè della Posta**, at Via Roma 51, Courmayeur (© **0165-842272**), is Courmayeur's most popular spot for an après-ski grog. Since it opened 90 years ago, it has been welcoming the famous and not so famous into its series of cozy rooms, one of which is grouped around an open hearth.

---

breakfast is served in a prettily paneled room off the lobby. There is an exercise room and a much-used sauna.

c.p. 75, 11013 Courmayeur-Entrèves. © **0165-869733**, or off season 335-6463533. Fax 0165-869744. www.lagrange-it.com. 23 units. Aug 4–Aug 25 104€–130€ ($120–$150) single; 130€ ($150) double; 150€ ($173) triple; 207€ ($238) suite. July 21–Aug 5 and Aug 25–Sept 1 93€–104€ ($107–$120) single; 104€ ($120) double; 130€ ($150) triple; 185€ ($213) suite. July 1–21 and Sept 1–30 52€ ($60) single; 80€ ($92) double; 104€ ($120) triple; 155€ ($178) suite. Rates include American breakfast. Free parking. AE, DC, MC, V. Closed May–June and Oct–Nov. **Amenities:** Bar; exercise room; sauna; bike rental; concierge; room service; in-room massage; babysitting. *In room:* TV, dataport, minibar, hair dryer (ask at desk).

GREAT DEALS ON DINING

Ristorante La Palud SEAFOOD/VALDOSTON   Come to this cozy restaurant, in the little cable-car settlement just outside Entrèves in the shadows of Mont Blanc, on Friday so that you can enjoy a wide selection of fresh fish brought up from Liguria. At any time, though, a table in front of the hearth is just the place to enjoy the specialties of the Valle d'Aosta: mountain hams, creamy *polenta concia* (with Fontina cheese and butter folded into it), and *cervo* (venison) in season. A selection of mountain cheeses is offered for dessert, and the wine list borrows heavily from neighboring Piemonte but includes local vintages.

Strada la Palud 17, Courmayeur. © **0165-89169**. Primi 6€–9€ ($6.90–$10); secondi 8€–20€ ($9.20–$23); fixed-price menus 16€–25€ ($18–$29; the pricier one includes wine). AE, MC, V. Thurs–Tues noon–3:30pm and 7:30–10:30pm.

Worth a Splurge

Maison de Filippo ✦ VALDOSTON   The atmosphere at this popular and cheerful restaurant in Entrèves is delightfully country Alpine, and the offerings are so generous you may not be able to eat again for a week. Daily menus vary but often include an antipasto of mountain hams and salamis, a selection of pastas filled with wild mushrooms and topped with Fontina and other local cheeses, and a sampling of fresh trout and game in season. Service is casual and friendly. In summer, you can choose between a table in the delightfully converted barn-like structure or one on the flowery terrace.

Loc. Entrèves. © **0165-869797**. www.lamaison.com. Reservations required. Fixed-price menu 40€ ($46; without wine). MC, V. Wed–Mon 12:30–2:30pm and 7:30–10:30pm. Closed June and Nov–Dec 20.

11

Liguria & the Italian Riviera

by Reid Bramblett

From the top of Tuscany to the French border, Italy follows a crescent-shape strip of seacoast and mountains that comprise the region of **Liguria.** The pleasures of this region are no secret. Since the 19th century, world-weary travelers have been heading to Liguria's resorts to enjoy balmy weather (ensured by the protective barrier of the Alps) and turquoise seas. Beyond the beach, the stones and tiles of proud old towns and cities bake in the sun, and hillsides are fragrant with the scents of bougainvillea and pines.

Liguria is really two coasts: The beachier stretch east of Genoa is known as the **Riviera di Levante (Rising Sun),** and the rockier, more colorful fishing-village-filled stretch to the west of Genoa is called the **Riviera di Ponente (Setting Sun).** Both are lined with fishing towns, including the remote hamlets of the Cinque Terre, and fashionable resorts, many of which have seen their heydays fade but continue to entice visitors with palm-fringed promenades and gentle ways. **Genoa,** with its proud maritime history, is a world apart from the easygoing seaside towns that surround it: Brusque and clamorous, it is one of the more history-filled, and least visited, cities in Italy.

1 Genoa: Sophistication & Squalor

142km (88 miles) S of Milan, 501km (311 miles) N of Rome, 194km (120 miles) E of Nice

With its dizzying mix of the old and the new, of sophistication and squalor, **Genoa (Genova)** is as multilayered as the hills it clings to. It is, first and foremost, a port city: an important maritime center for the Roman Empire; boyhood home of Christopher Columbus (whose much-restored house still stands near a section of the medieval walls); and, fueled by seafaring commerce that stretched all the way to the Middle East, one of the largest and wealthiest cities of Renaissance Europe.

It's easy to capture glimpses of these former glory days in the narrow lanes and dank alleys of Genoa's portside old town, where treasure-filled palaces and fine marble churches stand next to laundry-draped tenements. In fact, life within the old medieval walls doesn't seem to have changed since the days when Genovese ships set sail to launch raids on the Venetians, crusaders embarked for the Holy Land, or Garibaldi shipped out to invade Sicily in the 19th-century struggle to unify Italy. The other Genoa, the modern city that stretches for kilometers along the coast and climbs the hills, is a city of international business, peaceful parks, and breezy belvederes from which you can enjoy fine views of this dingy-yet-colorful metropolis and the sea that continues to define its identity.

However, be prepared to deal with what is probably the seediest port city in Italy. The back alleys—and plenty of main streets as well—teem with muggers, whores, and heroin addicts shooting up all night *and* all day. Always stick to the

A Taste of Liguria

No matter where you travel in this region, you will never be far from the sea. A truism, but a bit misleading because seafood is not as plentiful as you might assume here in the heavily fished north. What are plentiful are *acciughe* (anchovies), and once you try them fresh and *marinate* (marinated in lemon) as part of an antipasto, you will never underestimate the culinary merits of this little fish again. More noticeable than fish are the many fresh vegetables that grow in patches clinging to the hillsides and find their way into tarts (the **torta pasqualina** is one of the most elaborate, with umpteen layers of pastry; some restaurants serve it year-round, not just at Easter) and sauces, none more typical of Liguria than **pesto,** a simple and simply delicious concoction of basil, olive oil, pine nuts, and parmigiano ground together with mortar and pestle (hence the name). Ligurians are also adept at making fast food, and there's no better light lunch or snack than a piece of **focaccia,** flatbread that's often topped with herbs or olives, or a *farinata,* a chickpea crepe served in wedges. Both are sold in bakeries and at small stands, making it easy to grab a bite before you head out to enjoy the other delights of the region.

widest, busiest, most major roads you can find. It is telling that, in an attempt to scrub the city clean for the 2001 G8 conference, the authorities swept all the street denizens into makeshift jail cells and then welded 5m (15-ft.) steel cages across all access streets and alleys to keep the conference attendees in the historic center safe (for a while, they even considered having the meetings on a ship out in the harbor). These measures were only partly successful, and local officials are still tainted by the scandal that arose when the police shot and killed a fire extinguisher–wielding protester. Meanwhile, the port district has quickly reverted to its dingy, dangerous old self. Genoa is, to say the least, probably not going to win "favorite bit of Italy" on your list, but it is worth a visit.

ESSENTIALS

GETTING THERE   By Plane   Flights to and from most European capitals serve **Aeroporto Internazionale de Genova Cristoforo Colombo,** just 6km (3¾ miles) west of the city center (© **010-60151** central line, or 010-6015410 information; www.airport.genova.it). **Volabus no. 100** (© **010-5582414;** www.amt.genova.it) connects the airport with Stazione Principe and Stazione Brignole. Buses run to the airport every 20 to 30 minutes from 5:30am to 10:30pm and from the airport with the same frequency from 6:15am to 10:20pm; tickets are 3€ ($3.45) and can be bought on board the bus. The nearest airports handling overseas flights are at Nice, 187km (116 miles) west just over the border with France, and Milan, 137km (85 miles) to the north. Both cities are well connected to Genoa by superhighways and by train service.

By Train   It is important to know that Genoa has two major train stations, **Stazione Principe** (designated on timetables as Genova P. P.), near the old city on Piazza Acquaverde; and **Stazione Brignole** (designated on timetables as Genova B. R.), in the modern city on Piazza Verdi. Many trains, especially those on long-distance lines, service both stations; however, many other trains stop only at one, making it essential that you know at which station your train is scheduled to arrive and from which station it will depart. Trains (www.trenitalia.com)

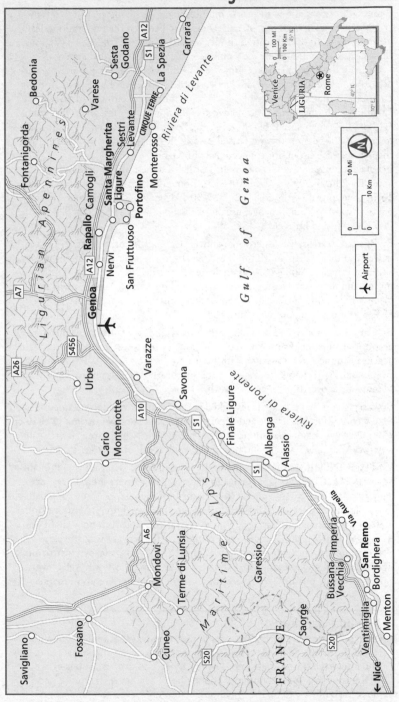

connect the two stations in just 6 minutes and run about every 15 minutes (1.50€/$1.75). City bus nos. 40 and 37 also run between the two stations, leaving from the front of each station about every 10 minutes (.75€/85¢); you must allow at least 20 minutes for the connection on Genoa's crowded streets.

Genoa is the hub for trains serving the Italian Riviera, with trains arriving and departing for **Ventimiglia** on the French border about every half-hour, and for **La Spezia,** at the eastern edge of Liguria, even more frequently, as often as every 15 minutes during peak times between 7am and 7pm (regional: 105 min., 4.25€/$4.90; high speed: 60–90 min., 6.90€–9.25€/$8–$11). Most of these trains make local stops at the coastal resorts (for those towns covered in this chapter, see each listing for connections with Genoa).

Lots of trains connect Genoa with major Italian cities: **Milan** (one to three per hour; 1½–2 hr., 7.90€–13€/$9.10–$15), **Rome** (hourly; 4½–5½ hr.; 35€/$40), **Turin** (one to two per hour; 1¾–2 hr., 7.90€–13€/$9–$15), **Florence** (hourly but nearly always with a change, usually at Pisa; 3–3½ hr.; 18€–20€/$20–$23), **Pisa** (hourly; 2–3 hr., 7.90€–13€/$9–$15).

By Bus   An extensive bus network connects Genoa with other parts of Liguria, as well as other Italian and European cities, from the main bus station next to Stazione Principe. While it is easiest to reach seaside resorts by the trains that run up and down the coast, buses are the only link to many small towns in the region's hilly hinterlands. For tickets and information, contact **ALI** (© 010-56474206; www.ali-autolineeliguri.it).

By Car   Genoa is linked to other parts of Italy and to France by a convenient network of superhighways. The A10/A12 follows the coast and passes through dozens of tunnels to link Genoa with France to the west (Nice is less than 2 hr. away), and Pisa is about 1½ hours to the southeast. The A7 links Genoa with Milan, a little over an hour to the north.

By Ferry   Port that it is, Genoa is linked to several other Mediterranean ports by ferry service. Most boats leave and depart from the **Stazione Marittima** (© 010-256682; www.stazionimarittimegenova.com), which is on a waterfront roadway, Via Marina D'Italia, about a 5-minute walk south of Stazione Principe.

VISITOR INFORMATION   The **main tourist office** is at Stazione Principe (© 010-2462633; www.apt.genova.it or www.genovatouristboard.net), open daily from 9:30am to 1pm and 2:30 to 6pm. Branches can be found at Cristoforo Colombo airport (© 010-6015247), open Monday through Saturday from 9:30am to 1:30pm and 2:30 to 5:30pm, or near the aquarium on Via al Porto Antico (© 010-2530671), open only in summer (hours vary year to year).

For regional information on Liguria, check out the official **www.turismo. liguriainrete.it** and the unofficial (but far more helpful) **www.hotelsgiovani. com**, run by the private "Committee of Young Hoteliers of Genova Province."

A Genoa Warning

Even locals are wary of back streets in the old city, especially after dark, in midafternoon, and on Sundays, when shops are closed and streets tend to be deserted. Purse snatching, jewelry theft, and armed robberies are all too common. Also, count your change here. I've never had more people consistently try to rip me off (shops, restaurants, even the public parking garages) anywhere else in Italy.

CITY LAYOUT   Genoa extends for kilometers along the coast, with neighborhoods and suburbs tucked into valleys and climbing the city's many hills. Most sights of interest are in the **old town,** a fascinating jumble of old palazzos, laundry-festooned tenements, cramped squares, and tiny lanes and alleyways clustered on the eastern side of the old port. The city's two train stations are located on either side of the old town, known as **Caruggi;** as confusing as Genoa's topography is, wherever you are in the old town, you are only a short walk or bus or taxi ride from one of these two stations. **Stazione Principe** is the closest, just to the west; from **Piazza Acquaverde** in front of the station, follow **Via Balbi** through **Piazza della Nunziata** to **Via Cairoli,** which runs into Via Garibaldi (the walk will take about 15 min.). Palazzo-lined **Via Garibaldi** forms the northern flank of the old town and is the best place to begin your explorations. Many of the city's major museums and other major monuments are on and around this street, and from here you can descend into the warren of little lanes that lead through the cluttered heart of Caruggi down to the port.

From **Stazione Brignole,** walk straight across the broad, open, buildingless space to Piazza della Vittoria/Via Luigi Cadorna and turn right to follow broad **Via XX Settembre,** one of the city's major shopping avenues, due west for about 15 or 20 minutes to **Piazza de Ferrari,** which is on the eastern edge of the old town. From here, **Via San Lorenzo** will lead you past Genoa's cathedral and to the port, but if you want to use Via Garibaldi as your sightseeing base, continue north from the piazza on **Via XXV Aprile** to **Piazza delle Fontane Marose.** This busy square marks the eastern end of Via Garibaldi.

FESTIVALS & MARKETS   In June, an ancient tradition continues when Genoa takes to the sea in the **Regatta Storica,** competing with crews from its ancient maritime rivals, Amalfi, Pisa, and Venice. The winner of the previous year's competition hosts the event, so your chances of witnessing the regatta during a June visit to Genoa depend on the fortunes of the previous year's boatmen.

Genoa adds a touch of culture to the summer season with an **International Ballet Festival** that attracts a stellar list of performers from around the world. Performances are held in the beautiful gardens of Villa Gropallo in outlying Nervi, an early-1900s resort with lush parks and an animated seaside promenade. Contact the tourist office in Genoa for schedules and ticket information. (Frequent trains connect Genoa and Nervi in 10 min. and run about every 20 min.) The tourist office also keeps tabs of the summer concerts staged at venues, many of them outdoor, around the city.

The **Mercato Orientale,** Genoa's sprawling indoor food market, evokes the days when ships brought back spices and other commodities from the ends of the Earth. Still a boisterous affair and an excellent place to stock up on olives, herbs, fresh fruit, and other Ligurian products, it is held Monday through Saturday from 7am to 1pm and 3:30 to 7:30pm (closed Wed afternoons), with entrances on Via XX Settembre and Via Galata (about halfway between Piazza de Ferrari at the edge of the old city and Stazione Brignole). The district just north of the market (especially V. San Vincenzo and V. Colombo) is a gourmand's dream, with many bakeries, *pasticcerie* (pastry shops), and stores selling pasta, cheese, wine, olive oil, and other foodstuffs.

GETTING AROUND   Given Genoa's labyrinth of small streets (many of which cannot be negotiated by taxi or bus), the only easy way to get around much of the city is **on foot.** This, however, can be a navigational feat that requires a good map. You can get a basic one for free at the tourist office, but it is woefully inadequate and lists only major arteries; purchase a more detailed map, preferably one with a good street index and a section showing the old city in detail, at a newsstand. Genovese are usually happy to direct visitors, but given the geography with which they are dealing, their instructions can be complicated. You should also be aware that Genoa's archaic street-numbering system seems to have been designed to baffle tourists: Addresses in red (marked with an *r*) generally indicate a commercial establishment; those in black are offices or residences. So, two buildings on the same street can have the same number, one in black, one in red.

By Bus   Bus tickets (1€/$1.15; valid for 90 min.) are available at newsstands and at ticket booths, *tabacchi* (tobacconists, marked by a brown-and-white T sign), most newsstands, and the train stations; look for the symbol **AMT** (© 010-5582414; www.amt.genova.it). You must stamp your ticket when you board a bus. Bus tickets can also be used on most of the funiculars and public elevators that climb the city's hills. Day tickets cost 3€ ($3.45).

By Taxi   Metered taxis, which you can find at cab stands, are an especially convenient and safe way to get around Genoa at night—or by day, for that matter, if you are tired of navigating mazelike streets or trying to decipher the city's elaborate bus system. For instance, you may well want to consider taking a taxi from a restaurant in the old city to your hotel or to one of the train stations (especially Stazione Brignole, which is quite a bit farther). Cab stands at Piazza della Nunziata, Piazza Fontane Marose, and Piazza de Ferrari are especially convenient to the old city, or call a **radio taxi** at © 010-5966. The initial charge is 3€ ($3.45), and each additional kilometer is .75€ (85¢). Expect to pay an additional 2€ ($2.30) for trips to and from the airport, any trip between 10pm and 6am, and on Sundays. There's a .50€ (55¢) fee for each piece of luggage.

SIGHTS TO SEE

Acquario di Genova (Aquarium of Genoa) (Kids)   Europe's largest
aquarium is one of Genoa's biggest draws and a must-see for travelers with children. The structure itself is remarkable, resembling a ship and built alongside a pier in the old harbor (the aquarium is about a 15-min. walk from Stazione Principe and about 10 min. from V. Garibaldi). Inside, more than 50 aquatic displays realistically re-create Red Sea coral reefs, pools in the tropical rainforests of the Amazon River basin, and other marine ecosystems. New in 2004 are exhibits on Italy's protected marine areas and a touching pool, as well as an Antarctic tank. These environments provide a pleasant home for sharks, seals, and just about every other known kind of sea creature. Even the displays are fun—one room is a forest of transparent columns eerily lit and filled with jellyfish; the playful seals and dolphins like to blow trick bubbles to entertain you; and there are small rays in a shallow pool you can pet. All the descriptions are posted in English. There's also a 10-minute 3-D film on ocean life (ask for a sheet with the narration's English translation).

Ponte Spinola. © 010-2345678. www.acquariodigenova.it. Admission 13€ ($15) adults, 11€ ($13) seniors over 65, 8€ ($9) ages 4–12, free for children under 4. Sept 1–June 30 Mon–Wed and Fri 9:30am–7:30pm, Thurs 9:30am–10pm; July to mid-Aug daily 9:30am–11pm. Last admission 90 min. before close. Bus: 1, 2, 3, 4, 5, 6, 7, 8, 12, 13, 14, 15.

Cattedrale San Lorenzo   The austerity of this black-and-white-striped
12th-century structure is enlivened ever so slightly by the fanciful French Gothic carvings around the portal and the presence of two stone lions. A later addition is the campanile, completed in the 16th century and containing at one corner a beloved Genoa artifact—a sundial known as L'Arrotino (the knife grinder) for

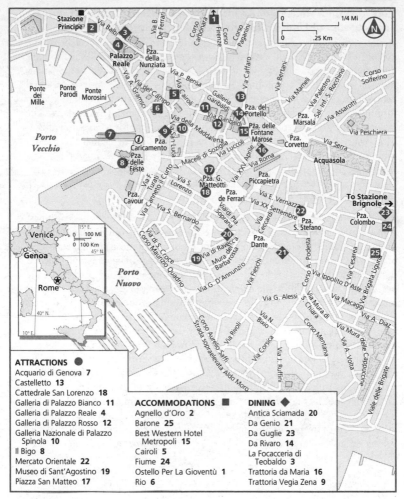

ATTRACTIONS ●

Acquario di Genova **7**
Castelletto **13**
Cattedrale San Lorenzo **18**
Galleria di Palazzo Bianco **11**
Galleria di Palazzo Reale **4**
Galleria di Palazzo Rosso **12**
Galleria Nazionale di Palazzo
  Spinola **10**
Il Bigo **8**
Mercato Orientale **22**
Museo di Sant'Agostino **19**
Piazza San Matteo **17**

ACCOMMODATIONS ■

Agnello d'Oro **2**
Barone **25**
Best Western Hotel
  Metropoli **15**
Cairoli **5**
Fiume **24**
Ostello Per La Gioventù **1**
Rio **6**

DINING ◆

Antica Sciamada **20**
Da Genio **21**
Da Guglie **23**
Da Rivaro **14**
La Focacceria di
  Teobaldo **3**
Trattoria da Maria **16**
Trattoria Vegia Zena **9**

its utilitarian appearance. In the frescoed interior, chapels house two of Genoa's most notable curiosities: Beyond the first pilaster on the right is an unexploded shell fired through the roof from a British ship offshore during World War II; and in the Cappella di San Giovanni (left aisle), a 13th-century crypt contains what crusaders returning from the Holy Land claimed to be relics of John the Baptist. Fabled tableware of doubtful provenance appears to be a quirk of the adjoining treasury: The plate upon which Saint John's head was supposedly served to Salome, a bowl allegedly used at the Last Supper, and a bowl thought at one time to be the Holy Grail. The less fabled but nonetheless magnificent gold and bejeweled objects here reflect Genoa's medieval prominence as a maritime power.

Piazza San Lorenzo. ℂ 010-2471831. Admission to cathedral free; treasury 5.50€ ($6) adults, 4.50€ ($5) students and seniors over 60, 11€ ($12) family ticket for 2 adults and 2 children. Cathedral: Mon–Sat 9am–noon and 3–6pm; Sun noon–6pm. Treasury: by half-hour guided tour only, Mon–Sat 9am–noon and 3–6pm. Bus: 1, 7, 8, 17, 18, 19, 20.

Sant'Agostino—Museo di Architettura e Scultura Ligure (St. Augustine Museum of Ligurian Architecture and Sculpture) ⓐ   The cloisters
of the 13th-century church and monastery of Sant'Agostino (most of which, except its two cloisters and a campanile, were destroyed in World War II bombings) are the evocative setting for an eclectic and fascinating collection of architectural fragments and sculpture. Roman columns, statuary, and architectural debris from Genoa's churches are scattered in what seems to be random fashion throughout the grassy monastery gardens and in a few bare interior spaces. The treasures here are the panels from Giovanni Pisano's crypt for Margherita of Brabant, wife of the German emperor Henry IV. She died in Genoa in 1312 en route to Rome for her husband's coronation as Holy Roman Emperor.

Piazza Sarzanno 35r. ⓒ 010-2511263 or 010-5572057. www.museosantagostino.it. Admission 4€ ($4.60), free for those under 18 or 65 and those with Card Musei. Tues–Fri 9am–7pm; Sat–Sun 10am–7pm. Bus: 17, 18, 19, 20, 31, 33, 35, 37, 40, 41; Volabus: 100.

Galleria di Palazzo Bianco (White Palace) ⓐⓐ   One of Genoa's finest
palaces, built of white stone by the powerful Grimaldi family in the 16th century and enlarged in the 18th century, houses the city's most notable collection of art. The paintings reflect the fine eye of the duchess of Galliera, who donated the palace and her art to the city in 1884. Her preference for painters of the northern schools, whom the affluent Genovese imported to decorate their palaces and paint their portraits, becomes strikingly obvious. Van Dyck and Rubens, both of whom came to Genoa in the early 17th century, are represented here with one painting each, as they are in the city's other major collections. One of the museum's most notable holdings is *Portrait of a Lady,* by Lucas Cranach the Elder. The collection also includes works by other European and Italian masters (Filippino Lippi, Veronese, Palma il Giovane, Caravaggio, Hans Memling, Jan Steen, Murillo, Ribera), including several Genovese masters who were the catalyst for the city's flourishing art movements—an entire room is dedicated to the works of Bernardo Strozzi, whose early-17th-century school made Genoa an important force in the baroque movement. The palazzo reopened in 2004 following extensive renovations; open hours weren't finalized at press time, so call ahead to confirm.

Via Garibaldi 11. ⓒ 010-5572013 or 010-5572203. www.museopalazzobianco.it. Admission 7€ ($8), free for those under 18 or over 65 and those with the Card Musei. Tues–Sat 9am–7pm; Sun 10am–7pm. Bus: 17, 18, 19, 20, 31, 37, 40, 41; Volabus: 100.

Galleria di Palazzo Reale (Royal Palace)   The Royal Palace takes its name
from its 19th- to early-20th-century tenants, the Royal House of Savoy, who greatly altered the 17th-century palace built for the Balbi family. The Savoys

---

A Money-Saving Tip

Genoa has recently expanded benefits for holders of the **Card Musei di Genova (museum card).** The card, available in 1- and 3-day versions (with or without free usage of the public transportation system), is good for one entry to each of about **20 of the city's museums.** A 1-day card is 8€ ($9) without transportation and 9€ ($10) with transportation. The 3-day card is 12€ ($14) without transportation and 15€ ($17) with transportation. The museum card—sold at tourist offices and the admissions offices of participating museums—will also get you a small discount on admission to the city's aquarium.

endowed the sumptuous surroundings with ostentatious frippery, covered with elaborate 17th- and 18th-century stuccowork and frescoes, most in evidence in the hall of mirrors, the ballroom, and the throne room. The rooms are filled with the dusty accouterments of the Italian royalty who once lived here (or at least used it as a home when they occasionally passed through). A lot of paintings by relative nobodies are interspersed with a few by Tintoretto, Luca Giordano (in the crushed-velvet throne room), and Van Dyck. The English placards explaining each room will help you identify them.

Via Balbi 10. © 010-2710236. www.palazzorealegenova.it. Admission 4€ ($4.60), 2€ ($2.30) 18–25, free for those under 18 or over 65. Cumulative ticket with Palazzo Spinola 6.50€ ($7). Tues–Wed 9am–1:30pm; Thurs–Sun 9am–7pm. Bus: 17, 18, 19, 20, 31, 37, 40, 41; Volabus: 100.

Galleria di Palazzo Rosso (Red Palace)   Another lavish 17th-century palace now houses, as does its neighbor the Palazzo Bianco, a magnificent collection of art. Many of the works—including many lavish frescoes—were commissioned or acquired by the Brignole-Sale, an aristocratic family who once lived in this red-stone palace. Van Dyck painted two members of the clan, Pauline and Anton Giulio Brignole-Sale, and their full-length portraits are among the masterpieces in the second-floor portrait galleries, whose ceilings were frescoed by Gregorio de Ferrari and Domenico Piola. *La Cuoca*, widely considered to be the finest work of Genovese master Bernardo Strozzi, and works by many other Italian and European masters—Guido Reni, Dürer, Titian, Guercino, and Veronese, among them—hang in the first-floor galleries.

Via Garibaldi 18. © 010-2476351. www.museopalazzorosso.it. Admission 7€ ($8), free for those under 18 or over 65. Tues–Fri 9am–7pm; Sat–Sun 10am–7pm. Bus: 17, 18, 19, 20, 31, 37, 40, 41; Volabus: 100.

Galleria Nazionale di Palazzo Spinola *&*   Another prominent Genovese family, the Spinolas, donated their palace and magnificent art collection to the city only recently, in 1958. One of the pleasures of viewing these works is seeing them amid the frescoed splendor in which the city's merchant/banking families once lived. As in Genoa's other art collections, you will find masterworks that range far beyond works of native artists like Strozzi and De Ferrari. In fact, perhaps the most memorable painting here is *Ecce Homo*, by the Sicilian master Antonello da Messina. Guido Reni and Luca Giordano are also well represented, as are Van Dyck (including his fragmentary *Portrait of Ansaldo Pallavicino* and four of the *Evangelists*) and other painters of the Dutch and Flemish schools, whom Genoa's wealthy burghers were so fond of importing to paint their portraits.

Piazza Pellicceria 1. © 010-2705300 or 010-2530450. www.palazzospinola.it. Admission 4€ ($4.60) adults, 2€ ($2.30) ages 18–25, free for those under 18 or over 65, 6.50€ ($7) cumulative with Palazzo Reale. Tues–Sat 8:30am–7:30pm; Sun 1–8pm. Bus: 17, 18, 19, 20, 31, 37, 40, 41; Volabus: 100.

HISTORIC SQUARES & STREETS

PIAZZA SAN MATTEO   This beautiful little square is the domain of the city's most acclaimed family, the seagoing Dorias, who ruled Genoa until the end of the 18th century. The church they built on the piazza in the 12th century, San Matteo, contains the crypt of the Dorias' most illustrious son, Andrea. The cloisters are lined with centuries-old plaques heralding the family's many accomplishments, which included drawing up Genoa's constitution in 1529. The church is open Monday through Saturday from 8am to noon and 4 to 5pm, and Sunday from 4 to 5pm. The **Doria palaces** surround the church in a stunning array of loggias and black-and-white-striped marble facades denoting the homes of honored citizens—Andrea's at **no. 17,** Lamda's at **no. 15,** Branca's at

no. 14. To get there, take bus nos. 18, 19, 20, 32, 33, 35, 37, 40, 41, 100, 605, 606, or 607.

VIA GARIBALDI ✦✦   Many of Genoa's museums and other sights are clustered on and around this street, one of the most beautiful in Italy, where Genoa's wealthy families built palaces in the 16th and 17th centuries. Aside from the art collections housed in the **Palazzo Bianco** and **Palazzo Rosso** (see above), the street contains a wealth of other treasures. The **Palazzo Podesta,** at no. 7, hides one of the city's most beautiful fountains in its courtyard, and the **Palazzo Turisi,** at no. 9, now housing the municipal offices, proudly displays artifacts of famous Genoans: letters written by Christopher Columbus and the violin of Nicolo Paganini (which is still played on special occasions). Visitors are allowed free entry to the building when the offices are open: Monday through Friday from 8:30am to noon and 1 to 4pm. To get there, take bus nos. 19, 20, 32, 33, 35, 36, 41, 42, 100, 605, or 606.

PIAZZA DANTE   Though most of the square is made of 1930s office buildings, one end is bounded by the twin round towers of the reconstructed **Porta Soprana,** a town gate built in 1155. The main draw, though, is the small **house** (rebuilt in the 18th c.) still standing a bit incongruously in a tidy little park below the gate, said to have belonged to Christopher Columbus's father, who was a weaver and gatekeeper (whether young Christopher lived here is open to debate). Also in the tiny park are the reconstituted 12th-century **cloisters of Sant'Andrea,** a convent that was demolished nearby.

VIEWS & VISTAS

The **no. 33 bus** plies the scenic **Circonvallazione a Monte,** the corniche that hugs the hills and provides dizzying views over the city and the sea; you can board at Stazione Brignole or Stazione Principe.

From Piazza Portello (off the eastern end of V. Garibaldi, just before the Galleria Garibaldi tunnel), an elevator carries you up to the **Castelletto belvedere,** which offers stunning views and refreshing breezes and provides a handy break during sightseeing in the central city for .50€ (60¢) each way, daily from 6:40am to midnight.

A similar, view-affording climb is the one on the **Granarolo funicular,** a cog railway that leaves from Piazza del Principe, just behind the railway station of the same name, and ascends 300m (984 ft.) to Porto Granarolo, one of the gates in the city's 17th-century walls. There's a parklike belvedere in front. (The cost is 1€/$1.15 each way, or you can use a bus ticket; it operates daily every 15 min. 7am–11:45pm.)

An elevator lifts visitors to the top of **Il Bigo,** the modernistic, mastlike tower that is the new landmark of Genoa, built to commemorate the Columbus quincentennial celebrations in 1992. The observation platform provides an eagle's-eye view of one of Europe's busiest ports for 3.30€ ($3.80) for adults, 2€ ($2.30) for ages 4 to 12, and free for children under 4. March through May and September, it's open Tuesday through Saturday from 10am to 6pm. June through August, it's open Sunday, Tuesday, and Wednesday from 10am to 6pm; Thursday through Saturday from 10am to 11pm; and Monday from 2 to 8pm. Winter hours are shorter.

Hour-long **harbor cruises** *(giro del porto)* on one of the boats in the fleet of **Cooperativa Battellieri dei Porto di Genova** (✆ **010-265712;** www.battellieri genova.it) provide a closer look at the bustle, along with close-up views of the

Lanterna, the 108m (354-ft.) lighthouse (tallest in Europe) built in 1544 at the height of Genoa's maritime might (you can ride to the top Sun afternoons only; visits leave from the Bigo at 2:30pm). Boats embark daily from Porto Antico, near the aquarium, and the trip costs 6€ ($7) for adults; it's free for children under 5.

ACCOMMODATIONS YOU CAN AFFORD

Genoa is geared more to business than to tourism, and as a result, decent inexpensive rooms are scarce. On the other hand, just about the only time the town is booked solid is during its annual boat show, the world's largest, in October. Except for the ones included below, avoid hotels in the old city, especially around the harbor—most are unsafe and prefer to accommodate guests by the hour.

Agnello d'Oro This converted convent enjoys a wonderful location—only a few short blocks from Stazione Principe, yet on the edge of the old city. And the dead-end side street in front ensures peace and quiet. A few of the lower-floor rooms retain the building's original 16th-century character, with high (rooms numbered in teens) or vaulted (rooms numbered under 10) ceilings. Those upstairs have been completely renovated in crisp modern style, with warm-hued tile floors and mostly modular furnishings. The tiled bathrooms are new and spotless, though many have only curtainless tubs with hand-held nozzles. Singles all come with those lovely extra-wide "French-style" beds. Some top-floor rooms come with air-conditioning and the added charm of balconies and views over the old town and harbor (best from no. 56). The friendly proprietor dispenses wine, sightseeing tips, and breakfast in the cozy little bar off the lobby.

Via Monachette 6 (off V. Balbi), 16126 Genova. ℂ 010-2462084. Fax 010-2462327. www.hotelagnello doro.it. 25 units. 75€ ($86) single; 90€ ($104) double. Ask about lower rates on weekends and in the off season. Rates include breakfast. AE, DC, MC, V. Parking 13€ ($15). Bus: 18, 19, 20, 30, 32, 34, 35, 37, 41, 54, 100, 605. **Amenities:** Bar; concierge; 24-hr. room service; nonsmoking rooms. *In room:* A/C (top floor), TV, hair dryer (4 rooms).

Barone Near Stazione Brignole, this family-run pensione occupies the high-ceilinged large rooms of what was once a grand apartment. And, a rarity in Genoa, it offers unusually pleasant accommodations at very reasonable rates. Marco, the young proprietor, affords a gracious welcome, pointing guests to nearby restaurants, telling them what not to miss, and joining them in the communal sitting room. Self-service espresso is available around the clock. The rooms are indeed baronial in size (some can be set up with extra beds for families) and are reached by elegant halls hung with gilt mirrors and paintings. While the eclectic furnishings are a bit less grand, many retain lovely touches like a stuccoed ceiling here (in most, actually) or a chandelier there. The beds are firm and comfortable, the linens are fresh, the TVs are hooked up with Sky TV, and the shared facilities are spotless. One technically bathroomless accommodation has a shower in the room, but you must share the hall toilets. In 2003, Marco renovated the communal bathrooms, and in 2004 he refurbished the guest rooms.

Via XX Settembre 2 (3rd floor), 16121 Genova. ℂ/fax 010-587578. www.hotelsgiovani.com. 12 units, 1 with bathroom (11 with shower, no toilet). 40€ ($46) single with shower, 49€ ($56) single with bathroom; 50€ ($58) double with shower, 58€ ($67) double with bathroom; 67€ ($77) triple with shower, 78€ ($90) triple with bathroom; 85€ ($98) quad with shower. No breakfast. MC, V. Free parking on street (ask for permit). Bus: Any to Stazione Brignole. **Amenities:** Bar; nonsmoking rooms. *In room:* TV, hair dryer (upon request), safe (in 1 room), no phone.

Best Western Hotel Metropoli Facing a lovely historic square just around the corner from the Via Garibaldi, the Metropoli brings modern amenities, combined with a gracious ambience, to the old city. No small part of the appeal of staying here is that many of the surrounding streets are open only to pedestrians, so you can step out of the hotel and avoid the onrush of traffic that plagues much of central Genoa. Guest rooms have somewhat banal and businesslike contemporary furnishings, but all were redone in 2004, and with double-paned windows and pleasing pastel fabrics, they provide an oasis of calm in this often unnerving city. The style of the renovated rooms is more or less the same, but the furnishings are nicer; the biggest difference is the newly refurbished bathrooms, now equipped with hair dryers, heated towel racks, and double sinks with lots of marble counter space.

Piazza Fontane Marose, 16123 Genova. (C) **800-820080** in Italy, or 010-2468888. Fax 010-2468686. www.bestwestern.it/metropoli_ge. 48 units. 87€–142€ ($100–$163) single; 100€–180€ ($114–$207) double; 116€–220€ ($133–$253) triple. Lower rates during slow periods. Rates include buffet breakfast. AE, DC, MC, V. Parking 20€ ($23) in nearby garage. Bus: 17, 18, 19, 20, 31, 37, 40, 41; Volabus: 100. **Amenities:** Bar; concierge; limited room service; laundry service; same-day dry cleaning; nonsmoking rooms. *In room:* A/C, TV, dataport, minibar, coffeemaker, hair dryer.

Cairoli Location is a bonus at this pleasant family-run hotel on the third floor of an old building a little ways south of Stazione Principe and near the port, the aquarium, Via Garibaldi, and the sights of the old city. The small rooms are extremely pleasant, with tasteful modern furnishings and tidy little bathrooms; double-paned glass keeps street noise to a minimum, and the new air conditioners will keep you cool. The friendly management leaves a little basket of snacks in your room (cookies, crackers, and Pringles) and has a soft spot for stray cats (four of them roam the place). In good weather, you can relax on a terrace covered with potted plants (compact no. 9 opens onto it). Room no. 14 is perfect for families, with two twin beds in the first room and a double bed in a back room separated by a curtain. The hoteliers are in the process of sprucing up some of the Cairoli's public areas, including the breakfast and reading rooms, and are also installing a small exercise room.

Via Cairoli 14, 16124 Genova. (C) **010-2461454.** Fax 010-2467512. www.hotelcairoligenova.com. 12 units. 47€–77€ ($54–$89) single; 73€–88€ ($84–$101) double. Breakfast 6€ ($6.90). AE, DC, MC, V. Parking 15€–20€ ($17–$23) in nearby garage. Bus: 18, 19, 20, 30, 34, 35, 37, 39, 40, 41. **Amenities:** Concierge; tour desk; car-rental desk; laundry service; same-day dry cleaning; nonsmoking rooms. *In room:* A/C, TV, dataport, minibar.

Fiume I don't include this choice as a memorable hotel experience. Rather, the Fiume is a serviceable budget option, clean, safe, and close to Stazione Brignole as well as to Genoa's intriguing Mercato Orientale food market and the profusion of food and wine shops around it. The desk staff in the brightly lit lobby can be brusquely efficient as they direct you to the rather run-down rooms, where the furnishings consist of little more than cotlike beds, tables, and functional chairs. Even so, everything—including shared facilities in the halls—is immaculate, and the travelers from around the world who stay here provide good company. This being a 19th-century palazzo, the second-floor rooms are more spacious, with higher ceilings than those on the first floor (no elevator). All rooms except a few singles have a shower and sink in the room, but toilets are shared, with the exception of those in two doubles and two singles.

Via Fiume 9r, 16121 Genova. (C) **010-591691.** Fax 010-5702833. 20 units, all but a few singles with shower (but no toilet), but only 4 with private bathroom. 30€–40€ ($35–$46) single with shower, 30€–60€ ($35–$69) single with bathroom; 30€–60€ ($35–$69) double with shower, 40€–70€ ($46–$81) double with bathroom. Breakfast not offered (there's a bar next door). AE, MC, V. Bus: Any to Stazione Brignole. *In room:* TV, hair dryer.

Rio   It's a bit of a dump, but it's a cheap, well-located dump! The Rio is wonderfully located amid the clamor and intrigue of the old city and just a few steps from the port and aquarium. In fact, the Rio provides just about the only decent accommodations so close to the old harbor area. (You'll want to keep your wits about you, though, when coming and going late at night.) The guest rooms tend to be large and are equipped with modern furnishings that do the job well enough, but bathrooms are hurting for an overhaul. *Tip:* Upper floors tend to be a bit nicer. Genoa's convention facilities are nearby, so reservations are essential at periods when the city hosts one of its trade fairs (many are held in Oct).

Via Ponte Calvi 5 (off V. Gramsci), 16124 Genova. ℂ 010-2461594. Fax 010-2476871. 42 units. 30€–60€ ($35–$69) single; 60€–80€ ($69–$92) double. Rates include breakfast. AE, MC, V. Parking 16€ ($18). Bus: 1, 2, 3, 7, 8, 54. **Amenities:** Bar. *In room:* TV, dataport, fridge (in some), hair dryer (in some).

GREAT DEALS ON DINING

Da Genio GENOVESE   One of Genoa's most beloved trattorias, handily situated near Piazza Dante in the old quarter, Da Genio is wonderfully animated. Local artists' works brighten the cozy dining rooms, which are almost always full of Genovese businesspeople and families who have been coming here for years. The assorted antipasti provide a nice introduction to local cuisine, with such specialties as stuffed sardines and *torte di verdure* (vegetable pie). While the menu usually includes a nice selection of fresh fish and some meat dishes (including delicious tripe or steak with porcini), you can also move on to some of the homey standbys the kitchen does so well, such as *spaghetti al sugo di pesce* (topped with a fish sauce) or an amazingly fresh *insalata di mare* (seafood salad)—though almost everyone starts off with *trenette al pesto* (small pasta twists in pesto). The wine list includes a nice selection from Ligurian vineyards.

Salita San Leonardo 61r. ℂ **010-588463.** Reservations recommended. Primi 7€–11€ ($8.05–$13); secondi 8.50€–14€ ($9.80–$16). AE, MC, V. Mon–Sat 12:30–3pm and 7:30–10pm. Closed Aug.

Da Guglie LIGURIAN   The busy kitchen, with its open hearth, occupies a good part of this simple restaurant, which serves this neighborhood near Stazione Brignole with takeout fare from a counter and accommodates diners in a bare-bones little room off to one side. In fact, there's no attempt at all to provide a decorative ambience. The specials of the day (which often include octopus and other seafood) are displayed in the window. Tell the cooks behind the counter what you want, and they will bring it over to one of the oilcloth-covered tables when it's ready. Don't be shy about asking for a sampling of the reasonably priced dishes because you can happily eat your way through Genovese cuisine here. *Farinata* (chickpea crepes), focaccia with many different toppings, gnocchi with pesto, *riso di carciofi* (rice with artichokes), and other dishes are accompanied by Ligurian wines served by the glass or carafe.

Via San Vincenzo 64r. ℂ **010-565765.** Primi 3.50€–7.50€ ($4.05–$8.65); secondi 5€–11€ ($5.75–$13). No credit cards. Daily noon–10pm.

Da Rivaro LIGURIAN/ITALIAN   Wonderfully located amid the Renaissance splendor of the nearby Via Garibaldi, this old institution does a brisk business with a loyal clientele from nearby banks and consulates, especially at lunch and in the early evening. The decor is pleasantly reminiscent of a ship's cabin, with inlaid wooden panels and long wooden tables lit by brass lanterns. Many of the attentive, white-jacketed waiters have worked here their entire careers. Ligurian classics, such as *trenette al pesto con patate e fagiolini* (pasta with pesto, potatoes, and beans) and a *zuppa da pesce* made with local fish, emerge from the kitchen, but the menu also ventures far beyond Genoa to include a wide range of pastas from other regions (many with tomato and cream sauces) and grilled meats.

Via di Portello 16r. ⓒ 010-2770054. Reservations recommended. Primi 8€–9€ ($9.20–$10); secondi 9€–13€ ($10–$15); fixed-price menu 25€ ($29). AE, DC, MC, V. Mon–Sat noon–3pm and 6–11pm.

Trattoria da Maria LIGURIAN   Maria Mante is something of a local legend and for decades has turned out delicious meals from her busy kitchen, attended by relatives young and old. Her cooking and the congenial ambience of the two-floor restaurant in the old city near Piazza delle Fontane Marose draw a crowd of neighborhood residents, students, businesspeople, and tourists of all nationalities. This unlikely mix sits side by side at long tables covered with red- or blue-checked tablecloths and engages in animated conversation, while the staff hurries around them and shouts orders up and down the shaft of a dumbwaiter. Daily specials and the stupendously cheap fixed-price menu of the day—which often includes *minestrone alla genovese, risotto buonissimo alla genovese* (rice stirred with a sauce; they also feel secure labeling their creamy gelato "buonissimo"), *zuppe da pesce* (a rich fish soup you must try if it's available), and such simple main courses as a filet of fish sautéed in white wine, or grilled sausages—are listed on sheets of paper posted to the shiny, pale-green walls. As befits a Genovese institution like this, the pasta with pesto sauce is especially delicious, as is *pansotti*, small ravioli covered with a walnut-cream sauce.

Vico Testadoro 14r (just off V. XX Aprile). ⓒ 010-581080. Primi 3€–3.50€ ($3.45–$4.05); secondi 4€–5.50€ ($4.60–$6.30); *menu turistico* 10€ ($12) with wine. MC, V. Sun and Tues–Fri 11:45am–2:15pm and 7–9:15pm; Mon 11:45am–2:45pm.

Trattoria Vegia Zena GENOVESE   In the *centro storico* near the old port (in an alley across from the aquarium), this lively, white-walled and wood-paneled room lives up to its name—dialect for "Old Genoa"—with expertly prepared Genovese dishes. Since the restaurant is very popular with Genovese from all over the city who consider this their favorite place to dine, you may well be asked to share one of the crowded tables with other diners. Pasta with pesto is excellent, followed by a fine selection of fresh seafood.

Vico del Serriglio 15r. ⓒ 010-2513332. Primi 6€–19€ ($6.90–$22); secondi 7.50€–25€ ($8.60–$29). MC, V. Tues–Sat noon–2:30pm and 7:30–10pm; Mon noon–2:30pm.

PASTRY & GELATO

The **Antica Pasticceria Gelateria Klainguti** 𝕽𝕽, on Piazza Soziglia 98r–100r (ⓒ 010-2474552), is Genoa's best bakery as well as its oldest—it was founded in 1828 by a Swiss family. One satisfied customer was the composer Giuseppe Verdi, who said the house's Falstaff (a sweet brioche) was better than his. This and a stupefying assortment of other pastries and chocolates, as well as light snacks (including panini), are served in a pretty rococo-style room or on the piazza out front. It's open daily from 8am to 7pm.

Add **Bananarama**, Via San Vincenzo 65r (ⓒ 010-581130), to your explorations of the many food shops and markets in the neighborhood near Stazione Brignole. Is this the best gelato in Genoa? The jury is still out, but the creamy concoctions are indeed memorable. Just as good are the simple *granites*, shaved ice with fresh fruit flavorings. It's open Monday through Saturday from 9am to 7:30pm.

Just off the waterfront and near the fairgrounds, the simple, no-frills **Cremeria Augusto**, Via Nino Bixio 5 (ⓒ 010-591884), is almost a mandatory stop in

Fast Food, Genoa Style

Fast food is a Genovese specialty, and any number of storefronts all over the city disburse focaccia, the heavenly Ligurian flatbread often stuffed with cheese and topped with herbs, olives, onions, vegetables, or prosciutto. A favorite place for focaccia, and so close to Stazione Principe that you can stop in for a taste of this aromatic delicacy as soon as you step off the train, is **La Focacceria di Teobaldo** ★, Via Balbi 115r (✆ **010-2462294**), open daily from 8am to 8pm; focaccia begins at .50€ (60¢) a slice.

Another Genovese favorite is ***farinata,*** a cross between a ravioli and a crepe made from chickpea flour that is stuffed with spinach and ricotta, lightly fried, and often topped with a cream and walnut sauce. Locals say this delicious concoction gets no better than it is at the two outlets of **Antica Sciamadda,** Via Ravecca 19r (✆ **010-200516**) and Via San Giorgio 14r, both open Monday through Saturday from 9am to 7:30pm; from 2€ ($2.30).

this part of the city. The house makes dozens of flavors of rich, delicious gelato fresh daily, and it is marvelous, but the specialty is crema, a frozen egg custard. It's open Sunday through Friday to 10pm.

GENOA AFTER DARK

The harbor area, much of which is unsafe even in broad daylight, is especially unseemly at night. Confine late-hour prowls in the old city to the well-trafficked streets around Piazza Fontane Marose and Piazza delle Erbe, where many bars and clubs are located anyway.

PERFORMING ARTS Genoa has two major venues for culture: **Teatro Carlo Felice,** Piazza de Ferrari (✆ **010-589329** or 010-591697; www.carlofelice.it), is home to Genoa's opera company and hosts visiting companies as well. **Teatro delle Corte** (✆ **010-5342200;** www.teatro-di-genova.it), on Piazza Borgo Pila near Stazione Brignole, hosts concerts, dance events, and other cultural programs.

BARS & CLUBS Open all day, **Brittania** at Vico Casana (just off Piazza de Ferrari) serves pints to homesick travelers from morning to night, but caters to a largely Italian crowd at night (✆ **010-2474532**).

New Yorkers will recognize the name and chic ambience from the branch of **Antica Cantina i Tre Merli,** at Vico Dietro il Coro della Maddalena 26r (✆ **010-2474095;** www.itremerli.it), which does a brisk business in Manhattan with several restaurants (two in downtown, one uptown). Here in Genoa, I Tre Merli operates several enotecas, and this one, with a location on a narrow street just off Via Garibaldi that makes it a safe nightspot in the old city, is delightful. A dark stone floor and walls of brick and stone provide a cozy setting, augmented by "refined country" style tables and chairs. You can sample the wide selection of wines from throughout Italy by the glass, and there is a full bar. The half-dozen each of primi and secondi are refined Ligurian and, along with the cheese and salami platters, make this a good spot for a late-night meal. It's open Monday through Friday noon to 3pm and 7pm to 1am, and on Saturday from 7pm to 1am.

Le Courbusier, Via San Donato 36 (© 010-2468652), opens early and closes late. This coffeehouse-cum-bar in the old quarter just west of Piazza delle Erbe is especially popular with students. The smoky room is perpetually busy, dispensing excellent coffee and sandwiches (from 3€/$3.45) as well as wine and spirits.

2 The Riviera di Ponente

San Remo: 140km (87 miles) W of Genoa, 59km (37 miles) E of Nice

SAN REMO

Gone are the days when Tchaikovsky and the Russian empress Maria Alexandranova joined a well-heeled mix of titled Continental and British gentry in strolling along San Remo's palm-lined avenues. They left behind an onion-domed Orthodox church, a few grand hotels, and a snooty casino, but **San Remo** is a different sort of town these days. It's still the most cosmopolitan stop on the Riviera di Ponente (Setting Sun), as the stretch of coast west of Genoa is called, catering mostly to sun-seeking Italian families in the summer and elderly Romans and Milanese who come to enjoy the balmy temperatures in the winter.

In addition to the gentle ambience of days gone by, San Remo offers its visitors a long stretch of beach and a hilltop old town known as La Pigna. For cosmopolitan pleasures, the casino attracts a well-attired clientele willing to try their luck.

San Remo is an excellent base from which to explore the rocky coast and Ligurian hills. So is Bordighera, a quieter resort just up the coast. With excellent train and bus connections, both are within easy reach of a full itinerary of fascinating stops, including Giardino Hanbury, one of Europe's most exquisite gardens; the fascinating prehistoric remains at Balzi Rossi; and Docleacqua, perhaps the most enticing of all the inland Ligurian villages.

ESSENTIALS

GETTING THERE   By Train   There are trains (www.trenitalia.com) almost hourly to and from **Genoa** (regional: 2½ hr., 7.70€/$9; high speed: 1¾ hr., 11€/$13). There are two trains per hour connecting with **Bordighera** (8–10 min.; 1.35€/$1.55). Trains from Genoa continue west for another 15 to 20 minutes to **Ventimiglia** on the French border (1.60€/$1.85). From Ventimiglia, you can continue across the border on one of the hourly trains to **Nice,** 40 minutes west.

By Bus   Riviera Trasporti buses (© 0184-592706; www.rivieratrasporti.it) run every 15 minutes between San Remo and **Bordighera** (20 min.; 1.70€/$1.95). Almost as many buses continue on to **Ventimiglia** (40 min. from San Remo; 1.70€/$1.95).

By Car   The fastest driving route in and out of San Remo is the A10 autostrada, which follows the coast from the French border (20 min. away) to Genoa (about 45 min. away). The slower coast road, S1, cuts right through the center of town.

VISITOR INFORMATION   The **APT tourist board** is at Largo Nuvoloni 1 (© 0184-59059; fax 0184-507649; www.rivieradeifiori.org or www.san remonet.com), at the corner with Corso Imperatrice/Corso Matteotti (exit the train station, cross the street, and walk to the left a few hundred ft.). It's open Monday through Saturday from 8am to 7pm and Sunday from 9am to 1pm. In

A Day at the Beach

Plunging into the Ligurian Sea in San Remo means spending some money. The pebbly beach below the Passeggiata dell'Imperatrice is lined with beach stations, where many visitors choose to spend their days—easy to do, since most provide showers, snack bars, and, of course, beach chairs, lounges, and umbrellas. Expect to spend at least 5€ ($5.75) for a basic lounge and up to 15€ ($17) for a more elaborate sun-bed arrangement with umbrella.

addition to a wealth of information on San Remo, the office dispenses information on towns up and down the nearby coast, known as the Riviera dei Fiori.

FESTIVALS   August 15, the **Feast of the Assumption,** is celebrated with special flair in San Remo, with the festival of Nostra Signora della Costa (Our Lady of the Coast). The Virgin Mary allegedly saved a local sailor from drowning, and she is honored with fireworks and a procession in medieval garb to her shrine on a hillside high above the town.

Since the 1950s, the **Sanremo Festival** (www.sanremo.rai.it; late Feb or early Mar) has been Italy's—and one of Europe's—premier music fests. It's sort of an Italian version of the Grammys, only spread out over several days with far more live performances—by Italian pop stars, international headliners, and plenty of up-and-coming singers, songwriters, and bands. "Volare" was Sanremo's first-ever Best Recording, and today if you peruse the CD collections of most Italian households, you'll find at least a few of the yearly compilation albums the festival puts out. The festival has spawned many other contestlike celebrations of film and music (international folk to *musica lirica*) throughout the year, but this is the big one, booking hotels up and down the coast months in advance. Call the tourist office if you want to try to score tickets.

STROLLING AROUND TOWN

Though San Remo has a municipal bus system, you should be able to get anywhere you want on foot. The train station is on the seaside and divides the commercial part of town from the resort and beach area. The tourist board is in front of the station, and just beyond that is the onion-domed **Chiesa Russa** (© **0184-531807**), more formally the Chiesa di Cristo Salvatore, where the Russian nobility who once favored San Remo worshipped. You can step inside for a view of the dark, icon-enriched interior. It's open Tuesday through Sunday from 9:30am to 12:30pm and 3:30 to 6:30pm; suggested donation is .50€ (60¢).

To the left as you leave the station is the beginning of the palm-lined promenade, the **Passeggiata dell'Imperatrice,** which skirts the narrow pebbly strand between the train tracks and the busy coastal road, passing any number of cramped beach stations. One of the more pleasant stops along the way is the **Giardini Comunali Marsaglia** (signposted AUDITORIUM FRANCO ALFANO), a small but luxuriant hillside garden that bursts with exotic flora (open daily dawn to dusk).

To the right of the station are the beginnings of Corso Roma and Corso Giacomo, San Remo's two main thoroughfares. Corso Giacomo will lead you past the **casino** (see below) and into the heart of the lively business district. Continue on it until it becomes Via Matteotti, which, after a block, runs into Piazza Colombo and the flower market. If you turn left (north) on Via Feraldi about midway down Corso Giacomo, you will find yourself in the charming older

Is Board Necessary?

Many hotels offer room-and-board rates that include breakfast, lunch, and dinner (full board or full pension), or breakfast and one of the other two meals (half board or half pension). Only in busy beach season (late July to early Aug) do many require you to take these meals, however. If you can procure a room without the meal plan, do so—San Remo has many excellent restaurants, and this is not a place where you have to spend a lot for a good meal.

precincts of town. Continue through the Piazza degli Eroi Sanremesi to Piazza Mercato, where Via Monta leads into the old medieval quarter, **La Pigna.** The hill on which this fascinating district is located resembles a pine cone in shape, hence the name. Aside from a few restaurants, La Pigna is today a residential quarter, with tall old houses overshadowing the narrow lanes that twist and turn up the hillside to the park-enclosed ruins of a **castle** at the top.

VISITING THE CASINO

Set intimidatingly atop a long flight of steps across from the train station—Corso degli Inglesi swoops around it off Corso Matteotti—San Remo's white palace of a casino (② **0184-5951;** www.casinosanremo.it) not only lords it over the center of town, but it's also the hub of the local nightlife scene. You can't step inside without proper attire (jacket for gents Oct–June) and your passport. From Monday to Thursday admission is free, but Friday through Sunday you must unburden yourself of 7.50€ ($9) to get in—and that's even before you hit the tables, which attract high rollers from the length of the Riviera. Gaming rooms are open daily from 2:30pm to 3am (to 4am on weekends). Things are more relaxed in the rooms set aside for slot machines, where there is neither a dress code nor an entrance fee. These rooms are open Sunday through Friday from 10am to 2:30am and Saturday from 2:30pm to 3am.

ACCOMMODATIONS YOU CAN AFFORD

Al Dom   This rambling, dark, old-fashioned pensione near the casino, city center, and harbor occupies the second floor of a grand 19th-century apartment house. The rooms, basically but nicely furnished with modern pieces and floral bedspreads, are carved out of former salons and tucked into the closed-off ends of ballroom-size hallways; no. 5 has a large balcony over the street. Tiny bathrooms (some of them modular units that resemble the public facilities you find in Paris and other cities) have been appended wherever they might fit. So, be prepared for the unexpected: You may well find yourself staring up at an ornately plastered ceiling from a metal-frame bed crammed next to a marble fireplace. In short, the surroundings may not be stylish, but they are memorable. Hopefully, you reception will be memorable as well, but for the right reasons: The family that runs the pensione can, by turns, be friendly and at other times downright jerks.

Corso Mombello 13, 18038 San Remo. ② 0184-501460. 13 units. 20€–30€ ($23–$35) single; 40€–60€ ($46–$69) double. Rates include breakfast. No credit cards. **Amenities:** Restaurant. *In room:* TV, no phone.

Paradiso ⭐⭐   Three generations of the Gaiani family have run this former villa, set in a pretty garden above the seaside promenade, as a hotel since 1926. Since then, the original villa has been topped off with several extra floors of very pleasant guest rooms, many of which have flower-filled balconies overlooking the sea (a room with a balcony costs slightly more). An understated elegance characterizes these relaxing surroundings. Guest rooms are extremely well maintained to retain the sort of old-fashioned comfort that brings a loyal clientele back year after year for their month by the sea. Furnishings are a homey collection of old armoires, armchairs, and upholstered headboards, and the tiled bathrooms, with large sinks and bathtubs, are luxuriously commodious. Cocktails are served in the comfortable, elegantly furnished salon in the evenings, or in the nicely planted garden in good weather. Guests can take meals in an airy and newly renovated Liberty-style dining room. The owners have added a pool and recently installed air-conditioning in every room.

Via Roccasterone 12, 18038 San Remo. © 0184-571211. Fax 0184-578176. www.paradisohotel.it. 41 units. 54€–105€ ($62–$121) single; 72€–140€ ($83–$161) double. Half board 62€–106€ ($71–$122) per person; full board 74€–119€ ($85–$137) per person. Rates include buffet breakfast. AE, DC, MC, V. Parking 8€ ($9) in hotel garage. **Amenities:** Restaurant; bar; outdoor pool; bike rental; concierge; tour desk; car-rental desk; courtesy car; 24-hr. room service; babysitting; laundry service. *In room:* TV, dataport, minibar, hair dryer.

Sole Mare 𝒢 Don't let the location on a drab side street near the train station put you off. This cheerful pensione on the upper floors of an apartment house is a delight and offers its guests a friendly welcome along with some of the best-value lodgings in the resort area. A lounge, bar area, and dining room are airy and spacious and flooded with light, with gleaming white tile floors, blond-wood furniture, and doors leading out to a wide terrace. The large guest rooms are also cheerful and are equipped with the trappings of much more expensive hotels—pleasant modern furnishings and soothing pastel fabrics, TVs and minibars, small but modern and well-lit bathrooms—and almost all enjoy sea views, about half from wide balconies. Recent renovations included the installation of air-conditioning in 18 of the 21 rooms, as well as construction of a new bar.

Via Carli 23, 18038 San Remo. © 0184-577105. Fax 0184-532778. www.solemarehotel.com. 21 units. 55€ ($63) single; 88€ ($101) double; 120€ ($123) triple. Half board (obligatory in Aug) 50€–63€ ($58–$72) per person. Continental breakfast 6€ ($6.90). AE, DC, MC, V. **Amenities:** Restaurant; bar; concierge; tour desk; car-rental desk; 24-hr. room service; babysitting. *In room:* A/C (in 18 rooms), TV, minibar, hair dryer, safe.

Villa Maria 𝒢𝒢 It's fairly easy to imagine San Remo's turn-of-the-20th-century heyday in this charming hotel incorporating three villas on a flowery hillside above the casino. The promenade is only a short walk downhill, yet the hubbub of the resort seems kilometers away from this leafy residential district. A series of elegant salons and dining rooms with parquet floors, richly paneled ceilings, and crystal chandeliers spread across the ground floor, and many of these public rooms open to a nicely planted terrace. The bedrooms, too, retain the grandeur of the original dwellings, with silk-covered armchairs and antique beds; many have balconies facing the sea. The bathrooms have old-fashioned details such as tubs with hand-held shower nozzles. Since rooms vary considerably in size and decor, ask to look around before you settle on one that strikes your fancy.

Corso Nuvoloni 30, 18038 San Remo. © 0184-531422. Fax 0184-531425. www.villamariahotel.it. 38 units. 42€–68€ ($48–$78) single; 64€–116€ ($74–$133) double. Rates include continental breakfast. Half board (required Easter, Christmas, and Aug 1–15) 53€–78€ ($61–$90) per person; full board 63€–94€ ($72–$108) per person. AE, DC, MC, V. Free parking inside garden. **Amenities:** Restaurant; concierge; babysitting; laundry service. *In room:* TV.

GREAT DEALS ON DINING
Antica Trattoria Piccolo Mondo 𝒢𝒢 *Value* LIGURIAN The attentive staff will make you feel at home the moment you step into the perpetually crowded rooms of this decades-old trattoria on a narrow side street near the waterfront in

the commercial district. The clientele is local, and they come here in droves to enjoy the comfortable atmosphere (which includes the furnishings installed when the restaurant opened in the 1920s) and the distinctly Ligurian fare—*verdura ripiena* (fresh vegetables stuffed with rice and seafood), fresh fish, and *polpo con patate* (octopus with potatoes). The menu changes daily to incorporate what is fresh in the markets, but it also includes excellent risottos, pasta dishes, and meat dishes that are standards. (The grilled veal chop topped with fresh mushrooms is delicious.)

Via Piave 7. © 0184-509012. Reservations recommended. Primi 7€–8€ ($8.05–$9.20); secondi 7€–12€ ($8.05–$14). No credit cards. Tues–Sat 12:30–1:45pm and 7:30–9:30pm.

Cantine Sanremese LIGURIAN

This cozy, publike restaurant devoted to the local cuisine is firmly planted in the center of the modern town, as if to suggest that old San Remo traditions are not to be discarded. Patrons share tables as they enjoy the wide selection of wine by the glass (from 1.50€/$1.70) and sample the offerings that owner Renzo Morselli and his family prepare daily. The best way to dine here is not to order a whole meal, but to sample all the dishes that tempt you. These may include *sardemaira,* the local focaccia-like bread, *torta verde* (a quiche of fresh green vegetables), and many kinds of soups, including a minestrone thick with fresh vegetables and garnished with pesto.

Via Palazzo 7. © 0184-572063. Reservations recommended. Primi and secondi 6.50€–12€ ($7.50–$14). AE, MC, V. Tues–Sun 10am–3pm and 5–9:30pm. Closed last 10 days of June and Nov.

Il Mulattiere ★★ Finds LIGURIAN

Anyone who visits San Remo should plan to visit this family-run trattoria in La Pigna, the oldest part of San Remo. Whether you come for lunch or dinner or just to enjoy a glass of wine, you'll probably first want to stroll around the surrounding quarter, an amazing warren of steep lanes clinging to the side of a hill. This two-floor eatery is as rich in character as its surroundings—the tables, covered with red-checked cloths, are overshadowed by antique farm implements (*Il Mulattiere* means "Mule Driver") and other rural artifacts. The menu is simple, featuring Ligurian specialties that change daily, and often includes delicious *crostini all'acciughe* (toasted bread topped with fresh anchovies), *zuppa al pomodoro* (a spicy soup of fresh tomatoes) or minestrone, and many fresh pastas. For a light meal, you can choose from an antipasto table laden with fresh vegetables and olives, and accompany your choice with a bowl of pasta.

Via Palma 11. © 0184-502662. Primi 4€–8€ ($4.60–$9.20); secondi 6€–8€ ($6.90–$9.20); *menu completo* 9.50€ ($11) includes antipasto and a primo. No credit cards. Thurs–Tues noon–3pm and 7:30–10pm. Closed last 3 weeks of Nov.

Ristorante L'Airone ★ LIGURIAN/PIZZA

With its pale gold walls and green-hued tables and chairs, this delightful, friendly restaurant in a pedestrian-only section of the city center looks like it's been transported over the border from Provence. The food, though, is definitely Ligurian, with a wide selection of fresh pastas, including gnocchi in pesto sauce, followed perhaps by a *grigliata mista* of fresh fish or grilled sole. For a more casual meal, light-crusted pizzas emerge from a tiled oven in the rear. In good weather, meals are served in small garden out back covered by a reed-thatched tent—and there are some tables on the (admittedly nothing special) piazza outside.

Piazza Eroi Sanremesi 12. © 0184-531469. Primi 6€–15€ ($6.90–$17); secondi 6.50€–18€ ($7.50–$21); pizza 4.50€–7€ ($5.20–$8.05); *menu turistico* 14€ ($16) without wine; *menu degustazione* 31€ ($36) without wine. DC, MC, V. Fri–Wed noon–2:30pm and 7:30–11:30pm (daily in summer).

THE CAFE & BAR SCENE

Agora Caffè, Piazza San Siro (no phone), which faces San Remo's cathedral, makes no claim other than that it's a comfortable watering hole, a function it performs very well. For foot-sore travelers, the terrace out front, facing the pretty stone piazza and cathedral of San Siro, is a welcome oasis. Sandwiches and other light fare are served late into the night, when an after-dinner crowd tends to make this one of the livelier spots in town. It's closed on Monday.

Wanderings through the center of town should include a stop at the handsome wine bar **Enoteca Bacchus** ★★ (V. Roma 65; © **0184-530990**), open Monday through Saturday from 10am to 9pm. This is where you can also stock up on olive oil and other Ligurian foodstuffs. Wine is served by the glass at a sit-down bar or at one of the small tables. You can accompany your libations with fresh focaccia, cheeses, vegetable tarts, and even such substantial fare as *buridda,* a dish of salted cod, tomatoes, and other vegetables.

3 The Riviera Levante: Camogli, Santa Margherita Ligure, Portofino

Camogli: 26km (16 miles) E of Genoa. Santa Margherita Ligure: 31km (19 miles) E of Genoa. Portofino: 38km (24 miles) E of Genoa

The coast east of Genoa, the **Riviera Levante (Shore of the Rising Sun),** is more ruggedly beautiful than the Riviera Ponente, less developed, and hugged by mountains that plunge into the sea. Four of the coast's most appealing towns are within a few kilometers of one another, clinging to the shores of the Monte Portofino Promontory just east of Genoa: Camogli, Santa Margherita Ligure, and little Portofino.

CAMOGLI

Camogli (Casa dei Mogli—House of the Wives) was named for the women who held down the fort while their husbands went to sea for years on end. The little town remains delightfully unspoiled, an authentic Ligurian fishing port with tall, ocher-painted houses fronting the harbor and a nice swath of beach. Given also its excellent accommodations and eateries, Camogli is a lovely place to base yourself while you explore the Riviera Levante and is a restful retreat from which you can easily visit Genoa, just 20 minutes away.

ESSENTIALS

GETTING THERE   By Train   One to three trains (www.trenitalia.com) per hour ply the coastline, connecting Camogli with **Genoa** (35–50 min.; 2.10€/$ 2.40), **Santa Margherita Ligure** (5 min.; 1.10€/$1.25), **Monterosso** (50–60 min.; 3.45€/$3.95), and other Cinque Terre towns.

By Bus   There is at least one **Tigullio** (© **800-014808** in Italy, or 0185-288835; www.tigulliotrasporti.it) bus an hour, often more, from **Santa Margherita.** Since the bus must go around and not under the Monte Portofino Promontory, the trip takes quite a bit longer than the train ride—about half an hour—and costs 1.10€ ($1.25).

By Boat   In summer, boats operated by **Golfo Paradiso** (© **0185-772091;** www.golfoparadiso.it) sail from Camogli to **Portofino** (8€/$9.20 one-way).

By Car   The fastest route into the region is the A12 autostrada from Genoa. Exit at Recco for Camogli (the trip takes less than half an hour). Route S1 along the coast from Genoa is much slower but more scenic.

VISITOR INFORMATION   The **tourist office** is across from the train station at Via XX Settembre 33 (©/fax **0185-771066;** www.camogli.it or www. portofinocoast.it). It's open Monday through Saturday from 9am to 12:30pm and 3:30 to 7pm (Mar–Oct it closes at noon in the morning and 6:30pm in the evening), and Sunday from 9am to 1pm.

FESTIVALS & MARKETS   Camogli throws a much-attended annual party, the **Sagra del Pesce** 👀, on the second Sunday of May. The town fries up thousands of sardines in a 4m (13-ft.) diameter pan and passes them around for free—a practice that is accompanied by an annual outcry in the press about health concerns and even accusations that frozen fish is used. Even so, the beloved event is well attended.

The first Sunday of August, Camogli stages the lovely **Festa della Stella Maris.** A procession of boats sails to Punta Chiappa, a point of land about 1.6km (a mile) down the coast, and releases 10,000 burning candles. Meanwhile, the same number of candles is set afloat from the Camogli beach. If currents are favorable, the burning candles will come together at sea, signifying a year of unity for couples who watch the spectacle.

EXPLORING THE TOWN

Camogli is clustered around its delightful waterfront, from which the town ascends via steep, staircased lanes to Via XX Settembre, one of the few streets in the town proper to accommodate cars (this is where the train station, the tourist office, and many shops and other businesses are located). Adding to the charm of this setting is the fact that the oldest part of Camogli juts into the harbor on a little point (once an island) where ancient houses cling to the little **Castello Dragone** (now closed to the public) and the 12th-century **Basilica di Santa Maria Assunta** (© **0185-770130**), with an impressively over-baroqued interior, open daily from 8am to 6pm. Most visitors, though, seem drawn to the pleasant **seaside promenade** 👀 that runs the length of the town. You can swim from the pebbly beach below and, should you feel your towel doesn't provide enough comfort, rent a lounge from one of the few beach stations for 5€ ($5.75).

ACCOMMODATIONS YOU CAN AFFORD

Augusta *(Value)*   This is an acceptable alternative if the Camogliese (see below) is full. More than a fallback, though, it's pleasant and convenient, with a handy location a short walk up a steep staircase from the harbor. The elderly couple and their son who run the pensione also operate the ground-floor trattoria, which serves as a sitting room for the guest rooms upstairs and makes it easy to enjoy a cup of coffee or glass of wine. The rooms are extremely plain, with new modular units and wood floors, but they are large and clean, have good-size bathrooms, and now have air-conditioning. Show this guidebook for 15 minutes of free Internet access. Ask for a room in front—those in back face the train tracks.

Via Schiaffino 100, 16032 Camogli. © **0185-770592.** Fax 0185-770593. www.htlaugusta.com. 15 units. 50€–65€ ($58–$75) single; 68€–86€ ($78–$99) double. Breakfast 6€ ($6.90). Show your Frommer's guide for a discount (especially during slow periods). AE, DC, MC, V. **Amenities:** Restaurant; bar; concierge; room service. *In room:* A/C, TV, dataport, safe.

La Camogliese *(Kids)* 👀   A lot of Genovese come out to spend the weekend in this friendly, attractive little hotel near the waterfront, and they appreciate it for the same simple charms that will appeal to travelers from farther afield. (In fact, given the hotel's popularity, it's always a good idea to reserve ahead, and essential on weekends.) Proprietor Bruno and his family extend a warm welcome to guests and are happy to help them navigate the logistics of visiting the different towns on the nearby coast (which is especially easy to do from here, since the hotel is at the bottom of a staircase that leads to the train station). Rooms are large, bright, and airy, and decorated in modern furnishings that include comfortable beds. Some have balconies, and while the house isn't right on the waterfront, it faces a little river and is close enough to the beach that a slight twist of the head usually affords a view of the sea (best from corner room no. 16B). Bathrooms are small but adequate. The proprietors remodeled the first floor in 2000 to add a breakfast room and overhaul the other rooms. They've also added several new beachfront rooms. Families may want to stay in the Camogliese's apartment (400€/$460 for a week's stay). The family also runs the beachfront restaurant of the same name just down the road (see below).

Via Garibaldi 55, 16032 Camogli. ℭ 0185-771402. Fax 0185-774024. www.lacamogliese.it. 21 units. 50€–85€ ($58–$98) single; 67€–97€ ($77–$112) double; 90€–120€ ($104–$138) triple. Rates include breakfast. AE, DC, MC, V. Parking 10€ ($12). **Amenities:** Outdoor pool; golf nearby; exercise room; concierge; salon; babysitting; laundry service. *In room:* A/C (in 10 rooms), TV, dataport, kitchenette (in apts), hair dryer, safe.

Worth a Splurge

Cenobio dei Dogi 𝄞𝄞   This Ligurian getaway sits just above the sea at one end of town and against the forested flank of Monte Portofino. The oldest part of the hotel incorporates an aristocratic villa dating from 1565; a chapel, still occasionally used as such, dates from the 17th century. Converted to a hotel in 1956, the premises now include several wings that wrap graciously around a garden on one side and a series of terraces facing the sea on the other. There's a pool and a private beach and several airy salons, including a lovely bar and lounge area and a glass-enclosed breakfast room that hangs over the sea. Both restaurants, which serve Ligurian cuisine, were renovated in 2004. The guest rooms vary considerably in size and shape, but all are furnished with a tasteful mix of reproduction writing desks, contemporary glass-top tables, and—especially in "standard" category rooms—island-style furnishings (rattan, bent bamboo headboards, and so on). Many overlook the sea and have balconies, and a few have terraces that lead directly to the pool. In most rooms, the bathrooms have sizeable counter space and luxurious fixtures.

Via Cuneo 34, 16032 Camogli. ℭ 0185-7241. Fax 0185-772796. www.cenobio.com. 106 units. 108€–151€ ($124–$174) single; 150€–205€ ($173–$236) standard double with garden view, 175€–244€ ($201–$281) superior double with garden view, 196€–281€ ($225–$323) standard double with sea view; 217€–311€ ($250–$358) superior double with sea view; 31€–41€ ($36–$47) triple supplement; 258€–348€ ($297–$400) junior suite; 361€–425€ ($415–$489) suite. Rates include buffet breakfast. Half-board supplement 35€ ($40) per person, full-board supplement 70€ ($81). AE, DC, MC, V. Free parking. **Amenities:** 2 restaurants (1 at beach); 2 bars; outdoor saltwater pool; 18-hole golf course (in Rapallo, 7km/4½ miles away); outdoor tennis courts (lit); exercise room and spa across street; watersports equipment; bike rental; concierge; tour desk; car-rental desk; secretarial services; salon; limited room service; massage (across street); babysitting; laundry service; dry cleaning. *In room:* A/C, TV, dataport, minibar, hair dryer, safe.

GREAT DEALS ON DINING

Bar Primula LIGHT FARE/DESSERTS   Camogli's most fashionable bar is on the waterfront, and it seems as if just about anything goes here. Drinking is taken seriously, as self-proclaimed "Capo Barman" Renato Montanari is well known in his trade. You can also enjoy a light meal (a pasta dish and seafood plate or two or are usually available, along with sandwiches, salads, and omelets), but many regulars come in for a cup of the delicious house espresso and dessert, which presents a difficult choice between the delicious ice cream and the pastries (if you're torn, try the sumptuous Camogliese chocolate rum ball–like concoction).

Via Garibaldi 140. ℂ **0185-770351.** Sandwiches 3.50€–4.50€ ($4–$5.75); dishes and other light fare 6€–10€ ($6.90–$12); gelato from 1.70€ ($1.95). AE, MC, V. Fri–Wed 9am–2am.

Ristorante La Camogliese 🦜🦜 SEAFOOD   You probably won't be surprised to find that the menu at this bright seaside spot, perched over the beach on stilts, leans heavily toward seafood. In fact, when the weather is pleasant and the windows that surround the dining room are open, you feel you are at sea (admittedly, a sea with piped-in pop music). This is one of the most popular and appealing restaurants in town. The hearty fish soup is a meal in itself, as are any number of pastas topped with clam and other seafood sauces. There is always a tempting array of fresh fish entrees, caught that day, on hand as well.

Via Garibaldi 78. ℂ **0185-771086.** Primi 6.50€–16€ ($7.50–$18); secondi 11€–21€ ($13–$24); fixed-price menu 24€ ($28). AE, DC, MC, V. Thurs–Tues (daily July–Sept) 12:30–2:30pm and 7:30–10:30pm.

SANTA MARGHERITA LIGURE

Santa Margherita had one brief moment in the spotlight, at the beginning of the past century, when it was an internationally renowned retreat. Fortunately, the seaside town didn't let fame spoil its charm, and now that it's no longer as well known of a destination as its glitzy neighbor, Portofino, it might be the Mediterranean retreat of your dreams—a palm-lined harbor, a nice beach, and a friendly ambience make Santa Margherita a fine place to settle down for a few days of sun and relaxation.

ESSENTIALS

GETTING THERE   By Train   Between two and three coastal trains per hour connect Santa Margherita with **Genoa** (regional: 50 min., 2.10€/$2.40; high speed: 30 min., 4.05€/$4.65), **Camogli** (5 min.; 1.10€/$1.35), **Rapallo** (3 min.; 1€/$1.15), and **Monterosso** (60–85 min., 3.45€–8.85€/$4–$10) of the Cinque Terre.

By Bus   There is at least one **Tigullio** (ℂ **0185-288834;** www.tigulliotrasporti.it) bus an hour to **Camogli** (30–35 min.; 1.10€/$1.35) and to **Rapallo** (10 min.; .80€/90¢), leaving from Piazza Vittorio Veneto. Buses also ply the stunningly beautiful coast road to **Portofino,** leaving every 20 minutes from the train station and Piazza Vittorio Veneto (25 min.; 1€/$1.15).

By Boat   Tigullio ferries (ℂ **0185-284670;** www.traghettiportofino.it) make hourly trips to **Portofino** (15 min.; 3.50€/$4 one-way) and **Rapallo** (15 min.; 2€/$2.30 one-way). In summer, there is a boat about 4 days a week to **Vernazza** in the Cinque Terre for 14€ ($16) one-way. Hours of service vary considerably with the seasons; schedules are posted on the docks at Piazza Martiri della Liberta.

By Car   The fastest route into the region is the A12 autostrada from Genoa; the trip takes about half an hour. Route S1 along the coast from Genoa is much slower but more scenic.

VISITOR INFORMATION   The **tourist office** is near the harbor at Via XXV Aprile 2B (ℂ **0185-287485;** fax 0185-283034; www.apttigullio.liguria.it). Summer hours are daily from 9am to 12:30pm and 3 to 6pm; winter hours are Monday through Saturday from 9am to 12:30pm and 2:30 to 5:30pm.

FESTIVALS & MARKETS   Santa Margherita's winters are delightfully mild, but even so, the town rushes to usher in spring with a **Festa di Primavera,** held on moveable dates in February. Like the Sagra del Pesce in neighboring Camogli, this festival features food—in this case, fritters are prepared on the beach and served around roaring bonfires. One of the more interesting daily spectacles in town is the **fish market** on Lungomare Marconi; this colorful event transpires from 8am to 12:30pm. On Fridays, cars are banned from Corso Matteotti, Santa Margherita's major street for food shopping, turning the area into an open-air **food market.**

EXPLORING THE TOWN

Life in Santa Margherita centers on its palm-fringed **waterfront,** a pleasant string of marinas, docks for pleasure and fishing boats, and pebbly beaches. Landlubbers congregate in the cafes that spill into the town's two seaside squares, Piazza Martiri della Liberta and Piazza Vittorio Veneto.

The train station is on a hill above the waterfront, and a staircase in front of the entrance will lead you down into the heart of town. Santa Margherita's one landmark of note is its namesake **Basilica di Santa Margherita,** just off the seafront on Piazza Caprera. The church is open daily from 8am to noon and 3 to 7pm, and is well worth a visit to view the extravagant, gilded, chandeliered interior.

ACCOMMODATIONS YOU CAN AFFORD

Annabella   The Annabella's nice proprietors manage to accommodate groups of just about any size in this old apartment that's been converted to an attractive pensione, with comfortable old modular furniture and whitewashed walls. Some of the rooms sleep up to four, and one family-style arrangement includes a large room with a double bed and a tiny room outfitted with bunk beds for children. None of the rooms has a private bathroom, but the four shared facilities are ample and hot water is plentiful. The three sons run the popular Cutty Sark pub/*paninocateca* near the train station at Via Roma 35.

Via Costasecca 10, 16038 Santa Margherita Ligure. ⓒ 0185-286531. www.hotelannabella.com. 11 units, none with bathroom. 41€–45€ ($47–$52) single; 62€–75€ ($71–$86) double. Breakfast 5€ ($5.75). No credit cards. **Amenities:** Room service (breakfast only). *In room:* No phone.

Fasce 𝄢𝄢𝄢   Aristide, whose grandmother built this small hotel, and his British wife, Jane, make great efforts to make their guests feel at home—they do, after all, live here themselves along with his parents—and as a result, they provide some of the most pleasant lodgings in Santa Margherita. Their hospitality includes the use of free bicycles and a laundry service (16€/$18 for a wash and dry). If you stay 3 nights or longer, they'll give you a free Cinque Terre packet with train times and two free tickets to go all the way to Riomaggiore and back. The surroundings are lovely: A broad staircase leads into the flowery, courtyard-like entryway, off which there's a pleasant lobby and breakfast/bar area; a roof terrace affords lovely views of the sea and town. The guest rooms are large, bright, and modern in design, with cheerful white laminate furnishings and many thoughtful touches, such as copious amounts of storage space, shelves around the beds on which to place reading matter, and in-room safes. Four rooms have balconies, and three accommodations (the triples and a quad) have folding beds, to make them perfect for families. With this many amenities at such reasonable prices, it's a good idea to reserve ahead.

Via Luigi Bozzo 3, 16038 Santa Margherita Ligure. ⓒ 0185-286435. Fax 0185-283580. www.hotelfasce.it. 18 units. 85€ ($98) single; 95€ ($109) double; 120€ ($138) triple; 140€ ($161) quad; 150€ ($173) family room. Rates include buffet breakfast. AF, DC, MC, V. Parking 16€ ($18). Closed Dec 8–Mar 15. **Amenities:** Bar; free bike loans; concierge; limited room service; laundry service; nonsmoking rooms. *In room:* TV, fax, dataport, minibar, hair dryer, safe.

Nuova Riviera 𝄢   The Sabini family acts as if its sunny, turn-of-the-20th-century, Liberty-style villa in a quiet neighborhood behind the town center is a private home and guests are old friends. Every room is different, and though eclectically furnished with pieces that look like they may have passed through a couple of generations of the family, most retain the high-ceilinged elegance of days gone by and have a great deal more character than you're used to finding in rooms at this end of the budget scale. The best have expansive bay windows. Modular furnishings mix with antiques, the beds are springy (very springy), and a few rooms get balconies; all rooms have ceiling fans. Bathrooms have been added to all units. There's a pretty garden out front and a homey, light-filled dining room where Signora Sabini serves breakfast with fresh-squeezed orange juice. A home-cooked, fixed-price dinner costs 15€ to 25€ ($17–$29) for just homemade pasta, salad, and gelato.

Their nearby **annex** has four very nice, simple rooms—one a large triple with balcony—which share two bathrooms. Also available is a ground-floor apartment with two double rooms, a living room, a kitchen, a terrace, a washing machine, and a refrigerator for four or five people. Credit cards aren't accepted at the annex; you'll have to pay cash.

The hoteliers are currently expanding to create a self-catering apartment with a kitchen for two to four people.

Via Belvedere 10/2, 16038 Santa Margherita Ligure. ℭ/fax **0185-287403**. www.nuovariviera.com. 9 units in main house; 4 units in annex across the street, none with bathroom. In main house: 74€–88€ ($85–$101) single with bathroom; 78€–98€ ($90–$113) double with bathroom. In annex: 50€–64€ ($58–$74) single without bathroom; 60€–74€ ($69–$85) double without bathroom; 80€–100€ ($92–$115) triple without bathroom. Lower rates for stays of 5 nights or more. Rates include continental breakfast (served in the hotel). MC, V (only at main hotel, but you'll get a 5% discount if you pay in cash); cash only in annex. Parking available on street. **Amenities:** Restaurant; bar; laundry service; nonsmoking rooms. *In room:* TV, hair dryer.

GREAT DEALS ON DINING

Trattoria Baicin ✪ LIGURIAN The husband-and-wife owners, Piero and Carmela, make everything fresh daily, from fish soup to gnocchi, and still find time to greet diners at the door of their cheerful trattoria just a few steps off the harbor. You can get a glimpse of the sea if you choose to sit at one of the tables out front. The owners/cooks are most happy preparing fish, which they buy fresh every morning at the market just around the corner; the sole, simply grilled, is especially good here, and the *fritto misto di pesce* constitutes a memorable feast. You must begin a meal with one of the pastas made that morning, especially if *trofie alla genovese* (a combination of gnocchi, potatoes, fresh vegetables, and pesto) is available. By ordering one of the fixed-price menus, you can get a nice sampling of the expertly prepared dishes. The owners are making plans to renovate the restaurant, so call ahead before you go.

Via Algeria 9. ℭ **0185-286763**. Reservations recommended. Primi 5€–7.50€ ($5.75–$8.60); secondi 8€–17€ ($9.20–$19); fixed-price menus 20€–22€ ($23–$25). AE, DC, MC, V. Tues–Sun noon–3pm and 7–10:30pm. Closed Nov–Dec 15.

Trattoria da Pezzi *Value* GENOVESE/LIGURIAN The atmosphere in this cozy little restaurant in the center of town near the market is pleasantly casual. Two whitewashed, tile-floored rooms are usually filled with local workmen and businesspeople, who invite newcomers to share a table when no other place is available. Service is minimal—the chef puts what he's prepared for the day on a table near the front door, you tell him what you want, and one of the staff will bring it to the table when it's ready. Focaccia, farinata, and other Genovese specialties are usually on hand, as are at least one kind of soup (the minestrone is excellent), a chicken dish, and grilled fresh fish.

Via Cavour 21. 𝄎 0185-285303. Reservations not necessary. Primi 4€–7€ ($4.60–$8.05); secondi 4€–13€ ($4.60–$14). MC, V. Sun–Fri 11:45am–2:15pm and 6–9:15pm. Closed 2nd week of Sept and 1 month late Dec to late Jan.

PORTOFINO

Portofino is almost too beautiful for its own good—in almost any season, you'll be rubbing elbows on Portofino's harborside quays with day-tripping mobs who join Italian industrialists, international celebrities, and a lot of rich but not so famous folks who consider this little town the epicenter of the good life. If you make an appearance in the late afternoon when the crowds have thinned out a bit, you are sure to experience what remains so appealing about this enchanting place—its untouchable beauty.

ESSENTIALS
GETTING THERE   By Train   Get off in Santa Margherita (see above) and catch the bus.

By Bus   The **Tigullio** bus (𝄎 **0185-288834;** www.tigulliotrasporti.it) leaves the train station and Piazza Vittorio Veneto in **Santa Margherita** every 20 minutes, and follows one of Italy's most beautiful coastal roads (25 min.; 1€/$1.15). In Santa Margherita, you can change for a bus to **Rapallo** (another 15 min.; 1.10€/$1.25).

By Boat   The best way to arrive is to sail to Portofino on one of the **Golfo Paradiso** ferries (𝄎 **0185-772091;** www.golfoparadiso.it) from **Camogli** (8€/$9.20 one-way), or on one of the **Tigullio** ferries (𝄎 **0185-284670;** www.traghetti portofino.it) from **Santa Margherita** (3.50€/$4 one-way) or **Rapallo** (5€/$5.75 one-way).

By Car   On a summer visit, you may encounter crowds even before you get into town, since traffic on the shore-hugging corniche from Santa Margherita, just a few kilometers down the coast of the promontory, can move at a snail's pace. In fact, given limited parking space in Portofino (visitors must pay obscene rates—roughly 4€/$4.60 per hour, 17€/$20 per day—to use the town garage), you would do well to leave your car in Santa Margherita and take the bus or boat.

VISITOR INFORMATION   Portofino's **tourist office** is at Via Roma 35 (𝄎/fax **0185-269024;** www.apttigullio.liguria.it). Summer hours are daily from 10:30am to 1:30pm and 2 to 7:30pm; winter hours are Tuesday through Sunday from 9:30am to 12:30pm and 2:30 to 5:30pm.

EXPLORING THE TOWN
The one thing that's free in Portofino is its scenery, which you can enjoy on an amble around the town. Begin with a stroll around the **harbor,** which—lined with expensive boutiques and eateries as it is—is stunningly beautiful, with colorful houses lining the quay and steep green hills rising behind them. One of the most scenic walks takes you uphill for about 10 minutes along a well-signposted path from the west side of town just behind the harbor to the **Chiesa di San Giorgio** (𝄎 0185-269337), built on the site of a sanctuary Roman soldiers dedicated to the Persian god Mithras. It's open daily from 9am to 7pm.

From there you'll want to continue uphill for a few minutes more to Portofino's **Castello Brown** (𝄎 0185-267101 or 0185-269046), built to ward off invading Turks. You can step inside the walls to enjoy a lush garden and the views of the town and harbor below. The castle is open daily from 10am to 7pm (to 5pm Oct–Apr); admission is 3.50€ ($4), and free for those under 13. There are great views back over the town. For some lovely views on this stretch of coast and plenty of open sea before you, continue even higher up through lovely pine forests to the **faro** (lighthouse).

From Portofino, you can also set out for a longer hike on the paths that cross the **Monte Portofino Promontory** to the Abbazia di San Fruttuoso, about a 2-hour walk from Portofino. The tourist office provides maps.

GREAT DEALS ON DINING

Portofino's charms come at a steep price. Its few hotels are expensive enough to put them in the "trip of a lifetime" category, and the harborside restaurants can take a serious chunk out of a vacation budget. Enjoy a light snack at a bar or one of the many shops selling focaccia, and wait to dine in Santa Margherita or one of the other nearby towns.

La Gritta American Bar LIGHT FARE   James Jones called this snug little room the "nicest waterfront bar this side of Hong Kong." Your praise might not go that far, but the bar is very attractive, very friendly, and far enough along the harborside quay to be a little less hectic than other establishments. Most patrons stop in for a (pricey) cocktail, coffee, or other libation (the floating terrace out front is perfect for a drink at sunset). Light fare, such as omelets and salads of tomatoes and mozzarella, are available to provide a relatively affordable meal.

Calata Marconi 20. © 0185-269126. Salads and other light fare from about 8€ ($9.20). AE, MC, V. Fri–Wed 9am–3am.

4 The Cinque Terre

Monterosso, the northernmost town of the Cinque Terre: 93km (58 miles) E of Genoa

Olive groves and vineyards clinging to hillsides, proud villages perched above the sea, hidden coves nestled at the feet of dramatic cliffs—the **Cinque Terre** is about as beautiful a coastline as you're likely to find in Europe, or anywhere else. What's best about the Cinque Terre (named for the five neighboring towns of Monterosso, Vernazza, Corniglia, Manarola, and Riomaggiore) is what's *not* here—automobiles, large-scale development, or much else by way of 21st-century interference. The pastimes in the Cinque Terre don't get much more elaborate than **walking** ⚡ from one lovely village to another along trails that afford spectacular vistas, plunging into the Mediterranean or basking in the sun on your own waterside boulder, and indulging in the tasty local food and wine.

Not too surprisingly, these charms have not gone unnoticed. American tourism especially has positively exploded in the past 5 years or so. Throughout summer (weekends are worst), you are likely to find yourself in a long procession of like-minded, English-speaking trekkers making their way down the coast, or elbow to elbow with day-trippers from an excursion boat. Even so, the Cinque Terre manages to escape the hubbub that afflicts so many coastlines. Even a short stay here is likely to reward you with one of the most memorable seaside visits of a lifetime.

ESSENTIALS

GETTING THERE   By Train   You often cannot coast directly into the Cinque Terre towns, as they are served only by the most local of train runs (www.trenitalia.com). You'll often find you must change trains in nearby **La Spezia** (one to two per hour; 8 min.; 1.30€/$1.50) at the coast's south tip, or in **Pisa** (about six daily; 75 min.; 4.55€/$5). This is true of the one to two trains per hour from **Rome** (4½–5 hr.; 28€/$32) or the hourly ones from **Florence** (2½ hr.; 8.20€/$9). There are direct trains from **Genoa** (one to two per hour; 1 hr. 40 min.; 4.95€/$6); many more from Genoa require a change in Levanto or Sestri Levanto, both a bit farther north up the coast from Monterosso.

By Car   The fastest route is via the A12 autostrada from Genoa, using the Corrodano exit for Monterosso. The trip from Genoa to Corrodano takes less than an hour, while the much shorter 24km (15-mile) trip from Corrodano to Monterosso (via Levanto) is made along a narrow road and can take about half that amount of time. Coming from the south or Florence, get off the A12 autostrada at La Spezia and follow CINQUE TERRE signs.

By Boat   Navigazione Golfo dei Poeti (© **0187-732987** or 0187-730336; www.navigazionegolfodeipoeti.it) runs erratic service from **La Spezia, Lerici,** and **Portovenere** (3–4 per day Mar 27–Nov 1), as well as once a day (late June to mid-Sept only) that starts at the Marina di Pisa and hits several northern Tuscan stops (Livrono, Marina di Carrar, Marina di Massa, Forte dei Marmi, Viareggio). These tend to be day cruises stopping from 1 to 3 hours in Vernazza before returning (though you can usually talk them into not picking you up again for a day or two). They charge about 11€ ($13) one-way, or 18€ to 28€ ($21–$32) round-trip.

GETTING AROUND

By Foot   The best way to link the Cinque Terre is to devote a whole day to hoofing it along the trails. See "Exploring the Cinque Terre," below, for details.

By Train   Local trains make frequent runs (two to three per hour) among the five towns. Some stop only in Monterosso and Riomaggiore, so check the posted "Partenze" schedule at the station first to be sure you're catching a local. One-way tickets between any two towns cost between 1€ ($1.15) and 1.50€ ($1.70).

By Car   A narrow, one-lane coast road hugs the mountainside above the towns, but all the centers are closed to cars. Parking is difficult and, where possible, expensive.

There are public **parking** facilities as follows: Monterosso has a big open dirt lot right on the seafront that costs 1€ ($1.15) per hour up to 3 hours, and 6€ ($6.90) for any length of time over 3 hours, up to a full day that ends at midnight; this means if you pick up your car the next day, your second day already began ticking at midnight, so you owe 12€ ($14). Practical upshot: First overnight costs 12€ ($14); each subsequent one costs 6€ ($6.90).

Free minibuses will carry you and your luggage from the parking facilities up above Riomaggiore and Manarola down into the respective towns. Riomaggiore has a garage at 1.80€ ($2.05) per hour and 17€ ($20) per day. Manarola has an open lot for 1.30€ ($1.50) per hour (hourly rate gets lower the longer you stay), 10€ ($12) for 1 day, and 18€ ($21) for 2 days (and, again, progressively less the longer you stay).

By Boat   From the port in Monterosso, **Navigazione Golfo dei Poeti** (© **0187-732987** or 0187-730336; www.navigazionegolfodeipoeti.it) makes about nine trips a day between Monterosso and Riomaggiore (30 min. one-way), all stopping in Vernazza and Manarola as well. A one-way ticket anywhere is a whopping 11€ ($13); round-trip tickets run 18€ to 28€ ($21–$32).

VISITOR INFORMATION   The **tourist office** for the Cinque Terre is underneath the train station of Monterosso, Via Fegina 38 (© **0187-817506** or 0187-817059; fax 0187-817825). It's open from Easter to early November and again at Christmas daily from 9:30 to 11:30am and 3:30 to 7:30pm. Even when it's closed or in the off season, posted outside the office is a handy display of phone numbers and other useful info, from hotels to ferries.

Websites to visit include **www.cinqueterrenet.com** and **www.aptcinque terre.sp.it.**

EXPLORING THE CINQUE TERRE

Aside from swimming and soaking in the atmosphere of unspoiled fishing villages, the most popular activity in the Cinque Terre is **hiking from one village to the next** ☆ along centuries-old goat paths. Trails plunge through vineyards and groves of olive and lemon trees and hug seaside cliffs, affording heart-stopping views of the coast and the romantic little villages looming ahead in the distance. The well-signposted walks from village to village range in degree of difficulty and the length of time it takes to traverse them, but as a loose rule, they get longer and steeper—and more rewarding—the farther north you go. Depending on your pace and how long you stop in each village for a fortifying glass of *sciacchetrà*, the local sweet wine, you can make the trip between Monterosso, at the northern end of the Cinque Terre, to Riomaggiore, at the southern end, in about 5 hours.

The walk from **Monterosso to Vernazza** is the most arduous and takes 1½ hours on a trail that makes several steep ascents and descents (on the portion outside of Monterosso, you'll pass beneath funicular-like cars that transport grapes down the steep hillsides). The leg from the **Vernazza to Corniglia** is also demanding and takes another 90 minutes, plunging into some dense forests and involving lengthy ascents, but is among the prettiest and most rewarding stretches. Part of the path between **Corniglia and Manarola,** about 45 minutes apart, follows a level grade above a long stretch of beach, tempting you to break stride and take a dip. From **Manarola to Riomaggiore,** it's easy going for about half an hour along a partially paved path known as the Via dell'Amore, so named for its romantic vistas (great to do at sunset).

Since all the villages are linked by rail, you can hike as many portions of the itinerary as you wish and take the train to your next destination. Trails also cut through the forested, hilly terrain inland from the coast, much of which is protected as a nature preserve; the tourist office in Monterosso can provide maps.

BEACHES The only sandy beach in the Cinque Terre is the crowded strand in **Monterosso,** on much of which you will be asked to pay 2.80€ ($3.20) each per hour for a beach chair or umbrella, 5€ ($5.75) per day for a chair, 10€ to 15€ ($12–$17) per day for two chairs with an umbrella, and 8€ ($9.20) for an hour in a pedal boat.

Guvano Beach is a long, isolated, pebbly strand that stretches just north of Corniglia and is popular with nudists (almost entirely men, many of whom are happy it's almost entirely men). You can clamber down to it from the Vernazza–Corniglia path, but the drop is steep and treacherous. A weird alternative route takes you through an unused train tunnel that you enter near the north end of Corniglia's train station. You must ring the bell at the gated entrance and wait for a custodian to arrive to unburden you of 2.50€ ($2.90), which is good for passage through the dank, dimly lit, 1.6km-long (1-mile) gallery that emerges onto the beach at the far end.

There's also a long, rocky beach to the south of **Corniglia.** It is easily accessible by quick downhill scrambles from the Corniglia–Manarola path. **Riomaggiore** has a tiny crescent-shape pebble beach reached by a series of stone steps on the south side of the harbor. Everywhere else, you're swimming off piers or rocks.

MONTEROSSO

The Cinque Terre's largest village seems incredibly busy compared with its sleepier neighbors, but it's not without its charms. Monterosso is actually two towns—a bustling, character-filled old town built behind the harbor and, separated by a rocky promontory, a relaxed resort section that stretches along the Cinque Terre's only **sand beach** and is home to the train station and the tiny regional tourist office. (Upon exiting the station, turn left and head through the tunnel for the old town; turn right for the newer town.)

The region's most famous art treasure is here: Housed in the **Convento dei Cappuccini,** perched on a hillock in the center of the old town, is a *Crucifixion* by Anthony Van Dyck, the Flemish master who worked for a time in nearby Genoa (you can visit the convent daily 9am–noon and 4–7pm). While you will find the most conveniences in citified Monterosso, you'll have a more rustic experience if you stay in one of the other four villages.

ACCOMMODATIONS YOU CAN AFFORD

Albergo Amici ✦✦   The aptly named Amici is unpretentious but extremely friendly. It's reached by a curving marble staircase lined with flowerpots and facing a delightful garden. While the hotel is not on the seafront (which is only a few minutes away by foot), the garden up at the top of the property and many of the rooms overlook the town and the sea beyond, and the location on a narrow street in the old town ensures quiet. The rooms, 10 of which were recently redone, are simply but tastefully furnished in blond-wood contemporary pieces and open onto balconies through French doors. Like most hotels in Monterosso, from June 15 to September 15, the Amici prefers (but doesn't absolutely require) that guests choose either half board or full board. Meals, served in a cavernous dining room, are adequate, but you'd do well to opt for the half-board plan so you can sample other restaurants throughout the region.

Via Buranco 36, 19016 Monterosso al Mare (SP). ✆ **0187-817544.** Fax 0187-817424. www.hotelamici.it. 38 units. 42€–63€ ($48–$72) single without bathroom; 90€–105€ ($104–$121) single with bathroom; 85€–115€ ($98–$132) double with bathroom. 55€–82€ ($63–$94) half board per person. Buffet breakfast 8€ ($9). MC, V. Parking 10€ ($12). Closed Nov 3–Dec 22 and Jan 7–Feb 20ish. **Amenities:** Restaurant; bar; children's center (Ping-Pong and billiards in garden); video arcade; dry cleaning. *In room:* A/C, TV, hair dryer, safe.

GREAT DEALS ON DINING

All the towns in the Cinque Terre have little shops like the **Enoteca Internazionale** ✦✦, where you can taste and purchase the local wines by the bottle or simply enjoy a glass of Cinque Terre D.O.C. (1.55€/1.80) or *sciacchetrà* (3.15€/ $3.60) on the premises. The selection here, in the bustling part of old Monterosso, includes olive oil pressed just down the street and jars of homemade pesto.

Foccaceria Il Frontoio SNACKS   Many patrons say this bustling shop, with a takeout counter and a few tables where you can dine on the premises, serves some of the best focaccia in Liguria. That's quite a claim, but suffice it to say that the freshly baked bread (especially when topped with fresh vegetables) is heavenly and provides one of the best fast meals around.

Via Gioberti 1 (off V. Roma). ✆ **0187-818333.** Pizza and focaccia from 1€ ($1.15). No credit cards. Fri–Wed 9am–2pm and 4–7pm. Closed Oct–Mar.

VERNAZZA

It's hard not to fall in love with this pretty village. Tall houses cluster around a natural harbor (where you can swim among the fishing boats) and beneath a castle built high atop a rocky promontory that juts into the sea (Mar–Oct daily 10am–6:30pm; admission 1€/$1.15). The center of town is waterside **Piazza Marconi,** itself a sea of cafe tables. Vernazza's only drawback is that too much good press has turned it into the Cinque Terre's ghetto of American tourists, in summer especially.

ACCOMMODATIONS YOU CAN AFFORD

Besides the Barbara below, you can rent one of **Trattoria Gianni Franzi's** 23 rooms spread across two buildings. Some come with a bathroom, some with excellent views up the coast, and all with a steep climb up the stairlike streets of the town, then up the stairs within the building—but all are worth it. Rates are 35€ ($40) for a single without a bathroom, 58€–62€ ($67–$71) for a double without a bathroom, 75€ ($86) for a double with a bathroom, and 98€ ($113) for a triple with a bathroom. Call © **0187-821003** or fax 0187-812228 to book, or stop by the trattoria's harborside bar at Piazza Marconi 5 when you arrive in town (which is closed Wed except during the busy summer months). They're closed from January 8 to March 8.

Albergo Barbara (Value)   This is the sort of place threatened by overpopularity and subsequent development of former backwaters like Vernazza: an exceedingly basic but clean and cheap hotel in an absolutely stellar location, in the center of the tiny harbor piazza with views over the fishing boats and the Mediterranean. This pleasant, bare-bones pensione on the two upper floors of a tall old house on the waterfront is at the top of four flights of broad stone steps (63 of 'em), and from there, many of the rooms are reached by an additional climb up a ladderlike spiral staircase. These efforts are rewarded, however, by an eagle's-eye view of Vernazza's harbor from almost every room. While the accommodations are basic, they are not without charm, with a pleasant smattering of homey furniture, cool tile floors, and a shower and sink. The seven rooms without a full bathroom share three clean and nicely equipped bathrooms. If no one answers the buzzer, step across the square to Taverna del Capitano and ask about one of their rooms.

Piazza Marconi 30, 19018 Vernazza. ©/fax **0187-812398.** 10 units, 3 with bathroom. 45€ ($52) attic double without sea view; 48€ ($55) attic double with askance sea view; 60€ ($69) double without sea view; 80€ ($92) large double (nos. 8 and 9) with full sea view. No credit cards. Closed late Nov to mid-Feb. *In room:* No phone.

GREAT DEALS ON DINING

Gambero Rosso (★★) SEAFOOD/LIGURIAN   It would be hard to find a more pleasant way to take in the scene on Vernazza's lively harborside square than to do so while enjoying the tasting menu on the terrace at this excellent restaurant. You will also be content ordering one or two choices from the a la carte menu—either way, you can explore some hard-to-find dishes such as *acchiughe* (fresh anchovies) baked with onions and potatoes, *ravioli di pesci* (a delicate fish ravioli), and *muscoli ripieni* (*muscoli* is the Ligurian word for mussels, known as *cozze* elsewhere in Italy; here they are stuffed with fresh herbs). Another specialty, the *grigliata mista* of freshly caught fish, is excellent. Any meal should be followed by the house *sciacchetrà* (the local sweet dessert wine) and accompanied by homemade biscotti. The stone-walled, stone-floored, timbered-ceiling dining room is a pleasant alternative when the terrace is closed.

Piazza Marconi 7. © **0187-812265**. Primi 7€–11€ ($8.05–$13); secondi 10€–15€ ($12–$17); tasting menus 38€–50€ ($44–$58). AE, DC, MC, V. Tues–Sun 12:30–4pm and 7:15–10:30pm (sometimes Mon in August). Closed Dec 15–Mar 1.

CORNIGLIA

The quietest village in the Cinque Terre is isolated by its position midway down the coast, its hilltop location high above the open sea, and its little harbor. Whether you arrive by boat, train, or trail (the last only from the south), you'll have to climb more than 300 steps to reach the village proper, which is an enticing maze of little walkways overshadowed by tall houses.

Once there, though, the views over the surrounding vineyards and up and down the coastline are stupendous—for the best outlook, walk to the end of the narrow main street to a belvedere that is perched between the sea and sky. More than these vistas, Corniglia is also the village most likely to offer you a glimpse into life in the Cinque Terre the way it was until a couple of decades ago.

ACCOMMODATIONS YOU CAN AFFORD

Da Cecio ★★ *Finds*   Proprietors Elia and Nunzio have converted the second floor of their old stone house in the countryside just 2 minutes outside Corniglia (on the road to Vernazza) into what we consider one of the Cinque Terre's most pleasant inns. The rooms are big, bright, and stylish, with dark wood–veneer headboards and furnishings. Most feature great views over the sea, olive groves, and the hilltop town (nos. 2 and 6 are on a corner with those vistas out both windows). They all have modern bathrooms with good box showers and, in a few, marble sinks. The sun-drenched rooftop deck or flowery terrace downstairs (which at mealtimes serves as an outdoor dining room for the excellent restaurant; see below) are the perfect places to idle away an afternoon. If a room is not available here, the proprietors will take you down to one of their four pleasant rooms in the village. For breakfast, they'll send you to their nearby bar, which has tables set out on the village's tiny main piazza.

19010 Corniglia. © **0187-812043**. Fax 0187-812138. simopank@libero.it. 12 units (4 in a *dipendenza* nearby). 50€ ($58) single; 60€ ($69) double; 80€ ($92) triple. Breakfast 10€ ($12). DC, MC, V. Free parking. Closed Nov. **Amenities:** Ligurian restaurant (see review below); bar. *In room:* TV, hair dryer, no phone.

GREAT DEALS ON DINING

Bar Villagio Marino Europa BAR   It would be hard to find a location more scenic than the one this simple outdoor bar enjoys, with stunning views up and down the coast from a hillside perch. Built to service guests at an attached bungalow village, the bar is also a welcome refuge for hikers on the Manarola–Corniglia path (at the Manarola end of the ramshackle tunnel of low buildings you pass through just beyond the Corniglia train station). The offerings don't get more elaborate than sodas and beer, panini, and ice cream, but you will certainly want to stop here at least once on your treks up and the down the Cinque Terre to take in the view.

19010 Corniglia. © **0187-812279**. Snacks from 1€ ($1.15); sandwiches from 2.70€ ($3.10). Mid-May to mid-Oct daily 8am–midnight. Closed winter.

De Mananan ★★ LIGURIAN   The pleasure of being in hilltop Corniglia is well worth the trek up to town, especially if the visit includes a meal at this tiny restaurant carved into the stone cellars of an ancient house. Agostino and Marianne, the husband-and-wife owners and chefs, draw on age-old local recipes and use only the freshest ingredients in their preparations. The results, posted on a blackboard in the one handsome vaulted room furnished with granite tables, are wonderful. Fresh vegetables from gardens just outside the village are grilled and mixed with herbs and smoked mozzarella as a simple appetizer, which can be followed by any of the hand-rolled pasta topped with homemade pesto or porcini. You can continue in this meatless vein with a plate of mussels, grilled fish, or fresh anchovies stuffed with herbs, but the few meat dishes on the daily menu are also excellent—especially the *coniglio nostrano,* rabbit roasted in a white sauce. Local wines accompany the meals.

Via Fieschi 117, Corniglia. © **0187-821166** or 0187-812320. Reservations recommended. Primi 4.15€–9€ ($4.80–$10); secondi 8.50€–13€ ($10–$15). No credit cards. Wed–Mon 12:30–2:30pm and 7:30–9pm.

Ristorante Cecio ♠ LIGURIAN Like the inn upstairs, the stone-walled, wood-beamed dining room and flower-filled terrace overlooking olive groves provide extremely pleasant surroundings. A nice selection of simple, homemade fare emerges from the family-run kitchen, including fresh pasta with a rich pesto or walnut sauce or *alla scogliera,* topped with fresh clams and mussels. Meat and fish are grilled over an open hearth. (Fish accounts for the high *secondi* prices listed below, but there's plenty less expensive than that.) Outside of peak meal-times, you can sit on the terrace and enjoy the view over a beer or glass of the house wine.

Corniglia. © **0187-812043.** Primi 6€–15€ ($6.90–$17); secondi 7€–30€ ($8.05–$35). MC, V. Winter Thurs–Tues 9am–3pm; summer daily 9am–4pm and 6:30pm–midnight. Closed Nov.

MANAROLA

Not as busy as nearby Riomaggiore or as quaint as its neighbor Corniglia, Manarola is a near-vertical cluster of tall houses that seem to rise piggyback up the hills on either side of the harbor. In fact, in this region with no shortage of heart-stopping views, one of the most amazing sights is the descent into the town of Manarola on the path from Corniglia: From this perspective, the hill-climbing houses seem to merge into one another to form a row of skyscrapers. Despite these urban associations, Manarola is a delightfully rural village where fishing and wine making are big business. The region's major **wine cooperative,** Cooperativa Agricoltura di Riomaggiore, Manarola, Corniglia, Vernazza e Monterosso, is here; call © **0187-920435** for information about tours.

ACCOMMODATIONS YOU CAN AFFORD

Manarola's **Ostello 5 Terre** (© **0187-920215;** fax 0187-920218; www.cinque terre.net/ostello) has cheap sleeps: 16€ to 19€ ($18–$22) beds in six-bed dorm rooms, or the same price per bed in four-bed family rooms with private bathroom—but you gotta rent the whole room. The hostel offers services such as kayak, bike, and snorkel rental; Internet access; and a cheap laundry. The only major drawback is the strict midnight curfew (1am in summer). It's closed from January 6 to February 15 and from November 4 to December 6.

Marina Piccola ♠♠ This cozy inn on the harbor in Manarola is a favorite with many travelers to the Cinque Terre, and it's easy to see why. Part of the premises, including the glass-enclosed seafood restaurant where you may be required to take half board or full board in the busy summer months, is right on the water, and many of the guest rooms in the tall house have sea views as well. Decor is a cut above that of most inns in the region—the welcoming lobby doubles as a sitting room, with divans surrounding a fireplace. Because one of the hotel's two buildings (the one above the restaurant) is right on the port, book ahead to get a room with windows opening onto fishing boats and the rocky shoals directly below, and the Tyrrhenean Sea spread before you. As for the small but serviceable rooms, old prints, homey faded floor tiles, light pine–veneer furnishings, and predominant Santorini colors of white and pale blue lend a great amount of charm. Rooms in the other building (the next up the hill, containing the hotel lobby) are done in a more country style, with nicer nut-brown, heavy wooden furnishings; flower-edged wallpaper; and fancy scrolled headboards. Even here, about half the rooms get a sea view over or around the side of the pink stucco of the first building (better views as you go higher up, but no elevator). In 2002, they installed TVs and air-conditioning. The aforementioned meals are excellent, a cut above most room-and-board fare. The only quibble with this otherwise pleasant hostelry is that the service can be somewhat scatterbrained and occasionally downright unfriendly.

Via Discovolo 38, 19010 Manarola. © 0187-920103. Fax 0187-920966. hotelmarinapiccola.com. 13 units. 83€ ($95) single; 105€ ($121) double. Half board 90€ ($104) single, 85€ ($98) per person double. Rates include breakfast. AE, DC, MC, V. Closed Nov. **Amenities:** Restaurant (local cuisine); bar.

GREAT DEALS ON DINING
Aristide ★★ LIGURIAN   In this old house up the hill from the harbor (just below the train station), diners are accommodated on a couple of levels of small rooms as well as on a covered terrace across the street. Many of these patrons live in the Cinque Terre or take the train here from nearby La Spezia because this long-standing trattoria is known for its heaping platters of grilled fish, *gamberoni* (jumbo prawns), and *frittura di mare* (a selection of fried seafood). The *antipasti di mare* includes a nice selection of octopus, clams, sardines, and other local catches, and serves well as a lighter meal. The house's white wine is from the hills above the town, and if the owner is in a good mood, he may come around after your dinner proffering a complimentary glass of *sciacchetrà*, the local dessert wine.

Via Discovolo 290. © 0187-920000. Primi 4.20€–7€ ($4.85–$8.05); secondi 6€–19€ ($6.90–$22); fixed-price fish menu 37€ ($43) with wine. AE, DC, MC, V. Tues–Sun noon–2:30pm and 7–9pm.

RIOMAGGIORE
Riomaggiore clings to the vestiges of the Cinque Terre's rustic ways while making some concessions to the modern world. The old fishing quarter has expanded in recent years, and Riomaggiore now has some sections of new houses and apartment blocks. This blend of the old and new works well—Riomaggiore is bustling and prosperous, and makes the most of a lovely setting, with houses clinging to the hills that drop into the sea on either side of town. Many of the lanes end in seaside belvederes.

From the parking garage, follow the main drag down. From the train station, exit and turn right to head through the tunnel for the main part of town (or, from the station, take off left up the brick stairs to walk the Via dell'Amore to Manarola).

That tunnel and the main drag meet at the base of an elevated terrace that holds the train tracks. From here, a staircase leads down to a tiny fishing harbor. Off to the left heads a rambling path that, after a few hundred yards, leads to a pleasant little **beach** of large pebbles.

ACCOMMODATIONS YOU CAN AFFORD
Villa Argentina   The only full-fledged hotel in Riomaggiore is in the newer section of town, on a hillside about a 5-minute walk (up a lot of stairs) from the center. This location affords astonishing views, which you can enjoy from most of the guest rooms, and provides a nice retreat from the tourist-crowded main street and harbor. A breezy, arbor-shaded terrace and a bar area decorated by

local artists off the lobby are the places to relax. And, while the tile-floored rooms upstairs will not overwhelm you with their character, they are large and pleasant, if blandly furnished, with ceiling fans and (all except room nos. 4–6 and 10) balconies featuring views over the town to the sea. In the past year, the owners have redone all the bathrooms and have added an elevator.

Via de Gaspari 187, 19017 Riomaggiore. ℂ **0187-920213.** Fax 0187-760531. www.hotelvillaargentina.com. 15 units. 77€–99€ ($89–$114) single; 94€–130€ ($108–$150) double; 100€–135€ ($115–$155) triple. Buffet breakfast 7€ ($8.05). Lunch or dinner in nearby restaurant 20€ ($23). No credit cards. Parking 8€–10€ ($9.20–$12). **Amenities:** Ligurian restaurant nearby; bar; watersports equipment rentals; concierge; tour desk; limited room service; babysitting (afternoons only); laundry service; nonsmoking rooms. *In room:* A/C (in some), TV, minibar, hair dryer, safe, no phone.

GREAT DEALS ON DINING

Riomaggiore's nightlife, such as it is, revolves around the **Bar Centrale,** smack in the middle of town at Via C. Colombo 144 (ℂ **0187-920208**), with tables set under a roofed wooden deck in the middle of the main drag, Devil's Kiss beer on tap, and a cheap ISDN Internet connection (.10€/10¢ per minute; 3€/$3.45 for a half-hour). It's open Tuesday through Sunday from 7:30am to 1am.

La Lanterna ⊛ SEAFOOD/LIGURIAN   From a table on the terrace here, perched only a few feet above Riomaggiore's snug harbor, you can hear the waves lap against the rocks and watch the local fishermen mend their nets. Seafood, of course, dominates the menu, with many unusual Ligurian-style dishes, such as *spaghetti al scoglio* (spaghetti with mussels and shrimp in a white-wine sauce) or *spaghetti ai ricci di mare* (with sea urchins). The antipasto of shrimp, smoked tuna, and grilled swordfish is excellent and can suffice as an entree. You should, however, make room for one of the house specialties, *chiche*—homemade gnocchi filled with seafood and topped with a spicy tomato sauce.

Riomaggiore. ℂ **0187-920589.** www.lalanterna.org. Primi 6.50€–8€ ($7.50–$9.20); secondi 9€–23€ ($10–$26). AE, DC, MC, V. Daily 11am–11pm (closed Tues in winter).

12

Southern Italy:
Campania & Apulia

by Lynn A. Levine

The province of **Campania,** rich in fertile volcanic soil deposited by the omnipotent and often menacing Mount Vesuvius, boasts some of the most breathtaking real estate in the world. The mystery and fascination of the Bay of Naples go back to the ancients, who claimed to have discovered the entrance to the underworld here. As a summer retreat for the wealthiest of Romans, the coastline from Naples to Sorrento was dotted with sumptuous summer villas, including those of many a retired Roman emperor. Although there's no disputing that the **Amalfi Coast** continues to captivate its visitors, this amalgam of fishing villages and holiday resorts has traded in some of its rural and pastoral charm in the name of mass tourism. Yet even at their most developed, the little towns along the formidable Amalfi Drive are an enchantment: perfect little pastel villages flowering in the limited living space between sea and cliffs. Dress to impress while strolling the twisting alleyways of the picture-perfect hillside town of **Positano,** or attend an evocative evening concert in the refreshing medieval hilltop retreat of **Ravello.** In **Naples,** you can mimic the privilege of the 18th-century court of the Bourbons in their royal palace while Caravaggio awaits in a museum. Between visits to baroque churches and Renaissance piazze, don't forget to sample a pizza in the very restaurant

that invented it. And from any of the mainland towns, the islands of the Bay of Naples beckon, from the seductive vertical cliffs of **Capri** to the rich volcanic and restorative springs of the spellbinding island of **Ischia.**

From a base amid the culture of Naples or sun-kissed **Sorrento,** you can day-trip to one of the most destructive forces in western history, **Mount Vesuvius.** A short train ride will take you to **Pompeii** and **Herculaneum,** two cities doomed to complete burial by the volcano's wrath in A.D. 79, frozen in time and offering an unparalleled glimpse into daily life almost 2,000 years ago. For even further past-life regressions, head to southern Campania, where you can wander amid the columns of some of the most intact Greek temples in the world in the forgotten 5th-century-B.C. colony of **Paestum.**

To the southeast is the heel of Italy's boot, peninsular **Apulia** (**Puglia,** *pool-*yah), that could easily be called Italy's "last frontier." Nowhere else in Italy is there a more precise balance of East and West, Greek and Roman, Byzantine and Lombard, and Arab and Norman. This is the land of sunflowers and Santa Claus, olive oil and *orecchiette* pasta, Romanesque churches and Swabian castles, whitewashed villages and pearly sands. Here you'll find a cultural melting pot unequaled in Italy (except for maybe Sicily), forming one of the country's most underrated,

The Amalfi Coast

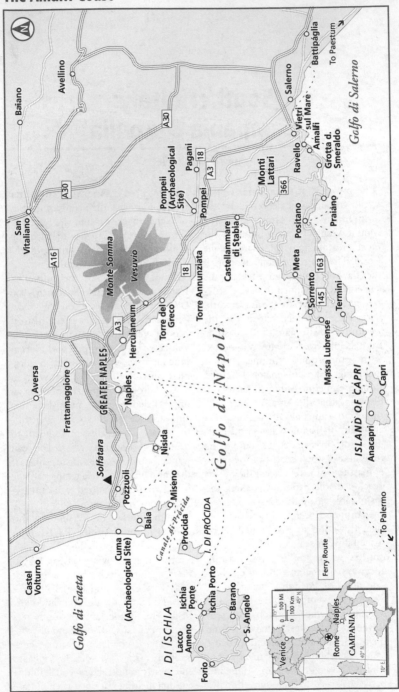

A Taste of Campania

The world owes Naples a great debt, if for no other reason than for the invention of the "plain" *pizza Margherita.* Naples had good stock to work with, as Campania is *the* center of mozzarella production in Italy, with fine *mozzarella di bufala* (buffalo-milk mozzarella) served in restaurants across the province (actually, on pizza you'll more often find *fiordi-latte* cheese, which is mozzarella made with cow's milk that holds up better to the heat of cooking). Mozzarella is a key ingredient in *gnocchi alla Sorrentina* (or any other pasta thusly named), a gooey mix of pasta, tomatoes, and cheese.

But since Campania is mainly coastal, some of its best cuisine is of a fishy nature. Any pasta or risotto *alla pescatora* (fisherman's style) or *ai frutti di mare* (literally "fruits of the sea") will be infused with a selection of seafood, generally some combination of *vongole* (clams), *cozze* (mussels), *ostriche* (oysters), *calamari* (squid), *polpo* (octopus), *gamberi/gam-beroni/scampi* (shrimp), *ricci di mare* (sea urchin), *aragostini* (crawfish), *aragote* (lobster), or *granchio* (crab). Any pasta cooked *al cartoccio* is basically the same sort of seafood dish, only this time all the ingredients are tossed together, wrapped in foil, and baked. Naples's most typical dish is *spaghetti con le vongole,* spaghetti tossed with the tiny, delicious clams found in the city's bay. You may find your fresh fish cooked *all'acqua pazza,* in "crazy waters," with baby tomatoes, white wine, and spices (often including capers).

Of Campanian **wines,** some of the best include Lacryma Christi, "Christ's Tears," grown on the slopes of Vesuvius by monks; Ravello's juicy local white; and the dry Greco di Tufo. In shops on Capri and along the Amalfi Coast, you'll find bottles of *limoncello,* a liqueur made with lemon zest and lots of sugar (best when drunk ice-cold).

---

underexplored, and undiscovered regions, and full of some of the country's most hospitable residents.

The sweeping natural preserve of the **Gargano Peninsula** provides the region with what little geographical variations can be found here, a rough highland that hides spectacular sea grottos pockmarking stunning bays. Camouflaged in olive orchards are the whitewashed medieval walls of **Ostuni** and **Otranto,** with their swirling baroque "new" centers and unspoiled beaches—you could travel as far as the rocky landscapes of the Salento and never once see a beach chair.

1 Naples: See It & Die

201km (125 miles) SE of Rome, 207km (128 miles) W of Bari

Un gran cassino, a rather coarse expression with its roots in the whorehouse, describes a great teeming noisy mess. It also describes **Naples (Napoli)** perfectly, showcasing the quicksilver southern Italian character at its warm, friendly best and its temperamental, frenzied worst. While one local will welcome you to his city like a long-lost relative, another is reaching into your pocket to relieve you of your wallet (pickpocketing of tourists is an ongoing problem). But these petty problems are just as much related to the cultural mix of citizens (and a swarm of illegal immigrants) that lends this paradox of a city some of its street-wise allure. Naples is not an easy city to love, but it's definitely worth the effort.

A Taste of Apulia

Apulia's trinity of homemade pasta shapes is *orecchiette* ("little ears" shaped like tiny, thick Frisbees), *cavatelli* (orecchiette rolled into a short tube), and *troccoli* (fat, square spaghetti). Any pasta served with *cime di rapa* comes with boiled turnip greens and is *very* Apulian. After "little ears," the quintessential Pugliese dish is *purè di fave con cicoria* (broad beans puréed and sided or mixed with boiled chicory). Other popular dishes include *spaghetti ricci di mare* (with sea urchin), *polpette al sugo* (meatballs in tomato sauce), and *braciola* or *involtino* (veal rolled up and stewed for hours in tomato sauce). Fresh ewe's milk *ricotta* is often salt-cured to form a hard, gratable variety called *ricotta dura, ricotta forte,* or *cacioricotta*—when invoked in a pasta sauce (sometimes called *mante-cati*), the hard ricotta is grated over a tomato puree.

Naples is generally unappreciated and undervalued, disregarded as seamy and squalid by Northern Italians and caricatured on tile in countless American pizza parlors. The historic grip of the Camorra crime family combined with a Byzantine bureaucracy doesn't help, and for years, Neapolitans have suffered from an insidious level of unemployment. In spite of the uphill climb, the city is experiencing a Renaissance, or so it would seem, given the visibility and quantity of civic improvements taking place around the city, and the resulting optimism is contagious.

The original Greek colony of Parthenope was founded on the tiny island of Megaris, today enclosed within the fortified walls of the **Castel dell'Ovo (Castle of the Egg).** Attracted by the charisma of the site, the Roman army descended upon the settlement in the 4th century, shifting the city inland and transforming it into a winter seaside resort and important cultural center for the likes of Virgil, Nero, Augustus, and Tiberius.

Piazza Plebescito, with its semicircle of columns opposite the imposing **Palazzo Reale,** was the crown jewel of 18th-century Renaissance Naples but had lost much of it luster. In 1994, prompted by the coming G7 Summit at the palazzo, local officials instituted a program to clean house, which resulted in the restoration of the piazza to its former, pedestrian-only, glory. As a cultural center, Naples remains the capital of the south, boasting a superb collection of artifacts in the **Museo Archeologico (Archaeological Museum),** a superior painting gallery at **Capodimonte,** and more than a handful of notable museums set within the imposing walls of medieval and Renaissance **castles** and downtown *palazzi* (palaces). Pompeii is reachable in minutes, while the breathtaking islands of **Capri** and **Ischia** hover on the horizon.

On the waterfront, with Mount Vesuvius as a backdrop, and connected to the mainland by a pedestrian causeway is **Castel dell'Ovo,** which fortifies a waterside neighborhood of trendy restaurants, cafes, and old apartment buildings, replete with laundry hanging out the windows. Known as **Borgo Marinari,** it's a magnet for those in search of a typical *al fresco* Neapolitan evening.

In spite of the wind-blown deluge of trash that continues to blight Piazza Garibaldi and Corso Umberto, we can forgive this most famous of landscapes on a sunny day. With breezes blowing off the bay and ramparts rising high above every corner of the city, the rewards of visiting this port town are innumerable.

Naples

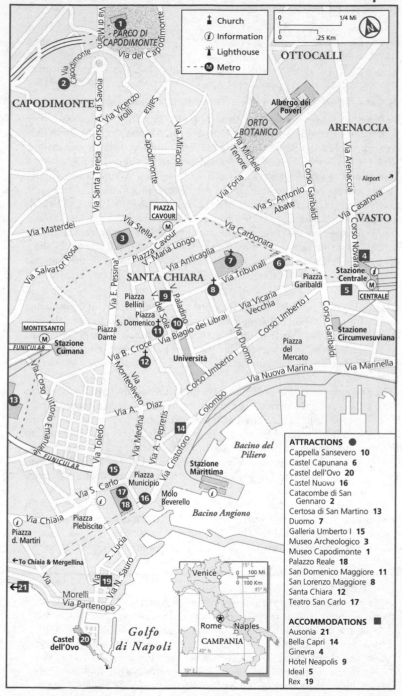

Legend:
- ✝ Church
- ⓘ Information
- 🕯 Lighthouse
- – –Ⓜ– Metro

Scale: 0 – 1/4 Mi · 0 – .25 Km

Map labels:

OTTOCALLI
CAPODIMONTE
ARENACCIA
Albergo dei Poveri
ORTO BOTANICO
Via di Miano
PARCO DI CAPODIMONTE
Via del Capodimonte
Via Capodimonte
Via Santa Teresa
Corso A. di Savoia
Via Vincenzo Irolli
Salita Capodimonte
Via Miracoli
Via Michele Tenore
Via Foria
Via S. Antonio Abate
Corso Garibaldi
Via Arenaccia
Airport
Via Casanova
VASTO
Corso Novara
Via Materdei
Via Stella
PIAZZA CAVOUR
Piazza Cavour
Via Carbonara
Via Maria Longo
Via Anticaglia
Via Salvator Rosa
Via E. Pessina
SANTA CHIARA
V. Paladino
Via Tribunali
Via Vicaria Vecchia
Piazza Garibaldi
Stazione Centrale
CENTRALE
Piazza Bellini
V. del Sole
Piazza S. Domenico
Piazza Dante
Via B. Croce
Via Biagio dei Librai
Via Duomo
Corso Umberto I
Corso Garibaldi
Stazione Circumvesuviana
MONTESANTO
FUNICULAR
Stazione Cumana
Via Montoliveto
Università
Piazza del Mercato
Via Marinella
Via A. Diaz
Via Toledo
Via Medina
Via A. Depretis
Via Cristoforo Colombo
Via Nuova Marina
Corso Vittorio Emanuele
FUNICULAR
Bacino del Piliero
Stazione Marittima
Via S. Carlo
Piazza Municipio
Molo Beverello
Bacino Angiono
Via Chiaia
Piazza d. Martiri
Piazza Plebiscito
To Chiaia & Mergellina
S. Lucia
Via N. Sauro
Morelli
Via Partenope
Castel dell'Ovo
Golfo di Napoli

Inset map:
Venice · 0 – 100 Mi · 0 – 100 Km · 15° E · 45° N · Rome · Naples · CAMPANIA · 40° N · 10° E

ATTRACTIONS ●

Cappella Sansevero **10**
Castel Capunana **6**
Castel dell'Ovo **20**
Castel Nuovo **16**
Catacombe di San Gennaro **2**
Certosa di San Martino **13**
Duomo **7**
Galleria Umberto I **15**
Museo Archeologico **3**
Museo Capodimonte **1**
Palazzo Reale **18**
San Domenico Maggiore **11**
San Lorenzo Maggiore **8**
Santa Chiara **12**
Teatro San Carlo **17**

ACCOMMODATIONS ■

Ausonia **21**
Bella Capri **14**
Ginevra **4**
Hotel Neapolis **9**
Ideal **5**
Rex **19**

ESSENTIALS

GETTING THERE   By Train   There are trains at least twice hourly **from Rome** (1½–2½ hr.; 14€–22€/$16–$25). If you plan on hopping directly onto a hydrofoil for Capri, or if you're staying at the Ausonia hotel (later in this section), get off at Naples–Stazione Mergellina. Otherwise, stay on until Naples–Stazione Centrale/Piazza Garibaldi. For rail information, call © **081-5534188.**

By Car   Follow the A1 from Rome. For parking, see "Getting Around," below.

By Plane   Naples's **Capodichino Airport** (© **081-7896385**) is served extensively both nationally and internationally. Domestically, **Alitalia's** (© **081-7093333**) network reaches the farthest, with daily flights arriving from Rome, Milan, Venice, Turin, Trieste, Genoa, Bologna, Palermo, and Catania. The privately run **Meridiana** (© **081-5526661**) arrives daily from Paris, Verona, Cagliari, and Milan. From points beyond the border, **Air Littoral** flies from Nice, **Transavia** from Amsterdam, **Lufthansa** from Munich, **Air France** from Paris, and **British Airways** from London. For information on international flight arrival and departure times, call the airport information line, © **081-7896259.** The airport is a 15-minute bus ride north of the center. The orange city bus line no. 14 shuttles passengers between the airport and Napoli's Molo Beverello via the train station in Piazza Garibaldi about every half-hour (1€/$1.15; last departure at 11:30pm).

CITY LAYOUT   Naples lies on the northern rim of the Bay of Naples, surrounded by low mountains struggling to contain the urban sprawl of the city along its slopes. You'll arrive in the dingiest corner of the city, **Piazza Garibaldi,** on the eastern edge of the center (hold your first impressions). From here, wide **Corso Umberto I** runs diagonally across the center toward **Piazza Municipio** at the main port, **Molo Beverello.**

The historic **old center** of Naples is bound by **Corso Umberto** on the south, **Piazza Cavour** on the north, **Via Duomo** on the east, and **Via Toledo** on the west. Through its heart runs **Spacca Napoli,** which translates loosely as "divide Naples in half." The name refers both to this historic district as a whole and to the arrow-straight street that runs down its center heading from east to west. The street changes names from **Via San Biagio dei Librai** to **Via Benedetto Croce,** to **Via Domenico Capitelli** (it's actually the old Decumanus Maximus, or Main Street, of the Roman city).

Across Via Toledo to the west lies the checkerboard of the **Quartiere degli Spagnoli,** a grid of narrow streets laid out by the Spanish viceroys along the bottom slopes of the Vomero hill. Its tall tenements are filled with lower-income housing, and while you can see some of the most genuine Naples life in this

---

A Ticket to Ride

The **giraNapoli,** a ticket to ride any of the city's means of public transport (bus, Metro, funicular, or the city portions of the rail lines), is available for 1€ at any *tabacchi* (tobacconists), most newsstands, and all Metro stops, funicular stations, and train stations. It's valid for **90 minutes,** during which time you can transfer between as many buses as you'd like, plus once to each of the other public transport systems (Metro, funicular), *but don't forget to validate it.* There's also a daily pass for 3€ ($3.45). See the sections on Pompeii and Sorrento for competitive transportation options for day trips from Naples.

A Travel Tip

The Naples daily paper *Il Mattino* has a page near the back listing the **current transportation schedules** for the entire province, including the state and private rail lines, buses, and ferries, as does the free bimonthly *Qui Napoli*, available at tourist information offices and most hotels.

area—ascending the winding stairs of the hill will put you practically in the living rooms of these people—be extra cautious; it is also one of the strongholds of the Camorra organized crime network. South of the Quartiere degli Spagnoli, Via Toledo spills into **Piazza Plebescito,** the heart of 18th-century Naples, with the royal palace and theater, and the docks just beyond.

West of the center is a trio of rather nice middle-class residential neighborhoods, starting with **Santa Lucia,** rising above Piazza Plebescito on the seaward slope of the Vomero. Beyond this is the long, wide, harborside park of **Chiaia,** with a few blocks of buildings climbing behind it up a small ridge. At the end of Chiaia are the docks and train station of the workaday zone of **Mergellina.**

GETTING AROUND   By Metro, Bus & Funicular   Naples's **Metro** is really a commuter rail line, though it is handy for visitors to zip from Mergellina (where there are some fine hotels) into the center, or from the train station direct to Naples's top sight, the Archaeological Museum.

You'll probably be using the **bus/trolley** system more often, and **Piazza Garibaldi,** in front of the central train station, is the hub for almost every bus in Naples. Most useful are the **R1 bus,** which circles endlessly around the heart of the historic center; the **R2,** which shuttles between Piazza Garibaldi/the train station down Corso Umberto to Piazza Trieste e Trento; and the **R3,** which connects Piazza Trieste e Trento and Piazza Municipio with the Riviera di Chiaia and Mergellina. To get to the hilltop neighborhoods like the Vomero, Naples has built several *funiculari* (cog railways). **Tram 1** runs from the western edge of Piazza Garibaldi (the far side from the train station) direct to the Molo Beverello ferry docks, but as it's always overcrowded and prone to petty theft, we don't recommend it.

By Car   Drive in Naples only if you are practicing for the demolition derby. Neapolitan motorists drive twice as fast and three times as aggressively as your average Italian, and while red lights seem to be considered optional in the rest of Italy, here they're considered a nuisance and ignored entirely. No city in Europe (except maybe Paris) is more stressful, aggravating, confusing, and downright dangerous to drive in.

Do yourself a favor and **park** as soon as you arrive in town. If you want to explore the Amalfi Coast by rental car, pick it up the day you leave Naples (or, better yet, take the train to Sorrento and pick up your car there). There are garages just south of the central train station at Via Ferraris 40 (© **081-264344**); near the center at Via Shelley 11, between Via Toledo and Piazza Municipio (© **081-5513104**); near the Molo Beverello ferry docks at Via dei Gaspari 14 (© **081-5525442**); and near the Mergellina docks and Mergellina train station at Piazza Sannazaro 142 (© **081-681437**). The major car-rental agencies have their offices at the train station, thoughtfully located near the entrances to the A1 (to Rome) and the A3 (to the Amalfi coast) autostradas.

By Taxi   Use only legitimate taxis, hired at the following locations, or call the Radio taxi numbers below. Taxi stands are at Piazza Garibaldi, Piazza Municipio,

Piazza Trieste e Trento, Piazza dei Martiri, Piazza Vittoria, Via Partenope, Piazza San Pasquale/Riviera di Chiaia, and Via Mergellina. Naples Radio taxi numbers are © 081-5564444, 081-5560202, 081-5515151, 081-5525252, and 081-5707070; or simply dial © 2525.

There are occasional reports of unscrupulous drivers trying to swindle unsuspecting tourists, so know these official rates: Rides cost an initial 2.60€ ($3), plus .05€ (6¢) for every 75m (246 ft.). There are supplemental charges for Sunday (1.60€/$1.85), rides between 10pm and 7am (2.10€/$2.40), luggage (.50€/60¢ per bag), calling ahead for a radio taxi (.77€/90¢, plus the metered distance to reach you). Fixed rates for the following rides apply (no supplements): 13€ ($14) train station to the airport; 16€ ($18) Molo Beverello to the airport; 9.50€ ($11) Piazza Municipio to Museo Capodimontel; and 9.50€ ($11) Molo Beverello to the train station.

VISITOR INFORMATION There are **tourist information desks** at the train station (© **081-268779**), the airport (© **081-7805761**), the Palazzo Reale at Piazza Plebescito (© **081-2525711;** fax 081-418619), Piazza del Gesù Nuovo (© **081-5523328**), and Piazza dei Martiri 58 (© **081-405311**). Before you go, log on to **www.inaples.it** for regularly updated information on the city, events, art, and culture.

FAST FACTS: Naples

Books **Feltrinelli,** at Via Tommaso d'Aquino 70 (just off V. Torino; © **081-5521436**), has travel books and novels in English (mainly Penguin classics) upstairs.

Consulates There's a **U.S. Consulate** on Piazza della Repubblica (© **081-5838111**) and a **U.K. Consulate** at Via dei Mille 40 (© **081-4238911**).

Drugstores There are **all-night pharmacies** around the **train station** (in the station itself, at Piazza Garibaldi 11, and at Corso Garibaldi 354), in the **city center** (at Piazza Municipio 54 and at Piazza Dante 71), in **Chiaia** (at Riviera di Chiaia 169, at V. D. Morelli 22, and at V. Carducci 21), and on the **Vomero** (at V. G. Merliani 27 and at V. Cliea 124). You can also dial © **1100** (Italian operators) for the addresses and phone numbers of the three closest open pharmacies.

E-mail & Snail Mail There are central **post offices** at Piazza Matteotti off Via Diaz (© **081-5511456**), in the main train station, and in the Galleria Umberto I (© **081-5523467**). All are open Monday through Friday from 8:15am to 7:15pm and Saturday from 8:15am to noon. Internet points are generally available in hotels; there are several located around the train station (try the call center opposite the McDonald's).

Emergencies Call © **113** for any emergency. Dial © **112** for the carabinieri to get emergency aid in English, French, and Spanish; to report a fire, call © **115**; for an ambulance, dial © **081-7520696**; for car breakdowns, dial © **116**.

Hospitals Anyone can head to the *pronto soccorso* (first aid) station of the nearest *ospedale* (hospital). Near the train station, the **Ospedale Ascalesi** is at Piazza Collenda/Via Pietro Colletta just off Corso Umberto I (© **081-2542111**). Just south of the train station at the harbor is the

Ospedale Loreto Mare, on Via Amerigo Vespucci (© **081-2542111**). In the city center there is the **Policlinico,** on Piazza Miraglia/Via del Sole just above Piazza San Domenico (© **081-5661111** or 081-7461111); also in the center is the **Ospedale Vecchio Pellegrini,** off Via Toledo on Via Porta Medina at the foot of the funicular up to the Vomero (© **081-2543475**). In Chiaia is the **Ospedale Loreto Crispi,** where Via Francesco Crispi changes names to Via Schipa at Via A. Mirelli (© **081-2547210**).

Laundry There's a coin-operated **laundromat** (© **338-8942714**) at Corso Novara 62–64 (1 block from the Hotel Ginevra), open daily from 8:30am to 8pm. The cost to wash and dry 7 kilograms (15 lb.) is 7€ ($8.05).

Safety The Camorra (Neapolitan Mafia) continues to control much of the city, and petty theft is rampant—though the rate of violent crime against visitors is, as in the rest of Italy, much lower than that of any U.S. city. In recent years, Naples has made great strides in cleaning up the city, but this is not a "go ahead" to let down your guard. Clutch your camera firmly (try to keep it out of view at all times) and keep a hand on your wallet. Women should avoid carrying bags with ineffectual magnetic closures; wear your purse straps diagonally, and proceed confidently. Be especially protective of your personal space, particularly around the train station, as pickpockets look for "accidental" body contact in order to separate you from your belongings. Avoid the tram.

The residential neighborhoods to the west—Santa Lucia, Chiaia, and Mergellina—are a bit safer, but not much so. Take comfort in knowing that even the locals are afraid to leave their cars on the street, so follow their example by parking in a garage—and don't leave anything valuable in the car.

EXPLORING NAPLES
IN THE CENTER

Museo Archeologico (Archaeological Museum) *★★* This is one of the most significant archaeological collections in Europe (certainly, southern Italy's best), the only absolutely required sight in Naples, and well worth 2 to 3 hours of your time. If you explore Pompeii without paying this museum a visit as well, you've missed out on half its riches. The best statues, mosaics, and wall paintings at Pompeii that hadn't already been carried off by looters were long ago removed from the archaeological site to be preserved here. Pompeii's artifacts, best seen *after* a visit to the site, are displayed alongside finds from across southern Italy as well as many from Rome itself (including the important and impressive statuary collected by the Farnese family). The museum is poorly labeled and in a constant state of metamorphosis, but be sure to search out these highlights throughout the collections.

The *Doriforo,* or *Policleto's Spearman* (a Pompeiian Roman copy of a 440-B.C. Greek original), is the most accurate surviving copy of a masterpiece by Policletus of Argo, one of the geniuses of Greek Golden Age sculpture. It represents Policleto's embodiment of the ideal human form, carved with exacting mathematical proportions and a perfect figurative balance. The **Pozzuoli Sarcophagus** is a well-preserved 3rd-century-A.D. Roman piece with a tumultuous high relief showing a seated, contemplative Prometheus creating Man surrounded by a swirl of deities and *putti* (cherubs).

Island-Hopping Made Easy

When shopping at Naples's Molo Beverello for a boat to Capri, Ischia, or Procida Island, there's no need to visit all the dock offices for the best price. **Ontano Tours** (✆ 081-5800341) is a central clearinghouse, located just to the left of the driveway leading into the dock area. This travel agency will book you on the next ferry or hydrofoil out, tell you which line it is, and sell you a voucher that you then carry to that line's dock office to trade in for a ticket—all at no extra cost.

The bulked-up and burly *Farnese Hercules* was excavated from Rome's Baths of Caracalla and is a fine example of the exaggerated 3rd-century-A.D. Athenian style of the sculptor Glykon. Discovered without legs, the statue had its limbs recomposed by a student of Michelangelo (Guglielmo della Porta) and preferred to the originals well after their rediscovery. Eventually, the originals were restored to their rightful owner, while della Porta's calves are relegated to an exhibit on the wall behind the statue.

Commanding the hall at the opposite end is the impressive *Farnese Bull,* the largest surviving sculpture of the ancient world. Standing 4m (13 ft.) high, this 2nd-century-A.D. Hellenistic work copies a 1st-century-B.C. original and tells the tale of Amphion and Zethos (the two nude men) avenging the maltreatment of their mother, Antiope (standing at the back), by tying her tormentor, Dirke (the woman about to get trampled), to the horns of a bull she was preparing to sacrifice. Remarkably, all of the figures were carved from a single, gargantuan block of marble.

On a mezzanine level between the ground and first floors (make sure you take the main sweeping staircase to gain access) is preserved the museum's most famous collection, the mosaics and paintings from Pompeii, including the slightly ruined but remarkably well-crafted *Battle of Alexander and Darius* ✸, discovered in the House of the Faun at Pompeii. This scene, with a highly advanced use of color and minuscule mosaic chips to render the figures as well as any painting, is probably a Roman copy of an original crafted within a few decades of the actual battle of Isse of 333 B.C., depicting Alexander astride his horse (on the left) giving chase to Darius, who's retreating in his chariot.

Among the paintings here, be sure you don't miss the portrait of a young woman wearing a gold filigree hair net and pausing with her stylus to her lips before returning to write in the wax volume she holds. This must have been a standard pose, for it appears again in the portrait of Paquio Proculo and his wife, a prosperous middle-class Pompeiian couple, probably bakers. This portrait was rather shocking when it was discovered, for it showed that interracial marriage was probably common (she appears to be European, he North African) in the ancient empire. The portrayal of these women is also intriguing, in that it implies ancient Pompeii enjoyed a great deal of equality: the first is probably writing poetry (an artist), the second possibly keeping the books for the couple's bakery (a businesswoman).

One of the more hyped-up exhibits in the collection is the **Gabinetto Segreto (Secret Chamber)** ✸✸. The gated entrance is accessible through the mosaic exhibit and guards a collection of sexually symbolic and not so symbolic paintings, mosaics, and artifacts recovered from the *lupinare* (brothel), as well as from the many private pleasure chambers of Pompeii. The visit is free, but since the capacity of the gallery is a mere 20 people at a time, you must reserve your time

Travel Tip: Napoli Artecard

Initially introduced for the Maggio dei Musei event (May at the Museums) and extended indefinitely due to popularity, the **Artecard** (www.campaniartecard.it) functions like the Eurailpass. It works like this: For 25€ ($29) (18€/$21) for children 18 to 25), the cardholder is entitled to 3 days of unlimited museum entrances, and all public transportation is free for the duration of the ticket. A 7-day ticket costs 28€ ($32) (21€/$24) for children 18 to 25), while a more limited ticket (entrance to two museums and transport within Napoli only) is available for 13€ ($15) (8€/$9.20) for children 18 to 25). Participating museums are Capodimonte, San Martino, the Archaeological Museum, Sant'Elmo Castle, the Royal Palace, and Castelnuovo. The Artecard is widely available, including at the airport, the train and Metro stations, and all of the museums on the circuit.

at the ticket window when paying for admission to the museum. Guided tours (in Italian) begin every half-hour, and the exhibit is well signed in both Italian and English. (For large groups, call ahead to reserve a guided tour in English.)

Piazza Museo/Piazza Cavour (at the northern edge of the city). (C) 081-440166. Admission 6.20€ ($7.15). Wed–Mon 9am–7:30pm. Bus: R1, R4, V10, 24, 42, 47, 110, 137. Metro: Cavour.

Santa Chiara ⊛ Santa Chiara is the most rewarding of Naples's churches. Built in 1328, altered in the 18th century to the baroque style, and half-destroyed by incendiary bombs in 1943, the church was restored as best as possible to its original Gothic state in 1953. The light-filled interior is lined with chapels, each containing leftover bits of sculpture or fresco from the medieval church, but the best three line the wall behind the High Altar. In the center is the towering, multilevel **tomb of Robert the Wise d'Angio,** sculpted by Giovanni and Pacio Bertini in 1343. To its right is Tino di Camaino's **tomb of Charles, duke of Calabria;** on the left is the 1399 **monument to Mary of Durazza.** In the choir behind the altar are more salvaged medieval remnants of frescoes and statuary, including bits of a Giotto *Crucifixion.*

Exit the church and walk down its left flank to enter one of Naples's top sights and the most relaxing retreat from the bustle of the city, the 14th-century **cloisters** ⊛. In 1742, Domenico Antonio Vaccaro took the courtyard of these flowering cloisters and lined the four paths to its center with arbors supported by columns, each of which is plated with colorfully painted majolica tiles, interspersed with majolica tiled benches. In the **museum** rooms off the cloisters is a scattering of Roman and medieval remains. On the piazza outside is one of Naples's several baroque spires, the **Guglia dell'Immacolata,** a tall pile of statues and reliefs erected in 1750.

Piazza Gesù Nuovo/Via Benedetto Croce. (C) 081-5526209, or 081-7971256 for museum. Admission to church and cloisters free; suggested museum donation 4€ ($4.60). Daily 9:30am–1pm; Mon–Sat 3:30–5:30pm. Bus: E1, R1, R3, R4.

Cappella Sansevero (Sansevero Chapel) ⊛ If you want the best example of how baroque can be ludicrously over the top, hauntingly beautiful, and technically brilliant all at once, search out the nondescript entrance to one of Italy's most fanciful chapels. This 1590 chapel is a festival of marble, frescoes and, above all, sculpture—in relief and in the round, masterfully showing off the considerable technical abilities and intricate visual storytelling of a few otherwise relatively unknown Neapolitan baroque masters. At the center is Giuseppe Sammartino's remarkable alabaster **Veiled Christ** ⊛⊛⊛ (1753), one of the most successful and convincing illusions of soft reality crafted from hard stone in the history of art, depicting the deceased Christ lying on pillows under a transparent veil.

Three **sculptures** on the walls stand out as well, including Francesco Celebrano's 1762 relief of the **Deposition** behind the altar; Antonio Corradini's allegory of **Chastity** (a marble statue of a woman whose nudity is covered only by a decidedly immodest, clinging, gauzy veil); and Francesco Queirolo's virtuoso allegory of **Despair,** represented by a man struggling with a net carved in marble.

Via Francesco de Sanctis 19 (near Piazza San Domenico Maggiore). © 081-5518470. Admission 5€ ($5.75). Wed–Mon 10am–8pm (to 5pm Nov–June). Bus: E1, R1, R3, R4, V10, 24, 42, 105, 105r.

San Lorenzo Maggiore   The greatest of Naples's layered churches was built in 1265 over a 6th-century basilica, constructed atop many ancient remains. The interior is pure Gothic, with tall pointed arches and an apse off which radiate nine chapels. Aside from some eye-popping inlaid marble baroque chapels, the highlight of the interior is Tino da Camaino's **canopy tomb of Catherine of Austria** (1323–25), daughter-in-law of Robert the Wise. It was here, too, in 1334, that Giovanni Boccaccio first caught sight of Robert of Anjou's daughter Maria, who inspired the "Fiammetta" in his writings.

San Lorenzo holds the best and most extensive (although still largely unexcavated) remains of the ancient **Greek and Roman cities,** currently open to the public. The foundations of the church are actually the walls of Neapolis's basilican law courts (this architectural type, the basilica, was adopted by the paleo-Christians as a general blueprint for their first churches). In the cloisters are bits of the Roman city's treasury and marketplace. In the crypt are the rough remains of a Roman-era shop-lined street, a Greek temple, and a medieval building.

Piazza San Gaetano 316. © 081-290580, or 081-2110860 for scavi. Admission to church free; scavi 3€ ($3.45). Mon and Wed–Sat 9am–1pm and 4–6:30pm; Sun 9am–1:30pm. Bus: E1, 42, 105, 105r.

Duomo (Cathedral)   The neo-Gothic facade of Naples's cathedral—built in the French Gothic style for Charles I in 1294 but rebuilt after a disastrous earthquake in 1456—was finished in 1905, but the central portal survives from the 1407 version. The 16 piers inside are made of 110 antique columns of African and Asian granite removed from nearby pagan buildings.

The third chapel on the right is the sumptuous 17th-century **Cappella di San Gennaro,** elaborately frescoed by Domenichino and, later, Giovanni Lanfranco, who completed the concentric clouds of saints and angels spiraling up the airy dome. Also here is a painting of **San Gennaro Exiting Unharmed from the Furnace,** by Giuseppe Ribera, showing a miracle by Benevento's persecuted bishop in A.D. 305, who survived both this roasting and being thrown to lions, only to be done in by an axe to the neck. Among the silver reliquaries you'll see is one of **St. Irene Protecting the City,** in which the saint holds a scale model of Naples circa 1733. The most venerable item in all of Naples, however, is the silver reliquary bust that preserves the head of the city patron, St. Gennaro. Stored behind the chapel altar are two immeasurably venerated vials of his coagulated blood. The vials are taken out for the **Miracolo di San Gennaro** ⊛ on the first Saturday of May, September 19, and December 16, amid much religious pomp and ceremony, whereupon the blood in the vials miraculously liquefies and then boils, only to liquefy again (Gennaro, incidentally, is the patron saint of blood banks). The speed with which the blood liquefies is a prediction of Naples's prosperity for the coming months. When the miracle occurs, the faithful line up to kiss the vials.

To the right of the High Altar are two chapels with staccato remnants of 13th- and 14th-century frescoes and an inlaid marble floor. The **Crypt of San Gennaro** (aka Cappella Carafa) beneath the High Altar is one of the greatest examples of Renaissance design in Naples, including the Cosmatesque-style tomb of Pope Innocent IV (1315). To the left of the High Altar is a chapel containing an *Assumption* by Umbrian master painter Perugino.

Off the left aisle is the entrance to the ancient **Basilica di Santa Restituta,** a pre-existing church built in the 4th century atop a Temple to Apollo, which is probably where the antique columns of the nave—rebuilt in the 14th century— come from. Luca Giordano's brush was active again here on the ceiling, but the highlight is the **baptistery** ✹ at the back. This domed cube of a room is the old- est building of its kind in Christian Europe, built in the 5th century and retain- ing impressive swatches of the original mosaics on the dome. From this little side church you can descend to the basement, where a few scraps of Greek and Roman streets, walls, and mosaics remain.

Via Duomo. ✆ 081-449097. Admission to church free; archaeological crypt and baptistery 3€ ($3.45). Daily 9am–noon and 4:30–7pm (crypt and baptistery close Sun at noon). Bus: E1, 42, 105, 105r.

ON THE WATERFRONT

Teatro San Carlo   San Carlo is one of the oldest, largest, and most respected opera houses in Italy, built (40 years before La Scala) under the auspices of Charles of Bourbon in 1737 (who didn't particularly care for opera but cared very much about his reputation as an enlightened patron of the arts). After a fire in 1816, the theater was rebuilt by Antonio Niccolini—who, it's said, filled the walls with terra-cotta vases to help give the performance space what is still widely regarded as the best acoustics in Europe. San Carlo reopened shortly after under the musical direction of Gioacchino Rossini, opening up its sumptuous audito- rium to premieres of operas by Rossini, Bellini, and Donizetti. **Tickets** (✆ 081- **7972331** or 081-7972412) run 8€ to 125€ ($9.20–$144), depending on the type of performance and where you sit.

Via San Carlo/Piazza Trieste e Trento. ✆ 081-7972111. Guided tours suspended indefinitely. Bus: R2, R3, C25, V10, 24, 105, 105r, 140.

Palazzo Reale (Royal Palace) ✹   Naples's royal palace had to be restruc- tured following Allied bomb damage in 1943, but it retains some sumptuous royal apartments and, in niches along the 18th-century facade, statues of the greatest kings from the eight dynasties that have ruled Naples: Roger (Norman), Frederick II (Swabian), Charles I (Angevin), Alfonso (Aragonese), Charles V (Austrian), Charles III (Bourbon), Joachim Murat (French Napoleonic), and Vittorio Emanuele II (Savoy and, ultimately, Italian).

Court engineer Domenico Fontana started construction of the palazzo in 1599 under the viceroy Ruiz de Castro, who wished to create one of the most glorious palaces in the kingdom of Spain's King Philip III. The core was finished by 1616, but in 1759 Ferdinando Fuga was brought in by Ferdinand IV to amplify the palazzo, including the addition of the ornate **Teatro do Corte,** built on the occasion of the king's wedding to Maria Carolina of Hapsburg (Marie Antoinette's sister) and decorated with papier-mâché sculpture. Also here are preserved 15th-century bronze doors from the Castel Nuovo, whose reliefs tell of Ferdinand of Aragon's feuds with the local barons (the cannonball jutting out of the bottom of one door is a testament to the battle waged by the French and Genoese navies in Naples's harbor). Written descriptions of each palatial room and its contents are available in English. Be sure not to miss the elaborate

Throne Room or Belsario Corenzio's ceiling frescoes in several chambers that depict the *Glories of the Spanish Monarchy.*

The expansive **Piazza Plebescito** 𝒢 in front of the royal palace is one of Naples's largest open spaces, laid out with a curving colonnade and equestrian statues of Charles III of Bourbon and Ferdinand IV in the early 18th century. At the center of the curve is the neoclassical church of **San Francesco di Paola** 𝒢𝒢𝒢, modeled after Rome's Pantheon in 1817 for Ferdinand IV, who ordered it built as an offering of thanks after he retook the city from Napoleonic troops.

Piazza Plebescito. 𝒞 081-5808326. Admission 4.15€ ($4.75), free for those under 18 or over 60. Mon–Tues and Thurs–Sat 9am–8pm; Sun and holidays 9am–8pm. Bus: R2, R3, C25, V10, 24, 105, 105r, 140.

Castel Nuovo (New Castle) & Maschio Angioino (Angevin Fortress) 𝒢𝒢
Though the core Maschio Angioino was built in the 13th century, the grand **triumphal arch** 𝒢𝒢 wedged between two massive 15th-century bastions is pure Renaissance. This unique adaptation of a triumphal arch was grafted onto the castle to commemorate Alfonso I of Aragon's arrival in the city in 1443. The highlights inside are the statues and frescoes from the 14th and 15th centuries in the **Cappella Palatina (Palatine Chapel)** 𝒢, a middling collection of paintings from the 15th to 20th centuries, and the huge **Sala dei Baroni** 𝒢𝒢, the grand hall where Naples's City Council still meets.

Piazza Municipio. 𝒞 081-7952003. Admission 5.15€ ($5.95). Mon–Sat 9am–7pm. Bus: R2, R3, C25, C82, C82b, V10, 24, 105, 105r.

Naples Underground *Kids*   Interred beneath the sidewalks and highways of Naples is another world, a city underground that would be impossible to explore in its entirety. During the Roman rule of Augusto, a project for the construction of an aqueduct was completed, creating a subterranean labyrinth 170km (105 miles) long. Over the years, the system of aqueducts has been altered and enlarged, even functioning as air-raid shelters during World War II. The guided visit touches the surface of this complex system of tunnels, homing in on particular points of interest that include **Greco-Roman remains.**

Visits are organized by both the Libera Associazione Escursionisti Sottosuoli (𝒞 081-400256; meet at Caffè Gambrinus) and the Associazione Napoli Sotterranea (𝒞 081-296944; meet in Piazza San Gaetano) on Saturday and Sunday. The latter also offers continuous admission daily (reduced hours off season; call ahead) at the entrance in Piazza San Gaetano Monday through Wednesday and Friday from noon to 4pm; Thursday from noon to 9pm; and Saturday, Sunday, and holidays from 10am to 6pm. Admission is 6.70€ ($7.70). The guided visit lasts 80 minutes. Add 20 minutes for the Roman theater.

IN THE HILLS
Museo Capodimonte 𝒢𝒢   Set in the green of Capodimonte Park high above the city is by far the best painting gallery in all of southern Italy. The National Picture Gallery consumes an 18th-century royal palace and is particularly strong on works from Old Masters representing all phases of the Renaissance and baroque periods. The core of the museum's holdings is the Farnese Collection, inherited by the Bourbon dynasty, along with the historical apartments and the china and majolica collections. Among the early Renaissance paintings is a simple and beautiful 1426 *Crucifixion* by Masaccio, and one of **Giovanni Bellini**'s masterpieces, his *Transfiguration* 𝒢 (1478–79). From the great **Raphael** we have *Portrait of Cardinal Alessandro Farnese* (who became Pope Paul III; 1511), a cartoon of *Moses and the Burning Bush* (1514), and the *Eternal*

Father. Representing the genius of **Michelangelo** is a cartoon of soldiers that he made as a study for his *Crucifixion of St. Peter* fresco in the Vatican.

There are High Renaissance pieces from Sebastiano del Piombo and **Correggio,** whose 1518 *Marriage of St. Catherine* is a finely studied classical work. **Titian** painted a whole gaggle of portraits of various Farnese cardinals in the 1540s, along with a provocative *Danäe* (1546) painted for Cardinal Alessandro Farnese (and probably using the cardinal's mistress as the goddess model), and the *Portrait of a Young Lady* (1546), which some scholars believe is a portrait of Titian's own daughter. **El Greco** contributes the haunting *El Soplón,* or *Youth Lighting a Candle with a Coal* (1575). There are many good **Mannerist** works from the brushes of Andrea del Sarto, Pontormo, Rosso Fiorentino, and Parmigianino.

After a breather of Flemish paintings (look especially for *The Misanthrope* and *The Blind Leading the Blind,* both 1568 works by **Pieter Bruegel**), the baroque takes over with a survey of the **Carracci** clan, including works by Agostino, Ludovico, and especially **Annibale Carracci,** who pokes fun at his arch-competitor Caravaggio by painting that artist's leering face on his rendition of a *Satyr.* **Caravaggio** got the last laugh, though, since art history books give but a paragraph to Carracci while filling pages with homage to Caravaggio's genius for composition and dramatic use of *chiaroscuro* (strongly contrasting light and dark areas), well evident in the ***Flagellation of Christ*** ✦ (1609) kept here.

Early baroque's greatest (and virtually only) female artist was **Artemisia Gentileschi,** whose rape as a teenager (and the subsequent highly public and sensational trial) may have later led her to turn her artistic lens often to the many examples throughout history, myth, and the Bible wherein women exact revenge upon men, as in this gallery's gory *Judith Beheading Holofernes.* **Luca Giordano** manages to give good compositional balance and use of light to baroque extravagance in his *Madonna del Baldacchino* (1686).

Pop into the small, excruciatingly elaborate Chinese-style **Salottino di Porcellana** for an excellent example of Italy's finest 18th-century porcelain, still being produced in a nearby factory (built in 1743) here on Capodimonte.

Parco di Capodimonte, Via Capodimonte. ② 081-7499111. Admission 7.25€ ($8.35; 6.20€/$7.15 after 2pm), free for those under 18 or over 60. Tues–Sun 8:30am–7:30pm. Bus: 24, 137, 110.

Catacombe di San Gennaro (Catacombs of San Gennaro) (Kids) These

wide tunnels lined with early Christian burial niches grew around the tomb of an important pagan family but became a pilgrimage site when the bones of San Gennaro himself were transferred here in the 5th century. Along with several well-preserved 6th-century frescoes, there's a depiction of San Gennaro from the 5th century A.D. whose halo sports an alpha and omega and a cross—symbols normally reserved exclusively for Christ's halo. The tour takes you through the upper level of tunnels, passing through several small early basilicas carved from the tufa rock. The cemetery remained active until the 11th century, but most of the bones have since been blessed and reinterred in ossuaries on the lower levels (closed to the public). The catacombs survived the centuries intact, but the precious antique frescoes suffered some damage when these tunnels served as an air raid shelter during World War II. *Note:* At press time the catacombs were closed for restorations; call before you go to see if they are open to the public.

Via Capodimonte 16 (enter around the left of the Basilica del Madre di Bonconsiglio and through the gate). ② 081-7411071. Bus: 24, 137, 110.

Certosa di San Martino ✦✦ This 14th-century Carthusian monastery

is famous for its fine church, peaceful cloisters, small painting gallery, and remarkable *presepio* collection of Christmas crèches. From here, the **views** ⓕ across the city below are fantastic, and alone worth the trip up.

The marble-clad **church** has a ceiling painting of the *Ascension* by Lanfranco in the nave, along with 12 *Prophets* by Giuseppe Ribera. Ribera also did the *Institution of the Eucharist* on the left wall of the choir, while Lanfranco painted the *Crucifixion* and Guido Reni the *Nativity* at the choir's back wall. In the church treasury is Luca Giordano's ceiling fresco of the *Triumph of Judith* (1704) and Ribera's masterful *Descent from the Cross.*

The vast **museum of *presepi*** houses dozens of Neapolitan Christmas crèches with an overall cast of thousands. These inspired peasant and holy figures have come out of the workshops of Naples's greatest artisans over the past 4 centuries. The modest **painting and sculpture gallery** houses 15th- to 18th-century works, including a few by Bernini, Caracciolo, and Vaccaro.

Next door to the monastery is the star-shape **Castel Sant'Elmo** (ⓒ 081-5784030), partially carved into the tufa of this strategic position above the city. The castle was built between 1329 and 1343 by the Angevins and enlarged in the 16th century. After a walk through the dark, resonant, medieval stone halls, the castle proffers a magnificent 360° panorama of Naples and its bay. The castle is open Tuesday through Sunday from 9am to 2pm; admission is 1.05€ ($1.20).

Largo San Martino/Via Tito Angelini (on the Vomero next to Castel Sant'Elmo). ⓒ 081-5781769. Admission 5€ ($5.75). Tues–Fri 8:30am–7:30pm; Sat–Sun 9am–11pm (to 7:30pm in winter). Funicular: Montesanto, then Bus V1 (or walk).

ACCOMMODATIONS YOU CAN AFFORD
NEAR THE TRAIN STATION

Ginevra   This family-run pensione three flights up in a charming palazzo offers the convenience and comfort difficult to find in a neighborhood so close to the train station. But access to transportation is one of the central draws of this pension-bordering-on-hotel (Pompeii, Herculaneum Sorrento, and Naples's historic center almost as easy as stepping out the front door). Almost all of the rooms in the older section have been redecorated and upgraded, a work-in-progress that includes renovated bathrooms and air-conditioning (otherwise, large fans are available on request). The five new rooms (nos. 25–29) that were added across the hallway are more typical of a three-star hotel (air-conditioning, TV, safe), thus the price tag of 80€ ($92) double and 110€ ($126) triple. The English-speaking receptionists (either the owner, Bruno; his son, Lello; or their partner, Luigi) make themselves available to their guests for reliable recommendations for what to do in town.

Via Genova 116, 80142 Naples. ⓒ 081-283210. Fax 081-5541757. www.hotelginevra.it. 14 units (5 to follow; 6 with shower). 35€ ($40) single without shower; 55€ ($63) double without shower, 65€ ($75) double with shower; 75€ ($86) triple without shower, 90€ ($104) triple with shower. Breakfast 5€ ($5.75). 10% discount with this book and payment in cash. **Amenities:** Car-rental desk; tour desk; Internet point; laundry (5€/$5.75). *In room:* TV.

Ideal   The name may be a bit of wishful thinking, but this large, clean budget standby is just 60m (197 ft.) from the train station (and a 10-min. tram ride from the ferry docks) and is indeed ideal if you plan on lots of day trips. Some of the tile floors are fantastically patterned, and the walls are decorated with simple stuccoes. A 1998 renovation installed new bathrooms in all rooms. Several rooms have terraces on the courtyard and are much quieter than those fronting traffic-choked Piazza Garibaldi. For 10€ ($12) extra per night, you can make use of the air-conditioning unit available in most of the rooms.

Piazza Garibaldi 99 (on the left side of the square as you exit the train station), 80142 Naples. ℂ 081-269237 or 081-202223. Fax 081-285942. www.albergoideal.it. 45 units. 50€–60€ ($58–$69) single; 75€–95€ ($86–$109) double; 100€–130€ ($115–$150) triple. 5% discount for Frommer's readers. Rates include breakfast. AE, DC, MC, V. Nearby parking in garage 15€ ($17). Metro: Naples Centrale. Tram: 1, R2, 14, 14r, 42, 110 (to Piazza Garibaldi). *In room:* TV.

IN THE CENTRO STORICO

Bella Capri   The uninviting side-street entrance to this neglected residential palazzo may put you off, but once you're under the warm glow of the green neon outside this welcoming sanctuary, things can only get better. Located in the vibrant heart of the city opposite the gulf, Bella Capri provides an unbeatable base for excursions just about anywhere, from ferry hops to the nearby islands, to the historic highlights of the city proper. There's even a bus directly to Pompeii across the street at the docks. A bayside room (nos. 2, 3, 4, and 5, the same ones with air-conditioning at 10€/$12 extra per night) includes an oversize door to a balcony overlooking the port; back rooms get a view of Mount Vesuvius. You may want to avoid no. 8, as it is opposite the entrance and participates forcibly in the rattle of all incoming phone calls and door buzzings. Call ahead to reserve, and have a 5€ ($5.75) coin ready to use the elevator (reimbursed).

Via Melisurgo 4 (stair B; 6th floor), 80133 Naples. ℂ 081-5529494. Fax 081-5529265. 9 units. 55€–65€ ($63–$75) single; 66€–82€ ($76–$94) double; 82€–100€ ($94–$115) triple. Rates include voucher for breakfast at corner bar. AE, DISC, MC, V. From airport or train station, take bus 3S directly to Molo Beverello; from Piazza Garibaldi, take bus 152 to Molo Beverello. *In room:* TV, no phone.

Hotel Neapolis 𝒢 *Finds*   This hotel is a great option for those wishing to make a dent in perusing the overwhelming architectural and historical patrimony concentrated in the historic quarter. Only a couple of years old, this crisp hotel located on the third floor of a historic palazzo is filled with modern hotel conveniences and a computer in every room. Aesthetically, the rooms are pleasingly simple, with clean and cool terra-cotta tile floors and the sparest combination of wooden and wrought-iron furniture. One of the rooms is accessible to travelers with disabilities. Besides free Internet access, the in-room computers allow you to use a database of tourist information on all of Napoli. If that weren't enough, the Neapolis will provide on request a debit card for use at selected neighborhood shops and restaurants.

Via Francesco Del Giudice 13, 80138 Napoli. ℂ 081-4420815. Fax 081-4420819. www.hotelneapolis.com. 19 units. 80€ ($92) single; 120€ ($138) double. AE, MC, V. Bus: 201 to Piazza Dante, then follow the arc to Port'Alba; the hotel is near the corner of Via Tribunale. **Amenities:** Bar; nonsmoking rooms. *In room:* A/C, TV, minibar, hair dryer.

Rex 𝒢   Set back from the harbor road, the 1960s Rex is another great bargain in Naples's tiniest area (it's directly behind the top hotels in town). Much of it has been refurbished, and the units have updated bathrooms, but the moldings and wallpaper still hint at the era in which it was built. Most accommodations are amply sized, while some don't get as much light as others. Half the rooms have balconies, but thanks to the double-paned windows, your sleep will be undisturbed. In high season, the hotel charges a 10€ ($12) fee per night for use of the air-conditioning.

Via Palepoli 12 (between V. Nazario Sauro and V. Santa Lucia), 80123 Naples. ℂ 081-7649389. Fax 081-7649227. www.hotel-rex.it. 34 units. 85€–105€ ($98–$121) single; 100€–125€ ($115–$144) double. Rates include breakfast. AE, DC, MC, V. Parking 12€–14€ ($14–$16) in hotel garage. Tram: 1, R3 (to the end of Galleria d. Vittoria tunnel), C25, 140 (to V. S. Lucia), 152. *In room:* TV.

IN MERGELLINA

Ausonia 𝒢 In the pleasant and safe neighborhood around the hydrofoil docks, the Ausonia is convenient for boats to Capri or Ischia, but you'll have to take a bus or Metro to get to the city center (walkable for die-hards). Porthole mirrors, ship's helm nightstands, and polished wood surfaces create a spiffy nautical theme, making you feel as if you're on a cruise rather than on land. Maritime living carries over to the curtainless showers and in spotlessly kept rooms, but happily not in the size of these relatively roomy accommodations. Its location at the back of a harbor-front building means you're cheated of an ocean view, but you're spared the traffic noise of the seaside boulevard. Instead, windows open onto the courtyard or a noisier back alley, and gauzy curtains graze the marble floors in the breeze.

Via Caracciolo 11 (at the Mergellina docks), 80122 Naples. ℂ 081-664536. Fax 081-682278. 19 units. 85€ ($98) single; 120€ ($138) double. Rates include breakfast. Possible 10% discount in low season. AE, MC, V. Parking 11€ ($13). Metro: Mergellina. Tram 1, R3, C16, C24, C21, 140 (to Mergellina). **Amenities:** Bar. *In room:* A/C, TV.

GREAT DEALS ON DINING

Quickie meals can be had nearest the train station (the pizza in the McDonald's-dominated complex to the left is actually pretty good), or you can get all the **picnic fixings** you need in the string of little shops lining the first block of Salita Santa Anna di Palazzo, off Via Chiaia. Treat yourself to at least one sit-down Neapolitan meal, and order anything with *mozzarella di bufala* any chance you get.

NEAR THE TRAIN STATION

Da Michele 𝒢 *Finds* *Kids* PIZZERIA If you don't mind the wait—and there will be one—head over to the most highly trafficked pizzeria in town. You'll be seated at a table set with paper placemats and hastily placed utensils and treated to anything but a sophisticated dining experience. Even the service will be rushed. But apparently the pizza is worth the wait because Michele's clients keep coming back for the dual offering of a simple Margherita or the marinara (with shellfish) over an authentic thick and spongy *"pasta Napolitana"* (thick crust). Indulge in extra cheese, and you're bound to come back at least two nights in a row.

Via Sersale 1 (follow V. Colleta from Corso Umberto). ℂ 081-5539204. Pizza 3.50€–4.50€ ($4–$5.15). No credit cards. Mon–Sat 10am–11pm.

Iris Caffetteria Restaurant and Pizzeria 𝒢 NEAPOLITAN I can't count the number of times I found myself at the train station and in need of a meal, only to look around distrustfully at the eateries lining Piazza Garibaldi. Thank the day I fell upon the Iris! This restaurant even won an award from the Associazione Cuochi Italiani for *"la fantasia ed esecuzione"* (creativity and execution). Nobody should pass up the *mozzarella di bufala* or the *polipo in cassuola* (octopus and tomato cooked in a casserole). Overcome your revulsion of the *pizza con bianchetti* (little eel-like white minnows with the eyes staring out at you)— this specialty of the house is actually pretty good. Iris also offers a *menu turistico* at 9.50€ ($11).

Piazza Garibaldi 121–125. ℂ 081-269988. Primi 2.50€–6.70€ ($2.85–7.70); secondi 3.60€–10€ ($4.15–$11). 10% discount for 2 or more with this book. AE, DC, DISC, MC, V. Sun–Fri noon–midnight or 1am. Closed for 3 unpredictable days in Aug.

IN THE CENTRO STORICO

'a Taverna 'e zi Carmela NEAPOLITAN/PIZZERIA This is a simple, down-to-earth, cozy family taverna conveniently located next to Le Fontane al

Mare and Piazza Vittoria. The walls are covered with pictures of the family posing with the odd Italian actor who has happened by, and bottles of wine casually line the shelves. Try a plate of their *linguini alle vongole* (in a clam sauce), with or without a dusting of Naples's infamously succulent tomatoes.

Via Nicolò Tommasea 11–12 at Via Partenope. ℂ 081-7643581. Primi 5€–6€ ($5.75–$6.90); secondi 8€–16€ ($9.20–$18). AE, DC, MC, V. Tues–Sun 9am–3pm and 6pm–midnight. Closed for 2 unpredictable weeks in Aug.

La Tavernetta *Value* NEAPOLITAN   This home-style eatery provides the intimate and down-to-earth osteria we all hope to find when exploring the back streets of a tourist destination. The food is as unpretentious and unadorned as the decor, offering the tried-and-true basics of Neapolitan cuisine like *spaghetti alle vongole* (in clam sauce), *salsiccia grigliata* (grilled marinated eggplant), and the ubiquitous (and for good reason) pizza Margherita. La Tavernetta is a great value, all the more for offering two lunch menus, at 5€ ($5.75) and 10€ ($12).

Via Sergente Maggiore 47 (the street opposite the Galleria Umberto 1). ℂ 081-413823. Primi 4€–5€ ($4.60–$5.75); secondi 4€–6€ ($4.60–$6.90); pizza 3.50€–4.50€ ($4–$5.15). MC, V. Daily 12:30–3pm and 7:30–11pm. Closed 2 weeks in Aug.

Osteria Castello 🔆 NEAPOLITAN   This dimly lit restaurant is the perfect example of the transformation of an osteria into a sophisticated and cozy dining experience. A tasty antipasti table at the entrance offers a selection of seasonal marinated vegetables, and two small rooms connected by a low doorway accommodate a scant 15 or 16 tables. Try a simple plate of *pasta al pomodoro* (in a fresh tomato sauce), followed by the *pesce spada* (swordfish) or a less copious potato *con provola* (with smoked cheese).

Via San Teresa a Chiaia 38 (between V. Cavallerizza and V. Martiucci, below Piazza Amadeo). ℂ 081-400486. Reservations suggested on weekends. Primi 5.50€ ($6.30); secondi 5.50€–18€ ($6.30–$21). MC, V. Mon–Sat 8pm–midnight (Sat lunch in summer).

Pizzeria Brandi PIZZA/NEAPOLITAN   Owned and operated by the same Neapolitan family for over 200 years, Pizzeria Brandi is Naples's most famous pizzeria and a local institution. Popular legend holds that it was on this very spot in 1889 that, in honor of a visit by the first queen of a newly unified Italy, the *pizzaiolo* concocted a patriotic pizza modeled after the colors in the country's new flag: white *mozzarella di bufalo,* red tomato sauce, and green basil. They named it after the queen herself and delivered it straight to the palace at Capodimonte, pioneering not only the first pizza Margherita, but also the first pizza to go. Although the hordes descend here just for the pizza (which is still pretty good), Brandi does offer pasta dishes like *linguine agli scampi* and some secondi as well, such as *scaloppine al limone.* Book ahead for one of the six outside tables, or content yourself with watching the activity at the open wood-fired oven.

Salita Sant'Anna di Palazzo 1–2 (just off V. Chiaia, 2 blocks up from Piazza Trieste e Trento). ℂ 081-416928. Reservations highly recommended. Primi 5.50€–9€ ($6.30–$10); secondi 6.50€–11€ ($7.50–$13). AE, DC, MC, V. Daily 12:30–3:30pm and 7:30pm–midnight. Closed Aug 14–16. Bus: R2, R3, V10, C22, C25, 24 (to V. S. Cairo/Piazza Trieste e Trento).

WORTH A SPLURGE

Ristorante Transatlantico NEAPOLITAN   This wonderful little harborside restaurant is a favorite among locals for its evocative location and characteristic meals, and many a visitor has discovered this spot, only to return here for an encore. Set on the edge of the marina alongside the Castel dell'Ovo, Transatlantico lets you choose between tables on the delightful laundry-draped piazza

---

Tips **Saving Money**

From April to October, in conjunction with the ferries and a few cooperating restaurants, **combination tickets** for day trips to the three nearby islands (Procida, Ischia, and Capri) are available for 24€ ($28), 26€ ($30), and 34€ ($39), respectively. Tickets include round-trip transport via hydrofoil or ferry, lunch at one of a limited selection of established restaurants, and the funicular (required for trips to Capri only, 1.30€/$1.50 value). Independently, the ferry or hydrofoil costs from 11€ to 17€ ($13–$20) round-trip, depending on which mode of travel you choose, so clearly, if you plan on eating a panino, you're better off going it alone. The one exception is the combo ticket to Capri, where a simple coffee in the main Piazzetta can break the bank, and where that three-course lunch (included in price of ticket) comes in handy.

---

or harbor-side to watch the local boys swimming or rowing around the marina. You can rely on a good pasta or pizza here, but the fish, although pricey, is excellent. Try it grilled or in the cold seafood salad accompanied by a local wine.

Borgo Marinari, Isola di Megaris. © 081-7648842. Primi 6.50€–16€ ($7.45–$18); secondi 8€–18€ ($9.20–$21). Fish sold by weight. AE, DC, MC, V. Wed–Mon noon–3pm and 7:30pm–midnight or 1am.

CAFES

The grande dame of Neapolitan cafes is the 1860 **Gran Caffè Gambrinus** *⚑*, Piazza Trieste e Trento (© **081-417582**), where intellectuals and writers as diverse as Gabrielle d'Annunzio and Oscar Wilde have gathered since 1860 under the stuccoes, silks, and frescoes of the Belle Epoque interior. The ambience is perfect for enjoying a cappuccino and *sfogliatella* (Naples's premier pastry, a cream-stuffed horn made of flaky millefeuille dough). There's an outdoor cafe with an elegant view of the Teatro San Carlo, the Royal Palace, and Piazza Plebescito, but the noise and fumes from the cars that roar down Via Toledo around the traffic circle at your back might induce you to stand (and save euros in the process) at the bar. The cafe is closed Tuesday and in August.

The pastry shop and bar **Scaturchio**, Piazza San Domenico 19 (© **081-5516944**), has also long been a favored spot to sample the rich bounty of Neapolitan pastry, though the setting is far less elegant (and prices a bit lower). You'll find the best gelato in town at **Gelateria della Scimmia**, Piazza Carità 4 (© **081-5520272**), established in 1934; and the **Gran Bar Riviera**, Riviera di Chiaia 183 (no phone), which opened in 1860 and claims to have invented the tartufo ice-cream ball.

2 Herculaneum: A Prelude to Pompeii *⚑⚑*

30km (19 miles) SE of Rome, 25km (16 miles) SE of Naples

The builders of **Herculaneum (Ercolano)** were still working to repair the damage caused by an A.D. 63 earthquake when Vesuvius erupted on that fateful August day in A.D. 79. But in contrast with Pompeii, which met its demise under a rush of piroclastic ash, Herculaneum was buried under more than 25m (82 ft.) of burning mud, sand, and rocks. About one-fourth the size of Pompeii, Herculaneum didn't start to come to light again until 1709, when Prince Elbeuf launched the unfortunate fashion of tunneling through it for treasures, more

Casa a Graticcio
(House of the Wooden Trellis) 8
Casa dei Cervi
(House of the Stags) 11
Casa del Bicentenario
(Bicentennial House) 1
Casa del Grande Albergo
(Large Inn) 9
Casa dell'Atrio a Mosaico
(House of the Mosaic Atrium) 10
Casa del Mobilio Carbonizzato
(House of the Charred Furniture) 3
Casa del Sacello di Legno
(House of the Wooden Cabinet) 4
Casa del Tramezzo di Legno/
Casa del Tramezzo Carbonizzato
(House of the Wooden/Charred
Partition) 7
Casa di Poseidon
(House of Poseidon) 2
Casa Sannitica
(Samnite House) 6
Palestra 13
Terme (Baths) 5
Terme Suburbane
(Suburban Baths) 12

intent on profiting from the sale of objets d'art than on uncovering a dead Roman town.

ESSENTIALS

GETTING THERE The private **Circumvesuviana rail line** (© 081-7722444) services Herculaneum (from Naples 8 min., 1.70€/$1.95; from Sorrento 50 min., 3.10€/$3.55), Vesuvius (same stop), Pompeii, and Sorrento (the latter two are covered later in this chapter). It leaves from its own station in Naples on Corso Garibaldi, just south of the central station, every 20 minutes. (You can also catch Circumvesuviana trains underneath the main Stazione Centrale itself; follow the signs.)

EXPLORING THE AREA

Pompeii gets all the press, but **Herculaneum** (© 081-7390963) is just as enthralling. Unlike workaday Pompeii, this ancient Roman city was a resort and retirement town for the rich, inauspiciously set on the shore under the menacing gaze of Vesuvius. Admission to Herculaneum is 10€ ($12); 3-day combination ticket costs 18€/$21 and also gets you into Pompeii, Oplontis, Stabia, and Boscoreale), and the site is open daily from 8:30am to an hour before sunset (last entrance 6pm Apr–Oct; 3:30pm Nov–Mar).

The archaeological site is considerably smaller than that of Pompeii. Herculaneum had about 5,000 inhabitants to Pompeii's 20,000, but the homes of the rich and famous, uncovered largely intact, were much more elaborate, extensive, and sumptuously decorated than those in its illustrious neighbor. Many still have their second stories. Floor mosaics, wall frescoes, ceiling stuccoes, and even wooden furnishings have all been preserved. Plenty of plebeian houses are mixed in as well, along with shops like the bakery, with its stone grain grinders set up in the backyard.

Although all the streets and buildings of Herculaneum hold interest, some ruins merit more attention than others. The **Terme (baths)** are divided between those at the forum and the **Terme Suburbane (Suburban Baths)** on the outskirts, near the more elegant villas. The municipal baths, which segregated the sexes, are larger, but the ones at the edge of town are more lavishly adorned. The **Palestra** was a kind of sports arena, where games were staged to satisfy the spectacle-hungry denizens.

The typical plan for the average town house was to erect it around an uncovered atrium. In some areas, Herculaneum possessed the forerunner of the modern apartment house. Important private homes to seek out are the **Casa del Bicentenario (Bicentennial House), Casa a Graticcio (House of the Wooden Trellis), Casa del Tramezzo di Legno** or **Casa del Tramezzo Carbonizzato (House of the Wooden/Charred Partition),** and **Casa di Poseidon (House of Poseidon),** as well as the **Anfiteatro (Amphitheater).** The finest example of how the aristocracy lived is the **Casa dei Cervi,** named the **House of the Stags** because of the sculpture found inside. Guides are fond of showing the males on their tours a statue of a drunken Hercules urinating. Some of the best houses are locked and can be seen only by permission.

For a long time, scholars believed that most of Herculaneum's elite had closed up their summer homes for the season or that inhabitants had time to escape, since only six bodies were found in the streets and houses (this compared to the 2,000 found at Pompeii). Then, in 1982, while excavating around the docks at what was the shoreline in ancient times, a worker discovered hundreds upon hundreds of bodies, scorched by volcanic gases right down to the bone, huddled in the dock houses under 18m (59 ft.) of hardened volcanic mud. Although the common understanding is that they died waiting for the boats to carry them to safety, the truth is that they likely perished from the sudden, blazing heat that preceded the mudslide: Most of the recovered bodies had their heads split open—a sign that their fluids heated up so much as to make their heads explode.

3 Pompeii & Its Amazing Ruins (★(★(★

20km (12 miles) SE of Naples, 15km (9½ miles) SE of Herculaneum, 33km (20 miles) NE of Sorrento

Though the ancient Oscan city of **Pompeii,** founded before the 6th century B.C., had its ups and downs, by the 1st century A.D. it was a Roman colony of 20,000 and a thriving, bustling seaport. It occupied a prime stretch of coastline southeast of *Neapolis* (Naples), just on the other side of that huge mountain called Vesuvius. After 14 years of hard work, Pompeii was just getting back on its architectural feet following the massive earthquake of A.D. 63. The columns of the forum had been re-erected, and villa owners had piled lime next to the last walls that needed replastering. They thought the worst was over.

At noon August 24, A.D. 79, the peak of Mount Vesuvius exploded, sending a mottled black-and-white mushroom cloud 19km (12 miles) into the air at twice the speed of sound, raining ash and light pumice down on the region. For 12 hours, the sheer force of the eruption kept the cloud aloft. Some Pompeiians fled. But more than 2,000 bodies have been uncovered at Pompeii—these souls

Mt. Vesuvius: Contents Under Pressure

Though one of the smallest and least regularly active volcanoes in the world, the infamous Mt. Vesuvius, inspiration for Dante's *Inferno*, is one of the most destructive. The only active volcano on continental Europe, the broad, 1,264m-high (4,214-ft.) cone of Mt. Vesuvius dominates the Bay of Naples from the northeastern shore. Its unexpected eruption in A.D. 79 buried the Roman cities of Herculaneum and Pompeii in ash and mud, but its activity has been sporadic ever since—the last time it even put on any mild fireworks was back in 1944.

To visit the surprisingly calm, rather plain gravel-filled depression that is Vesuvius's crater, take the Circumvesuviana train from **Naples** or **Sorrento** to the Ercolano stop, from which a special bus (② **081-7392833**) travels five times daily up to the Colle Margherita parking lot (55 min.; 4€/$4.60 round-trip). A guide (② **081-7775720**; 6.50€/$7.45) will walk you the 15 minutes from here to the crater's rim, an austere landscape with unparalleled views across Campania on clear days. Buses leave the parking lot six times daily between 8:30 and 3pm; the last bus back to Ercolano leaves at 4:30pm. Additionally, the **Parco Nazionale del Vesuvio (Vesuvius National Park)** (② **081-274200**; www.laportadelvesuvio.it) administers a network of trails, offering guided tours and summertime hikes by startlight (and flashlight). A nighttime visit costs 10€ ($12), and reservations are necessary.

---

probably thought the enormous cloud hanging over Vesuvius was just smoke, and saw no need to leave. When the cloud finally collapsed, the horror engulfed the city before anyone could run more than a few feet. Pompeii was buried by a pyroclastic flow, a superfast rush of hot ash and pumice with an undercurrent of rock and burning gases, all of which came barreling down the mountain like a tidal wave, the force ripping the doors and roofs off houses, fusing metal house keys to skulls, and dismembering human bodies.

The 17-year-old Pliny the Younger was across the bay at the time, and he saw "a cloud of unusual size and appearance . . . like an umbrella pine." His uncle, the famed writer Pliny the Elder, fared worse. When he saw the volcano go, he took some boats to try to evacuate friends from a village on the shore below the mountain. The elder Pliny dictated his impressions to a scribe as they sailed, but the great author succumbed to the poisonous gases while ashore and suffocated.

ESSENTIALS

GETTING THERE   By Train   From **Naples,** take the half-hourly private **Circumvesuviana** train (② **081-7722444;** www.vesuviana.it) *toward Sorrento* and get off at POMPEII–VILLA DEI MISTERI (27–40 min; 2.20€/$2.55). The train passes through **Ercolano** (20 min; 1.70€/$1.95). It also runs to or from **Sorrento** (20 min; 1.80€/$2.05).

Note: There are four Circumvesuviana lines; only the one headed for Sorrento stops at the ruins. Also, one of the two lines headed to Sarno diverges just before the site and also features a stop called "Pompei," but this is for the modern town, *not* the archaeological site, so make sure you pay attention to the destination marker on the lead car as well as on the platform departures board. The bar in the train station will let you **store your luggage** for 3€ ($3.45) per bag for up to 12 hours. Turn right out of the station, and the entrance to the site is just a

---

Travel Tip: The Unico Ticket

Campania's new system of ticketing makes getting around one of Italy's most archaeologically important regions a snap. The **Unico** (www. unicocampania.it), a new system of ticketing based on *fascie* (zones), provides a wide array of choices for transportation in and around the region of Campania, from Pozzuoli and Campi Flegrei to the north of Naples as far south as Sorrento. Day-trippers from Naples to Pompeii or Sorrento should pay particular attention to fascia 3 and fascia 5. While a round-trip ticket from Naples to Pompeii costs 4.40€ ($5.05) on the Circumvesuviana line, the fascia 3 (4.50€/$5.15, valid for 1 day) adds the flexibility of stopping at Herculaneum, for example, as well as unlimited transportation within the city of Naples. The Unico ticket is available at any *tabacchi* (tobacconists), most newsstands, and all Metro stops, funicular stations, and train stations.

---

few hundred feet down on your left. A 5-minute walk past the site entrance down this road leads to modern Pompei.

By Bus SITA buses (© 081-5522176 or 081-6106711) leave from Naples's Molo Beverello near the Tirrenia Lines pier (30 min.; 1.60€/$1.85) for Pompeii, continuing on to Positano and Amalfi.

VISITOR INFORMATION The **ticket booth** at the archaeological site will give you the free map and all the information you need to explore the excavations at Pompeii. There's also a **tourist office** in modern Pompei at Via Sacra 1 (© 081-8507255; fax 081-8632401; www.uniplan.it/pompei/azienda), open Monday through Friday from 9am to 2:30pm, and Saturday and Sunday from 9am to 2pm.

EXPLORING THE ANCIENT CITY

Pompeii wasn't buried entirely; in fact, the top floors of many houses poked above the new ground level. But between survivors returning to dig for personal belongings, the inevitable looters, and later farmers plowing their fields over the site, these building tops were shorn off. Within a few generations, incredibly, Pompeii was forgotten. In 1594, the architect Domenico Fontana was building an aqueduct through the area when he struck the ruins of Pompeii quite by accident. Most of the excavations have been carried out since the 18th century. Admission to Pompeii is 10€ ($12; combination ticket with Herculaneum, Oplontis, Stabia, and Boscoreale 18€/$21), and the site is open daily from 8:30am to an hour before sunset (last entrance 6pm Apr–Oct; 3:30pm Nov–Mar). Audioguides to the site are available at the entrance for 6€ ($6.90), with discounts for multiple rentals.

The **archaeological site** 옳옳옳 (© 081-8610744; www.uniplan.it/ruins) is now enclosed and takes a full day to explore. At the very least, it takes 4 hours to pop into the major sights. The roads are made of stone slabs, rutted deep with centuries' worth of wagon wheels. At most intersections are crosswalks of raised stepping stones—so citizens wouldn't have to step in the mucky, muddy streets. Besides the public buildings and mansions highlighted below, Pompeii is full of buildings that may be more pedestrian but are just as fascinating for the insight they offer into daily life in an ancient Roman city. Poke around to find the shops with counters still in place and paintings describing the wares sold, bakeries with

Antiquarium **1**

Basilica **3**

Casa degli Amorini Dorati
(House of the Gilded Cupids) **13**

Casa dei Vettii (House of the Vettii) **12**

Casa del Fauno (House of the Faun) **11**

Casa del Menander (House of Menander) **18**

Casa del Poeta Tragico (House of the Tragic Poet) **9**

Casa di Venere in Conchiglia
(House of Venus in the Shell) **19**

Cattedrale (Cathedral) **20**

Foro (Forum) **5**

Lupanare **14**

Odeon (Teatro Piccolo) **17**

Teatro Grande **16**

Terme del Foro (Forum Baths) **8**

Tempio di Apollo (Temple of Apollo) **4**

Tempio di Giove (Temple of Jupiter) **7**

Tempio di Venere (Temple of Venus) **2**

Tempio di Vespasiano (Temple of Vespasian) **6**

Thermae Stabiane (Stabian Baths) **15**

Villa dei Misteri (Villa of the Mysteries) **10**

millstones and brick ovens in the backyard, even fast-food parlors with deep bowls set into the counters where prepared food was kept hot.

The **Foro (Forum)** ⚅, the central square of any Roman city, sits a few blocks up from the entrance. Around the edges you'll see that there was once a two-story colonnade, its 141m (462-ft.) length oriented so that, ironically, "scenic" Mount Vesuvius serves as a natural backdrop. At the northern end of the eastern edge is a small room with a countertop embedded with bowl-shape depressions of increasing sizes. The Forum was also a central marketplace, and to forestall arguments between buyer and seller, these were used as the city's standards of measure.

Plaster casts of bodies are located just past the measuring table in an enclosed building. During the early excavations, archaeologists realized that the ash had packed around dying Pompeiians and hardened almost instantly. The bodies decayed, leaving just the skeletons lying in human-shaped air pockets under the ground. Holes were drilled down to a few and plaster was poured in, taking a rough cast of the moment of death. Some people writhe in agony. A dog, chained to a post, turns to bite desperately at his collar. One man sits on the ground, covering his face in grief.

Exit the Forum onto Via dell Abbondanza, detouring left down Via del Teatro to see the **Teatro Grande,** a 2nd-century-B.C. theater that could seat 5,000. Under the stage lay a reservoir so that water would flood the area during mock naval battle scenes (some suggest the water also helped amplify the acoustics

Touring Tips

To get a detailed background of Pompeii, it's worthwhile to invest 9€ ($10) in a nice guidebook full of color photos at the gift shop *before you explore*. If you have a large family or small group, you may want to splurge on hiring a registered guide for about 75€ ($86). It's hard to escape the sun at Pompeii, and the dust is everywhere, so bring a hat with a brim and sunblock. If you forgot your bottled water, there's a decent cafeteria tucked at the back of the site. Be prepared for crowds, especially on weekends (on average there are 4,700 visitors a day; up to 22,000 people come here on holidays). Or, you can completely forgo the sunstroked experience and step back in time with "Pompeii by Night," a multimedia voyage back to the sights and sounds of the dramatic moments leading up to and in the wake of the eruption. For information on nighttime tours, contact **Pompeii by Night** ((C) 081-8575347; reservations: 081-8616405; www.arethusa.net).

during performances). Nearby on Via Stabiana is the **Odeon** or **Teatro Piccolo,** a much smaller theater (seating 1,000) used mainly for concerts. The **Casa di Menander (House of Menander)** has painted scenes from the Trojan cycle in some rooms, and a floor mosaic of the Nile in the peristyle. Members of the family that lived here were all found together, huddled in one room, killed when the roof caved in on them.

Past the intersection with Via Stabiana along **Via dell Abbondanza** marks the site of the "New Excavations," undertaken since 1911. Many of the houses on both sides of this street retain their second stories. While those on the north/left side haven't been excavated much beyond the facades, those on the right have. And unlike in much of the older, more famous excavations (north of the Forum; we'll get there in a minute), many of the frescoes, mosaics, and statuary have been left in place rather than shipped off to a museum.

Among the houses along this street, be sure you pop into the **Casa di Octavio Quartius (House of Octavius Quartius),** with lots of good frescoes and replanted gardens; and the **Casa di Venere in Conchiglia (House of Venus in the Shell),** with a large wall painting of the goddess stretched out on a clamshell. Near the end of the street, turn right to walk through the **Grand Palestra**—a huge open space shaded by umbrella pines where the city's youths went to work out and play sports (many came here seeking shelter from the eruption; their skeletons were found huddled in the corner latrine)—to the **Anfiteatro (Amphitheater).** Built in 80 B.C., this is the oldest amphitheater in the world. It could hold 12,000 spectators, who, according to the records, were just as wont to break into a brawl in the stands as watch the gladiators fighting on the field below.

Return down Via dell Abbondanza to Via Stabiana. On the northwest corner sit the **Thermae Stabiane,** a series of baths with stuccoed and painted ceilings surviving in some rooms, and a few glass caskets with more twisted plaster cast bodies of Pompeii victims. Head up Vico del Lupanare on the other side of these baths to the acute intersection with the overhanging second story, the **Lupanare.** This brothel left nothing to the imagination. Painted scenes above each of the little cells inside graphically showed potential clients the position in which the lady of that particular room specialized. Until a few decades ago, only male tourists were allowed in to see it.

Continuing north to the heart of the Old Excavations, stop by the **Casa dei Vettii (House of the Vettii),** one of the most luxurious mansions in town (it belonged to two trading mogul brothers) and in a wonderful state of preservation. Behind a glass shield at the entrance is a painting of a little guy with a grotesquely oversized male member—here shown weighing the appendage on a scale. This was not meant to be lewd, but rather was a common device believed to ward off evil spirits and thoughts. Painted putti (cherubs) dance around the atrium while the rooms are filled with frescoes of mythological scenes and characters. Don't miss the Sala Dipinta, where a black band around the walls is painted with cherubs engaging in sports. The **Casa del Poeta Tragico (House of the Tragic Poet)** is closed, but between the bars of the gate you can still see the most famous mosaic in Pompeii: a fearsome chained dog with a spiked collar and the epithet *Cave Canem* (Beware of the Dog). The nearby **Foro Terme (Forum Baths)** retain ribbed stucco on some ceilings and a strip of tiny telamons along one wall.

Walk north along Via Consolare to exit the ruins (hold on to your ticket) and follow the path for 5 minutes to the suburban **Villa dei Misteri (Villa of the Mysteries)** ★★★, which you get into on the same ticket. Built around the 2nd century B.C., this villa was converted into a center for the Dionysian cult, and the walls are gorgeously and skillfully painted with life-size figures engaging in the Dionysian Mysteries of an initiate (though these paintings have helped modern scholars guess at the nature of these rites, we still don't know exactly what was involved). The scenes play out against a background of such deep, intense red that the color used is still called "Pompeiian red."

ACCOMMODATIONS YOU CAN AFFORD

Villa dei Misteri   This remains the bland roadside inn of choice for die-hard archaeology buffs who want to sleep a stone's throw from the excavations (the entrance is a 2-min. walk downhill with the Circumvesuviana at the halfway mark). Once you get past the cement war casualty exterior, the amply sized rooms are pleasant enough, with balconies, shiny tile floors, well-worn but serviceable furnishings, and updated bathrooms. The mattresses, however, still rest on lazy-springed cots. An outdoor pool ringed with statues (open late May–Oct) does wonders for the hotel's appeal.

Via Villa dei Misteri 11, 80045 Pompei (NA). © 081-8613593. Fax 081-8622983. www.villadeimisteri.it. 33 units. 54€–62€ ($62–$71) single or double; supplement for A/C 11€ ($13) per day. Breakfast 5.50€ ($6.30). AE, DC, MC, V. Free parking. Located ¼ mile from site entrance and train station; turn left upon exiting station. **Amenities:** Restaurant; bar; outdoor swimming pool. *In room:* A/C.

A GREAT DEAL ON DINING

Zi Caterina ★ CAMPANIAN   Among the countless glorified pizza joints with polyglot menus on modern Pompei's main drag, Zi Caterina stands out for its solid cooking and reasonable prices. The cavernous single room, antiqued with lots of wood, can get noisy with the arrival of the strolling troubadour strumming his guitar. The delicious *risotto alla pescatora* is heavily laden with shellfish, calamari, and shrimp, and the *gnocchi alla Sorrentina* is also good. Secondi tend to be fishy as well, with a beach platter of *saut di frutti di mare* (clams, oysters, and mussels) or *baccalà* (dried salt cod), but landlubbers can always order *coniglio alla cacciatora* (rabbit stewed with tomatoes and mushrooms).

Via Roma 20, about a 10- to 15-min. walk to Pompei center. © 081-8507447 or 081-8631263. Reservations recommended. Primi 5.50€–8.50€ ($6.30–$9.75); secondi 6€–13€ ($6.90–$15). AE, DC, MC, V. Wed–Mon noon–11pm.

4 The Isle of Capri ★★★

4.8km (3 miles) off the tip of the Sorrentine peninsula

The isle of **Capri** (*Cap*-ree) embodies images of sophisticated international stars like Grace Kelly, Rita Hayworth, and Jacqueline O draped with billowy chiffon scarves and hidden behind oversize sunglasses. Sure, it's still possible to rediscover the celebrity luster that put this magnificent island outcropping on the map; it's just a little more difficult for those of us on a budget, and practically impossible as a day excursion. Still, lacking the Hollywood glamour of its earliest years, Capri manages to glisten, thanks to at least the consistent presence of Prada- and Ferragamo-sporting socialites milling around Capri's infamous main piazza in capris and colorful strappy sandals.

Most of Capri is blanketed in lush green foliage, an Eden of oleander, jasmine, and bougainvillea spilling over the walls of the white cube houses. Stunning for its exquisite natural beauty and exhausting scenic walks that wind leisurely down toward swimming holes and luminescent grottos, this tiny island of sharp lava rising dramatically above the sparkling surfaces of deep blue and green waters is, more than anything, an outdoor lover's paradise.

Capri's sheer physical beauty has attracted sun seekers for millennia, from Roman emperors to modern-day hedonists. Homer certainly chose his spot well when he designated this island as the home of the mythical Sirens, beautiful but monstrous flesh-eating women who lived on the offshore rocks and sang an irresistible song to lure ancient sailors to their doom. Capri's allure today is still just as strong, though the only doom you're likely to face these days is the damage done to your wallet.

Up a switchback road and occupying the opposite half of the island is Anacapri, the town center more representative of the origins of the islanders, with its tranquil walkways and open vineyards characteristic of provincial Italy.

Most visitors pop over on the ferry in the morning, fork over the euro for a quick row through the Blue Grotto, gawk at the obscene prices in Capri boutiques, and end up lunching in an overpriced cafe on the Piazzetta, missing entirely the magic and mystery of the island. By day, especially in summer, Capri witnesses a tourist crush that veritably sucks the enjoyment right out of the island. If at all possible, spend the night. As the day-trippers leave on the 5pm ferry, the sounds and scents of Capri creep out of hiding and locals come together to reclaim the island. Spend the evening strolling down a quiet cobbled alleyway as the skies turn a seductive purple, and take your extra day to visit Capri's sibling village, Anacapri, hike the undeveloped side of the island, or ride the chairlift up Monte Solaro for a panoramic sweep of the bay.

ESSENTIALS

GETTING THERE   By Ferry or Hydrofoil   Companies providing *aliscafo* (hydrofoil) service from Naples include **Caremar** (② **081-8370700;** www. caremar.it), **NLG** (② **081-8370819**), and **SNAV** (② **081-4285555**), all of which leave from the Molo Beverello dock. **SNAV** also operates service from the Mergellina docks to Capri. The ride takes 40 minutes and costs 12€ ($14). If you're really pinching pennies, Caremar runs a fast ferry service from Molo Beverello to Capri, which, at half the price (5.50€/$6.30), takes more than twice as long. **Linee Marittime Partenopee/LMP** (② **081-8073024;** www. consorziolmp.it) runs 50-minute hydrofoils from Sorrento for around 9.50€ ($11); Caremar runs a fast ferry (20 minutes) for 5.80€ ($6.65).

Ferries cost about half the hydrofoil rate but take about three times as long. Caremar and LMP run *traghetti* (ferry) lines out of **Naples**'s Molo Beverello.

From elsewhere along the Amalfi Coast, several companies run limited ferries (from Salerno 130 min., 11€/$13; Amalfi 90 min., 11€/$13; and Positano 50 min., 10€/$12) and hydrofoils (from Positano 30 min.; 13€/$15), but these are generally offered as day trips departing once in the morning and returning sometime in the late afternoon.

If you're staying in Capri, take the **funicular** (© 081-8370420) up to the center of town, from where you'll have to walk to your hotel, since almost all of Capri is pedestrian only. The last funicular up coincides with the arrival of the last Caremar ferry from Naples, so choose your carrier wisely.

A one-way trip on the funicular costs 1.30€ ($1.50); if you plan on doing a lot of running around, the tickets are good for all buses as well; there's a 1-hour option (2.10€/$2.40) as well as a daily ticket (6.70€/$7.70). Ticket offices issue reusable magnetic cards for a mandatory refundable supplement of 1€ ($1.15) as long as, at the end of your stay, you return the card in good condition.

Because of the effort involved in hauling your bags, most hotels provide the services of a porter at an extra charge of about 2.50€ to 5€ ($2.85–$5.75) per bag. Porters are located at the port opposite the entrance to the funicular. (*Note:* When departing, you must specify service from the hotel to the docks—unless you want your bags to wait for you in the main piazza.)

Buses run every 30 minutes between Marina Grande (via Capri) and Anacapri; add on waiting time to actually board the bus at the ferry docks (lines are unimaginable July–Aug). The bus stop is defined by a group of handrails near the exit to the marina (behind the taxi stand); since more than one route departs from here, be sure to get in the correct line. Luggage is looked at disapprovingly, as it takes up valuable rider space. If you can't take the heat, go ahead and splurge for a convertible taxicab (10€–15€/$12–$17) or stay at one of the hotels that provides free pickup service at the docks.

GETTING ORIENTED   Capri's transportation hub is **Marina Grande,** the busy, touristy main port sitting at the base of the island's soaring cliffs. A bus or funicular will take you up to Capri center, the main town and home to most of the boutique shopping, posh hotels, chic nightlife, and Beautiful People. The heart of Capri (the town) is **Piazza Umberto I,** called by everyone the **Piazzetta,** sprouting a handful of narrow passages and cobbled lanes away from the fray. On the other side of Capri, down the backside of the cliffs, is **Marina Piccola,** a smaller yachting port consisting of several beach establishments and restaurants. Capri and the two ports occupy the narrowest part of the island, from which a mountain rises in either direction.

Halfway up the larger of these, Monte Solaro, sits the village of **Anacapri,** Capri town's historic rival but today the cooler, calmer, cheaper, and more bucolic of the two towns. Saying that Anacapri is less crowded than Capri fails to convey the crush of Capri's Piazzetta, but if any village life survives on this touristy island, it's in Anacapri.

GETTING AROUND   Capri town is completely off limits to motor vehicles (as is Anacapri's old center, but this is less of a problem, being essentially one street). In Capri, buses depart from the roundabout at Due Golfi; in Anacapri, you can hop on either at the main Piazza Vittoria or farther down the road at Piazza Caprile. **SIPPIC** buses (© 081-8370420) provide regular service (generally every 20–30 min.) between Marina Grande (via Capri) and Anacapri,

Marina Grande and Marina Piccola, Marina Grande and Damecuta, and Marina Piccola and Anacapri, with connections possible at the roundabout just before the entrance to Capri. **Staiano Autotrasporti** (© 081-8371544) runs service between Anacapri and the Grotta Azzurra, and between Anacapri and Faro di Punta Carena from Anacapri's depot on Via de Tommaso. Buy your tickets at the funicular's ticket window, when boarding the bus, or at any *tabacchi* (tobacconists).

Although bus service is comprehensive, its infrequency, combined with high demand, translates into long waits, making this an iffy replacement for independent wheels like a scooter. Most convenient for day-trippers is **Oasi Motor Rent** (closed Sun), located at Marina Grande, Via Cristoforo Colombo 47, up the road past Bar Corallo (© 081-8377138). For those staying in Anacapri, they also have a shop on Piazza Caprile 3A, at the very far end of town before the road heads out to Faro (© 080-8372444). For those staying in Capri, **La Custodia,** Via Roma 68 at the rotunda (© 081-8375863), is the most convenient, and they're also open on Sunday. La Custodia also has an outlet in Anacapri at Traversa Carlo Ferraro (© 339-2085475). For both agencies, expect to pay around 30€ ($35) for a half-day and 45€ ($52) for a full day, gasoline and helmet (required by law) included.

By Taxi   Those colorful 1950s convertibles are highly seductive. You can often bargain, but to go anywhere usually costs a minimum of 10€ ($12). Take advantage of those stagnant lines for the bus by asking some strangers to chip in, and the total cost goes down. There are stands in Capri on Piazza Martiri d'Ungheria, in Anacapri on Piazza Vittoria, and at the docks of Marina Grande and Marina Piccola. You can also call for one in Capri at © 081-8370543 or in Anacapri at © 081-8371175.

CAPRI'S SCENIC WALKS 🎯🎯🎯   Day-trippers who arrive, shop, and do the requisite lap around the main Piazzetta before heading out are setting themselves up for major disappointment. The natural beauty of Capri remains its most seductive draw, so plan to take advantage of at least one of the island's gorgeous walks. Keep in mind that the majority of the paths have a significant grade to them or a noteworthy number of steps (or a combination of the two); be sure you're up for the challenge and well hydrated. The Greek-era **Scala Fenicia** connects Anacapri with Marina Grande, a half-hour hike that requires you to walk a good part of the way along the main road. If you don't mind a little vertigo, you may want to tackle the 700 steps going down, rather than up, the hill. From Capri, you can easily stroll down to Marina Grande in about 15 minutes or to Marina Piccola via scenic **Via Krupp** in 20 minutes. From Anacapri, you can reach the Faro in 20 minutes or the Blue Grotto in half an hour. From Capri center, you can follow the path to the **Arco Naturale** (a natural mega-arch), then backtrack down, down, down, and around to **Faraglioni.** (The problem is getting back up; you can hop on Restaurant da Luigi's private boat back to Marina Piccola for 3€ ($3.45) per person; skip the food, though, as it's overpriced and underportioned.) More recent is the new path that connects Faro with the Blue Grotto, a scenic hike that skirts the western edge of the island and takes about 2 hours.

VISITOR INFORMATION   There's a little **tourist office** along the right side of the ferry dock (© 081-8370634) that fills up as the ferries empty out, so you may want to take advantage of the tiny **satellite offices** in Capri, Piazza Umberto I, open Monday through Saturday from 8:30am to 8:30pm, and Sunday from

9am to 1pm and 2:30 to 6pm (© **081-8370686**); or in Anacapri, Via Giuseppe Orlando 19a (just off Piazza Vittoria), open Monday through Saturday from 9:45am to 1:30pm and 2 to 5:30pm (© **081-8371524**). The tourist office puts out a free map of the island; they also offer a more detailed one for 1€ ($1.15)—highly recommended if you plan to take any of the scenic hikes.

Capri OnLine (**www.capri.it**) is the best website for general info on Capri and its businesses, and includes links to the official tourist office website (**www.capritourism.com**).

FESTIVALS   The festival of Capri's patron saint, **San Costanzo,** traditionally opens with an all-out procession on May 14 behind a silver reliquary bust of the saint (people stand on their balconies and strew flower petals on the bust as it passes). The statue is carried to the church of San Costanzo in Marina Grande until 2 days later, when the procession resumes up to Capri. The festivities continue throughout the week with community-sponsored concerts and other events. Anacapri throws its own version to honor its patron saint, **St. Antonio di Padova,** on June 13. Nonreligious events take place the first week of January, when **folklore groups** perform on the main piazzas of Capri and Anacapri. And on Friday at 7:45pm from June to August, The Villa Axel Munthe (© **081-7640737**) hosts free **sunset concerts.**

EXPLORING THE LAND OF THE SIRENS

Grotta Azzurra (Blue Grotto) ★★   Capri's greatest claim to fame is this long, low sea cavern whose water glows a brilliant, awe-inspiring blue from the effect of light refracting through the entrance tunnel. Although the scandalous wallet-gouging admission gets you only a 3-minute row through, the walls echoing unromantically with a half-dozen boats full of tourists with their oarsmen spewing out facts (occasionally true) or, even worse, attempting to sing, this natural phenomenon is a must-see. The oarsmen often point out a tunnel in one of the cave's walls, claiming that it is connected with the villa of Tiberius above, when, in fact, it is unremarkably a natural fissure that leads nowhere. The Roman villa above did, however, use the cave as a nymphaeum, and several statues were discovered at the bottom.

To get to the Grotta Azzurra, you can either take a local bus (15 min.) from Anacapri to the land entrance or hook up with a boat excursion from the Marina Grande docks (1 hr.; add 5€/$5.75 or 6€/$6.90, depending on which company you go with).

No phone. Admission 4€ ($4.60) plus 4.30€ ($5) for private rowboat into cave. Daily 9am–5pm. Limited hours in winter.

Villa Jovis (Tiberius's Villa) ★★   Set majestically at the top of a 293m (961-ft.) sheer bluff above the sea, this is but one of 12 villas that Roman Emperor Tiberius built on his favorite island. You can clamber around the half-decayed walls that once defined the imperial apartments, baths complex, and servants' quarters, but none of it is in very good shape—come more for the romantic setting than the archaeology. Built into the ruins right on the cliff's edge at what is called the Salto di Tiberio (Tiberius's Leap) is the tiny 17th-century church of Santa Maria del Soccorso, which treats you to a great sweeping view across the Bay of Naples.

Rome's second emperor, Tiberius rose to power as an army general. After 12 years on the throne, he got tired of the political infighting of Rome and semiretired to his beloved Capri. A gruff, dour man, he was swift in meting out punishments; prudently modest in refusing most honors during his reign; tough to get along with, second-guess, or bribe; and probably a little too fond of dallying with young boys and girls.

Tiberius spent his final 10 years throwing banquets on the island and communicating imperial decrees to the mainland by signaling with flashing lights. For centuries, we moderns have taken the famous ancient chronicler Suetonius's depiction of the emperor as gospel truth, which is why Tiberius has gone down in history as the man who, sitting in judgment at this cliff-top villa, ". . . ordered his victims, after prolonged and skillful torture, to be thrown into the sea before his very eyes. Below, a company of sailors beat them with boat hooks until the life was crushed from their bodies."

Had Suetonius lived today, he probably would have been a reporter for *Hard Copy*. There is little doubt his reports were greatly exaggerated, if not outright fabricated. The worst of Tiberius's crimes were letting the empire founder a bit while he was on his island retreat and naming his certifiably deranged nephew Caligula as heir.

Follow signs from Capri's Piazzetta up Via di Botteghe (a 40-min. hike). No phone. Admission 2€ ($2.30). Daily 9am to 1 hr. before sunset.

Villa Axel Munthe (Villa San Michele) 𝕮𝕮   The Swedish autobiographer, bird fancier, and selfless doctor Axel Munthe (1857–1949) had a love of Capri and an eye for tremendously magical views. He built his classically inspired villa to capitalize on vistas and naturally frame the essences of Capri's beauty, whether it be crumbling walls overflowing with bougainvillea, arbored paths centered on copies of Greek bronzes, ancient columns supporting whitewashed Gothic arches, miniature temples hidden in lush gardens, or a bust-lined balustrade spanning breathtaking panoramas of the island and azure waters. Inside, the villa is filled with archaeological knickknacks and memorabilia of the good doctor and his famous book, *The Story of San Michele*.

Via Axel Munthe (a continuation of V. Capodimonte), Anacapri. ☎ 081-8371401. Admission 5€ ($5.75). May–Sept 9am–6pm; Oct 9:30am–5pm; Nov–Feb 10:30am–3:30pm.

San Michele 𝕮   This 18th-century church is floored with a fantastical studied majolica representation of *Adam and Eve in the Garden of Eden* (1761), filled with remarkable detail and dozens of exotic plants and beasts. You can get an overall view from the choir loft.

Piazza San Nicola, Anacapri. ☎ 081-8372396. Admission 1€ ($1.15). Daily 9am–2pm and 3–5pm.

Monte Solaro 𝕮𝕮   At 584m (1,916 ft.), Monte Solaro is Capri's highest point, sporting a romantically ruined little 1806 British castle (built medieval style) that offers dreamy island vistas and a **panorama of coastal Italy** 𝕮 that on clear days stretches as far as Calabria to the south and north almost to Rome. The chairliftlike *seggovia* takes 12 minutes to get up there; the steep walk takes an hour (the walk down, through the Valley of Santa Maria a Cetrella, is a pleasantly scenic workout).

Seggovia (chairlift) at Via Caposcuro 10 (off Piazza d. Vittoria). ☎ 081-8371428. Chairlift 4.50€ ($5.15) one-way, 6€ ($6.90) round-trip. Wed–Mon Mar–Oct 9:30am–7:15pm; Nov–Feb 10:30am–3pm; last ticket sold 15 min. prior to closing.

FUN IN THE SUN & SHOPPING

BEACHES   Although Capri is an internationally known island resort, don't expect great sandy beaches. Most of the island is sharp volcanic rock plunging into the azure waters, making for a spectacular dip in the crystalline waters—but rough on tender hands and feet. Snorkeling, too, can be rewarding, and there

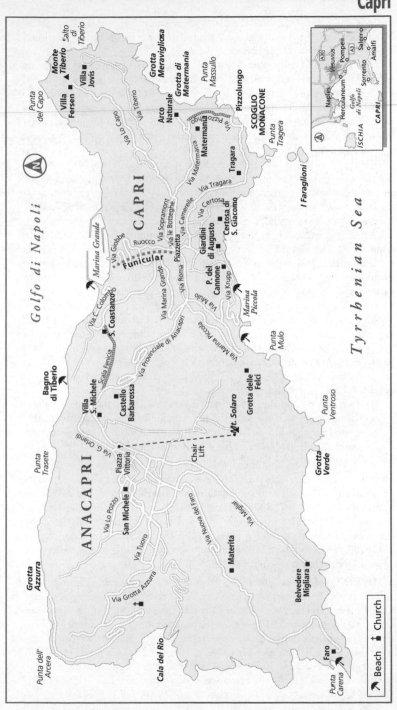

Golfo di Napoli

Tyrrhenian Sea

Monte Tiberio
Salto di Tiberio
Villa Jovis
Villa Fersen
Punta del Capo
Via Lo Capo
Via Tiberio

Grotta Meravigliosa
Grotta di Matermania
Arco Naturale
Punta Massullo
Pizzolungo
SCOGLIO MONACONE
Via Pizzolungo
Matermania
Via Matermania
Punta Tragara
Tragara
Via Tragara

CAPRI
Via Sopramonte
Via le Botteghe
Via Camerelle
Via Certosa
Certosa di S. Giacomo
Giardini di Augusto
Via Giobbe
Ruocco
Piazzetta
Via Roma
P. del Cannone
Via Krupp
Via Marina Grande
Via Mulo
Marina Piccola
Marina Grande
I Faraglioni
Punta Mulo

FUNICULAR
Via C. Colombo
S. Coastanzo
Bagno di Tiberio
Scala Fenicia
Via Felicia
Via Provinciale di Anacapri
Via Marina Piccola
Punta Ventroso

Villa S. Michele
Castello Barbarossa
Grotta delle Felci

ANACAPRI
Via G. Orlandi
Punta Trasete
Piazza Vittoria
Chair Lift
Mt. Solaro
San Michele
Via Lo Pozzo
Via Tuoro
Via Nuova del Faro
Via Migliar
Materita
Grotta Verde

Grotta Azzurra
Via Grotta Azzurra
Belvedere Migliara

Cala del Rio
Punta dell' Arcera
Faro
Punta Carena

Naples
Vesuvius
Pompeii
Herculaneum
Golfo di Napoli
Sorrento
Salerno
Amalfi
A3
A30
ISCHIA
CAPRI

🏖 Beach   ✝ Church

are indeed a few places around the island where you can spread out your towel. Beach lounges and umbrellas are for hire at all of the main "beaches," at around 9€ ($10) or 10€ ($12) per person.

There's a scrap of pebbly beach just to the right of the ferry docks at **Marina Grande,** but it's crowded, a bit dirty, and really best only as a last-resort "I need a swim" bathing spot. Capri's best beach for the past 2,000 years has been the **Bagni di Tiberio,** about a 20-minute walk west from Marina Grande. There's a pebble-and-sand shore, lots of sun worshippers and rocks to lie out on, and a crumbling wall to remind you that even Tiberius, capitalizing on the spot, built a small bath complex here.

Marina Piccola has several restaurant/bathing establishments right on the water—mostly rocks and piers with pools and decks for tanning. Even better, out on either side of the little port are modest rocky beaches: to the east under a Saracen tower, to the west surrounding the stony spit known as **Scoglio delle Sirene.** According to legend, these were the very rocks from which the flesh-eating Sirens sang irresistibly to lure sailors to their deaths. Homer's hero Odysseus prudently stuffed his crewmen's ears with wax and lashed himself to the mast of his boat as they passed the rocks, so as not to be tempted. However, when he heard the Sirens' seductive song, Odysseus fell under their spell and begged to be untied so he could rush to them; luckily for him, his crewmen refused.

A bus ride or 20-minute walk from Anacapri (down V. Nuovo del Faro, off Piazza Caprile) takes you to Lido del Faro at **Punta Carena** (© 081-8371798; take the bus from Anacapri piazza direct), a lovely watering hole tucked into a rocky cove. The raw terrain is scattered with private rowboats. With your back to the hideously modern nearby lighthouse, you get a view out over rocks to azure waters. Watch where you set your feet, though; these rocks support colonies of spiny sea urchins.

Best of all are the "beaches" at **Punta Tragara,** framed by the huge *faraglioni* (rocks slicing up through the water). The boat ride here is spectacular, cutting between the faraglioni just as Odysseus did; but walking the steep path from Capri center, doable in about a half-hour, is just as breathtaking.

BOAT TRIPS   A **cruise around the island** 𝕣𝕣𝕣 is a splendid way to see Capri's rocky perimeter and many sea-level grottoes (the Blue Grotto is just the most famous). As of this writing, only **Gruppo Motoscafisti** (© 081-8375646) and **Laser Capri** (© 081-8375208) circle the island, in a 90-minute excursion (11€/$12 and 9€/$10, respectively) that leaves you wanting more. Both run the excursion to the Grotta Azzurra by sea (6€/$6.90, in addition to the 8.30€/$9.55 admission and rowboat into the cave), as well as excursions from Marina Grande to Faraglioni (9€/$10).

SHOPPING   The most popular Capri purchase is *limoncello,* that wonderful, sugary lemon liqueur, best when consumed close to freezing in an icy shot glass. Luckily, it can also be one of the cheapest souvenirs you can buy. You pay more for the funky shape of the bottle than for the amount of booze inside. You can get sample-size gift bottles for as little as 3€ ($3.45), but for your own consumption, you may want to shell out 8€ to 10€ ($9.20–$12) for ¾ liter. To buy the brand tossed back by Gorky, Krupp, and Axel Munthe, head to the shop run by their supplier's grandkids, **Limoncello di Capri,** Via Roma 79 (© 081-8375561), in Anacapri at Via Capodimonte 27 (© 081-8372927).

Staying on the aromatic end of shopping, Capri is a wonderfully scented island, and the **perfumes and colognes** sold here reflect it. You can find some good bargains at the popular **Carthusia,** Via Camerelle 10 in Capri; Via Capodimonte 26 in Anacapri (© 081-8370368). The store's Aria di Capri concoction of orange, lemon, mimosa, and peach was developed in the 17th century by the monks at the nearby *certosa* (Carthusian monastery). You can also tour the store's tiny lab at Via Giacomo Matteotti 2b.

Capri's other famous product is handmade strap **sandals**—but don't try to hike the island in them. The famous bijou-studded footwear pounded out at **Canfora,** Via Camerelle 3 in Capri (© 081-8370487), will run you a whopping 100€ ($115). For the best bargains, head to **Vincenzo Faiella**'s shop on Capri's Via Vittorio Emanuele 49 (no phone), where cloth and rope shoes and slippers start at 25€ ($29). My favorite cobbler is old Antonio Viva, who sits outside his Anacapri shop **L'Arte del Sandolo Caprese,** at Via Giuseppe Orlandi 75 (© 081-8373583), and proclaims gently through his mustache, "We make these shoes the artisan's way. We make them with heart." Antonio has the widest selection of handmade slippers on Capri, and his work goes for 35€ to 75€ ($40–$86).

ACCOMMODATIONS YOU CAN AFFORD

The isle of Capri is no secret to vacationers, so room vacancies, especially in a more affordable price range, are rare, if not nonexistent. Book as far in advance as possible, and be prepared for rejection. Below is a longer than average list of possibilities, to counter this problem. High season usually runs from mid-June to September, and, unless otherwise noted, this seasonal variance is reflected in the price ranges listed for hotels below.

IN CAPRI TOWN

Belsito   This converted 18th-century house run as a hotel and restaurant by Liliana and Mario Tarantino is removed from the town bustle and very tranquil, yet still just a lovely 10-minute stroll (uphill) from Capri's main piazza. Sadly, the aging structure, outdated linoleum-floored rooms, and dreary sateen bedcovers give the impression that the cleanliness is merely superficial, so I would stay here only assuming nonvacancies at all of the other recommendations below. On the positive side, rooms are small but bright, and the beds won't punish your spine. Room nos. 22 to 27 have views over the arc of Capri, the sea, and the mass of Monte Solaro, while the balance of rooms do not have a view or indeed much light, but are cheaper. There's a rooftop terrace where everyone can enjoy sweeping vistas and, in high season, a dip in the hotel's aboveground swimming pool.

Via Matermania 9–11, 80073 Capri (NA). © 081-8370969. Fax 081-8376622. www.hotelbelsito.com. 13 units. 83€ ($95) single; 180€ ($210) double. Lower rates off season. Rates include breakfast. AE, DC, MC, V. Closed Nov. **Amenities:** Restaurant; aboveground swimming pool (July–Aug only). *In room:* No phone.

La Tosca *(Value)*   This charming villa is hidden on one of Capri's back alleys, surrounded by bird song and seemingly a world away, yet only a 5-minute stroll from the tourist crush of the Piazzetta. Ettore Castelli and his Connecticut-born wife have been improving La Tosca since taking it over in 1997, and although the rates have practically doubled since last year, it's still one of the best values in town. The most recent round of renovations can be seen in updated bathrooms, bright tile flooring, and matched furniture, and all rooms have gracious high ceilings. For view value, room nos. 47 through 51 are the best, with small terraces overlooking the nearby monastery to the sea and the *faraglioni*. The rooms get smaller as they go up in number; after no. 49, trees begin to block much of the view. You can take breakfast privately on your own terrace or communally on the patio amid jasmine and rose bushes.

Via Dalmazio Birago 5, 80073 Capri (NA). ℂ/fax **081-8370989**. www.latoscahotel.com. 12 units. 40€–80€ ($46–$92) single; 63€–125€ ($72–$144) double. Rates include breakfast. MC, V. Closed late Oct to mid-Mar. From the tourist information office in the Piazzetta, follow Via Vittorio Emanuele to Via Federico Serena; turn right onto Via Dalmazio Birago. **Amenities:** Concierge; car-rental desk; 24-hr. room service; in-room massage; babysitting; laundry service. *In room:* A/C, hair dryer, safe.

Worth a Splurge

Villa Krupp 𝄞𝄞𝄞 Villa Krupp is set like a crown jewel of old-world style atop the Giardini d'Augusto at the end of a path that winds up amid the umbrella pines. Its breezy back hill location is very quiet, but still convenient to Capri's shopping and restaurants and Marina Piccola's beach below. An old favorite of Russian intellectuals (Lenin lodged and Gorky lived here), the Krupp's rooms have period or antique-style furnishings on tile floors, updated bathrooms, and firm beds. The larger and more expensive nos. 18 to 21 are the best in the house, with high ceilings, small chandeliers, hair dryers, and killer terrace views over the monastery and the wooded slopes of Monte Tuoro to *faraglioni* and the sea. Smaller, cheaper doubles look over the white-cube tumble of Capri's houses. Most rooms have air-conditioning, and guests can sit in the TV solarium to read and gaze out at the trees and bits of sea peeking through.

Viale Giacomo Matteotti 12 (a long but pleasant path up from the main road), 80073 Capri (NA). ℂ **081-8370362**. Fax 081-8376489. 12 units. 80€ ($92) single; 120€–150€ ($138–$173) double. Rates include breakfast. MC, V. Closed Nov–Mar 31. **Amenities:** Bar; room service (7–10am); laundry service. *In room:* Hair dryer.

IN ANACAPRI

Biancamaria The family-run Biancamaria, a spacious and decorous hotel right in the center of town, has an old-fashioned attitude (they turn away scruffy backpackers). Rooms are generally big and are furnished with ultramodern veneer furnishings, contemporary tile floors, small easy chairs, and not-so-terrible floral bedspreads. Better yet are the huge bathrooms featuring heated towel racks and hair dryers. Rooms with the view of Monte Solaro have small terraces over the town's main drag, which *does* quiet down late at night. For even more silence, request a sea-view room with French doors opening onto a fantastic panorama of the Bay of Naples.

Via Giuseppe Orlandi 54, 80071 Anacapri (NA). ℂ **081-8371000**. Fax 081-8372060. hotelbiancamaria@ capri.it. 25 units. Apr–May and Oct 130€ ($150) double; June–Sept 150€ ($173) double. Rates include breakfast; 10€ ($12) supplement for A/C. AE, MC, V. Closed Nov–Mar. **Amenities:** Bar; 24-hr. room service; dry cleaning, babysitting. *In room:* A/C, TV, hair dryer, safe.

Il Girasole 𝄞 Nestled amid vineyards and olive groves, and just a 10-minute stroll from Anacapri, the family-run Girasole has changed dramatically from the student pensione of a few years ago. Rooms are now bungalows opening onto the terrace (nos. 8, 9, and 12), with summery accommodations of tile floors, functional furnishings in wicker or wood, modern (if not minuscule) bathrooms, and good beds. On lazy days, you can take a dip in the pool or lounge around the bricked terrace garden with views over the island to the Bay of Naples. Rates can fluctuate wildly (and are often spontaneous), so bargain, bargain, bargain. Internet access is available.

Via Linciano 47, 80071 Anacapri (NA). ℂ **081-8372351**. Fax 081-8373880. www.ilgirasole.com. 24 units. 80€–96€ double in low season; 80€–350€ ($92–$400) double in high season. Breakfast 3€–8€ ($3.45–$9.20). AE, MC, V. A 5- to 10-min. walk from Anacapri. Call from Marina Grande or before your ferry departs, and they'll come pick you up for 10€ ($12) for 2 people. Otherwise, ride the Anacapri bus to the end of the line and follow signs along the footpath. **Amenities:** Bar; outdoor swimming pool; Jacuzzi; shuttle service; massage; babysitting. *In room:* A/C, satellite TV, hair dryer, safe.

Loreley   This family-run hotel has three very redeeming characteristics: It's centrally located, Michele and his father are both warmly hospitable and helpful, and the price is right. Room renovations have introduced fresh tile and updated plumbing. Expect soft beds (the way I like them), white cotton linens you love to sink into, and a mishmash of institutional chairs and tables. Balcony doors welcome a little fresh air at night. In season, breakfast is served in the entry courtyard under a flowering trellis.

Via Giuseppe Orlandi 16, 80071 Anacapri. ℂ 081-8371440. Fax 081-8371399. www.loreley.it. 14 units. 60€–80€ single; 80€–120€ ($92–$138) double; 100€–150€ ($115–$173) triple. Rates include breakfast. MC, V. Closed Nov to Easter. *In room:* TV, safe.

Villa Eva 𝒜𝒜 *Kids*   This is one of the island's best inns, an exotic tropical paradise amid lush gardens. The accommodations—small bungalows nestled in the nooks and crannies of the grounds—are a perfect getaway for the regulars who book for weeks at a time. An outdoor pool flanked by a rustic breakfast bungalow peeks through the greenery, guarded by a lazy St. Bernard whose bark is worse than his bite. The place is run by the husband-and-wife team of Vincenzo and Eva Balestrieri, and most of the comfy furnishings were built by Vincenzo. As if painting the decorative artwork on the walls and personalizing the structures with majolica tiles weren't enough, he also installed thoughtful touches like mosquito screens and architectural details like wood beams or tiny *bifore* windows.

Via la Fabbrica 8, 80071 Anacapri (NA). ℂ 081-8371549. Fax 081-8372040. www.villaeva.com. 15 units. 85€–100€ ($98–$115) double; 110€–140€ ($126–$160) triple; 140€–190€ ($126–$220) quad. Rates include breakfast. AE, MC, V. Cash payment only for fewer than 3 nights. Closed mid-Nov to Feb. A 10- to 15-min. walk out the far end of Anacapri toward the Blue Grotto; call from Marina Grande for directions. If possible, someone will pick you up; or take the Blue Grotto bus from Anacapri and ask the driver to let you off for a 2-min. walk. **Amenities:** Bar; outdoor swimming pool (May–Oct).

Worth a Splurge
San Michele 𝒜𝒜   This converted 19th-century villa, sequestered behind a great wrought-iron gate and surrounded by lawns and gardens, has all the trappings of aristocracy. Rooms are characterized by high ceilings and marble and terra-cotta surfaces, with terraces or balconies that enjoy either sea or mountain views. Redecoration of the rooms has freshened up formerly dowdy quarters; try to book one of the renovated rooms, which benefit from a complete overhaul of the bathroom facilities, windows, and flooring. The bonus is the huge pool in the garden, sculpted into the surrounding greenery—normally an unaffordable amenity in these parts. The San Michele hosts sporadic summer concerts and recitals.

Via Giuseppe Orlandi 1/3/5, 80071 Anacapri. ℂ 081-8371427. Fax 081-8371420. www.sanmichele-capri. com. 60 units. Doubles: 140€–155€ ($160–$175) Apr 4–30 and Oct 1–31; 155€–172€ ($175–$200) May 1–July 31 and Sept 1–30; 165€–180€ ($190–$210) Aug and Easter. Rates include breakfast. Half- and full pension available. Reduced rates for stays over 10 days. AE, DISC, MC, V. Closed Nov to Easter. **Amenities:** Restaurant; 2 bars; outdoor swimming pool; 24-hr. room service; laundry service; dry cleaning. *In room:* A/C (in half; 10€ supplement), TV, minibar, hair dryer, safe.

GREAT DEALS ON DINING
Island cuisine is mostly Campanian, relying heavily on fish, but one dish deserves to be singled out. Invented here in the 1950s for calorie-counting vacationers, the *insalata caprese*—often just called the *caprese* and now served in restaurants throughout Italy—is a salad of fresh tomato slices and mozzarella

topped with torn basil and some cracked black pepper. If ever the mozzarella is fresh or *di bufala* (made from buffalo milk), **order it.** You won't get anything quite this fresh or this amazingly good.

There's no lack of overpriced, poor-quality snack bars in Capri. For a good quick bite, your best bet is to pop into a local *alimentari* (grocery shop) and make your own panino or small picnic. For a treat, stop by **Sfizi di Pane,** a short stroll from the Piazzetta at Via Le Botteghe 4 (© **081-8370160**), to sample some of Ottavio Serena's outstanding pastries and breads (closed Sun afternoon). Or head over to **Raffaele Buonacore,** straight under the arch of the Piazzetta, to Via Vittorio Emanuele 35 (© **081-8377826**), where you can choose from a daunting selection of towering quiches, salads, pastas, pastries, and gelato.

AROUND CAPRI

Al Grottino CAPRESE/ITALIAN   The "Little Grotto" is one of our fanciest choices, the sort of place where the waiter debones your fish tableside and good Italian and French vintages supplement the local table wine. It has changed little since the days that Ted Kennedy, the Gabor sisters, and Igor Stravinsky dined in the single room of tightly spaced tables under a stuccoed, vaulted ceiling. Wine flasks, photos of famous patrons, and a rose on every table complete the decor, while a dozen foreign tongues (mixed with some local dialect) and the clamor of the adjacent kitchen set the tone. *Agnolotti al pomodoro caprese* (giant ravioli of cheese and ham topped with fresh baby tomatoes and torn basil) and *risotto alla pescatora* (rice infused with shellfish and tiny squid) make excellent first courses. For the secondo, you can order *involtino alla Napoletana* (veal roll stewed in tomatoes) or *mozzarella in carrozza* (fresh mozzarella on toast fried to a golden brown). But Al Grottino's strong suit is fresh fish; try it cooked *all'acqua pazza* (with tomatoes, white wine, and spices).

Via Longana 27 (standing on the Piazzetta with your back to the Duomo, duck through the tunnel/alley in the center). © 081-8370584. Reservations highly recommended. Primi 7€–10€ ($8.05–$12); secondi 7€–17€ ($8.05–$20). AE, DC, MC, V. Daily noon–3pm and 7pm–midnight. Closed mid-Nov to mid-Mar and Tues in Oct.

Ristorante Pizzeria Longano ⭐ *(Value* CAPRESE/PIZZA   This is probably one of the best values in Capri, apart from packing your own picnic. The lack of pretension combines with a charming stone arched dining room; lucky couples will time their arrival just right to coincide with the availability of one of the handful of tables set under parapet-style windows overlooking one of Capri's countless views. The back room can get a bit smoky, so abstainers may want to sit at one of the tables near the entrance. The ample menu lists a seemingly endless choice of pizzas and other favorites like *penette Nerana* (little penne with sautéed zucchini) and *linguini ai frutti di mare* (seafood linguini). Diners bored with the *bistecca alla griglia* have an alternative in the tasty *pollo alla cacciatore* (chicken parts cooked in olive oil and herbs).

Via Longano 9, Capri (from the piazza, under the arch below the Municipio on the left). © 081-8370187. Primi 5€–12€ ($5.75–$14); secondi 6.50€–12€ ($7.45–$14). AE, DC, MC, V. Daily noon–4pm and 7:30pm–midnight.

Verginiello *(Value (Kids* CAPRESE/SEAFOOD/PIZZA   Verginiello sits steps below the post office along the path leading down the Marina Grande, offering delicious food at optimum value. The outer dining room enjoys a panoramic windowed view of the Gulf of Naples, while the adjacent dining area is a covered garden, with a small courtyard space where the children can work off some energy after finishing their meal. Tables are pleasantly packed to the gills with

Italians, especially on weekend evenings, and service a bit overwhelmed by the overflow. By the look of the ample portions, it's easy to see why. Start with a plate of the *risotto al pescatore* (seafood risotto), and follow that with the house specialty, grilled seafood (notice the open grill as you enter). Meat-eaters will be equally pleased with the *bistecca ai ferri* (grilled steak) and the *scaloppine al Marsala* (veal Marsala). Verginello also offers a 15€ ($17) menu for lunch.

Via Lo Palazzo 25 (10 or so steps down from the post office). ℭ 081-8377140. Reservations imperative on weekends. Primi 4.50€–9.50€ ($5.15–$11); secondi 7.50€–18€ ($8.60–$21) and up for fish. AE, DC, MC, V. Daily noon–4pm and 7pm–midnight.

AROUND ANACAPRI

Al Nido d'Oro *(Value)* *(Kids)* CASARECCIA CAPRESE/PIZZA   Make no mistake: This ain't fine dining or a tourist restaurant with a view. This is one of the few places locals like to keep to themselves, with pizza takeout on one side and families crowding the eight tables of the other room in the early evening, giving way to couples and small groups after 9:30pm. Caprese dialect sets the tone while the busy chef in the kitchen whips up heaping plates of simple, filling, fragrant home cooking. The *ravioli caprese* gets you pasta pockets stuffed with ricotta and basil, while the *penne con crema di carciofi* is in a flavorful creamy artichoke sauce. Secondi are basic: *scaloppina al limone* and the overwhelmingly popular *frittura di calamari* (fried squid). You can also enjoy pizzas such as *pizza capricciosa* (topped with tomato, mozzarella, prosciutto, mushrooms, olives, capers, and Parmesan).

Via de Tomasso 30–32. ℭ 081-8372148. Reservations not accepted. Primi 5.50€–9.50€ ($6.30–$11); secondi 6.50€–20€ ($7.45–$23). Thurs–Tues noon–3pm and 8pm–midnight (from 7pm in winter). Closed Jan 20–Feb 20.

Il Cucciolo *★★* CAPRESE   Tucked away on a back path off the road to the Blue Grotto, Il Cucciolo offers abundant portions of quite excellent food on a terrace surrounded by lush greenery and views of the Bay of Naples below. The *caprese* salad is excellent, as are the *pennette alla contadina* (minitube pasta in a savory sauce of onions, Parmesan, and lean pancetta). For the secondo, try *pollo marinato alla griglia* (succulent marinated and grilled chicken—ask for the special "Argentina" sauce) or fresh *pesce alla griglia*. Head over in the evening, when the candlelight adds to an already romantic ambience and when the walk back to town will allow you to work off the guilt, but be sure to call ahead because the dining room closes frequently for family celebrations.

Via la Fabbrica 52. ℭ 081-8371917. Reservations recommended. Primi and secondi 8€–20€ ($9.20–$23). AE, DC, MC, V. Tues–Sun noon–2:30pm; daily 7–11:30pm. Closed late Oct to Easter. Take the bus to Blue Grotto and ask to be let off at the turnoff (from where it's another 20m/67 ft.); or take a 20-min. walk from Anacapri.

Il Solitario *★★★* *(Value)* CAPRESE   The clientele in this garden trattoria is likely to be half regulars on a first-name basis with the chef/owner and half tourists here for the second time, fending off the insistent stares of the owner's little dog, Pedro. The house dish is ravioli stuffed with fresh cheeses and is deservedly the most popular menu item. Also good are the *gnocchi alla Sorrentina*, *tagliolini all'aragosta* (ribbons of egg pasta with tomatoes and baby lobsters), and *cannelloni caprese* (ricotta- and spinach-stuffed pasta tubes). For secondi, sample the simple omelet with mozzarella or the *spiedini di carne mista* (shish kebabs of beef, sausage, and rabbit). Reserve ahead in nice weather for the best seating out on the back terrace, where the low, hanging vines of an arbor shade little tile-topped tables.

Via Giuseppe Orlandi 96 (on the main road in town). (© 081-8371382. Reservations recommended. Primi 4.50€–10€ ($5.15–$12); secondi 6.50€–12€ ($7.45–12); *menu turistico* 8€ ($9.20) or 13€ ($15) without wine. AE, DC, MC, V. Tues–Sun noon–3pm and 7:30pm–midnight (daily June 21–Sept 21). Closed Nov–Mar.

5 The Emerald Isle of Ischia ⓐ

After scouring the Amalfi Coast for the unspoiled innocence described in the book, Anthony Minghella, director of *The Talented Mr. Ripley,* disqualified the real thing until he stumbled on **Ischia,** a luxuriant island spa. Ischia, pleasantly devoid of the polish and glitz that has become the Amalfi coast, remains untainted by the overdevelopment that plagues the mainland coast and forgotten by visitors caught in the undertow toward Capri. Ischia may not have the show-stopping sheer cliffs of Capri or the drama of the Amalfi Coast, but it does have consistently stunning views, ample pristine beaches, and decadent thermal centers for the best in guiltless self-indulgence. As the resort of choice for Italians, Ischia maintains its quiet authenticity (all bets are off in Aug).

Known as the **Emerald Isle,** this island is no secret—Ischia is mentioned in Homer's *Iliad* as well as Virgil's *Aeneid*—but the influx of mostly British and German tourists hasn't been enough to spoil the forthcoming and earnest nature of the Ischians. Ischia still retains much of its agricultural quality, boasting the production of the first D.O.C. (Denominazione di Origine Controllata—meaning it's quality controlled by the State) wine in the country. The marinas still bustle in the earliest hours of the morning, as local fishermen prepare their nets for the day's work.

The island comprises six municipalities, with the village of Ischia, sitting atop an ancient crater, serving as the capital. The island is home to an abundance of curative **thermal waters and mineral springs.** Beneath all that restorative bubbly is a volcanic system whose eruption in 302 B.C. transformed the original ancient settlement into a natural lake. The lake was opened up in 1854 and transformed into a port by Ferdinand II, now enveloped by modern-day **Ischia Port.** Ischia Port revolves around **Via Vittoria Colona,** a progressive avenue of cafes, smart boutiques, and beauty and thermal spas. A 15-minute walk (more, if you stop to shop) down the road will lead you to **Ischia Ponte,** named for the long pedestrian bridge connecting the mainland to the islet and the 15th-century **Castello Aragonese** ⓐ, built by Alfonso d'Aragona, king of Spain, on the foundations of an earlier 474 B.C. fortress. On the island's southern section is the village of **Sant'Angelo,** whose dramatic cliffs and unspoiled waterfront facades rival the jaw-dropping views of Capri. **Mount Epomeo** can leave you breathless, not only for the 90-minute hike uphill, but for the perfect panorama of the island that will be your reward. Or you can simply spend a week of complete decadence and utter self-indulgence, scheduling your day around massages, mudpacks, and meals—the perfect vegetative beach vacation you've always dreamed of.

ESSENTIALS

GETTING THERE & GETTING AROUND   By Ferry or Hydrofoil   The *aliscafo* (hydrofoil) from **Naples** takes 40 minutes and costs 11€ ($12); the *traghetto* (ferry) takes about 1 hour and 20 minutes and costs about half that. Both **Caremar** (© **081-8370700;** www.caremar.it) and **Alilauro** (© **081-5527209;** www.lauro.it) run hydrofoil and ferry service from both the Molo Beverello and Mergellina docks.

By Bus   SEPSA buses (.95€/$1.10 for 90-min. pass; 4€/$4.60 for day pass) circle the island clockwise (CD) and counterclockwise (CS), departing from the terminus in Piazzale Trieste, behind the port. C7 circles from the port to the causeway at the Castello Aragonese (stopping far outside the pedestrian-only area 11am–1pm daily and on Sun). You can also catch a bus to specific points toward the center of the island; check with the tourist information office for schedules and destinations. Buses run every 20 minutes, but since services overlap, it's unlikely you'll have to wait very long to get where you're going.

By Taxi Those farcical three-wheeled Ape (*Ah*-pay) minitrucks you may have spotted on your travels have been transformed into utilitarian public transport, but it's going to cost you. The minimum fare for stepping foot into one of these babies is around 10€ ($12). Travel light or take the bus.

By Rental Car/Scooter There are dozens of auto- and scooter-rental offices on the left bank of the port (exit the ferry and continue on foot to the left). That imposter of a tourist information office across from the ferry landing also manages a scooter and auto-rental service, at prices slightly higher than the others. Expect to pay in the area of 20€ to 25€ ($23–$29) per day for a scooter and from 35€ ($40) per day for a car (rates increase in Aug). Most rental agencies are closed November through March.

By Water Taxi A water taxi and excursion service is run by the **Cooperative Rimessaggio Barche Ischitana,** Via Pontano 7 (next to the Miramare Hotel; ℂ/fax **081-984854**). The cooperative is open 24 hours June through August, cutting back to an 8am-to-8pm schedule during the shoulder season and closing altogether in the height of winter. Prices vary according to distance, from about 2€ ($2.30) per person to get to Scogli di Sant'Anna up to about 50€ ($58; maximum three people) to Istmo di Sant'Angelo. A relaxing half-day *giro dell'isola* (tour of the island) will cost you around 15€ ($17) per person, allowing you swimming stops at some astoundingly beautiful spots while you circle the island. They also rent boats with or without a captain.

VISITOR INFORMATION All the services you'll need are crowded around the port. There's an **official Azienda Turismo** next to the unmistakable hydrofoil and ferry ticket office (ℂ **081-5074211**), open daily from 9am to 2pm and 4 to 7pm. You can change money or withdraw cash using your ATM card at the Banco di Napoli (walk left from the ferry landing) at Via Iasolino 34.

THINGS TO SEE & DO

Castello Aragonese ⭐⭐ The fortress occupies an exceptionally picturesque islet connected to the "mainland" by a narrow causeway. Begin your visit at the summit, reachable via elevator, and work your way down through the **terraced gardens** and medieval paths that echo with the sounds of the nearby camouflaged chicken coop. From the upper terraces (where there is also a cafe), the grounds open onto a breathtaking **view** of the Gulf of Naples. Worth seeing are the ruins of a 14th-century Romanesque **cathedral,** altered in the 18th century with the addition of baroque elements. The restored **crypt** exhibits some astonishingly well-preserved frescos and religious icons in the various chapels. Beyond the **Casa del Sole,** the heavy gates and massive gratings of the **prison** detained political prisoners, particularly those martyred during the Italian *Risorgimento.* At the upper reaches of the outcropping is the **convent,** founded in the 16th century and abandoned in 1818 upon the king of Naples's secularization decree. Beneath the convent is a **Cemetery of the Poor Clares,** two confined cellars lined with, well, latrines . . . upon which the corpses were seated (the holes, rather than seats, allowed the fluids to drain). This ghoulish display served as a place of meditation for those among the living, until the bones putrefied and were piled up in the charnel house.

Piazzale Aragonese, Ischia Ponte. (℃) 081-992834. Admission 8€ ($9.20). Mar–Nov and 1 week between Christmas and New Year's daily 9am–7pm.

La Mortella   La Mortella, home and creative refuge to the late English composer William Walton, began as a stark and arid stone quarry. While Walton toiled about in his studio, his wife, Susana, with the tireless help of renowned landscape architect Russell Page, created the lavish botanical gardens that now consist of over 1,000 Mediterranean and tropical plants enveloping the property. The gardens and studio are open to visitors now, and **classical vocal recitals** are performed every Saturday and Sunday (free with park admission) in combination with a yearly workshop for singers. Susana continues her labor of love, from personally supervising the addition of rare or endangered species to the gardens, to hand-feeding the hummingbirds in the aviary. **Victoria's House,** a tropical greenhouse named after the resident giant Brazilian water lily *Victoria Ammazonica* (time your visit around the automatic sprinkler mist), was one of the exhibitions invited to the prestigious Chelsea Flower Show in 2000.

Via Francesco Calise 35. (℃) 081-986220. www.ischia.it/mortella. Admission 10€ ($12). Apr–Nov Tues, Thurs and Sat–Sun 9am–7pm. Take the La Mortella bus from Ischia Port to the La Mortella bus stop; entrance is about 15m/50 ft. from the turnoff.

BEACHES & WATERWORKS

With 34km (21 miles) of alternating pine woods and *spiagge* (beaches), and a total of eight thermal springs and innumerable mineral springs, you'll be hard-pressed to find something to do that doesn't involve getting wet. Halfway between Ischia Port and Ischia Ponte beckons the **Spiaggia dei Pescatori,** littered with colorful fishing boats and buoys and with postcard views of the Castello Aragonese. On the opposite side of the island is the **Spiaggia di Citara,** spreading out under the protection of the majestic headland of Punto Imperatore. The fishing village of Sant'Angelo lies at the southern tip of the island, with the **Spiaggia dei Maronti** extending several kilometers to the east. Sant'Angelo spills into the sea by way of a narrow strip of sand flanked on both sides by the sea and ending in the great green rock of La Roia at **Punta Sant'Angelo.**

If your budget won't allow you accommodations in a hotel with its own thermal spa, you'll definitely need to sample some of the *giardini termali* **(thermal gardens),** private establishments charging a basic entrance fee of anywhere from 20€ to 25€ ($23–$29) for the day (half-day rates available). The fee generally includes use of the thermal pool, dressing rooms, sauna, and whirlpool, along with access to the beach and a beach chair. The **Giardini Poseidon Terme** in Forio ((℃) 081-907122) is the largest and most hyped destination on the island, with an entrance fee of 25€ ($29) for use of its 17 outdoor and 3 indoor thermal pools. You also get to wander around the peaceful and enchanting gardens, or make use of one of the many curative treatments available. It's open daily April through November 8:30am to sunset.

The **Parco Termale Castiglione,** Via Castiglione 36, Casamicciola Terme ((℃) 081-982551), is slightly more characteristic of Ischia's numerous thermal gardens; it also has a full-service spa, including medical checkup, various massages, and decadent beauty treatments (peelings, pedicures, waxings, facial treatments). The park is open daily April through November from 9am to 7pm. (From the Ischia Port bus terminal, take bus no. CS or no. 2 to the second stop, about .8km/½ mile.)

If you've only got a couple of hours, the Ischia Thermal Center, Via Delle Terme, 15, at Ischia Porte (© **081-984376**), is the people's choice, offering year-round access to thermal waters (11€/$13), mud baths (28€/$32), a menu of massages (12€–43€/$13–$50), and a whole host of diagnostic therapies and cosmetic treatments.

For those on the prowl for a really local experience (the numerous German tourists notwithstanding), head down to **Sorceto,** where the scorching volcanic heat of the island's bowels meets with the cool salty waters of the Mediterranean. *Beware:* The water closest to the beach is too hot to handle; instead, you must scramble out a bit on the (slippery!) rocks until you reach a more temperate thermal mixture. There's a bar on-site and a dubiously accredited "resident" masseur, providing mud facials and other services at a modest price. From Panza, follow the connecting road down about 600m (1,968 ft.) forking left; then take the stairs down to the cove. Note that this hike is not for the weary or unfit, as you will be heading back down the mountain to sea level (and back up).

ACCOMMODATIONS YOU CAN AFFORD

Aragonese   Located on a sloping residential road above the pedestrian center of Ischia Ponte, the Aragonese offers a compromise between value and simplicity. The hotel is fronted by a garden-enclosed thermal swimming pool, the focal point for all of the inn's accommodations. Rooms are more indicative of basic guest quarters, with antique furniture and tile floors. Bathrooms are spacious and pleasantly old, yet are outfitted with practical box showers. The clientele at the Aragonese is mostly German couples on package tours, but that doesn't diminish the appeal of this family-owned and -operated Ischian gem.

Via GB Vico 76 (at Via Cartaromana), 80070 Ischia Ponte (NA). © 081-992431. Fax 081-981491. www.hotel aragonese.it. 25 units. 38€ ($44) single; 70€ ($80) double. Rates include breakfast. Half pension 5€ ($5.75) extra and obligatory in Aug. AE, MC, V. Closed Nov to Easter. **Amenities:** Restaurant; bar; thermal swimming pool; tour desk. *In room:* No phone.

Il Monastero ★★ *Kids* Occupying the former Convent di Clausura, Il Monastero sits high atop the castle grounds, affording panoramic views over the communal terrace from every room. In keeping with the spartan lifestyles of its former inhabitants, the hotel accommodations boast high arches, whitewashed walls, and loads of character, while the bathrooms are unexpectedly modern and utilitarian. The dining room is small and cozy, much like a trattoria in the countryside, but it still maintains the monastic reticence of all those years ago. To get up to the pensione, go to the castle's ticket window and have the employee call up and announce your arrival; you will be provided with a pass.

Castello Aragonese 3, 80070 Ischia Ponte (NA). ©/fax 081-992435. www.castelloaragonese.it/main.htm. 21 units. 75€ ($86) single; 110€ ($126) standard double; 122€ ($140) superior double. Rates slightly lower off season and include breakfast. AE, DC, MC, V. Free parking at base of castle. Just past castle museum entrance, turn right to access the elevator; exit elevator to the right past the Chiesa dell'Immacolata; the hotel entrance is to the left opposite the gift shop. **Amenities:** Restaurant; bar; tour desk; car-rental desk; babysitting. *In room:* A/C.

Terme Oriente ★ Occupying a mansion in the center of Ischia Port, the Hotel Terme Oriente strikes you as elegant in a sort of colonial way. Gorgeous ceramic tile floors are everywhere, and most rooms come with a spacious balcony. The house is surrounded by porches and terraces on all sides: There's a rear garden with an outdoor thermal pool and a panoramic rooftop terrace with two iron-rich hydromassage tubs (no extra charge). You can also sign up for a regimen of curative treatments (including acupuncture, reflexology, aerosol inhalation

Cruising Down the Amalfi Coast

The Amalfi Coast is one of Europe's greatest scenic wonders. High on the cliff side, the **Amalfi Drive** ⊛⊛⊛ road winds dizzily along the coast, a marvel of engineering and one of the world's best white-knuckle thrill rides outside of an amusement park. This 50km (30-mile) stretch of crinkled coastline between Sorrento and Salerno offers breathtaking scenery as you make your tortuous, winding way from one gorgeous sea cove into the next, past craggy inlets so sheer and deep they almost qualify as minifjords. High, tree-swathed cliffs on your left plunge tumultuously into the azure waters below you. Scraps of beaches, terraced groves of giant lemons, and some of the most inviting, relaxing, and picturesque small towns in Italy punctuate the coastline's inlets and headlands.

The bougainvillea-crowned and jasmine-scented villages of the Amalfi Coast range from pricey resort towns to old-fashioned fishing hamlets. Among the dozen or so communities strung along the coast is a trinity of required stops: posh Positano, historic Amalfi, and garden-filled Ravello. In between you'll find everything from the Emerald Grotto sea cave to the ceramics of Vietri sul Mare. Many people on a day trip take the bus from Sorrento to Amalfi, then turn around to come back, but the most spectacular, least-developed sections of the coast lie east of Amalfi en route to Salerno. Information on specific towns is detailed below. *Note:* While riding down the Amalfi Coast, fight for a seat on the right side of the vehicle. You'll get the best view—and worst case of vertigo (unless you're coming from Salerno north, in which case you'll want to sit on the left).

The **bus** ride down the Amalfi Coast is one of the world's cheapest carnival rides, and by far the one with the most stunning scenery. The skilled drivers take on the stressful job of navigating the twists and turns, leaving you free to focus your camera and gasp in awe (and a bit of terror) as each bend brings vistas even more spectacular than the last into view and the side of the giant blue bus swings out over the edge of the cliff, giving you the sensation of dangling high above the sparkling waters.

---

treatments, and physiotherapy) or rehabilitation services for, among other ailments, arthritic problems and spinal and back ailments. Of course, this may mean that you'll be sharing the Jacuzzi with elderly overweight and undertanned tourists. The hotel arranges musical entertainment nightly, although with its restaurant putting out food this respectable, you may not need any coaxing to dine in.

Via delle Terme 9/11, 80077 Ischia Porto (NA). ℂ/fax **081-991306.** www.ischia.it/oriente. 80 units. 70€ ($80) double in high season. Rates include breakfast and dinner. Rates lower Sept–July. 14€ ($16) discount for breakfast only. 10€ ($12) per person supplement Aug 7–28. Spa packages available. AE, MC, V. **Amenities:** Restaurant; bar; spa; 2 rooftop Jacuzzis; concierge; tour desk; car-rental desk; 24-hr. room service; massage; babysitting; laundry service; dry cleaning. *In room:* TV, refrigerator, hair dryer, safe.

GREAT DEALS ON DINING

If you thought that eating in Italy had become abnormally expensive, wait till you get to Ischia. But all is not lost. **Da Ciccio,** near the port (Via Porto 1; no

Unflinching **SITA** (© 081-5522176) bus drivers make the drive down the Amalfi Coast from Sorrento to Amalfi (there are also connections from Naples). Buses leave about hourly from in front of Sorrento's train station (buy your tickets at the station newsstand outside the exit). The Amalfi Drive itself skirts **Positano** (35 min.), with the bus stopping twice (the second stop, "Sponda," is closer to the heart of town and the beach). The bus continues on to stop above **Praiano** (another 20 min.) and **Conca dei Marini** (15 min. past Praiano); it ends up in the center of **Amalfi** at the port (10 min. from Conca and 85 min. from Sorrento). It's a commuter bus, so while you can hop on and off, you must buy a new ticket for each leg (see individual sections for exact fares). From Amalfi, hourly SITA buses run through Atrani up to **Ravello** and back (25–30 min.; 1€/$1.15), while other SITA buses run at least hourly through Atrani, Maiori, Minori, and **Vietri sul Mare** (1 hr. from Amalfi; 1.60€/$1.85), to end in **Salerno** (10 min. from Vietri, .95€/$1.10; or 70 min. from Amalfi, 1.60€/$1.85).

If your stomach is strong enough and you're up to the task, you can take these curves from behind the wheel of your own **car,** but concentrating on the road (and not losing your lunch) will definitely detract from the event. If you are determined to take your life into your own hands, you can drive yourself along the twisting, death-defying Amalfi Coast down the **SS163** from Sorrento to Salerno. Buses blare their horns when rounding blind, outside curves so you'll know they're coming. Be prepared for inevitable delay: When there's not enough room for the bus to pass, chaos (and congestion) ensues, with masses of gesticulating locals getting involved to figure a way out of the mess. Chances are, you'll have to back up along with everybody else. **Tra.vel.mar.** (© 089-872950) services the Amalfi Coast with six or seven daily **boat** connections among Sorrento, Positano, Amalfi, and Salerno. Both **Caremar** (© 081-8073077) and **Linee Marittime Partenopee** (© 081-8071812), a cooperative of area ferries and hydrofoils, provide limited service to Capri from the Amalfi Coast (see the specific sections for time/fare listings).

phone), has an array of light food (stuffed eggplant, vegetables, sandwiches) and a comfortable back room where you can sit and eat without paying that annoying Italian cover. It's open daily from 8 to 11pm, but keep in mind that as the day wears on, the selection diminishes.

Halfway between Ischia Porto and Ischia Ponte at Piazza Degli Eroi is **Calise** (© 081-991270), which is guaranteed to satisfy almost any craving. It's a bar, a gelateria (some of the best on the island), a *tavola calda* (head down the sloping walkway to the basement level for gourmet food you can afford), a pasticceria (*baba al rhum al limoncello* is an island specialty) and, on summer evenings, a concert venue. It's open daily 6am to 4am.

Coco ISCHIAN It's a bit unconvincing, this quintessential tourist spot in the shadow of the castle, but who'd expect the food to be so good? Another local eatery that specializes in fish, Coco puts out a fantastic *frittura mista,* with calamari and baby whiting as fresh as the day they were born. The kitchen puts out the island's specialty of *coniglio alla cacciatore* (rabbit in tomato and spices) as well. The primi are exceptional, faultlessly executed traditional recipes like *spaghetti alle vongole* (with clam sauce), although you could easily fill up before the meal begins on antipasti like *fiori di zucca* (fried zucchini flowers) and marinated anchovies. The nearby castle ramparts loom above, making this a scenic and extremely romantic spot.

Piazzale Aragonese 1, Ischia Ponte. © 081-981823. Primi 4.50€–12€ ($5.15–$14); secondi 6€–10€ ($6.90–$12) and up for fish. AE, DC, MC, V. Daily 12:30–3:30pm and 7:30pm–midnight. Closed Wed in winter.

WORTH A SPLURGE

Ristorante Alberto Sul Mare ✮✮ CREATIVE ISCHIAN Unaware of the sublime dining experience that awaits, rarely do day-trippers make it to this side of Ischia Lido. A family-run establishment and a team effort, Ristorante Alberto combines whimsical and inventive recipes along with exuberant hospitality. In this beachside shack, diners can enjoy sea views through the walls of glass giving onto the sea, it's not surprising that fresh fish dominates the menu. If you like your fish raw, start with *the marinati misti,* a variety of raw or marinated local fish in lemon or balsamic vinegar. Or throw caution to the wind and start with the *linguini all'aragosta,* prepared with male lobster, said to be the tastier of the species, over a bed of pasta bought fresh daily from the *granaio.* A tasty secondo would be the *spigola in salsa di pere* (fish in a pear sauce). With the sun's receding rays turning Procida Island a burnt orange, you'll probably want to drag out your meal as long as possible, leaving you to indulge in the house tiramisu.

Via Cristoforo Colombo, on the opposite side of Bagno Lido. © 081-981259. Primi 12€–18€ ($14–$21); secondi 16€ ($18), fish by weight around 25€ ($29) per person. AE, DC, MC, V. Daily noon–3pm and 7:30pm–1am. Closed Nov–Mar.

6 Sorrento: Hear the Sirens Call ✮

48km (30 miles) SE of Naples, 8km (5 miles) NE of Capri, 17km (11 miles) W of Positano

Sorrento may not have the fishing-village charm (or inflated prices) that you'll find in Positano or Amalfi, but it offers a good central location (with connections for major highways and transport routes) for touring the Amalfi Coast, abundantly accessible shopping, and a genuinely unspoiled picture of a vibrant Italian seaside town.

A cheerfully modern city perched on the cliff tops high above the Bay of Sorrento, Sorrento's ancient allure lies in the sweeping picturesque bays, the narrow alleyways of the old town, and the ancient and endless stone stairways leading down to crystal-clear waters. Those mythical femme fatale Sirens certainly made an impression, leaving their legacy in the very name Sorrentum, which has drawn pleasure-seekers as far back as antiquity—wealthy Romans who left a legacy of crumbling aqueducts and cisterns, along with a smattering of villas occupying the most coveted panoramic positions along the coast.

Sorrento never gained status as a major trading port, but that didn't stop the Longobards or the Normans from asserting their might here, albeit in a relatively hands-off fashion. Not so the Turks, who, in 1558, sacked the town and carted much of the local population back to Constantinople as slaves. In a classic case of closing the barn door after the horse, the city walls were fortified, but Sorrento's streak of bad luck continued soon after with the arrival of a plague that swooped down and killed over 2,000 people throughout the peninsula. It wasn't until the 19th century that the city was able to regain her momentum as a tourist destination, regaining enough appeal to attract such illustrious figures as Lord Byron, John Keats, Walter Scott, Charles Dickens, and Wolfgang Goethe—it was even here that Wagner met Nietzsche and Ibsen completed *Peer Gynt*. Significantly, these personalities had at their disposal a richer level of hospitality than our budgets allow, so don't expect the same experience depicted by their portrayals.

ESSENTIALS

GETTING THERE   By Train   From Naples, the private **Circumvesuviana rail line** (© 081-5368932 or 081-7722444; www.vesuviana.it) runs efficiently every half-hour or so from 5:09am to the last train at 10:42pm. It stops at Herculaneum (1.70€/$1.95), Pompeii (2.20€/$2.55), and Sorrento (80 min.; 3.10€/$3.55), with numerous stops in between. *Tip:* At 6.40€ ($7.35), the regional Unico day ticket (buy the zone, or *fascia*, 5) will get you from Naples and back on the Circumvesuviana and includes unlimited travel within the city of Naples for the duration of the ticket.

By Car   From Naples, take Route 18 to Castellammare di Stabia, where you transfer over to the SS145 to Sorrento.

By Ferry/Hydrofoil   The **Linee Marittime Partenopee** cooperative (© 081-8781430) runs two connections daily to and from Amalfi (9.50€/$11) and Positano (9€/$10). **LMP** also oversees four ferries daily from Capri (© 081-8071812; 40 min.; 7€/$8.05) and frequent hydrofoils (20 min.; 9.50€/$11), in addition to twice-daily hydrofoils from Positano (9€/$10). From Capri, **Caremar** (© 081-8073077) runs ferries three times a day (40–50 min.; 5.80€/$6.65).

By Bus   **Autolinee Curreri Service** (© 081-8015420) runs four buses daily from Napoli's Capodichino Airport (1 hr.; 5.20€/$6) and two Marozzi buses daily from Rome's Tiburtina Station (© 06-44249519; 4 hr.; 15€/$17). **SITA** (© 081-5522176) buses run along the coastal road between Amalfi and Sorrento, passing through Positano and Priano (optimistically 85 min.; 3.15€/ $3.60).

GETTING AROUND   By Bus   The historic center around Piazza Tasso is walkable, but for longer stretches and to avoid the endless stairs down to the harbor—or, worse, up—orange buses run from around 7am to around 11:30pm. From the station, **Bus D** runs to Piazza Tasso (city center) and Corso Italia (the main drag). **Bus A** runs from Piazza Tasso out to Via Capo (where you'll find lots of hotels). **Buses B and C** run from Piazza Tasso down to Marina Piccola (the ferry dock) and back again. Tickets cost 1€ ($1.15) and must be bought before boarding the bus (tickets are sold at several booths at Marina Piccola and in *tabacchi*). A taxi from the Marina Piccola to the train station will run you about 10€ ($12).

By Rental Car   Since Sorrento makes such a good base, picking up a car or scooter here (rather than fighting the traffic in Naples) can make a lot of sense. The most reputable agencies, roughly in order from cheapest to most expensive, are **De Martino** (Auto Europe), Corso Italia 253 (© 081-8782801); **Sorrento/Sixt Rent a Car,** Corso Italia 210A (© 081-8781410); and **Avis,** Viale Nizza 53 (© 081-8782459). All except Avis also rent scooters—as does **Jolly Rent A Scooter,** Via Fuorimura 29 (© 081-8781719)—for around 27€ ($31) for 4 to 5 hours, and around 38€ ($44) per day, including gas, with discounted rates for multiple-day rentals.

VISITOR INFORMATION   Sorrento's **tourist office** is inside the Circolo dei Forestieri club just down from Piazza San Antonio, at Via Luigi de Maio 35 (© **081-8074033;** fax 081-8773397). It's open Monday through Saturday from 8:30am to 8pm May through September, and from 8:45am to 2:45pm and 3:30 to 6:30pm October through April. If you arrive by boat, take the orange bus up to Piazza San Antonio and walk back to the gated entrance across the street on your right.

Check your e-mail at the **Internet Café** at Via Fuorimura 20D, near Piazza Tasso (© **081-8074854**). It's open daily from 10:30am to 1:30pm and 4:30pm to 1am.

Leave your luggage at the kiosk down at the marina for 1€ ($1.15) per bag.

FESTIVALS   In honor of **Good Friday,** the town hosts a solemn Byzantine procession. In July and August, Sorrento hosts both a **classical music festival** in indoor and outdoor venues across town, and an **international film festival** that, although lacking the star quality of Cannes or Venice, is beginning to gain a certain following.

WHAT TO SEE & DO IN SORRENTO

Sorrento's sights include the 14th-century **cloisters of San Francesco** (now an art school) on Via Vittorio Veneto. The former convent stands on a system of interlaced arcades typical of Sicilian Saracen architecture. A closer inspection reveals elements recycled from pagan temples.

The neighboring public gardens of the **Villa Comunale** offer great views down to the marina and up the coastline. There's also a small museum at the east end of town, the **Museo Correale di Terranova,** Via Correale 50 (© **081-8781846**), open Monday and Wednesday through Friday from 9am to 2pm (Sat–Sun to 1pm). The collections include lots of locally inlaid wood furnishings, majolica, porcelain figurines, Neapolitan baroque paintings (plus a Rubens), marvelous views over the gardens to the Bay of Sorrento, and crumbling bits of Roman statuary to remind you of the city's venerable, if little visible, heritage. Admission is 5.15€ ($5.90).

If you're not convinced of Sorrento's allure, some of the best sightseeing happens along the streets of the old town. Italians out for a *passeggiata* head to modern Corso Italia and the parallel and cobbled Via San Cesareo, the old Decumanus Maximus of the Roman town. While tourists and locals mill about the streets in the late afternoon, peering into shops cramped with *objets* of inlaid wood or locally fired ceramics, the town elders gather under the 15th-century loggia of the **Sedile Dominova** at the corner of Via San Cesareo and Via Giuliano to play Italian card games under the 18th-century frescoes (be sure you filter back amid the bar umbrellas on the tiny piazza out front to glimpse the Sedile's majolica dome growing weeds).

BEACHES & BOAT CRUISES   Although Sorrento is a seaside town, don't come here expecting beaches. While the water's a bit cleaner than along most of the bay, swimming is mainly off piers jutting out over the rocks, plus a few tiny pebble beaches that charge admission. An elevator ride down from the town (look for these elevators along V. Marina Grande) will take you near the water's edge.

Because of its optimum location, Sorrento is a great base of operations for day trips to Capri and Ischia, as well as short hops down to Positano and Amalfi. You can also sign up with one of the companies down at the marina for day-long minicruises (20€/$23) that might include Capri's Faraglioni, Li Galli, one of the coast's infamous grottos.

ACCOMMODATIONS YOU CAN AFFORD

It's certainly possible to find accommodations in one of the budget hotels that line Corso Italia from the train station to the town center. But you can get significantly better quality at competitive rates if you make the effort and walk a little farther. You can also find a number of cheaper hotels along **Via Capo,** the ultrascenic cliff-top road leading out the far end of town.

Corso   Located in the fringes of the historic center, the family-run Corso is now a three-star hotel, with prices to match. Its biggest selling point is also its greatest drawback: Sorrentine life passes below your street-side window along the car-trafficked main drag of Via del Corso. The plain accommodations feature exceedingly firm beds, the usual modular furnishings, and generous proportions, though the overall effect can be a bit bland. Room nos. 52 through 55 have tiny mostly-for-show balconies that overhang quiet, pedestrianized Via San Cesareo. If you can't score one of these, go for nos. 62 to 65, deprived of the view, but still on the building's quieter back side.

Corso Italia 134 (½ block beyond Piazza Tasso), 80067 Sorrento (NA). © 081-8071016. Fax 081-8073157. www.hoteldelcorso.com. 26 units. 90€ ($104) single; 120€ ($138) double; 160€ ($184) triple. Rates include breakfast. AE, DC, DISC, MC, V. Parking 10€–12€ ($12–$14) in nearby garage or lot. Closed Dec–Jan. **Amenities:** Bar. *In room:* A/C, satellite TV, hair dryer.

La Tonnarella 🌟🌟   Rising cliffside high above Sorrento Bay, the vista-blessed Tonnarella gives the coastal road to Amalfi an auspicious beginning. Sharing the grounds with gardens of citrus, the hotel is the best of Via Capo's inns, offering first-class amenities and decor at criminally low prices. Persian runners spill down over the rich parquet floors, antiques fill the halls, and though it's only a 10- to 15-minute walk from town, you'll feel like a tourism fugitive in a coastal hideaway. The brightly tiled rooms sport an odd mix of 19th-century chairs and modern built-in headboards. Some of the bathrooms are getting on in years, but many are *modernissimo,* with hyperspray showers and heated towel racks. Book the suite and you can take advantage of the Jacuzzi, in-room VCR, and Internet access. There's a pleasing abundance of pine-shaded terra-cotta terraces—some public, others attached to rooms such as nos. 1 to 4, whose windows take in the full sweep of the bay (book ahead for a room with view). The picture-window restaurant, with open balconies, could almost be recommended separately for its plump ravioli and fresh fish. There's an elevator (or stairs through a verdant gorge) down to a little private pebble beach, open from May to September.

Via Capo 31, 80067 Sorrento (NA). © 081-8781153. Fax 081-8782169. www.latonnarella.com. 21 units. 145€–160€ ($165–$184) double; 170€–225€ ($195–$259) triple; 250€ ($288) suite. Rates include breakfast. AE, MC, V. Free parking. Closed Jan–Feb. Bus: A from Piazza Tasso. **Amenities:** Restaurant; bar; tour desk; 24-hr. room service; babysitting; laundry service. *In room:* A/C, TV, hair dryer, safe.

Loreley et Londres 🌟   This hospitable 100-year-old pensione is the most popular of Sorrento's budget hotels, despite the 10- to 15-minute walk from town and lack of phones or air-conditioning. The hotel, well covered by the guidebook industry and word-of-mouth, sits on the cliff's edge. Accommodations are very well worn, with mismatched functional furniture and a few near-antiques, featuring tile floors (some with painted designs), bathrooms with curtainless showers, cool breezes, and medium-soft beds. Most have at least a balcony, and in the case of no. 14, which has its own wraparound patio, the terrace is almost as large as the room. Most rooms (the best are nos. 11–13) get at least part of the remarkable view sweeping from Sorrento and its marina around the bay to Vesuvius, but a few are on the road. Everyone enjoys the panorama

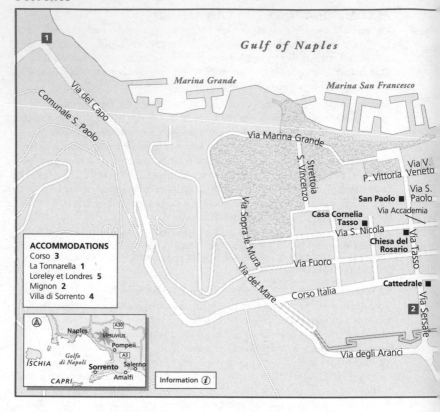

ACCOMMODATIONS
Corso **3**
La Tonnarella **1**
Loreley et Londres **5**
Mignon **2**
Villa di Sorrento **4**

from the bamboo-shaded terrace, where you take meals in high season. An elevator takes you down to a little bar and a private swimming pier.

Via Califano 2, 80067 Sorrento (NA). © 081-8073187. Fax 081-5329001. 28 units. 74€ ($85) single; 87€ ($100) double; 108€ ($124) triple; 134€ ($155) quad. 8€ ($9.20) breakfast. Half pension available. DC, MC, V. Parking free behind hotel. Closed Nov to Easter. (It's a long walk from Piazza Tasso or the station; no bus makes the trip regularly.) **Amenities:** Restaurant; bar. *In room:* No phone.

Mignon Located under a stone arch on one of the older back streets in Sorrento, Mignon picks up the overflow from the Loreley, which is owned and operated by the same local family. The hotel, convenient to the station and located just off the main drag, makes up for its lack of a view with reasonable prices and sensible decor. Late risers should request rooms at the back, which face the garden and courtyard, because rooms on the street facing the Chiesa del Cattedrale get the full force of the ringing church bells. Book early; rooms fill up in summer.

Via Sersale 9, 80067 Sorrento (NA). © 081-8073824. Fax 081-5329001. www.sorrentohotelmignon.com. 23 units. 93€ ($107) double; 120€ ($138) triple. Rates lower off season and include breakfast. MC, V. *In room:* A/C, TV.

Villa di Sorrento The comfortably sober Villa di Sorrento is excellently located just half a block up a tree-lined street from Piazza Tasso. As befits an upscale inn, the wood-framed beds are large and firm, and the bathrooms are modern. Some rooms are smallish, but the air-conditioning and other amenities

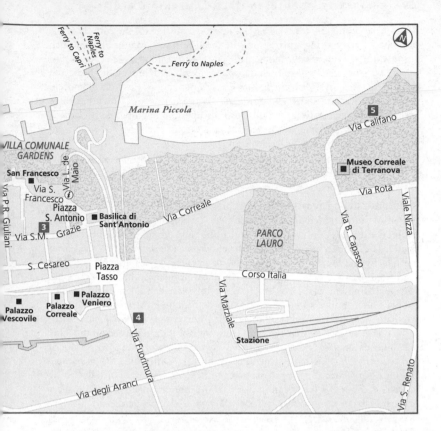

more than make up for it. Paintings or prints decorate the walls, and a few near-antiques give most rooms a touch of class. Nos. 41 and 42 have terraces with the best views over red-tiled roofs. If you splurge by opting for the breakfast—not bad, but not worth 9€ ($10), either—you'll enjoy the vaulted dining room beyond a sofa-scattered sitting room.

Via Fuorimura 6 (½ block north of Piazza Tasso), 80067 Sorrento (NA). ℂ 081-8781068. Fax 081-8072679. 21 units. 84€ ($97) single; 148€ ($171) double. Rates lower off season and include breakfast. AE, DC, MC, V. Parking 20€ ($23) in nearby lot. *In room:* A/C, TV, hair dryer.

GREAT DEALS ON DINING

If you're suffering from carb overload, head over to **Angelina Lauro,** a self-serve cafeteria and bar in Piazza Angelina Lauro 39–40 (ℂ **081-8074097**), where you can fuel up on a refreshing selection of alternatives that will get you through the meal without even one slice of bread. Expect to spend 3€ ($3.45) on a vegetarian casserole of escarole, currants, pignoli nuts, and mozzarella cheese, and up to 8€ ($9.20) for pork chops. Angelina Lauro is open Wednesday through Monday 8am to midnight. Worth a mention also is **Da Franco,** a homey *panetteria* and pizzeria at Corso Italia 265 (between Piazza Tasso and Piazza Angelina Lauro; ℂ **081-8772066**), with masses of hanging prosciutto beckoning the passersby.

Da Gigino SORRENTINA/PIZZA   Although all of Sorrento's restaurants cater to tourists, this one has a loyal local following as well; the TV in the corner adds a neighborhood-joint touch. Most opt to sit outside on the cobbles of the tiny side street, enjoying a pizza from the wood-burning oven or a primo such as *scialatielli ai frutti di mare* (homemade pasta with seafood), *gnocchi verdi provola e gamberi* (potato-and-spinach dumplings tossed with provolone cheese and shrimp), or, as always, *gnocchi alla Sorrentina* (a rich, gooey casserole of gnocchi baked with tomatoes under a lid of mozzarella and Parmesan). The primi shine here, but the straightforward secondi don't disappoint, including the *grigliata di pesce* (mixed fish grill) and *pollo arrosto con patate* (roast chicken sided with bland potatoes you could just as well do without).

Via degli Aranci 15 (just down from Corso Italia). ℂ 081-8781927. Reservations recommended. Primi 5.50€–10€ ($6.30–$12); secondi 7€–17€ ($8.05–$20); pizza 5.50€–9€ ($6.30–$10). AE, MC, V. Daily noon–3pm and 7–11pm. Closed Tues Sept–June.

Ristorante della Favorita O'Parrucchiano ⋆⋆ SORRENTINA   Under a thicket of vines and lemon and orange trees, in botanical gardens with greenhouse-like terraces, you won't even notice the tour groups dining beside you. Founded as La Favorita in the late 19th century by a seminarian snatched from the fold by the love of a young girl (*o'parrucchiano* is Neapolitan dialect for "parish priest" and was added later by local regulars), the restaurant has remained family-managed ever since. While the place can boast celebrities like Sophia Loren, Andy Warhol, and Vittorio de Sica as former patrons, its vast popularity has led to neither price gouging nor compromised quality. Most seafood dishes, since they change with daily availability, are printed on the "chef recommends" menu. Look for *scialatielli ai frutti di mare* (pasta with seafood) and *involtini di pesce spada* (swordfish roll-ups). Otherwise, try *cannelloni "Favorita"* (pasta leaves wrapped around meat fillings and baked), followed by *scaloppina di vitello alla Sorrentina* (veal scallops under tomato sauce and slices of mozzarella) or *filetto al pepe rosa* (beef filet with pink peppercorns).

Corso Italia 71–73. ℂ 081-8781321. Reservations recommended. Primi 5.50€–10€ ($6.30–$12); secondi 7€–13€ ($8.05–$15) and up for fish. MC, V. Thurs–Tues noon–4pm and 7pm–midnight (daily May–Nov 15).Closed Jan–Feb.

7 Positano: A Posh Resort ⋆⋆

56km (35 miles) SE of Naples, 16km (10 miles) E of Sorrento, 266km (165 miles) SE of Rome

Nestled in the cleavage of two intersecting mountains, **Positano** positively drips off the cliff face, its white and pastel buildings crowned by the green and yellow majolica-tiled cupola of the Duomo. Its stunning position, public passageways draped in bougainvillea, and simple living are characteristic of Campania's coastal charm—not bad for a humble fishing village of coarse volcanic origins. Risen from the ashes after several centuries, Positano served for decades as a jet-set playground—everyone from Picasso and Stravinsky to John Steinbeck, Liz Taylor, and Sir Laurence Olivier vacationed here. Positano's popularity among trendsetters even introduced several fashions to the world, including the bikini (polka-dot, in 1959).

Positano may still be a world-class destination full of glamour, but seekers of the legend are becoming more prominent. Instead, the Spiaggia Grande hosts an unremarkable gathering of vacationers unfazed by the high ticket prices on everything from a beach lounge (10€/$12) to a few slices of tomato (6€/$6.90). Nevertheless, Positano maintains its position as a tony resort with fine beaches, swanky shops, and languorous, terraced cafes. It's a must-see before the last vestiges of craftsmanship and gastronomy give way to the endless deluge of overpriced ruffled linen dresses, interspersed with the expected surfeit of beachwear and the rare splendid collection of antiques or locally crafted ceramics.

ESSENTIALS

GETTING THERE Once you arrive in town, be it by bus, car, or ferry, you're still only halfway there, since getting to any hotel will most likely involve a trek up a hill or an endless set of stairs. If you're willing to drop 4€ to 6€ ($4.60–$6.90) per bag, all you have to do is yell, "Porter!" and a handsome man with a mechanical trolley will come to the rescue (**Carovana Facchini,** Piazza dei Mulini; ℂ **089-875310**).

By Bus SITA (ℂ **081-5522176**) buses run up and down the coastal road between Naples and Salerno, offering one of the best, if not tortuous, hair-raisingly scenic rides in Italy. There's more than one stop in Positano along the highway, so if you're headed to the beach or the center of town, get off at the stop marked "Sponda," but take the Chiesa Nuova stop if you're staying at Pensione La Rosa dei Venti. The fare from Naples (leaving from next to the Tirrenia pier at Molo Beverello) is 3.15€ ($3.60); from Amalfi, it's 3.15€ ($3.60); and from Sorrento, it's 1.20€ ($1.40).

The orange "Interno Positano" minibus will run you from Chiesa Nuova down the wide, looping Viale Pasitea to Piazza dei Mulini at the heart of town (1€/$1.15, paid on the bus), leaving half-hourly from 9am to midnight (an earlier bus leaves at 7:50am). The bus makes its way down and around through the more reasonable heights of Positano, a welcome respite for the traveler weary of lugging baggage up and down narrow steps.

By Car From the north, take the Autostrada del Sole to Naples, then follow signs for the Salerno–Reggio Calabria highway. Exit at Castellammare di Stabia, then follow signs for Positano. My best advice is to leave your car in the first lot available, and expect to pay anywhere from 3€ to 4€ ($3.45–$4.60) per hour and 22€ to 30€ ($25–$35) per day, depending on the size of your car. There's limited street parking (coins only; 8am–8pm) along the road that winds down into Piazza dei Mulini, but you can park for only up to 3 hours at a time.

By Ferry Tra.vel.mar. (ℂ **089-873190**), the cooperative of hydrofoil companies, intersperses several daily ferries with fast boats to Positano from Amalfi for 11€ ($13) round-trip and six daily from Salerno (70 min.; 12€/$13; hydrofoils cost about 2.50€/$3 more). They also run a 9:30am and 10am hydrofoil to Capri (return 4:25 and 5pm; 50 min.; 6€/$6.90).

VISITOR INFORMATION There's a small **tourist office** at Via Saracino 4, in front of the Duomo in the heart of town (ℂ **089-875067;** fax 089-875760), open Monday through Friday from 8:30am to 2pm and Saturday from 8:30am to noon (8am–8pm Mon–Sat in summer). More than just a repository for brochures, the office is staffed with people ready to give advice—they'll also help you find a room in town if you're having trouble.

EXPLORING THE AREA

Once you've seen the baroque majolica-tiled dome of the 13th-century **Santa Maria Assunta** church, you've finished with the historic sights of Positano. But the real sightseeing here is wandering the twisting and scenic alleyways near the port, window-shopping at the boutiques, and sipping aperitifs at one of the beachside bars while scoping out celebrities.

BEACHES Unmistakably at the heart of town is the **Spiaggia Grande.** Much of the beach is taken up by bathing establishments (chair and umbrella rental

10€/$12 for the day) and boat-rental agencies, but about half of the beach is free of charge. From the dock next to Spiaggia Grande, Via Positanesi d'America wraps around the headland to Positano's quieter half above **Fornillo Beach.** It's calmer and less trendy than Spiaggia Grande, but you'll get unspoiled beauty in exchange for the pebbles. Again, the far right end is free; otherwise, an umbrella and chair will cost you about the same.

BOAT EXCURSIONS   You can rent boats from **Noleggio Barche Lucibello** (© **089-875032**) right on the beach: Sea kayaks cost 5.50€ to 8€ ($6.25–$9.20) per hour; rowboats and paddle boats cost 11€ ($13) per hour, 34€ ($39) per day; motorboats cost 30€ to 50€ ($35–$58) per hour, 130€ to 250€ ($150–$288) per day (this last for boats accommodating up to eight passengers). Also on the beach (located on the pier) is **Blue Star** (© **089-811888**), with much the same equipment and prices as Lucibello. They also rent jet skis for 25€ ($29) per 15 minutes and easy-to-navigate rubber boats for 40€ ($46) per hour. This outfitter also runs a 2-hour tour to the entrance of the **Emerald Grotto** (12€/$14 per person, not including entrance fee; info below), and a half-day trip to the Emerald Grotto, along with a swim at **Li Galli** islets (18€/$21). Night excursions are available.

ACCOMMODATIONS YOU CAN AFFORD

California ★★★   The California is installed in a 17th-century palazzo poised above street level just 5 minutes from the beach. All of the rooms sport balconies with a sea view, and four have high frescoed ceilings. Most bathrooms have large tubs surrounded by fresh tile and newish fixtures, and rooms are furnished with a collection of antiques, many of which belonged to owner Maria's grandmother. There are five additional airless, windowless, unrenovated rooms at the rear, but frankly, the 100€ ($115) price tag isn't worth the trade-off, unless you need only a place to sleep. Continental breakfast is included, with the option of add-ons like eggs, bacon, and yogurt.

Via Cristoforo Colombo 141, 84017 Positano (SA). © **089-875382.** Fax 089-812154. www.hotelcalifornia positano.it. 12 units. 140€–150€ ($160–$173) double; 165€–175€ ($190–$200) suite. Rates include breakfast. AE, DC, MC, V. Free parking. Closed mid-Nov to Feb. Get off SITA bus at La Sponda and walk downhill. From the port, head up to Piazza dei Mulini and turn uphill; the hotel is on the left. *In room:* A/C, TV, minibar, hair dryer.

La Bougainville ★ *(Value)*   Centrally located on the hill just above Piazza dei Mulini, the Bougainville offers clean, friendly accommodations and small but gracious common areas at just the right price. Rooms at the front have panoramic views of the sea, while rooms at the back tend to be dark and a bit claustrophobic, due to the high placement of the window. Room no. 10 has a large terrace overlooking a garden, and no. 12 lacks the sea view but is a bit larger and is graced with a window overlooking an inner courtyard. The hotel is one flight up (with rooms up another flight) and there's no elevator, so pack light and bring a bag with straps.

Via Cristoforo Colombo 25, 84017 Positano. © **089-875047.** Fax 089-811150. www.bougainville.it. 14 units. 65€–70€ ($75–$80) single; 75€–90€ ($86–$104) standard double, 90€–120€ ($104–$138) double with view. A/C supplement 12€ ($14). Breakfast 7.50€ ($8.60). AE, DC, MC, V. Closed Nov–Mar 15. Get off SITA bus at La Sponda and walk downhill. From the port, head up to Piazza dei Mulini and turn uphill; the hotel is on the left. *In room:* A/C.

La Rosa dei Venti   Around Positano's headland to the west, in a quieter pocket of town that retains an echo of the old village feel, this pensione offers a comfortable stay in a friendly, family-run establishment. The main negative in staying here is that it's about a kilometer (half-mile) walk along Positano's internal road to get to any of the action, and a hefty workout down (and up) the cliff's characteristic yet daunting staircase to get to the beach. The Rosa dei Venti is relatively new, so the rooms are fresh, albeit modest. They're also sizeable, decorated simply with solid-colored tile floors; each unit enjoys a garden terrace overlooking the sea. One room is actually a studio efficiency with an attached kitchen, with a 15€ ($17) supplement to cover the cost of gas and cleanup.

Via Fornillo 40, 84017 Positano. ©/fax **089-875252**. www.larosadeiventi.net. 6 units. Low season 100€ ($115) double; high season 150€ ($173) double. Breakfast 5€ ($5.75). AE, MC, V. No parking. SITA bus to Chiesa Nuova, and internal bus to the grotto, then follow walkway up to the right. *In room:* A/C, TV, fridge, hair dryer.

La Tavolozza *Value* *Kids*   Offering a scant six units (including two self-catering apartments), the family-owned La Tavolozza residence gives visitors with kids the breathing room to enjoy an affordable vacation without sacrificing space or character. Rooms in the small structure are reached by way of narrow and gleaming tiled corridors, the most coveted of which are those facing the sea, offering views from gracious balconies. Room size varies greatly, as do the bathrooms (some have open floor showers, others have bathtubs), while the two large apartments benefit from expansive terraces and self-catering kitchens. All rooms have a private bathroom, although, in some cases, the bathroom is directly across the narrow hallway. And unlike at other typical "residences," room towels are changed daily. Breakfast includes freshly squeezed orange juice.

Via Cristoforo Colombo 10, 84017 Positano (SA). ©/fax **089-8755040**. celeste.dileva@tiscalinet.it. 6 units. 85€–110€ ($98–$126) double. Breakfast (on request) 10€ ($12). No credit cards. *In room:* No phone.

Villa Rosa *★★*   Across the street from famous Hotel Le Sireneuse and up an endless flight of steps lined with bougainvillea, Villa Rosa offers twice the view at one-quarter the price. The large, high, vaulted square rooms are quiet (no. 11 even has frescoes), and all are graced with large terraces draped in vine-strewn arbors. There are postcard views of Positano and bits of the harbor and sea. The mattresses are orthopedic, the furnishings peasant style, and the bathrooms functional yet modest. My favorite feature (next to breakfast being served on your private terrace) is the decorative tile ceramic floors, polished to a glistening white and a pure delight for bare feet. Owners see an elevator in the hotel's future, but for now, you'll have to be in good cardiac shape. If there's no room at the inn, the owners can offer the same hospitality and identical decor close to the beach at their *dipendenza,* **La Tartana,** at Via della Tartana 5 (© **089-875645** or 089-812193; www.villalatartana.com). It has 12 units with the same amenities and rates.

Via Cristoforo Colombo 127, 84017 Positano (SA). ©/fax **089-811955**. www.villarosapositano.com. 12 units. 130€–140€ ($150–$160) double. Rates include breakfast. AE, DC, MC, V. Parking in public garage. Closed Nov–Feb. Get off the SITA bus at La Sponda and walk downhill. From the port, head up to Piazza dei Mulini and turn uphill; the hotel is on the left. **Amenities:** Concierge; room service (8am–10pm); laundry service. *In room:* A/C, TV, fridge, hair dryer, safe.

GREAT DEALS ON DINING

Da Vincenzo POSITANO   Although it's less than central, the few minute's walk up the internal road towards Fornillo fails to keep the guests away from this family-owned trattoria. The tables lining the street are probably best in the evening, when fewer vehicles are passing by. The alternative is characteristic enough: The back wall of one of the internal dining rooms is the cliff face, giving the sense that you are dining in a cave. For starters, try the homemade *penne* *all'arrabbiata,* followed by a flavorful *agnello alla griglia* (grilled lamb steak) or the cheesy eggplant Parmesan.

Viale Pasitea 12/178. ⓒ 089-875128. Primi 7.50€–11€ ($8.60–$13); secondi 8€–16€ ($9.20–$18). AE, MC, V. Daily 1–4pm and 7:30pm–midnight.

Il Brigantino and Internet Cafe SNACKS & SANDWICHES Located just below the Duomo and just steps from the beach, Il Brigantino fills a much-needed vacuum, providing a small selection of tasty bites along with the traditional selections of a local bar, including a bottle of Cristal Champagne for a mere 200€ ($230). Internet and e-mail junkies can get a fix at one of five computer stations lining one wall, opposite the bar formed out of the hull of a fishing boat. A handful of battened-down tables face a large-screen TV at the back of the bar for keeping up on the latest news or World Cup scores.

Via del Saracino 35. ⓒ 089-811055. Sandwiches 2.50€ ($2.85). E-mail 2.50€ ($2.85) 1st 20 min. MC, V. Daily 9am–2am.

Lo Guarracino ⓡ POSITANO/PIZZA A quiet, cliff-hugging path wraps around the fortress towers to this seaside trattoria/pizzeria in a scenic 5-minute stroll, and you'll know you've arrived by the bougainvillea-shrouded entrance unobtrusively to the right. The food is genuinely tasty, even more so when you're tucked into a table at the edge of the terrace, where the sound of the crashing sea and the dreamy views of the Galli islets beyond, with ranks of floating fishing boats, will tweak your appetite. Surprisingly, Lo Guarracino has resisted the temptation to keep up with local inflation, bucking a common practice by eliminating entirely the charge for *pane e coperto* (that mysterious sum tacked on to the end of your bill for simply walking in the door). The pizzas are quite good if you want something light and quick, or go local with linguine *ai ricci di mare* (with sea urchin) or homemade gnocchi Sorrentina. Unless you opt for something basic like a *scaloppina al limone,* the proximity of the sea guarantees you'll be following up with something fishy, like *pesce spada* (grilled swordfish steak) or *calamari alla griglia* (grilled calamari).

Via Positanesi d'America 12. ⓒ 089-875794. Reservations recommended. Primi 8.50€–14€ ($9.75–$16); secondi 9€–20€ ($10–23); pizza 7.50€–9€ ($8.50–$10). AE, MC, V. Daily noon–3pm and 7:30–11pm. Closed Nov to Easter. From the port, follow the stairs up and around La Saracena toward Fornillo Beach.

Zagara ⓕinds SNACKS & SANDWICHES This stylish and comfortable bar/pasticceria offers a haven from those drawn-out afternoon carb overloads that leave you passed out on the beach like a bloated siren. On the lunch menu is a selection of panini and pizza slices, along with a tempting array of creamy pastries and exotically named gelato. They also offer a tantalizing selection of *granite* (flavored ices)—perfect for a sweltering afternoon. The outdoor deck in the rear overlooks the gorge and is covered in lush citrus greenery and perfumed by large wrought-iron citronella candelabras. Service may be a bit harried, a small price to pay for a quick sit-down bite.

Via dei Mulini 10. ⓒ 089-875964. Panini 3€–4€ ($3.45–$4.60); soft drinks 3€ ($3.45). MC, V. Daily 7:30am–midnight.

WORTH A SPLURGE

Donna Rosa ⓡⓡⓡ INVENTIVE CAMPANIAN The food at this countryside trattoria located high above Positano blows away the competition down in town. Attention to detail, from using the freshest of ingredients and making pastas and desserts by hand, to a thoughtful presentation on your plate, is impeccable. Start with the *ravioli ripieni di arragosta,* delicately flavored dumplings stuffed with lobster. To sample a variety of the kitchen's bounty, order a primo of *trittico,* a trio of pastas perhaps including *pappardelle funghi porcini e gamberi* (wide noodles with porcini mushrooms and shrimp), or *ravioli del Marchese* (stuffed with pumpkin in a sauce of fused butter, crisped sage, and Parmesan). Fresh fish is an excellent choice for a secondo, accompanied by a perfectly refreshing house white wine. The kitchen is open to view—always a sign of honest cooking—as are the cooking classes that the family conducts sporadically. And although it's almost deserted at lunch when everyone's down at the beach (but you can be up here in the cool breezes), nighttime packs it full until long after midnight. Definitely worth the journey.

Via Montepertuso 97–99 (a village in the hills above Positano). (© 089-811806. Reservations recommended. Primi 6.50€–35€ ($7.45–$40); secondi 9€ ($10) and up to 30€ ($35) for lobster; tasting menus 45€ ($52) and 65€ ($75). AE, DC, MC, V. Apr–Sept daily 7pm–midnight; Wed–Sun 12:30–3pm. Closed Tues in winter and Jan to 1 week before Easter. Bus to Montepertuso every 2 hr. from Via Colombo; for lunch, take the 10:20am or schoolchild-packed 12:20pm. If you reserve ahead, they might be able to pick you up in Positano.

POSITANO AFTER DARK

At the far end of Spiaggia Grande is the dance club **Music on the Rocks** (© 089-875874; www.musicontherocks.it; open Apr–Sept; 15€ cover), carved into the cliff side and overlooking its own section of beach. Catch a boat to nearby Praiano and the hottest club of the coast, **Africana** (© 089-874042), another sea-level grotto, this one with a transparent dance floor with watery sinkholes (which fishermen sometimes come to dredge while the party's going on). You must book ahead at **Agenzia Viaggi Positour** (© 089-875555) or **Music Station Quicksilver** (© 089-811963) for the boat (10€/$12 round-trip) that leaves at 11:30pm from the Pontile Lucibello dock at Spiaggia Grande, to return at 3am. Both clubs open nightly from June to August and weekends in May and September, and close the rest of the year.

EN ROUTE TO AMALFI

About 16km (10 miles) beyond Positano is its sister hamlet of **Praiano,** also a trendy resort (only much smaller and still little known), with a majolica-domed church. If you're making the trip by sea, keep your eyes peeled for the Madonna Col Bambino di Praiano, a rock formation rising from the cliff face that mimics the image of the Madonna and Child, and another that resembles a great pharaoh.

Past the village of Furore, the bus pops out of a tunnel to take a bridge across one of the coast's most dramatic gorges, the **Vallone del Furore.** At kilometer marker 24, outside the fishing community of Conca dei Marini, are the stairs (or elevator) down to the **Grotta dello Smeraldo (Emerald Grotto).** This cavern was originally formed above sea level by the volcanic activity that affected the whole region (notice the stalactites and stalagmites, which can't form in sea grottoes). Mysteriously sunken deep in the water is a ceramic crèche, on which the effect of light refracting an emerald green is unusually mystical. Admission is 5€ ($5.75; plus the cost of the excursion boat to get there; see individual sections for info). The grotto is open daily from 9:30am to 3:30pm.

8 Amalfi: A Modest Seaside Village (★(★

61km (38 miles) SE of Naples, 18km (11 miles) E of Positano, 34km (21 miles) W of Salerno, 272km (169 miles) SE of Rome

The modest seaside village of **Amalfi,** tacked tastefully onto the cliff side, will surprise you initially: Long a legendary tourist destination and home of movie stars (Sophia Loren kept a home on the hill), it might be at least *bigger.* But not even the decades-long tourist crush has turned this once-great maritime port sour; rather, Amalfi retains the charm that has earned it the dubious honor of gracing the tile walls of many a New York pizzeria.

The whitewashed streets of Amalfi are full of history, recalling a time in the Middle Ages when it rivaled Genoa, Pisa, and Venice as a trading behemoth. Amalfi's connections with the Orient (mainly Constantinople) led it to introduce to Europe such novelties as paper, carpets, and the compass—though Amalfi holds that they themselves invented the latter, having gone so far as to erect a statue in the middle of the piazza in honor of hometown boy Flavio Gioia (who more than likely just perfected it).

At its height in the 11th century, Amalfi had a population of 70,000 and dominated the Tyrrhenian Sea. But the Normans moved here in 1131, and soon after, Pisa swept in not once, but twice, to trounce its rival. The final blow came in 1343, when a one-two punch of tidal waves and earthquakes slumped much of the grand city into the sea. Amalfi is now a much-reduced little resort town of 6,000 inhabitants, but left over from its glory days are a spectacular Duomo and the Tavole Amalfitane, the Western world's first maritime code, a set of laws that continued to rule trade and the sea until 1570.

ESSENTIALS

GETTING THERE **SITA buses** run frequently and efficiently (except for the inevitable road blockage at those tight curves) up and down the Amalfi coast, from **Sorrento** (2.10€/$2.40) to **Salerno** (1.65€/$1.90). Piazza Flavio Gioia is the hub for all buses, including those for excursions to **Ravello** (1€/$1.15) and **Positano** (3.15€/$3.60). SITA buses also run to **Napoli** (3.15€/$3.60) via the autostrada. Tickets can be purchased in a number of establishments around the terminus; just look for the blue SITA insignia.

Ferries arrive and depart regularly to and from **Sorrento** (9.50€/$11), **Positano** (6€/$6.90), and **Salerno** (5.50€/$6.30). For information and reservations, call the **Tra.vel.mar** cooperative at ✆ **089-873190,** though it's just as easy to pick up the tickets at the dock.

If you've come by **car,** you'll just be carrying around dead weight because local traffic laws prohibit the circulation of vehicles during specified times daily, effectively closing the town (for those compliant) to traffic for extended periods. Diehard drivers can park at the lot in town for 3€ ($3.45) for the first hour and 2.50€ ($2.85) hourly thereafter, but most hotels offer parking either free or in conjunction with a nearby lot for around 15€ ($17) per day.

VISITOR INFORMATION The **tourist office** (✆ **089-871107;** fax 089-872619) is hidden at the back-left corner of a lovely little courtyard inside Corso Roma 19, up the slope past Piazza Gioia.

AMBLING THROUGH AMALFI

The star of Amalfi is the 13th-century **Duomo** ⚓, on Piazza del Duomo, its magnificent Lombard-Norman facade of striped arches, Gothic tracery, interlocking arches, and glittering mosaics rising majestically at the top of a mighty set of 62 stairs. Towering over it on the left is a 13th-century bell tower with a majolica-tiled drum surrounded by four smaller drums. Simeon of Syria crafted the cathedral's massive bronze doors (whose panels feature crosses and saints inlaid with silver) in Constantinople in 1066. Like other great maritime powers, Amalfi stole itself a saint from the Holy Land in the 12th century. This is why the body of St. Andrew the Apostle lies under the altar and why 30 days prior to the sacred "feasts" of June 27 (patron festivities for St. Andrew) and Christmas, the venerable saint's head is exposed in a glass reliquary atop the tomb. A side entrance to the left of the main entrance gives access (2.50€/$2.85; open daily 9am–5pm) to the crypt via the Chiostro del Paradiso (Cloisters of Paradise), tiny Saracen-style cloisters from 1263 composed of interlocking and superimposed pointed arches forming a complex pattern above the colonnade.

Off Corso delle Repubbliche Marinare (the road east along the harbor), upstairs in the municipal buildings that surround a small piazza, is a tiny **Museo Civico** (free admission), which preserves the original *Tavole Amalfitane* outlining the oldest maritime code in the world.

Up the main road past the Monastery of St. Basilio, Via Pietro Capuano becomes Via Marino del Giudice and finally Via delle Cartiere, where you'll find the Museo delle Carte (Paper Museum), Via delle Cartiere 23 (© **089-8304561**), with its representation of an almost-extinct breed of purveyors of **local traditional paper.** There is no way to determine how many paper mills once dotted Amalfi's Valle dei Mulini, but if the patronage of such illustrious clients as the Vatican is any indication, we can only assume that there would have been a supply to meet the demand. The Paper Museum, located in a medieval paper mill just a 5-minute walk from the center of Amalfi, provides a historic window into the traditional craft through demonstrations and the preservation of centuries-old hydraulic wheels, wooden mallets, paper presses, and pulp vats. It's open daily from 10am to 6pm from March through October; and Tuesday through Sunday from 9:30am to 3pm from November through February. Admission and demonstration are 3.50€ ($4).

HITTING THE BEACH & A BOAT EXCURSION   Amalfi's **beach,** right in the center of the port off Piazza Flavio Gioia, isn't much to write home about, but it's convenient, the pastels of Amalfi are at its back, and the water is exceptionally clear. A lounge chair and umbrella will cost you a sizable 14€ ($16) per day. You can rent a canoe on the beach closest to the parking lot at **Andrea Beach** (© **089-872956**) for only 5€ ($5.75) per hour. Jolly Signor Rosa at **Da Rosa** (at the far end of the port; © **089-872147**) rents **rowboats** (8€/$9.20 per hour; 25€/$29 per day) and **motorboats** (from 30€/$35 for 2 hr. to 100€/$115 for 7 hr., depending on the horsepower; rates include gas); boats hold up to four people.

From the docks, excursion boats leave according to demand daily from 9am to 3pm for **trips to the Grotta dello Smeraldo** (see above) for 10€ ($12), not including the admission fee of 5€ ($5.75). The round-trip jaunt lasts about 1 hour. By land, **SITA** runs service from Piazza Gioia to Conca dei Marini, 5km (3 miles) away, where you can get an elevator down to the cave.

ACCOMMODATIONS YOU CAN AFFORD

If you're willing to wing it, **Divina Costiera Travel,** across from the SITA depot (© **089-872467**), will find you a place to stay at no charge. They'll also hold your luggage for 3€ ($3.45) per bag, if you want to have a look at your options for yourself.

Albergo Lidomare *(Finds*   The Lidomare is tucked into a quiet courtyard opposite the Duomo, occupying a 14th-century palazzo Ducale (or Ducal abode) that retains the character and grace of a bygone era. Floor-to-ceiling bookcases line the entrance foyer, which leads to the guest rooms. Rooms are spare and simple but unusually spacious. Bathrooms are modern and functional; two are equipped with a Jacuzzi tub or hydromassage shower. Double-glazed windows allow optimum enjoyment of the rooms facing the busy seafront, while rooms on the courtyard have a small balcony.

Largo Duchi Piccolomini 9, 84011 Amalfi (SA). © 089-871332. Fax 089-871394. www.lidomare.it. 15 units. 50€ ($58) single; 99€–110€ ($115–$126) double. Rates include breakfast. Discounts for payment in cash. AE, MC, V. *In room:* A/C, TV, fridge, hair dryer, safe.

Amalfi Located in a back corner of whitewashed streets just off the main drag, the Amalfi is a hands-on enterprise managed by a capable team of seven siblings, along with their husbands and wives. The hotel itself is basic, with spare and functional light-toned wood furnishings on broad tile floors. Some rooms overlook the narrow white alleys surrounding the hotel (no. 406 has a view of the dome's drum), while others face the pretty gardens whose orange trees provide the fruit for your breakfast juice. There's a pretty good **restaurant** on the roof terrace, with views of the historic center and a shaded garden patio perfect for reading a book as the sun dips in the sky.

Via dei Pastai 3, 84011 Amalfi (SA). © 089-872440. Fax 089-872250. www.starnet.it/hamalfi. 40 units. 90€ ($104) double. Rates include breakfast. Half pension 15€ ($17) extra. AE, MC, V. Parking in public lot. About halfway up the main road in town, look for a sign pointing up a stair/street off to the left. **Amenities:** Restaurant. *In room:* TV.

La Conchiglia *(Finds* The main attraction of this simple yet charming family-owned pensione is the lush natural setting on a beachfront outcropping at the far northern end of the marina. Rooms are old and unrenovated, a feature that makes the rooms upon close inspection seem a little dingy, while the basic bathroom and shower setups offer more of the same. But the setting is secluded and natural, and you can spend your days lounging on the hotel's private beach (use of lounges and umbrellas included in price of room). The pensione opens its shady outdoor restaurant in July and August.

Lungomare dei Cavalieri (at the far end of the port), 84011 Amalfi (SA). ©/fax 089-871856. 11 units. 100€–120€ ($115–$138) double. Rates include breakfast. Closed Nov–Mar 1, excluding Christmas.

Residence The faded, harbor-front facade doesn't bode well, but upstairs in the guest quarters, the Residence is decidedly more upscale than you might expect. A large vaulted dining room has a shaded terrace overlooking the beach, statues in niches, and a swirling central wrought-iron staircase. The rooms, all with balconies, are nicer than the price would suggest, and five of them even have Jacuzzis. Many have patterned tile floors, updated bathroom fixtures, oils on the walls, and pleasantly unobtrusive furniture mixed with some antiques. Rooms at the front are filled with the traffic sounds of Amalfi Drive below by day (and Vespa-mounted teens by night), but they also have a great view of the beach and port for people-watching. Side rooms overlook the slightly quieter road leading into Piazza del Duomo. During slow periods, rates can go as low as 100€ ($115) double.

Via delle Repubbliche Marinare 9, 84011 Amalfi (SA). © 089-872229. Fax 089-873070. www.residence hotel-amalfi.it. 27 units. 115€–125€ ($130–$144) double; 150€–160€ ($173–$184) triple. Ask for low-vacancy rates. Rates include breakfast. AE, MC, V. Parking 18€ ($21) in nearby garage. Closed mid-Oct to Easter (but open all year if demand exists). **Amenities:** Restaurant (July–Aug). *In room:* TV.

GREAT DEALS ON DINING

Don't come to Amalfi looking for bargains. Several beachfront establishments offer the added pleasure of the sound of lapping waves, but the hard-to-find trattorias are bound to be more characteristic of the countryside. For a quick bite, head to **Porto Salvo** off Piazza del Duomo (under the arch to the port; © 089-872445), where an enormous slice of potato pizza or a panino is 4€ ($4.60).

Da Barraca CAMPANIAN/SEAFOOD A real bargain gem, this restaurant is the only one on a truly typical piazza in Amalfi, surrounded by the fruit stands, butcher shops, and *alimentari* (neighborhood grocery stores) that ensure your food will be fresh. In cooler weather, you can sit under the fishing nets of the glassed-in veranda listening to records of Neapolitan guitar music. The meat-stuffed cannelloni are hearty, with cracked pepper for a spicy edge, while the perfectly cooked gnocchi alla Sorrentina and *farfalle vongole e rughetta* (bow-tie pasta with clams and rughetta) are also worthy. Secondi include scaloppine al Marsala, an omelet with mozzarella, or roasted fresh fish. The waiters are perennially harried, but give them time and, while you wait for the bill, enjoy a *profitterole al limone* (pastry stuffed with lemon cream).

Piazza degli Dogi (off the left of Piazza del Duomo, duck under the arched street and bear right). © 089-871285. Reservations recommended. Primi 7€–9€ ($8.05–$10); secondi 8€–13€ ($9.20–$15). AE, MC, V. Daily noon–3pm and 7pm–midnight.

Il Tarì ★★ *Value* AMALFITANA/PIZZA   Il Tarì's two packed rooms on Amalfi's main street are separated by low arches that do nothing to stem the flow of humanity drawn by the friendly atmosphere and reasonable prices. It's a bit cozier than Da Maria down the block, despite the noisy babble in a half-dozen tourist tongues that keeps the atmosphere lively. The pizza has excellent crust—try it topped *à la Tarì*, with mozzarella, prosciutto, Parmesan shavings, and arugula. If you'd prefer pasta, dig into the local specialty *scialatielli*, either *con frutti di mare* (seafood) or *con pomodoro, melanzane, e mozzarella* (a rich gooey mix of tomatoes, eggplant, and mozzarella). Secondi are less exciting, with a list of the same old *scaloppine* (veal cooked with herbs), *calamari in umido* (stewed octopus), or the somewhat more successful *pesce al cartoccio* (fish baked in foil). There are also several low-priced alternatives like omelets, cheeses, and salads.

Via Pietro Capuano 9–11 (a continuation of V. Cavour, the main road into town). © 089-871832. Reservations recommended. Primi 5.50€–11€ ($6.30–$13); secondi 5€–14€ ($5.75–$16); pizza 3.50€–9€ ($4–$10). AE, MC, V. Wed–Mon 11:30am–3pm and 7–11pm.

9 Ravello: A Retreat for Celebrities ★★

275km (171 miles) SE of Rome, 66km (41 miles) SE of Naples, 29km (18 miles) W of Salerno

Poised between sea and sky, the mountain retreat of **Ravello** rests on a verdant terraced plateau between two steep valleys carved by the Rivers Dragone and Regina. At only 6km (3¾ miles) from Amalfi and 347m (1,138 ft.) up in the hills, this pocket-size town of profuse flowering vines and sweet-scented landscapes bursting with color makes a marvelous escape from the tourist crush of the sun-worshipping towns down on the coast.

Ravello flourished in the 5th century, thanks to its commercial links with Sicily and the Orient, whose influence can be seen in town monuments like the Arab-Sicilian style of the bell tower of the Church of San Michele and in the Villa Rufolo's Moorish cloisters.

In an earlier era, the beauty and tranquillity of Ravello provided inspiration to such artistic greats as Richard Wagner, who upon seeing Villa Rufolo declared the discovery of his "Klingsor Garden," the setting for the second act of *Parsifal*. Ravello was also immortalized by the English painter William Turner, whose sketches of this lofty Garden of Eden can be seen at the Tate Gallery in London.

Almost every bend in the narrow alleys and stone steps opens to another eye-popping vista, either down into the **Valle del Dragone (Valley of the Dragon)**, a deep and lush terraced ravine strewn with white houses and small hamlets, or over the distant eastern stretch of the Amalfi Coast. Crumbling villas whose grounds and lush pleasure gardens have become public parks provide most of the attractions, leaving you to do little more than relax and smell the scent of bougainvillea and jasmine that permeates the morning air.

While exploring the coast from Ravello will require a trip into Amalfi (for bus transfers or ferry excursions), the scarce commercialism, compulsory inactivity, and crisp summer evenings of Ravello will certainly make the added effort worth your while.

ESSENTIALS

GETTING THERE/GETTING AROUND   SITA minibuses run from Amalfi's Piazza Flavio Gioia to Ravello (1€/$1.15). Service is limited to once an hour, resulting in buses packed with day-trippers to or from Amalfi, so once you arrive up in Ravello, you may never come down. Ideally, the trip takes under 15 minutes, but during rush hour, expect unparalleled gridlock at the coastal road turnoff. The bus lets you off just outside the tunnel-like gate into town.

VISITOR INFORMATION   There's a **tourist office** at the unmistakable Piazza del Duomo under the left side of the cathedral (© **089-857096;** fax 089-857977). The office is open Monday through Saturday from 8am to 8pm (to 7pm Oct–Mar).

WHAT TO SEE & DO

A constant assault of the natural perfumes of lilies, lemons, bougainvillea, and pine fabricates the perfect settings for the series of chamber music, orchestra, and soloist **concerts** that run throughout the year. In July, the music of Richard Wagner (another Ravellophile) is celebrated with performances by the likes of Plácido Domingo, conducted by Zubin Mehta and backed by world-class orchestras from Israel, London, Moscow, and so on. The Villa Rufolo (see below) sponsors a series of outdoor concerts, but seating for 2,700 still can't support the demand for the annual sunrise concerts that take place on August 10 and 11. For info, contact the **Ravello Concert Society** (© **089-858149;** www.ravelloarts.org).

Duomo   Ravello's Romanesque cathedral was built in 1076. The central **bronze doors** ⟨✦⟩ were cast in 1099 in Constantinople and feature 54 disarmingly simple low-relief panels of archers, warriors, and Bible scenes. Inside are a pair of gorgeous 12th-century **marble pulpits** ⟨✦⟩. The Pulpit of the Gospel on the right side of the nave is carried on the backs of three sets of splendid lions; both pulpits are inlaid with mosaics of swirling designs, Christian symbols, and fantastic mythical beasts (look for the whale swallowing Jonah on the left). The small museum displays Renaissance busts, late Imperial cinerary urns, and more medieval carvings and bits of mosaic.

Piazza del Duomo. Admission to church free; museum entrance 2€ ($2.30). Daily 9:30am–1pm and 3–7pm.

Villa Cimbrone ⟨✦✦⟩   Getting to Villa Cimbrone is half the fun, down a stepped alley open to the verdant valley below. The parts of the 1904 villa you can explore are full of cryptlike nooks and cloistered crannies. The grounds are a huge playground of palms, magnificently spreading umbrella pines, ivy-clad walls, hidden flower gardens guarded by statues, panoramic terraces lined with busts, and vertigo-inducing cliff-top vistas from tiny templelike gazebos.

At the end of Via Santa Chiara (take V. San Francesco out of Piazza del Duomo). No phone. Admission 5€ ($5.75) adults, 3.50€ ($4) for those under 12. Daily 9am–7:30pm.

Villa Rufolo ⟨✦✦⟩   The villa itself was started by the powerful Rufolo family in the 11th century and served as a residence for several popes. The Saracen and

Norman motifs were added in later generations—take a moment to enjoy the Moorish cloisters, with their sharply pointed arches and interlacing patterns. The rooms of the restructured central villa are now used for art exhibits, and the surrounding grounds—filled with intimate flowering gardens set into the extensive villa ruins above a spectacular view down the eastern Amalfi Coast—are the backdrop for excellent outdoor concerts. This is only appropriate, since, upon seeing this tropical paradise in 1880, composer Richard Wagner exclaimed, "The magical garden of Klingsor has been found!" and, inspired, went on to complete the second act of *Parsifal.*

Piazza Duomo. ⓒ **089-857657.** Admission 4.50€ ($5) adults, 2.50€ ($3) for those under 12 or over 65. Daily 9am–8pm (some days it closes at 4pm).

ACCOMMODATIONS YOU CAN AFFORD

Garden ⁄ᴠᵃˡᵘᵉ   With only 10 rooms, all but 1 of which enjoy sweeping coastal views at bargain-basement rates, the Garden rarely sees a vacancy. It's conveniently located on a terrace below the bus stop just outside the pedestrian-only center (sounds iffy, but it's not), which ensures an effortless arrival and departure without the slightest compromise. Blue-tinted rattan furniture and clean tile floors keep the rooms looking cheerful, and bathrooms all have a good amount of breathing space. The attached restaurant gets the same stunning panorama as the rooms and, with a half-pension rate of 70€ ($80) per person, is a bargain for guests.

Via Boccaccio 4, 84010 Ravello (SA). ⓒ **089-857226.** Fax 089-858110. www.starnet.it/hgarden. 10 units. 105€ ($120) double. Rates include breakfast. AE, MC, V. Closed Nov 15–Feb. **Amenities:** Restaurant; bar. *In room:* TV, hair dryer.

Villa Amore ⁄ᶠⁱⁿᵈˢ   This gorgeous spot on the hilltop has a spectacular view of the valley and mountains—but you'll have to get there first. Forever run by a pair of kindly ladies, Villa Amore is quite a climb above the main piazza, but that only makes it feel more like a hidden retreat. By now, the beds have lost much of their firmness, and the phones aren't direct dial, but most bathrooms are updated and well maintained. The tile floors are scattered with rugs, the place is heated in winter, and there are abundant breezes to part the curtains in summer. All rooms have small terraces; from second-floor rooms the vista is unobstructed, but downstairs you have to peek past a little flowering garden. The setting is quiet as can be. Breakfast is served on the panoramic terrace. If you simply can't bear the thought of hauling your luggage up and down stepped alleyways, then take advantage of the panoramic terraced restaurant for lunch or dinner.

Via dei Fusco 5 (a cross street of V. Santa Chiara), 84010 Ravello (SA). ⓒ/fax **089-857135.** 16 units. 56€ ($64) single; 90€ ($104) double. Rates include breakfast. MC, V. Half- and full pension available. **Amenities:** Restaurant; laundry service; nonsmoking rooms. *In room:* Hair dryer, safe.

WORTH A SPLURGE

Villa Maria ⁄ᶠⁱⁿᵈˢ   Villa Maria, converted from a 1935 private home, offers a taste of the refined elegance enjoyed by Ravello in past centuries. An old-fashioned salon off the entrance, where a grand chandelier hangs over an antique silver tea setting, sets the tone. Floor tiles in the rooms are richly patterned, the walls are hung with quality prints and oils, and the period furnishings mix with the odd futon couch. Firm mattresses rest on genuine box springs backed by antique wooden or brass headboards, and many of the ample bathrooms feature Jacuzzi tubs and multiple-jet showers. Almost all of the rooms enjoy some type of outdoor access or view, enhancing the luxurious tone of this spectacular location. Only nos. 6 and 7 have garden views rather than vistas down the Valle del

Dragone to the sea. Guests can use the parking facilities and outdoor pool at the inn's nearby recommended three-star sister hotel, the **Giordano** (same contact info; 129€–155€/$150–$178 double). Villa Maria's garden restaurant, recommended below, is one of the town's best, so you may also want to inquire about the hotel's meal plans for guests.

Via San Chiara 2 (follow V. San Francesco toward the Villa Cimbrone), 84010 Ravello (SA). ℂ 089-857255. Fax 089-857071. www.villamaria.it. 26 units. 175€ ($200) single; 215€ ($247) double; 270€–435€ ($310) suite. Rates lower in winter. Rates include breakfast. AE, DC, MC, V. Free parking at nearby sister hotel. **Amenities:** Restaurant; use of pool at Hotel Giordano; concierge; tour desk; car-rental desk; 24-hr. room service; laundry service; dry cleaning; nonsmoking rooms. *In room:* A/C, satellite TV w/pay movies, minibar, hair dryer, safe.

GREAT DEALS ON DINING

Cumpá Cosimo 🌟🌟 CAMPANIAN   Beloved culinary matriarch Netta Buttone presides over these wood-beamed dining rooms, effusively displaying her joys of cooking and providing her guests with a memorable evening. Cumpá Cosimo has been a Ravello institution for more than 70 years—Bogie and Jackie O were once customers, and Gore Vidal still pops in every now and again. Ingredients come from the family farm, concocted into the likes of *gnocchi alla Sorrentina,* marvelous *crespolini alla Cumpá Cosimo* (pasta crepes layered with prosciutto and cheese, then rolled and baked), *fusilli al pomodoro,* and cheesy *maccheroni al forno.* The best way to sample the bounty is the *piatto misto della casa,* seven sampler-size portions of Netta's primi, each better than the last. Secondi include *coniglio alla cacciatore* (rabbit with tomatoes and olives), *agnello scottaditto* (delicious lamb chops), and fresh fish. For dessert, try one of Netta's storied soufflés, or a peach or fig from the family orchards.

Via Roma 44–46. ℂ 089-857156. Reservations highly recommended. Primi 8€–16€ ($9.20–$18); secondi 10€–27€ ($12–$31; up to 40€/$46 for *zuppa di pesce*). AE, MC, V. Daily 12:15–3:30pm and 6:30pm–midnight. Closed Mon Nov–Dec 10 and Jan 8–Feb. Left at Duomo, hidden behind hanging beads on your right immediately after the arch.

WORTH A SPLURGE

Villa Maria 🌟🌟🌟 CAMPANIAN   Villa Maria scores twice, with both the best splurge hotel and the finest restaurant in town. The dining terrace, which overlooks the hamlets of the Dragone Valley, is shaded by spreading tree branches and filled with the strains of classical music from hidden speakers. The waiter will suggest the specialties of the day, but if you can't choose from among the mouthwatering array of primi, order the *trittico,* a sampler of the chef's proudest recipes that includes *soffiatini* (crepes with local cheese and spinach) and perhaps *ravioli del pescatore* (seafood-stuffed ravioli in a red clam sauce). Follow that with the *pescato del giorno all'acqua pazza* (baked fish with tomatoes, olives, and parsley). Up in the mountains and this close to the sea, you can bet on fresh fish and local game. The hotel also sponsors cooking courses.

Via Santa Chiara 2. ℂ 089-857255. Reservations highly recommended. Primi 7€–11€ ($8.05–$13); secondi 10€–22€ ($12–$25). AE, DC, MC, V. Daily 12:30–3pm and 7:30–10:30pm. Closed Tues Oct to Easter.

10 Paestum & Its Greek Temples 🌟

42km (26 miles) S of Salerno, 100km (62 miles) SE of Naples, 304km (188 miles) SE of Rome

Poseidonia, or the City of Poseidon, was founded in the 6th century B.C. by Greek colonists from Sybaris. It went about its business unremarkably as the Roman colony of **Paestum** from 273 B.C. until around 79 B.C., when a series of eruptions from Mount Vesuvius resulted in the silting up of the city's river.

These swamplands brought about a malarial plague that decimated the population, and in the midst of a decline during the 9th century, the citizens of Paestum didn't know whether to flee to the hills from the brutal Saracen invaders or the mosquitoes.

Despite legends of a lost city, Paestum was all but forgotten until the 18th century, when a bunch of local farmers, working to build a road through the area, stumbled across three incredible **Greek temples** jutting out of the landscape, surrounded by blue-gray mountains. The rest is bureaucratic history.

You'll need about 2 hours for a leisurely visit of the archaeological area, plus another hour for a visit to the museum, making the site doable as a day trip from Naples or the Amalfi Coast. But despite the monotony of the place after hours, you may want to schedule in as many meals as possible down here in mozzarella country, for the most exquisite *mozzarella di bufala* 🌟🌟🌟 (made from the milk of local buffalo) and ricotta you will ever have the good fortune to taste.

ESSENTIALS

GETTING THERE   By Train   Only local trains (*diretto* or *regionale*) stop at Paestum. **From Naples,** there are eight daily runs (90 min.; 4.65€/$5.35). **From Salerno,** nine daily trains (headed to "Paola") stop at Paestum (35 min.; 2.70€/$3.10).

By Bus   SCAT buses (📞 0974-838415) from **Salerno** (📞 089-226604) are more frequent than trains (four per day; none on Sun) and let you off right at the museum in front of the archaeological site (50 min.; 2.10€/$2.40). They leave Salerno from Piazza della Concordia at the waterfront, a few blocks down from the train station (and a few blocks over from where the Amalfi Coast SITA buses stop).

By Car   From Naples, follow the A3 to the Battipaglia exit and follow the S18 to Paestum. From Salerno, take provincial road 175 south.

GETTING AROUND   Paestum occupies a flat agricultural plain in the middle of nowhere, the only signs of civilization being the postcard stands, hotels, and restaurants drawn by a tourist site. From the train station, you can bargain with a taxi driver for the trip to your hotel (don't go over 5€/$5.75). Otherwise, head out of the station and continue straight under the arch—part of the ancient city wall—at the intersection. After a 15-minute, 1km (½-mile) stroll, the road ends at the archaeological site and Albergo delle Rose. The museum, main site entrance, and tourist office are about 15m (49 ft.) to the right. For the Hotel Helios, Nettuno restaurant, Porta della Giustizia site entrance, and, eventually, the beach, turn left; then take the first right for another 5-minute walk.

VISITOR INFORMATION   There's a **tourist office** near the museum at Via Magna Grecia 155 (📞 0828-811016; fax 0828-722322). It's open Monday through Saturday from 8am to 2pm.

EXPLORING ANCIENT GREECE IN CAMPANIA

Scavi (Archaeological Site) 🌟🌟   Amid the grasses stained with poppies and crisscrossed by the low stone walls that outline the remains of the ancient city rise three mighty temples, all of which still go by their erroneous old names. The modestly sized **Basilica** was actually a **Temple of Hera,** built in 530 B.C. and the oldest temple at Paestum. Next door is the enormous and strikingly well-preserved **Temple of Neptune** 🌟, in reality probably dedicated to Apollo or Zeus, built in 450 B.C. and one of the three most complete Greek temples in the world. Its pediments and entablature are virtually intact atop 14 9m-high

(30-ft.) fluted columns down each side, 6 each across the front and back, and a cella in the center divided by two more rows of smaller columns. Farther off in the site is the **Temple of Ceres,** more likely a temple to Athena, and the midget of the bunch, built around 500 B.C. and preserving, along with all 34 of its columns, some architrave and large chunks of its pediments. The temples of Hera and Neptune have been swathed in scaffolding for restoration work, and there's no word as yet on when they'll be unveiled.

Via Magna Grecia. (✆ 0828-811023. Combo ticket with museum 6.50€ ($7.45); independently 4.50€ ($5.15). Daily 9am to 1 hr. before sunset (as early as 3:30pm in late Nov, 7:30pm June–July). Closed 1st and 3rd Mon of every month, May 1, Dec 25, and New Year's Day.

Museo Nazionale (National Museum) 🕏🕏   Along with archaic Greek sculpture and vases, this museum preserves a great series of **metopes** (carved reliefs) from a nearby sanctuary of Hera, which depict scenes from Homeric myth and women dancing to honor the goddess. The museum's **Tomb of the Diver** 🕏 paintings from 480 B.C. are the only surviving examples of ancient Greek painting in the world. Aside from their namesake image of a bronzed youth diving into a blue sea (a symbol of the journey to the afterlife), these paintings focus on a homoerotic banquet scene in which the revelers play at games and musical instruments (and at flirting) while reclining on couches.

Via Magna Grecia. (✆ 0828-811023. Combo ticket with archaeological site 6.50€ ($7.45); independently 4.50€ ($5.15). Daily 9am–6:30pm. Closed 1st and 3rd Mon of every month, May 1, Dec 25, and New Year's Day.

ACCOMMODATIONS & DINING YOU CAN AFFORD

True bargain hunters can head to Paestum's budgeteer crash pad of choice, the **Albergo delle Rose,** Via Magna Grecia (✆ 0828-811070), located almost directly opposite the main entrance to the ruins. The small, plain, functional doubles upstairs go for 52€ ($60) with bathroom and breakfast, and the restaurant downstairs serves tasty cheap pizza, an outstanding *caprese* salad, and other Campanian dishes.

Hotel Helios   Nothing if not convenient, this contemporary hotel across from a secondary archaeological site entrance sports spacious, whitewashed rooms in a series of low, white buildings set in gardens around a pool and shaded terrace. Although about half of the rooms have been outfitted with ultramodern bathrooms with Jacuzzi tubs, they're still a bit bland in their functional modernity, with dully upholstered sofas and practical floor lamps. In the open spaces of the public rooms are a small bar and stylish restaurant with plate-glass views of the busy kitchen.

V. P. di Piemonte, 84063 Paestum (SA). (✆ 0828-811451. Fax 0828-721-047. 25 units. 78€–83€ ($90–$94) double. Rates include breakfast. AE, DC, MC, V. Parking free. **Amenities:** Restaurant; bar; outdoor swimming pool. *In room:* A/C, TV, minibar.

Ristorante Nettuno ITALIAN   Paestum's best, and certainly most scenic, lunch remains at this 18th-century country villa, converted to a restaurant in the 1920s and often taken over by entire busloads of tourists. It's wedged between the parking lot and archaeological site entrance, with a glassed-in patio a scant 150m (492 ft.) from the temples. Arrive or book early to get that prime view of the ruins, but if you find the crowds milling about the souvenir stands and into the site distracting, you can retreat to the grandly arched interior. The house dish is *crespolini* (baked pasta crepes wrapped around fresh mozzarella studded with prosciutto), or start with *stracciatella* (egg-drop soup with Parmesan) before sampling their *cotoletta alla milanese* (breaded veal cutlet) or *pollo al forno* (oven-roasted chicken).

Via Principe di Piemonte (in the archaeological zone). © 0828-811028. Reservations recommended. Primi 6€–10€ ($6.90–$12); secondi 6€–16€ ($6.90–$18). AE, DC, MC, V. Tues–Sun 12:30–3pm. July–Aug sometimes open evenings and on Mon.

11 The Gargano Peninsula ★★ & Tremiti Islands

237km (147 miles) NE of Naples, 39km (24 miles) NE of Foggia

Originally an island, the **Gargano Peninsula,** a rugged and surging landmass forming a spur above the heel of Apuglia, was connected to the mainland by deposits carried down from the Apennines. The resulting formations are mountainous steppes that descend dramatically into the sea, perforated by glittering caves of emerald and blue, and largely accessible only by boat. Ancient fishing villages have grown into resort towns like **Vieste,** with its long beaches and a 13th-century cathedral dominating a whitewashed historic center, and **Mattinata,** a simple agricultural town surrounded by kilometers and kilometers of olive groves. In the center of the promontory is the **Foresta Umbra** ★, the largest leafy forest in Europe and a cool shaded retreat protecting a host of endangered species.

The **Tremiti Islands** comprise an archipelago of mini-islands, including the isle-mountain of San Nicola (capped by the 11th-c., half-ruined abbey of Santa Maria a Mare) and the pine-forested **San Domino,** where Roman Emperor Augustus's granddaughter Julia died in exile. The surrounding waters have been declared a marine preserve—good news for fish and scuba enthusiasts, with dives up to 45m (148 ft.) in lukewarm waters amid swarms of fish and spectacular red and yellow corals thriving offshore.

As a primarily industrial port town, **Manfredonia**'s only redeeming factor is that it hasn't yet succumbed to an overwhelming tourist influence, not that that would do it any harm. The city's main monument is its 13th- to 16th-century **Castello Svevo-Aragonese,** undergoing restorations as of this writing and housing a **museum** ★ (© 0884-587838) that boasts a fantastic collection of funerary steles whose carvings reflect the whims of the day. The museum is open daily from 8:30am to 7:30pm (ticket office closes at 7pm; in summer the museum adds Sat evenings 8–11pm) and is closed the first and last Mondays of the month. Admission is 2.50€ ($2.85) for adults, half-price for ages 18 to 25, and free for those under 18 or over 65.

The Gargano has also long been a destination of religious pilgrimages, turning formerly forgotten towns into Las Vegas look-alikes, especially on religious holidays. Monte Sant'Angelo manages to maintain its dignity in and around the **Basilica San Michele Arcangelo** (© 0884-561150), a church assembled over the centuries atop a grotto where St. Michael the Archangel miraculously appeared to a local bishop in A.D. 490. This consecrated spot was once so important it was an obligatory stop on the road to the Holy Land. Notice the **marble statue of the saint** ★ carved by Andrea Sansovino in the 16th century. Entrance to the cave/basilica is free, but there is a fee of 3€ ($3.45) to visit the crypt, during which a minimum of five people must be accompanied by a (non-English-speaking) guide.

Nearby is the 9th- to 15th-century **castello** (© 0884-565444), restored and embellished by Frederick II, who lived here with Bianca Lancia, mother of Manfredi and Enzo, his two illegitimate sons. Your kids might be creeped out but delighted by the fly-infested dungeons, making the admission of 1.55€ ($1.80) worth your while. The castle can be visited daily from 9am to 7pm in summer, 9am to noon in winter. (Reservations are suggested in high season.)

Ultimately, the Gargano offers an undisturbed and always scenic escape from life, and most visitors head straight for the crystal-clear waters along one of the numerous and painfully lovely rocky coves. If you're planning to drive the coast in search of a refreshing swim, be aware that you'll have to pay, and possibly lunch, at one of the dozens of campsites signposted along the roadside. While you're sweating, keep in mind that 40km (25 miles) can take 2 to 3 hours and that much of the road rides the upper reaches of the cliffs and, sadly, out of sight of the coastline. Plan your trip for the spring or early fall, for landscapes of irises in bloom and wondrous wild orchids of purple and green.

ESSENTIALS

GETTING THERE   Unless you're already in Apuglia and approaching from the direction of Bari, the unexciting provincial capital of **Foggia** will most likely be your gateway into the Gargano region. There are five **Eurostar trains** daily from **Rome** (3½ hr.; 31€/$35) or, if you're counting every euro, one Intercity night train (5 hr.; 21€/$25). From **Bari,** you can either hop on one of the half-hourly trains (90 min.; from 6.70€/$7.70) or on the ultracomfortable Eurostar, which stops in Foggia on the way to Rome (1 hr. 15 min.; 14€/$16). If you're coming from **Napoli** Central, you'll have to change in Caserta for a Eurostar or Intercity train to Foggia (19€/$22); depending on how good your connections are, total travel time can vary from 2 hours and 20 minutes to 5½ hours. Less of a hassle and equally comfortable is the bus service run by **C.L.P. Bus Line** right from the center of **Naples**'s Piazza Garibaldi (✆ 081-269966) to Foggia's train station/transport hub (2 hr.; 9€/$10). Buy your tickets on board; buses leave 13 times a day, 6 times on Sunday.

Ferrovie del Gargano (✆ 0881-772491) runs both bus and train service, and **SITA** (in Foggia ✆ 0881/773117) runs frequent daily connections (service is drastically reduced to **Manfredonia** [45 min.; 2.30€/$2.65 on Sun]) from **Foggia**'s train station, the logical gateway into the Gargano. A few buses continue up the coast to Vieste (another 85 min.; 3.10€/$3.55).

GETTING AROUND   In addition to connecting Manfredonia to Vieste, **Ferrovie del Gargano** (✆ 0881-772491) and **SITA** (✆ 0881-773117) make frequent connections to Monte Sant'Angelo (40–60 min.; 3.85€/$4.40), San Giovanni di Rotondo (40–60 min.; 3.10€/$3.55), and Mattinata (40 min.; 1.30€/$1.50). Remember that service is greatly reduced (or nonexistent) on Sunday.

If you have a **car,** the SS89 will get you from Foggia to Manfredonia, where the highway begins to follow the scenic and winding Gargano coastline, in under 30 minutes. Easier on the stomach and more captivating than the land approach to the northern reaches of the peninsula are the changing vistas as seen by sea. **Adriatica,** in Vieste (✆ 0884-708501; in Manfredonia ✆ 0884-582520; www.adriatica.it), runs daily hydrofoil service from Manfredonia to the Tremiti Islands, departing at 8am and returning at 5pm June through September (departs half-hour earlier in Aug; 2 hr.; 21€/$24; half-price for kids), with a stopover in Vieste (21€/$24 round-trip for those not going to the islands). Adriatica also runs daily service in June, July, August, and September from Vieste to San Nicola, upping frequency to three times a day in August (1 hr.; 14€/$16; half-price for kids). A public skiff runs between San Nicola and San Domenico every 10 minutes (5 min.; 1€/$1.15).

VISITOR INFORMATION   **Manfredonia**'s tourist office is located upstairs at Corso Manfredi 26 (✆ 0884-581998; fax 0884-583295) and has general

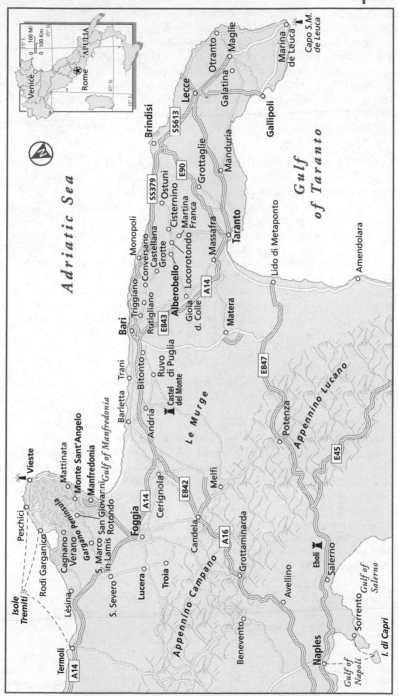

Adriatic Sea

APULIA

Venice

Rome

Isole Tremiti

Termoli

A14

Lésina

S. Severo

Lucera

Troia

Benevento

Avellino

Salerno

Eboli

Sorrento *Gulf of Salerno*

Naples

Gulf of Napoli

I. di Capri

Rodi Garganico

Peschici

Vieste

Cagnano Varano

Gargano peninsula

S. Marco in Lamis

San Giovanni Rotondo

Mattinata

Monte Sant'Angelo

Manfredonia

Gulf of Manfredonia

Foggia

A14

Cerignola

E842

Candela

A16

Grottaminarda

Appennino Campano

Melfi

Potenza

Appennino Lucano

E45

E847

Matera

Amendolara

Barletta

Trani

Bitonto

Andria

Ruvo di Puglia

Castel del Monte

Le Murge

Bari

Triggiano

Rutigliano

Conversano

Castellana Grotte

Alberobello

Gioia d. Colle

Locorotondo

A14

Monopoli

Ostuni

Cisternino

Martina Franca

Massafra

Taranto

Lido di Metaponto

Gulf of Taranto

Manduria

Gallipoli

Grottaglie

SS379

E90

Brindisi

SS613

Lecce

Galatina

Otranto

Maglie

Marina de Leuca

Capo S.M. de Leuca

E843

information on the Gargano region. The office is open Monday through Saturday from 8:30am to 1:30pm. **Vieste's** tourist office is on Piazza Kennedy, where Via Fazzini becomes Corso Italia (© **0884-708806;** fax 0884-707495; www.viesteonline.it), and is open year-round Monday to Saturday 8am to 2pm. During the summer, the office reopens Monday through Saturday from 4 to 9:30pm and Sunday from 9am to 1pm. For more detailed information on the **Foresta Umbra,** contact Ecogargano, located in a cabin on the otherwise empty road through the center of the forest (© **0884-565444** or 0884-565579). The Gargano towns have also banded together on the Internet at **www.gargano.it/citta** (in Italian).

ACCOMMODATIONS & DINING YOU CAN AFFORD

When the entire Gargano was declared a natural reserve, all building projects came to a halt, leaving the region with a tourist infrastructure that caters more to travelers in RVs. The coastline from Mattinata to Vieste is smattered with campgrounds with or without bungalows that sound more charming than they are. Many of these campsites sit on their own private beach, which is good enough reason to stay there, since none of the beaches accessible from the high promontory is public (this is where a private boat rental comes in handy). Below are the best options from which to explore the region, from industrialized Manfredonia to minuscule Mattinata and beyond. It would be difficult to confuse Manfredonia with a seaside resort town, but as far as transportation connections go, it can't be beat. Vieste comes in at an easy second, since you can avoid the tortuous road up from Manfredonia by hopping on the hydrofoil. Remember that the farther away from Manfredonia you go, the more isolated you will be.

IN MANFREDONIA

Gargano   One of a sparse handful of hotels in and around town, the Gargano is your typical 1970s beach hotel, with plaid carpets to add texture to a primarily blue-and-white Mediterranean color scheme. The straightforward modular room furnishings aren't too much worse for wear, but who cares with a sea view from your balcony over the treetops of the palm-lined promenade? The hotel's saltwater pool is a treat until the sun sets behind the building, when you can move to the well-tended lobby or outdoor terraces for a late-afternoon aperitif. When dinnertime rolls around, it's only a 10-minute seaside stroll to the castle and main drag on Corso Manfredi, but don't turn your nose up at the hotel restaurant; it offers the best meal you'll get in town.

Vle. Beccarini 2 (at the north end of town on the main shore drive), 71043 Manfredonia (FG). © 0884-587621. Fax 0884-586021. 46 units. 80€ ($92) single; 110€ ($126) double. Rates include breakfast. MC, V. Parking 11€. **Amenities:** Restaurant; bar; outdoor swimming pool; concierge; dry cleaning. *In room:* A/C, TV, hair dryer, safe.

IN MATTINATA

Baia delle Zagare   Located on one of the more scenic spots along the Mattinata-Vieste coastline, this bay is featured in all the marketing brochures of the region. Horse-shape *faraglione* and *piramide* rock formations slice through the surface of the water, and there are enough nearby marine caves to keep you occupied for some time. The resort is sensitively tucked amid the pines high above the private beach, which is accessible via either an elevator down through the rock or, for the heartier, by stairs. Mediterranean cottages dot the landscape, and the result is a welcoming, well-tended, and rustic getaway. The only downside is that getting here without a car is nearly impossible. Book early because the convention center fills beds fairly regularly.

71030 Mattinata. ℂ 0884-550155. Fax 0884-550884. www.hotelbaiadellezagare.it. 150 units. 60€–88€ ($69–$101) per person. Rates include breakfast. Half- (18€/$21) or full pension (24€/$28) obligatory in Aug. AE, MC, V. Free parking. Closed from Sept 22 to end of May. Drive 11km/6¾ miles north of Mattinata on the road to Vieste. **Amenities:** Restaurant; 2 bars; outdoor swimming pool; tennis court; soccer field; volleyball court; salon; baby club; laundry service; dry cleaning; disco; cinema. *In room:* A/C, TV, minibar, hair dryer.

IN VIESTE

Hotel Seggio   Vieste's 17th-century town hall, tucked halfway up the hill of the old quarter, is now home to the Hotel Seggio. Although rooms vary greatly, most have functional furnishings and, sadly, time-weary beds. Some are low ceilinged and poorly lit, but almost all accommodations are fairly large, and about half have water views. The choice room, no. 104, has windows on two sides, a high wooden ceiling, and a terrace overlooking both the sea and the postcard-size square below. The stone-walled restaurant has a medieval flair and Pugliese menu. There's a sofa-filled bar area for piano music after dinner some nights. Set into the cliffs below are a tiny pool and a cement pier over the shallow, sandy waters, accessible via an elevator from the hotel down to the private beach.

Via Vieste 7/Piazza Seggio, 71019 Vieste (FG). ℂ 0884-708123. Fax 0884-708727. www.emmeti.it/Hseggio. 30 units. 70€–130€ ($80–$150) double; half- or full pension required July 27–Aug. Sea view 10% extra. Rates include breakfast. AE, DC, MC, V. Limited free parking; additional parking 5€ ($5.75) per day. Closed Nov–Mar. **Amenities:** Restaurant; bar; outdoor swimming pool; small fitness room; 24-hr. room service; laundry service; dry cleaning; private beach. *In room:* A/C, TV, minibar, hair dryer, safe.

A CASTLE EN ROUTE TO BARI 🏰🏰🏰

Frederick II's 1240 masterpiece of octagonal proportions, the **Castel del Monte** (ℂ 0883-569997), commands a 534m (1752-ft.) hilltop in the solitude of the Pugliese countryside, rising above wheat fields and olive groves in its pale honey-gray stone and geometric perfection. No documentation survives to tell us the history of the castle, but its unique design and location rule out such possibilities as fortress or hunting lodge. The best-supported hypothesis is that the castle served as some type of astronomical observatory; in fact, when the sun is at its zenith, the shadows projected on the walls correspond to the changing signs of the zodiac, as well as to the measurements of the castle. Corroborating this is Frederick II's affinity to cultures of the East, including the "infidels," who were intellectually light-years ahead of the West in terms of science (another revolutionary feature of the castle is the existence of baths and toilets). Later used as a prison, the castle was left to decay until the end of the 19th century, when the locality of Andria sold it to the State for the bargain price of 25,000L (13€/$15 in today's money). Private guides through the castle are provided free of charge (plus a donation at your discretion) by the City of Andria; look for the kiosk near the entrance to the site marked COMUNE DI ANDRIA.

Admission is 3€ ($3.45) for adults, free for kids under 18. The castle is open daily from 10am to 1:30pm and 2:30 to 7pm; the ticket window closes a half-hour before. The castle is closed Christmas and New Year's Day.

The castle sits along the **SS170bis** 20km (12 miles) from the town of **Andria** (tourist info: ℂ 0883-592283). With or without a car, you'll have to pass through the town of Andria, where public transportation to the castle outside of the summer months is nonexistent. But even in the height of summer, bus service from Andria is kept to a minimum (1€/$1.15). For those throwing caution to the wind, a taxi will run a steep 30€ ($35) or so round-trip.

To get to Andria, take a twice-hourly train **from Bari,** or 1 of 23 (9 Sun) SITA buses **from Trani** (1.30€/$1.50).

12 Bari

138km (86 miles) SE of Foggia and the Gargano

The second-largest city in southern Italy, **Bari** was founded even before the Greeks landed in Apuglia and has been an industrial and commercial powerhouse ever since.

The city earned itself a bad rap due to a high rate of petty crime, but if you lived this close to your neighbors, you'd probably raise some hell, too. The **Città Vecchia (Old City)** is the medieval heart of Bari, characterized by improbably narrow alleyways and thin curtains that barely succeed in creating privacy for those within. Tables and chairs are set out on the street until the early hours of the morning, as people chat and smoke or gather around an open grill for a triangle of moist fried polenta. Local entrepreneurs are taking advantage of the area by opening stylish bars and eateries in archaeologically outstanding spaces. At night, the castle ramparts light up with activity, when the large piazzas with views of the marina fill with the overflow from the crowded bars and cafes.

Bari is also the home of Santa Claus—or, rather, the bones of St. Nicholas. Stolen from their penultimate resting place in the bishop's hometown of Myra in Asia Minor, the saint's bones are sheltered in Apulia's first grand Romanesque church here in Bari.

GETTING THERE   By Train   Daily trains run twice an hour from **Foggia** (67–100 min.; 6.70€–14€/$7.70–$16). Six daily trains (that pass through Foggia) run from **Rome** (4½ hr.; 31€–36€/$36–$41).

The **Bari Centrale station** (✆ 080-5240148) is on Piazza Aldo Moro, in the middle of the modern city and only a 5- to 10-minute walk to the Città Vecchia. This station is serviced by national FS trains (from points north you'll be passing through Foggia), plus several private lines, including the **Ferrovia Bari Nord** (ticket office on the left of Piazza Aldo Moro as you exit the main rail station; ✆ 080-5213577). The private **Ferrovia del Sud-Est** (✆ 080-5462111) services Alberobello and the Valle D'Itria (see "Alberobello & the Land of the Trulli," below), as well as Lecce.

By Bus   There are only two daily **SITA** buses from **Manfredonia** (2 hr. 15 min.; 6.70€/$7.70; none on Sun; www.sitabus.info) and five **Maco** (✆ 081-200380; www.marinobus.it) buses daily from **Napoli's** Piazza Garibaldi (2–3 hr.; 19€/$22). In Bari, buses arrive and depart at the back of the train station at Largo Sorrentino opposite the exit to the train station's underground passage. Taxis should be waiting (insist on running the meter *before* you get in the car). Otherwise, take the underground passage to the main entrance to the station, and catch either a bus or a cab (or walk) to your final destination.

The **SITA office** is at the edge of town, Via Bruno Buozzi 35 (✆ 080-5741800), but you can get tickets and info at the **Marozzi office** (✆ 06-4076140 in Rome, or 080-4322882 in Bari), a division of SITA, at Corso Italia 3 (at the corner of Piazza Aldo Moro). Marozzi runs service daily from Rome's Stazione Tiburtina, departing at 10am, 11am, 3:30pm, and midnight (2½–3 hr.; 28€/$32), stopping in Bari before continuing on to Brindisi and Lecce.

By Car   Bari is on the SS116 from Trani and Barletta, and the A14 highway from Foggia. From Manfredonia, just follow the coastal road until it merges with the SS116.

VISITOR INFORMATION   The **tourist information office** is at Piazza Aldo Moro 33A (✆ 080-5242244 or 080-5242361), on the right side of the square as you exit the train station. Its limited hours are Wednesday and Saturday 9:30am–12:30pm, with extended hours in summer. For train and bus tickets or other services that require a travel agent, there's an Agenzia 365 inside the train station (© **080-5289082**).

SIGHTS TO SEE

San Nicola ✪✪   Bari built the first great Norman Romanesque church in Apulia in 1087 to house the earthly remains of St. Nicholas, today mythologized as Santa Claus but originally a 4th-century Turkish bishop renowned for his piety, kindness, and miracles, including the re-memberment and resurrection of three children after they had been chopped up with a butcher's knife and pickled in brine. St. Nick's tomb is in the **crypt** below the main altar, where a service is most likely in progress (and where here, at least, the saint is depicted with dark skin). It's best not to circulate during prayer, but you can find a vacant corner from which to examine the Byzantine and Romanesque capitals carved with lions, griffins, and peacocks. Near the right entrance is a **pillar** said to have miraculous healing powers, unfortunately enclosed within an iron grating. The legend goes that after the pillar was found floating in the Tiber, the Bishop of Myra had it sent to his church on the Mediterranean, where it stood for 7 centuries. The column miraculously appeared in Bari in 1098 and was finally erected in the crypt, where it is still a magnet for hopeful pilgrims.

The church's **central portal** is an especially fine marriage of Arab, Byzantine, and native styles, with carved decorations and a griffin-crowned gable whose columns are supported by two worn bulls. Inside the apse sits the **Bishop's throne,** crafted in 1098 with telamones supporting the legs.

Piazza San Nicola. © **080-5211205**. Free admission. Daily 7am–noon and 4:30–7pm.

Cattedrale (Cathedral) ✪   Built about a century after the church of San Nicola, the cathedral is a striking Romanesque edifice, with a tall bell tower and an octagonal drum. The **facade** has more recent embellishments, including baroque canopies over the doors and a modern rose window. The **pulpit** is a curious cobbling together of 13th-century fragments. Bits of **mosaic** flooring from an earlier 8th-century church survive in the transept alongside some medieval **frescoes.** In the sacristy is a precious **Byzantine scroll** in typical medieval Beneventan script. The illustrations are upside down so that they would be visible to the congregation as the scroll was unrolled.

Piazza dell'Odegitria. No phone. Free admission. Daily 7am–noon and 4:30–7pm.

Museo del Castello Svevo & Gypsoteca ✪✪   The massive bastion standing today was instrumental in re-establishing Bari's fortunes as an independent and thriving cultural and trade center in the 13th century. In the 16th century, the castle was expanded by the Aragonese, when Isabella of Aragon and her daughter, Bona Sforza, took up residence here and transformed it into a Renaissance showpiece fit for a king. Under the Bourbons, the castle was neglected, serving once again as a fortress, a prison, and army barracks, until its final tour of duty during the French revolution.

The structure alone is interesting enough, if not a bit barren. In the "minors" tower, so-called because of its use as a prison for juveniles in the mid–19th century, is a 13th-century Gothic portal decorated with a magnificently engraved lunette arch. The Renaissance (inner) courtyard has an interesting double-arched loggia whose columns support capitals decorated with sculptures of eagles and acanthus leaves. The castle houses the **Gypsoteca,** a collection of plaster casts and architectural remnants taken from ancient Apulian monuments, in addition to a small permanent collection that includes some good 15th-century frescos and what was probably a portrait in stone of Frederick II. The castle also occasionally hosts temporary exhibitions; check with the tourist information office or keep an eye out for billboard advertisements.

Piazza Frederico II di Svevia. ℂ 080-5286111. Admission 2€ ($2.30). Tues–Sun 8:30am–7pm.

Pinacoteca Provinciale (Provincial Picture Gallery)   This small collection is marked by some good pictures by medieval and baroque Pugliese painters; the Neapolitan school (including several by Luca Giordano); Venetian works by Bellini, Paolo Veronese, and Tintoretto; and some fine folk art (ceramics, *presepio* figurines) and canvases by local 19th-century artists.

Via Spalato 19 (off Lungomare N. Sauro). ℂ 080-5412421. Admission 2.55€ ($2.95) adults, .50€ (55¢) students. Tues–Sat 9:30am–1pm and 4–7pm; Sun 9am–1pm. Closed holidays.

ACCOMMODATIONS YOU CAN AFFORD

Bari is a business town, leaving very little choice for the middle-of-the-road budget traveler. If you're having trouble lining up a room, stop at the train station **tourist office.**

Moderno   Probably the best value in Bari, the Moderno is more residence than hotel, the result being that the rooms are cleaned twice a week rather than daily (plus, of course, before a new guest moves in). Accommodations are all miniapartments featuring modern bathrooms and kitchenettes; even the singles are spacious. The furniture is standardized, the beds predictably saggy, but the prices are excellent, and it's convenient for day tripping (the train station is just around the corner).

Via Crisanzio 60, 70122 Bari. ℂ 080-5213313. Fax 080-5214718. 45 units. 45€ ($52) single; 65€ ($75) double. MC, V. Parking 16€ ($18) overnight (extra charge for daytime). *In room:* A/C, TV, fridge, kitchenette.

WORTH A SPLURGE

Boston   You pay for the level of comfort at this businessperson's hotel, located halfway between the train station and the historic district. Most rooms are cut to a modest size, and the comfort level is everything an executive might require. The well-built modular furnishings have suede accents. While windows are fairly soundproof, you may want to request a room on the back *cortile* (courtyard) to escape the bus and traffic noise. Ask for lower rates on weekends and in August.

Via Piccinni 155, 70122 Bari. ℂ 080-5216633. Fax 080-5246802. www.bostonbari.it. 70 units. 60€ ($69) single; 110€ ($126) double. Rates include breakfast. AE, DC, MC, V. Parking 15€ ($17). **Amenities:** Concierge; car-rental desk; 24-hr. room service; babysitting; dry cleaning. *In room:* A/C, TV w/movies, minibar, hair dryer.

GREAT DEALS ON DINING

La Credenze   BARESE/PUGLIESE   Although La Credenze has an attractive and ample menu, customers come here to entrust themselves to the care of Cosimo, the affable optometrist-cum-restaurateur. With the wave of a hand, your table will be buried under a parade of antipasti, including *cozze ripieni* (stuffed mussels), *panzelottini* (wonderful little fried cheese triangles), and a variety of fish proudly served *crudo* (raw). Not for the faint of heart is the *braciola,* in Bari, a thick slice of horsemeat stuffed with garlic, cheese, and cubes of lard, once a recipe for the poor and now enjoying a renaissance as a Saturday night treat.

Via Verrone 25. ℂ 080-5244747. Reservations suggested. Primi 6€ ($6.90); secondi 6€–8€ ($6.90–$9.20). DC, MC, V. Thurs–Tues 1–3pm and 8:30pm–midnight. Closed June–Aug.

Taverna Verde 😋 BARESE/PUGLIESE It pays to book ahead here since Bari families treat it as a sort of dining room away from home, filling the tables with three generations and lots of noisy chatter. Although there's a good selection of regional and national wines, a giant beer is the beverage of choice to accompany *pappardelle alla taverna verde* (wide noodles with tomatoes, mushrooms, and prosciutto), *spaghetti alle cozze* (with mussels), or *orecchiette alla barese* (in a ragu with turnip greens). As a nice change of pace, there are several light secondi, such as an *omletta al prosciutto* or *crostino di mozzarella al prosciutto* (a log of alternating mozzarella and bread slices, toasted and topped with prosciutto). More substantial fare includes *filetto di manzo al pepe verde* (beef filet with green peppercorns) and the ever-popular *frittura di pesce mista* (mixed fried fish).

Largo Adua 19 (on Lungomare Nazario Sauro). © 080-5540870. Reservations recommended. Primi 4.50€ ($5.15); secondi 5€–10€ ($5.75–$12). AE, DC, MC, V. Mon–Sat noon–3pm and 7:30pm–midnight. Closed Aug 14–24 and Dec 24–Jan 6.

13 Alberobello & the Land of the Trulli ★★★

63km (39 miles) SE of Bari

Hidden in plain sight is the fairy-tale village of **Alberobello,** an otherworldly cityscape of cone-shaped houses called *trulli,* where, at any moment, you may be greeted by a mob of pointy-eared elves in green shoes. Well, not exactly. But once amid the mystery and romance of the *trulli,* you'll think you're under some kind of magic spell.

Alberobello comprises a pair of low hills that house two sizable neighborhoods composed of some 1,000 *trulli*—ancient mysterious dwellings forming a vision so unique and well preserved that the entire town has been declared a national monument. For this reason, Alberobello has become the de facto capital of the region, even if it's not the largest town among those in the enchanting fairy-tale landscape of the Itria Valley.

Italy's oddest example of idiosyncratic vernacular architecture, a *trullo* is a single-room, whitewashed cylindrical structure with a conical roof made of dark, flat rocks fixed—without mortar—into a dry roof made of piled-up stone refuse. No one is sure where the *trulli* came from, though there are plenty of theories. One novel idea is that, during the Aragonese rule, the locals used them to avoid taxation; when they saw King Ferdinand's tax man coming, they'd just collapse the roof, rendering the structure "unfinished," and hence nontaxable. Plausible, but questions remain as to why similar ancient structures appear in eastern Turkey and in Syria.

As you might expect, Alberobello sees its share of tour buses whose arrival encourages the manufacture of tacky backlit plaster *trulli* and other useless memorabilia. Many visitors are seduced into purchasing a tablecloth or set of hand towels typical of the exquisite hand-woven textiles (at extortionist prices) produced in the region.

The crowds tend to swarm around the boutiques, leaving these marvelous cobbled lanes empty once the sun goes down, and allowing the local elderly to emerge from their own private *trulli* for a bit of fresh air and late-night chatter.

ESSENTIALS

GETTING THERE The **Ferrovia del Sud-Est** private rail line (© 080-5462111) from **Bari** to Taranto services the Itria Valley Monday through Saturday, with 14 to 16 trains daily stopping at the Grotte di Castellana (1 hr.;

2.60€/$3), **Alberobello** (95 min.; 3.60€/$4.15), Locorotondo (104 min.; 4€/$4.60), and Martina Franca (110 min.; 4€/$4.60). There are no trains on Sunday, and only limited bus service into and out of the secondary provincial hub of Martina Franco.

By Car   From Bari or Brindisi, take State Highway 16 to Monopoli, passing through Fasano on the way to Alberobello (once you arrive, follow yellow signs for ZONA TRULLI).

VISITOR INFORMATION   Alberobello's **tourist office** is in the Casa d'Amore *trullo* at Piazza Ferdinando IV (© **080-4325171;** fax 080-9325706). The office is open Monday through Friday from 9am to 1pm and 3 to 8pm, Saturday and Sunday from 9am to 8pm (possibly shorter hours in winter).

WHAT TO SEE & DO

Alberobello is rather touristy, but with two swatches of the whitewashed townscape made almost entirely of cone-topped dwellings, the roofs dotted and topped with ancient, symbolic "knobs," it is a sight to behold, lost in the low-lying olive groves of the Itria Valley.

Don't be put off by the town's central parking lot: Bordering this access area is the slope known as **Rione Monti,** the larger of the two *trullo* zones, with blindingly white stone pedestrian streets and character to spare. Although most of Rione Monti's *trulli* now house souvenir or crafts stands, the character of the zone is not compromised. But if you want to see a more genuinely residential *trullo* zone, head across the parking area, behind Piazza XXVII Maggio through Piazza Plebescito, for the **Aia Piccola** district.

The 18th-century **Trullo Sovrano,** on Piazza Sacramento, was the only *trullo* built with two stories. Originally a seminary, it was bought by a local family who returned from America with modest riches and set it up as a house. The admission of 1€ ($1.15; half-price for kids under 12) includes a free guided tour through rooms decked out as they would have been two generations ago. It's open daily 10am to 1pm (9am in Aug) and 3 to 7pm.

A CAVERN EN ROUTE TO ALBEROBELLO 🖈🖈🖈

The **Grotte di Castellana** (© **080-4965511** or 080-4998211; www.grottedi castellana.it) is one of Italy's most spectacular cave systems, glittering with crystals and filled with wondrous rock formations spread throughout a series of massive caverns and long narrow tunnels formed by an ancient underground torrent. The first great chamber is almost 60m (197 ft.) deep, with a naturally formed oculus at the top open to sunlight and rimmed with streamers of vegetation.

Throughout the underground system are groupings of colossal stalagmites, formations in the shapes of a wolf, a camel, an owl, a serpent, and (of course) a Madonna in miniature, near a rocky congregation of faithful kneeling in prayer.

The short, 1-hour, 1km (½-mile) tour gives you a taste for this underworld, but it's worthwhile to take the 2-hour, 3km (1¾-mile) tour that includes the most stunning sight of the caverns, the fabulous **Grotta Bianca.** The calciferous water seeping through it has so few impurities that the crystalline stalactites and stalagmites it has formed shine a brilliant white.

The longer tour (in English, high season only) costs 13€ ($15) and leaves at 11am and 4pm; the shorter English-language tour, which costs 8€ ($9.20), leaves at 1pm and 6:30pm. If your schedule doesn't coincide with these times, you can catch one of the long (hourly 9am–noon and 3–6pm; 10am and noon only in low season) or short (hourly) tours that are guided in Italian. The caves are open daily from 8:30am to 1pm and 2:30 to 7pm, and are closed for Christmas and New

Year's. The drop in temperature is sudden and drastic, getting as low as 9°C (48°F) in the main cave, so bring a sweater.

To get there by car from Bari, take the SS16 to the Conversano Cozze exit and follow signs. From Taranto, take the A14 to Gioia del Colle, then follow signs for Putignano and finally for Castellana, or take the FSE train to the site entrance (six departures daily from Bari, excluding Sun).

ACCOMMODATIONS YOU CAN AFFORD

Albergo Sant'Antonio ⭐ *(Kids)* This converted seminary served as summer quarters for young clerics until the 1970s, when it was vacated and ultimately left in neglect. The arrival of UNESCO to Alberobello infused a breath of life into the building, where wayward pilgrims to this preserved wonderland can hole up for more than reasonable prices. Accommodations are expectedly austere yet comfortable—guests are greeted with restored wooden shutters and window details, along with shiny earth-toned tile floors and functional enclosed box showers. Most rooms look out on the cloisters, providing a peaceful reminder of Sant'Antonio's roots.

Via Isonzo, 8/a, 70011 Alberobello (BA). ℂ/fax **080-4322913**. www.albergosantantonio.com. 21 units. 36€–42€ ($41–$48) single; 52€–67€ ($69–$77) double; 70€–86€ ($80–$99) triple; 83€–104€ ($95–$120) quad. Rates include breakfast. MC, V. **Amenities:** Concierge; car-rental desk; 24-hr. room service; babysitting; dry cleaning. *In room:* TV, hair dryer.

Trullidea ⭐⭐ *(Kids)* Here you have the chance to sleep in a bona fide *trullo*, most of them smack on the prettiest street of the historic district. Guido Antionetta's idea was simple but brilliant: help preserve the *trulli* zone by renovating and opening up uninhabited structures as miniapartments. The more desirable units have atmospheric stone floors, wood beams crossing the inside of the conical roofs, sturdy peasant-style furnishings, fireplaces (25€/$29 supplement), and kitchenettes (10€/$12 supplement)—ask when you reserve for one of these. Bathrooms are disappointingly basic, given the charm of the actual *trulli*. *Trulli* are naturally cool in summer and warm in winter—but the space heaters and fireplaces help.

Via Monte Nero 18, 70011 Alberobello (BA). ℂ/fax **080-4323860**. www.trullidea.com. 25 *trulli* apts (sleep 2–6 each). 78€–92€ ($90–$106) double; 93€–114€ ($107–$133) triple; 114€–129€ ($133–$150) quad. Rates include breakfast. Half- and full board available. AE, MC, V. *In room:* No phone.

A GREAT DEALS ON DINING

Le Ulivi ⭐⭐ *(Value)* PUGLIESE   Not a foreigner in sight: That's how I like my meals when I travel around Italy. And that's what you'll get at this popular local family restaurant on the outskirts of Alberobello. The house specialty is the *pizza saporita* (with arugula, fresh tomato, mozzarella, and the local *cacioricotta* cheese)—and one of the highlights of my trip to Puglia. The *affetato*—their plate of sliced local meats—is also a standout, but beware: They use horsemeat for the (sinfully good) *bresaola*. The *bistecca di vitello* (veal steak) offers a memorable taste of an exceptionally rare cut of meat. Le Ulivi has outdoor seating for warmer evenings; otherwise, it's frequently SRO, with hungry guests lining up at the door waiting for a seat.

Corso da Popoleto, 15. ℂ **080-4323796**. Primi 4€–8€ ($4.60–$9.20); secondi 4€–10€ (4.60–$12). MC, V. Thurs–Tues 1–3:30pm and 7:30–11pm. Exit Alberobello, following signs for Putignano at the roundabout. Pass under the bridge and make the immediate right (slightly hidden). The restaurant is on the right.

Ristorante Trullo d'Oro ⭐⭐ PUGLIESE/ITALIAN   One of the more highly recommended favorites in town, Trullo d'Oro takes up a complex of *trulli*, providing not only killer atmosphere, but good food as well. You can sample three of

Ferries to Greece

Throughout the centuries, the shores of Apulia have launched more ships than Helen of Troy. She'd blanch today if she were forced to embark at Brindisi, where almost every doorway in town that isn't a pizza joint is a smarmy travel agency. Not actually hailed as a tourist destination, Brindisi acts as a magnet for voyagers on their way to or from Greece, and those transients not necessarily interested in the city's paltry (but lovely, if not for their location) medieval monuments. Few are aware that ferries to Greece also depart from infinitely more inviting Bari, a city that is equally, if not more easily, reachable, and certainly more charming.

Superfast Ferries (© 080-5211416; www.ferries.gr/sff), on Corso Antonio De Tullio, leave from **Bari** four to six times daily to both **Igoumenitsa** (9 hr.) and **Patras** (15 hr.). Although the low price of a chilly deck seat may be appealing (61€/$70 in low season; 96€/$110 in high), this might be a good time to pony up for a bed in a dorm (98€/$113 low season; 140€/$160 high) or, better yet, a cabin. Depending on the services you ask for, the latter will set you back from 119€ ($137) all the way up to 380€ ($437) for a first-class cabin.

Otherwise, both **Med Link Lines** (© 0831-561580), at Corso Garibaldi 100, and **Hellenic Mediterranean Lines** (© 0831-528531; www.ferries.gr/hml), down the street at Corso Garibaldi 8, depart from **Brindisi** for **Patras** and **Corfu**. A spot on the deck runs between 23€ ($26) and 29€ ($33), a reclining seat costs 25€ to 49€ ($29–$56), and a spot in a cabin (capacity two to six people of the same gender) with shower and toilet costs from 41€ to 170€ ($47–$195) per person, depending on the season. Strintzis Lines' **Blue Star Ferries,** at Corso Garibaldi 65 (© 0831-562200; www.ferries.gr/strintzis), and **Hellenic Mediterranean Lines** make the trip from **Brindisi to Corfu** (8 hr.; HML continues on to Igoumenitsa, arriving 2 hr. later). Depending on the season, a ticket will cost anywhere from 31€ ($36) for a spot on the deck in low season (55€/$63) in high season) to a maximum of 135€ ($155) for a deluxe cabin in high season (minimum price for a bed in a 4-person cabin with toilet and shower is 67€/$77).

Purchase your tickets at any reputable travel agency or, better yet, from the ferry companies themselves, which are conveniently situated near the harbor port. Some rail passes like Eurail get you the travel free, *but you must still reserve and pay for a cabin or deck chair.* Pick up *Frommer's Greece* for more information on these and other destinations.

---

the most traditional primi with the *assaggini dello chef*, perhaps including *spaghetti al trullo* (with fresh tomatoes, arugula, and Parmesan), *orecchiette alberobellesi* (in ragu topped with savory bread balls), and *purè di fave con cicoria* (fava purée with chicory). If the huge portions of *assaggini* were almost too much, go easy with *melanzane ripiene* (stuffed eggplant); otherwise, dine on *capretto ai carboni* (kid cooked over coals) or the regionally popular *arrosto misto* (mixed meat roast).

Via Felice Cavallotti 29. © 080-4321820. Reservations recommended. Primi 7€–9€ ($8.05–$10); secondi 8€–15€ ($9.20–$17). AE, DC, MC, V. Tues–Sat noon–3pm and 8–11:30pm; Sun noon–3pm. Closed Jan.

14 Ostuni ★

75 km (47 miles) SE of Bari, 35 km (22 miles) NW of Brindisi

A medieval gem of lone baroque portals and labyrinthine alleyways, **Ostuni,** also known as the **Città Bianca (White City),** sits atop one of seven hills high above a landscape of silvery olive groves. Its silhouette is enchanting: a whitewashed cluster of unadorned cube houses that conceals a tangle of lanes, stairways, and courts, and a 15th-century **cathedral,** whose facade gracefully marries Romanesque, Gothic, and Venetian elements. The huge Goldomagno/baroque **archway** in front of the cathedral is so artfully crafted that you might easily be deceived into thinking that you're at the Bridge of Sighs in Venice.

A handful of unblemished **sandy coves** 3km (1¾ miles) in length only help to boost the magnetism of this very special place.

Not to be outdone by Venice, Ostuni has a tradition of hand-painted glass, so you may want to check out the lamps and aperitif sets displayed the entire length of Via Cattedrale.

ESSENTIALS

GETTING THERE   By Train   Trains run at least hourly from Bari (about 1 hr.; 7.10€–8.25€/$8.15–$9.50) and Lecce (40–65 min.; 7.10€–8.25€/ $8.15–$9.50). The station is located about 3km (1¾ miles) outside the historic center, so you'll have to take one of the local orange buses to Piazza Libertà (about every half-hour; 1€/$1.15) to begin your *passeggiata* around the old city.

By Bus   From Rome, hop on one of the three **Marozzi buses** (© 06-4076140 in Rome, or **080-5741800** in Bari) bound for Bari and continuing on to Brindisi and Lecce.

By Car   Take the Ostuni exit of the Bari–Brindisi state highway. From Alberobello, follow the two-lane road following signs first to Locorotondo, then Cisternino, and finally Ostuni.

GETTING AROUND   There's only one intraurban **bus,** running a circular route from Ostuni's station to Piazza Libertà in the town center. If you're headed to the beach, take the bus marked VILLANOVA (1€/$1.15) from Piazza Libertà (the one with the column near the hugely baroque Palazzo di Città).

VISITOR INFORMATION   The **tourist office** is located steps from Piazza Libertà, behind the Palazzo di Città on Corso Vittorio Emanuele 39 (© **0831- 307219**). Request a copy of their color-coded map of the old city (Città Vecchia), showing walking tours into medieval streets according to historic, architectural, or scenic interest.

ACCOMMODATIONS YOU CAN AFFORD

Tre Torre *Value*   Located on the road out of Ostuni toward the beach, this hotel, run by three women, is the only reasonable option if you're on a budget but still want to stay in town. Although the hotel is about 40 years old, recent renovations guarantee a level of cleanliness without having sacrificed any of its old-world charm. Rooms are simple yet comfortable, with tile floors and area rugs, which get rolled up around beach season to keep them sand free. As of this writing, not all of the rooms had been redone, so you may want to confirm the state of the bathrooms to avoid the one whose shower resembles a kitchen sink in the floor. Otherwise, the bathrooms are in good shape, and 9 of the 15 rooms that have a bathroom also come with a TV and a minifridge.

Corso Vittorio Emanuele 298, Ostuni 72017. (C) **0831-331114**. 15 units, most with bathroom. 36€ ($41) single without bathroom, 41€ ($47) single with bathroom; 48€ ($55) double without bathroom, 54€ ($62) double with bathroom. AE, MC, V. Free parking on street. **Amenities:** Restaurant; bar; free pickup from station. *In room:* No phone.

GREAT DEALS ON DINING

Ostuni is a gourmand's paradise, with wonderfully typical Ostunese trattorias like the **Restaurant Club Spessite,** Via Brancasi 43 ((C) **0831-302866**), a converted 17th-century oil mill, open Thursday through Tuesday from 6pm to 1am. It's a teeny venue for local fare like *orrecchiette*, fava purée, and chicory at more-than-fair prices. You'll wind up paying a bit more at **Porta Nova,** Via Gaspare Petrarolo 38 ((C) **0831-338983**), open Thursday to Tuesday 1 to 3pm and 8pm to midnight. Its panoramic terrace and *cucina casereccia* attract a stream of famed Italian actors and singers. Located behind the cathedral, **Osteria del Tempo Perso,** Via Tanzarella Vitale 47 ((C) **0831-303320**; open daily from 5:30am–12:30am), serves up good quality at fair prices. Avoid visiting on Wednesday, when all of these restaurants are closed. They also close for lunch during much of the summer, when most everyone is down at the beach.

15 Lecce: The Florence of the Baroque (★)

143km (89 miles) SE of Bari, 85km (53 miles) E of Taranto

Not unlike the rich pedigree of most of Italy's lower boot, **Lecce**'s ancestry dates back to a prehistoric settlement and runs the gamut through Greeks, Romans, Byzantines, Normans, and Bourbons. Thanks to an early leaning toward scholarship, Lecce earned itself the title of the Athens of Apuglia (it's still home to one of Apulia's two universities). But the name that stuck still defines the city's artistic heritage: the Florence of the baroque. The swirls and cornucopias of this late Renaissance style are reflected in Lecce's basilicas, churches, and chapels, but also in the massively decorated portals to the old city and various private residences. Lecce's historic center is crowded with a legacy of these ecclesiastical excesses because much of the creative impulses would have remained unexpressed, were it not for the benefaction of the Church. The municipality has done its homework, as many of the major baroque attractions have explanatory plaques (in Italian and English) out front. You can visit them at night, when the best sights are floodlit and the piazzas come alive with people out for their evening *passeggiata* or one of the city's free summer concerts.

ESSENTIALS

GETTING THERE   There are twice-hourly **trains** from **Bari** (2 hr.; 7.50€–12€/$8.60–$14) that pass through **Brindisi** (23–43 min.; 2.30€–8.25€/$2.65–$9.50), and six daily trains from **Rome** (6½–9½ hr.; 33€–44€/$37–$51), passing through Bari and Brindisi as well. The train station is within easy walking distance of the main baroque sights of the old city.

   Marozzi (in Lecce (C) **0832-303016**), a division of SITA, runs service daily from Rome's Stazione Tiburtina (departures at 7am, 11am, and 3:30pm), stopping at **Bari's Estramurale Capruzzi** (2½–3 hr.) and **Brindisi's Viale Regina Margherita** (30 min.). The price is 37€ ($43) for all or a portion of the journey. Marozzi also makes the 13½-hour trip from **Pisa** (7:30pm; 60€/$69), passing through **Florence** (8:15pm; 55€/$63; leaving from the SITA bus station) and **Siena** (9:30pm; 50€/$58; leaving from the train station). If you're driving, Lecce is on the fast-moving **SS613** from Brindisi.

VISITOR INFORMATION The **main tourist office** is at Via Monte San. Michele 20 (© **0832-314117;** fax 0832-310238), but the central information office is near the Duomo on Via Vittorio Emanuele, open Monday through Friday from 9am to 1pm and 5 to 7pm, and Saturday from 9am to 1pm. Their map of the old city is especially useful in identifying the old city gates and other sights of major importance.

SIGHTS TO SEE

Lecce's center revolves around broad **Piazza Sant'Oronzo,** which preserves the lower levels of a 1st-century-B.C. **Anfiteatro Romano (Roman Amphitheater),** much of which is still buried under Santa Maria delle Grazie at the piazza's southeastern end. At the square's center is an **ancient Roman column,** topped by a copper statue of the patron, St. Oronzo, which was cast in Venice. The column's original home was Brindisi, where, as one of a pair, it marked the end of this stretch of the Appian Way. In fulfillment of a promise made during the plague of 1656 (aided, no doubt, by the fact that lightning had recently felled the thing), the column was brought to Lecce by its citizens. Nearby is the **Sedile,** serving as the town hall when it was built in 1592 until 1851.

The greatest of Lecce's baroque facades, **Santa Croce** 👫👫, on Via Umberto, was built between 1549 and 1679, a time span that explains the relative sobriety of the facade's lower half compared to the top-heavy and fantastic exuberance of Giuseppe Zimbalo's work above. The balustrade is supported by a series of telamones, each representing a symbol of paganism. Notice the figure of the "infidel Turk," against which the papacy and the empire combined forces in an unprecedented union at the victorious Battle of Lepanto. Supported by the balustrade are cherubs, which expand on this theme of triumph over evil. Next door is the long and only slightly more subdued facade of the **Palazzo del Governo,** formerly a Celestine convent.

Hiding off Via Vittorio Emanuele is one of Lecce's other gorgeous baroque corners, the enclosed L-shaped **Piazza del Duomo** 👫👫👫. This piazza, intentionally designed with only one way in as a defensive measure, wows the visitor as much for its starkness (especially on a lonely summer Sun) as for its grandeur. Giuseppe Zimbalo rebuilt the 12th-century **Duomo** in 1570, giving it a 68m (223-ft.) bell tower and two facades: on the main entrance and around on the right transept, tucked into the other half of the piazza's L where it faces down the **Palazzo Vescovile** (1420–1632). Adjoining the cathedral is the Palazzo del Seminario, designed by Giuseppe Cino, who also built the piazza's picturesque central well.

SHOPPING

The province of Lecce has been a *cartapesta* (papier-mâché) center since at least the 17th century, so if you're looking for artistically crafted additions to your crèche, here's the place to stock up. Perhaps the best artisan studio is that of **Claudio Riso** and his brothers at Via del Tufo 16 (off V. Federico d'Aragona; © **0832-242362**). They produce remarkably detailed figures (starting at 30€/$35) of everyday 18th-century Lecce life that have won them international prestige. Another noteworthy *bottega* is that of **Maurizio Ciafano,** Via Carlo Russi 10 (© **0360-740906**), where three young men work hard in their tiny space to create peasant figures carrying bundles of twigs or wine jugs, for around 15€ ($17) a figure. If you're looking for more variety, check out the **Mostra Permanente dell'Artigianato Salentino,** Via Rubichi 21 (© **0832-246758**), where you can peruse traditional crafts from across the province: small-town ceramics, cast iron, Lecce-made stone carving, and papier-mâché.

GREAT DEALS ON DINING

Cucina Casareccia 🏗🏗🏗 PUGLIESE HOME COOKING   Concettina Cantoro makes coming to this spare, humble osteria like coming home for dinner. The place doesn't even have a name, just a sign that says HOME COOKING, but Concettina's culinary fame has spread—she's gone to Boston and New York to cook typical Pugliese dishes for top chefs. Concettina is a surrogate Leccese mamma to all her clients, from local regulars—some of whom are daily patrons—to the few lucky tourists who make it here. Let her take charge of your meal, offering a menu strong on local specialties such as purée of fava beans with wild chicory, a potato-mussels-and-zucchini salad, *polpette* (meatballs), and *sagna 'ncannulata* (tagliatelle rolled into rough spirals under a tomato and ricotta sauce).

Via Costadura 19 (a road running north off the Villa Comunala gardens). 🕿 0832-245178. Reservations recommended. Fixed-price menus 13€ ($15) and 18€ ($21). MC, V. Tues–Sat 12:45–3pm and 7:30–10:30pm; Sun 12:45–3pm. Closed end of Aug for 10 days and Dec 22–Jan 6.

Guido e Figli 🏗🏗 *Value* *Kids* PUGLIESE/ITALIAN/PIZZA   The low stone vaulting is atmospheric enough, but most patrons head straight back to the self-service area, where neighborhood regulars, the Sunday paper in hand, partake of the same items as those served in the main restaurant at half the prices. The *orecchiette alla Guido* (Lecce's large whole-wheat orecchiette in a tomato sauce with minimeatballs, eggplant, and Parmesan) isn't bad, nor are the *fusili gran gusto* (pasta spirals with shrimp and salmon) or *parmigiana di melanzane* (a tomato, eggplant, and cheese casserole). Secondi include *polpette e messicane* (two types of meatballs), *pollo al forno con patate* (oven-roasted chicken with roast potatoes), and *lumache* (snails) cooked however you like them (assuming you like them). Service is friendly but can drag, another reason to head straight to the back. Their popular **tavola calda** branch (a cafeteria sort of place), around the corner at Via San Trinchese 10 (🕿 **0832-300802**), also has outdoor tables on a pedestrian street off the main Piazza Sant'Oronzo.

Via XXV Luglio 14. 🕿 0832-305868. Reservations recommended. Primi 5.50€–7€ ($6.30–$8.05); secondi 4.50€–7€ ($5.15–$8.05); pizza 3.50€–7€ ($4–$8.05). AE, DC, MC, V. Tues–Sun noon–3pm and 7:30pm–1am. Daily in Aug. Closed July 1–15.

13

Sicily

by Lynn A. Levine

Expectations of Sicily are inevitably tainted by images of car bombs and surprise Mafia hits in reruns of *The Godfather* and its sequels. But if anything in these movies' depictions of this terrible triangle is accurate, it's the intense imagery: from the pastoral hills and wrinkled peasants, to some of the most beautiful temples and amphitheaters of Magna Graecia, to the medieval stone cities tinged with the majestic pink glow of the setting sun. Even the island's iconography has always been radical: Phalaris, the tyrant of Agrigento, was notorious for his cruelty and not above dining on infants to make his point.

Times have certainly changed, and Cosa Nostra's methods have become much more discreet. Yet beyond the lore, few are truly aware of Sicily's ridiculously rich cultural heritage, of its penchant for craftsmanship, and of its culinary treasures.

Well off the coast of Italy's mainland, Sicily is the largest island in the Mediterranean, enjoying the benefits of a whopping average of 2,500 hours of sunlight per year. An archaeological tour of the island will take you to some of the ancient world's most spectacularly sited temples (Agrigento, Selinunte, Segesta) and theaters (Siracusa, Taormina, Segesta), remnants of powerful **Greek** outposts in the Mediterranean. You can see the **Roman** legacy in the sumptuous mosaics of Agrigento's Piazza Armerina and Taormina's Greco-Roman Theater, and the **Arabic Saracens'** founding of their capital at Palermo in the 9th century left regal pointed arches and graceful domes. The **Normans** came along in the early 11th century and set up a highly advanced monarchy incorporating the best of Greek, Arabic, Roman, and Celtic fashions. Under such enlightened rulers as **Roger II** and the Hohenstaufen emperor **Frederick II**, Sicilian literature came into its own a full 200 years before Dante, laying a linguistic minefield for territorial disputes between Sicilians and Florentines for having founded the Italian language. Frederick II was such a wise ruler and committed patron of the arts that he earned the nickname *Stupor Mundi* ("Wonder of the World") for ushering in an era of artistic, scientific, cultural, and intellectual prosperity. The Normans left the northern coast (Cefalù, Palermo, Monreale) scattered with perfectly balanced Norman cathedrals and Arab-style palaces filled with some of Europe's most gorgeous mosaic cycles. The marriage of **Ferdinand of Aragona** to **Isabelle of Castille** opened Sicily's doors to **Spanish** rule, but under the viceroys and later the **Bourbons,** Sicily pretty much languished through the Renaissance, gearing up instead for a baroque fest during which native architects and sculptors rebuilt churches, palaces, and even entire cities after a series of devastating earthquakes. It wasn't until 1860 that Sicily joined Italy, and it wasn't until the 1980s and 1990s that the organization we call the Mafia began to lose its dominance (but not its presence) over corrupt local governments (see "Men of Honor," below).

Throughout these struggles, each civilization took advantage of and perhaps benefited by the natural defenses of the island's isolation and topography. And if Sicilians consider themselves only nominally part of Italy, this sense of autonomy may be coming to an end. In the summer of 2002, the Italian government approved an ambitious bridge-building project for the Straits of Messina aimed at boosting Sicily's participation in Italian and European trade, one that will inevitably alter the very character of the island. If there's ever a time to go, it's now. In return, Sicily will show you its treasures: pagan festivals, puppet shows, and ancient mystical lore that's now indistinguishable from fervent Christian piety, symbolized in all-or-nothing feasts in honor of a city's patron saint. If you're looking for fabulous beaches, aside from those mentioned here, your selection will be somewhat limited, as much of Sicily's prime coastline has been given over to industrial pursuits. For ancient ruins, medieval magic, and traditional village charm, you've come to the right place. Sicily alone could easily fill a guidebook, but here, I barely have space to cover the highlights. If you try to see everything, you'll see nothing, so pace yourself well—and don't forget to stop and smell the sunflowers.

ESSENTIALS

GETTING THERE   By Train   If you buy a train ticket from a mainland city to anywhere in Sicily, the train will head south to **Villa San Giovanni** in Calabria and then board the ferry for the crossing to Messina with you on it, so just sit tight. There are daily trains from **Rome** (7½–9 hr. on the Intercity or Eurostar, plus travel time from Messina to your final destination) passing through **Naples** (6 hr.) into Messina's **Stazione Marittima** or **Stazione Centrale** (© 090-714935). The latter is connected by train to points west and south as well as to the ferry docks. For information on through trains to Sicily, contact any **FS office;** in Palermo, call © **091-6161806** for passenger information and © **091-6033088** for car rail transport information.

By Bus   SAIS Autolinea Diretta (© **800-920900,** 051-242150 in Bologna, 055-215155 in Florence, 090-771914 in Messina, 091-6166028 in Palermo; www.saisautolinee.it) provides a 13-hour bus ride that leaves Bologna's bus station on Monday, Wednesday, and Friday at 4pm (62€/$71), stopping at both Florence's Piazza Adua (5:30pm) and Piazza Certosa (5:45pm) and arriving in Messina's Piazza della Repubblica at 6am. A **SAIS Trasporti** bus from **Rome** (c/o Agenzia Viaggi Eurojet, Piazza della Repubblica; © **06-4743980; www. saistrasporti.it**) on its way to **Agrigento** (13½ hr.; 39€–45€/$45–$52) also passes through Messina. You can get local tickets and information by contacting SAIS: in **Messina,** Agenzia SAIS Autolinee, at Piazza della Repubblica 6 (© **090-771914**); in **Catania** at Via d'Amico 181 (© **095-536201**); in **Caltanissetta** on

---

Tips Travel Tip

Those medieval hilltop towns may be magical, but you'll have to get there first. Historic centers are generally closed to vehicular traffic, requiring a whole lot of footwork—much of it up and down stone staircases and severely inclined roads. This kind of activity may not be suited to everyone, especially with the midday sun beating down, and in an effort to cram in as much as possible, not all tour operators are sensitive to this. Do your research, and pace yourself.

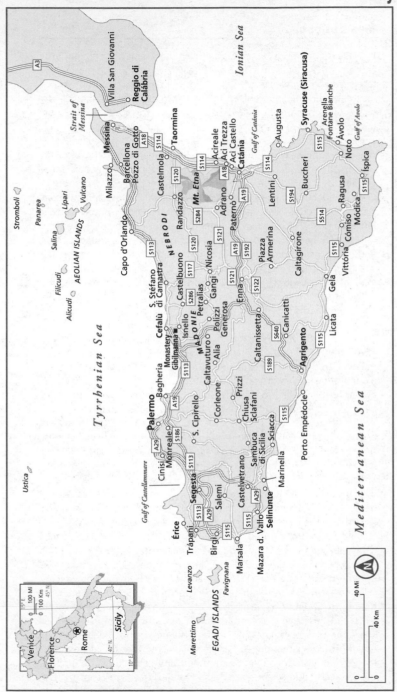

Men of Honor

In Sicily, they don't call it the Mafia (from the Arabic *mu'afah* or "protection"); they call it Cosa Nostra (literally "our thing," but more accurately "this thing we have"). Its origins are debated, but the world's most famed criminal organization seemed to grow out of the convergence of local agricultural overseers working for absentee Bourbon landowners—hired thugs, from the peasant workers' point of view.

Members of the Sicilian Mafia—or "Men of Honor" as they like to be called—traditionally operated as a network of regional bosses who controlled individual towns by setting up puppet regimes of thoroughly corrupt officials. It was a sort of devil's bargain with the national Christian Democrat party, which controlled Italy's government from World War II until 1993 and, despite its law-and-order rhetoric, tacitly left Cosa Nostra alone so long as the bosses got out the party vote.

Men of honor trafficked in illegal goods, of course, but until the 1960s and 1970s, their income was derived mostly from funneling state money into their own pockets, running low-level protection rackets, and ensuring that public contracts were granted to fellow *Mafiosi* (all reasons why Sicily has experienced grotesque unchecked industrialization and modern growth at the expense of its heritage, invaluable real estate, and the good of its communities). But the younger generation of Mafia underbosses got into the highly lucrative heroin and cocaine trades in the 1970s, transforming the Sicilian Mafia into a major player on the international drug-trafficking circuit—and raking in the dough. This ignited a clandestine Mafia war that, throughout the late 1970s and 1980s, generated lurid headlines of bloody Mafia hits. The new generation was wiping out the old and turning the balance of power in their favor.

This situation gave rise to the first Mafia turncoats, disgruntled ex-bosses, and rank-and-file stoolies who opened up and told their stories, first to police prefect Gen. Alberto Dalla Chiesa (assassinated in 1982) and later to crusading magistrates Giovanni Falcone (slaughtered in 1992) and Paolo Borsellino (murdered in 1992), who staged the "maxi-trials" of *Mafiosi* that sent hundreds to jail. The magistrates' murders, especially, garnered public attention to—and, perhaps for the first time, true shame regarding—the *dis*honorable methods that defined the new Mafia.

On a much broader and, in many ways culturally important, scale, it's these young *Mafiosi*, without a moral center or check on their powers, who have driven many Sicilians to at least secretly break the unwritten code of *omertà*, which translates as "homage" but means "silence," when faced with harboring or even tolerating a man of honor. The Mafia still controls much of Palermo, the small towns south of it, and the provincial capitals of Catania, Trapani, and Agrigento. Throughout the rest of Sicily, though, its power has been slipping, notwithstanding the indelible print left on the island's citizens that leaves them suspicious and closemouthed about even the most innocuous subjects. But the heroin trade is a far cry from construction schemes and protection money, and the Mafia is swiftly outliving its usefulness *and* its welcome.

Via Collajanni (© **0934-564072**); and in **Agrigento** at Via Ragazzi del'99 (© **0922-595933**). Reservations are required for seats on SAIS Trasporti, making the trip daily at 8am, 7:30pm, and 9pm from Rome (c/o Tiburviaggi, Piazzale FS Tiburtina; © **06-44245905**) to **Messina** (9½ hr.; 34€/$39; Piazza della Repubblica 6; © **090-771914**), on its way to **Taormina** (10 hr.; 33€/$38; © **0942-625301**), **Catania** (11½ hr.; 41€/$48; © **095-536201**); and **Siracusa** (12½ hr.; 45€/$52; Via Trieste 28; © **0931-66710**). There's a 10€ ($11.50) discount on the price of all round-trip tickets for returns within 10 days.

By Car Ferry   The car ferry from Villa San Giovanni in Calabria to Messina on Sicily runs like clockwork. When you exit the highway, just follow the lanes indicated by the pictogram of a boat with a car in it. When you see everyone parking haphazardly in an open lot to hop out and run into a little building, that's your cue to do the same to buy your ticket (take your car-rental form in with you; they'll need documentation of the license plate). The ferry runs every 20 minutes or so and costs from 17€ ($19.55), depending on the size of your car. The crossing takes 25 minutes. Foot passengers pay a mere 1€ ($1.15). For car ferry information, contact **Tourist Ferry Boat s.p.a.** in Messina (© **090-3718510**) or in Villa San Giovanni (© **0965-751413**).

VISITOR INFORMATION   The **main tourist office** in Palermo (see later in this chapter) has information on the entire island. The island's official website is **www.regione.sicilia.it/turismo**. On the **Volcano Etna page** (www.volcano etna.com), you can learn all you want to know about one of the world's most active volcanoes.

1 Passing Through Messina

237km (147 miles) E of Palermo, 683km (423 miles) SE of Rome, 469km (291 miles) S of Naples

Sicily's primary port and third-largest city doesn't offer many attractions aside from swordfish dinners and a pair of Caravaggios in the **Museo Regionale,** Via della Libertà 465 (© **090-361292;** bus: nos. 76 or 81; admission 4.50€/$5.15). In fact, thanks to excellent through-connections to points south and west, you can pretty much stay on whatever mode of transportation you've chosen until you reach your final destination. In the event that you find yourself in Messina with a few hours to kill, there's a **provincial tourist office** outside the **Stazione Marittima (Port)** at Via Calabria 36 (© **090-675353** or 090-675675), open Monday through Thursday from 8am to 1:30pm and 3 to 6pm, and Friday and Saturday from 8am to 1:30pm.

If you get stuck overnight, try the simple and reliable **Hotel Cairoli,** Viale San Martino 63 (©/fax **090-673755**). It has 59 units: 47 with bathrooms and all with phones, air-conditioning, and TVs. Doubles without bathrooms go for 50€ ($58); those with bathrooms are 80€ ($92). For a dining experience where you'll be the only nonregular, head just below Via La Farina for ultra-Messinese cuisine at **Trattoria Al Padrino,** Via Santa Cecilia 54 (© **090-2921000**), open Monday through Saturday from 12:30 to 2:30pm and 8 to 10:30pm.

2 Cefalù ⟨★

165km (102 miles) W of Messina, 70km (43 miles) E of Palermo

Nestled between a dramatic headland and a naturally sheltered bay, **Cefalù** (*chay-fa-loo*) is an enchanting, if compact, medieval town and a lovely place to unwind. At first sight, Cefalù can be a bit discouraging: modern concrete apartments with red rooftops sandwiched between the foothills of a towering mountain and a naturally sheltered bay. But the pearl is hidden deep within, easily overlooked at the base of an irregularly formed rocky promontory that served as an effective defense against potential invaders during the 11th and 12th centuries. The *centro storico* (historic center), which, blissfully free of traffic, is tidily laid out on the tip of a small cape, is protected by a medieval system of construction employing tight alleys that provided little access from the sea. The sweeping curve of the coastline extends southwest, revealing an expansive and wonderful sandy beach that gives way in both directions to secluded rocky coves and picturesque *faraglioni* (cliffs).

The 5th-century-B.C. Greeks left a few vases for the museum, and Roger II gave the town a mighty **Norman cathedral** whose authority over the main piazza gives you a viable excuse for partaking (several times) of the Italian evening rite, the *passeggiata*. Cefalù is also a viable base for excursions to nearby Palermo, Mount Etna, or Taormina (anything else is a bit far for a day trip), but after a day or two, there's little else to do but while away the hours at the beach or on the romantic boat-strewn bay.

ESSENTIALS

GETTING THERE   By Train   There are 10 trains daily from **Rome** (10½–12 hr.; 47€–67€/$54–$77) and from **Naples** (8½–11½ hr.; 38€–51€/$43–$58). Be sure to check your departure location, as some trains leave from Rome's Tiburtina Station and from Naples's Campo Flegrei Station rather than from Roma Centrale/Napoli Centrale.

There are at least hourly trains from **Palermo** (45–75 min.; 3.85€–4.85€/ $4.40–$5.50) and 10 to 12 trains daily from **Messina** (2½–4 hr.; from 7.90€– 9.25€/$9.10–$11). For local train information, contact the **train station** at © 0921-421169.

By Car   Construction of the A20 highway from Messina ran out of funding years ago, making the 46km (29-mile) stretch between Sant'Agata to Castelbuono a much longer drive than it needs to be. If you're driving from Messina, you'll have to drop to the parallel old coastal SS113 (expect traffic); coming from the other direction **(Palermo),** though, the A20 *is* complete. The *centro storico* is closed to traffic during business hours, so once you arrive, you may want to look for a parking spot along the *lungomare* (ocean drive) or in the often fully occupied Piazza Cristoforo Colombo adjacent to the historic quarter.

VISITOR INFORMATION   The **tourist office** (© 0921-583847; fax 0921-586338) is in Piazza Castelnuovo 34. It's open Monday through Saturday from 8:30am to 2pm and 3 to 7pm. There are information booths at the train station and on Piazza Garibaldi, open Monday through Saturday from 9am to 1pm and 5:30 to 9pm (in winter, the hours may be shorter or they may close altogether).

STROLLING THE TOWN & CLIMBING THE MOUNTAIN

Corso Ruggiero is the quaint and lively pedestrianized main drag of Cefalù, lined with shops and modest medieval *palazzi* (palaces) and prime real estate for the evening *passegiata*. A leisurely stroll leads you to **Piazza del Duomo,** a palm-shaded, cafe-lined square serving as a stage for the monumental twin-towered facade of the **Duomo** ✿ (© 0921-922021), a Norman architectural masterpiece magnificently set against the foot of the towering cliffs. Roger II built this first of Sicily's western-style cathedrals in 1131, supposedly in thanks after his ship found shelter here during a violent storm. By 1166, they'd put the finishing touches on the altar mosaics, fantastic Greek–Byzantine creations featuring a mighty *Christ Pancrator* in the curve of the apse with outstretched hands. Local lore says that although nine workers had been hired for the creation of the mosaic, 10 men were present during the actual inlaying, so the face of Jesus, whose eyes follow you from any point within the church, is said to have been done by an angel. The cathedral is open daily from 8am to noon and 3:15 to 7:30pm (later in summer).

From the edge of the Duomo square, Via Mandralisca leads down to the **Museo Mandralisca** at no. 13 (© **0921-421547**). Be sure to take a look at the family's restored glass-enclosed **oil warehouse** on your way into the small museum whose sparse treasures include a 4th-century-B.C. vase showing a tuna vendor and customer haggling, and Antonello da Messina's smirking *Portrait of a Man* (ca. 1460s). Admission is 4.15€ ($4.75); it's open daily from 9am to 1pm and 3 to 7pm (in summer 9am–7pm or later).

Continue down Via Mandralisca to Via Vittorio Emanuele, turn left, and head to the large opened wrought-iron gate marked **Discesa Fiume,** leading right down to the **Lavatorio** (washroom). This small enclosed courtyard was used as a laundromat during the Arab époque and takes advantage of a natural freshwater spring. The washroom is complete with stone basins and wedge-shaped scrubbing slabs. Head the other way down Via Vittorio Emanuele to glimpse into the dock-front rooms on the left where fishermen mend their nets, and finally turn left into the little **fishing wharf** itself, where the pebbly beach is filled with sun-bleached wooden boats and (in summer) suntanned swimmers. The uneven row of waterfront boathouses with their yawning Gothic arches was used for scenes in the Oscar-winning film *Cinema Paradiso,* and the washed-out colors of the ancient facades are as poetic as ever.

If you have a hankering for a steep climb, you can tackle the hearty 291m (954-ft.) hike up the **Rocca** (wear shoes with good tread for the slippery walk down). An hour should provide plenty of time for a brisk walk straight up and down, but allow enough time to enjoy the sunset from the **panoramic position** above Cefalù Bay. To get there, follow the yellow sign from Corso Ruggiero through the alleyway and up a set of iron stairs, continuing up until you spot the railed stairway on the left. About halfway (at the outer fortress wall), the path splits. Steps to the right lead the long way up to the overgrown foundations of a 13th-century **Byzantine fortress** at the very top of the mountain. The path to the left leads past ancient cisterns and remnants of medieval houses (and a long, picturesquely crenellated wall) to the **Tempio di Diana (Temple of Diana),** a tiny chapel of a monument, one of the oldest structures left standing in Sicily. Neglected, overgrown, and in dire need of a pooper-scoopering, this Greek-era temple rests on foundations from the 9th century B.C. The temple, made of huge stones fitted together, is hauntingly isolated, with just of a few of its doorways surviving. A path to the right above the temple leads steeply to the mountaintop fortress.

ACCOMMODATIONS YOU CAN AFFORD

Cefalù is a compact and picturesque town on the beach. Even so, as a pool rather than a beach person, I prefer secluded accommodations on the outskirts, even when the train tracks pass just beyond my door. No matter where you choose to stay, be prepared for funny-tasting tap water that never truly gets hot.

Astro   This modern hotel is in the new part of town, 5 minutes' walk from the *centro storico* and two blocks from the beach. In exchange for the lack of an elevator, the management provides squeaky-clean rooms (the maid proudly pulled the bed away from the wall to prove that nothing gets "swept under the rug here"). The simple, contemporary-style rooms have oils on the walls, nice modular furnishings, a few scattered Persian rugs, and plenty of elbow room. The main downside to this exceedingly friendly hotel is the considerable noise on the two sides that face the street, especially during the rush-hour motorcycle procession. The hotel restaurant is on a terrace off the sidewalk, although the street's so busy this may actually be a drawback.

Via Roma 105, 90015 Cefalà (PA). C 0921-421639. Fax 0921-423103. www.astrohotel.it. 30 units. 54€ ($62) single; 76€–160€ ($87–$184) double; 15€ ($17.25) per person half-pension supplement required in Aug. Rates include breakfast. AE, MC, V. Free parking in adjacent lot. (Turn left out of station. The street ends in 3 blocks at V. Roma and the hotel.) **Amenities:** Restaurant; bar; use of private "Smart Car" (electric) in city; bike and boat rental (car, bikes, and boat free for guests in superior rooms); children's play room; room service (breakfast only); private beach. *In room:* A/C, TV.

Baia del Capitano 🔧 *(Kids)* Isolated from Cefalù's modern center, the Baia del Capitano provides a piece of paradise for those seeking solitude. The location also offers a bit of rural charm, as you have to pass through a slightly overgrown gravel road to access the picturesque and private rocky beach below. There's also foot access to a pebble beach 10 minutes away. Without sacrificing charm, the rooms are noticeably more welcoming than those at most of the other places in town, with the additional pleasure of a small terrace overlooking the pool. There's bus service (1.50€/$1.70) about every 2 hours between the hotel and Cefalù's center. In summer, an outdoor garden becomes a barbecue and Sicilian folklore show.

90015 Contrada Mazzaforno/Cefalù. C 0921-420003. Fax 0921-420163. www.baiadelcapitano.it. 46 units. 75€–120€ ($86–$138) single; 95€–118€ ($109–$135) double. Rates include breakfast and reflect seasonal fluctuations. Special rates for families and newlyweds. AE, MC, V. Free parking. Exit the state highway to the right, then make an immediate left and follow signs. From the train station, a taxi costs 7.20€ ($8.30). **Amenities:** Restaurant; bar; outdoor swimming pool; tennis courts; watersports; children's playground; 24-hr. room service; laundry service. *In room:* A/C, TV, hair dryer, safe.

La Giara 🔧 *(Kids)* The only hotel in the historic center is the sort of place where repeat guests hug the owners good-bye when checking out. An elevator scoots you up to the newly renovated midsize rooms with air-conditioning, minibars, hair dryers, and VCRs. Units on the street are a bit noisier, but most rooms overlook tiny Arab courtyards and narrow Saracen alleys. The roof terrace gets lots of sun and views of the city roof tiles, with the top half of the Duomo rising under the Rocca a few hundred feet away. Guests can use space on a private beach. The owners are very proud of the city and its history and traditions, especially in the kitchen, which also offers an "organic corner" in its adjoining restaurant. La Giara also rents out three studio apartments, of which two are the two-room type for up to five people.

Via Veterani 40 (between the Duomo and the harbor), 90015 Cefalù (PA). C 0921-421562. Fax 0921-422518. www.hotel-lagiara.it. 24 units. 45€–110€ ($52–$126) single; 53€–130€ (61–$150) double. Rates reflect seasonal changes. AE, MC, V. **Amenities:** Restaurant; bike and boat rental; children's playroom; room service (breakfast only). *In room:* Cable TV.

GREAT DEALS ON DINING

Considering that historic Cefalù occupies such a small area, there are certainly plenty of places to eat. If you're absolutely set on sticking to your budget, skip dinner on the bay-side terraces and walk to the fringes along the beach. But even here along the lungomare, don't be so smug and convince yourself that you've exited the tourist trap. Even oceanside trattorias need to unload yesterday's fish, so if you'd like to avoid food poisoning, stick to the old reliable pastas and pizzas.

La Brace INNOVATIVE SICILIAN   The service can be interminably slow and the owner slightly overwhelmed by the flow of people at the oldest restaurant in town, but Le Brace remains popular among locals as well as visitors. Co-owner Dietmar Beckers's Dutch influence must be in the more creative dishes, such as *involtini di melanzane* (eggplant wrapped around tagliatelle and ricotta, then baked under tomatoes and Parmesan), and roast beef over ricotta with balsamic vinegar, though the eggplant rolls would have been better served hot and the roast beef would have been tastier as a carpaccio. Perhaps these innovations are a bit of a stretch for these Italian cooks, so it's advisable to stick to sure bets like *spaghetti alla crudaiola* (with garlic, capers, tomatoes, and basil), *spaghetti con gamberi e pesce spada* (with shrimp and swordfish), or *tagliatelle con funghi porcini* (with porcini mushrooms). Prices include the usual *pane, coperto,* and *servizio* (bread, cover, and service), leaving you to splurge on that *banana Le Brace,* a banana doused with orange liqueur, baked in foil, and topped with whipped cream.

Via 25 Novembre 10 (off Corso Ruggero). ℂ **0921-423570.** Reservations required for dinner. Primi 6€–7.50€ ($6.90–$8.60); secondi 7€–13€ ($8.05–$14.95). AE, DC, MC, V. Tues–Sun 1–2:30pm; Wed–Sun 7–11pm. Closed Dec 15–Jan 15.

Vecchia Marina ⭐⭐⭐ *(Value)* SICILIAN   Popular among locals and a magnet for visitors in the know, Vecchia Marina boasts a romantic location and an outstanding execution of typical Sicilian cuisine. But if you arrive late and find all the waterside tables occupied, the not-so-shabby consolation prize is a narrow dining room elegantly framed under a single-vaulted ceiling. Fresh pasta is featured in the *pasta fresca con sarde fresche,* a local favorite with an intense flavor. Another typical local dish is the appetizer of *bottarga di tonno,* salty smoked tuna roe mashed and formed into rolls that are sliced and served with lemon and toast. The mixed grilled fish tastes like it just landed in the boat, except that the fishermen actually delivered it live to the dining room's centerpiece holding tank. Oysters, clams, and mussels are also alive in tanks. With all this bounty, it'll be hard to leave room for the *cassata,* a sweet pie of creamy ricotta topped with white frosting.

Via Vittorio Emanuele 73–75 (near Piazza Cristoforo Colombo). ℂ **0921-420388.** Reservations suggested for dinner. Primi 7€–9€ ($8.05–$10); secondi 7€–15€ ($8.05–$17). AE, MC, V. Daily noon–3pm and 7–11:30pm. Closed Tues Nov to Easter.

3 Palermo: Sicily's Capital ⭐⭐⭐

70km (43 miles) W of Cefalù, 237km (147 miles) W of Messina

"You ain't seen Italy until you've seen Palermo" was the mantra at my neighborhood Italian bakery, and though there's no debating the grandeur of the city's sights and there's no doubt about my baker's prejudice, I must say I agree. Aside from harboring some of Sicily's greatest palaces, churches, and art museums, Sicily's capital has a decidedly local flavor: It's a city of puppet theaters, vibrant local markets, and mobile street vendors breaking decibel levels with popular musical selections. Palermo also houses its share of immigrants and the debris that usually accompanies them; frequently unsightly by day and often seedy by night, neighborhoods like those around the train station and the Vecchio Borgo make Palermo a tough place to love.

Palermo hasn't had an easy history. Founded by the Phoenicians, conquered by the Romans, briefly absorbed by Byzantium, and later appropriated as the Saracen capital, **Palermo** lived its "Golden Age" under Norman and Swabian rule. Roger II, along with Frederick II and successive kings, succeeded in blending the city's heritage of architectural styles, resulting in richly ornamented basilicas, luxuriant gardens, and Eastern-style arches and arcades. Other layers were added by later empires: The Hohenstaufen and Angevin kings brought the Gothic to Palermo, while the Bourbons of Naples gave Palermo a definite baroque tradition, even if, during 6 centuries of Spanish and Bourbon rule, only one king, Charles V, ever set foot on Sicily. (This hands-off approach effectively dropped Palermo into the clutches of the Mafia, creating problems that have plagued the city ever since.)

For those unaccustomed to the sensory overload of rubble and trash-filled alleys in the Old City and around Palermo's Vucciria market, it might be a stretch to appreciate the city as the diamond-in-the-rough responsible for producing such a rich collection of gloriously stuccoed oratories, glittering 12th-century mosaics, and world-class art museums. To see Palermo's highlights—the churches, markets, and art museums of the Old Center, the Cappella Palatina—plan at least 2 days, and don't forget to tack on a day for a leisurely trip to nearby Monreale.

ESSENTIALS

GETTING THERE   By Train   There are nine trains daily from **Rome** (about 13 hr.; 52€–71€/$60–$81). Five trains daily make the trip from **Naples** (about 10 hr.; 43€–55€/$49–$63), 13 to 16 trains daily from **Messina's Stazione Marittima** (about 4 hr.; 11€–15€/$12–$18), and at least hourly trains from **Cefalù** (50–75 min.; about 4€/$4.60). Almost all trains pull into the **Stazione Centrale** (✆ 091-6167514 or 091-616806) at the foot of Via Roma (*don't* get off at the suburban Stazione Notarbartolo).

By Bus   SAIS lines, Via P. Balsamo 16 at Piazza Stazione, Palermo (✆ 091-6166028), run seven buses daily (five on Sat, four on Sun) from **Messina's** Piazza della Repubblica (3 hr. 15 min.; 20€/$24), and hourly buses from **Catania** (✆ 095-536168; 2 hr. 40 min.; 19€/$22), leaving from both the airport and the Via d'Amico 181 in Piazza Stazione. **Cuffaro lines,** Via P. Balsamo 13 (✆ 091-6161510), run seven buses daily from **Agrigento** (2 hr.; 6.90€/$7.95). **Segesta lines,** Via Paolo Balsamo 26 (✆ 091-6167919), run buses every half-hour (13 times on Sun) from **Trapani** (1 hr. 45 min.; 7.40€/$8.50). From **Rome's** Tiburtina station, there's a daily 9:30pm **Segesta lines** bus (✆ 091-6167919; 12 hr.; 41€/$47).

By Car   Palermo lies on the coastal A20 autostrada that travels the 237km (147 miles) from **Messina** through **Cefalù** (though you'll have to detour part of the way onto the old SS113 road due to an unfinished stretch in the superhighway). From Catania, much of the A19 autostrada cuts through the center of Sicily, but it'll be a relatively quick 208km (129 miles). There are **parking** garages at the train station at Piazza Giulio Cesare 43 (✆ 091-6168297) and near the port at Via Guardione 81 (✆ 091-322649). There's a 24-hour garage in the new city (between the Politeama theater and Ucciardone prison) at Via Archimede 88 (✆ 091-581658).

By Ferry   SNAV (✆ 081-7612348 in Naples, or 091-6118525 in Palermo) runs a 4-hour hydrofoil from **Naples** daily at 9am and 5:30pm (52€/$60 in low season to 77€/$88 in July–Aug) but only from April to October. The return to

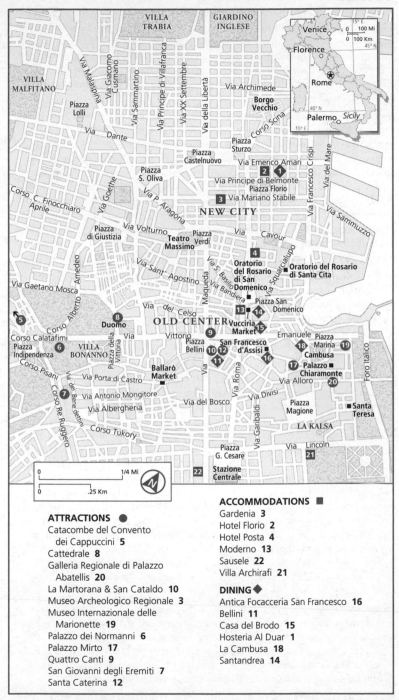

Palermo

VILLA TRABIA

GIARDINO INGLESE

VILLA MALFITANO

Piazza Lolli

Via Malaspina
Via Giacomo Cusmano
Via Sammartino
Via Principe di Villafranca
Via XX Settembre
Via della Libertà

Via Dante

Via Archimede

Borgo Vecchio

Corso Scina

Piazza Sturzo

Piazza Castelnuovo

Via Emerico Amari

Piazza S. Oliva

Via Principe di Belmonte
Piazza Florio
Via Mariano Stabile

Corso C. Finocchiaro Aprile

Via Goethe

Via P. Aragona

NEW CITY

Via Francesco Crispi
Via del Mare
Via Sammuzzo

Piazza di Giustizia

Via Volturno

Teatro Massimo

Piazza Verdi

Via Cavour

Via Sant' Agostino

Via Maqueda
Via S. Basilio
Via Bandiera
Via Squarcialupo

Oratorio del Rosario di San Domenico

Oratorio del Rosario di Santa Cita

Via Gaetano Mosca

Amedeo

Via del Celso

Piazza San Domenico

Via Alberto

Duomo

OLD CENTER

Vittorio

Vucciria Market

Emanuele

Piazza Marina

Corso Calatafimi

Piazza Indipendenza

VILLA BONANNO

Via della Vittoria

Piazza Bellini

San Francesco d'Assisi

Cambusa

Piazza Foro Italico

Corso Pisani

Corso Re Ruggero
Via dei Benedettini

Ballarò Market

Via Porta di Castro

Via Roma

Palazzo Chiaramonte

Via Alloro

Corso Tukory

Via Antonio Mongitore

Via Albergheria

Via del Bosco

Via Garibaldi

Via Divisi

Piazza Magione

Santa Teresa

LA KALSA

Piazza G. Cesare

Via Lincoln

Stazione Centrale

0 1/4 Mi
0 .25 Km

Venice
Florence
Rome
Palermo Sicily
0 100 Mi
0 100 Km

ATTRACTIONS ●

Catacombe del Convento dei Cappuccini **5**
Cattedrale **8**
Galleria Regionale di Palazzo Abatellis **20**
La Martorana & San Cataldo **10**
Museo Archeologico Regionale **3**
Museo Internazionale delle Marionette **19**
Palazzo dei Normanni **6**
Palazzo Mirto **17**
Quattro Canti **9**
San Giovanni degli Eremiti **7**
Santa Caterina **12**

ACCOMMODATIONS ■

Gardenia **3**
Hotel Florio **2**
Hotel Posta **4**
Moderno **13**
Sausele **22**
Villa Archirafi **21**

DINING ◆

Antica Focacceria San Francesco **16**
Bellini **11**
Casa del Brodo **15**
Hosteria Al Duar **1**
La Cambusa **18**
Santandrea **14**

Naples leaves Palermo at 9am and 5:30pm. Year-round, **Tirrenia** (© **199-123199,** or 091-6021111 in Palermo; www.tirrenia.com) runs a first-class-only ship that makes the 11-hour trip nightly, departing Naples at 8:45pm and arriving in Palermo at 7:45am. Cuccettes accommodate two to four people and cost from 66€ ($76) for a spot in a quad without a window. Tickets can be purchased directly at the Tirrenia window in Naples or at any travel agency posting the Tirrenia sticker. Rates are lower off-season.

By Plane   Palermo's **Aeroporto Falcone-Borsellino** (© **147-865643** toll-free, or 091-7020313 for information), also called Punta Raisi, is 30km (19 miles) west of the city center on A29. There are daily direct flights in from all of Italy's major cities and from London, Barcelona, and Frankfurt. The **Prestia & Comandè bus** (© **091-580457**) heads to central Palermo every 30 minutes from 6:30am until the arrival of the last scheduled flight, and costs 4.65€ ($5.35), making stops at Piazza Ruggero Settimo and at the train station. If you're laden with luggage, you can catch a taxi for about 30€ ($35; that's the regular fare plus an obligatory and totally legal 7.75€/$8.90 supplement; add 1.55€/$1.80 for nights plus .25€/30¢ per bag).

CITY LAYOUT   Central Palermo is divided into a **Centro Storico (Old City)** to the south and a **Città Moderna (New City)** to the north by **Via Cavour.** There are two main north-south roads. **Via Maqueda/Via Ruggero Settimo** starts just left of the train station and crosses Via Cavour at the central **Piazza Verdi,** also called **Teatro Massimo** after the theater at its center. Roughly parallel to Via Maqueda to the east is **Via Roma,** a busier and more commercialized boulevard that starts directly across from the train station.

Old Center   Corso Vittorio Emanuele runs east-west through the heart of this area. It crosses Via Maqueda at the **Quattro Canti (Four Corners),** neatly dividing the Old Center into traditional quadrants. To the southeast of this intersection lies **La Kalsa,** once the Saracen Emir's walled quarter for his and other Arab nobles' palaces. These were later replaced with medieval palazzi and baroque oratories, but the neighborhood was badly bombed during World War II. Although still relatively degraded, it is beginning to make a comeback. Though many of Palermo's central sights are here, it's one of the more dubious areas after dark and probably not the best place to base yourself if you're squeamish. To the southwest of Quattro Canti lies the residential **Alberghiera,** home to the vast Ballarò market and more bombed-out zones, and also less than safe after dark. The center's northwest quadrant is **Sincaldi;** aside from the Capo market, it holds relatively little of specific interest to the visitor. Finally, the northeast **Amalfitani** district is the smallest of the quarters (La Cala harbor intrudes to fill half of it), home to the Vucciria fish market. It's so small that the Via Roma division down its middle helps keep the zone less mazelike, a bit brighter, and more commercially oriented.

New City   The center of this grid of easily navigable, broad roads is **Piazza Castelnuovo/Politeama,** where Via Maqueda (now called V. **Ruggero Settimo**) crosses **Via Emerico Amari.** We're more interested in the hotel-, bar-, and restaurant-filled southern half of the New City—centered on such streets as the wide **Via Mariano Stabile** to the port and the pedestrian-only **Via Principe di Belmonte**—than in the sprawling urban residential section to the north.

GETTING AROUND   **By Bus**   Palermo's bus system is modern and efficient, with the **major central lines** routed down Via Roma, Via Maqueda, and Corso Vittorio Emanuele. The most useful **hubs** are the Stazione Centrale/Piazza

Giulio Cesare (the train station), Piazza Indipendenza (behind the royal Palazzo dei Normanni at the end of Corso Vittorio Emanuele), Piazza Verdi/Teatro Massimo, and Piazza Castelnuovo/Politeama. A **bus ticket,** available at most newsstands and *tabacchi* (tobacconists), costs .80€ (90¢) and is valid for 90 minutes; an all-day pass is 2.60€ ($3). Tickets on the Red and Yellow buses are slightly cheaper, at .50€ (55¢).

By Metro   Mostly a commuter railway, Palermo's metro (© **091-6161806**) basically doesn't go near the major tourist sites. Take the bus.

By Taxi   To call a taxi, dial © **091-513311,** 091-513374, 091-225455, or 091-225460. There are taxi stands at the train stations as well as at Piazza Verdi (Teatro Massimo), Piazza Ruggero Settimo (Teatro Politeama), and Piazza Indipendenza. Taxis cost 3.10€ ($3.55), plus 2.05€ ($2.35) for the first kilometer and .65€ (70¢) per kilometer after that. Make sure the meter is always on and running.

VISITOR INFORMATION   There's a **tourist office** in the main train station (© **091-6165914;** www.aapit.pa.it), open Monday through Friday from 8:30am to 2pm and 3 to 6pm, and Saturday from 8:30am to 2pm (Sat evening and Sun hours may be added; call ahead). Besides the city map, make sure you ask for a copy of *Palermo & Provincia Live,* a bimonthly publication with lots of handy tourist information plus an events calendar. The main office, at Piazza Castelnuovo 34 (© **091-583847;** fax 091-586338), is a little less harried and has a few more pamphlets, as well as lots more information on not only the province and day-tripping possibilities, but also all of Sicily. There's a branch at the airport as well (© **091-591698**). The official website for the province of Palermo is also chock-full of useful information (**www.palermotourism.com**).

A FESTIVAL   Palermo's blowout festival, U Fistinu, the **feast of patroness St. Rosalia,** takes place on July 14 and is celebrated with costumed processions and a fantastic fireworks display over the harbor.

FAST FACTS: Palermo

American Express   The local Amex representative is at **Giovanni Ruggieri e Figli,** Via Emerico Amari 40 at the corner of Via La Masa (© **091-587144**). It's open Monday through Friday from 9am to 1pm and 4 to 7pm, and Saturday from 9am to 1pm. To report a lost card, dial © **800-018839.**

Bookstores   By far the best selection of books in English is at **Feltrinelli,** Via Maqueda 395 (© **091-587785**).

Consulates   The **U.S. Consulate** is at Via Vaccarini 1 (© **091-305857**). The **U.K. Consular representative** is at Via Cavour 117 (© **091-326412**).

Emergencies   For general emergencies, call the carabinieri at © **112.** For the city **police,** dial © **113;** for an **ambulance,** © **118** or 091-306644; for **fires,** © **115;** for **road assistance,** © **116.**

Hospitals   The emergency room closest to the center is at the **Ospedale Civico** (© **091-6661111**), off Via Carmelo Lazzaro (in the upper-left corner of the tourist office map). Take bus no. 108 from Politeama or Piazza Indipendenza, or bus no. 246 from the train station. *Warning:* It's not the most modernized hospital, out in no-man's land beyond empty lots and dirt roads. The people at the main emergency desk are the ones who can help you, despite the sign that tells tourists to go to some other office down around the corner (they'll just send you back to the main desk). For an ambulance, dial ℂ **118** or 091-306644.

Mail & E-mail The **main post office** (with fax service) is at Via Roma 322 (ℂ **091-321507**), open Monday through Friday from 8:15am to 6:30pm and Saturday from 8:30am to 1:30pm. There are branches at the **train station** (no phone), open Monday through Saturday from 8:30am to 1pm, and at the **airport** (ℂ **091-6519239**), open Monday through Saturday from 8:10am to 1:20pm.

There's **an Internet cafe, Internett@mente,** at Via Sammartino 3A, near Piazza Amendola and the Politeama Theater (ℂ **091-6121174**), open Monday from 2 to 8pm and Tuesday through Saturday from 10am to 8pm. **The Internet Shop,** Via Napoli, 32/34 (ℂ **091-584146**), is open Monday through Saturday from 10am to 8pm.

Police Dial ℂ **113** for the carabinieri (national police force) and ℂ **112** for the city police.

Safety Palermo is not the safest of Italian cities, with the crime problems of both a big city and a port town, but it isn't much more dangerous than Big Town, USA, either. Yes, there's a strong Mafia presence, but despite splashy headlines and Hollywood imaginations, you're not going to be caught in some kind of goodfellas crossfire. You should be more worried about common thievery and **rampant pickpocketing;** take the necessary common-sense precautions, don't flash valuables, and keep your camera inconspicuous and firmly in hand. Most of the Old Center is a bit dicey, especially after dark—steer clear particularly of the southern half of the Old Center: La Kalsa, the Alberghiera, and around the train station. Stick to Via Roma and Corso Vittorio Emanuele at night. Most of the New City is as safe as any Italian city.

Transit Information The city bus company is **AMAT** (toll-free ℂ **167-018378** or 091-6902690).

SIGHTS TO SEE

Galleria Regionale di Palazzo Abatellis ✿ This is one of the best art museums in Sicily, well worth an hour or two of your time. The ground floor of this 15th-century, Catalan-Gothic-meets-Renaissance palazzo contains the sculpture collection, including one room devoted to Francesco Laurana (look for his bust of Eleonora of Aragon) and another room to a passel of Madonnas by the Gagini clan. Also down here is the 1449 fresco of the *Triumph of Death* ✿, by an unknown but clearly warped hand (possibly Flemish or from the school of Pisanello). The skeleton of death rides an emaciated horse, felling with his arrows an undue number of bishops and popes.

Upstairs is the painting gallery, starring works by Sicily's greatest Renaissance master, Antonello da Messina, including his signature masterpiece, the ***Madonna Annunziata*** ✿. This is an "Annunciation" scene from the angel Gabriel's point of view, wherein a quiet, delicately featured Mary interrupted at her reading stretches out her hand to us from under the voluminous pyramid of an intensely blue shawl. Also be on the lookout for the incredibly detailed 16th-century

A Sightseeing Tip

August sees many Palermo sights locked up and the custodians of smaller churches and stuccoed chapels ordered to hang up their keys for a month. However, some of the major sights actually keep longer hours, reopening from 8:30 to 11pm or so; ask the tourist office for a list.

Malvagna Triptych, by Mabuse; Pietro Novelli's early-17th-century Mannerist *Madonna and Child in Glory;* and Franccsco Solimena's *Return of Joseph's Brothers.*

Via Alloro 4. © 091-6230011. Admission 4.50€ ($5.15). Combo ticket with Palazzo Mirto 5.15€ ($5.90) or with archaeological museum 6.20€ ($7.15). Mon–Sat 9am–1pm; Sun 9am–12:30pm; Tues and Thurs 3–7:30pm. Bus: 103, 105, 139, 225, 824.

Palazzo Mirto   Most of Palermo's glorious and famed 18th- and 19th-century palazzi are rotting behind their massive doors, but this one is open to the public for a glimpse into the lifestyle of Palermo's wealthy caste of centuries past. The noble Filangeri-Lanza family lived in this palace from the 17th century until 1982, and it's furnished exactly as it was in the 19th century, when it included many 17th- and 18th-century pieces. Don't miss the tiny Chinese-style room with its remarkable *trompe l'oeil* ceiling.

Via Merlo 2 (off Piazza Marina). © 091-6164751. Admission 2.50€ ($2.85) adults, free for those under 18 or over 60. Combo ticket with Palazzo Abatellis 5.15€ ($5.90). Mon–Sat 9am–7pm; Sun and holidays 9am–12:30pm. (Also open some evenings in summer.) Bus: 103, 105, 139, 225, 824.

Museo Internazionale delle Marionette (International Museum of Marionettes) ☆ *Kids*   This is one of the world's largest collections of puppets, inventively documenting a cultural and artistic craft heritage that spans the globe from Javanese stick puppets, Indonesian silhouettes, the Turkish "shadow play," and Chinese dolls to Neapolitan *Pulcinella* (Punch and Judy) hand puppets and, of course, Sicilian marionettes—many displayed against original stages and backgrounds.

Marionette shows were Sicily's poor man's theater over the past few centuries, telling tales of Charlemagne and the adventures of his knights, as well as swashbuckling Saracen pirate stories and even opera. No visit to Sicily is complete without attending a show, and on Fridays at 5:30pm (5.20€/$6; 1.05€/$1.20 last Fri of the month), the lights dim and these artistic creatures come to life as warriors in battle or fire-eating dragons. For other puppet plays, see "Palermo After Dark," later in this section.

Via Butera 1 (off Piazza Marina). © 091-328060. Admission 3€ ($3.45). Mon–Fri 9am–1pm and 4–7pm. Closed last 2 weeks in August. Bus: 103, 105, 139, 225, 824.

Quattro Canti (Four Corners) & Piazza Pretoria ☆   Quattro Canti is the nickname for old Palermo's dead-center intersection. Each of the four corners of the intersection is sculpted into elaborate concave corner facades, each containing three sculptural levels stacked atop fountains. The lower level symbolizes the seasons, the middle level contains statues of the four Spanish kings of Sicily, and the upper section is adorned with statues of the patronesses of the city: Santa Cristina, Sant'Oliva, Sant'Agata, and Santa Ninfa. Today the site is choked by heavy traffic and its facades are blackened by pollution, but a recent cleaning has uncovered a glimmer of the grandeur the Quattro Canti must have enjoyed during Palermo's theatrical 17th century.

> **Tips Saving Money**
>
> The purchase of a 2-day combination ticket will gain you access to the
> Archaeological Museum, the Palazzo Mirto, and the Palazzo Abatellis for
> 7.75€ ($8.90), a savings of about 2€ ($2.30). Tickets are available at the
> ticket windows of any of the three sites.

Just south of this intersection, off Via Maqueda, is the raised pedestrian
Piazza Pretoria, centered on a Mannerist **fountain** sculpted for a Florentine
villa in the 1550s but rejected by its commissioners. Palermo bought the thing
and set it, piece by piece (644 in all), proudly at city center, though the local
populace, scandalized by the racy nude figures and lewd glances these statues
were throwing each other across the water jets, promptly renamed it the
Fontana della Vergogna (Fountain of Shame). This hasn't stopped them from
making it a 24-hour sight, dramatically floodlit at night. Alas, the circular fountain is currently visible only through a disappointing peephole, as it's completely
encased in a huge wooden barrel for restorations.

Clearly, Palermo didn't make the Jubilee deadline for restoration, so if by
divine providence the church of **Santa Caterina** capping the piazza's east end has
finally reopened when you visit, pop inside for one of the most elaborate
baroque marble-and-stucco interiors in Palermo. If it's still closed, content yourself with the grand baroque interior of **San Giuseppe dei Teatini,** on the southwest corner of the Quattro Canti (enter from the front on Corso Vittorio
Emanuele or the side on V. Maqueda). Aside from the dome frescoes by Borremans, there's not much to single out inside, but the scale and richness of the decorations make it stand out.

The intersection of Corso Vittorio Emanuele and Via Maqueda. Bus: 101, 102, 105.

La Martorana (aka Santa Maria dell'Ammiraglio) & San Cataldo 🎔🎔

La Martorana may have submitted to a number of disfiguring modifications, but
this mosaic church and its next-door neighbor, San Cataldo—that of the little dark
pink domes—are still some of the finest works of Sicilian architecture. Enter La
Martorana under the surviving 12th-century bell tower of lithe columns and cor-
rugated archways, where you can still make out the original Greek cross layout.
Aside from some minimal baroque redecoration and 1717 frescoes by Borremans,
the interior is pure glittering gold-back mosaic, done between 1140 and 1155 by
the finest artists imported from Constantinople. Notice the dedicatory mosaic of
George of Antiochia—whose generous donation made the church possible—at
the feet of the Virgin Mary, and the symbolic crowning of Christ by Roger II.

In sharp contrast, the only thing the little Arab/Byzantine church of San
Cataldo got for decorations are those pink, mosquelike domelets and some
crenellations ringing the top. Although San Cataldo served for a time as a post
office in the 18th century, today the interior has been stripped wonderfully bare
again, a quiet stony vault whose trio each of aisles, apses, and domes are lit
through the traditionally Islamic stone latticework of the small windows.

Piazza Bellini 3 (next door to Piazza Pretoria). 🕿 091-6161692. Free admission. La Martorana: Mon–Sat
8:30am–1pm and 3:30–7pm; Sun 8:30am–1pm. San Cataldo: Mon–Fri 9am–3:30pm; Sat–Sun 9am–1pm.
Bus: 101, 102.

Cattedrale (Cathedral) 🎔   Palermo's cathedral is not the city's greatest
church; rather, it's a hodgepodge of styles uncomfortably knitted together. The

original 1185 Norman structure (visible in the towers and apses at the east end), was constructed on the oldest and most sacred part of Palermo, replacing a Muslim mosque. Over time, additions and restorations modified the original structure, from the 15th-century Catalan-Gothic overhaul, to the incongruous 1801 baroque dome inflicted upon it by Ferdinando Fuga (who also revamped the interior).

The entrance is partway down the right aisle, through the well-crafted **Catalan-Gothic porch,** with 15th-century wooden doors and a column on the far left, salvaged from the 9th-century mosque that once stood here (carved with a worn Arabic inscription from the Koran). Once inside, to your left are the dark, gated-off chapels containing a block party of **Norman royal tombs,** housing the mortal remains of, among others, **Emperor Frederick II** in the left-front sarcophagus and, partially obstructed, the mosaicked canopy tomb of **Roger II** behind him.

The **former High Altar** sculptural ensemble by Antonello Gagini has since been dismantled and dispersed throughout the church. Its statues line the nave, a bit still serves as the main altar, and three reliefs and an *Assumption* reside in the second chapel of the left aisle. In the Santa Rosalia chapel, in a 17th-century silver urn, are the **ashes of the patron saint** of Palermo. The seventh chapel on the left has a nice *Madonna* statue by Francesco Laurana.

One of the most interesting things about the interior is the **meridian** line transecting the floor of the nave near the altar, central to a system of time-telling instituted in 1794 by astronomer Giuseppe Piazzi in order to bring Sicily up to European standards. The meridian is made of an opening in the roof of a lateral cupola and a long line of brass, bordered by the symbols of the zodiac.

Don't bother paying to visit the boring collection of tombs in the **crypt,** but the **treasury** is worthwhile for the nifty, 12th-century bejeweled caplike crown that Frederick II's wife, Constance of Aragon, was wearing when her tomb was opened in the 18th century.

Corso Vittorio Emanuele. ℂ **091-334376.** Free admission to church, crypt .50€ (55¢), treasury .50€ (55¢). Church: Mon–Sat 7am–9pm; Sun 8am–1:30pm and 4–7pm. Treasury: Mon–Sat 9:30am–5:30pm. Bus: 104, 105.

Palazzo dei Normanni (Palace of the Normans) & Cappella Palatina (Palatine Chapel) 🏵🏵   Most of the royal palace itself—built by the Saracens and enlarged by the Normans (Roger II and Frederick II both held court here) and again later by the Aragonese—has been closed for years. Among the visitable sections are the **royal apartments**—little to write home about—and the not-to-be-missed mosaicked **Sala di Re Ruggero,** one of the few rooms retaining its original Norman look and swathed in details of stylized beasts.

Even with the palace closed, the tour buses line up, bringing visitors to file into Palermo's most stunning sight, the Byzantine Greek mosaics of the **Cappella Palatina** 🏵🏵🏵, built by Roger II in the 1130s. It takes the form of a tiny basilica, every inch covered in rich religious mosaics symbolically glorifying the enlightened reign of Roger II. The craftsmanship is exquisite, using not only gold-backed tesserae, but also silver mosaic tiles to cause the softly lit surfaces to sparkle and gleam in a kaleidoscope of saints and Old Testament characters. The mosaics on the nave walls date from a bit later (1150s) and exhibit a more Roman styling, while the mosaicked *Christ with Sts. Peter and Paul* above the Norman throne are 15th century. The unexpected *muqarna* design—a traditionally Islamic motif—on the ceiling, carved in Lebanese cedar, is surprising considering its placement in a church, but indicative of the multiplicity of character of not only Palermo, but all of Sicily.

Piazza Indipendenza. (C) 091-7054317 palazzo, or 091-7054879 Cappella Palatina. Free admission. Palazzo: Mon, Fri, and Sat 9am–noon. Cappella Palatina: Mon–Fri 9–11:45am and 3–4:45pm; Sun 9–10am and noon–1pm. Bus: 104, 105, 108, 109, 110, 118, 304, 305, 309, 318, 327, 339, 364, 365, 368, 380, 389.

San Giovanni degli Eremiti ☆☆   One of the city's most romantic spots is this ruined 12th-century church and monastery complex on the Albergheria's western edge, whose five unmistakable Arab-Norman red domes are often used as a symbol of the city. The simple church is set amid luxuriant gardens of palm, Indian fig cacti, and citrus and pomegranate trees, where little paths lead to the evocative remains of 13th-century cloisters and into a small rectangular building that was once a mosque.

Via dei Benedettini (at V. Antonio Mongitore). (C) 091-6515019. Admission 4.50€ ($5.15). Mon–Sat 9am–7pm; Sun 9am–12:30pm. Sometimes closed Sun in winter. Bus: 109, 108, 305, 318, 368.

Catacombe del Convento dei Cappuccini (Capuchin Catacombs & Convent) ☆☆   This is one of the most macabre yet fascinating sights in Italy, a subterranean house of the dead for only those entitled (read: rich) enough to afford such an extravagant "burial." The monks began preserving their dead here in 1599, but it soon became fashionable, and sections were created for the wealthy (men and women separate), priests, professors, and children. The plaster-walled network of high, lit tunnels is crammed with the fully dressed, mummified bodies of some 8,000 dead Palermitani dangling from hooks, some preserved in lime or arsenic, but most simply dried out by the naturally controlled climate. The last entombment was in 1920, when 2-year-old Rosalia Lombardo was mummified using a secret chemical injection method that has kept her so remarkably preserved (if a little sallow) she's dubbed the "Sleeping Beauty." But even in death, gravity takes its toll, and many of these aristocrats have simply lost their heads over it.

Via Cappuccini 1 (many blocks up from Piazza Indipendenza). (C) 091-212117. Obligatory "donation" of at least 2€ ($2.30). Daily 9am–noon and 3–5pm. Bus: 327 from Piazza Indipendenza.

Museo Archeologico Regionale (Regional Archaeological Museum) ☆   Palermo's archaeology museum gathers artifacts from across Sicily, from prehistoric times through the Romans, including one of the most comprehensive collections of Etruscan artifacts in the world. It's not a sizeable collection, but it is rich and worth at least an hour of your time. The highlight is the **metopes of Selinunte** ☆, a series of decorative friezes—the only ones in Sicily decorated with sculpture—that show a development from the 6th-century-B.C. archaic style to the more classically inspired 5th-century-B.C. metopes from Temple E (see the section on Selinunte, later in this chapter). Among the rest of the collections, look for the 6th-century-B.C. **oinochoe vase** from the Etruscan town of Chiusi (Tuscany), one of the most elaborate pieces of Etruscan *bucchero* (blackened earthenware) in existence. Among the Roman bronzes are a 3rd-century-B.C. **ram** and a **Heracles fighting a stag** that may have served as the centerpiece for a Pompeiian villa's fountain.

Via Bara all'Olivella 24 (between Piazza Verdi and V. Roma). (C) 091-6116805 or 091-6620220. Admission 4.50€ ($5.15). Combo ticket with Palazzo Abatellis 6.20€ ($7.15). Daily 9am–1:45pm; Tues–Wed, and Fri 3–6:45pm. Bus: 101, 102, 103, 104, 107, 122, 124.

Sanctuario di Santa Rosalia & Monte Pellegrino ☆☆   Looming impressively over north Palermo and thankfully protected as parkland, the sheer cliffs and green cradles of trees covering the 600m (1,968-ft.) **Monte Pellegrino** headland make it look more like it belongs at Yosemite or in some Japanese silk painting than in Sicily. This mountain has seen Paleolithic cave art (casts of

Street Markets—The Best Free Sightseeing in Town

Markets are an integral part of Palermo life and a colorful sight not to be missed. Vendors hawk potbellied silvery fish next to Levi's jeans, spiny sea urchins, bootleg CDs, olives from barrels, and succulent fruits and vegetables picked directly from the vine. Bring your camera (but little else), and guard it well. Close to a dozen markets are in town; here are the best.

Even if you're in town for just a day, the **Vucciria** should be on your list of top sights. Originally a meat market (the name is a bastardization of the French *boucherie*), today it comprises dozens of fish stalls and vegetable stands as well as a few enotecas where you can rub elbows with unshaven regulars for a .25€ (30¢) glass of wine. The market is sunk below the surrounding streets (head down the stairs just up V. Roma from its intersection with Corso Vittorio Emanuele), and some good old-fashioned trattorie hidden here serve the freshest fish in town. This most famous of Palermo's markets has gotten a bit touristy in recent years, but it's still a sight to behold.

More ebullient these days is the sprawling **Ballarò,** in the Albergheria quadrant, spreading roughly from Piazza Carmine to Piazza Casa Professa and Piazza Santa Chiara. It, too, is mainly a food market, but with a better balance of veggies, meat, cheese, and dry goods mixed in among the fish stalls, plus a section selling cut-price clothing and toys.

The **Capo** market has two parts: a long line of mainly **clothing** stalls snaking down the middle and sides of Via Bandiera/Via Sant'Agostino in the city center; and the Via Porta Carini/Via Beati Paoli **food** section off Via Volturno, where many of the streets have been reduced to dirt roads between the buildings and awnings; sometimes it's hard to tell whether you're indeed in a major European city or a North African casbah. Lastly, a treasure trove of **antiques** stalls await you in the short, shady **Piazza Peranni,** behind the bishop's palace off Corso Vittorio Emanuele, but this last breaks down and locks up in the early afternoon.

which are in the archaeology museum), a 3-year battle during the first Punic War between Rome and Carthage, and hordes of Christian pilgrims for the past 4 centuries.

Santa Rosalia, a niece of William II, lived and died as a religious hermit here on the mountain. In 1624, during a vicious plague, she appeared in a vision to a man and showed him the cave where her remains lay unburied. Palermitani carried these relics through the town to give them a consecrated burial, whereupon the plague stopped and Rosalia was swiftly granted patron-saint status. Her cave was outfitted with pews and a baroque foyer to become the popular pilgrimage chapel **Sanctuario di Santa Rosalia,** where the holy water flows from plastic cooler jugs and all the merchandise in the gift shop has been blessed for your convenience. In the cave sanctuary itself, thin spikes of flattened steel cobweb hang from the ceiling like some conceptual modern sculpture—they're to channel the watery mineral drippings from would-be stalactites away from the heads of the devout and collect them as a holy, miraculous liquid.

Hikers may want to reach the sanctuary as the pilgrims have done for the past 4 centuries, by trekking up Monte Pellegrino through a scenic path fragrant with jasmine (about 1.5km or just under a mile) to the top, or, with the opening in 2000 of the asphalt road, by car.

Via Pietro Bonanno (14km/8½miles north of the city center). ℭ 091-540326. Free admission. Daily 7am–7pm (you have to pop in between frequent Masses). Bus: 812. The asphalt road to Via Monte Ercta was reopened in 2000, but Via Bonanno remains closed as of this writing. To reach the ancient pilgrimage road, take bus 139 from Palermo's train station or 837 from Piazza Politeama and get off at the entrance to the old road.

ACCOMMODATIONS YOU CAN AFFORD

Gardenia   Salvatore Genduso is proud of the renovations in his hotel, especially of the fact that the Gardenia has earned three-star status. What was formerly a worn but comfortable pensione has been transformed into a crisp and spacious collection of rooms sporting modular wooden furniture, bedspreads, bed linens embroidered with hotel initials, and parquet floors contrasting with Persian-style area rugs. The bathrooms are all freshly renovated, though the removal of safety mats in the shower stalls means you'll have to be extra careful not to slip. The upper-floor rooms share a wraparound terrace that has been sectioned off to provide some privacy, with the rooms farthest away from the reception enjoying a glorious view of the mountain.

Via Mariano Stabile 136, 90139 Palermo. ℭ 091-322761. Fax 091-333732. www.gardeniahotel.com. 16 units. 65€ ($75) single; 90€ ($103) double; 130€ ($150) triple. Breakfast 5€ ($5.75) per person. AE, DISC, MC, V. Parking in private garage 15€ ($17). Bus: 101, 102, 103, 104, 107, 124. *In room:* A/C, TV.

Hotel Florio *(Value*   Located in the former moldy Principe di Belmonte pension, Hotel Florio was reopened in the winter of 2001–02 under new management. The changeover reveals freshly renovated bathrooms and improved, if not still rather basic, sleeping quarters. There's still no air-conditioning, but the mold is gone, replaced by a bright and welcoming lobby entrance. The location couldn't be more convenient: The pedestrian-only Via Principe di Belmonte, lined by shops and outdoor cafes, is just steps away from the transportation hub of Piazza Castelnuovo and within walking distance of most of the historic center.

Via Principe di Belmonte 33, 90139 Palermo. ℭ/fax **091-6090852**. 15 units. 55€ ($63) single; 75€ ($86) double. Rates include breakfast. MC, V. Free on-street parking. *In room:* No phone.

Hotel Posta   Posta has been family run since 1921 and, despite its lackluster decor, has been a favorite of Italian actors and writers (including Nobel Prize–winner Dario Fo) for years. Everything was redone in 1998, from the modern wood veneer to the white-lacquer furniture, so in exchange for the dreariness, you get sparkling white tile floors, comfortably large rooms, and a central location. The downsides to this excellent central choice are that the paint and lacquer are chipping in spots, and with the city's major thoroughfare just a narrow block away, there is some background traffic noise mixed with those Palermo sirens—but at least it isn't right under your balcony.

Via A. Gagini 77 (parallel to V. Roma, between Piazza San Domenico and V. Cavour), 90133 Palermo. ℭ 091-587338. Fax 091-587347. www.hotelpostapalermo.it. 27 units, 22 with bathroom. 80€ ($92) single; 100€ ($115) double. Rates include breakfast. AE, DC, MC, V. Parking 7.80€ ($9). Bus: 101, 102, 103, 104, 107, 122. **Amenities:** Bar; car-rental desk; 24-hr. room service; babysitting. *In room:* A/C, TV, hair dryer.

Moderno *(Value*   Signore Consalez has been running his tight ship for 40 years and attributes his success to a rigid no-nonsense policy: If he doesn't like the looks of you—even with a reservation—he'll send you and your grubby attire off to sleep on a bench at the train station. If approved, you get to stay in immaculate, modestly sized rooms with shower stalls that glisten and smell faintly of pine. The fourth floor (there's an elevator) has two lucky rooms with a sea view. If you've booked for an extended stay, you may get breakfast thrown in for free.

Via Roma 276 (at V. Napoli), 90133 Palermo. ℂ **091-588260**. Fax 091-588683. 38 units. 60€ ($69) single; 80€ ($92) double; 100€ ($115) triple; 110€ ($126) quad. AE, DC, MC, V. Bus: 101, 107. **Amenities:** Bar. *In room:* A/C, TV.

Sausele   This family-run inn would stand out anywhere in Palermo, let alone in this wasteland behind the train station. You'll be greeted at the reception desk by an amicable staff and their very protective but benign German shepherd, both of whom will escort you past a collection of tchotchkes brought back by the late Signore Sausele on his travels through Asia and Africa. The rooms come with newish wood modular furnishings, high ceilings, and strikingly clean linoleum or tile floors. While rooms on the street can be a bit noisy, those overlooking the courtyard are blissfully quiet. There's a living room–style TV lounge with antiques and white doilies, plus a rustically cozy breakfast room.

Via Vincenzo Errante 12, 90127 Palermo (exiting the train station, turn left, then left again onto Via Oreto, then right). ℂ **091-6161308.** Fax 091-6167525. www.hotelsausele.it. 36 units. 49€ ($56) single; 78€ ($90) double; 105€($121) triple. Breakfast 6€ ($6.90) per person. AE, DC, MC, V. Parking in nearby garage 12€ ($14). Bus: Any to Stazione Centrale. **Amenities:** 24-hr. room service. *In room:* A/C, hair dryer.

Villa Archirafi 𝔎 *(Kids)*   Villa Archirafi is yet another dull exterior that hides the bright decor within. Located near the train station but not *too* near, the hotel borders the *centro storico* and sits only blocks away from the botanical gardens (Orto Botanico). At the back of the lobby, a ground-floor door opens onto a flowery terra-cotta patio. Inside, a narrow staircase (or you can take the elevator) leads up to the guest quarters. Rooms are cheerfully decorated with yellow, blue, and red plaid bedspreads covering firm beds, and the bathrooms sport marble and shiny fixtures. They even installed soundproof windows with internal motorized shades. If you book one of the updated rooms on the first floor, you'll be sacrificing views of the botanical gardens. The suite, at 30% more than the regular rate, is made up of two large rooms, including a kitchenette and large terrace, a reasonable option for families.

Via Lincoln 30, 90133 Palermo. ℂ **091-6168827.** Fax 091-6168631. 33 units. 60€ ($69) single; 90€ ($103) double. Breakfast 6€ ($6.90). MC, V. Free parking. Turn right outside of the train station and walk 5 blocks. **Amenities:** Bar. *In room:* A/C, TV, hair dryer.

GREAT DEALS ON DINING

Thanks to centuries of cross-cultural invasions, Palermo offers a variety of restaurants, from Tunisian to African to Arabic. Naturally, there's plenty of pasta and fish on the menus, but when you simply can't stomach another sit-down meal, head over to the **Mercato Vucciria** (see above). Hidden behind hanging beads, these "ad hoc" eateries do look somewhat intimidating, and you're sure to pay more than your wine-swigging neighbor, but you won't get much more authentic than this. For those unwilling to brave this level of authenticity, the streets across from the Teatro Massimo, especially along **Via Bara all'Olivetta** and **Via dell'Orologio,** are good for bars, trattorias, or pizzerias.

Antica Focacceria San Francesco 𝔎 *(Value) (Kids)* SANDWICHES/POOR MAN'S FARE   This Palermitano institution has been stuffing customers with stuffed focaccia sandwiches and other cheap eats since 1834 in a high-ceilinged space that resembles nothing so much as an old-fashioned train-station waiting room. A huge central counter proudly displays trays of deep-dish *focaccie* fresh from the oven and a bubbling cauldron of steaming *milza* (spleen). A second counter expands the menu to include primi like lasagna, minipizzas, and salads, but these blander options are not really the reason to come here. Regulars usu-ally order a beer and two dishes each, the most popular being *arancie* (giant fried rice balls filled with ragout, peas, and cheese) and split, stuffed *focaccie*, best served *maritata* (with spleen, heart, ricotta, and hard caciocavallo cheese). The squeamish can order the *schietta* (with ricotta and hard caciocavallo cheese only) or *con panelle* (with chickpea fritters).

Via Allesandro Paternostro 58 (on Piazza San Francesco d'Assisi). ℂ 091-320264. Panini and primi 2.50€–8€ ($2.85–$9.20). No credit cards. Daily 10am–midnight. Bus: 103, 105, 225.

Bellini SICILIAN/PIZZA   Spread on the piazza in front of the floodlit domes of La Martorana, Bellini has one of the choicest locations in Palermo: set into the entryway of the recently revived Bellini theater. It is undoubtedly more pop-ular for its outdoor cafe than for its menu, though the pizza is reliable. There's live keyboard music on summer evenings.

Piazza Bellini 6 (off V. Maqueda). ℂ 091-6165691. Reservations recommended. Primi 5.50€–10€ ($6.30–$12), secondi 8.50€–11€ ($9.75–$13) and up for specials; pizze 3.50€–8€ ($4–$9.20). MC, V. Wed–Mon noon–3:30pm and 7pm–midnight (daily June–Sept). Bus: 101, 102, 104, 105.

Casa del Brodo 𝒶𝒶𝒶 SICILIAN   Recommended by countless barmen, trashed by a family of visiting Americans, and confused with a similarly named neighboring establishment by a British guidebook, the verdict is finally in: *"Si mangia veramente bene!"* (The food's great!) Affectionately named "Brodino" by the Palermitani and a favorite hangout for post-theater actors and artists, Casa del Brodo began as a simple workingman's stop for ample bowls of boiled meats. Over a hundred years later (and still a father-son business), the restaurant has evolved into an elegant yet unpretentious Sicilian dining experience, although if you're truly adventurous, you can still order the *lingua in salse varie* (cow's tongue). The antipasto spread is difficult to resist and easily a meal in itself (don't pass up the little fried sardine balls), while the seafood risotto is best described as an abundant cornucopia of shellfish over a few (exceptionally tasty) grains of rice. Get there close to opening time; otherwise, forget about getting a table.

Corso Vittorio Emanuele 175. ℂ 091-321655. Reservations highly recommended. Primi 5€–8€ ($5.75–$9.20); secondi 5.50€–15€ ($6.30–$17). AE, DISC, MC, V. Summer Mon–Sat 12:30–3:30pm and 7:30–11pm; winter Wed–Tues 12:30–3:30pm and 7:30–11pm.

Hosteria Al Duar 𝒶 *(Value* *(Kids* TUNISIAN/ITALIAN   Homesick Tunisians and hungry Palermitani come here for one thing only—the gut-busting *completo tunisiano*, perhaps Palermo's best dining deal. The full menu is a conga line of North African specialty stews and couscous dishes, attracting regulars with a hankering for the *merghes* (veal sausage with Tunisian spices) or the *sceptie* (veg-etable balls of potato, eggs, and greens). Julietta and Simone have created a comfy home away from home in this long, air-conditioned room hung with bat-tered pots and pans and brightened by hand-painted Tunisian plates. You will surely have no room left for the cream pudding, but order it anyway, as it's made with warm milk straight from the cow. If you're not in a Tunisian mood, there's plenty of standard Italian fare as well.

Via Ammiraglio Gravina 31–33 (between V. Principe di Scordia and V. La Masa; don't confuse with V. Benedetto Gravina). No phone. Primi 3.50€–6.50€ ($4–$7.45); secondi 6.50€–8.50€ ($7.45–$9.75); com-pleto tunisiano 9.30€ ($11) with wine. MC, V. Tues–Sun noon–3pm and 7pm–midnight. Open Mon in sum-mer. Bus: 101, 102, 103, 104, 106, 107, 108, 124, 134, 164, 806, 812, 824, 833, 837.

La Cambusa 𝒶𝒶 *(Finds* SICILIAN   Set near the shadows of the immense rub-ber trees of the Garibaldi Gardens, La Cambusa provides the perfect "getaway" to a vast yet quiet corner of the city. Although the menu is limited, it's sufficient enough to have a loyal following who fill the tables by 1:30pm. This close to the marina, you'd be wise to order fish, with your pick of the catch of the day in the cold display, preceded by the *fettucine Cambusa* (fresh pasta with zucchini, shrimp, and cherry tomatoes in a white saffron sauce) or the *bucatini con le sarde alla bottarga* (thick, hollow spaghetti with sardines and topped with grated compressed fish roe). For those looking for a lighter meal, you can pretend to eat less at the ample antipasto buffet.

Piazza Marina 16. ℂ 091-584574. Primi 4€–9€ ($4.60–$10); secondi 6€–8€ ($6.90–$9.20); antipasto buffet 5€ ($5.75) as an appetizer or 8€ ($9.20) as a meal. AE, MC, V. Tues–Sun 1–3pm and 8–11pm.

Santandrea *(Finds)* INNOVATIVE SICILIAN/SEAFOOD   Family run and casually classy, Santandrea is all about candlelit tables on a small Palermo piazza of half-decayed buildings and a forgotten church facade (in winter, they retreat beneath terra-cotta ceilings). Instead of a menu, waiters recite in delicious detail the daily offerings based on the freshest ingredients from the market. The excellent *antipasto misto* is heavy on the seafood. The *spaghetti con bottarga e aragosta* (lobster and dried, grated fish roe) is excellent, as are the fresh tagliatelle with mullet, shrimp, capers, and black olives or in a pesto of zucchini leaves, toasted pine nuts, and sun-dried tomatoes. Roasted or grilled fish is the most popular main course, like *tonno all'agredolce* (sweet-and-sour tuna with mint and onions) or *spigola con asparagi selvatici* (with wild asparagus grown on the premises), though a mix of grilled meats is also tempting. The desserts are all made in-house. Still little-known among foreigners, this place is popular with Palermitani, so book ahead, especially in summer.

Piazza Sant'Andrea 4 (south of Piazza San Domenico). ℂ 091-334999. Reservations highly recommended. Primi 6€–8€ ($6.90–$9.20); secondi 8€–14€ ($9.20–$16). AE, DC, MC, V. Wed–Mon 1–3pm and 8pm–midnight. Closed Jan. Bus: 101, 102, 103, 104, 107.

WINE & DESSERTS

Palermo is still filled with old-fashioned **wine shops.** The market areas are great places to seek out these joints. A favorite watering hole for many an arid throat is in the Vucciria, the **Taverna Azzurra,** Via Maccheroni 9 (no phone), where Nino will hook you up with a .25€ (30¢) shot of wine or a bottle of hearty, frosty Forst beer for .50€ (55¢).

You can find great Sicilian **pastries**—including the rich Sicilian candied-fruit *cassata* cake and treats made of marzipan almond paste that for centuries has been artistically shaped to mimic fruits, vegetables, and other foods (sometimes even whole plates of spaghetti) in miniature—at **Peccatucci di Mamma Andrea,** Via Principe di Scordia 67 (ℂ **091-334835**); or at **Spinnato il Golosone,** Piazza Castelnuovo 16 (ℂ **091-329220**) or Via Principe di Belmonte 107–115. On All Soul's Day, sweets shops flood with *pupi a cera* (delicious marzipan figures of knights and ladies). Spinnato il Golosone makes some rich and memorable flavors of ice cream. If you're in the neighborhood of La Kalsa, head to a legendary favorite in the city wall across from the harborfront, **Gelateria Ilardo,** Via Foro Italico 11/12 (near Porta dei Greci; no phone).

PALERMO AFTER DARK

Extremely proud of having checked the advance of the local Mafia, Palermitani are quick to say how far their city has come with regard to safety. But the truth is, you just won't want to be hanging around after dark in many parts of Palermo. You can consider most of the narrow streets of the old center off limits at night, especially to women, but even men will find themselves fending off advances from prostitutes (both male and female) in Piazza Kalsa, the

Alberghiera, and around the train station or first few blocks of Via Roma. Stick to the New City, which is perfectly safe, and Piazza Verdi and Piazza Castelnuovo, which are both generally full of people.

Palermo's selection of classical arts rivals that of any major European city. The restored **Teatro Massimo,** Piazza Verdi (© **800-655858** or 091-6053315; www.teatromassimo.it), takes its rightful position as presenter of the official season of **theater, music, opera,** and **dance** in a historic venue. (Guided visits inside the theater are available Tues–Sun 10am–4pm.) From November to May, the **Politeama Garibaldi,** Piazza Ruggero Settimo (© **091-6053315**), stages concerts and ballets, while at the concert hall of the Sicilian Symphonic Orchestra in **Teatro Golden,** Via Terrasanta 60 (© **091-305217**), internationally acclaimed soloists team up with leading conductors. The tourist office has detailed schedules of everything going on in town (pick up the *Palermo & Provincia Live* pamphlet here), including lists of restaurants and cafes presenting live music in the summer.

For an early evening of traditional fun for all ages, hunt down a *teatro dei pupi* (marionette theater) to watch professional puppeteers stage elaborate stories from the Charlemagne/Orlando sagas or tales of Saracen warriors. For a long time, this was the poor Sicilian's version of theater—colorful and rousing enough to have survived and established itself as a cultural institution. The **Museo Internazionale delle Marionette** (see "Sights to See," earlier in this chapter) puts on shows every Friday at 5pm from September to July. **Mimmo** puts on 5:30pm shows Saturday and Sunday on Via Bara 52 (© **091-323400**), while over at the Palazzo Asmundo, on Via Pietro Novelli (across from the Duomo), the **Argento** (© **091-6113680**) puts on scheduled performances.

If all you want to do is kick back with a beer or sink a spoon into a gelato, head to **Via Principe di Belmonte** (between V. Ruggero Settimo and V. Roma), a pedestrian strip lined with **bars and cafes,** many of which have outdoor seating in nice weather, a few with live pianists. Or head to **Kursaal Kalhesa** (Foro Umberto 1, unmarked entrance just south of the old gate leading to Piazza Kalsa; © **091-6167630;** www.kursaalkalhesa.it), a cultural center rising from the rubble of the restored Antico Palazzo di Seta (Old Silk House). The building, actually a 15th-century section of the old city fortress walls, features fabulous high stone ceilings and a tranquil raised garden courtyard. The center also does duty as a cafe and wine bar, a bookstore (Italian language only), and a cocktail lounge. An adjoining travel agency offers bike rentals and other travel assistance. The center is open Tuesday through Thursday from 10:30am to 12:30am, Friday and Saturday from 10:30am to 1am, and Sunday from 11am to 4pm.

A SIDE TRIP TO CATTEDRALE DI MONREALE ✫✫✫

Perched majestically on the hillside 8km (5 miles) south of Palermo is the home to Europe's greatest medieval mosaic cycle: the **Cattedrale di Monreale,** the last and greatest of Sicily's Norman cathedrals in the town of the same name. If you do only one thing in Palermo, do this. The polychrome scenes on a shimmering gold background literally carpet the walls, arches, and apses. When Palermo's British bishop Walter of the Mill started building the downtown cathedral, young William II decided in 1174 to exert his independence from that ecclesiastical potentate by raising his own cathedral outside the city. His intention was to surpass the Duomo in Cefalù and at least match the splendor of Constantinople's Santa Sophia on Norman land. His efforts proved more than adequate, in one of the most visually sumptuous day trips you can take anywhere in Italy.

> **Tips Free Museum Days**
>
> The city's experimental closing of the *centro storico* to traffic on the first Sunday of every month was so successful that they've extended it to every Sunday, freeing the entire zone of exhaust fumes and noise pollution. Making the event even more attractive to visitors, admission is free on the first Sunday of every month to the following museums: Galleria Regionale Siciliana, Museo Archaeologico Salinas, Palazzo Mirto, and San Giovanni degli Eremiti.

Even if you have only 1 day in Palermo, spend half of it here; nothing in town can compare.

Few people don't gasp in awe when they enter this cathedral, swathed with 6,430 sq. m (69,212 sq. ft.) of luminous **mosaics** consisting of 130 panels plus an innumerable collection of isolated series. The glittering interior competes with St. Mark's of Venice as the most mosaicked church in Christendom—only less well lit, since few visitors arrive with sufficient coins to feed the 11 1.05€ ($1.20) light boxes. Many panels do stand out, like the Old and New Testament scenes of the central nave, but none more magnificently than the 20m (66-ft.) all-embracing *Christ Pantocrater* in the main apse, whose gaze, thanks to an optical illusion, appears to follow yours from anywhere in the church. The two side apses are dedicated to St. Paul (left) and St. Peter (right). The restored **wood ceiling** of the nave is gorgeous, too, as is the marble inlay work on the **floor,** but don't forget to admire the sculpture work: Especially noteworthy are the Corinthian capitols depicting heads of converted pagans (notice the cross on the capitol above the heads). On the way out, take a closer look at the main portal, framing a splendid 12th-century **bronze door** crafted by Bonanno Pisano.

The attached monastery preserves the beautiful and serene **cloisters,** an Islamic and Byzantine festival of pointed arches supported by twin columns, each pair different from the last: some carved or twisted, some plain, and many inlaid with colored marble and gold mosaic chips in geometric patterns. Every column capital, too, is unique, carved in a beautifully symbolic medieval style with mythological figures and religious scenes. Even with the bused-in tour groups, these cloisters manage to retain a relaxed, contemplative air, helping make this day trip a double escape from the urban chaos of Palermo.

The **Duomo** itself (© 091-6404413) is free and open daily from 8am to noon and 3:30 to 6:30pm. The **Tesoro del Duomo (Treasury)** is hidden behind a red velvet curtain to the left of the altar; admission is 2.50€ ($2.85), and it's open daily from 9:30 to 11:45am and 3:30 to 5:45pm. You can get a peek of the cloisters backed by a panorama of the Conca d'Oro (Golden Basin, referring to the Gulf of Palermo) from the terrace through a door at the back of the nave (terrace admission: 1.55€/$1.80), but you may prefer to visit the actual cloisters (© 091-6404403), open Monday through Saturday from 9am to 6:30pm, and Sunday and holidays from 9am to 1pm. Admission is 4.50€ ($5.15).

For ridiculously large portions of home cooking at remarkably low prices, try the huge **La Fattoria** restaurant, just below town on the main road from Palermo at Via Circonvallazione di Monreale 26 (© 091-6401134). It serves an excellent *cannelloni alla casalinga* (homemade pasta leaves wrapped with meat and ricotta, topped with tomatoes and cheese, then baked) and a tasty *pollo al*

Tips Preparing for the Sunday Lock-Down

Most places in Italy are closed on Sunday, and that includes *tabacchi* (tobacconists). If you plan on going anywhere by bus on Sunday, and especially if you plan to go to Monreale, buy your bus tickets the day before. In a pinch, you can pick up tickets at the newsstand/kiosk in front of Teatro Massimo.

---

forno (oven-roasted chicken). Pizza is served as well. Hours are Tuesday through Sunday from noon to 1am (daily July–Aug). Credit cards are not accepted.

GETTING THERE   Take **bus no. 389** from Palermo's Piazza Indipendenza right to the cathedral. Monreale has a **tourist office** to the left of the cloisters entrance on Piazza V. Emanuele (© **091-6466070**), open Monday through Saturday from 9am to 1pm and Tuesday and Thursday again from 3:30 to 5:30pm, but you're better off stocking up on printed material at the tourist office in Palermo (the Monreale office can provide you with a detail-rich map of the mosaics, however).

THE GREEK RUINS OF SEGESTA EN ROUTE TO ERICE ★★

The temple and theater of ancient Egesta are two of the most beautifully sited classical monuments in the world, set in the middle of nowhere on the rolling hills of the Sicilian countryside. Settled by the Elymi, a people said to have come from Troy, **Segesta** exhibits quintessentially classical features in its 5th-century-B.C. **Doric temple,** perched at the lip of a wide ravine surrounded by a high natural amphitheater of verdant hills. Of the main cities settled by the Elymi, Egesta, rival city of Selinus (Selinunte; see below), was the most powerful, exerting its influence over its sister cities, Erice and Entella, probably in no small part due to the commercial and spiritual implications of its sulfur springs. The city was probably destroyed by Saracen invaders (note the excavations of what may have been the first mosque in Sicily, on the summit of Mount Barbaro, above the theater).

The nearby theater is chipped out of a mountaintop with a sweeping vista across the lush landscape to the Gulf of Castellammare. Undergoing restoration since October 1999, the theater is roped off and accessible only from one restricted platform, making the hike up hardly worth the effort. Before you go, check on whether it has once again begun to serve as the stage for **classical plays** (for tickets and information, call © **0924-951131**). But even with the tour-bus crowds and modern highways nearby, Segesta remains one of the most magical corners of Italy.

Admission to the site is 4.50€ ($5.15). It's open from 9am to an hour before sunset; in summer, it's open until 6pm on show days. The site is wedged between the A29 autostrada from Palermo to Trapani and the old SS113 road (exits from both). There's limited service into Segesta. Trains from **Palermo** (two morning departures daily; 2 hr.; 5.05€/$5.80) stop at the train station Segesta Tempio, about a 1km (⅔-mile) walk from the site.

If after the short hike up to the temple you're too pooped to make it the 1km (⅔ mile) up the hill to the theater, a shuttle outside the cafe/ticket office/souvenir stand (© **0924-952356**) leaves every half-hour. Tickets for the shuttle are on sale in the cafe and must be purchased in advance. They're good for the ride up and back, so don't hike up without a ticket expecting to hitch a free ride down.

4 Erice ★★

112km (69 miles) W of Palermo

Located atop a headland that rises almost vertically above the Trapani plain, **Erice** is an enchanting medieval city of narrow and labyrinthine cobbled streets, rich in mythology, splendid landscapes, and romance. The protection provided by this dramatic and solitary hilltop was a natural magnet for the Elymi, who, after migrating to nearby Segesta, established their spiritual center on the foundations of this impenetrable native Sicani city. Significantly, the city is laid out along the lines of a mystical triangle, with a 13th-century **Norman castle** constructed over the remains of an ancient temple dedicated to the supreme mother goddess, known as Astarte by the Carthaginians, Aphrodite by the Greeks, and Venus Erycina by the Romans.

This thrilling mountaintop setting 743m (2,437 ft.) high conceals flowering courtyards, dozens of medieval structures, and views of majestic Monte Cofano rivaling anything you'd see in Capri. Nevertheless, the exhilarating and windy ride up will set you back at least 30 minutes, making this anything but a convenient base for day trips off the mountaintop. Undeterred by either the effort to get there or the tourist-gouging prices (equaling prices in Taormina), tourists and honeymooners swarm to this landlocked promontory to steep in an environment little changed over the centuries. Adding to the mystique are the clouds that frequently rise (yes, rise) to an altitude great enough to allow them to "descend" upon the narrow cobbled streets, and the times when the only sound is the clip-clop of your soles on the ancient stones. Stay at least one night, when, devoid of raucous groups and school kids, Erice is at its most enchanting.

FESTIVALS   On Good Friday, there's a street **procession of the *misteri* ★,** a parade of sculpted scenes (some are papier-mâché) of the Passion. From late July to early September, the churches around town host a **festival of medieval and Renaissance music,** and in December a Sicilian **folk music festival** comes to town.

ESSENTIALS

GETTING THERE   By Train or Bus   To get to Erice by public transportation, you must pass through the hideous provincial capital of Trapani 14km (8⅔ miles) below Erice on the coast. There are eight to nine trains daily from **Palermo** (2–4 hr.; 6.25€/$7.20) to Trapani. Also from Palermo, **Segesta** (© 0923-20066) runs half-hourly buses (105 min.; 7.40€/$8.50). **Lumia** (© 0922-596490) runs four buses (one Sun) from **Agrigento** (3–4 hr.; 9.50€/$11) to Trapani. From Trapani, the **AST** bus (© 840-000323 or 0923-23222) to Erice makes 10 runs daily on weekdays and 2 on weekends (40 min.; 2€/$2.30).

By Car   Follow A29dir from Palermo or Segesta to the first Trapani exit, then continue along the signposted switchback road up the mountain. If you're arriving by car and staying at the Edelweiss or Moderno, it's best if you park in the lot along the road up to Erice (free, in spite of the "attendant"), as you'll surely crash your car if you attempt to navigate the windy narrow medieval streets— or, worse, crash into a 1,000-year-old building.

VISITOR INFORMATION   The **tourist office** at Viale Conte A. Pepoli 11 (© **0923-869388;** fax 0923-869544) is open Monday through Friday from 8am to 2:30pm.

STROLLING THROUGH ERICE

Erice has plenty of medieval hill town character, and the best way to enjoy it is simply to wander the back streets. If you need an agenda, the tourist information office (or your hotel) can provide you with a brochure listing the numerous historic churches you will encounter as you amble through alleys set with strategically placed flowering vines and pots, baroque balconies, and medieval shop fronts (today, private home entrances).

One excellent church is the **Duomo (Chiesa Matrice)** ✹✹✹, built in 1314 with a fine Gothic porch. The neo-Gothic interior, open from 8am to noon and 4 to 7pm, has a Domenico Gagini *Madonna* on the right aisle. The 15th-century **bell tower** sometimes opens its staircase; at the top, you get a great view over the town in one direction and a panorama across the Gulf of Trapani and the Egadi Islands on the other.

Make sure you head to the southwest corner of town, where you'll find the **Villa Balio gardens**—shaded by thick shrubbery laid out in the 19th century when Count Agostino Pepoli reconstructed the Norman castle in their midst. Beyond the gardens, a path along the cliff's edge leads up to Erice's highest point, the **Castello di Venere** ✹✹, today little more than crumbling Norman-era walls surrounding the sacred site where the Temple to Venus once stood. Piercing the walls are several windows and doorways with spectacular views across the countryside.

ACCOMMODATIONS YOU CAN AFFORD

Edelweiss   Comfortable, friendly, and family run, this pensione is tucked away in a quiet corner of town off Piazza San Domenico. It's a simple place whose large rooms have patterned rugs on tile floors and sometimes a few choice architectural elements like a column-flanked archway (room no. 106). The beds aren't the firmest, but they will do. Some accommodations come with an adjacent room for a third bed—great for families. Six rooms have sea views, four from balconies (though the vista itself is best from the top-floor room nos. 115 and 118). If business is slow, they'll let the half-pension requirement slide.

Cortile Padre Vincenzo, 91016 Erice. ℂ **0923-869158** or 0923-869420. 15 units. 61€ ($69) single; 82€ ($94) double. For stays of longer than 1 day in Aug, obligatory half-pension 60€ ($70) per person. Rates include breakfast. MC, V. *In room:* TV.

GREAT DEALS ON DINING

Almonds feature prominently in Erice cooking, which is otherwise dominated by Trapanese cuisine like couscous covered with a fish stew.

Monte San Giuliano ✹ TRAPANESE/SEAFOOD   Tucked away in a stone courtyard beyond a medieval double gate is Monte San Giuliano, serving some of the best food in Erice. Its fair prices and terrace setting make it stand out, so you may want to book ahead for a seat on the walled flagstone terrace. Try the pungent *pasta con sarde* (pasta with sardines), the savory *busiati San Giuliano* (pasta in an almond pesto with tomatoes, eggplant, and Pecorino added), or the ubiquitous *cuscus alla trapanese* (couscous doused in fish broth and ladled with the meat of various whitefish). Follow it up with *pescespada al salmorgiano* (swordfish with marjoram) or *zainetto dello chef* (beef rolled around tomatoes, mozzarella, and eggplant, then roasted). The desserts here are divine.

Vicolo San Rocco 7 (off Corso Vittorio Emanuele). ℂ **0923-869595.** Reservations highly recommended. Primi 5€–7.50€ ($5.75–$8.60); secondi 7€–10€ ($8.05–$12). AE, DC, MC, V. Tues–Sun 12:30–3pm and 7:30–11pm. Daily July–Aug. Closed Nov 3–16 and Jan 7–16.

Osteria di Venere *✶✶* SICILIAN/TRAPANESE Having never before noticed a "guarantee of hygiene" sticker on a restaurant's storefront, I wasn't sure whether I should feel secure to dine here or dubious about all the other places I've eaten. Nevertheless, this one-room restaurant has a touch of refinement that makes it popular with locals who turn out for the finely observed Sicilian recipes. Luckily, you can dabble in much of it via the *tris di primi,* a trio of pastas that may include pappardelle with shrimp and tuna, ravioli in cream sauce, or *casarecce* prepared *all'Ericino* (with an almond/tomato pesto) or *alla venere* (with eggplant, tomatoes, swordfish, and mint). Secondi run from the expected *involtini alla siciliana* (veal rolls) and fresh fish to more inventive dishes like *calamari ripieni* (stuffed squid).

Via Roma 6 (at Piazza San Giuliano). *✆* 0923-869362. Reservations recommended. Primi 5€–8€ ($5.75–$9.20); secondi 7€–12€ ($8.05–$14). MC, V. Thurs–Tues 12:30–3pm and 8–11pm.

PASTRIES & RUGS

Erice is renowned for two products: pastries and hand-woven rugs. The former is a craft developed and refined by various orders of nuns based in Erice from the 14th to the 18th centuries. The tradition is carried on by the *pasticceria* founded by **Maria Grammatica** in 1950 at Via Vittorio Emanuele 14 near Piazza Umberto (*✆* **0923-869390**), where you'll find sugary almond treats kissed with lemon or citrus juices and made famous by *Bitter Almonds,* the cultural cookbook she co-wrote with Mary Taylor Simetti.

Local **rugs,** about a half-meter-wide (1⅔ ft.) with colorful basic geometric designs in zigzags and diamonds, were traditionally woven from textile leftovers. The best weavers still use scraps on their hand-worked looms, although they also turn their artisans' hands to more innovative designs using first-rate threads and a range of dyes. These woven rugs cost between 50€ and 125€ ($58–$144).

5 Selinunte & Its Temple Ruins *✶✶*

120km (74 miles) S of Palermo, 98km (61 miles) SE of Erice, 90km (56 miles) NW of Agrigento, 88km (55 miles) SE of Trapani

The westernmost outpost of Greek territories in Sicily, **Selinunte** was founded in the 7th century B.C., enjoying a brilliant, if short-lived, existence as an important and powerful capital. Selinunte got rich quick, built a series of outstanding temples to prove it, and then was defeated by Carthage not once, but twice, definitively in 250 B.C., only to fade into malaria-borne obscurity until the 16th century.

One of the most striking things about this archaeological site is the sheer quantity of ruins, stretched out over 284 hectares (701 acres) wedged between the impossible blue of the Mediterranean and a natural plain of hills covered in wildflowers, clumps of low bushes, and the odd lone tree. For the most part uninhabited until the 16th century, the ancient capital city remains uncorrupted by modernity—a few re-erected rows of columns standing on two plateaus backdropped by the wild celery *(selinon)* for which the city is named.

Selinunte's modern support town is **Marinella,** a fishing village turned modest beach resort that has in the past decade boomed from a single road with a few hotels to a thriving little town flanking the eastern edge of the site.

ESSENTIALS

GETTING THERE Getting to Castelvetrano by Train or Bus The gateway to Selinunte is Castelvetrano, a city undistinguished except for the magnificent

Selinunte Tips

You'll need the better part of a day to visit the archaeological site of Selinunte, much of it spent in solitary walks along the picturesque glades. If you're short on time or physically unable to cover the territory, you can save the hike between the East Hill and the Acropolis by driving to the entrances; both zones are served by a parking lot. Be sure to avail yourself of the toilets *outside the main gate,* fill up on carbohydrates before you go, wear a hat and sunscreen, and carry enough water to withstand the relentless rays of the sun.

Ephebe of Selinunte, a 460-B.C. bronze tomb statuette, moved here in 1997 from Palermo's Museo Archeologico Regionale. Located about 23km (14 miles) inland from the ruins, Castelvetrano receives 13 trains daily (seven on Sun) from **Trapani** (68–83 min.; 4.25€/$4.90) and five to seven trains daily (one direct, the others entailing an iffy change at "Alcamo Diramazione" with just a 3-min. window to transfer; 2 hr. 45 min.; 5.85€/$6.70) from Palermo.

To bus it, contact **AST** (© **840-000323,** or 0924-47392 in Castelvetrano), which runs four daily buses from **Trapani** (95 min.; 5.30€–8.50€/$6.10–$9.75 round-trip) through Castelvetrano on the way to Agrigento. **Lumia** lines (© **0922-596490;** www.autolineelumia.it) will also carry you here from **Agrigento** three times daily (once on Sun; 2–2½ hr.; 6.60€/$7.60) and lets you off near the hospital on Via Marinella (wait for the local bus to the ruins across from the Bar Selinus). **Salemi** (© **091-9811120;** www.autoservizisalemi.it) runs a direct bus from **Palermo** to Castelvetrano eight times Monday through Saturday and two on Sunday (2 hr.; 6.40€/$7.35).

Getting to the Site   From Castelvetrano's train station, the *linea urbano* **bus** makes the 20-minute run to Marinella/Selinunte only five times daily (four on Sun), dropping you off across from the site entrance. Purchase tickets (.80€/90¢) either on the bus or at the Bar Selinus across from the hospital and near the train station). The last departure back to Castelvetrano currently leaves at 6:40pm; check with the friendly tourist information office at the entrance to the site for schedule changes before you find yourself stranded. In July and August, an infrequent shuttle bus from outside the archaeological site winds through Marinella. By **car,** the roads are well marked from SS115. From Castelvetrano, just take Via Marinella out of town; the road becomes SS115 and branches left into SS115d.

VISITOR INFORMATION   The **tourist office** at the parking lot/site entrance (©/fax **0924-46251**) is staffed by knowledgeable, helpful, and jolly Italians. They hand out an indispensable site map. Hours are Monday through Saturday from 8am to 8pm, and Sunday from 9am to noon and 3 to 6pm. If you're short on cash, don't put your money on finding a cash machine—the only place you can fill up is at the **money exchange** arm of the post office in Marinella.

A FESTIVAL   In summer (when there's sufficient funding), there's a series of **nighttime performances amid the ruins,** usually at Temple E. These can range from classical plays like *Oedipus Rex* to Southern U.S. gospel, or from productions of *A Chorus Line* to modern dance. Call the **Agenzia Mondo Servizi** in Castelvetrano (© **0924-904555**) for information and tickets.

EXPLORING THE TEMPLES

Selinunte's archaeological site (℡ 0924-46277) is split between two zones: the **East Hill** temples right behind the ticket office and arrival center—nearest to Marinella and boasting the largest temples—and the **West Hill/Acropolis,** picturesquely sited overlooking the sea. Admission is 4.50€ ($5.15); hold on to your ticket to get into the separately fenced West Hill. Selinunte is open daily from 9am to 1 hour before sunset.

Selinunte's temples lie in scattered ruins, the honey-colored stones littering the ground as if an earthquake had struck (as one did in ancient times). Some columns and fragments of temples are still standing, with great columns pointing to the sky. Parts of the zone have been partially excavated and reconstructed as much as is possible with the bits and fragments remaining. All the temples are known simply by letters, since no one is certain to which god any one was dedicated. All have descriptive plaques to provide background; most date from the 6th and 5th centuries B.C.

Near the entrance, the Doric **Temple E** contains fragments of an inner temple. Standing on its ruins before the sun goes down, you can look across the water that washes up on the shores of Africa, from which the Carthaginian fleet emerged to destroy the city. **Temple G,** in scattered ruins north of Temple E, was one of the largest erected in Sicily and was also built in the Doric style. The ruins of the less impressive **Temple F** lie between Temples E and G. Not much remains of Temple F, and little is known about what it was.

After viewing Temples G, F, and E, all near the parking lot at the entrance, you can get in your car and drive along the Strada dei Templi west to the Acropolis. You can also walk there in about 20 minutes. The site of the western temples was the **Acropolis,** which was enclosed within defensive walls and built from the 6th to the 5th centuries B.C.

The most impressive site here is **Temple C,** which towers over the other ruins and gives a good impression of what all the temples might have looked like at one time. In 1925, 14 of the 17 columns of the temple were re-erected, and today, behind scaffolding, efforts have been set into motion to reconstruct even more of the temple. This is the earliest surviving temple at ancient Selinus, having been built in the 6th century B.C. and probably dedicated to Hercules or Apollo. The pediment, ornamented with a clay Gorgon's head, lies broken on the ground. Also here is **Temple A,** which, like the others, remains in scattered ruins. Hippodamus of Miletus laid out the streets of the Acropolis along classical lines, with a trio of principal arteries bisected at right angles by a grid of less important streets. The Acropolis was the site of the town's most important public and religious buildings, and it was also the residence of the town's aristocrats. If you look down below, you can see the site of the town's harbor, now an arid stretch of beachfront property. After all the earthquake damage, you can only imagine the full glory of this place in its golden era.

ACCOMMODATIONS & DINING YOU CAN AFFORD

Lido Azzurro   This beachside crash pad sits at the heart of Marinella's minuscule main drag, across from its own beach and restaurant. The management makes up for the scarcity of amenities with good old friendliness, *plus* the bulk of the rooms have balconies with views of the Mediterranean. The place is kept tolerably clean, the beds aren't *too* soft, the modular furnishings aren't too worn, and the prices are still reasonable. The management may want to pour some baking soda down the bathroom drains, though. The **restaurant** 🍴🍴 is definitely worth a stop, having upgraded both ambience and quality from its previous incarnation as a pizzeria. Expect the most velvety of olive oils (made from their own orchard), delectable antipasti, and fresh fish.

Via Marco Polo 98, 91020 Marinella (TP). ©/fax **0924-46256.** 14 units. July–Aug 44€ ($51) single, 55€ ($63) double; Sept–June 37€ ($43) single, 50€ ($58) double. Rates include breakfast. AE, MC, V. Street parking. No amenities.

6 Agrigento & the Valley of the Temples (★(★(★

129km (80 miles) S of Palermo, 175km (109 miles) SE of Trapani, 90km (56 miles) SE of Selinunte, 256km (159 miles) W of Siracusa

"The most beautiful city of mortals," said the poet Pindar when describing the great city of **Akragas (Agrigento).** These words ring true as you cross the Morandi Viaduct into the **Valle dei Templi (Valley of the Temples),** over an open expanse of flowering fertile hills and the pale peach tones of the imperial Tempio della Concordia (Temple of Concord) crowning the highland in the distance. Of the original 10 Doric temples built on the ridge below the new city line, parts of 9 are still visible in various states of ruin, except for the Temple of Concord—one of the best-preserved Greek temples in the world.

The ancient Greek colony of Akragas was founded around 581 B.C. and flexed its muscle around 570 B.C. under the leadership of one of the cruelest despots of them all, the tyrant Phalaris. Born locally, Phalaris is remembered more for his barbarism—notably, his taste for babies and the invention of the bronze grated bull, a means of torture in which his victims were slowly roasted over an open flame—than for his contribution to the city's fortunes. Under the tyrant Theron, the city continued to prosper, attracting the greatest artistic and cultural minds of the day. Subsequent years saw Agrigento submitting to the humiliation of numerous invasions, from recurrent Carthaginian sackings, to defeat by the mighty Roman Empire in 210 B.C. Renewed prosperity during the Imperial Age relied heavily on the production of wine and grain, making use of its bustling port (now San Leone) and transforming a beaten Agrigento once again into a destination for the likes of Strabo, Ptolemy, and Pliny. Agrigento now makes headlines, thanks to an ongoing State war against the Mafia, concentrated around these parts.

The best way to approach a visit to the area is to plan a bridge of 2 days. This will allow you to devise a plan of attack that will maximize time away from the blight of tour buses and still allow you time to witness one of the most breathtaking and romantic sunsets you will ever see. To beat the crowds, visit the upper temples near sundown, when the grounds once again become a solitary sight and the floodlights flicker on to bathe the temples in a golden glow. Save the lower temples (the area with the entrance fee) for the following morning, but get there before 10:30am because tour groups will by then have completed the first half of their visit, which began at the upper gate. Plan on a full day for a visit to the Archaeological Museum, the Insula Romana, and the Valley of the Temples, and be prepared to cover expansive distances on foot (again). If your time is limited, just hit the temples. With any spare time, head up to the modern city (notwithstanding the eyesore of 600 concrete condominium monstrosities illegally erected under the overwhelming presence of the Mafia) to take in a leisurely itinerary of Norman, Gothic, and Arab sights and spend a few hours shopping and dining.

ESSENTIALS
GETTING THERE   By Train   There are five trains daily from **Palermo** (2 hr.; 6.70€–9.85€/$7.70–$11) and five to eight trains from **Catania,** direct or

with a transfer at Caltanissetta Xirbi (3½–4½ hr.; 9.20€/$11). The **Agrigento Centrale station** (© 0922-26669) is on Piazza Marconi, just down the steps from Agrigento's central Piazzale Aldo Moro. Don't get off at the suburban station Agrigento Bassa.

By Bus   Buses arrive at Agrigento's depot at Piazzale Rosseli just steps away from Piazza Vittorio Emanuele, where you can also pick up a local bus (see "Seeing the Valley of the Temples," below) to the archaeological zone. **Lumia** lines (© 0922-596490) run Monday through Saturday three times a day (once on Sunday) from **Castelvetrano** (the **Selinunte** stop; 2¼ hr.; 6.60€/$7.60) and from **Trapani** (4¼ hr.; 9.50€$11). **Cuffaro** (© 091-6161510) runs seven daily buses from **Palermo** (2 hr.; 6.90€/$7.95). The Agrigento-based **Camilleri-Lattuca & Argento** (© 0922-471886) runs buses four times a day from **Palermo** (2 hr.; 6.90€/$7.95), leaving at 1:30pm, 2:30pm, 5pm, and 7pm. **Autolinea Licata** (© 0922-401360; 2 hr.; 8€/$9.20) runs two buses from Palermo's airport. **AST** (© 091-6208111) provides a shuttle between 7am and 8:45pm from **Catania**'s airport to Catania's train station (15 min.); **SAIS** (© 0922-595933) has hourly runs (fewer on Sun) between 11am and 9pm from **Catania**'s train station and Agrigento (2½ hr.; 10€/$12); the SAIS office is behind the booth on Via Ragazzi 99.

Bus nos. 1, 2, and 3 run from in front of the train station down Via dei Templi into the Valley of the Temples. You can get off at the Museum/Insula Romana or stay on all the way to the Posto di Ristoro (aka Piazzale dei Templi), a pricey cafe/souvenir stand at the entrances to the two temple zones. Stops on this route are not obligatory, so be sure to alert the bus driver when you want to get off.

By Car   Agrigento lies on the coastal SS115, which you can follow from Castelvetrano near Selinunte or from Siracusa (the latter drive is interminable, passing by industrial panoramas worthy of the New Jersey Turnpike). From Palermo, take the SS121/SS189.

VISITOR INFORMATION   In Agrigento, five unrelated local offices deal with provincial, local, municipal, and regional information. You'll find the best information about the site, or at least the most willing staff, at the little Posto Ristoro **booth** (© 0922-26191) in the parking lot near the entrance to the archaeological site. It's open daily from 8:30am to 7pm (shorter hours in winter; also expect the booth to be closed for "coffee breaks"). There's an adjacent **money change** booth. If you need help with accommodations in town, there's an **Ufficio Informazioni Turistiche** (©/fax 0922-20454) above the train station just behind Piazzale Aldo Moro at Via Cesare Battisti 15, your first left off Via Atenea. For a **taxi**, call © 0922-26670 or 0922-21899.

A FESTIVAL   The temple zone is even more lovely than usual in early February during the **Festival of Almond Blossoms**, a folkloric harvest celebration with music, flag tossing, and traditional foods.

SEEING THE VALLEY OF THE TEMPLES
MUSEO ARCHEOLOGICO REGIONALE (REGIONAL ARCHAEO-LOGICAL MUSEUM) 𝕽𝕽𝕽   The rich collection of temple leftovers, pottery fragments, and even prehistoric findings in this museum (© 0922-497111) make it one of the most important archaeological museums in all Sicily. The entrance is past the little garden of the San Nicola (see below), along a catwalk over the Roman **Comitium**, a 4th-century-B.C. assembly arena (originally a Greek Ekklesiasterion), and past the **Oratorio di Falaride (Oratory of**

Phalaris), a funerary monument said to have been built above the first tyrant's palace. Among the painstakingly classified and labeled items is an outstanding collection of superbly painted vases spanning the 6th to 3rd centuries B.C. in room no. 3. Room no. 6 is devoted to the Temple of the Olympian Zeus (see below), along with the museum's most striking exhibit, a reconstituted 8m (26-ft.) giant *telamon* 𝕽—sculpted male figure—stacked up against one wall in its original position as a supporting column. In the rest of the museum, look for the 2nd-century-B.C. alabaster sarcophagus of a child, carved with happy childhood moments and a touching death scene; the 5th-century-B.C. **Efebo (Ephebe),** a masterpiece of masculine features and feminine lines; and the 5th-century-B.C. painted krater from Gela showing a battle with the Amazons. Admission is 4.50€ ($5.15; combination ticket with the temple archaeological site 6€/$6.90). The museum is open daily from 9am to 1:30pm and Wednesday through Saturday from 2 to 6pm (last ticket sold ½ hr. before closing).

Next to the entrance to the museum is **San Nicola,** a small Norman church built on the foundation of Greco-Roman ruins. Inside is the **Sarcofago di Phaedra (Sarcophagus of Phaedra),** a Roman-era work dating to the 2nd or 3rd centuries, and an enamel-on-wood **Crucifix** above the altar. The church, recently reopened to the public, is open from 10am to 2pm Monday through Saturday from September to June.

INSULA ROMANA (ROMAN QUARTER) 𝕽   Across from the museum is the Roman–Hellenistic Quarter, over 10,000 sq. m (107,639 sq. ft.) of excavated urban living, inhabited as far back as the 2nd century B.C. and covered by some wonderful 4th-century Roman polychrome floor mosaics. You can see some terra-cotta storage vases still stuck in the mortar. It's worth a walk through the grid for a look under those glass huts at mosaic floors laid out as rhomboids, magical symbols, and gazelles. Admission is free; the quarter is open daily from 9am to 1 hour before sunset and is across the street from the Museo Archeologico Regionale (through a less-than-obvious gate). Bring a picnic lunch.

TEMPLES   Down the road, you'll arrive at the main attraction of Agrigento—a series of 5th-century-B.C. Doric wonders surrounded by olive and almond trees (© 0922-20014). To the right of the road, past the ticket booth, are the massive, jumbled remains of the **Tempio di Zeus Olimpio (Temple of Olympian Zeus),** or **Olympieion.** At 110 by 52m (361 by 171 ft.), this is the largest Doric temple ever attempted, begun in 480 B.C. but left unfinished when the Carthaginians invaded in 409. Earthquakes and wars brought some of it down but, sadly, most of the stones were carted off as building materials for the construction of the nearby wharf of Porto Empedocle.

It's hard to fathom the sheer size of the thing—little remains other than a weedy mound of ancient cut rubble—but here are some ciphers to help. Each column was over 17m (56 ft.) high and 4m (13 ft.) thick at the base—there's half of one capital sitting near the top of the rubble pile. Lying in the dust nearby is a worn replica of one of the *telamones,* or columns carved as a man (the original is in the museum up the road). This 8m (26-ft.) giant took up less than half the height of the columns (never mind adding in the steps, pediment, and roof). Beyond is a pile of cut blocks with U-shaped grooves, which were used to help haul them into place.

Surging above the far end of the sacred hill are the four remaining columns of the **Tempio di Dioscuri (Temple of the Dioscuri).** Probably dedicated to the earth gods Demeter and Persephone, the temple dominates an area dating to the first generation of settlers, pockmarked with the remains of round altars, *bothroi* (sacred wells used for sacrifice and libations), and an agora.

Admission to the archaeological site is 4.50€ ($5.15; combination ticket with the archaeological museum is 6€/$6.90). It's open daily from 8:30am to 1 hour before sunset.

THE TRIO OF TEMPLES 🏛🏛🏛   The postcard trio of temples is up off the east/left side of Via dei Templi, balancing atop a wide ridge with a wash of olive groves spilling down on the Agrigento side and a partially man-made cliff falling toward the sea on the other. Nearest the lower entrance of the valley are the ruins of the **Tempio di Ercole (Temple of Hercules),** the oldest shrine here (500 B.C.). Most of it is in piles, but eight 10m (33-ft.) columns have been re-erected and you can scramble about the remains of the *cella* (the sacred central chamber of the temple).

Just up the road, past a **paleo-Christian necropolis** (closed to visitors as of this writing) with tombs honeycombed into the rocky ground and tunnels under the road, is the spectacular **Tempio della Concordia (Temple of Concord).** Raised in 430 B.C., this is the best-preserved and most complete temple in the Greek world outside the Theseion in Athens and the Temple of Hera at Paestum. In the days when pagan temples were being burned and razed, this temple survives mostly intact because Agrigento's bishop converted it into a church in the 6th century. Thanks to classically minded 18th-century purists, the temple was restored to its original state, although it was probably at this point that the name "Concord," taken off an unrelated inscription on one of the stones, stuck. The cella and 34 Doric columns all still stand, supporting an architrave and miraculously complete entablatures on both ends. The temple is in such good shape, they've fenced it off to keep us from stomping all over it.

The road continues to slope up, past ancient city walls on the right perforated with Byzantine tombs, to the broken-toothed **Tempio di Hera (Temple of Hera),** also incorrectly called the Temple of Juno. It was built around 450 B.C. at the very edge of the cliff, probably as a mirror image to the one just below. Twenty-five of its 34 columns remain standing, with bits of the entablature intact on one end, while the blackened walls of the cella stand as a reminder of the temple's destruction by fire at the hands of the Carthaginians. The temple is partially disfigured by scaffolding and remains closed indefinitely, for fear of another landslide at its edge like they had in 1976. A low, stepped wall on the far side makes (wind notwithstanding) an ideal spot to picnic with the panorama of temples before you.

ACCOMMODATIONS YOU CAN AFFORD

Concordia 🏛 *Value*   If you aren't forking over the dough for the Villa Athena (see below), call here first. The Concordia is an eternal Agrigento favorite, an inexpensive family-run inn with by far the warmest reception in town. Although the cots are lazy-springed and the bathrooms cramped, the modest-size rooms are kept clean, the modular veneer furnishings are nice enough, and the stuccoed walls are repainted regularly. Some rooms have air-conditioning. Best of all, you get to take advantage of the terrific lunch menu at their trattoria, La Forchetta (see below).

Piazza San Francesco 11, 92100 Agrigento. 📞/fax **0922-596266.** 30 units. 25€ ($29) single; 45€ ($52) double. Rates include breakfast. AE, DC, MC, V. Take Via Pirandello (left parallel to V. Atenea), which becomes Via San Francesco; the hotel is about 150m (492 ft.) down on the left. *In room:* TV.

WORTH A SPLURGE

Villa Athena ✩✩✩   The rates at this gem make its inclusion in this guide a tough call. But this 18th-century villa just may have the most fantastic location of any hotel in Italy: right inside the archaeological zone and across an olive grove from the Temple of Concord, whose practically perfect Doric profile is framed by the windows of half the rooms (best from room nos. 302–304 and 202–206). If you can tear your eyes off the ancient splendor, you'll see that the carpeted rooms are smallish but comfortable, with genuine beds and mattresses and nice functional pieces, but without the location, certainly not worth the price tag. Several restaurant and bar spaces are set into terraced gardens that overlook the temple, plus a pool at the base for washing off the dust of a day. Book far in advance for this romance, particularly if you want one of the coveted temple-facing rooms with a terrace, especially during summer.

Via dei Templi 9, 92100 Agrigento. ⓒ **0922-596288.** Fax 0922-402180. www.athenahotels.com. 40 units. 130€ ($150) single; 210€ ($240) double. Rates include breakfast. AE, DC, MC, V. Free parking. Take Via Petrarca (or bus 1, 2, or 3), following signs into the archaeological zone; it's a private drive to the left after the museum (ask the bus driver to let you off). **Amenities:** 2 restaurants; bar; outdoor swimming pool; concierge; tour desk; car-rental desk; 24-hr. room service. *In room:* A/C, TV, minibar, hair dryer.

GREAT DEALS ON DINING

If you're planning a day at the temples, pack a lunch because there's nothing worth eating at the sandwich bar at the site anyway, and whatever is leftover by the bus crowds is ridiculously expensive. Most of the hotels near the archaeological zone have first-class restaurants, but even these cater to the demands of an international clientele with international wallets. For *nonna's* cooking, you'll have to head to Agrigento's *centro*.

AGRIGENTO CENTRO

La Corte degli Sfizi SICILIAN   La Corte degli Sfizi occupies both an indoor cantina space and a peaceful garden courtyard (in the palazzo opposite the entrance) with a wooden deck and hanging lights for meals alfresco. To entice the masses, the amiable owner offers a tourist menu, drinks included, for a mere 15€ ($17). The menu is über traditional, topped off by the pre-eminent *cavatelli alla Norma* followed by an order of grilled fish, brought in fresh from the waters off the beachfront hamlet of San Leone.

Cortile Contarini 4 (perpendicular to V. Atenea, near the end). ⓒ **0922-20052.** Primi 4.50€–6.50€ ($5.15–$7.45); secondi 4.50€–6.50€ ($5.15–$7.45); fish dishes 7€–10€ ($8.05–$12). AE, DISC, MC, V. Fri–Wed noon–3pm and 7–10:30pm; daily July–Aug.

La Forchetta ✩✩ *Value* AGRIGENTESE/SICILIAN   La Forchetta has grown from its humble osteria roots, but one thing hasn't changed: It still serves the best food in town at prices that can't be beat. Gone is the bare room where locals filed in and grabbed their own bread from the kitchen. Now you get bona fide ambience (seven tables amid pine paneling and historic photos) to go with your meal, and tourists have become the major clients, at least in summer. The prices, however, have stayed low, and, if anything, the food's improved. The judiciously spicy *penne pirandello* (pasta with tomatoes, sausage, pepperoncino, and cream) is delicious, as is the *pasta del giorno* (pasta of the day), which is usually made with fish or eggplant. Secondi are simple, be it a *panata siciliana* (breaded steak) or a *cotolette di agnello arrosto* (roast lamb chop).

Piazza San Francesco 11. ⓒ **0922-596266.** Reservations recommended. Primi 4.50€–6.50€ ($5.15–$7.45); secondi 6€. MC, V. Mon–Sat noon–3pm and 7–11pm; Sun 7–11pm (summer only).

EN ROUTE TO SIRACUSA: THE MAGNIFICENT MOSAICS OF PIAZZA ARMERINA

In the hamlet of Casale outside the small city of Piazza Armerina lies the **Villa Romana del Casale** ⭐⭐⭐ (© **0935-680036**), a 4th-century villa carpeted in some 11,521 sq. m (122,974 sq. ft.) of the most extensive, intact, and colorful ancient mosaics in western Europe, and certainly in all of the Roman world. Situated on the heights of inland Sicily's hills, Piazza Armerina was destroyed by William I for the treasonous hospitality its people gave to rebel barons and was then rebuilt by William as a patrimony of 12th-century churches and baroque palaces. While most visitors make a beeline from the train station to the mosaics on the fringes of town, the "modern" Piazza Armerina, with its narrow, winding cobbled lanes and a concentration of **baroque monuments** ⭐ in the *centro storico*, is charming enough to hold your interest for at least an afternoon.

ESSENTIALS

GETTING THERE   No matter where you're coming from, you'll have to change buses in Enna. **SAIS** (© **0935-500902**) handles the connections from Enna to Piazza Armerina (40 min.; 2.60€/$3) nine times daily, as well as connections into Enna from Palermo (90 min.; 7.75€/$8.90) and Catania (1 hr., 40 min.; 6€/$6.90). The trip gets a little complicated from Agrigento because of an additional connection in Caltanisetta and is practically undoable from Siracusa, requiring two bus companies and as many transfers. In these last two cases, it'll be worth your time and money to rent a car for the day or make it an overnight trip.

Once in Piazza Armerina, the B bus (.80€/90¢) makes the 15-minute run to the Villa Imperiale at Casale hourly (look for buses marked PIAZZA ARMERINA/MOSAICI SERVIZIO URBANO) from 9 to 11am and 4 to 6pm (return trips hourly 9:30–11:30am and 4:30–6:30pm).

VISITOR INFORMATION   Piazza Armerina has a friendly **tourist office** inside the palazzo at the top of Via Cavour (© **0935-680201;** fax 0935-684565), open Monday through Saturday from 8am to 2pm.

SEEING THE MOSAICS

Villa Romana del Casale ⭐⭐⭐   Still shrouded in mystery is the identity of the wealthy patrician and patron of this vast country villa and surrounding complex. Experts cite clues, and lots of 'em, suggesting that this was the hunting lodge of Maximanus, Diocletian's co-emperor. Beginning with the former grand entrance, the faint remains of a main triumphal arch and dual troughs for horses intimate the stature of the head of the household. Also look for the recurring **heart-shaped emblem**—often resembling Mickey Mouse ears and symbolic of Hercules—and the **"coat of arms"** for the emperor, aka Massimiliano Hercoleo.

More interesting than the clues is the notion that the villa's 40 sumptuously decorated rooms represent less than 50% of the area yet to be excavated, with the kitchens and stables still buried under the now-hardened mud deposits left by a disastrous 12th-century flood. Ironically, it was this very event that has allowed these remarkable mosaics to survive in such a state of preservation, blanketed as they were for centuries in a moist protective layer.

The current visit begins with an overview of the extensive system of heating and water supply for the baths. Notice the craftsmanship of the pavements inside the baths' tiled rooms (probably attributable to North African artisans), which exhibit early attempts at perspective through the use of darkened areas around the feet to represent shadows. This being a hunting lodge, many of the scenes involve big-game hunting and other sports, no more spectacularly than in the **Great Hunt,** a mosaic scene undulating for 60m (197 ft.) in a catalog of animals found throughout the ancient empire. Most are shown being captured alive and herded onto the ships that will carry them to Rome to be sacrificed in stadium spectacles (look for the North African lion, rendered extinct by such Roman excesses). Note that the sunken areas of the corridor, caused by the flood mentioned earlier, resulted in an area of mosaics even more vivid than those in adjacent areas. In the nearby *palestra* (gym), you'll see a **Chariot Race** held at Rome's Circus Maximus (another clue to the ownership of the villa), complete with cheering fans. But the most famous scene is hands-down the **Ten Bikini Girls,** a lineup of female athletes either working out at the gymnasium or competing in various events and clad in strapless bikinis. Part of an earlier layer of geometric flooring, dating to the Byzantine era, is left exposed in the corner. At this point, the catwalk leads outside to an elliptical peristyle and into the **triclinium,** a three-apsed dining room decorated with the **Twelve Trials of Hercules** (two more clues: the shape of the building and the decorative theme). The peristyle featured a central basin indispensable during these extended gluttonous food orgies—often lasting for days—when Roman high society would make room for the constant supply of delicacies by regurgitating the last course.

The path back into the private apartments leads first to the children's rooms, especially amusing for their pint-size versions of the main halls' majestic scenes and a red disc **alphabet** translated into both Greek and Roman. Finally, be on the lookout for the mosaic **erotic couple** 🕱 stealing a kiss in one side room. This is where the master of the house would sneak away for illicit rendezvous, but by the pristine state of preservation of the entire series, this room apparently didn't see much action.

6.4km (4 miles) SW of Piazza Armerina, off SS117 bis. 🕾 **0935-680036.** Admission 4.50€ ($5.15). Open 8am to 30 min. before sunset (ticket office closed 1–3pm). By car from the city center, follow Viale Libertà (which becomes V. Manzoni, then SS117 bis) to the intersection with the Ristorante da Battiato. Turn left and follow the signs for I MOSAICI.

A GREAT DEAL ON DINING

Pepito RUSTIC SICILIAN   It's amazing what table linens and cloth napkins can do. Pepito is simple without being bare, but even neighborhood trattorie are expected to display a minimum amount of propriety, after all. It's welcoming without being overbearing, and there's an upstairs dining area for those looking for a more elegant setting. Expect hearty mountain dishes like the tasty *coniglio alla cacciatore* (rabbit with artichokes and olives in a sauce of tomatoes and white wine), and a small but pleasingly fresh "Wendy's Fixins"–type table for the antipasto spread. This far inland, you'll need to give advance notice for the paella alla Valenciana—well worth the planning.

Via Roma 140 (near the corner of V. Sturzo). 🕾 **0935-685737.** Primi 4.50€–6.50€ ($5.15–$7.45) secondi 5€–8€ ($5.75–$9.20). AE, MC, V. Wed–Mon 9am–midnight.

7 Siracusa 🕱🕱🕱

256km (159 miles) E of Agrigento, 87km (54 miles) S of Catania, 330km (205 miles) SE of Palermo, 182km (113 miles) S of Messina

One of the most influential, powerful, and culturally rich cities in Magna Grae-cia, modern-day **Siracusa (Syracuse)** benefits from a perfect seaside location, a thriving trading port, and some fantastic ruins—including one of the world's largest intact Greek theaters. Siracusa was settled by Greeks from Corinth in 733 B.C. and almost immediately began a systematic suppression of and expansion to neighboring territories. With a perfect location at the center of the Mediterranean world, Siracusa eventually fell under tyrant rule. By 480 B.C. it had become the most important center in Sicily and a major political and military player among the most powerful civilizations in the Mediterranean, to the great displeasure of Athens and Carthage. At its height, Siracusa welcomed such greats as Archimedes, whose mathematic genius ultimately led to the city's defeat at the hand of the Romans in 212 B.C.

Some 2,700 years later, as the heir to an incredible artistic and archaeological patrimony, Siracusa offers the visitor a singular look into the ancient world, as well as a window into the Sicily of yore. Several implausibly juxtaposed ruins stand amid dusty cobbled streets and crumbling facades, but as the allure of history becomes a significant impetus for renovations, that picturesque snapshot is bound to fade into obscurity.

If you can actually find a vacant room, Siracusa is a good place to slow down and catch your breath for a day or two. It has plenty of top-notch sights to keep you busy, and the zone where you should base yourself—the laid-back and historic zone of Ortigia—supports a wonderful array of cafes, seaside strolls, and alfresco restaurants. And an overnight visit to Siracusa will allow you to take advantage of the city's sights with enough spare time to wander amid the mythical bounty of the morning market.

ESSENTIALS

GETTING THERE   By Train   From **Palermo,** you can take one of five daily trains through **Catania** (3½–4 hr.; 11€/$13), from where there are at least hourly runs (85 min.; 4.65€–6.05€/$5.35–$6.95) on to Siracusa or through **Messina** (about 4 hr.; 11€–15€/$12.65–$17.25); from where there are at least hourly runs to Siracusa (3–4 hr.; 8.75€–12€/$10–$14). If you buy a "through ticket" from Palermo, you'll save around 3€ to 4€ ($3.45–$4.60). **Siracusa's station** (© 0931-67964 or 0931-66640) is on the mainland, .8km (½ mile) west of the *centro storico* and south of the archaeological zone.

By Bus   Only **Interbus,** Via Trieste 28, Siracusa (© 0931-66710 in Siracusa, or 095-532-716 in Catania), currently services Siracusa on long-distance routes, so if you're headed out from a provincial town on another bus service, you'll have to change to Interbus in one of the major cities listed here. Interbus runs continuous daily service departing from both **Catania**'s airport and Catania's train station (1¼ hr.; 4.10€/$4.70; reduced service on weekends). It runs two to three buses daily to and from **Palermo** (3 hr.; 13€/$15; reduced service on weekends). You can also hop on a **SAIS bus** (© **800-920900; www.saistrasporti.it**) in **Rome**'s Piazza della Repubblica for a 7:30am departure that will get you into Siracusa at 10pm that night (14½ hr.; 45€/$52).

By Car   From **Piazza Armerina,** follow the scenic, twisting, fragrant SS124 through the mountains. From **Agrigento,** take this hideous stretch of SS115 all the way. From **Palermo,** take the A20 autostrada east toward Cefalù, exiting onto the A19 through Enna and the interior to where it hits the SS114 just south of Catania, and follow that into Siracusa. From **Messina,** you can follow the coastal SS114 all the way through **Taormina** and **Catania** to Siracusa.

GETTING AROUND   City **buses** cost .80€ (90¢) and make circular routes. Most start and end at Piazza della Posta just over the bridge on Ortigia. Although line nos. 21 to 23 stop at the train station and continue to Ortigia,

Travel Tip: The Antico Mercato

Dating to 1899, the restored Antico Mercato, Via Trento 2 (© 0931-449201), is designed in the style of a typical Arab covered market, with lofty rooms connected to an enclosed arcade set around an open central courtyard. The space is now an invaluable resource for tourists: Services include a bookstore and bike rental (4€/$4.60 per hour; 13€/$15 per day), tourist information office, bar/cafeteria/tearoom, and Internet access. Chairs are set up in the courtyard around a baroque fountain and shaded by canvas umbrellas, providing the perfect ambience for some downtime or for a series of special events (**www.anticomercato.it**).

these run infrequently; you're better off turning left out of the station and walking a few blocks to Piazza Marconi (aka Foro Siracusiano), where just about every line passes. From here, it's an easy 5-minute walk down Corso Umberto to Ortigia. For a **taxi,** dial © **0931-69722,** 0931-60980, or 0931-64323.

VISITOR INFORMATION   Make a beeline to the **Antico Mercato** (see above) before heading to any of the official tourist information offices around town. Meanwhile, there's a **tourist office** on Ortigia at Via Maestranza 33 (© **0931-464255;** fax 0931-60204), open Tuesday through Friday from 8:30am to 1pm and 4:30 to 7pm, and Monday and Saturday from 8:30am to 2pm. There's also an office in modern Siracusa at Via San Sebastiano 45 (© **0931-67710** for the desk, 0931-482100 for the main office; fax 0931-67803), across from the San Giovanni catacombs. June through September, hours are Monday through Saturday from 8am to 7pm and Sunday from 9am to 1pm; October through May, hours are Monday through Saturday from 8am to 2pm and 3 to 6pm. Finally, there's an **info kiosk** at the entrance to the archaeological zone at **Largo Anfiteatro** (© 0931-60510), open daily from 8:30am to 7pm (they may close during *riposo* in winter). For information before you go, log on to **www.apt-siracusa.it** or **www.flashcom.it/aatsr.**

FESTIVALS & MARKETS   Siracusans parade a statue of their patron **Santa Lucia,** an opulent figure of solid silver, around with pomp and ceremony on December 13 and again the first two Sundays in May. The city also sponsors summertime **performances in the ancient Greek theater** (even years only). These tend to be of classical plays translated into Italian (some of which even premiered in this very theater 2,500 years ago). Tickets can be purchased at the theater, or call toll-free within Italy (© **800-907080**). Tickets in the general seating area cost 15€ to 35€ ($17–$40); reserved seats cost 35€ to 77€ ($38–$88), depending on the performance and location. Check with the box office for deep discounts on seats at weekday performances. Information on performances is available via the Istituto Nazionale (© **06-44292627;** fax 06-44260260; www.indafondazione.org) or on Siracusa's tourist website (**www.apt-siracusa.it**).

SEEING THE ARCHAEOLOGICAL ZONE ON THE MAINLAND

Archaeological Park of Neapolis ⭐⭐⭐ *(Kids*   This vast archaeological park contains Siracusa's greatest concentration of ruins. It's divided into three main sections: the *latomie* (stone quarries), the Greek theater, and the Roman amphitheater, all of which you can see in about 2 hours. The first two are together beyond the main gate. Hold on to your ticket, for upon exiting the

Greek theater/latomie area, you backtrack up the souvenir stand–lined road to enter the amphitheater area, where you must again present your ticket.

Along the entry path past the Roman amphitheater area (see it on the way out), you'll see on your left the few columns still standing and the long stone base of the 3rd-century-B.C. **Altar of Hieron II.** At 196 by 23m (643 by 75 ft.), it's the longest altar ever built and was used for sacrifices of entire herds of cows. Veer right onto the path down to the **Latomia del Paradiso (Paradise Quarry),** an ancient quarry now overgrown with a jungle of orange and lemon trees. Along the back wall is a narrow cavern 23m (75 ft.) high, 64m (210 ft.) deep, and only about 7.5m (25 ft.) wide. Used as a prison for the survivors of the Athenian army after their defeat in 413 B.C., the cave was later dubbed by Caravaggio the "Ear of Dionysius"—due to either its pointy shape, like the ear on a satyr, or its remarkable acoustics, which amplify even the quietest whisper. According to local legend, these remarkable acoustics allowed the tyrant Dionysius to spy on his captives by listening through a crack in the cave's roof (further conjecture theorizes the space as a former cistern).

Next door to the "ear" is the cordoned-off **Grotta dei Cordari (Ropemaker's Cave),** a wide quarry fissure romantically filled with water and maidenhead ferns. Its preservation is in a precarious state, so it is closed to visitors.

Return to the ticket office and take the left path, which leads to the stark white curve of the **Teatro Greco (Greek theater)** ⭑⭑⭑, whose 137m (449-ft.) diameter makes it one of the largest in the world. Built in the 5th century B.C. and later expanded, its 42 rows of seats were hewn directly out of the living rock, and probably saw the first productions of some of Aeschylus's plays. The Romans, who felt serious drama was to be taken only in moderation, adapted the theater so they could occasionally flood the stage and have tiny mock sea battles.

Summer productions (mostly classical plays) are still staged at the theater—great if you can attend one, but don't be crushed if you can't: During the 2 months of performances, the theater is blanketed in steel railings and gray wooden planks, diminishing significantly the impact of the site, naturally backed by a scrim of pine trees and azure sea. At the top of the *cavea* are niches that once contained little votive altars, plus a little niched pond that collects the cold water flowing from an ancient aqueduct—temporarily boarded up during show season because the actors complain of the distraction created by the running water.

On your way out of the site, stop into the 1st-century-A.D. **Anfiteatro Romano (Roman Amphitheater)** ⭑, where Siracusans once held bloody gladiator fights and the like when they tired of the plays at the Greek theater. It, too, is used today for productions (mainly musicals) in the summer, when bright red poppies bloom against the green wash of the overgrown seating sections.

Largo Anfiteatro, off Corso Gelone/Viale Teracrati. ✆ **0931-66206.** Admission 4.50€ ($5.15). Combo ticket with museum 6€ ($6.90). Combo ticket with museum and Palazzo Bellomo 8€ ($9.20). Daily 9am to 1 hr. before sunset (site closes at 5pm when there are performances). Bus there: 1, 4, 8, 11, 12, 15, 21, 22, 23, 25. Bus back: 2, 3, 8, 11, 12, 14, 26.

Museo Archaeologico Paolo Orsi (Archaeological Museum) ⭑⭑⭑

This fantastic museum is one of Italy's top archaeological collections and by far the best in Sicily. It would be a worthwhile stop simply for the aesthetic beauty of many pieces, but the well-documented exhibits make it invaluable for understanding the Greek and other cultures of ancient Sicily.

Section A covers the island's southeastern corner during prehistoric times, kicking off with a pair of articulated dwarf elephant skeletons found in nearby caves. A closer look at the skulls, and it's easy to see why many academics believe that their odd shape and large central nasal passage led the local ancients—who surely stumbled across them—to invent the myth of the one-eyed, cave-dwelling giant called Cyclops. But the best part of the prehistoric section is the remains left by humans, a collection of tools, ceramics, and sculptures that open a window onto the richness of Sicily's Stone and Bronze Age cultures.

Section B covers Siracusa and its province in all its ancient Greek glory. The highlights include a terra-cotta statue of a goddess nursing twins (550 B.C.); the headless *Venus Landolina,* an Imperial Roman copy of a 2nd-century-B.C. statue that's a lesson in both anatomy and aesthetics; the museum's mischievous mascot, a 6th-century-B.C. terra-cotta Gorgon grinning and sticking his tongue out; and cases full of 5th- and 4th-century-B.C. votive statuettes dedicated to Demeter/Ceres and Kore/Persephone, to whom there was apparently a temple across the street (workers breaking ground for the huge Sanctuary of the Madonna discovered it a few decades back).

Section C contains the best remains from Magna Graecia settlements across eastern Sicily, including decorated vases from Gela spanning the 6th and 5th centuries B.C., an enthroned goddess from 6th-century-B.C. Grammichele, and a trio of rare 7th-century-B.C. wooden statues found near Agrigento. Look for the spectacularly carved 4th-century sarcophagus from the Catacombe di San Giovanni (San Giovanni catacombs).

Viale Teocrito 66. ℭ 0931-464022. Admission 4.50€ ($5.15). Combo ticket with Archaeological Zone 6€ ($6.90). Combo ticket with Archaeological Zone and Palazzo Bellomo 8€ ($9.20). Daily 9–1:30pm and Mon, Wed and Fri–Sat 3:30–7:00pm. Shorter hours in winter. Bus there: 1, 4, 8, 11, 12, 15, 21, 22, 23, 25. Bus back: 2, 3, 8, 11, 12, 14, 26.

Catacombe di San Giovanni (Catacombs of San Giovanni) 𝘈𝘈 (Kids

What is now the ruined church of San Giovanni was a potters' cave in Greek times, but once St. Paul came here to preach, it became serious holy ground, topped by a 6th-century basilica until it was knocked down by the Saracens. The church was rebuilt by the Normans in the 12th century and once again ruined when a 1693 earthquake shook it to the ground, but, not dissuaded, locals grafted a baroque structure onto the ruins. The Siracusans gave up after a 1908 earthquake destroyed it once and for all, leaving the roofless Norman walls and half an apse as they were, romantically sprouting flowers and weeds. It's still consecrated, and marriages and summer Sunday services take place around a sarcophagus-like altar.

A guide will whisk you through the original 6th-century Greek-cross crypt, with remnants of frescoes and capitals from the Byzantine and Norman eras, including the purported column where Siracusa's first bishop, San Marziano, was flogged to death. But the real treat is the catacombs, the only set of Siracusa's many early Christian subterranean burial grounds currently open to the public. There are some 20,000 tombs down here, niched into tunnels that honeycomb the earth connecting former Greek cisterns (recycled by early Christians into chapels). Along with rows of graves that once housed extended families, you'll see a few faded frescoes and early Christian symbols etched into stone slabs.

Via San Giovanni alle Catacombe (between the archaeological park and museum). ℭ 0931-67955. Admission 3.50€ ($4). Wed–Mon 9am–1pm (Apr–Oct 2:30–4pm). Bus there: 1, 4, 8, 11, 12, 15, 21, 22, 23, 25. Bus back: 2, 3, 8, 11, 12, 14, 26.

EXPLORING THE HISTORIC QUARTER

Just across the Ponte Umbertino bridge is the islet of **Ortigia,** home to the original settlers of Siracusa. Visitors crossing the bridge are greeted by the shaded

Piazza Panciale, the end of which opens up into Piazza XXV Luglio, a traffic circle bounded on the east by a sunken archaeological zone that sprouts a few Doric column stumps; a long, low set of stairs; half a wall; lots of weeds; and a few palm trees. This is what remains of the early-6th-century-B.C. **Temple of Apollo,** the first Doric temple in Sicily.

If you manage to find yourself here during the morning hours, follow the white cloth awnings of the local market to Piazza Pancali for a look at what Mother Nature is capable of. Carry lots of 1€ ($1.15) coins and brace yourself to choose among an abundance of **local produce** the likes of which you've never seen: enormous lemons, nuclear-size zucchinis, strawberries the size of racquet balls, succulent cherry tomatoes, and stacks of mussels garnished with lemon halves and girthy local tuna.

Make your way to the oblong, cafe-lined Piazza del Duomo at Ortigia's center to the **Duomo** 𝔊 (8am–noon and 4–7pm), adapted by the Byzantines and then the Normans from a 5th-century-B.C. **Temple to Athena.** The interior is marvelously simple, a honey-colored world of sacred quiet that feels about as close as stepping back in time and into an ancient temple as you're ever going to find. To convert the Greek temple to a church wasn't hard: They just punched archways through the cella to make it into a nave, and filled in the spaces between the 19 giant Doric columns from the temple's peristyle (all a bit askew from a 1542 earthquake) to make the outer walls of the aisle. Aside from Andrea Palma's 1728 to 1754 baroque facade, the cathedral remains essentially medieval and plain (baroque additions in the interior were stripped away in the 1920s). Look in the first chapel on the right for a baptismal font recycled from an ancient marble font resting on 13th-century bronze lions. Along the left aisle are four statues by the **Gagini** family workshop (three between the second to fifth columns and a *Madonna della Neve* up near the end of the aisle) and a painting on wood with a gold background of *St. Cosimo* attributed to **Antonello da Messina.**

Just down Via Picherali from the south end of the piazza, you'll find the harborside Largo Aretusa, whose centerpiece is the lovely little sunken pond containing the **Fonte Aretusa,** Siracusa's most famous mythological site. Half a dozen Greek poets wrote the tale of the nymph Aretusa, who was bathing in the Alpheus River in Greece one day when the god of that river took a liking to her. She begged for deliverance from his persistent amorous advances, and Artemis in pity turned the nymph into a spring, allowing her to escape underground. She traveled under the sea to emerge here in Siracusa, but Alpheus was hot on her heels and came gushing out in the same spot, mingling his waters with hers for eternity. They used to say you could toss a goblet into a spring at Arcadia in Greece and it would pop up here. Today the font still flows softly from its grotto into the pond, planted with puffy-headed, willowy papyrus (supposedly a gift from Egyptian ruler Ptolemy II) and swimming with fish and ducks. Shops selling sheets of papyrus "paper" can be found in the surrounding streets, especially Via Capodieci.

The **Palazzo Bellomo,** just up Via Capodieci at Via Roma, was built between the 13th and 15th centuries. It features a Catalan–Gothic staircase and courtyard, and is home to the **Museo Regionale di Arte Mediovale e Moderna (Regional Museum of Medieval and Modern Art; ✆ 0931-69617).** Its two stellar works are Antonello da Messina's highly ruinous but still exquisitely painted *Annunciation* (1474) and Caravaggio's moody *Deposition of Santa Lucia* (1608). Other standouts include medieval and Renaissance sculptures on the ground floor—among them a *Madonna* by Domenico Gagini—and a comical early-17th-century painting of angels ferrying the Madonna's house across the sea to Loreto with baby Jesus perched on the roof. Eighteenth- and 19th-century carriages, livery, furnishings, and ceramics, including a 15th-century Spanish/Moorish faience plate patterned in metallic reddish gold, round out the collections. Admission is 5€ ($5.75; combo ticket with archaeological museum and Archaeological Zone 8€/$9.20; combo ticket with museum only 6€/$6.90). It's open Sunday 9am to 12:30pm, Tuesday through Saturday from 9am to 1:30pm, and Wednesday and Friday from 3 to 7pm. Check for expanded afternoon and evening hours in July and August.

ACCOMMODATIONS YOU CAN AFFORD

Domus Mariae 🌟🌟   In 1995, the Suore Orsoline turned part of their old convent into a quietly stylish, modern hotel, located on the quiet coastal road on the far side of Ortigia. Half the rooms have balconies that front the sea, and a few feature fold-out couches that make them great for families. Rooms are large—even the singles are spacious—with built-in units and patterned rugs on tile floors. Bathrooms are modern and like new, with pristine finishes and marble-top sinks. Those sea-view rooms, the kindly reception desk, and all these comforts make this upscale nunnery worth the splurge. Keep in mind, however, that rooms are cleaned only every second day. The hotel now offers visits and excursions to little-visited nearby towns as well as shuttle service to and from the beach; for information, inquire at the reception desk or visit their website.

Via Vittorio Veneto 76 (on the east side of Ortigia, just below V. Mirabella), 96100 Siracusa. ℂ/fax **0931-24858.** www.sistemia.it/domusmariae. 12 units. 110€ ($126) single; 135€–150€ ($172) double. Rates include breakfast. AE, DC, DISC, MC, V. **Amenities:** Bar; fitness bike; tour desk; 24-hr. room service; babysitting; laundry; dry cleaning; nonsmoking rooms. *In room:* A/C, TV, minibar, hair dryer.

Gran Bretagna 🌟🌟   A comprehensive updating of the entire hotel, which was originally constructed as a patrician home, may have plastered over most of the building's 19th-century character, but it has done nothing to conceal the comfort or friendly nature of the staff. An automatic glass door greets guests at street level, revealing a steep flight of marble stairs up to the hotel (the reception desk is halfway up the 1st flight, where you can leave your bags). In keeping with the style of the original building, rooms are gracious in size, with rich brocaded draperies, innocuous modular furnishings, and lofty ceilings. A few rooms even have frescoes—nos. 2 and 3 just around the light fixture, but in huge, family-perfect no. 7, the whole ceiling is painted. In originally bathroomless rooms, bathrooms are fairly compact but functional and closed off behind a space-saving sliding door. On your way to breakfast, which is served in the sky-lit atrium on the ground level, notice the glass-enclosed remains of the Spanish bastions just below the floor.

Via Savoia 21 (on Ortigia, near Piazza XXV Luglio), 96100 Siracusa. ℂ **0931-68765.** Fax 0931-449078. www.hotelgranbretagna.it. 17 units. 73€ ($84) single; 100€ ($115) double; 125€ ($144) triple. Rates include breakfast. AE, MC, V. Closed mid-Nov to early Dec. *In room:* A/C, TV, minibar, hair dryer.

GREAT DEALS ON DINING

Il Cedro 🌟🌟 *Value* TRATTORIA/PIZZERIA   You wouldn't expect such a reasonably priced outstanding meal this close to the "uptown" crowd along the lungomare, but it's always refreshing when a meal exceeds your expectations. Huge canvas umbrellas shade the courtyard tables, and there's a cozy dining room for cooler weather. The quality of the shellfish is irreproachable, making the delicate flavors of the *antipasto Cedro* (mixed seafood salad) or the smoked swordfish come to life. The *linguine Cedro ai frutti di mare* in a slightly tomato-based garlic sauce is divine, but if you've had enough fish, try Cedro's impossibly delicious invention of *garganelli con panna e mandorle* (screw-shaped pasta in a light cream-and-almond sauce). Finish the meal with their exceptional homemade *limoncello,* which is neither too sweet nor too syrupy.

Via Capodieci 49, summer entrance also around the corner on Via Maniace 3 (off Largo Aretusa). © **0931-465860.** Primi 5€–9€ ($5.75–$10); secondi 6.50€–13€ ($7.50–$15). AE, DISC, MC, V. Thurs–Tues noon–3pm and 7:30pm–1 or 2am.

Zza ✶✶✶ *Value* SIRACUSANA Warm, dry-brushed, gold-hued walls crowned by a large archway house Zza's 14 or so tables spaciously distributed beneath the high ceilings. The menu is a true representation of local cuisine—it's even written in the local dialect—translated into both English and standard Italian. Start the meal off with a plate of *che cac o cciuli* (artichoke spread on toasts) followed by the delicious *sfizi di mari nostru* (spaghetti cooked in foil with shrimp, calamari, and mussels). For the secondo, stick with the local specialty and order the *piscispada co'limuni* or *c'orancia* (swordfish with your choice of a lemon or orange sauce). Zza also offers alternatives like *spiedini di fummaggi e viddura arrustitui* (grilled cheese and vegetable kebabs) or frittatas. Leave room for a pizza dolce (filled with lemon cream) or for the creamy *budino di pistachio* (pistachio pudding).

Via Roma 73–75–77 (behind the Duomo). © **0931-22204.** Primi 5€–7.50€ ($5.75–$8.60); secondi 5€–7.75€ ($5.75–$8.90). AE, DC, MC, V. Tues–Sun noon–3pm and 8–11pm.

8 Mount Etna: The Forge of Vulcan ✶✶✶

Mount Etna is the biggest, baddest volcano in Europe and one of the largest in the world, 3,297m (10,814 ft.) of massive molten energy that dominates all of eastern Sicily with a menacing unpredictability. Etna's active crater is constantly blowing a thin yet steady trail of smoke, as if relishing a quality Cuban cigar. You know her temper is flaring by the white mushroom cloud that emerges, inevitably turning an ominous black before blowing its top in bright red jet streams of molten lava and ash. Etna's show of fireworks plays to an appreciative audience about every 10 days or so, depositing its lava flows harmlessly into an enormous and isolated crater. But every few years, it goes into a dangerously violent volcanic fit. In 1989, at the summit, a new crater grew over 99m (325 ft.) in just a month. From 1991 to 1993, it erupted almost continuously, and in 1998, 8 months of violent activity culminated in an eruption that spewed ash almost 1.5km (a mile) into the air, closing Catania's airport and covering the mountain with a fresh layer of pumice and lava. Her fury was last unleashed in 2003. Etna's lava flows have threatened, and occasionally actually swallowed, several of the small towns that brave the danger to take agricultural advantage of the rich volcanic soil, making the locals rather nervous.

But it's there, and visitors still must climb it. The most popular arrival point by car is the **Rifugio Sapienza,** a base station at the 1,890m (6,199-ft.) mark more than slightly disfigured by the infestation of souvenir shops, postcard stands, and snack bars. There's a tourist information office at the far end of the parking lot to the right (© **095-911505**).

GETTING TO THE VOLCANO

From almost any major town in Sicily, you can count on the local travel agencies offering day excursions to Mount Etna. Prices vary according to the jumping-off city; just check around town for these tour offerings, or ask your hotel concierge for information.

BY CAR   Take the Catania–Messina **A18** autostrada to the **Giarre** exit and follow signs for **Santa Venerina,** then **Zafferana Etnea** and **Etna Sud.** You'll be rewarded by a fertile and verdant path that winds up the mountain (an **alternative** approach via **Nicolosi** will take you through an entirely different landscape—a monotone and barren terrain of dark volcanic detritus). Driving north on Catania's Tangenziale Highway, take the exit for Gravina di Catania, heading in the direction of Nicolosi–Etna Sud.

BY BUS   You can catch the **AST** bus (© **095-7230511**) from Catania (2½ hr.; 4.75€/$5.45 round-trip), currently leaving at 8:15am Monday through Saturday; the return bus leaves the Rifugio at 4pm. On Sunday, the bus departs Catania at 8:30am and returns from the Rifugio at 4:30pm.

GETTING TO THE CRATER

The 2003 eruption seems to have forced **Funivia dell'Etna** (© **095-911158;** www.funiviaetna.com), the organization that used to administer the cable car up to an access point for the crater, to suspend its activities. When the 2001 eruption fried the cable car, Funivia dell'Etna responded by offering off-road Mercedes or IVECO turbo minibuses up as far as conditions would allow. Perhaps by the publication of this book, Funivia dell'Etna will have resumed at least a minimum service. One can only hope: On a clear day, the vistas from up here encompass all of Sicily, but most certainly you'll be eyeing the spectacular former active crater of the **Valle delle Bove,** an enormous yawning cleft measuring 18km (11 miles) around and almost 1,200 extremely steep meters down (3,936 ft.), scooped out of the southeast slope. Much of the lava flows this century have found their way safely into this channel, away from inhabited soil.

9 Taormina ★★★

134km (83 miles) N of Siracusa, 48km (30 miles) S of Messina

Dominating the surrounding headland from atop a richly fragrant and flowering hilltop is **Taormina,** the crown jewel of Sicily. Together with its sibling resort, Giardini-Naxos, Taormina accommodates over 50% of Sicily's tourism, a fact all too evident during the crushing summer months. The **Teatro Greco-Romano (Greco-Roman Theater)** serves as a backdrop to the hedonistic tendencies of mass tourism and Hollywood glitterati alike. Its dizzying concentration of hotels, one more gracious than the next, almost all cling to the rock face and feature terrific terraces that face mighty Etna and the sea. Taormina has been a favorite over the years of everyone from Greta Garbo, who returned every spring for 30 years, to D. H. Lawrence, whose inspiration for his feverishly sensual *Lady Chatterley's Lover* was, according to local rumor, based on his own wife's dalliances with a Sicilian mule driver. But in spite of the hoards clamoring for their share of paradise, Taormina remains a spot of extraordinary beauty, with its hidden stairways, medieval palazzi, tiny churches, and breathtaking panorama.

Taormina is the legacy of Greek settlers blown fortuitously into Punto Schisò, at the south end of Giardini-Naxos, by an unexpected crosswind as early as the 8th century B.C. The site was eventually built up into the thriving center of Naxos, an orderly city of gridded streets doomed to annihilation at the hands of the terrible tyrant Dionysius in 403 B.C. Those citizens not massacred or sold as slaves managed to find refuge up the hill, founding a colony along the steep and impregnable hill. Centuries later, Taormina is a vision of loveliness, with the perfect blend of polish and pleasure. The main drag of Corso Umberto showcases

Taormina

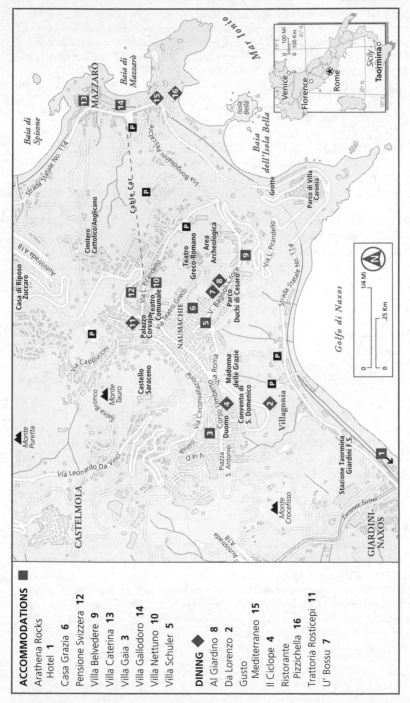

ACCOMMODATIONS ■

Arathena Rocks
   Hotel **1**
Casa Grazia **6**
Pensione Svizzera **12**
Villa Belvedere **9**
Villa Caterina **13**
Villa Gaia **3**
Villa Gallodoro **14**
Villa Nettuno **10**
Villa Schuler **5**

DINING ◆

Al Giardino **8**
Da Lorenzo **2**
Gusto
   Mediterraneo **15**
Il Ciclope **4**
Ristorante
   Pizzichella **16**
Trattoria Rosticepi **11**
U' Bossu **7**

an endless parade of eye-opening architecture, culinary crafts, and couture, while the pebbly beach, accessible via a funicular or a series of leg-cramping steps down to sea level, provides a poetic reprieve from life's concerns. Laze under a striped umbrella overlooking the ruins of an ancient fortress, then head back in time to graze and gaze along Corso Umberto.

ESSENTIALS

GETTING THERE   By Train   There are 12 to 13 trains daily from **Siracusa** (2–3½ hr.; around 9.50€/$11) and hourly ones from **Messina** (35–65 min.; 3.05€/$3.50). There are also three daily trains from **Rome** (8½–10 hr.; 33€–43€/$38–$49) that pass through **Naples** (6½–8 hr.; 23€–33€/$26–$38). The train station, **Taormina-Giardini** (© 0942-51026 or 0942-51511), is down on the SS114 coastal road. A local bus makes the 15-minute trip up to Taormina twice an hour between 7am and 12:30am for 1.20€ ($1.40). (Don't take this bus if you're booked at the Arathena Rocks Hotel, Villa Gallodoro, or Villa Caterina.) Once you arrive at the bus depot in Taormina, it's about 457m (1,500 ft.) uphill to the Villa Nettuno and a short cab ride up to any of the other hotels.

By Bus   SAIS (© 800-920900) has daily departures to the Taormina–Giardini–Naxos train station from Rome (10 hr.; 33€/$38).They also make the trip about hourly (60–90 min.) to Taormina from **Catania,** beginning at the airport and making stops in the city before continuing on to Giardini-Naxos and then Taormina. Bus service runs less frequently on Sunday and costs 4€ ($4.60). You'll have to change buses in Catania if you're headed in from **Siracusa** (2 hr. 45 min. total; 7.40€/$8.50, not including fare after transfer) or from points beyond.

There's an Interbus ticket booth at the bus station just outside the town gate on Via Pirandello (© 0942-625301) and one down at the Taormina-Giardini train station.

By Car   Taormina is above the coastal A18 autostrada (and its parallel, SS114) from Messina to Catania and Siracusa.

VISITOR INFORMATION   The **tourist office** is in the Palazzo Corvaja on Largo Santa Caterina (© **0942-23243;** fax 0942-24941; www.comune. taormina.it). If you're lucky, they won't have run out of the handy and colorful local map that clearly highlights a series of walks in and around the town. Otherwise, you'll have to be satisfied with the basic map and a steely smile. Useful, however, is the fact that all of the train and bus schedules in and out of town are posted on the wall.

An **Internet cafe** keeps shop hours across from the Municipio on Corso Umberto 214 (© **0942-628839**).

FESTIVALS & MARKETS   In May, there's a festival to show off **traditional Sicilian carts and costumes.** There are **concerts and performances** in the Greek theater and churches around town from June to September. And in July and August, Taormina hosts an **international film festival.** There's a daily morning **market** on Via Cappuccini.

PASSEGGIATA DESTINATIONS

The single most popular activity in Taormina is simply strolling along the main drag, **Corso Umberto,** window-shopping, people-watching, and occasionally getting caught in the middle of a marching-band parade. The east end of Corso Umberto is anchored by Largo Santa Caterina, home to **Palazzo Corvaja,** a fine 14th-century example of local masonry style, which highlights gray limestone walls with black-and-white lava trim. The staircase in the pretty little courtyard leads up to the **Museo Siciliano d'Arte e Tradizioni Popolari (Sicilian Museum of Art and Popular Traditions),** a small collection of Sicilian folk art and crafts. Admission is 2.50€ ($2.85), and it's open Tuesday through Sunday from 9am to 1pm and 4 to 8pm.

Via Teatro Greco leads to Taormina's only required sight, the 3rd-century-B.C. **Teatro Greco-Romano (Greco-Roman Theater)** ✦✦✦ (© **0942-23220**), a drama in and of itself. Carved into the mountainside in the traditional Greek style, the *cavea* (curved seating) enjoys sweeping vistas of the coastline, the mountains of Calabria across the straight and mighty Mount Etna in the near distance. Why the Romans thought they could improve on the majesty of Mother Nature is beyond me, but in the 2nd century A.D., they were compelled to brick up the back wall, creating a system of claustrophobic underground passageways with low barrel vaults constructed of local stones. The view of the sea would have been completely eliminated but for a millennium of seismic activity, which has opened up a cragged window in the *scena* that once again allows for a magnificent sea view. Admission is 4.50€ ($5.15); the theater is open from 9am until an hour before sunset.

Walk back to Largo Santa Caterina and around the right side of its eponymous church to see a section of curving seats belonging to the **Odeon,** a modest Roman-era theater currently growing weeds. Continuing up Corso Umberto, turn left down Via Naumachie to see the **Naumachie,** a 120m (394-ft.) brick wall of 5m (16-ft.) niches that formed a wall between an Imperial Roman gymnasium and an ancient cistern. A bit farther up the Corso is the town center, **Piazza IX Aprile,** a communal living room built as a terrace with a view over the Ionian Sea from the railing bounding one side. Lined with pricey cafes and brimming with visitors and caricature artists, it's the best place to sit back with a cappuccino and enjoy the relaxed, resortlike ambience of Taormina.

Pass under the 12th-century **clock tower,** and you'll be in the medieval section of town, where Corso Umberto eventually spills into **Piazza del Duomo.** The battlemented Duomo sports six huge antique pink marble columns inside and free concerts many summer evenings. The square's centerpiece is a fantastical 1635 fountain atop which perches a copy of the odd two-legged female centaur, a Greek mythological creature whose meaning or function no one quite seems to understand—ironically, Taormina made it the town mascot.

With a bit of enthusiasm and a lot of energy, head up the hillside staircase for increasingly unobscured panoramas and ultimately the sanctuary of the **Madonna della Rocca,** a tiny 17th-century church carved into and built onto an outcropping.

HITTING THE BEACH

Sitting unceremoniously at the base of the cliffs is **Mazzarò,** the seaside beach resort also known as Taormina Bassa. A *funivia* (cable car; © **0942-23906**) links Mazzarò with Taormina Alta (entrance at V. Pirandello, between the bus depot and the gate into town) and runs every 15 minutes from 8am to 1am (1.60€/$1.85 one-way; 2.70€/$3.10 round-trip).

At the bottom and exiting the funivia to the right, past the Capo Sant'Andrea headland, is the region's loveliest cove, where twin crescents of beach sweep from a sand spit out to the minuscule **Isola Bella** ✦✦✦ islet. Locals say that Isola Bella once was the home of an Italian *principessa* who had her home built over the remains of ancient rock dwellings. Hidden on this scenic islet are over 40 rooms and two swimming pools, both fed with seawater by way of a pump located in a stone well on the southern side of the sandbar. Because of the pebbles, this beach may be slightly unkind to your delicate little feet, but what a small price to pay for crystalline water and the natural beauty of what is actually a natural preserve. You can set yourself up at the **Lido Mendolia Beach Club** (© 0942-625258), where you can rent lounges and umbrellas (5€/$5.75 per person per day); restore yourself at your choice of restaurant, snack bar, or gelateria; or lay out a towel along the sandbar.

If, instead, you turn left out of the funivia, duck into one of those narrow stone staircases that will lead you over the train tracks and down to the beach to **Lido Il Delfino** (© 0942-24528). Here an umbrella and chair run 6€ ($6.90) per day and paddle boats rent for 10€ ($12) an hour—great for a miniexcursion around Capo Sant'Andrea, passing by a few grottoes with excellent light effects on the seaward side toward Isola Bella. Show them this book, and they'll give you a 20% discount. To the right of Il Delfino is **Lido La Pigna** (© 0942-24464), a much more posh beach establishment owing to gracious service, including towels and free minibus service to the beach. Lounges and umbrellas go for 6€ ($6.90). The attendants will bring you as many coffees as you like and let you run a tab for the day (a nice tip will get you a front-row seat for the next day). Check for their business card at local hotels for a 20% discount.

North of Mazzarò are the scenic rock fortress of **Spisone** (frequented by gays but popular in general); long, wide beaches; and **Letojanni.** A local bus leaves Taormina for Mazzarò, Spisone, and Letojanni, and another heads down the opposite coast to Giardini. No matter where you lay your towel, you'll have the chance to hop on one of the many **roving fishing boats** near the shoreline, shaded by a romantically utilitarian sun umbrella that advertises minitours of the area waters. They'll take you to some of the area's most infamous caves (if you see unmanned paddle boats near a cave's entrance, you'd be prudent to knock before entering) and as far south as Punto Capo Taormina for a sweeping view of Punto Schisò and the built-up resort of Giardini-Naxos. The boat ride lasts about 40 minutes and costs 15€ ($17).

ACCOMMODATIONS YOU CAN AFFORD

It's hard to believe that a town so obscenely crammed with hotels can fill up, but in summer it does, even down below at Mazzarò and at nearby and sprawling Giardini-Naxos. Obviously, the high demand keeps prices high, but so does the quaintness quotient, especially up in Taormina proper. Book well in advance, and don't show up here looking for vacancies at the last minute.

TAORMINA ALTA

Casa Grazia   Casa Grazia's Signora welcomes you with open arms, and you'll be hard pressed to tear yourself away from her tremendous warmth and hospitality. The house, unobtrusively located down a central street, is small, but it's as crisp and well kept as any three-star establishment. Even the marble bathrooms are pristine, glimmering as if freshly installed, except that they're over 10 years old. There's a roof terrace with views over Taormina, but keep in mind that the staircase is narrow and that there are lots of levels. Casa Grazia is no secret, and with so few rooms, it'll take an act of God to get you in there, but it's definitely worth the try.

Via Iallia Bassia 20, 98039 Taormina (ME). © 0942-24776. 5 units. 40€ ($46) double; 55€ ($63) triple. No credit cards.

Pensione Svizzera *Value*   This dignified three-story pink-washed stone house teeters on the sea-facing edge of Via Pirandello, conveniently located between the funicular and the bus depot. Sea-facing rooms take full advantage of its position, while a convivial flowering garden provides solace for those in rooms without. The pensione is by no means luxurious, but rooms now have air-conditioning, and under the management of the Swiss-born head of the household, you can count on everything being crisp and clean. The showers are potentially messy, though, with unruly shower curtains and only a 2-inch porcelain lip separating the water from the bathroom.

Via L. Pirandello 26, 98039 Taormina. © 0942-23790. Fax 0942-625906. www.pensionesvizzera.com. 22 units. 60€–90€ ($69–$104) single; 80€–120€ ($92–$138) double. MC, V. Rates include breakfast. Free parking available. **Amenities:** Bar; free shuttle to hotel beach; 24-hr. room service; babysitting; laundry service. *In room:* A/C, satellite TV, hair dryer, safe.

Villa Gaia   Staying at this cozy little hotel in the heart of town is like moving in with a local family—or like moving into the kids' room for a night. It's located in an antique palazzo, only steps from the lively main drag of Corso Umberto. The entire pensione was renovated in 2000, giving a fresh look to the mix of florals, statues, and mismatched furniture. The orthopedic beds are a little soft but not bad, and almost all rooms have a terrace or balcony: The view from nos. 5, 7, and 8 gets in a bit of the sea and Etna via private terraces, while nos. 1 through 4 share a long communal terrace. Breakfast is served in a small garden shaded by mandarin orange and grapefruit trees.

Via Fazzello 34/Piazza Carmine 6 (turn up Salita Badia Vecchia staircase from Piazza del Duomo), 98039 Taormina (ME). ©/fax 0942-23185. www.hotelvillagaia.com. 15 units. 50€–80€ ($58–$92) single; 85€–100€ ($98–$115) double. Breakfast included in rates in Aug; otherwise 7.50€ ($8.60) per person double; 10€/$12 singles). Reduced rates off-season. MC, V. Limited free parking. *In room:* A/C, TV, minibar, hair dryer.

Villa Nettuno 🄀 *Value*   Villa Nettuno is a gracious family house turned pensione, managed with loving care by Maria and Vicenzo Sciglio and assisted by their son, Antonio. The location is handy—between the bus stop and town gate and just across from the cable car to the beach, while perched high enough to afford a sea view from all except three rooms. The Sciglios are in the process of upgrading, but because they insist on keeping prices low (thank the no-agency policy), the process may be lengthy. The Nettuno offers a healthy amount of Taormina's 19th-century class, from the antiques-filled salon and the wandering paths and stairs of the colorful statue-studded gardens. Climb to the peaceful gazebo temple at the summit of the gardens for an outstanding vista from Etna across the sea to Calabria.

Via Pirandello 33, 98039 Taormina (ME). © 0942-23797. Fax 0942-626035. 13 units. 30€–40€ ($34–$46) single; 50€–70€ ($58–$80) double. Breakfast 4€ ($4.60). MC, V. Parking in public lot. Closed some weekdays in Jan.

Villa Schuler 🄀🄀   Nestled within its own fragrant terraced gardens, the Villa Schuler looks over the Ionian Sea from a premier site below Piazza IV Aprile. Gerardo Schuler's grandfather built it to be a private home, but the family has run it as a hotel since 1905. Sea-view rooms look across the flowery and palm-shaded gravel terrace where most guests take their breakfast. (V. Roma runs directly below this terrace, meaning garden-view rooms are slightly quieter, though smaller and less attractive.) The addition of a panoramic elevator adds to the appeal of this hotel, where accommodations are fitted with modular furniture mixed with antiques. Most rooms have balconies; nos. 29 through 32 on the top floor share a terrace with a vista from the Greek Theater to the coast. There's access to nearby tennis courts for a nominal fee and free shuttle service to the beach, along with a free chair and umbrella (May–Nov). If you plan on sticking closer to home, they provide free bikes for tooling up and down the sometimes steep hills.

Piazzetta Bastione/Via Roma, 98039 Taormina (ME). © 0942-23481. Fax 0942-23522. www.infoservizi.it/hotels/taormina.htm or www.villaschuler.com. 26 units. 88€ ($101) single; 110€–124€ ($126–$143) double; 160€ ($184) junior suite. 20% discount from mid- to end of Mar, June 28–July 26, and Nov 2–16. AE, DC, MC, V. Limited parking; reserve for 8€ ($9.20) per day. Closed mid-Nov to mid-Mar. Turn left off Corso Umberto on Scesa Morgana just before Piazza IV Aprile. **Amenities:** Bike and scooter rental; concierge; tour desk; car-rental desk; 24-hr. room service; in-room massage; babysitting; laundry service. *In room:* A/C, TV, hair dryer, safe.

Worth a Splurge

Villa Belvedere 🌟🌟🌟   Christian Pécaut's hotel has remained a favorite for three generations, thanks to a friendly reception desk, professional maintenance, and old-fashioned style. The terra-cotta floors support firm beds and a variety of furnishings, all functional but with a touch of class, and bathrooms are embellished with local tiles and all the modern conveniences. Most rooms have slivers of balconies to enjoy views over the neighboring public gardens to the sea. The top-floor rooms have small terraces from which you can glimpse Mount Etna (these are also air-conditioned, as are rooms on the back, which have double-paned windows to block noise from the street). The flowering property is terraced down the hillside (elevators included), with the pool at the lowest level sprouting a palm tree from its center.

Via Bagnoli Croci 79, 98039 Taormina (ME). © 0942-23791. Fax 0942-625830. www.villabelvedere.it. 47 units. 70€–128€ ($80–$146) single; 90€–164€ ($104–$186) double used as single; 120€–198€ ($138–$229) double. Rates include breakfast. MC, V. Parking 5.50€ ($6.30). Closed Nov 15–Mar 13 (sometimes open Dec 18–Jan 10). **Amenities:** Outdoor swimming pool; 24-hr. room service; babysitting; laundry service. *In room:* A/C, TV, hair dryer.

TAORMINA MARE/MAZZARO

Villa Caterina   You can tell by the pristine Mediterranean garden and flawless terra-cotta patio that this is actually somebody's home, but more than that, it is a verdant oasis sunken into the hill and surrounded by trees. The yellow tile floor and brown bathroom tile recall the 1950s, with a local *artigianato* wrought-iron headboard thrown in for good grace. The location is convenient to (but not immediately on top of) the beach as well as the cable car to Taormina Alta, and after a day in the sun, what better to do than to write postcards under the lemon tree?

Via Nazionale 155, 98039 Mazzarò (ME). © 0942-24709. www.hotelvillacaterina.it. 9 units. 98€–108€ ($113–$125) double. Discounts for longer stays. No singles. Rates include breakfast. No credit cards. Free parking in small lot. Closed Nov to Easter. (Turn left out of the funicular; the pensione is up the road on your right. If you're arriving by Interbus, get off at the Sea Palace and continue up the road for about 90m/300 ft.) *In room:* No phone.

Villa Gallodoro (Value   Kudos to the Gallodoro for providing the best balance of quality and price in a characteristic 1920s house that's practically on the beach. The rooms are in pristine condition, as are the bathrooms, where tiled shower partitions gleam with bright white grout. Double-glazed windows and doors block out the noise from the train below, but keep in mind that anywhere in Mazzarò you're going to hear some engine noise. The original stone arches provide a contrast to the pink stucco of the exterior, which is flanked on two sides by sun terraces and on the third by a lovely overgrown garden cafe, which sometimes doubles as a restaurant.

Via Nazionale 151 (next to the Sea Palace), 98039 Mazzarò (ME). ℂ/fax **0942-23860**. 15 units. 45€ ($52) single; 80€ ($92) double. V. Free parking. Closed Nov to Easter. **Amenities:** Bike/scooter rental; room service (7am–midnight). *In room:* A/C, TV, no phone.

GIARDINI-NAXOS
Arathena Rocks Hotel ℛ *(Value)*   Arathena Rocks Hotel takes full advantage of its secluded position on the furthermost tip of Punto Schisò, overlooking the black lava rock formations that essentially constitute the hotel's private "beach." But above the salt water is a gracious sun terrace laid with lava stone featuring a refreshing outdoor pool. It shares the hotel's grounds with a garden fit for nobility, bursting with the scent of freshly cut grass and flowers. The accommodations are no less gracious, with hand-painted Venetian-style pieces interspersed with tasteful antiques and Oriental rugs. Rooms off the garden and parking lot have air-conditioning. A shuttle runs twice daily between the hotel and Taormina Alta.

Via Calcide Eubea 55, 98035 Giardini-Naxos. ℂ **0942-51349**. Fax 0942-51690, www.hotelarathena.com. 49 units. 52€–55€ ($60–$63) per person double. Add 12€ ($14) for obligatory half board July–Aug. From the train station, a taxi will run around 10€ ($12). **Amenities:** Bar; outdoor swimming pool; 24-hr. room service; laundry service; dry cleaning.

GREAT DEALS ON DINING
TAORMINA ALTA
Al Giardino SICILIAN/ITALIAN   Friendly Sebatiano Puglia really cares about his simple, tasty dishes. There are only a dozen small tables scattered on the patio out front, shaded by an awning dripping with flowers, so call ahead if you want one. The only drawback is the occasional car that whizzes by (but other than that, the sole sound is bird song from the public gardens across the street). His *spaghetti alla carbonara* is great, as is the *paglia e feino alla bolognese* (strands of green and yellow pasta tossed with a meat sauce). For a secondo, try the *omlette al prosciutto* or the *involtini alla rusticana* (veal rolls stuffed with cheese and skewered with lemon slices and Sicilian sausages before being grilled).

Via Bagnoli Croci 84. ℂ **0942-23453**. Reservations recommended. Primi 6.50€–8€ ($7.45–$9.20); secondi 8.50€–13€ ($10–$15). AE, MC, V. Wed–Mon noon–2:30pm and 7:30–11pm. Closed Nov.

Il Ciclope ℛℛ *(Value)* SICILIAN/ITALIAN   Although it looks awfully touristy, with its shaded terrace fronting the main drag in the medieval part of town, Il Ciclope is actually quite good. Salvatore Sturiale's restaurant serves simple-looking dishes bursting with flavor, like the *rigatoni alla ciclope* (just spicy enough, with ham, tomatoes, hot and black peppers, and oil), *fettucine con pescespada* (with swordfish, olives, and pistachios), *cuscinotto alla polifemo* (veal rolled with mozzarella, prosciutto, and mushrooms; breaded; and coated with an herbed cream sauce), and *bocconcini di vitellina alla turiddu* (almost a veal stew, with olives, tomatoes, pancetta, onions, pepperoncino, and basil). Call ahead for a street-side table, or take your chances.

Piazzetta San Leone 1 (on Corso Umberto). ℂ **0942-23263**. Reservations recommended. Primi 5.50€–8.50€ ($6.30–$10); secondi 7.50€–12€ ($8.60–$14). DC, MC, V. Daily 11:15am–3pm and 7–10:30pm. Closed Wed in winter.

Trattoria Rosticepi ℛℛ *(Finds)* SICILIAN   Located just outside the periphery of the high-profile tourist traps, Rosticepi bucks the trend by providing great-tasting, low-priced, honest fare in an unadorned setting. The absence of an outdoor cafe and low foot traffic ensure that only the well informed drop by.

Traditional recipes top off the menu, but since it's likely you'll be visiting more than once, you may want to try the *linguini alla crema di astice* (linguini in a lobster cream sauce) or, on the heartier side, the *escalope Rosticepi* (creamed scalloped veal with mushrooms and green pepper).

Via S. Pancrazio 18, just beyond Porta Messina, down the hill on the left. ℂ 0942-24149. Primi 5€–10€ ($5.75–$12); secondi 8€–10€ ($9.20–$12). MC, V. Thurs–Tues 1–3pm and 8pm–midnight.

U' Bossu 🌟🌟 *Value* SICILIAN   Historic opera recordings mix with Mariah Carey in this superlative hole in the wall—why Enzo's place isn't better known is beyond me. It has killer prices (especially for Taormina), a friendly staff, quaint trattoria decor (plants, garlic ropes, and bunches of peppers hanging from wood beams in a candlelit room), and rather excellent food. Still, the tourists manage to find it, so either go early or book ahead for one of the nine tables arranged around a great antipasto buffet. And plan to spend the evening if the restaurant is full, as the service can be excruciatingly slow. The primi are flavorful works of art, from the *spaghetti alla mafiosa* (with tuna and tomatoes) to the *casareccia alla turiddu* (homemade pasta with tomatoes, cream, capers, olives, baked ricotta, and eggplant). The best secondo is *involtini "U' Bossu"* (veal rolls), though the swordfish *alla Messinese* (with olives and capers in a tomato broth) is great, too. By all means, don't miss Enzo's terrific homemade pepperoncino liqueur.

Via Bagnoli Croci 50. ℂ 0942-23311. Reservations recommended. Primi 6€–7€ ($6.90–$8.05); secondi 7€–18€ ($8.05–$21). DC, MC, V. Tues–Sun noon–3pm and 7:30–11:30pm; open Mon evenings mid-June to Aug. Closed Nov 15–Dec 20 and Jan 10–Mar 20.

Worth a Splurge

Da Lorenzo 🌟🌟🌟 SICILIAN   Forget about slipping on your swimsuit after a meal at Da Lorenzo, where you'll fight to clear your plate of what is essentially food of *Travel & Leisure* caliber. And with any luck, you'll have arrived at the corner table on the terrace in time for an unexpected light show over at nearby Etna. For starters, dig into a plate of varied smoked fish and carpaccio (on request, there are also individual selections like octopus and tuna). My favorite primi are the *gamberoni al curry con riso* (curried prawns and rice) and the flavorful and not overly rich ravioli *ai carciofi* (in a delicate artichoke-cream sauce). The *cordon bleu al Gorgonzola* (a good-quality steak with blue cheese) seems to be a house classic, but expect to be stuffed well before the arrival of the secondo. Try to leave room for one of their homemade desserts and a refreshing finisher of mandarin liqueur. Da Lorenzo also has the best selection of Italian wines in all of Taormina.

Via Roma 12 (near the San Domenico Hotel). ℂ 0942-23480. Primi 6.50€–9.50€ ($7.45–$11); secondi 9.50€–28€ ($11–$32) and up for fish. AE, DC, MC, V. Thurs–Tues 12:30–2:30pm and 7:30pm–midnight. Closed a month in winter.

TAORMINA MARE/MAZZARO

Gusto Mediterraneo *Value* TAKEOUT SICILIAN   This little take-away spot is just a short walk from the lidos to the left of the funivia and Isola Bella, perfectly positioned as it is for when those lazy beach munchies get hold of you. If you've timed it so that none of the local shopkeepers is taking up the lone two tables (rigged from wine barrels and boxes of timber), you'll be able to eat the hot dishes hot. The food is outstanding—exactly what you'd prepare in your own kitchen—from stuffed focaccia to *insalata riso* to a simple and healthful grilled chicken sandwich (a great option if you want to bring a bit back to your beach towel).

Mazzarò (up the hill toward Isola Bella). No phone. Salads and sandwiches 2.60€–5€ ($3–$5.75). No credit cards. Daily 10am–9pm. Closed Tues in May and Nov to Easter.

Ristorante Pizzichello ⓖ SICILIAN   I guess this is what would be considered your local "dive," although this crooked old shack keeps a respectable face with great food and white tablecloths. The ceiling is hung with crab traps and netting, a nod to their working fisherman clientele. Have a plate of their *frittura mista* (mixed fried shrimp, calamari, and whatever else is available) with a cold beer, or sample the *zuppa di cozze e vongole* (mussel-and-clam "soup"), then sit back and enjoy the incomparably fabulous views of Isola Bella and Taormina Alta.

Spiaggia Isola Bella (next to the boats). No phone. Primi 4.50€–8.50€ ($5.15–$10); secondi 5.50€–11€ ($6.30–$13). No credit cards. Daily 12:30–3pm; Sat–Sun 7:30pm–midnight.

Index

Great Trips Like Great Days Begin with a Plan

FranklinCovey and Frommer's Bring You *Frommer's Favorite Places* Planner

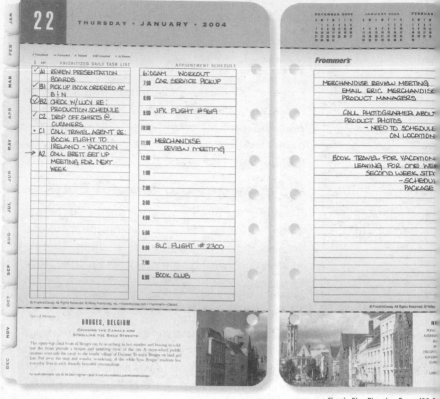

Classic Size Planning Pages $39.9

The planning experts at FranklinCovey have teamed up with the travel experts at Frommer's. The result is a full-year travel-themed planner filled with rich images and travel tips covering fifty-two of Frommer's Favorite Places.

- Each week will make you an expert about an intriguing corner of the world
- New facts and tips every day
- Beautiful, full-color photos of some of the most beautiful places on earth
- Proven planning tools from FranklinCovey for keeping track of tasks, appointments, notes, address/phone numbers, and more

Save 15%

when you purchase Frommer's Favorite Places travel-themed planner and a binder.

Order today before you next big trip.

www.franklincovey.com/frommers
Enter promo code 12252 at checkout for discount. Offer expires June 1, 2005.

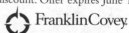

Frommer's is a trademark of Arthur Frommer.

FROMMER'S® COMPLETE TRAVEL GUIDES

Alaska
Alaska Cruises & Ports of Call
American Southwest
Amsterdam
Argentina & Chile
Arizona
Atlanta
Australia
Austria
Bahamas
Barcelona, Madrid & Seville
Beijing
Belgium, Holland & Luxembourg
Bermuda
Boston
Brazil
British Columbia & the Canadian
  Rockies
Brussels & Bruges
Budapest & the Best of Hungary
Calgary
California
Canada
Cancún, Cozumel & the Yucatán
Cape Cod, Nantucket & Martha's
  Vineyard
Caribbean
Caribbean Ports of Call
Carolinas & Georgia
Chicago
China
Colorado
Costa Rica
Cruises & Ports of Call
Cuba
Denmark
Denver, Boulder & Colorado
  Springs
England
Europe
Europe by Rail
European Cruises & Ports of Call

Florence, Tuscany & Umbria
Florida
France
Germany
Great Britain
Greece
Greek Islands
Halifax
Hawaii
Hong Kong
Honolulu, Waikiki & Oahu
India
Ireland
Italy
Jamaica
Japan
Kauai
Las Vegas
London
Los Angeles
Maryland & Delaware
Maui
Mexico
Montana & Wyoming
Montréal & Québec City
Munich & the Bavarian Alps
Nashville & Memphis
New England
Newfoundland & Labrador
New Mexico
New Orleans
New York City
New York State
New Zealand
Northern Italy
Norway
Nova Scotia, New Brunswick &
  Prince Edward Island
Oregon
Ottawa
Paris
Peru

Philadelphia & the Amish
  Country
Portugal
Prague & the Best of the Czech
  Republic
Provence & the Riviera
Puerto Rico
Rome
San Antonio & Austin
San Diego
San Francisco
Santa Fe, Taos & Albuquerque
Scandinavia
Scotland
Seattle
Shanghai
Sicily
Singapore & Malaysia
South Africa
South America
South Florida
South Pacific
Southeast Asia
Spain
Sweden
Switzerland
Texas
Thailand
Tokyo
Toronto
Turkey
USA
Utah
Vancouver & Victoria
Vermont, New Hampshire &
  Maine
Vienna & the Danube Valley
Virgin Islands
Virginia
Walt Disney World® & Orlando
Washington, D.C.
Washington State

FROMMER'S® DOLLAR-A-DAY GUIDES

Australia from $50 a Day
California from $70 a Day
England from $75 a Day
Europe from $85 a Day
Florida from $70 a Day
Hawaii from $80 a Day

Ireland from $80 a Day
Italy from $70 a Day
London from $90 a Day
New York City from $90 a Day
Paris from $90 a Day
San Francisco from $70 a Day

Washington, D.C. from $80 a
  Day
Portable London from $90 a Day
Portable New York City from $90
  a Day
Portable Paris from $90 a Day

FROMMER'S® PORTABLE GUIDES

Acapulco, Ixtapa & Zihuatanejo
Amsterdam
Aruba
Australia's Great Barrier Reef
Bahamas
Berlin
Big Island of Hawaii
Boston
California Wine Country
Cancún
Cayman Islands
Charleston
Chicago
Disneyland®
Dominican Republic
Dublin

Florence
Frankfurt
Hong Kong
Las Vegas
Las Vegas for Non-Gamblers
London
Los Angeles
Los Cabos & Baja
Maine Coast
Maui
Miami
Nantucket & Martha's Vineyard
New Orleans
New York City
Paris

Phoenix & Scottsdale
Portland
Puerto Rico
Puerto Vallarta, Manzanillo &
  Guadalajara
Rio de Janeiro
San Diego
San Francisco
Savannah
Vancouver
Vancouver Island
Venice
Virgin Islands
Washington, D.C.
Whistler

Frommer's® National Park Guides

Algonquin Provincial Park
Banff & Jasper
Family Vacations in the National
   Parks

Grand Canyon
National Parks of the American
   West
Rocky Mountain

Yellowstone & Grand Teton
Yosemite & Sequoia/Kings
   Canyon
Zion & Bryce Canyon

Frommer's® Memorable Walks

Chicago
London

New York
Paris

San Francisco

Frommer's® With Kids Guides

Chicago
Las Vegas
New York City

Ottawa
San Francisco
Toronto

Vancouver
Walt Disney World® & Orlando
Washington, D.C.

Suzy Gershman's Born to Shop Guides

Born to Shop: France
Born to Shop: Hong Kong,
   Shanghai & Beijing

Born to Shop: Italy
Born to Shop: London

Born to Shop: New York
Born to Shop: Paris

Frommer's® Irreverent Guides

Amsterdam
Boston
Chicago
Las Vegas
London

Los Angeles
Manhattan
New Orleans
Paris
Rome

San Francisco
Seattle & Portland
Vancouver
Walt Disney World®
Washington, D.C.

Frommer's® Best-Loved Driving Tours

Austria
Britain
California
France

Germany
Ireland
Italy
New England

Northern Italy
Scotland
Spain
Tuscany & Umbria

The Unofficial Guides®

Beyond Disney
California with Kids
Central Italy
Chicago
Cruises
Disneyland®
England
Florida
Florida with Kids
Inside Disney

Hawaii
Las Vegas
London
Maui
Mexico's Best Beach Resorts
Mini Las Vegas
Mini Mickey
New Orleans
New York City
Paris

San Francisco
Skiing & Snowboarding in the
   West
South Florida including Miami &
   the Keys
Walt Disney World®
Walt Disney World® for
   Grown-ups
Walt Disney World® with Kids
Washington, D.C.

Special-Interest Titles

Athens Past & Present
Cities Ranked & Rated
Frommer's Best Day Trips from London
Frommer's Best RV & Tent Campgrounds
   in the U.S.A.
Frommer's Caribbean Hideaways
Frommer's China: The 50 Most Memorable Trips
Frommer's Exploring America by RV
Frommer's Gay & Lesbian Europe
Frommer's NYC Free & Dirt Cheap

Frommer's Road Atlas Europe
Frommer's Road Atlas France
Frommer's Road Atlas Ireland
Frommer's Wonderful Weekends from
   New York City
The New York Times' Guide to Unforgettable
   Weekends
Retirement Places Rated
Rome Past & Present

Travel Tip: He who finds the best hotel deal has more to spend on facials involving knobbly vegetables.

Hello, the Roaming Gnome here. I've been nabbed from the garden and taken round the world. The people who took me are so terribly clever. They find the best offerings on Travelocity. For very little cha-ching. And that means I get to be pampered and exfoliated till I'm pink as a bunny's doodah.

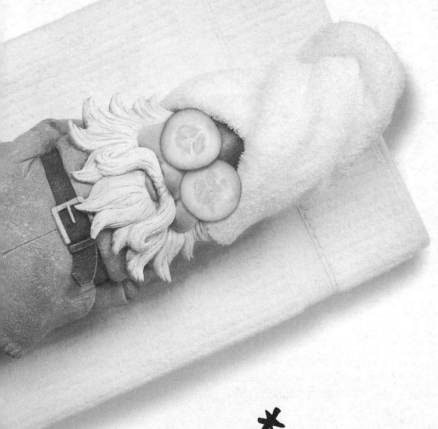

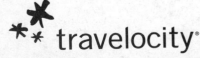

1-888-TRAVELOCITY / travelocity.com / America Online Keyword: Travel

Travel Tip: Make sure there's customer service for any change of plans — involving friendly natives, for example.

One can plan and plan, but if you don't book with the right people you can't seize le moment and canoodle with the poodle named Pansy. I, for one, am all for fraternizing with the locals. Better yet, if I need to extend my stay and my gnome nappers are willing, it can all be arranged through the 800 number at, oh look, how convenient, the lovely company coat of arms.

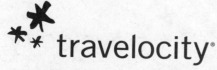